Developing Managers and Leaders

*Perspectives, Debates
and Practices in Ireland*

Developing Managers and Leaders

Perspectives, Debates and Practices in Ireland

**Thomas N. Garavan, Carole Hogan
and Amanda Cahir-O'Donnell**

Gill & Macmillan

Gill & Macmillan Ltd
Hume Avenue
Park West
Dublin 12
with associated companies throughout the world
www.gillmacmillan.ie

978 07171 4035 0

Index compiled by Cover to Cover
Print origination in Ireland by Carole Lynch

The paper used in this book is made from the wood pulp of
managed forests. For every tree felled, at least one tree is planted,
thereby renewing natural resources.

A CIP catalogue record for this book is available
from the British Library.

Table of Contents

Part One

Part Two

Part Three

Part Four

Acknowledgements

We would like to acknowledge the support, encouragement, advice and contribution of a number of individuals and organisations in helping us to complete this text. In particular, we would like to thank the following:

- Kim O'Mahony, Quality Officer, Information Technology Division, University of Limerick
- Mike McDonnell and Wendy Sullivan, Chartered Institute of Personnel and Development, Ireland
- Dr Claire Gubbins, Research Fellow, University of Limerick
- Hugh Fisher, Director, Training Connections, Dublin
- Zeita Lambe, Training Specialist, IBM Ireland
- John Conway, HR Director, AIB Capital Markets
- Avril Farrell, Head of Learning and Development, AIB Capital Markets
- Janet Mooney, HR Learning Manager, AIB O&T
- Damian Lenagh, HR Director, Dublin Airport Authority
- Celeste McCloskey, Head of Organisational Capability, Dublin Airport Authority
- Robert Hilliard, Director of Dublin Airport, Dublin Airport Authority
- Sinead Heneghan, Director, Irish Institute of Training and Development
- Denise Banks, Training and Development Manager, Accenture Ireland
- Tom Jordan, Executive Coach, OPD
- Jo O'Donoghue, Publisher, Currach Press
- Michael Gaffney, Human Resource Development Decisions
- Jonathan O'Mahony, University of Limerick
- Eugene Dalton, Learning and Development Specialist, Group HR, ESB.

A number of organisations and individuals provided data and materials that enabled us to prepare the case scenarios that appear at the beginning of each chapter. In particular, we would like to thank the following:

- First Data's Approach to Leadership Development: Designing a Leadership Model – Ciara McCluskey, Senior Manager, Learning and Development, Ernst and Young
- Quinn Direct: Managing Training and Development in a Call Centre – Dr Christine Cross, Lecturer in Human Resources and Organisational Behaviour, University of Limerick
- Fexco: Developing Organisational Leadership Capability in an Entrepreneurial Company: A Blended-Learning Approach – Pat Salisbury, Human Resource Director, Fexco Ireland
- Developing a Competency Framework in Stryker Corporation – Julie O'Mahony, Learning and Development Specialist, Stryker Orthopaedics
- Managing Talent at Dell Computers: Scaling Employee Potential – Liam Haigney, Business Process Improvement Manager, EMEA HR, Dell Computers
- AIB (ROI): Implementing Multisource Feedback for Management Development – Dr Alma McCarthy, Lecturer in Human Resource Development, NUIG
- Using Development Centres to Develop Managers in AIB Capital Markets: A Best Practice Approach – Avril Farrell, Head of Learning and Development, AIB Capital Markets

- Developing a Culture of Succession in First Trust Bank: Starting with Junior Management – Bernie Braniff, Head of Learning and Development, AIB Group UK plc
- Senior Management Development at ESB – Michael Loughnane, Manager, Leadership and People Development, ESB Group
- Establishing a Formal Mentoring Programme at Bausch and Lomb Ireland – Jackie Roche, Training and Development Specialist, Bausch and Lomb, Waterford
- Dick Spring: A Case of Informal Learning – Dick Spring, Director, Fexco Ireland
- Focusing on Individual Development at Ernst and Young Ireland – Ciara McCluskey, Senior Manager, Learning and Development, Ernst and Young
- Developing the Top Team through Executive Education: Avocent Partnering with the Kemmy Business School – Professor Donal Dineen, Dean, Kemmy Business School, University of Limerick
- Developing Graduates at Kerry Group plc – Adrian Grey, HR Director, Kerry Group
- Managing Strategic Change through Business Scorecard and Workshop Processes at Sonopress – Linda Coughlan, Human Resources Director, Arvato Digital, Dublin
- Developing a Global Virtual Learning and Development Team within Hewlett-Packard – Aidan Lawrence, Workforce Development Director, Hewlett Packard
- Excellence through People: Implementing a National Standard for Learning and Developing in Ireland – Aileen Murphy, Lecturer in Hospitality Management, Waterford Institute of Technology.

We would also like to thank colleagues in our respective organisations and those individuals who have been most helpful and supportive of our efforts. These include: Breda Ahern, Dr Paul Aitken, Sabrina Amodeo, Damaris Anderson-Supple, Claire Armstrong, Gordon Armstrong, Bridie Barnacle, Naomi Birdthistle, Naoise Blake, Patricia Bossons, Hamish Brown, Mick Byrne, Kevin Cahill, Ronan Carbery, Mary Carroll, Noreen Clifford, Pamela Cole, David Collings, Jeanne Colvin, Patricia Conroy, Pat Costine, Christine Cross, Dom Crotty, Eleanor Curtis, Dr Elizabeth Curtis, Collette D'Arcy, Yvonne Delaney, Faye Doherty, Helena Downey, Sarah Downing, Jennifer Doyle, Julie Elliott, Fintan Fanning, John Fitzgerald, Rita Foley, Veronica Gannon, Sinead Gaynor, John Gorman, Alan Grey, Paddy Gunnigle, Alison Hardingham, Bruce Harley, Brid Henley, Noreen Heraty, Amanda Horan, Breiga Hynes, Sean Kane, David Kearney, Anne Kiely, Judy Kinnane, Dr Cyril Kirwan, Jonathan Lavelle, Paddy Lavelle, TJ McCabe, Sarah MacCurtain, Christine Maloney, Sinead Marron, Bridie Matthews, Anthony McDonnell, Elaine McGleenan, Dave McGuire, Bernadette McMahon, Juliet McMahon, Finnoula McNamara, Anne McNeely, Kevin Meehan, Bridget Milner, Sarah Moore, Michael Morley, Eilish Moylan, Aileen Murphy, Michele Murphy, Tony Murphy, Ciara Nolan, Fergal O'Brien, Mike O'Brien, Maria O'Connell, Carol O'Connor, Karl O'Connor, Peter O'Connor, David O'Donnell, Deirdre O'Dwyer, Anne O'Loughlin, Grace O'Malley, Nial O'Reilly, Michelle O'Shea, Bob Patterson, Jill Pearson, Morgan Pierse, Ineke Powell, Jamie Power, Peter Quinn, Bill Rainey, Jackie Roche, Andrew Rock, Patricia Rooney, Enda Ryan, Kathy Ryan, Valerie Shanahan, Craig Skelton, Ger Slattery, Patrick Sutton, Elizabeth Switzer, Margaret Swords, Patricia Treacy, Tom Turner, Joe Wallace, Emma Walsh, Karen Whelan, Phil Wolsey.

We would like to acknowledge the contribution of Marion O'Brien, Aoife O'Kelly and Emma Farrell of Gill & Macmillan and Jane Rogers for helping to bring this work to fruition.

Finally, we would like to thank our families – Margaret, Jim, PJ, Gerard, Rita and Mary B (Garavan); Martin, Hugh and Brian (O'Donoghue); Keelan and Conor (O'Donnell); and TJ and Carmel (Cahir).

TG, CH, A. C-O'D, February 2009

Author Profiles

Thomas N. Garavan is Professor and Associate Dean, Postgraduate Studies and Executive Education, Kemmy Business School, University of Limerick. He teaches HRD, Training and Development, and Leadership Development. He is author of more than 100 academic articles, Editor in Chief of the *Journal of European Industrial Training* and Associate Editor of *Human Resource Development International*. He is a member of the Board of Directors of the Academy of Human Resource Development.

Carole Hogan is Director and Principal Consultant at Carole Hogan Associates. She has more than 27 years' experience in consulting and researching. Her particular areas of expertise are: management and leadership development; programme design, delivery and evaluation; developing executive coaching and mentoring relationships; team and organisational development. Carole is currently a doctoral candidate focusing on the area of management learning and development.

Amanda Cahir-O'Donnell is the Founding Director of TIO Consulting Ltd, which specialises in Learning and Management Consultancy. She has over 20 years' experience in developing managers, leaders and teams across diverse industry sectors. Previously, she established and led the Learning and Development Function in AIB Capital Markets. She is a Chartered Fellow of the CIPD and a Fellow of the IITD. Amanda's areas of expertise include: management and leadership development; executive coaching; mentoring; team development; and organisational development.

Preface

In contemporary organisations management and leadership development practices continue to evolve. Managers and leaders are a highly influential group in terms of creating high-performance organisations, and leadership strength is considered essential to improved competitiveness and future growth. Organisations that take a strategic approach to management, leader and leadership development produce higher-quality leadership talent and have greater competitiveness in the marketplace. Best-practice organisations are characterised by the intensity and quality of their management, leader and leadership interventions and investments. They do much the same as other organisations but with greater consistency and more prioritisation.

The growth in management, leader and leadership development is an international phenomenon. In the USA, for example, surveys reveal that organisations now pay more attention to leadership development and allocate greater resources to it. Managers are typically the decision-makers with regard to the opportunities afforded by new technologies; they are pivotal in how proactively and effectively change is managed; and they are particularly instrumental in creating an organisational culture of development. Surveys in Europe reveal that the top companies are more likely systematically to develop their leaders and prepare them for future challenges. The systematic development of managers and leaders has a positive influence on a range of organisational outcomes, although it may take a substantial period of time to produce returns: it can take up to twenty years for a leader to acquire all the skills needed to solve complex organisational problems. Development is therefore progressive in that the manager will proceed from relatively simple situations to those that require complex knowledge. The kinds of experience that promote development at one point in a leader's career are different from those that may be beneficial at a later stage.

Not all organisations pay adequate attention to the development of managers and leaders. Some, especially small and medium-sized enterprises (SMEs), neglect the training and development of managers and leaders, or it becomes a casualty of cost-cutting. It is considered a cost rather than an investment, and where it is undertaken it is piecemeal, not sufficiently strategically integrated and rarely systematically evaluated. Some studies have highlighted the weakness of links between business strategy management and leadership development strategy in SMEs. Small firms often produce rigid development plans that are not responsive to changing business strategies. They tend to be inward-focused and centred on the demands of the immediate business environment.

There is a mixed picture of management and leadership development in Ireland. Large organisations are generally committed to and invest more in management and leadership development, but SMEs show significantly less commitment. Indigenous firms (both large and small) are less effective than multinational companies (MNCs) in aligning their management and leadership development initiatives with business strategy. They tend to carry out management and leadership development on an ad hoc basis. Management and leadership development has moved up the list of priorities in MNCs, and a growing number of organisations see it as an essential part of wider human resource management (HRM) and development strategy.

We currently know a great deal about the factors that shape management, leader and leadership development in organisations. It is in the application of this knowledge that organisations fall short. There is an abundance of literature highlighting the shifting priorities of organisations. Poorly designed HRM and leadership development systems, and outmoded assumptions about how leaders develop, cause organisations to implement ineffective leadership development interventions. Organisations frequently assume competency models to be static rather than dynamic, while in reality competency models can quickly become outdated because of changes in the organisation's environment. Best-practice organisations take proactive approaches to building leadership talent. Leadership requirements vary according to situation and level in the organisation. The requirements of a start-up organisation differ from those of a mature organisation and from those of an organisation that has experienced a fundamental transformation. Similarly, there are major differences between leadership at functional, business unit and chief executive levels. Organisations often take a unitary approach to leadership development across different levels and situations. Those occupying top positions frequently ignore their own development: chief executives and directors are less likely than their junior colleagues to participate in management and leadership development initiatives.

Management, leader and leadership development are ambiguous and potentially contradictory concepts. They can have different meanings for different stakeholders in an organisation. Managers frequently consider management, leader and leadership development to be concerned solely with attending training courses and external seminars. Middle managers often view management and leadership development as being about managing their careers. Senior managers often focus on the strategic contribution of management and leadership development. At a societal level, the focus is on the development of a society that effectively harnesses human potential and builds knowledge. At this level there will also be a concern that managers continue to learn and are socially responsible. These differences suggest that the search for a universal paradigm or model of management, leader and leadership development is futile. It may be more useful to understand how these processes operate in diverse situations and what contribution these processes can make to individuals, organisations and societies.

Evidence of Management and Leadership Development: Best Practice or Best Principles?

The notions of best principles and best practice are controversial. Studies of management, leader and leadership development indicate that organisations have distinct and unique processes and there is doubt about whether or not they can be duplicated. However, a number of fundamental principles of effective management leader and leadership development can be articulated:

- **Support of Top Management:** Effective management and leadership development requires top management or CEO support to be effective. In reality, this support is frequently absent. Companies with CEO support and involvement show higher financial returns than those whose top management is less involved.
- **Involvement of the Board of Directors:** This is even more significant than top management support. We believe that the board has a duty to ensure that the organisation has a pool of well-developed leaders who have the capacity to execute the strategies of the organisation. It can make a major contribution in mentoring senior managers, participating in development programmes and formulating management and leadership development processes and strategies.

- **A Focus on Developing the Total Management Pool:** We have observed that a number of organisations prioritise their management and leadership investment, focusing on the top ten to fifteen per cent of their current leadership population. This strategy is acceptable as far as succession to the top team is concerned, but it can leave weaknesses at other levels of development. All managers should have an opportunity to participate in ongoing development, though the intensity of this development may vary. High-potential managers and leaders are likely to need more intensive levels of investment in development, but not at the expense of other 'solid' performers. Strong companies will have a leadership bench strength which has depth and breadth.
- **A Diversity of Leadership Development Interventions:** Research undertaken by the Corporate Leadership Council indicates that feedback and relationship-focused development are important for leadership development. This is followed in importance by on-the-job experience. The most important feature of this is the amount of decision-making authority managers have. Organisations must consider the strength of their total leadership bench.
- **Selecting the Right Practices and Implementing them Correctly:** Establishing the right approach is complex, and depends on many factors, including the life cycle stage of the company, its culture and structure, and the external environment. Most fundamental is the strategic direction of the organisation. When appropriate practices are selected they need to be implemented thoroughly. The best companies execute their leadership development effectively. Three aspects of execution are important: 1) synergies between different practices; 2) the degree to which the espoused practices are actually utilised; and 3) the extent to which their effectiveness is measured. Accountability is important. The best companies hold managers and leaders accountable for the success of development initiatives. Accountability means accountability for the development of the team as well as the development of oneself and can be incorporated into performance management and rewards.

Key Assumptions About Management and Leadership Development

Assumption 1: Effective leadership requires a combination of ability, skill and motivation. Skill and ability will be ineffective without a strong motivation to perform, which in turn is a function of self-confidence and willingness to perform. Self-confidence derives from a leader's ability to influence, and self-motivation determines the leader's capacity to motivate others. Managers and leaders who are skilled in motivating others are less aggressive, less critical and have greater emotional stability. A long line of research indicates that the extent to which leaders influence their followers is related to self-confidence, but in order to be an effective leader it is also important to possess the capacity to motivate others. Judge and Bono (2000), for example, found that warmth, trust, altruism and emotional stability are the most significant predictors of effective leadership. Other studies have found that effective leaders are less likely than others to be critical or aggressive in their behaviour.

The practitioner literature focuses on the ability of leaders to 'move' people. This is often referred to in more academic literature as the ability to inspire others with a vision of the future to which they can aspire. To express and communicate this vision with enthusiasm, leaders are expected to be optimistic and energetic and to have the requisite communication skills.

Assumption 2: Management and leadership development involves components of selection and socialisation. Organisations need to select people who have the potential to become leaders, taking into consideration both ability and motivation to lead. Management and leadership development needs to pay attention to the socialisation dimension of both processes, which enable the manager/leader to understand the values of the organisation and to function effectively within it.

Assumption 3: Experience is a central component of effective management and leadership development. Managers and leaders are better able to cope with abstract situations when they have experience of similar situations. Experience also contributes to self-confidence and self-efficacy. Kotter (1988) found that, in retrospect, managers viewed practical experience as a most important process in their preparation for leadership positions.

Assumption 4: Managers and leaders learn from observing the behaviour of others. Bandura (1995), for example, found that leaders learn a great deal from observing other leaders. This is important because it expands the number of opportunities for learning a complex range of behaviours, which occur in situations that are too complex to be simulated in formal development interventions.

Assumption 5: There are critical periods in an individual's life when various skills that contribute to management and leadership are shaped more emphatically than at other times. These include childhood experiences in the home, at school and at social events. Zaleznik (1992), for example, found that crucial experiences included the absence of a father at home, whereas Kotter (1988) found that the development of managers and leaders was influenced by early management experiences. Popper and Mayseless (2003) suggested that the world view of leaders is largely formed by their operational experience and, most significantly, at the beginning of their entry into key managerial roles.

There are many myths about management and leadership development, most frequently expressed by managers with little or no commitment to their own development. Three myths in particular are found in the discourse of managers: that good leadership is common sense; that good leaders are born, not made; and that effective leadership is developed in the 'school of hard knocks'. Figure 1 looks in more detail at these myths.

Figure 1: Three Common Myths Concerning Management and Leadership Development

Myth 1: Effective Leadership is no More than Common Sense

This myth is the idea that the possession of common sense is the only requirement needed to be an effective leader. The basic weakness of this myth is the definition of 'common sense'. To practitioners it may mean a body of practical knowledge about life, but one of the challenges is to know when common sense applies and when it does not. If leadership consisted primarily of common sense, organisations would have little difficulty in finding leaders, but research tells us that this is not the case. This suggests that common sense itself is not sufficient for effective management and leadership development.

Myth 2: Leaders are Born, not Made

There is a school of thought that suggests that leadership is in the genes. This view is supported by research that indicates that cognitive abilities and personality traits are partly innate and that these characteristics may enhance or limit the manager or leader. Another school of thought takes the view that it is life experience that makes the leader. It is possible that both views are correct, because both innate characteristics and experience are important in explaining the behaviour of leaders.

Myth 3: Leadership is Developed in the School of Hard Knocks

This myth challenges the notion that it is possible to develop managers and leaders through formal training and education. It argues that that the only way leadership can be developed is through experience. We take the view that both formal development interventions and experience are necessary to develop effective managers and leaders. It is more appropriate when discussing the contribution of formal development interventions to consider the types of intervention that are appropriate. Leadership development plays a critical role and specific interventions can enhance a leader's ability to understand the relevance of key lessons derived from experience. Formal leadership development interventions provide potential managers and leaders with frameworks within which they can examine particular leadership situations. They provide leaders with the opportunity to use multiple perspectives as well as skills to help them to become better leaders.

Distinctive Text Features

This textbook has a number of important features:

- Streamlined text in eighteen chapters with particular focus on strategic management and leadership development of global leaders, the integration of management and leadership development with succession management and talent management practices and development issues related to different contexts and groups.
- Case scenarios that place the student/practising manager in a decision-making role with regard to selecting management development strategies, designing development activities and implementing management and leadership development so that it will contribute to the success of the organisation.
- Research focus notes giving guidelines to organisations and managers on how to implement and contextualise management and leadership development practices.
- Multiple perspectives that examine different levels of analysis, in addition to the perspectives of managers as individual learners. Drawing on international research, we consider individual, team and country organisational perspectives.
- Current practices are identified, but we are conscious that context will determine the effectiveness of these practices. We do specify the issues that should be considered in order to ensure successful management and leadership development.
- Discussion and application questions at the end of each chapter challenge students and managers on topics addressed in the chapter. These will provide immediate feedback on understanding.

Organisation of the Book

Throughout this book, we use the terms 'management development' and 'leadership development' interchangeably, although we discuss the conceptual and practice differences between the two concepts in Chapter One. We also introduce the concept of leader development, but for the remainder of the book we combine this concept with leadership development. Many development processes in organisations focus on the development of both management and leadership skills.

The book is divided into four major parts. Part One comprises three chapters in which we summarise key concepts and theories relating to management, leader and leadership development, the context of leadership development and the nature of management and leadership. Chapter One, which is conceptual in nature, considers the scope and purpose of management, leader and leadership development. In Chapter Two we provide a detailed consideration of the key internal and external factors that serve as a context in which managers and leaders operate. Chapter Three considers the nature of managerial work and theoretical views on leadership. Material from recent debates in leadership research is also included in this chapter.

Part Two of the book focuses on organisational aspects of management and leadership development, including the positioning of management and leadership in organisations, the structure of leadership development activities, the use of competency-based approaches to leadership development, and talent management processes. Chapter Four outlines the characteristics of strategic management and leadership development and the various decisions that organisations need to make to ensure that management and leadership development contribute to strategic objectives and are aligned with other human resource strategies. Chapter Five focuses on how organisations can structure and manage their leadership development, emphasising policy, structures and stakeholder dimensions. Chapter Six looks at the advantages and limitations of competency-driven models and the issues organisations need to face when these are used to drive leadership development. Chapter Seven focuses on talent management and succession management in organisations, with particular emphasis on the development issues that emerge from these processes.

Part Three focuses on management and leadership development interventions and processes. Chapter Eight considers formal interventions such as personal growth-based, skill-based and feedback-based programmes. We also pay particular attention to action learning and management or leadership education. Chapter Nine focuses on formal job assignments and the characteristics of various special projects, acting up and secondments. Chapter Ten examines formal developmental relationships and identifies the spectrum of developmental relationships in organisations. Chapter Eleven looks at informal management and leadership development processes such as reflection, peer conversations and informal coaching and mentoring.

Part Four of the book focuses on various aspects of management and leadership development for different groups and contexts. Chapter Twelve considers individual development and self-managed learning, highlighting the challenges of this type of learning for organisations and the role of learning contracts in managing self-development processes. Chapter Thirteen outlines career development processes, emphasising the challenges of organisationally directed career development activities that are focused on the individual. Chapter Fourteen describes and evaluates the role and efficacy of development processes in enhancing team effectiveness and the competencies of executives. Chapter Fifteen discusses development issues associated with female managers, entrepreneurs, CPD for managers and small-firm development issues. We also highlight leadership development issues in voluntary organisations and for mid-career managers. Chapter Sixteen focuses on collective approaches to management and leadership development, discussing how concepts such as the learning organisation, organisational learning, knowledge management and leadership can be used to develop managers and leaders. Chapter Seventeen discusses the issues involved in developing an international and global cadre of managers and leaders, and the challenges involved in developing expatriate managers and in ensuring that the competencies of managers are appropriate for international tasks. Chapter Eighteen, the final chapter, focuses on comparative aspects of management and leadership development, exploring how different world views influence our thinking about what constitutes management and leadership development and whether there is convergence or divergence in management and leadership development thinking and practices across countries.

PART ONE

Chapter One

Understanding Management and Leadership Development

Outline

Learning Objectives

Opening Case Scenario

Management and Leadership Development: The Same or Different?

Distinguishing Management, Leader and Leadership Development

Why Should Organisations Invest in Management, Leader and Leadership Development?
- Characteristics of Managers' and Leaders' Jobs
- Strategic Fit and Competitive Advantage
- Leadership Development and Organisation Socialisation
- Leadership Development, Succession and Talent Management

Perspectives on Management, Leader and Leadership Development
- The Beardwell and Holden Model

- Talbot's Typology of Management and Leadership Development
- The Mabey Model
- Burgoyne and Reynolds' Arena Thesis

A Piecemeal Approach
- An Open Systems Approach
- A Relational Approach
- A Critical Theory Perspective

A Dynamic Approach to Management and Leadership Development

Leadership Development as Sustainable Development

Holistic Management and Leadership Development

Conclusion

Summary of Key Points

Discussion Questions

Application and Experiential Questions

OPENING CASE SCENARIO

First Data's Approach to Leadership Development: Designing a Leadership Model

First Data Corporation is a global payments company which provides electronic commerce and payments services worldwide. It has approximately 3.5 million merchant locations, 1,400 card issuers and millions of customers. It seeks to add value for its customers by ensuring it is easy, fast and secure for customers (people and businesses) to buy goods and services using virtually any form of payment. It provides credit, debit and smart cards, issues store value cards and provides merchant transaction-processing services. It also provides internal commerce solutions, money transfer services, money orders and cheque processing and verification services. First Data has operated in Ireland for the past ten years. Its Irish headquarters are located in Dublin, where it employs a total of a thousand people.

The First Data leadership model is based on its core business beliefs and values. These core beliefs emphasise a single company approach, performance, leadership and innovation. The organisation places a strong emphasis on operating as a single entity in order to ensure unity of purpose and economies of scale. This unity of purpose ensures that leadership behaviour is consistent across the organisation. Performance is an essential requirement of the organisation. There is a strong emphasis on ensuring that leaders understand what is expected of them and that they demonstrate abilities above and beyond their current role. Leadership starts at the top. Senior executives and managers are expected to embrace key behaviours and use those behaviours to motivate performance. Innovation is valued within First Data. Leaders are expected to be innovative and to inspire innovation in others.

First Data adopted a systematic approach to developing its leadership model, identifying key leaders within the organisation who demonstrated effective leadership. Managers were interviewed about their leadership skills and actions and, from those interviews, the organisation identified key behaviours. First Data senior executives were involved in identifying competencies that they considered vital to the organisation's future success. It also looked at other high-performance organisations and identified how they approached leadership. The leadership model which evolved is based on four key themes: a leader's demonstrated ability to mobilise and manage talent in his or her organisation; a leader's ability to drive and inspire high performance; a leader's ability to focus and innovate, including the need to know about trends external to the organisation and to assess their impact on First Data; and a leader's ability to align, to develop strategic partnerships across the organisation and with its customer base. Each theme was then used to specify a cluster of competencies which leaders are expected to demonstrate. The behaviours associated with each competency are broken down into four levels: baseline, intermediate, advanced and mastery. Baseline behaviours are considered to be core to performance and emphasise the tactical and short term. At the other end of the spectrum, mastery level behaviours are more aspirational and focus on the organisation and its strategic direction. Leaders who have achieved the mastery level are consistently able to demonstrate the behaviours identified at the three previous levels.

Each competency cluster was given a precise definition and included a number of specific competencies. In turn, each competence component was defined in terms of its core focus, its key dimensions, and it included a behaviour scale which highlighted the depth of the competency. For example, the 'mobilise' cluster included three competencies: inspirational leadership or the capacity of the leader to communicate a compelling vision; developing people, which is the capacity to take ownership and value the development of others; and managing talent, which focuses on the leader's capacity to build organisational capacity. The 'drive' cluster included three competencies: drive for experience, which is defined as the leader's drive to improve performance and achieve excellence; impact and influence, which focuses on the skills of the leader deliberately to influence others; and organisational savvy, which refers to the skills of the leader to leverage insight into the organisation to get things done. The focus/innovate cluster included two competencies: 'scanning', which involves the leader's curiosity to research issues within and beyond his/her line of business; and developing creative solutions, which focuses on the extent to which the leader generates creative solutions to meet business needs. The align cluster indicates the need to develop a global mindset and customer partnership competencies. A global mindset is defined as the extent to which the leader can adapt his or her behaviour and business decisions in accordance with corporate and country cultures. Customer partnership emphasises the abilities of the leader to partner with customers to achieve business results.

The leadership model is not a stand-alone concept, but is integrated with a range of other human resource management processes. It is used in recruitment and selection as a tool to assess internal and external leadership candidates and as a framework for integrating new leaders. It is also used for the purposes of development. This includes matching a leader's skills to position requirements and helping the organisation understand how best to develop its leaders in order to meet the future needs of the organisation.

This model has had a major impact on the development of managers in First Data. It serves as a framework for the organisation's development initiatives. It is used as a tool for coaching and mentoring leaders, and it is the foundation of the organisation's 360-degree feedback process. It has helped to shape the organisation's approach to succession and talent management. It is useful as a metric for assessing and evaluating current and future capability gaps, as a basis to help leaders determine performance and potential level of leaders and as a basis to manage performance and formulate a talent management strategy.

Talent management and succession planning are given particular focus in this bespoke model. They are designed to evaluate the organisation's talent readiness for strategy execution; to understand talent requirements, both short and long term; to assess leaders regarding results, behaviours, potential and development priorities; to identify critical roles; to assess current incumbents' capabilities and potential; to assess retention risk by determining the likelihood of turnover and its impact on the business; to identify opportunities to acquire leaders with growth potential who can add strategically required skills and capabilities; and to create organisation and individual talent action plans with a focus on accountability.

First Data has created a talent forum and succession management process in order to ensure the effective implementation of the leadership model. This involves the business unit leader meeting with the human resource generalist to establish goals and priorities for the talent forum. The leader and HR generalist then meet with the leader's direct reports to communicate process, timeline, roles, responsibilities and data collection requirements. Leaders then send out communications to direct reports and their employees, identified as participants in the talent forum, to outline timelines and requirements. Direct reports are then expected to complete organisation and employee assessments of leaders identified as participants, complete individual talent profiles and self-assessments. The business unit leader hosts the talent forum or review. The leader and his/her direct reports will be required to discuss organisational strategy, talent requirements and individuals within the organisation. Talent forums begin in the fourth quarter of the year and continue into the second quarter of the following year. The information gathered is sent to the executive committee, which culminates with the CEO's talent forum. The findings of the talent forum are presented to the board of directors during their summer meetings. The organisational development function facilitates the talent forum process and then works on a one-to-one basis with individuals on their development plans.

QUESTIONS

Q.1 What approach does First Data take to the development of managers or leaders? Explain your answer.

Q.2 What do you see as the strengths and weaknesses of First Data's approach to ensuring that it has a supply of talented leaders in the future?

Q.3 Using the ideas presented in Table 1.9 (see p. 27), analyse which particular frame(s) is/are evident in the First Data case scenario.

Management and leadership are contested concepts. Some commentators consider them to be one and the same, whereas others define management and leadership as complex, interrelated but distinct concepts. Most of the earlier writings talked about management rather than leadership. They focused on explaining management in terms of key financial activities and behaviours which have a task orientation. Leadership, in contrast, tends to be defined in terms of vision, motivation and a people orientation. The term leadership is now considered to be superior to the concept of management. There is considerable evidence in practice that management and leadership are interchangeable activities that are not easily defined. The practitioner literature does suggest that both concepts share some distinct elements. The field of management and leadership development makes distinctions between management, leader and leadership development.

This chapter is essentially theoretical in nature. We distinguish management development from leader and leadership development. The chapter highlights a range of related concepts that are used by practitioners and academics. We suggest a possible synthesis by identifying the common features of these activities. The chapter provides a rationale for investment in management, leader and leadership development and explores in detail a number of models of management, leader and leadership development.

Management and Leadership Development: The Same or Different?

The question of whether management and leadership are distinct concepts is contested. Cunningham (1986), for example, identified three different viewpoints on the relationship between leadership and management. The first position assumes that leadership is one competence among a range required for effective management. A second position advocated by Bennis and Nanus (1985) suggested that the two concepts are separate but related, whereas the third position sees the two concepts as partially overlapping. There is evidence, amongst academics at least, of a bias to distinguish leadership conceptually from management, usually at the expense of the latter. Management as an activity and concept is often viewed as a 'second-class citizen', something which is very transactional in nature.

Since the 1980s the majority of scholars trying to understand transformational leadership have sought to differentiate between leading and managing and to understand leading as something distinct and separate from managing. We will focus in detail on transformational leadership in Chapter Three. Kotter (1996) argued that leaders and managers are distinct in their roles and functions. He considered management to be concerned with planning and organising, whereas leadership is concerned with creating value, coping with change and helping organisations to adapt in turbulent times. Two other recent contributions likewise emphasised that the concepts are different. Boydell *et al.* (2004) considered management to be about implementation, order, efficiency and effectiveness. They defined leadership as being concerned with future direction in times of uncertainty. Boydell and his colleagues argued that although management may be sufficient in an organisation in times of stability, it is insufficient when organisational conditions are characterised by complexity, unpredictability and rapid change.

Kent *et al.* (2001) focused on identifying three key differences: purposes, products and processes. These differences are illustrated in Table 1.1. We have added three additional dimensions of potential difference.

Table 1.1: Differences between Leading and Managing

Leading	Managing
Purpose • To create direction and the unified will to pursue it through the development of people's thinking and valuing their involvement	*Purpose* • To determine and compare alternative uses and allocation of resources and to select the alternative which is most effective towards accomplishing or producing a product, end or goal

Leading	Managing
Products • The establishment of trust towards a purpose or end • The creation of social orderliness to carry out that trust • Higher states of behaviour and thinking in terms of principles, values and ethics	*Products* • The provision of resources, organised effort and awareness of performance and progress towards goals • The creation of a desired model of combining people with other resources • The creation of the most energy-effective way of dealing with the causes of events and situations in order to accomplish a purpose tied to a particular situation
Processes • Creating vision, aligning people within a team, managing their 'self', recognising and rewarding, communicating meaning and importance of the vision	*Processes* • Planning, organising, controlling and co-ordinating
Values • Leaders value flexibility, innovation and adaptation • Leaders are concerned with what things mean to people and then try to get people to agree about the most important things to be done • Leaders are people who do the right things	*Values* • Managers value stability, order and efficiency • Managers are concerned with how things get done and try to get people to perform better • Managers are people who do things right
Outcomes • Leadership seeks to produce organisational change through the development of vision, communication of vision and motivation of people to attain the vision • Strong leadership can disrupt order and efficiency • Strong leadership can create change that cannot be implemented	*Outcomes* • Management seeks to produce predictability and order through operational goals, action plans, timetables and resources • Strong management can discourage risk-taking and innovation • Strong management can create bureaucracy without purpose
Focus • Leadership is a multidirectional influence relationship between a leader and a follower with the mutual purpose of accomplishing change	*Focus* • Management is an authority relationship between a manager and subordinate

Source: Adapted from Kent, Crotts and Aziz (2001)

The contrasts reveal that while the two processes are distinct, they cannot effectively work without consideration of each other.

A UK study conducted by IDS (2003) argued that management and leadership roles are different and demand different competencies. They went so far as to argue that managers and leaders are usually quite different types of people. This latter notion is somewhat controversial. For the purposes of this book we will use the terms 'manager' and 'leader' interchangeably to indicate people who occupy positions in which they are expected to perform leadership roles in addition to key management tasks. We consider management and leadership from both social influence and specialised role perspectives. Management and leadership can be performed solo or be shared and distributed. Both concepts include rational and emotional processes.

We recognise that a person can be a leader without being a manager, and vice versa. We do not, however, make the assumption that leaders and managers are different types of people. It is more helpful to focus on the notion that leading and managing are conceptually different processes. We follow the viewpoint which has emerged in contemporary debates that the success of a manager in modern organisations necessarily involves some elements of managing and leading. The integration of the two concepts is complex and currently remains unresolved. We also suggest that some of the distinctions made are both arbitrary and subjective and that there is no single 'correct' definition of either management or leadership.

It is therefore more appropriate to consider the competencies that are necessary to perform both managing and leading functions. The competent leader or manager has the ability to employ these competencies 'situationally'. We think it appropriate to acknowledge the integrative nature of the two processes. Table 1.2 presents a synthesis of leading and managing competencies.

Table 1.2: Leadership and Management Competencies

Leadership Competencies	Management Competencies
Visualising Greatness • Thinks strategically • Demonstrates appropriate risk-taking and innovation • Sees, in his/her mind's eye, what could be achieved • Emotes enthusiasm and inspiration	*Planning and Organising* • Determines long-term objectives and strategies • Decides how to use personnel and other resources
Creating and Empowering the 'We' • Builds teams • Develops others • Appropriately involves others in decision-making • Creates ownership/commitment in others • Delegates responsibility	*Informing* • Disseminates information about decisions and plans • Answers requests for information *Representing* • Tells others about the organisational unit and its accomplishments • Provides a fair accounting of subordinates' ideas and proposals
Communicating for Meaning • Communication is principle- and value-based • Communicates in facts, values, and symbols • Makes communicating for meaning a priority • Takes required time to explain why something is important	*Problem-Solving* • Identifies and analyses work-related problems to identify causes and solutions • Acts decisively to implement solutions and resolve problems or crises
Managing Oneself • Maintains an even temperament • Keeps personal energy high • Is self-confident • Maintains focus, persistence and constancy of purpose	*Conflict Managing* • Encourages and facilitates the resolution of conflict • Encourages co-operation and teamwork

Leadership Competencies	Management Competencies
Care and Recognition • Publicises people's effort and successes • Focuses on the positive and recognises positive progress • Cares about others • Recognises and rewards people frequently and appropriately	*Monitoring* • Gathers information about work activities and progress toward goals • Evaluates the performance of individuals and the work unit *Consulting and Delegation* • Encourages suggestions, inviting participation in decision-making • Allows others to have substantial responsibility and discretion in decisions *Networking* • Develops contacts with people who are a source of information and support • Maintains contacts through periodic interaction, visits, calls, etc. *Clarifying* • Assigns tasks, provides direction, etc. • Communicates job responsibilities, task objectives, deadlines and expectations

Sources: Adapted from Kent, Crotts and Aziz (2001); Yukl, Wall and Lepsinger (1990)

Distinguishing Management, Leader and Leadership Development

We find that the literature makes conceptual distinctions between management, leader and leadership development. Management development includes management education and training and places an emphasis on acquiring specific categories of knowledge, skills and abilities designed to enhance task performance in managerial roles. Day (2000) suggested that management development focuses on the application of existing and proven solutions to known problems. Management development is often associated with a deficit in management skill and competency. Mintzberg (2004) suggested that management development is a pull activity in which organisations draw on whatever they find appropriate to enhance the skills of their manager pool. Increasingly there is a move towards customisation, where organisations carry out management development as an in-house activity with specially selected context and development strategies.

Leader development focuses on the individual and the development of intrapersonal skills. Day (2000) suggested that leader development places emphasis on individual-based knowledge, skills and abilities. Leader development activities place emphasis on development of self-awareness, self-reflection and self-motivation. Zand (1997) suggested that these capabilities enable the leader to acquire personal power, enhance knowledge and trust. Leader development facilitates the leader to construct an independent identity and a unique understanding which facilitates differentiation from other leaders.

Leadership development is defined as focusing on enhancing the collective capacity of managers to engage effectively in leadership roles and practices. McCauley *et al.* (2004) distinguished between leadership roles and processes. Roles refer to both formal and informal roles, whereas processes enable groups of people to work together. Leadership development enhances the capacity for groups of managers to cope with unique and novel problems. It places emphasis on the development of capacity in anticipation of future challenges. Day (2000) suggested that management development differs from leadership development in that it focuses on performance in formal roles and believes that the development processes are for position and organisation-specific activities.

On the other hand, leadership development focuses on social capital, i.e. the building of relationships to enhance organisational performance. Day suggested that leadership development activities should focus on the interaction between the leader and the social and organisational context. It is therefore a complex process with a strong focus on the development of relationships.

Day (2000) suggested that leadership development emphasises integration rather than differentiation (Table 1.3).

Table 1.3: Summary of Differences between Management, Leader and Leadership Development

Development Target			
Comparison Dimension	Management Development	Leader Development	Leadership Development
Capital Type	Human	Human	Social
Emphasis	Differentiation	Differentiation	Integration
Model	*Organisational* • Task specific • Organisation specific • Performance in management roles	*Individual* • Personal power • Knowledge • Trust	*Relational* • Mutual respect • Trust and networking • Commitments
Skills/ Competencies	*Time and Task Management* • Prioritising • Management of time • Delegation *Problem-solving* • Problem identification • Generation of alternatives • Evaluation of alternatives *Decision-making* • Selection of alternatives • Resourcing • Implementation of decision	*Self-awareness* • Emotional awareness • Self-confidence • Self-image *Self-regulation* • Self-control • Trustworthiness • Personal responsibility • Adaptability *Self-motivation* • Initiative • Commitment • Optimism	*Social Awareness* • Empathy • Service orientation • Political understanding *Social Skills* • Building relationships • Team orientation • Customer relationship management • Change champion • Conflict management
Strategies	Job assignments Hardship experiences In-house training programmes Management education programmes	360° feedback Coaching/mentoring Development centres Personality profiles	Mentoring Networking Action learning Team development

We present a selection of definitions of management, leader and leadership development in Table 1.4. These definitions illustrate how ill-defined and variously interpreted these concepts are. Historically, the definitions reflect a shift in our thinking about management and leadership processes and the emergence of human resource development (HRD). HRD has broadened our thinking concerning the purposes of management, leader and leadership development and the strategies that are appropriate to achieve the objectives of each activity. Many definitions view managers as resources and consider management development to be driven by functional performance rationale. Few of the earlier definitions emphasised learning. They considered management, leader and leadership development activities as activities that are done with managers, rather than as activities that enable managers and leaders to generate meaning and understanding.

Table 1.4: Definitions of Management Leader and Leadership Development

The systematic improvement of managerial effectiveness within an organisation, assessed by its contribution to organisational effectiveness.	1971	Morris
A conscious and systematic decision-action process to control the development of managerial resources in the organisation for the achievement of organisational goals and strategies.	1975	Ashton, Easterby-Smith and Irvine
An attempt to improve managerial effectiveness through a planned and deliberate learning process ... that function which, from deep understanding of business goals and organisational requirements, undertakes the following: a) to forecast needs, skill mixes and profiles for many positions and levels; b) to design and recommend the professional, career and personal development programmes necessary to ensure competence; c) to move from the concept of 'management' to the concept of 'managing'.	1977	Training Services Agency (cited in Mumford 1997)
...the whole, complex process by which individuals learn, grow and improve their abilities to perform professional management tasks.	1986	Wezley and Baldwin
An attempt to improve managerial effectiveness through a planned and deliberate learning process.	1987	Mumford
I define 'management development' as the management of managerial careers in an organisation context. I define a 'managerial career' as the biography of a person's managerial work life (and I define 'managing' as the creation and maintenance of practical meaning in organised activity).	1988	Burgoyne
... those processes which engender enhancement of capabilities whilst leaving scope for discretion, creativity and indeterminacy.	1989	Storey
Management development can be viewed as a process (consisting of planned and unplanned activities and experience) that helps managers in an organisation to develop their experience, ideas, knowledge, skills, relationships and personal identity, so that they can contribute to the effective development of their organisation.	1990	Temporal

Management development is a term which embraces much more than simply education or training. It is that entire system of corporate activities with the espoused goal of improving the performance of the managerial stock in the context of organisational and environmental change.	1992	Lees
The complex process by which individuals learn to perform effectively in managerial roles.	1994	Baldwin and Padgett
We use the term 'management development' to describe management education, structured training and also more informal processes such as mentoring and self-development.	1997	Thomson *et al.*
An attempt to improve managerial effectiveness through a learning process.	1997	Mumford
A legitimately targeted and dynamic initiative that can enhance the management block of human capital skills.	1999	Lepak and Snell
The central challenge of management development is to control and manage the learning process of managers, focused on individual development and career success and/or reaching organisational goals.	2001	Van der Sluis-den Dikken and Hoesksema
Management development (MD) is defined as the system of personal practices by which an organisation tries to guarantee the timely availability of qualified and motivated employees for its key positions. The aim of MD is to have at its disposal the right type of manager and specialists at the right moment.	2001	Jansen and van der Velde
Management development is … a multi-faceted process in which some aspects are easier to identify and measure than others.	2001	Thomson, May, Storey, Gray and Iles
The complex process by which individuals learn to perform effectively in managerial roles.	2001	Paauwe and Williams
The pursuit of order and predictability in organisational performance.	2002	Mabey
Facilitates the achievement of a fit between management resources and the long-term strategy of the company.	2003	Morley and Heraty
The definition used for management development … includes both the personal and career development of an individual manager (i.e. attendance at formal development programmes, seminars, conferences and also informal learning through methods such as coaching and mentoring, etc). It also includes management education, which is achieved through formal undergraduate/postgraduate qualifications.	2004	O'Connor and Mangan

... We may define appropriate management development as a dynamic capability or as a learned pattern of collective activity through which the organisation systematically generates and modifies its routine in the pursuit of encouraging and developing managers to balance efficiency and adaptiveness.	2005	Espedal

A number of additional observations on these definitions include the following:

- They espouse a unitary conception of organisations. They consider the organisation to have clear goals and objectives that are understood and accepted by all stakeholders. This may not necessarily be a realistic assumption. Burgoyne and Jackson (1997) have argued that a pluralist rather than a unitary perspective may be more appropriate.
- Many definitions assume the existence of medium and large organisations that can offer the level of sophistication required to deliver formal management and leadership development.
- Definitions frequently fail to acknowledge the contribution of wider life experience and 'situated' learning and development. They fail to acknowledge the complex and uncertain nature of managerial work.
- Chia (1996) argues that the tendency to view organisations as objective, independent entities is misplaced as an idea. It is more appropriate to view organisations as constructed of shared experiences and language which are used to make sense of experience.

Management, leader and leadership development have different meanigs from a number of other related concepts such as management training and education. Mintzberg (2004) referred to management education as a push activity undertaken by business schools. It focuses on the development of theories and concepts and educates students and potential managers outside the practice into which they are subsequently hired. These programmes are typically intense and disconnected from an organisational context. Some education programmes have elements of customisation, but they tend to draw elements from a generic pool of strategies and modules.

Management training is located between management education and development. It is increasingly a short-term and highly instrumental activity. Managers frequently attend management training because of a perceived need. It is often associated with a deficit in management skills and techniques. Although these programmes do contain elements of customisation, they may draw on materials produced by business schools. Management development was characterised by Mintzberg as a pull activity in which organisations draw on whatever they find appropriate to further the development of their manager pool. Increasingly there is a strong move towards customisation. This means that organisations carry out this activity in-house with specially selected context and development strategies.

Table 1.5: Distinctions Between Management Training, Management Education, Self-Development, Organisation Development and Career Development

	Management Training	Management Education	Self-Development	Organisation Development	Career Development
Purpose/ Focus	• Focuses on the development of technical knowledge and skills, and management techniques • Development of individuals to meet the current demands of their job	• Focuses on the development of manager's/leader's analytical skills and conceptual skills • Strong focus on business functions and a cross-disciplinary approach	• Focuses on the development of an individual's personal goals and aspirations • Usually instigated by the individual • Might not be related to organisational needs	• Focuses on the development of organisational structures, culture and systems • Strong focus on the enablement of organisational change	• Can focus on individual or organisation or both • The development, implementation and monitoring of career goals and strategies
Processes/ Strategies	• Frequently formal and structured • Frequently done by trainers, consultants and various institutions • Strong focus on immediate transfer of skill to work situation • Usually programmes of short duration	• Frequently highly structured programmes of longer duration • Managers are frequently educated outside the context they are subsequently hired into • High intensity programmes with some elements of customisation • Most common model is an MBA programme	• Preparation of personal development plans • Strong emphasis on individual decision-making • Individual devises own programme of development activities • Strong emphasis on development of self-awareness	• Action-based methodology • Strong emphasis on use of surveys and feedback processes • Team and organisation-wide interactions with experimentation • Use of a change agent internal or external to the organisation	• Strong emphasis on the use of career instruments and psychometric assessment • Balancing of individual and organisational needs • Preparation of plans of varying lengths

	Management Training	Management Education	Self-Development	Organisation Development	Career Development
Prerequisite Conditions	• Opportunities to transfer skills and techniques to job situations • A job role with sufficient complexity and variety • Willingness by organisation to invest in training activities	• Strong motivation and self-confidence to learn in an educational setting • Strong analytical ability to meet the demands of the programme	• Self-motivation and self-confidence • Confidence to take initiatives designed to develop individual • Expertise and external support in careers	• Knowledge of corporate objectives and culture • Creation of a sense of purpose and willingness to change • Commitment to a long-term process of development	• Career clarity and strong self-awareness • Motivation to plan and identify future career options • Organisational support for career development

Self-development is most often conceptualised as a process driven and managed by the individual, while career development usually seeks to integrate individual and organisational perspectives and focuses on the short, medium and longer term. Organisational development tends to focus its activities on the team and organisational levels. The agenda is set primarily by organisational concerns.

All of these development activities share a number of common features: assessment, challenge and support. McCauley *et al.* (1998) argued that these three elements have two primary purposes: first, to motivate the individual to focus attention and effort, and second, to provide the raw material or resources for learning and development.

Assessment: The developmental activities outlined in Table 1.6 (see p. 15) all rely on rich data. Assessment at the individual and organisational level is important because it provides an understanding of the position of the individual or organisation at this point in time. It provides evidence of current effectiveness and performance levels and helps to clarify the learning opportunity or need. It enables the individual and/or organisation to benchmark future development. It also helps people to engage in self-assessment and reflection. There are many sources of data which enable the development of self-awareness, including: self, peers in the workplace, bosses, employees, family, customers, suppliers and experts. The process through which this data is collected and interpreted can vary in terms of formality. We will consider formal feedback processes in more detail in Chapter Eight.

Challenge: The development concepts are characterised by stretch or challenge. The research evidence is consistent in telling us that people like consistency. They become comfortable and this leads to habitual ways of thinking and acting. Development activities that involve degrees of challenge force people out of their comfort zones and create a situation where people begin to question their skills, frameworks and approaches.

Challenging assignments fulfil a number of important functions in the context of the development concepts defined in this chapter. They enable managers to develop new capacities that they will require if they are going to be successful in new roles. Managers are likely to feel challenged when they encounter situations that demand skills and abilities that exceed current capabilities. Challenges are likely to develop where there is ambiguity and confusion. Some challenges require new values and thinking; they require the individual to change attitudes and respond in a different way. Leaders respond positively to difficult or stretch goals. They may work harder or smarter.

Support: If people do not receive support in the form of confirming messages, or there is insufficient encouragement to change, the potential of the developmental experience will be reduced. Support performs a number of important functions in the context of development. Each developmental concept contains some elements of support. Support helps managers to handle the struggle and pain of developing and enables them to remain positive and see themselves as capable of dealing with challenges. Support is a key factor in maintaining motivation to learn and to grow. There is evidence that support can contribute to increased self-efficacy in learning. Managers with higher self-efficacy are more likely to exert more effort to master challenges. Support serves as an important social cue and a key learning resource. Where managers talk to others about their learning, they have an opportunity to confirm and clarify the lessons that they have learned.

Why Should Organisations Invest in Management, Leader and Leadership Development?

This is a complex question and it raises important issues about why it is important to single out managers for special consideration. There is evidence that organisations invest considerably in the development of managers. This holds true for many different sectors and organisation types. Management and leadership development becomes more important as the organisation increases in size. In the Irish context, the evidence suggests that multinational companies are leaders in investment in management and leadership development. Organisations invest in management and leadership development for a multiplicity of reasons, including the need to support business strategy, the individual, business performance situation and succession planning. These purposes are often conflicting and make significant demands of management and leadership development activities.

Table 1.6: Key Development Agendas of Management, Leader and Leadership Development

Self-Awareness
- Understanding self or awareness of personal strengths and weaknesses.
- Understanding which situations bring out the best in a manager and which are more difficult to manage.
- Developing manager insight into why they have certain traits and preferences.
- Helping managers/leaders understand how they can be most effective in their roles.

Self-Confidence
- Frequently cited outcome of management, leader and leadership development interventions.
- It helps managers understand their abilities and enables clarification of what they have to offer the organisation.
- Increased self-confidence enables managers and leaders to perform effectively in difficult situations and deal with complex leadership challenges.

To Think Differently/Creatively
- Development enables managers and leaders to take a broader and more complex view of situations.
- Enhances the systems thinking ability of managers to deal with ambiguity and complexity.
- Enables managers to think 'outside the box', move beyond current assumptions and frameworks.
- Enhances capacity to contribute novel insights to address problems and opportunities.

To Develop Networking Skills
- Develops interpersonal and networking skills and helps leaders become more successful in influencing peers, building teams and networking with customers.
- Develops cultural sensitivity for leaders working with managers from different cultures.
- Enables managers to work effectively in a range of social settings and to be confident in a range of interpersonal situations.

To Enhance Learning Ability
- Enhances the learning capabilities of managers to develop new attitudes and ways of thinking.
- Develops motivation to learn and ability to develop skills in learning how to learn.
- Develops increased awareness of how the manager learns new perspectives in relation to learning.

Mabey and Salaman (1995) and Lees (1992) argued that development activities are designed to address four specific agendas: 1) functional performance, 2) political reinforcement, 3) compensation and 4) psychic defence. The functional performance perspective represents the more conventional viewpoint. It argues that management development is concerned with developing the knowledge, skill and attitudes of individual managers. It assumes that the relationship between investment in management development and individual performance is direct and uncomplicated. A political reinforcement purpose focuses on the reinforcement and propagation of skills and attitudes valued by senior managers. It makes an assumption that senior managers have made a correct diagnosis and selected the appropriate solution. A compensation purpose postulates that organisations can use management development as a reward strategy. It makes the assumption that managers will value management development and view it as motivational strategy. It also assumes that the provision of management will enhance the commitment of managers to the objectives of the organisation. A psychic defence purpose postulates that organisations provide management development as a safety valve for management anxieties. It assumes that managers experience anxieties concerning their ability to cope with jobs and careers. This typology of purposes clearly stretches the scope of management development beyond the conventional. Lees and Mabey's multiple purposes or frames are presented in Table 1.9.

The purpose of management and leadership development can vary over time. A study published by CIPD in 2002 argued that the purpose of management development is to deliver the current business model and to contribute to developing future business models. It focuses on the supply of current and future managerial capability. We will now explore in more detail some of the justifications that are made by individuals and organisations for investment in management, leader and leadership development.

Characteristics of Managers' and Leaders' Jobs

It is argued that managers and leaders carry a different and more complex burden than other employees. They are accountable and responsible for ensuring that employees have the knowledge and skills required to perform their jobs and ensure that human resources are appropriately integrated so the organisation can achieve its objectives. Managerial work is rather fragmented, ad hoc and challenging. Doyle (2000) argued that managers find themselves in a cycle of demands, expectations and challenges. Managerial effectiveness is complex and difficult to explain. To understand a manager's job fully, one first needs to understand the context in which the manager and the organisation operate. Specific aspects of context that are relevant include the strategic direction of the organisation, its technology, its human and financial resources and structure. This complexity raises important skill needs and demands for managers and suggests that the majority of managers may not initially have the profile of competencies necessary for the role. Investment in management and leadership development therefore represents an important strategy in enabling managers to cope with complexity and ambiguity.

EXHIBIT 1.1

The Leadership Skills Strataplex

Mumford, Campion and Morgeson argue that leadership skills are stratified by organisational level. They formulate the term 'strataplex' to capture the stratified and complex nature of leadership requirements, suggesting four triangles representing four categories of leadership skill requirements. Dotted lines indicate the skill requirements at different organisational levels. The area subsumed in each successive triangle suggests the amount of leadership skill that will be required at each job level.

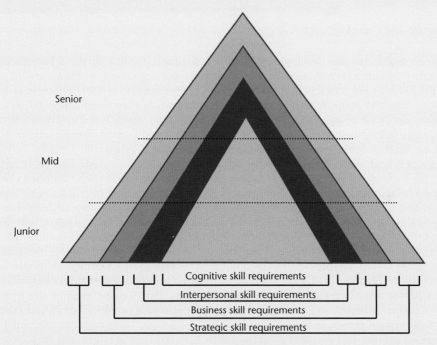

They identify four categories of skills that are required in different proportions at different levels of management:

- **Cognitive skills:** Cognitive skills represent the foundation of leadership. These skills are defined in terms of basic cognitive capabilities and learning capacities and are integral to effective leadership. Typical skills include writing, active listening and reading comprehension. Another cognitive skill focuses on the capacity to adapt and learn. This skill is facilitated by active learning which enables leaders to work with new information and understand its implications. Active learning skills enable leaders to deal with dynamic and non-routine situations.

- **Interpersonal skills:** Interpersonal skills focus on the need for the leader to interact with and influence others. It is a complex cluster of skills. Examples include social perceptiveness, negotiation skills, persuasion skills and skills that enable the co-ordination of actions.
- **Business skills:** Business skills focus on skills related to specific functional areas. These skills provide the context in which managers and leaders carry out their work. Typical business skills include the management of physical resources, the management of human resources and functional resources and skills in operational analysis.
- **Strategic skills:** Strategic skills are conceptual in nature and enable leaders to understand complexity, deal with ambiguity and articulate a vision of the future. Strategic skills are a complex, difficult to develop category and include such skills as visioning, systems understanding, problem analysis, root cause analysis and the selection of solutions.

Mumford, Campion and Morgeson found that jobs at higher levels of the organisation have significantly greater overall leadership requirements. Cognitive and interpersonal skills are required to a greater degree than business and strategic skills. Business and strategic skills are in demand at high levels of management. Cognitive skills do not, however, diminish in importance at higher levels of leadership. The more fundamental skills serve as a foundation for the development of the more complex leadership skills. Leadership development initiatives should focus on the continual refinement of existing skills as well as the development of new skills.

Source: Mumford, Campion and Morgeson (2007)

Strategic Fit and Competitive Advantage

Management and leadership development has a role to play in facilitating the achievement of fit between managerial resources and the strategy of the organisation. Management and leadership development provides organisations with the potential to outperform competitors. However, in order to be effective it must be coupled with other human resources practices such as selection, performance management and talent management. There is debate about whether or not strategy influences management development, which represents the more conservative position, or whether management development can influence strategy.

Management and leadership development can be considered as initiatives designed to enhance the managerial skill pool and make it unique and valuable. Lepak and Snell (1999) suggested a human resource architecture that is premised on the idea that not all employees possess knowledge and skills of equal strategic importance. They advocate internalisation, which refers to the continuous internal development of employees who possess unique skills and capabilities that are highly valued by the organisation and that are not readily available externally. It is appropriate to have a strong internalisation focus on managers.

Management and leadership development has a lot to offer in terms of improving strategic decision-making. Garavan *et al.* (1999) noted that for an organisation to be successful, it is vital that people are integrated with the firm's strategy. This linkage enables the firm to achieve sustained competitive advantage. This point is also supported by Boxall and Purcell (2003), who argued that it is imperative in today's dynamic business environment that organisations achieve and preserve a successful fit between their strategy and their human resources. Strategic management and leadership development should be seen as an integrated part of a firm's competitive strategy; hence the fundamental objective is to ensure that as innovations and products are developed managers possess the necessary skills, abilities, knowledge and attitudes to implement the required strategy successfully. Hussey (1988) argued that in order for management development to contribute to the attainment of organisational objectives, it needs to focus on organisational needs, which implies that development needs have to be related to an understanding of the organisation's aims, strategy, the business environment and the desired firm culture.

Numerous commentators emphasise the need to link management and leadership development with strategy. Seibert *et al.* (1995) noted that the aim of aligning management development with strategy is to enable the organisation to anticipate the skills that will be essential to managers in the future and to develop them in advance of them being required. Winterton and Winterton (1997) suggested that effective alignment of management and leadership development with business strategy would result in signgicant financial improvements.

Traditional management and leadership development focused on individual effectiveness, whereas management and leadership development programmes linked to business strategy are focused on organisational effectiveness. The new approach is to 'analyse the organisation's ability to implement strategy and deal with business challenges' and then to implement development interventions to address those weaknesses; hence the organisation will gain a better understanding of its external environment. Aligning management development with strategy may have a positive effect for HRD practitioners. They may find it easier to justify management development budgets because 'the content of management development relates specifically to the organisation's vision, its operating strategies and its short-term objectives'.

Thomas and Ramaswamy (1996) stressed the importance of achieving a fit between managerial characteristics, management development and strategy. They suggested that if a correct fit is not achieved it will have negative performance implications for the organisation, because it will result in conflict between the competencies of the organisation and the decisions taken by managers.

Despite the evidence advocating a link between management and leadership development and strategy, many organisations continue to make the mistake of not integrating their management and leadership development activities with the overall strategic goals of the organisation. Miller (1991) noted that in the UK 'few companies have yet integrated it into their strategic planning process'. Winterton and Winterton (1996) noted that the percentage of UK business organisations in which management development was explicitly linked to organisational strategy increased from 34 per cent to 54 per cent in a six-year period. This led Storey *et al.* (1997) to declare that management and leadership development had gone through a revolution and 'the whole concept of management development has shifted'. However, it is still unclear whether management development 'may at last be fulfilling its role as a strategic tool for organisations and growing in significance as a contributor to enhanced organisational performance'. In terms of aligning management and leadership development with strategy, it would seem appropriate to quote a party slogan: 'a lot done, more to do'.

The link between management and leadership development and business performance is consistently highlighted. As we shall explore in Chapter Four, it is often more talked about than proved. The arguments made for alignment are, however, convincing. Siebert and Hall (1995) argued that effective alignment will ensure that the organisation is able to anticipate the skills that are essential to ensure that it grows. Winterton and Winterton (1997) anticipated that effective alignment would result in both better business performance and higher profitability. Management, leader and leadership development activities have traditionally focused on individual effectiveness, whereas a strategic approach seeks to make explicit links between investment in development activities and organisational effectiveness. A strategic approach, which we consider in detail in Chapter Four, advocates that organisational effectiveness should start with an analysis of an organisation's ability to implement its strategy and deal with business challenges that lie ahead. Development activities that address both weaknesses and opportunities can then be designed and implemented.

Achieving fit between managerial characteristics and competencies and management and leadership development strategy is a particular challenge for organisations. Inappropriate fit will probably have negative performance implications for the organisation. Development strategies need to take account of fit at the strategic level and at the level of the manager, or there may be conflicts between the competencies required by the organisation, the decisions taken by managers and the strategies selected to develop managers.

Even though there is evidence highlighting links between management and leadership development and strategy, many organisations invest in development activities that are not related to the strategic goals of the organisation. Scientific and rigorous evidence is difficult to find: the majority of the evidence is based on self-reports. Studies by Miller (1991), Winterton and Winterton (1996), Storey, Edwards and Sisson (1997) and Conway and Guest (2002) highlight that organisations in the UK and Ireland have made progressive improvements in making explicit links between development and business strategies.

Mabey and Finch-Lees (2008), among others, highlight that management and leadership development has experienced a revolution and it may now be fulfilling its role as a strategic tool to achieve growth and profitability. Whether management and leadership development is effective depends on how it is viewed. It may be viewed as part of a wider HRM package and it may be posited that there is a universal 'recipe' for achieving success. Alternatively, it may be considered from a contingent perspective, whereby management and leadership development is packaged to address the contingencies of the organisation.

Leadership Development and Organisation Socialisation

The attention paid to organisation socialisation has increased significantly in recent years. Organisation socialisation represents the learning process by which newcomers develop attitudes and behaviours that are necessary to function as a fully fledged member of the organisation (Ardts *et al.* 2001). Management, leader and leadership development can be used as a means of transmitting organisational culture and values. It can be used as a strategy to socialise managers into a particular corporate ethos and match their personal values with those of the organisation. One of the problems with hiring new managers is that they may not be well-prepared for their task and new identities as managers, but will still be expected to propagate the organisation's values. 'Attitudinal structuring' can greatly help an organisation to instill its values into managers and build a common identity.

It has been suggested that having such a purpose for management and leadership development helps to maintain order and minimise chaos in organisations. This is especially true for large organisations. Lees (1992), however, warned of the dangers associated with this approach. It may help managers to work better together as a team, but it may also discourage innovation and diversity of thinking. The challenge facing organisations in this respect is how to achieve an appropriate balance between instilling similar values and beliefs in managers and encouraging a certain degree of independent thinking.

A more contemporary approach, known as 'reverse socialisation', was advocated by Paauwe and Williams (2001). The logic behind this approach is to recruit managers from outside the organisation rather than internally. Organisations may implement this strategy in order to change an existing culture and/or to introduce fresh thinking. However, most organisations rely on traditional forms of socialisation because they are often concerned about the risks inherent in reverse socialisation.

Leadership Development, Succession and Talent Management

Succession and talent management have become an increasingly important part of successful organisational growth. Organisations now pay attention to ensuring that they have the right people with the appropriate skills, attitudes and behaviours in the right place to meet organisational needs (Aitchison 2004). These processes frequently focus on the perceived need to grow managers internally (Garavan *et al.* 1999). In this case, the responsibility for management, leader and leadership development rests firmly with managers themselves. It is largely up to managers to decide exactly what is necessary to facilitate self-development. Most of this development is assumed to happen in the real work context rather than through formal interventions. Organisations that place a strong emphasis on succession planning tend to have a 'make' rather than 'buy' approach to human resourcing. They believe that in the long run this will give them competitive advantage over rivals who focus on buying in talent.

Succession and talent management are considered crucial both from an external and an internal perspective. Viewed externally, it is an indicator of the degree to which leadership is focused on the future. The quality and outcomes of the process are important indicators of the future health of the organisation. Internally effective succession planning is a key driver of manager retention. Retaining talented managers is critical given the limited supply of such individuals in the labour market. Where organisations are explicit about the capabilities sought in future leaders, they create a 'cultural glue' that becomes part of the employer brand (Aitchison 2004). McMaster (2002) emphasised the need for such planning in an increasingly tight labour market. He asked: why recruit managers when you can identify, train and promote talent from within?

Table 1.7 provides a summary of the key arguments in favour of investment in management development.

Table 1.7: Reasons for Investment in Management, Leader and Leadership Development

- A strategy to engineer, create and shape organisation change and, in particular, to manage culture change
- A motivational tool to encourage managers to accept the need to change their attitudes and improve their knowledge and skills in order to perform more effectively
- A strategy to facilitate organisational renewal and to grow leadership and fulfil the organisation's mission
- A process to ensure organisational vigour, create a competitive edge, develop a flow of talent and enhance the lives of people in the organisation
- A means of obtaining the best fit between managers' and leaders' capabilities and attitudes and the organisation
- A tool in pursuit of quality, cost reduction and profitability through a focus on excellence
- A strategy to forge a common identity, philosophy and management style
- A system to draw input from the organisational environment in the form of human resource and organisational diagnoses and to create outputs in the form of developed managers
- A means to enable the organisation to anticipate the skills that will be essential to managers in the future, thereby assuring competitive advantage
- A strategy to enable the organisation to maintain order and minimise chaos

Sources: Adapted from Antonacopoulou (1999), Aitchison (2004), Lees (1992), Seibert *et al.* (1995), Garavan *et al.* (1999)

Perspectives on Management, Leader and Leadership Development

There are divergent views about the nature of management, leader and leadership development, and the literature contains a multiplicity of perspectives, conceptualisations and models. We focus here on explaining a number of frameworks that will help an understanding of competing interpretations of management, leader and leadership development.

The Beardwell and Holden Model

Beardwell, Holden and Clayton (2004) argue that management and leadership development can be understood from the perspectives of strategy, style and outcomes.

Management and Leadership Development as Strategy

After the publication of critical reports in both Ireland and the UK in the late 1980s and early 1990s, management and leadership development began to move up organisations' agendas. Organisations are now more willing to invest in leadership and to show more commitment to the development of managers. There is some debate about the extent to which management and leadership development can help organisations to achieve their strategic objectives. This debate has focused on inputs that management and leadership development can make, including the possibility of a significant contribution to talent and succession management.

The notion that managers and leaders contribute to competitive advantage is a strong theme within a strategy framework. Significant advantages can derive from the expertise of leaders and their adaptability, which allows organisations some degree of strategic flexibility. Management and leadership development can also enhance the commitment of managers and leaders to the organisation's business plans and goals.

Management and Leadership Development as Style

Management and leadership development can be analysed from a style perspective. This concerns the extent to which it is considered 'hard' or 'soft' in its intent. It is considered a 'hard' activity when, for example, it emphasises the utilisation of managers and is closely aligned with the strategic goals of the organisation. Some leadership development initiatives are used to ensure that the organisation is lean and efficient. In this case there is a strong emphasis on cost minimisation. This approach pays little attention to the priorities and perspectives of individual managers.

'Soft' approaches place more emphasis on the needs of individual managers. The organisation's agenda comprises trust, commitment and communication. Organisations that practise 'soft' approaches are more likely to implement development strategies that emphasise self-awareness, individual development planning and customised development interventions such as coaching and mentoring. In practice, 'soft' and 'hard' approaches sometimes overlap.

Ulrich, Younger and Brockbank (2008) proposed an alternative style typology. He focused on practitioner roles within HR and identified four roles the management development practitioner can adopt. The first involves the specialist taking on the role of 'employee champion'. This requires the management development specialist to articulate the perspective of manager and ensure that individual needs are addressed in management and leadership development provision. The practitioner essentially operates in a service and support capacity and it is unlikely that management and leadership development is perceived to add value. This role derives form the welfare tradition of HR.

Kirkbride (2003) argued that management and leadership development practitioners frequently adopt this role. It is manifested in the concern of specialists to receive positive participant feedback. They focus on the needs of individuals rather than the more general needs of the organisation. At the most basic level specialists spend time providing training and development that managers want or need. This style of management and leadership development often results in interventions that are safe and non-threatening.

Ulrich and Kirkbride identified a second style of administrative expertise, in which the specialist focuses on process efficiency, the needs of the organisation and supporting line managers. This style involves providing standardised management and leadership development practices and services. Success is measured by the ability of specialists to deliver high-quality development at the lowest cost. This style directs specialists towards an operational role. They will spend a great deal of time on venue booking, sending out joining instructions and issuing pre-work. Their work will also include elements of training, record-keeping and data analysis. This style may be adopted by specialists starting out in their career or may be appropriate where management development is at an early stage in the life cycle of the company.

The third style posits that specialists act as 'agents for change'. They are expected to add value to the organisation. The 'agent for change' role focuses on people rather than process and the specialist is expected to focus on people as a collective resource. This involves identifying opportunities for change and implementing change. Specialists will be expected to demonstrate skills in facilitation, coaching and championing change.

The fourth style requires specialists to act as a 'strategic partner', which will be discussed in more detail in Chapter Five. The essential requirement of this style is for specialists to become fully contributing members of the top management team. They are expected to bring expertise in management and leadership development to the top table and to demonstrate how management and leadership development can add value and supply the organisation with a source of competitive advantage. Kirkbride (2003) argued that specialists would need to spend a significant amount of their time interacting with key decision-makers in the organisation, although Staunton and Giles (2001) argued that in reality few specialists are able to operate at this level.

Management and Leadership Development as Outcome

An outcome approach focuses on the outcomes that derive from investment in management and leadership development. Management and leadership development has the potential to impact on individual and organisational performance but this is a contested issue, as we will explain in Chapter Four.

The work of Huselid (1995) and West and Patterson (1997) suggested that management and leadership development was in isolation unlikely to result in significant outcomes for organisations. A bundle of HR practices that includes management and leadership development is likely to be more effective.

The measurement of the impact of management and leadership development on organisational performance is problematic. There is a range of opinions about the measures that should be used to evaluate its impact and the relative importance of management and leadership development when it is combined with other HR practices. A major question concerns the causal relationship between investment in management and leadership development and organisational performance. Does investment in management and leadership development lead to better individual and organisational performance or is it the case that the best-performing organisations are more likely to invest in management and leadership development?

Talbot's Typology of Management and Leadership Development

Talbot (1997) utilised the conceptual framework proposed by Kolb (1984) to suggest four approaches to management development: abstract conceptualisation (the traditional model); active experimentation (the project and consultancy model); concrete experience (the competence model); and reflection (reflective practitioner personal development model).

The Traditional Model (Abstract Conceptualisation)

An abstract conceptualisation approach focuses on a model of management as an organisational function rather than as a function of individual managers, and places considerable emphasis on formal management education as the primary approach to management and leadership development. The approach assumes that management and leadership can be taught in classroom settings, and embraces knowledge and skills in areas such as strategy, functional management and management skills. Managers are expected to know something about all aspects of management and to learn analytical skills, which are best developed through academic instruction. Development depends on external experts who have key knowledge and expertise, and the knowledge of theory and cognitive skills are core attributes of effective management.

The Action Learning, Project and Consultancy-Based Model (Active Experimentation)
An active experimentation approach takes the view that the best opportunities for learning occur in the workplace. Projects, which may be based on familiar or unfamiliar tasks and settings, are central to this approach. The action learning and project consultancy approach uses other strategies such as consultancy assignments and self-managed learning initiatives. The emphasis in all these strategies is on active experimentation, and peer learning, self-knowledge and self-assessment, rather than expert knowledge or opinion, are highlighted. It emphasises questioning skills and the ability to challenge existing practices, develop new practices and deal with new problems in context-specific ways.

The Competence Approach (Concrete Experience)
We discuss the competence and competency approach in more detail in Chapter Six. This approach rests on a number of important assumptions:

- The competencies that make up managing are relatively independent of one another.
- It is possible to identify key outputs from the utilisation of managerial competencies.
- The possession of managerial competence is an important factor in ensuring increased organisational effectiveness.
- Managerial competence represents a stabilising influence in organisations.
- The demonstration of a competence is not impacted by a manager's perceptions of context. Competence operates independent of context.
- The demonstration of a competence by a manager operates independently of competencies demonstrated by peers, direct reports and superiors.
- Managerial competences can be acquired and demonstrated across a wide range of situations.

A competence approach values practice and evidence of practice and considers management theory of little value. It is a pragmatic approach and shows concern for cognitive development and intellectualism.

The Reflective Practicum and Professional Development Model (Reflection)
A reflective practice approach emphasises development by means of guided and supervised practice, a concept that refers to a setting designed for the task of learning a practice. The characteristics of the setting approximate to the practice world. This approach emphasises professional and tacit knowledge acquired through a hierarchical, guided mentoring system as the key to development. It has a strong retrospective emphasis and differs from an action approach, which is more prospective and peer-group focused. It differs from the competence approach by virtue of its strong emphasis on reflection and development. Unlike the traditional approach, it emphasises tacit and uncodified knowledge rather than the coded and conscious knowledge transmitted in an academic setting.

Table 1.8: Talbot's Model of Management and Leadership Development

Aspect of Kolb's Learning Cycle	Description	View of Leadership Development	Advantages	Disadvantages
Abstract Conceptualisation	• Traditional management education and MBAs. • Focuses on theory and educating the manager on a broad range of topics. • Excellent for building manager's knowledge and broadening perceptions. • Focuses more on individual personal development than organisational performance.	• Considers education the core and foundation phase.	• Educated managers are better able to network and solve problems more effectively. • Broadens the perspectives of managers.	• Focuses too much on theory as opposed to practice. • Contains too much analysis and prescription as opposed to learning how the organisation really works. • Can be very costly to implement where the organisation has large pool of managers.
Concrete Experience	• Competence approach focuses on the experience of the manager, e.g. through job rotation/ temporary placement. • Learning and assessment is central to manager's performance. • Management goals of the organisation considered more important than personal development of the individual.	• Considers LD to focus too much on theory and not enough on what managers actually work at. • Believes formal LD is ancillary to concrete experience.	• Allows for clear objectives to be set and worked towards. • Learning can be assessed through clear objectives	• Favours the practical manager above the intellectual manager. • Competency approach can be inappropriate if the analysis undertaken is incorrect or faulty.

Aspect of Kolb's Learning Cycle	Description	View of Management Development	Advantages	Disadvantages
Active Experimentation	• Learning within the organisation usually while at work. • Includes action learning. • Rejects traditional leadership development and the role of formal knowledge and opinion. • Objectives of the organisation considered more important than personal development of the individual.	• Formal leadership development secondary to actual experience. • Development on the job provides the best opportunities to develop managers.	• Facilitates problem-solving through self-questioning and decision-making. • Real learning takes place in the role.	• Ignores the abstract conceptualisation part of Kolb's cycle which would leave many managers lacking in formal knowledge.
Reflective Observation	• Learning through reflection on a manager's own work. • Advocates that the manager reflects critically on practice and learns from this. • It focuses on the personal development of the manager.	• Formal leadership development provides a foundation for reflection.	• Encourages the manager's use of tacit knowledge. • Enhances the impact of each of the other parts of the cycle. • Inexpensive for the organisation as managers learn by doing.	• For effective use of this approach, close supervision of the learning manager is required. • Reflection on practice is a powerful concept, but very difficult for the busy manager to find the time to do.

Source: Adapted from Talbot (1997)

The Mabey Model

Mabey (2003) suggested that human resource development and, by extension, management and leadership development, can be framed in a number of ways. He draws on the work of Bolman and Deal (1997) and identifies four possible frames: structural, human resource, political and symbolic. Mabey made a very important contribution to our understanding of the variety of lenses through which it is possible to analyse management and leadership development. Table 1.9 below provides a summary of these concepts when applied to management and leadership development.

The Structural Frame

This represents a dominant discourse in the current management and leadership development literature. Management and leadership development is primarily about enhancing the capability of managers in order to achieve the strategic objectives of the organisation.

Management and leadership development is designed to address gaps in current performance and it is likely that most of the provision will be structured and formal. We will explore the notion of fit in greater detail in Chapter Four. However, it is sufficient to say at this point that a key role for management and leadership development is to ensure that the organisation's structure and leadership capabilities are aligned to the external environment. Many organisations work within a structural frame but, as we will see later in this chapter, it is possible to question the underlying rationality of this frame or consider it to be unreliable.

The Human Resource Frame

The focus of the human resource frame is on understanding the exchange between what is required by the organisation and what the manager has to offer. In the management and leadership development context, the emphasis is on the needs and priorities of the individual manager. Development is likely to be less structured and more customised. It may include activities such as a consultancy project, a stretch assignment or mentoring/coaching support. It is very much influenced by the ideas of Rogers (1986), who advocated freedom of choice in respect of what is learned and how it is learned. The task of the organisation is to develop conditions that are conducive to individual learning. This frame finds expression in concepts such as self-directed development.

However, the reality for many organisations is that leadership development provision has an organisational focus, with the result that organisations ultimately control what managers learn. Mabey (2003) criticised a human resource frame for its lack of attention to the political dimensions of management and leadership development.

Table 1.9: A Frames Approach to Management and Leadership Development

	Structural Frame	HR Frame	Political Frame	Symbolic Frame
Derived From	• Intellectual capital theory • Open-systems theory • Contingency theory	• Social, psychological theories which inform learning theory • Resource-based view of the organisation	• Resource-dependent theory • Critical management theory • Application of process theory	• Institutional theory • Symbolic interactionism
Central Proposition	• Focus on organisation • LC serves to maximise employee capabilities to achieve organisational objectives (means-end calculation) • Performance imperative superior to all others	• Focus on individual • Individualistic aspects of learning highlighted through acknowledgment of learner autonomy and intrinsic motivation • LD as a vehicle for mutual exchange between what the organisation needs and what the individual has to offer	• Focus on power and politics • LD assumed value-free and desirable for all stakeholders, but divergence of interests inherent between stakeholders in organisations • Argues that all organisational activities and processes reflect aims of dominant coalitions of interests	• Focus on reinforcing organisational values • Organisational culture consists of values, beliefs and rituals • Organisational processes, including decision-making, are cultural in nature • LD can be utilised as a self-reinforcing cultural mechanism

	Structural Frame	HR Frame	Political Frame	Symbolic Frame
Assumptions of Framework	• Organisations are dynamic, goal-directed, bounded and rational entities • People exist to 'serve' the organisation and are compliant • Needs and interests of organisation and employee are compatible • Employees have the capability and willingness to learn • LD goal is to achieve equilibrium	• Organisations provide continuous learning opportunities for individuals to develop themselves through the facilitation of a learning culture • Utilisation of opportunities is contingent on the individual employee's motivation to learn. • LD goal is to tap talents of employees for the greater good of the organisation	• Pursuit of order and predictability in organisational performance is influenced by power distribution within the organisation • Performance imperative replaced by the elevation of partisan rights • Politicking can occur at multiple levels and within or through any LD activity whether formal, informal or non-formal	• LD goal is to enable the organisation to increase its legitimacy as perceived by its internal and external stakeholders
Purposes and Type of LD	• To address the internal performance gap; to achieve organisational 'fit' with external environment • Conformist in nature and supports dominant organisational ideology • Structured and formal interventions to facilitate continuous learning, orchestrated by the organisation	• To maintain employee motivation and satisfaction • Embedded learning within daily routines serves as a resource mobility barrier which is difficult to imitate • Although individual goals predominate, LD is conformist in nature and supports dominant organisational ideology • LD interventions can be formal and structured • Acknowledges that learning can also occur through informal and incidental learning strategies • Idea of continuous learning process therefore dominates	• Primarily viewed by dominant coalitions as ways to achieve increased power, influence, and/or legitimacy through the acquisition of unique or novel knowledge and skills • Bounded emancipation challenges dominant organisational ideology in favour of those who wield sufficient power	• To communicate cultural messages about what is important, thereby creating organisational solidarity and cohesion • Conformist in nature and supports dominant organisational ideology • Use of symbols and stories that have currency in the organisation • Diffused through formal and informal learning experiences • Cultural change programmes focus on this frame.

	Structural Frame	HR Frame	Political Frame	Symbolic Frame
Implications for LD Practitioners	• Accurate identification of knowledge and skills gaps which need to be addressed of paramount importance • How to motivate and develop employees to retain their expertise?	• Accurate identification of ways in which employees and organisations acquire new knowledge, skills and behaviours to reinforce the learning capacity of the organisation	• An understanding of how socially divisive unequal power relations in an organisation can be reinforced through LD is imperative (for example, specific target populations)	• Primary consideration is how to construct 'reality' through utilisation of stories and symbols in tandem with content of initiative to reduce diverse interpretations and reinforce desired organisational message
Evaluation Strategy	• Analyse impact on the way people perform • Assess LD outcomes in terms of increased productivity, efficiency and profitability for the organisation	• Analyse impact on ongoing organisational processes • Assess LD outcomes in terms of increased employee creativity and ingenuity, which optimise organisational learning capacity	• Analyse who has achieved dominance and empowerment through LD activities • Assess degree to which multilevel synergies have been achieved within the organisation – are these constructive or destructive?	• Assess the degree to which cultural norms have become embedded throughout the organisation
Critique	• Most identifiable framework, although criticised as unrealistic because: • Unitarist assumption fails to acknowledge multiplicity of interests and politicking which exists within organisations • This depends on ability of LD professionals to translate business priorities into appropriate LD goals or to analyse external environmental imperatives.	• Provides insight into goals and methods of learning • Assumes individual learning serves exclusively organisational purposes which means that the organisation remains in control of the learning process • Little attention paid to competing interests of stakeholders or political dimensions of training	• Pluralist assumption acknowledges differing and competing stakeholder interests in organisations • Questions the LD performance imperative • Little empirical evidence to systematically track multiple levers of power and influence	• Provides explanation through the use of cultural norms as to why certain LD interventions encounter approval or irrational resistance • Little empirical evidence available which utilises the framework as a basis for analysis of LD

The Political Frame

The political frame represents a less frequently discussed perspective in the management and leadership development literature. Mabey considered it a useful perspective from which to understand and explain why and how management and leadership development happens. It suggests that organisations, political arenas and coalitions of interest form around particular beliefs and perceptions of reality. Discussions concerning management and leadership development are based on power. Management and leadership development is provided, therefore, to meet the needs and interests of certain groups. The frame highlights that many organisational processes are irrational, ambiguous and uncertain. It questions the performance imperative of the structural frame. It recognises that motivation for management development is derived from a multiplicity of forces and processes.

The Symbolic Frame

The symbolic frame also challenges the rationality of organisational decision-making. It is less preoccupied with the performance imperatives, focusing instead on the meanings that are attached to management and leadership development. It suggests that management and leadership development is a social construction that is as much about meaning as it is about content, and represents a strategy through which the organisation can communicate the culture of the organisation. Mabey also viewed management and leadership development as a strategy for conferring status and initiating managers into the elite. It is arguable that many of the ideas underpinning talent-management processes fit within a symbolic frame.

Turnbull (2002) highlighted that the symbolic frame is infrequently used to understand management and leadership development processes.

Burgoyne and Reynolds' Arena Thesis

Burgoyne and Reynolds (1997) argued that a majority of management and leadership development models advocate a unitary perspective. This, they suggested, oversimplifies the process of management and leadership development in organisations. They saw too much preoccupation with behavioural issues and insufficient focus on the cognitive and symbolic dimension of management and leadership development. There is too much focus on the ideal and not enough on the reality.

The arena thesis is pluralist, and conceptualises management and leadership development as having conflicting purposes, perspectives and values. The concept of an arena has six key characteristics:

- It represents a place where differences between stakeholders are discussed, fought over, contested, reconciled and reconfigured.
- The arena is visible in that it is possible for other parties to become aware of the key differences and why they occur.
- The arena is accessible in the sense that observers can become participants and they achieve awareness of the issues that they want to be involved in.
- Individuals take on 'roles' and 'scripts' which influence how conflict is manifested and resolved. These roles and scripts are an important feature of organisations.
- The staging of these activities, having regard to both location and time, can have an important influence on how they are resolved.
- It is possible to manage the arena. This can be achieved through ensuring that differences are aired and that opportunities for compromise and synergy are not lost.

An arena thesis has perhaps its most significant contribution to make in helping us understand why management and leadership development programmes are supported or resisted. It is likely that various stakeholders may coalesce around a particular issue or group of issues and that elements of both convergence and divergence will always exist. It is possible for different stakeholders to support a particular management and leadership development initiative for entirely different reasons.

A central concept of an arena thesis is that of legitimacy, which Burgoyne and Reynolds defined as a 'set of constitutive beliefs that are the primary driver for institutional processes'. It is viewed as a mechanism to control actors and constrain conflicts between different stakeholders. Table 1.10 suggests a list of reasons why different stakeholders might support or block a management and leadership development initiative.

Table 1.10: Organisational Stakeholders' Rationale for Supporting or Blocking a Management and Leadership Development Intervention

Stakeholder	Rationale for Supporting	Rationale for Blocking
Managers or Potential Managers as Participants	• Opportunity for personal development • Improved employability and marketability • Opportunity to get away from the workplace • Recognition of importance of individual to the organisation • Potential springboard for promotion	• Have too much work and too little time for development • Perceive development as a waste of time or energy • Fear learning and lack interest in learning • Have little interest in career advancement
Direct Reports	• Expectation of better-quality supervision and leadership • Recognition that the team is important to organisational effectiveness • Strong personal commitment to learning	• Resist organisational change • Do not value leadership or supervision • Perceive learning and development as a waste of time and money • Perceive that the prescribed development initiative is inappropriate
Peers	• Perceive the intervention as a possible means of participating in development • Intervention may address team performance problems • Believe in the value of learning and development	• Believe that internention will result in an excessive workload due to manager absence • Perceive that the peer manager is preferred for advancement • In order to prevent a peer from participating in the development activity • View development as a waste of time and money • Believe that development should focus on the team rather than the individual

Stakeholder	Rationale for Supporting	Rationale for Blocking
Line Managers	• Want a quick solution to performance problems • View learning and development as an incentive for the team • View learning and development as a measure of commitment of organisation to the employees • Concerned with the bench strength of the management team	• View learning and development as a waste of time and money • Production or target takes priority over development • Have little interest in learning and development • Believe that the best learning is day-to-day experience • Consider the intervention to be inappropriate
Top Team or Senior Managers	• View management and leadership development as a mechanism to convey particular messages to managers • Committed to developing the leadership bench strength of the organisation • Believe in the potential for improved financial performance • Wish to demonstrate action to other stakeholders	• Do not see a link with the bottom line • View the solution as inappropriate • Has limited interest in management and leadership development • Intervention not consistent with the views of the top team • Too much focus on cost-efficiency rather than effectiveness • Unwilling to be accountable for management and leadership development
The Board	• Wishes the company to be viewed as an employer of choice • Perceives intervention as concrete means of demonstrating support for managers • Communicates a strong message to the organisation • Strong concern with succession and talent process • Concerned with improved financial performance	• Views development as an overhead • Does not fully understand the concepts of management and leadership development • Views management and leadership development as disruptive to organisation • Not concerned with image in the labour market
External Consultants	• Major financial opportunity • Helps to build customer base and reputation • Potential for further opportunities within the organisation	• Inadequate financial opportunity • Client is not sufficiently prestigious • Limited further business opportunities • Future of the programme could undermine credibility of consultant

A Piecemeal Approach

Commentators are critical of the piecemeal and fragmented way in which many organisations approach management and leadership development. Burgoyne (1988) and Mole (1996), for example, criticised organisations for having an off-the-shelf approach to delivery of management development. A piecemeal approach represents an easy solution to a particular problem, rather than a commitment to a long-term and embedded strategy.

A piecemeal approach is typically found in organisations that have resource constraints, lack awareness of the potential of management and leadership development and focus on once-off development initiatives. This fragmented or discrete approach to management development is commonplace in SMIs in Ireland. Commentators argue that such an approach is a significant contributor to the failure of management development to meet expectations. Mumford and Gold (2004) considered this approach to be a waste of investment, time and effort. It may also lead to a situation where the commitment of managers to development can be undermined.

Piecemeal approaches to management and leadership development have a number of common characteristics:

- The lack of a management and leadership development infrastructure. It is not linked to business strategy and there is a lack of overall direction or philosophy underpinning its provision. Where management and leadership development does exist, it is not strategically integrated.
- It will focus almost exclusively on the needs of the organisation. It is unlikely to address the needs and learning aspirations of individuals and groups.
- Development provision is largely confined to a narrow range of strategies, i.e. formal off-the-shelf internal or external programmes which are generic in nature.
- Espoused support may exist for management and leadership development. This can arise out of the belief that it is a good thing to be doing. It may occur irrespective of organisational needs.
- Management and leadership development initiatives are more likely to be wasted because they are more likely to be used as solutions to the wrong problem.
- There is a lack of common vision among those responsible for management development. Some managers may view management and leadership development as central to their job, whereas others may see it as peripheral or even, perhaps, a nuisance.
- There is a lack of systematic evaluation, with the result that future initiatives also lack direction and clearly defined objectives.

It can be difficult for organisations to break out of piecemeal approaches. Molander and Winterton (1994) suggested that it is necessary to focus on the organisation rather than simply getting the attention of individual managers. It will usually require an organisation-wide assessment of the learning culture and the identification of elements which need to be changed.

An Open Systems Approach

A systems perspective provides a framework for understanding and managing the interactions and interdependencies that are characteristic of organisations. Doyle (1995; 1997) was a major proponent of the systems perspective. He argued that it is possible to view management and leadership development as a sub-system that operates within a wider organisational system. Management and leadership development has a continuous and dynamic interaction with a variety of internal and external variables.

Figure 1.1 on page 34 shows how a systems perspective can be used to understand the operation of management and leadership development in organisations. It illustrates that doubts about the value of investing in management and leadership development may be negatively reinforced by questions concerning the credibility of the management and leadership development specialist. These perceptions are further reinforced by the perceived incapacity of the specialist to think strategically and work within the politics of the organisation.

A central premise of an open systems perspective is that management and leadership development consists of both systems and process elements. It is composed of identifiable components that interact with one another. Inputs are transformed by various processes which, in turn, lead to outcomes such as increased individual and organisational effectiveness.

Figure 1.1: Negative Causal Loops Undermining the Efficacy of Management Development

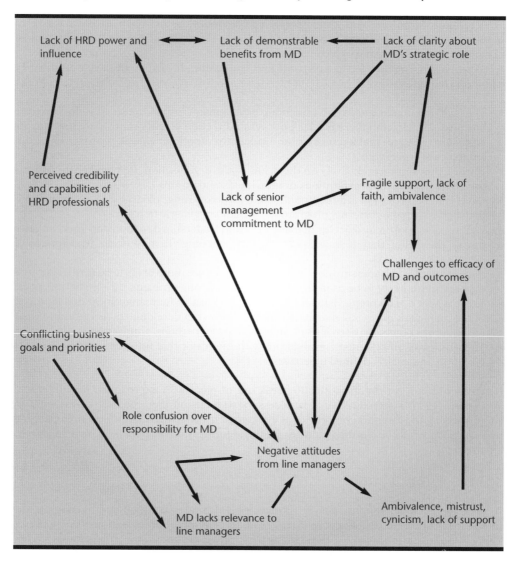

An open systems perspective highlights a number of significant inputs. These include the cultural sub-system, which is made up of prevailing ideologies, values and beliefs within the organisation. Some organisations may use management and leadership development interventions as strategies to reinforce or change the cultural sub-system. Other key input components include the strategic objectives of the organisation, the psychological contracts of managers, existing skills and knowledge, and the technological and structural sub-system. An open-systems approach reinforces the idea that management and leadership development is integrated with and therefore mutually dependent upon other organisational subsystems, activities and processes.

It enhances our understanding of management development in organisations in a number of ways:

- It helps to reveal how the organisational context impacts on the management and leadership development process. It is likely to lead to a more rigorous and detailed assessment of the impact of particular development initiatives.
- It has the potential to help practitioners to develop a set of strategies, policies and plans that are customised to the organisational context and reflect the core values and philosophy of the organisation.
- It reinforces the notion that if you develop managers you are also developing the organisation. An open-systems approach makes more explicit the ways in which management development contributes to overall organisational and individual effectiveness.
- It reinforces the notion that management development initiatives need to be adaptable, flexible, proactive and responsive in the face of organisational change and turbulence.

A Relational Approach

Doyle (2000) suggested that organisations are evolving a more contingent perspective on management and leadership development, which advocates the shaping of management and leadership development by strategic concerns. He contended that organisations have focused too much on process issues at the expense of achieving a more sophisticated understanding of the factors impinging on management and leadership development. Table 1.11 summarises the key characteristics of a relational approach.

Table 1.11 Key Characteristics of the Relational Approach

- Pluralist arena. Diversity acknowledged and managed. Learning and development become more situated and contextually based.
- Recognition of the messy and complex nature of organisational change. Social, political and emotional issues are significant and have to be addressed. The focus is on developing wider change expertise and the ability to cope in rapidly transforming contexts.
- Control is devolved to different stakeholders. Developers must build political and social relationships. Greater awareness and skill in 'managing' as well as 'doing' development.
- Clearer delineation of roles and expectations agreed amongst stakeholders. Ownership is dispersed. LD professionals act as internal consultants. Tighter control over stakeholder responsibilities and performance.
- Criteria and measurement broadened to include a heightened awareness of the significance of softer dimensions. Success judged in wider context of 'managing' the organisational system.

A relational model suggests important implications for management and leadership development practice:

- It advocates the need for a more collaborative and shared approach. This approach has the capacity to capture a diversity of inputs and exchanges that occur between key stakeholders. Burgoyne and Jackson (1997) highlighted significant variation in interpretation of development goals and outcomes. Various stakeholders may also differ on the relative importance of different competencies. A relational approach has the effect of politicising the management and leadership development process. It suggests that the leadership development specialist needs to develop the skills to engage successfully with the politics of the organisation.
- It suggests a need to manage the diversity of stakeholder interests. The specialist may have to challenge current views and be more conceptual and systemic in his/her analysis.

It requires that specialists ask challenging questions about the level of commitment to development and how that commitment can be secured.

- The specialist needs to adopt management and leadership strategies that are pragmatic. Walton (1999) suggested that the specialist may have to use 'nudging strategies' which involve searching for points of leverage or entry. It may involve the specialist making attempts to overcome negative perceptions and barriers. Some commentators have described this strategy as customer-oriented. It involves ensuring that the outcomes of management and leadership development are aimed at delivering meaningful and attractive benefits to stakeholders. The articulation of benefits is, however, insufficient. It also requires political activity to gain support for development initiatives.

- Leadership development specialists must understand the unique context within which they operate. The analysis of context may reveal that it is a waste of time to invest in development due to the negative environment which already exists.

- A relational perspective brings power to the forefront. The specialist will only be successful where he/she can obtain and deploy sufficient power and combine these actions designed to build credibility and confidence to challenge how things are done in the organisation.

EXHIBIT 1.2

Focus on Research: Are Leaders Portable?

When a company hires a CEO from General Electric – widely considered in the USA to be a training ground for top-notch executives – the hiring company's stocks spike instantly. But not all GE alumni deliver on their promise; context is a crucial factor. When a company hires a new executive, it gets a bundle of abilities and experience. Some general management techniques transfer well to other environments, but those specific to a given company don't transfer as well. Executives from GE can, however, be relied upon to have first-rate general management skills, which accounts for the market reaction.

The different types of skills and experience which may shape performance in one job and influence performance in another include: *strategic human capital*, the individual's expertise in cutting growth, or cyclical markets; *industry human capital*, meaning technical and regulatory knowledge unique to an industry; and *relationship human capital*, the extent to which an individual manager's effectiveness can be attributed to his experience working with colleagues or as part of a team. The advantages conferred by these skills are likely to transfer between similar environments.

But even gifted executives with superlative management training don't make the best CEOs. Companies need to look beyond the corporate pedigree, however fabled. The types of skills and likely portability are better indicators of a successful match. Groysberg, McLean and Nohria (2006) highlight five different types of human capital: general management, strategic, industry relationship and company specific. General management human capital consists of the management skills to utilise a range of resources. It includes leadership and decision-making capabilities in addition to functional expertise. General management human capital is portable; however, managers are expected to develop these skills when they take on a new role or job.

Strategic human capital is the most portable of management skills. But the skills required to control costs to maintain a competitive edge in a price war are not the same as those needed to improve the top line in a growing business or balance investment against cashflow to survive in a cyclical business. These can be of no business advantage if the skills required by the company don't match the skills of the manager. John Trani is a case in point. When he left GE for Stanley Works after a long period of growth, the required skill set was different and Trani was unable to deliver the cost-cutting measures the company needed. However, a perfect match was made when Carolos Ghosn moved from

Michelin; having turned around their fortunes in Brazil and overseen the Goodrisk–Uniroyal acquisition, he became CEO at Nissan, reviving the nearly bankrupt firm by knowing exactly where and when to cut costs.

Industry human capital is another management skill. It consists of technical, regulatory and customer knowledge unique to an industry. Relevant industry experience has a positive impact on performance in a new job, but these skills don't necessarily transfer between industries. The most successful stories are from those who moved between companies in the same industry. For example, Pepsi's managers often go to other food or beverage companies, while executives from IBM or Motorola usually stay in hi-tech industries. Industry expertise includes business relationships with people like suppliers, which can offer advantage. It also includes familiarity with a customer set. When AMIS hired Christine King in 2001 they cited her relationship with customers as a great asset. Transferring between industries is a large risk, entailing a steep learning curve, a factor companies in crisis should bear in mind during the hiring process.

Relationship human capital, the social power developed over the course of a career, including ties to other executives, can prove a valuable asset. Key relationships often come from company experience and research showed that GE executives fared better when they were followed by other GE alumni. There are numerous examples of new executives populating teams with former colleagues. But an executive's social capital can help in other cases, for example in the sharing of best practice between GE and Allied Signal.

Company-specific human capital skills include tacit knowledge about a company that is generally thought to be non-portable. It includes knowledge about routines, procedures, corporate culture and informal structures. But CEOs may have an advantage over other employees by having the authority to modify the existing management system to their satisfaction. When John Trani was CEO at Stanley Works, he could have implemented some of GE's celebrated management techniques. This worked well for Stephen Bennett at Intuit who developed a leadership course, overhauled performance evaluation and worked for greater clarity in the company budgets.

When star executives leave companies, they are leaving an environment in which they are effective. The more closely the new environment resembles the old, the greater chance of success in the new position. This should be a factor considered by managers who leave jobs, as certain company-specific skills will be irrelevant in a new position. High-profile managers come at a premium, so as well as looking at corporate pedigree, hiring companies would be well advised to assess fully the portfolio of transferable human capital possessed by each CEO candidate. If the fit is less than perfect, some adjustment time will need to be allowed and some changes may be necessary to accommodate the newcomer, whether in leadership or in business systems. With careful attention to detail, a hiring company can do well wherever it sources its talent.

Source: Groysberg, McLean and Nohria (2006)

QUESTIONS

Q.1   What role can management, leader and leadership development play in developing the different forms of human capital discussed in Exhibit 1.2 above?

Q.2   What types of approaches or strategies would you suggest to develop each type of human capital?

A Critical Theory Perspective

A critical perspective on leadership development has emerged in recent years. This perspective urges a critical and reflective approach and endorses the importance of using different theoretical lenses to achieve a better understanding of the complexity, ambiguity and paradoxical nature of management and leadership development. A critical perspective views management and leadership development as a discourse and emphasises the varied conflicting purposes of management and leadership development. It highlights how management and leadership development can be perceived as both productive and repressive. It rejects the notion of a single objective truth and, as a consequence, rejects any one perspective on management and leadership development. Instead it views management and leadership development as a multifaceted concept which lacks stability across both time and space. A critical perspective focuses on revealing the unspoken dimensions of management and leadership development in organisations.

Critical perspectives challenge the conventional thinking on management and leadership development which has focused on refining manager skills and developing organisational capabilities to ensure that organisations operate effectively. It challenges rational organisation practices and replaces them with more democratic and emancipatory management development practices. It questions orthodoxy and emphasises the need for self-reflection and the empowerment of individuals to bring about change, and it recognises that organisational practices are not, in fact, rational but are characterised by messiness, complexity and irrationality (Sambrook 2004).

The argument that management and leadership development has an emancipatory dimension is challenging. It arises because there is an inherent tension between reconciling the needs of individuals and those of organisations. It raises the question of whether the purpose of management and leadership development may be to free managers from the control of the employment relationship. It also focuses on identifying what lies behind the dominant imagery and icons of management and leadership development. What, for example, is the underlying purpose of individual development plans? Is it about performance or development? At a more fundamental level, a critical perspective seeks to address what we mean by management and leadership development. There is a tendency to take its meaning for granted. What does it mean for those managers who are exposed to management and leadership development? Table 1.12 provides a summary of six perspectives of management and leadership development and the questions they pose.

Table 1.12 Discourses On Management and Leadership Development

Perspective	Key Questions for Management Development
Political	• Who are the stakeholders involved in management and leadership development? • Who influences management and leadership development and in what ways? • Who gains from management and leadership development? • Whose interests do management and leadership development specialists meet?
Iconoclastic	• What lies behind the dominant imagery and language of management and leadership development? • Is management and leadership development concerned with learning or performance? • To what extent is management and leadership development concerned with personal development? • What myths prevail concerning management and leadersip development?
Investigative	• What do we actually mean by 'management and leadership development'? • How can we investigate what we actually mean by management and leadership development? • How do we question those who decide what management and leadership development should mean?

Perspective	Key Questions for Management Development
Epistemological	• What constitutes knowledge in the context of management and leadership development? • What methodologies are accepted in constructing our understanding of management and leadership development?
Revelatory	• What is the truth about management and leadership development? • How is management and leadership development talked about? • Is there a single truth about management and leadership development?
Emancipatory	• How do we reconcile the needs of individuals or organisations? • Do management and leadership development processes promote the potential to emancipate? • Whose needs do management and leadership development practitioners serve?

EXHIBIT 1.3

Theoretical Perspectives Relevant to Understanding Management, Leader and Leadership Development in Organisations

Theory	Description	Prescriptions for Management and Leadership Development
Resource-Based Theory	The resource-based view of the firm argues that all a firm's attributes can be considered as resources, including all assets, capabilities, competencies, organisational processes, information and knowledge. The resource-based approach can be viewed as a continuing search for competitive advantage through the creation, acquisition and utilisation of unique firm resources. The theory addresses the central issue of how superior performance can be attained relative to other firms in the same market and posits that superior performance results from acquiring and exploiting unique resources of the firm. Sustained competitive advantage is generated by the unique bundle of resources at the core of the firm. The resource-based view describes how business owners build their businesses from the resources and capabilities that they currently possess or can acquire. It emphasises that only resources that meet the four criteria of Value, Rareness, Inimitability and Non-substitutable firm-specific capabilities can delivery competitive advantage.	• Key management and leadership development themes – learning contracts, competency investment and lifelong learning investment. • Management and leadership development can be used by organisations to achieve value and uniqueness in a strategic context. • Internal capabilities can be developed into a source of competitive advantage. • Organisation needs to drive the development of internal capabilities • Management and leadership development can be used strategically to achieve the desired behaviours. • Management and leadership development can be used to develop both hard and soft skills and abilities. • Management and leadership development focuses on differentiating leaders from others. • Management and leadership development must transmit knowledge and skills and articulate the social and behavioural norms of the organisation. • Effective LD is defined in terms of the acquisition of prerequisite skills, knowledge, abilities, attitudes and values in order to meet the demands of the competitive environment.

Theory	Description	Prescriptions for Management and Leadership Development
Resource- Based Theory *contd.*		• As organisational goals and objectives are ambiguous and the means of achieving these goals are often uncertain, the agenda for management and leadership development may be to provide for a broader range of skills, attitudes, behaviours and abilities.
Human Capital Theory	The basic idea of human capital theory is that human capital induces productivity and that more human capital implies a higher productivity which, depending on whether the investment in human capital is general or specific, may be rewarded on the labour market by higher wages. Acquisition of human capital can take place during initial education or during the career. Investment in human capital can take place throughout a person's career on the job or off the job. Human capital theory looks at the rewards of investment in education and training and is concerned with relating measurable investments in human capital to monetary rewards to indicate labour market success.	• Create a learning culture where knowledge creation and action can flourish. • Core competencies embedded within a given philosophy and organisation culture. • Continuous investment in training, education and development strategies to keep ahead of competitors. • Managers invest in their own employability through learning processes, experience, project work and a range of career-enhancing strategies. • Firms utilise bonding mechanisms to bind managers to the organisation. • Invest in basic training, continuous professional development activities and post-experience education programmes, project learning and planned job experiences.
Learning Network Theory	Learning network theory is a theory about the organisation and development of learning systems. Learning systems in work organisations are analysed in a network approach to organisations. They are subject to tensions, which arise from their dual orientation: an orientation towards the development of human potential (humanity) and an orientation towards the development of the work process (work relevance). Learning Network Theory offers a frame of reference for analysing the tensions between humanity and work relevance and provides leads for handling such tensions. A learning network operates in every organisation. Learning networks are not limited to network-type organisations, matrix organisations or team-based organisations. People learn in every organisation, even in a hierarchical one or a chaotic one, and the learning network merely represents how the learning is organised. A learning network consists of the various learning activities organised by the members of the organisation.	• Improve capacity for learning by individuals. • Create different ways of generating and using knowledge through networks and other learning methods. • Create a work environment that stimulates and supports collective learning. • Acknowledge the role of informal and non-formal leadership development processes.

Theory	Description	Prescriptions for Management and Leadership Development
Psychological Contract Theory	Psychological contract theory focuses on the nature of the employment relationship. It argues that the modern psychological contract is transactional in nature and focuses on specific monetary economic exchanges which are short-term, such as working longer hours and accepting new job roles in exchange for more pay or job-related training. It may also be relational in nature, in which case it focuses on loyalty and discretionary behaviour in exchange for job security, financial rewards and training and development. In this relational exchange, the individual comes to identify with the organisation and there is a higher degree of mutual interdependence. This relationship can be associated with the experience of more progressive human resource practices and is seen to lead to a more positive state of contract and improved employee and business performance. Under the new psychological contract, there are no long-term expectations but a commitment of the organisation to provide employees with the best training and development and this will allow employees to find new jobs in case the company should have no further requirement for their skills and services. The HR practitioner is an agent for the organisation when dealing with the psychological contract. The agent sells the idea of employability to its employees.	• Facilitate delivery of the deal for both employer and employee. • Develop proactive and lifelong learning and career development activities. • Invest in generic and advanced competencies. • Facilitate the creation of positive employee perceptions of the psychological contract. • Contribute positively to outcomes such as job satisfaction, organisational commitment and citizenship, motivation and job involvement. • Regularly evaluate management and leadership development at performance review time and at times of renegotiation of the psychological contract. • Establish exchange programmes, job relations and mentoring relationships to facilitate information sharing and enable the transfer of information. • Take opportunities to learn and become more marketable and to move jobs if necessary.
Social Capital Theory	Social capital theory focuses on structure, networks and action. The social structure consists of people with varying levels of resources and with varying levels of authority. The measure of their resources and authority is determined by their place within the social structure. The second aspect of social capital is the relationship type: weak ties or strong ties. There exist 'valued resources' that can be accessed within this network. Mutual agreement through persuasion rather than authority or coercion dictates the actor's participation and interaction. The search for valued resources explains the existence of relationships, what these resources are, why they are important and why people interact with each other. The third aspect is the motive or motivation of individuals to engage in social networks. Instrumental action motives include investing, seeking out, mobilising relations and connections that may provide access to social resources.	• Create social career ladders and mentoring programmes. • Conceptualise the market in terms of social networks and actors. • Share knowledge to create new learning. • Encourage informal learning between individuals at all levels in organisations. • Improved career outcomes when social capital leads to knowledge-sharing. • Utilise the knowledge of all organisation members. • Allow all managers to work and learn across boundaries. • Improve organisational effectiveness through relationship-building, skill and competence development. • Make more effective use of development processes such as training needs analysis and feedback processes.

Theory	Description	Prescriptions for Management and Leadership Development
Chaos Theory	Chaos was most commonly used as a popular pseudonym for dynamic systems theory which describes itself as 'recurrent, random-like and a periodic behaviour generated from deterministic non-linear systems with sensitive dependence on initial conditions of the system'. The core properties of the chaotic system are: consciousness, connectivity, indeterminacy, emergence and dissipation. Chaos is seen as a lens and the 'thing' of organisational reality itself; it cannot tell one what is to be seen, only how one can see it as clearly as possible. Chaos is essentially neither a model nor a theory but a fundamental way of seeing, thinking, knowing and being in the world.	• Develop a learning organisation whereby the organisation enables the learning of its members to create positively viewed outcomes such as change and innovation. • Allow organisations and its members to be capable of adapting, changing, developing and transforming in response to the needs, wishes and aspirations of people. • Encourage learning that will enable collectives to enhance capacity to create and change. • Change the way individuals and organisations think about learning and development. • Informal, incidental and proactive learning are still very much part of chaotic systems. • Create a network of communities of commitment and communities of practice.
Agency Theory	Agency theory explains how to best organise relationships in which one party (the principal) determines the work, which another party (the agent) undertakes. Agency relations are problematic to the degree that: a) the principal and agent have conflicting goals; and b) it is difficult or expensive for the principal to monitor the agent's performance. A principal–agent relationship involves the entrusting of duty or authority by the owner (the principal) to another party (the agent) to act on the owner's behalf. The use of the word entrust is somewhat misleading because the principal does not trust the agent to act in his best interest, but assumes that the agent is opportunistic and will pursue personal interests which are in conflict with those of the principal. Contracts are used to govern such relations and efficient contracts align the goals of principals and agents at the lowest possible cost. Costs can rise from providing incentives and obtaining information (e.g. about the agent's behaviour and/or the agent's performance outcomes). With agency theory the probability that self-interested or opportunistic behaviour will occur is dependent on the amount of control the principal has over the agent's activities and the degree of information asymmetry which exists between agent and principal. Low principal control over the agent and high information asymmetry in favour of the agent allows the agent great discretion to pursue his or her own interests. To counter the agent's propensity to engage in	• Investment in firm-specific training more likely to be utilised. • Bond the employee to the organisation. • Organisation needs to drive the development of internal capabilities. • Short-term focus when selecting management and leadership development interventions. • Leadership development may be used to manage the relationship between principals and agents.

Theory	Description	Prescriptions for Management and Leadership Development
Agency Theory *contd.*	opportunistic behaviour, the principal should monitor the behaviour of the agent, or provide incentives to align the interests of the agent with his own.	
Social Identity Theory	Social identity theory is a theory of group membership and behaviour. A sub-theory of social cognition, social identity theory developed with the purpose of understanding how individuals make sense of themselves and other people in the social environment. Individuals derive a portion of their identities from their membership and interactions within and among groups. Social identity is a concept with enduring (core) and (peripheral) components evolving in a reciprocating process between the individual and the group. It is an ongoing process of interaction between the individual and the focal group (in-group) and between the individual and other groups (out-groups). It is a process, not an entity or label. This processual nature helps to explain the complex and dynamic nature of identity in social interactions. The resulting identity, in effect, depends on the situation and the relative strengths of internal and external categorisation at the time. The emphasis on process recognises the relational, dynamic, contextual and constructed nature of social identity.	• Management and leadership development activities should address group behaviour issues. • Management and leadership development is influenced by group dynamics and social processes. • Social identity theory has important implications for the way in which managers are socialised and the use of manager role models. • Leadership development involves processes of social interaction and collective identity.
Social Con-structionism	Social constructionism focuses on social interaction. It acknowledges a dynamic interaction between the learner's tasks and the instructor. Learners create their own truth as a result of their interaction with others. The task or problem becomes the interface between the instructor and the learner. Social constructionism emphasises the importance of culture and context in understanding what is happening in society and constructing knowledge based on this understanding. It acknowledges the uniqueness and complexity of the learner and argues that responsibility for learning should increasingly reside with the learner. The learner should be actively involved in the learning process. Developers, according to this theory, adopt roles as facilitators, not instructors. The context in which learning occurs is central to understanding the value of learning.	• Management and leadership development is an active process of dynamic interaction. • The manager creates a personal vision of the truth that is tested through dialogue with others. • Managers engage in situation-specific tasks that facilitate development. • The background culture and language of the manager are integral parts of the learning process. • Each manager has a unique learning agenda based on his/her personal development objectives.

Theory	Description	Prescriptions for Management and Leadership Development
Leadership Complexity Theory	Leadership complexity theory provides a framework to understand leadership as an enabler of the learning, creative and adaptive capacity of complex adaptive systems in knowledge-producing organisations. Leadership complexity theory focuses on context, which it defines as an ambience that spawns a given system's dynamic persona. Leadership is socially constructed in and from this context. History and time are important issues. The theory distinguishes between leadership and leaders. Leadership is an emergent, interactive dynamic that produces adaptive outcomes. Leaders are individuals who act in ways that influence this dynamic and its outcomes. The theory postulates that leadership complexity occurs in the face of adaptive challenges rather than technical problems. These adaptive challenges require new learning, innovation and patterns of behaviour. Technical problems, on the other hand, can be solved using existing knowledge.	• Management and leadership development must take consideration of the mechanisms and contexts through which change occurs. • Development processes are essentially non-linear in nature, changeable and unpredictable. • Development occurs through interaction and the nature of development outcomes are complex and difficult to understand. • The challenge of leadership development is to ensure that leaders are adaptive and that they possess the competencies to solve complex problems and integrate new learning into their repertoire of skills.
Gift Exchange Theory	Gift exchange theory postulates that the exchange of gifts between two parties represents a special type of social exchange. Gifts seek to strengthen the ties between the parties. The exchange of gifts is governed by a set of rules. When the relationship is positive, less emphasis is placed on the actual resources being exchanged. The social context of the parties is the most fundamental issue. Gifts may have emotional significance to a recipient that is considered equivalent to a more impressive gift given to the other party. The focus is not on calculating the monetary value of the gift. The relationship is characterised by its personal nature. The parties develop mutual empathy and there are frequent interactions between the parties. The relationship itself is then indefinite, with a high potential for trust between the parties. The types of resources exchanged are likely to be both tangible and intangible. The key rules of the gift exchange are: 1) a gift should consider the recipient's personal needs and feelings; 2) the parties should avoid discussing the gift exchange balance sheet; 3) parties avoid making explicit their expectations of the gift exchanged; 4) each party acts appreciatively when a gift is presented;	• Management and leadership development can be framed as a gift exchange. • Management and leadership development is a gift that increases a manager's stock of marketable skills which can be translated into a higher salary. • The employer who pays for the manager's development will frame these resources as a gift. • The manager is likely to perceive that his/her personal needs are being considered by the employee. The manager will likely feel more secure given that the employer has paid for skills that make him/her more marketable. • The manager will reciprocate by creating discretionary extra role behaviours that go beyond the core job tasks. • The co-operation of the manager will benefit the employer. Managers who are co-operative take into account the interests of the employee. • Managers who receive management and leadership development investment by their employer are likely to be more productive and committed. It reduces the likelihood that the employer will lose the investment due to the manager leaving.

Theory	Description	Prescriptions for Management and Leadership Development
Gift Exchange Theory *contd.*	5) the recipient of a gift should ensure sufficient time delay before reciprocating the gift to the other party; and 6) the equilibrium of exchange between the parties is always dynamic.	

A Dynamic Approach to Management and Leadership Development

The majority of approaches to management and leadership development are reductionist in nature. They emphasise both structure and process. Recently academics have focused on a more dynamic and adaptive approach to development. This approach to development has as its starting point the notion that, because human beings are complex, adaptive entities, these characteristics are also inherent in their management and leadership development and careers. Drawing on the work of, amongst others, Savickas and Lent (1994) and Block (1993), it is possible to identify a number of characteristics which describe a dynamic theory of management and leadership development:

- Managers continually reinvent their careers, moving freely among and within roles. Management and leadership development is a complex process. It requires participation in the give and take of the outside world. Managers build relationships that are complex and dynamic.
- Management and leadership development is an entity within the entity of the individual, but it also exists in the context of relational networks. These networks consist of education, occupations, roles, cultures and organisational processes and represent ongoing relationships that are affected by the character of each development activity.
- The development of a manager is a component of that manager's entire life experience and of the entire work system. Because development is part of a relational network and these networks are in continual open exchange, development occurs. This development may be sought by the manager or the manager may have little choice.
- Each manager's development pattern makes sense only in the context of that manager's life and the specific dynamics of the environment and the internal dynamics of that manager. The development of each manager is a series of choices that resonates for the individual and can only be fully understood in terms of that individual.
- Random and, in some cases, small events can lead to major development. These changes can thrive due to particular conditions in the workplace or life of the manager.

Dynamic and non-linear perspectives of management and leadership development are in their infancy but, at a theoretical level, they have the potential to provide us with interesting insights concerning the process of development. They do suggest that change is inevitable and not always comfortable. Managers are likely to experience ambiguity and chaos. This suggests that managers should focus on the development of generic, transferable competencies. This theoretical perspective also suggests that management and leadership development is an individual process and that the willingness to make changes and meet challenges is an opportunity for development.

Leadership Development as Sustainable Development

Another emerging perspective argues that the purpose of leadership development should be to contribute to sustainable development. Wade (2006) suggests that sustainable development is both a value and a broad framework of thinking, and that leaders in organisations should strive to develop competitive advantage based on a strong commitment to business principles and sustainable development. Leaders with a sustainable development mindset exemplify competencies that reflect a breadth of vision and an external mindset. The challenge for leadership development is to develop in leaders a capacity to:

- Identify key trends and influences that are of strategic importance to the organisation and to use the insights gained to enable strategic growth
- Balance the short and longer term
- Ensure the integration of environmental and social factors in both strategic and operational decision-making
- Demonstrate visible leadership in creating a culture that facilitates innovation, enables diversity and decisiveness and creates challenge
- Build long-term relationships with internal and external stakeholders and engage with their values and priorities.

The development of leadership must be embedded in an organisation. It needs to focus on collective actions of common value across the organisation. Figure 1.2 provides an illustration of a sustainable leadership development framework.

Figure 1.2: A Sustainable Development (SD) Framework for Leadership Development

Objective	Activity	Medium	Agent
Awareness and Understanding	**Communicating** • Key messages • Latest updates • Best-practice examples	• SD e-portal • Newsletters, e-letters • Shell report • Resource library	• Corporate centre • Businesses • Functions
Working Knowledge	**Skilled Training/ Learning** • SD presentation packs • SD case studies • SD best-practice guides • SD modules/events • SD e-learning tools	• SD workshops • SD master classes • Chronos (e-learning) • Leadership assessment and development • Training/coaching interventions	• SD advisers • Subject experts • Self-directed • Programme managers
Mastery and Advocacy	**Beyond Training** • Active learning • Experienced people • Functional leadership • Competency profiling	• SD networks • Cross-posting • Career planning • Competencies	• Businesses • HR planners • SD advisers • SD practitioners

Holistic Management and Leadership Development

Shefy and Sadler-Smith (2006) argue that effective leadership development is based on an approach that embodies balance and harmony, focuses on relationships and avoids the tension of opposites. They suggest six principles that characterise a holistic approach:

- **Quieting the Mind:** This is defined as a state of contemplation and quiet. Managers are required to let go of tension, doubt and expectation as a prerequisite to see through and into the essence of things. This suggests that managers can develop new insights, become more effective with less effort, and allow their intuitions to emerge. Managers who are free of past experiences and prejudices become more effective and attuned to others.
- **Harmony and Balance:** The holistic perspective argues that the essence of management lies in the manager's chi and in enabling that chi and the chi of others to flow. In a management and leadership development context, this might arise through the development of self-motivation in skills and the skills to motivate others. Holistic thinking advocates that managers should avoid extremes.
- **Relinquish the Desire to Control:** This suggests that managers should develop an understanding that it is not always possible to control, to manipulate or to predict. Managers should be skilled in accepting a lack of control and use personal power instead. This suggests empowering others in decision-making and task performance. Managers should give power to others and they will be more fulfilled.
- **Transcend the Ego:** Managers should strive to increase self-awareness and understand that the conflict of the self represents the key challenge. Holistic leadership development argues that if one's self-awareness is enhanced, people will follow naturally. Managers are challenged to transcend the ego and be aware of strengths and weaknesses.
- **Tenderness:** Managers need an anchor or a centre of gravity. This includes the requirement to be functionally flexible and possess values that provide an anchor for honesty and integrity. This suggests that managers need a frame of reference in times of crisis or pressure. Strong contriteness provides the manager with greater self-confidence and presence.
- **The Power of Softness:** Holistic management and leadership development suggests that the 'tough' manager is an outdated stereotype. The holistic perspective suggests openness, softness and flexibility. Managers who demonstrate these attributes will be more effective in difficult and unpredictable situations.

Table 1.13: Assessing the Development Potential of Your Managers and Leaders: Key Questions for Organisations

Thinking Beyond the Boundaries

Definition:

The application of conceptual ability to broach questions and to think in a big picture way. It involves the disposition to look beyond the role and make connections with other areas.

Key Questions:

Does the manager in his or her thinking make useful connections that are beyond the scope of the job or role?

Has the manager the capacity to think in a creative way about big questions?

Has the manager the capacity to make complex issues relatively simple and grounded in reality?

Curiosity and Eagerness to Learn

Definition:

A natural curiosity and eagerness to learn and take in new challenges, which is evident in the manager's willingness to ask questions that push the boundaries.

Key Questions

Does the manager display behaviours which indicate a willingness to go beyond what is normally expected in the job?

Does the manager display a willingness to take on different and challenging job assignments?

Does the manager attend unusual development activities?

Does the manager show a willingness to take risks in the interest of learning?

Social Understanding and Empathy

Definition:

This consists of a desire and ability to understand others and to see the individual in his/her entirety.

Key Questions

Does the manager demonstrate effective listening skills, ask appropriate questions for purposes of clarification and make considered conclusions?

Is the manager continually motivated to understand others?

Does the manager treat others with respect and make positive evaluations of others?

Does the manager possess the capacity to bring out the best in others?

Emotional Balance

Definition:

This characteristic focuses on the manager's emotional balance, emotional resilience and degree of optimism.

Key Questions

How does the manager respond emotionally when things do not go as planned?

Does the manager possess the capacity to recover and learn quickly from mistakes?

Is the manager willing to seek out constructive criticism and improve performance as a result?

Does the manager pursue actions that are in the interests of the team as a whole?

Other Key Issues in Considering Development Potential of Managers and Leaders

Are the organisation's growth factors or criteria recognisable early in a manager's career?

Are growth factors useful to many leadership roles in organisations?

How much time and resources are required to develop the desirable competencies?

Conclusion

Management and leadership development has a range of meanings, purposes and outcomes. It is possible, at a conceptual level, to differentiate management and leadership development from other processes such as organisation development, management education and training and career development. For our purposes we recognise there are differences in emphasis, but for the purposes of the book we treat them as part of a wider system of development initiatives that can be implemented by individuals and organisations. We distinguished between management, leader and leadership development. A multiplicity of lenses or frames exists through which management and leadership development may be understood. There is much that is debated and contested within the field. Definitions and perspectives on management and leadership development will influence approaches and methods adopted in practice. The notion of management versus leadership is widely highlighted. Leadership is often assumed to be a superior activity to that of management. Management tends to be viewed as a transactional activity, whereas leadership is focused on change and relationships.

Individuals and organisations invest in management and leadership development for a multiplicity of reasons. These reasons are sometimes complex and problematic. The more conventional view suggests that the purpose of management and leadership development is primarily to improve organisational performance and success. This has led in particular to the emergence of strategic management and leadership development, which argues that management development should be linked in some way with organisational strategy.

Management, leader and leadership development has in the past focused on formalised and structured approaches. We highlighted the tendency to write about management and leadership development as a process with large-scale organisation and sophisticated resources and systems. This model does not fit all organisation types. Nor does it account for more informal and situated development processes.

Management and leadership development is an ongoing process. It is grounded in personal development, a process that never ends. It is also embedded in experience. It is well established that managers and leaders expand their experience over time and that they therefore learn continuously. Development is related to experiences which can enhance self-awareness. Development processes are characterised by a sense of challenge, appropriate support and personal insight. The most effective management and leadership development will be embedded in an organisational and individual context. The process focuses on the expansion of a manager's capacity to be effective in a variety of management and leadership roles.

Summary of Key Points

In this chapter, the following key points have been made:

- 'Management' and 'leadership' are complex and potentially problematic concepts. This complexity explains the variety of meanings that academics and practitioners attach to each concept.
- Management and leadership development can focus on managers collectively or individually. It has aims that focus on the development of capabilities and competencies consistent with the context (strategic, cultural and environmental).
- Numerous approaches to management and leadership development exist, ranging from the more conventional to the unorthodox. We identified piecemeal systems and strategic approaches as more conventional approaches. We considered more contemporary approaches, such as critical and dynamic approaches to management and leadership development.
- Management and leadership development needs to consider the perspectives of different stakeholders, including managers, top management, the board, peers and subordinates.
- The purposes of management and leadership development are many and potentially conflicting. They often have to be negotiated and reconciled.
- Organisations invest in management and leadership development to develop self-awareness, self-confidence, networking skills and competencies and to contribute to the strategic success of the organisation.

■ Discussion Questions

1. Is it possible to design management and leadership development interventions that can accommodate both individual and organisation expectations?

2. What assumptions are made concerning the concepts of management and leadership and what implications do they have for development?

3. What factors should be taken into account when deciding on different approaches to management and leadership development?

4. How can critical perspectives on management development be reconciled with conventional organisational perspectives?

5. Is it possible to reconcile the many potentially conflicting purposes of management and leadership development?

■ Application and Experiential Questions

1. Do some research in an organisation of your choice or your current organisation. What are the main purposes of management and leadership development in the organisation? How does it reconcile individual and organisational priorities? What problems have arisen in delivering management and leadership development?

2. Put yourself in the position of a manager or senior executive. Why would you invest in management and leadership development? How would you use management and leadership development to manage risk in the external environment?

3. In groups of three, represent a consulting firm. You have been asked to prepare a proposal for a leadership development programme for young graduate managers. What purposes would you prioritise? What steps should the company take to ensure that the initiative is a success? Present your ideas in class and justify why you should be given the contract.

Chapter Two

The Context of Management and Leadership Development

Outline

Learning Objectives

Opening Case Scenario

The Wider Business Environment
- Globalism or Globalisation

Hyper-Competition and New Organisational Forms
- Structural Transformation
- A Virtual Organisation
- Downsizing and Delayering
- The Knowledge-Based Economy
- New Technologies
- Business Ethics, Social Accountability and Governance

Changing Demographic Trends, Work Values and Attitudes
- An Ageing Workforce
- Participation of Women in the Workforce and in Management
- Dual-Career Families
- Work–Life Balance Issues

Emerging Management Trends
- Management of Diversity
- New Team Concepts
- Total Quality Management, Integrated Manufacturing and Re-Engineering
- High-Performance Work Systems
- The Psychological Contract and Discretionary Behaviour
- Strategic Alliances: Mergers, Takeovers and Acquisitions
- The Emergence of Service Work and Emotional Labour

New Ways of Thinking about Managing and Leading
- Post-Modernism
- The New Science

Conclusion
Summary
Discussion Questions
Application and Experiential Questions

Learning Objectives

After reading this chapter you will be able to:

- Define and explain how factors in the external environment impact on management and leadership development.
- Explain how key management trends and directions in the utilisation of human resources are challenging traditional assumptions concerning management and leadership development in organisations.
- Analyse the role of international issues such as global competition, global sourcing of management talent and international culture in devising strategies and policy on management and leadership development.
- Describe trends such as changes in demographics, employee values, attitudes and changing organisation structures and the challenges they present for managers and leaders in organisations.

OPENING CASE SCENARIO

Permanent TSB: The Story of a Merger

The Irish Life and Permanent Group was created in 1999 out of a merger of Irish Life plc and Irish Permanent plc. The merger brought together two organisations with distinct financial strengths: Ireland's largest home loans provider and Ireland's largest insurance company. Prior to the merger, both companies had 20 per cent of the market share in their respective markets.

Irish Permanent was established in 1984 as a mutual building society. In 1992, it established Irish Permanent Finance Limited to provide personal and auto loans. This represented a conscious effort to diversify its product range. In September 1994, Irish Permanent became a public company and obtained a licence from the Central Bank to carry on banking activities. It also acquired Prudential Life of Ireland, which was then renamed Irish Progressive Life Assurance Company Limited, a company involved in the life assurance and provisions business, and Guinness & Mahon (Ireland) Limited, which provided private banking services. In 1996 it acquired Capital Home Loans Limited, a mortgage-lending company operating in the United Kingdom.

The Irish Life Assurance Company was established in 1939 as a result of the amalgamation of a number of Irish and British life assurance companies. The Irish Minister for Finance acquired a 90 per cent holding in the company. In 1990, Irish Life plc was established with a public listing on the Irish and London Stock Exchanges in July 1991. As a result of the listing, the Minister's holding was reduced to 33 per cent. In 1995 this was disposed of. Irish Life plc conducted business in Ireland, the USA and the UK. Its key products were in the areas of life assurance, pensions and investments.

The merger was designed to create a leading personal finance provider in Ireland. Irish Permanent gained access to Irish Life's comprehensive range of products, its distribution network and its customer base. Irish Life gained access to Irish Permanent's extensive branch and agency network. In December 2000, the Irish Life and Permanent Group made a successful bid to acquire TSB Bank, which was formed in 1992. The merger of the bank with Irish Life and Permanent was viewed as a route that best served the long-term interests of TSB stakeholders. Acquisition also created a 'third banking force' in the Irish market, which was to be known as Permanent TSB. The vision of Permanent TSB was to offer real value, excellent customer service and product options. According to the then Chief Executive of Permanent TSB, Harry Lorton, it aimed to set new benchmarks in the financial services industry. Strategically, the merger represented a major step forward and, while the merger was strategically real, there were many overlaps which presented problems for the merged organisation.

A key decision in making the merger possible was the agreement by Irish Life and Permanent to approach the integration with the clear objective of creating the 'best of both' organisations. A programme of change was initiated to enable the organisation to achieve a successful merger. This programme set out clear objectives and a clear statement of where the merged organisation wanted to go. Over a hundred people were drawn from various parts of the two organisations to work together, first to understand each other's business in detail, and, second, to begin designing the new organisation. This also provided the first indication of how the two organisations would work together, given that each had its own distinct culture and tradition. Initial contacts were promising. The team set clear and demanding objectives and created a positive working environment. Staff who worked on the integration process moved back into the organisation and acted as ambassadors for the integration process.

The merger had a significant impact on staff. Although the organisation had anticipated that there would be fewer people working in the bank in the future, it was not simply a matter of identifying 2,000 employees who would have to go. It was agreed that there would be no compulsory redundancies. Various voluntary schemes were put in place to encourage early retirement. Staff also found themselves being asked to consider moving location to fill vacancies in other areas. The merger encountered problems in dealing with the unions. A total of seven unions represented staff from the different organisations and there was considerable disagreement concerning terms and conditions of employment. Management made a mistake by not appointing an HR manager of the retail division at the time of the merger. This resulted in a protracted industrial relations battle about working hours. Staff from TSB Bank quickly became disillusioned because they perceived that TSB management had little influence on strategic planning. They also believed that the merger was not necessary. Staff had particular grievances concerning the quality of the space and facilities in merged branches. This resulted in bitter exchanges in the branches and led to a dramatic increase in the level of customer complaints. The merger was also hampered by management deciding which managers would be appointed without a sufficiently transparent selection process and the differing terms and conditions of employment for the combined staff. Staff complained about the limited knowledge of each other's products. This was further complicated by the introduction of new products, some of which were a combination of existing products.

Ultimately, the merger process did not address a key issue of a successful merger, i.e. 'the difficulties staff encountered in adjusting to a new culture and ethos'. Inconsistency in branch manager appointments was particularly problematic. This contrasted with the executive selection process, which was viewed as considerably more transparent. The process was too drawn out, due largely to procrastination about finalising new terms and conditions of employment. This led to staff mistrust in management. The company ultimately placed more emphasis on the short-term appeasement of the financial markets and analysts and there was a major concern that the merger be perceived as an immediate success. They did not focus sufficiently on the people management and development issues.

QUESTIONS

Q.1   What mistakes do you think were made in facilitating the merger?

Q.2   What role could management and leadership development processes have played in this scenario?

Managers and leaders are being challenged to operate in a complex and dynamic external environment. Managers are required to understand how to lead and to realise why employees at work behave in particular ways. This requires an understanding of the dynamic context within which managers operate. The tasks and roles of a manager are evolving all the time and the context within which managers work is in continual flux. A host of environmental changes have converged to produce particular challenges for managers and leaders.

This chapter discusses those environmental factors that impact on management and leadership development processes in organisations. Important external influences which have implications for the roles of managers and leaders include managing globalisation, dealing with downsizing, addressing business ethics issues, understanding and responding to changing organisation structures, exploring new technology and new developments in management thinking.

Managers and leaders are also challenged by issues such as work–life balance, the increased individualisation of the employment relationship, new challenges in respect of managing careers and psychological contracts and a range of management trends such as diversity, team working, human resource outsourcing, managing mergers and acquisitions, re-engineering and quality management initiatives.

This chapter is structured as follows: the wider business environment, including new organisational forms and competitive dynamics; worker values and attitudinal trends, including demographic and managerial trends; the changing dynamics of the employment relationship; career concepts, trust, job insecurity, work–life balance and individualisation of the employment relationship, and international developments.

The Wider Business Environment

Globalism or Globalisation

Globalism is defined as global competition, which is characterised by networks of international linkages and which creates an interdependent global economy. Globalism has arisen as a result of increased competition, foreign direct investment and global alliances. Global companies are less drawn to specific locations and they are likely to spread their operations throughout the world. Increasingly, they source and co-ordinate resources and activities in a manner that ensures greater flexibility. Smaller companies are impacted by global competition and network involvement. As terms, globalism or globalisation are used interchangeably with a range of other concepts such as internationalisation, westernisation and modernisation. Scholte (2001) suggested that the following activities and themes can be included in the concept of globalisation:

- Global communication, including electronic mass media and telecommunication
- Global markets, including products and sales strategies
- Global production, including production, sourcing and production chains
- Global organisations, including corporate strategic alliances and governance agencies
- Global consumers, including the world as a single place, symbols, events and subsidiaries
- Global finance, including bankers, bonds and the insurance business
- Global social ecology, including the atmosphere and biosphere.

Held *et al.* (1997) suggested that globalisation is 'not a singular condition, but a linear process'. They highlight five key themes:

- Different countries are developing along different pathways to the market economy. Globalisation impacts on them differently.
- Globalisation does not impact on all aspects of economic life. Local labour market-intensive services and public services are largely unaffected by world markets.
- Globalisation is not homogenous. There are differences between regions, localities and nation states.
- US business culture is not necessarily being copied throughout the world. The emergence of globalisation does not result in convergence of national culture.
- Globalisation does not necessarily lead to the decline of the nation state.

Definitions of globalisation distinguish between those that emphasise quantitative versus qualitative linkages between countries. In the former, often called the 'strong globalisation thesis', the emphasis is placed on major changes in the pace of growth in the linkages between countries. This includes significant growth in trade and foreign direct investment, information exchange and deregulation. In the case of the latter, globalisation is defined as growth in the functional integration of national economies. This definition argues that the ties between countries are becoming stronger in a more intangible way.

Globalisation is driven by powerful economic factors, including market, cost and competitive factors. Examples of market factors include the growth of common customer preferences, largely created by successful global branding. In terms of cost, globalisation is said to offer the advantages of economies of scale and standardisation. Examples include cost advantages in advertising, material sourcing and economies of scale due to larger market potential.

Globalisation tends to elicit a broad range of responses. Critics argue that globalisation has and will continue to increase the North–South divide, widening the gap between rich and poor people. Global companies are allowed to exploit developing nations and have the potential to cause significant damage to the natural environment. People have become increasingly aware of their cultural and ethnic identity. There is an insistence that cultural differences should be recognised. Global companies have increasingly come to recognise that new business opportunities can be secured through catering for local tastes and adjusting their strategies and policies to suit local employment practices.

Globalisation suggests that employment has become more volatile because of the increased sensitivity to institutional shareholders, which legitimises the sense of risk and uncertainty that prevails in the workplace. It has also promoted more contingent work. Globalisation has exerted and will continue to exert a significant influence on the content of work. Specifically, it has reduced the requirement for manual work and fostered new kinds of skills such as those found in customer service work and call centres. It has enabled managers to work across spatial boundaries with an increased use of forms of virtual teamworking.

A particular aspect of globalisation concerns outsourcing and offshoring. Organisations have discovered that costs can be cut through outsourcing. Outsourcing transfers work to places where labour costs are lower. Lower labour-cost economies, such as China, Brazil and India, can compete on lower costs and, as a result, they can compete in world markets. They have made manufacturing capabilities a commodity. Increasingly, outsourcing is not restricted to manufacturing and production. White-collar, professional and knowledge work is increasingly offshored.

Outsourcing has changed the way managers manage and lead people. They are more frequently having to manage temporary, freelance and contract workers. This means, in some cases, having to manage employees who are less committed and demonstrate less loyalty to the organisation. The major challenge for managers is that of engaging these freelance employees.

Globalisation has important implications for the careers of managers. It requires managers who are skilled in operating and managing a global business. Managers are expected to have skills in managing subsidiaries, the transfer of knowledge and the development of marketing. Deresky (2000) suggested that companies that desire to be globally competitive will need continuously to develop managers and leaders who have foreign operational experience. They will need skills in managing people from other cultures and they need to understand how to do business in other countries.

Hyper-Competition and New Organisational Forms

The competitive reality for many organisations is that they are dealing in a commercial world which is variable and unpredictable. Sparrow (2002) used the concept 'hyper-competition' to describe the evolving commercial environment. This environment is characterised by a speed of change far greater than has previously been the case. Illinitch *et al.* (1996) suggested that hyper-competition has four characteristics: 1) market situations fraught with uncertainty; 2) a diverse range of global players; 3) rapid and unpredictable technological change; and 4) widespread price wars and continuous and endless reorganisation. Child (2005) suggests that the key features of what they termed the 'new world' include: a fast-changing economy; continually evolving business strategies; short product life cycles; changing customer needs; a global market place; and thousands of potential competitors. Child suggests that the consequences of these changes include a shift from an environment in which firms occupy competitive space to one in which competition is a war and success depends on anticipating market trends.

Changing competitive dynamics have important strategic, structural and managerial implications. Organisational survival will no longer be achieved through the adoption of defensive business strategies. Organisations will be increasingly required to develop and exploit new capabilities that will enable them to be attractive to the market. They will need to be aggressive in their strategic posture and attack competitors' existing strengths. Hyper-competition requires that organisations be flexible in areas such as strategy, work organisation and deployment of competencies. Managers and leaders are expected to be skilled in restructuring organisational processes within a short timespan.

Hyper-competition has major implications for the quality of managers and leaders. Organisations will need to find managers who are comfortable working in organisations that regularly downsize and expand in different directions. Managers will be expected to manage people during frequent periods of structural change and reorganisation. They need to be confident and skilled to cope with situations of rapid growth and rapid decline. Managers will be increasingly expected to work in organisations or parts of organisations that are temporary in nature or project based. One of the most significant implications of hyper-competition concerns the emergence of new organisational forms to ensure the required level of flexibility.

Organisational forms can be defined as a combination of strategy, structure, internal control and co-ordination mechanisms that enable the organisation to function effectively. Commentators highlight four key elements of organisational restructuring and the emergence of new organisational forms:

- **Downsizing:** This means reducing the size of the workforce and achieving production targets with fewer employees.
- **Externalisation:** This refers to the outsourcing of activities that are not considered central to the organisation's production process. Outsourcing strategies are considered to offer firms significant cost and flexibility advantages.
- **Delayering:** This refers to the elimination of key layers in the organisation's hierarchy. Delayering is frequently perceived as a strategy to enhance decision-making processes and increase the flow of communication.
- **Devolution:** This process refers to the pushing down of responsibility for decision-making and problem-solving to core workers and junior managers in the organisation.

These various changes in organisational form make significant demands on managers. Managers are expected to be able to respond rapidly to changing conditions. They are expected to ensure that customer expectations are met while at the same time matching the supply and quality of labour with demand cycles. They are expected to restructure and reorganise work in order to gain productivity increases.

Organisation structures are also changing as a result of advances in information technology. One consequence is that the distinctions between management and other employee categories have become blurred. Employees have become more empowered: information is more often shared in team settings and structures have become significantly less hierarchical. Managerial status is increasingly de-emphasised, combined with a rise in the use of rotating leadership roles. These changing dynamics have significant implications for the competency and skill requirements of managers and leaders.

Structural Transformation

Four particular structural transformations have emerged in recent years, which have significant implications for the skills of managers and leaders:

- **Unbundled Structure:** This structural form represents an outsourcing model in which many traditional support services are outsourced to consultants and vendors, providing the organisation with significant advantages. It allows the organisation the opportunity to redeploy resources to areas of greater flexibility. It provides developing managers with opportunities to acquire broader managerial competencies. These new core units provide managers with opportunities to manage high-impact employees, manage change and manage supplier–vendor relationships.
- **Network or Virtual Structure:** The term 'network organisation' is used to describe a structure with multiple autonomous units. It is similar to an unbundled structure in that the organisation creates a network of smaller entities driven by the need to outsource or create joint-venture arrangements to perform tasks more effectively. The term 'virtual organisation' is also used to describe a situation where there is a strong reliance on

outsourcing and a need to respond to customer needs very quickly. Allred, Snow and Miles (1996) suggested that network structures make particular skill demands of managers, including: partnering skills such as networking and negotiating; relationship management skills such as managing customer or internal partner needs; and referral skills, which include solving problems through referral to the appropriate part of the network.

- **Cellular and Respondent Structures:** Cellular structures consist of groups of small technology-oriented units that maintain relationships over time. Managers in these units are responsible for managing technical professionals and several units may join forces on various projects for which they have the correct combination of skills and abilities. Managers in cellular-type structures are expected to have a strong technical knowledge, be skilled in handling cross-functional issues, adopt more collaborative styles of leadership, be flexible and possess strong self-management skills. Respondent structures tend to be defined as entrepreneurial units designed to provide customised services. The manager of such a unit is required to be entrepreneurial in focus and to make decisions quickly. Managers in this situation are provided with opportunities to develop as generalists.

The emergence of new organisational forms has significant implications for the careers of managers. Traditional vertical careers are in decline. Managers are now expected to make sideways moves across organisations. Snow, Miles and Coleman (1992) suggested that managers will have to change their career several times and that they will be required to develop new skill sets.

A Virtual Organisation

The concept of the virtual organisation raises the possibility that managers will no longer be employed by a single employer. Managers will instead become portfolio managers, doing a range of jobs for different employers. This scenario suggests the decline of a long-term employment relationship and the emergence of more contingent forms of employment. The evidence so far suggests that the long-term employment relationship is still prevalent. Many managers still seek permanent employment. Commentators such as Montoya-Weiss, Massey and Song (2002) and Maznevski and Chudoba (2000) highlighted that newer forms of employment bring a decrease in commitment, which may lead to disruption and poorer organisational performance.

The various organisational forms that have emerged in recent years have allowed organisations to become more flexible. Managers have played an important role in achieving this. Managers are expected to be highly skilled, adaptable and creative. Sparrow (1998) argued that organisations have been repackaging the tasks, duties and responsibilities that are considered jobs. This includes redesigning the content, changing the way in which managers interact with one another and reshaping the competence and commitment required of managers. Exhibit 2.1 summarises what Sparrow and Marchington (1998) called the seven simultaneous flexibilities in organisations.

EXHIBIT 2.1

Characteristics of the Seven Simultaneous Flexibilities in Organisations

1. **Numerical flexibility**, where the battle concerns who owns (and therefore has some legal obligation to) the employment relationship. Does the job need to be within the internal labour market, or can it be sufficiently controlled through outsourcing, peripheral forms of employment or the use of various associate relationships?
2. **Functional flexibility**, an organisation's ability to deploy employees between activities and tasks to match changing workloads, production methods or technology. The battle concerns the roles and competencies deemed appropriate for the job. When the new package of elements, tasks and duties are considered, does the job need to be staffed by a multiskilled individual, are there new core competencies that must be delivered, or are there important cross-business process skills that must be acquired?
3. **Financial flexibility**, where the battle concerns the reward–effort bargain to be struck with the job-holder. What is the best balance between the type and nature of reward and the delivery of performance? Could a more efficient wage–effort bargain be struck by the use of performance-related pay, gainsharing, or cafeteria benefits?
4. **Temporal flexibility**, where the battle is the need for continuous active representation on the job. What time patterns should the job be fitted into and will employees be able to achieve the highest levels of customer service and performance throughout these time patterns? What is the role, for instance, of flexitime, nil hours or annual hours?
5. **Geographical flexibility**, where the battle is around the ideal location of the job and its constituent tasks. Does the job need to be carried out in specific locations, or is there latitude for homeworking, or even operating through virtual teams?
6. **Organisational flexibility**, where the battle concerns the form and rationale of the total organisation and its design, into which the job may be fitted. Does the organisation operate as an ad-hocracy, a loose network of suppliers, purchasers and providers, or a temporary alliance or joint venture?
7. **Cognitive flexibility**, where the battle concerns both the mental frames of reference and the level of cognitive skills required to perform the job effectively. Does the job require people with a particular sort of psychological contract? What sorts of strategic and cognitive assumptions cannot be tolerated?

Source: Sparrow and Marchington (1998)

Downsizing and Delayering

Downsizing, which began as a short-term management strategy in the mid 1980s, has become a relatively permanent feature of organisations. It is now largely driven by global competitive pressures, new technology and, in particular, the demands of customer requirements, including database-driven marketing. Child (2005) defines downsizing as the planned elimination of positions and jobs. It may arise from the outsourcing of certain non-core activities and/or from the retrenchment of the organisation's activities.

The literature makes a distinction between 'reactive' and 'strategic' downsizing. Reactive downsizing typically refers to situations where the organisation makes across-the-board reductions in employee numbers in response to short-term economic conditions. It is often considered a crude form of downsizing because it fails to consider unique competencies and areas of special knowledge that may be relevant to the organisation in the future. It is simply a cost-cutting measure. Employee costs can make up thirty to eighty per cent of total business costs (Casio 1993).

Strategic downsizing, on the other hand, is designed to support the organisation's long-term strategy. It may come about as a result of the implementation of lean production, business process re-engineering and other organisational structuring initiatives. Strategic downsizing starts from the position that it is an appropriate strategy to move the organisation forward and make significant structural reforms.

Delayering is advocated as a strategy to simplify the organisation's structures and enhance its competitive strength and decision-making processes. Delayering may be associated with downsizing, but this is not always the case. Delayering tends to have its greatest impact at managerial level. It is likely to reduce opportunities for promotion and to restrict career choices. Although it may offer managers opportunities to assume greater responsibility, there is evidence that, on the whole, its consequences can be negative.

Downsizing and delayering, in general, can have potentially negative consequences for organisations. Excessive downsizing can lead to 'organisational anorexia'. This results in the depletion of key experience, skills, competencies and knowledge. Survivor syndrome is also an important issue. Managers who remain may be shattered by the experience and trust levels may be significantly eroded. Manager commitment may take a downward spiral.

Downsizing can have major negative effects on 'corporate memory' (Burke 1997) and employee morale. It has the potential to destroy knowledge networks and cause a significant loss of knowledge (Littler 2000). Fisher and White (2000) suggested that downsizing can seriously impact the learning capacity of organisations. Downsized organisations provide fewer formal management development opportunities to managers. Managers may, however, set extra responsibilities. They also recruit fewer staff externally and, as a result, the organisation's skill capacity can 'hollow out'.

EXHIBIT 2.2

Downsizing – Explanations and Strategies

Three dominant theories have been used to explain the attractiveness of downsizing strategies: economic, institutional and socio-cognitive. The dominant theory has been the economic perspective.

1. **Economic Theory:** This views downsizing as being caused by a search for productivity and efficiency, as a response to organisational decline or as an attempt to increase profitability, i.e. a rational attempt to manipulate performance. This stream of research has examined the financial outcomes of downsizing and established the link to productivity, profitability and stock price. This perspective has been questioned as more evidence emerges to indicate that it has failed to deliver the financial benefits expected.
2. **Institutional Theory:** This argues that social conventions impel the pursuit of downsizing and views it as 'good initiative'. Managers conform to this view in order to gain legitimacy. Downsizing decisions are seen as cloned and learned responses to uncertainty, reinforced by the rewards that exist within the internal career system, with external professionals now voicing fewer objections to the pursuit of downsizing. The proportion who believe the process has 'gone too far' fell from fifty-two per cent to thirty-nine per cent from 1966 to 1997.
3. **Socio-Cognitive Theory:** This approach focuses attention on managers' mental models of downsizing and how these models are constructed. Managers' decisions to downsize are based on shared mental models that define the causes and effects of downsizing and indicate that it is an effective way of conducting business better, faster and smarter, even though objective data might show that downsizing strategies may be implemented on false assumptions of efficiency.

Source: Zhao, Rust and McKinley (1998)

Downsizing Tactics

Downsizing Tactic	Characteristics	Examples
Workforce reduction	• Aimed at headcount reduction • Short-term implementation • Fosters a transition • Buyout packages • Layoffs	• Attrition/natural wastage • Transfer and outplacement • Retirement incentives
Organisation redesign	• Aimed at organisation change • Moderate-term implementation • Fosters transition and, potentially, transformation	• Eliminate functions • Merge units • Eliminate layers • Eliminate products • Redesign tasks
Systematic redesign	• Aimed at culture change • Long-term implementation • Fosters transformation and new organisational forms	• Change responsibility • Involve all constituents • Foster continuous improvement and innovation • Simplification • Downsizing: a way of life

Source: Cameron *et al.* (1991)

The management of downsizing initiatives presents significant challenges for managers. They need skills in communication and the management of change. They also have to manage procedural justice issues related to selection for redundancy. Managers need to give consideration to how to manage the workforce that remains. In particular, managers face the challenge of moving the survivors away from negative reactors towards the challenge of change and opportunities for growth.

Delayering is conducive to the decentralisation of initiative and to empowerment. Applegate (1995) suggested that delayering makes it easier, in some cases, to introduce better communication and teamworking processes.

The Knowledge-Based Economy

The concept of the knowledge-based economy advances the idea that knowledge creation is the most significant source of economic growth. The *Global Competitiveness Report* (2005) argued that the new economics of knowledge depends largely on the quality and management of human resources. Five dimensions of knowledge are highlighted in this report.

- Knowledge has the potential to accumulate over time. It is an important engine of economic growth. The proportion of knowledge workers in an economy and their levels of knowledge are considered critical.
- Knowledge is different from information. Information is codifiable, 'know why', and 'know what', whereas knowledge tends to be tacit and is embedded in people and contexts. It is the 'know how'.
- Knowledge is embodied in databases. This has resulted in organisations seeking to protect their intellectual property and offshore some of this knowledge work to emerging economies.

- Knowledge possesses the capacity to spill over and to be localised. Breakthrough ideas created by one firm spill over to other firms in the local region. Cappelli (1999) suggested that the clustering of knowledge-intensive firms has important implications for the career opportunities of managers.
- The diffusion of knowledge is facilitated through the emergence of knowledge networks. These networks are particularly viable in the diffusion of tacit knowledge. These networks are based on trust.

One of the consequences of the emergence of the knowledge-based economy is the knowledge-based firm. These firms are differentiated from other forms of organisation by their ability to bring together the knowledge of specialists in an effective manner. Specifically, they have the capacity to identify and acquire new knowledge with greater speed, intensity and focus than other organisations. They can also assimilate this new knowledge quickly into current routines and processes. Child and McGrath (2001) suggest that they also have the capacity to transform knowledge by developing it and fusing it with existing knowledge. They then exploit this newly transformed knowledge either by leveraging existing learning competencies or by developing new competencies.

The possession of superior knowledge and the organisational ability to use it represent a significant source of competitive advantage due primarily to the difficulties competitors encounter in imitating knowledge. Organisations have implemented knowledge management initiatives in order to capture this knowledge. Many of these initiatives have produced mixed results due primarily to cultural and people issues.

Exhibit 2.3 presents a typology of knowledge found in organisations.

EXHIBIT 2.3

A Typology of Organisational Knowledge

- **Embrained Knowledge:** This knowledge relies on conceptual and cognitive skills and is commonly referred to as knowing about something. It has an abstract character and involves higher-level reasoning and understanding. It is theoretical in nature.
- **Embodied Knowledge:** This knowledge is acquired through action. It is commonly referred to as 'know how'. Embodied knowledge is acquired through working on something, face-to-face interaction and discussion through emotional engagement. Embodied knowledge is rooted in a specific context and, as a result, is not easily transferable to other contexts.
- **Encultured Knowledge:** This refers to the process by which people share culture. It is dependent on the sharing of a common language and on the negotiation of meaning.
- **Embedded Knowledge:** This type of knowledge is located in organisational routines or capabilities. It can be located in systems of relations such as technology, the roles people perform and routines that organisations use. Embedded knowledge is systemic and context-determined.
- **Emoded Knowledge:** This is frequently referred to as information and is more easily transmitted than embedded knowledge. It is knowledge abstracted from context and it can be selective in the meaning it conveys.
- **Knowing:** This refers to the process of becoming something. It focuses on the process of change.

Source: Cummings and Worley (2001)

The emergence of knowledge-intensive firms and the corresponding emergence of knowledge workers raises significant challenges for organisations, including the management and development of expertise and the facilitation of knowledge-sharing.

Knowledge workers may be less willing to participate in knowledge management initiatives due to the power and status that can be derived from possessing specialist knowledge. Hislop (2004) pointed out that organisational knowledge is tacit and personal in character. It is built up over time and employees may be unwilling to participate in organisational knowledge management initiatives if they perceive that this involves giving away a significant source of power and status. Furthermore, the extent to which employees are willing to participate in knowledge management initiatives is related to the nature of the employment relationship. Conflicts may arise concerning who has ownership of the knowledge and how it is used. Table 2.1 presents a summary of the organisational factors that influence managers' attitudes to organisational knowledge management initiatives.

Table 2.1: Organisational Factors that Influence Attitudes of Managers to Organisational Knowledge Management Initiatives

Organisational Factor	Explanation
Knowledge Availability	• To what extent do managers and employees have the necessary tools, manuals and information they need to do their job? • What procedures are in place for managers to access training when they need it?
Collaboration and Teamwork	• Is teamwork encouraged and facilitated within the organisation? • Does the organisation provide places for people to meet informally? • Does the organisation ensure that time is set aside for managers to share and learn from one another?
Information Sharing	• Does the organisation encourage managers to leverage best practice and share new ideas? • Are best practices leveraged across departments or units?
Information Systems	• Does the organisation have the necessary systems in place to collect and store information? • How effective are information systems in making information available to employees?
Innovation	• To what extent are new ideas welcomed? • Are employees encouraged to find new and better ways to do work? • Does the organisation solicit employees' inputs in solving problems? • Do senior executives and managers work in partnership with employees and value their perspective?
Organisation Culture	• How open is the culture and does it facilitate knowledge sharing? • Does the organisation culture articulate clearly what the organisation stands for and how it works? • Does the organisation have too many rules and procedures and too much administrative machinery?
Connectivity with Customers	• Does the organisation encourage the formation of enduring relationships of trust with customers? • Does the organisation have mechanisms for involvement of customers in knowledge-sharing?

The growth of the knowledge-based economy, corresponding knowledge management initiatives and the emergence of knowledge workers have major implications for managers and leaders. Managers have a key role to play in creating and supporting an organisation culture conducive to knowledge sharing and its use and development. There is debate concerning whether managers have the capacity to create and manage cultures. The more pessimistic position appears to be that, unless the organisation implements knowledge management initiatives compatible with the existing culture, these initiatives are likely to fail.

Management and leadership development is considered one of the more important HRM policy areas that can be used to support knowledge management initiatives. Hunter *et al.* (2002), for example, argued that the provision of appropriate management and leadership development interventions is most appropriate when the knowledge management strategy is focused on building the social capital of its managers and knowledge employees. Garvey and Williamson (2002) pointed out that the most valuable management training and development initiatives are those designed to encourage reflexivity, learning through experimentation and skills in conducting critical dialogues with peers and employees.

Knowledge workers need to be managed in distinctive ways. Horowitz *et al.* (2003) suggested that there are distinctive bundles of HR practices that are effective in motivating and retaining knowledge workers. These HR practices make significant demands of managers. They require that managers provide high levels of autonomy and interesting work tasks, and that they ensure significant opportunities for self-development. Autonomy is very important to knowledge workers. Research has found that knowledge employees liked to have autonomy in the projects they worked on, the type of training and development initiatives they undertook, the work patterns they chose and the way in which performance goals were set. Knowledge workers demand continuous development. Knowledge employees place a high priority on the amount of development available and the types of needs that it addresses. Some employees and managers consider the provision of such opportunities potentially a double-edged sword. A lot of knowledge work is both intangible and invisible and is therefore difficult to measure.

Alvesson (2000) argued that managers have a key role to play in ensuring the retention of knowledge employees. They have a particular role in the development of a sense of organisational identify. He distinguished between instrumental-based and identification-based loyalty. Instrumental-based loyalty works on the premise that the knowledge employee will remain loyal to the employer as long as specific personal benefits are available. This represents the weakest form of loyalty. Identification-based loyalty is based on the knowledge employee having a strong sense of identity with the goals and objectives of the organisation. Identification-based loyalty can be developed through: 1) the creation of a set of values with which the knowledge worker identifies; 2) the creation of a strong sense of identification with a team; and 3) through a combination of both approaches. It has been argued that the development of interdisciplinary teamwork meets a number of knowledge worker needs. These teams must be permitted a considerable degree of autonomy in what they do and how the various capabilities are utilised.

New Technologies

Technology has emerged as an important factor in explaining how organisations manage work, where managers actually work and the way in which they manage. Technology has resulted in a number of important outcomes for organisations. In some cases it has led to deskilling. It has created the knowledge worker, led to the emergence of telecommuting and distributed work, and posed significant challenges for organisation structures and communication.

New technology has resulted in significant productivity gains for organisations. It has, as a result, led to the elimination of workers. A particular consequence is deskilling, where skilled professional workers and craftsmen have had their job content eroded. Most modern forms of work involve the use of information technology. This has resulted in managers having to acquire the competence to use these technologies.

Technology has impacted on where managers live and work. New technology has facilitated telecommuting and distributed work. In some cases managers no longer have to commute long distances to the workplace. They can telecommunicate, meet online and manage virtual teams. Some commentators (Ware 2005) suggest that managers are even more connected to their workplace as a result of new technology. They are constantly checking emails, downloading documents and working outside normal hours. In some cases, managers have become addicted to both technology and work.

Technology has facilitated the distribution and sharing of information, and the development of knowledge networks and collaborative work. Producers and consumers can now collaborate in the production of goods and services. Technology has altered communication processes in organisations. Employees, as a result, have more access to senior managers. Middle-level managers are becoming increasingly irrelevant in the organisation hierarchy. Employees have become more powerful because they have access to knowledge networks. Malone (2004), for example, suggested that organisations have become less bureaucratic and more democratic. He suggested that the style of managers must evolve from 'command and control' to 'co-ordinate and cultivate'. Senior managers are increasingly required to be in touch with the ground floor. Leadership is also increasingly distributed throughout the organisation.

At an organisational level, new technologies have facilitated the development of interdependence between organisations. Child (2005) pointed out that organisations have used new technology to develop networks with customers and suppliers. Networked companies have the capacity to outperform more conventional companies. New technology provides organisations with new possibilities in terms of technology-centred flexibility. This refers to the flexibility of manufacturing systems. Beach *et al.* (2000) suggested that technology or manufacturing flexibility can be evidenced in five different senses:

- The ability of a manufacturing system to adjust volumes of production
- The ability of an organisation to produce a certain mix of products
- The ability of a system to change the mix of a certain set of products
- The ability to deal with changes in the design of existing products
- The ability to deal with new products.

In the Irish and UK context, a mixed picture emerges concerning the adoption and operation of technology by organisations. The slower-than-anticipated rates of adoption can be explained in terms of failures in and problems with the technological hardware itself. Likewise, the relative lack of success is related to managerial failure and incompetence and the inappropriate design of flexible organisation structures.

New communication technologies have enabled organisations to externalise their operations. The research indicates that, with information technology, independent operations are cost-effective. IT enables the development of partnerships with suppliers and other contributors to the value chain. These advantages, if they are to be accrued, require managers to be skilled in organising the support of relationships and flows of information across boundaries. Managers are increasingly required to manage boundary relationships, work through external networks and manage outsourcing. Managers are increasingly spending their time on the management of trust between network members and on facilitating co-ordination. Managers are required to manage velocity. This includes issues such as internal communication, supplier and competitive interchange, changes in strategic conditions, and greater uncertainty and ambiguity.

Business Ethics, Social Accountability and Governance

Business ethics is a contemporary and problematic issue for organisations, managers and leaders. Various scandals have adversely affected the reputation of managers and executives and have led to the suggestion that large corporations possess too much power. Lefkowitz (2006) suggests four descriptive paradigms of ethical challenges which are faced by managers.

- *The opportunity to prevent harm*: Managers are frequently privy to policy decisions that may involve harm or wrongdoing. Managers may be motivated not to act by a sense of loyalty or some other self-serving objective.
- *Temptation*: This involves the contemplation of a self-serving action that is potentially unjust, deceitful or that can cause harm to others.
- *Role Conflict*: This involves having competing obligations or responsibilities to two or more individuals or organisations.
- *Values Conflict*: This involves situations where managers face conflicting personal values of equal importance.

Exhibit 2.4 presents a categorisation of immoral behaviour.

EXHIBIT 2.4

Categorisation of Immoral Behaviour

- **Incivility**: Rude or hostile behaviour. This consists of interpersonal actions that violate norms of conventional social behaviour. It includes discourteous or insulting behaviour. If the behaviour is particularly hostile, it may be unethical.
- **Organisational Misbehaviour**: This behaviour is targeted at the organisation rather than the individual. It may include theft, defacing company property, bad-mouthing the organisation, sabotage or fraudulent criminal behaviour. These actions are unethical, depending on the motivation of the person doing them.
- **Unethical Behaviour**: This category involves unintentional ethical transgressions, due to failure on the part of the manager to appreciate the moral implications of the situation, and intentionally unethical actions instigated on behalf of the organisation, such as deceptive sales practices.

A fundamental question arises concerning who has responsibility for the ethical behaviour of organisations. Some commentators consider it the primary responsibility of directors and senior managers. However, others take the view that everyone in the organisation shares responsibility for his or her part in the business. Tonge *et al.* (2003) argued that a key determinant of an ethical culture of an organisation is the example set by senior management. It has been found that the problem of poor adherence to business ethics is related in part to managers' lack of personal ethics.

It has been suggested that the creation of a society in which business values are considered to be central has generated demands that business behaves better. This incorporates the idea that business has a responsibility to be a better citizen. There is evidence that many corporate mission statements and ethical codes pay lip service to virtues such as integrity and fairness and address these issues to a variety of stakeholders. In some case, the enthusiasm for ethics comes about as a result of a scandal which damaged the organisation's reputation. In other cases, it is used as a marketing tool. The majority of ethical codes tend to concentrate their attention on external stakeholders, in particular customers, and fail to address the responsibilities managers have to internal stakeholders.

A related argument concerns the social responsibility and accountability of firms. Corporate social responsibility is difficult to define. Winstanley, Woodhall and Heery (1996) suggested that it involves every aspect of society on which a company has an impact. Particular strands within this broad definition include concern for the environment, the impact of business on the communities in which it operates, and labour rights. Most definitions of corporate social responsibility indicate that responsible organisations are expected to go beyond their legal obligations. Mellahi and Wood (2003) suggested that most businesses see corporate social responsibility and business ethics as niche issues. Some businesses are still hostile to these concepts.

Corporate governance came to the fore in the 1990s, due in the main to the emergence of corporate scandals involving directors in public companies promoting their own interests, either illegally or at the expense of the shareholders. Models of governance tend to focus on the shareholder or the wider stakeholders. The shareholder or Anglo-American model focuses on the obligation to serve shareholder interests, whereas the stakeholder or continental European model promotes an external orientation and emphasises the continuous balancing of shareholders and stakeholder interests. Table 2.2 provides a summary of both perspectives.

Table 2.2: Contrasting the Anglo-American and Continental European Models of Governance

Levers	Anglo-American	Continental European
Transparency	Financial; investor-based	Spread of director interests
Remuneration	Options, bonus-based additional to salary but performance-driven	Salary, status, promotion, security of tenure
Loyalty	Oneself, profession	Organisation
Values	Self-generated wealth	Public good
Conduct	Self-disciplined, codes of conduct as models	Legislation
Identity	Own initiatives; self-developed; mobility	Community or organisational; broader-based initiatives; less mobile
Risk assessment	Executive, non-executive director responsibility; needs attention; formally given attention	Executive, external director responsibility; needs attention; formally given attention

These models place a demand on the leadership of organisations to ensure that there are external non-executives in place who have a range of functional and sectoral experience. They are also expected to have independence of mind and be experienced in leading during times of change. They must also possess the strength to offer an unwelcome opinion or to challenge where it is necessary. New organisational forms have, in general, de-emphasised hierarchy in favour of horizontal team-based relationships. These new forms do raise important issues for corporate governance. The first concerns the dilution of top-level control that arises from devolution. Problems also emerge from the growing use of network partnerships and other forms of strategic alliance.

Table 2.3: Business and Organisational Challenges: Implications for Management and Leadership Development

Issue	Key Issues	Leadership Issues	Leadership Development Challenges
WIDER BUSINESS ENVIRONMENT			
Globalisation	• Global competition is increasingly the norm for many organisations • The challenge of the local versus the global • Globalisation has driven the need to focus on costs and to be competitive • Increased use of outsourcing and off-shoring	• Managers and leaders need to think in a more global way • Need to understand and work in different cultural contexts • Clear need to design organisation structures that are suitable to the global environment	• Increased need to develop managers and leaders who have foreign operational experience • Need to develop skills in a culturally sensitive way • Greater use of international assignments and expatriate managers • Development initiatives for working in complex structures
HYPER-COMPETITION AND NEW ORGANISATIONAL FORMS			
Structural Transformations	• Flatter organisational structures • Increased use of matrix arrangements • Use of temporary organisations for special projects	• Greater need for autonomy and responsibility • Greater clarity on areas of responsibility • Working with experts from different disciplines and areas	• Develop leader and manager skills in generating commitment and trust • Develop communication skills and skills in foreign languages
Virtual Organisations	• People in different locations and different organisations working together • Greater global co-operation on joint projects	• Linkages needed between independent employees • Greater need for communication and different modes of communication	• Develop skills in communicating the corporate culture • Develop cultural awareness and sesitivity
Downsizing and Delayering	• Strong focus on costs and efficiency • Greater use of empowerment and flexible job descriptions • Greater need to align business with the competitive environment	• Managing and leading with fewer resources • Managing change programmes	• Skills in dealing with uncertainty and resolving ambiguities

Issue	Key Issues	Leadership Issues	Leadership Development Challenges
HYPER-COMPETITION AND NEW ORGANISATIONAL FORMS (*contd.*)			
The Knowledge-Based Economy	• Knowledge is increasingly used as a source of competitive advantage in organisations • Introduction of knowledge management systems • The emergence of knowledge workers who have unique management requirements • Initiatives designed to capture tacit knowledge and develop expert systems	• Need for managers to develop an understanding of how to manage knowledge workers • Need to leverage HR practices to optimise the contribution of knowledge workers • Role of leaders in facilitating the retention of knowledge workers and the promotion of loyalty	• Leaders need to develop skills in managing organisational knowledge • Leaders need to be proficient in developing others • Develop team-working skills and interdisciplinary team-working initiatives
New Technologies	• Enterprise-wide data systems more commonly used • Greater use of distributed PC/Intranet-based technologies • Use of technologies to speed up production processes • Use of statistical process control (SPC) • Use of technology to facilitate e-commerce opportunities	• Need to be comfortable with new technologies and become technologically proficient • Development of partnerships with specialists who develop systems • Management of technically proficient staff who are likely to be young and business-savvy	• Develop skills in monitoring the environment for technological opportunities • Use multiple technologies to keep people informed • Develop skills in strategic thinking, thinking creatively and data analysis
BUSINESS ETHICS, SOCIAL ACCOUNTABILITY AND GOVERNANCE			
Ethics	• Strong focus on personal ethics and values • Increased external regulation of the activities of business • Greater focus on the use of social responsibility programmes • Strong emphasis on governance issues and avoiding conflicts of interest	• Performance of leaders and managers judged by external regulators • Greater need to act ethically and have a strong set of moral values	• Develop knowledge of ethical issues facing business • Assess leaders'ethical awareness and develop ethical principles

Issue	Key Issues	Leadership Issues	Leadership Development Challenges
CHANGING DEMOGRAPHIC TRENDS, WORK VALUES AND ATTITUDES			
Ageing Workforce	• Increased use by organisations of older employees • Evidence of higher productivity and commitment from older employees	• Provision of development opportunities • Need for more flexibility and adaptability in leadership styles and approaches • Challenges to younger managers when interacting with older employees	• Develop skills in managing older employees • Develop skills and knowledge of diversity issues
Women in Management	• Increased participation of women in senior management • Changing expectations and different styles of managing amongst female managers	• Development of confidence to work in predominantly male environments	• Develop understanding amongst managers of the contribution of female managers
Dual-Career Families	• Design of work arrangements to suit the needs of dual-career couples • Retention issues for dual-career couples	• International assignments issues for dual-career couples • Provision of day-care and child-rearing facilities to accommodate dual-career couples	• Provide leadership development and international assignments opportunities for dual-career couples
Work–Life Balance	• Increased focus on managing work–life balance • Implementation of alternative and more flexible work arrangements such as flexitime and home-working • Increased use of technology to facilitate new working arrangements	• Implementation of strategies to integrate work and caring responsibilities • Management of employees who work from home	• Be flexible in the provision of leadership development opportunities

Issue	Key Issues	Leadership Issues	Leadership Development Challenges
EMERGING MANAGEMENT TRENDS			
Management of Diversity	• Greater need to cope with cultural, gender and language differences • Implementation of diversity awareness programmes and diversity training	• Management of conflicts that may arise due to cultural differences • Need to capitalise on diversity for the advantage of the organisation	• Include diversity issues in management, leader and leadership development initiatives • Develop foreign language and cultural sensitivity skills
New Team Concepts	• Project teams and taskforces are increasingly commonplace • Greater use of multicultural teams • Geographically dispersed team structures	• Need to ensure that there is buy-in to projects • Greater need to have role clarification • Leaders need to emphasise the bigger picture and understand their leadership role	• Develop skills in team management, team decision-making and project management • Understand the value of team-working in the organisation
TQM/Integrated Manufacturing	• Strong focus on continuous improvement and organisation-wide quality initiatives • Use of concepts such as SPC and re-engineering concepts	• Need to secure involvement and commitment to quality • Teams need to stay focused on quality improvement goals	• Understand customer relationships and satisfaction • Develop team-working skills
High-Performance Organisations	• Increased adoption of high-performance management practices in organisations • Use of high-performance practices to achieve competitive advantage	• Leadership style and approach are important aspects of high performance • Issues around the use of HR strategies and change interventions	• Develop skills in the use of sophisticated HR strategies and practices • Develop skills in aligning conflicting priorities and creating distinctive capabilities
Changing Psychological Contracts	• Changing expectations such as flexibility • Greater customisation of HR strategies • Emergence of i-deals and continuous renegotiation of employment relationships	• Management of individuals who have different expectations • Leader is fundamental in facilitating retention and building commitment to organisation	• Develop opportunities for rising or emerging leaders • Develop skills in managing star talent and high performers • Develop skills in coaching, giving feedback and leader-led development

Issue	Key Issues	Leadership Issues	Leadership Development Challenges
EMERGING MANAGEMENT TRENDS (*contd.*)			
Strategic Alliances	• Increased use of mergers and strategic alliances • Understanding of mission and vision issues related to mergers and strategic alliances	• Understanding of cultural issues that arise from mergers • Management of change and conflicts • Sensitivity to different organisational traditions	• Develop skills in valuing differences, sharing responsibilities and developing trust • Develop skills in working effectively within and across organisations
Service, Work and Emotional Labour	• Increased use of call-centre models and customer-interaction work • Service standards are increasingly a measure of competitiveness • Customer has an increasingly important role to play in shaping how work is performed	• Management of service workers is complex because leadership style will impact on the quality of service provided • Emotional maturity and intelligence of managers is increasingly important • Managers play a significant role in shaping employee attitude	• Develop emotional intelligence and emotional management strategies of employees • Develop skills in 'managing' self-management teams • Develop skills in handling service conflicts and interpersonal encounters
NEW WAYS OF THINKING ABOUT MANAGING AND LEADING			
Post-Modernism	• Advocates changing notions of what it means to be a leader or manager • Emphasises the significance of discourse and the potential for multiple, co-existing and competing interpretations of management and leadership	• Leadership must accommodate different interpretations and concepts of managing people • Need to understand the interplay of power and potential for dominance of the most powerful	• Leadership development is about the way people talk about development • Leadership development is anything that enables the leader to be effective in the leadership role
The New Science	• Challenges our assumptions concerning certainty, linearity and predictability in management • Organisations are not fixed entities but are flexible and self-managing	• Leadership is a relational process because information flow is facilitated through relationships • Strong focus on trust, inclusion, respect and a concern for the person	• Role of leaders is to articulate vision and values • Develop coaching and feedback skills • Develop skills in understanding the core beliefs of followers

Changing Demographic Trends, Work Values and Attitudes

One of the most significant factors impacting on organisations and the tasks of managers and leaders is changing demographics. Particular demographic trends include the ageing of the workforce, increasing workplace diversity, the emergence of the 'net generation', changing work values, the increased participation of women in management, dual-career families and work–life balance issues. These changes require managers and leaders to rethink current management practices to match the changes that are taking place.

An Ageing Workforce

The median age of working employees has increased significantly over the past ten years. The baby-boomer generation is moving towards retirement age. There is evidence that a significant proportion of employees will opt for early retirement. Organisations are experiencing a shortage of skills and workers resulting from a combination of factors, including an ageing workforce, lower birth rates and an increasing number of younger people delaying work in favour of higher education. The effects of an ageing workforce in organisations are considerable. They are losing skills and knowledge when experienced workers retire. There is increased competition for a younger workforce, which has led some commentators to suggest that there is a war for control (Farnham 2005).

The age structure of the working population has important implications for the availability of knowledge workers and the provision of development opportunities. It suggests that, to utilise the maximum potential contribution of all employees, organisations have to be imaginative in adopting appropriate development strategies. Management and leadership development initiatives need to promote adaptability and flexibility in managers' behaviours and enable them to meet the challenges of the changing business situation. Burke and Ng (2006) suggest that a significant priority for organisations concerns the successful transmission of knowledge from the older generation of managers to the next generation. This may be achieved through the adoption of mentoring programmes and pairing older managers with younger protégé managers, which will help to provide younger managers with unique access to the experience and perspectives of older managers. Younger managers could also benefit from development opportunities that focus on personal and career issues.

Participation of Women in the Workforce and in Management

One of the most significant changes in the last twenty years concerns the feminisation of the workforce. Women's employment is, however, characterised by both horizontal and vertical segregation. Women are still found in the lower levels of organisations, although there is increased participation in first- and middle-level management positions. Black women are even more under-represented at higher levels of management. Women in Europe currently represent about five per cent of managing directors and chief executives. Women are far more likely to be in part-time work and to occupy temporary posts; therefore they have less job security. There is evidence that women are increasingly interested in senior management positions.

Hackim (1960) studied the experiences of women in the labour market. She argued that women are disadvantaged in the workplace because their differing needs mean that they do not face the labour market with one voice. Table 2.4 presents an analysis of women's work-style preferences. This table indicates that twenty per cent of women are home-centred, twenty per cent are work-centred and sixty per cent make up a diverse group who wish to combine work and family without either taking priority.

Table 2.4: Women's Work Style Preferences

Home-Centred	Adaptive	Work-Centred
20% of women (range 10% – 30%)	60% of women (range 40% – 80%)	20% of women (range 10% – 30%)
Family life and children are the main priorities throughout life. Gender-traditional individuals who accept the gendered division of labour in the home	Diverse group including women who want to combine work and family without either taking a priority, as well as career drifters (women with no definite idea about the life they want but who respond to opportunities and modify goals quickly) and women with unplanned careers	Pursuing stereotypical male careers and work histories. Includes childless women or women with children treated as 'weekend hobby'. Main priority in life is employment or equivalent activities in the public arena; politics, sports, art, etc.
Prefer not to work	Want to work, but not totally committed to work career	Committed to work or equivalent activities
Qualifications obtained for intellectual dowry	Qualifications obtained with the intention of working	Large investment in qualifications and training for employment in other activities
Responsive to social and family policy	Very responsive to all policies	Responsive to employment policies

Source: Hakim (1996)

There is compelling evidence to indicate that women are generally under-represented in management positions in Ireland and the UK. The research evidence generally indicates that women are well represented at junior management level. There are few women at chief executive level (Davidson and Cooper 1992; Vinnicombe and Colwill 1995). The glass ceiling is still a problem for women at higher levels of management in Ireland and the UK. Women have suffered a degree of ghettoisation in their managerial roles. Female managers are more frequently found in the banking, retail and hospitality sectors, usually at lower- and middle-management levels. They frequently occupy positions in the 'softer' areas, such as customer services, relationship management, human resource management and training and development. Ohlott, Ruderman and McCauley (1994) argued that women run risks because they find themselves in softer roles. They are likely to be stereotyped and, as a result, organisations are likely to retain them in these roles. Woodall and Winstanley (1998) suggested that women face many barriers when forging a career in management. To be successful, women have to enter management at an earlier stage than men. They must gain experience in core management functions, be continuously employed, work long hours, be geographically mobile and conform to male-oriented promotion criteria. Some women lack confidence and competitiveness, and might not have a career orientation. Some employers have implemented work arrangements designed to attract talented female managers. Such approaches include part-time schemes, flexi-time, flexi-scheduling and home-working.

Dual-Career Families

An issue related to the increased feminisation of the workplace is the growing number of dual-career families. The number of families with two wage-earners has increased rapidly in the last ten years. Organisations are challenged to provide work arrangements to accommodate such families, including day care and sick child care programmes. Such services have the potential to reduce absenteeism, lower management turnover and increase productivity. However, such services may engender resentment from employees who do not need them.

Baruch (2004) argues that women try to delay having children in order to avoid the damaging effects of a career break on progression within the managerial hierarchy. One of the most frequently cited issues in relation to dual-career couples concerns international assignments. Harvey (1997), for example, found that their dual careers present obstacles to their readiness and willingness to accept international assignments. It is very difficult for spouses in professional and managerial positions to find suitable roles elsewhere.

Work–Life Balance Issues

The structure of work is better suited to the needs of men than women (Thesing 1998; ILO 1998). Furthermore, the concept of a managerial career is also gendered. Drew and Murtagh (2005) argue that senior management culture impacts upon women in two particular ways. It tends to ignore women's responsibility to their family. This manifests itself in the timing of meetings that prove problematic for female managers with families. Second, women's life cycle patterns of work and childminding are incompatible with a senior management career. The career stage, when there are significant demands at work, also coincides with peak child-rearing years. Box 2.1 highlights four theoretical perspectives on work–life balance.

Box 2.1: Four Theoretical Perspectives on Work–Life Balance

Institutional Theory: The adoption of work–life balance policies is predicted to vary according to size, sector, unionisation and industry. Organisations conform to and reflect the normative pressures in society (changes in wider societal value systems), depending on the extent to which they have to maintain a sense of social legitimacy. The organisations most likely to conform to pressures to introduce work–life balance policies are large private sector firms (because of their high visibility) and public sector organisations (because of their accountability to the electorate). Organisations that compete in the same industry come under pressure to imitate these practices for fear of damaged reputation among suppliers, customers and existing workers. Organisations with union presence are also exposed to more scrutiny and are therefore more likely to conform.

Organisational Adaptation Theory: Although organisations must respond to societal norms and expectations, how these expectations become known, recognised and taken on board by managers is more important. The processes through which organisations recognise and interpret the changing world around them are important, and the perception and interpretation of societal norms are influenced by the values of senior management. Therefore, in addition to size, sector, unionisation and industry as predictors of take-up, the gender composition of the workforce (more female staff employed), reliance on gender composition of the workforce (more female staff employed), reliance on high-skilled workers who are difficult to replace, and work designs that already allow employees much latitude in the manner and pace with which they carry out tasks will all be associated with more attention to work–life balance.

High Commitment Theory: There is a link between the organisation's HR strategy and its adoption of family-friendly employment practices. Work systems and worker–management relationships that improve

---

employee commitment to the organisation revolve around the introduction of innovative HRM practices that facilitate co-operation between managers and workers, and an opening up of management decisions to scrutiny by employees. Organisations can enhance commitment by showing that they understand the conflicts that can arise between work and other aspects of life and can tolerate flexible work practices that allow employees to balance these competing demands.

Situational Theory or Practical Response Theory: Organisations act more simply and respond most directly to the pressures of immediate circumstances. Work–life balance practices have grown in response to traditional pressure towards profitability and productivity, as well as difficulties in recruiting and retaining a high-quality labour force. Work–life balance policies are introduced where the organisation sees a direct link between them and a solution to problems of absenteeism, staff turnover and unfilled job vacancies. Broader shifts in the composition of the workforce, such as an increase in the number of female employees, require adjustments to existing labour practices.

Source: Wood (1999)

The work–life balance debate has arisen largely from the intrusion of work into home life. Hochschild (1997) argued that home life is being taken over by work. He suggested that organisations face a new experience in which the workplace is being changed into a more home-like environment. He suggested a feminisation of the workplace, but a masculinisation of the home. Sparrow and Cooper (2004) argued that the modern employment relationship is a negotiation designed to establish boundaries around the attention and presence of an employee. Organisations are increasingly required to adopt policies that co-ordinate and integrate work and non-work dimensions. Felstead *et al.* (2002) suggested that organisational work–life initiatives take three forms:

- Strategies to integrate employment with caring responsibilities
- Strategies designed to reconcile the balance between paid employment and the need to have time off work
- Policies that allow managers more opportunities to work from home.

While some organisations implement work–life flexibility options, very few managers, male or female, feel that they can be availed of. Thesing (1998) suggested that taking up such opportunities could convey the idea that managers are not committed to their careers. Wajcman (1999) found that women at the higher end of the managerial hierarchy do not opt for work–life balance options. This arose primarily from the negative way in which senior women perceived that they would be viewed by the organisation. Drew, Murphy and Humphreys (2003) found that the take-up of work–life balance initiatives by senior managers in Ireland was very low. It was almost non-existent amongst male managers. Drew did find that Irish organisations were more conscious of the need to accommodate work–life balance issues. Irish organisations faced a challenge in transforming their cultures to ensure that fairness existed and that work–life balance policies were accessible to all employees.

Emerging Management Trends

In recent years, a host of managerial trends have emerged that impact on managerial work and on organisations. These trends include the management of diversity, new team concepts, total quality management, lean manufacturing, business process engineering, managing the aftermath of mergers and acquisitions, high-performance work systems and the management of professionals.

Management of Diversity

Workplace diversity refers to a situation where an organisation's workforce is made up of people with different human qualities or who belong to various cultural groups. Loden (1996) distinguished between primary and secondary dimensions of diversity. Primary dimensions include age, race, ethnicity and sexual orientation. Secondary dimensions include work style, communication style, language, religion, education and style level.

Recent research studies lend support to the idea that a focus on diversity can add value to organisations and contribute to competitive advantage. Richard (2000) suggested that diversity can enable organisations to meet the needs of diverse customers. Diverse employees can help an organisation build better relationships with customers by making them feel connected to the organisation. When organisations support diversity, managers feel more valued for what they can bring to the organisation. Diversity helps to develop greater organisational flexibility.

Diversity issues have a number of important leadership implications. Konrad *et al.* (2000) found that executives from different countries had different values and attitudes. They suggested that to lead effectively in a diverse, global environment, leaders need to be aware of cultural and subcultural differences. Cultural differences have major implications for leadership style. The perception of how behaviour is perceived differs from culture to culture. Forlin and Dans (1997), for example, suggested that in some cultures such as the USA, the UK and Ireland, it is considered appropriate to criticise a subordinate in private. However, in collectivist cultures such as Japan, this type of leader behaviour would be considered inconsiderate. The expectation is that people will receive criticism from peers rather than directly from leaders. Chemers and Ayman (1993) advocated that leaders must develop personal characteristics that support diversity. They identify four particular characteristics:

- A personal, long-range vision that recognises and supports a diverse organisational community. Leaders must be aware of the need to express their vision through symbols and rituals that reinforce the value of a diverse culture.
- Leaders need a broad knowledge of the dimensions of diversity and an awareness of multicultural issues. This knowledge needs to be put into action by using inclusive language and demonstrating respect for differences.
- Leaders need to be open to change. They must be willing to accept criticism and change their behaviour if necessary.
- Leaders should be prepared to take an active role in mentoring and empowering employees so that they can use their unique abilities.

New Team Concepts

Work teams and new team concepts have become popular in leading global companies. Katzenbach and Smith (1992) defined a work team as 'a small number of people with complementary skills who are committed to a common purpose, performance goals and an approach for which they hold themselves mutually accountable'. Team structures have a number of benefits, including enhanced decision-making, improved performance and quality and enhanced flexibility. However, they can pose problems. Sundstrome, DeMeuse and Futrell (1990) found that teams can be problematic due to issues of team leadership and developmental issues.

Virtual and global teams present significant challenges for leadership. Virtual teams have members who work closely together even though they are based in different locations (including different countries) and may even be in different time zones. Typically, they have members from different countries who work across organisational boundaries. Leaders in virtual teams do not have available the normal methods with which to monitor team members. Bell and Kozlowski (2002) suggested that virtual team leaders have to trust team members to do their jobs without constant supervision and that they need to focus more on results than on the means of accomplishing them. They identified four strategies that leaders must utilise in order to manage and be effective in leading virtual teams. These are presented in Exhibit 2.5.

EXHIBIT 2.5

Leadership Issues in Leading Virtual Teams

Selection of Team Members
- Team members need to have strong technical knowledge and responsibilities to work effectively in a virtual environment.
- Small virtual teams tend to be more cohesive and work together more effectively.
- Members will usually come from diverse backgrounds and viewpoints.

Build Trust by Building Connections
- Virtual team leaders need to work hard at establishing connections between team members.
- There is a need for initial face-to-face interaction if trust is to be quickly established.
- Leaders should have frequent intense meetings that allow teams to go through key stages of team development rapidly.
- Team development, in a virtual team context, is best established through bringing team members to the same place at the same time.

Establish the Ground Rules
- Team members need to understand both team and individual goals, deadlines and expectations.
- Goal setting enables team members to monitor their own performance and regulate their behaviour appropriately.
- Virtual teams need to agree on communications etiquette. This will include issues such as time limits for responding to emails and the degree to which it is appropriate to criticise team members openly.

Use of Technology
- Leaders should, where possible, use face-to-face communication sessions that are rich in achieving understanding.
- Leaders should schedule regular times for people to interact online.
- Team members should be trained in the use of electronic communications. Issues need to be made more explicit when the communication is online.

Virtual teams are increasingly used in a global context. Global teams are work teams, made up of culturally diverse members, who live and work in different countries and co-ordinate some or all of their work activities on a global bias. The challenges provided by virtual teams are magnified in the case of global teams. Building trust is a significantly greater challenge when team members have culturally different norms and values. Govinderajan and Gupta (2001) suggested that communication barriers are particularly problematic. These include language differences, tone of voice, dialect, semantics and accent. They found that senior leaders considered building trust and overcoming communication barriers the two most difficult leader tasks in achieving global team success.

Total Quality Management, Integrated Manufacturing and Re-Engineering

Total quality management and other continuous improvement initiatives continue to be utilised by organisations, typically by those that have to manage the pressures of world-class competition. TQM is a term that encapsulates many ideas, including the articulation of a strategic vision, benchmarking, employee empowerment and team building, committed leadership, customer involvement and a systems view of quality improvement.

TQM initiatives have the potential to increase the importance of management and leadership development initiatives. TQM concepts challenge leaders to facilitate major change, empower direct reports, institute team-based initiatives and articulate to employees a vision of quality and their role in achieving quality.

Niven (1993) argued that TQM can lead to goal displacement in which TQM becomes an end instead of a means. Managers tend to blame employee empowerment for slower decision-making. Blackburn and Benson (1993) suggested that TQM, with its top down overtones, gives very limited employee empowerment and it may also have an air of surveillance, whereby the performance of employees is monitored. They argued that the role of middle managers can become unclear and confused, which creates conflict. Because TQM is centralised, service departments compete with rather than collaborate with TQM initiatives. Wilkinson and Wilmot (1995) suggested that it has placed significant pressures upon managers to organise the work of employees in more profitable ways.

Organisations have also adopted new approaches which streamline manufacturing. These include advanced manufacturing technology (AMT), just in time (JIT) and computer-aided manufacturing (CAM). These systems, when combined with managerial processes, have the potential to provide significant gains in productivity, greater dissemination of information and greater collaboration in problem-solving. They challenge managers to develop high-level problem-solving capabilities. Organisations which adopt new manufacturing processes are also more likely to give more emphasis to management and leadership development and make greater developmental use of performance management. Snell and Dean (1992), for example, found that these organisations were more selective in hiring managers and were more proactive in preserving their investments in managerial skills.

Business process re-engineering is widely practised in organisations. This initiative is directed at achieving significant savings by eliminating unnecessary activities and consolidating work. Re-engineering initiatives demand greater cross-functional co-ordination and the crossing of organisational boundaries. Such initiatives often disrupt existing power relationships and may lead to organisational delayering. Re-engineering initiatives fail where there is a lack of support from top management. They entail a significant time commitment from senior managers as well as extensive communications with employees. The elimination of jobs may result in a significant increase in the workload of managers.

High-Performance Work Systems

The concept of a high-performance organisation or work system is one of the more recent concepts to emerge in the management literature. This concept seeks to understand why some organisations are winners and others are losers. This question has led researchers to identify the factors that determine high performance. Table 2.5 summarises some of the key research findings to date, which are shaping the notion of a high-performance organisation or work system.

Table 2.5: What are the Keys to the High-Performance Organisation?

Researcher	Prescriptions
Quader and Quader (2008)	• Emphasise collective decision-making and communication of core values • Leadership which provides a guiding vision and stretch goals • Continuous learning, creation of employee empowerment and a sense of ownership • Place value on courage and fire in the belly • Utilise global benchmarks of excellence • Encourage entrepreneurship and innovation
Holbeche (2008)	• An emphasis on employment security • Selective hiring of new personnel • Implementation of self-managing teams • Decentralisation of decision-making • Extensive training and development activities • A reduction in status distinctions and barriers
Foster and Kaplan (2001)	• Focus on transformation rather than incremental change • Place emphasis on abandoning outdated structures and rules • Adopt new decision-making processes, control systems and mental models • Create new businesses
Hailey, Farndale and Truss (2005)	• Quality information available to employees • Develop employee's ability to interpret information • Provide employees with the latitude to use their skills • Extend benefits to all categories of employees
Holbeche (2004)	• Focus on organisational changeability • Create a knowledge-rich context for innovation • Create a boundary-less organisation • Stimulate people to sustainable levels of high performance • Become a great place to work • Become a values-based organisation
Flood *et al.* (2005)	• The use of structured, standardised interview processes • Systematic evaluation of performance • Extensive/intensive training in company-specific skills • The provision of relevant operating performance information • The provision of relevant strategic information

The term 'high-performance organisation or work system' is complex. It has a variety of meanings:

- The first meaning suggests that it is associated with the concept of high-commitment management or high-involvement management. This first meaning also incorporates notions of total quality management. Lawler, Mohram and Ledford (1995) defined the concept to include human resource and operational initiatives which can guarantee both higher productivity and competitiveness. This meaning suggests that the essence of a high-performance organisation combines high-commitment management, quality assurance and inventory strategies.

- A second meaning focuses on shifting the emphasis from employee attitudes and commitment, and incorporating issues such as the structure of work, performance management, skill formation and pay satisfaction. This meaning suggests that high performance must be targeted directly rather than indirectly through a focus on employee attitudes. A strong feature of this meaning is the emphasis on performance-related pay, something which is not considered by the high-commitment model of the high-performance organisation or work system.

Some commentators have suggested that the concept of the high-performance organisation is as much about marketing as about any fresh conception concerning how an organisation can operate. Holbeche (2004) is a strong proponent of the high-performance organisation model. She identified some of the factors that make a positive difference to productivity and facilitate the achievement of sustainable high performance. She suggested that six factors or inputs are relevant:

- *Organisational Changeability*: This is conceptualised to include strategies to develop flexibility, speed and learning.
- *Knowledge-Rich Contexts*: This is defined as the implementation of strategies to stimulate business breakthroughs and continuous improvement.
- *Boundaryless Organisations*: This dimension focuses on the maximisation of potential synergies and includes cross-boundary working activities.
- *Discretionary Effort*: This dimension focuses on creating the conditions where employees are willing to give discretionary effort and achieve sustainable levels of high performance.
- *A Positive Work Environment*: This concerns the creation of conditions that make the organisation a great place to work. It includes employee needs for work–life balance, development opportunities and career growth.
- *A Values-Based Organisation*: This concerns the implementation of strategies that enable the organisation to connect with employees and other stakeholders at a deeper level of meaning. Employees are making greater demands for more open, democratic and ethical leadership styles.

These characteristics bring into focus the important role of leadership and the contribution of development initiatives to creating the appropriate leadership style. The high-performance model emphasises the role of the leader in maximising the organisation's capabilities. Gabel (2002), for example, suggested that the success of managers and leaders at all levels is contingent on their ability to manage situations from a position of being 'caught in the middle'. The effective leader understands that individuals in organisations will have conflicting views on key issues, and understands these perspectives. Collins (2001) suggested that leadership at five levels is needed for corporate success. There is a growing scepticism concerning the power of the top executive to bring about significant change. Collins suggested that, at Level 1, leadership focuses on the highly capable individual who makes productive contributions through talent, knowledge, skills and positive working behaviours. Level 2 focuses on the contributing team member who has important capabilities to bring to the achievement of team objectives. Level 3, the competent manager, focuses on organising people and resources towards the achievement of predetermined objectives. At Level 4, the leader emphasises the need to foster commitment and the vigorous pursuit of predetermined objectives. The Level 5 executive focuses on building organisational greatness through a blend of personal humanity and professional will. This executive is totally committed to furthering the organisation's interests.

EXHIBIT 2.6

Focus on Research: Designing High-Performance Jobs

There has been much research conducted on building and sustaining high-performance organisations and high-performance teams. However, consider a scenario where there is a compelling vision and mission for the business and a clear strategy on how to achieve its aims, but the implementation of the strategic plans is very poor. Unit leaders don't seem to collaborate; new products are delayed; customers are dissatisfied; and profit margins are being eroded. There is a possibility that critical jobs have not been structured to achieve the business's strategic objectives.

There are four dimensions or spans to every manager's job:
1. *Control:* Resources over which a manager has decision rights.
2. *Accountability:* Measures used to evaluate a manager's performance.
3. *Influence:* The extent of the network of people with whom a manager must interact and whom one must influence to do one's job.
4. *Support:* Assistance that a manager can expect from people in other areas.

Each span can be adjusted to become wider or narrower. If the organisation can structure critical jobs to achieve the right balance between the four spans, talented individuals will be able to contribute at their highest level. The reverse is also true. For example, if managers are made accountable for delivering certain results without having the necessary resources or influencing power, this can lead to problems in strategy execution.

The span of control for a manager's job needs to be based on an organisation's strategy for delivering value to the customer. For example, in Nestlé (food company) regional business managers need a wide span of control so that they can customise products as per the company mission to satisfy regional tastes. Second, the span of accountability needs to be based on what behaviours the organisation wants to encourage in their leaders. For example, in a highly regulated environment that requires strict compliance managers will need a narrow span of accountability.

The span of control and the span of accountability are mutually dependent. So should the two spans be equally wide or narrow? In high-performing organisations, the answer to that question is an emphatic *no*. The span of accountability (goals to be achieved) is explicitly set wider than the span of control (resources available to the manager) to force managers to exhibit entrepreneurial behaviour. In this way, managers are forced to think creatively to succeed without having all the necessary resources at their disposal.

The third span (influence) is based on a job's interdependence with other jobs. Influencing, as a skill, has become critical for leaders in today's complex organisational environment. The more the leader must cross boundaries and encourage others to assist him or her, the wider the span. In order to increase a span of influence, a manager can become responsible for stretch goals, report to multiple bosses or manage a virtual team.

The fourth span of job design is support, and this should be based on how much commitment the leader needs from others to deliver the goals. For example, traders in a financial environment will need only a narrow span of support to achieve results, as they are principally self-reliant. This span also depends on the company's culture and values. For example, in Hewlett Packard teamwork (supporting others) is strongly encouraged and promoted.

When job spans are misaligned, the company's goals will not be delivered. One scenario that can ensue is a *crisis of resources*, when the supply of resources is clearly inadequate for the specific job. This is most likely to happen when the senior leaders are over concerned with control, influence and accountability and have not adequately considered support. A wide span of support can compensate for a relatively narrow span of control. Another scenario that can arise is a *crisis of control* when job spans are not properly calibrated. In this case, the supply of resources exceeds demand, which can lead to missed opportunities and wasted resources. The more dynamic the marketplace, the more challenging it is for managers to ensure alignment of the four job spans to enable the business to reach its goals.

Source: Simmons (2005)

QUESTIONS

Q.1 How should leaders approach designing high-performance jobs?

Q.2 Reflecting on the article, do you think that your job is designed to enable you to achieve your optimum performance?

Table 2.6: High-Performance Work System Terminology

High-Performance Work Systems (HPWS) are often touted as corporate saviours by their practitioners. However, the term covers several distinct approaches, some of which are more successful than others in increasing organisational performance, and a substantial amount of jargon. Aspects of HPWS include:

- Participatory Work Organisation (PWO): Systems that are designed to allow a greater level of participation by non-managerial employees in everyday decision-making. Includes self-managed teams and workplace-level employee involvement programmes.
- Commitment Enhancing Human Resource Management (C-HRM): HR practices that are designed to increase affective commitment to an organisation. Includes intensive training, work–life balance programmes, profit-sharing, job security, selective recruitment and dissolution of status discrimination between workers and management.
- Quality of Work Life (QWL): Programmes that are designed to increase employee perception of quality in working life and job. Often a combination of PWO and C-HRM functions.
- Total Quality management (TQM): A system that espouses increased empowerment through the management of quality in an organisation. Includes greater distribution of information and substantial management training.
- Lean Production (LP): A process that is intended to increase organisational performance by the division and allocation of tasks to teams that are responsible for efficiently achieving preset targets.
- Self-Managed Teams (SMT): A system designed to reduce organisational hierarchies by placing many managerial functions under the control of semi-autonomous groups that are responsible for planning, implementing and completing tasks. Ideally, SMTs are also in charge of developing their own performance standards, setting and meeting deadlines and deciding which resources they require for successful project completion.

The Psychological Contract and Discretionary Behaviour

The psychological contract has emerged as a major concept in the management and human resource management literature. The concept is contested, but it is generally defined as being concerned with an individual's subjective beliefs, as shaped by the organisation, and with the nature of the exchange relationship between the individual employee and the organisation. Sparrow (1996) argued persuasively that the psychological contract underpins the work relationship and provides a basis for capturing and understanding many complex organisational phenomena. The most common discussion of psychological contracts focuses on those that are transactional and those that are relational. The former are based on a short-term relationship, whereas relational contracts are long-term and based on trust and mutual respect. Arnold, Cooper and Robertson (1997) suggested that, under a transactional contract, the employee offers long hours, broader skills and greater acceptance of change in return for higher pay and rewards for higher performance. Some commentators such as Guzzo and Noonan (1994) suggest that psychological contracts can contain elements that are transactional and relational in nature.

Hutchinson, Kinney and Purcell (2002) expanded our thinking on the psychological contract by arguing that the crucial factor linking HR practices to performance is the way in which these practices trigger discretionary behaviour on the part of employees. They define discretionary behaviour as a set of choices that employees make concerning the speed, core innovation and style of job delivery. Discretionary behaviour lies at the heart of the employment relationship. The employment relationship is indeterminate in that it is difficult to specify both its content and outcomes. The employee has a choice concerning how conscientiously they will carry out a job: he or she can, for example, withdraw discretionary behaviour.

The prime drivers of discretionary behaviour are ability, motivation and opportunity. Employees must possess the necessary abilities and the corresponding motivation to apply these abilities. However, there must also be opportunity to engage in discretionary behaviour. These opportunities may be derived from the job itself, the team or the wider organisational context. The concept of discretionary behaviour has important implications for the way in which managers and leaders perform their roles. It suggests important skill issues in respect of the extent to which line managers are skilled in delivering human resource management practices. Line managers are increasingly expected to be the deliverers of human resource policies and strategies. They make them a reality and bring them to life. Hutchinson, Kinney and Purcell (2002) highlighted that, whereas policies are usually found in written form and are therefore more clear cut, it is in the practice of these policies that managers are more likely to be challenged. This study highlighted the crucial differences between espoused and enacted policies and concluded that what happens in reality deviates considerably from that which is espoused.

The way in which line managers manage human resources is, in itself, discretionary. Managers vary considerably in how much attention they give to human resource issues. The discretionary behaviour that managers demonstrate is strongly associated with leadership. Local leadership is what gives HR policy a life and existence in the organisation. A significant dimension of line managers' discretionary behaviour concerns the extent to which they discuss development needs and provide coaching and guidance opportunities. The effective management of discretionary behaviour by managers requires a significant level of support. They have expectations in respect of training, development and future careers. They have to balance short-run and long-run performance expectations and there is a strong need for leadership at the centre of the organisation.

Strategic Alliances: Mergers, Takeovers and Acquisitions

The definition of a merger or acquisition is relatively straightforward. An acquisition occurs when one firm acquires a controlling interest in another firm. A merger, on the other hand, occurs when two firms join forces by combining operations and assets under a single ownership structure. Mergers are therefore viewed as the combination of approximate equals, whereas acquisitions may be hostile and imply the purchase and subsequent control of the acquired firm by the acquirer. Mergers and acquisitions are a major feature of the modern business landscape. These alliances are usually strategic in that they are formed to help the strategic partners realise their strategic objectives on a basis that can be achieved better in co-operation than in isolation. Such alliances are not a transient phenomenon. Contractor and Lorange (1988) suggested that there are seven more or less overlapping objectives for strategic alliance formation:

- The reduction or sharing of risk
- Achievement of economies of scale for rationalisation
- Facilitation of technology exchange
- Pre-emption, counteraction or co-option of competition
- As a strategy to overcome government-mandated trade or investment barriers
- Facilitation of initial international expansion of inexperienced firms
- They may combine contemporary competencies as well as assisting diversification.

Figure 2.1 presents a summary of strategic alliances. Strategic alliances pose a number of important challenges for managers and leaders. If one particular member of the alliance dominates the alliance, it may be possible for the partner to manage it as a single organisation.

Figure 2.1: A Summary of Strategic Alliances

Category	Type	Characteristics
Partnerships between Non-Competing Firms	International Expansion Joint Venture	• Established to overcome trade or investment barriers • Created to facilitate initial international expansion to territories where risks are high
	Vertical Partnerships Joint Venture	• Consist of alliances between firms that operate at two successive stages within the same value chain • Usually formed to achieve quasi-vertical integration advantages • They allow firms to rationalise through specialising on core competencies or share new technology development costs
	Cross-Industry Agreements	• May combine contemporary confidences as well as assist diversification • May be used to pre-empt competition in a new field
Alliances Between Competitors	Shared-Supply Alliances	• Formed to achieve economises of scale and to reduce risk by sharing R&D costs
	Quasi-Concentration Alliances	• May be established to co-opt or counter competition as well as reduce risk by sharing R&D costs
	Competitive Alliances	• Usually formed to achieve strategic synergies. • They are potential competitors who seek to gain benefits by pooling contemporary strengths

In cases where the alliance is a relatively balanced one, the challenge is to find ways to reconcile different structures, styles and cultures. Managers of joint ventures can experience conflicting pressures. The manager may experience conflict with the parent company. These conflicts, where they are incompatible, may produce role conflict. The severity of role conflict is likely to be more pronounced when the alliance manager has to satisfy the needs of two equally strong parent companies that have competing priorities. It is likely that experience, management development and education will be of value in helping to deal with this situation; however, the consequences of role conflict may be poor decision-making, stress and burnout. The literature is replete with suggestions concerning how to minimise role conflict in strategic alliance situations. These include clarifying and backing the general manager's authority; creating special liaison positions to facilitate the development of a common policy position and assist greater understanding; and establishing mechanisms to resolve conflict.

A major challenge for managers in the context of strategic alliances is the potential clash between partner cultures. Each partner in the alliance will have its own unique organisational culture. Where the alliance is cross-border in nature, these cultural differences will be further complicated by national cultural differences. These cultural differences require careful management by managers and leaders. Managers are likely to encounter difficulties in areas such as attitudes towards authority, relationships, uncertainty and time.

- **Authority:** This problem is likely to be manifest in local staff demonstrating reluctance to take responsibility and exercise authority. This may result from differences in organisation size and from their locations in emerging economies.
- **Relationships:** There are cultural differences in how people regard personal or friendship ties. This is known as the universalism versus particularism debate. In a universalism context, friendships are not considered important, whereas particularism would suggest that friendship ties are important.
- **Uncertainty:** This dimension focuses on attitude to risk. Risk-averse cultures are likely to focus on control and certainty and utilise formal rules. Risk-prone cultures are more likely to encourage innovation, deviant ideas and behaviours.
- **Time:** Cultures differ in their attitude to time. Some cultures view time in a more flexible way than others. It is also likely that corporate and national cultures may differ in the extent to which they adopt a long- or short-term orientation. Such differences can lead to mistrust and fundamental disagreement over policy decisions and managerial practices.

Boris and Jemison (1989) suggest that 'the amount of energy and time needed to merge two organisations resembles the planning and execution of the invasion of Normandy. It results in a clash of cultures from many elements attempting to work together towards the end.'

EXHIBIT 2.7

Perspective on Theory: I-Deals or Idiosyncratic Deals

Rousseau, Ho and Greenberg define i-deals as 'voluntary, personalised agreements of a non-standard nature, negotiated between individual employees and their employers, regarding terms that benefit each party'. They argue that i-deals have a number of important characteristics.

- *Individually Negotiated:* I-deals result from an individual negotiation process. The market power of the employee and the value placed on the employee by the employer will determine who sets the terms of the deal.

- *Unique Terms:* The terms of the deal will be unique to the individual employee and they will differ from other employees in similar positions. These unique terms may be the result of perceived inequality and injustice.
- *Benefits for both Employer and Employee:* I-deals are intended to address the priorities of both the employee and the employer. The benefits to the employee are premised on the value that the employee has to the employer.
- *Varied in Scope:* I-deals will vary considerably. They may contain individual elements that are different, or the total package may be unique.

Employees have a major role to play in creating and negotiating aspects of their employment. They can be negotiated prior to employment or they may be ex-post i-deals. However, i-deals are negotiated in contexts where some employment terms are standard to all employees. Therefore the potential of an employee to negotiate unique conditions is a sign of the employee's contribution to the organisation.

Three particular dimensions of i-deals are important: the strategic value of the employee to the organisation; the timing of i-deals; and the implications of repeated bargaining.

- *Strategic Value of Employees:* Employees who recognise that they are valued by the organisation are in a better position to assert their preferences and power when bargaining for i-deals. Firms that engage in the negotiation of i-deals have a particular strategic need for the employee's knowledge and skill.
- *The Timing of I-Deals:* Employees or potential employees can negotiate i-deals at two time periods: during the recruitment process or after the relationship has been established. The timing of the negotiation will depend on the employee's perception of their negotiation strength. At the time of recruitment it will depend on the employee's perceptions concerning successful negotiation. Labour market conditions will dictate the extent and dynamics of the negotiation process once the employee is in employment. If the employee possesses skills that are in significant demand in the labour market, it is to be expected that he or she will engage in the negotiation of i-deals. It is likely that an employee will focus more on negotiating deals ex-post rather than ex-ante because the employee will receive signals and information concerning his or her value. I-deals may also be used as a way of rewarding employees for their performance contributions and loyalty to the organisation.
- *Repeated Bargaining:* It is likely that where an employee has a lengthy employment relationship there will be repeated bargaining. These successive deals may reflect adjustments, and they may also reflect attempts to up the ante and get more from the employer. These repeated bargaining sequences may change the meaning of the deal over time. Each subsequent deal may become less special. It is also possible that employees who repeatedly negotiate may diminish or damage their reputation in the organisation.

The specific terms of i-deals will vary considerably. The terms may range across issues such as pay, travel opportunities, mentoring, development, education and personal support. Some of the resources that form the terms of the deal may be highly tangible, whereas others may be more abstract or intangible. The intangibles may include higher quality employee–supervisor relationships, more job scope and responsibilities, participation in special projects or high-profile events in the organisation.

Source: Rousseau, Ho and Greenberg (2006)

The Emergence of Service Work and Emotional Labour

Many employees and managers now work in the services sector. These service jobs require, in many cases, direct interaction with customers. This type of work requires significant emotional labour. Employees and managers are expected to present their emotions and manage their behaviour in order to comply with the service ethos of the organisation and to create positive perceptions of service in the mind of the customer. Morris and Feldman (1997) highlighted that service standards are frequently incorporated in the rules of employment and in performance appraisal processes.

Service work has a number of important characteristics. The customer has a major role to play in shaping how the work is performed. The customer articulates key expectations and makes the key determination concerning whether performance standards are met. Fuller and Smith (1996) suggested that the customer may, in some cases, act as a co-producer. In other cases, the customer may be enlisted by the organisation to supervise employees jointly. The involvement of customers in the service delivery process has resulted in organisations taking proactive steps to manage employee behaviour. Leedner (1996) suggested that the employee's 'looks, works, personality, feelings, thoughts and emotions' are considered aspects which should be managed.

Hochschild (1990) made an important distinction between emotional work and emotional labour. Emotional work describes the act of attempting to change an emotion and how it is displayed in everyday life. She argued that people conform to particular feelings and rules that define what is emotionally appropriate. Emotional labour, she considered, exists when a profit motive underpins the performance of emotional work within an organisation. Emotional labour has as its essence the containment of an outward countenance in order to produce a particular emotional state in others. Hochschild argued that people tend to use one or two types of techniques: 'surface' and 'deep' acting. Surface acting involves pretending to experience emotions that are essentially not genuine whereas deep acting involves something more sustained and genuine.

Driver (2003) suggested that employees not only accept but expect some level of organisational control of emotional expression. Emotional labour is in many cases low-paid, low-status work. It is also predominantly carried out by women. O'Brien (1994) suggested that women are inherently more skilled in the performance of emotional labour.

The concept of emotional labour has important implications for the management of human resources. A fundamental issue concerns variability in service provision and the lack of buffers between production and consumption. Service is perishable, and produced and consumed simultaneously. It is also variable in nature. Customer demands are often unusual and require different skills and dispositions from the service provider. The control of service delivery is complicated because of the day-to-day variability in employee attitudes and behaviours. Organisations increasingly use tight rules of interaction to narrow the scope for variability. This has the effect of restricting opportunities for employee discretion. Wharton (1996) suggested that employees are expected to display emotions in a public way that they do not feel privately. Some organisations have used invasive forms of control to ensure that service delivery is controlled. Batt and Moynihan (2004) suggested that organisations use computer technology to monitor the speed of work, the level of downtime and the quality of the interaction between the employee and the customer. Employees are also expected to follow tightly scripted dialogue with customers and to work to detailed instructions.

Organisations tend to organise service work in particular ways. Herzenberg, Alic and Wial (1998) suggested four particular approaches. Each work system has distinct implications for managerial and employee behaviour. The four systems have the following characteristics:

- **Tightly Constrained:** In this scenario, jobs are narrowly defined. Skill requirements are low and technology is used to control the pace of work. This type of work is often stressful with the result that there is a high staff turnover.
- **Unrationalised Labour-Intensive:** In this scenario, skill and knowledge requirements are low and there are few, if any, training- and career-development opportunities. The majority of learning takes place on the job, through informal peer interaction. The level of service provided often depends on the employee's sense of obligation.
- **Semi-Autonomous**: In this scenario, employees perform work that cannot be easily monitored or controlled. The work is subject to greater variation. It is also more complex and demands firm- or employee-specific skill and knowledge. There is a higher level of investment in training and development and career opportunities are more widely available.
- **High-Skilled Autonomous:** This scenario involves a work system that is built around professional qualifications and skills. There is a large amount of formal and informal on-the-job learning. The work performed tends to be complex in nature, highly non-routine and intangible. Fewer opportunities exist for tight supervision, monitoring and control. The self-motivation of the employee emerges as a critical issue.

Table 2.7 presents a summary of each service work system and implications of each for leadership development.

The management of service employees is complex. The way employees are managed will impact on the quality of the service provided. Ashkanasy and Daus (2002), for example, highlighted that, through a process of 'emotional contagion', positive expressions of emotions by front-line employees can create favourable impressions in customers' minds. A major challenge facing managers concerns how best to monitor employee performance without being too intrusive. Some organisations have implemented initiatives designed to instil values of good customer service in their employees. Managers are expected to play a major role in 'shaping' employee attitude. They use strategies which promote self-control and encourage participation in teamwork. Wharton (1996) argued that part-time employees are likely to find their jobs more satisfying when attention is paid to the 'fit' between the demands of the job and the employee's personality characteristics. Batt (1999) found that self-managed teams are associated with higher service quality, because when employees are provided with greater discretion they are likely to offer better service quality. Furthermore, employees who receive support from their immediate managers are more likely to report higher levels of job satisfaction.

Table 2.7: Implications of Service Work Systems for Training and Leadership Development

Service Work Systems	Implications for Leadership Development
Tightly Constrained	• Very little emphasis on training due to tight prescription of tasks and tight supervision • Managers use control-oriented management strategies • Development will consist of task-management skills • Very little emphasis on formal education and credentials • Few internal job moves or opportunities for job-based development
Unrationalised Labour-Intensive	• Focus on informal on-the-job development • Few opportunities for stretch and development of job breadth • Low to moderate focus on education and credentials • Relatively loose supervision of tasks

Service Work Systems	Implications for Leadership Development
Semi-Autonomous	• Emphasis on formal education and credentials • Moderate levels of on-the-job development • Internal job moves are important for supervisors and managers • Task supervision is moderate; some discretion given to employees
High-Skilled Autonomous	• Significant emphasis placed on formal education and credentials • Internal job moves and broadening of development important for managers • Relatively little task supervision • Strong emphasis on the development of flexible management styles

New Ways of Thinking about Managing and Leading

So far in this chapter we have considered a range of external and internal forces that have implications for managing and leading processes in organisations. In this final section, we focus on two issues that derive from the world of ideas. 'Post-modernism' and the 'new science' have the potential to disrupt established thinking about leadership and the practice of management and leadership by individuals and organisations.

Post-Modernism

Post-modernism is difficult to define and explain, but in a management and leadership context it is often associated with non-quantitative and narrative approaches to leadership. The post-modern approach stresses the importance of organisational stories as small narratives, but defers the choice of taking sides in determining which of them is really true. Instead, it explores the stories and other narratives as discourses, looking at what makes them possible and asking what their effects are.

However, this explanation does not fully come to grips with what it truly represents. Hassard (1993) suggested that it can potentially refer to an epoch, a period of historical time, a continuation or a disjunction with the past, or an epistemological position. Clegg (1990) focused more on the epochal interpretation in emphasising what constitutes the modern organisation. He considers post-modern organisations to be flexible, with highly differentiated, demarcated and deskilled jobs.

As an epistemological position, post-modernism tends to assume that truth is tactical and socially construed. It challenges established thinking. The post-modern approach blurs the boundaries of what we consider as leadership. Leadership is seen as existing only in the ways in which it is talked into being. Post-modern leadership is whatever people do when they talk in ways that people recognise as leadership. It turns the concept of leadership on its head and stresses that leaders are servants. We will focus more on these concepts in Chapter Three.

Post-modernism has significance for the practice of management and leadership development. It recognises that multiple and competing views of management and leadership development are legitimate. It suggests that management and leadership development processes are conducted through the interplay of power relationships and potential for the dominance of the most powerful. It encourages managers to engage in self-reflection and to be critically suspicious of one's own interpretations.

Post-modernism highlights the significance of discourse. There are many discourses identifiable in the field of management and leadership development. Our discussion in Chapter One highlights that multiple, co-existing and competing interpretations of management and leadership development exist. This suggests that, in the future, we will encounter new interpretations of management and leadership development.

The New Science

'New science' challenges some of the key assumptions of Newton's mechanistic notion of the universe, which essentially assumed that certainty, linearity and predictability are essential elements of the universe. Traditional social science defines organisations as controlled and capable of measurement. The new science clarifies how individuals can act independently and still contribute in an orderly and unified way, and emphasises the concept of auto-process. This suggests that a system produces its own organisation and maintains and constitutes itself in a space. It is also defined as a tendency for living systems to renew themselves and regulate the reward process so as to maintain the true integrity of the system.

The new science postulates that organisations are open systems which possess the capacity to evolve into states of greater organisation, complexity and order. Open systems need information in order to evolve. The capacity for self-organisation requires a dialogue between the internal organisational environment and the external environment.

Leadership is considered a relational process because information flow is facilitated through relationships. The new science emphasises that leadership must show a concern for trust, inclusion, respect and a concern for the whole person. Relationships represent the key building blocks of an effective organisation. New science rejects the idea that total organisational control is possible, although it believes that leaders have a key role to play in shaping behaviour and have the capacity to shape the overall feel and structure of the organisation. Table 2.8 presents a summary of the principles that emerge from the new science perspective.

Table 2.8: The New Science and Leadership Development: Some Principles

- Life in organisations is full of paradoxes. Leaders need to have a level of comfort and confidence with ambiguity. They learn to ask the right questions. They can influence organisational life, but they do not ordain it.
- Leaders must put their heads above the chaos of organisational life and understand its contradictions. They must adopt a balcony perspective.
- Leadership is about coping with change. Leaders assist followers in experiencing organisational change as a productive activity.
- Vision and values serve as organisational elements and allow leaders to behave in particular ways. A vision has the potential to wrap the organisation in a value-laden field whereby individuals can view themselves and others in certain ways and act consistently with these values. A vision represents the essential nature of an organisation.
- An essential element of leadership concerns the ability to understand the core beliefs and values of followers. Listening to followers represents an essential skill of leadership.
- Leaders have a teaching and coaching function. A key task is to teach and coach followers to both accept and apply the vision. Teaching and coaching processes strengthen the attraction of vision and values.
- Autonomy and order are necessary to ensure viable organisations. Leadership ensures that principles are articulated. Leaders must ensure that individuals can be creative and make choices. Leaders focus on stewardship rather than control and ownership.

Conclusion

This chapter explored a number of contextual factors that shape management and leadership development. A key to understanding management and leadership development lies within its context. The wider socio-economic, political and cultural context of management and leadership development is complex and dynamic. Various elements of context have multiple and often competing implications. This suggests that the purpose and concept of management and leadership development is a contested terrain.

A host of challenges faces managers and leaders today. Managers and leaders are challenged by a range of external factors, including globalisation, downsizing, employee diversity and new technology. Managers are expected to adjust to a more competitive global economic environment. To meet the challenges posed by intense competition, organisations have downsized, developed and decentralised. They have adopted more flexible forms and have implemented a range of change initiatives such as business process re-engineering, lean production, learning organisations and cultural change programmes. The boundaries between work and non-work are now more blurred and employees are now more likely to be female, to work part-time and to work away from the workplace.

These challenges have brought the significance of management and leadership development to the fore. Specific elements include the management of careers, employability and flexibility. Managers are increasingly required to be self-directed in their careers. They need to possess competencies that have a value in a multiplicity of contexts. They must have both the confidence and the skill to manage ambiguity, show vision, encourage discretionary effort and utilise a range of leadership styles and approaches. They are less likely to rely on control and directive aproaches. They need to understand the role of values and vision and utilise these to create value for the organisation.

Summary

In this chapter, the following key points have been made:

- Management and leadership development is embedded in its context. This context is complex and dynamic.
- Managers and leaders are challenged by globalisation and its associated challenges such as downsizing, delayering and decentralisation.
- Managers and leaders now operate in organisations that are less hierarchical in nature and they have adopted more flexible forms.
- Managers and leaders are increasingly challenged by waves of organisational change. They are exposed to initiatives such as total quality management, business process re-engineering and lean production.
- The boundaries between work and home are more blurred. Managers and leaders must now operate across organisational boundaries.
- New forms of work organisation demand new management and leadership strategies. Management and leadership development must meet these challenges through balancing the demands of organisations and managers.
- Our notions of what constitutes management and leadership development have changed. Leaders are expected to take the strategic view and to deal with complexity. Leadership development focuses increasingly on values and stewardship.

■ Discussion Questions

1. What assumptions and hypotheses underpin our discussion of context in this chapter?

2. What wider business environment changes do you see having the greatest impact on managers and leaders in your organisation?

3. Organisations have become increasingly concerned with the utilisation of human resources. How does this issue impact on what managers and leaders do?

4. The majority of new management initiatives focuses on the leader's ability to manage waves of organisational change. What competencies do the manager and leader need to manage change effectively?

5. What impact do post-modern theories have for how we view leadership and management processes in organisations and the way in which leaders are developed?

■ Application and Experiential Questions

1. Conduct some research on the global business environment of a specific company. What are the most recent developments affecting its business? How have these developments impacted on management and leadership development?

2. Select a company and gather information on its diversity initiatives. What are the key policy objectives? How do those initiatives impact on management and leadership development in the organisation?

3. Working in groups of three or four, prepare a presentation in which you outline the implications of outsourcing and off-shoring for leadership. What implications do they have for global leadership development specialists?

Chapter Three

Understanding Managers and Leaders in Organisations

Outline

Learning Objectives
Opening Case Scenario

The Nature and Characteristics of Managerial Work

The Content of Managerial Work
- The Characteristics Approach
- The Roles Approach
- The Process Approach

Explaining Leadership in Organisations
- Who are Leaders and What is Leadership?
- The Trait Approach to Leadership
- The Skills Approach to Leadership
- The Style Approach to Leadership
- Contingency Approaches to Leadership

The New Leadership
- Charismatic Leadership
- Transformational Leadership Approaches
- A Social-Network Approach to Leadership
- Ethical Leadership
- Change and Strategic Leadership
- Emotional Intelligence and Leadership

Post-Modern Leadership Approaches
- The Narcissistic Leader
- Post-Heroic Leadership
- Level Five and White-Water Leadership
- The Leader as Servant
- Stewardship
- Leadership Substitutes
- Thought Leadership
- Shared or Dispersed Leadership
- Self-Leadership and Individualised Leadership
- Spirituality and Leadership

Contemporary Debates on Leadership
- Gender and Leadership
- Cross-Cultural Dimensions of Leadership

Can Managers and Leaders be Developed?

Conclusion
Summary of Key Points
Discussion Questions
Application and Experiential Questions

Learning Objectives

After reading this chapter you will be able to:

- Describe and evaluate the key roles and activities of a manager's job.
- Understand different approaches to analysing a manager's job.
- Describe the key differences between managerial traits and skills.
- Describe and evaluate alternative explanations of leadership.
- Describe the main characteristics of the 'new' leadership.
- Evaluate the role of emotional intelligence in the development of leadership.
- Evaluate whether there are differences between men and women as leaders.
- Evaluate cross-cultural influences in leadership and what they mean for development.
- Describe and evaluate the arguments for and against the notion that it is possible to develop managers and leaders.

OPENING CASE SCENARIO

Leadership in the Aviation Industry: Michael O'Leary and Willie Walsh

Michael O'Leary is the Chief Executive of Ryanair, one of Europe's most successful low-fare airlines. When it was founded in 1985, it was a full-service conventional airline with two classes of service. However, during its first five years of business it experienced major turbulence, five chief executives were dismissed, and it accumulated significant losses. In the early 1990s its survival was seriously in question. As a result it restyled itself as a low-fares, no-frills carrier and modelled itself on Southwest Airlines. Tony Ryan, the founder of the airline, appointed a new management team, headed by Michael O'Leary, who by all accounts was a reluctant recruit. O'Leary set about transforming the airline. In a few short years he affected a major turnaround in the fortunes of the company. In 1997 Ryanair was floated in an initial public offering (IPO) on the Dublin stock exchange and on NASDAQ. It dropped its cargo services and, without the need to load and unload cargo, it reduced its turnaround time from 30 to 25 minutes. O'Leary cites on-time performance and baggage handling as key priorities for customers. Ryanair has a strong record on both aspects.

As a leader, Michael O'Leary is controversial. He has been described as 'buccaneering', 'loud-mouthed' and as possessing 'an instinctive hostility'. He has little tolerance of passengers connecting from one flight to another and he is not concerned that customers cannot work out the rules. His mission is to re-educate Europeans about air travel and he is quick to capitalise on the misery of competitors. He is, however, equally recognised as a genius, an innovator, a builder of teams and a great visionary. He demonstrates many of the characteristics of the classic entrepreneur. He identifies opportunities and pursues them relentlessly. He is considered more of an ideas man than a manager, but at the same time he has the skills to bring discipline to a business. He is continually praised for his prudent decision-making and for his careful management of publicity. He has demonstrated an uncanny ability to pull off publicity stunts and will not think twice about taking out full-page adverts that are critical of government ministers and competitors. He acknowledges that he can be confrontational, but he also suggests that he is upfront concerning what Ryanair offers. He has been exceptionally critical of the Dublin Airport Authority and BA. He argues that they are run by people who 'know everything about airports except how to run them'. He acknowledges that he is disliked by the media because he is perceived as an arrogant, rich bully boy. He has described British Airways as 'expensive bastards' and travel agents as 'f*****s'. However, in America he is considered a business genius. He has been nominated by various American magazines, including Fortune magazine, as one of the most powerful and influential men in the business world. He is considered a leader who has transformed the airline industry. His drive to win is admired in the American media, as is his ruthlessness and his need to be the ringmaster. O'Leary demonstrates many of the characteristics of the charismatic leader. He can be a showman, and he can be dramatic and aggressive. It is all driven by the will to win and to fight when it is to the advantage of Ryanair.

Willie Walsh first entered the airline industry in 1989 when he became a cadet pilot with Aer Lingus. He gradually worked his way up through the ranks and into flight operations. In 1988 he became the Chief Executive of Futura, Aer Lingus's chartered airline in Spain. In 2000 he was named the Chief Financial Officer of the airline and became Chief Executive of Aer Lingus in 2001. He left the airline in 2005 to become Chief Executive of British Airways plc.

Walsh very quickly made an impact at Aer Lingus. He cut costs by thirty per cent and got rid of business class on shorter routes. He sold off a significant proportion of the airline's corporate art collection, which raised over €400,000. Although his initial steps were met with opposition, especially from the trade unions, he earned the respect of the Irish government and senior management colleagues within Aer Lingus. He is considered to be bright and personable, and is well liked and respected within the industry. He is also considered very single-minded and shows a high level of tenacity in achieving his goals. His efforts at Aer Lingus produced results. In 2002 the company posted an operating profit of €63.8m, which represented a rebound from a loss of €35.5 million in 2001. In 2003 he achieved operating profits of €83 million.

Walsh's bold actions eventually got him into trouble with the government, the unions and industry. His stance on job losses led to a stand-off with the unions which in 2002 led to a three-day lockout. He had a row with the Exporters' Association due to his decision to axe short-haul cargo routes. In 2004 he made it known that he wanted to explore the possibility of a management buyout. This proved too much for the Irish government. The Taoiseach Bertie Ahern attacked him in the Dáil, accusing him of trying to cash in on the airline. Walsh resigned when the government refused to budge on the buyout issue.

Many people consider that Willie Walsh was in the right place at the right time. He was significantly removed from traditional, conservative leadership, which is typically found in large state-owned firms. Walsh's leadership style has been described as 'personable', and he has been described as a risk-taker and an entrepreneur. He has demonstrated skills at bargaining and is good at spotting an opportunity. He does not believe in half measures. He introduced a large number of risk-taking and innovative changes during his early tenure as CEO. These included a pay freeze for pilots, fleet reductions and increased utilisation of the current fleet, concentration on direct web marketing, better revenue management techniques, commission reductions and a reduction in business fares of more than fifty per cent. These were difficult changes to sell, but he achieved success with all of them. He articulated a very clear vision to stakeholders and demonstrated that it could be achieved. He produced major profitability and, during his tenure, he significantly remade Aer Lingus.

Walsh joined BA in 2005. Since taking over he has increased BA's investment in newer and better first-class and club world cabins and enhanced the airline's already substantial in-flight services. In 2007 he committed BA to buying both the Boeing 787 Dreamliner and Airbus's giant A380. He has also focused on controlling costs. Many critics claim this cost cutting resulted directly in the disastrous launch of Terminal 5 at Heathrow. Walsh has admitted that the T5 opening 'was not our finest hour', and he delayed the final move of BA's international flights to T5 until the autumn of 2008. He also sacked two top BA executives who were in charge of planning T5's opening, and refused to take a $1.5 million bonus. Overall, his relatively short tenure at BA has produced more positive than negative outcomes: he has achieved strong annual profits and the payment of the first shareholder dividend in seven years.

QUESTIONS

Q.1   What do you see as the similarities and differences in the leadership styles of these two leaders?

Q.2   Who would you consider the most effective leader?

The study of managerial work has preoccupied academics as far back as the beginning of the last century. Taylor (1911), for example, described the role of management as concerned with identifying and utilising the best way to control work and eliminate waste. Fayol (1916) was the first researcher to describe the basic managerial functions as: planning, organising, co-ordinating, commanding and controlling. He added to these categorisations at a later stage to include three additional functions: staffing, directing and budgeting. These role descriptions are now viewed as classic types, although they tell us very little about what managers actually do on a day-to-day basis.

There is a long tradition of research on management and leadership, and research on the nature of managerial work and leadership has taken two parallel paths. Much of the research on managerial work has focused on defining, measuring and developing managerial competencies. The topic of management work is, however, given less consideration than explanations of leadership in organisations. Explanations of leadership are many and varied. The field is characterised by various strands of debate. Research on leadership in organisations has in the past focused primarily on explaining leadership in terms of abilities, behaviours and the skill to articulate a vision. Contemporary theories of leadership, however, focus on notions such as post-heroic leadership, the leader as servant, stewardship, leadership substitutes and though leadership. These various theoretical perspectives have different prescriptions for leadership development. In this chapter we explore both traditional and contemporary explanations of leadership. We also address a very pertinent question in the context of this book: 'Is it possible to develop managers and leaders?'

The Nature and Characteristics of Managerial Work

Traditionally, the job of the manager involved the direct management of a team of people. This situation may no longer apply. There is evidence that many managers are more often individual contributors or 'singletons'. They do not have direct control over teams, but they have a significant role to play in supporting others. Managerial work is diverse. Traditionally, managers were viewed, for example, as planners, communicators and organisers. Increasingly, they are described as 'team leaders', 'the managers and developers of talent', 'coaches' and 'project managers'.

Two schools of theory exist on management. The empiricist perspective attempts to address the question: What do managers do? This theoretical perspective is generally associated with Mintzberg (1973), Kotter (1990) and Stewart (1991). These theorists examined managerial behaviours and practices and developed prescriptive theories of what managers should do. Mintzberg (1973), for example, used observation to describe the characteristics of managers' jobs and to categorise the various roles that they perform. The essentialist perspective, on the other hand, seeks to identify the 'essence' of management and explores the relationship between the various functions that managers perform. This tradition is associated with the traditional theorists such as Taylor and Fayol, who sought to identify a single best way.

Mintzberg suggested that there are three components of a manager's job: the frame, the agenda and the context. The frame of the job refers to its purpose, perspective and position. He defined purpose as what a manager is attempting to do. The perspective refers to how the organisation considers the role to fit into the business. Mintzberg (1994) argued that managers interpret their jobs differently, depending on their personal style and the context. Managers will also vary on how they do things, depending on the sharpness or clarity of their frame or mindset. The agenda refers to the process by which the manager figures out what to do and how to cope with ambiguity and uncertainty.

Working out the agenda may take time. The context refers to the situation within the department, the wider organisation and external to the organisation. The external context is likely to be more problematic and may require the manager to network and scan the environment.

The Content of Managerial Work

Researchers who have examined the job content of managers have adopted three perspectives: the characteristics, roles and process approaches.

The Characteristics Approach

This approach involves observing the tasks that managers perform and grouping them into meaningful categories. In the classic study of managerial work, Mintzberg (1975) identified several characteristics of a manager's job:

- Managers work long hours. The idea that managers work a thirty-five-hour week is a myth. With developments in technology, it is not uncommon for managers to engage in work seven days a week.
- Managers are busy people. Mintzberg found that managers were overworked. This is perhaps even truer today. There is a lot of evidence to indicate that downsizing and lean production approaches have created extra work for managers. Delayering has also resulted in managers having to do the work of two or three people.
- The manager's work is fragmented and done in short bursts. In contrast to the classic idea that managers perform work in a systematic manner, the empirical evidence indicates that managerial work is varied and mixes the important with the trivial. Managers are required to shift gears frequently.
- Managers are frequently interrupted. Managers are now exposed to instant communication, they are increasingly self-managed and they are in charge of all their communications. Managers appear to enjoy interruptions to their work and much of what they do tends to be superficial.
- Managers like action. Managers tend to enjoy the 'here and now'. They like the stimulus-response approach. Mintzberg found that managers like tasks that are current, specific, well defined, routine and concrete.

- Managers spend most of their time with other people. Managers spend little time on thinking tasks, in particular strategising. They spend most of their time in meetings.
- Managers spend a considerable amount of time with external contacts. This is increasingly the case, and external contacts might include suppliers, suppliers' associates and managers in other businesses.

Stewart (1975) conducted a similar study in the UK. She found that managers' work was not really confined to the themes of classical theorists. Instead, their work largely comprised interacting with others, working in a brisk and continuous fashion. She found substantial variety in managers' jobs and that personal choices affected what they did and prioritised.

McCall, Morrison and Hannan (1978) reviewed the results of a number of observational studies. They concluded that particular elements were consistently present. Managers tend not to be reflective planners; they have high activity levels which involve long hours of work; managers perform poorly in accurately estimating how they spend their time; they engage primarily in oral communication, have many contacts internal and external to the organisation and are continuously involved in information-gathering.

Although the characteristics approach is useful, it tells us little about how managers perform their work and how their skills should be developed. More fundamentally, the characteristics approach is not effective in explaining the relationship of the various managerial activities with each other.

The Roles Approach

This approach can be supported by using observational or empirical techniques. The observational approach is illustrated by Mintzberg's managerial roles categorisation: interpersonal (figurehead, leader, liaison); informational (monitor, disseminator, spokesperson); and decisional (entrepreneur, disturbance handler, resource allocator and negotiator). Taylor's five functions of management, which include planning, organising and control, were also based on an observational approach. These categorisations are popular, but they are not effective in describing what managers actually do. They say little concerning the interrelationships between the various roles and they lack specificity.

The empirical approach to managerial role analysis focuses on the use of questionnaires that are completed by managers themselves and/or by others with whom they work. Researchers frequently use the management position description questionnaire. This approach is useful, but it has failed to provide detailed descriptions of managerial work.

The evidence suggests that the nature of managerial work will vary according to the manager's place in the hierarchy. Typically, in large organisations, a distinction is made between senior, middle and first-line or supervisory management. Middle management roles have changed in a number of interesting ways. Mintzberg (2004) and Burack, Hochwarter and Mathys (1997) suggested that middle managers have the following characteristics:

- They are increasingly more generalist with greater responsibility for a wider range of tasks.
- They have acquired a wider span of control. They are required to manage a greater diversity of staff.
- Their performance and that of their teams has become more visible and can be monitored more systematically due to the increased use of information technology. They have therefore more accountability for performance.
- They are required to be strategic in focus. They are expected to know what is going on in other parts of the organisation and to be conscious of the dynamics of the external environment.
- They are required to have greater skill flexibility. They must demonstrate a larger number of competencies.

Woodall, Edwards and Welchman (1997) conclude that middle management roles have become more complex; they involve elements of strategy and have more defined and specific accountabilities than before. Organisations also have a smaller number of middle managers.

Supervisory or first-line roles are commonplace in organisations. They have increased visibility in organisations today. Storey (1995) suggested that people in these roles carry out a greater diversity of human resource roles and that their tasks have become more defined and visible in the managerial hierarchy. First-line managers or supervisors carry out a multiplicity of tasks, but they are increasingly required to balance the technical dimensions of the job with more people-focused elements. This latter trend has placed a focus on the need to develop supervisors' managerial capabilities. There is evidence that organisations are investing considerably more resources in developing first-line supervisors (Garavan, Collins and Brady 2004).

Figure 3.1: The Competent Manager: A Model of Effective Performance

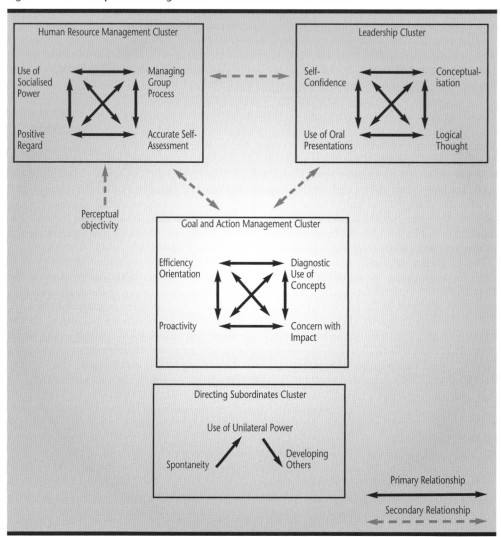

Source: Boyatzis (1982)

The Process Approach

Researchers have attempted to overcome the limitations of the characteristics and roles approaches through the development of process models that take account of relevant competencies and constraints involved in managerial work. Three process models that are relevant to the discussion of management and leadership development are: the integrated competency model; the four-dimensional model; and Mintzberg's integrated model of managerial work.

- **Integrated Competency Model:** This model was developed by Boyatzis and colleagues (1982). It was based on interviews with more than two thousand managers in twelve organisations. The model focuses on managerial competencies rather than on the roles that managers perform and it suggests six categories: human resource management, leadership, goal and action management, direction of subordinates, focus on others and specialised knowledge. Figure 3.1 shows the specific competencies included in each cluster. Boyatzis suggested that the human resources, leadership, and goal and action clusters are the most central to effective managing. This model made an important contribution to describing the managerial role in terms of competencies that explain effective performance. It also focused on the relationship between these competencies. As we shall see in Chapter Six, competency-based approaches are extremely popular as a basis for management and leadership development organisations.

   Schoenfeldt and Steger (1990) criticised the Boyatzis model. They considered it to be based on a narrow range of measurement devices, resulting in an incapacity to measure and reveal all of the traits, skills and knowledge needed for effective managerial performance. Barrett and Depinet (1991) criticised the use of behavioural event interviews as the basis for data collection. This method asks managers to describe three job incidents they felt were effective and three job incidents they considered ineffective. Barrett and Depinet specifically criticised the appropriateness of this method to measure a competency as defined by Boyatzis. Boyatzis's definition contains elements that are unconscious in nature, and therefore managers may be unable to describe them. Barrett and Depinet also criticised the model on more technical grounds, specifically the validation process used to support the model.

- **The Four-Dimensional Model:** This model was proposed by Schoenfeldt and Steger (1990). It was derived from the use of a range of data collection methods, including diaries, interviews, performance-appraisal documentation and observation. The model suggests that a managerial role is characterised by particular functions, roles, relational targets and styles. The functions consist of forecasting and planning, training and development, persuasive communication, influence and control, functional expertise and administration. The model suggests four roles and five relational targets. The roles specified are innovator, evaluator, motivator and director. The five relational targets are peers, self, subordinates, supervisors and external. The model does not specify the number of managerial styles. The model postulates that managers interact with various relational targets, carrying out an assortment of functions by performing specific roles. They perform these roles and functions in a manner consistent with their managerial style. The model provides a conceptual basis on which to view the role that a manager performs within a specific organisation. It also identifies the competencies managers need to perform effectively. The model is, however, not well researched and there is limited support for its validity.

- **Mintzberg's Integrated Model of Managerial Work:** Mintzberg (1994) proposed an integrated model based on empirical work in a wide variety of roles and organisations.

Mintzberg brought together what has been learned about managing in a more holistic and integrated way. Figure 3.2 illustrates Mintzberg's integrated model. He argued that three dimensions are important: the person in the job; the frame or structure of the job; and how to manage at three different levels of management.

Figure 3.2: Mintzberg's Integrated or Well-Rounded Model of the Managerial Job

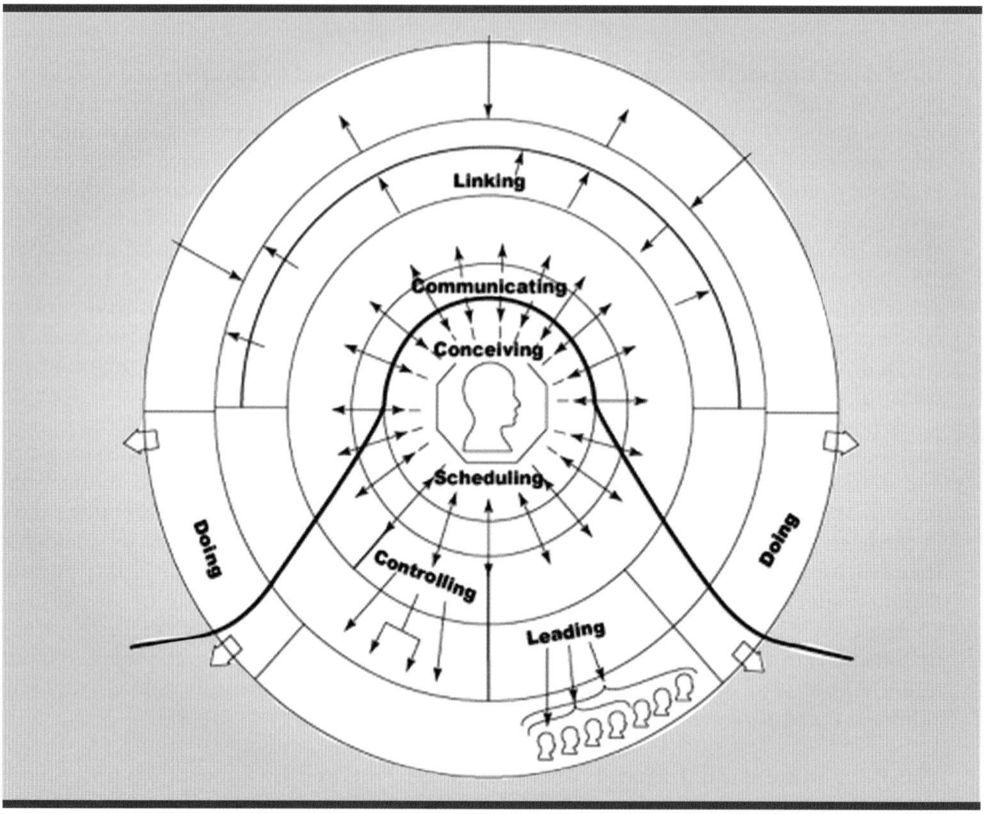

Source: Mintzberg (1994b)

Individuals come to the managerial role with personal histories, which include knowledge, experience, values, competencies and mental models. These elements of personal history combine to influence the individual's managerial style. The second component focuses on the frame of the job. Mintzberg argued that individuals create a frame for the job – a mindset that includes elements of strategy and vision. Managers focus on a purpose; in other words, they focus on what they are trying to do or achieve. Managers also adopt a perspective. This represents the overall approach to the management of the team. An additional component focuses on positions, which includes the location of the department in its environment, the specific products or services it provides and the processes used to deliver the service. The frame can be imposed by senior management or left to the discretion of the manager. The frame adopted has important implications for the set of issues that the manager addresses as well as how the manager's time is allocated.

The next component of the model focuses on the actual behaviours that managers exhibit. Mintzberg suggests three levels of evoking action: managing through information, managing through people and managing through direct action. Managers perform all these, but the level a particular manager actually prefers is an important determinant of managerial style.

Traditionally, managers were considered 'doers'. They were expected to get involved in the action. The modern manager, as an individual contributor, will be involved in projects and problem-solving. However, managers with direct reports also 'do' because they feel their judgement is necessary and they want to keep in touch with the work of the department or section. Mintzberg argued that managers manage through people both internally and externally. The internal role involves leading and the external role involves linking. They lead on a one-to-one basis by motivating and mentoring and they lead at a group level by building and sustaining the team. Managers manage externally through networking.

When the manager focuses on managing through information, the manager is two steps away from managerial action. Mintzberg considers the use of information for communications and controlling purposes. Communication refers to the collection and dissemination of information, whereas controlling refers to the use of information as a means of directing action.

Mintzberg's ideas are particularly instructive in terms of management and leadership development. His model reveals that a manager's job cannot be practised as a set of independent parts. The model emphasises that managers are people and that the job of managing is complex and multifaceted. It highlights that management and leadership development should focus on developing the whole person. Organisations should therefore endeavour to design management and leadership development interventions that are integrated with day-to-day work. They should provide the opportunity to reinforce and refine what has been learned in the context of performing the work.

EXHIBIT 3.1

Perspectives on Theory: Explaining the Nature of Managerial Work

Agenda-Driven Model (Carroll and Gillen 1987)
Carroll and Gillen advocated that managers have task and goal agendas. These agendas are influenced by a multiplicity of factors: organisational and unit plans; policies and procedures; problems and tasks assigned by others; the manager's own values and belief systems; perceptions of the organisational environment and job constraints, demands and choices. The model postulates that as agendas crystallise or change, managers undertake activities to carry out managerial functions. Managerial performance is impacted by the knowledge base, the competencies of the managers and the efficacy of the key management functions.

A Meta-Theoretical Model (Tsoukas 1994)
Tsoukas sought to explain the evidence on managerial work. He suggested four perspectives to explain the work of the manager: management functions; manager task characteristics; management roles; and management control. A management functions perspective suggests that the essence of management can be distilled into a set of functions that organisations must carry out. The management tasks perspective argues that while there are management functions, they are carved out differently according to context. Therefore managers have different discretion levels over resource allocation. Management tasks are fluid, unstandardised, interdependent and contextual. The management roles perspective focuses on different roles that managers performs such as interpersonal and informational. The management control perspective focuses on the structural and institutional

basis of managerial power rather than the superficial aspects of managerial behaviour. Tsoukas concluded that management consists of a four-layered structure corresponding to the four perspectives.

Structuralist Model (Hales 1999)

Hales argues that a manager is responsible for a well-defined area of work and for those who work in the area. Managerial responsibility is embedded and constrained by the resources, cognitive rules and moral rules of the social systems in which managers find themselves. Managers, because of the precarious nature of their work, are forced to draw upon and reproduce the resources of a system and its cognitive and moral rules, to affirm themselves and their position in that system. In affirming themselves, managers engage in generic activities. Hales envisages an inward-looking managerial cadre that justifies its own existence by turning to self-created social rules or norms.

Demands, Constraints and Choice Model (Stewart 1982)

Stewart developed her model to explain why managers holding similar jobs have widely different perceptions about their work. She proposed three new categories to describe aspects of managerial jobs: demands, constraints and choices. Demands consist of what a manager has to do; constraints consist of internal and external factors that limit what the job-holder can do; and choices are about what the job-holder can do, but doesn't have to do. These three dimensions change over time and in different situations. Stewart also postulated that managers bring to a job their own demands and perceptions of their choices. The interplay between the job characteristics and the characteristics of the manager accounts for variations in managerial work.

Strategic Exchange Perspective (Watson 1994)

Watson suggested that management is essentially a human social craft which requires the ability to interpret the wants and thoughts of others and the facility to shape meaning, values and human commitments. If managers are to be effective, they must make sense of the complexity that dealing with people entails. Managers generally believe that they can shape their organisation and, in doing so, they make sense of their own identities. Managers, according to Watson, have a desire to remain in control all the time. But this involves control of circumstances rather than of subordinates per se. Managers continually enhance symbolic and material things, while interacting with other individuals, groups and their external environment. These exchanges are not random but pertain to the interests, purposes and objectives of the parties involved. They are strategic exchanges in that managers know what exchanges are in their interest.

Competing Values Framework (Quinn et al. 1991)

Quinn described four management models that he claimed reflect the dominant viewpoint of their respective era: the rational goal model; the internal process model; the human relations model; and the open systems model. The competing values framework depicts the relationship between the four models along two axes (Figure 3.3, page 105). The vertical axis ranges from flexibility to control and the horizontal axis from internal to external focus. Each quadrant in the figure contains one of the four models. Quinn argues that organisations need to acquire the ability to move to any quadrant when needed or simultaneously exist in all four. Managers should be competent in eight roles. These eight roles are based on twenty-four managerial competencies. The roles envisaged by the model are facilitator, mentor, innovator, broker, monitor, co-ordinator, director and producer.

Managers are increasingly required to operate in complex and ever-changing environments; to manage a diverse workforce; to manage virtual teams; and to manage in a cost-conscious environment. There is an increased emphasis on credibility and trust. The trends influencing managers are many and varied, and are summarised in Table 3.1. Managers must manage what, on the face of it, looks like many conflicts or dichotomies. This includes managing stability and change, the big picture and the operational, focusing on the present as well as the future, dealing with the well defined and the ambiguous, balancing control and empowerment, creating a collective identity, as well as encouraging diversity. Many of these activities require seemingly contradictory skills. These challenges highlight the importance of continuous learning and development. Specific aspects of development include self-awareness, the development of networks of quality relationships and the skills to develop individuals and teams.

Figure 3.3: Competing Values Framework

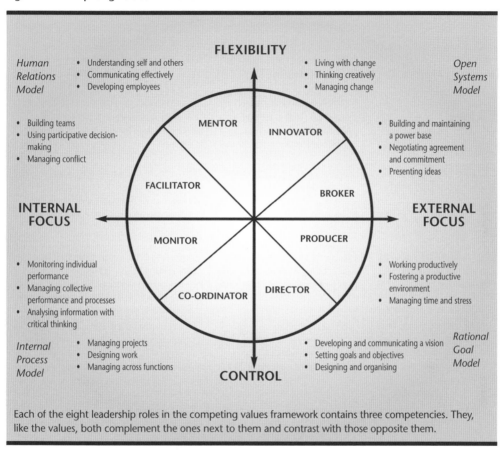

Each of the eight leadership roles in the competing values framework contains three competencies. They, like the values, both complement the ones next to them and contrast with those opposite them.

Table 3.1: Challenges for Managerial Work: Consequences for Managers

Old	New	Consequences for Managers
Stable, predictable environment	Changing, unpredictable environment	From routinisation to improvisation, adaptability and flexibility
Stable and homogenous workforce (or at least the workforce was treated as such)	Mobile and diverse workforce	From one-size-fits-all styles to multiple styles

Old	New	Consequences for Managers
Capital and labour-intensive firms	Knowledge-intensive firms	From machine and industrial relations models of organisations to learning models of organisations
Brick-and-mortar organisations	Brick-and-click (or just click) organisations and e-commerce	From managing relationships face-to-face to managing relationships through communication technologies (e.g. telecommuting)
Knowledge and product stability	Knowledge and product obsolescence; mass customisation	From routinisation to improvisation, adaptability and flexibility
Knowledge in the hands of a few	Knowledge in the hands of many (in large part due to advances in information and communication technologies)	From manager as expert and information broker to manager as a creator of a context that enhances collective learning
Stability of managerial knowledge and practices	Escalation of new managerial knowledge and practices	From a focus on learning to a focus on learning and unlearning; from uncritical acceptance of managerial knowledge to becoming wise consumers of managerial knowledge
Technology as a tool for routine tasks (data processing era)	Escalating information and communication technologies (knowledge and relationship era)	From using technology primarily for routine tasks to using technology as a key leadership resource for wide-scale organisational and societal changes
Economies of scale	Mass customisation, cycle time, speed	From routinisation to improvisation, adaptability and flexibility
Local focus	Local and global focus	From one-size-fits-all styles and standards to multiple styles and standards
Bureaucracy	Networks	From command and control to relationship building; from autonomy to interdependence; from clear to permeable boundaries inside and outside the organisation
Managers as fixed cost	Managers as variable cost	From security to pay for performance
Predictable career trajectories	Multiple careers	From employment to employability
One-breadwinner families	Dual and triple career families	From an emphasis on traditional family and work roles to an emphasis on fluid family roles, flexible work schedules and work/life integration

Explaining Leadership in Organisations

Organisations and researchers are obsessed with leadership. However, we still seem to know relatively little about the defining characteristics of effective leadership. The study of leadership has a history stretching back over centuries (Collingwood 2001). This research has covered a broad spectrum, from trait models to behaviour models to contingency theories. More recently, the focus has been on transactional versus transformational leadership models. In the following sections, we focus on a number of theoretical perspectives and explain their implications for management and leadership development. We also focus on more contemporary or post-modern perspectives and we give consideration to the topics of narcissistic leadership, gender and cross-cultural aspects of leadership.

Who are Leaders and What is Leadership?

The traditional view argued that leaders were born and not made. However, Drucker (1996), while to an extent agreeing with that proposition, argued that born leaders do exist but are rare and that leadership, therefore, can and must be learned. He also contended that leaders come in all sizes and shapes, with differing personal characteristics. He suggested that the most effective leaders need the following: they must get results; they must be visible and set an example; and they must understand leadership as a responsibility.

Handy (1995b) argued that organisations have, in many cases, dropped the term 'manager' in favour of terms such as 'team leader', 'project co-ordinator', 'lead partner' and 'facilitator'. This change reflects the fact that organisations have evolved and require more fluid leadership characteristics and skills capable of functioning effectively in decentralised, organic structures. Manz and Sims (1989) suggest that four types of leader are found in organisations. These are: strong man; transactor; visionary hero; and super leader. They differ in terms of their focus, the basis of their power, their behaviours and the roles they expect of followers.

Table 3.2: Four Types of Leader: A Typology

	Strong Man	Transactor	Visionary Hero	Super Leader
Focus	Commands	Rewards	Visions	Self-leadership
Type of Power	Position/Authority	Rewards	Relational/ Inspirational	Shared
Source of leader's wisdom and direction	Leader	Leader	Leader	Mostly followers (self-leaders) and then leaders
Followers' response	Fear-based compliance	Calculative compliance	Emotional commitment	Commitment based on ownership
Typical leader behaviours	• Direction • Command • Assigned goals • Intimidation • Reprimand	• Interactive goal-setting • Contingent personal rewards • Contingent material rewards • Contingent reprimand	• Communication of leader's vision • Emphasis on leader's value • Inspirational persuasion	• Becoming an effective self-leader. Modelling self-leadership • Creating positive thought patterns • Developing self-leadership through reward and constructive reprimand • Promoting self-leading teams • Facilitating a self-leadership culture

Source: Manz and Sims (1989)

Leadership was traditionally boxed into managerial jobs at the top end of the traditional organisational hierarchy, but the view now prevails that leadership is necessary at all levels. Stodgill (1974), for example, suggests that three particular forms of leadership are required: 1) formal leadership, which is responsible for orchestrating, integrating and resourcing activities; 2) ad hoc leadership; and 3) leadership capability in every organisational member.

Fiedler and Garcia (2005) define leadership as a relationship between an individual and a group, based on power and influence, which enables the group to achieve a predetermined goal. They argue that there is a need to take the model of the organisation into account. The modern organisation is flatter and relies on teams and networks. Therefore, organisations need to avoid unidimensional ways of developing leaders. Cooper (2005) suggests that we may be moving towards a new leadership model, fuelled by the changing nature of work and new technology. He suggests a new leadership paradigm that places less emphasis on traditional activities such as planning, compliance and reaction, and more on vision, change, commitment, extra discretionary behaviour and proactivity. Kakabadse and Kakabadse (2005) suggest a similar viewpoint. They advocate the need for discretionary leadership and consider the older models inadequate. They include the notion of cadre or shared leadership in their conception of leadership in the organisation. Starkey and Tempest (2005) berate the legacy of late twentieth-century management which was based on individualism and greed. They consider the challenge to be concerned with building social capital. They view leadership as rooted in trust, loyalty, connectivity and communication. Grint (2005) concludes that, by its very nature, leadership is extremely difficult to define. He suggests that it is an 'essentially contested concept'. He suggests a four-fold typology to understand leadership. This serves as a heuristic model which captures a significant number of current and past definitions of leadership.

Table 3.3: Grint's Typology of Leadership

Leadership in Person	Leadership by Result	Leadership as Position	Leadership as Process
• Person-based • Who are leaders? • Traits approach • Personality • Characteristic • Charisma	• What leaders achieve • Distinguish between coercion and leadership • Not restricted to authoritarian or unethical leaders • Focus on results versus methods	• Spatial position in organisation • Leader in charge • Leadership in front • Where do leaders operate?	• How leaders get things done • Act like leaders • Recognise leaders by behavioural processes • How leadership works • The practices through which they lead • We can distinguish leaders from non-leaders by the things they do

Source: Adapted from Grint (2005)

The Trait Approach to Leadership

The most basic and, for a considerable period of time, the conventional viewpoint was the assumption that good leadership resides in the innate abilities of certain individuals who are considered 'born leaders'. Particular emphasis was placed on identifying the specific characteristics or traits that constitute the behaviour of good leaders. Trait theory was attractive because it offered ways to measure the strength of leadership qualities, and proposed that good leadership would be guaranteed by selecting individuals with the appropriate positive traits for the role. This poses a particular challenge in a management and leadership development context. It assumes that leaders cannot, by and large, be trained and developed. It also assumes that leadership and management are inextricably separate activities, requiring different qualities.

Northouse (2004) suggested that the trait approach is intuitively appealing. It fits neatly with the idea that leaders are 'out front' and 'leading the way'. It reinforces the idea that leaders are different and that these differences can be explained in terms of the traits they possess. It focuses solely on the leader and ignores the situation and characteristics of followers. It has the advantage of helping to explain the make-up of the leader, in particular how certain personality traits explain leadership effectiveness.

The trait approach is bedevilled by a very significant challenge. It is extremely difficult to define the traits that leaders are actually born with. How can we be sure that they have not acquired these traits? Figure 3.4 highlights a range of traits that are associated with effective leadership, but none of these can be specifically identified as traits that people are born with. Some commentators criticise the trait approach because it tends to be masculine and potentially glorifies uncaring behaviour. Manz and Sims (1992) have suggested that a particular variant of the trait approach is the 'strong-man' model. It tends to glorify the tough image of authority in which the leader has superior strengths. This image or notion is still prevalent in some organisations.

Figure 3.4: Traits Associated with Effective Leadership: Some Recent Studies

Charin and Colvin (1999)
- Integrity, maturity and energy
- Business acumen or a deep understanding of the business
- A strong profit orientation
- Acumen in judging people, leading teams, coaching and growing people
- Skill in engendering trust, sharing information and listening effectively
- Curiosity, intellectual capacity and a global mindset
- Superior judgement
- An insatiable appetite for accomplishment and results
- A powerful motivation to grow and convert learning into practice

Peterson, Smith, Martorana and Owens (2003)
- A high level of conscientiousness with a concern for legality and sense of control over the environment
- Strong emotional stability with team cohesion, intellectual flexibility and leader dominance
- Strong agreeableness with team cohesion and power decentralisation
- Strong extroversion with leader strength (dominance)
- Strong openness with team risk-taking and intellectual flexibility

Deloitte & Touche (2000)
- Ability to make difficult decisions
- Ability to lead a company during a crisis
- Trustworthiness
- Honesty
- Intelligence and brains

Sources: Charin and Colvin (1999); Peterson *et al.* (2003); Deloitte & Touche (2000)

Kirkpatrick and Locke (1991) made a strong case for the view that certain traits are consistently associated with effective leadership, but they concluded that no fixed set of traits can be said to constitute good leadership.

Ultimately, however, the trait approach is limited because of its failure to take situations into account. It is difficult to isolate specific traits and consider their impact without considering first of all the influence of the situation. The notion of a universal set of leadership traits identified in isolation from the context in which the leadership occurs is difficult to sustain. The trait approach is also criticised because it has resulted in highly subjective interpretations of the 'most important' leadership traits.

The Skills Approach to Leadership

The skills approach takes a leader-centred perspective on leadership but, unlike the trait approach, it places emphasis on skills and abilities that can be learned and developed. It posits that knowledge and skills are necessary for effective leadership. Its origins can be traced to a classic article published by Robert Katz in the *Harvard Business Review* in 1955. He addressed leadership as a set of developable skills. It took many years for the approach to take hold, although in the early 1990s a number of research studies emphasised the need for a skills-based model of leadership. Katz initially proposed that the skills-based approach include three skills: technical, human and conceptual. It is important for leaders to possess all three skills. However, depending on the situation, some skills are more important than others.

Mumford *et al.* (2000) proposed a capability model of leadership which examines the relationship between a leader's knowledge and skills and leadership effectiveness. They argue that many individuals have the potential for leadership and that leadership capabilities can be developed through education and experience. Mumford and his colleagues' skills-based model is composed of five different components: competencies, individual attributes, leadership outcomes, career experiences and environmental influences. The model specifically highlights three key competencies that account for effective performance in the leadership role. They are problem-solving skills, social judgement skills and knowledge. Problem-solving skills are a leader's creative ability to solve new, unusual and ill-defined organisational problems. Social judgement skills relate to the capacity to understand people and social systems. They are necessary for leaders to work with others. Knowledge means the accumulation of information and the mental structures used to organise that information. Mumford *et al.* postulated that knowledge results from having developed an assortment of complex schemata for learning and organising data.

The skills model also emphasises four individual attributes that have an impact on the development of leadership skills and knowledge. It distinguishes between general cognitive ability and crystallised cognitive ability. The former focuses on the leader's intelligence, whereas the latter refers to intellectual ability that is learned or acquired over time. It represents the store of knowledge that the leader acquires through experience. The model also considers motivation and personality important. It suggests that leaders must be willing and motivated to tackle complex problems and be prepared to lead. The model also proposes that personality has an impact on the development of leadership skills. The skills approach is essentially descriptive in that it provides a framework which enables or facilitates an understanding of effective leadership. The skills model represents one of the few approaches that places skills development in a central role. It considers learned skills to be a key feature of effective leadership performance at various managerial levels. It provides strong guidance concerning the content of leadership development programmes and a structure that helps to frame the curricula of leadership development interventions.

The skills model does, however, have relatively weak predictive power. It has had little success in explaining how various combinations of skill impact on leader performance or how skills are linked to effective leadership. The model offered by Mumford *et al.* is not strictly a purely skills model; it includes other variables that are important in explaining leadership. The model is based on studies in large organisations, and it is unclear how appropriate the model is to other organisational settings.

The Style Approach to Leadership

The style approach emphasises the behaviour of leaders. It focuses on how the leader acts rather than on his or her personal qualities. The majority of the early research falls into two camps: whether the leader's style is dictatorial or authoritarian, or consultative, democratic and participative. The style approach is much studied and includes the Ohio and Michigan studies, Blake and Monton's Managerial Grid and Likert's System 4 Approach. The majority of these models sought to provide different categorisations of style. The more authoritative approaches were associated with scientific management, whereas the participative and democratic styles were associated with the human relations school.

The style approach provides a framework which can be used to assess leadership in task and relationship dimensions. It describes various components of leadership behaviour. It suggests that leaders need to be more task-oriented in some situations and more relationship-oriented in others. It also acknowledges that some subordinates like a lot of direction, whereas others like to be empowered.

The style approach has made a significant contribution to our understanding of leadership. It has broadened the scope of leadership and has shifted the emphasis away from the concept of personality as a key element of leadership. The style approach incorporates the behaviours of leaders and what they should do in different situations. The task and relationship behaviour dichotomy has proved to be valuable. In any situation, the leader is acting out both task and relationship behaviours. The task for the leader is to achieve an appropriate balance between these two behaviours. The style approach has strong educational appeal. It provides various typologies and categorisations which can be used in training and development situations. Leaders can assess their behaviour and determine whether or not their leadership style should be changed or adjusted. There is a lot of evidence to indicate that many management and leadership development programmes are structured around the style approach. Typically, this involves giving managers self-report questionnaires to complete. Participants then use the outputs of these questionnaires to assess the effectiveness of their overall leadership style.

The style approach does have its critics. Yukl (2002), for example, suggests that research on leadership styles is contradictory and does not adequately show how leadership style is associated with leadership effectiveness. The approach has failed to find a universal style of leadership. It has proved ineffective in explaining what universal behaviours are associated with effective leadership. There is a tendency for style categorisations and typologies to suggest that the leader will be most effective when he/she is high on task and relationship. It fails to acknowledge that certain situations may require high task behaviour and others are better with low task and high relationships.

Contingency Approaches to Leadership

Contingency approaches take into account the significance of the situation or context in which the leader functions. Contingency approaches focus on identifying particular contextual situations and identifying the style of leadership appropriate to each. Contingency theory is normative in nature in that it assumes that, for a given situation, there will be one identifiable best leadership style. The theories are valuable because they illustrate the variability and complexity of situations and emphasise the futility of one best approach.

Table 3.4 Characteristics Associated with Individual and Collective Strategic Leadership

Determining the Firm's Purpose and Vision
- The strategic leader must possess the skills to provide a strong statement of vision and direction and to articulate the key steps to be taken to reach that end.
- A strong vision will make sense to all organisation members and stretch their imagination, while still being perceived as being within the bounds of possibility.
- Visions are best defined through a process of discussion and involvement of all key stakeholders.

Exploiting and Maintaining Core Competencies
- For the strategic leader, core competencies represent the resources and capabilities that give a firm competitive advantage over rivals.
- Strategic leaders consistently work on applying core competencies in ways that will ensure that significant advantages are achieved.
- Strategic leaders focus on developing the knowledge base of the firm and fostering a culture of innovation.

Developing Human Capital
- Strategic leaders view employees as critical resources on whom many core competencies are built and through whom competitive advantage is exploited.
- Strategic leaders understand the importance of investing in human resources to derive the optimum competitive advantage from human resources.
- Strategic leaders seek to create a community of employees rather than a group of employees working for a firm.

Sustaining an Effective Organisation Culture
- Strategic leaders understand the organisation's culture and use it as a context to develop and implement strategies.
- Strategic leaders are skilled at shaping the organisation's culture and use it as a source of competitive advantage.
- Strategic leaders understand that strong and well-aligned cultures need to be dynamic and to move forward continuously.

Emphasising Ethical Practices
- Strategic leaders understand the importance of ethical practices and display ethical qualities that have the capacity to inspire others. They also focus on developing an organisational culture in which ethical practices are the norm.
- Strategic leaders focus on ensuring that decision-making processes result in outcomes that benefit stakeholders.
- Strategic leaders focus on meeting stakeholders' legitimate claims. Employees will demonstrate practices that are accepted as ethical.

Establishing Balanced Organisational Controls
- Strategic leaders are able to design control systems which facilitate innovation, flexibility and commitment.
- Strategic leadership requires a deep understanding of the strategic context, the competitive environment and the unique features of the business.

Source: Ireland and Hill (2005)

Contingency theory postulates that situations can be characterised by assessing three factors: leader–member relations, position power and task structure. These situational factors, in combination, determine how favourable various situations will be in organisations. It posits that certain styles will be effective in certain situations.

Contingency theories are well supported in the literature. Peters, Hartke and Pohlmann (1985), for example, suggested that contingency theories represent a valid and reliable approach to explaining leadership effectiveness. Contingency theories are valuable because they emphasise the significance of the relationship between the leader's style and the demands of the situation. They highlighted the importance of context rather than trait or skill. Contingency theory suggests that leaders do not need to be effective in every situation. This implies that a major development task for organisations should be to select and place leaders in situations that match their leadership style.

Two main criticisms of contingency approaches are to be found in the literature. It is argued that contingency theories do not present a cumulative set of ideas. Each theory tends to select different contingency factors and, in some cases, these factors are not sufficiently explained. Likewise, the contingency factors are not explained in terms of the organisation's structure, technology and size. These are factors that are likely to influence leadership effectiveness.

Contingency theories are less valuable in explaining what organisations should do when there is a mismatch between the leader and the situation. Their principles do not include the idea that organisations should develop leaders to adopt their styles to various situations. Instead, they advocate that leaders should engage in situational engineering, which means changing the situation to fit the leader. It is possible that the situation may not be easily changed to match the leader's style.

Contingency approaches have two significant implications for leadership development. Training and development for management and leadership skills needs to incorporate the use of tools and techniques that enable managers to analyse context. Leaders should develop skills in matching techniques to the situation. The contingency approach suggests that leadership can change hands in response to changing circumstances. This notion of leadership change has implications for management structures and individual careers.

The New Leadership

The new leadership era is generally considered to have started in the 1980s. Its distinguishing features are a move away from the trait, style and contingent models, and a focus on leadership as a socially constructed process. It is also premised in the notion of transformational change. Leadership actions are viewed as attempts to shape and interpret situations, influencing a common interpretation of reality for followers. We will explore a number of examples of the new leadership, including charismatic leadership, transformational leadership, social-network approaches to leadership, ethical leadership, change and strategic leadership and emotional-intelligence perspectives on leadership.

Charismatic Leadership

Charismatic leadership is generally defined in terms of a leader's influence over followers, and the character of the leader–follower relationship. Conger and Kanungo (1987) suggested that particular dimensions of leadership behaviour include: articulating a compelling vision; communicating high performance expectations; demonstrating self-confidence; providing exemplary role model behaviour; expressing confidence in the skills and abilities of followers to achieve goals; and emphasising the importance of collective identity. Charismatic leaders are also proficient in articulating innovative strategies, displaying creative behaviours, taking personal risks and showing sensitivity to followers.

Charismatic theory tends to focus on aspects of personality and behaviour. In his theory of charismatic leadership, House and Shamir (1993) suggests that charismatic leaders act in unique ways that have charismatic effects on followers. Charismatic leaders are dominant and self-confident; they have a strong desire to influence others and a well-developed sense of their own moral values. These characteristics ensure that the leader is a strong role model, demonstrates competence, articulates goals, expresses confidence and arouses motivation. There are several effects that are the direct result of charismatic leadership. These include: trust in the leader's ideology, unquestioning acceptance, affection toward the leader, identification with the leader, increased confidence and heightened goals. Shamir, House and Arthur (1993) extended charismatic leadership theory. They postulated that charismatic leaders transform followers' self-concepts and seek to link the identity of followers to the collective identity of the organisation.

Adair (2003) suggests that charismatic leadership is about creating and communicating vision, having a passion and dynamism that drives the leader, and engaging the enthusiasm and efforts of the followers. Conger (1999) suggested that it includes the abilities to take a long-term view and to inspire trust and confidence, which unlocks talent and enables the achievement of exceptional performance.

Charismatic theories of leadership make a distinction between socialised and personalised charismatic leadership. Socialised charismatic leadership emphasises the development and empowerment of followers, low Machiavellianism, non-authoritarianism, strong internal beliefs and high self-esteem. Personalised charismatic leadership, in contrast, focuses on the exploitation of others, high dominance and authoritarian behaviours. These behaviours are counterproductive. Furnham suggests that this variant of charismatic leadership relies on emotional manipulation and may be ethically suspect. He argues that it may engender less desirable characteristics in followers, such as a high level of individual dependence on the approval and support of the leader. Conger (2004) suggested that it may encourage followers to stray beyond the boundaries of what might be considered ethical in an effort to impress the leader.

Transformational Leadership Approaches

Transformational leadership is popular in the contemporary management literature. It gives particular emphasis to visionary leadership. Typically, transformational leadership is contrasted with transactional leadership. Transactional leadership focuses on leadership as essentially concerned with supporting, directing and co-ordinating the work of others. Transactional leadership relies on a leader's capacity to negotiate appropriate follower behaviour. Alimo-Melcalf (1995) found that men were more likely than women to adopt transactional styles. Transactional leadership is not concerned with initiating dramatic change, but rather with fine-tuning what goes on in the organisation.

Some researchers draw a distinction between transformational and charismatic leadership. Bass (1990), for example, suggested that a leader may be charismatic without being transformational. Charismatic leadership represents one component of transformational leadership. Whereas Bass considered charisma as a necessary but not sufficient element of transformational leadership, Conger and Kanungo (1987) argued that charisma is a unique and distinct element and the only aspect of leadership that is extraordinary or outstanding.

Transformational leadership is concerned with motivating others by transforming their individual self-interests into the goals of the group. It focuses on creating a vision, communicating it and finding the symbols and experiences to support it. Alimo-Metcalfe (1995) suggested that there is a female version of transformational leadership which focuses on the creation of a 'sense of belonging, inclusiveness and connectedness with others in the organisation as well as its goals'. Men who use the transformational approach focus on autonomy and separation in pursuing organisational goals. Legge (2005) argues that the appeal of transformational leadership lies in its association with the 'American Dream'.

Transformational leadership has a certain attractiveness. It treats leadership as a process that occurs between followers and leaders. This suggests that leadership is not the sole responsibility of a leader, but emerges from the interplay between leader and follower. Arguably, followers gain a more prominent position in the leadership process. Bryman (1992), for example, suggested that the attributes of followers are instrumental in the evolving transformational process. Transformational leadership theory places a strong emphasis on followers' values and needs as well as the growth of followers. Avolio (1999) argued that transformational leadership is morally uplifting because it focuses on motivating followers to transcend their own self-interests for the good of the team and the organisation.

Criticisms of transformational leadership are many. They tend to emphasise issues such as the excessive, almost evangelistic, role accorded the transformational leader. Transformational leadership theory has strongly promoted the view that leadership and management are distinct activities. Bass and Avolio (1993) considered transformational leadership to be elitist and anti-democratic. It gives the impression that the leader is acting independently of the followers and putting his/her views and priorities above the needs of followers. Transformational leaders have the potential to be directive and authoritarian. It is argued that only a few dynamic and charismatic people can be transformational leaders. The theory holds out little promise for leadership development.

Coopey (1995) argues that there is the potential for transformational leaders to believe in their own 'greatness'. He suggests that transformational leaders need to be sufficiently self-reflective and have the capacity to distance themselves from adulation.

A Social-Network Approach to Leadership

Balkundi and Kilduff (2005) suggest that a social-network approach is based on four key ideas. First, leadership can be understood as social capital that collects around certain individuals. Second, individuals can invest in social relations with others; they can structure their social networks and they can reap benefits from these relationships. Third, embeddedness in social networks involves paradox: some social relations may be difficult to perceive accurately and to manage. Fourth, although the social structure of the organisation determines opportunities and constraints for emergent leaders, it is not within the control of any individual.

A social-network approach to leadership consists of a number of key elements:

- *Leaders' Cognitions*: A key starting point for this perspective is the notion that leaders' cognitions about social networks influence the 'ego networks' that surround each leader. The network cognitions of leaders will impact the extent to which they occupy strategically important positions in the organisational network. Where leaders have accurate perceptions of the informal influence network, this can be a source of power.
- *Centrality in the Network*: Individuals who are central in the immediate network around them, and in the larger networks that connect them to others inside and outside the organisation, are likely to acquire expert power and access to powerful people. The challenge is to be in the centre of every important network. This may be difficult to achieve.
- *Knowledge of Relationships*: The extent to which a leader is effective depends on: a strong knowledge of the relations between actors in the organisation; the extent to which such relationships involve embedded ties; the extent to which individuals are extracting value from their personal networks to facilitate organisational goals; and the extent to which the social structure of the organisation includes differences between different factors.

This suggests that the leader must have a deep knowledge of the existence, nature and structure of ties.
- *Social Intelligence and Management of Others' Perceptions*: Social-network theory postulates that to be an effective leader requires strong social intelligence and the skill to manage perceptions. Some leaders perceive situations more accurately than others. Leaders can suffer from cognitive distortions, which prevent the emergence of effective leadership. Leaders can develop cognitive network schemas that influence their capacity to build coalitions. To do this effectively, the leader must understand multiple and complex factors in the organisation. Leaders who possess accurate perceptions are most likely to be effective in managing the perceptions of others.

A social-cognitive approach to leadership advocates that, essentially, leadership is about the management of social relations. Leaders make cognitions concerning patterns of relationships and use these to form and maintain social ties. Through a variety of actions and interactions, the leader accomplishes his or her goals.

A network approach to leadership has value in that it draws attention to social relations. It focuses on the perceptions of leaders and the way in which actions are embedded in their perceptions of networks. Leaders have the capacity to generate and use social capital, depending on how well they perceive social structures and on the actions they implement to build connections within important groups.

Ethical Leadership

There is currently a lot of interest in ethical leadership particularly on the academic front. For example, Heifetz (1994), Ciulla (2003) and Johnson (2001) have explored the nature of ethical leadership. Heifetz (1994) emphasised how leaders help followers to confront conflict and to effect changes from conflict. He placed a strong emphasis on values. He argued that leadership involves the use of authority to help followers deal with value conflicts. He also suggested that one of the key duties of a leader is to assist followers in struggles with change and personal growth.

Burns (1978) suggested that a primary role of the leader is to increase awareness of ethical issues and to enable followers resolve conflicting values. Burns emphasised that leadership is a process, not a set of discrete acts. He views leadership as a process of mobilising power to change social systems and transform organisations. Moral or ethical leadership involves both the moral elevation of individual followers and collective efforts to achieve change.

Greenleaf (1977) suggested that service to followers is the primary responsibility of leaders and the essence of ethical leadership. He suggested that service to followers comprises a number of key components. These include nurturing, defending and empowering followers. The servant leader has a duty to defend right and to stand for what is good, even when such a position is not in the financial interests of the organisation. Greenland considered that social responsibility is one of the key challenges facing organisations and that it should be one of the organisation's major objectives.

There is clearly a growing interest in ethical or moral leadership, but there is considerable disagreement concerning how it should be defined. Kanungo and Mendonca (1996) suggested that cognitive socio-moral development theory is a useful source of insight into the qualities of moral leadership. They suggested that the highest stages of moral development focus on openness to multiple perspectives, voices and paradigms. Moral leaders possess a sense of irony and a preference for power that is exercised diagonally in a spirit of mutuality and awareness enhancement. They found, however, that few, if any, leaders reach this stage. Snell (2000) argued that while many leaders will not reach advanced stages of moral development, they can contribute to a moral ethos and existing socially responsible objectives.

Ethical leadership is a timely and relevant concept. There is evidence of a strong demand for moral leadership in society and a strong argument to be made that ethics must be seen as an important component of leadership development. Relatively few theories of leadership actually incorporate this dimension. Leadership has an influence dimension that distinguishes it from other types of influence. It also has a strong values component.

Some commentators make a distinction between those leaders who do things to encourage and promote ethical behaviour and those who oppose unethical activities and decisions. Both approaches are important and can be used by the same leader. Nielsen (1989) suggested that leaders can promote an ethical climate by setting clear standards, setting an example of ethical behaviour, recognising and rewarding ethical behaviour by followers, taking personal risks to avoid moral solutions and helping others to find fair and ethical solutions to problems. Opposition to unethical practices can include such things as speaking out publicly against unethical and unfair policies, refusing to accept assignments that are unethical and refusing to share in the benefits of unethical activities.

Change and Strategic Leadership

Change and strategic leadership are more recent perspectives on leadership in organisations. They focus on the relationship between leadership and the ability of the organisation to manage and deliver significant organisational change. Kotter (1996) suggested that a significant number of change initiatives fail because the nature of leadership behaviour required to deliver success was not available. Although change leadership is still in an evolutionary stage, contributions by Albers (2008), Gill (2006) and Higgs and Rowland highlight the potential of this perspective. Much of this literature still overlaps with the transformational leadership perspective in that contributors emphasise the role of the leader in framing and mobilising followers by articulating a compelling utopian vision. Channer and Hope (2001), for example, suggested that the leader's role in transformational change involves planning, mobilising, organising, building a vision, taking personal risks, sending out the right signals, holding course and, in particular, making the tough calls. The change literature also highlights the emotional dimensions of change leadership. It draws attention to characteristics such as handling anxiety, being assertive and coping with psychological overload.

Higgs and Rowland (2001) investigated the competencies required of the change leader. They identified a distinct set of leadership competencies which are associated with the process of implementing major change successfully. These competencies are:

- **Articulating the Case for Change:** This involves engagement with others in recognising the need for change.
- **Creating Structural Change:** This involves ensuring that the proposed change is based on a deep level of understanding of the key issues and ensuring that it is supported with a consistent set of tools and processes.
- **Engaging Others:** This competency focuses on the process of engaging with followers and building commitment for the change.
- **Implementing and Sustaining Change:** This focuses on the development of effective plans and ensuring that effective monitoring and review processes are put in place.
- **Facilitating and Developing Capability:** This competency emphasises the skill of ensuring that followers are challenged to find their own answers and that they are supported in doing this.

Change leadership theory has yet to make a distinct contribution and find its place within the broader leadership field. It has strong links with both transformational leadership and the emotionality intelligent leader perspectives. There is clearly a recognition that change places a unique strain on the leadership of a business.

Strategic leaders are differentiated by their contribution to shaping the strategic future of organisations. Proponents of strategic leadership suggest that strategic leaders usually have risk-cognitive maps that permit them to deal with complex organisational and environmental challenges. Boal and Hooijberg (2000) suggested that the essential features of strategic leadership are absorptive capacity, adaptive capacity and managerial wisdom. Absorptive capacity involves a capability for knowledge capture and utilisation. Adaptive capacity is the potential for change, which is linked to strategic flexibility. Strategic leaders possess managerial wisdom. They are sensitive to change in the external environment and to the behaviours of others. This latter idea is akin to emotional intelligence. It should, however, be pointed out that the characteristics which differentiate effective strategic leaders from others is not yet fully defined. Table 3.4 (page 112) suggests characteristics of individual and collective strategic leadership.

Emotional Intelligence and Leadership

Mayer and Salovey (1995) were amongst the first to introduce the concept of emotional intelligence. They defined emotional intelligence as the ability 'to monitor one's own and others' feelings and emotions, to discriminate among them, and to use this information to guide one's thinking and actions'. However, it was Goldman (1995), in a very popular book, *Emotional Intelligence: Why it Can Matter More than IQ*, made the ideas of Mayer and Salovey more acceptable. Goldman developed a now well-accepted model of emotional intelligence (Exhibit 3.2).

EXHIBIT 3.2

Dimensions of Emotional Intelligence

Personal Competence: These competencies determine how we manage ourselves:
- *Self-Awareness*: knowing one's internal states, preferences, resources and intuitions
- *Emotional Self-Awareness*: recognising one's emotions and their effects
- *Accurate Self-Assessment*: knowing one's strengths and limits
- *Self-Confidence*: a strong sense of one's self-worth and capabilities
- *Self-Management*: managing one's internal states, impulses and resources
- *Self-Control*: keeping disruptive emotions and impulses in check
- *Trustworthiness*: maintaining standards of honesty and integrity
- *Conscientiousness*: taking responsibility for personal performance
- *Adaptability*: flexibility in handling change
- *Achievement Orientation*: striving to improve or meeting a standard of excellence
- *Initiative*: readiness to act on opportunities

Social Competence: These competencies determine how we handle relationships:
- *Social Awareness*: awareness of others' feelings, needs and concerns
- *Empathy*: sensing others' feelings and perspectives, and taking an active interest in their concerns
- *Organisational Awareness*: reading a group's emotional currents and power relationships
- *Service Orientation*: anticipating, recognising and meeting customers' needs
- *Social Skills*: adeptness at inducing desirable responses in others
- *Developing Others*: sensing others' developmental needs and bolstering their abilities
- *Leadership*: inspiring and guiding individuals and groups
- *Influence*: wielding effective tactics for persuasion
- *Communication*: listening openly and sending convincing messages
- *Change Catalyst*: initiating or managing change
- *Conflict Management*: negotiating and resolving disagreements
- *Building Bonds*: nurturing instrumental relationships
- *Teamwork and Collaboration*: working with others towards shared goals; creating group synergy in pursuing collective goals

Higgs and Dulewicz (1999) from Henley Management College popularised emotional intelligence in the UK. They suggested three key components:

- **The Drivers** (Motivation and Influencing): These traits have the capacity to drive leaders towards achieving goals which are set at a high level.
- **The Constrainers** (Conscientiousness and Emotional Resilience): These traits have the potential to act as controls and curb the potential excesses of the drivers.
- **The Enablers** (Self-Awareness, Interpersonal Sensitivity and Influence): These traits are important because they facilitate performance and help the leader to succeed.

All the models argue essentially that emotional intelligence operates in a different part of the brain and works in harmony with one's intellectual components. Leaders who have high levels of emotional intelligence possess the capacity to work more effectively and harness their emotions. They are better able to communicate, to understand other people's emotions and to influence others.

Supporters of emotional intelligence suggest that leaders who possess it are better at resolving workplace conflict, are better negotiators and make more effective leaders. Dulewicz and Higgs (2002) suggested that not every manager needs to have emotional intelligence, but that managers should be aware of it in others, and value it.

An emotional-intelligence perspective therefore argues that leadership success cannot be explained by IQ alone. It is the combination of IQ and emotional intelligence (EQ) that makes the most significant contribution. Emotional intelligence is relevant to an understanding of leadership effectiveness. Mayer and Salovey (1995), for example, suggested that it has the potential to help leaders cope with complex problems, make better decisions, be more conscious about how to use time effectively, manage crises effectively and adapt their behaviour to the situation. Self-awareness helps leaders to understand their own needs and how they will react to certain events. Strong self-regulation is linked to better emotional stability and information processing in difficult, stressful situations. It also helps leaders to maintain a sense of optimism and enthusiasm about a change initiative when faced with obstacles. Empathy is also an important dimension of a leader's emotional intelligence. Emotional intelligence is associated with strong social skills that are necessary for the leader to establish co-operative interpersonal relationships (Steiner 1997). Wong and Law (2002) found that emotional intelligence was related to follower job satisfaction and performance. Specific development interventions can facilitate the learning of emotional intelligence. Dulewicz and Higgs (2003) suggested that it requires sustained personal development. This development will derive from the leader reflecting on individual behaviours which are exhibited in different situations, consciously practising different behaviours and actively seeking feedback on how those behaviours are understood and received by others. The role of feedback is considered important. The leader has to consider the following: What did other people feel? How did they feel about the outcomes of decisions and actions? How could the outcomes have been improved in terms of the resolution of feelings? What has the leader learned from the situation which can help in dealing with future issues? Most commentators are in agreement that formal training programmes are not effective. Emotional intelligence is best developed through an assessment process combined with detailed feedback and development planning.

There is some debate concerning whether emotional intelligence can be learned. Goldman suggested that long-established development methods emphasise cognitive learning. He also speculated that managers are more likely to resist being told that they need to control their mood. Goldman suggested that a particularly effective approach, in a leadership context, is to use multisource feedback combined with a development plan. Higgs and Dulewicz (1999) suggested that some components of emotional intelligence can be learned using established learning methods such as personal development initiatives. These can be used, for example, to develop self-awareness, sensitivity and influence. However, some elements are more resilient and enduring. These include motivation, emotional resilience and conscientiousness. The development approach may therefore need to be more innovative and focus on developing 'coping strategies' to minimise the impact of weaknesses.

There is some scepticism as to whether the possession of emotional intelligence is the critical factor in explaining leadership effectiveness. Goldman claimed that approximately ninty per cent of star performers' success is attributable to emotional intelligence. Woodruffe (2001) suggested that it is misleading to equate EQ with a specific proportion of performance. Many measures of emotional intelligence are considered unreliable. Overall, an emotional-intelligence perspective on leadership is useful because it points out that some of the competencies required by leaders are rooted in emotional skills. It elevates emotionally based competencies to a level where they are as important as technical ability.

EXHIBIT 3.3

Focus on Research: Leadership that gets Results

There are six distinct leadership styles: *coercive, authoritative, affiliative, democratic, pacesetting* and *coaching*. Leaders with the best results do not rely on any one style, but move seamlessly between all of them, tailoring their style to the situation, so switching flexibly is well advised. A good analogy is a golfer with a bag of clubs, who selects a club on the basis of the shot.

To look at the impact of the different leadership styles, we will first define the most important factors in the working environment or 'climate'. *Flexibility* concerns how free employees are to innovate unencumbered by red tape; their sense of *responsibility* to the organisation, the nature of *standards* that people set; the sense of accuracy about performance feedback and the aptness of *rewards*; the *clarity* people have about mission and values; and, finally, the level of *commitment* to a common purpose.

Coercive leaders demand immediate compliance. Their style is 'Do what I tell you', and it is motivated by the drive to achieve, initiate and control. This is a good approach in a crisis, to kick-start a turnaround or deal with problem employees, but the overall effect on a business climate is negative. Flexibility is reduced by the destruction of new ideas. Responsibility evaporates, and the reward system is affected, as people need to take pride in their work. Clarity and commitment suffer when people are not shown how their work contributes to the work of the organisation as a whole.

The authoritative style mobilises people towards a vision; it says 'come with me'. It comes from self-confidence, empathy and being a change catalyst. This style works best when changes require a new vision, or when a clear direction is needed. The authoritative leader is a visionary who motivates people by showing them their role in the bigger picture, getting them to understand why what they do matters. Standards and rewards are made clear to all, which strengthens commitment, and people have freedom to innovate. Powerful though it is, this approach does not work in every situation. When working with peers more experienced than the leader, they might perceive it as pompous. A leader who tries to be authoritative and comes across as overbearing will undermine the egalitarian spirit of the team.

The affiliative leader creates harmony and builds emotional bonds. His or her style says: 'People come first' and this leader is motivated by emphasis on empathy, building relationships and communication. This style is effective in healing rifts in a team, and in motivating people through stressful periods. While its overall impact is positive, it should not be used alone. Its exclusive focus on praise can allow poor performance to go uncorrected. When people need clear directives this approach is unhelpful, so many leaders use it in conjunction with other styles.

The democratic style forges consensus through participation. It says 'What do you think?' It comes from motives of collaboration, team leadership and communication. It is most effective in reaching group agreement, or in getting input from valued employees, especially when the leader is uncertain and needs guidance. Its impact is positive. This type of leadership builds trust, respect and commitment and, by allowing people to have a say in decisions which affect their goals, it also boosts flexibility and responsibility. However, this style has some disadvantages. It can lead to endless cycles of meetings in a bid to reach consensus.

The pacesetting style sets high performance standards by saying to employees 'Do as I do now'. The motives are similar to the coercive style: conscientiousness, drive to achieve and initiative. It is helpful in getting quick results from a highly motivated and competent team, but the impact is negative overall. Used long-term, many employees feel overwhelmed by the emphasis on excellence, and morale drops. Communication is often unclear. Flexibility and responsibility suffer because employees believe that they cannot be trusted to take initiative.

A coaching style develops people for the future and says 'Try this'. It is motivational because it focuses on developing others, and on empathy and self-awareness. Used effectively, it helps an employee to improve performance or develop long-term strengths, and the overall impact is positive. However, it fails when employees are resistant to learning, or when the leader lacks the expertise to help followers. Sometimes managers are unfamiliar with or inept at coaching, particularly when it comes to giving feedback.

The most successful managers switch between these styles and choose the approach best suited to the situation. A common problem is that managers often feel confined to one style. One solution to this is to employ another person on your team who is more competent in the style that is absent, but a far more effective solution is for managers to work actively on expanding their leadership repertoire. To do this they must first look at themselves and their emotional strengths and weaknesses. So, if you are mostly a pacesetter, lacking the affiliative style, you need to work on your empathy and relationship-building skills. The payoff is in the results.

Source: Goleman (2000)

QUESTIONS

Q.1 What implications do the arguments in Exhibit 3.3 have for management and leadership development?

Q.2 How can organisations develop managers who can switch between styles and choose the best style for the situation?

Post-Modern Leadership Approaches

We include a number of approaches in this category, largely because they reject some of the traditional thinking on leadership. They advocate that leadership is not necessarily 'heroic', but is instead a widely dispersed activity. Post-traditional leadership ideas accommodate the viewpoint that leadership can be dispersed throughout teams. Many recent theories are premised on the emergence of globalisation, and discontent with leadership in organisations due to corporate failures and the tendency to run companies through committees and boards. Post-modern approaches de-emphasise the idea that one single leader is responsible for setting the direction and vision of the organisation.

New approaches to leadership are now practised in organisations. Organisations are tapping the spiritual or emotional side of people's personalities. The notion of 'macho' transformational leadership is less effective where organisations wish to capture the tacit knowledge of employees. Organisations are increasingly involved in networks with suppliers, customers and competitors. These situations demand different styles of leadership which focus on sharing information and building trust. Another line of research suggests that organisations do not need heroic leaders simply because they have lots of exemplary followers. These followers challenge the very idea of leadership and leaders may feel challenged by them because they are active, independent and critical thinkers.

This set of challenges has led to the emergence of new leadership concepts. These include the narcissistic leader, post-heroic leadership, level-five leadership, white water leadership, the servant leader, stewardship, leadership substitutes, thought leadership and spiritual, shared and self-leadership. These ideas fit within a post-modernist perspective, which we highlighted in Chapter Two. Post-modernist thinking suggests that leadership is whatever people do when they talk in ways that people recognise as leadership.

The Narcissistic Leader

This narcissistic leader represents a critical response to the rhetoric of the transformational and visionary leaders. Fineman (1993) suggested that many leaders have a vision which is not of the organisation or of the future, but of themselves. Callaghan (1997) argued that many leaders suffer from narcissism, which manifests itself in three basic behaviours: they must be something more than they are; their value as people is dependent upon the image that they project; and they view other people as objects who must be manipulated. Downs (1997) suggested that narcissistic leaders exhibit behaviour which produces a dearth of values, careful image management, an absence of both empathy and loyalty and an obsession with personal gain.

Brown (1997) conducted some of the more innovative conceptual thinking on the basic features of narcissism and how it impacts at different levels on organisations. Table 3.5 presents a summary of the main traits of narcissistic leaders and their implications for individuals, groups and organisations. Sandowsky (1995) examined narcissism in the context of charismatic or transformational leaders. His basic argument was that these leaders possess major symbolic power. Followers tend to idolise this type of leader because they view the leader as an omnipotent archetype, a heroic stereotype, a value-driven, virtuous leader or a mystic. He warns, however, that transformational leaders often promote visions that reflect their own sense of grandiosity, and they sweep others along with their grand ideas. The transformational leader may expect followers to defer to him or her and to accept without question the leader's view of reality. Sandowsky also highlights the potential for the charismatic leader to diminish the self-worth of others or make the follower totally dependent on the leader's approach.

Table 3.5: Narcissism in Organisations

Narcissistic Trait	Level of Analysis		
	Individual	Group	Organisation
Denial	Individuals deny the reality of market demands and resource constraints, facts about themselves and features of past occurrences.	Groups deny facts under the influence of groupthink and through denial myths.	Organisations deny facts about themselves through spokespeople, propaganda campaigns, annual reports and myths (e.g. abilene paradox).
Rationalisation	Individuals rationalise action, inaction, policies and decisions.	Groups offer collective rationalisations for their activities, their structures and behaviour, their decisions and their status.	Organisations provide rationalisation that structure thought and *post hoc* justify their actions, inaction and responsibility.

	Level of Analysis		
Narcissistic Trait	Individual	Group	Organisation
Self-aggrandisement	Individuals engage in fantasies of omnipotence and control, exhibit grandiosity and exhibitionism, create cultures in their own image, narrate stories that flatter themselves, make nonsensical acquisitions, engage in ego-boosting rituals, and write immodest autobiographies.	Groups use myth and humour to exaggerate their sense of worth, have fantasies of unlimited ability when under stress and engage in exhibitionist social cohesion ceremonies.	Organisations endow themselves with rightness, make claims to uniqueness, commission corporate histories and deploy their office layouts and architecture as expressions of status, prestige and vanity.
Attributional egotism	Individuals blame external authority for their personal plight and narrate stories that contain self-enhancing explanations.	Groups collectively attribute the failure of their decisions to external factors.	Organisations (or management groups) use annual reports to blame unfavourable results on external factors and attribute positive outcomes to themselves.
Sense of entitlement	Individuals are exploitative, lack empathy, engage in social relationships that lack depth, and favour their own interests over those of shareholders.	Groups use songs and humour and ceremonies to express a sense of entitlement.	Organisations are structured according to a principle of entitlement to exploit. Organisations assume entitlement to continued successful existence.
Anxiety	Individuals suffer internally, need stability and certainty, experience deprivation and emptiness, are paralysed by personal anxiety and tension, and struggle to maintain a sense of self-worth.	Management groups are prone to anxiety. Groups such as nurses and social care workers suffer from particularly high levels of anxiety.	Organisations suffer from lack of moral and social standards and alienation, requiring shared culture, moral order, a common sense of purpose, leadership attempts to secure commitment, and the broader distribution of work responsibilities.

Source: Adapted from Brown (1997)

Post-Heroic Leadership

Post-heroic ideas emerged in the 1990s, largely due to the work of Bradford and Cohen (1984). They identified a new form of leadership which has elements of transformational leadership, but which places a strong emphasis on managers developing their subordinates. The post-heroic leader is the 'manager as developer'. This leader approaches every situation as an opportunity to develop both his/her subordinates and himself/herself. Another version of post-heroic leadership was proposed by Heifetz and Laurie (1997). They argued that the leader's work is increasingly focused on coping with a 'multiplicity of adaptive challenges'. Leadership is therefore the work of many people in one organisation. The challenge facing leaders is to mobilise or influence employees to adopt new behaviours, challenge and change their own behaviours, and take personal responsibility for managing change.

Nicoll (1986) argued that the idea of a 'hero or saviour' leader is largely mythical. He suggests that leaders need to think of themselves as engaged in action, dialogue or 'shared' leadership. Leadership is a mutual, interactive process. Bennis (1997) likewise challenged the heroic notion. He suggested that the distinction between 'leader' and 'hero' has in many cases become blurred. Leadership is not necessarily an inherently individual phenomenon.

Table 3.6 summarises some of the principles associated with post-heroic leadership compared with modern and pre-modern leadership.

Table 3.6: Key Principles of Post-Modern Leadership versus Modern and Pre-Modern Leadership

Pre-Modern Leaders/ Leaders as Masters	Modern Leaders/ Leaders as Panoptics	Post-Modern Leaders/ Leaders as Servants
• **Master**: Head of the work institution. Owner of the slaves, serfs and tools. • **Authoritarian**: Enforces unquestioning obedience through authoritarian rule over subordinates. • **Slave Driver**: A leader oversees the work of others. A real taskmaster. • **Tyrant**: Sovereign and oppressive control over other people. • **Elite**: Leaders are regarded as the firmest or most privileged class and are usually drawn from such classes. • **Ruler**: Leaders govern and rule over other people.	• **Panoptic**: Leader gazes on everybody, Big Brother style. Bentham's principle of the Panopticon is central here: power should be visible and invisible. • **Authoritarian**: Final evaluator of performance and quality. • **Network of Penal Mechanisms**: Penal mechanisms are little courts for the investigation, monitoring and correction of incorrect behaviour followed by the application of punishments and rewards to sustain normalcy and reinforce leader's power. • **Organisational**: Lots of divisions, layers, specialities and cubbyholes to cellularise people. Leader sits at the top of the pyramid. • **Top**: The head boss, the top of the hill, and the highest-ranking person. • **Inspector**: In charge of surveillance, inspection and rating of everyone else. • **Centralist**: All information and decisions flow up to the centre and back down to the periphery.	• **Servant**: The leader is the servant to the network. Leaders serve people who, in turn, serve customers. Differentiates self from the people. • **Empowers**: The leader empowers participation in social and economic democracy. • **Recounter of Stories**: Tells the stories of company history, heroes and futures. • **Visionary**: Without vision, we perish. • **Androgynous**: Male and female voices. • **Networker**: Manages the transformation and configuration of the diverse network of teams spanning suppliers to customers. • **Team Builder**: Mobilises, leads and develops a web-work of autonomous teams.

Level Five Leadership and White-Water Leadership

Jim Collins (2001) argues that leadership has five levels: level 1 is individual ability; level 2 is team skills; level 3 is managerial capability; level 4 is leadership as traditionally concerned with a strong emphasis on heroism, performance and the celebrity CEO; and level 5 is what

Collins describes as the extra dimension, a blend of personal humanity and professional will. Level 4 consists of putting the company and the contributions of others above self and level 5 consists of staying power, commitment and a willingness to make tough decisions. Collins argues that Level 5 leadership represents the antithesis of the egocentric celebrity of CEOs.

There is evidence of a link between effective leadership and humility. The Industrial Society (1999) in the UK reported a research study in which leaders were asked to complete a self-rating, while four ratings were obtained anonymously from their immediate reports and peers. The best leaders tended to be more modest in their self-rating, whereas the less effective leaders had an inflated sense of their own abilities.

While, Hodgson and Crainer (1996) suggested that future leaders need to be able to cope with uncertainty and turbulence. They proposed five skills essential to white-water leadership:

- **Difficult Learning:** Leaders must possess the skill to identify and learn the things that the individual or organisation finds hard to learn.
- **Maximising Energy:** Effective leaders have a capacity to handle ambiguity and to harness the energy both in themselves and others.
- **Resonant Simplicity:** Effective leaders posses the ability to capture the essence of an issue in a way that will resonate with the rest of the organisation.
- **Multiple Focus:** Effective leaders possess the capacity to balance the short and long term in an effective way.
- **Mastering Inner Sense:** Effective leaders must possess the capacity to be comfortable using intuition when there is an absence of reliable data.

The Leader as Servant

Although Boje and Dennehey (1999) put forward a servant model of leadership, the term 'servant leader' was first used by Greenleaf (1997). Servant leaders possess the following capacities: to learn, to demonstrate empathy, to help people cope with emotional suffering and pain, to be sensitive to what is going on, to be good conceptually and show foresight, to show commitment to the growth of people and to be concerned with building community.

Boje and Dennehey (1999) took this approach a step further. They made an important distinction between the leader as servant and the leader as panoptic master. They viewed the leader essentially as a servant to the network, who empowers others, tells stories, articulates vision, networks and is a team builder. They also make the point that the leader is androgynous, meaning that the leader must be able to speak in both male and female voices.

Stewardship

The notion of stewardship is associated with Block (1993). He suggested that stewardship is about 'a willingness to be accountable for some larger body than ourselves' and that it is about service over self-interest and a willingness to be accountable without choosing to control the world. Block's central idea is the notion of partnership. This he defined as the principle of placing control close to where the work is done.

The notion of stewardship is premised on four requirements:

- **Exchange of Purpose:** This suggests that each person at every level of the organisation has responsibility for defining vision and values. Purpose gets defined through a process of dialogue.
- **The Right to Say No:** Block contends that every individual has the right to say no. He does acknowledge, however, that others have the right to tell you what to do.

- **Joint Accountability:** Accountability becomes widely distributed and is linked to the reward system. This indicates that bosses are no longer responsible for the development, learning and career of their subordinates.
- **Absolute Honesty:** Block sees this as an essential requirement. It reflects the ethical leader.

Leadership Substitutes

Kerr and Jermier (1978) argue that leadership is sometimes not important by virtue of the existence of leadership substitutes and neutralisers. They define a leadership substitute as something that, by its presence, makes leader behaviour unnecessary. Well-educated subordinates are more likely to be self-directed and to desire autonomy. This minimises the need for leadership. A leadership neutraliser is something that, by its absence, prevents the leadership behaviour from being important. Organisations may look for leadership substitutes in situations where leaders are not effective and few other possibilities exist to develop or hire them. Organisations frequently use leadership neutralisers, such as removing rewards from the control of leaders or taking managers out of promotion processes. Kerr and Jermier make the point that their approach represents a 'true situational theory of leadership' because it raises the possibility that, in some situations, the role of the leader is replaced by something else. They view effective leadership as an ability to supply subordinates with guidance and positive feelings.

Thought Leadership

McCrimmon (2005) suggests that thought leadership is based on the power of ideas to transform how people think. He argues that it represents a significant departure from conventional, positional leadership and that it champions new ideas rather than managing people for goal attainment. It is a type of leadership that is distributed throughout the organisation but is unlike shared leadership, where a person is usually in charge of a team.

Thought leadership has a number of important characteristics:

- It is the promotion of new ideas through, for example, logical argument, inspirational appeal and/or factual demonstration.
- It can be directed up and down the organisation and can be demonstrated by any employee in the organisation.
- It is fast changing, ephemeral and egalitarian and is therefore not the preserve of a small number of people.
- It has the capacity to change how people think, but it does not necessarily have to lead to action.
- Thought leadership is creative, but it does not necessarily lead to innovation in a collective sense.
- It depends on technical rather than more personal characteristics. It can also come from outside the organisation and is therefore not confined to people known to each other.
- Thought leadership is organic and can therefore emerge in a wide range of situations. It differs considerably from conventional leadership, which is more mechanistic in form.

Thought leadership falls neatly into post-modernist notions of leadership, which suggests that all perspectives are legitimate and that leadership consists of anything that people conceive it to consist of.

Shared or Dispersed Leadership

Proponents of shared leadership include Fletcher and Kaufer (2003) and Pearce and Conger (2003). Shared leadership ideas challenge the notion that leadership resides in one person. It raises the notion that leadership should be considered as a group-level phenomenon. Shared leadership models are premised on a number of important ideas, as described below. Leadership as a set of practices can, and should, be enacted by people at all levels in an organisation, not just those at the top. Leadership is an interdependent activity, which emphasises collective achievement, shared responsibility and the importance of teamwork.

Shared leadership emphasises that leadership is a social process. It is dynamic, multi-directional and collective in nature. Shared leadership focuses on the team or unit as a whole and examines patterns of social interaction. It de-emphasises the notion of hierarchy and instead focuses on fluid rather than static interaction. Followers play a key role in influencing and creating leadership.

Shared leadership focuses on learning for both the individual and the organisation. It highlights the need to create conditions where collective learning can occur. It places emphasis on greater self-awareness, openness, and an ability to respond to the learning needs of others.

Shared leadership ideas challenge traditional leadership development approaches. Many traditional leadership development initiatives are based on the notion of the leader as an independent entity, and development as a process of moving towards independence. Shared leadership requires a different type of development experience, specifically an experience that facilitates the development of relational skills and the skills to contribute to the development of others. Shared leadership theories challenge the idea that the leader can be understood as separate from his or her personal life.

Self-Leadership and Individualised Leadership

Self-leadership and self-management approaches have many applications in high-performance organisations and self-managed teams. Self-leadership is defined as a set of strategies that an individual uses to influence or improve his/her behaviour and actions. Where self-leadership can be encouraged, it raises the possibility that leaders can be eliminated or can engage in other activities. Markham and Markham (1998) suggested that there is a possible trade-off between increased self-leadership for individuals and increasing a group's ability to manage itself.

Individualised leadership focuses on the one-to-one relationship between a leader and a specific direct report. Each relationship is conceptualised in terms of the leader's investments in and returns from subordinates and vice versa. Dansereau *et al.* (1998) defined investments as what one party gives to the other party. A key role for the leader is to provide support to the direct report. Such an individualised approach suggests that the leader will negotiate the degree of giving and receiving.

Table 3.7: Leadership Substitutes, Neutralisers and Enhancers: Managerial Leadership Problems and Effective Coping Strategies

Leadership Problems	Enhancer/Neutralizer	Substitutes
Leader doesn't keep on top of details in the department; co-ordination among subordinates is difficult.	Not useful.	Develop self-managed work teams; encourage team members to interact within and across departments.
Competent leadership is resisted through non-compliance or passive resistance.	**Enhancers:** increase employees' dependence on leader through greater leader control of rewards/resources; increase their perception of leader's influence outside of work group.	Develop collegial systems of guidance for decision-making.
Leader doesn't provide support or recognition for jobs well done.	Not useful.	Develop a reward system that operates independently of leader. Enrich jobs to make them inherently satisfying.
Leader doesn't set targets or goals, or clarify roles for employees.	Not useful.	Emphasise experience and ability in selecting subordinates. Establish group goal-setting. Develop an organisational culture that stresses high-performance expectations.
Leader behaves inconsistently over time.	**Enhancers:** these are dysfunctional. **Neutraliser:** remove rewards from leader's control.	Develop group goal-setting and group rewards.
Upper-level manager regularly bypasses leader in dealing with employees, or countermands leader's directions.	**Enhancers:** increase leader's control over rewards and resources; build leader's image via in-house champion or visible 'important' responsibilities. **Neutralisers:** physically distance subordinates; remove rewards from leader's control.	Establish group goal-setting and peer performance appraisal.
There is inconsistency across different organisational units.	Not useful.	Increase formalisation. Set up a behaviourally focused reward system.
Leadership is unstable over time, leaders are rotated and/or leave office frequently.	Not useful.	Establish competent advisory staff units. Increase professionalism of employees.
Incumbent management is poor; there is no heir apparent.	**Enhancers:** these are dysfunctional. **Neutraliser:** assign non-leader to problem managers.	

Source: Howell *et al.* (1990)

Spirituality and Leadership

Spirituality and its relationship with leadership is an emerging theme in leadership studies. Spirituality is advocated as freedom to enhance organisational learning, build communities and act as a basis for connection with others at work. Leaders have a major role to play in instilling a spiritual sense into the organisation. Fry (2005) defines spiritual leadership as values, attitudes and behaviours that facilitate the process of motivation of self and others, so that they have a strong sense of spiritual survival.

Spiritual development in organisations can be facilitated by appropriate development interventions. Some organisations offer development programmes which enhance the leader's spirituality and facilitate the development of workplace spirituality. Proponents of a spirituality approach to leadership suggest that it offers the possibility of increasing individual effectiveness. It allows people to be more effective and facilitates value congruence.

EXHIBIT 3.4

Focus on Research: First, Break All the Rules: What the World's Greatest Managers do Differently

This is a very practical book by Buckingham and Coffman which is based on analysis of research conducted by the Gallup Organisation over twenty-five years ago. Firstly, Gallup statistically reviewed a million or more employee surveys that it had on file to examine what distinguished effective work units from less effective units. Secondly, Gallup reviewed interviews that it had conducted with 80,000 managers to identify what made themselves and their work units effective. The unit of analysis was the work unit and the first line manager, not the entire organisation. This is what makes it so useful for manager, and supervisors.

Early in the research project, Gallup identified the differentiating factor between work unit performances as follows: the way the manager of the unit behaves. As the adage goes, employees don't leave organisations, they leave their direct managers. The research identified twelve elements (known as the 'Gallup 12') that have a significant impact on work unit performance, including the following: employees know what is expected of them; they work for someone who cares about them; their development is encouraged; they have the opportunity to do every day what they do best. These are factors that lead to employee engagement.

Further investigation into this phenomenon of 'how the manager of the unit behaves' demonstrated that there was not a single way of being an effective manager. In fact, there was great variability in the behaviour of great managers. What they shared in common was the following key insight: get the best out of people in terms of a personal best, and that will differ greatly between individuals. The implication is that not all people have unlimited potential and it is OK to 'play favourites' based on individual talents. This is, of course, breaking the conventional rules of management.

So how can this insight be applied in the workplace? Effective managers hire for specific critical talents:
1. Striving - Why people do what they do.
2. Thinking – What are people's critical choice points when they make a decision?
3. Relating – How people relate to each other.

These talents are not learnable because they are not knowledge or skill. They are formally defined as recurring patterns of thought, feeling and behaviour. In other words, it is just as important to hire for 'fit with the team' as for demonstrated values such as knowledge and skill.

The second activity of effective managers is how they set expectations. Great managers determine 'what' has to be achieved but not 'how' it is to be done. This allows room for individual initiative and creativity to shine.

Third, great managers focus on employees' talent strengths, since weaknesses in the talents noted above cannot be addressed. Matching the right people to the right jobs is a key competency of effective managers. This means that not everyone can be treated equally: talented individuals are put into jobs that maximise their talents.

The fourth tactic of great managers is to find the best fit for every individual. The implication of this practice is that when an employee is in a role that maximises his/her talents, he/she should not necessarily be moved or promoted out of the role. This is described as '… create heroes in every role'. The authors argue that time in the role is the only route to excellence. The flip side of this coin is that line managers should not keep someone in a role that is clearly the wrong fit.

QUESTIONS

1. What are the features that distinguish great managers from their peers?

2. Looking at the three critical talents, do you think that there are any talents missing from the list?

Table 3.8: Theories of Leadership: Propositions for Management, Leader and Leadership Development

Theory/Approach	Key Propositions	Management, Leader and Leadership Development Implications
Trait Approach	• Effective leaders share common characteristics that cause them to behave in certain ways. • These traits may be psychological or sociological in nature. • The traits that appear to be most important include intelligence, ability, self-confidence, dominance, sociability and persistence.	• Development has a rather limited role to play. • Teaching new traits is not easy because traits are very difficult to change. • Traits are often considered to be relatively fixed concepts which therefore limits the value of leader and leadership development interventions.
Skills Approach	• This approach highlights skills rather than traits or qualities of leaders. • The skills approach focuses on acquisition of knowledge and competencies necessary to achieve goals. • Leaders require technical, human and conceptual skills in order to be effective. • The importance of these skills varies depending on the level of management.	• The skills approach envisages that it is possible to develop the skills necessary to be effective leaders. • The task of development is first to identify key-skill gaps and to design an appropriate development programmes to address these needs.

Theory/Approach	Key Propositions	Management, Leader and Leadership Development Implications
Style Approach	• Style approaches have primarily focused on characteristics of the leader, follower and task. • Style theories focus on behaviour rather than values. • Style theories focus on task and people-orientation styles and suggest that the leader adjusts the style depending on task and follower characteristics. • Style approaches suggest that people-centred behaviours are more effective in getting results.	• The style approach focuses on the development of the leader. • The task of leader development is to increase awareness of leader style and to enhance the leader's overall leadership style. • Development interventions have a major role to play in enhancing the effectiveness of leaders.
Contingency Approach	• Contingency theories suggest that there is no one best style of leadership. • Successful leaders use different styles according to the nature of the situation and the followers. • Different contingency theories of leadership emphasise different aspects of the situation.	• The task of development processes is to develop leaders' situational sensitivity or their ability to read a situation. • Development can also enhance the flexibility of leaders or their ability to change behaviours according to situational needs.
Charismatic Leadership	• Charismatic leadership focuses on the characteristics of leaders that attract and inspire followers. • Charismatic leaders articulate values that shape the organisation. • Charismatic leaders are sociable and open, have impressive physical appearance and may adopt unconventional behaviours.	• Leader and leadership development has a relatively limited role to play. • It may have a role in shaping the values and beliefs of leaders.
Transformational Leadership	• Transformational leadership focuses on raising the motivational state of leaders and followers. • Transformational leaders have strong values and are concerned with justice and equality. • Transformational leaders empower followers to think independently, creatively and critically.	• Key focus of leader development is to increase self-efficacy, self-worth, competence, autonomy and risk-taking. • Self-awareness can be enhanced to self-assessment, multi-source feedback processes and developmental assessment centres.
Social Network Approach	• Leadership is understood as social capital that collects around certain individuals. • Leaders invest in social relations with others. • Leaders have the capacity to structure their networks to secure relationship benefits. • The social structure of the organisation determines networking opportunities and constraints.	• Leadership development interventions can be used to develop networking skills and knowledge of relationship building. • The challenge for leaders is to develop their confidence to network and to utilise networks to their advantage.

Theory/Approach	Key Propositions	Management, Leader and Leadership Development Implications
Ethical Leadership	• Ethics is central to leadership because of the nature of the process of influence. • Ethical leaders show respect for each other, they serve others and they make decisions which are just and honest. • Ethical leadership focuses on building community.	• Leader and leadership development interventions can enhance the awareness that ethics plays in leadership. • Leader development can help leaders to understand and strengthen their own leadership. • Leadership development can educate leaders concerning the benchmarks of ethical leadership.
Strategic Leadership	• The primary focus is on strategic development. • Strategic leadership focuses on shared vision, a global mindset and strategising. • Strategic leaders monitor the culture and ensure that its values support the organisation's mission and vision.	• The challenge for leader and leadership development is to develop a strategic mindset and skills. • Development can be used to enhance visionary, problem-solving and strategy implementation skills.
Emotionally Intelligent Leaders	• Emotionally intelligent leaders possess the capacity to understand and manage themselves, their thoughts and feelings, strengths and weaknesses and to plan effectively to achieve their personal goals. • Emotionally intelligent leaders have skills in understanding other people, displaying empathy, recognising individual differences, and they possess strong interpersonal intelligence.	• Leader development interventions can help provide leaders with personal insights and accurate self-assessment. • Leadership development can be used to enhance leaders' self-confidence and provide leaders with strategies for self-control.
Shared Leadership	• Leadership can be enacted by people at all levels in an organisation. • Leadership is a social process which is dynamic, multi-dimensional and collective in nature. • It focuses on learning for both the individual and the organisation.	• Shared leadership challenges traditional leadership and leader development. • There is a strong emphasis on developing leadership at all levels and the development of relationship and developing other skills. • It should develop leaders in a context which includes non-work life.

Source: Buckingham (2006)

Contemporary Debates on Leadership

Two contemporary issues of relevance to leadership development concern themes of gender and national culture. There is a widespread recognition that gender has a significant role to play in understanding leadership. Various explanations have been put forward for the relatively smaller proportion of women than men in senior leadership positions. Likewise, national cultural differences are increasingly relevant to the leadership debate. Today, leaders are tasked more often with the job of communicating the organisation's vision to a multi-cultural and diverse workforce and therefore leaders need to be more sensitive to national cultural differences.

Gender and Leadership

Gender currently represents an important preoccupation of leadership research and practice. We will address gender and leadership development issues in Chapter Fifteen, but our focus in this section is on gender issues and leadership. Wilson (1995) pointed out that the study of leadership has rarely included gender and gender roles as organisationally significant variables. She argued that leaders seem to be not only male, but quite masculine with it. The research on women leaders and managers has focused on a number of questions, specifically: Can women be leaders? Do male and female leaders differ in their behaviour and effectiveness in organisations? Why do so few women leaders reach the top? We will briefly consider these three questions.

Can Women Become Leaders?

There is evidence in Ireland, Europe and the US that a greater proportion of women are taking on leadership roles compared to the 1990s, but this does not reflect their overall proportion in the labour force. Women and people of ethnic origin are major sources of untapped value in organisations. Women occupy the lower levels of management. Sellers (2002) pointed out that at the very top of major corporations there is an absence of women. This occurs because, as women move into their mid- to late thirties, they have a greater need to balance work and life. The incidence of women owning and running their own companies is increasing. Pofeldt (2002) found that in the US, women have started businesses at twice the rate of men, even though only five per cent of venture capital and three per cent of government contracts are awarded to women. African-American women represent the largest group of black women in management and are surpassing African-American men in executive and managerial positions.

Do Female and Male Leaders Differ in their Behaviour and Effectiveness?

This is a complex question. The most significant variation appears to exist in respect of behaviour. Eagly, Karau and Makhijani (1995) found that female and male managers do not differ in their overall effectiveness early in their careers. Similarly, they have essentially the same aptitude for leadership, motivation for leadership, commitment and job satisfaction. Tharenou, Latimer and Conroy (1994) found, however, that women may be evaluated differently. This has major implications for training and development opportunities, challenging job assignments, the existence of mentors and promotional prospects. Female leaders were significantly undervalued when they worked in male-dominated settings. Male and female managers differ in the steps they must take to be promoted.

Rosener (1990) reported research indicating that male and female leaders tended to describe their management style differently. Men perceived themselves as transactional leaders and viewed performance as a series of transactions. Women tended to be more transformational in their descriptions of leadership style. They described their leadership style as interactive, participative, energising and focused on relationship rather than authority. Denmark (1993), in a US study, found that women were perceived to be more democratic than men and they encouraged more participation. She also found that when women acted more autocratically, they were viewed more negatively by both men and women. Women who occupied leadership positions traditionally held by men were devalued by male evaluators.

Women perceive power differently from men. They view it as liberating rather than as a means of controlling or as a dominating force. Pringle (1994) suggested that men are more likely to maintain distance from their subordinates. They are also more likely to be task-oriented, instrumental and dominant. Women are more likely to describe their style in terms of empowerment. Eagly and Wood (1991) found that women's social skills tend to be stronger than men's and that women leaders' preferred style is co-operative, or what they call 'web leadership'.

Goffee and Scase (1992) argued that the preferred managerial styles of both men and women are influenced by prevailing fads and fashions about effective management. They suggested that when assertiveness was highly popular, female managers surveyed claimed to be tough, aggressive, firm and assertive. They also found that a leader's appearance influences the way people respond to them.

There is also agreement that leadership and managerial roles will be defined in a more masculine or feminine fashion, depending on the organisational context. Micco (1996), for example, found that despite organisational obstacles, women leaders perform effectively, and that men and women performed equally effectively in delegating authority. However, women outperformed men in conflict resolution, work quality, capacity to deal with change, idea generation and motivation of others. Men were, however, better at dealing with pressure. Gendron (1995) found that women performed more effectively in planning and decisiveness.

Overall, there are few differences between male and female leaders concerning effectiveness. Style differences do exist. Women tend to be more evaluative and less autocratic. They have also been shown to be more effective in middle-management positions, where there is a greater requirement for co-operation and networking.

Women in Top Management

As a general trend, women have made significantly less progress in reaching top management positions. Ragins, Townsend and Mattis (1998) suggested multiple explanations for this. One explanation concerns the 'pipeline theory', which argues that women are not in managerial positions long enough for natural career progression to occur. They also put forward two other explanations: women lack general management or line experience; and women are less suited to executive demands than men. There appears to be limited support for the pipeline theory. Gallagher (1996), for example, found, in a study of seventy executive women, that the average length of time they took to reach that position was 11.5 years. This compared to less than nine years for men.

There is support for the second explanation. Hurley, Fagenson-Eland and Sonnenfeld (1997) found that top executives had worked in a wide range of positions and departments. The timing of line and staff functions appears to be a more important issue. Line and staff experience needs to come earlier in the female manager's career. There is little support for the third explanation, namely that women are unsuitable for leadership positions. Female managers perform very effectively in leadership roles. Tharenou, Latimer and Conroy (1994) suggested that the most significant factors concern the lack of career encouragement and training opportunities for women.

The dearth of women in top management positions is multi-dimensional. Organisational, interpersonal and personal barriers are important. Of particular importance, organisational barriers include inhospitable corporate cultures, a preference for gender similarity as a basis for promotion decisions, the disregard and inaction of CEOs, lack of development opportunities and higher standards of performance and effort required from women. Particular interpersonal barriers include male prejudices, stereotyping, lack of emotional and interpersonal support, exclusion from informal networks, and lack of male mentors. On a personal level, two critical factors are highlighted: work-home conflicts and lack of political savvy.

The research on the gender dynamics of leadership is important. It is interesting to observe that leadership theories have pretended gender neutrality or displayed a form of gender blankness. Differences in leadership style can be attributed to specific feminine qualities. These feminine qualities are perceived as 'inferior' and compare less favourably with the traits and characteristics possessed by men. Some commentators hold the view that women will always stand to lose, given male managers' perceptions about leadership traits. There is also the criticism that a focus on gender can become the only or the primary identifying attribute, rather than viewing gender as one of the many attributes that impacts on the contribution of employees.

EXHIBIT 3.5

Focus on Research: When Should a Leader Apologise and When Not?

An apology is generally expected from a person who has hurt someone else, perhaps even unintentionally. 'I'm sorry' is generally seen by the injured party as an admission of error and regret and a placatory statement.

But a leader speaks to and for their followers. Their actions and behaviour have broad implications. When a leader apologises, the act of apology is carried out at institutional level, which becomes public record. It is a high-risk move for the leader, their followers and their institutions. Clearly then they should not apologise often, lightly or without good reason. Refusal to apologise can be smart or suicidal. Readiness to apologise can be seen as a sign of strength or weakness. A successful apology can transform enmity into triumph, while a failed apology can bring ruin to the individual and the organisation.

Tavuchis (1991) wrote that apologies speak to acts that cannot be undone 'but cannot go unnoticed without compromising the current and future relationship of the parties'. From this we have a general principle that leaders will publicly apologise if they calculate that the costs of doing so are lower than the costs of not doing so.

There are four main reasons why leaders apologise publicly; the first three reasons are rooted in self-interest, and the last is primarily ethical, extended because it is the right thing to do.

- Individual purpose: The erring leader publicly apologises to encourage their followers to forgive and forget.
- Institutional purpose: People in a company err and the leader apologises on their behalf to restore cohesion within the group and maintain their reputation.
- Inter-group purpose: One or more parties within a company commit a wrongdoing that affects an external party, and the leader apologises publicly to ask forgiveness and seek redemption.
- Moral apology: The leader feels genuine remorse for a wrongdoing committed at the individual or institutional level.

A good apology is genuine and timely. First, there is an acknowledgement of the mistake or wrongdoing, the acceptance of responsibility, an expression of regret and a promise that it will not be repeated. In 1982 seven people died when cyanide was inserted into Tylenol capsules. Although the crisis was precipitated by a random individual rather than Johnson & Johnson, they assumed responsibility immediately. James Burke, the CEO, advised the public not to consume the products, production and advertising stopped and there was a product recall at a cost of $100 million. He also went public on America's *60 Minutes*. Vouchers were offered in return for already purchased products, and he promised more secure packaging to avoid a future crisis. Marketing experts had written off the Tylenol brand but within a year, and with new tamper-resistant packaging, it had regained ninety per cent of the market share. The company and the brand emerged from the crisis with their reputation enhanced. From this example we can see that good apologies usually work.

Some leaders refuse to apologise, but it's risky to protest innocence against obvious evidence. When Merck's drug Vioxx was linked to about 139,000 heart attacks, some fatal, the CEO, Gilmartin, refused to apologise and refused to address the issue at all. He eventually left the company without assuming responsibility or expressing regret in any way. We cannot be sure why he stonewalled. Perhaps he felt that he had nothing to apologise for, or was worried by the impact an apology would have on other members of the company, or it could have been self-interest and a desire to protect his reputation. On his own calculations maybe he felt that the risk of apologising was greater than the risk of not doing so, or he could have been advised by lawyers that silence was the best option. But overall his approach in this instance failed. Interestingly, it did not prevent a litigation process, widespread redundancies within the company and the closure of several plants, so it is hard in this instance to see how an apology could have worsened this situation.

There are disadvantages to a public apology. While it can sometimes moderate a customer's anger, it can also strengthen negative perceptions of the brand. It can also be risky since not everyone requires an apology, and often a public apology informs previously unaware customers about a problem, and they may in turn think, 'Hey, I didn't know you were doing that kind of stuff'. But generally a good apology in a timely fashion is more likely to ameliorate a situation than to exacerbate it. Academic research shows that leaders are more likely to overestimate the cost of apologies and underestimate the benefits. Apologies often defuse the anger of the wronged party, and if litigation proceedings ensue they often lead to quicker settlements. The more severe the injury, the more important the apology in resolving the conflict.

When you or your people mess up, there are some questions that can frame your approach as you decide whether or not to apologise publicly:

- What function would it serve?
- Who would benefit from an apology?
- Why would an apology matter?
- What happens if you apologise publicly?
- What happens if you don't apologise?

In summary, some answers to the question 'When should a leader apologise?':
- When doing so is serving an important purpose.
- When the offence has serious consequences.
- When it is appropriate that the leader assume some responsibility for the offence.
- When no one else can get the job done.
- When the cost of saying something is less than the cost of staying silent.

Unless one or more of these conditions apply, no good reason exists for the leader to apologise. An apology that is misguided can do more harm than good. When an apology is obviously in order, though, even a partial apology can help both sides of the dispute. Similarly, when an apology is needed but not forthcoming, resentment can fester and difficulties escalate.

Source: Kellerman (2006)

QUESTIONS

Q.1 Is it reasonable to expect that leaders should apologise? Justify your answer.

Q.2 What skills are required of the leader to make an effective apology?

Cross-Cultural Dimensions of Leadership

Cross-cultural leadership research is in its infancy. Hofstede (1992) argued that theories of leadership which purport to be universalistic are, in fact, shaped significantly by the fact that they were developed by US theorists. The majority of US theories tend to advocate participation in decision-making, but it remains at the manager's discretion to extend this participation. Hofstede suggested that this notion is consistent with the medium power distance that typifies US culture. Dorfman (1993) suggests that given the culture-boundedness of leadership theories, a key question is raised concerning the applicability of these theories to different cultures. Dorfman also contended that increased globalisation makes it imperative to learn about effective leadership in different cultures. There is support for the proposition that leaders, in order to be effective, must understand how people in different cultures understand them and interpret their actions.

National cultural values influence the attitudes and behaviours of managers and leaders. They are internalised by managers who grow up in a particular culture. Adler (1997) indicated that cultural values, as internalised by managers, will influence their attitudes and behaviour in ways that they may not be conscious of. We currently know a number of things concerning cross-cultural differences in leadership:

- Dorfman (2003) found that American managers use more participative leadership than managers in Mexico or Korea. This finding must, however, be interpreted with caution, given that questionnaire designs present significant interpretation problems.
- Podsakoff *et al.* (1986) found that positive reward behaviour is important to leadership in different cultures. However, there are significant cultural differences in the types of behaviour that are rewarded and the types of rewards that are used.
- Smith *et al.* (1989) found differences in the way managers communicate directions and give feedback to subordinates. American managers showed a strong preference for face-to-face meetings, whereas Japanese managers tended to use written memos and to channel negative feedback through peers.
- Scandura, Von Glinow and Lowe (1999) found that where leaders demonstrated supportive behaviour, it significantly influenced subordinate satisfaction in the US, but not in Jordan and Saudi Arabia. These countries display a stronger preference for structuring behaviour.
- Dorfman *et al.* (1997) found that there was a stronger preference for directive leadership behaviour in Mexico and South Korea than in the US.
- House *et al.* (2004) found that particular traits and behaviours are highly relevant across many cultures. These are personal integrity, and visionary, inspirational, decisive and diplomatic behaviours. Other behaviours tend to vary more significantly across cultures. These include ambition, comparison, dominance, formality, independence, logic, risk-taking and status. Team-oriented behaviours are more effective in cultures that are collective. Participative behaviours are more relevant in cultures with low power distance and lower avoidance of uncertainty and are more relevant in cultures that have a high-performance orientation.
- Westwood (1992) suggested that a paternalistic style of leadership is characteristic of Asia. This style works best in cultures that have high power distance. These cultures tend to prefer more directive and autocratic styles of leadership.

Table 3.9 provides a summary of cultural clusters. These differences suggest that the design of leadership development programmes for a culturally diverse group of managers is challenging. Formal training programmes may not necessarily represent the most effective way to develop global leaders. Work experience and international assignments are much more effective. International assignments are increasingly used for high-potential managers as a strategy to develop their global leadership mindset. We give more detailed consideration to these issues in Chapter Seventeen. They are derived from the GLOBE study.

Table 3.9: Cultural Clusters Classified on Societal Culture Practices

Cultural Dimension	High-Score Clusters	Mid-Score Clusters	Low-Score Clusters
Performance Orientation	Confucian Asia Germanic Europe Anglo	Southern Asia Sub-Saharan Africa Latin Europe Nordic Europe Middle East	Latin America Eastern Europe
Assertiveness	Germanic Europe Eastern Europe	Sub-Saharan Africa Latin America Anglo Middle East Confucian Asia Latin Europe Southern Asia	Nordic Europe
Future Orientation	Germanic Europe Nordic Europe	Confucian Asian Anglo Southern Asia Sub-Saharan Africa Latin Europe	Middle East Latin America Eastern Europe
Humane Orientation	Southern Asia Sub-Saharan Africa	Middle East Anglo Nordic Europe Latin America Confucian Asia Eastern Europe	Latin Europe Germanic Europe
Institutional Collectivism	Nordic Europe Confucian Asia	Anglo Southern Asia Sub-Saharan Africa Middle East Eastern Europe	Germanic Europe Latin Europe Latin America
In-Group Collectivism	Southern Asia Middle East Eastern Europe Latin America Confusion Asia	Sub-Saharan Africa Latin Europe	Anglo Germanic Europe Nordic Europe
Gender Egalitarianism	Eastern Europe Nordic Europe	Latin America Anglo Latin Europe Sub-Saharan Africa Southern Asia Confucian Asia Germanic Europe	Middle East
Power Distance	Southern Asia Latin America Eastern Europe Sub-Saharan Africa Middle East	Latin Europe Confucian Asia Anglo Germanic Europe	Nordic Europe

Cultural Dimension	High-Score Clusters	Mid-Score Clusters	Low-Score Clusters
Uncertainty Avoidance	Nordic Europe Germanic Europe Confucian Asia Anglo	Sub-Saharan Africa Latin Europe Southern Asia Middle East Latin America	Eastern Europe

Source: House *et al.* (2004)

Can Managers and Leaders be Developed?

We have observed throughout this chapter that there has been much debate over whether leadership and management are different and whether leadership is a skill, a trait or innate behaviour. The view of contemporary researchers and educators is that leadership is both a skill and a behaviour that exhibits that skill. This dual perspective has generated debate concerning whether or not leadership can be developed.

There is a lot of evidence of leadership education and training initiatives in industry and business schools. These trends suggest that leadership is an important issue for managers to learn about.

A review of academic opinion and the opinions of management gurus indicates the belief that leadership can be learned. Handy (1992), for example, suggested that leadership skills cannot be taught, but they can be learned, discovered, fostered and allowed to grow. He stipulated four conditions that are necessary for this to happen: the manager or leader must have the opportunity to change things, to demonstrate initiative, experiment and make mistakes; the manager must possess self confidence; the manager or leader needs to have a broad perspective and not be blinkered by a narrow range of experience; and, finally, the manager or leader must be respected and trusted, but not necessarily loved.

Conger and Toegel (2003) suggested that 'work experiences, job assignments, special projects, role models and education, all play a role in leadership development'. They acknowledged that not everyone can become an outstanding leader, but all leaders will benefit from development. Bennis and Nanus (1985) argued that leadership is something that can be both learned and taught. Sadler (2003) made a distinction between leadership and management capability. He considered it relatively easier to develop managerial skills than leadership skills.

There is even greater controversy concerning whether leadership can be taught in a formal context. The most frequently articulated viewpoint is that some dimensions of leadership can be taught, but this is contingent on both the learner and the development context. London (2002) suggested that if leadership is defined to include knowledge, skills and attitudes, then it is possible to teach it. He argued that many elements of leadership knowledge can be delivered through either formal training or, more appropriately, through life experience and development processes. We are inclined to the viewpoint that while leadership itself may not be easily taught, the competencies of leadership can be developed. They must, however, be developed in a particular context. Context is critical in explaining how leaders behave and learn. Conger and Toegel (2003) suggested that the ideal leadership development programme will consist of three elements: specialist developers who have an in-depth knowledge concerning leadership; a group of company executives who are accepted role models for leadership and can provide appropriate frameworks for action; and, finally, professional trainers who have experience in experiential and feedback methods. Many formal leadership development interventions consider leadership as a set of portable knowledge skills and attitudes. This comment reflects the contemporary viewpoint that leadership can be developed in a multiplicity of ways.

It is therefore possible to state that management and leadership development interventions can be used to develop particular capacities of managers and leaders. Strong support exists for the viewpoint that it is possible to develop leaders' self-awareness, self-confidence and ability to view issues from a broader, systematic point of view. We have highlighted throughout this chapter that leadership is a social process. This suggests that management and leadership interventions can also be used to enhance interpersonal and social skills. These are important because the ability to work within social systems is a fundamental capacity for leaders and managers. Increasingly, management and leadership interventions are used to enhance the ability to learn. Leadership development helps managers and leaders to recognise when new behaviours, skills and attitudes are called for. Conger and Benjamin (1999) argued that an important feature of leaders is their ability to instil a learning mindset throughout the organisation. Useem (1998) suggested that it is important for leaders to have a viewpoint or vision which is teachable. Leaders must possess the skills to articulate that vision in a form that others can readily learn and transmit.

Some commentators suggest that the literature has created a false dichotomy by distinguishing between leadership and management. Some suggest that leaders' roles are closely associated with managers' roles and use the terms interchangeably. Others, in particular Zaleznick (1977), suggested that managers and leaders differ in motivation, personal resources and in how they think and act. We are of the viewpoint that the distinction has pedagogic value. At a conceptual level, it is useful to consider leadership as different from management. We do, however, for the purposes of this book, consider that the terms can be used interchangeably.

We premise this book on the view that management and leadership can be developed. Aspects of management and leadership are, however, innate and there may be limits to the contribution of formal development interventions. The contemporary view is that management and leadership skills are best acquired throughout a combination of formal classroom-based learning combined with practical experiential learning experiences.

Conclusion

We have considered various aspects of management and leadership in this chapter. Management work is inherently varied, fragmented, reactive, disorderly and political. Several features of the organisation affect the nature of managerial work. These are the level of management, lateral interdependence, crisis conditions, the size of the organisation unit and its stage in the organisational life cycle. The nature of managerial work is being altered by trends such as globalisation, workplace diversity, technological change and the emergence of new forms of organisation.

Leadership is an elusive concept and takes on a variety of forms, depending on the situation. Large, complex organisations require different kinds of leadership processes than smaller organisations. Leadership research has focused on attempts to identify the traits of effective leaders. Research has also looked at contingency approaches and the interaction between the leader and followers. Contemporary theories of leadership have emerged out of changes in the business environment. Environmental turbulence and uncertainty, combined with changing attitudes to business by society, has led to disillusionment with traditional views of leadership. The leaders of the twenty-first century are expected to exercise influence without the backing of hierarchy. They are expected to demonstrate high ethical standards, show humility and be open to learning. They are expected to value people and show concern for personal as well as professional development. Contemporary notions of leadership include the leader as servant, the leader as steward, and leaders who possess a paradoxical combination of humility on the one hand and assertiveness and learnedness on the other.

Our notions concerning how leaders learn have also changed. The work of managers and leaders increasingly involves an understanding of the dynamic nature of management and leadership processes as well as the social context in which they are applied. Managers and leaders are expected to develop a broad and diverse range of skills, abilities and cognitive frameworks. They must also possess the ability to change these frameworks. Learning and critical reflection are challenges in which managers and leaders must engage. These can be developed through appropriate leadership development interventions.

Summary of Key Points

- Managerial work is complex and multidimensional. It is characterised by social interaction, external networking, short timeframes and highly fragmented work activities.
- Leadership is a social process involving interaction between people who offer leadership and people who accept the offer and act as followers. Leadership takes a variety of forms that depend on different situations.
- The effective leader tends to share decision-making and responsibility. The effective leader is also considered a visionary who possesses the skills to develop a shared vision with his or her followers. Leaders are expected to be concerned with values.
- Leadership involves both a concern for task and a concern for people's needs, aspirations and expectations. There is no single way to be effective in all situations. Leadership style will vary according to the situation.
- It is possible to develop the competencies of leadership. This development can take place in a multiplicity of ways.

■ Discussion Questions

1. What does the research tell us about managerial work? How does it differ from the theoretical perspectives of classical management thinking?

2. Compare and contrast contingency theories with trait theories of leadership. What implications do they have for management leadership development processes?

3. What do you see as some of the problems associated with charismatic and transformational leadership?

4. The new leadership theories challenge the way we should think about leadership development. Evaluate this statement.

5. Given current trends towards empowerment and self-managed leadership, how important will leadership development be in the next ten years? Justify your answer.

■ Application and Experiential Questions

1. Select an individual who you think is an effective leader. In your opinion, what factors or attributes contribute to that individual's effectiveness as a leader? How could individuals be trained to develop more of the attributes you identified in your target leader?

2. Reflect on three of the most significant debates discussed in this chapter for an individual responsible for developing leaders in an organisation, or for your organisation. List them and explain why these three debates are important. Describe how you would translate these debates into action for members of the organisation.

3. Does your organisation celebrate heroic leaders? Is there any evidence of a dispersed leadership model? What factors may support the introduction and/or extension of this model of leadership?

PART TWO

CHAPTER FOUR
A Strategic Approach to Management and
Leadership Development

CHAPTER FIVE
Structuring and Managing Leadership Development
in Organisations

CHAPTER SIX
Management and Leadership Competency Models

CHAPTER SEVEN
Managing Talent and Succession in Organisations

Chapter Four

A Strategic Approach to Management and Leadership Development

Outline

Learning Objectives

After reading this chapter you will be able to:

- Define strategic management and leadership development and describe how it can be practised in organisations.
- Explain specific ways in which management and leadership development can be linked to organisational goals and strategies.
- Describe and evaluate a number of conceptual models explaining the relationship between leadership development and business strategy.
- Evaluate the concepts of best practice, strategic leadership and management and leadership development.
- Explain the main drivers for and barriers to strategic management and leadership development in organisations.
- Describe some of the practical steps that need to be taken to ensure that a strong case is made for strategic management and leadership development in organisations.

OPENING CASE SCENARIO

Quinn Direct: Managing Leadership Development in a Call Centre

Quinn Direct is part of the highly diversified and successful Quinn Group of companies. It began operation in Ireland in 1996. It is involved in the insurance market and currently has over 350,000 customers in Ireland and the UK. It is the fastest growing insurance company in Ireland: customer numbers doubled between 2004 and 2007 and its profits grew by over fifty per cent in a two-year period. Currently, Quinn Direct is in the top three in the motor and commercial liability insurance industry in Ireland. Overall, since 2002 it has achieved growth rates averaging thirty per cent in headcount, customer numbers, sales turnover and profit. This growth is likely to continue with its expansion into the UK market.

The company is quite media shy. However, the general manager of Quinn Direct, Colin Morgan, recently said, 'We are very pleased with the performance of the business since 2005 and, in particular, with the growth in premium income we generated across all business lines in Ireland and the UK. 2005 has been a highly significant year for Quinn Direct as we completed ten years of growth. We commenced operations in 1996.'

Quinn Direct is split into three key areas: Private Lines, Commercial Lines and Claims. Private Lines deals with personal car and home insurance; Commercial Lines deals with employers; and Claims deals with the settling of claims on policies. Quinn Direct settles claims faster than its competitors, taking an average of fourteen weeks to settle a claim compared to the competitors' average of forty weeks.

As one of its strategic goals, the organisation intends to 'continue to invest in our committed and dedicated workforce, which we believe is our most valuable asset'.

The organisation has a well-established and integrated training and development function. It has a formal training and development strategy and clear goals and objectives are established for each year. The organisation's training and development manager reports to the financial services director. At an operational level, the strategic goals are translated into key performance indicators which form part of each department's goals. Department managers' performance goals are linked to these goals. The training and development strategy is agreed by senior management and is formally documented each year. The key objectives for the training and development department reflect a range of concerns, including: ensuring that all managers are developed to meet the needs of their current roles and that there are appropriate career paths and corresponding development initiatives to match these paths. The organisation does not, however, have in place a strategic training and development plan setting out the general direction that training and development will take over the medium to long term. Its absence is primarily due to the pace of growth within the organisation rather than a lack of understanding of the importance of a strategic approach to training and development.

The HR manager and the training and development manager are involved in the development of the business strategy and its core objectives. The organisation adopts a flexible approach to the training and development budget. They adopt the maxim, 'if we need to do it, we need to do it'. Investment in leadership development makes up a significant proportion of the training and development budget. Line managers' involvement is an important component of the organisation's approach to training and development.

Identifying leadership and development needs is undertaken systematically. The manager's direct manager has a key role to play in identifying needs through the yearly performance appraisal process. The training and development manager and his team collect the information from the appraisal forms and, in discussion with line managers, agree on leadership development priorities. Quarterly follow-ups are conducted with each line manager and where new needs are identified, these are included in the training and development plan. Each team leader receives a monthly email from the training and development department, investigating where there are additional development requests. The training and development department uses this collated information to design a series of training programmes. These are set out in a brochure and calendar which is published twice a year.

Quinn Direct places a strong emphasis on the use of career paths for all categories of staff, but particularly for managers and team leaders. Career paths consist of a combination of career development activities, promotional ladders and educational support. A strong emphasis is placed on encouraging all employees and managers to participate in learning and development. The organisation offers a range of qualification-based programmes, which are focused in particular on developing first-line management. Quinn Direct has a strong relationship with the Institute of Leadership and Management and offer certificates in team leadership and an introductory certificate in management. These custom-designed programmes are delivered by trainers from the accrediting bodies and are conducted in house. Managers and team leaders are required to take six modules in the following topics: developing yourself; communication; and managing the team. The organisation provides mandatory training in insurance for all managers to ensure that they comply with regulatory requirements.

Quinn Direct places a strong emphasis on benchmarking its leadership development against standards within and outside the call centre sector. Each year it compares its performance with the annual CIPD Training and Development Survey and it uses these bench marks to monitor progress. This survey alerts the organisation to new developments being undertaken by other organisations. Quinn Direct has spent a considerable amount of time benchmarking its graduate training programme with both sector-specific and non-sector-specific examples. The training and development manager uses personal networking as a way of finding information on current training and development practices. Quinn Direct has achieved the Experience Excellence through People Award, and was recently reassessed and successfully retained it. Although the majority of leadership development activities are conducted in house, the organisation also makes use of coaching, mentoring and one-to-one training and development activities. Course delivery times are varied and tailored to the requirements of the business. They can range from two-day courses to one-hour training sessions. The shorter sessions enable managers and supervisors to be released for training. This flexible delivery structure enables the organisation to schedule when managers and supervisors are going to be on training sessions.

The training and development function within Quinn Direct is ISO accredited and is subject to an external training audit. The ISO auditor has audited the training function on two occasions in the past three years. He has, for example, taken a specific programme, examined how it is developed and delivered, and interviewed participants who completed the programme. All training and development programmes are evaluated at reaction level. There is a strong focus on the learning design and delivery. In the case of management and leadership development, Quinn Direct seeks to identify the outcomes for both the organisation and the individual. The company acknowledges that outcome evaluation is difficult to undertake on management and leadership development. It is difficult to find statistical evidence which indicates how the development has impacted on call centre performance. The training and development department interview team leaders who complete the coaching programme. They also interview a team member to identify behavioural changes when the manager returns to the workplace. They use statistical data on the team's performance to assess the impact of the changed coaching style on the performance of call centre team members. Quinn Direct acknowledges that it needs to tighten up its evaluation processes. Management and leadership development is in a state of evolution in Quinn Direct. It has grown organically to meet the needs of the business in the next three years, and the company anticipates that there is scope to develop better systems and become more strategic in its approach.

QUESTIONS

Q.1   How strategic is Quinn Direct's approach to managment and development?

Q.2   Suggest a strategy which Quinn Direct could use to evaluate the effectiveness of its training and development activities.

Strategic management and leadership development aims to ensure that the organisation identifies and mobilises competent management and leadership talent to perform at a level necessary to implement successfully and in some cases formulate the strategies of the organisation. The way in which an organisation formulates and implements its strategies plays a key role in determining management and leadership development priorities, plans and strategies. Strategic management and leadership development is much discussed in the literature, but there is less evidence that organisations practise it. Many organisations implement management and leadership development in a reactive fashion. Business priorities are usually the key trigger for management and leadership development, but it less often shapes corporate and business strategies. Effective strategic management and leadership development makes an impact at all stages of the strategic development process. This chapter considers the nature of strategic management and leadership development. We examine a number of conceptual models that can help explain the relationship between business strategy and leadership development, and highlight the gap between the theory and practice of strategic management and leadership development. We examine how this can be overcome so that organisations can make informed choices about leadership development strategies and link them more effectively to business strategies.

Defining Strategic Management and Leadership Development

Surprisingly, there are relatively few definitions of strategic management and leadership development. Woodall and Winstanley (1998) noted the tendency of traditional management and leadership development to overlook the more dynamic views of business strategy and to operate at a more tactical level. Burgoyne (1989) and Mumford (1993) articulated the relationship between strategy and management and leadership development. Burgoyne advocates an evolutionary logic which progresses gradually from a practically non-existent relationship to a more integrated view of strategic management and leadership development. Mumford suggests that three strategic relationships exist. Type 1, informal managerial, includes accidental learning processes which occur naturally in connection with other managerial activities. Management and leadership development is an unstructured activity and it does not have clear developmental objectives. Type 2, integrated managerial, refers to opportunistic processes, where natural managerial activities are structured in such a way as to make use of currently available learning opportunities. Management and leadership development activities are planned and are subsequently reviewed as learning experiences. Type 3, formalised development, focuses on planned learning processes which take place away from normal managerial activities. Management and leadership development activities have definite development objectives and they are based on clear, explicit intentions. Both authors emphasised the strategic integration of management and leadership development. Burgoyne was concerned with the depth of integration and with the evolution of management and leadership development as an activity to a point where it is fully strategic in focus. Mumford placed more emphasis on a multiplicity of integration forms.

Luoma (2005) suggests that it is possible to integrate both models. He proposes an alternative model which differentiates between sporadic, reactive and integrative management and leadership development. He describes each type as follows:

- **Sporadic management and leadership development (MLD):** MLD is unco-ordinated and the target setting is vague. Line organisation ownership of MLD initiatives is weak. The content of MLD is only loosely coupled with specific development needs or future aspirations of the organisation. Learning benefits individuals rather than the organisation.
- **Reactive MLD:** MLD is used as a response to identified problems or anticipated failures in performance. MLD follows technological, financial or product/market-related

considerations of strategy. There is some consistency in various MLD initiatives, which represent mainly formal learning. MLD is designed to benefit the organisation rather than individuals.

- **Integrative MLD:** Various MLD initiatives, formal and non-formal, form an integrated whole. MLD focuses on the key elements of current strategy and/or addresses previously unidentified solutions or problems that might lead to novel strategies. MLD's input in business strategy is sought intentionally. MLD benefits both individuals and the organisation.

We place considerable emphasis in this book on the strengthening of the strategic link between strategy and management and leadership development. Burgoyne (1989) cautioned that it is a long-term and resource-intensive process. It requires organisations to focus on the development of systems and processes as well as developing cultural and climate dimensions. He suggested that these need to be integrated or joined together by a strong corporate identity and future direction. Seibert *et al.* (1995) focused on the development of a clear strategic intent in the organisation, as well as strategic processes that are participatory and ever-changing.

Strategic integration of management and leadership development is appropriate only after it has progressed through earlier stages of development. Barid and Meshoulam (1988) argued that a partial determinant of the effectiveness of management and leadership development is the degree to which it matches the organisation's developmental stage. Management and leadership development often fails to play a major role in the organisation's strategy formulation processes because of the planning deficiencies of management and leadership development specialists, who are frequently action-oriented, focusing on the problem-solving and tactical decision-making components of their role. Strategic integration requires the specialist to think in terms of the organisation as a whole and the relationships between the organisation and the factors that impact on it within its environment. This is sometimes a difficult task for the in-house management development specialist to undertake.

Table 4.1 provides a summary of issues that the organisation may need to consider. Luoma (2005) suggests three requirements for maximising the return on investment in strategic management and leadership development. These requirements are:

- Making the case for investment in managerial talent.
- Making the connection between business planning, organisation and management and leadership development.
- Managing the management and leadership development process by getting the implementation right.

Table 4.1: Evolving Towards Strategic Management and Leadership Development

1. **Management Involvement:** Ranges from a focus on administration to a full integration of management and leadership development considerations in all management decision-making.
2. **Management of the Function:** Includes the structure of the leadership development function and the planning, allocation and control of resources. The structure may vary from very loose or non-existent to complex matrices and/or decentralised.
3. **Portfolio of Leadership Programmes:** Ranges from relatively simple programmes such as management induction and management skills programmes to more complex and sophisticated leadership development processes such as mentoring, developmental planning, multi-source feedback and stretch development initiatives.
4. **Skills of Professionals:** Management and leadership development professionals need appropriate skills. Basic programmes and simple information systems require basic skills. The addition of complex programmes and growth in size requires more advanced, differentiated and specialised skills.

5. **Information Technology Capacity:** Information tools range from manual record-keeping to sophisticated distributed systems with modelling capabilities and talent management processes to advanced forecasting and simulation based on statistical tools.
6. **Scanning the External Environment:** In the initial stage, because of pressures involved in start-up, top management does not systematically assess and react to the environment. At the strategic integration stage, top management is very aware of the internal and external environments and their links with leadership development strategy. It remains flexible and adjusts to opportunities and risks that arise, and to what competitors are doing on leadership development.

Source: Adapted from Barid and Meshoulam (1988)

Definitions and models of strategic management and leadership development stress contribution to realising organisational goals and strategies. Management and leadership development has a collective character: the majority of models emphasise organisational capability and performance rather than the capability and performance of individual managers. Strategic management and leadership development is clearly a choice for organisations; it will therefore be influenced by the attitudes and values of top management. It does, however, assume necessary insights concerning the diagnosis of and preconceptions about what is needed from management and leadership development. It is not, however, without tensions. Woodall and Winstanley (1998) were conscious of this tension in their model of integration and differentiation. Integration stresses compatibility with the aims and objectives of the organisation, a proactive consensus on objectives, and direction from the top. Differentiation emphasises compatibility with individual objectives and future careers, self-managed development processes, enabled choices to suit career, learning styles, personality and contextual factors and a bottom-up approach. It is likely that organisations that practise strategic management and leadership development will need to balance both perspectives.

Linking Management and Leadership Development to Strategic Human Resource Management

To be effective, strategic management and leadership development must be one component of a bigger, embedded strategic human resource management philosophy. Grattan *et al.* (1999) suggested that this will include vertical and horizontal links. Vertical links focus on connecting SMLD to SHRM and business strategy. Horizontal links focus on coherently connecting management and leadership development initiatives to each other and to operational HR activities. Such links will need to be mutually reinforcing.

A number of studies have focused on the relative priority given to management and leadership development when compared with other SHRM areas. Tyson (1995), for example, found that succession management and leadership development were the best documented of all HR activities. Companies ranked management and leadership development high on their strategic agenda, and many adopted it in conjunction with organisation development as strategic policy levers. Grattan *et al.* (1999) found that management and leadership development and organisation development were viewed as long-term processes. Leadership development initiatives were strongly linked with other HR strategies, as well as with business strategy. Leadership development tended to concentrate on the development of future leadership cadres. These development initiatives were based on a future needs analysis, derived from an assessment of very broad strategic drivers. Specific aspects of management and leadership development were emphasised more strongly than others. The focus was primarily on the development of high-fliers at the expense of solid and mid-range performers.

Stiles (1999) examined how transformational change is managed in large organisations. He found a very strong focus on competency frameworks, which emphasised leadership quality, leadership and team development. Managers received intensive training in coaching, feedback and counselling. Middle managers were involved in cross-functional teams. They provided feedback on change initiatives to senior management.

Mabey and Ramirez (2005) argue that management and leadership are key dimensions of progressive SHRM. The systematic development of leadership is linked to other HR strategies, but it is their internal fit rather than the number of practices that is important. This clearly highlights that strategic management and leadership development consists of an internally coherent set of processes. In practice, this is often difficult to achieve due to a range of factors, which will be considered later in this chapter.

EXHIBIT 4.1

Key Assumptions of Strategic Management and Leadership Development (SMLD)

Assumptions	Consequences	Implications for Action
• There is an existing overarching mission statement specifying organisational commitment to learning; SMLD initiatives are linked with and supported by organisational policies, systems and resource provision.	• Mission statement shapes organisational vision, corporate strategy, organisational plans and SMLD vision. • Linking the organisation's mission to planned learning experiences through SMLD ensures that, if the value of SMLD is questioned, the value of the organisation is also questioned. • Emphasises the proactive long-term nature of strategic SMLD.	• SMLD interventions need to be planned and conscious; unplanned and functional experiences cannot be strategic unless explicitly linked to strategy. • SMLD needs to be linked to SMLD systems and collaborative career-planning processes. • The organisation should implement systems which facilitate periodic review and/or revision of the organisation's mission statement and, as a result, influence corporate SMLD strategies and policies.
• Environmental planning and scanning by senior management is timely, accurate and realistic and interpreted in terms of implications for learning.	• L&D plans and policies flow from the organisation's strategic plan which is influenced heavily by the process of environmental scanning. • Ensures that SMLD plans and policies are timely, accurate and realistic to facilitate achievement of the strategic priorities of the organisation.	• SMLD needs holistic and systematic planning processes. • SMLD specialists should understand the implications of internal and external context.
• Planning processes are formal, systematic and holistic and integrated with the corporate plan as well as emergent and flexible SMLD processes.	• SMLD activities shape and support the achievement of clearly articulated organisational goals and are enhanced by the identification of links and information-sharing inherent in the planning process. • SMLD is supported by complementary SMLD activities, e.g. SMLD implications arising from HR plans and forecasts are considered.	• SMLD should develop mechanisms to feed into strategic processes and capture emergent processes. • SMLD specialists should strive to align SMLD strategies and activities with the wider policy framework. • Mechanisms need to be put in place which enable the SMLD specialist to participate in corporate strategy sessions with other managers.

Assumptions	Consequences	Implications for Action
		• SMLD specialists need to articulate an SMLD vision, mission statement and statement of values. • SMLD specialists need to consider the extent and depth of expertise needed to implement solutions to achieve corporate strategy.
• All major plans are weighted in terms of human skills available to implement them and alternative ways to obtain these skills.	• SMLD is not a panacea providing solutions for all problems. It is an appropriate solution to knowledge, skills and attitude issues. • The 'where' and 'how' of obtaining the skills required are considered at the outset of policy formation and planning processes.	• Employees have a responsibility to evaluate their own skills and development needs. • SMLD specialists need sophisticated mechanisms to understand organisational and individual level learning needs. • SMLD specialists should be concerned to use training and development resources in an effective manner.
• Outcomes of SMLD activities produce added value for the organisation and are enhanced by a recognition of the role of cultural 'fit'.	• Organisational and work processes are integrated across units and knowledge shared across boundaries. • Learning is perceived as a core strategic competency for the organisation. • The emphasis is on evaluation of the suitability, feasibility and acceptability of SMLD policies, plans and practices. • Organisation culture is supportive of feedback, open communications, participation and continuous learning in particular.	• Effective evaluation processes, including cost-benefit analysis, need to be introduced. • SMLD specialist needs to be clear on the criteria to be used when evaluating the SMLD function.
• People at all organisational levels share responsibility and accountability for learning activities. • Senior management actively supports learning and the SMLD specialist works in partnership with line management and the HR function.	• Planned learning is considered an essential component of every employee's job. • An organisational culture of continuous learning permeates throughout the organisation and provides a positive climate for SMLD. • Line management best placed to assess learning needs. • Line management has a legitimate input to SMLD plans and policies, facilitating systematic identification of SMLD needs. • Top management ensures commitment to, responsibility for and ownership of SMLD activities.	• Line manager commitment and involvement is critical to successful SMLD. • SMLD specialist needs to develop mechanisms that facilitate regular networking with members of the organisation. • There is a need to ensure clear definitions of roles, responsibilities and policies. • How can the SMLD specialist engage with and involve the top team in the formulation of SMLD strategies and policies? • Individuals should have responsibility for the development of others.

Assumptions	Consequences	Implications for Action
• SMLD is a core element of the performance expectations of line management. • Management and leadership development professionals are skilled and confident enough to deliver.	• Managers, supervisors and employees are evaluated on the degree to which they simultaneously develop themselves and others. • Reward and career progression decisions are contingent on the extent to which development criteria are satisfied.	• Responsibility for development should be incorporated into the performance management processes. • Effective SMLD specialists should adopt strategic partner-type roles.

Exhibit 4.1 summarises our understanding of the key dimensions of strategic management and leadership development. These dimensions confirm that management and leadership development is linked to business plans and strategies through core competencies. General and personal competency development is insufficient in itself. Commitment is required from senior management to ensure that management and leadership development initiatives are implemented. Leadership development initiatives must focus on global competencies, and individual development must take place within the context of organisational learning. Corporate culture shapes, and is shaped by, leadership development initiatives, and there must be a supportive developmental climate in which executives feel confident to tackle unstructured problems and solutions. It should, however, be pointed out that this picture of SMLD may not be applicable in more stable situations. Table 4.2 provides a list of questions that organisations should ask when considering their capability for strategic management and leadership development.

Table 4.2: Perspective on Practice: Assessing an Organisation's Overall Capability for Strategic Management and Leadership Development

- Does the organisation have an understanding of the skills and competencies it needs to execute its growth objectives?
- What processes does the organisation have in place to enable it to identify, assess and develop the next generation of managers and leaders across its business units?
- What specific development plans does the organisation have in place to develop its high-potential talent?
- How much flexibility does the organisation possess in terms of deploying its managers and leaders to avail of emerging opportunities and challenges?
- Does the organisation possess the agility to move its managers and leaders around without creating significant disruption to other parts of the organisation?
- What strengths does the organisation possess at executive level?
- Does the organisation need managers and leaders who are skilled to operate in a complex global environment?
- To what extent do current leaders of the organisation demonstrate a high level of commitment to the development of managers and leaders?
- To what extent does the organisation hold its managers accountable for identifying and developing managerial talent?

Conceptualising Strategic Management and Leadership Development

Strategic management and leadership development can be considered from a number of perspectives: a competitive strategy framework; the strategic human resource activity typology; strategic types theory; and strategy-making modes theory, amongst others. We briefly evaluate each of these models and their prescriptions for management and leadership development.

Competitive Strategy Perspective on Management Development

An organisation's competitive strategy requires different skill sets, competencies and role behaviours. The role behaviours and competencies required of managers provide a rationale for a relationship between competitive strategy and management development practices.

Strategists generally make a distinction between three types of competitive strategies: cost leadership/reduction; innovation or differentiation strategies; and quality enhancement strategies. Different management and leadership development strategies and activities are required for each set of strategies. Table 4.3 provides a set of management development prescriptions for each competitive strategy.

Table 4.3: The Relationship between Competitive Strategy and Management and Leadership Development Practices

Competitive Strategy	Focus	Management and Leadership Development Implications
Cost Reduction Strategies	• Short-term focus • Risk-averse behaviours in organisations • Strong results orientation • Predictability and standardisation • Rule-based organisation culture	• Limited investment in management development • Narrow and specialised job roles • Narrow and specialised career paths • Management development, where it exists, will focus on current priorities
Innovation Strategies	• Co-operative employee behaviours • Strong orientation towards the longer term • Strong degree of comfort with ambiguity • Promotion of risk-taking behaviours • Highly creative organisation culture	• Strong emphasis on teamwork and team development • Generalised managerial competency development and broad career paths • Flexible and innovative management development processes • Strong emphasis on career planning and the development of manager employability • Sophisticated management appraisal systems
Quality Enhancement Strategies	• Emphasis on the quality of production and service processes • Emphasis on risk reduction • Predictability and robustness of processes and systems • Emphasis on meeting a narrower segment or providing a single product/service	• Managers will have longer-term security and guaranteed psychological contracts • Extensive management training and development programmes • Broadly defined managerial roles and participative decision-making processes

Organisations that adopt innovative competitive strategies are more likely to place an emphasis on team-development processes, sophisticated management appraisal systems, broad career paths, the development of generic management competencies and continuous investment in management and leadership development. Organisations that pursue cost-cutting, competitive strategies are less likely to invest in management and leadership development. They are also likely to emphasise narrow managerial roles and specialised career paths. Organisations that pursue quality enhancement competitive strategies are likely to value longer-term employment relationships, extensive investment in management training and development, flexible managerial roles and participative decision-making.

A Strategic Human Resource Activity Typology

Speaker (2000) proposed a conceptual typology of human resources which has many applications in management and leadership development. The typology categorises human resource activities in two dimensions: 1) whether they are relational or transactional in value; and 2) whether they have high or low strategic value. Management and leadership development activities that are transactional in nature tend to be administrative and impersonal. The performance of these activities does not demand much in terms of human involvement and, in many organisations, they are likely to be computerised. Relational management development activities, on the other hand, are complex and require high levels of human input, including interpersonal skills, political and cultural awareness and sensitivity. Focusing on the strategic value dimensions, certain management development activities are likely to have a direct impact on the organisation's ability to implement its competitive strategies, whereas others may have a more indirect impact.

Exhibit 4.2 applies the model to management and leadership development. While we have placed activities in various quadrants, it should be noted that the value of the various activities is likely to vary according to the specific characteristics of the organisation. Examples of activities in the low strategic value/transactional quadrant include such management development activities as collecting management and leadership development records and preparing evaluation results of management development. These activities do not have an immediate impact on the organisation's ability to implement various strategies. They are, however, important to the management and leadership development function and need to be performed in a timely and cost-effective manner.

It is unlikely that senior management will view these activities as strategically important, and they are unlikely to get involved in them unless there is a problem. Where they are performed poorly, they are likely to undermine the credibility of the management and leadership development function. It is generally accepted that the function must perform these activities well before it starts to focus on more high-impact strategic activities. Some of these low strategic and more transactional activities could be outsourced.

Activities in the high strategic value/relational quadrant are likely to have a more direct impact on an organisation's ability to implement its competitive strategy successfully. Examples of activities are executive and top-team programmes, coaching and mentoring processes, fast-track management development and action-learning projects. Excellence in these management and leadership development activities is likely to provide organisations with a source of competitive advantage and, because they are politically sensitive programmes based on relationships developed over time, they are less likely to be outsourced. Managers and senior executives are likely to place a lot of importance on the activities in this quadrant.

EXHIBIT 4.2

Strategic Typology of Management and Leadership Development Activities

High Value Transactional
- Management training programmes
- Succession planning and talent management processes
- Development activities around regulatory requirements
- Management education programmes

High Value Relational
- Executive and top team development interventions
- Action learning projects
- Coaching and mentoring programmes
- Fast-track management development programmes
- Job and hardship assignments
- Multi-source feedback programmes

Low Value Transactional
- Administration of management development activities
- Records of management development
- Preparation of management development brochures
- Preparation of management development evaluation results

Low Value Relational
- Identification of management development needs
- Preparation of individual development plans and career-development plans
- Conduct of management development evaluation

Several management and leadership development activities fall within the high strategic value/transactional quadrant. We postulate that these activities are likely to affect the organisation's competitive position. Typical examples include succession planning and talent management. Such planning activities are necessary to ensure the availability of key managers to implement business strategies in the future. The fourth quadrant (low strategic value relational) may include a range of developmental activities that are of low value in strategic terms, but which demand substantial relationship skills, including trust, confidentiality and a focus on the needs of the manager. We have included management development activities such as individual development planning, career development plans, needs identification processes and feedback programmes in this quadrant. These activities are necessary in order to ensure that long-term relationships with managers are sustained. These activities make a positive contribution to manager morale and ensure good citizenship behaviour. It is also arguable that these activities are a reflection of good corporate citizenship.

A Typology of Management and Leadership Development Systems

The work of Sonnenfeld and Peiperl (1988) has some very useful applications to the field of management and leadership development. This framework focuses on two important dimensions that have a direct relevance: source of managerial labour supply, and assignment and promotion criteria. Exhibit 4.3 presents a conceptualisation of the framework applied to management and leadership development.

EXHIBIT 4.3

Strategic Management and Leadership Development

External ↑

Source of Managerial Labour Supply

Internal ↓

Fortress
- HR strategy: low sophistication
- Management development strategy: some development for core employees
- Essentially reactive in approach
- Psychological contract: relational but subject to layoffs
- Business strategy: highly competitive organisations

Baseball Team
- HR strategy: buy talent where necessary
- Management development strategy: fast track with emphasis on job assignments
- Psychological contract: transactional with emphasis on employability
- Business strategy: innovation strategies

Club
- HR strategy: retention of managers
- Slow progression and focus on team contribution
- Management development strategy: development of internal talent.
- Focus on development of generalist competencies
- Psychological contract: strong relational contract
- Business strategy: cost leadership

Academy
- HR strategy: development of talent
- Extensive investment in management development
- Management development strategy: complicated career paths
- Psychological contract: relational but low tolerance of poor performers
- Business strategy: product innovation and low-cost production

Group Contribution ←——— **Assignment and Promotion Criteria** ———→ **Individual Contribution**

Organisations categorised in the club quadrant tend to pursue low-cost production and focus on controlling costs. They tend to have a short-term focus and place a strong emphasis on predictability and control, the maintenance of quality and consistency of service. When these organisations invest in management and leadership development, they focus on the internal development of talent and promote from within. There is an expectation that managers will remain with the organisation for the long term. The psychological contract is strongly relational in nature. Managers are developed as generalists, career paths are generally slow, and there is a focus on team contribution.

Companies in the baseball team category tend to pursue innovation strategies. These organisations seek to foster conditions that facilitate risk-taking, co-operation, creativity and a long-term investment in managers. Organisations in this category will invest in the development of their managers. They are also concerned to develop managers for current and future roles and there is strong emphasis on varied career paths. These organisations seek to emphasise on-the-job and workplace development interventions and will want a strong relationship between business strategy and management development. Baseball team organisations are also likely to buy talent and to develop managers through rapid assignment changes. Performance management processes are results-focused and it is often the case that the positions of those who have been passed over for promotion are excised from the organisation.

Organisations in the academy quadrant are something of a hybrid in strategic terms. They seek to be both product innovators and producers and may focus on a particular niche in the marketplace. There is a substantial emphasis on development, but the organisation will buy in managerial talent when necessary. The organisation will adopt 'make' and 'buy' approaches to ensure that it has the necessary managerial capability. There is likely to be extensive investment in management development combined with elaborate career paths.

Organisations in the fortress quadrant operate in highly competitive markets and are very vulnerable to the external environment. They tend to adopt very passive approaches to management and leadership development. They may invest in core managers in an effort to retain them.

Strategy-Making Modes and Management and Leadership Development

Hart (1992) produced a typology of five decision-making modes which are now accepted as providing a strong theoretical explanation of how strategic decisions are made in organisations. Exhibit 4.4 outlines each mode and its implications for the strategic contribution of management and leadership development.

EXHIBIT 4.4

Strategy-Making Modes of Management and Leadership

Mode	Characteristics	Implications for SMLD
Command	• Strategy made by strong individual leader and a few top managers • Strong emphasis on analysis and option evaluation • Other managers are the executors of strategy • Business environment is relatively simple to understand • Typically found in small organisations	• Strong emphasis on functional rather than strategic management development • Management development tends to make limited contribution to a strategic management • Overall commitment to management development

Mode	Characteristics	Implications for SMLD
Symbolic	• Top management creates a clear and compelling vision • Long-term vision can be translated into specific targets • There is an implicit control system in the form of shared values • Suited to a dynamic external environment • Typically found in larger organisations	• Some commitment to strategic management and leadership development • Limited emphasis on formalised planning of development • Management and leadership development used to develop values and reinforce the culture • Strong emphasis on customisation of development initiatives
Rational	• Emphasis on formal strategic planning with written strategic and operational plans • Upward sharing of data and high level of information processing and analysis • Detailed plans and well-developed control systems are in place • Found in large organisations defending established strategic positions • Relatively stable business environment	• Management and leadership development is used to facilitate implementation of strategy • Very little investment in strategic management and leadership development • Management and leadership development based on thorough analysis and the development of formal programmes • Focus more on management techniques than on leadership
Transactive	• Strong strategy making based on interaction and learning • Little focus on predetermined plans • Strong emphasis on cross-functional communications, feedback, learning and dialogue with key stakeholders • Strategic approach is iterative • Tends to adopt various initiatives • Top management is concerned with facilitation and linking outcomes over time to determine strategic direction • Suitable approach for larger firms operating in complex environments	• Strong emphasis on experimenting with alternative management and leadership development • Management and leadership development emphasis is strategic • Strong level of commitment to using development to facilitate learning • View management and leadership development as a long-term initiative
Generative	• New ideas emerge upwards from entrepreneurship • Top managers encourage experimentation • New strategies emerge through innovative activist • Strategy is continuously adjusted to reflect the outcomes of high-potential innovations • Suitable for highly turbulent environments and businesses operating in fragmented and complex markets	• Large amount of experimentation with management and leadership development • Strong commitment to strategic as well as functional management and leadership development • Very strong commitment to all things strategic • Managers are expected to be innovative, flexible and creative

Strategic management and leadership development can play a significant role in facilitating the achievement of strategic objectives, as well as the strategic management competencies and processes of the organisation. Different strategic decision-making modes have implications for management and leadership development activities, as well as the contribution of these activities to business strategy. Some of the decision-making modes, in particular the command and rational modes, provide less space for strategic management and leadership development. Others, such as symbolic, transitive and generative modes, suggest a more expansive contribution for SMLD.

Patching's Management and Leadership Development Grid

Patching (1998) suggested a model of SMLD which combines the purpose of SMLD and different levels of specificity to the organisation. The purposes of SMLD can focus on either success through change or success through alignment (Exhibit 4.5). The model suggests four variations of management and leadership development in organisations.

EXHIBIT 4.5

Patching's Management and Leadership Development Grid

	Specificity to the Organisation	
	High	**Low**
Success Through Change	**Transformational** • Focus on giving the organisation competitive advantage • Management and leadership development driven by corporate strategy • Management and leadership development used to develop a new culture • Strong management vision of the role of management and leadership development	**Exploratory** • Focuses on achieving innovation and learning through innovation • Drawn by a strong entrepreneurial focus • Management and leadership development can be used to develop strategic management capabilities • Focus on informal as well as formal development initiatives
Success Through Alignment	**Specific Capabilities** • Management and leadership development focuses on developing management competencies of value to a specific organisation • Management and leadership development used to defend the competitive position of the organisation • Competencies developed have major strategic value	**Generic** • Management and leadership development emphasises the need to develop competencies that are of value in any organisation • Competencies developed do not contribute to competitive advantage • Competencies will therefore contribute to the employability of managers

Transformational management and leadership development focuses on providing the organisation with a competitive advantage and is driven by top management vision and corporate strategy. It places a strong emphasis on the development of a new culture and focuses on the critical business success factors. Exploratory management and leadership development focuses on the facilitation of innovation and the promotion of learning through experimentation. It is usually driven by strong entrepreneurial thinking and is frequently used to develop strategic management capability. Generic management and leadership development focuses on the development of competencies which are valuable to managers in any kind of organisation. These competencies may not contribute to strategic advantage. Specific capabilities-focused management and leadership development emphasises leadership competencies which are required for a particular organisation and helps it to defend its competitive position. Patching suggested that many different management and leadership development strategies are appropriate for each quadrant, but he advises that the selection of strategies should focus on one quadrant to avoid confusion.

Brown's Business Environment Model of SMLD

Brown (2004) proposes a model of SMLD which acts as a guide to the selection of development interventions that are appropriate to the nature of the business environment and the focus of the leadership development initiative (Exhibit 4.6).

EXHIBIT 4.6

Business Environment Model of Management and Leadership Development

| | Nature of External Environment | |
	Static	Dynamic
Organisation	• Planned management and leadership development linked to business objectives • Development of detailed competency frameworks • Strong focus on use of formal development methods • Management and leadership development directed primarily at senior management • Use of management and leadership development to implement strategy	• Management and leadership development driven by vision, values and core competencies • Major use of change initiatives, action learning projects and experimentation • Adoption of broad competency frameworks and performance management systems • Strong senior and middle management in management and leadership development
Individual	• Development of an internal menu of modules to address generic competencies • Emphasis on the development of the whole person • Use of external programmes for more generic and unusual needs • Major emphasis on developing the employability of managers	• Development of meta competencies • Strong usage of networking and action learning • Strong focus on self-development and working in teams • Use of management and leadership development to cope with new technical knowledge

The framework proposes that organisations operating in dynamic and complex external environments need to approach management and leadership development by acquiring high-level broad competencies, promoting informal and work-based approaches to management and leadership development, involving middle managers in the process and encouraging teamwork. There is a need to emphasise process aspects of SMLD. Development initiatives at the individual level are likely to be collaborative in nature and to provide managers with adaptability and flexibility. Managers are likely to have technical and professional knowledge requirements which can be enabled through self-development processes. Planned management and leadership development initiatives are more difficult to organise because of the speed of change and the complexity of the business environment. The shaping of SMLD will be influenced by broad concepts such as vision, values and core competencies and driven by organisation-wide change initiatives and systems. Where competency frameworks are used, they will be broad, emphasising teamwork, creativity, flexibility, visionary leadership and change management.

Strategic management and leadership development in organisations operating in environments that are more static and simple will have a significantly different character. There is likely to be a greater focus on the centralised planning of management and leadership development initiatives. The slower rates of change make it possible to plan development interventions in more detail. The organisation is likely to be characterised by greater formality and bureaucracy. This suggests that less emphasis will be placed on informal management and leadership development initiatives. They are also likely to be less valued. Organisations operating in dynamic business environments are likely to place more emphasis on whole-person development, and may use development interventions that place emphasis on feedback and the development of personal awareness. Strategic management and leadership development is likely to be more concerned with strategy implementation rather than formulation. Middle managers are likely to have a less active role in shaping the leadership development agenda.

A Strategically Aligned Framework of Management and Leadership Development

Clarke, Butcher and Bailey (2004) proposed a discriminating approach to SMLD that is based on two sets of variables: the population to be developed (targeted or inclusive), and the content of the leadership development initiatives (individualised or corporate-consistent). They identified four distinct approaches that are not mutually exclusive. It is possible to find all four approaches used in the same organisation. They applied the framework to both the strategic positioning of management and leadership development and to managers' career development (Exhibit 4.7).

- *Tailored*: This quadrant focuses on highly targeted and individualised promotion. It is a structured approach to management and leadership development, driven by talent and succession management processes that target star performers. The focus is on individualised development initiatives that are designed to nurture talented managers. Because the development needs of talented managers are likely to be unique, the challenge for leadership development specialists is to have expertise in matching needs with a wide range of development strategies. The development focus is long term and future oriented, with the possibility of sourcing the development intervention outside the organisation if it is more cost-effective.
- *Programme*: This quadrant focuses on management and leadership development initiatives that address groups of managers. Development needs are identified through a series of planned and consistent needs development strategies that are driven by corporate business needs. In a career development context, managers who are identified

as high-potential managers may require more tailored and targeted development interventions. To balance the focus of development interventions, managers should be provided with a high degree of personal development and opportunities to experience other business situations. These experiences will allow managers to enhance their visibility and credibility across the organisation.

- *Self-Motivated*: This quadrant focuses on management and leadership development which is inclusive and individualised. This approach has no prescribed methods or content. Development opportunities are open to all managers, depending on their individual motivation. Managers are expected to manage their own development. Career development initiatives are likely to be focused on acquiring external knowledge and the development of strategic leadership. The role of the leadership development specialist is to stimulate and support managers to participate in development. For senior executives, development challenges should contain a high degree of personal challenge.
- *Generic*: This quadrant focuses on corporate-focused, consistent leadership development initiatives. This approach is driven by a need to improve specific organisational capabilities and is likely to cascade down through different levels of management. Leadership development opportunities are available to all managers. In the context of career development, it is important at early career stages to focus on the development of internal organisational knowledge, including culture. A generic development approach is more likely to emphasise the short term and special projects as well as leadership development programmes.

EXHIBIT 4.7

A Strategically Aligned Framework of Management and Leadership Development

Who? What?	Targeted Individuals	Inclusive (all talent in organisation)
Individualised Content	**High Potential Tailored** • Strong focus on developing star talent • Talent has a major impact on business success • Individualised or customised strategies • Strong focus on individual performance assessment	**Self-Motivated** • Strong emphasis on self-directed development • Managers have significant control over their development • Managers and executives need challenge and variety to sustain development initiatives • Focus may be on generic rather than company-specific competencies

Who? What?	Targeted Individuals	Inclusive (all talent in organisation)
Corporate Consistency	**High Potential Programme** • Individuals identified as high-potential managers will require more targeted development • Strong focus on providing personal development to generate greater self-awareness • Emphasis on consistency of approach rather than individualisation	**Generic Programme** • Focus on the development of internal organisational knowledge such as culture • Focus on short-term development priorities and assignments • Forced to move to a longer-term approach and to look at more generic competencies

These various perspectives or models of the role of SMLD and its relationship to business strategy suggest a number of pointers in helping us to distinguish strategic management development from functional management development. Strategic management and leadership development tends to emphasise the development of abilities to manage change, competencies in strategic management and the development of entrepreneurial behaviour. It also plays a role in the redefinition and reformulation of corporate strategy, the facilitation of innovation and creativity, the shaping and modification of culture and the development of managers who are change agents. Functional management and leadership development emphasises the improvement of current job performance, the enhancement of a manager's capability to handle a larger role and the identification of succession possibilities. Functional management development also contributes to the building of teams and networks and the preparation of managers for job moves.

SMLD is characterised by sensitivity to the external environment, the strategic direction of the organisation and the organisation's human resource system. These models show that organisations need to be discriminating in the selection of leadership development initiatives. They need to make conscious links between business strategy and management and leadership development strategy. The frameworks highlight that leadership development specialists and other stakeholders need high levels of organisational and personal awareness, to take a business rather than a HR view of the organisation, and to be sufficiently critical of the value and limitations of various leadership development strategies. Exhibit 4.8 (page 166) provides a list of questions that organisations should ask concerning the strategic alignment of management and leadership development activities.

Achieving Strategically Aligned Management and Leadership Development Questions for Organisations and Leadership Development Specialists

- Where do the organisation's current leadership development strategies sit in the various frameworks?
- What do current external environments demand and what conditions support that position?
- Is it possible to demonstrate that current leadership development strategies create a real payback for the business?
- What particular factors or criteria are most important in making management and leadership development initiatives strategically aligned? Is the organisation consistently concerned with an individualised approach, the present or the future?
- How can development professionals work more effectively with other HR specialists?
- Do all relevant stakeholders understand the strategic relevance of current approaches to management and leadership development?
- What development activities do we currently undertake that are different from our competitors?
- What values and beliefs about leadership development are driving our current provision?
- Does the organisation understand how changes in the business environment and strategy will impact on the focus and positioning of management and leadership development?

Management and Leadership Development: Business and Individual Performance Effects

One of the most significant arguments for investment in management and leadership development is that it can directly improve manager performance and, as a result, also improve corporate performance. Lees (1992) stated that this assumption is 'the cornerstone of much of the current management and leadership development debate'. A functional performance argument operates at numerous different levels of analysis and depths of intervention. We focus here on the business and individual levels. It should be noted that attempts to evaluate the impact on business as well as the individual impact of leadership development have produced inconsistent and disappointing results. The measurement of links between investment in leadership development, individual performance and business performance are problematic. Seibert *et al.* (1995) surveyed twenty-two US companies and found it difficult to establish links between business strategy and management and leadership development strategy. They attributed this to three factors. First, leadership development functions tend to be internally focused rather than focused on the customer and the business environment. Second, they tend to devise somewhat rigid management and leadership development plans that are not always responsive to changing business strategies and the environment. Third, they suggested that there is a false dichotomy between developing leaders and conducting business, which is viewed retrospectively as the task of the leadership development function and line managers. McClelland (1973) suggested that one of the biggest obstacles to management and leadership development is that managers tend to link it with enhanced individual effectiveness rather than organisational effectiveness. Hirsch and Reilly (1999) found that the biggest challenges to showing a link with organisational effectiveness came not from the formal documented corporate plans, but from changes within the planning cycle. Development needs are generated by specific change projects or high-level messages from senior managers. Furthermore, formal corporate strategic plans frequently have little to say about people. Even when organisational capabilities were identified, it was difficult to link them directly with skills. Organisations encounter difficulty in identifying how skills at an individual level can be aggregated up at corporate level to demonstrate that leadership development initiatives have made a difference to business performance.

Burgoyne, Hirsh and Williams (2003) suggested that establishing a direct micro link between leadership development and business performance is difficult because of the model used. This is frequently expressed in the following way: Corporate strategy — key competencies — to competency-based leadership development — to enhanced corporate performance.

Leadership Development as Part of a Suite of HRM Practices

Management and leadership development is often studied as one of several HRM practices that may explain business performance. This approach suggests that is the bundle of HRM practices that is important. Becker and Huselid highlighted that as organisations add more HRM practices they will reach a point where significant performance improvements are achieved. This point is reached when there is a critical mass of HRM practices. There is a growing body of evidence on the general (macro) association between good human resource management practices and organisational performance (Box 4.1). A study conducted for the CIPD by Chaulakin (2001) concluded that people management strategies contribute to business performance improvement. A number of practices, or sets of practices, such as the development of skills and empowerment, are strongly related to business performance.

Box 4.1: Leadership Development Combined with other HRM Practices and Business Performance

- Pfeffer (1994) and Becker and Huselid (1998) found associations between certain HRM practices and superior business performance, although there was considerable variation in explanations of how these links might operate.
- Richardson and Thompson (1999) and Guest *et al.* (2000) concluded that, while there did seem to be some association between progressive or 'high-performance' HRM practices and organisational performance, a causal link had not yet been proved.
- Leadership development is quite often included as one of the HRM practices seen as possibly contributing to business performance. Pfeiffer, for example, listed management training and development as usually measured in very simple terms in these studies, most often as training spent or proportion of employees receiving training.
- Patterson *et al.* (1997), in a large-scale longitudinal study in the UK, grouped training with other practices affecting the acquisition and development of skills (selection, induction, training and management development). This group of HR practices were found to have a strong influence on productivity. A combination of human resource practices explained productivity far more conclusively than strategy, emphasis on quality, application of technology and R&D expenditure.
- Dearden *et al.* (2000) used longitudinal data from the UK Labour Force Survey and industry-level productivity data which demonstrated that investment in training and management development increased the value of each worker in productivity terms far more than the cost in increased wages.

Specific Impact of Investment in Management and Leadership Development

Research suggests a possible positive link between investment in leadership development and organisational performance. Leadership development is not often the employment practice most strongly associated with organisational performance. However, a few studies have examined the impact of management and leadership development on organisational performance (Box 4.2).

Box 4.2: Investment in Management and Leadership Development and Business Performance: The Evidence

- Winterton and Winterton (1996) highlighted a link between management development and organisational performance in a study of sixteen UK organisations, especially where such development was competence-based and linked to overall strategy.
- DTZ (1998) examined 127 firms using TEC-related management-development activity. Although 63% could identify an impact of this development on business performance, only 18% felt this was definite and direct and under 9% could quantify this impact.
- Mabey and Thomas (2000) used large surveys to examine changes between 1996 and 2000 in a matched sample of organisations. They found that those reporting improvements in management and leadership development also reported improved financial performance relative to others in their sector. They emphasised the importance of such activity being linked to business strategy.
- Thompson *et al.* (2001) found that the majority of HRD managers felt that management development activities achieved their objectives, although client managers were somewhat more critical. The same pattern was evident in a question about the impact of management and leadership development on the organisation. 81% of HRD managers felt the impact was medium or high compared with 61% of client managers. Perceptions were stronger in organisations with higher commitment to management development and more centralised approaches.
- Thompson (2000) found that company performance in over 600 aerospace establishments was not related at all to total management and leadership development spend, but that high-performing firms spent more of their management and leadership development budget on people management skills (27% of spend) than low-performing firms (9% of their spend).
- Lee *et al.* (2003) assessed the impact of management training and development on financial savings for organisations. They found a strong positive relationship.

Some researchers suggest that leadership development represents an important factor in attracting and retaining managers. Winter and Jackson (1999), for example, suggested that organisations frequently offer opportunities for part-time study to attract managers to the organisation.

Impact of Leadership Development on Manager Skill and Performance

Mabey and Ramirez (2005) argue that leadership development programmes vary widely. Furthermore, industrial learning outcomes remain the primary focus on leadership development programmes. Box 4.3 summarises the findings of these studies.

Some studies have investigated the performance gain to individuals from investment in leadership development. Collins and Holton (2004) conducted a major analysis of the impact of investment in leadership development on individual level expertise and performance. The majority of leadership development initiatives were formal interventions. They found that leadership development will impact on firm productivity where it is strategic and consistent and where managers believe that it has the potential to produce financial and productivity gains for the organisation. Their study was comparative and involved firms from six European countries.

Burgoyne, Hirsh and Williams (2003) speculated that where the organisation trains the total management population, it is more likely that this will have a strong impact on management performance. They suggest, however, that the leadership development provision needs to be relevant to the strategic focus of the business. Martin, Pate and Beaumont (2001) compared managers in a company in Scotland who had undertaken formal educational courses while at work with those who had not. This study indicated that formal management development did lead to improvements and innovations; these changes were often communal in nature and strongly influenced by the extent of departmental integration.

Overall, the evidence of the performance impact of leadership development on both individuals and organisations is fragmented. The majority of the research studies have focused on formal development interventions. There is little evidence on the performance outcomes of coaching, mentoring, feedback interventions and on-the-job development. These are commonly used leadership development interventions and are considered by many organisations to be leading edge.

Best Practice or Best Principles of Management and Leadership Development

The concept of best practice is contested in the management and leadership development literature. The primary objection to the concept is that no single best practice is replicable across companies, sectors or geographies. A key issue is the design and implementation of leadership development practices that are unique and context-specific. It may, therefore, be more appropriate to define best practices as practices that differentiate the organisation at a particular point in its strategic development. However, the research to date reveals a number of principles that hold firm, irrespective of the context. The focus on principles may prove more useful because it places more emphasis on key assumptions that need clarification and discussion that organisations must make for practices to be effective. Burgoyne and James (2003) suggested that these principles fall into three categories: strategic imperatives, strategic choices and evaluation.

- **Strategic Imperatives:** Burgoyne and James (2003) suggested that strategic leadership development should be driven from the top with specialist support. It is then more likely to drive and support the organisation. Second, leadership development initiatives must reflect the concepts of leadership held by the top team and the chief executive. These concepts will have a direct impact on the style of leadership development undertaken, as well as the development interventions used. Third, leadership development needs to reflect the culture in which it is embedded. There is well-established support for the theory that CEO involvement is central to effective leadership development. Effron, Greensdale and Salob (2005) go so far as to indicate that CEOs must be accountable for the development of their leaders.

  The credibility of those responsible for leadership development is crucial. The capacity of the specialist to execute leadership development is considered critical to success. The specialist must have a strong understanding of the philosophy of leadership espoused in the organisation. Heifetz and Laurie (1997) found that this understanding was a key determinant of the leadership practices embedded in the organisation. This suggests that certain practices are in, and others are out. Ibarra (1993) has highlighted that, because of these tacit leadership concepts and implicit assumptions about leadership, certain groups may not be supported in the leadership development process. Box 4.4 suggests a number of techniques that can be used by specialists to gain buy-in for leadership development.

- **Strategic Choices:** Burgoyne, Hirsh and Williams (2003) advocated that strategic choices should involve decisions about a clearly articulated framework for leadership and career development. This framework should: be transparent and fully understood: strive to achieve a balance between formal and informal development opportunities, as well as between developing leadership talent internally and recruiting talent externally; consider using business schools and other resources; devise competency frameworks that fit the organisation and link leadership development with other HR practices.

   These best-principle ideas are well supported in the research. Conger (1993) suggested that leadership development must be customised if it is to achieve specific corporate objectives, not just generic capabilities. Others point to the need to use active learning methods with real challenges, using real time to solve them. The importance of linking leader development to business objectives is well supported. The research highlights that learning methods must contextualise learning and that the development of leaders and the development of the business go hand in hand.

- **Evaluation:** There is a need for an explicit approach to evaluation that involves a review of leadership development strategy against key strategic imperatives and a commitment to evaluate practice. This suggests a number of initiatives, such as real-time feedback, behaviour modification and sharing results. The latter involves the development specialist making a decision on the relevant metrics to share with various stakeholders. These should be proactively updated and shared with stakeholders who are concerned with the outcomes of leadership development.

Drivers of and Barriers to Strategic Management and Leadership Development

We have already highlighted a number of factors that are likely to drive strategic leadership development in organisations. Table 4.4 summarises these drivers and barriers. We focus here on barriers that the literature suggests are important.

Table 4.4: Drivers of and Barriers to Strategic Leadership Development in Organisations

Driver	Barrier
Planned (or deliberate) strategy	Emergent strategy
High commitment to strategic planning	Low commitment to HR strategic planning
MLD coherent with business strategy and objectives	Fragmented MLD responses to strategic issue
MLD seen as lever for transformational change	Short-term focus of business; failure to invest in long-term initiatives
Good links between line and HRD management	Inward-looking HR departments
Championship of CEO, vision for MLD communicated	Lack of emphasis on HR in corporate strategy
Analysis of MLD needs derived from strategies	Difficulty translating strategic issues into MLD interventions
Identifying organisation-specific core competencies and meta-competencies	Mindset of managers, emphasising individual effectiveness. Narrowly defined competency frameworks
Responsive MLD and flexible competencies to meet dynamics of strategy	Rigid plans of HR: static or retrospective nature of competencies
MLD through projects, on-the-job methods, integrated with management work	MLD divorced from real issues and implementation
Supportive learning environment	Learning organisation ideas difficult to achieve in practice

Translation of Corporate Strategies into SMLD Strategies

The process of translating corporate objectives into leadership development strategies is a complex one. Some organisations have identified specific core competencies or meta capabilities required by the organisation. Some, however, tend to focus on the individual rather than on collective competence. Competency frameworks can be static and are not capable of dealing effectively with the dynamic nature of strategy.

Poor Evaluation of Leadership Development

Leadership development activities are poorly evaluated. Cairns (1997) suggested that a lack of clear objectives and the difficulty of establishing quantifiable results present the main barriers. The types of evaluation methodologies used tend not to be sophisticated enough to capture the complexity of leadership development outcomes. Frequently, evaluation criteria are selected which lead to inappropriate evaluation results. Collins and Holton (2004) suggested that organisations need to incorporate organisation-level outcomes in their evaluation strategies, or they will experience difficulty in determining the overall effectiveness of leadership development interventions.

Concerns about the Capability of Development Specialists to Deliver

The research evidence raises doubts concerning the capability of leadership development specialists to deliver and add value to the organisation. Meldrum and Atkinson (1988), for example, found that line managers did not have confidence in leadership development specialists, or in the ability of HR generally, to deliver. They found line managers had particularly negative perceptions about the capacity of HR and leadership development professionals to be effective role models, to influence the business on the value of leadership development and to think strategically about leadership development. The incapacity to think strategically about leadership development is a recurring theme. Mole (1996) found that leadership development professionals were biased towards efficiency and systems rather than innovation and strategic thinking. Thomson *et al.* (1997) suggested that leadership development specialists did not think creatively about leadership development and were not setting the agenda for leadership development in organisations.

Confusion Concerning the Nature of Leadership and its Distinction from Management

We explored this distinction in Chapter One, but, in an organisational context, it is typical to find terms such as 'business leadership', 'supervisory management', 'management training' and 'leadership development'. These terms are used interchangeably, suggesting that specialists in many cases have not considered whether they are conceptually different. Barker (1997) argued that, because there is a lack of a coherent theory of leadership and its significance for business performance, it is unlikely that practitioners will fully understand these conceptual distinctions when organising leadership development activities.

EXHIBIT 4.9

Reasons why Organisations do not Invest in Management and Leadership Development: The Views of Irish Leadership Specialists

- **Leadership development is not a top management priority.** The primary reason why management training efforts are often inadequate, poorly handled, or even neglected, is because leadership development is frequently not a top management priority. It can be viewed as a 'nuisance', a 'distraction' or even a 'bother' when more pressing 'hot' issues are at hand. When it is not seen as priority, it can easily be set aside in the short-term heat of battle and the longer-term negative consequences can fail to be recognised until serious problems emerge.
- **Over-reliance on trial-and-error learning.** Organisations place an over-reliance on on-the-job leadership development or trial-and-error learning. This approach can be very costly with unpredictable side effects as managers 'learn as they go' or 'muddle along' or 'shoot in the dark' when trying to develop the skills they need to survive on the job and lead their operations forward. The real problem with trial-and-error learning is that when managers make errors, the consequences can be unforeseen, large, costly and unpredictable.

- **Unwillingness to take the time to train/educate**. Time constraints can prevent leadership development from being effective or even conducted at all. This may be a symptom of ineffective HR planning or unexpected personnel changes. If organisations do not anticipate development needs and allocate sufficient time to develop managers, these efforts will be too rushed to be effective or foregone altogether. Managers are frequently willing to work additional hours if the activity is perceived either to help them be more successful in their careers or to make it easier for them to get their work done. Managers at all levels will put the time into development if they are required and encouraged to do so.
- **Organisations assume managers are already competent**. Organisations frequently assume that their managers already possess the knowledge and skills they need to perform their jobs at a satisfactory level. They believe the manager is either 'ready to go' or can quickly learn the skills required. Although effective managerial selection/promotion procedures should increase this likelihood, the assumption is a dangerous one. There is no substitute for proper orientation and training for a new management position, regardless of the manager's level in the organisation. Because demands on managers and associated skill sets change over time, selection/promotion procedures can only be one part of the solution.
- **No accountability for leadership development**. Because there is no accountability for the development of managers, these practices often fall into a state of neglect or disrepair. Without accountability for leadership development and a connection to the organisational reward system, upper-level managers and human resource professionals will focus their efforts on other matters where rewards for performance and effort are more evident and short term in nature.
- **Reluctance to spend money**. When organisations do not want to spend money on development to prepare managers to succeed, job performance suffers. Failing to develop managers properly can produce a wide variety of organisational problems. These problems, which are caused by inadequate training, are often much more expensive to the organisation than the initial cost of leadership development.
- **Lack of formal and systematic leadership development processes**. When an organisation fails to develop formal leadership development processes, leadership development is handled in a piecemeal or ad hoc fashion that prevents the organisation from developing a first-rate process. While formal development can include off-site or classroom work, most training and learning takes place on the job through a combination of planned new experiences, ongoing feedback, coaching, formal performance appraisal and reviews and a host of other experience-based learning tools. The key is not just to have a formal programme, but also to make sure it is implemented in a systematic fashion, i.e. it supports a clearly defined desired set of learning objectives and skills to be developed by the manager in question.
- **Unclear leadership competencies**. Another barrier to effective leadership development exists when organisations are unclear on the competencies needed to perform the managerial jobs effectively. Organisations fail to develop a clear idea of what skills a manager needs in order to succeed in his or her job/organisation. This finding has far-reaching HR ramifications in terms of effective job analysis, recruitment, selection, promotion, succession planning, career development, performance appraisal and compensation practices. Without a clearly defined set of competencies for a specific management position, most HR practices will suffer.
- **Assumption that leadership development is solely the manager's own responsibility**. Many organisations assume that leadership development is solely the manager's own responsibility. They believe that it is up to their managers to figure out what they need to be doing, what they do not know, or what new skills they need. It is also up to the managers to fill perceived gaps in competency through some combination of outside reading, tapping into professional support networks for advice, taking formal university classes and/or attending seminars in their own time. Unfortunately, these assumptions can be unrealistic. How likely is it that a manager will be able to know what they do not know or have the time outside their demanding jobs and personal responsibilities to get the training they need? Is it likely that all managers will be able to accomplish these objectives with equal effect? In fact, many managers fear asking for help because such a request is often perceived as a sign of weakness or incompetence and could lead to the loss of their position.
- **Lack of specialist developers**. After a long period of ineffective leadership development, or none at all, the organisation's 'bench strength' becomes anaemic and there is no one around to perform the necessary training or well enough steeped in organisational or process knowledge to pass on the necessary information or to model or train the skills. In this case, the organisation may have to go outside the organisation and hire experts with specialist development knowledge.

Making the Business Case for Investment in Management and Leadership Development

We conclude this chapter with a consideration of the practice issues that leadership specialists and other relevant shareholders need to consider in order to make an effective business case for strategic management and leadership development and to secure the necessary resources.

Making Leadership Development Strategic

We have emphasised throughout this chapter that leadership development should be linked with organisational strategy and structure, and aligned with HR strategies. Seibert, Hall and Kram (1995) highlighted three discrete links that can be realised in practice. These are: 1) the link between the business environment and business strategy, 2) the link between business strategies and the organisation's leadership development strategy, and 3) the link between leadership development strategies and leadership development activities. They found that organisations pay most attention to the first and third links, but the second link was poorly operationalised. This arose because leadership development specialists and wider human resource development functions were too focused on internal rather than external issues. Seibert, Hall and Kram proposed four guiding principles of value to leadership development specialists in making effective strategic links.

- Refocus the role of HR and that of leadership development specialists. This involves viewing the primary role as implementing strategy and the secondary role as developing managers and leaders.
- Rethink the nature of leadership development. This involves using job-based experiences as the central development activity, with classroom activities viewed as secondary. This does, however, require that job-based experiences are effectively managed and that they address the strategic needs of the organisation.
- Engage in opportunistic behaviours. Leadership development activities need to be flexible and open to respond to changing business needs. This involves a significant mindset change, moving away from rigid programmes towards more customised leadership development.
- Provide support for experience-based development. This involves focusing on the development climate of the organisation and putting in place supports to ensure that managers take control of their development.

Burack, Hackwalker and Mathys (1997) offered an alternative proposal. They suggested that effective strategic leadership development:

- Ensures a consistent link between leadership development and business strategies
- Implements development activities which cut across hierarchical and functional boundaries
- Focuses on a global orientation and incorporates cross-cultural dimensions in development activities
- Places a priority on individualised learning within a wider organisational learning context
- Is constantly aware of the influence of the organisation's culture and ensures that leadership development fits within, creates or supports the desired cultures
- Implements leadership development activities that are career focused
- Builds leadership development on empirically determined core competencies.

These ideas are not blueprints for success, but they have the potential to make leadership development more relevant and credible.

Timing Strategic Management and Leadership Development

Timing is a major issue in effective strategic management and leadership development. Leadership expertise develops slowly over a period of ten years or more. Initially, leaders enter the leadership role as novices. They have a limited understanding of the basic concepts required to understand the work, the organisational context and leadership roles. Leaders at the initial stage of their development are likely to be presented with more structured activities and problems early in their leadership career, which draw on their technical and social skills. At this stage of development, initial training and socialisation are important for the novice leader to understand the organisation's vision, its culture and norms.

Mumford *et al.* (2000) suggested that for leaders to guarantee their development, they must first elaborate their knowledge base and achieve more 'real world' experience. Second, they must begin independently to tackle leadership problems. They suggest that at this stage of the leader's career, it is important to provide the leader with supervisory responsibilities with limited direction. This will prove invaluable for skill development. Key development challenges at this stage focus on ensuring that the leader is committed to organisational goals and to others. Third, this type of experience enables the leader to move on to solve more complex problems, develop creative skills, cope with novelty and build a foundation of critical thinking. This type of leadership development challenge demands that managers undertake assignments that present novel challenges and that the leader works with others who have different perspectives on an issue. Finally, effective leaders must have the skills to generate solutions to complex problems and to make good judgements concerning their workability. They are also expected to be skilled in working with stakeholders, developing a vision and thinking long term. These requirements present significant development challenges. Mentoring by senior leaders will have value, as will complex stretch assignments that involve challenging organisational problems and demand autonomy, risk-taking, ongoing environmental scanning and developing long-term solutions.

Mumford *et al.* (2000) estimated that it may take up to twenty years for a leader to reach the point where he/she can solve complex, novel problems (Figure 4.1). This indicates that developments are progressive, moving from simple situations to situations that require the integration of knowledge. The kinds of leadership development experiences that facilitate skill development in the early part of a career are fundamentally different from those required at later career stages. Box 4.6 (page 180) presents some questions in respect of the timing of development and the most appropriate development interventions.

Figure 4.1: Conceptual Model of Leader Development

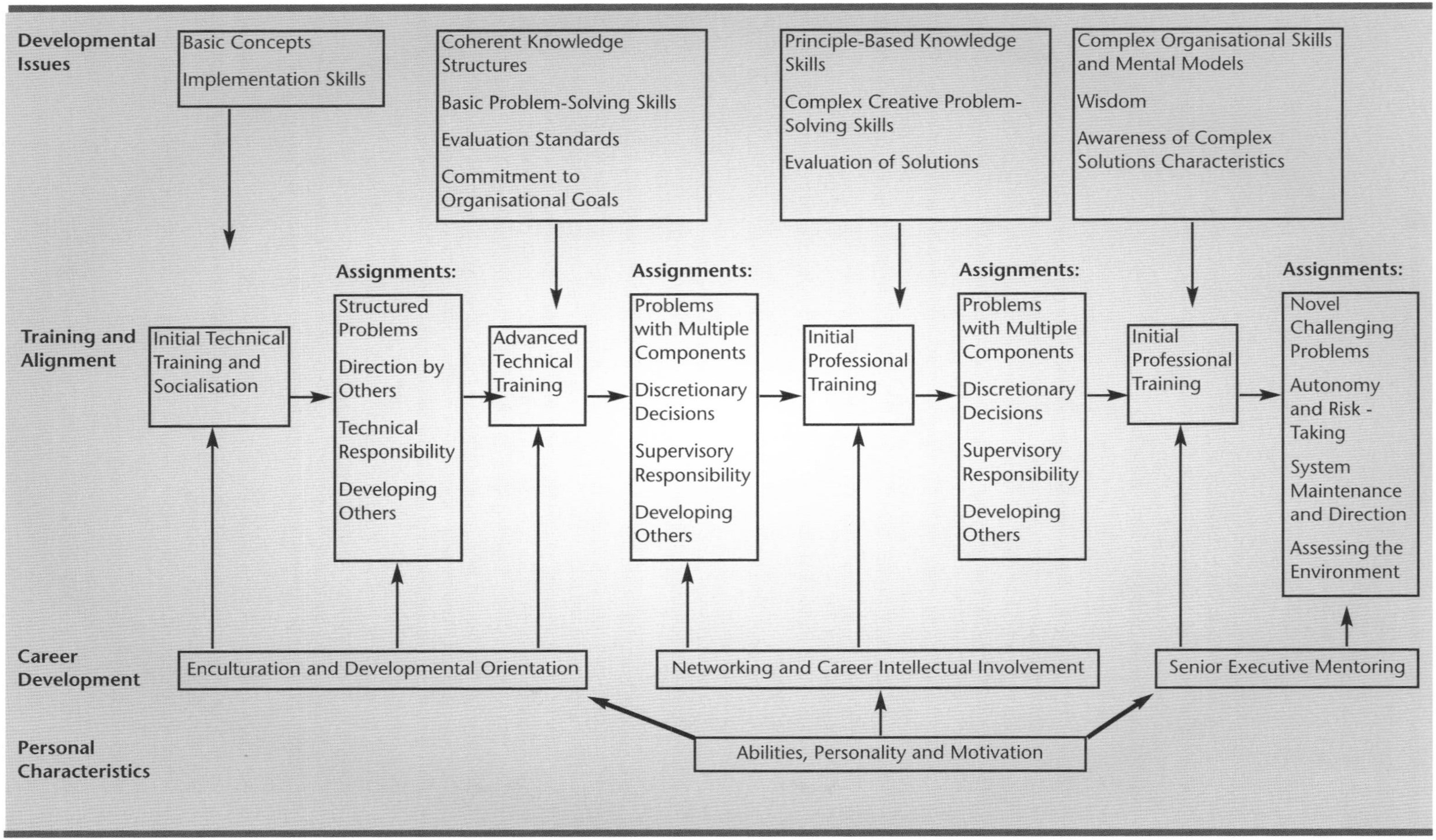

EXHIBIT 4.10

Leader-Led Development (LLD): Reality or Utopia?

According to the Corporate Executive Board, the key to ensuring that the organisation has a supply of talented leaders is to develop senior leaders' ability and willingness to engage in LLD. They acknowledge that organisations struggle to achieve a situation where leadership development is driven by leaders themselves rather than the L&D function. They suggest six incentives that organisations should consider using to drive LLD.

- *Make incentives proportional to the intended outcomes:* The types and amount of incentives that are linked to LLD should be in line with the outcomes that are expected by the organisation.
- *Set explicit organisation-wide expectations for LLD*: Learning and development functions have a responsibility to articulate clear performance expectations and define the desired outcomes for LLD. Leaders should have an understanding of the types of activities that will drive the development of others. Leaders should understand that they will be held accountable.
- *Provide development for senior leaders*: It is important for leadership development or L&D functions to prepare leaders to take on the development of others. They need to understand what constitutes effective LLD and then provide leaders with skills to assess their direct reports, peers and reporting managers.
- *Stipulate a clear time line for LLD assessment*: Leadership development of the L&D function should set clear time lines for the assessment of LLD effectiveness. Leaders should be given time to improve their effectiveness.
- *Support and resources*: Effective LLD requires that leaders are provided with the necessary support and training resources.
- *Effective LLD versus business performance*: LLD is a core leadership responsibility but it does not come at the expense of business performance.

The Corporate Executive Board has found that the most effective LLD occurs when leaders are open to development and they ensure active follow-through. Effective leaders openly acknowledge their need for improvement and take proactive steps to transform weaknesses into strengths. They are also more likely to follow through on development feedback that they require. A major challenge for organisations that wish to move towards an LLD model concerns the creation of a culture of LLD. A strong LLD culture values learning and teaching. The organisation creates visibility around developmental role models who inspire others to be more active coaches of their direct reports. Culture change is an incremental process, but it needs to have some early wins to generate greater momentum, thereby contributing to long-term, lasting gains. Organisations should provide a flexible architecture that makes it possible for leaders to get involved in leading and coaching.

LLD is reciprocal. It involves both the senior leader and the rising leader. The senior leader, according to the Corporate Executive Board, should:

- Place less emphasis on traditional performance-type assessment and instead give rising leaders guidance and feedback to enable them to ask the right questions rather than providing them with the answers.
- Introduce rising leaders to other leaders and emphasise the importance of relationships for development. It is important that development plans include relationship-based learning strategies and multi-source feedback processes.
- Senior leaders should use their organisational knowledge to provide rising leaders with insights concerning who they should know in the organisation. The senior leader should leverage his/her relationships to ensure contacts and connections.
- Senior leaders should create compelling and challenging career paths for rising leaders. They should ensure that roles are sequenced to facilitate the development of competencies.

- Rising leaders need the right amount of stretch and leverage in their development tasks. This may include dealing with uncertainty, handling failing projects or taking on greater responsibility.
- Rising leaders should be given the scope to reflect and synthesise what they have learned from key development experiences.
- Senior leaders should focus on ensuring that rising leaders make their potential known to others, providing them with opportunities to be promoted.
- Senior leaders should be open with rising leaders about their own development needs and objectives. It is important for them to know that senior leaders also receive coaching and feedback from other leaders.
- LLD is based on a productive relationship and appropriate management style. It is important that rising leaders are treated with respect and fairness and that they are provided with room to make decisions.
- Senior leaders need to be strong in articulating their vision to the rising leader.

The rising or developing leader must also demonstrate particular behaviours and values if LLD is to become a reality in organisations. The rising or developing leader within an LLD model is expected to:
- Maintain a productive relationship with his or her manager. This includes respecting the decisions of the manager and helping them improve their functional/technical knowledge.
- Demonstrate openness to development. This includes openness to new ideas, acknowledging the need for improvement and actively soliciting feedback.
- Actively follow through on development opportunities. The rising manager must consistently demonstrate a willingness to act on input concerning coaching and developmental suggestions received from the manager.
- Request assignments that build on long-term capabilities. Rising managers should be proactive in requesting stretch assignments and in getting exposure.
- Seek out development opportunities in the current role. The current role should be a primary focus for development for the rising manager. This may include additional assignments and projects that contribute to both performance and development.
- Build a comprehensive understanding of key organisational players. Rising managers should ask senior managers for guidance before making contact with other managers in the organisation.
- Consistently focus on developing relationships with other leaders. Development can occur through relationship building which is sustained and of high quality.
- Engage in reflection on key learning experiences. It is important to schedule time with senior managers to develop key insights into what the rising manager has gained from the development assignment.
- Promote accomplishments: rising managers need to keep their reporting manager aware of key achievements so that potential is understood.
- Solicit coaching and feedback. Feedback is important in development. It opens up possibilities and enhances self-awareness.

In summary, LLD is not a panacea. It represents another way of thinking about leadership development in organisations. It recognises that for leadership development to become sustainable it must be led by the leaders themselves rather than by L&D departments.

Source: Corporate Executive Board (2006)

Preparing the Business Case

An initial challenge for the leadership development specialist in preparing a strong case for investment in strategic leadership development involves forming a view on the main challenges facing the business. It is important to understand how senior managers and the top team view these challenges as well as the financial context of the business. The specialist needs to speak to key managers in the organisation and get answers to the issues highlighted in Box 4.6.

Performance
- What are the most important business performance imperatives facing this organisation, and which three are the most urgent?

Strategy
- What is the overall strategy of your business?
  - To what extent is your strategy based on:
    - Stretching aims?
    - Specified opportunities?
    - The capabilities of your organisation?
  - How is it affecting the performance of your business?
  - What, in the way managers think about strategy, is helping and/or hindering you in addressing the performance challenges for your business?
- To what extent is your strategy visible in action?
  - Do managers know when to turn business down?
  - Can people take appropriate initiatives with confidence?
  - Can people at the operating level articulate your strategy?
  - Is this reflected in feedback from customers and competitors?
- Has your strategy changed recently to take creative advantage of new opportunities and/or threats in the wider environment, or new corporate goals?
- What is it about strategy that would need to be different in order to address the performance imperatives you've identified?

Operations
- How well do your business processes work? What are the strengths and weaknesses of your:
  - Product/service delivery?
  - Product/service development?
  - Quality-assurance processes?
  - Sales activities?
  - Marketing activities?
  - Customer-service activities?
  - Materials management activities?
  - Financial management activities?
- Are you using a framework for continuous improvement in your operational and business activities? How well is this framework working?
- What is it about operations that would need to be different in order to address the performance imperatives you've identified?

Leadership
- Looking at the changes that are needed in the performance of the business overall, where is the need most urgent and most important:
  - In what 'leadership' means in your business?
  - In how managers and employees think, relate and act?
  - In your strategy development and business planning processes?
  - In the innovation process (i.e. the way change is managed)?
  - In the way managers use HR management processes?

Organisation
- Looking at the changes that are needed in the performance of the business overall, where is the need most urgent and most important:
  - In roles, responsibilities, authorities, expected contributions?
  - In teamworking and partnerships within and between departments or locations?
  - In teamworking and partnerships with external organisations?
  - In the communications infrastructure?
  - In the hierarchy?
  - In work design?
  - In processes for designing and changing organisation?
  - In management control systems (e.g. finance)?
  - In information and knowledge sharing?
  - In the way conflict is managed?
  - In the culture and climate of the business?

The leadership development specialist must develop a compelling rationale for investment in management and leadership development. This requires a clear understanding of the most important and urgent strategic issues for the organisation and of their performance implications. It also requires a careful consideration of the best opportunities for a leadership development intervention. The CIPD (2002) recommended that the specialist needs to analyse the organisation and people capability outcomes that are preconditions for success. This requires an analysis of capabilities required at organisational, group and individual level. An essential requirement here is the generation of a shared view of short- and long-term performance gaps. The CIPD suggests that the appropriate vehicle to achieve this is a business, organisation and management review (BOMR). This enables key stakeholders to think about the relationships between business and performance imperatives (Box 4.7).

Box 4.7: A Business, Organisation and Management Review Framework

The **first part** of the review will normally be a discussion of:
- The challenges facing the business in its competitive markets
- The key strategies that will enable the enterprise to succeed and the specific targets and goals for the planning period
- The current and future business model(s) for the particular business and the organisational and management capabilities that will enable the business to deliver the strategies/respond to the challenges
- The actual performance of the organisation and any major performance shortfalls/gaps
- The organisation and how well it is working, including a review of business and management processes, roles, responsibilities and relationships.

From the definitions of the strategies, performance goals and actual performance, you can then:
- Identify the 'gaps' forecast in longer-term performance or strategy delivery, and distinguish which of them are likely to have their roots in the capabilities and characteristics of the organisation
- Identify any shortfalls in short-term performance that have organisational roots.

The **second part** will include a review and identification/discussion of:
- The appropriateness and effectiveness of key teams and business functions
- Key managers – performance, problems, potential and development needs

---

A key outcome of the review process is agreement on key leadership development priorities. Once these priorities have been agreed, it is necessary to prepare a detailed plan and strategy to tackle them. A strong case will indicate who has responsibility for achieving the key goals and priorities. It is important that stakeholders are continuously involved. The issue of evaluation is vital and the initial case needs to specify the types of measures and processes that will be used to track success.

Conclusion

Strategic management and leadership development emphasises a deliberate long-term orientation, and specific and strategically linked development interventions. The way in which an organisation formulates and implements its business strategies plays a key role in determining leadership development priorities. Key elements of successful strategic leadership development include commitment from top management, senior backing through written processes and strategies, alignment with the cultural context and human resource strategies, and a commitment to evaluation processes that ensures leadership development is of a high quality and remains business-focused. Strategic management and leadership development has a collective dimension in that it focuses on the organisation's capability and performance rather than the capability of individual managers. We have emphasised throughout this chapter that strategic leadership development requires a supportive development climate to be effective. It also requires that specialists understand the leadership philosophy of senior executives and select leadership interventions that are compatible with this. Most important of all, management and leadership development activities must reflect the business's stage of development.

Summary of Key Points

- Strategic management and leadership development is linked to business plans and strategies through core competencies.
- Leadership development activities are complex to design because of a multiplicity of factors leading to significant change in the external environment.
- Strategic management and leadership development emphasises collective capability and, consequently, there are tensions with individually oriented leadership development activities.
- Leadership development specialists need to articulate a business case for investment in leadership development. This must involve discussions with key stakeholders.
- Management and leadership development should be based on a best principles approach. These principles are sensitive to context.

■ Discussion Questions

1. Explain why it is difficult to achieve strategic management and leadership development in organisations.

2. Why is it important for leadership development specialists to understand the business environment of the organisation? How can they do this?

3. Describe some of the steps that can be taken to achieve senior management buy-in for strategic leadership development.

4. How might leadership development specialists address some of the reasons why organisations fail to deliver on management and leadership development?

5. What are the advantages and disadvantages of a 'best principles' approach to strategic leadership and development?

■ Application and Experiential Questions

1. Select an organisation with which you are familiar with or in which you work. Prepare a short report setting out the business case for leadership development.

2. Design a set of criteria which you could use to evaluate the contribution of strategic leadership development to organisation success. Suggest how you could go about designing an evaluation process to ensure that your results are valid.

3. In groups of three or four, role-play a meeting between yourself (leadership development specialist) and a group of senior managers at which you are discussing an agenda item about whether to invest in a specific leadership development programme. Senior management are considering postponing the programme due to poor quarterly business results.

Chapter Five

Structuring and Managing Leadership Development in Organisations

Outline

Learning Objectives

After reading this chapter you will be able to:

- Describe and evaluate the design considerations to be taken into account when structuring management and leadership development in organisations.
- Evaluate a number of structural options that are appropriate for management and leadership development.
- Describe the steps that need to be followed when formulating management and leadership development policy.
- Describe and understand the issues to be considered when selecting leadership development strategies and planning leadership development activities.
- Identify and analyse the variety of methods that can be used to identify management training and development needs.
- Explain the decisions that need to be made to evaluate management and leadership development effectively.
- Evaluate the advantages and disadvantages of e-management and leadership development.

OPENING CASE SCENARIO

Fexco: Developing Organisational Leadership Capability in an Entrepreneurial Company: A Blended-Learning Approach

Fexco is a privately owned company that was established in 1981 by Brian McCarthy. It is an entrepreneurial venture which has grown into a multi-faceted company, operating global payments through a diverse range of products, including Western Union, money transfer, dynamic currency conversion, VAT refunds, stockbroking, call centres, international corporate payments and travel-related services. The company has operations in Ireland, UK, Spain, Malta, Australia, Lapland, Denmark, Sweden, USA and Dubai. In 2000, First Data purchased a twenty-five per cent shareholding in Fexco. Fexco has a strong focus in its business model on a culture of transparency, long-term business relationships, commitment to the best and a focus on people as employees, clients and partners. It has acquired core competencies in treasury management, innovation, seeing the invisible and technology-driven transaction processing. It has continued to grow, both through developing its product range and through acquisition. This growth path highlighted the need for management and leadership competency development to meet growth projections. Many of the organisation's 1,200 staff members developed within their day-to-day work and business and were not exposed to development planning processes or structured management and leadership development interventions.

As in many entrepreneurial ventures, management and leadership development activities were typically informal and occurred on the job. Although this type of development was valuable, it did not occur at a sufficiently fast pace for the company to remain competitive. In 2002, senior management identified the requirement for management to be enhanced in two ways: management needed to have a more holistic set of competencies in order to be fit to compete in a significantly more competitive competency gap between directors; and senior management needed to be significantly improved.

Fexco worked with an experienced training and development consultant in order to develop a programme that met the needs of the organisation and ensured real performance improvement. When the organisation started to think about an appropriate management development intervention, it knew that it needed to have a programme that facilitated its senior managers to become proficient business managers. The programme needed to address the development of competencies as well as developing managers' confidence to enable them to take the next step. In order to meet this brief, the HR director worked in close collaboration with the training consultant in order to put together a design which was sustainable, given the organisation's resources, and which contributed to the development of the collective leadership capability of the organisation. The final programme had a number of important key elements: an intensive developmental assessment process that was based on a defined set of competencies, specifically developed to meet the long-term needs of Fexco; and a programme consisting of five modules spread over a ten-month period. The key theme of this programme was to awaken participants to their leadership potential and to provide development around strategy, customers, leadership, managing, proactivity and initiative and an understanding of the organisation's culture. A mentoring and coaching process was also put in place to help participants address development issues of relevance to their work circumstances, and a work-based project was designed using the principles of action learning.

Fexco took great care in selecting the participants to ensure that, for each module, multiple business units were represented. This had the advantage of creating a better and more holistic business understanding as well as presenting networking opportunities for managers. The role of HR in shaping the process was also highlighted. The perception of HR as a business partner has significantly changed through their active involvement in the design and delivery process of this bespoke programme.

The developmental assessment centre was the starting point of the programme. Each developmental assessment centre consisted of twelve participants and six professionally trained observers. The centre included exercises, questionnaires, role plays and simulations, which enabled observers to gather detailed behavioural observations which were then communicated to participants during one-to-one feedback processes. The feedback was then used to prepare individual development plans.

The structured programme, consisting of five modules, was externally accredited. The five modules reflected a range of strategic and operational issues facing the business. These modules were held off site, and there was a strong emphasis on experiential learning throughout. This included case studies, role plays, in-tray exercises and organisational analysis exercises. A strong emphasis throughout the taught component of the programme was the concern to address the organisation's culture. The programme had participants working in different business units and it was extremely important for them to have opportunities to analyse the overall organisational culture, to network and support each other. Participants valued the opportunity to get to know one another and build relationships across the organisation.

Networking and support were also reinforced through the coaching and mentoring processes. When it came to mentoring, a senior manager would typically meet with his or her mentee after each module. The senior manager acted as a 'wise head', offering both new perspectives and practical advice. The HR function had a key role to play in matching mentors and mentees. The coaching element was delivered by the external consultants. It was designed to help participants to stay on track with their development. Reinforcement of new skills, models and insights was an essential part of what is called 'learning that sticks'. The coaching process ensured that each manager reviewed what he or she had learned and brought into focus any particular aspects of individual development that needed attention. The skills of the coach in these circumstances was to help managers build awareness of what they needed to review or practise and to agree with those being coached how they might apply particular skills or learning to their own situation. In many cases, managers had a broad range of skills before they started the programme, but, in some cases, they were not aware of them. The mentoring and coaching elements helped managers to recognise their own potential and realise their leadership energy.

The work-based project was a fundamental component of the programme. The project component was based on principles of action learning, and participants used a range of methodologies and models to analyse strategic projects which were generated by executive management. Each project team took the project area and defined its scope. They frequently used the SCORE model (symptoms, causes, outcomes, resources and effects) in order to have a framework around which to consider a particular outcome they wanted to achieve. When participants became clear about what it was that they wanted to happen and recognised the effect that such an outcome would have, it became easier for them to see how to address the problem. This and other models helped participants to identify the causes of any problems they had and to identify the resources needed to achieve the results they required. The action-learning projects brought the learning into sharp focus and ensured that participants made direct links between new skills and business results. Participants worked on the project throughout the programme. They developed skills in strategic thinking, complex problem analysis, and skills to help them persuade, influence and negotiate more effectively. Managers presented the projects to a team of directors and were involved in implementing change in the organisation. The overall programme was managed by a high-profile steering group consisting of the chairman, managing director and two non-executive directors.

Fexco learned a lot from the programme, which helped to reinforce a number of important principles and practices of leadership development, and placed strong emphasis on self-reflection, self-appraisal, guided reading, seeking out honest and accurate feedback from a wide variety of sources, working on current needs of the organisation and utilising projects as a vehicle for significant strategic learning. The programme design placed a significant burden on the shoulders of individual managers. The success of the programme was contingent on the willingness of managers to engage in self-reflection, to seek feedback and to keep their knowledge base up to date.

QUESTIONS

Q.1 Evaluate how Fexco approached management and leadership development.

Q.2 What lessons can be learned from Fexco's blended learning approach?

The demands on the management and leadership development function in organisations are considerable. Many firms have expanded internationally and those that have not face considerable competition from abroad. Leadership development processes in organisations have become complex and, as a result, the management and leadership development support function has grown in complexity. The structuring of the management and leadership development function must parallel other aspects of business. It has to interface with multiple customers and stakeholders and manage complexities arising from geography or product and service characteristics. It must be flexible, without adding costs, and it must build strong relationships while aligning its activities with customer requirements. This chapter considers the types of decisions that organisations have to make when structuring and managing leadership development activities. Organisations must take into account a particular set of factors, such as the life cycle of the organisation, the characteristics and philosophy of the HR function, the existing leadership development specialist capabilities, the business strategies and market characteristics of the organisation. The leadership development function will not be effective in influencing stakeholders if it has not considered how best to structure and manage its own activities.

Structuring the Leadership Development Function

The leadership development function should be structured in such a way that it is capable of handling complexity and can serve a wide range of business needs. It must also be concerned to keep itself visible to the client and have the capacity to both co-ordinate its activities and collaborate with customers or stakeholders.

Key Design Considerations

The structuring of an effective leadership development function requires consideration of these important issues:

- *Focusing on Strategic Issues*: The strategic imperatives of the organisation represent the primary consideration. Some commentators have suggested that, in order to be strategically focused, the leadership development function must be project-based rather than function-based. It must have the capability to assemble teams or individuals quickly around needs and opportunities. It also needs the capacity to disassemble these teams and move on to new projects and activities. A key focus of the individual responsible for leadership developments should be the strategic agenda.
- *Distributed Leadership Considerations*: Some learning and development functions have sought to create greater strategic alignment within the team by giving specialists leadership responsibility for a particular area of the business, or a particular process. Such a distribution of leadership enables a better understanding of the business. It means that the person with overall responsibility for leadership development does not have to be involved in all initiatives. They have the confidence of knowing that the team has both the responsibility and the capability to take care of the business. They can also trust that the line-of-business issues will be factored in when decisions are made about leadership development. A distributed leadership approach is likely to reduce some of the line-of-business/specialist function tensions that may emerge in more centralised approaches. Such a distributed leadership approach requires a cohesive leadership development team and this model may not be feasible for the smaller organisation.
- *Leadership Team Capabilities*: The capability of the leadership team is a key consideration in selecting a structural model. Important elements are the expertise base of the team, their credibility within the organisation, the quality of their dialogue with the lines of business and their decision-making track record. It is important that the team possesses

the capacity to collaborate and leverage its expertise. Increasingly, leadership development specialists are being selected from operational areas and a premium is put on their business and management experience over their leadership development expertise. Some organisations use job rotation within the HR or leadership team in order to create more effective peer relationships (Lawler *et al.* 2006). They also rotate leadership specialists into more senior generalist roles in order to build general management skills and foster better relationships with business line staff.

An Internal Consultancy Model

Under this arrangement, the management and leadership development function will operate as an internal consultancy. This consultancy function may be centralised or decentralised. In large organisations, it is possible that a central team of leadership development professionals may exist who provide services to business units. Alternatively, the specialist may be permanently located in the business unit with a small, centrally located core that is more strategically oriented.

The internal consulting function will achieve its credibility through a history of interactions with the business. The consultant is expected to have a deep and detailed understanding of the business, including its culture, language and strategies, and to have a strong focus on the corporate agenda.

This structural arrangement is not without its problems. The internal consultant may be faced with the challenge of how best to balance central with localised needs. The leadership development effort may become fragmented simply because each business unit may begin to pursue its own agenda, regardless of the corporate-wide approach to leadership development. It is possible that the consultant in a decentralised model may suffer from a lack of understanding of the role within the business unit. Trust issues may arise and the consultant may lack the power at a local level to action projects and proposals. A centralised approach may be more valuable in terms of gaining ongoing senior management support for leadership development.

A Strategic Business Partner Model

The term 'business partner' is used loosely to cover a multiplicity of ideas from strategic to administrative to consultancy. Business partnering involves the restructuring of HR and leadership development into three specialist sub-functions:

- *Shared Services*: This is a single, usually large, unit that handles many of the transactional aspects of leadership development. A shared services remit is to provide low-cost, effective administration. We discuss its application to leadership development later in this chapter.
- *Centres of Excellence*: These consist of small teams of experts with specialist knowledge of leading-edge leadership development solutions. The role of centres of excellence is to deliver competitive business advantage through leadership development innovations.
- *Strategic Partners*: These are leadership development professionals working closely with business leaders, influencing strategy and steering its implementation. The task of the strategic partner is to ensure that the business makes the best use of its leadership capability.

The business partner model developed in response to the fear that lines of business perceived HR and leadership development functions to have become too centralised, too disconnected from the business and too inward-focused on issues of low importance to the managers (Exhibit 5.1). Three key pressures are leading the move towards business partnering in the leadership development context.

- *Competitiveness*: Leadership development has increasingly become central to competitiveness. It is required to ensure that leaders are skilled, motivated, flexible, creative and challenging.
- *Increased Expectations*: Organisations increasingly expect more from the leadership development function. Leadership development is expected to contribute to strategy, to facilitate the execution of business plans and to deliver results.
- *Reduction in Costs*: Multinational organisations increasingly see business partnering, particularly the shared services component, as a way of reducing costs. Large functions are often targets for cutbacks, so it is important to show bottom-line business benefits.

EXHIBIT 5.1

The Business Partner Model Applied to Leadership Development

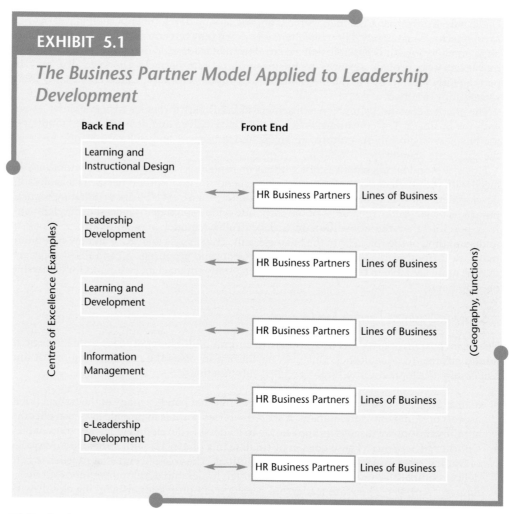

Holbeche (1999) suggested that a business partner as a leadership development specialist will work alongside senior managers and provide the link between business and organisational strategies. The specialist provides support and challenges to the senior team while, at the same time, developing credible management and leadership development initiatives. It is envisaged that the business partner will have a seat at the executive table and will be viewed as an equal partner in making strategic decisions about the business. It is likely that the specialist will have responsibility for a wider brief than leadership development and talent management. It may also include elements of organisational design, strategy development and planned organisational change. The business partner model operates at a strategic level and demands a skill set of the job-holder which provides him/her with the capacity to influence change at a strategic level. Kenton and Yarnall (2005) suggest that the business partner focuses on delivering to the business by having a strong holistic overview and a long-term perspective. Business partners are required to play many roles successfully. They are expected to work alongside managers in the business, they build and maintain effective relationships and build good internal networks across the business. Businesses partners are expected to maintain a business focus and to demonstrate effectiveness through creating and leading change.

The business partner model is, therefore, very challenging for the leadership development specialist. It is likely to operate more successfully in large organisations. A CIPD study (2003) found that a large number of HR professionals are increasingly engaged in strategy issues. They are required to have credibility as business partners, but many feel poorly skilled for their roles. A lack of business knowledge and strategic tools represent important skill gaps. Garavan, Shanahan and Carbery (2008) found that business partners may have less effective people skills. They do not possess the assertiveness, self-confidence and openness to others required to be successful in the role. Harrison (2005) provides a useful summary of the role dimensions that business partners are required to perform.

EXHIBIT 5.2

Role Dimensions of the Business Partner Role in the Context of Management and Leadership Development

- *Partner others*: build effective working relationships inside and outside the business so that leadership development strategies work on the ground and new initiatives gain the support they need.
- *Achieve results*: promote leadership development activity that supports the business and the learners, work with others to monitor and evaluate its outcomes and spread awareness of the value-adding contribution that the leadership development function provides.
- *Remember the people-performance framework*: without the right organisational context, people cannot or will not use their learning and skills for the benefit of the business. Help to build commitment and a learning culture in the workplace through partnerships and expertise.
- *Travel around*: move about the organisation, establishing a live and proactive presence in the business, expanding and deepening business knowledge and cementing valuable relationships.
- *Never be complacent*: use partnerships as a vehicle for own learning as well as that of others, stimulating professional development and generating new knowledge to make the leadership development function leading edge.
- *Ensure professional and ethical practice*: respect the values of others, building on diversity of whatever kind in order to produce rich learning experiences with access for all employees to opportunities to develop their performance and potential.
- *Raise awareness*: ensure that managers and all employees know about the big leadership development issues facing the organisation and the part they can play in tackling them.

A strategic business partner model is not without its problems. It can create tensions between the business and the centre and it challenges the skills of leadership development specialists. Four particular challenges are highlighted:

- *Who Owns the Client*: A business partner model poses a significant tension between the generalist and the specialist perspectives. It leads to problems concerning who owns the client. The business partner will likely determine when centralised leadership specialists should be brought in. Specialists often feel that they are brought in too late, after the leadership agenda is set, and that they have little scope to shape the project. Centralised specialists frequently feel that they cannot work directly with clients when business partner models exist. Harrison (2005) suggests that business partners tend to use specialists in a very selective way and, as a result, they become frustrated and believe that their capabilities are not properly utilised. The reality is that the business partner is in control. He/she owns the relationship, co-ordinating the work, assembling the team and accessing resources outside the team when necessary. This leaves the specialist out on a limb. Furthermore, not all business partner leadership specialists make an effective switch to working on leadership development, organisational development and the management of talent. They frequently find it difficult to measure their success. They tend to spend a lot of their time becoming indispensable and important in the eyes of their clients. This may sometimes be at the expense of their colleagues.

- *Dealing with the Conflict between the Transactional and the Transformational*: Business partners are expected to deliver high-end leadership development. They frequently find themselves having little slack to respond to complex needs and situations. As a result, they are less able to provide strategic and organisation development type interventions. This has led some organisations to have less confidence in the business partner model and to buy in external consultancy for complex and specialist projects. As a result, organisations that have adopted the business partner model of leadership development delivery are still struggling with how to make it work well.

- *Balancing Business and Business-Wide Priorities*: The business partner model presents a challenge in terms of getting the right balance between line-of-business initiatives and wider enterprise or corporate-level initiatives. Business partners are expected to have a different set of priorities from those in centres of excellence. Achieving this balance can lead to conflict and frustration on the part of the business partner. Corporate leadership initiatives are often criticised because they do not demonstrate an understanding of the needs of the business. This can result in programmes from the centre being sabotaged. An important element of the relationship concerns who funds the leadership development initiative. Frequently, the business partner may identify a leadership development need and then engage with a central specialist to provide a solution. The centre may consider that the development initiative has value across the business and may bring in business partners from other lines of business to leverage it. These business partners may not put the initiative high in their agenda and may be less inclined to participate in an initiative that is of little value to their own businesses.

- *Organising the Leadership Development Team*: The business partner model requires that a significant majority of leadership development staff are dedicated to line-of-business work. This can reduce the capacity of the leadership development team to move quickly when opportunities arise and when needs surface elsewhere. The line of business may be very reluctant to see their business partner participate in other initiatives at enterprise or corporate level. Business partner models, therefore, may inhibit the capacity of the leadership development team to reconfigure itself. It locks up talent on line-of-business initiatives, with the result that corporate-wide leadership development initiatives suffer.

Box 5.1: Adopting Business Partnership Models of Leadership Development: Manager Guidelines

Preparing for Business Partnering

- Build an understanding of partnering with the leadership development function to underpin good business decisions. Ensure that specialists are well informed about, and are openly discussing, partnering.
- Work with the senior training and development or HR team to define a vision containing practical principles and clear, realistic goals.
- Identify the common obstacles to achieving effective partnering:
  - Line managers without the skills or desire to take on more or do things differently.
  - Poor, expensive or slow transactional leadership development services and intranets.
  - Leadership development professionals with little skill or experience to succeed as business partners.
  - The absence of a consistent business strategy with which leadership development can work.
  - A leadership development agenda that is set independently of the business.
- Engage all of the development team in the vision, principles and goals. Looking at the forthcoming year, activities include:
  - Looking at who will do what, and how they will work together as a team.
  - Identifying success measures and publicity. Assessing how leadership development will demonstrate added value.
  - Considering how partnering will be 'sold' to line managers.

Selecting and Developing

- Provide detailed information on what business partnering involves and how these roles differ from more traditional leadership development specialist roles.
- Clearly articulate the skills and knowledge requirements, in particular in-depth knowledge of the partnership business. It is likely that a number of learning and development competencies will now be less important.
- Place a strong focus on competencies related to building influential relationships, contributing to strategy development, providing leadership development solutions and demonstrating added value.
- Provide comprehensive development to ensure that business partners receive a comprehensive understanding of the specific business.
- Focus on ensuring that the business partner can 'hit the ground running'. They need to deliver success to ensure credibility with the line.

Strengthening Partnering

- Ensure that the performance measures business leaders use are widely available and are discussed. Use meetings to explore business performance problems and successes.
- Check every day with a few senior leadership and development professionals how (their part of) the business is performing, what the hot issues are and what is being done. This will ensure that leadership and development professionals get around the business and ask questions.
- Ask to be involved from the outset in the business planning process. Get the key meetings in diary and see that training and development professionals are well prepared for those meetings. Never put them in a position where they are simply responding to business plans.

- Set the personal objectives of strategic HR partners to be those of their line-manager customers.
- Arrange appraisals so that training and development specialists are appraised jointly by their manager and their line-manager customers. Use 360-degree feedback to collect a broad range of views.
- Build teamwork within leadership development team through joint projects, knowledge-sharing, away-days, peer-coaching and celebrating successes. Where partnering seems to be faltering, get all the leadership and development specialists involved in addressing the problem.
- Make leadership development a role model for others' functions and for benchmarking the leadership development against competitors' teams.
- Maintain an ongoing debate about how leadership development is performing. Ask the organisation's leaders, line managers, HR professionals and other functions. All specialists should be listening to, and responding to, their stakeholders.

A Shared Services Approach

This is usually included as a component of business partnering. According to Ulrich (1995), the impetus for a shared services model has resulted from the intersection of five key concerns: productivity, re-engineering, globalisation, service and technology. Demands for productivity have required managers to do more with less through better models of delivery. It is argued that a shared services model enhances productivity by pooling key services.

A key feature of a shared services model is that the activities involved are available to a number of business units. The customer defines the level of service and decides which services to take up. This model presupposes central provision in that it combines or consolidates leadership development services throughout various business units into one unit. Shared services may focus on transitional- or transformational-based services. It is likely that leadership development will have a number of transactional-based services which are administrative in nature. It is perhaps more difficult to include more transformational-type leadership development services into a shared services model.

A shared services model, in the context of management and leadership development, has some potential in that it can achieve economies of scale by bundling together key leadership development services. Some commentators consider it to be an attempt to centralise leadership development and make it less responsive to local conditions. Table 5.1 summarises some of the key success factors and limitations of a shared services approach.

Table 5.1: Key Success Factors and Limitations of a Shared Services Approach to Management and Leadership Development

Key Success Factors	Key Limitations
• Must keep in mind that management and leadership development has a number of different customers. • Must have explicit agreement concerning what services will be delivered and what the key deliverables will be. • Need to spend time considering how various management and leadership development processes fit together. • Do not rely on one mechanism to deliver management and leadership development services.	• The shared services model may be viewed as a way of losing boring administrative tasks, but this is the wrong way to consider the model. • The model may present the business unit with a disparate set of services without consultation and involvement of the line. • The dilemma of efficiency versus choice is a problem. It forces the line manager to accept responsibility for key management and leadership development activities.

Key Success Factors	Key Limitations
• A shared services model does require the devolution of some management and leadership development activities to the line. • The organisation will need to pay high attention to the monitoring of service quality. • It is important that customers understand the principles and values behind the shared services model. • The shared services centre must not lose sight of the culture of particular business units.	• Managers may perceive the model as a mechanism for dumping work on them with insufficient support. • It is possible that the providers of the service may become distant from the people they service. • Many service centres have suffered from promising too much and not being able to deliver on time. • Some customers consider a shared services model a faceless, depersonalised experience.

Devolution of Management and Leadership Development

A devolved model advocates that line managers should have the primary responsibility for managing management and leadership development. Many management and leadership development specialists consider this option to be risky and potentially doomed to failure due to a lack of commitment on the part of line managers to put management and leadership development sufficiently high on the agenda. Under this arrangement, it is likely that line managers will perform a lot of the operational and tactical aspects of management and leadership development, with the more strategic aspects being dealt with by a small core of management and leadership development specialists at the corporate centre. Harrison (2005) suggests that a devolved model, for example giving line managers responsibility for management and leadership development, will only work effectively if certain preconditions exist. These are as follows:

- **Vision and Strategy:** The organisation will need a very clear statement of vision and strategy on management and leadership development. This strategy will need to be strongly integrated both horizontally and vertically. The management and leadership development vision will require a strong level of commitment from senior management. Top management will need to be proactive and consistent in espousing support for management and leadership development.
- **Management and Leadership Development Objectives:** The organisation will need to devise management and leadership development objectives that can be effectively executed by line managers. It should be feasible to translate these objectives into practical plans for implementation.
- **Clearly Defined Policy:** The organisation should have in place an explicit and formalised policy framework on management and leadership development. This statement should set out clear guidelines on the various roles in management and leadership development policy.
- **Performance Management Processes:** The performance management process of the organisation will need to incorporate management and leadership development criteria into the objectives that are set for managers. It is important that the rewards that managers receive are based partly on how well they carry out their management and leadership development responsibilities.
- **A Clear Management and Leadership Development Structure:** The organisation will require a clear statement of all the management and leadership development roles within the organisation. It is important that the key stakeholders have a clear understanding of their management and leadership development tasks, and are competent, committed and have the power to carry them out.

- **A Strong Learning Culture:** The culture of the organisation needs to be well developed in that it contributes to conditions where manager actions are supported and valued.

Outsourcing Leadership Development

Outsourcing has become an important topic of research and an equally important decision for organisations to make in an HR and leadership development context. The outsourcing of management and leadership development, combined with other training and development, has become a reality for many organisations. A distinction is made between outsourcing and contracting out. Outsourcing is a long-term arrangement to provide management and leadership development, whereas contracting out is more of a once-off arrangement where a leadership development consultant is provided, largely on the basis of need. The reasons for the outsourcing of leadership development are both strategic and operational. Greer, Youngblod and Gray (1999) observed that HR outsourcing decisions are frequently a response to a demand for reduced costs. Outsourcing is also viewed as a way of liberating leadership development professionals within the client organisation to enable them to perform a more strategic and consultative role. The outsourcing of leadership development is also viewed as an effective way of bypassing organisational politics. In the leadership development context, outsourcing may represent an extension of a partnership approach, in this case with external partners.

An outsourcing model is likely to be used in conjunction with some of the models described earlier in this chapter. Outsourcing enables organisations to build a small, expert core of leadership development specialists who have the opportunity to work in internal and strategic partner-consultant roles. The organisation can then buy in the services that it requires. This gives the function significant levels of flexibility to respond to unusual needs and provide a customised/specialised service to the business. Many organisations have implemented service-level agreements to ensure that external providers meet specific quality standards and develop a positive and continuous relationship with the organisation.

Outsourcing arrangements can be structured in a number of ways. Kates (2006) suggests the following arrangements:

- *Internal (or Captive) Shared Services Centre*: This is most likely only an option for a large company. Essentially it involves offshoring without outsourcing. If the organisation has sufficient scale internally, this approach enables it to retain control over its leadership development process.
- *Joint Ventures*: These arrangements can be used where there is a desire to build a long-term relationship between the parties.
- *External Co-Sourcing*: This may be an option for a group of small organisations who agree to pool their operations. It is appropriate where each organisation can agree on common issues.
- *Vendor Co-Sourcing*: In this arrangement, the organisation will retain control of leadership development activities while letting go of detailed operations and systems.
- *Re-Badging*: This approach involves transferring the leadership team to the vendor along with all of the processes. This approach ensures that there is no loss to business continuity.
- *Business Transformation Outsourcing*: In this approach, the vendor will form a strategic relationship with the client organisation to influence leadership development in the organisation. The vendor will take ownership and operational responsibility for leadership development.

There is a lack of clarity concerning the effectiveness of outsourcing. One danger with the outsourcing of leadership development is that the service provider may have a vested interest in standardising all parts of the services in order to achieve economies of scale across clients.

Standardisation has the potential to result in the loss of the client's unique organisational characteristics. Pickard (1998) suggested that problems may arise from a mismatch in culture between the host operation and the supplier. Where the outsourcing service is delivering poor quality, the cost of switching or bringing the service back in house may be considerable. Although the outsourcing of administrative and transactional aspects of leadership development may be feasible, it may not be an appropriate model for transformational leadership development activities. It is also arguable that leadership development is a service that is co-produced with top management and line managers. Leadership development professionals are being asked to provide unique solutions. This suggests, in the leadership development context at least, that outsourcing should be used in conjunction with an internal leadership development team that focuses on core competencies and produces development solutions in partnership with the external services provider.

Outsourcing has major implications for in-house leadership development professionals. It may lead to job losses, but it also creates a need to monitor and evaluate the service provider's performance. It will require the reorganisation of the leadership development team. Leadership development staff can manage the outsourcing relationships, but there is the possibility of work intensification because these specialists may still be relied upon by colleagues to provide the service. Where leadership development activities are outsourced, it may result in fewer career development opportunities for in-house specialists, especially those who have specialist rather than generalist skills.

The outsourcing of leadership development activities has important implications for line managers. Vernon *et al.* (2000) found that the most common pattern of policy decision-making in European organisations involved sharing responsibilities between HR specialists and line managers. Line managers no longer merely implement leadership development decisions, they shape them. The outsourcing of leadership development may therefore be inconvenient to line managers. Instead of having leadership development specialists to call on when they need assistance, they will find that HR outsourcing providers are likely to be located in a different place. The service provider may not fully understand the line manager's specific needs and may not have an effective working relationship. Some of the advice that the line manager requires may be difficult to provide via electronic communication. Box 5.2 summarises key advantages and limitations of outsourcing in a leadership development context.

Box 5.2: Advantages and Limitations of an Outsourcing Model for Management and Leadership Development

Advantages

- Provides flexibility and enables the function to customise its solutions to the business.
- The organisation can make cost savings because the services may be cheaper.
- Enhances the credibility of the leadership development function where it establishes relationships with quality external providers.
- Aspects of leadership development can effectively be outsourced to consultants.
- Know-how and expertise that is not available in the organisation can be purchased.

Limitations

- Undermines specialist management and leadership development expertise in the organisation.
- Leads to the fragmentation of the leadership development function.
- It needs to be managed carefully so that the external provider delivers a customised solution to the organisation.
- It should not be done simply for short-term cost gains and headcount reductions.
- The decision to outsource may be made too quickly without sufficient analysis of the level of service required.
- It can lead to a loss of local knowledge and processes which now reside with an outsource provider.

Where the decision is made to outsource, the leadership development team should exert its influence over the selection of a vendor. It is important in the leadership development context to select a partner who can ensure a significant on-site presence. Marchington *et al.* (2004) suggested that leadership development work is relational in nature. It is highly customer-facing and requires substantial interaction with line managers as learners. It requires that the outsource partner has an understanding of organisational processes and it is a mission-critical activity. Table 5.2 outlines the key decisions that the organisation needs to make before it considers an outsourcing model of leadership development purposes.

Table 5.2: Outsourcing Leadership Development Activities: Key Decisions

Initial Considerations
- Achieve a full understanding of existing leadership development service provision. This includes cost base, responsibilities and level of service.
- Achieve a full understanding of future requirements.
- Speak to other organisations that have used outsourcing providers and understand their satisfaction level with the service.
- Consider issues of 'fit' with potential service providers. This includes cultural fit as well as geographical issues.

Design of Internal Organisation to Manage the Vendor
- Need to give detailed consideration to the design of the future internal organisation to monitor, control and manage the vendor.
- If there is a scale issue it may be appropriate to establish the dedicated unit within the leadership development team.
- Consider the degree of contractual flexibility and the preferred contract length.

Managing the Transition
- A phased transition is necessary if the organisation desires business continuity and effective skill transfer.
- Select an executive sponsor who is responsible and accountable for the outsourcing process.
- It may be appropriate to select a transition manager who has responsibility for creating and implementing plans and managing a transition team (where one is appointed).

Continuous Improvement and Flexibility
- Build in mechanisms that facilitate continuous improvement. Devise systems to ensure that there is regular review.
- Ensure that there is sufficient leadership development expertise within the organisation to ensure a strong strategic-level contribution.

A Solutions Centre Model

Hammonds (2005) suggests that the business partner model is a transitional design. A solutions centre has an important additional characteristic: a matrixed group of leadership specialists that represent the delivery engine of a centre of excellence, combined with a front-end business partner approach (Exhibit 5.2). The solutions centre model differs from a business partner model in a number of ways:

- Business partner models tend to have multiple layers of generalists with relatively common skill sets. The solutions centre model emphasises small teams of leadership specialists, with a variety of skills, who carry out transformational leadership development activities.
- Specialists function in the roles of customer relationship managers. The solutions centre may have just one person serving a function or whole line of business.
- Leadership development specialists highlight their expertise, but they do not usually deliver the work. Instead, they link up with external providers and other internal business functions to deliver the required solution.

- The solutions centre will contain a robust middle, consisting of groups of specialists who are matrixed by function, line of business and geography. These staff can be assembled into teams relatively easily and focus on categories of managers and leaders. The solution centre has the capacity to support both vertical and horizontal dimensions of organisations in equal measure.

EXHIBIT 5.3

The Solutions Centre Model Applied to Leadership Development

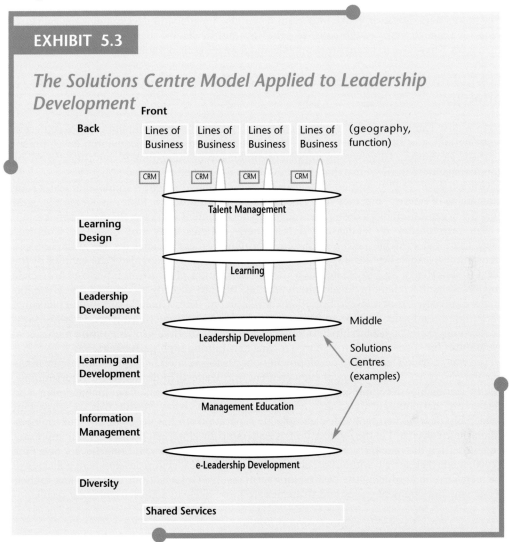

Kates (2006) makes a strong case for the flexibility and adaptability of a solutions centre model. Specifically, she argues the following:

- It possesses the ability to configure teams simultaneously around multiple issues that mirror the complexity of work in the organisation.
- It allows the leadership development team to be more strategic, to identify patterns, analyse trends and consider options. It can take a global perspective.
- It allows work to originate anywhere and therefore deals with potential conflicts and tensions.

- It enables the organisation to assign resources to important priorities and ensures greater effectiveness and relevance.
- It acknowledges that the delivery of leadership development in organisations is a combination of both the transactional and transformational and that transactional work does not have to be outsourced.

The model does, however, make important demands of leadership development specialists. It requires them to make tough calls, to prioritise and to defend these decisions to business managers. They have to be highly adaptable and manage considerable amounts of complexity.

Formulating Management and Leadership Development Policy and Strategy

In formalised and written form, management and leadership development policies represent a strong indicator of the strategic importance of management and leadership development in the organisation. However, an important dimension of this policy is that it is 'owned' by top management in the sense that they have formally agreed a written policy.

Gratton *et al.* (1999) argues that leadership development policy statements are strong statements of interest, but they may not represent actual practice. Policy statements suggest that the organisation has a desire for leadership development to be systematic and consistent.

The formulation of leadership development policies does not occur in isolation. Organisational strategies and human resource management policies are key influencers in determining leadership development policies. Mabey (2002) recognised the validity of the 'best fit' approach, and suggested that the differentiation of strategic intent must precede any decision on leadership development policies. We have already mentioned that HRM has many dimensions that relate to leadership development. These include succession planning, recruitment and selection, performance management and reward systems. Organisations increasingly focus on leadership development as a means of, first, growing future managerial candidates for succession, but also as a means of retaining high performers.

The way in which leadership development policy is formulated has significant implications for the perceived effectiveness of management and leadership development interventions. Many leadership development policies are created in isolation. The management and leadership development specialist frequently generates what he/she sees as important leadership development activities, completely separate from the needs of key stakeholders. Manager involvement in the formulation of leadership development policy plays an important role in setting the management and leadership development agenda. Longenecker and Fink (2000) made it clear that, without capable leadership, most leadership development policies will be ineffective in producing the desired long-term results. Organisations that are clear in their leadership development policy and strategies are more likely to achieve significant results.

Content of the Leadership Development Policy

A question arises immediately as to which should come first: the leadership development policy or the leadership development strategy? Initially, we discuss the policies simply on the basis that they serve as the link between organisational strategy and management and leadership development strategy. Organisations formulate leadership development policies for a multiplicity of reasons. We suggest the following as key reasons:

- To clearly define the relationship between the organisation's strategic objectives and its commitment to management and leadership development.

- To provide operational guidelines to key stakeholders in the organisation. These guidelines may focus on the identification of responsibilities and desired roles for leadership development.
- To provide information to managers on the organisation's philosophy and approach to leadership development.
- To raise the profile and status of management and leadership development in the organisation.

When formulating policy, the leadership development specialist should take into consideration the strategic objectives of the organisation, its size and prevailing culture, its wider HR policies, past and current management and leadership development practices, the expectations of managers and the calibre of specialist leadership development staff.

Leadership development policies should be customised to meet the needs of the organisation. It is better to have a planned and formal approach to the development of leadership development policy. Policies which emerge out of the unsystematic growth of decisions, rules and procedures and which are designed to deal with particular issues, tend to produce bad policy. It results in a piecemeal development of policy which does not reflect the wider organisational context. Ad hoc policy development can result in major inconsistencies and undermine the credibility of management and leadership development. Box 5.3 provides examples of policy statements for management and leadership development.

Box 5.3: Examples of Policy Statements for Management and Leadership Development

- To diagnose organisational problems within, between and across departments. To design, develop and help implement appropriate solutions that enhance the company's efficiency, effectiveness and capability.
- To promote and develop a managerial culture which:
  - Emphasises achieving results rather than carrying out processes
  - Requires managers to manage rather than be administrators
  - Shows impatience with poor performance, conformity and the status quo
  - Gives power to line managers to win the business
  - Emphasises satisfying external and internal customer needs
  - Experiments and trusts, and lets go of excessive control
  - Displays flexibility and allows those best placed to take decisions and action
  - Responds to the company's real financial and business environment
  - Recognises and optimises its asset value in all its employees
  - Tries to reach new standards of excellence and constant improvement.
- To specify the ideal manager profile appropriate for future success, as an input to:
  - Appointment and promotion decisions
  - The identification and auditing of managerial talent
  - The design of training and development strategies, initiatives and programmes.
- To design, implement and monitor the use of appropriate means of performance management, including appraisal, with respect to:
  - Objective-setting
  - Appraisal interview skills
  - Personal development plans
  - Documentation
  - Processes
  - Feedback
  - Ratings
  - Rewards.

- To endorse the use of a wide variety of imaginative and positive developmental and learning opportunities within departments, including:
  - Enlarging job responsibilities
  - Undertaking special projects
  - Taking part in task forces
  - Reorganising work arrangements
  - On-the-job guidance and coaching
  - Mentoring
  - Access to appropriate learning material
  - Work shadowing
  - Temporary job swaps with colleagues
  - Short off-the-job training courses
  - Educational studies
  - Internal and external secondments
  - Private counselling on personal matters
  - Complete change of job role.
- To design, plan, organise, conduct and evaluate in-house, off-the-job manager, management and leadership development education and training programmes which enhance personal, inter- and intra-group competence, solve managers' real business problems and extend their personal vision.
- To sponsor and organise the use of external training and education provision where appropriate.
- To encourage and provide the means of managers' access to relevant professional management literature, conferences, programmes and networks, which will keep them abreast of developments in their field. Scan the external world of management and thereby the means by which the company can continually update its management aspirations.
- To help plan managers' careers. Be a resource for career advice to individual managers. Advise top management on job rotation plans for managed experience. Plan and ensure key succession capability at senior levels. Ensure that decisions about who to retain and who to release take account of managerial talent as well as other considerations.

Devising a Management and Leadership Development Strategy

The actual development of management and leadership development strategy immediately poses an integration problem. It is generally accepted that a management and leadership development strategy should achieve both horizontal and vertical integration.

Horizontal Integration: This concerns the extent to which management and leadership development practices are integrated with other HRD and HRM practices. This alignment process does, however, pose a number of specific challenges:
- Is it possible that current HR strategies are of poor quality and not focused on the current and future needs of the organisation?
- How do changes in any dimension of management and leadership development strategy impact on other HRD and HRM practices?
- How will poor integration undermine other HRM and HRD processes?
- Is it prudent to have management and leadership development as a stand-alone activity?

Vertical Integration: This concerns the extent to which management and leadership development strategy integrates with overarching HR strategy and with business strategy. Vertical integration appears to be an evolutionary process, but a number of questions arise:

- How explicit and of what quality are business strategies and is it wise to have tight vertical integration of management and leadership development strategy?
- Does tight vertical integration have the potential to put management and leadership development into a reactive role simply involved in strategy implementation, but not involved in strategy development?
- At what level of strategy is integration desirable? Is it a corporate, divisional or functional strategy?
- Should the focus on integration occur over the short or longer term?

The question of integration, both vertical and horizontal, is complex. Hendry (1995) advocated two approaches to the integration problems: tight- and loose-coupled approaches. Tight-coupled models place emphasis on a close interconnection between business strategy and management and leadership development strategy. This approach may be feasible where there is a clear and detailed business strategy in place that is agreed by all stakeholders. A loose-coupled approach, on the other hand, advocates that management and leadership development specialists working in business partnerships produce plans that respond to the needs of the business units. These plans are also in line with the overall strategic goals of the business. A loose-coupled approach is considered more feasible for most organisations because it provides the specialist with greater flexibility.

The formulation of management and leadership development strategy involves consideration of a number of issues:

- **Formation of a Team:** This team should have wide representation, including not only management and leadership development specialists but other key stakeholders who have the capacity to put forward interesting ideas concerning management and leadership development strategy.
- **Reviewing the Organisation's Overall Approach to Leadership Development:** This involves consideration of a number of complex issues. These include: current position and management and leadership development practice; the organisation's current management performance; the organisation's culture and climate; current management and leadership development policies; and processes and links with other HR activities and processes. Each area suggests a multiplicity of questions that need to be asked. Box 5.4 provides a comprehensive list of these questions.

Box 5.4: Reviewing Management and Leadership Development Strategy: Critical Agenda Questions

On Present Position and Practice
- What are our unit's strengths and weaknesses? What are its opportunities and threats?
- What management and leadership development are we currently carrying out?
- How are management and leadership development needs/performance needs currently analysed and established?
- What are we achieving?
- What feedback do we receive from our customers (e.g. learners and their bosses)?
- What are our managers' current perceptions and expectations of what we provide?
- What are our current forward commitments?
- Are we given any targets?
- How generous a budget are we allowed? What proportion of company revenue is spent on training?
- What resources and facilities do we have or could be expected to have?
- How do we balance management and leadership development to solve known problems with opening doors to new possibilities?

- What are our standards for leadership development?
- How does the line get involved in management and leadership development (e.g. support, mentoring, coaching)?

On the Organisation's Management Performance
- What is currently holding back the organisation?
- What are the main obstacles to managers doing a better job?
- How skilled are we at analysing these wider management performance issues?
- What access do we have to these wider management performance issues?
- How good is teamwork in and across departments?
- How well qualified, in formal terms, are our managers for the tasks they need to perform?
- How capable are our managers, viewed generally?
- Have we any aggregate performance data (e.g. from appraisals or competency analyses)?

On the Organisation's Culture, Values and Style
- How important are managers' qualifications in this organisation?
- What is the working climate like?
- What issues cannot be discussed?
- How important are means versus ends in this organisation?
- How free and diverse is management style and behaviour?
- Has the company taken a view on the competence-based approach for management?
- What sort of people 'get on'?
- What do people get picked for?
- What factors are formally built into appraisal?
- What is the bottom line?
- How easily are people satisfied around here?
- How far down the road is the company as a learning organisation?
- What recognition is given to team performance versus individual performance?
- Is management and leadership development seen as something the company provides or something managers do for themselves?
- Are any management groups deemed beyond need of our management and leadership development services?
- How does the organisation's culture need to change?

Corporate Culture, Values and Style
- Does the organisation have a distinct culture or culture shift it wishes to promote?
- Is development expected to and able to lead this?
- Is there a core requirement for all managers in order to generate a distinctive corporate style?
- How good is the fit between the development culture and the organisation's culture?
- How important in the company are managerial qualifications such as MBAs?

On HR and Employment Matters
- How does our labour market affect our hiring or losing of talented managers?
- What company employment policies and practices have an impact on training?
- Are there any new policy needs for management and leadership development (e.g. management and leadership development vouchers, OU sponsorship)?
- What performance management and appraisal processes interact with training?

On Politics and Processes in Organisation
- What access do we have to our board's strategic business plan?
- What is in that plan that could have a bearing on training?

- Do we want to be involved in national initiatives (ETP, national management and leadership development awards, lead bodies)?
- What are our publicity channels? How well do they work for us?
- How high profile do we want management and leadership development to be seen to be, inside and outside?
- How is management and leadership development evaluated at macro and micro level?
- What is our brief? What are our boss's expectations? How long have we got?
- Who is to be involved in this review process? How private is it?
- How are we expected to present our new management and leadership development strategy?
- What are the important political issues to be recognised?
- What are the painful political issues that will have to be confronted?
- Who are our most powerful allies who can support new strategies for development?
- Where do we need improved access? How might we achieve it?
- How much freedom do we have to change leadership development's role and develop new strategies?
- What are the biggest organisational obstacles to us achieving the aims of leadership development?

Business Direction and Needs
- How can development best support our company's business plans and chosen direction?
- How can development best respond to general trends in the business world?
- What particular current company problems can development directly try to solve with its activities?

Target Learners
- What current level of capability is there generally in our company's managers?
- What competence do we need to develop?
- How and how much do we want managers to take responsibility for their own development?
- On what groups, levels and disciplines do we need and want to expend most effort?
- What are our highest and lowest priorities?

Practical Responses by Leadership Development
- Where can line management expertise be home grown, and where will it have to be hired?
- What skills do we have in the development function and what do we need?
- What should be resourced inside and what should be resourced outside?
- Where can development expertise be home grown, and where will it have to be hired?
- What should the terms of reference be for the leadership development function?
- How should development organisationally relate to other HR specialities?
- How can we balance traditional learning methods with modern, open-learning approaches?
- How can we reinforce learning interventions with other complementary organisational action?

Image
- What image do we and/or the leadership development function currently have that may need to be worked on?
- How high a profile should we give development, inside and outside?

Selecting Management and Leadership Development Interventions

The precise leadership development intervention will depend on the leadership development strategies chosen. It is important, however, to consider the balance of interventions chosen, as well as their potential to enhance organisational performance. The choice of development interventions will also be determined by financial resources, the maturity of management and leadership development in the organisation, and the capabilities of the leadership development team. Exhibit 5.4 provides a conceptualisation of development strategies based on their centrality to business strategy and their potential impact on business performance. We will pay particular attention to these different strategies in Chapters Eight to Eleven.

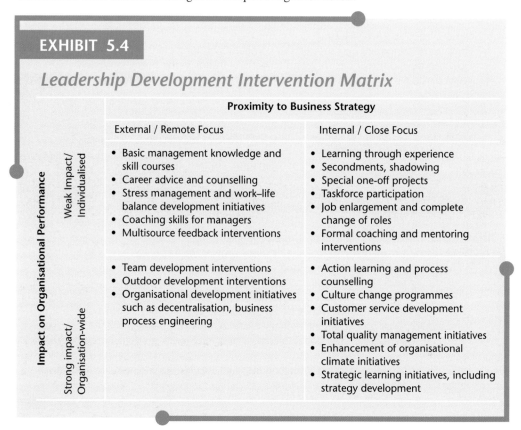

EXHIBIT 5.4

Leadership Development Intervention Matrix

	Proximity to Business Strategy	
	External / Remote Focus	Internal / Close Focus
Weak Impact/ Individualised	• Basic management knowledge and skill courses • Career advice and counselling • Stress management and work–life balance development initiatives • Coaching skills for managers • Multisource feedback interventions	• Learning through experience • Secondments, shadowing • Special one-off projects • Taskforce participation • Job enlargement and complete change of roles • Formal coaching and mentoring interventions
Strong impact/ Organisation-wide	• Team development interventions • Outdoor development interventions • Organisational development initiatives such as decentralisation, business process engineering	• Action learning and process counselling • Culture change programmes • Customer service development initiatives • Total quality management initiatives • Enhancement of organisational climate initiatives • Strategic learning initiatives, including strategy development

Impact on Organisational Performance

Formulating Leadership Development Plans

An organisation's leadership development plan represents a detailed statement of the management and leadership development activity that will take place in a given period. This plan will usually be derived from priority leadership development needs, the available resources for leadership development and current management and leadership development policy guidelines.

Planning processes may be centralised or customer-facing. Leadership development activities are frequently planned in a centralised fashion. This involves the preparation of an agreed and detailed plan covering the entire managerial population with articulated plans catering for the specific needs of graduates and high-potential managers, and taking account of diversity issues. A centralised planning approach focuses on ensuring that:

- Management and leadership development considerations are taken into account when the business strategy is formulated.
- Management and leadership development forms an integral part of the wider human-resource plan.
- Management and leadership development activities at the business unit level are suited to the needs of the business.
- Management and leadership development specialists adopt a collaborative approach to planning to ensure that key stakeholders are brought into the plan.

Centralised approaches suffer from critical weaknesses. The overall plan may not be sufficiently sensitive to the needs of specific business units. It may ignore the input of important stakeholders and, as a result, be perceived as not sufficiently customer-facing. It tends to assume that there is agreement amongst stakeholders on specific priorities and that stakeholders are sufficiently skilled and confident to influence plans.

In contrast, a customer-facing approach focuses on continuously achieving an excellent service to all leadership development's different customers. It is premised on the leadership development specialist working in a close-knit, proactive collaboration with the business. Specialists are expected to have a full understanding of the business and be comfortable addressing strategic and operational issues. It advocates a more flexible approach to planning rather than having one plan for a specific duration. It requires the specialist to combine the development of strategy and planning in a continuous and creative way, and therefore mirrors the emergent view of strategy. Such an approach makes significant demands on the leadership development specialist, but it is acknowledged that it has potential to increase the perceived value of management and leadership development in the organisation. Where organisations adopt a more centralised approach to planning, they will likely give consideration to the planning elements that are presented in Exhibit 5.5.

EXHIBIT 5.5

Elements of a Management and Leadership Development Plan

- Details on a calendar basis (monthly, quarterly, half-yearly) of each department's learning and development requirements by job classification and by number of managers involved.
- Details on a monthly, quarterly, half-yearly, etc. basis of the projected leadership for staff not permanently allocated to a department (e.g. three graduate trainee managers).
- Specification, against each item of development, of the standard to be achieved, the person responsible for seeing that it is implemented, the strategy to be used (e.g. self-development, on-the-job coaching, internal or external course), how much the intervention will cost, its duration, when it will take place and its target completion date.
- A summary of the organisation's and each department's budget allocation for leadership development: this may be divided into leadership development that is continuing and to which the organisation is already committed, e.g. craft trainees who are part way through their apprenticeships, and other training.
- Possibly a sum set aside for additions to the organisation's learning resource centre or for the development of material to be used over the organisation's intranet.

Managing Stakeholder Relationships

Strategic management and leadership development requires that the leadership development specialist does not operate solo. The specialist needs to forge relationships with both internal and external stakeholders, and devise mechanisms to involve stakeholders in leadership development decision-making processes. The involvement of the top team, line managers and individual learners is driven by a multiplicity of factors, such as:

- The devolution of leadership development responsibilities to line managers and individuals.
- The growth in developmental appraisal processes and individual development planning.
- The growth in formal mentoring and coaching processes.
- Workplace-based assessment of managerial competence.
- Increased involvement of senior management in managing learning in organisations.

These changes challenge the leadership development specialist to ensure effective alignment of development activities with business priorities.

EXHIBIT 5.6

Securing and Sustaining Top Management Support for Management and Leadership Development

Role of Top Team	Facilitating Factors	Inhibiting Factors
Ownership/ Resources	• Articulate a clear vision for management and leadership development • Understand and value the contribution of management and leadership development to strategy • Commit resources to the development of managers at all levels	• View management and leadership development as a cost rather than investment • Fail to understand the nature and processes of management and leadership development • Inhibit or prevent management and leadership development initiatives in the organisation
Participation	• Demonstrate behaviours consistent with the development agent • Participate as developers and learners in management and leadership development • Reward strong development behaviours of managers	• View management and leadership development as something done to junior managers • View the training and development function as the key driver of management and leadership development • Fail to develop own skills and competencies
Feedback	• Stipulate requirement for management and leadership development to be evaluated • Give feedback and listen to findings • View learning as a means of shaping strategy	• Fail to provide resources for the evaluation of management and leadership development • Fail to listen to criticism, feedback and value continuous improvement

The Executive Team

The executive team has a primary role to play in championing leadership development through defining the organisation's strategy and establishing leadership development policies. This indicates that the executive team is instrumental in both driving the perceived importance of leadership development and also, more fundamentally, in determining the policies, strategies and resources that enable leadership development to flourish. Blanchard and Thacker (2007) highlight that active top-management support is necessary in order to create a high level of commitment to development on the part of middle and junior line managers. If management and leadership development is to be a strategic activity, it requires that the executive team view it as a proactive strategy, an investment rather than a cost. Storey, Mabey and Thompson (1997) emphasised that relationship with corporate strategy and board support are the most crucial factors in ensuring that leadership development happens.

Smith, Mabey and Thompson (1999) argued that one of the reasons for under-investment in leadership development by SMEs is the lack of a champion at senior management level. Senior managers frequently take the view that it is the responsibility of individual managers to undertake leadership development. Antonacopoulu (1999) suggested that recognition of the importance of leadership development by senior management is not in itself a guarantee that it will actually happen. Leadership development budgets are often used as a political tool and leadership development is itself a political process because of its inter-relationship with performance management, promotion and rewards (see Exhibit 5.6).

Line Managers and Leadership Development

The involvement of line managers in leadership development has always been highlighted in the literature. This is viewed as both positive and negative. In terms of positive aspects, it is considered a good idea that the line manager takes responsibility and accountability for leadership development. Gibb (2003) suggested that managers have a key role in becoming more proactive about leadership development. They should expect and help their managers to learn and develop. The argument is also made that leadership development will be of better quality if line managers are more directly involved. They are considered to be more familiar with both organisational needs and the roles that individual managers play. Line managers have a more proximate view of the issues than leadership development specialists. Involvement of line managers in leadership development has the potential to lead to a transformation of line managers themselves. It is frequently highlighted that line managers have poor leadership skills, but taking on leadership development responsibilities will force them to become more competent. This will enable the enhancement of the quality of the leadership cadre in the organisation as a whole. The involvement of line managers in leadership development can therefore contribute to broader organisational change and transformation of the organisation (see Exhibit 5.7).

The involvement of line managers in leadership development, however, is problematic. Line managers have many duties and may lack time and enthusiasm for leadership development. They may not be experts in leadership development. Involvement in leadership development may also dilute the line manager's generalist management focus. There may also be tensions between the line and leadership development specialists concerning the transfer and completion of leadership development. The possibility exists that the line manager may be too reliant on leadership development specialists to deal with the transformational aspects of leadership development. They frequently argue that they have responsibility and accountability for leadership development, but little authority. Gibb (2003) raised the possibility that there will be less leadership development taking place if line managers are made solely responsible for it. He also suggested that there is little reason to believe that line managers can be better developers than leadership development specialists. Line managers are likely to be less objective and accurate in determining leadership development needs. They can be less skilled at coaching and facilitating development. They are also likely to be less adept at evaluating leadership development initiatives. A significant barrier to involvement of line managers in leadership development is the possibility that it marginalises specialists. Gibb (2003) suggested that the specialist role will become transformed as line managers take on more responsibility. Specialists, however, may fear that they will be isolated or excluded from the leadership development process. Where leadership development specialists are very powerful, it may result in managers taking on less responsibility. It is clear that it is a difficult balance to strike. Lynton and Pareek (2000) suggested that it is perhaps naïve to assume that the relationship between a line manager and his/her team can be a good guide to the quality of leadership development. They suggest that responsibility for a manager's development should lie in part with a neutral third party. The line manager's direct report relationship may involve conflict of interest and the line manager may not be in a position to resolve this.

The extent and nature of line management involvement in leadership development will be influenced by cultural norms. Even where strong support is demonstrated by the line manager for management and leadership development, it may often be skills-centred and exclude support for other leadership development interventions. Development initiatives that are more developmental/strategic-focused and less quantifiable in terms of outcomes may be given a lower priority. This focus on the more operational aspects can result in the compartmentalisation of management and leadership development.

EXHIBIT 5.7

Managing Line Manager Involvement in Leadership Development

Role of Line Management	Facilitating Factors	Inhibiting Factors
Ownership/ Resources	• Value management and leadership development as contributing to enhancing job performance • Buy in to the values of management and leadership development • Support calls for resources for management and leadership development	• Place too much focus on short-term performance at the expense of development • Advocate a production rather than a development philosophy • Block the allocation of resources for management and leadership development activity
Participation	• Articulate own management and leadership development needs • Engage in coaching and mentoring processes • Create opportunities for learning and transfer of learning	• Refuse to update own skills and competencies • Do not contribute to the development of a developmental climate • Fail to perform coaching and mentoring roles
Feedback	• Support the systematic evaluation of management and leadership development • Encourage feedback and solicit feedback • Act on feedback and support continuous improvement	• View management and leadership development as a waste of time • Fail to listen to feedback and/or act upon it • Lack openness to criticism

From the perspective of the individual manager, management and leadership development plays an important part in their career development. Management and leadership development represents an important source of information and guidance in relation to the portfolio of competencies relevant to current and future roles. It can also be used as a means of facilitating a better understanding of the forces and influences acting upon managers' job performance. Managers frequently have negative perceptions of and attitudes towards management and leadership development. This is often based on the results of previous negative experiences of management, unmet demands for management and leadership development and the extent to which the organisation encourages or does not encourage individuals to develop and grow.

For managers, the organisation's perspective dominates the way management and leadership development is perceived. Organisations view management and leadership development as a mechanism through which they can communicate the symbols of the organisation's culture and the management behaviours considered acceptable. There is evidence to indicate that managers may not always view management and leadership development as a learning experience. Antonacoponlou (1999) suggested that a multiplicity of factors underpin the perceptions of managers and their willingness to pursue development. These include the culture of the organisation, reflected in the value placed on learning and development, the implicit and explicit messages indicating the organisation's expectations and the amount of learning opportunities available in the organisation. Managers have particular expectations concerning how management and leadership development can be a valuable learning experience. These include providing assistance to managers in their own development by identifying their weaknesses and providing information on how to improve, developing the manager as a person through enhancement of knowledge and understanding of the self and context, providing confidence and insight concerning how to increase knowledge, and preparing managers in advance of unexpected future development. It is clear that while managers are concerned with the organisational agenda, individual managers also have personal agendas or sets of priorities which can be significantly different from each other.

Identifying Management and Leadership Development Needs

The identification of leadership development needs represents an important process dimension of effective management and leadership development. Analyses of development needs play a central role in achieving the appropriate alignment between strategy, management and leadership development policy and actual management performance. Without an effective analysis of development needs, management and leadership development policy will exist independently of the actual requirements of the organisation. Three levels of analysis are typically identified: organisation, operational and individual. The last of these three is the one most frequently undertaken by organisations. However, the individual level may prove less effective without proper analysis of the other levels. Ford and Noe (1987) highlighted six specific objectives of the needs assessment process. These include answering questions such as: Who needs to learn what? What does the manager need to learn? At what depth does the manager need to learn? What are the priority learning needs? How can we get buy-in to the learning? The assessment of managerial learning needs is therefore a set of answers to the right questions asked systematically by the right people.

A shift has occurred in recent years away from specialist-driven approaches to learner-centred approaches. In contrast to the more traditional specialist-focused approach, a learner-centred approach puts the learner at the centre of the process and keeps him/her there, while systematically reviewing the other relevant organisational issues to create a complete picture of what the manager needs to learn. The process begins by looking at the manager's job and asking questions about job responsibilities and tasks. The questions then move to consider broader issues which focus on tactical and strategic dimensions of the job. Traditional approaches tended to focus on the system instead of keeping the learner central to the process.

Task and Skill Taxonomies for Managers

A lot of published work has attempted to identify taxonomies of managerial and leadership competencies. These studies go back as far as the mid-1980s. Powers (1987), for example, used a job competency assessment approach to identify the competencies of effective managers. He identified five clusters: 1) goal and action management, 2) directing subordinates, 3) human resource management, 4) leadership, and 5) focus on others. Whetten and Cameron (1999) identified and interviewed a large sample of highly effective managers in a variety of firms. They found that managerial effectiveness was associated with three personal skills: developing self-awareness, managing stress and solving problems creatively; and four interpersonal skills: communicating supportively, gaining power and influence, motivating others and managing conflict. The study findings emphasised that the competency areas overlap and managers have to rely on all skill areas in order to be effective in a managerial role.

Luthans, Hodgetts and Rosencrantz (1988) made a detailed observation of forty-four managers in a variety of organisations. They identified four categories of competencies: communication, traditional management, networking and human-resource management. They found that the most significant differences between successful and unsuccessful managers lay in networking activities such as external communication, socialising and politicking. McCall, Lombardo and Morrison (1988), in a project initiated by the Centre for Creative Leadership, conducted in-depth interviews with eighty successful managers. They identified ten managerial skill categories.

There is evidence that many organisations use competency models of some sort. Hogan and Warrenfelz (2003) concluded that virtually every managerial competency model falls into one of four major categories:

- **Intrapersonal Skill:** These are leadership competencies and behaviours that are associated with how managers adapt to stress, have goal orientation, and adhere to rules. These skills and behaviours do not involve interacting with others; they are therefore considered the most difficult to change.
- **Interpersonal Skills:** These are skills that involve direct interaction, such as communication and building relationships with others. These competencies are considered easier to develop.
- **Leadership Skills:** This category includes motivation and development of others, supporting change and a range of skills and behaviour concerned with building teams and getting results through others. These skills and behaviours are more easily developed than the skills and behaviours associated with the first two categories.
- **Business Skills:** This category includes vision, strategy and management skills, such as developing plans and focusing on results. These skills and competencies are often developed through MBA and formal management training programmes. They are the easiest of the four categories to learn.

We will explore leadership development competencies in Chapter Six.

A range of techniques is available for conducting training needs analysis with managerial populations. These include observation, questionnaires and consultation with subject-matter experts, interviews, multisource feedback, developmental assessment centres and performance management processes. We will give detailed consideration to performance management, multisource feedback and development assessment centres. However, we will also discuss some of the more conventional approaches, such as interviews, surveys, etc.

Conventional Approaches: Surveys are a common method of needs assessment with management populations. Surveys have perhaps reached a level of saturation through overuse. They do, however, offer a number of advantages. They can gather a lot of information from a large population of managers, and there is an established statistical procedure with which to analyse the data. Surveys are relatively easy to administer and large samples can help to reduce certain biases. They are, however, slow to administer and the results obtained might not be very insightful in terms of identifying development needs. It is often the case that follow-up may be required to clarify responses. Managers are not very prompt in responding to questionnaires. Where the development specialist considers the questionnaires are appropriate, four key decisions need to be made. Should the questionnaire collect factual information or opinions or a combination of both? Should the questionnaire be personally administered or mailed out? Is it necessary to conduct a pilot study? What statistical methods are appropriate for analyses?

Interviews and focus groups are useful methods with which to collect information concerning the development needs of managers. Interviews provide the management and leadership development specialist with a number of options. Interviews can be conducted with senior managers who are in a position to understand the collective development needs of a group of managers. It is also possible to conduct interviews with individual managers to get self-reports of development needs. Group interviews or focus-group methodology can be implemented. Interviews have a number of important advantages in the context of the identification of development needs of managers. They allow managers the opportunity to convey their views and feelings more completely than do surveys. Focus groups permit the immediate synthesis of ideas, they help build support for a specific development initiative and ensure that managers are part of the solution. Focus-group interviews allow for follow-up discussion with individual managers. The potential downside is that interviews and focus groups do take up a considerable amount of time and they demand particular skills of the management and leadership development specialist. Rossett (1987) argued that focus groups offer such significant advantages that they are one of the most useful methods of gathering information about organisational and individual manager training and development needs.

Managerial training and development needs assessment can also be conducted through observation. Observation can generate highly relevant information about the work setting of the manager. It does, however, demand a considerable amount of time, and the management development specialist must have both process and content knowledge. Because of the time involved, relatively few managers can be observed. Observation can be subject to serendipity in that sometimes a particular event occurs and sometimes it does not. The very presence of the observer can contaminate the outcome.

Performance Management Appraisal: Performance appraisal is an appropriate technique to use in the identification of management development needs. It is a powerful tool in the context of management and leadership development. It is in itself a developmental intervention. Delahaye (2000) argued that the engagement between manager and direct report can bring about significant development. It serves as a mechanism to identify development issues as well as a strategy to evaluate the impact of developmental activities. For performance appraisal to be effective in a needs identification context, it is necessary to recognise that performance appraisal has both administrative and developmental components. It requires that the manager give a significant level of priority to the developmental aspects as well as the evaluation of performance. Typically, the more sophisticated performance appraisal systems have three important features:

- Managers use some form of scale to rate how well a target leader has accomplished specific objectives.
- Managers also rate leaders on dimensions that the organisation considers to be important. These include issues such as integrity, communication, impact, leadership, etc.
- Managers rate the overall performance and/or promotability of the leader and identify development issues.

We must, however, acknowledge that the administrative and developmental components of performance appraisal are conflicting in nature. The developmental component requires the appraising manager to undertake the role of helper and supporter rather than that of judge and jury. Managers become confused by conducting both dimensions simultaneously. They become confused by the expectation that they must conduct them but, at the same time, keep them separate. Some commentators recommend that they be conducted at different times. Woodall and Winstanley (2003) argued that if a performance appraisal process includes a requirement that individual development plans are to be prepared and discussed, managers can make effective decisions concerning the skills and competencies that need to be developed.

Multisource Feedback: Multisource feedback has become a popular method with which to identify the development needs of managers. Bracken, Timmreck and Church (2002) pointed out that management development specialists and managers have in the past assumed that self-appraisal by managers was the most accurate survey information concerning strengths and weaknesses. This view has changed. Proponents of multisource feedback argue that its strength lies in the breadth of sources both internal and external to the organisation. Judge, Lock and Durham (1997) argued that managers use multisource feedback to promote self-awareness of skill strengths and deficiencies.

Multisource feedback is valuable in the context of identifying a manager's strengths and weaknesses. It should, however, be built around an organisation's competency model, which should describe the leadership behaviours necessary for organisational success. The evidence suggests that multisource feedback is very valuable in giving the manager 'how' feedback. 'How' feedback focuses on how managers should act in order to get better results. The feedback derived from the system must be translated into specific goals and development plans. The multisource feedback process should give managers lots of ideas on what and how to improve, but it requires post-feedback action in order to be effective. Overall, multisource feedback is valuable in a needs identification process because it gives managers more balanced feedback and it allows managers to see themselves as others see them.

Development Centres: Development centres have grown in popularity as a method of managerial development needs identification. They may represent the most sophisticated way available of assessing management and leadership development needs. The purpose of development centres is to assess, identify and develop leadership potential. Development centres have the potential to highlight behavioural tendencies that can be difficult to assess using more conventional methods.

Development centres operate on the basis of multiple observers, observations and methods. Typically, they involve between three and six observers and eight to ten participants. Participants are required to work through a combination of methods such as simulations, tests, role-play and self-report personality inventories. Information is brought together from all of these methods using a competency framework as the method of organisation. Participants receive detailed feedback as well as identification of skill or competency gaps.

Participation in a development centre can change the self-assessment that managers make about their strengths and weaknesses. They must, however, be highly structured and the combination of methods must be appropriate to measure the competencies included in the development centre. Like multisource feedback data, development centres must be supported with development planning interventions and individualised interventions to address the development issues that arise. We will discuss development centres in more detail in Chapter Seven.

Evaluating Management and Leadership Development Activities

The evaluation of management and leadership development is complex and not always conducted in a comprehensive way. Organisations, as a rule, tend to emphasise a functional performance rationale for investment in management development. This rationale posits that there is a direct relationship between management development and individual and organisational performance. This indicates why organisations are concerned that management and leadership development initiatives should be formally evaluated and, where possible, should be subject to return on investment methodology. Organisations typically measure the impact of management development through simply recording the average number of development days per annum. This is, however, considered to be both an imprecise and possibly misleading measure. It tells us little about the effectiveness of different management development methods or the quality of the development undertaken.

Studies reporting the specific impact of management and leadership development in quantifiable terms are difficult to find. Attempts to identify the distinctive benefits of investment in management development are useful for policy-making purposes, as well as justification of the investment. They are, however, time-consuming to undertake and there is a temptation not to do anything large scale.

The specific difficulties associated with the evaluation of management and leadership development are many, but four specific difficulties are highlighted:

- The majority of evaluation models are better applied to a training rather than a management and leadership development context. Management and leadership development activities can take different forms, from formal to informal, and many of the evaluation models are geared towards the evaluation of formal development interventions.
- Managerial work is contextual. This usually means that even where a manager develops new skills, there may be difficulties in implementing what has been learned due to barriers of an organisational or individual nature.
- The learning preferences of managers have an impact on the value they derive from management and leadership development.
- The outcomes of management and leadership development are likely to accrue long-term. Many organisations want a quick fix and evaluate development interventions too quickly.
- It is sometimes difficult to get managers to participate in scientifically designed evaluation programmes. They often find it burdensome to complete questionnaires and participate in interviews. It can prove difficult to get a pre-measure of managerial performance, which is necessary in order to show changes in both skill and performance.
- Return on investment studies are costly to undertake. They are best used for a high-profile leadership development initiative. They are time-consuming to undertake and require the application of a rigorous methodology.

Bernthal and Wellins (2000) argued that organisations should use appropriate measures to evaluate the contribution of leadership development. They suggested a comprehensive test of lead and lag measures (Exhibit 5.8).

EXHIBIT 5.8

Lead and Lag Measures Appropriate to Evaluate Leadership Development

Lead Measures	Lag Measures
• Increased job satisfaction and engagement ratings • Increased perception of growth opportunities • Increased percentage of high potentials completing development plans • Executive review board established with clear understanding of process and roles • High potentials' perception of value regarding the succession process • Percentage of participation in learning and development activities • Percentage of leaders registered in the mentoring network	• Increased percentage of high-potential leader retention • Increased leadership diversity • Increased performance relative to strategic goals • Lower percentage of external hires for key positions • Fewer key positions without ready successor • Higher HR strategic-value creation ratings (e.g. from executive team, stakeholders) • Positive ROI from action-learning projects

We will now focus in our discussion of evaluation of leadership development on return-on-investment issues. Phillips (1997) positioned ROI as a fifth level of evaluation and builds on Kirkpatrick's framework. According to Phillips, ROI is calculated as the net programme benefit divided by the programme cost x 100.

ROI (%) = Net Programme Benefits / Programme Costs x 100

Considering an ROI for leadership development is complex and potentially costly to do. Specific problems that are likely to be encountered include the following:

- Isolating the impact of the leadership intervention from other contextual factors that could influence the results.
- Determining the costs of the leadership intervention and converting the results of leadership development into financial results.

Costing the leadership intervention: In costing the intervention, it is important to distinguish between indirect and direct costs. Costs associated with the design of the intervention are prorated over its anticipated lifespan. Direct costs associated with the intervention are usually calculated as part of the specific intervention being measured. Phillips (1997) indicated that the fully allocated fixed-costs model should be used. This suggests that organisations need to include a charge for the fixed assets associated with the development intervention. This is appropriate in a leadership development context because of its link to strategic drivers in the organisation.

Converting the results of leadership development into financial benefits: This is a very challenging task in a leadership development context. It will begin with some decision on the metrics or measures to be used in the calculation. This could include sales, response time and quality. Some of these, however, are not discrete performance measures. They pose particular problems when trying to assess the impact of individual leadership development and job-based development interventions. It may be necessary to use more subjective estimates of business impact. However, this should not be done in isolation. It is important to talk to stakeholders in order to secure a fuller picture.

Isolating the effects of the leadership intervention: This is a very significant challenge when an ROI analysis is conducted on leadership development activities. It is very rare that organisations will use a quasi-experimental design and therefore the specialist will have to deal with the 'real world'. It may be necessary to get estimates from managers themselves, from line managers and from the executive team. This will serve to enhance the credibility of any subjective analysis that is undertaken. It is important to err on the conservative side and not make any over-ambitious claims. Box 5.5 suggests questions that should be asked when conducting ROIs for leadership development.

Box 5.5: Conducting ROI for Leadership Development: Questions for Leadership Development Specialists

- What particular leadership intervention should be chosen to demonstrate ROI?
- At which point in time should the ROI calculation be undertaken?
- How has the financial quantum of the results been calculated?
- What level of confidence does the specialist have in the calculation of financial benefits?
- What percentage of business performance or improvement is directly attributable to the leadership intervention?
- What level of confidence exists in the estimate of the costs of the leadership intervention?
- How should the key organisational stakeholders be included in the ROI process?
- Is it prudent to conduct an ROI for all leadership development interventions or is it better to select a high-profile programme to conduct ROI?
- Do the costs and resources involved in conducting the ROI justify its value to the leadership development specialist?
- How should the results of the ROI be communicated to key stakeholders?

E-Leadership Development

Electronic human resource systems are being used with increasing frequency in organisations. Therefore, interest has arisen in the notion of e-leadership development. It is possible to define e-leadership development as spatially segregated, technically networked, technically supported, with shared performance of leadership development tasks through at least two human or technical actors (Kabst and Strohmeier 2006). We will explore some of these characteristics as they apply to leadership development.

- *Spatial Segregation*: This indicates that the learners are not in the same place. However, this does not have to be always the case. They could be working in the same room.
- *Technical Networking*: This is an essential feature. Information technology enables learners to be technically networked, irrespective of where they are located. E-leadership development processes can be separated in both time and space.

- *Technical Support*: This assumes that the technology will perform certain parts of the task either fully or partially. This includes simple email as a leadership development tool.
- *Shared Tasks Between at least Two Learners*: The sharing of learning processes between two managers is a necessary requirement.
- *Performing Leadership Development Tasks*: This suggests that e-leadership development is essentially geared towards more transactional aspects of leadership development.

The question arises concerning whether e-leadership development represents a substitute or a useful addition to conventional leadership development. It is unlikely to replace conventional leadership development if its methodologies cannot be extended to all leadership development activities. It is possible that, for technical reasons, it will be limited to certain aspects of leadership development activity. A significant amount of leadership development, such as coaching, mentoring and formal leadership development programmes, cannot be conducted that effectively through e-leadership development.

E-leadership development is premised on the idea that greater responsibility for development can be given to the learner. Stone, Stone-Romero and Lukaszewski (2006) suggest that three factors are important in explaining the acceptance of e-leadership development.

- *Information Flows*: The use of e-leadership development is likely to change information flows in the organisation. This may include increasing the organisation's capacity to access and disseminate coded information such as talent management ratings, competency profiles of individuals, career paths and individual development planning processes. These systems enable managers to have rapid access to that information.
- *Social Interaction*: E-leadership development systems are likely to modify social interaction systems within the organisation. A particular concern is that such systems often substitute electronic communication for face-to-face interactions, which are a fundamental part of a majority of leadership interventions. This lack of interaction has potential implications for the quality of informal leadership development, teamwork and collaborative learning processes. Cardy and Miller (2005), for example, posit that e-leadership development systems may decrease the degree to which leaders understand role requirements and it may influence the level of trust that exists between managers at different levels.
- *Perceived Control*: An important issue which may undermine the effectiveness of e-leadership development concerns the extent to which they are used to control the behaviours of managers. Stone, Stone-Romero and Lukaszewski (2003) suggested that electronic systems have the potential to limit the freedom of managers and therefore they may be resisted. Managers may resist e-leadership development systems that keep track of how much development time they have put in and the amount of time spent on specific leadership development links. A primary goal of leadership development is to ensure alignment with organisational goals. Junior managers and supervisors may feel threatened by an e-leadership development system because it makes many of their skills and roles redundant. It is likely that such systems might provide useful feedback, but this may not compensate for the reduction in autonomy.

It is likely that e-leadership development systems have both positive and negative aspects for organisations. It perhaps makes more sense to use blended leadership development systems, i.e. systems that combine e-leadership development systems with proven leadership development processes. Blended leadership development processes have the potential to reduce some of the fears concerning perceived losses of freedom and control in organisations. Blended leadership development systems do require a complex and varied leadership specialist competency set, including the following:

- The ability to devise leadership development strategies that integrate traditional and electronically mediated features.
- Skills in relationship building and stakeholder management, so that a community of practice on blended leadership development can emerge.
- Project management skills in the implementation of blended learning leadership development programmes.
- Instructional design skills to ensure the effective integration of e-learning components, multimedia delivery and blended learning methodologies.
- Web development skills, so as to develop interactive electronic codes and tools such as discussion forums and just-in-time leadership development modules.

Box 5.6 provides examples of eight electronically supported learning approaches that can be used in an e-leadership development context.

Box 5.6: Electronically Supported Learning Approaches Useful for e-Leadership Development		
Medium	**What is it? When Should it be Used?**	**Live or Self-Study**
Webinars (Live E-Learning)	Live Internet-based education, conducted through a browser, taught by an instructor or subject-matter expert. Typically includes slides and a small amount of animation. This medium works very well for special topics, online demonstrations, guest lectures and other less interactive training events that are two hours in length or shorter. It is not a full replacement for classroom education because there is far less interactivity. It is very scalable, however, and can accommodate hundreds of students. Interactivity can be improved by opening up Q&A and letting students open up the phone lines for questions and discussions. You should consider it a 'tell' medium, however, not a 'learn' medium.	Live and Self-Study
Courseware (Web-Based)	Internet-based courseware, largely consisting of graphics, text, some audio, and some interactivities and assessments. Self-paced and run from a PC or other browser. There are many different types of web-based courseware, but for the purposes of this book we group courseware into basic courseware, simulations, CD-ROM courseware and rapid e-learning courseware. Courseware is the most traditional aspect of e-learning, and has been traditionally built in 'chapters' with various amounts of interactivity possible. The term 'interactivity' refers to exercises and tests that encourage learners to try what they have learned and see the effect of their actions. The 'tell' and 'try' approaches both work here. The limitation of courseware is that it can be very expensive to build, expensive to maintain, and alone does not give enough interactivity to hold learners' interest for new topics and in-depth high-level learning.	Self-Study

Medium	What is it? When Should it be Used?	Live or Self-Study
Simulations (Application, Business, Process)	Scenario-based courseware, typically run on a PC or through the Internet, providing the learner with a real world to play in. Simulations fall into three categories: application, business and process. The purpose of simulations is to give the learners a self-study approach where they can directly try the material and experience what happens. An application simulation, for example, enables learners to use a piece of software and see how it behaves, so they learn how to execute certain functions. A business simulation enables learners to change a business or personal scenario in some way and see what happens. Process simulations enable the same in either technical or business processes.	Self-Study
CD-ROM-Based Courseware	CD-ROM-based courseware is very different from web-based courseware. It fulfils many of the same goals, but is often developed to take advantage of video and other local capabilities on users' PCs. The main difference is that it runs 'offline' whenever a user wants, without needing access the Internet. The primary difference between this item and courseware is that CD-ROM-based content typically assumes that the student will run all the content on a local PC, and therefore has much more bandwidth to use. You can easily take courseware designed for the Internet and run it on a PC, and this eliminates the need for the network. But true CD-ROM designed content (typically older titles) have more video, interactivity and rich media (audio) built in. Media-rich CD-ROMs are very expensive to build and are very useful for video-based training where audiences are young, new to the company, or not highly educated – and you need to give them a lot of images and very little text. CD-ROM technology requires some kind of PC player and a PC with a minimum amount of memory and speed to run correctly, so when you develop this type of content you must determine the minimum PC configuration you will need.	Self-Study
Rapid E-Learning Courseware (PowerPoint-Based)	There is a special form of courseware built on PowerPoint. We are identifying this separately because it is a big growth area and this type of medium has very different characteristics and applications from traditional courseware.	Self-Study

Medium	What is it? When Should it be Used?	Live or Self-Study
Rapid E-Learning Courseware (PowerPoint-Based) *contd.*	It is very new. This medium takes PowerPoint based content and publishes the slides, animations and usually audio in a web-based format that can be delivered on the Internet. In most cases, the content is converted to Flash, a technology that runs on virtually every PC without the need for any plug-ins. These tools have the added benefit of letting subject-matter experts author their own content. They remove the web development from the middle of the content development process, which is a huge time and financial saving. With some tools, you can also add assessments and standard tracking technology to the courseware, so you can actually create a true courseware. However the programmes are limited in their interactivity and levels of assessment.	Self-Study
Internet-Delivered Video	This is a video replay delivered through the Internet, typically played through Real Player or Windows Media Player. This medium drives high bandwidth and is growing in usage, but is often limited by deployment efficiencies. Early e-learning consisted of instructor-led training delivered through this medium, which proved to be an ineffective solution. Despite the potential for this solution, most learners do not have a consistent high-bandwidth connection that can be relied on for this medium. If you believe you have a demonstration or physical image that should be shown by Internet-based video, create it as an optional 'module' or hint that special exercise learners can choose to skip it if they are working from a low-bandwidth location. You will dramatically lower completion rates if you force learners to watch a painfully slow video that may not run correctly. Remember that plug-ins are required for video and that you must specify in advance which formats you will support. Typical formats include Real Audio/Video, Windows Media and streaming technologies like Akamai, which can improve delivery speed. A warning here: do not try to use 'talking heads' as video on the web. The talking-head instructor video was an early attempt to put existing content onto the web. It largely fails because the low bandwidth, small screen size and small images (faces are usually small and the screen shows a lot of background) make for a very unappealing experience.	Self-Study

Medium	What is it? When Should it be Used?	Live or Self-Study
EPSS (Electronic Performance Support Systems)	EPSS represents a category of technology often referred to as 'online help'. These systems are designed to help individuals complete a certain task by giving them electronic performance support. These systems are very expensive to build but have huge returns on investment for large audiences in applications like call centres, order-processing and technical support. They are not 'training' *per se*, but rather performance support or on-the-job assistance, e.g. trainerslearning.com. EPSS systems are not covered in detail in this book, but are presented here because some online courseware evolves into EPSS solutions. An EPSS system serves a different need than traditional blended learning; it is designed as a performance support tool to help someone complete a task at the time needed. Training, by contrast, is typically used to teach someone how to do something in advance. If you are building content that is starting to look like an online help system, then you may be building an EPSS system and not even know it. EPSS systems are very powerful, expensive to build and can be justified for large production environments as a support tool to complement training. They do not, however, replace training, because they do not give learners any context, theory or business-process education in the task or topics they need to understand.	Self-Study
Offline Video (Videotapes)	Videotapes are the first attempt to turn classroom training into self-study training. Typically, they are recordings of actual classes, with the video shot to include the instructor's face, blackboard, flip chart, and often other materials. They do not work on small computer screens, but on a TV set: in this way they can be useful. Few companies can successfully leverage these libraries widely, largely because the video is not shot for use in a self-study format. In order to be useful, video for the web must be very close to a person's face, large, and surrounded by interesting visual images. Shooting video from the web is a different video shot and can be useful for small topics and demonstrations, but requires specialised skills.	Self-Study

Conclusion

This chapter discussed a number of issues associated with establishing strategic management and leadership development in organisations. We focused on explaining the practical steps that need to be taken to ensure that management and leadership development is professionally organised. Management and leadership development needs to be addressed at the strategic level. It is important that senior management support is given, both in the form of written management and leadership development policies, and in making sufficient resources available for leadership development. Two fundamental components of an effective management and leadership development process involve the systematic diagnosis of development needs and the design of evaluation processes to ensure that management and leadership development provision is of high quality and business-focused. How management and leadership development activities are structured and positioned in the organisation is an important consideration for the leadership development specialist. The organisation should select an arrangement that enables the leadership development specialist to lead as well as manage leadership development activities. Management and leadership development activities should be both horizontally and vertically integrated. These forms of integration focus on relationships with other human resource management activities and the strategic priorities of the organisation.

Organisations have a number of options when it comes to the identification of management and leadership development needs. In addition to the standard or more traditional methods, such as surveys and interviews, methods more sensitive to the dynamics of the managerial role include multisource feedback, development centres and performance appraisal. The evaluation of management and leadership development activities is both complex and resource-intensive. Traditional evaluation methods may not be deemed appropriate because they do not capture the complexity of leadership development outcomes and the contextual nature of managerial work.

Summary of Key Points

In this chapter, the following key points have been made:

- Management and leadership development can be used as a strategic tool to help organisations implement organisational strategies. Managers, through their actions and decisions, can also impact on incremental change in the organisation.
- Management and leadership development policy represents a strong statement by the organisation of its intentions in respect of developing managers. Policy contributes to positive perceptions concerning the value of management and leadership development and it clarifies the roles of key stakeholders in the management and leadership development process.
- Management and leadership development strategy should be customised to meet the needs of the organisation's managers and it should reflect the culture and values of the organisation.
- Organisations have a number of options around which to structure management and leadership development activities. These vary from the more traditional, internal consultancy model to a shared-services approach.
- The assessment of management and leadership development needs requires judgement concerning the performance of the manager and the manager's current and future skill gaps.
- The selection of needs identification processes requires the organisation to consider who will make judgements concerning the needs, how this will be done and how the validity of the decisions made will be enhanced.

- Organisations expect that management and leadership development activities represent a valuable investment. Proving this, however, is difficult. Evaluation has multiple purposes, including proving, improving the quality of intervention, learning and influencing key stakeholders.

■ Discussion Questions

1. Management and leadership development should be aligned to corporate strategy. What do you see as the main issues to be considered in achieving this alignment?

2. How appropriate is it for managers to identify their own management and leadership development needs?

3. To what extent should management and leadership development be evaluated simply as an act of faith?

4. Strategic partner models pose significant challenges for the leadership development specialist. Discuss.

5. What factors should you consider when formulating a management and leadership development strategy for a large organisation?

■ Application and Experiential Questions

1. Think of a leadership development intervention that you are familiar with. How would you calculate its ROI? What costs would you include? What unit of results measured would you use? How can this unit of measurement be converted into financial benefits? How would you isolate the effects of leadership intervention from other factors?

2. Select a leadership development programme with which you are familiar. How did you go about identifying the leadership development needs? What role did the learners play in the needs identification process? Overall, how would you rate the effectiveness of the needs identification process you undertook?

3. In two groups of three or four, prepare for a debate on the following motion:
   'Organisational performance may be explained not by the leadership development practices that are reportedly in place, but by the context and the way the practices are implemented.'
   One group should prepare the case for and the other the case against this motion.

Chapter Six

Management and Leadership Competency Models

Outline

Learning Objectives

After reading this chapter you will be able to:

- Understand the terms 'competence' and 'competency' and the different approaches to understanding leadership competencies in organisations.
- Provide a rationale for the use of competency frameworks in management and leadership development.
- Understand the underlying assumptions of competencies and the extent to which they are of value.
- Understand the methods that can be used to identify and measure competencies and competence.
- Critique leadership competencies and understand their advantages and limitations in a management and leadership development context.
- Understand the decisions that organisations need to make when introducing competency-based approaches to leadership development.

OPENING CASE SCENARIO

Developing a Competency Framework in Stryker Corporation

Stryker Corporation operates in the medical device industry, developing, manufacturing and marketing surgical and medical products for the global market. Stryker Corporation employs about 14,000 people worldwide, throughout Europe, Canada, Japan, Latin America and the Pacific Region (Hong Kong and China). The headquarters are in Kalamazoo, Michigan, USA. Stryker operates in a highly decentralised manner through seventeen manufacturing and distribution divisions, for example: orthopaedics; trauma; spine; biotech; instruments; endoscopy; and medical. Each division has a specific specialist field. In 2003, Steve MacMillan joined Stryker as President and CEO, and, in the same year, Stryker Howmedica Osteonics became Stryker Corporation as part of a global branding exercise.

In 1998, Stryker Corporation established a plant in Cork. This state-of-the-art manufacturing and development facility, which was established to provide surgeons with a portfolio of hip, knee and shoulder implants, focused on product and procedural innovation. Stryker ensures that it has the right procedure and the right implant for the right patient. It is a flat-structured organisation and currently employs approximately 350 people. The leadership team is representative of nine manufacturing business units or cells that operate on the factory floor, each of which has a team leader who is a member of the leadership team. Each cell has a different function with its own goals and objectives, which are ultimately guided by those of the company. Every team leader is responsible for all members of their cell, in which there are two groups: support staff and team members. In addition to the business unit team leaders, there is also a representative from each of the following departments on the leadership team: HR, IT, Finance, Quality, R&D, Central Facilities and Distribution. The HR department consists of eight team members who perform the following functions: HR manager, employee relations, compensation and benefits, payroll administration, recruitment and selection, training and development, HR administrator and reception duties.

The mission of Stryker is to be the recognised leader in global orthopaedics and to build intense customer loyalty. This business objective is supported by a strong statement of core values, which focus on integrity, accountability, open communication, quality, individual respect, commitment and innovation. These values served as a guide and foundation for the company development process.

Stryker Orthopaedics decided to introduce a competency approach to management and leadership development in order to reinforce the organisational culture, link people performance and behaviours to business objectives, support organisational change processes, enable the assessment and development of leaders to provide the organisation with competitive advantage, promote a common language for the discussion of leadership capabilities and adopt systematic, specific and objective assessment methods.

The company recognised the potential benefits of competencies in view of the future threat of competition from Eastern Europe and Asian countries, such as China and Japan. Therefore, a need emerged to change the way they operated. Furthermore, Stryker realised that a fundamental change was required to its HR model, because the traditional HR model – for example, hiring employees, putting them through training and leaving them to their own devices to perform their role – no longer works in today's world. Therefore, the HR model needed to be aligned to the business model to drive business performance improvement and create a high-performance workforce, achieved by employees who would become focused on organisational objectives. At an individual level, the defined knowledge, skills and behaviours for each role should be linked with the performance review process; thus competencies would become the standard to work towards, ensuring strong recognition to drive human performance through an integrated HR model.

The competency development process was facilitated utilising two external consultants. They interacted with key stakeholders in the organisation to facilitate the development of a generic competency model. The consultants conducted a series of intensive workshops to gather data on how leaders perform their work and the competencies required to be effective performers. In order to get the process going, the organisation agreed on a definition of a competency. They defined a competency as consisting of 'knowledge, skills and behaviours which enable performance excellence'. The data gathered through the workshop process was content-analysed independently by each consultant and by members of the HR and learning team. They were each asked to suggest a categorisation of the competencies revealed by the data. The various categorisations were then shared and, from this process, an overall competency categorisation emerged. The organisation made two fundamental assumptions concerning the competency model: expectations of leaders change as they move throughout their career and their tenure in the job as leader; and as they enter the role, they are expected to 'learn the ropes', demonstrate their abilities and absorb the organisation's culture. As the leader gains experience, he or she is expected to make an impact by working through others. The final stage of development involves leading through vision. Stryker defined this stage of development as requiring the following competencies: to build a strong network and use that network to achieve results; to stimulate others through ideas and knowledge; to provide direction to the organisation; and to drive critical business opportunities and develop a strategic perspective.

The organisation assumed that people could be trained in each competency specified in the model. However, it also acknowledged that it was less easy to train people in the ability component. Development interventions are not the complete solution to the enhancement of competencies. The final competency model generated identified nine generic and two technical competencies. The generic competencies focused on: business knowledge and strategic knowledge; customer engagement; teamworking and developing others; communication and influencing; leadership; problem-solving and decision-making; planning and prioritising; continuous improvement; and managing change. The technical competencies were: technical expertise; and knowledge of regulation, compliance and legislation.

Stryker Orthopaedics then developed an extensive training and development programme to provide managers with an understanding of the basic concept of competencies. They also implemented a personal development planning process to enable managers to identify key competency gaps and plan customised leadership development solutions. The organisation's performance management system was redesigned to integrate and use the competency framework. This was done on a phased basis because managers initially found it difficult to understand what the competency model meant for their roles and performance.

QUESTIONS

Q.1 What do you see as the advantages of a customised approach to the development of a leadership competency model?

Q.2 What do you see as the key limitations of a competency-based approach to leadership development for an organisation like Stryker Orthopaedics?

The concepts of competence and competency are increasingly used in many organisations. Competencies are viewed as an increasingly versatile and powerful concept to underpin human resource management practices and to drive management and leadership development activities. Competencies have become a critical issue in developing a pool of managerial talent that can contribute to the achievement of competitive success. The adoption of competencies has significantly influenced the way in which leadership development is undertaken. Competencies reflect the multiplicity of roles that managers and leaders typically play in organisations. Managerial performance depends on how well these multiple roles are performed. However, competencies are not without their critics. Organisations are initially drawn to competencies, but become discouraged by the resources required to implement them effectively. They are fashionably in keeping with contemporary concepts such as competitive advantage, the protean career and employability. These concepts place significant responsibility for development on managers themselves.

Competency approaches are considered most appropriate in situations where there is a need to develop clearly defined standards of performance, and where there is a desire to link management and leadership development with strategic imperatives.

This chapter considers the use of competencies in management and leadership development. We explore different approaches to managerial performance and explain the concepts of competency and competence. We examine various conceptualisations of competency and discuss key differences between rationalist and interpretativist approaches to understanding competencies. We outline and evaluate the key issues that organisations need to consider when developing competency frameworks for managers and outline and evaluate the contribution of competency-based approaches to management and leadership development.

Historical Evolution of the Competency Approach

The emergence and development of the competency movement has a more than thirty-year history. Harvey (1991) suggested that organisations traditionally operated in relatively stable and predictable environments. Development consisted of moving managers through a series of job moves in order to acquire job experience. There was little emphasis on measuring individual differences. Bos (1998) suggested that the emergence of competency in the management and education discourse can be attributed to two movements: developments in business organisations; and developments in education.

Developments in Business Organisations: Assessment centres were first introduced in the early 1970s. These initially focused on measuring managers against underlying performance dimensions in the selection process. However, over time, they switched to identifying person-focused variables for the selection and development of managers. In 1973 McClelland published an article, 'Testing for competence rather than for "intelligence"', which many consider the starting point of the competency movement. He argued that IQ tests were poor at predicting successful management performance. He made a case for the assessment of competencies and developed the Behaviour Event Interview as a way of identifying who had potential for management and leadership. Spencer and Spencer (1993) proposed a competency dictionary that distinguished superior from average managers.

Initially, competencies were developed for specific organisations and were very carefully designed. Hollenbeck, McCall and Silzer (2006) suggest that this rigour did not continue and it led to a deterioration in the quality of organisational competency models. Since the early 1990s, various authors have sought to define competencies and, in recent years, competency models have been approached in a strategic context. The idea of core competency emerged, particularly with the work of Prahalad and Hamel (1995).

Developments in Education: Educational organisations have also focused on competencies. Mulder (1998) argued that their development in education can be traced back to humanistic-based leader education and competency-based feedback education. It is, however, difficult to ascertain exactly when they became popular in the education context. The development of work competencies in an educational setting has led to many questions: Can competencies be developed outside the work context? Are different competencies required for the novice and the experienced manager and, most fundamental of all, can competencies be taught? There is no doubt that educational organisations have increasingly taken on the competency challenge and it has raised fundamental questions concerning how best to develop managers.

Understanding Managerial Performance in Organisations

A key to understanding the contribution of competencies concerns the nature of managerial performance. Managerial performance is complex. It takes place in a unique social and cultural context which is linked to immediate task requirements. The notion of context is fundamental to understanding managerial performance, but it is understood in different ways. Three particular approaches – job-focused, person-focused and role-focused – are highlighted.

- **Job-Focused Approaches:** Job-focused approaches emphasise the identification of the key tasks of managerial work. This approach works on the assumption that the job can exist independently of the job-holder. This approach is highly functional and is common in HR and training practices in Ireland, UK and Europe. Burgoyne (2002) suggested that a job-focused approach is highly centralist because of its emphasis on skills rather than output standards. Cole (2002) suggested that functional analysis approaches are not particularly appropriate for management and leadership positions because they do not capture the complex dynamic context in which managerial performance is manifested. Job-focused approaches place too much emphasis on the notion that managerial jobs are relatively similar. Cheng, Dainty and Moore (2003) argued that management is essentially a creative activity. At the supervisory level, precise job functions can be specified, but at top management level this is a much more complex process. Soft attributes such as creativity, sensitivity and flexibility are intangible and difficult to measure. A concept of competencies which focuses on the tasks inherent in jobs is limited and inflexible. It fails to provide sufficient guidance to make assessments of senior leader competence. It stipulates that competences are micro and specific.

- **The Person-Focused Approach**: The person-focused approach conceptualises a manager's performance in terms of how it relates to personality, values and other individual attributes. This approach views competencies as macro in nature and argues that the manager has the ability to deal with non-routine and complex situations. It envisages that competencies are generalisable and portable. Brown (1993) suggested that macro competencies are of particular significance to the performance of complex managerial work that is typically required at higher levels of management. The person-centred approach envisages a concept of competencies which is intangible, dynamic and essentially elusive. Henderson (1993) suggested that the person-focused approach has merit in that it views managers not simply as performers, but as reflective actors. The imposition of rigid standards is not conducive to creativity and initiative.

- **Role-Focused Approach:** The role-focused approach understands managerial performance by studying the social and cultural context in which performance is undertaken. Holmes and Joyce (1993) described this approach well when they suggested that job performance concerns the enactment of a role that emerges through the interaction between the job-holder and other managers in the social situation. A role-focused approach places emphasis on demands made of the individual manager and the extent to which the manager accepts them. It highlights the degree to which a manager's performance meets standards set by him/herself and others. A role-focused approach is grounded in the reality of the manager's situation and rejects universal models which are context-free. It recognises that individual performance is influenced by culture and values, the actions of co-workers and leader behaviour. Any attempt to understand performance must be understood in the reality of the individual manager's situation. This approach highlights the contingent nature of managerial work.

Defining Competence and Competency

The definitions of 'competence' and 'competency' are problematic and complex. There is confusion concerning whether there is a distinction between these terms. The National Council for Vocational Qualifications (UK) defines competence as the ability to perform a range of work-related activities and skills, displaying the knowledge and understanding which underpins such a performance. Boyatzis (1982) suggests that 'competence' refers to all aspects of the job that have to be performed competently, whereas competency is defined as what managers need to bring to the role in order to perform its key dimensions to the required level of competence. Many definitions make a reference to the notion of performance. This standard may be defined as 'high performance' or 'the achievement of work objectives'. Eraut (1994) suggested that the everyday use of the term 'competent' includes some aspects of performance referencing. It tends to be considered a characteristic of a manager rather than a statement concerning the range of a manager's competence. Marsick, Watkins and Wilson (2002) suggested that it is best to view competence as what a manager knows and can do in ideal circumstances.

The term competency is used in multiple ways. One notion refers to 'core competencies'. These consist of various capabilities in the organisation's value chain that enable it to excel and be better than its competitors. Core competencies are considered to be central to the strategic direction of the organisation. In the management and leadership development context, the term 'competency' is generally understood to denote ability and capability. It is possible to distinguish between non-behavioural and behavioural competencies in this context. Non-behavioural competencies focus on acquired knowledge, skills and attitudes. Behavioural competencies focus on the definition of excellent behaviour associated with management and leadership. Figure 6.1 highlights different notions of competency.

Figure 6.1: Different Perspectives on the Notion of Leadership Competency

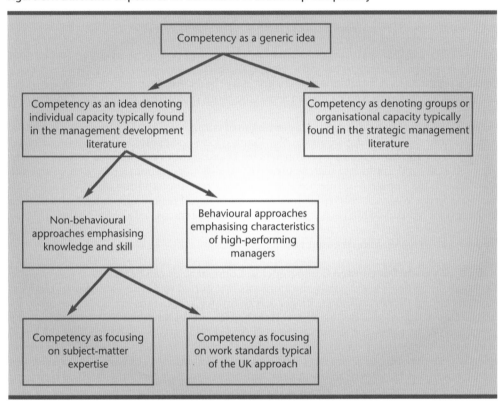

Competencies in a management and leadership development context are conceptualised as individualised and distinct from the core competencies of the organisation. Management and leadership development specialists tend to use the term 'behavioural competencies' because they want to describe how managers behave when they perform managerial and leadership roles. These different discourses reveal the confusion that permeates the leadership competency debate.

Inside-Out and Outside-In Approaches to Defining Leadership Competencies

The inside-out approach focuses on defining dimensions of competency. The literature suggests five important dimensions, which we will now consider:

Personal versus Task Dimensions: This is often referred to as the US versus the UK approach to competency. The personal competency approach focuses on skills and characteristics that explain performance. Derous (2000) defined competence as: 'an underlying behavioural dimension or characteristic that can result in effective or superior performance, depending on context, organisation, environmental factors and job-specific characteristics. The task approach focuses on the essential elements of the task to be performed.'

Bergenhenegouwen (1996) argued that managers should possess a range of both personal competencies and task competencies to perform effectively. They must also possess the vision to encourage the development of personal and task competencies in subordinates. Such a perspective allows employees to share a common vision of the organisation and permits organisations to link resource requirements to business strategies. However, competency models do not specify the balance between these two sets of competencies. This represents a significant drawback, because it, in turn, inhibits the potential of management and leadership development efforts to correct any imbalance between these two sets. Currie and Darby (1995) posited that the competency models fail to provide a weighing system that would allow organisations to prioritise competencies. Consequently, all competencies carry equal importance. A production manager may be more focused on task-orientated competencies, whereas a sales manager may be more concerned with enhancing person-orientated competencies.

The balance between person- and task-orientated competencies will vary according to the organisation and industry context. Nordhaug (1998) suggested that person-centred competencies can be called meta-competencies because they encompass a broad range of personal skills and aptitudes, such as creativity, ability to communicate and to co-operate with others, the capacity to tolerate and master uncertainty and the ability to adjust to change. Van der Wagen (1994) highlighted the importance of person-orientated competencies in the service industry, which is heavily dependent on customers and service quality. This led her to suggest that the focus of future research should be on the development of competency frameworks to match industry segments.

Individual versus Distributed Competencies: Competencies can be viewed as belonging to one single individual. Increasingly, the emphasis has shifted to the development of teams at all levels within the organisation (Prager 1999). Strategic decisions are no longer taken by individuals acting alone, but by teams. Kakabadse and Anderson (1993) argued that the prevalence of mergers, the focus on product and service quality and customer care and orientation suggest that teams, not individuals, are now the unit of focus for learning interventions. Boam and Sparrow (1992) suggested that organisations should consider top teams in terms of bundles of competencies, rather than seeking out individuals who each fit a desired competency profile. Overmeer (1997) predicted that bringing together individuals, who have conflicting norms of performance, may result in the creation of an organisation-based action bias. Organisational success is often contingent on the proper cohesion of top team members and the mix of competencies that these individuals possess. Examples of behavioural competencies essential for organisational success include: good interpersonal relationships among team members; the capacity for openness and willingness to discuss issues; high levels of trust among team members; discipline and cohesion in decision-making; the capacity to discuss and understand both long- and short-term issues.

While studies reveal that the correct identification and implementation of generic team competencies can lead to more effective outcomes for the organisation, there are few guidelines on the individual competencies that team members should possess and the optimum mix of individual competencies within a team.

Specific versus General Competencies: Definitions of competency range from the specific to the general. Specific definitions are narrow in scope and may focus on a specific task in a specific context. These definitions have little or no transferability to other tasks or contexts. General competencies are defined much more broadly. They may comprise competencies for a category of manager, or for a particular profession. These definitions suggest that competencies have general application and are not context-specific, and may be so general as to prove difficult to operationalise for management and leadership development purposes. The majority of managerial competency models focus on generalisable behaviours and attitudes and it is assumed that managerial behaviours in all sectors are based on three role sets that Mintzberg (1973) appropriately defined as interpersonal, informational and decision-making. Turner and Crawford (1994) suggested that the possession of generic managerial competencies may be insufficient to differentiate between average and high performance. It may be necessary to focus on specific functional and technical competencies to distinguish excellent senior manager performance. This debate suggests that organisations need to move beyond sole reliance on generic managerial competencies to include more specific technical competencies. This requires organisations to adopt a more holistic approach to the development of competencies.

The employability debate raises a number of important questions with respect to the issue of general versus specific competencies. Feldman (1996) pointed out that competency development, in the form of seeking out opportunities to develop generic competencies, enhances an individual's employability. However, others argue that generic competencies are changing rapidly, causing a sharp decline in the lifespan of many competencies. Both employers and managers must invest in competencies which are in line with prevailing business and technological trends.

Increasingly, managers are taking responsibility for their own development. They should ensure that the bundle of competencies they acquire makes them uniquely marketable in meeting the high-skill requirements of employers. In this regard, the transferability of competencies has attracted much attention. The competencies developed in one job may be helpful, or even essential, for successful performance in other jobs (Greenhaus and Callanan 1994). Managers with highly transferable competencies are not bound to the organisation, as their competencies are portable and can be used to good effect in different organisations. In contrast, managers with low transferability of competencies are less employable, because they are bound by their present employer's organisation-specific skills, which may not be effective in other employment (Hirsch and Jackson 1996).

Levels of Competency versus Competency at a Level: This distinction is construed in a number of ways. Levels of competency may refer to certain amounts of competence. Thijsen standards refer to a minimum competence that is necessary to perform a task or role. It is often associated with graduate managers or newly appointed supervisors. Likewise, Boyatzis (1982) distinguishes between threshold and differentiating competencies. Threshold competencies tend to be generic in nature and apply to most managerial roles. Examples include problem-solving and decision-making, communication and influencing. Differentiating competencies refer to competencies that distinguish superior from average managers. These competencies are more organisation-specific. Examples include customer focus and global mindset. Competency can also be considered at one particular level. This suggests that competency is a delineating point, for example differentiating novice from expert.

Technical versus Non-Technical Competencies: The majority of competency definitions contain elements such as knowledge, skill, attitude, values, personality and so forth. The question arises whether those elements can be taught and developed. Spencer and Spencer (1993) tackled this issue through the Iceberg Model. This model distinguishes between observable and non-observable elements of competency. Know-how and transferable skills form the top. At the bottom of the iceberg lie the less visible elements. These attributes include social role, self-image, values, traits and motives. These are said to control surface behaviours. The more hidden dimensions are less easy to develop because of their stability and may need to be explored during the selection process. Parry (1996) distinguishes soft from hard competencies. Hard competencies include specific job-related knowledge and skills, whereas soft competencies are focused more on personality, values and styles.

The outside-in approach, in contrast, focuses on how the concept of competency relates to or is differentiated from other terms. For example, it argues that the concept of competency differs from terms such as ability, skill and performance. Stoof *et al.* (2002) highlighted five key distinctions that can be made between the concept of competency and other terms.

Competency versus Skill, Knowledge and Attitude: Skills have been viewed as task-centred (Parry 1998), and best suited to routine or programmed tasks associated with stable organisational environments. They are manifested in overt behaviour elicited or triggered by these tasks, thus demonstrating organic properties (Kanungo and Misra 1992). In contrast, competencies are associated with intelligent functioning and cognitive activities, are needed for non-routine tasks indicative of complex, volatile environmental conditions, and are more generic than skills, making them transferable. They are dependent on the individual to be enacted. Finally, competencies do not necessarily imply an underlying skill (Antonacopoulou and Fitzgerald 1996).

Attempts to distinguish between competence and attitudes have centred on demonstrating how managerial competence contributes to the formation of certain attitudes. Competence is thought to be closely related to self-efficacy because self-perceived competence develops in part as a result of feedback following successful task performance (Stone and Stone 1985); a feature shared with self-efficacy. Self-efficacy or self-beliefs about capability are considered central to understanding motivation and level of performance (Bandura 1990) and would appear to be associated with self-perceived competence (Arnold and Mackenzie-Davey 1992).

Few efforts have been made to distinguish knowledge from competence or competency. Knowledge and competency are very similar terms. Knowledge is often considered in relation to business school curriculum content and knowledge-based competencies are understood as knowledge of subject matter (McLagan 1997), ranging from the more specific and concrete to the broader, more general or more abstract. The synonymous use of knowledge and competency is coupled with the virtual absence of any effort to better define these terms and distinguish between them. Treating knowledge as a competency is an extension of previous assumptions upon which the competence approach is based (Vaill 1989); in this case viewing knowledge and performance as positively related to each other.

Competency versus Performance: Competency and performance are also confused. Bartlett and Ghoshal (1997) suggested that competence is a quality possessed by an individual as a result of training, whereas performance is an expression or demonstration of that competence in some particular circumstance. Jeris and Johnson (2004) referred to the term competent as meaning the standard required to perform an activity or function successfully. To be competent means performing to professional or occupational standards. Winterton and Winterton (1999) suggested that competency is about potential to perform, whereas performance is about situated behaviour. Gonzi, Hager and Athanasou (1993) made the point that performance is usually observable, whereas competency is not directly observable but is inferred from performance.

Competency versus Qualification: Competent managers are not necessarily qualified. Qualification is associated with standards and certificates. It is considered a kind of objective indication that a manager has the minimum requirements for the job. Some commentators suggest that competency includes the notion of qualification. Ellström (1998) suggested that qualification is a representation of competency and is a sub-area of competence.

Competency versus Capability and Ability: The distinction between possession of competencies, capability and ability are difficult to articulate. Capability is often defined as characteristics of a person that are not necessarily used in the management task. The manager may not be aware that he/she possesses such capability. Ability can be used to refer to the capacity to acquire managerial competencies.

Competency versus Expertise: Dreyfus and Dreyfus (1986) suggest that a competent manager is someone who is between a novice and an expert, but it is generally very difficult to distinguish between competency and expertise.

Rationalist and Constructivist Approaches to Competency

We highlighted earlier in this chapter three perspectives on managerial performance. These are clearly reflected in discussions about competencies. Rationalist approaches are based on scientific principles and reflect a job-focused approach to performance. They consider competency to be an attribute-based phenomenon. Human competence is considered to consist of a specific set of attributes that managers use to accomplish their work. Competencies are context-free and can be used in a wide range of activities. Competencies are described in a way that is independent of the manager and are viewed as human attributes or work activities. Sandberg (1994) distinguishes between three rationalist approaches: worker-oriented approaches, work-oriented approaches and multimethod-oriented approaches. Table 6.1 provides a summary of competency definitions organised by type or approach.

Table 6.1: Definitions of Competency: Different Perspectives

Worker-Oriented Definitions
- The behavioural characteristics of an individual that are causally related to effective and/or superior performance in a job. This means that there is evidence to indicate that possession of the characteristic precedes and leads to effective and/or superior performance in the job (Boyatzis 1982).
- An underlying characteristic of an individual that is causally related to criterion-referenced effective and/or superior performance in a job or situation (Spencer and Spencer 1993).
- A high performance or H-competency is a relatively stable set of behaviours that produces superior workgroup performance in more complex organisational environments (Schroder 1989).

Work-Oriented Definitions
- 'Competency is a knowledge, skill, ability or characteristic associated with high performance on a job, such as problem-solving, analytical thinking or leadership. Some definitions of a competency include motives, beliefs and values' (Mirabile 1997:75).
- 'A competency is a cluster of related knowledge, skills and attitudes that affects a major part of one's job (a role or responsibility) that correlates with performance on the job, that can be measured against well-accepted standards, and that can be improved via training and development' (Parry 1996:50).
- 'A competency is an underlying characteristic of an individual that is causally related to criterion-referenced effective and/or superior performance in a job or situation. Underlying characteristic means that the competency is a fairly deep and enduring part of a person's personality and can predict behaviour in a wide variety of situations and job tasks. Causally related means that a competency actually causes or predicts behaviour and performance. Criterion-referenced means that the competency actually predicts who does something well or poorly, as measured on a specific criterion or standard' (Spencer and Spencer 1993:9).

- Occupational competencies: the ability to perform the activities within an occupation or function to the level of performance expected in employment (Management Charter Initiative 1990). The ability to perform the activities within an occupation (Nordhaug and Gronhaug 1994). An action, behaviour or outcome, which the person should be able to demonstrate (Training Standards Agency 2000).
- 'Human competence … is displayed behaviour within a specialised domain in the form of consistently demonstrated actions of an individual that are both minimally efficient in their execution and effective in their results' (Herling 2000:20).
- Competency is about micro-sized job characteristics, skills, knowledge and motives of the employee that have been causally related to superior managerial performance (Hammond 1989).
- The glue that binds the organisation together, taking a holistic view of people, purpose, process and and performance (Wynne and Stringer 1997).
- The concept of competence is related to the dynamics of higher education, resulting from the contemporary urge for co-operation between education and labour organisations in order to establish a competitive workforce (Barnett 1994).
- The potential capacity of an individual or collective to handle successfully (according to laid-out criteria, formal or informal, as set out by someone else) certain situations or handle a certain job or task. The ability to perform the activities within an occupation.

Multidimensional Definitions
- The ability to apply knowledge, understanding, practical and thinking skills to achieve effective performance to the standards required in employment. This includes solving problems and being sufficiently flexible to meet changing demands (NCVQ 1997).
- The skills, knowledge and understanding, qualities and attributes, sets of values, beliefs and attitudes which lead to effective managerial performance in a given context, situation or role (Woodall and Winstanley 1998).
- 'Competence [is the] ability to handle a situation (even unforeseen)' (Keen 1992:115). 'Competence is a compound, made up of different parts just like the fingers of a hand {i.e. skills, knowledge, experience, contacts, values, and also coordination, which is located in the palm, and supervision, symbolised by the nervous system)' (Keen 1992:112).

Worker-Oriented Definitions: Worker-oriented definitions place emphasis on the attributes possessed by managers in the form of knowledge, skills, attitudes and personal traits required for effective performance. Boyatzis (1982) argued that job competencies are underlying characteristics which are generic. He placed particular emphasis on the generic or context-independent nature of competencies and adopted an empirical method to determine the characteristics of managers that enabled them to be effective performers. Spencer and Spencer (1993) followed a similar tradition and suggested that competencies include: 'motives, traits, self concepts, attitudes or values, content knowledge or cognitive or behavioural skills – any individual characteristics that can be measured or counted reliably and that can be shown to differentiate significantly between superior and average performers, or between effective and ineffective performers' (Spencer and Spencer 1993:4).

Worker-oriented definitions are behavioural in focus. Questions arose concerning how generalisable these competences are. Cseh (2003) indicated that different cultural contexts influence how competencies are understood.

Perspective on Research: Understanding Competencies for Leadership in Organisations

Garonzik, Nethersell and Spreier (2006) found that senior manager roles tend to fall into one of three types: operational, advisory and collaborative. Operational roles are more traditional roles. They control resources and are very focused on results. They have to perform constant balancing acts and need to possess strong self-confidence. Advisory roles provide advice and support in specific areas. They are seldom directly accountable for results. They implement policies and provide expert advice. They use influence and organisational knowledge to make things happen. Collaborative roles are hybrid in nature and have emerged from flatter, matrix-type structures. They have accountability for results, but have little direct operational control. They work through others. These leaders draw on the competencies of their advisory and operational peers. They need a strong understanding of organisations and they need the competencies to influence. Garonzik, Nethersell and Spreier found that some managers have more strategic roles, whereas others are more tactical. Different competencies are required at different levels. The study findings indicated that, as the complexity and sophistication of the role increased, successful leaders demonstrated a wider repertoire of leadership and influence skills, along with more integrity and organisation-specific competencies. Tables 6.2 and 6.3 summarise these research findings.

Table 6.2: Leadership Role Matrix

	Leadership Trait	Operational Role	Collaborative Roles	Advisory Roles
Strategic	Global Enterprise Leadership	Top leaders of large, complex international organisations, typically publicly traded, high-profile conglomerates that span diverse technologies.	n/a	n/a
	Enterprise Leadership	Leads all aspects of business to generate results. Typically the highest-level leadership role in a diverse enterprise with multiple business units, lines and markets.	n/a	n/a
	Strategy Formation	Focused on the achievement of bottom-line results where global or business-critical objectives must be achieved. Typically more complex general manager or sales roles.	Develops and delivers strategically important programmes critical to the organisation's mission through co-ordination and direction of diverse resources over which direct control is not exercised.	Focuses on the alignment and integration of strategies for a function that is a critical driver of business success. Partners in determining business strategy and provides strategic advice that supports the achievement of critical business objectives.

	Leadership Trait	Operational Role	Collaborative Roles	Advisory Roles
	Strategic Alignment	Focuses on the achievement of bottom-line results where product and marketed developments demand significant change to current business capabilities. Typically general manager or sales roles.	Defines and delivers specific and measurable long-term programmes and results through a complex network of resources and partners over whom direct control is not exercised.	Focuses on the alignment and integration of policy in a strategically important and diverse area. Provides advice and guidance that support the achievement of major business objectives. Seen internally as thought leader.
	Strategic Implemen-tation	Integrates and balances operational or sales resources to extend current business capabilities, ensuring that market demands are met in the short and medium term. Manages a large, complex operating unit to pre-determined requirements.	Delivers specific, measurable results across a broad, complex area through a network of diverse resources and patterns over which direct control is not exercised.	Focuses on the translation and application of policy in diverse although usually related areas.
Tactical	Tactical Implemen-tation	Manages defined resources to ensure achievement of clearly specified objectives such as volume, cost, quality and service to meet schedule and customer requirements.	Delivers specific measurable results in a discrete, defined area through a network of internal and external resources and partners over whom direct control is not exercised.	Focuses on the translation and application of policy in a specific functional area.

Table 6.3: Leadership Competencies

	Leadership Trait	Operational Role	Collaborative Roles	Advisory Roles
Strategic	Global Enterprise Leadership	• Symbolic leadership • Externally focused • High level of social responsibility • Focused on building top team and organisational capability • Unique competencies related to values or strategy	n/a	n/a

Leadership Trait	Operational Role	Collaborative Roles	Advisory Roles
Enterprise Leadership	If top CEO: • High level of teamwork • Wide range of sophisticated or unique competencies based on organisation Otherwise: Same as level below, plus • High levels of integrity, coaching and customer focus	n/a	n/a
Strategy Formation	Competencies from level below, plus • Strategic focus with broader, longer-term view • Higher levels of developing others • Sophisticated influence strategies based on in-depth understanding of others and of organisation's policies	• Networks and builds relationships • Takes a strong leadership role • Greater level of organisation commitment; models loyalty • Encourages development and provides feedback • Integrity	(Insufficient data due to small sample size for this role and level)
Strategic Alignment	Competencies from level below, plus • Focuses on providing strong visionary leadership • Willing to apply rules flexibly	• Seeks information to support decisions, negotiate and influence others • Most likely to seek input of others • Integrity	• Broad and strategic business perspective (understanding the organisation in the market) • Complex influence skills based on deep understanding of people, organisation and business • High integrity
Strategic Implementation	Competencies of level below, plus • Demands high performance from the team • More likely to act consistently with values and beliefs	• More initiative than preceding level • More likely than other collaborative managers to set challenging goals	• Continues to focus advice and service on the larger organisation • Continues to model loyalty to the organisation • Coaches and develops others • More likely to take a leadership role than at preceding level

Leadership Trait	Operational Role	Collaborative Roles	Advisory Roles
Tactical Implementation	• Focuses on business results • Focuses on own team, coaching, supporting, gaining input • More likely to take on challenges than peers in other roles	• Demonstrates responsive rather than proactive initiative • Demonstrates pattern recognition more than insight	• Focuses on service to the larger organisation • Models loyalty to the organisation • Manages subordinates one-on-one rather than as a team • Accepts need for flexibility

(The left margin of this table is labelled vertically: **Tactical**)

Work-Oriented Definitions: Work-oriented approaches focus on the identification of work activities that are essential to achieving work objectives. The definition proposed by the Management Charter Initiative in the UK, for example, takes work as its point of departure and focuses on occupational activities. These lists do not of themselves indicate the attributes required to accomplish such activities. Winterton and Delamare-Le Deist (2004) called this a functional approach. The functional or work-oriented approach focuses on identifying occupational standards for key roles, which are then broken down into units of competence. These are further sub-divided into elements of competence. For each element, performance criteria are specified with appropriate range indicators. The competence of individuals is assessed against actual performance in the workplace. This approach is also used in some European countries, e.g. Germany. Nordhaug and Grunhaug (1994) envisaged a notion of competency which focuses on the ability to perform the activities found within an occupation. Tolley (1987) suggested that work-oriented approaches place strong emphasis on the performance requirements for job positions rather than the characteristics of job-holders. Work-oriented definitions tend to assume that these characteristics already exist. Bell and Dale (1999) criticise the work-oriented approach because of its inability to capture many informal outcomes of work. Winterton and Delamare-Le Dist (2004) suggested that work-oriented approaches have inadequate theoretical underpinnings: they focus on the demonstration of competence rather than the way in which knowledge is acquired.

Table 6.4 summarises key differences between worker- and work-orientated approaches.

Table 6.4: Differences in Definition of Competencies: The European versus the US Approach

Basis for Difference	European Approach Work-Oriented	US Approach Worker-Oriented
Purpose	Assessment and certification of employees	Development of competencies to enhance performance
Focus	Focus on job/individual characteristics and skill accumulation	Focus on individual behaviour and attributes
Procedure to Develop	Produce performance standards for job functions and professions	Produce descriptions of excellent behaviour and attitudes to define standards

Basis for Difference	European Approach Work-Oriented	US Approach Worker-Oriented
Role of Organisational Context	Context is not as significant as professional area and specific job functions	Context defines the behaviours and traits required
Conceptualisation of Work/Individual	The characteristics of the work are the point of departure	Greater emphasis on the individual than on specific tasks
Methodological Approach	More multimethod and quantitative	Rationalistic and positivistic
Scope	Competencies are specific to professions	Competencies are specific to organisation
Measurement	Documentation of evidence of work activities and experiences denotes evidence of competency	Quantitative measurement and identification of a correlation between possession of attributes and work performance
Role of Assessor	Formally assessed by external assessor to determine level	Assessment of performance of job supervisors and job incumbent
Perspective of learning advocated	Constructivist perspective of learning	Cognitive perspective of learning

Multidimensions Definitions: Multidimensional approaches draw on the best of worker- and work-oriented approaches. It is, however, difficult to find examples of the multidimensional approach in the literature. Veres, Locklear and Sims (1990) used a multidimensional approach to assess the ideal competencies of members of the police force. Their descriptions consisted of forty-six personal attributes, which were expressed in the form of statements of knowledge, skill and attitudes that corresponded to twenty-three police attributes. The work activities and the personal attributes were then quantified in percentage terms as they related to police work.

Holton and Lynham (2000) offered another example of a multidimensional approach. They identified six 'competency domains' related to the performance of the organisation at process level and individual level. These domains were broken down into 'competency groups' and then further divided into 'sub competencies'. At the organisational level, they proposed strategic thinking and strategic stewards. At a process level, they suggested two competency domains, process management and process planning. At the individual level, they proposed employee performance and employee appraisal as the two key competency domains. These competencies are based on functional job-related standards, but they are clearly underpinned by behavioural competencies.

Cheetham and Chivers (1998) proposed a multidimensional model comprising five sets of interconnected competencies. Their model proposed the following:

- Cognitive competencies, including underpinning theory and concepts as well as informal tacit knowledge gained experientially.
- Functional competencies (skills or know-how), which they define as those things that a job-holder should be able to perform.
- Personal competencies, which are defined as relatively enduring characteristics of the manager that are related to superior performance.

- Ethical competencies, which are defined as personal and professional values and the ability to make ethical decisions in the workplace.
- Meta-competencies, which focus on the ability to cope with uncertainty and included learning and reflection.

Winterton and Delamare-Le Deist (2004) suggested that the French approach to competencies is multidimensional in nature. It focuses on knowledge, functional competence and behavioural competencies.

Rationalist versus Constructivist Approaches: Rationalist approaches have dominated the discourse on competencies. These approaches do have limitations, in particular their inability to capture what constitutes competence. The descriptions emerging from rationalist approaches are general and sometimes abstract. Jacobs (1989) suggested, for example, that Boyatzis' model does not always generalise. He concludes that different managerial jobs require different competencies. Rationalist approaches place too much emphasis on quantitative measures and do not capture the complexity of managerial work and competence in work performance. Sandberg (1994) suggested that definitions of competence may confirm a researcher's own model competence rather than capturing the manager's competence.

Constructivist approaches to competency argue that rationalist approaches overlook the ways managers interpret and experience their work. They view competencies as integrating worker and work from one key entity. Competency, therefore, is constituted by the meaning the work has for the manager through his or her experience of it. Interpretative approaches are context-rich and focus on capturing the manager's experience of work. The interpretativist approach is not popular in managerial practice and would be a difficult sell to many organisations. A small number of constructivist approaches are found in the academic literature. Dreyfus and Dreyfus (1986) found that the attributes used to accomplish performance are not context-free, but are integrated with particular types of work situations regardless of the level of competence acquisition. The attributes of effective performance are, in many cases, tacit in nature. Giddens (1984) suggested that work activities are performed in practical consciousness, which consists of what managers know tacitly about how to proceed. The tacit dimension represents an important contribution of the constructivist approach. There is a lot of evidence to indicate that how managers work differs significantly from descriptions in manuals. The attributes used in managerial work are context-depicted because of managers' ways of experiencing that work. Interpretative approaches do not explain how individual attributes are integrated into work performance.

Stoof et al. (2002) suggested that it is not necessary to achieve a precise definition of competency within a constructivist approach. The key issue is viability or the notion that the definition should be adequate to the situation in which it is used. They highlighted three variables that increase the viability of a definition of competency.
- *People*: The construction of a competency definition is frequently a team-based activity, but individuals are likely to have different interpretations of the meaning of competency. It is important to recognise that such differences exist and to agree on a definition that is acceptable to the team.
- *Goals*: The way in which a definition of competency is found depends on the goal of the definition. What is the definition going to be used for? Is it a redefinition of a role, development or leadership competencies? Competency definitions that are too global in nature may not be workable.
- *Context*: Context refers to the broader organisation. This raises questions concerning what the organisation does. For what organisational processes will the definition be used? Any definition should fit organisational processes and should be comprehensible to key stakeholders.

EXHIBIT 6.2

Perspective on Practice: A Situationalist or Constructivist Perspective of Competency Development

The competency literature generally adopts a universalist approach and applies it in a deductive way. Competency models are usually defined in a top-down way, through the use of generic descriptions that have application to different contexts and work situations. This approach is, however, questioned by some academics, for example Capaldo, Iandoli and Zollo, who highlight that the increased standardisation using a top-down approach produces a paradox: organisations end up with competencies that are similar, whereas the literature highlights the need to have distinctive competencies. The descriptions which are produced using the top-down approach tend to be very general and do not prove useful to leadership development specialists. The authors argue for a situationalist approach, which recognises that competencies are influenced by organisation culture, the extent and nature of social interaction and the unique ways in which people make sense of their jobs in organisations. Therefore, what constitutes competency is determined by the social context in which competencies are advocated and developed over time.

Capaldo, Iandoli and Zollo suggest that competency can be defined in this way: 'An individual ability or characteristic that is activated by a worker, together with personal, organisational or environmental resources to cope successfully with specific work situations.'

They define individual abilities and characteristics as personal attributes such as skills, know-how and traits. Resources are the means for action and include relationships and facilities. These are made available to the individual, the organisation or the external environment. Job situations are defined as spaces of action and include behaviours and results. Competencies, according to this approach, are manifest in two ways: when the performance that results from certain behaviour is considered by a customer to be above average; and when the performance is achieved through unexpected or surprising behaviour. This emerging competency is one that the organisation does not realise it has, but employees have developed it through individual learning and it is designed to cope with new or unexpected work situations.

The mapping of competencies using a situationalist model provides a number of challenges to organisations and requires a methodological approach which elicits contributions from employees. Job-holders describe their own and others' superior performance. The elicitation of these descriptions requires a high level of interaction between the analyst and organisational members. Three key issues need to be addressed:

Types of information to be collected: The analyst will need to identify salient job situations which are used by the job-holder to frame his/her work. A work or job situation focuses on describing how an employee or manager interprets a task, the commitment the employee has to undertaking the task, the behaviour exhibited and activities undertaken, the network of customers and the available resources. The task of the analyst is to provide a description of a competency which highlights how managers experience their daily work, how they interpret the outcomes of their action and how they create meaning through their interaction with other members of the organisation.

Information sources: The sources of information used by the analyst are represented by the job-holder. Job-holders provide the elements necessary for the analysis. These information sources are filtered through the subjectivity of the job-holder. The job-holder provides a great deal of information on the dimensions of the competency. It is also useful to get the viewpoint of other organisational members on a given role. They can express specific expectations through their interaction with the individual who performs that specific role. The authors suggest that the analyst should identify a network of organisational members who act as organisational observers. They should have expressed expectations concerning the role and include the employee, the direct supervisor and one or more peers or collaborators. This multi-source approach enables the analyst to secure an understanding of the whole set of job situations for a particular role.

Techniques for analysing and mapping explanatory discourse: The analyst needs to select techniques that enable the elicitation of explanatory discourse. This can be done through semi-structured interviews and test analysis technique (argument analysis). During the interview the analyst elicits an overall evaluative judgment about the performance of an individual performing a given role. The analyst then explores the reasons for this judgement. The interview will then develop according to the answers provided by the observer. The questions will seek more detailed explanations until the analyst achieves an appropriate level of understanding. This protocol is used with each information source.

Each interview can be analysed using argument analysis technique. This approach identifies arguments and the reasons that the interviewees provided to explain their excellent performance. The technique identifies the key claims, the evidence for the claims and any linguistic expressions limiting the validity of a claim.

Data acquired through this interview process is coded to identify the most relevant information. This will include descriptions of job situations, the relevance of each situation to the overall job, short descriptions of individual characteristics and resources. The analysis process should ideally be undertaken by a team who worked through the data to identify recurring job situations, individual characteristics and resources. This enables the team to build shared definitions and achieve inclusive definitions of the competency.

Source: Capaldo, Iandoli and Zollo (2006)

The Value of Competencies in a Leadership Development Context

Consensus exists concerning why organisations should consider competency frameworks as part of management and leadership development activities. They should, however, be considered as part of a wider approach to human resource management and change. The research highlights that organisations should consider the following:

- Increased performance demands and competencies can be used as a mechanism to establish appropriate performance standards. Changes in structures and roles and competencies are an appropriate framework within which to define skills and behaviours.
- Competency frameworks should not be used retrospectively. An organisation needs to define the competencies required for future success. Organisations should avoid the pitfall of including ill-defined characteristics which have no measurable impact on manager performance.
- Organisations should draw on internal and external models of best practice in order to enhance an awareness of current change initiatives. It is also important to benchmark practices with others found in similar organisations.
- Line management should have a stake in shaping necessary leadership competencies.
- Competency initiatives should be considered on a pilot basis.
- It is useful to consider using competency frameworks as a basis for experience and success. It is also important to make sure that time frames are realistic and that pilot programmes are initiated in a positive environment.

Table 6.5 provides a summary of the main advantages and disadvantages of competencies for management and leadership development.

Table 6.5: Advantages and Disadvantages of a Competency Approach to Management and Leadership Development

Advantages	Disadvantages
• Competency has no time limit; individuals can learn at their own pace • Enterprises have the opportunity to shape their own competency model • Competency models help align individual and business needs • Ageing labour force has encouraged national government to invest in lifelong learning and competencies • Competency approaches such as the NCVQ in the UK allow certification for achievement of competency in certain tasks, skills or job roles/education • Competency can lead to greater efficiency and outputs for industry • Competency models for delivery of education can lead to a more valid delivery of education suitable for industry and working life • Competency models develop all levels, not just the hierarchical level • Competency does not reinforce the status or hierarchical level in the workplace • Some competencies are readily recognisable, i.e. knowledge, skills and abilities • Competencies can help teams achieve extraordinary things, e.g. climb Mount Everest • The absence of agreement on what competency actually is allows a degree of autonomy to shape one's own model • Competency models can achieve best practice in selection, recruitment, appraisal, staff retention, development, special projects teams. Delivery of valid educational programmes and greater efficiency in national economies can be achieved • Cultures with strong individual development values, e.g. Scandinavia, USA, are more likely to embrace competency • Competency models complement the idea of development and employability for workers	• Disagreement as to what competency actually is • Because of the vagueness of the definition, there is possibly too much flexibility to call other management instruments competency • Can be time-consuming and costly to develop • Some individual competencies are difficult to measure, e.g. iceberg theory (traits and motives) • Competencies are regarded as overly bureaucratic and elaborate • Notions of competency are often those of the researcher • Transferability of competency models to other organisations is difficult • Competency models in some cultures are seen as a control instrument for capital over the workers, e.g. the Netherlands • Some companies do not have a competency ethos • Some competency models do not have validity for other situations, i.e. education vs industry • Sometimes HRD and competencies are seen as a 'fix-it' shop for incompetent staff • Competencies of interpersonal skills are often incorrectly used in job advertisements to make the job sound interesting • Employees are often selected for interpersonal competencies over technical competencies, employers taking the view that the technical side is easier to teach • Selection for interpersonal over technical competencies could be detrimental to technical competency in the long term • Perspectives on competency can be a problem, i.e. those with a T&D background think that competency can be taught

Sparrow (2002) suggested that competencies have both content and process benefits for management and leadership development. Specific process benefits include:

- Involvement of line managers in the identification of competencies and the design of assessment and development interventions can result in stronger ownership of leadership development.
- The process of developing competency frameworks helps to create a shared understanding of the types of leadership required in the organisation.
- Competencies enable more informed decisions about resourcing issues. This can include decisions concerning whether to buy or to develop managerial talent.

- Competencies provide a language for self-development and self-assessment by managers and represent a good basis for coaching and other developmental relationships.
- Competency frameworks are valuable in generating information on the development of successful teams and they represent a tool for establishing a development culture.

EXHIBIT 6.3

Assumptions Underpinning Leadership Competency Models

Hollenbeck, McCall and Silzer (2006) identify the four assumptions that underpin leadership competency models:

- A single set of characteristics describe effective leaders: Competencies have the potential to predict managerial behaviour which, in turn, predicts leadership effectiveness. A challenge to this view is that it represents a strategy to leverage the experience, lessons learned and knowledge of effective leaders in the interest of developing future leadership talent.
- Competencies are independent of each other and of context: This assumption is challenged on the grounds that competencies are interrelated. Furthermore, strengths can be weaknesses and the overall effectiveness of a leader depends on various combinations of competencies. The key challenge concerns the use of the competencies in a particular context to achieve results.
- Competencies represent the most appropriate framework to think about leadership effectiveness: There is evidence that competency frameworks have enhanced the overall status of leadership development in organisations. They give leadership development specialists desirable visibility and allow them to talk the language of senior managers. Managers are most likely attracted to competency models because they are based on their experiences and they make some logical sense. Competency models are a good way to start talking about leadership development.
- Competencies should be the basis of HR systems: Competency models are increasingly used for selection, training, performance management, rewards and leadership development. However, the general viewpoint is that it is the way in which human resource systems are implemented that counts rather than the underlying model. Competency models are, at best, a very strong organising framework for bundles of HR practices. They give these practices a sense of coherence.

Identifying Leadership Competencies

Competency identification and assessment are controversial issues. Considering criticisms about the validity and the reliability of identification processes (Burgoyne 1989; Collin 1989; Jubb and Robotham 1997), many of the assessment methods are strongly based on positivistic traditions and reflect scientific principles. Work-oriented approaches advocate methods such as the job element method, whereas worker-oriented approaches advocate personal profiling. Multidimensional approaches do not advocate any particular method, but suggest the use of multiple methods.

The literature on competency identification is strongly positivistic in orientation. It assumes a causal relationship between underlying characteristics of competence and superior performance. The research evidence, however, reveals mixed evidence of this relationship. Early work by Boyatzis (1982), for example, found that, where a relationship exists, it could at best be described as associational. Parker and Wall (1998) took a more definite position, arguing that no systematic relationship exists between the possession of particular competencies and performance outcomes. More recent research reveals a more positive picture of the beneficial role of competencies in individual and group performance improvements. The Competitiveness White Paper (DTI 1995), for example, argued that management performance can be improved through the development of standards and qualifications for management that are also linked to development and training opportunities. In a comprehensive study of competency-based management development in sixteen organisations, Winterton and Winterton (1996) reported major improvements in individual performance attributable to the effective use of competency frameworks.

Work-oriented models view competencies as recognisable in terms of job-specific outcomes. It follows that the competencies required for a job or role are assessed through an analytical process called functional analysis. It is envisaged that such a top-down process will yield a set of items including the job's key purpose and key roles. Each is broken down in turn into units of competence, which are then referred to by elements of competence and performance standards. UK and Irish organisations use a variation of the work-oriented approach, in which they try to ascertain the manner in which the components of competence interact. The UK competency system, for example, views competence as consisting of three basic components: task, task management and the job environment.

Worker-oriented models view measurement as concerned with generating lists of behaviours or personal attributes that relate to effective role performance. Essentially, the problem is that, in order to measure something, one needs a yardstick. Consequently, where alternative models of competence exist, it is difficult to arrive at a universal understanding of a notion of competence that is amenable to measurement for the purposes of benchmarking levels of competency across industry sectors.

Specific Methods Used to Identify Competencies

Organisations have a number of options when they take on the task of identifying competencies. These include observation, self-description reports, interviews, focus groups and surveys. Each method has unique strengths and weaknesses:

- **Observation:** Observation involves a specialist observing and recording the activities of the manager. This will provide details about activities, but it does not indicate the relative importance of the work over its difficulties. Observation is useful, but when used in isolation it is of limited value. Observation is challenging in a managerial context because a lot of work consists of making decisions. It follows that many managerial processes are not open to direct observation (pure observational data will generally need to be supplemented by some form of interviewing). Observation is a time-consuming activity and is subject to various observational errors. This latter problem may highlight validity problems with the data collected and for this reason it is unwise to rely solely on observation-derived data.
- **Self-Description Reports:** Self-description reports require the manager to compile an account of their activities. This is usually accomplished through the use of diaries, logs or a written account completed over a specified time period. This approach offers a significant advantage in that it does not require the management development specialist to gather the information. The specialist will, however, need to interpret the data. It is a potentially subjective approach in that it relies on the manager to compile information accurately. The manager may over-emphasise or de-emphasise certain aspects of the job.
- **Job Analysis Interview:** The job analysis interview is a frequently used technique. Goel (1988) defines a job analysis interview as a meeting between two or more people for the purpose of evaluating information about a job or role. It is a very useful approach in a managerial context because it is both flexible and potentially valid. This latter

characteristic is, however, dependent on the skills of the interviewer. Interviews are flexible in that they can range from highly structured to semi-structured questions. More structured approaches will yield more useful and comparable information. A structured interview approach will use pre-prepared questions. However, it is important to allow for some elements of flexibility. The interviewer should allow for the use of more supplementary questions which arise out of the content of the interview. It is important to note that job analysis may not be very effective in identifying the softer components of the managerial job, such as the measurement of behaviour, attitude, intuition and creativity.

- **Focus Groups:** Focus groups have become increasingly popular. They are essentially group interviews in which a moderator guides the interview while small groups discuss the topics that the interviewer raises. What participants in the group contribute during the discussion represents the essential data. Focus groups typically consist of between six and eight participants. The moderation may be carried out by the management-development specialist. Three factors need to be considered when using focus groups in a competency identification process: budgetary, ethical and time concerns. Ethical concerns are very important because the process may involve issues around confidentiality of data. It is critical that clear ground rules are set with the group. Merton, Fiske and Kendall (1992) suggested four criteria for effective focus group operation: 1) they should cover a large range of topics; 2) the should produce data which is specific; 3) they should encourage interrelations which facilitate the emergence of feelings; and 4) they should consider the manager's background in relation to his/her responses. Once data is gathered, it needs to be carefully analysed in a structured and systematic way. Focus groups are, however, subject to the operation of group processes and therefore the outputs may be subject to biases.

- **Surveys/Questionnaires:** The conduct of individual interviews with a large sample of managers is both time-consuming and costly. An alternative is to use a questionnaire or questionnaires in combination with a sample of follow-up interviews. Questionnaires offer significant advantages in that they can be circulated to a large group of managers. They can also be analysed in a relatively short period of time. Questionnaires can take a range of formats (e.g. a multiple-choice format, which allows managers to choose one item from a list of options, or an open-ended format, which allows managers to compile the questionnaire in their own words). It is also possible to use a ranked or rating format. Ranking formats allow the manager to prioritise a list in a particular order, whereas a rating format requires the manager to assign points to each alternative using a prescribed scale. Questionnaires need to be long enough to gather the required information, while at the same time not being so long that the manager will be discouraged from completing them. They tend to elicit a relatively poor response rate, unless respondents are interviewed, and the sample who respond may be biased. It is important to note that the design of a robust questionnaire is a complex process.

- **Critical Incident Technique:** This approach is very popular amongst US academics and leadership development practitioners. Flanagan (1954) originated the idea. It requires managers to pinpoint the key incidents in a task which result in either effective or ineffective performance. This has the potential to provide detailed information concerning how the job is conducted. Although the critical incident technique has value on its own, it is perhaps most effective when it is combined with other methods. Some commentators have suggested using it in combination with the repertory grid technique. This approach asks managers to describe features of work behaviour and to explain which features contribute to effective work performance. The choice of incident made by the manager, as well as the manager's description of his/her actions, can be subjective, and this has implications for the usability of the outputs. The evaluation of a manager's performance is subjective in itself and generally, in critical situations, it is difficult to predict individual behaviour (whether of high performance or average performance) and consequently the future consistency of behaviour is difficult to predict.

Table 6.6 provides a summary of each method and its effectiveness.

Table 6.6: Methods Used to Identify Management Competencies

Method	Researchers	Process	Effectiveness
Direct Observation	Boam and Sparrow (1992); Mirabile (1997)	• Employees are asked to perform a number of critical tasks. • Observers record the tasks being performed, which in turn form the basis of competencies	• Relatively cheap to implement and not time-consuming • Provides a clear picture of the observable elements • Not effective when observing mental processes, e.g. decision-making • Subject to observer error
Critical Incident Technique	New (1996); Thomas and Mabey (1994)	• Involves clarifying the differences between average and superior performers • Interviews with the job holder, supervisor or other relevant person • Participants asked to describe particular job incidents • Process is repeated a number of times • Individuals must describe what behaviours were displayed, who was involved and the outcome	• Ability to capture unusual behaviours • Involves key individuals in the job process • Requires a long data-collection process • Requires critical knowledge of the position • Capacity to identify good and bad behaviours
Job-Competency Assessment Method	Spencer and Spencer (1993); McClelland (1973)	• A team is formed to identify the skills and knowledge required • Team conducts interviews to identify attributes of outstanding performers • Data used to develop a competency model • Expert panels validate the model to determine its effectiveness	• Data can be collected in an effective manner • Useful to identify functions of individual jobs • Tends to focus on job functions and overlook personal attitudes • May take some time to analyse data and generate an outcome

Method	Researchers	Process	Effectiveness
Expert Panels	Spencer and Spencer (1993); Cockerill and Hunt (1995); Boam and Sparrow (1992)	• Selection of a panel of in-house experts and others who have superior knowledge • Panel observes employees performing tasks and identifies a list of competencies that they consider relevant to job • List is prioritised to identify those who require priority development	• May give the process legitimacy and credibility within the organisation • May have difficulty pulling together a panel of appropriate experts • Suitable for larger organisations • A tendency to miss out on certain competencies
Structured Interviews	Goel (1988); Armstrong (2006); Moser and Kalton (1971)	• A conversation between interviewer and manager • Designed to elicit certain information • May vary in structure • Based on the use of questions	• Potential to gather lots of detailed information • Suitable with smaller samples of managers • Depends on the effectiveness of the interviewer • Subject to interviewer or interviewee bias
Surveys / Questionnaires	Bell (1993); Cohen and Manion (1989)	• They vary both in structure and format • They have a particular question order • They are generally non-labour-intensive • They gather the same type of information from different managers	• May have a poor response rate • Are effective in analysing large managerial population • Require specialist design and analysis expertise • Have the advantage of confidentiality
Focus Groups	Morgan (1997); Fiske and Kendall (1990)	• Consists of a group interviewing technique • Facilitated by a moderator • Consist of small groups of managers • Moderator works from a pre-determined set of discussion topics	• Require professional moderators to be effective • Have the potential to gather large amounts of information • Are time-consuming, costly and slow • Require specialist analysis skills

Measuring Competence: The Challenge for Organisations

The measurement of competencies is also a complex and controversial topic. First of all, it depends on whether the focus is on behavioural or output-based definitions of competence. This continuum raises the immediate question of what we are seeking to measure.

A behavioural or worker-oriented approach is often characterised as a soft approach. This perspective provides many challenges to those managers who wish to measure behaviour. It includes a very diverse set of elements such as motives, traits, self-concepts, content knowledge, cognitive and behavioural skills. These intangible elements are essentially perceptual and subjective. Behavioural competencies are derived from a process of criterion validation, in which competencies are derived from the behavioural standards of excellence displayed by top-performing managers.

An output or work-oriented approach to competencies focuses on concrete output measures. Output measures are derived from a process of criterion referencing. Criterion-referencing competencies focus on standards of actual work performance as a means of distinguishing competence.

The measurement of competencies assumes first that competence exists and second that it can be measured objectively. Debate arises concerning whether attempts to measure competence are based on a mistaken belief that such a thing exists as an unchanging, measurable entity. A static view of competencies is considered unrealistic. Competences consist of much more dynamic elements, indistinguishable from the environment within which they operate. Competencies, therefore, are shaped by the system that purports to measure them as independent variables. The measurement of competence involves making a value judgement based on the assumption that competence is a linear combination of behavioural performance characteristics. We will focus on two approaches to measurement: behaviourally anchored rating scales (BARS) and conventional rating scales.

Behaviourally Anchored Rating Scales (BARS)

Behaviourally anchored rating scales rate the competence of managers by comparing actual observed behaviours with numerically rated behavioural descriptions. BARS generally contain between five and nine points, three or four of which are usually marked by behavioural descriptions. These points have been differentiated using other techniques such as critical incident. Those behavioural descriptions are then used by managers as scale anchors to determine the extent of the competency. The scale-anchor description serves as a guide and is not to be considered prescriptive. In the context of competency measurement, it is unwise to have descriptions that are too specific. Box 6.1 provides a summary of guidelines that managers should consider when constructing a BARS for use in managerial competency assessment.

Box 6.1: Guidelines for the Construction of BARS

- Begin each anchor sentence with an action verb. Use the active voice and try to describe observable behaviours.
- The anchor sentence should be between five and ten words long.
- Keep the BARS simple. It should be used to measure one behaviour at a time. This makes it easier for the respondent to answer and helps eliminate uncertainty.
- Try not to use words such as 'and'/'or' because they may indicate the presence of two separate thoughts.
- Avoid judgemental expressions such as 'effective' or 'excellent' because these words are not objective.
- Make sure to address the rater.
- Use words such as 'demonstrate' and 'show' sparingly. These words tend to indicate that the description is not sufficiently thought through.

BARS do have a number of advantages that make them appropriate for managerial competency assessment. Boam and Sparrow (1992) suggested that well-designed BARS should display objective, psychometric properties. BARS define what a specific score means in terms of observable behaviour and are therefore considered a reliable and valid means of measuring competence. BARS have the potential to increase the objectivity of the measurement process. They can reduce the amount of rater error. Where managers are involved in the design of BARS, this can help to engender ownership and to increase enthusiasm for the measurement process.

The outputs of BARS can be used to generate specific feedback. Baron (1988), for example, found that increasing the specificity of feedback that managers give to ratees led to enhanced role clarity and greater satisfaction with the process. BARS are also considered useful in making more accurate assessments, independent of situational factors, because they concentrate on the measurement of behaviour rather than output.

It is likely that BARS-based competency measurement will be susceptible to rater errors such as halo and leniency. Halo effects are positive, whereas leniency effects are negative. There is also the suggestion that the degree of rater agreement is not significantly enhanced by the use of BARS. BARS methodology does not make allowances for situational constraints that may be influencing observable behaviours. The methodology also suffers from the problem of rater error. It is likely that there will be blurring between the categories of motives, traits, behaviours and outputs. It may be difficult to isolate and measure these specific elements individually. There is also the pragmatic consideration that BARS methodology is very costly to develop.

Conventional Rating Scales

The aim of conventional rating scales is to produce overall scores that are comparable with the scores of other managers in similar roles. Unlike the BARS scale, conventional scales are anchored not by behaviours but by alternative descriptions of intensity, such as levels of agreement, importance, effectiveness or frequency. It is argued that conventional scales are suitable for the measurement of traits, motives and outputs. It is claimed that they lend a degree of objectivity to competency measurement.

Research suggests that there are four rateable dimensions to implement. These are:

- **Intensity:** This refers to the intention or personal characteristic as reflected by the competencies or the actions that are taken in carrying out the intention.
- **Complexity:** The number of things, data, concepts or people that are taken into account by the rater.
- **Time Horizon:** The extent to which a situation is projected into the future and to which action is taken based on the anticipation of the future.
- **The Size of the Impact:** The number and position of people impacted upon and the size of the problem addressed.

Box 6.2 provides guidelines concerning the development of rating scales.

Box 6.2: Guidelines for Developing Rating Scales

- It is important to know what competence looks like at each rated level. Conventional scales do not describe the situation at each rated level. There should be an awareness and consensus among managers of what each level looks like. Where this consensus does not exist, it is likely that conventional scales will be less effective.

- Keep the description of the scale category simple. It is best to stick to one behaviour or output at a time. It is wise to subdivide competencies into individual behaviour. This will ensure more accurate measurement.
- Use scale categories that are relatively independent of each other. If they are interdependent, it will create confusion.
- Use an even number of behavioural ratings. This will help ensure that managers do not take the neutral category. Six category levels are perhaps more effective than, say, three. They provide a wider range.
- An excessive number of rating levels should be avoided. Nine or more rating levels are considered too cumbersome. It is likely that managers will ignore the two or three lowest levels in this case.
- It is important that managers are trained in the use of the scale. It is likely that managers will use gut feeling where there is insufficient training. Training can help to ensure that the scales is used in a similar way for different rates.

Rating scales have benefits in the context of the measurement of competence, but the most significant difficulty concerns the lack of differentiation among a large pool of managers. It is likely, in this case, that low averages and rater error will occur. Where a simple one-dimensional rating scale is used, it will be difficult to distinguish one manager from another. Where two or more sub-levels are used together, the amount of detail gained about competence is enhanced. Ward (1997) recommends the use of a combination of current judgements of competence with judgements of expected competence. He also suggests the weighting of effectiveness with importance.

Introducing Leadership Competency Models

Organisations need to give careful consideration to a number of issues when introducing leadership competency models. These issues focus on resources, clarity of definition of competencies, the divergence of individual and organisational needs, conflicts with other HR strategies and what type of competency model to select.

- **Resource Intensive:** The introduction of competency-based approaches are resource intensive. This approach requires considerable time, energy and cost to implement effectively. A robust and well-resourced management development strategy is required in order to both initiate and support the process. Competency-based approaches require a considerable amount of support from line managers, individual managers and training and development specialists. Organisations frequently underestimate the role and function of continuous support mechanisms for competencies.
- **Achieving Clarity over Definition of Competencies:** This proves to be a challenging problem, both intellectually and politically. The preparation of competency definitions and questions requires a large number of questions to be addressed. The training and development function needs to be clear concerning the types of competencies that are required and these competencies need to be properly defined. Sometimes organisations over-compensate on different issues and produce competency descriptions that are too flexible and too detailed. This can give rise to unanticipated and inappropriate interpretations. Currie and Darby (1995) suggested that a generic competency approach presents problems for organisations. The first relates to the definition of competence. The generic approach makes the assumption that managerial skills are general in nature. Competency distinctions frequently encounter difficulties in making distinctions between high- and lower-performing managers. Organisations may lack the skills to assess the

softer dimensions such as assertiveness, creativity, sensitivity and intuition. Many organisations invest too much time on the assessment of competencies and not enough on their development. Competency models can add too much complexity and bureaucracy.

- **Divergence between Individual and Organisational Needs:** The competencies required by the organisation to meet particular business objectives may be significantly different from those required by individual managers. This is a problem often experienced by organisations that implement competency-based approaches. Individual managers are more likely to focus on the development of a portfolio of competencies that are valued in the market place as well as in the organisation. Managers may place more emphasis on portability of competencies, whereas organisations are interested in organisation-specific competencies.

- **Conflicts with Other Training and HR Strategies:** Competency-based approaches, because of their strong emphasis on the future, may conflict with more immediate training and development needs. Competency-based approaches have a tendency to concentrate on professional and technical competencies, whereas organisations may be more concerned with competencies for specific functions. Some organisations use competencies for performance appraisal and reward purposes, in addition to management development. Where such links exist, managers may be slower to acknowledge competency weaknesses. This can emerge as an important conflict because organisations may perceive pressure to reward competencies.

- **Is it Possible to Train for All Competencies?:** This is a complex but frequently encountered question that organisations are faced with when considering the introduction of a competency-based approach. The development of the more technical competencies is relatively straightforward, but the development of the behavioural-type competencies will vary from manager to manager. Not all managers possess the same development potential.

- **Selecting the Most Appropriate Model:** Organisations invest a great deal in developing competency frameworks. They may begin with a more general off-the-shelf model, or they may develop a model from scratch. Three key issues are important when developing the most appropriate model:
  1. What types of leadership roles are appropriate for the competency model? The organisation may seek to develop a model which has application to a variety of leadership roles. It may, on the other hand, wish to develop models which are specific to particular functions, business units or levels of management.
  2. Should the competency model focus on current or future requirements? This question requires that organisations need to develop an understanding of how the leadership context will change in the future. This is a difficult task for organisations that have not fully defined their strategic direction.
  3. How should acceptance of the model be ensured? This suggests that managers need to be involved in the generation and implementation of data related to the development of the competency model. Involvement in the design process is likely to engender greater acceptance. Buy-in is enhanced when the model is integrated into career systems, performance management processes and reward systems.

Box 6.3 presents some questions that the management development specialist should consider when developing a competency-based approach to management development.

- Does the organisation intend using the approach for external and internal benchmarking purposes?
- How will a competency-based approach raise the profile of management development in the organisation?
- How does the approach align with the organisation's other training and development initiatives?
- How does the approach align with other human resource management practices?
- What wider benefits will the approach bring to the organisation?
- How flexible will the approach be? Is flexibility an important priority?
- What strategic needs of the organisation will a competency-based approach address?
- Will the approach have implications for succession planning and career development?
- How much of a shift will a competency approach represent for the organisation?
- What competencies are the most cost-effective to include in the approach?
- What are the most useful development strategies to develop particular competencies?

Competency-Based Approaches to Management and Leadership Development: Theoretical Issues

Organisations frequently face a dilemma: do they adopt macro competency-focused approaches which are perceived to be removed from daily life, or do they adopt a more micro competency- or job-focused approach, which Mangham (1990) suggests is normative and geared towards the development of 'identical' managers, as we have argued. Competency frameworks emphasise a functional view of management and propose models that seek to identify the ideal combination of knowledge, skills, attitudes and experiences. If managers possess these attributes, they will be superior performers. Competencies tend to be advocated as a route to superior performance. However, to focus solely on competencies as the basis on which to develop rounded, competent managers is somewhat unrealistic. Context is very important in explaining the potential contribution of competencies to managerial performance. Cheng, Dainty and Moore (2003) illustrated how organisational context is relevant. They proposed three scenarios:

- Managers may be encouraged to develop a level of performance superior to existing performance in order to contribute to a superior organisational performance. The emphasis will be on an incremental improvement in performance that will contribute to a new cultural set-up.
- Organisations may use competencies to support a strategy of building manager performance to superior levels in order to deal with organisational expansion.
- Organisations experiencing significant organisational transformation may use competency-based approaches to ensure a speedy development of superior performance in a selected group of managers.

These scenarios suggest that organisations require different performance improvements. Other aspects of context which competency-based approaches often fail to consider include the emphasis placed on teamwork, the uncertainty of the organisation's environment and the rate of change in the environment.

The issues of power and control are central to discussions of leadership competency. A developmental, humanist approach argues that the notion of competencies can be both liberating and empowering – an equalising force in the context of management and leadership development. Competency models suggest that managers should be provided with a high degree of self-control and self-regulation on the basis that such committed managers will work actively to achieve the objectives of the organisation. A more utilitarian perspective suggests that the management of employees leads to the creation of organisational competitive advantage. This position is characterised by tight management control, close direction and presentation of required competencies. It also advocates the concept of 'fit' between strategic objectives and competencies possessed by managers. The power relations that exist within the competency approach do not, however, reflect developmental humanism, but everything that developmental humanism is not. Competency frameworks present a dilemma in that managers wishing to be considered competent are, in effect, forced to reshape and reinterpret themselves, to reconfigure their experience in order to match the specific demands of the competency discourse. Even the assessor, where there is one, lacks autonomy because of the requirement to make judgements within a specified vocabulary and to maintain appropriate records. Competencies are a key organisational tool to instil consistency in behaviour and attitude across the organisation.

A competency approach fits comfortably within a strategy/structure/systems model of organisations and consequently may have questionable value in contemporary post-modernist notions of leadership and more person-focused development perspectives. Indeed, a fundamental premise underpinning utilitarianism, the idea of strategic integration, is somewhat problematic in itself because it lacks precision both at a theoretical and at a measurement level. It does, however, represent a common justification for the utilisation of leadership competencies in organisations. A utilitarian perspective poses a number of dilemmas for management and leadership development, specifically the need to justify management and leadership development in strategic terms and to treat managers in a rational and quantitative way. It may result in very narrowly defined, short-term learning activities at the expense of more developmental learning. The advocacy of utilitarian-instrumentalist notions of competencies are associated with learning initiatives designed to contribute to bottom-line performance, so this means that line managers' efforts will concentrate on revenue-producing learning at the expense of ensuring that managers are fully developed and retained.

There are also epistemological tensions associated with the use of competencies in management and leadership development activities. Competency frameworks espouse a rationalistic, positivistic perspective and make some important assumptions about work and behaviour. Competency tends to be an attribute-based concept relating to a specific set of attributes that managers utilise to perform work. Those who perform effectively are considered to have a superior set of competencies. There is a strong bias towards considering notions of competency in a context-free way. This is manifest in prescriptions about how possession of specific competencies can lead to high performance, irrespective of the organisational context within which they are utilised. Competency can be viewed as an atomistic, mechanistic, bureaucratic concept.

Cockerill and Hunt (1995) suggested three distinct perspectives: 'traditionalists', 'inventors' and 'scientists'. For traditionalists, the use of leadership competencies is based on the behaviour of the most successful managers or employees in the organisation. They view successful job performance in terms of speed of career advancement. Traditionalists advocate the use of the characteristics of quickly promoted individuals as the basis for the development of an organisation's competency model. Inventors focus on predicting what an organisation and its attitudes will be in the future and consider this to be the most effective way of identifying appropriate managerial behaviours. The outcome of this perspective is the creation of competency based on imaginary future organisations. The scientific perspective places emphasis on identifying, measuring and developing behaviours that will distinguish individuals who continuously outperform others. It advocates that there are generalisable high-performance competencies that distinguish high-performing from average-performing employees.

Descriptions of competency do not factor in the characteristics of the human agent. In particular, they give little consideration to when competencies are used, how they are used and the moderating influence of personal characteristics on their usage. Sandberg (2000) uses the term 'indirect descriptions of competency' to characterise a situation where the typologies advocated reflect the researcher's own models rather than capturing employees' notions or models of competence.

While the intention, if not the practice, is to use leadership competencies derived from national standards, the definition of these competencies is often based on rationalistic job analysis techniques, rather than more context-focused techniques. One alternative, the phenomenological approach, has made only modest impact to date. However, this literature postulates the view that our understanding of competence and competencies cannot ignore the internal organisational context, the role of the employee and their experiences of work. The tacit dimension is to the fore (Tyre and Von Heppel 1997; Fielding 1988). This contrasting tradition suggests that it is not the competencies themselves that are significant, but it is the way the manager experiences work that is fundamental to his/her competence. Competence, this perspective suggests, must therefore be internally rather than externally framed.

The emergence of a post-modernist lens has some value. It is argued that post-modernism, by embracing chaos and complexity, offers a coherent explanation of the unpredictable, uncertain and uncontrollable nature of the modern business environment. Free from the overarching ideological claims of positivism, it leaves open the possibility that competencies may need to be adjusted to take account of a range of contextual factors and, as a result, competency frameworks may differ from one organisation to another (Cockerill 1989).

The competency debate is not always sure what it wants to be. Three strands are evident: competencies as characteristics of individuals; competencies as characteristics of organisations; and competencies as a mode of discourse between education and the labour market. The first perspective essentially relates to characteristics of individuals. There are, however, differences in emphasis, the most important of which relates to whether these characteristics can be learned or whether they are innate. The dominant view is to emphasise the trainability dimension of competency and the potential contribution of workplace learning activities to the development of competencies (Eraut 1994: Fletcher 1992). A more traditional view emphasises that competencies and competence are given. Characteristics such as emotion, attitude and cognition originate from innate abilities and therefore cannot be learned; they can only be developed (Klink, Van Der Boon and Bos 2000). A related perspective is the notion that competencies do not relate to capacities, but instead to the willingness and ability of the employee to use his/her capacities in specific situations (Spencer 1983).

Conceptualisations of competencies as characteristics of the organisation take as their starting point the view that human competencies are a key resource available to organisations. The origins of this notion of competencies can be attributed to the work of Prahalad and Hamel (1990), who analysed the competitiveness of organisations and attributed it to the possession of core competencies. They postulated that organisations can possess unique clusters of factors that allow it to be competitive and that human capital is one of those factors. Resource-based perspectives of the firm utilise the notion of competencies in this fashion. They conceptualise the organisation as a collection of competencies and draw attention to issues of learning, including knowledge accumulation and experience. Cappelli and Singh (1992) suggested that competent employees have the potential to create competitive advantage, where such competencies are firm-specific and are difficult for competitors to imitate.

The issue of how firm-specific leadership competencies are is a controversial point. Boon and Van der Klink (2001) suggested that many organisations possess very fixed and rather stable list of competencies and do not engage in efforts to produce a set of firm-specific descriptions or take proactive steps to develop these competencies. While it is appropriate to conceptualise competencies in this way, this approach is problematic to implement in practice because it is very difficult to find the appropriate level of context specificity in the descriptions of competencies. They either come as lists with very broadly defined competencies or are so detailed and reductive as to be of limited pragmatic value.

A further consideration is whether competency frameworks should be based on current organisational priorities or should be future-oriented and derived from an organisation's vision statement. Such a dualistic choice is dependent on whether one views competencies as a tool enabling organisational change through direct communication with employees or as a behavioural modelling mechanism to deal with current organisational problems and difficulties. Those who are labelled 'inventors' would advocate a focus on future competencies.

Some commentators consider it to be an inappropriate conceptual stretch of the competency concept to regard it as a characteristic of the organisation. One problem that immediately arises is the variation in terminology used. Selznick (1957) used the term 'distinctive competence'. Teece (1990) talked about 'dynamic capabilities'. Prahalad and Hamel (1990) suggested the term 'core competencies', and Kamoche (1996) suggested 'human-resource competencies'. These definitions range from narrow, specific descriptions to very broad ones that can be somewhat tautological; capabilities are defined in terms of competence, and competence is then defined in terms of capability. The empirical support for core competencies at the organisational level lags significantly behind the theoretical development of competency frameworks. The notion is solid at the macro-theoretical level, but stands relatively unsupported by micro-theoretical models and empirical research. The theory would suggest that management and leadership development activities represent a vital, if not pivotal, component of organisational success and strategy. However, there is no systematic evidence of a transformation of management learning activities by organisations on either side of the Atlantic as a result of resource-based perspectives.

Conclusion

Leadership competencies have become an important aspect of leadership development. They are viewed as a critical component in ensuring that managers can realise their full potential while developing comprehensive management development systems and providing growth opportunities. As concepts, competencies are problematic and yet they are insufficiently differentiated from related concepts such as individual characteristics, skills and knowledge. The use of competencies in a management development context facilitates a continuous and well-integrated approach to management development. It is also an approach which offers advantages in areas such as personal development, greater promotability, employability and manager performance.

Leadership competency models consider the development of competence not in terms of any set programme of learning; the issue is not whether the employee is trained, but whether the employee can do what is required by the role, function, job or profession. How the competency is developed is unimportant. It is argued that competency has no time limits: individuals develop and acquire competencies at their own pace. Managers are considered to be not yet competent rather than incompetent. Notions of competency are advocated as egalitarian and premised on the view that, given the right motivation, circumstances and practice, anyone can develop almost any set of competencies. In a leadership development context, the notion of competency is based on the job, rather than on common standards of performance achievable in the workplace.

Summary of Key Points

- A competency-based approach sits comfortably within current thinking on careers and human resource development. There is an increased emphasis on personal responsibility for development. This approach also reflects a resource-based theory of the firm.
- Competency-based approaches are used by organisations because they help align managers' capabilities to business strategies and give the organisation a competitive advantage.
- When defining competencies, it is important to differentiate between competency and competence. Competencies are considered what managers need to be able to do to perform a role effectively, while also linking together the notion of what has to be done and to what standard of competence.
- Competency-based approaches are complex and resource-intensive. They require careful consideration and need to be implemented in a structured and systematic way.
- Leadership competency models should be designed to reflect context and the way in which managers enact their roles.

■ Discussion Questions

1. Suggest some arguments for the use of a competency-based approach to management development.

2. Is it possible to develop all leadership competencies? Explain.

3. What issues need to be considered when identifying and measuring the existence of competence in managers and leaders?

4. What suggestions would you make to ensure that a competency-based approach to leadership development adds value to the organisation?

5. What do you see as the future of the competency-based approach in management and leadership development?

■ Application and Experiential Questions

1. Review the competency model of two organisations with which you are familiar. What assumptions do these models make about leadership behaviours? How trainable are the various competencies described in the models?

2. Think about your own competencies as a manager or leader. How would you rate your competencies? Which of the competencies outlined in Table 6.2 can you develop further? What leadership development interventions are appropriate to enhance these competencies?

3. Conduct an informational interview with a leadership development specialist. Some of the questions you might ask include:
   1) What competencies do they need to perform their job?
   2) What has changed in their job over the past five years?
   3) Where do they see leadership competencies going in the next five years?

Chapter Seven

Managing Talent and Succession in Organisations

Outline

Learning Objectives

After reading this chapter you will be able to:

- Understand the concepts of talent and succession management and how they differ from each other.
- Understand why the management and development of talent has become a major strategic priority for organisations.
- Understand the types of decision that organisations have to make to integrate management and leadership development with talent management processes.
- Outline the succession management issues that arise for senior management, top teams and CEOs.
- Understand the issues that arise in the effective implementation of talent management.

OPENING CASE SCENARIO 1

Managing Talent at Dell Computers: Scaling Employee Potential

Dell is a global company operating in thirty-four countries in three world regions, with about 35,000 employees and $30 billion in sales. Dell is organised along geographic lines to include the Americas, Asia-Pacific and Japan, and Europe/Middle East/Africa (EMEA). Corporate headquarters is in Round Rock, Texas, which is also the regional headquarters for Dell America. Each region has its own regional headquarters and its own assembly plants and supply networks. Regional headquarters include Bracknell, UK for EMEA, Hong Kong for Asia-Pacific and Kawasaki for Japan. Dell EMEA is made up of more than 12,000 people in twenty-eight sites in twenty-four countries. These include sales and service centres and the European manufacturing facility in Limerick, Ireland. Dell's business activities are organised in each region around different customer segments. These vary somewhat, but generally include: 1) relationship (large corporate) customers; 2) home and small business (sometimes called transaction customers); and 3) public sector (government and educational) customers. Product development is largely centralised in the US and the same base products are sold worldwide. These products are customised for different regional and country markets with appropriate power supplies, keyboards, software and documentation. Other functions such as IT and e-commerce applications usually originate in the US and are then adopted with necessary modifications in the other regions. Manufacturing processes are constantly being upgraded, and the newest plant, wherever it is located, is usually the most advanced. Improvements developed for new plants are implemented as much as possible in existing plants. Dell makes extensive use of call centres, both for sales and technical support.

Dell has a passion for winning in every aspect of its business. Because of this, Dell believes that the effort of reaching for more and better is not negotiable. Continuous improvement is part of Dell's DNA and drives its efforts to be a greater company and a great place to work – in short, to cultivate a winning culture. A winning culture requires talented individuals working as a team with a commitment to common values and a collective determination to execute a shared vision. It focuses on encouraging personal accountability, maintaining a high standard of ethics and integrity, and building a workforce with diverse backgrounds, skills and potential.

Talent management represents a core component of Dell's human resource strategy. The strong focus on globalisation, product leadership, the customer experience and the winning culture places a strong emphasis on both leadership and talent management processes. Dell has programmes in place designed to address key talent, provide career development and develop leaders who have the flexibility to be future-focused, proactive and strong strategic thinkers. In order to make systematic assessments of talent, Dell focuses on identifying managers' career potential, identifying opportunities and managers' abilities to scale within the organisation. The scaling call is determined on the basis of past performance and is undertaken by the management team and manager's direct report. The scaling call rating signals a manager's potential to grow, to perform a role of greater scope and complexity. Dell uses specific criteria and categories to scale a manager and to identify talent potenial and rating. These include decisions concerning whether a manager or executive has global capability, is promotable, should be developed in his or her current role or developed laterally; whether the manager should stay in his or her current role; and whether the manager should be managed out of position or whether it is too soon to make a judgement concerning the manager. Managers with global corporate talent potential will probably lead a regional or global function or business unit within a period of three to five years. These managers will already be executives. Assessment is based on a consistent record of exceeding performance targets and a capacity to demonstrate strong leadership behaviours, and it reflects the organisation's culture. This manager or executive will have the capacity to learn quickly and be proactive in seeking out learning opportunities. Global talent will make up a very small proportion of Dell's pool of managers. Within the category of global talent, managers may be deemed to have key talent or to be exportable. Key talent represents the next generation of leaders within the organisation and therefore the organisation should take systematic steps to influence their career development. Key talent managers have the potential to lead within a two-year period, whereas a manager or executive classified as exportable is ready for movement inside or outside the region function or line of business. The organisation will also factor in the risk of the manager leaving the organisation in the short to medium term.

Managers who are considered promotable are growing faster than the demands of the current position. These managers will have achieved significant results and have the potential for both skill-broadening and taking on a role with significantly more responsibility. Promotable managers will, most likely, have taken on additional work or assignments and performed them to a very high level. They consistently demonstrate strong leadership behaviours and possess strong intellectual ability. Managers who are categorised as having development potential in current roles or in a lateral move are performing well in their current roles, with the scope to grow further or the possibility that a lateral move will provide additional learning and development opportunities. A manager who makes a lateral move is unlikely to take a position with significantly greater scope and responsibility within the next twelve months. Managers who are rated as contributing in their current roles are meeting the expectations of the role, but there is scope for further development. This manager might experience performance issues if the role were to grow or expand. The manager is comfortable with the current level of complexity. Managers who are categorised as needing to be managed out of their current position are not currently keeping pace with demands. Their current skills would be best utilised in a role with narrower scope and ultimately they may be managed out of the organisation if performance does not improve. Managers who fall into this category are given special help in the form of a performance improvement plan, a development plan or a transaction plan.

The scaling process is a complex one that places a strong level of responsibility on managers. It takes place on an annual basis, however, and is a time-bound assessment. Strong emphasis is placed on communicating that the scaling decision is not an evaluation of current performance, but a judgement made at a particular time concerning the manager's potential to grow and contribute in the future. It is likely that managers will sometimes find it difficult to avoid discussing performance issues and the potential exists to get into a full-blown performance discussion. The model is strongly related to the Dell leadership competency model. This scaling process does not necessarily mean immediate promotion. The emphasis is first and foremost on broadening and enhancing skills and then on having managerial talent available to fill positions when they become available. These are necessary in a fast-changing global environment.

Developing a Culture of Succession in First Trust Bank: Starting with Junior Management

First Trust Bank is a wholly owned subsidiary of Allied Irish Banks. In July 1991 the merger of AIB Group's interest in Northern Ireland with those of TSB Northern Ireland created First Trust Bank. This was viewed as an opportunity to build a major new banking organisation in Northern Ireland. The organisation provides retail and commercial banking services in Northern Ireland where it maintains fifty-eight branches and 1,500 staff. This operation provides a full range of banking services including current accounts, loans/overdrafts, mortgages, deposits and investments. Like most European countries, the Northern Ireland financial services market is highly developed in its customer usage patterns and competitive structures. In the late 1990s, First Trust Bank was facing serious challenges as economic conditions, an increasing knowledge of financial matters, technological developments and other non-bank financial institutions providing competitive services meant that previously loyal customers were beginning to shop around. For the organisation to sustain its business, remain competitive, retain existing staff and attract the right kind of new staff, it was necessary to have world-class HR policies and processes in place.

In order to succeed in a highly competitive global marketplace, organisations need to be able to make changes quickly. Employees must be able to acquire and assimilate new knowledge and skills rapidly. In order to sustain competitive advantage, organisations like First Trust must outperform competitors and reward shareholders on a consistent basis. At the most senior levels within First Trust there was collective recognition that investment in people was essential to maintaining competitive advantage and was First Trust's key differentiating resource. In early 2004, a succession management exercise was undertaken. At that time the officer population, the first-line level of management within the organisation, was recognised by senior management as a strong potential cadre of management: they could become the future leaders within the organisation.

While there is recognition of the importance of providing ongoing visible support and encouragement for succession within First Trust, it occurs in a sporadic way. First Trust is at the early stages of developing a succession management process which will likely take a further two to three years to become an essential part of the organisation. In order for this to happen there is a need to move away from a replacement planning model to a situation where the organisation has a pool of talented individuals within the organisation. The organisation recognises that this can be achieved by positioning succession as a developmental process that is open to more candidates through a process of self-selection. However, First Trust must also develop the notion, amongst its manager and potential manager population, that progression to the next level requires the development of specific competencies. Succession practices need to be fully integrated with internal selection processes and the performance management process.

Effective succession practices require the development of a succession culture. Currently the organisation has a silo mentality, but it is recognised that good succession involves acknowledging the need to develop talented individuals and broaden their skills base rather than being afraid of losing a talented performer. This requires talented individuals to be nurtured and released to avail of new job experiences in other areas of the organisation. The human resource function will play a major role in facilitating the process, but management have perhaps the greatest responsibility. Management will play a significant part in reducing the barriers created by a functional structure. They will need to be visibly supportive but also be held accountable for ensuring that succession decisions are taken on a systematic basis. In order to make a case for the development of a succession culture, First Trust will focus in the short term on developing specific HR metrics which relate succession to business performance.

QUESTIONS

Q.1   Contrast the approaches and situation of Dell Computers and First Trust with respect to talent and succession management.

Q.2   What problems or issues would you expect to encounter in an organisation starting out to implement talent and succession management processes?

Talent management has emerged as an important strategic issue for many large organisations and for multinational and global companies in particular. These organisations strive to align their talent with the organisation's vision, goals and business strategy. The success of business strategy execution is largely dependent on people and particularly on the quality of leadership talent. Numerous research studies illustrate that organisations that focus on improving their total human capital system, rather than specific components of it, tend to perform better. Organisations that perform better consider their managers and leaders to be a source of competitive advantage and this belief influences how the business is managed.

Talent management, as a concept, originated in the USA as a result of a major study by McKinsey consultants, who examined the impact of how organisations managed their leadership talent on corporate performance. It was originally used to describe the recruitment of an organisation's most valuable employees. Its meaning has broadened to include the attraction, selection, development and retention of top-class talent. Top-class talent represents the top ten per cent of the organisation's manager population. Talent management is broader in scope than management and leadership development because it incorporates other domains of human resource management such as recruitment and retention. Some commentators suggest that talent management has supplemented succession management. However, the differences between talent management and succession management are difficult to identify. At this stage, we suggest a rather simple distinction. Talent management tends to focus on the 'cream of the crop', whereas succession management focuses on the total population of managers, but we will identify how succession management represents a variant of talent management. Most organisations practise some form of succession management. Talent management is more likely to be practised in multinational and global companies. Both sets of practices have, however, become popular as a result of the competitiveness of the managerial labour market and the costs associated with hiring and developing managers. Organisations tend to use these sets of practices for senior managers or future leaders. We argue that managers at all levels, and not just those at the top, need to be managed and developed as a talent pool.

Initially we focus on defining both talent management and succession management, highlighting key similarities and differences. We discuss and evaluate the rationale for introducing both sets of practices in organisations. Most of this chapter focuses on the practices involved in designing talent management and succession management systems and the role of leadership development processes in ensuring effective talent and succession management. We highlight the special considerations that apply to talent management and succession management for top chief executive officers (CEOs) and general managers (GMs) and conclude with a discussion of some of the problems associated with talent and succession management ideas.

Defining Talent and Succession Management

It is difficult to get a precise definition of talent management. It is used interchangeably with terms such as 'talent strategy', 'human resource planning' and 'succession management'. Definitions tend to focus on either the individual or the organisation. The definitions in Exhibit 7.1 illustrate these levels of analysis.

Individual-Focused and Organisation-Level Definitions of Talent Management

Individual-Focused Definitions

Talent describes a well-rounded manager with 'a sharp strategic mind, leadership ability, emotional maturity, communication skills, the ability to attract and inspire other talented people, entrepreneurial instincts, financial skills and the ability to deliver results'. (Michaels, Handfield-Jones and Axelrod 2001:x)

An attempt to ensure that 'everyone at all levels work to the top of their potential' (Redford 2005:20)

'The talent inherent in each person, one individual at a time.' (Buckingham and Vosburgh 2001:18)

Organisation-Level Definitions

'Ensure the right person is in the right job at the right time.' (Jackson and Schuler 1990:235)

'A deliberate and systematic effort by an organisation to ensure leadership continuity in key positions and encourage individual advancement.' (Rothwell 1994:6)

'Managing the supply, demand and flow of talent through the human capital engine.' (Pascal 2004:12)

'Talentship is concerned with increasing the success of the organisation by improving decisions that impact or depend on talent resources.' (Boudreau and Ramstad 2005)

Three definitions suggest that both individuals and organisations need to develop a new talent mindset because leadership talent is mission critical. Lewis and Heckman (2006), in a major contribution, suggest these particular variants of talent management:

Talent Management as Human Resource Management: This requires an organisation to manage its HR processes and ensure that they contribute to the development and advancement of leadership talent. Olsen (2000), for example, believed that the challenge is to ensure that staffing, recruitment and development processes can be converted into an enterprise-wide human talent attraction and retention process. The key requirement is to ensure the horizontal integration of human resource practices.

Talent Management as Succession Management: This variant defines talent management as a set of organisational processes designed to ensure an effective flow of human resources, including leadership resources. It is largely what is traditionally called succession planning or management. A succession management approach places strong emphasis on forecasting leadership requirements and managing the flow of leaders through a sequence of positions in the organisation. Succession management is not confined to managerial groups. Typically it focuses on the total workforce, identifying skills and the demand and supply of employees.

Talent Management as the Management of Talent in a Generic Sense: This variant suggests that organisations need to think about the management of talent generally, not simply with regard to positions or organisational boundaries. It suggests that organisations need to implement disciplined talent management processes using rigorous continuous assessment and development methods. In the leadership context, this variant takes two forms: the management and development of high-potential talent, or what are described as the 'stars' or the high potentials; and the management and development of talent generally, including top performers and mid-range performers. The star notion suggests that leadership talent possesses the capacity to differentiate organisations and give them strategic advantage.

For the purposes of this chapter, we make a distinction between talent management as managing and developing star performers and talent management as succession management. They share processes in common, but the points of difference focus on the objectives and priorities of each activity. Table 7.1 provides a summary of key distinctions.

Table 7.1: Managing Talent Management as Managing and Developing Star Performers and Talent Management as Succession Management

Criterion	Talent Management as Management and Development of Star Performers	Talent Management as Succession Management
Aims	• Concerned with efforts to devote special attention to managing best-in-class talent • Development of high-performing or high-potential managerial talent • Focusing on managerial talent that is strategically important to the organisation's future • Using scarce developmental resources where they will give the best return • Terminating managers who are poor performers	• Aims to increase the talent pool of the organisation generally • Providing increased opportunities for high-potential employees • Enhancing of an employee's ability to respond to changing work demands • Identifying replacement needs as a means of targeting necessary training and development • Encouraging the advancement of diverse groups in future jobs within the organisation
Identification	• How will the organisation's success be improved through the availability of a talent pool? • Implementation of talent segmentation to ensure the logical differentiation of talent pools by their importance to strategic success • Identification of pivotal talent pools who have the potential to enhance competitive success • Focus on a cyclical, continuous process of identifying future leaders • Identification and specification of a core set of leadership competencies	• Identification of a talent pool, multiple potential successors and multiple potential promotions • Development of formal selection and multiple assessment criteria • Development of manager capability in identifying talent • Use of competency models to clarify what type of talent the organisation wishes to build • Ensure the hands-on involvement of the CEO and other senior leaders in the identification process
Leadership Development Strategies	• Use specific individualist development plans for each manager • Use developmental experiences that involve increased responsibility and stretch • Focus on the use of special job assignments and action-learning activities • Select development strategies based on potential contribution of the manager or leader • Build a viewpoint that high-potential talent is a shared resource rather than owned by specific mangers	• Devise clear development plans tailored to individual needs and succession opportunities • Mandate development planning and follow-up as part of succession process • Use job rotations and other work-related projects for development • Tie manager bonuses to commitment to and participation in development • Use leadership development initiatives to build shared competencies for the future • Provide the right development to build competencies in the organisation

Criterion	Talent Management as Management and Development of Star Performers	Talent Management as Succession Management
Criteria of Effectiveness	• Key question concerns how much development processes have contributed to the capacity and actions of managers in talent pools • How many leadership development activities and programmes do we get for our investments? • Evaluation of effectiveness is an ongoing process – short cycle	• Set specific goals for success in planning programmes and measure progress against them regularly • Evaluation process is usually conducted on a yearly basis • Focus on making sure that the succession process works to build leaders at all levels over time

Talent Management as the Management of High-Potential Leadership Talent

The notion that talent management is concerned with the management of high performers is a controversial one, but it is one that organisations implement. It is based on the view that organisations take proactive steps in the leadership development context to implement processes for their high-potential managers or leaders. Some commentators suggest that it is not strategic, but we contend that it can be strategic in nature, provided it is based on an organisation-wide strategy to acquire, cultivate, retain and manage top leadership talent needed to execute business strategy. It should describe the competencies required of the best in the organisation. Its goal is to ensure that the organisation has the right managers with the right skills and expertise available at the right time and in the right place. It can be conceived as a three-phase process consisting of:

- **Building a Talent Strategy**: This requires the organisation to document an action plan on how it intends to get and prepare its managers to execute the business strategy effectively. The action plan consists of a mix of projects for acquiring, consulting, developing, rewarding and organising talent.
- **Implementing Talent Strategies**: This stage focuses on designing and implementing the projects identified.
- **Monitoring Talent Management Implementation**: This phase focuses on determining the results of major talent management initiatives.

What actually constitutes top talent is problematic. It may include executive management, team leaders, directors/vice-presidents and A-player managers. It may also include future business leaders with more strategic capabilities than just operational excellence skills, plus specialist talent with the capacity to execute business integration projects. These examples illustrate the lack of a concise definition. The definition of top talent will be influenced by historical and cultural features of the organisation. The talent management literature suggests that it is best to define talent in a fluid way to reflect changes in the business. Talent management represents an attempt to provide a coherent framework and to integrate different initiatives to develop top talent. It has both values and process components, which can be summarised thus:

- **Ethics:** Talent management emphasises the need to create a 'talent mindset' in the organisation. This mindset may be exclusive or broadened to incorporate the notion that everyone has potential worth developing.
- **Focus:** Talent management places emphasis on the organisation knowing which jobs make a difference and making sure that the right managers hold those jobs at the right time.

- **Positioning:** Talent management is a management, not an HR initiative, which starts at the top of the organisation and cascades through the management levels.
- **Structure:** Talent management places considerable emphasis on the creation of tools, processes and techniques that enable the identification and development of talent.
- **Systems-Focused:** Talent management focuses on a longer-term approach and the holistic integration of various strategies and initiatives.

Talent management as the development of stars rests on a number of assumptions that are open to challenge, but it does have a clear prescription for management and leadership development processes. Organisations should invest in development based on the manager's actual and potential contribution to organisational success.

Proponents of a talent management approach argue that it represents an advance on succession management in that it seeks to reframe talent within organisational strategy, performance processes and development initiatives. It focuses on the development of a collaborative point of view concerning how talent is connected to organisational success. Boudreau and Ramstad (2005) consider it to be a concept that facilitates a discourse of quality concerning talent decisions. This has the effect of embedding talentship within the organisation's processes and culture. There is a significant opportunity for organisations to achieve crucial and sustained competitive advantage through the talents of its human resources.

Critics of this notion of talent management exist. Pfeffer (2001) is one of its most trenchant critics. He takes the view that talent management is an inappropriate organisational process and that the negative consequences far outweigh its advantages. We will return later in this chapter to Pfeffer's arguments. However, we now summarise the main assumptions of talent management as the management of star talent in Exhibit 7.2.

EXHIBIT 7.2

Assumptions of Talent Management as the Management of Star Talent

- **Assumption 1:** The need for innovation and competitive advantage makes it imperative to recruit outstanding managerial and leadership talent.
- **Assumption 2:** The identification, detainment, development and retention of outstanding talent are major sources of competitive advantage.
- **Assumption 3:** There is a limited talent pool capable of rising to senior management positions so organisations face fierce competition when recruiting the best.
- **Assumption 4:** Organisations must take proactive steps to make themselves attractive to exceptional talent.
- **Assumption 5:** Modern recruitment and selection processes make it possible to predict the star performers of the future.
- **Assumption 6:** Organisations should encourage diversity in order to recruit the best.
- **Assumption 7:** Exceptional talent needs to be exposed to stretch developmental experiences early in his/her career.
- **Assumption 8:** Talent leaders produce better organisational performance.
- **Assumption 9:** The responsibility of the organisation is to do all they can to ensure that the leadership pool is as talented as possible.
- **Assumption 10:** Talent management is a central component of the business and part of the ongoing role of senior executives.
- **Assumption 11:** Senior executives should constantly take active and bold steps to attract and develop top leadership talent.

Talent Management as Succession Management

Some organisations will seek to implement a type of talent management which focuses on the total management pool. This variant is therefore broader in scope than others. Succession management focuses on the total management and non-management pool and is designed to ensure that, through planned development activities, organisations make proactive attempts to ensure continuity by cultivating talent at all levels within the organisation. Succession management is not just about finding replacements. It is also about developing talent and building sufficient bench strength. It is concerned with preserving the organisation's institutional memory as retained in the heads of veteran managers at all levels who possess specialised knowledge about how things are done, what works well and what needs to be done.

The classic definition of succession management was provided by Leibman (1996):

> '*A means of identifying critical management positions, starting at the levels of project manager and supervisor and extending up to the highest positions in the organisation.*'

Fiebman acknowledged that succession management is concerned with ensuring that the organisation has flexibility in lateral moves. He included the development of management skills as a key component of succession management, but qualifies this by arguing that the development must be aligned with organisational objectives. Hirsch (2002) suggested that succession management focuses on the process by which one or more successors are identified for key posts and career and development moves are planned for these successors. She considered that succession management sets a broader resourcing and development process. Succession management, therefore, is used to describe a wide variety of activities involving the planning of leadership resources within the organisation. It is a structured process that incorporates notions of identification and preparation of succession. The structured component indicates that it is not a just-in-time approach or simply ad hoc in nature.

The majority of the literature on succession management has as its focus executive-level succession. Spencer and Spencer (1993) argued that it can be applied to key jobs at any level, including those below the jobs that managers currently hold. They believed that in an era of downsizing and organisational change, it can be difficult to sustain all managers in their present positions. It is now generally accepted that effective succession management should address critical backups and individual development in any job category, including human resources in professional, technical and operative categories. This extends the definition of succession management beyond the managerial ranks and suggests that the aims of succession management are concerned to match the organisation's available current talent to its needed future talent and to enable the organisation to meet both strategic and operational challenges. Rothwell (2005) argues that succession management is a way of ensuring the 'continued cultivation of leadership and intellectual talent'. He also includes the concern to manage the important knowledge assets of the organisation. Exhibit 7.3 highlights the assumptions that underpin talent management as succession management.

The general distinction between the two variants of talent management considered here rests on the notion that talent management is associated with initiatives to devote special attention to a key group of managers. Succession management has a wider brief. It focuses on non-managerial as well as managerial employees and is not limited to top-of-the-house development. Succession management does not simply focus on investing money where the returns are likely to be most significant. Both processes suggest proactive initiatives in that they seek to ensure the continuity of leadership by cultivating talent from within the organisation through planned development activities. They focus on linking the development of talent to organisational strategic priorities and involving departments and potential successors as process co-owners. There is also the need to communicate openly and make the process as transparent as possible.

Assumptions of Talent Management as Succession Management

- **Assumption 1:** Organisations should focus on all managerial talent and manage underperforming managerial talent.
- **Assumption 2:** Managers increasingly need to make their own career decisions; therefore there needs to be a balance between organisational and individual aspirations.
- **Assumption 3:** Organisations should develop leaders for roles rather than jobs and ensure pools of talented managers.
- **Assumption 4:** Organisations need a certain amount of new blood to bring in new ideas and approaches; therefore it is important to balance insiders with outsiders.
- **Assumption 5:** Organisations should seek to link succession within business plans, but this may not be easy to achieve.
- **Assumption 6:** The talents of women and ethnic minorities should be properly developed.
- **Assumption 7:** Succession management should encourage lateral moves as well as traditional vertical movements.

Implementing Talent Management Processes in Organisations

There are a lot of opinion-based articles which frequently make an emotional case for the adoption of talent management practices. Although it is difficult to provide hard, direct evidence, the available evidence does highlight their value at executive or CEO level. In general, the data suggests that between forty and sixty per cent of US organisations adopt formal talent and succession management processes. Development Dimensions International (DDI) estimated in 2003 that sixty-four per cent of organisations implemented effective succession and talent management processes (Bernthal and Wellins 2003). When talent management practices are done well, they add tangible value to the organisation (Becker and Huselid 1998). Individual practices do not systematically address the management of talent.

Talent and succession management processes should enable organisations to formalise the process of preparing managers to fill key positions in the future. The emphasis is on the creation of talent pools rather than the simple identification of key successors. This provides organisations with choices associated with this idea, and talent and succession management processes enable organisations to put in place enhanced opportunities for high-potential managers. These managers are considered to have significant potential for advancement. Talent and succession management processes should enable organisations to identify appropriate strategies to accelerate the development of high-potential managers. They will also facilitate the retention of this category of manager and enable managers and other employees to realise their career plans. This suggests that talent and succession management should serve individual as well as organisational needs.

Talent and succession management processes can be used to improve the morale of managers by facilitating promotion from within. It is argued that promotions from within enable the organisation to utilise the skills and abilities of managers more effectively. Promotion is generally valued as an important incentive. Capelli (2001) and Gilmore (1988) suggested that talent and succession management processes help managers to respond more effectively to changing environmental demands. Talent processes can be used to prepare managers and leaders to respond to changing environmental conditions. Managers and leaders play a key role in transforming the ambiguity and uncertainty of the external environment and translating it into appropriate statements of vision and operational strategy.

Recent research by Garavan, Shanahan and Carbery (2008) reveals that there is a 'significant positive correlation' between an organisation's ability to develop senior executives internally and its confidence in its ability to meet future growth needs. Organisations with a good selection of highly capable executives, who are definitely senior-management material, are frequently the organisations that also have a strong, well-organised programme to develop high-potential employees. The two activities that have the greatest impact in developing these high-potential employees are developmental 'stretch' assignments with a company, and the personal involvement of the chief executive in driving the process.

The survey also reveals a corresponding significant negative correlation between an organisation's need to hire outside leaders and its confidence of meeting future growth needs.

How to Identify and Nurture Talented Managers

The survey highlights what respondents consider the most effective methods of identifying and nurturing talented employees who have leadership potential. The most effective techniques are considered to be:

- Defining leadership abilities based on the strategic challenges confronting the organisation.
- One-on-one coaching or mentoring for high-potential individuals.
- Allocation of resources for leadership development.
- Making the development of talent a strategic priority for the organisation.

The survey also investigates the personality characteristics organisations would be likely to look for in current staff members if they were assessing them for future leadership potential.

A striking aspect of the findings is that, in the current business climate, organisations appear to value personal leadership traits more highly than business-oriented capabilities when seeking future senior executive material. The following characteristics are regarded as especially important:

- An ability to build strong relationships both internally and externally.
- Openness to change and growth.
- Courage to make the decisions that feel 'right'.
- An ability to motivate and inspire others.
- A strong level of self-confidence.

Other principal findings of the survey are:

- 71% of respondents expect to hire 25% or more of their leaders from the outside over the next five to seven years.
- 57% of all organisations surveyed have been formally identifying and developing high-potential talent for less than three years.
- The larger organisations surveyed have been formally developing future leaders for significantly longer than the smaller ones.
- 62% of all organisations surveyed tell particular individuals that they are perceived to have high potential, but many say that the conversations happen informally and inconsistently.

Finally, on the question of the specific resources organisations use as tools to develop future leaders, the following are regarded as most important:

- An actively involved chief executive.
- Giving high-potential individuals new, significant roles that really stretch their abilities.
- Encouraging senior executives to enter mentoring relationships with high-potential individuals.
- Providing high-potential individuals with coaching relationships within the organisation.
- Providing high-potential individuals with external executive education programmes.
- Leaders and top executives will be held accountable for the retention of managers and key employees. The survey suggests that all managers will be rewarded for their retention rate accomplishments.
- A substantial proportion of an organisation's management development budget will be devoted to equipping leaders with the talent to be effective retention leaders.
- Organisations will increasingly select leaders based on their retention leader capabilities and talents.
- Management and leadership development metrics will increasingly be used to document their impact on turnover and retention imperatives.

We focus here on a number of issues that organisations should consider when implementing talent management practices, and their implications for leadership development.

Making Talent and Succession Management Strategic

Lewis and Heckman (2006) argue that talent management in either of the forms discussed in this chapter is not necessarily strategic. They suggest that proponents of talent management do not offer guidance to enable organisations to determine how resources should be allocated in order to identify leadership talent and to successfully manage and develop that talent in a strategic context. They also challenge whether the idea of categorising leadership talent into performance categories is strategic in nature. They suggest that it ignores an important reality. Certain roles may require competent performers and organisations may prioritise certain competencies over others. In an ideal world, talent and succession management should fit and link with the organisation's strategic priorities, culture, human resource strategies and development processes.

Rothwell and Kazanas (2003) suggested that organisations can adopt one or more approaches to achieving integration between strategic processes and talent and succession management. These are summarised in Exhibit 7.4. Ashton and Morton (2005) suggest that many organisations have failed to achieve effective links between talent management and strategy. They suggest that these organisations have failed to answer the following questions:

- Why are you doing talent management? Is it for the individual, the organisation, or both?
- What do you mean by talent and talent management?
- What are your propositions for attracting and retaining talent?
- How do you manage and use the talent your organisation needs?
- How are internal roles and resources deployed appropriately to support talent management?
- How is talent management integrated across HR processes and with business planning and strategy execution processes?

These are complex questions which are often not given sufficient time and consideration to answer.

Integrating Talent and Succession Management with Strategy

Approach	Characteristics
The Top-Down Approach	• The organisation's strategy drives talent and succession management processes. • Leaders are identified using systematic processes driven by the top team. • Talent and succession management processes support the successful implementation of strategy. • The chief executive is responsible for developing and implementing both sets of plans.
The Market-Driven Approach	• Talent and succession management processes are driven by the needs of the marketplace. • The organisation analyses the dynamics of the market place and identifies the talent implications. • The organisation may buy in the talent and/or develop it internally.
The Career Planning Approach	• Career planning processes are used as the mechanism to link talent and succession management processes to strategic plans. • Individual managers examine their own development plans in consultation with senior managers. • Managers assess their own career goals using the organisation's strategy as the context. • Managers and leaders make decisions concerning how they can best contribute to organisational needs. • Managers are also concerned with how they can improve their own advancement.
The Futuring Approach	• Talent and succession management processes are the mechanism for anticipating talent needs stemming from the corporate strategy. • Talent and succession management processes are used to scan external environmental conditions. • Talent and succession management processes are used to match the organisation's internal talent to the dimensions of the external environment.
The Rifle Approach	• Talent and succession management processes are focused on dealing with specific problems that currently exist through the organisation. • This approach is essentially reactive and tends to focus on the parts but ignore organisation-wide talent and succession management processes.

Talent and succession management processes help organisations to shape their approach to management and leadership development. Kester (2004) suggested that the strategic choices for growth adopted by organisations have major implications for the approach to leadership development. Organisations that pursue product- or service-innovation strategies will use talent management processes to develop deep leadership bench strength. The development challenge will be to ensure that leaders have sufficient cross-business exposure and that they have exposure to customers' organisations. Process innovators place a lot of emphasis on developing managers who possess both processes and managerial competencies. They may acquire leadership capacity from outside the organisation and they require leaders to have an understanding of technological issues and a deep knowledge of business and industry domains. Organisations who are delivery innovators view the task of talent management as being concerned with developing leaders who are culture change agents and who have acquired deep consumer-focused general management experience. They are also likely to search for skills/knowledge from other industries. Finally, organisations that are business model innovators like to develop leaders who are risk-oriented and who have extensive external relationship management competences. This discussion suggests that talent and succession management processes can be used as a driving force to justify a particular approach to management and leadership development. Table 7.2 summarises the implications of talent and succession management ideas for management and leadership development.

Table 7.2: Implications of Talent and Succession Management for Management and Leadership Development in Organisations

Proactive Planning	• Effective talent pool management focuses on developing a series of feeder groups up and down the entire leadership pipeline. • Management and leadership development initiatives must move forward with a clear sense of what results must be delivered. • Management and leadership development initiatives must be based on an analysis of current strengths and weaknesses. • Management and leadership development must challenge the status quo.
Ongoing Dialogue	• Management and leadership development processes must move away from the annual organisation review. • Effective management and leadership development requires an ongoing dialogue. • Decisions about management and leadership development must be based on ongoing processes with results checked on a continuous basis.
Recognition of the Policies of Talent Management	• Political issues are an inevitable element of decisions concerning management and leadership development. • Management and leadership development decisions inevitably raise the question of who owns the talent. • Management and leadership development practices and policy must challenge the situation where executives evaluate their own managers in overly positive terms and suppress information concerning the best leaders in an effort to hold on to the key staff.

Role of CEO	• Management and leadership development is a matter of corporate culture. The CEO sets the norms by investing time and energy in driving the process.
	• The CEO should articulate the principles and philosophies that guide management and leadership development.
	• CEOs should articulate principles concerning:
	  – Expectations concerning the differentiation of talent
	  – The role of line leaders in the development of managers
	  – Movement of managers across business and functions
	  – The role of diversity in management and leadership development
	  – Hiring for potential rather than hiring for position
	  – The role of management and leadership development specialists.

The Assessment of Potential	• The assessment of potential is problematic and controversial because development potential is difficult to measure. • An objective evaluation of past accomplishments is an important component in determining a leader's competency. • Multisource methods of assessment are more effective than reliance on a single source.
Assessing and Developing Talent	• Assessment and development are skills that must be learned by leaders in real time. • The process should be based on a common vocabulary and a single set of standards which is shared. • The assessment and development of talent should be a process driven by the CEO.
Executives should not develop their own Successors	• Executives should be accountable for development, but not for developing their own replacement. • Every executive vacancy should be viewed as an opportunity to search broadly across the organisation for the best available candidates.
Early Differentiation Matters	• Early differentiation of talent is necessary in order to allocate service development resources to the targets with the greatest return. • Development interventions that have the most significant impact on developing future general managers give target candidates increasing levels of responsibility. • The path to senior and top management is a series of varied experiences that occur at key crossroads. These crossroads are: manage self, manage people, manage managers, manage a function, manage a business, manage GMs and manage an enterprise. • Leadership development occurs from real and sustained accountability at each career crossroads.
Role of Accountability and Feedback	• In effective talent management, risks are taken to move managers through assignments. These assignments should be accompanied by accountability and feedback. • Development assignments should be accompanied with clear expectations concerning results and clear time in positions for developing managers.

Role of Management Development Specialist	• The development specialist can contribute to the development of leadership through the generation of robust data and hold well-held views concerning development
	• The specialist should provide internal and external professional assessment resources to support line-management judgment concerning leadership potential
	• The specialist must exert strong control over the practices that govern selection for development. This ensures the integrity of the process
	• The specialist should avoid dominating development decisions and direct the dialogue back to the leadership team
	• Specialists should be as transparent as possible concerning their philosophy on development

Source: Adapted from Kester (2004:32-44)

Integration of Talent Management with Human Resource Management Activities

The integration of talent management with other HR activities is important. Talent management tends to cut across traditional HR solos or specialisms. Proper integration helps to ensure that talent management is facilitative and that it reaches down the organisation. Ashton and Morton (2005) suggest that talent management presents a number of challenges and they identified key priorities for HR. These include:

- Rethinking/establishing the talent focus – talent definitions, values/principles, business context and talent market trends.
- Positioning talent management – strategic or tactical, decisions, actions and how talent processes are designed/delivered.
- Integrating talent and business – TM systems and alignment with the strategic management process and annual/quarterly operating plans.
- Leading the talent focus – the quality of leadership focus, direction and defined talent roles.
- Examining culture and talent mindset – common language, consistent messages, cultural attributes and negative influences.
- Assessing capability and accountability – defining talent capabilities, accountabilities for talent, quality/frequency of talent conversations and talent measures/evaluation.
- Process design and implementation – people/technology issues, success rates from talent processes and process shortcomings/failures.
- Assessing talent performance – improved talent development, realising potential, talent deployment and talent performance.
- The talent agenda – keeping this agenda fresh and responsive through continued support, consistent interpretation, regular discussions, etc.
- Reviewing talent management – to establish how well you compare with other organisations or business units/function internally in talent focus, delivery and shortcomings.

Best Principles Talent and Succession Management Processes

We discussed the appropriateness of the best practice approach to leadership development in Chapter Four. Our conclusion was that it may be best to talk about particular principles that hold up irrespective of context. We have identified four principles that emerge from the research:

- **CEO and Board Leadership:** The CEO and board of directors are actively involved in developing leadership talent. The more active the involvement of the CEO, the more effective the organisation rates its efforts in developing talent. Senior management involvement is a key enabler in the successful development of leader quality and bench strength. Board involvement needs to be visible. This may involve board members visiting with high potentials at their location and making concerned efforts to get to know the manager on a personal level. Active CEO and board involvement will likely ensure that there is a stringent focus on developing leaders at both corporate and business unit levels.
- **Differentiation of High-Potential Talent:** The best organisations formally identify high-potential leaders. They also communicate to high potentials that they are labelled as high potentials. Where a high potential resigns, a counter offer is made within twenty-four hours to that high potential, at any level within the organisation. Leaders are charged with retaining the high potentials in their departments. High potentials have increased access to and interaction with senior leaders. This usually happens through participation in special projects. Organisations also implement talent showcases where high-potential leaders present to the board at meetings. The majority of best-practice organisations regularly grow high potentials' capabilities through developmental assignments. There is a strong focus on the use of internal leadership training and potential assignments. Such organisations consistently use internal coaching and mentoring with their high potentials.
- **The Right Initiatives Done Right:** The best companies have a deep insight concerning the unique type of leadership that the business and corporate culture demands. They align talent development practices with organisational goals. Leadership development starts with strategy and competencies. The majority of organisations that are categorised as best practice have leadership and competency models that match the business strategy. These competencies are integrated into HR and development practices, such as performance management, selection for development assignments and succession. The best organisations offer a greater range of development opportunities to leaders. They also execute their leadership practices very effectively.
- **Accountability:** The best organisations hold leaders accountable for building leadership quality and depth. The less successful organisations tend to hold the HR department accountable. Leaders are measured on both their leadership behaviour and the improvement in their behaviours over time. Leaders are accountable for developing others.

EXHIBIT 7.5

Focus on Research: The Destructive Potential of Overachievers

The drive to achieve is a major driving force in a business, but it can also be hugely destructive. By relentlessly focusing on tasks and goals, a company can damage its performance by relegating the needs of its people.

Overachieving leaders tend to command and coerce to get results – stifling subordinates. They often take shortcuts, and the cycle of communication breaks down. They forget to relay vital information to others and remain oblivious to others' concerns. This demolishes trust, undermines morale and erodes confidence in management. A short-term relentless achievement drive can have long-term effects. Performance of the team suffers and they risk missing the goals which initially began the achievement-oriented behaviour.

Too intense a focus on results also impacts on public trust. As profits grow, confidence in big businesses have slid. For example, Enron's Jeffrey Skilling is an example of a classic overachieving leader, driving for results without caring how they were achieved. Managers competed against colleagues, and once he praised an executive for developing a new product he had forbidden her to work on. For every Skilling who makes the headlines there are others who don't but who still cause huge harm.

The single-mindedness encouraged by overachieving breeds undesirable behaviours. Consider Frank, who was so target focused that he ran roughshod over his colleagues. He became arrogant, aloof, demanding and never listened to others. Within four years the company was in disarray, people were threatening to leave and he was eventually fired. The career of Jan, a brilliant lawyer, was terminally stalled by her mean-spiritedness and inability to tolerate people less ambitious than herself; she was relegated to a small satellite office to work on cases alone.

Successful leadership is dependent on the leader taking time to motivate and empower others, rather than becoming overwhelmed by their own drive to succeed. Controlling achievement overdrive is one of the most important aspects of management. Be less coercive and more collaborative. Influence rather than direct. Focus more on people and less on results.

But the drive to achieve is hard to resist. Most people, particularly in Western cultures, are taught from early childhood to value achievement. Accomplishment becomes associated with feelings of excitement and happiness.

David McClelland, a famous Harvard psychologist, defined achievement – meeting or exceeding a standard of excellence or improving personal performance – as one of three personal drivers. The other two are affiliation, maintaining relationships; and power, which involves being strong and influencing others or having an impact on others. The power motive came in two forms: the leader draws strength both from controlling and from weakening people. His research showed that all three motives were present in varying degrees in everyone, and gave rise to certain needs and behaviours. Meeting these needs led to a repetition of the associated behaviours regardless of whether a desirable outcome was attained. McClelland originally believed that of the three factors achievement was the most crucial to the success of a company, but he also recognised its negative side – the use of Machiavellian tactics in which the end justifies the means. In his later work he argued that the most effective leaders were those primarily motivated by socialised power and those who helped others to be successful.

There are six main styles of leadership, and each style has its own strengths and limitations:
- *Directive:* entails strong (sometimes coercive) behaviour. This approach is useful in a crisis, but overuse stifles employees.
- *Visionary:* focuses on clarity and communication.
- *Affiliative:* emphasises harmony and relationships, works well when helping an employee with a personal crisis, but it generally works best in tandem with the visionary, participative or coaching style. It is rarely effective alone.
- *Participative:* is collaborative and democratic.
- *Pacesetting:* is characterised by personal heroics – often meaning that leaders are going out and doing deals themselves rather than building their organisations, and is exhausting for everyone in the long term.
- *Coaching:* focuses on long-term development and mentoring.

The good news about overachieving leaders is that they work hard to achieve a goal, even if it is to manage their achievement drive. The first step is to identify the problem behaviours and to adopt positive new behaviours, or to redirect the overachievement drive into interests outside work.

In the early 1990s, CEO Lou Gerstner aimed to regain IBM's market dominance by transforming the managerial approach. He sought out leaders who would orchestrate and enable rather than command and control. He knew that the organisation had to move away from the relevant culture of pacesetting and individualism. Two years ago, in a re-calibration of the competency model, IBM replaced it with a collaborating and team leadership environment. Although the motives of the managers had not changed (they were still high achievers) their behaviours had. The coaching styles had increased by seventeen per cent while the pacesetting had decreased by five per cent.

Of course a high achievement drive is a source of strength, but companies have to learn when to draw on it and when to draw it in. The challenge for managers today is to find an approach to leadership that uses socialised power to control achievement.

Designing Talent and Succession Management Processes

We now turn to the practice-level decisions that organisations and senior management need to consider when designing talent and succession management processes. These include linking these processes to the strategic goals of the organisation, deciding on the scope of both processes, developing a talent hierarchy, communication and dissemination, considering the extent of individual discretion, and evaluating the process. Handfield-Jones, Michaels and Axelrod (2001) mapped out some of the key elements of effective talent and succession management processes. We take up some of the themes highlighted in Table 7.3 and discuss how they may be tackled by organisations.

Table 7.3: Elements of Effective Talent and Succession Management

Danger Signs	Signs of Progress	Signs of Achievement
Disciplined Talent Management		
A focus only on obvious successors in succession planning exercises	Some discussion of incumbents' performance	Clear identification of A, B and C performers in each talent pool
Lists of high-potential people, but little action	Consultation of list when vacancies occur	Written action plans for each high potential's development and retention
Belief that there are no poor performers	Admit that there are likely to be some poor performers, but avoid doing much about it	Act decisively on poor performers by improving or replacing them
Hold no one except HR accountable for talent management	Evaluate managers on how well they manage their staff	Hold leaders directly accountable for developing their talent pool
Creative Recruitment and Retention		
Empty rhetoric about being a good employer to work for	Think about the EVPs for each type of talent	Understand the strengths and weaknesses of the EVPs for each type of talent and plan to strengthen them
Hire only at entry levels and grow only from internal hires	Occasionally bring in senior or specialist people from outside	Recruit a steady flow of talent at all levels
Go to the same sources for recruiting talent	Experiment with new sources, but look for similar backgrounds	Creatively tap new pools of talent, looking for essential capabilities
Have high and consistent attrition rates among managers	Analyse attrition data by department and type	Know the attrition rates of A, B and C performers and understand why they are leaving, performing or underperforming

Danger Signs	Signs of Progress	Signs of Achievement
Thoughtful Executive Development		
Leave the job assignments of managers to the manager who hires them	Suggest some candidates from the high-potential list or job-posting system	Involve leadership teams on every assignment decision, seeking to optimise these across the company
Recruit most qualified candidate with no discussion of development	Stretch people, but not in the context of any development plan	Thoughtfully consider the development needs of each assignment and the development needs of each candidate
Assume that the best way to develop people is by throwing them in at the deep end	Provide formal feedback through appraisal once a year	Embed candidate feedback and coaching into the routines of the organisation and the jobs of leaders
Invest in training driven by top-down assessments of candidates and then only in response to immediate needs, threats or crisis	Offer regular but basic programmes for management development and leadership, usually off-the-job	Offer integrated management/leadership learning programmes for each transition point of managerial careers

Making the Link with Strategic Objectives

The majority of writings stress the importance of linking talent and succession management processes clearly and explicitly to the organisation's long-term strategic objectives. The assumption exists that the organisation's strategic plans will directly inform future human resource needs and will provide guidance concerning the promotion and development needs of those who are likely to be promoted. There is an assumption that top management will support the talent and succession management processes. This support should be active and visible. Rothwell (2005) argues that who should make the final decisions in talent and succession management depends on the approach used. He suggests that where organisations use a top-down approach, all decisions are made at the highest level. Senior management, or the top team overall, decide on all of the key issues, usually supported by a leadership development specialist. Typically, senior and top management will make decisions concerning how competence and performance will be assessed, how future competence and potential will be identified and what development activities are considered appropriate. In contrast, a bottom-up approach is generally directed by individuals lower in the organisation, usually through individual career plans. Top managers then act on decisions made at lower levels. It is likely that a combination approach will be used in most organisations.

Two particular theoretical frameworks that explicitly link talent management with business strategy were proposed by Stewart (1997) and Boudreau and Ramstad (2005). Stewart suggested that leadership talent can be classified according to its value and how difficult it is to replace. Certain talent pools are easily replaced because they do not add unique value; they can be easily trained and/or it is easy to automate what they do. Managers are unlikely to fall into this category. It is possible that organisations may require managers who have very specialist skills yet do not add value to customers. Leaders are most likely to be in the high-value, difficult-to-replace quadrant. This framework has value in that it requires that the organisation looks at external labour and is therefore sensitive to the external conditions that it has to deal with. The model is, however, a reactive model in that talent management responds to strategic conditions and goals already defined by the organisation.

Boudreau and Ramstad (2005) take on the challenge of understanding how strategy contributes to strategic decision-making. They argue that it is necessary to develop a decision science that enables organisations to make decisions about their talent resources. They propose the HC Bridge ® Decision Framework. This suggests that talent management must be identified at three levels of analysis: impact, effectiveness and efficiency. Impact refers to the strategic impact of a changing leadership talent pool. It seeks to answer the question: what impact will improvements in the depth of leadership talent have on the organisation's ability to achieve priority strategic goals? This, they suggest, requires the organisation to differentiate talent. Effectiveness refers to the extent to which various leadership development initiatives impact on the performance and behaviour of leadership talent. Leadership development activities can address the capacity of leadership talent and/or the practice that this talent uses. It is important to combine effectiveness and impact criteria in order to see the true contribution of leadership development initiatives. Efficiency is the amount of activity generated from an investment in leadership development. Boudreau and Ramstad suggest that to focus on efficiency without consideration of effectiveness and impact can result in low-cost leadership development (Figure 7.1).

Figure 7.1: HC Bridge® Decision Framework

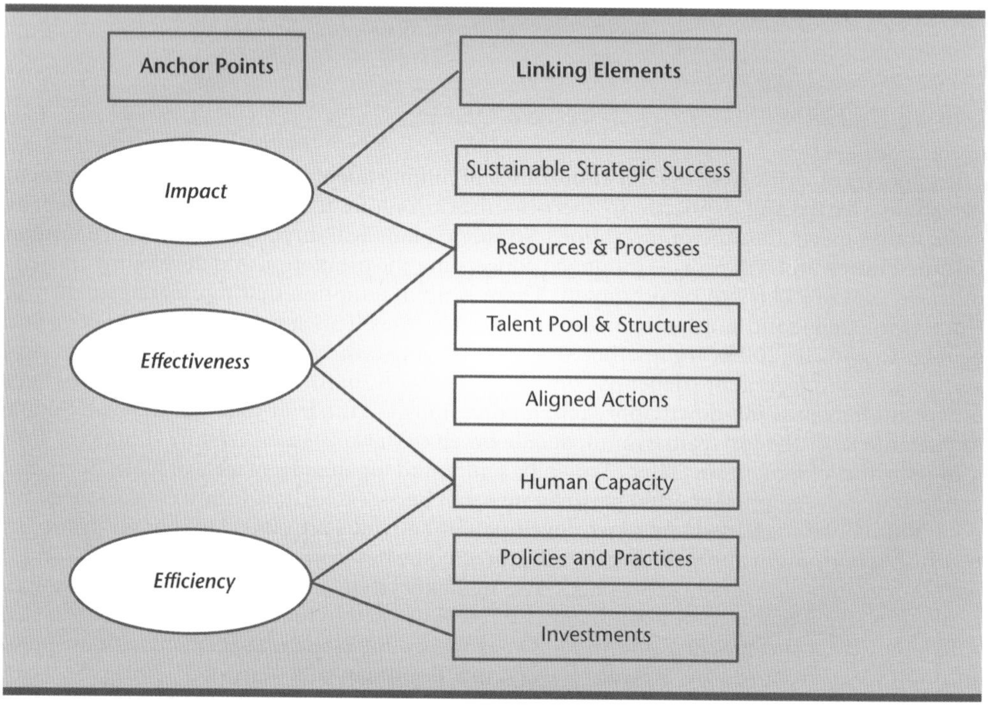

Source: Boudreau and Ramstad (2005)

Bergeron (2004) suggested that in order to build a talent strategy it is necessary to achieve a deep understanding of business context and its interdependencies. She suggested a number of questions that need to be asked. These are presented in Exhibit 7.6.

EXHIBIT 7.6

Understanding Your Business Context and Interdependencies

- What value does your business deliver to its customers?
  - What is the strategic purpose and direction?
  - What is the organisation trying to achieve and aspiring to become?
  - Why do customers choose to do business with you rather than with your competitors?
- What are the core business processes in which your organisation must excel in order to deliver customer value and how do you measure the effectiveness of these key business processes?
  - What core business processes enable your business to deliver customer value?
  - What are your measures of success for the key processes?
  - How are you performing against your priorities?
- What key capabilities must we have as an organisation to deliver value to customers?
  - What knowledge, skills and behaviours are most needed to execute core business processes and to deliver value to customers?
- What value does your organisation offer its employees?
  - What kind of culture, work environment and underlying value system do you need?
  - Why do employees join and stay with your organisation?

The framework is based on the notion that the customer value proposition will drive the core business processes and these will in turn drive talent needs. The employee value proposition focuses on the employee perspective and ensures that the organisation has considered issues of attracting and retaining talent.

Who Should be Included in Talent and Succession Management Processes?

This represents a fundamental decision for organisations. It centres on who should be included in talent and succession management processes. If we take the more narrow construction of talent management advocated by Berger and Berger (2004), for example, it is clear that it will focus only on the managerial population and then only on those who have the potential to contribute most to the organisation. In general, talent and succession management processes may be specialised or generalised. Specialised programmes target the high-potential leadership population and focuses on continuity. A more generalised programme will focus on managers in all categories.

A strategic approach to answering this question focuses on the identification of missing organisational capabilities. The organisation should systematically identify talent gaps between what it currently has and what it needs for the future. This process requires honesty, because organisations may be slow to fully recognise the extent of deficiencies. A more complete picture will be achieved from the broad input of key stakeholders. Stakeholder involvement will ensure a broader range of innovative ideas, diverse opinions and increased commitment to the implementation of the plan.

Categorising Management and Leadership Talent

A talent management approach, in particular, advocates that organisations should invest in development based on the manager's potential contribution to the organisation. Berger and Berger (2004), for example, suggested that the essence of talent management is the development of the best. What constitutes the best is itself a fluid concept. Brown and

Hesketh (2004), for example, suggested three phases of thinking concerning what represents the best. During the 1990s the key criterion was suitability, which focused on a manager's capacity to get the job done. This, in reality, meant meeting the ever-growing expectations of employees. The concept of ability has, however, shifted to a downgrading of technical skills in favour of social skills and personal characteristics.

Table 7.4: What Constitutes the Best Talent?

Criterion	1990s	2000s	Main Reasons for Change
Suitability	The basic competence 'to get the job done'. In some jobs an almost exclusive emphasis on personal, transferable skills, even within more 'technical' fields. Technical competence no longer enough	Remains essentially the same although with a greater emphasis on 'readiness' or the 'commercially savvy self'. Individuals have to show greater levels of business awareness and acumen alongside the personal and social skills that are necessary to get the job done	Highlights the continuing tension within modern organisations between the management of talent and short-term profitability. Greater emphasis on cost-cutting and 'quick wins' to a focus on oven-ready graduates who are 'billable within six months'
Capability to Proactivity	*Capability* – about the identification of future leaders and individuals who can 'add value' through their 'raw talent' and 'charismatic' personality	*Proactivity* – the demonstration of raw talent is no longer sufficient, although it remains important. Organisations want people who have demonstrated the capacity to get things done. People who have lots of 'get up and go' tailored to the competence profile of the organisation	Highlights the paramount importance of individual performance and contribution to the bottom line. As for suitability, it also reflects the importance that is now attached to hitting the ground running
Acceptability	Emphasis on the 'social fit' between the individual and the organisation	'Social fit' and 'personal chemistry' include a focus on clients and customers, along with colleagues. Also more emphasis on an appropriate narrative of employability	Highlights the increased emphasis on client focus and customer information. It also reflects the importance of networking and managerial activities beyond the physical confines of company premises

Intellectual ability and potential are important, but these need to be grounded and applied to the strategic needs of the organisation. Organisations are increasingly focusing on proactivity or drive and commitment. Proactivity focuses on the manager regulating his or her career, including creating and maintaining a career mentality. Fit or acceptability has also emerged as an 'important issue'. Organisations are increasingly concerned to recruit managers who best fit with the social norms of the organisation. The notion of 'fit' is itself ambiguous, but it appears to be about personal confidence in high-pressured social situations.

Both Berger and Berger (2004) and Brown and Hesketh (2004) suggest two very interesting classifications of talent. The latter authors are more cynical in their analysis and recognise the difficulties in making such categorisations. They do, however, acknowledge that organisations use a variety of assessment tools to achieve this objective of particular categorisation, which we summarise in Table 7.5.

Table 7.5: Categorisation Talent and its Developmental Implications (Berger and Berger)

Category	Characteristics	Development Implications
Super Keepers	• Leaders whom the organisation works to keep • Consists of 3% to 5% of the organisation • They consistently demonstrate superior performance • They have very high career expectations and may be expected to be treated as stars	• Require the most significant investment in leadership development • Scope to be given global stretch and leadership assignments • Need to give a strong emphasis to the planning of their careers • Development initiatives must be focused on matching their competencies to the strategic requirements of the organisation
Backup Support	• They make a continually effective contribution to the organisation • They represent approximately 25%-30% of the leadership population • They possess clearly demonstrated leadership capabilities • They exceed expectations for both job accountabilities and core competencies • Their impact on the organisation is less dramatic than super shapers	• Can be developed to take on roles of a divisional or global level • Will benefit from stretch assignments and hardship experiences • Need to manage training and development carefully because they are a significant group in the organisation
Solid Citizens	• These leaders make up 65% of the organisation • They meet expectations in terms of core competencies • They possess the capability to manage processes and may be able to lead others • Potential to take on managerial roles that do not involve the management of people	• Develop further to perform current roles and potential stretch of current roles • Consider the possibility of lateral moves • May benefit from mentoring and coaching processes to sustain contribution to organisation
Misfit Managers	• Consist of between 3%-5% of the manager population who do not fit into the organisation • They do not perform to the required level • They have potential to be given special development with close supervision	• Reassign them to other work where they may show an improvement in performance • May have to make a decision concerning their future in the organisation

A super keeper is defined as a manager who has demonstrated superior performance. This manager will also embody the core competencies of the organisation and has inspired others to achieve superior performance. Berger and Berger (2004) were of the view that no more than three to five per cent of managers can be classified as super keepers: it is assumed that the organisation cannot afford to lose this type of manager. They also acknowledge that it is necessary to have backup support. They therefore include the development of highly qualified backup managers for key positions as a key component of talent management. Highly qualified backup managers are essential for organisational continuity. These positions must not remain vacant for any length of time. No more than eight to twelve per cent of an organisation's managers fall into this category.

Berger and Berger recognise that a significant proportion of an organisation's managerial population will have consistently high performers or what they term solid citizens. Consistent high performers (keepers) are managers who exceed performance expectations and possess the competence to help other managers to perform. They typically make up 20%–25% of the organisation. The majority of managers are therefore categorised as solid citizens. The aim of development with this group is to ensure a consistent contribution. All organisations will have a small percentage (typically no more than 5%) of misfit managers. It is possible that a management development intervention may be appropriate in order to get the manager back on track. If we are to follow the ideas promulgated by talent management, it is clear that the position of this category of manager should be terminated.

We will now move on to look at Brown and Hesketh's (2004) typology (Figure 7.2).

Figure 7.2: Employers' Mental Constructions of Talent

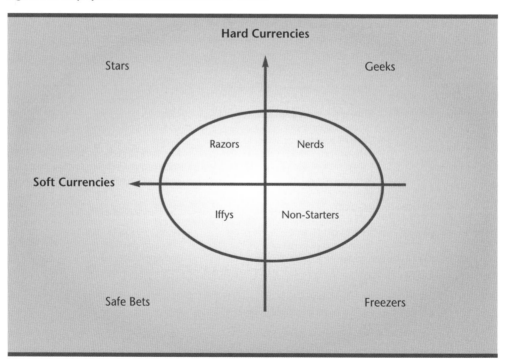

The vertical axis represents the way in which employers evaluate the hard currency or qualifications and formal achievements of managers. In selection processes, this is often done through a rolled summary of the manager's curriculum vitae. The horizontal axis represents the soft currencies or the personal and aesthetic skills of managers. These are often assessed using assessment and development centres, multisource feedback and psychological testing. The inner circle represents the fine line between success and failure. The key categories in this typology are described in Table 7.6:

Table 7.6: Typologies of Talent

- **Stars:** These managers have high levels of ability, intellectual achievement and excellent soft skills, including interpersonal sensitivity, persuasiveness, emotional resilience, teamworking and people skills. They are the complete package and are included in the top 10%.
- **Safe Bets:** This manager is a 'safe pair of hands' who will do a good job and has the potential to shine in the future. This category, however, may represent a gamble for the employer because they may be strong in analytical skills but weak on drive and proactivity.
- **Geeks:** This individual is not necessarily managerial material, but many managerial jobs in the knowledge economy require managers who have a high level of technical ability but who are not necessarily strong on interpersonal and leadership components.
- **Freezers:** These individuals do not perform well on assessment processes. They may have skills, but there is little to observe and they lack the social confidence that is an essential requirement for success.

Razors	**Nerds**
• This category demonstrates the thin line between success and failure. They are perceived to be over the top. • They can be arrogant, pushy and try too hard to impress. • In team situations, they dominate conversations.	• This potential manager lacks social confidence. They have strong technical knowledge but they lack the ability to apply that knowledge in social situations. • They represent a difficult development challenge for organisations. May perform most effectively in individual contributor roles.
Iffys	**Non-Starters**
• This group of potential managers lack commitment, business awareness and sufficient intellectual horsepower. • May initially appear as plausible, but they do not deliver on that promise. • They do not possess strong employability and are not effective at demonstrating a breadth of knowledge.	• This group are not 'at the races' in terms of management potential. • They may have an interest in becoming managers, but they lack the insight and personal attributes to be managers.

Developing the Talent Management Plan

An effective talent management plan will focus on four key issues: acquisition, cultivation, retention and organisation.

- **Acquisition:** This aspect of the plan focuses on how the organisation will secure talented managers to perform key roles in the organisation. It will articulate clearly the mix of acquisition strategies that the organisation proposes to use and the criteria on which judgements will be made concerning the appropriateness of the talent.
- **Cultivation:** This aspect addresses how the organisation will continue to develop its managerial talent. It will include some description of future needs and the strategies that

are appropriate to develop those needs. The cultivation component has a strong focus on developing the next generation of executives.

- **Retention:** This aspect focuses on the recognition of talent performance and the rewards for results. It will include actions that focus on both formal and informal recognition and reward.
- **Organisation:** This aspect focuses on the setting of clear goals and cascading them through the organisation. It will focus on how work is defined and organised, how information and communication slows and how strategy changes.

It is important that the talent plan speaks to the managers. This will be achieved by highlighting career development opportunities, the quality of the work environment, opportunities to influence, and recognition and reward programmes. It is important to manage expectations concerning the talent plan. It must demonstrate a sense of focus and the identification of key priorities.

Communication and Dissemination: There is a substantial convergence of opinion that talent and succession management processes need to be discussed openly. It is generally recommended that the process should be as transparent as possible. It is widely acknowledged that open communications is challenging for organisations that will have to deal with managers who are not part of the talent pool. It is generally argued that it is in the best interest of both managers and organisations that communications should be open about these matters. This arises out of recognition that the processes are essentially collaborative and that managers have a stake in the process and should be provided with the opportunity to inform its development.

Rothwell (2005) argues that the degree of communication depends on the organisation's culture. It is sometimes the case that organisations carry out talent and succession management processes in secret. In this scenario, managers made decisions concerning potential without the input of the manager concerned. Decisions concerning whom to develop and the approach to take are limited to a need-to-know basis. Top managers become the sole owners of talent and succession management processes and communicate little about how they operate. This approach therefore runs counter to good-practice prescriptions.

Extent of Individual Discretion: This issue concerns the extent of the involvement of managers in making assessments concerning performance and potential. Where decision-making processes are top-down, they ignore individual career goals. In these situations, managers identify the best candidates regardless of the views of managers. This approach is now considered to be outdated given that leaders are now more focused on managing their career and that there is an increased emphasis on work-life balance issues. The more contemporary best-practice approach is to involve managers in discussions concerning their development and career expectations. This approach seeks to balance organisational talent and succession needs with individual career goals.

Ongoing Evaluation of Processes: There is a need for ongoing evaluation. Because of the investment involved, it is important to determine return on investment and to communicate the results proactively. It is important to develop appropriate measures to enable this evaluation process to be undertaken. Examples of measures that can be used include: the extent to which leadership job openings can be filled from the internal pool; the average number of qualified candidates for each leadership position; the number of positions with two or more 'ready now' candidates; and the retention rate of the succession post.

It is also important that talent and succession management processes are designed to be flexible. They need to be evaluated to ascertain how responsive they are to changes in organisational needs, both current and future. There is evidence that talent and succession management processes may become too administratively intensive. Effective talent and succession management processes have a number of characteristics which ensure their success. They should:

- Display a clear recognition that the creation and containment of organisational alignment is a journey, not a one-off event.
- Identify a talent champion who should be a board member or CEO.
- Develop, implement and monitor the talent strategy using a stakeholder perspective.
- Challenge existing organisational capabilities so that the talent plan addresses key gaps.
- Strive for simplicity when implementing and monitoring the plan.
- Support the plan with resources, organisational visibility and communication.

Figure 7.3 illustrates the components of a talent management system.

Figure 7.3: An Integrated Talent Management System

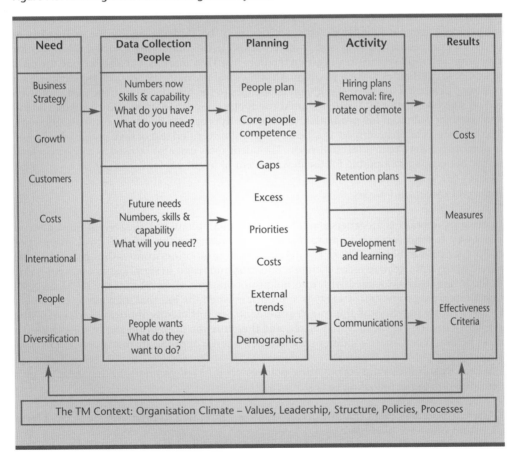

Management and Leadership Development Issues: Implications of Talent and Succession Management

We will now concentrate on the discussion of specific management and leadership development issues that arise from the implementation of talent and succession management processes. These include the leadership bench strength, the role of internal promotion processes, the preparation of individual development plans and the use of internal leadership development strategies.

Making Decisions about Bench Strength

We define bench strength as the capacity of an organisation to fill key management vacancies from within. When organisations test bench strength, they make determinations concerning how well the organisation is able to fill key positions quickly and from within. There is a lack of scientific rigour to the bench strength testing process. Some suggestions include the preparation of replacement charts, the administration of questionnaires and the analysis of previous records. A replacement chart can help identify roles for which no internal replacement can be identified. This activity may be undertaken by the management development specialist. It may also involve the specialist conducting a survey asking senior executives who will replace key position incumbents. This analysis will also include the ratio of available candidates to each position. An analysis of previous records will highlight which positions presented the most significant challenges to the organisation in the past. Rothwell (2005) suggests that organisations should conduct a talent show to identify available talent, analyse their potential for promotion and discuss appropriate developmental assignments. The outcome is often described as a 'beauty pageant or verified test of high potential matched to appropriate developmental challenges'. The talent show can also be used as a device to hold senior managers accountable for the development of talent pools.

Internal Promotion Policies

Internal promotion is a cornerstone of organisational talent and succession management processes. It represents an important strategy in managing the psychological contract of high-potential employees. There is evidence that a promotion-from-within policy has the potential to motivate managers, facilitate retention and result in significant cost savings due to the lower costs associated with internal promotion processes. Rothwell (2005) suggests that an internal promotion strategy is appropriate when the internal manager is competent to meet eighty per cent of the role requirements, is sufficiently motivated to accept the responsibility for the vacancy that arises, and therefore the promotion can be filled within a short period. Where these conditions are not met, it is not appropriate to use promotion from within.

When organisations are formulating policies on internal promotion, they need to give consideration to the following issues:

- Give a clear statement that the organisation is committed to promoting managers from within whenever possible.
- Define clearly the internal promotion process that will be followed and the mechanism of job-posting.
- Explain clearly the business reasons for having such a policy.
- Explain the conditions under which it may be necessary to select an external candidate.
- Put in place processes that will enable legal and other challenges to be addressed professionally.

Preparation of Individual Development Plans

Personal or individual development plans are a very effective tool to enable managers to narrow the gap between what they have in terms of competencies and future competency requirements. An individual development plan combines elements of learning, a performance contract and a career-planning tool.

- **Learning Contract:** This is an agreement to learn that seeks to balance individual and organisational needs. It is a collaboratively produced document.
- **Performance Contract:** This is an agreement between a manager and a reporting manager to achieve an identifiable and measurable performance. It focuses on future performance improvements and is usually linked to the performance-appraisal process, if one exists.
- **Career-Planning Tool:** This component of the development plan identifies specific career goals and specifies career strategies to realise them.

The Corporate Leadership Council (2001) identified the development plan as the second most influential development strategy. However, to be effective, it must be built around a development model which is grounded in real-world experience. The plan needs to be customised and to include appropriate job assignments. Stringer and Cheloha (2003) suggested that a development plan operates at two levels. At the organisational level, it helps to ensure that the next generation of leaders possesses the competencies required by organisational strategy. At the personal level, it forces individual leaders to focus on what needs to be done in order to develop. Bossidy and Charan (2002) and Collins (2001) suggested that the most effective development strategies are those that emphasise the development of plans focused on the skills and behaviours necessary for the achievement of corporate strategy. However, they caution that while organisations identify the most appropriate development strategies in their development plans, they fail to implement them effectively. Table 7.7 summarises some of the characteristics of an effective individual development plan.

Table 7.7: Characteristics of an Effective Development Plan

Characteristic	Features
Personalised and Personal	<ul><li>Personalisation involves the identification of a manager's unique set of development needs.</li><li>Managers must start from a particular point with an acknowledged set of strengths and development priorities.</li><li>Development actions should apply uniquely to the manager involved.</li></ul>
Emphasis on Specific Development Needs	<ul><li>Do not deal with surface symptoms but look at what lies behind or beneath particular behaviours.</li><li>The development plan must address real issues and consider these issues in terms of current and future consistency.</li></ul>
Practicality	<ul><li>Key issues are the meaningfulness of the plan and its potential to work.</li><li>Plan should reflect the key priorities and not be over-ambitious.</li></ul>
Focus is on On-the-Job Learning	<ul><li>Leadership is learned through actual experience; observation is not enough.</li><li>Leaders learn most of their skills through key tasks, interactions with others and personal partnerships.</li></ul>

Characteristic	Features
Ownership	• Leader must have complete commitment and buy-in. • Ownership and agreement are essential prerequisites for the future implementation of the plan. • The leader should create the plan because this will engender more responsibility for implementing it.
Living Documents	• An effective plan places the future leader in situations that provide learning opportunities. • Effective development plans include an array of on-the-job experiences, assignments and high visibility opportunities. • The plan includes activities which stretch emotional limits, foster risk and innovation and move the leader to a new phase of development. • The plan is dynamic and can cope with unplanned-for development opportunities.
Strong Emphasis on Coaching and Personal Feedback	• Well-designed plans will include a sounding board and an effective coaching relationship. • Feedback elements need to be grounded in reality and the manager needs to be given honest feedback. • More senior managers are, however, less likely to get candid feedback.

Source: Adapted from Stringer and Cheloha (2005)

Various processes are required to effectively implement a development planning process. Rothwell (2005), Garavan, Hogan and Cahir-O'Donnell (2003) and Stringer and Cheloha (2003) suggest the following elements of good practice:

- **Be Strategic in Targeting Specific Groups**: Following the principles of talent management, organisations should focus initially on high-potential populations. This group has the potential to realise a significant investment for the organisation.
- **Focus on Multiple Developmental Feedback**: Organisations should use multiple sources to assess the strengths and development needs of managers. Self-assessments of development have a tendency to be biased. Multiple assessments utilising 360-degree surveys or development centre processes offer significant advantages in terms of the range of competencies they assess and the depth and coverage of feedback.
- **Focus on Feedback Processes**: Feedback is an essential prerequisite for the preparation of a development plan. Feedback needs to be shared with the manager. The manager needs to be given sufficient time to assess the feedback process, which should be initiated as soon as the feedback is collected. This feedback session is of critical importance in helping to determine the content of the development plan.
- **A Collaborative Process**: The best plans are likely to be produced as a result of a collaborative process. This process is likely to involve the future leader, his/her boss, the management development specialist and perhaps an external coach. These parties need to collaborate in order to make sense of both the development context and the development opportunities. The plan should be time-focused and include developmental actions that focus on the short, medium and long term. The plan should account for the fact that development opportunities are difficult to predict and may be undermined by events in the wider organisation. This suggests that a review process is necessary in order to realign and reconsider the plan contents.

Internal Leadership Development Strategies

Effective leadership development and the development of talent take place in a specific organisational context. A fundamental component of the talent management process concerns the development of a culture of learning and the creation of awareness of the need for development amongst current and potential leaders. An additional component concerns the selection of development opportunities that are significantly stretching and developmental. An important question in the context of a talent management strategy concerns the creation of awareness of development amongst leaders and the engendering of support for development. Leaders contribute to the talent management process by developing their awareness of performance and competencies, by developing a motivation to change and by enhancing their skills to develop people.

Table 7.8 summarises some of the actions that leaders can take to facilitate the talent management process.

Table 7.8: Making Leaders Accountable for the Development of Future Leaders: Some Guidelines

Issue	Tactics
Awareness of Job-Performance Issues	• Be willing to provide objective feedback on performance. • Provide personal, positive performance feedback. • Give corrective performance feedback when necessary. • Be willing to provide the leader with feedback that is confirming.
Awareness of Competencies	• Focus on strengths and weaknesses and skills that need to be developed. • Be prepared to seek an expert concerning assessment of strengths and weaknesses.
Motivating Change	• Be clear concerning what constitutes excellent performance. • Communicate clear criteria for promotion and career advancement. • Communicate to the leader their value to the organisation. • Provide significant financial and non-financial incentives to motivate leaders to learn and develop.
Building New Competencies	• Be willing to spend time with the potential leader and give personal coaching. • Arrange coaching with others, both inside and outside the organisation. • Have future leaders work with a role model. • Be a friend to the leader and be a source of stability and wisdom. • Have the leader work on a project that requires a highly visible delivery. • Be candid in your assessment of what has been delivered. • Seek out development opportunities throughout the organisation.

Source: Adapted form Stringe (2002); Corporate Leadership Council (2001)

EXHIBIT 7.7

The Leadership Pipeline: How to Build a Leadership-Powered Company

Charan, Drotter and Noel advanced the concept of the leadership pipeline. The model takes a long-term approach to the development of leaders. It is premised on the following ideas: the demand for leadership has grown with economic performance, but the supply of leadership has not kept pace; organisations are finding it increasingly difficult to find leaders with the right skills; local leadership has become a prized commodity in order to manage the balance between global and local issues; and many companies do not yet recognise the importance of leadership development to business strategy.

The authors argued that leadership is required at all levels in the organisation. They viewed potential as a dynamic process and suggested that individuals pass through six leadership passages:

- *Passage 1:* Managing Self to Managing Others: The early focus on the potential manager's skill development is to earn 'promotable' status. These skills include planning and a range of personal and professional behaviours. The aim of the first passage is to enable the potential manager to move from being productive to making others productive and developing relationships in all directions. Potential managers frequently encounter difficulty in giving up what they do successfully.
- *Passage 2:* Managing Others to Managing Managers: This passage is rarely addressed as a formal step in organisations' leadership development processes. In this passage managers must be pure managers and no longer individual contributors. The challenge for the organisation is to select people who can make the transition, assign them appropriate management tasks, coach them effectively and manage their performance. The manager begins to recognise the importance of coaching and to value management work over technical expertise.
- *Passage 3:* Managing Managers to Functional Managers: This transition can be the most difficult one to accomplish. Managers during passage three are expected to manage outside their own experience, take other functional areas into account and compete for resources. The manager is expected to adopt a broad, long-term perspective. Functional managers develop maturity through on-the-job coaching and they will devote time to strategy and communication issues. They will focus on the business.
- *Passage 4:* Functional to Business Manager: This passage is often the most challenging and the most satisfying phase of a manager's career. The development challenge is to ensure that the manager has a profit perspective, is able to think both short and long term and has exposure to lots of new and unfamiliar responsibilities. Managers who successfully navigate this passage will develop respect for staff functions, and trust and accept advice and feedback from functional managers. Business managers are expected to cope with complexity but at all times understand how the business makes its money.
- *Passage 5:* Business to Group Manager: A business manager values the success of his/her own business, whereas a group manager values the success of other people's businesses. Group managers must become proficient at managing capital allocations between competing businesses. They must make a successful move from business strategy to portfolio strategy. The key skills are the ability to manage complexity, handle bigger decisions and to assess and cope with risk. They must also think in terms of the industry and be skilled in assessing business managers, their teams and culture. This passage represents a key testing ground for future CEO candidates.
- *Passage 6:* Group to Enterprise Manager: This passage focuses on the further development of group manager skills. The focus is on changing values. The enterprise manager must be a long-term visionary thinker while developing the strategies and mechanisms to drive short-term performance in line with long-term strategy. The enterprise manager needs to be proactive, outward-looking and feel comfortable focusing on the 'whole'. He/she must also assemble a team of high-achieving and ambitious direct reports and must be an effective communicator who inspires people at all levels of the organisation.

Building this pipeline requires a long-term and customised approach to leadership development. Managers must be held accountable for their own development as well as that of others.

Source: Charan, Drotter and Noel (2001)

Organisations have two distinct choices in respect of leadership development: an internal development versus a buy strategy. Internal development is defined as a set of leadership development activities sponsored by the organisation that are designed to enhance leadership capability. Rothwell (2005) makes a very useful distinction between six different types of internal development strategy:

- **Who-Based Internal Leadership Development Strategies:** This category of learning strategies focuses on matching high-potential leaders with leaders who have particular or specific talents. The manager with responsibility for development may have a particular management style or may possess specific expertise or abilities which can be passed on to the high-potential leader candidate.
- **What-Based Leadership Development Strategies**: These strategies focus on giving high-potential leaders exposure to work situations that facilitate the development of specific skills or competencies. These special experiences or work situations could include projects, committee or task-force participation and job assignments that are associated with novel or problematic activities. These strategies have the potential to both enhance the high potential's capability and increase visibility in the organisation.
- **When-Based Leadership Development Strategies:** These learning events are designed to give the high-potential leader candidate exposure to time pressures. The leader may be required to complete a task to a very tight deadline or secure a contract by a specific date. This strategy may also incorporate some element of hardship.
- **Where-Based Leadership Development Strategies**: These development strategies focus on giving high-potential candidates exposure to specific locations and/or ventures. It may involve the organisation sending the high-potential manager on an international assignment so as to give him/her exposure to a particular business culture. It may also include an assignment to a manufacturing or customer interface site. This strategy is most likely appropriate where the organisation has a multinational or global network of locations. It seeks to broaden the cultural skills of the high-potential manager candidate as well as provide experience in a number of value-chain activities.
- **Why-Based Leadership Development Strategies**: These learning strategies focus on providing the high-potential leader candidate with exposure to learning initiatives that involve mission- or strategy-driven change. They could entail the high-potential leader getting involved in a major continuous improvement initiative, a start-up process or a benchmarking activity.
- **How-Based Leadership Development Strategies**: These leadership development strategies focus on providing the high-potential leadership candidate with an in-depth how-to knowledge of different dimensions of the business. The leader may work in finance for a period of time, followed by manufacturing and sales experience. These strategies usually involve placing the leader in an area where he or she is unfamiliar.

Table 7.9 summarises the characteristics of each strategy and when it is appropriate.

Table 7.9: Internal Leadership Development Strategies

Strategy	Characteristics	When Appropriate	When Inappropriate
Who-Based Strategies	• Matching the high potential with an experienced manager • Focus on a developing manager who is a good role model • May involve elements of coaching and Mentoring • May have elements of planning	• For pairing up unlikely individuals on occasions • For building top-level ownership • To facilitate an understanding of organisational policies • To facilitate current progression	• For the development of specific skills
What-Based Strategies	• Exposure to specific types of experiences • Includes wide variety of work-based learning activities • May involve specific complex tasks	• When the project or assignment has sufficient development potential • When the work activities involved are directly related to future work • When the lack of experience is specified in the form of a learning contract	• When the lack of experience does not represent a sufficient stretch • When it is used to fill a staffing problem • When the assignment is not of sufficient duration to facilitate learning
When-Based Strategies	• Providing the high potential with time-based development activities • Testing the high potential to deliver on a complex task • Focuses the enhancement of stress- and time-management strategies	• When the high potential is at a point where he/she has to move to the next level • When the high potential has developed a good track record on more positive learning tasks	• To find out the high potential • When there is insufficient prior development activity • When the high potential is a novice
Where-Based Strategies	• Provides the high potential with international experience • May also involve putting the high potential in a special context to gain experience	• When the leader requires a knowledge of cross-cultural issues • When the leader needs to be expert in various elements of the organisation's value chain	• Not appropriate unless it is well-planned and it is clearly identified what the participant will learn • Should not be used simply to give the high potential leader international experience

Strategy	Characteristics	When Appropriate	When Inappropriate
Why-Based Strategies	• Development interaction focuses on change initiatives and mission-driven initiatives • May enable the high potential to develop skills in innovation and benchmarking • Usually involves short- to medium-term assignment	• To provide the leader with special skills that may not arise in the normal day-to-day duties • To develop accountability of the manager for specific areas of change	• Where the strategic issue is not strategic at all, but focuses on a short-term micro level issue
How-Based Strategies	• Focus is on the development of special knowledge and expertise • Involves planned organisational moves and lengthy job assignments • Provides high potential with opportunity to acquire knowledge of particular areas of business	• Where the leader needs to develop technical expertise • To address a significant weakness in the competency profile of the leader	• Just to get the leader to fill in for some other manager • Must be based on a recognised skill gap

Box 7.2: Adopting a Developmental Approach to Talent and Succession Management

The model still used in many companies is the military chain of command, or 'dead men's shoes'. The person with potential may not be waiting for one specific opening, but the opportunity pool is as limited as the talent pool. Depth of experience is highly valued. This model is most common in organisations that operate through functional silos. The alternative model assumes that talent is owned by the organisation, not by individual businesses, and moves designated high flyers around frequently to ensure they gain breadth of experience. Much less common than either of these is the organisation that offers people a choice, at different periods in their careers, of whether to enter a closed or open talent pool, and builds bridges between these – yet, for many people, this is a much closer reflection of the career progression they would like.

Implicit in many organisations' view of the talent pool is the philosophy of 'up or out'. Yet there are many reasons why people may wish to broaden their capabilities by horizontal career moves (for example, to allow for a period of high demand from their non-work lives). Going up may enable an individual to expand their leadership competence, but moving sideways can result in building cross-disciplinary operational skills, which are an ideal platform for more rapid subsequent progression and which may be highly valuable to the organisation. Moreover, the 'up or out' philosophy is discriminatory and therefore both wasteful and, in many countries, illegal. People from minority or disadvantaged groups appear to have different career trajectories than people from the dominant group, with longer intervals between promotions at early stages of their careers and shorter intervals once they enter senior management. Mentoring can help both the individual and the organisation by enabling the individual to make both the personal and business case for a non-vertical career path.

A Pragmatic Way Forward

So what can organisations do to improve the efficacy of their processes? Some of the issues to consider include:

- *Making sponsorship a more open and managed process*: Sponsors play a very different role from mentors and coaches. The modern version of a sponsor is an informed senior manager who takes on the long-term responsibility for balancing the career needs of talented individuals against the evolving needs of the business. He/she ensures that an appropriate range of moves is available for the individual and that the person's progress is not obstructed by line managers who want to hang on to their best people.

- *Stop putting people into boxes*: The negative side to putting people in boxes is that the box becomes a cell, from which it is difficult to break out. Labelling people may prevent them and other people seeing them differently in different circumstances. It is remarkable, for example, how many apparent middling performers, perceived to have low potential for promotion, become different people under a different boss who has different beliefs about them. The same principle may also apply to star players who die on the vine when they move out from the protection of a powerful boss.

- *Adopt a more systemic view of performance*: A systemic view sees performance as the outcome of both the individual's capabilities and the context in which they operate. Changing the environment may encourage talented people to apply themselves more and in original ways, which will be of far more value than dragooning them into a 'pipeline'. At the simplest level, a manager, who had been dropped from the high-flyer pool because he was judged not to be a sufficiently strategic thinker, negotiated one day a week at home to work without interruption. Six months later, his devastating analysis of the business IT strategy led to a total rethink of this aspect of the business. Two things had changed: he had gained the time to reflect; and he had been helped to use reflective space by occasional conversations with a mentor, who enabled him to tap into skills that were already there but had been suppressed by the working environment.

- The role of coaches and mentors increasingly includes helping the individual to create and negotiate with the organisation a development plan that is both imaginative and sustainable. In reflective space, it is possible to question both one's own and other people's perceptions, to envisage a range of parallel futures and to work to personal growth strategies that are simultaneously focused and highly flexible. In this way, it is not necessary to wait until the next formal performance/development review to react to changing opportunities – either the individual or the organisation can take the initiative.

- *Continually re-examine the qualities and experience required for significant roles*: Singapore Airlines, which has for decades moved its talented people into functions of which they have little experience, nonetheless always appointed a finance person to run the finance function. When the company finally took the plunge and appointed an engineer to the role, it worked extremely well. The experienced executive was better able than any of his predecessors to separate himself from the functional detail and remain strategic. There is also evidence that the most effective HR directors are typically people who have joined the function after a few promotions from line positions.

- *Managing the process of helping people build track record*: Intelligent use of project teams creates opportunities for people to demonstrate what they can do outside their normal box. Giving people tasks outside their previous experience within the project team grows both organisational and individual capacity. Making this practice work, however, typically demands a radical overhaul of how project teams are assembled and how the project team leader is trained. Making development of participants an equal or near equal measure of success of the project team is an essential part of this overhaul.

A Role for Coaches and Mentors

Important roles for the coach or mentor include:

- Helping the talented individual identify unconventional, less obvious moves and make the case for these. Again, a systemic approach is valuable here. The newly promoted manager does not work in isolation. Making their success and their learning a team responsibility does not work in isolation and changes the whole dynamics of the situation. The coach or mentor can help them plan how to engage the team in this way but, equally, there is a requirement for the organisation to create appropriate expectations in the team before the manager joins.

- Assisting the talented individual to establish better and wider networks inside and outside the organisation and to manage those networks effectively. More a mentor role than a coach role, network development can be both passive and active. In the active sense, it involves making introductions and suggesting people who the talented individual should contact. In the passive sense, it involves working with people to develop the skills of networking and manage personal credibility. Some organisations have specifically introduced mentoring programmes to help bright but unnoticed people to become known and therefore to enter the running when new opportunities arise.

- Providing a resource for reflecting upon wider issues of identity, personal values and personal goals. The keys here are a safe environment in which to open up this dialogue and the skills to maintain dialogue at a much deeper level than is possible in most other working conversations.

- Helping the talented individual extract more value from their current role. It is very easy for the coaching or mentoring conversation to concentrate on the next job the person wants. Yet there is usually a great deal of learning in the current job, if the person knows how to look for it. It is not uncommon for mentoring to help someone who is desperate to move on to recognise 'unfinished business' in their current role and take an extra six months or so to consolidate a skill that will prove invaluable to their subsequent career as a leader.

The integration of succession planning with both coaching and mentoring is an inevitable outcome of the modern organisation's need to manage its talent pool in a way that more realistically reflects the dynamics of its workforce and its markets. If each is to support the other, however, they must be managed with more skill and flexibility than is the norm.

Source: Clutterbuck (2005)

Talent and Succession Management for CEOs

CEO talent and succession management is complex and the cost of a mistake in succession can be significant. Even for the most experienced people, leadership at the top is difficult for new CEOs. The job role brings with it a significant degree of uncertainty and a high failure rate. The Centre for Creative Leadership (Martin 2007) estimated that forty per cent of new CEOs fail in the first eighteen months. Watkins and Marsick (2003) found that, when promoted from within, less than half of the leaders who reached the number two spot who expected to achieve the CEO position actually ended up in that position. A large number of organisations are now going outside their ranks to hire a successor. Ciampa (2005) suggests that the criteria for judging a successful CEO are complex and sometimes difficult to explain. He suggests three sets of capabilities that are important:

- **Senior Management Best Practice:** This refers to the ability to prioritise the things that make a difference in operational terms. It includes such issues as prioritising, the use of time, developing people and delegating the right tasks. The CEO needs to have these capabilities in a form that is subtly different from that of senior managers. Some of these differences are presented in Table 7.10.
- **Managing the Political Environment:** The research indicates that effective CEOs have the capacity to generate active peer support. Executives who are politically aware are very effective at finding ways for their strengths to be reflected on others. This means that they do not need to shine the spotlight of attention too brightly on themselves.
- **Personal Style:** Effective CEOs do not necessarily make a big deal of the success they have achieved. They manage to give credit to the success of others without diminishing their own position.

Table 7.10: The Characteristics of Effective CEOs

	The Good Candidate	The Elite Candidate
Management Savvy	• Knows what is required operationally for short-term results • Motivates others to do it • Uses time well • Prioritises among issues that are all important • Frequently delegates tasks • Has a history of developing subordinates and exporting talent • Organises and mobilises talent toward most significant problems • Pushes people to achieve more than they think they can	• Avoids jumping in personally to solve problems others can handle • Makes the right judgements about what to expend energy on • Maintains control of the key decisions and a full pipeline of talented people • Makes people feel appreciated and stay loyal
Political Intelligence	• Accurately reads political currents • Understands patterns of relationships quickly in an unfamiliar environment • Builds relationships with peers and subordinates • Makes sure the CEO and the board know what he or she is capable of doing	• Isn't labelled 'political' • Recognises how relationships are likely to affect early success • Gets peers and subordinates to go out of their way to help • Doesn't seem self-serving
Personal Style	• Is a star performer • Is intense and driven to excel • Is hardworking, usually putting in more time and effort than peers do • Enthusiastically backs initiatives that will help the business succeed • Is a leader among peers • Understands new ways of doing things and makes important connections	• Makes success look effortless • Allows others' performance to be recognised too • Manages energy to stay on the 'rested edge' and to avoid the 'ragged edge' • Knows when to hold back and when to let go • Enables peers to improve their performance • Stays grounded and makes sure basic needs are met while mastering new concepts

Determinants of CEO Succession

A considerable number of factors explain CEO succession in organisations. Specific factors include:

- *Board-Detailed Issues*: Power and political issues within the organisation are important in explaining the appointment of a CEO. These include the size of the board, the number of outside directors, the number of directors appointed by the CEO and whether the CEO is also the chairman of the board. Outside successors are likely to be demographically similar to the board and dissimilar to the predecessor CEO (Zajac and Westphal 1996). In times when the organisation is performing effectively, outside directors used their heirs apparent to prevent incumbent CEOs from abusing power, and during times of poorer performance they used their power to initiate the exit of heirs apparent to diminish the impact of incumbent CEOs.
- *Performance of the Firm*: Datta and Guthrie (1994) found that power growth and profitability are associated with the selection of an outsider CEO. Other research finds that poor organisational performance is associated with external successors, where the CEO leaves before retirement age.
- *Leader Characteristics and Actions*: This group of factors relate to tenure, managerial ability and efficiency, and the career background of the leader. Canella and Shen (201) found that firm-specific skills developed during the company tenure of the heir apparent will increase the likelihood of promotion to CEO and decrease the likelihood of exit.
- *Characteristics of the Firm*: Factors that come into play here include the research and development intensity of the firm, the organisation's corporate strategy and the firm size. High R&D intensity is associated with successors who are well educated and possess a technical background (Datta and Guthrie 1994). Corporate strategy is, however, not as effective in predicting the CEO's career specialisation. Hollenbeck (1994) found that the size of the firm is related to outside succession. They also found that outsiders extract a premium from the organisation and have a mandate for change. Where there are many potential candidates whose achievements are known, this will have an impact on the ability of the heir apparent to outshine others.
- *Succession Management Activities*: Fiegener *et al.* (1996) compared succession planning in family and non-family firms in the USA. They found that CEOs in family firms preferred developing personal relationships with their successors and also between the successor and important stakeholders. They were not inclined to view experience in other firms as important to succession preparation. CEOs in non-family firms preferred external and less personal forms of succession preparation, such as university performance and executive development seminars.

The overall conclusion to be drawn is that CEO succession is complex and explained by many internal and external variables. Succession of a CEO is a difficult task for organisations to undertake and should be handled carefully.

Managing CEO Succession

CEO talent and succession management should be driven by the board. The board's role, therefore, has a number of dimensions.

- The board should ensure that a succession planning process is always in development and that a plan is always in place. Therefore, in the event of something untimely happening, a replacement can be acquired very quickly.

- It is best to identify a specific successor. Having multiple successors has the potential to lead to a disruptive horse race which could have a negative impact on the organisation.
- The board should sign off on any designation of internal candidates or any succession planning initiatives. It is important that the current CEO understands that the board will make the ultimate decision.
- Once the successor is appointed, the board should ensure that all aspects of the contract are communicated to subsequent boards.
- The board should ensure that the selection process is conducted fairly and that the actual selection is not simply left to the CEO.

CEOs may frequently delay talent and succession management practices in the interests of maintaining their current position. It is also likely that boards may encounter a range of other problems, including:

- The lack of a clear transmission strategy and the lack of a clear exit strategy for the incumbent executive.
- The inability of the internal candidate to assume the position. The heir apparent may not be ready or may be unwilling to take the position.
- The organisation may experience the departure of others in the organisation who considered themselves to be ready for the position but have not been designated by the board as the heir apparent.

Box 7.3 sets out a number of questions that the board should consider in the context of CEO succession.

Box 7.3: CEO Talent and Succession Management: Key Questions

- What should the board do to ensure a successful succession?
- How should the leadership development issues for the successor be handled?
- How should the board work with the current CEO during the process?
- What criteria distinguish a strong CEO candidate?
- What role should be played by an executive search agency?
- When should the board consider external candidates?
- Should competition be encouraged among potential CEO candidates?
- How should development plans and succession timelines be implemented?
- What kinds of post-succession assessment should be undertaken to identify potential problems early on?

Development Issues for CEO Talent Management

The importance of developing CEOs is highlighted in numerous studies. The Corporate Leadership Council (2000), for example, suggested that the best-practice companies grow general managers and CEOs through well-planned experiences that expose them to a multiplicity of customers, functions, business models, geographic and cultural environments. These development initiatives are sustained for a significant period of time. Eichinger and Lombardo (2002) suggested that CEO and general manager (GM) development should focus on stretch job assignments, not coaching, mentoring or formal development processes. Potential general managers need to be stretched by complex job assignments over long periods of time. Arons and Ruh (2004) identified specific characteristics of these job stretch assignments and moves. Organisations should:

- Delegate real responsibility and hold potential GMs accountable for sustained results. Development should occur under pressure.
- High-potential leaders need to be tested and organisations should take overseeing risks in those who succeed.
- High-potential leaders should participate in function and general business assignments early in their careers.
- Organisations must prepare managers with smaller moves in order to make one or more substantial upward moves.
- Organisations should consider non-obvious job moves for key high potentials while at the same time considering the risks involved.
- Organisations should avoid moves that have unclear development goals and avoid adopting a one-size-fits-all approach to careers.
- The nature of general management roles varies considerably, even within a single large organisation. This presents major challenges when designing career paths and development opportunities.
- High-potential leaders are demanding. They expect some form of rationale to underpin job moves. Many organisations struggle to provide a clear rationale or template for job moves.

Kesler and Kirincic (2005) have conducted extensive research on development and talent management for general managers. Six particular findings emerge from their study:

- The roles that general managers perform are complex. General managers manage a diversity of functions and activities and they require different competencies depending on the context. Factors such as sales volume, headcount managed and assets control are of little value when considering the development moves for potential GMs.
- Many organisations have a lack of clarity concerning the developmental value of various leader roles. They have not worked out the talent pipeline and the transitions that managers must successfully navigate in order to be ready to take on the GM role.
- High-potential leaders are very ambitious and seek clarity concerning their future prospects for advancement. Organisations frequently fail to provide this clarity.
- Many general manager potentials focus on the more tangible aspects of the job and think narrowly about career paths. They focus primarily on moves within their division or group. Their bosses often think in a similarly narrow fashion. On the other hand, managers feel dead-ended and unclear about their future opportunities.

Kesler and Kirincic (2005) suggest five general manager archetypes. These archetypes apply to all organisations and lines of business and are based on three criteria:

- **Ability to Manage Complexity:** This criterion focuses on the intellectual abilities required for success in a leadership role. The management of complexity is viewed as a key differential. Kesler and Kirincic view it as hard-wired and therefore less amenable to development.
- **Motivational Requirements:** This criterion focuses on the motivation of the high potential to demonstrate breadth and depth of interest in multiple functions, rather than focusing on functional activities.
- **Competencies:** This criterion includes knowledge, skill and personal requirements. This component is highly amenable to development. It is best achieved through timely job moves that ensure extensive exposure.

Talent development for leaders needs to be integrated with talent selection and retention processes. It should involve the organisation engaging top leaders in defining the nature of general manager work and the future development needs of the business and producing development roadmaps to guide effective talent management. The Leadership Council

suggests that leaders with potential should move across the different GM types and businesses early in their careers. High potentials should remain in key positions for two to four years and move when successful results have been achieved. High-potential leaders need to have individualised development plans that are developed collaboratively with their boss.

EXHIBIT 7.8

General Manager Archetypes

	Manages a Function/Product		Manages a Business		Manages Multiple Businesses	
Criteria	Product or Market Segment GM	Functional GM	SBU GM		Multi-Business GM	Group GM
Operating Focus	Product, service or market segment with P&L ($75-350m revenue), focused on all facets of product management and development.	Major operating unit with multiple functions with P&L ($5-6b revenue) focused on corporate strategy execution.	Stand-alone strategic business unit with all functional accountabilities and full P&L (with variations in $ volume).		Stand-alone strategic business unit with multiple products or services, often in multiple divisions or SBUs.	Multiple SBUs with consolidated P&L. Responsible for external stakeholders and policy.
Organisation Managed	Product management. Product development. Sourcing. Customer management.	Multiple functions, typically including pooled sales and distribution functions and support roles.	All business functions represented, excluding legal and treasury.		All business functions represented.	Multiple SBUs. Group staff functions. Strategic planning.
Decision Authority	Product positioning and plans. Product development portfolio. Pricing with committee oversight. Customer (external) escalation and issue resolution.	Direct impact on external customers. Pricing within set corridors. Buy-side purchase decisions. Staffing. Recommends physical plant.	Same as product GM and functional GM with additional authority and less oversight.		Same as product GM and functional GM with limited oversight.	Same as SBU GM with very high degrees of autonomy across multiple business models.

Manages a Function/Product		Manages a Business		Manages Multiple Businesses	
Criteria	Product or Market Segment GM	Functional GM	SBU GM	Multi-Business GM	Group GM
Impact on P&L	High impact on expenses. Some impact on bookings.	High impact on specific volumes with material impact on business results.	High impact on all operating income elements. ROI targets.	Very high impact on all operating income elements. ROI targets.	Total accountability for all operating income elements for the long term.

Issues in Talent and Succession Management

Talent management is still a relatively underdeveloped area of human resource management. The very notion of talent itself is problematic. Michaels, Handfield-Jones and Axelrod (2001) defined talent as the sum of a person's abilities. This includes characteristics such as skills, knowledge, experience, intelligence, judgement, attitude, character and drive. It also includes characteristics such as motivation and ability to learn. They suggested that given the nature of talent, managers and leaders must be continuously inspired to do their best and teams of managers must be properly aligned and motivated to deliver collective performance. Organisations must possess the ability not only to recruit, but also to cultivate, develop and retain talent.

A key concern of talent management is to achieve integration of a range of activities and integration with business strategy. Global companies in particular place emphasis on the integration of talent management functions. The integration process is challenging and advocates of talent management underestimate the difficulty. Particular challenges include those that are organisational, cultural, technological and global in nature. Truly integrated talent management seeks to combine sourcing, recruiting, selection, development and retention within the business process. If integration is achieved, it brings with it a number of benefits (highlighted earlier). The barriers can include:

- **Organisational:** The evidence indicates that inconsistencies occur in how business units and divisions apply the philosophy and role of talent management. There is often a lack of cohesion among business units and difficulties are encountered in ensuring that talent management goals are clearly communicated.
- **Cultural:** Cultural barriers within the organisation may inhibit the effectiveness of the talent management process. Managers may not be aware of the organisation's talent management system's functions and capabilities.
- **The Self-Fulfilling Prophecy, Working in Reverse**: The talent literature consistently emphasises identifying the top ten per cent. It also suggests that the bottom ten per cent should be removed from the organisation or helped to improve. Pfeffer (2001) questions whether it is possible to produce such categorisations. He considers the process of labelling to be detrimental because the very labelling of managers will impact on their performance and identifying a few as stars will cause the majority to perform below potential.
- **Failure to Consider Systemic and Cultural Influences on Performance**: Talent management focuses organisations on individuals at the expense of the entire

organisation. As a result, organisations ignore the moderating influence of both cultures and systems that impact on performance.

- **Losing the War for Wisdom**: Pfeffer (2001) suggested that organisations might be better off hiring 'wise' rather than 'smart' people. Wisdom is of greater value to the organisation because it enables the organisation to take action even if it has doubts concerning what it knows. He suggests that smart people may not necessarily listen and learn. They may not show respect and may view less smart managers with contempt. The ability to learn from others depends on not thinking that you are superior and have nothing else to learn.

EXHIBIT 7.9

Focus on Research: Growing Talent as if your Business Depended on it

In general, a company's board of directors does not perceive the level of risk attached to not having a robust talent management process in place. This process includes succession planning and leadership development programmes, which result in having the right leaders in the right jobs at the right times. Unfortunately, a lack of integrated leadership development will be revealed when a company crisis emerges and, by then, it is already too late.

This risk can only be mitigated by creating an integrated leadership development programme which is designed to meet the needs of the specific company. This type of programme is not a series of ad hoc initiatives to develop managers, but an integrated programme of development that involves the board of directors, senior executives and line managers. Leadership development needs to be everyone's responsibility. Through this type of company-wide engagement, leadership development will be aligned with the strategic priorities of the business.

An integrated leadership development programme becomes a key element of a company's value proposition. This enables the business to attract talented leaders, establish current bench strength and future requirements and boost shareholder confidence in the organisation. This type of leadership programme is very difficult for competitors to replicate and it therefore becomes a basis of competitive advantage.

However, the reality is that many companies attempt to develop their leaders in a piecemeal way, following the latest management fads. For example, companies may try to bring in mentoring and coaching through a training intervention, without real buy-in at the top of the organisation or thought to the ultimate outcome. Year on year, a lot of money is spent on ad hoc leadership development which may not be linked to the company's overall strategic objectives. This is a wasted investment for the individual and the organisation.

Successful organisations adopt an integrated approach to leadership development, beginning with succession planning. Therefore, succession planning should drive leadership development and not the other way around. Interestingly, successful CEOs in large corporations find it very challenging to plan their own exits. The term 'succession planning' can be considered taboo by CEOs. Despite overall agreement of the importance of talent management in general, in a survey of twenty CEOs in large organisations conducted by Cohn, Khurana and Reeves (2005), almost half the respondents did not have a succession plan for VPs and above. Building strong leadership pipelines is dependent on succession planning by the CEO and leaders at least three levels below that. This is a nettle that CEOs must grasp. Starbucks is an excellent example of succession planning in action, demonstrated from the CEO downwards.

Contrary to the popular myth amongst executives, leadership development is not just a role undertaken by the HR department. The board should assume high-level ownership and accountability for the talent pipeline in the organisation. As the board is not directly involved in day-to-day operations, it can objectively review leadership development systems and bench strength. Leadership is not a 'soft' HR issue. Growing leaders is a real business issue in successful organisations. Executives themselves are measured and rewarded by how well they develop talent within the organisation. HR's role is to enable the entire organisation to own leadership development. HR can assist in the application of best practice.

Effective leadership development programmes ensure that future leaders have an opportunity to work in a range of the company's divisions. The benefit of this is that talent is shared throughout the organisation and rising stars can create excellent networks and be continually challenged. Future leaders will be motivated through continuous learning and talent will be retained.

QUESTIONS

Q.1 What is the role of the board of directors and the CEO in leadership development?

Q.2 Reflecting on Exhibit 7.9, how would you begin to design a formal leadership development programme?

Pfeffer (2001) and Groysberg, Nanda and Nohria (2004) argued that talent management ideas create zero-sum contests in organisations and the succession of one manager or unit is at the expense of another. They make five very powerful arguments that organisations need to consider:

- Organisations that continually look externally for stars de-emphasise the activities of insiders, who become demotivated and leave. This can create an image that the company will 'hire and fire', which can create hiring difficulties in the future.
- In order to hire external stars, managers have to give the process considerable attention. Therefore, in order to rationalise this effort, they place higher value on talented outsiders and ignore insiders. This is called the 'neglect of prophets in their own land' syndrome.
- To focus primarily on individual talent plays down the need to focus on the organisation as an entity. It ignores a lot of research which highlights the need to focus on collective leadership development.
- Talented stars have the potential to become arrogant and to believe in their invulnerability. This can result in these managers engaging in unethical behaviour because of their inability to listen.
- Stars often do not share because they are wary of being uprooted from a supportive context and placed in a context which may be less supportive.

EXHIBIT 7.10

Focus on Research: The Risky Business of Hiring Stars

Groysberg, Nanda and Nohria (2004) completed a study of 1,052 star stock analysts who worked for seventy-eight investment banks from 1988 to 1996. Their definition of 'star' was taken as someone ranked by *Institutional Investor* magazine as one of the best. Their survey shows that when a company hires a star, the performance of that person plunges and they don't stay long-term with the organisation, despite the huge salaries that firms have paid to lure them away from their rivals. The group the star works with also decline in function and the company's market value falls. The study concluded that companies should, in fact, channel their efforts into home growing talent of their own.

When companies hire stars, three things happen:

- First, the star's lustre fades. When someone leaves the company where they became a star they cannot transfer the firm-specific resources that contributed to their success. As a result, the star must un-learn the system they have been accustomed to and re-learn a new system, which could take years. Their learning efforts are often hampered by the people around them, and they avoid the star, cut off information to them and refuse to work with them. The star is often slow to adopt new approaches to their work and unwilling to adapt to fit in with the new organisation. Once stars leave a job, they keep moving between the highest bidders.
- Second, the group performance slips. The appointment of a star is often demoralising for co-workers, resulting in personal conflicts and communication breakdowns. They are also demotivated by the star's promotion from outside the company. The head of research at one bank likened the hiring of a star to an organ transplant, a procedure in which any number of complications can arise, and one which is not always successful.
- Third, the company's valuation suffers. In spite of the positive publicity companies get when they hire a star, investors see the appointment as value-destroying. In 1994, for example, every hiring announcement by Bear Stearns, Merrill Lynch and Salomon Brothers resulted in a fall in their stock prices. This negativity can be put down to three reasons: investors believe that rivals are blinded by star status to the extent that they overpay to get them; they assume that stars leave a company at their peak and they are therefore past their best when they leave; and investors interpret the move as indication that a company is beginning a hiring spree.

The organisation a star is in makes them perform well. Few stars would change companies if they understood the extent to which their performance is tied to the company they work for. The biggest performance drop in the survey was seen in stars who moved from larger companies to smaller companies, and lost many of the company resources which had contributed to their success. The company is, therefore, a large part of the reason why stars become and stay stars. Most hiring companies underestimate the degree to which stars' success depends on company-specific factors:
- *Resources and Capabilities:* Only after a star quits do they realise the extent to which they were empowered by the company's reputation and how much its financial and human resources allowed them to do the things that mattered.
- *Systems and Processes:* Corporate procedures and routines contribute in many ways to star success.
- *Leadership:* In most companies, bosses give talented employees the resources and support they need to become stars.
- *Internal Networks:* By encouraging people to forge relationships across functions and disciplines, companies help them deliver better results.
- *Training:* While attending in-house training programmes may not add market value to stars, it helps them perform better within the organisation.
- *Teams:* Despite their egos, stars know that one of their defining features is the quality of their co-workers.

Companies usually adhere to three people-development philosophies. Most firms hire hard-working people, and don't do much to develop or train them, but focus instead on retaining the high-level stars they recruit from outside. Others recruit smart people and develop some into stars, knowing that they may lose them to rivals. Only a few corporations recruit smart people, develop them into stars and do everything possible to retain them, and in business this is the only viable strategy.

If it is absolutely necessary to hire a star, a company must never forget the stars they already have.

Brown and Hesketh (2004) suggest that it is wrong to consider talent in the abstract. Talent is historically contingent. It rests on being seen to have specific competencies that others do not exhibit. The pool of talent is artificially limited by organisations for reasons of market reputation, rather than because of limitations in supply. Talent management places too much emphasis on the capacity of modern selection methods to identify talent and predict potential. The productivity of managers depends on context, which is difficult to predict before entering the workplace. Bartlett and Ghoshal (2001) highlight the high failure rate among managers in adapting to new jobs. The focus on a universal competency leadership profile does not capture the range of abilities, skills and styles and their embeddedness.

Talent management has yet to develop as an academic discipline. Some commentators suggest that it is an attempt to repackage standard solutions to human resource challenges. It does have potential to contribute to the organisation, provided it is based on explicit links to strategy and does more than simply respond to strategy.

Conclusion

Talent and succession management processes have major implications for management and leadership development. As a term, talent management originated in the USA. In recent years, its meaning has shifted to include the identification and development of managers and leaders who are considered essential to the organisation and who will fill key positions.

Talent management as a process is wider than management and leadership development in that it covers attraction and retention. In another way it is a narrower process in that it focuses on a high-potential group, whereas management and leadership development focuses on the development of all managerial resources and non-managerial staff who are expected to demonstrate leadership.

Talent management processes represent a particular focus for the management and leadership development resources of the organisation. Organisations should invest in development based on the manager's actual and/or potential contribution. It also argues that the retention of high-performing managers and leaders is important. Talent management processes have important implications for leadership development processes, in particular the need to make decisions about bench strength, the development of internal promotion policies, the preparation of individual development plans and the selection for internal leadership development strategies.

CEO succession is a complex process for organisations. The failure and subsequent departure of a CEO is a costly misadventure for an organisation. It is one of the board's most important functions and the leadership development function has an important role to play in communicating development needs and helping the potential successor to develop a clear plan for succession.

Summary of Key Points

In this chapter the following key points have been made:

- Talent and succession management processes are an important dimension of management and leadership development. Both processes are concerned with enhancing the leadership capability of the organisation.
- Talent and succession management is used to describe a wide variety of activities involving the planning for key transitions in leadership within organisations.
- Talent and succession management are potentially highly politicised processes, and therefore they need to be planned and managed in a fair and transparent way.
- Talent and succession management processes are not to be considered in an ad hoc or just-in-time fashion. The identification and preparation of leadership talent is a long-term and ongoing process.
- Leadership development processes can contribute to talent and succession management by mandating development planning processes, creating development plans tailored to individual needs and succession opportunities and implementing a variety of work-based development initiatives.

- CEO succession requires the active involvement of the board in specifying a process and identifying the successor, and in specifying appropriate criteria and development strategies.

■ Discussion Questions

1. In what ways can management and leadership development processes contribute to the management of talent?

2. What do you see as the main advantages and limitations of an individual development plan?

3. How can an organisation make talent management strategic?

4. Why is CEO succession a complex activity for most organisations?

5. To what extent is talent management considered a process that may lead to a lack of teamwork in organisations?

■ Application and Experiential Questions

1. Find an organisation that currently practises talent management. What are the main reasons for implementing a talent management approach to leadership development? What variant of talent management is implemented? How effectively is it linked to strategy?

2. If you were to design the perfect CEO succession management process for your organisation, how would you do so and what would you include? How would you know it was effective?

3. Divide yourselves into two groups. One group should prepare a case for talent management and the other a case against it. You have twenty minutes to prepare your case and ten minutes for each group to present its arguments.

PART THREE

CHAPTER EIGHT
Formal Management and Leadership
Development Interventions

CHAPTER NINE
Using the Job to Develop Managers and Leaders

CHAPTER TEN
Using Formal Developmental Relationships to
Develop Managers and Leaders

CHAPTER ELEVEN
Informal and Incidental Management and
Leadership Development

Formal Management and Leadership Development Interventions

Outline

Learning Objectives

After reading this chapter you will be able to:

- Describe the main formal leadership development interventions that can be used by organisations.
- Explain the characteristics of formal management and leadership development interventions and how they differ from informal interventions.
- Provide a justification for using formal interventions in a management and leadership development context.
- Describe and evaluate the aims of conceptual and skill-based programmes and describe the different learning strategies that can be used.
- Evaluate the contribution of personal growth programmes to management and leadership development.
- Explain the characteristics of development centres and evaluate their effectiveness.
- Explain the objectives of feedback-based management and leadership development interventions and describe different types of feedback processes.
- Describe the characteristics of action-learning programmes and explain how to design an effective action-learning programme for management and leadership development.
- Evaluate the contribution of management and leadership education and explain the characteristics and contribution of corporate universities.

OPENING CASE SCENARIO 1

AIB (ROI): Implementing Multisource Feedback for Management Development

AIB (ROI) division consists of the group's retail and commercial activities in the Republic of Ireland. It also includes other specialist areas, such as credit cards, finance and leasing products, direct banking, home mortgages and other services. AIB has had a very strong commitment to the development of its managers and it has a dedicated learning and development division that co-ordinates management and leadership development activities for the ROI division. Current leadership development activities are driven by a competency infrastructure, which places a strong emphasis on the development of a set of organisation-specific and generic competencies necessary for competitive advantage. These competencies, when fully developed in managers, enable high performance and career management. The competency model is supported by a career framework strategy. Key elements of this strategy include an enhanced performance management process and a suite of individual role profiles and accountabilities. Each role profile identifies the core and role-specific competencies required to perform assigned tasks to the desired standard.

The AIB (ROI) competency model comprises eleven behavioural competencies. Each competency consists of five levels which are described by behavioural indicators and which are assessed using a range of processes such as performance management, skills analysis and multisource feedback processes (360-degree feedback). The content of each competency is defined to reflect the current and future strategic direction of AIB. Competencies focus on customer relationship management, results focus, teamwork, people management, time and task management, problem-solving and decision-making, leadership, communication and influencing, change and innovation, continuous learning and strategic thinking and application.

AIB (ROI) uses multisource 360-degree feedback as one development strategy to identify competency gaps and to identify management and leadership development strategies. The process implemented by the organisation is for developmental purposes only. It is confidential to individual participants and is not linked to performance appraisal. Its purpose is to provide managers with detailed feedback on how they match the competency model. Individual development needs can be identified and a tailored individual development plan prepared to address these needs. The feedback, which is facilitated by an external consultant, focuses on four key aspects of the manager's profile: key strengths, which are evident to the manager and which are rated highly by others such as the boss, peers and subordinates; hidden strengths, which are competencies unknown to the manager but rated highly by other raters; development needs, which are known areas of underperformance and are confirmed by less favourable ratings from other raters; and performance blind spots, which are development needs of which the manager is largely unaware.

The process of introducing the 360-degree feedback programme was thorough and systematic. The organisation initially briefed all managers on the purposes of the feedback process and the methodology used by the organisation. A strong focus was placed on development. This purpose was reinforced in all communication with the key stakeholders. The next major decision involved the selection of the rating instrument. The organisation decided to use a questionnaire, which was purchased from an external provider. It was modified to reflect the organisation's competency profile and piloted on a small group of managers to test its effectiveness. Having decided on the instrument, the organisation then focused on choosing the raters. Participants were given the scope to select their raters. They could select up to ten raters, of whom a minimum of three were direct reports and three were peers. Feedback from self and reporting managers was also included in the process. The feedback process did not include external customers. The decision to allow the self-selection of raters is potentially controversial, due to the tendency of managers to choose raters who will be more lenient in their ratings. Questionnaires are completed online and sent to the external consultant for computation. An electronic system of administration proved more efficient, because the data could easily be aggregated using customised software. It enabled the efficient generation of reports. The analysis of the data is undertaken by the external consultants. They provide ratings on each behaviour in column format and the ratings from each rater are placed in categories. This allows the manager easily to compare how he/she is rated by various raters and to compare his/her score with other ratings. The data is also presented in graphical format and managers can immediately see how the various ratings fall in relation to one another. The report format allows for comments from different rating sources to be reported. The source of the comments is not identified.

When the data is processed, participants attend a leadership development feedback session, undertaken by a trained consultant. The feedback process includes a workshop component where the manager can discuss his or her feedback and its significance with an external facilitator. Participants have the option of discussing their feedback in groups, if they wish. The feedback process is followed by an individual development planning process. Feedback recipients should be able to identify priority improvement areas and skill gaps and identify possible developmental options to address these. The bank allocates a coach or mentor, who assistes in preparing the development plan, to each participant. The learning and development function then engages with participants in order to ensure that appropriate development solutions are identified and implemented.

AIB (ROI) places a lot of emphasis on training both the raters and the ratees. Raters are trained on the key components of the process and the various forms of rating errors that can occur. Ratees are trained on how to accept negative feedback and the wider set of stakeholders receive training on the purposes of the feedback and the types of support necessary to make it effective. Feedback recipients use the feedback to document and implement development plans. There is high acceptance of the feedback. The process reduces the potential for personal bias which can exist in manager-only feedback. The implementation process demonstrates that managers seek and need feedback to help them develop and improve. It is sometimes a challenge to find managers who feel comfortable enough to provide honest feedback and/or to understand the responsibilities and problems of managers to provide useful, meaningful feedback.

Multisource feedback can address this feedback gap and ensure that feedback is aligned to the overall leadership competency model. The initial implementation process was not without its problems. Some managers were sceptical about the purposes of the feedback. Direct reports used the process to provide negative feedback and feedback which lacked balance. Managers were sometimes concerned about the confidentiality of the information gathered and, in some cases, may not have taken full ownership of development. The problems associated with multisource feedback are outweighed by the many benefits that come about for both individuals and organisations.

Using Development Centres to Develop Managers in AIB Capital Markets: A Best Practice Approach

AIB Capital Markets is a division of AIB Group, the leading banking and financial services organisation in Ireland. It comprises global treasury, investment banking and corporate banking businesses. The division employs 2,500 staff and operates worldwide through offices in Ireland, the UK, the US, Europe and Asia-Pacific. AIB Corporate Banking has approximately 500 qualified professionals focused on providing a full range of banking services to top-tier corporations. AIB Investment Banking comprises seven distinct businesses committed to customer service and creativity in product development and delivery. AIB Global Treasury offers a centralised treasury service for the AIB Group. Its primary goal is to manage funding and liquidity for AIB Group, as well as monitoring interest rates and market risk.

AIB Capital Markets took its most significant steps to enhance leadership development in 2000. It appointed a manager with responsibility for learning and development and set about establishing a learning and development team. This team initially consisted of two people. By 2004, the team had grown to eight professionals with responsibility for learning and development. Two early actions served to establish a strong foundation for later development initiatives. The new learning and development manager implemented a training and development audit throughout the organisation. This questionnaire-based audit was designed to collect perceptions of the conditions that facilitated and inhibited training and development. In addition, it identified what managers and other stakeholders perceived to be the key training and development needs in the organisation. This audit proved valuable for generating discussions concerning training and development. It provided the HR team with a snapshot of the key training and development issues facing the organisation. It was a very relevant first step because it moved training and development up the organisational agenda within Capital Markets. The audit highlighted in particular the need to implement a more focused and strategic approach to leadership development.

The HR team launched a Leadership Through People initiative, which was instrumental in shaping the focus on management and leadership development in the organisation. It was aimed at developing best-in-class people management and leadership practices across Capital Markets. A fundamental component of the initiative was the development of a robust competency framework covering both leadership and management competencies, as well as technical competencies. It was envisaged that this framework would act as a foundation for role profiles: competency-based recruitment, competency-based interviews, performance management, career development and learning and development. The organisation utilised a strong scientific and empirical approach to the development of its competency model. It engaged in extensive external research and benchmarking of best practice combined with detailed internal data gathering and analysis. Focus groups were held with senior managers to define the high-level leadership competencies required by the organisation, given its strategic priorities, and its competitive position as the leading provider of banking and financial services. Working groups across the business areas then worked on these competencies and fleshed out the detail. Business involvement was considered key to ensuring that the final competency model reflected the strategic priorities of the business and encapsulated all levels and all roles within the organisation. It was also important that the language used to describe the competencies was appropriate for AIB Capital Markets. The initial competency model consisted of eighteen competencies with five levels, clustered under four key areas: management and developing self; managing work; managing and developing people; and strategic focus and leadership. Following a significant period of trial, that model was later refined and simplified to include eleven competencies. In addition to the development of a leadership competency model, information was also gathered to facilitate the development of a guide to over a hundred technical competencies reflecting the complexity of the work processes and technology used in Capital Markets.

Capital Markets took time to consider the best way of providing the manager population with feedback on its current strengths and weaknesses, and how it matched the competency model. It worked with a group of external consultants to design a customised leadership development centre (LDC) to suit the competency model and reflect the organisational culture of AIB Capital Markets. The LDC was designed to be a solely development-focused intervention. It provided managers with a snapshot of their proficiency in each competency, highlighting strengths and development issues. It also provided participants with a rating of strength on each competency. Unlike more traditional leadership development centres, which tend to rely on observational and self-report assessments, the final design incorporated a personality questionnaire and managerial critical reasoning tests. The initial LDC design was piloted on thirty managers and significant changes were made to its sequencing and management. All observers were external to the organisation. They were fully trained in competency assessment and in recording behavioural observations.

Each LDC is one day in duration and it typically involves twelve participants. At the development centre, participants undertake one role play based on an influencing upwards and/or a feedback-giving session. They also participate in a team consensus exercise aimed at assessing team skills, people management skills and problem-solving and decision-making competencies. They complete a team in-tray exercise designed to assess forward thinking, customer relationship management, change and innovation and leadership competencies. They work in small groups of four for each team exercise. Their behaviours are observed and assessed on criteria derived from the competency descriptions. At the conclusion of the development centre activities, results of the tests, personality profiles, role plays and team exercises are entered into a spreadsheet to facilitate discussion by observers and to help focus on key development issues for each participant. Observers meet as a team to discuss each participant and then submit their behavioural observations for inclusion in the feedback report. Within four weeks of the LDC, recipients receive a detailed one-to-one feedback session on their strengths and development priorities.

The feedback session lies at the heart of the leadership development centre. This session typically lasts up to two hours. The feedback is conducted by an external facilitator who explains the purpose of the centre, emphasises the confidentiality of the process and reinforces the developmental focus of the process. The participant and the facilitator then discuss the behavioural observations, the ability scores and the key personality traits highlighted in the personality profile. The discussion will typically focus on contextual issues facilitating or inhibiting development, the career aspirations of the participant, their motivation for development and the specific development agenda highlighted in the centre. The participant and facilitator agree what should be recorded on the summary sheet, which is sent to the participant's line manager. The participant is encouraged to be proactive in arranging a meeting with his or her line manager to discuss development issues and prepare an individual development plan.

The learning and development team play a key role in facilitating the developmental planning process. They organise a half-day development planning workshop, facilitated by an external consultant. This workshop includes an analysis of learning styles, discussion of the development centre outcomes, and discussion of appropriate development strategies. In addition, the collated results arising from the process are used by the learning and development team to identify and build on key areas of competency strength and to plan for areas that need development. Once these issues are prioritised, the learning and development team designs or sources tailored development interventions that will address specific gaps or build on current competency strengths. This ensures that investment in leadership development is targeted at priority areas and that provision is relevant and valued. The leadership development centre is at the heart of AIB Capital Markets' leadership development process. Key to its success is the perception and insistence that it is purely development-based, with no link to selection or rewards. The leadership development model, including the competencies and development centre, has provided a common language for managers to facilitate discussions concerning their development and that of their direct reports. The organisation is now at the stage of inviting managers to repeat the leadership development centre so that they can establish their current level of proficiency and identify how they have developed in the interim. This allows the learning and development team to update and re-tailor its development offerings, but it also provides an excellent tool for measuring the return on investment from its leadership development initiatives. The development centre enables AIB Capital Markets to develop extremely capable managers who fit well with its corporate culture, as well as developing its bench strength at competent performance level.

QUESTIONS

Q.1   What advantages do leadership development centres and multi-source feedback have in an organisation such as AIB Group?

Q.2   What lessons can be learned from the two case scenarios concerning the implementation of formal management and leadership development processes in organisations?

Formal development programmes have always been an integral part of management and leadership development and, for many organisations, they represent the backbone of their development initiatives. They are also the subject of considerable debate, both by academics and practitioners within organisations. Some organisations favour the use of more formal development interventions; others place greater weight on experience-based and informal development practices. Some invest considerable time and financial resources in implementing formal management and leadership development interventions. Traditionally, formal development interventions utilised lectures, group discussions and case studies to facilitate the development of managerial talent. Formal development interventions have, in the main, been based on a metaphor of learning as acquisition. This metaphor characterises the process of learning as concerned with the acquisition of knowledge, skill, values, attitudes, behaviour or competency. Increasingly, the metaphor is shifting to one of learning as participation. Learning, in this case, means belonging to a community of practice; it is the process of becoming a full member of the community of practice. There is a growing recognition that managers learn best by actually doing things that are of practical relevance to them. This has led to changes in the content and process of formal management and leadership development. We focus on a number of formal interventions in this chapter. Conger's (1992) classification of leadership development programmes provides a useful framework around which to structure this chapter. He suggested the following categorisation: conceptual and skill building programmes; personal growth programmes; feedback-intensive programmes; and action-learning programmes. We will also focus on formal management education programmes, or what is now called executive education.

Rationale for Formal Management Leadership Development Interventions

Leadership development must be considered from the dual perspectives of the individual manager and the organisation. From the perspective of the manager, organisational restructuring, downsizing and delayering has resulted, in some cases, in the death of the traditional career. Viney, Adamson and Doherty (1997), for example, highlighted the need for managers to develop transferable skills. New deal 'psychological contracts' have focused managers on seeking out opportunities for learning. Development opportunities are perceived as strategies to develop more transferable competencies and to remain marketable and employable. Managers have exchanged improved performance for the provision of additional development experiences. Managers do not necessarily view formal development interventions as a basis for advancement or progression. They see them as more about the manager maintaining value in the labour market. Baruch (2006) suggests that the landscape of leadership development has changed. He identifies a shift to manager-focused leadership development initiatives, but cautions that the organisational perspective should not be ignored or underestimated.

Organisations rely increasingly on human as opposed to physical capital in a knowledge-based economy. Organisations view investment in leadership human capital as a means of responding quickly and effectively to environmental changes. Garavan (2001) suggested that managers are an essential resource for organisations. Formal development interventions have the potential to enhance the development of organisational competencies. Specific aspects of competency that are increasingly valued by organisations include work planning, organising and reconfiguring resources, dealing with crises, taking risks, problem-solving and decision-making competencies. The possession of organisational competencies helps organisations achieve competitive advantage. Manager recruitment and retention is a knock-on effect of the provision of formal leadership and development opportunities. Managers are attracted to organisations that offer best-practice formal learning opportunities. These are also a motivator for managers to perform beyond expectations. Organisations tend to make significant investments in formal leadership development programmes when the economy is good but, when things are less certain, the pendulum swings the other way. Baruch (2006) suggests that the values of the organisation will determine how it views leadership development. Where the focus is primarily on organisational strategy, organisations will implement organisation-focused leadership development practices, whereas if they seek to balance organisational and individual perspectives, they will provide leadership development opportunities that enhance employability for managers as well as enabling them to develop organisationally critical capabilities.

Defining Formal Leadership Development Interventions

A polarisation exists, in academic terms, between formal and informal management and leadership development. In practice, these distinctions are often not clearly defined; however, there have been numerous attempts at an academic level to make a distinction between them. Enos, Kehrhahn and Bell (2003) suggested that formal leadership development occurs in the absence of action on the job, where learners engage in lectures, discussions, simulations, role plays and other instructional activities. Formal leadership development activities are typically sponsored by the organisation and target specific populations and competencies. Table 8.1 provides a summary of definitions of formal learning and development.

Table 8.1: Contemporary Definitions of Formal Learning and Development

Author(s)	Formal Leadership Development
EC (2001) Communication on Lifelong Learning	Development typically provided by an education or training institution, structured (in terms of learning objectives, learning time or learning support), and leading to certification. Formal learning is intentional from the learner's perspective.
Eraut (2000)	There are five features or characteristics of formal development: • A prescribed learning framework • Organised learning event or package • Presence of a designated teacher or trainer • Award of a qualification or credit • External specification of outcomes.
Garavan *et al.* (2002)	Formal development refers generally to 'intentionally constructed learning activities that are generally considered to come within the domain of HRD'.
Cedefop (2001)	Formal development comprises learning that occurs within an organised and structured context (formal education, in-company training), and that is designed as learning. It may lead to a formal recognition (diploma, certificate). Formal development is intentional from the learner's perspective.

These definitions indicate that formal leadership development tends to be 'planned processes' that are characterised as distinct from normal managerial activity. These definitions make other significant claims for formal development: unambiguous development objectives; structured interventions; ownership by the developer rather than the manager, learning that can be disconnected; and an artificial learning environment.

Scribner and Cole (1973) argued that much research and theorising about learning has focused on formal learning and development activities. They stated that:

> As enlightenment-based rationality and science were applied to learning, ways were sought and developed to improve upon the supposedly more primitive and simple everyday learning. Formal learning, when effectively provided, was assumed to have clear advantages. It opened up the accumulated wisdom of humankind, held in the universities. This sort of accumulated, recorded and propositional knowledge allowed each generation to know more and better than their predecessors, as science (or art) advanced. Furthermore, such knowledge was generalisable – it could be used or applied in a wide range of contexts and circumstances. In contrast, everyday knowledge was believed to be context-specific. Thus, the principles of mathematics can be used in any context where numerical values are relevant. On the other hand, learning to play darts only equips a person to use numbers in that very restricted setting. (Scribner and Cole 1973:26)

As formal learning opened up high-status knowledge and was equated with education in schools and universities, non-institutional formal learning was overlooked or dismissed. Earlier research suggests or considers formal and informal development as opposite ends of a learning spectrum. Table 8.2 presents some key differences. Boundaries or relationships between formal and informal learning can only be understood within specific, defined contexts.

Table 8.2: Differences between Formal and Informal Leadership Development

Dimension	Formal	Informal
Process	Structured	Incidental
Approach	Didactic, teacher-controlled, pedagogic	Democratic, none, formative
Pedagogue	Trainer	Negotiated, student-led, work colleague
Assessment	Summative	Negotiated
Location	Business school or classroom	Workplace and non-work context
Setting	Time restricted, specified curriculum, objectives and outcomes	Open-ended, few time restrictions, no specified curriculum, no pre-determined learning objectives
Purposes	Designed to meet externally determined needs	Learner determined and initiated
Content	Acquisition of expert knowledge/understanding/analysis	Development of something new or integration of learning
Focus	Proposition or vertical knowledge, high-status knowledge	Everyday practice, workplace competence
Metaphors	'Jug and Mug' 'Teacher and Student'	'Watercooler Wisdom' 'Coffee Table Discussion'

Source: Adapted from Malcolm, Hodkinson and Colley (2004), Garavan *et al.* (2003) and *Bureau for Business Practice* (1999).

A more contemporary viewpoint considers formal and informal leadership development not as competing paradigms, but as two sides of the same learning process. Furthermore, it is difficult to make a clear distinction between formal and informal leadership development because there is often a crossover between the two. It is arguable that, in an organisational context, formal and informal leadership development interventions reside in different places. Formal development programmes are typically managed and organised by a management or leadership development specialist or training and development function, whereas informal development occurs naturally through day-to-day managerial work processes or activities.

Efimoa (2002) suggested that this separation has resulted in a variety of learning support efforts in organisations that are often not related or aligned. It results in duplicated or contradictory interventions, unnecessary costs and lost learning opportunities. We take the view that, in the context of management and leadership development, formal and informal learning activities are interrelated, contributing in different ways to building leadership knowledge and competency. Formal development interventions are the most widely used to develop managers; however, a significant proportion of managerial learning takes place informally through work activities. We will give more detailed consideration to informal leadership development in Chapter 11.

Conceptual and Skill-Based Leadership Development Programmes

First of all we distinguish between conceptual and skill-based programmes. Conger (1992) and McCauley (2002) suggested that conceptual programmes focus on cognitive understanding of what is involved in the tasks of leadership and management and what it takes to be effective in these roles. Conceptual programmes focus on theory issues and are frequently provided by the executive education divisions of universities. Conger (1992) suggested that many organisations use conceptual programmes as a basis for introducing managers and potential managers who have relatively limited managerial or leadership experience to managerial and leadership ideas. The content of conceptual programmes tends to be generic and focuses on strategic planning, marketing operations, finance and human resources.

Skill-building programmes focus on a narrow set of skills, but may also focus on the development of a wider set of managerial and leadership competencies. Skill-building programmes are typically delivered in modular form and use a combination of instructional strategies designed to provide participants with specific information, opportunities to observe a skill in action, opportunities to practice the skill and to develop strategies to enable them to carry out the skill in the workplace. Gist and McDonald-Mann (2000) suggested that a significant proportion of skill-building programmes focus on the development of interpersonal skills and provide managers and leaders with self-regulation processes and strategies to acquire and maintain those skills.

Both conceptual and skill-based programmes may be provided in house or outside the organisation and typically utilise a range of methods that are appropriate to the prescribed learning objectives. Conceptual programmes rely on lectures, presentations, case studies and discussions. Skill-based programmes use demonstrations, role modelling, role playing, group exercises, simulations and video tapes. We discuss some of these learning methods, but it is important to understand that their appropriateness depends upon the nature of the learning objectives specified by the organisation.

Lectures, Talks and Presentations

Lectures, talks and presentations represent a staple part of many management and leadership development programmes. However, they are often used in inappropriate circumstances and are unsuitable for skills-type objectives. Woodall and Winstanley (1998) suggested that lectures, talks and presentations are often dismissed as representing the least effective in terms of transfer and skills development. Gibbs, Habeshaw and Habeshaw (2002) defined the lecture as 'forty to fifty-five minutes of largely uninterrupted discourse with little or no discussion between a participant and leader, other than listening and note taking'. House (1996), however, envisaged a more interactive lecture format and suggested that it is an effective learning method, especially for adults. An interactive lecture typically presents information, but it also engages managers in questions, discussion and exploration, and this interactive format does allow managers to tailor the information to their needs.

The lecture method does have its place in a management and leadership development context. It is an effective way of transferring information and data and may be very suitable for a conceptual-type leadership development programme. A skilled lecturer can use the method very effectively and use it to stimulate, enthuse, explain and challenge. Many management gurus have built reputations on an ability to engage with an audience.

The lecture method is widely criticised as a learning tool in a management and leadership development context. It places too much emphasis on one-way communication and perpetuates the traditional authority structure of organisations. It is less effective in facilitating transfer of learning and individualised training. It provides relatively little potential in facilitating attitudinal and behavioural changes, which are often important objectives of both conceptual and skill-based leadership development programmes. Managers frequently like to share ideas because, without dialogue, they may not be able to put things into a conceptual framework or make sense of them. The lecture method is clearly less effective in facilitating this dialogue process.

Burke and Day (1986) conducted a meta analysis which suggested that critics may be too harsh on the lecture method as an approach for management and leadership development. They found that there were positive learning effects of the lecture method, both when used alone and when used in combination with other methods such as role playing and discussion. They also found that role playing and lecture methods were equally effective in developing managerial skills. Significant advantages may be gained from supplementing the lecture with other methods such as discussion and role play. These are particularly effective combinations when abstract or procedural learning material is presented as part of a conceptual-type programme. It is clear that lectures, talks and presentations will continue to be used in management and leadership development programmes for the foreseeable future.

Case Studies

A case study is defined as a depiction of a situation which is written specifically for development purposes. It typically provides managers with information describing a situation, how the situation was handled and the outcome. The role of the trainer is to instruct participants to critique both the situation and the outcome. Using knowledge, conceptual models and personal experience, the participant will decide on what was done appropriately and what could have been done differently. Cases tend to vary in the degree to which they represent a convergent or divergent approach. The former allow for a specific best-practice interpretation, whereas the latter allow a variety of interpretations, insights and debate.

The case study method is extremely popular and frequently used in management and leadership development programmes. In some situations, the method is used in in-house programmes with case material generated from real-life company situations.

The merits and demerits of case studies in management and leadership development are much debated. Case studies provide managers with experience in solving problems. They are also valuable in helping managers to generate principles of good practice. They can be used to illustrate theories and techniques, but their effectiveness is dependent on how they are introduced and the skills of the trainer. They are very effective icebreakers, practice opportunities and tests of managers' learning. The provision of practice opportunities and opportunities for thinking is particularly relevant to both conceptual and skill-based leadership programmes. Alden and Kirkhorn (1996) suggested that, while case studies are useful in making managers aware of previously unrecognised issues, they are often most valuable as an opportunity for skill practice. They are particularly useful for practising complex skills such as questioning assumptions, generating alternative solutions, exploring ambiguity and thinking analytically. These are skills which form part of the majority of both management and leadership development programmes.

Burgoyne and Mumford (2001) suggested that the potential of the case method for developing managers in 'learning how to learn' is under-utilised. Case studies are less suitable for the transfer of knowledge; they may be perceived to be not realistic and, for some managers, may lack credibility. The case study method is also criticised because it has the potential to foster groupthink, focus too much on the past, reinforce passivity on the part of the learner and reduce the learner's ability to draw generalisations. Andrews and Noel (1986) suggested that cases often lack the level of complexity and sense of immediacy that managers expect in learning situations. Managers sometimes get caught up in the details of a situation at the expense of the bigger picture and of the conceptual issues that are the central focus of the case study. Argyris (1986) specifically criticised the case study in a management and leadership development context. Cases may undermine the learning process by not leading managers to question assumptions and may foster too much dependency on the facilitator. The facilitator should create a situation in which participants are free to confront themselves and each other without defensiveness. This allows managers to question whether their ideas are consistent with their actions.

In summary, case studies can be very effective in management and leadership development, provided the facilitator encourages managers to question and explore assumptions. It is also critical that the leader can provide a reasoned and logical rationale for developing a course of action, rather than simply focusing on finding the right solution.

Role Plays

Van Ments (1999) defined a role play as a situation of 'asking someone to take on the role of imagined people, real people and themselves' in a situation that focuses on people interaction. Managers are provided with the parameters of the role, which may be detailed or vague. The role play is usually designed to allow managers to enact behaviour and then review it in the light of their experience and feedback from others. Role plays reflect reality, but they provide managers with only some details about a hypothetical situation. As a result, they allow a wide range of behaviours to unfold during the exercise. The most significant learning emerges from responding to what evolves during the role play itself. Role plays are frequently used to develop managers' affective and interpersonal skills in situations such as coaching, interviewing, conflict management, assertiveness, negotiation and influencing.

The value of the role play method is enhanced when combined with a feedback session following the role play. It may also be appropriate to videotape the role play in order to allow for more detailed feedback to the manager and to encourage dialogue and reflection.

The role play method has a number of limitations. Some managers may feel intimidated by the requirement to perform in front of peers and/or to take on a persona that is different from theirs or challenging for them. This limitation can be overcome where the facilitator sets up the process and emphasises the safety of the learning environment, explains the scenario in detail and gives encouragement to the participants. Managers may perceive the role play method to be artificial and may not therefore take it seriously. This places the responsibility on the facilitator to reinforce the key learning that can be derived from participation.

Business Games and Simulations

The term 'simulation' is a catch-all term for a range of methods, including business games, in-tray exercises and practical tasks. Simulations are designed to offer participants a realistic representation of various aspects of leadership, including setting direction, building relationships, problem-solving and decision-making. Simulations usually start with a set of detailed information about a fictitious organisation, which may include an organisation chart, financial details, a description of various departments and an explanation of problems facing the organisation. Participants may be assigned a role or they may self-select one. In the business game scenario, participants are required to run the fictitious company. This includes the identification of priorities, problem-analysis and decision-making. On completion of the simulation, participants engage in self-appraisal and receive feedback on both the content and process aspects of the simulation.

A particular type of simulation used in management and leadership development programmes is the in-tray or in-basket exercise. The goal of this method is to assess participants' abilities to establish priorities, plan, gather relevant information and make decisions. Managers are required to make decisions in an allotted time period. The exercise is usually timed tightly so the manager must make quick and accurate decisions under pressure. Managers are evaluated on a number of criteria, including the quality of the decisions made, the ability to prioritise and the ability to absorb the information contained in critical documents.

Business games and simulations are used widely in management and leadership development programmes organised in house and externally. Keys and Wolfe (1988) reported that business games are effective in developing strategic skills. Specifically, in-tray exercises are effective in improving managerial effectiveness. Thornton and Byham (1982) found that they were also successful in predicting managerial effectiveness. Woodall and Winstanley (1998) highlighted that business games are effective for both teamworking and cognitive awareness. They are particularly effective in developing strategic awareness, getting managers to think about the total business rather than the department or function, and in developing teamwork.

Simulations are valuable for the purpose of management and leadership development because they are very flexible. They are suitable for a range of situations, including the development of personal and interactive skills; developing greater self-awareness; opportunities to learn under realistic organisational conditions; and where there are uncertain and conflicting decision situations.

Business games and simulations are criticised because they lack the realistic complexity and richness of information found in real organisational situations. Thornton and Cleveland (1990) highlighted that organisational history, social factors, organisational culture and the risks associated with alternative decisions are difficult to replicate in simulations. This significant limitation may impact on the level of learning transfer which occurs. They also criticised games and simulations for an over-emphasis on the use of quantitative analysis at the expense of qualitative judgement and interpersonal issues. Mumford (2003) suggested that simulations are less effective at dealing with theory or knowledge. They need to be used in conjunction with other methods which present theories and models which can be applied in the exercise.

Personal Growth Leadership Development Programmes

Conger (1992) suggested that personal growth leadership development programmes are based on the assumption that leaders who have a deep understanding of their strengths, talents, dreams and aspirations will act to address and fulfil them. This category of programmes is becoming increasingly popular as a form of management and leadership development. Programmes with personal growth orientation take two forms: outdoor development programmes and developmental assessment centres.

Outdoor Leadership Development Programmes

Outdoor, outward bound and adventure experiences have grown in popularity as a strategy to develop managers and leaders. Wagner, Baldwin and Roland (1991) distinguished 'wilderness-centred' from 'outdoor-centred' programmes. Wilderness-centred programmes involve white-water rafting or canoeing, or exercises in the wilderness where a team lives and works outdoors for up to a week at a time. This type of programme may be low or high impact. Low-impact programmes rarely get above eye level. Equipment typically includes simple props or permanently installed 'low ropes' courses. High-impact programmes, on the other hand, involve structured activities taking place well above the ground and include many 'high ropes' activities such as rock climbing.

Outdoor-centred development programmes involve a base camp, and participants live and eat indoors. There may be specific outdoor events or initiatives, depending on the objectives of the programme. Participants usually go through events in small groups, followed by discussion or debriefing. This latter activity is carried out by a trained facilitator whose role is to bring out the learning from each activity and link this learning back to the workplace.

Outdoor development activities are essentially designed to provide task-centred experiences that in some way reflect those found in the workplace. Lewis and Williams (1994) suggested that they are based on the assumption that individuals and groups often behave in ways that are similar or the same irrespective of whether they are in a workplace or in a wilderness setting. Outdoor programmes do allow for the introduction of more complex situations, incorporating a broader range of environmental factors, such as the transparent effects of participants' decisions and actions.

The majority of these activities are built around Kolb's Learning Cycle. Ewert (1989) suggested that they are a particularly suitable format for the application of experiential learning. He suggested that there are five conditions in the design of these programmes:

- *A High Level of Engagement*: Outdoor programmes can involve real-life activities with risk and excitement. This raises the attention and enjoyment level of managers above purely visual and verbal learning.
- *Shared Meaning*: Programmes typically include exercises that are shared and group-focused. It is common to have a series of such activities. This helps the evolution of shared meaning.
- *Co-Operation*: Outward-bound programmes emphasise teamwork and co-operation. This complements the competitive and individualistic behaviours found in many organisations.
- *Dissonance and Uncertainty*: The majority of complex management learning situations involve some degree of risk, fear and uncertainty. These conditions are replicated in outward bound programmes.
- *Managerial Tasks*: Tasks typically included in the outward bound programmes draw on various skills such as planning, prioritising and organising, conducted in unfamiliar environments.

Outdoor development programmes may improve managers' team and interpersonal skills, and they may produce change in the attitudes and behaviours of participants. Marsh, Richards and Barnes (1986, 1987) found that participation in an adventure learning programme resulted in enhanced self-concept, while Ewert (1989) found that some participants experienced anxiety. Baldwin, Wagner and Roland (1991) found that outdoor development programmes had a modest impact on perceptions of team awareness and effectiveness in addition to enhanced individual problem-solving. They found little change in trust levels or self-confidence. Better results may be achieved where complete managerial teams participate. The quality of the facilitation is also important. McEvoy, Cragun and Appleby (1997) suggested that the potential payback to organisations can be higher where the programme is tied more explicitly to the strategic vision and direction of the organisation.

Participants often experience real feelings and emotions in outward bound activities. They are not simply role playing and they have few or no opportunities to hide from the experience. The high impact of an emotional experience is significantly less likely in a conventional in-house programme. In many outdoor programmes, participants experience physical risk and therefore they must come out of their comfort zone. When faced with these risks, managers are more likely to confront their own limitations and analyse their behavioural choices. This level of personal questioning and emotional involvement is typically not found in more low-risk outdoor programmes. Managers are often forced to break out of their old paradigms and patterns of thinking and to experiment with some unique methods of problem-solving. The outcomes of the various activities are typically uncertain and the problem-solving takes place outside normal hierarchical constraints.

Many of the characteristics of outdoor development programmes that contribute to an effective learning environment may also present problems. They are expensive and time-consuming. They require an appropriate off-site location as well as appropriate accommodation. Clements, Wagner and Rowland (1995) suggested that they need to be repeated on a regular basis. They should not be viewed as a 'one-off' developmental experience and they require consistent follow-up. They also found that there may be a lack of managerial support for participants. Participants may sometimes view them as 'fun' experiences. This will negatively impact the level of transfer to the workplace.

Outdoor management and leadership development programmes focus on developing self-confidence, overcoming fears and working as a team. They can contribute to better understanding and tap inner psychological resources. There is a strong element of learning with and from others and, if combined with skilled facilitation of reviews and feedback, the development outcomes can be significant. Outdoor development programmes are less appropriate for learning the cognitive elements of functional management.

Leadership Development Centres or Developmental Assessment Centres

Leadership development centres or developmental assessment centres are the second form of personal growth programme. They represent a specific application of assessment centre methodology. Wilson (1996) suggested that leadership development centres can adopt five different formats: 1) development centres based on multidimensional psychometric profiling, 2) development centres based on work trialling, 3) development centres linked with rites of passage and mentorship, 4) development centres based on self-development principles, and 5) development centres as experiential online development processes.

Leadership development centres have a number of important features which make them appropriate for personal growth purposes, but there is confusion concerning what different purposes leadership development centres serve. Jackson and Yeates (1993), for example, found a range of terms were used in practice, such as 'development programme', 'career evaluation programme', 'development workshop', and 'fast-track development centre'. Organisations tended to use development centres for multiple purposes, including recruitment, fast-track promotion, assessment of high-potential managers and feedback. Bolton and Gold (1994) suggested that some organisations combine purposes and this can cause confusion amongst participants. Woodruffe (2000) suggested that if they are to be used for development purposes, it is important that the information generated is used for development purposes only and not to make decisions concerning promotion or selection. To use its outputs for unarticulated purposes will significantly undermine the effectiveness of the development centre and lead to cynicism amongst those selected to participate.

Particular features of leadership development centres that differentiate them from the traditional assessment centre include the following:

- **Exercises**: Leadership development centre methods should include personality and aptitude tests as well as exercises and simulations. Jackson and Yeates (1993) found that development centres typically include a mix of the following activities: group discussions involving problem-solving discussions and negotiations; presentations prepared during the centre process or based on preparation before the centre; role play, where the participant adopts a difficult role personality; questionnaires and ability tests; individual exercises designed to provide feedback and assist the participant in identifying development needs; and the preparation of a development plan. Managers like a variety of methods and a combination of exercises with more observational methods.

The nature of the exercises influences the quality of assessor ratings. The amount of instruction given to participants will influence the quality of judgements made. If the centre uses well-trained role players, this will help assessors observe relevant behaviours in exercises. The order in which assessors see participants, relative to exercises, has significant implications for the ability of assessors to give an assessment of a participant's strengths and weaknesses. As a basic requirement, the exercises must provide assessors with an opportunity to observe enough behaviours so that they are not pressured into making snap judgements. Many exercises are selected and designed because they have good face validity, rather than for their capacity to demonstrate behaviour, attitudes and skills. Many exercises are selected to reflect job content. This has both positive and negative dimensions. It is an effective way of revealing a participant's capacity to perform effectively on job- or role-relevant tasks, but it may result in a false picture of the participant's traits and strengths. The number of exercises is important in ensuring that all of the relevant job behaviours are represented. The effectiveness of the development centre will be influenced by the number and variety of exercises rather than the overall time spent observing participants.

- **Goals**: Kudish, Ladd and Dobbins (1997) suggested that the goals of leadership development centres vary. They can range from the identification of participants' development needs, to the formulation of personalised developmental recommendations and action plans, to skills development based on feedback from assessors and participants and on-site practice. Development centres work on the assumption that participants will accept and act upon the feedback. The extent to which they act on the feedback, and are motivated to pursue developmental activity, is dependent on how they perceive the quality of the assessors. Participants like ratings to be consistent with the values and norms espoused by the organisation. Staufenbiel and Kleinmann (1999) found that assessors do not judge exclusively on the basis of the competency dimension, but take into account the fit of the development issue with the culture of the organisation

  If participants do not understand the feedback, or do not accept it, it is unlikely that they will react positively to it and participate in further development activities. Participants are more likely to engage in development activity where they perceive that the development centre has face validity and is job related. Kudish and Ladd (1997) found that acceptance of developmental feedback was related to exercise, realism, feedback favourability and perceived assessor expertise. Participants receive both attribute or competency feedback and exercise feedback. Thornton *et al.* (1999) found that participants react favourably to both types of feedback, with no real differences in the extent to which participants perceive the attribute-based or exercise-based feedback to be more accurate or useful.

- **Ownership**: Ownership emerges as a crucial issue for the effectiveness of leadership development centres. Mumford and Gold (2004) suggested that a key signifier of the intended purpose of a development centre concerns the ownership and use of data and the feedback generated. If the purposes are solely developmental, then it is important that ownership of the data is primarily with the participant. Organisations may be interested in cumulative or general trends, but the individual reports are owned by each development centre participant. This raises important issues concerning how the data is actually used. Should the participant be encouraged to share the data with his/her superior? Does the culture of the organisation promote or hinder data sharing? What role does the management-development specialist have in encouraging the development centre participant to use the data for developmental purposes? How does the organisation handle issues concerning the content of individual reports?

- **Competency Frameworks**: An effective development centre should be based on a well-defined competency framework, which should not be too detailed. The number and quality of the dimensions to be rated will influence the quality of the judgement made by centre staff. In general, it is better to rate a small number of conceptually independent competencies which can be clearly operationalised and which have good opportunity to be revealed during the various exercises. It is also useful if a variety of competencies are rated. Typically, many organisations adopt competency frameworks that are too detailed and contain too many competencies. These competencies tend to overlap, with the result that assessors find it difficult to isolate their existence in the various exercises. Zaal (2002) suggested that organisations need to give careful consideration to which competencies to include in the development centre. Some of the behaviours included in competency descriptions, especially those related to personality, are more resistant to change than others. It is also important to separate trait-like features from skills. Trait components of competencies are relatively stable characteristics of a person.

- **Assessors**: Assessors play a crucial role in determining the quality of the outcomes derived from the development centre. A number of aspects influence the effectiveness of the assessor in providing quality outputs. These are the capability of the assessor to make quality judgements, including the motivation to provide quality judgements, and the opportunity to observe. This highlights the significance of empathy training for assessors. This training should include issues related to person perception, interpersonal judgment, information processing and decision-making. Motivation to provide quality judgements is also important. Development centre assessors are highly motivated and generally volunteer for the assignment. Centres should use a system that integrates observations, where assessors have an opportunity to justify their point of view regarding each participant's score. Assessors sometimes have to provide face-to-face feedback to participants.

- **Source of Assessments**: It is best to use assessments from multiple sources, which may include peer-ratings, self-ratings, ratings by role players and assessor ratings. The type of assessor appears to be important. Sagie and Magnezy (1997) compared ratings of psychologists and managerial assessors. Trained psychologists provided more accurate and comprehensive ratings than managers. Assessor ratings are more valuable than self-ratings. Self-ratings tend to be based on information not generated as part of the development centre; and they tend to be higher. There is research support for including all rating sources. Role players have an important contribution. They can give accurate assessments, but this depends on whether they are active or passive in style. When role players perform an active role, they significantly enhance the convergence of ratings given by assessors. Self- and peer-ratings are appropriate for development centre processes because they may engender stronger perceptions of ownership on the part of participants. They may also enhance the perceived fairness of the ratings and feedback provided.

- **Feedback and Written Report**: Typically, a well-designed development centre will include an oral feedback session. This should be highly interactive in nature. The objectives of this session are to explain the feedback focus on getting participant acceptance, deal with any issues that arise and build commitment to personal development planning. It is appropriate to provide an initial feedback session and repeat it some time later when the participant has reflected on the data. The feedback provider needs to be trained to deal with different responses and to focus the participant on the developmental components.

    The quality of the feedback will depend on how it is derived. It is important to combine the outputs of exercises and personality data. This allows the feedback giver to address skill needs in a more rounded and comprehensive fashion. The commitment of the participant to pursue further development depends on the interaction of a range of factors, including the credibility of the feedback giver, the quality of the feedback, the involvement of the individual's manager and the perceived availability of development opportunities. The written report provided to participants should be extensive and detailed. It should, where possible, prioritise the development issues and provide a summary of key strengths and development needs.

Well-designed leadership development centres have a valuable contribution to make to the management and leadership development processes. Burke and Day (1986) suggested that managerial employability can be enhanced when the manager has had an opportunity to reflect holistically on learning opportunities. It should be emphasised that the concept of employability is potentially problematic for both the individual and the organisation, because of the potential conflict between the needs of the organisation to develop specific, often time-limited, capabilities that are unique to that organisation and the needs of the manger to develop transferable skills. Wilson (1996) suggested that development centres should be designed to offer the organisation a distinct advantage and, at the same time, facilitate managers in planning their future development.

Woodruffe (1993, 2000) highlighted a number of advantages of leadership development centres:

- They have the potential to enhance the motivation of the manager to participate in development activity and are in line with a move towards lifelong and continuous development.
- They are very compatible with competency-based approaches to management and leadership development. Competencies are increasingly used by organisations.
- Development centres are based on the premise that managers take ownership of their development. This is a positive trend and reduces the dependency that managers may have on organisations to drive development.
- Where the development centre design includes elements of self-rating, these facilitate self-assessment and enable participants to consider career, development and work issues in a more holistic manner. They also facilitate feedback from peers and may act as a basis for the development of a network of support.
- The outputs of development centres are more acceptable to participants than those of other methods such as multisource feedback.

Leadership development centres are, however, expensive, time-consuming and exceptionally labour-intensive. They are expensive simply because they involve hiring facilities, selecting and training assessors, operating the development centre, and planning feedback and development planning processes. It is imperative that assessors are systematically trained. The process will not be perceived as robust unless all those involved are professionally prepared. The credibility and procedural justices of the development centre outputs will be undermined by a poor design process.

A CIPD (2005) research report suggested that that leadership development centres are primarily utilised by large companies. There is also evidence of growth in peer-development centres that represent a move away from the more hierarchical leadership development centre process. There are logistical and expertise problems involved in organising centres in smaller organisations. The content of centres needs to be frequently updated and there are opportunities for development centres to make increasing use of integrated technologies, such as intranets, to conduct assessments.

Feedback-Based Leadership Development Interventions

Feedback-based leadership development interventions are primarily built around a multisource or 360-degree process, but may also include development centre processes of the type described in the previous section. Feedback-based programmes typically include some form of feedback inventory and they use fellow participants and peers to provide in the moment or delayed feedback. They usually conclude with some form of development planning process. Follow-up development activities may also be an integral part of the programme design. McCauley (2002) distinguished between multisource feedback and feedback-intensive programmes. We will concentrate primarily on the former, but will briefly address some of the design issues associated with feedback-intensive programmes. We are solely interested in the use of multisource feedback for developmental purposes.

Multisource Feedback Processes

McCarthy and Garavan (2001) suggested that multisource feedback processes have become popular due to the conflux of three particular factors: the desire to empower employees and provide them with opportunities to appraise their managers; the desire to increase the quality of feedback and provide more balanced feedback in the context of flatter organisational structures; and the opportunity to reinforce good management behaviours by allowing managers to see themselves as others see them. Chappelow (1998) suggested that organisations may use multisource feedback processes for a multiplicity of purposes. Some organisations view it as a key component of the development of individual managers and leaders. In some cases, it may be used with special groups such as high-potential managers and graduates starting out on their managerial careers. Organisations may use multisource feedback as a way of determining managerial team strengths and development needs. This can be achieved by compiling individual feedback reports into an aggregated team profile. Organisations may use multisource feedback initiatives as a basis to broaden manager awareness of valued behaviours. Toegel and Conger (2003) reported a dramatic rise in multisource feedback processes as part of leadership development programmes for mangers and executives. These processes are usually built around a set of leadership competencies. A set of leadership competencies is fundamental to a formal multisource process (Tyson and Ward 2004).

An important assumption of multisource feedback is that management performance varies across contexts and that managers may behave differently with different constituencies. Multisource feedback acknowledges differences across sources in the organisation in observing a manager's performance. Day (2000) suggested that, in a development context, the growing popularity of multisource feedback processes is related to the desire to achieve better self-understanding. He also suggested that it is a practice that many of the 'most-admired' firms have adopted. Multisource feedback, in a developmental context, is valuable because it is a useful tool for building intrapersonal competence in the form of self-knowledge and increased self-awareness of the manager's impact on others. If multisource feedback processes are implemented in a professional way, they can lead to enhanced relationships between managers and, as a result, better teamwork. Their primary contribution focuses on the enhancement of the human capital of managers.

Typically, a multisource feedback process involves collecting perceptions about a manager's behaviour and the impact of that behaviour from the perpectives of the manager's boss, subordinates, peers, and internal and external customers, among others. It will also include self-assessments (McCarthy and Garavan 2001). It is a contrived method of providing a flow of feedback to managers regarding their work behaviour and developmental needs. In order to be effective, the process must be combined with skill development opportunities.

Table 8.3 provides a summary of the issues to be considered when implementing a multisource feedback process.

Table 8.3: Implementing Multisource Feedback in Management and Leadership Development

Selection of Data Collection Instrument
- Consider the purpose of the MSF and the target population.
- The business need should drive the decision concerning the kind of instrument to select.
- Managers need different kinds of feedback at different times in their careers, e.g. skill priorities, strengths and weaknesses.
- Consider the psychometric properties of the instrument. It should be professionally developed and tested.
- Consider whether to use a standardised instrument or have a customer designed instrument.
- The use of a standardised instrument may save on costs, but a customised instrument may better suit the needs of the organisation.
- It may also be possible to customise an existing instrument.

Collection of Data
- Selection of raters: should select raters who have an opportunity to observe the manager in action.
- Need to address the question of who selects the raters. Does the manager select raters or are they selected independently? It may increase buy-in to have the participants select the raters.
- Need to generate a sample of one boss, five peers and five direct reports.

Rater Anonymity
- The organisation needs to take steps to protect the privacy of raters. If the feedback is not perceived to be anonymous, raters may be reluctant to participate in the process.
- Questionnaires should be designed so that participants have no way of identifying who said what.
- The requirement to give written comments will likely result in the loss of anonymity.
- There is evidence, however, to suggest that participants give more attention to written comments than numerical data.

Data Confidentiality
- The data belongs to the participant. It should never be used in any way without the consent of the participant.
- Breaches of confidentiality will undermine the process and lead to a lack of trust.

Preparation of Participants
- All participants involved in the feedback process should be prepared for that role.
- The purpose of the process and the expected outcomes should be fully explained.
- Participants should be trained on how to interpret the data.

Feedback
- How the feedback is delivered will depend on the type of instrument used.
- The feedback may be delivered one-to-one. This approach requires a skilled facilitator who has a thorough understanding of the assessment instrument.
- The one-to-one session should be long enough to allow time to deal with potential emotional reactions and lack of acceptability of the data.
- The facilitator should seek to get buy-in for the data and explore how the participant intends to use it.
- Group feedback sessions can also be used to prepare participants for the interpretation of the feedback.
- Participants tend to play particular attention to the degree to which their ratings agree with the ratings of others.

Creation of a Development Plan
- An important outcome of a multisource process is the preparation of a development plan.
- The plan should prioritise the key development needs and identify appropriate development strategies.
- The plan should specify clear objectives and include a timescale for review.

As we have emphasised, multisource feedback processes have the potential to enhance managers' self-awareness. Wimer (2002) suggested that if managers are armed with better self-awareness, they can make important changes in their behaviour and maximise their learning opportunities. Multisource feedback processes have the potential to prevent career derailment, provided the manager acts on the feedback. A major strength of multisource feedback, when used in a development context, is that it represents more than one point of view on a manager's development needs and provides a broader and more comprehensive picture of the manager's strengths and weaknesses. Chivers and Darling (1999), in a study of six organisations, found that it was primarily used for development and was not linked in any way with reward and promotion. The purposes of the multisource feedback process must be made very clear. Managers must not suspect that it serves a political agenda. Otherwise, cynicism, ambivalence and negativity will result. Multisource feedback can make a significant contribution to management and leadership development initiatives, provided there is meaningful follow-up. Managers will need to be in a situation where they can make development decisions and have sufficient development opportunities.

What managers do with the feedback is important. Walker and Smither (1999) pointed out that managers who met with direct reports to discuss their improved feedback demonstrated greater performance improvement. Perceived organisational support enhances the usefulness of direct-report feedback over and above the overall favourability of the feedback. Bailey and Austin (2006) found that managers receiving negative feedback may not necessarily demonstrate constructive reactions. Managers who receive negative feedback are those most in need of a development intervention, but Bailey and Austin found that the feedback may work better for high-performing managers. They caution that negative feedback needs to be handled sensitively. The self-efficacy of the manager appears to be crucial in explaining how feedback is interpreted. Organisations, therefore, need to give more support to those managers in the form of interpretation and development planning.

A concern exists that multisource feedback may be used for the dual purpose of development and appraisal. It is dangerous to use one tool and one data-gathering process for both purposes. This weakens the process and, in particular, its ability to deliver its developmental objectives. If the aim of multisource feedback is developmental, then ownership of the data by the recipient is crucial. Ghorpade (2000) suggested that the gains from multisource feedback are considerable and that changes in behaviour brought about by such programmes can be immediate. An important factor that determines the effectiveness of feedback is the accountability of participants: are they willing to develop personal learning goals, generate development plans and take appropriate action?

With respect to the issue of ratee accountability, Toegel and Conger (2003) stated: 'for learning and improvement of management performance to occur, ratees should know in advance that they are held accountable for the use of feedback. Skilful facilitation of the feedback intervention, follow-up activities that enhance the perception of accountability, development of action plans for personal growth, tracking of results over time, commitment to behaviour change in public, and participation in training that is closely linked to feedback results have positive effects on learning from 360-degree feedback.'

Finally, Toegel and Conger (2003) suggested that there should be a more qualitative approach to increase the development potential of 360-degree feedback, as it encourages managers to move closer to their personal development goals. Feedback recipients need to reflect on the data because, in order for development to take place, managers need to feel psychologically safe and to own their multisource evaluations.

Feedback-Intensive Programmes

Guthrie and Kelly-Radford (1998) defined feedback-intensive programmes as having both depth and breadth. This translates as meaning that feedback is rich, deep and comprehensive; it comes from many sources and reflects many attributes. They identified several features of feedback-intensive programmes:

- The programme is classroom-based and may last for between three to five days.
- It takes place away from the workplace.
- The feedback is intensive and comprehensive because it comes from multiple perspectives utilising various instruments and experiences.
- The feedback is deep in that it goes beyond skills behaviour to focus on values and preferences and integrated surface behaviours with underlying personality traits.
- The feedback process is consistent over the duration of the programme.
- The programme provides participants with concepts and models for reflecting on various aspects of leadership.
- The programme climate is relationship-based and support-intensive.

Feedback-intensive development interventions combine three key elements: assessment, challenge and support, with participants immersed in a rich process of learning about themselves. Participants on the programme became a community of learners who grow to trust and challenge each other.

Feedback-intensive leadership interventions will consist of a number of pre- and post-programme activities, in addition to the programme itself. Typical pre-programme activities include: responding to a number of essay-type questions; interviewing superiors to get their views on effective leadership in organisations; completing a variety of personality assessments, attitude surveys and questionnaires about current leadership challenges; and completing rating forms by bosses, peers and subordinates in the form of a multisource process. These various instruments are then analysed and incorporated into feedback reports which are delivered at appropriate times during the programme. Post-programme activities are designed to give participants support as they continue to reflect on what they have learned about themselves. Two aspects of support are used: goal setters and peer-group support. On the last day of the programme, participants indicate whom they wish to contact about their goals. They are also encouraged to stay in contact with their peers, who provide a strong source of ongoing support.

Table 8.4 provides a summary of issues to consider when designing a feedback-intensive leadership development programme.

Table 8.4: Characteristics of Feedback-Intensive Leadership Development Programmes

Assessment
- Use well-validated and reliable multi-assessment instruments.
- Ensure that a variety of sources are included in the data, including some external to the organisation.
- Ensure that the process has integrity, particularly in relation to the anonymity of raters and the confidentiality of participants.
- Select experiences that surface managers' leadership strengths and development needs in real time.

Challenge
- Incorporate learning methodologies that capture the diversity in learning styles.
- Experiment with the use of unfamiliar activities and ensure a good, diverse mix of participants.
- Devise the programme content to reflect reality and ensure that the issues are salient to managers.

Action Learning Leadership Development Programmes

There has been a considerable growth of management and leadership development programmes based on action learning principles in recent years. Action learning is considered by some commentators to be a theory of adult learning rather than an approach to management and leadership development. It is based on the idea that people learn best from their experience of doing something, and makes a number of other important assumptions about how adults learn.

- People will only learn when they are motivated to learn. This motivation must be intrinsic. Effective learning is therefore self-directed, voluntary, intentional, purposeful and active.
- A significant proportion of learning is episodic rather than continuous. Learning typically takes place in short, intense bursts, which absorb a considerable amount of the learner's attention.
- People typically feel the urge to learn when they are faced with significant problems and difficulties that they would like to overcome.
- Learning can be blocked by a predisposed mental set formed by previous experience. People learn best when they have the opportunity to question their basic assumptions and review and reassess their previous experience. Learning, therefore, consists of both recognition of what is already known and the assimilation of new knowledge.
- Learning and revision of mental sets is easier when it happens in a safe environment. This function can be performed in a learning-set situation by an advisor or facilitator. The role of the facilitator is not to teach but to design, shape and create conditions that enable learners to understand their past experience and mental sets, review those mental sets and recognise the need for change.

Action learning has three mutually reinforcing purposes: to help managers make progress on a problem or opportunity; to help managers develop skills in coping with other ill-defined problems in the future; and to encourage team-based learning. Mumford and Gold (2004) suggested that action learning represents a middle ground between the informal, unplanned, accidental learning processes and the formal, planned, deliberate management and leadership development that are typically used in organisations. Action learning processes seek to capture the benefits of both planned and unplanned learning. Action learning is considered most suitable when real organisational problems are used as the basis for learning and there is a preference for learning from experience. It has the potential to challenge the status quo and encourage generative learning. Mumford (2003), a strong advocate, suggested that it encourages managers to cross over boundaries, share experiences and develop a common understanding. Most fundamentally, it encourages managers to take action in a controlled way and review what happens.

In a typical action learning programme, managers are exposed to theories of knowledge and asked to apply this knowledge to a project of significant complexity. Effective projects focus on major strategic or complex issues that involve a number of stakeholders. Marsick

(1990) suggested that, as managers are working on the project, they meet in groups with a facilitator or adviser, discuss their understanding of the project and question various theories and concepts as they apply them to the project. The aim is to discover new ways of thinking and to develop creative alternatives to solve the problem. They then engage in a process of action and thought feedback, through which they gain a deeper level of knowledge that they can use when faced with similar problems in the future.

Action learning programmes are utilised more extensively in the UK than in the US. Marsick and O'Neill (1999) suggested that their use has evolved in a number of different directions: as a component of an individual development programme; as part of an organisational change initiative; or as part of an ongoing strategy for organisational change. There is a good deal of research to highlight their effectiveness. Mumford (2002) and Pedlar (1997a) reported that managers found learning in areas such as teamwork, communication, facilitation skills, self-confidence and self-awareness and networking skills. Table 8.5 provides a summary of the issues that organisations should consider when using an action learning approach for management and leadership development.

Table 8.5: Using Action Learning for Management and Leadership Development: Guidelines for Practice

Selecting the Problem or Project
A number of questions need to be addressed at this initial stage:
- Will the project or problem involve managers in significant change?
- Is the proposed project feasible in terms of timescale, resources, management skills and experience?
- Are the risks of failure significant enough to stimulate action?
- Is the problem project one that is sufficiently complex to require imaginative and creative solutions?
- To what extent will managers be exposed to different perspectives and ways of learning?
- Are senior members of the organisation fully committed to the action learning programme?
- Does the organisation have the commitment and power to implement changes emerging from the action learning process?

Characteristics of Appropriate Problems
- *Be real and significant*: Key stakeholders in the organisation must be sufficiently concerned about the problem. The problem must be critical, complex and urgent.
- *Involve the managers in action as well as diagnosis*: Managers should be required not only to diagnose and propose actions, but also to implement them. This has implications for the timescale and amount of commitment that managers can give to the process.
- *Be challenging*: The problem should be something which managers have not previously experienced and addressed.
- *Be defined in some way*: The problem must be capable of definition, however lightly or loosely.
- *Provide potential for learning*: The problem must provide managers with significant learning potential. All members of the learning set must be able to make a contribution.

Forming the Learning Set
- Participating managers need to be carefully selected.
- The level of personal interest of the participants is an important criterion.
- The diversity of participants is an important issue. This includes skills, personal qualities, professional and departmental experiences and learning styles.
- The team should share a broadly common age range and work experience and be at a similar level in terms of career progression.
- The challenge inherent in the problem must be broadly similar for all participating managers.
- Participants should understand team dynamics and functioning.

Agreeing the Ground Rules
- Behavioural ground rules should address issues such as the commitment of participants, confidentiality, timekeeping, quality of air time, openness and enabling behaviour.
- Typical ground rules which may be set include the following:
  - Making attendance at set meetings a priority
  - Making an effort to complete on time any actions agreed by the team
  - Maintaining confidentiality in respect of the project
  - Taking personal responsibility for the outcome of the project team and for learning.
- The facilitator should encourage participants to debate and agree the ground rules and then have them distributed to all set members.

Conducting the Meetings
- Meetings perform a number of important functions in action learning: members can share perspectives on the problem; they allow members to support and challenge each other; members can question each other's current understanding of the problem; and they allow participants to set reviews.
- Set meetings typically go through the stages of catching up, agenda setting, progress reporting, problem-solving and review.
- Members are encouraged to ask questions in order to foster questioning insight. A good question is designed to open up participants' perspectives on the problem.

The Learning Set Adviser
- The role of the learning set adviser is to encourage involvement, enable learning to take place, manage time and encourage participation from quieter members.
- Effective learning set advisers should have a strong tolerance of ambiguity, a capacity to be open and frank, and to be patient, a desire to ensure that people learn, and empathy with the problem and set participants.
- The set facilitator should also have a good understanding of the micro politics of the organisation, and have the ability to summarise and draw the bigger picture and the ability to question oneself.

The effectiveness of action learning for the development of management and leadership skills is dependent on the type of project selected, the composition of the action learning set and the quality of the facilitation provided. If the project is very narrowly defined, managers may develop skills that have limited application beyond that project. Projects must be both complex and challenging in order to enhance leadership skills significantly. Marsick (1990) found that action learning works best when project teams are composed of managers of diverse backgrounds. This gives participants exposure to different viewpoints and perspectives.

Management and Leadership Education Programmes

Senior managers are increasingly expected to develop entrepreneurial skills to inspire innovation and acquire international, multicultural experience. Some of these skills cannot be developed through traditional management and leadership development interventions. Burgoyne and Reynolds (1997) highlighted the growth in management and leadership education and the number of business schools in universities providing formal education for managers and executives. Management and leadership education is now considered an inextricable component of an organisation's management development initiatives. Table 8.6 provides a summary of the role of management and leadership education and its relationship to management and leadership development. Talbot (1997) and Zuber-Skerrit (1995) posited that management education falls under the broad umbrella of management development. The majority of academic contributors in the field advocate an integrated approach to management and leadership development that incorporates management education as a vital component (Talbot 1997; Van de Sluis and Hoeksema 2001).

EXHIBIT 8.1

A Partnership Approach to Executive Education

Mintzberg (2004) is sceptical about the ability of business schools and what he calls traditional academic approaches to develop in managers the distinctive competencies they require to contribute to competitive advantage. He also questions the value of the MBA alone as a preparation for leadership effectiveness. He challenges in particular programmes that allow participation of potential managers who have never managed. Brownell argues that given the need to incorporate experience and organisational context, it becomes important for executive education to involve a partnership approach. She identifies five activities in which business educators must engage if they are to contribute to the development of managers' distinctive competencies:

- *The Admission Process:* Educators need to recognise the importance of distinctive competencies in the graduate admission process. The admission process should be designed to assess each applicant based on specific criteria. To perform this role effectively, it will be necessary for educators to dialogue with organisations to ensure that the admission criteria reflect the needs of organisations.

- *Course Talent and Industry Guests*: Where the course content reflects the distinctive competencies required by organisations, course graduates are better set up to take on the leadership challenges that face the organisation. Course content issues are likely to be reflected in the use of innovative teaching methods and real-life case studies. Industry guests have the potential to provide significant inputs which enhance and develop distinctive competencies. They provide examples of the lived experience. Vivid examples from managers can help prospective leaders understand how distinctive competencies contribute to leadership effectiveness.

- *Out-of-Class Leadership Experiences*: Participants who have limited managerial experience will gain considerably from carefully designed out-of-class leadership experiences. These experiences may include projects that address real problems in organisations. Students may spend a term working on a relevant issue in an organisation in order to acquire some of the distinctive competencies they require for leadership effectiveness. Internships and mentorships can also be provided to students to enable them experience real-life work situations. This allows organisations to observe a potential leader's distinctive competencies in a real work setting.

- *Travel Abroad*: Travel abroad is particularly important to develop intercultural understanding and global awareness. International experience is particularly important in developing cultural sensitivity, open-mindedness and global awareness. Students can experience cultural diversity at first hand and learn to understand the competencies required for working in a different culture.

- *Research Partnerships*: The world of business increasingly recognises that there is value in collaborating with business schools on mutually beneficial research activities. Executives within organisations can bring their most relevant and pressing problems to the attention of researchers who formulate appropriate research projects to address them. It may also be feasible for organisations and business schools to work as a part of a consortium to share problems and research findings.

Source: Brownell (2006)

Table 8.6: Definitions of Key Meanings of Management Education and Management and Leadership Development

Author	Management Education (MEd)	Management and Leadership Development (MLD)
Fox (1997)	Described MEd as 'a subset of higher education', delivered by educational institutions and in constant receipt of academic criticism and evaluation. Delivered using traditional teaching methods. Focus is on theory and increasing the manager's knowledge – his/her 'know what' and 'know why'.	Portrayed MLD as a 'subset of Human Resource Development (HRD), which tends to be delivered by the private sector, whether internally developed management development or provided by external consultants. Uses wide range of teaching methods, from workshops to weekends away. Focus on practical management and augmenting manager's skills and know how.'
Hilbert (1995)	Labelled MEd as the 'external approach' to the development of managers as it includes external providers who use seminars, certificate programmes, MBAs etc. Hilbert contended that MEd broadens the manager's mind.	Identified MLD as the 'internal approach' to developing managers that uses several types of internal courses and those delivered by professional trainers and consultants. Courses are of a bespoke nature, designed by the organisation to train the manager in organisation-specific skills.
Talbot (1997)	Suggested that MEd is the process of developing knowledge, as opposed to competence and skills that are developed in management training and management experience. The knowledge developed surrounds management, business and organisation.	Proposed that MLD is a combination of management training, management experience and management education. Also includes less typical learning systems like performance appraisal and reward systems.
Zuber-Skerritt (1995)	Emphasised the theory focus of traditional MEd, especially the MBA.	Referred to MLD as a generic term that incorporates MEd with other forms of management training.

There are numerous ways of discussing approaches to management education. For example, management education can be categorised in terms of 'high-waste' and 'low-waste' approaches. The high-waste category refers to programmes of management education that do not add significant value to the manager and the organisation. The low-waste category programmes do add value. Crotty and Soule (1997) categorised executive education as university-based or in house: some organisations arrange in-house education programmes that are supplied by a local education provider.

Many commentators suggest that the traditional management education model and, in particular, the MBA approach, do not deserve the status they seem to have amongst executives. Mintzberg (2004) argued that managers cannot learn to be managers through disconnected theories and case studies. Others hold the view that MBAs succeed in improving managers' analytical skills and inflating their egos, but very little else. Talbot (1997) acknowledges the necessity for MBAs to continually attempt to bridge the gap that exists in the MBA programme between theory and practice. He rates European MBAs as better than their US counterparts because they insist on a significant work-experience component as a prerequisite to entering the programme. They also engage with a much broader education programme.

Hilgert (1995) has specifically analysed the executive MBA. He found that it broadened graduates' perspectives and developed a 'big-picture' perspective on their work. Most graduates experienced a transition in their outlook from specialist to generalist and the majority of graduates reported an increase in self-esteem and greater personal development. Fox (1997) contended that management education develops critical analytical skills, particularly in the disciplines of management. Kretovics (1999) measured the learning outcomes of an MBA programme and found that it added significant value. Managers reported greater job satisfaction, improvement in performance and commitment to the organisation. Vickers (2000) postulated that management education liberates the mind and enhances managers' resourcing power in a time where intelligence and knowledge are of paramount importance. Each stakeholder may drive or hinder management education in a number of ways. Table 8.7 gives an overview of the positive and negative dimensions associated with each stakeholder.

Table 8.7: Multiple Perspectives on Management Education

Responsible Party	Positive Aspects	Negative Aspects	Attitude to MEd
Individual (self-directed)	Individual manager responsible for own development, thus personal development is central. Manager's self-esteem/job satisfaction all increase. Commitment to organisation may increase as a result.	Not all managers will participate. Finding time for management development can be difficult if manager does not have the support of own manager. Management development may not hold much benefit for the organisation.	Favours traditional MEd and MBAs more than any other MLD approach as enables individual build on won social capital as well as develop organisational management skills.
Team (learning guided by direct manager)	Management development driven by own team will help the manager in dealing with the challenges faced as part of normal workload. Finding time to engage in management development should be problem-free as manager has buy-in of his/her own team.	This type of MLD may not fulfil the development needs of the individual manager, which would lead to discontent and could result in the manager going to another organisation. Even though team level needs are met, strategic organisational needs may not be.	Team-driven MLD, generally does not favour traditional MEd or MBAs as there is no direct benefit for the team. MEd approach viewed as taking manager's time for personal development.

Responsible Party	Positive Aspects	Negative Aspects	Attitude to MEd
Organisation (designed by top management team)	Organisationally driven MLD will be in line with the organisation's business strategy and will help managers contribute to achieving organisational goals.	Often creates a conflict between the MLD and the organisation's desires and individual manager's desires. May neglect to build the manager's social capital and employability.	This type of MLD favours competency approach or active experimentation approach above traditional MEd approach. MEd focuses on individual development for the benefit of the manager. Learning may not be in line with organisation's business strategy.
Multifaceted source (360-degree feedback)	If multifaceted approach such as 360 degree is used – extremely balanced driver of feedback is taken from subordinates, peers, superiors and self.	Can tend to over-relate training to performance and competencies expected of the manager, which may become obtrusive in designing effective management development.	Equally balanced approach to all types of MLD, including traditional MEd. Input from the individual manager and peers means the traditional MEd approach is viewed favourably. This is balanced by the superior's input, most likely culminating in a holistic approach to MLD.

The most significant criticism of management education concerns the theory–practice divide. Burgoyne and Reynolds (1997) suggested that management education has been extremely slow to adapt and evolve at a pace that meets the needs of the corporate world. Zuber-Skerritt (1995) suggested that the gap between industry and academics renders management education excessively theoretical and lacking in relevance to industry. There are problems in measuring the impact of management education. The assessment of improvement in a manager's performance is often dependent on the subjective opinions of superiors. Horwitz (1996) suggested that traditional management education has tended to overlook the significance of cultural diversity as part of its curriculum.

Corporate Universities

A significant number of organisations have concluded that leadership development strategy is best achieved through the formation of a company academy or college in which all managers at certain levels are required to undertake a specific curriculum. Corporate universities have been established by companies such as GE, IBM, Motorola, Lexus and McDonalds. These universities have a specific mission focused on the organisation's leaders' key development needs and preferred ways of doing things. Paton, Taylor and Storey (2004) suggested that a corporate university is best understood as an approach to enable various forms of work-related leadership development to be undertaken. They identify three distinctive features of corporate universities:

- *Corporate-Level Strategic Focus*: Corporate universities focus on corporate and strategic issues. They seek to ensure that leadership development initiatives add value.
- *Strategic Alignment of Leadership Development*: This approach allows the organisation to systematically control its leadership development initiatives and ensure that they reflect

strategic priorities and focus on current business issues, so that managers are developed in a cost-effective and timely manner.

- *Enhance the Quality of Leadership Development*: They focus on strategic learning, on consistency in the provision of leadership development, the use of appropriate learning designs, the use of technology to deliver leadership development and the use of blended leadership development strategies.

Figure 8.1: A Typology of Executive Learning Initiatives provided by Corporate Universities

	Open Programmes	Customised Programmes
Long-Term / Broadening	• Focus on the development of generic managerial capabilities • Emphasise general managerial learning programmes • Assume portability of competencies	• Focus on the development of culture and strategy • Focus strongly on the development of top teams and strategic capability • Focus on the development of long-term capability and resilience
Short-Term / Focused	• Focus on the provision of issue-based programmes • Provide skills-based workshops • Provide self-developed and skills awareness programmes	• Development initiatives are action-focused and project-focused • Provide organisational consultancy in respect of strategy and structure
	Individual Development	**Organisational Development**

Typically, the faculty of corporate universities are drawn from the business world and they are trained in the design of learning programmes. They place a strong emphasis on leadership formation in the sense of ensuring that leaders and potential leaders are exposed to company-specific learning experiences early in their career. These experiences are consistently reinforced throughout the leader's career. Critics argue that this standardised curriculum can lead to problems such as detachment from the reality of business decisions and unresponsiveness to organisational needs. Eurich (1990) suggested that corporate universities have value in that they transmit knowledge to managers and leaders in a standardised way, but there is a need to keep pace with changes in approach and the changing circumstances of business.

Table 8.8: Perspective on Practice: Guidelines for Establishing a Corporate University

- Start by clearly and demonstrably aligning your CU to the corporate vision, strategy and organisational culture.
- The buy-in of your most senior management is crucial. Without their financial support, moral sponsorship and steering, as well as their physical presence in the CU concept, the CU is unlikely to succeed.
- Be clear about the range of your clientele. Is the CU just for senior and line managers or will it also include parts of the supply chain or customer base?
- Clearly support innovation in your organisation – be it projects to change the processes and systems of the company or mechanisms for sharing knowledge with direct bottom-line impacts.
- The resources you require in order to make an impact on your customers are a combination of clear strategic thinkers as well as didactic specialists. Your flexibility increases with outsourced specialist providers. However, beware of creating an overhead!

- May be useful initially to focus on the top team and provide interventions that are strategically linked.
- Make individuals responsible for their own learning – create systems to help them evaluate what they need to meet their personal and business objectives and drive learning as much as possible on the job.
- Help individuals to understand the link between their development and that of the business in which they work. Get teams faced with a business problem to use this as the focus for learning key skills.
- Measure your progress in both non-financial and financial terms. This helps clarify expectations for a variety of stakeholders, both internal and external.
- Always be able to give examples of how the CU adds value to your organisation. Remember that demonstrable alignment with the vision and strategic goals makes the difference!

Conclusion

Management and leadership development skills can be developed in a number of ways. We have focused in this chapter on formal programmes. Formal programmes are widely used to improve leadership capability in large organisations. Most formal development programmes are designed to enhance generic skills and behaviours that improve managerial effectiveness. Formal programmes are typically targeted at first line and middle management categories, and universities tend to provide executive education programmes aimed at senior management and executives. Senior management and executives are also more likely to participate in feedback programmes and programmes designed to enhance personal growth. Action learning programmes are typically directed at middle manager groups and focus on developing teamworking, problem-solving and strategic skills. Outdoor development programmes involve physical activities performed by a group of managers in an outdoor setting. The purpose of outdoor development is personal growth and teambuilding. Personal growth focuses on increased self-awareness of feelings and behaviour. The development activities are designed to increase self-confidence, risk-taking and willingness to give and receive trust. Leadership development centres utilise multiple methods to measure managerial effectiveness and provide feedback for future development. They typically use intensive measurement and assessment processes. The outcomes of these programmes include enhanced self-awareness, identification of training and development needs and the preparation of development plans. Development centres can facilitate the enhancement of leadership skills. Research on the effectiveness of formal development interventions is mixed. Most of the research studies fail to establish whether enhanced effectiveness is the result of these interventions or the result of other supporting processes.

Summary of Key Points

In this chapter, the following key points have been made:

- Organisations are investing significant resources in formal development interventions designed to enhance management and leadership capabilities.
- Formal management and leadership development programmes include five basic types of programme: conceptual programmes, skill-building programmes, feedback-intensive programmes and action learning. We also included formal management education programmes as an important component of management and leadership development.
- Conceptual and skill-building programmes fall within what are traditionally considered management training programmes. They focus on thinking and skill aspects of management and leadership development.
- Personal growth programmes rest on the assumption that effective leaders are aware of their personal talents and aspirations and that they will take proactive steps to achieve them.

- Feedback-oriented programmes focus on assessment and feedback processes and make use of psychological inventories to help leaders develop greater self-awareness.
- Action learning programmes focus on the use of complex projects that involve many stakeholders. They usually involve managers working in teams, using questioning, action and feedback processes.
- Management education represents a vital component of formal management development. Management education is usually provided by educational establishments, but it may be organised externally or in house.

■ Discussion Questions

1. What conditions facilitate and inhibit formal management and leadership development interventions in organisations?

2. What are the similarities and differences between multisource feedback and leadership development centres?

3. What is action learning and how is it relevant for management and leadership development?

4. What are the objectives and common assumptions of outdoor development programmes?

5. Why would an organisation consider executive education or management education as a way of developing managers and leaders?

■ Application and Experiential Questions

1. If you were to design a multisource feedback programme for senior managers or leaders, what questions would you ask initially? What design considerations would you take into account? How would you implement the feedback process?

2. What are some of the factors you would take into account when designing an action learning project? For which category of manager do you consider this method most appropriate? What factors could potentially undermine the effectiveness of action learning?

3. Assign groups of students the task of identifying various criteria by which formal leadership development methods may be evaluated. The groups should achieve consensus about the prioritisation of these different criteria. The class as a whole can share views about each group's prioritisation, as well as the extent to which there are unique or similar criteria across the different methods.

Chapter Nine

Using the Job to Develop Managers and Leaders

Outline

Learning Objectives

After reading this chapter you will be able to:

- Explain what is meant by a job assignment in the context of management and leadership development.
- Explain some of the conditions and situations in which it is appropriate to use job assignments for management leadership development purposes.
- Describe the different types of job assignment and explain when they are appropriate.
- Describe and evaluate the advantages of learning from difficulties and mistakes.
- Evaluate the effectiveness of shadowing, secondments and acting-up as management and leadership development strategies.
- Describe some of the practice-level decisions that need to be made in order to make different types of job assignment effective.

OPENING CASE SCENARIO

Senior Management Development at ESB

ESB (Electricity Supply Board) is a statutory corporation, 95 per cent owned by the Government of Ireland, with the remaining shares held by an employee share plan trust. It is the leading company in the energy utility sector in Ireland, and employs a total of 8,330 people (including temporary and part-time staff). The organisation has experienced major changes in the past ten years as it evolved from a monopoly electricity company to a group of companies involved in electricity generation, supply, worldwide consultancy and international investment. These changes have, in the main, been driven by competition. The Commission for Energy Regulation required that the different parts of ESB become more distant and re-engineered from each other.

ESB has had a long and well-respected tradition of investment in training and development. It has a policy that each staff member is offered training and development to help them at three levels of development: immediate job needs levels; expanding job requirements; and personal development needs. ESB has well-established policies on continuous professional development (CPD) and supporting educational opportunity for staff members who have not had the chance to obtain formal qualifications.

One of the consequences of major structural changes within the organisation has been the need for managers to develop skills to manage particular businesses rather than to focus on ESB as a company in its entirety. The Executive Director Team (EDT) and the sixty-six senior managers within ESB had a particular need to become a tightly knit senior management team.

ESB made the decision at the early stages that its senior leadership development programme should be organised by a business school with an international reputation and that the intervention should address strategic cultural and team dynamic issues. In order to select the best school, ESB identified ten schools with the potential to deliver the programme, it researched best practice in senior management and executive development, and initiated a tendering process. Nine business schools submitted proposals, which were evaluated on their potential understanding of the requirements of the organisation, the quality of faculty, previous experience, the extent to which the content addressed corporate and business issues, creativity in the learning design, the opportunity for project-based and experiential learning, the proposal for programme evaluation, the price and the international ranking of the school. A shortlist of three schools was made and the final selection was based on an assessment of the impact of the programme, the integration between the key design elements and the extent of best fit with the organisation. Once the decision was made, ESB engaged with the school to decide on the final design of the programme. This included a detailed needs analysis.

Prior to the start of the programme, participants completed the 'Denison Survey of Corporate Culture'. This questionnaire provides a snapshot of how participants perceive the characteristics of an organisation's culture. This formed the basis for a discussion on the organisation and its future. Participants focused in particular on elements where the organisation scored low. These included flexibility and change, sharing a common perspective, understanding customer needs, and innovation and risk-taking. Participants also completed a problem-solving inventory which was based on a model developed by Heppner and Peterson (1982). This inventory helps participants to understand their preferred ways of problem-solving and learning about new things. It highlighted participants' focus or emphasis on various stages of the problem-solving cycle and provided a perspective on both group and individual problem-solving approaches. This information was used to construct project teams.

The programme designed for the Executive Development Team was three days in duration. Day one focused on big-ticket challenges facing the company, individual leadership styles and capabilities. The programme for senior managers consisted of two modules: module one was four days and module two three days in duration. There was an eight-week gap between each module. Each module focused on individual and organisation level issues. The individual level emphasised the development of a personal model of leadership, and the organisation level focused on looking back at the success of the organisation from five years ahead. Projects were a fundamental component of the programme. Participants were divided into ten cross-functional teams. They worked on a specific project for an eight-week period and presented their findings at the end of module two. The programme for senior managers made extensive use of case studies, and the formal element of the programme sought to balance the emphasis on the individual and the organisation. In seeking to develop a personal model of leadership, participants completed a questionnaire that focused on lifelong learning (what, when and how people have learned) and a leadership pathways questionnaire which assessed strengths, weaknesses and underdeveloped talents, as well as linking development needs and personal vision with the capabilities needed to deliver the strategy of the organisation. Participants shared the outputs of these questionnaires in small groups and then used this reflection and discussion to develop their own personal model of leadership.

Stretch projects were an important component of the programme. The projects were selected by the Executive Director Team. Each project had an EDT member as a sponsor. The role of the sponsor was to prepare an initial project outline following a structured template. The project team then completed a more detailed 'Project Initiation Document'. The key outputs of the project were presented on the final day of the programme. Six months later, the sponsors presented progress reports to the full group of participants. The project topics chosen were varied, but all focused on key strategic and mid-range strategic issues facing the organisation. Examples of projects included: optimising generating plant performance; customer service improvement by internal service providers; developing a corporate structure for one business; competitor analysis of one business; and developing a framework for enhanced business performance.

The programme was evaluated at level one: reactions of participants to the programme. No measurement of ROI was conducted. The programme did contain a number of elements considered best practice, but lack of time and resources meant a full evaluation was not undertaken. Given the level of the programme, ROI would prove problematic because of the difficulty involved in unbundling the development intervention as one of many inputs and linking it to a series of business performance outputs. This is one area in which ESB would like to improve. ESB did, however, identify a number of important lessons which will facilitate the effective design of such programmes in the future. These include the following: involving the top team in selecting the provider and conducting the needs analysis; ensuring that the CEO is present and visible during the programme; listening to the experts and designing the programme with them; starting with the top team when delivering the programme; establishing the quality of the faculty rather than the provider, which is key; facilitating conversations between senior managers; and placing a lot of consideration on the pre-course work.

QUESTIONS

Q.1 Critically evaluate the approach taken by ESB to develop its senior managers.

Q.2 How would you redesign the programme to incorporate job assignments or special projects? What impact might these have?

The job of the manager offers numerous opportunities to learn from tasks and experiences. The nature of managerial work has changed significantly, making it difficult for organisations to plan long-term development strategies for their managers. Therefore, using the job as a developmental tool makes practical and theoretical sense because the opportunity is immediate. The modern manager is expected to survive and thrive in chaos and uncertainty, and formal learning and development interventions are no longer considered entirely relevant in today's fast-paced world. Some experts criticise formal management and leadership development as being no longer relevant and some of the development strategies have been described by Handy *et al.* (1987) as 'too little too late for too few'.

A strong case can be made for combining work and learning, which suggests that experiential practice approaches to learning are highly relevant for learning from current and new situations, problems and relationships. Traditionally, management and leadership development focused on rational reductionist models and theories transferred in traditional classroom situations; however, the development of managers needs to expand beyond its traditional boundaries and into the real environment of the workplace. Vaill (1996) argued that prevailing forms of development for leadership do not contribute to the effectiveness of managerial practice.

This chapter focuses on a number of strategies that enable the manager to learn and develop in the context of their practice. We first of all consider when it is appropriate to use job assignments in a management and leadership development context and the factors that facilitate and inhibit their use in organisations. We then focus on evaluating the appropriateness and effectiveness of specific types of job assignment.

What are Job Assignments and When Should Organisations Use Them for Development?

Job assignments are not a single method, but a range of different job-based approaches that facilitate the development of managers and leaders. Ohlott (2004) suggested that the term 'job assignment' can be used to describe the entire job. It can be a new project or it can mean responsibilities added to a current or new job. She highlighted that the assignment is not necessarily assigned. A manager may seek out an assignment or volunteer to undertake one.

Job assignments are not necessarily developmental in focus. Ohlott (2004) suggested that a job assignment should stretch the manager; it should push them out of their comfort zones and challenge them to think differently. Similarly, Lombardo and Eichinger (1989) examined factors that make job assignments developmental. They suggested eleven characteristics (Exhibit 9.1).

EXHIBIT 9.1

Charactertics of Challenging Developmental Job Assignments

- The challenge has the potential to be successful or to end in failure and has high visibility in the organisation. Managers can be more focused and motivated when they perceive that the stakes are high and they could potentially fail.
- The manager is expected to drive change and learn fast by being held responsible for the success of the project.
- The assignment requires the manager to deal with all types of people outside their zones of comfort and operation.
- The manager is put under a lot of personal pressure caused by extra hours, travel pressures and highly charged situations.
- The job challenge involves cross-functional influencing situations where the manager has limited coercive powers and has to negotiate successful outcomes.
- The manager has to cope with new solutions, again outside their zone of comfort.
- The challenge involves high visibility and monitoring from senior managers who have power over the manager's career prospects.
- It includes building an effective team from scratch.
- The challenge has a major strategic component and stretches the intellect.
- It also involves dealing with different types of bosses with good and bad characteristics.
- There is an absence of a key element that will ensure the success of the project.

Source: Lombardo and Eichinger (1989:3)

McCauley *et al.* (1994) described developmental job assignments as those originating from initiating change, taking on higher levels of responsibility and developing the skills to influence others in situations where managers have limited formal authority to do so. McCall (2004) asserted that one of the best ways of learning how to lead is by getting relevant experience, and suggested that the experience that matters is based on challenging assignments, e.g. start-ups, turnarounds and substantial increases in the scope and scale of responsibility, exposure to other people (usually either exceptional or terrible superiors – people don't seem to learn much from mediocre bosses), hardships (e.g. making mistakes or getting fired), and personal events (most significant in work experience). However, while this experience is crucial, it does not always follow that people will learn relevant lessons, or even learn anything, from the experience. Organisations need to focus on ways of assessing appropriate developmental job-related experiences and ensure that the right managers are exposed to these experiences and given the appropriate levels of support in order to learn from such experiences. A number of categories of job assignment can be identified.

Job assignments based on change initiatives: The manager can be tasked with starting the job without any prior structures or support (Dechant 1990; McCall, Lombardo and Morrison 1988). The manager is expected to cope with ambiguity and to motivate and energise others to assist in the project. This challenge can take managers outside of their zone of comfort and encourage them to interact with their environment without a pre-prepared script. They are expected to adapt to change and be capable of acquiring the relevant skills and competencies to cope with the new job, often without the traditional support structure. McCauley *et al.* (1994) suggested that the assignment might have a clear goal, but the role could be loosely defined. This gives the manager scope to determine how the goal is to be achieved. The manager has to dig deep into his/her personal resources to approach situations innovatively and with high levels of self-efficacy. The manager can learn to tackle problems creatively and develop more effective and flexible leadership styles (Davies and Easterby-Smith 1984).

Job assignments based on assuming higher levels of responsibility: McCauley *et al.* (1994) suggested that taking on higher levels of responsibility is a task-related source of job challenge. The manager can be empowered and motivated to develop stronger managerial competencies in order to cope with the extra responsibility. Again, the manager is stretched to assume a higher-level approach in the job.

Job assignments based on influencing others without having authority: Managers can be asked to engage in projects that involve working in cross-functional, inter-organisational teams where they have no formal authority. This can be extremely challenging because managers have to rely on their influencing and negotiation skills to achieve the project objectives. Managers are required to bring about major organisational change, even though they do not have formal authority. The core challenge is to ensure that others will respond to their needs. These challenges are evident, for example, in action learning sets where peer groups of managers work together on a specific project. They work in conditions that are unfamiliar to them, which leads to tension based on fighting for supremacy.

Job transitions, obstacles and challenges: Jobs that involve a transition such as a change in work role, or a change in job content, status or location, may provide opportunities for development. Job transitions provide the manager with exposure to new and novel situations and require him/her to develop new behaviours and skills. The job transition may also influence the motivation level of a manager, who may be driven to achieve high performance standards and prove to peers, superiors and subordinates the amount of value added.

Job obstacles also represent an important development opportunity. These adverse learning situations might include a boss who is difficult to manage, a lack of support from manager peers or a difficult downsizing situation. These situations can have both positive and negative effects. The skills of the manager will determine how well he/she copes with the associated discomfort. Yukl (2002) suggested that a challenging situation that is risky in terms of decision-making provides opportunities for development. The extent of development will be determined by the complexity of the challenge and the extent to which the manager works without guidance and support. Challenging situations require managers to seek different information, view problems in different ways, learn new skills and achieve better self-awareness. Success in handling challenging tasks is related to success in leadership roles.

Poell, Van Dam and Van Den Berg (2004) highlighted a number of issues in respect of the learning potential of jobs. There is a tendency to believe that increased autonomy will lead to more learning. However, this is not always the case. Some managers find it difficult to cope with too much autonomy. It may lead to frustration, stress and burnout. Job transitions, in particular, may increase uncertainty and feelings of anxiety. These stress reactions may interfere with learning. Competency systems prescribe the need for a manager to be capable of rapid change and development and able to tolerate ambiguity. Changes in the organisation's environment, coupled with changes in the manager's environment and the existence of a developmental culture, all create opportunities for development (Davies and Easterby-Smith 1984).

Conditions for development related to a job move are particularly obvious when a manager is moving from a specialist management role to a general management role. This might involve adding a people management dimension to a role where the manager becomes responsible for a team of people. This will involve the need to develop a range of people management competencies. This can be a major challenge for a manager who is technically competent yet lacks empathy with people. The organisation needs to provide development strategies for this manager that involve more than the 'sink or swim' mentality which could contribute to the failure of a manager in this instance and even to the loss of a manager to the organisation. A manager has to develop a high level of self-awareness and perception in order to develop the relevant strategies to cope.

What can the organisation do to help the manager transition effectively during the job move? The move from one job to another, especially if it is a promotion, often presents challenges to a manager, who is given increased responsibility and is required to make decisions in conditions of risk and uncertainty. Revans (1978:21) argued that managers will develop most effectively by 'taking tough decisions and by implementing them with probity'. However, organisations need to ensure that they oversee these job moves and that a manager has the necessary supports when the situation gets too challenging. Davies and Easterby-Smith (1984) suggested that managers are more likely to respond to development opportunities if they initiate or control the development moves themselves. Managers develop primarily through confrontations with novel situations and problems for which their existing repertoire of behaviours is inadequate and they have to develop new ways of dealing with these situations. McCauley *et al.* (1996) found that job moves or job transitions can motivate a manager to demonstrate competence to significant stakeholders, and the higher the level of unfamiliarity with the scope of the job the greater the potential for learning.

In summary, job assignments have value in a management and leadership development context. They have been identified as particularly helpful to enable managers to learn about building teams, how to be better strategic thinkers and how to gain valuable persuasion and influence skills. Day (2000) suggested that job assignments have value when the manager is given sufficient latitude to try out different leadership approaches as part of the developmental role. There must be intentionality; otherwise the focus will be on performance rather than development. Many developmental job assignments lack intentionality. There is too little emphasis on development. Some assignments are more developmentally focused than others. The linking of specific job assignments with desired developmental goals is likely to enhance the intentionality and effectiveness of job assignments.

Table 9.1 highlights how managers can develop managerial and leadership skills through different dimensions of job assignments.

Table 9.1: Using Job Assignments to Develop Management and Leadership Competencies

Job Assignments' Characteristics	Challenges	Examples of Assignments	Key Competencies Developed
Job Transitions • Change in work role, job content, level of responsibility or location	• Handling new and different responsibilities • Changes in level, function or employer • Increased scope of assignment • Moving from line job to staff job	• Taking on a co-ordinating role in a project team • Taking a general management job • Managing a completely different department, e.g. moving from HR to production	• Problem-solving • Facilitating, team problem-solving • Learning to influence upwards and laterally
Creating Change • Change mandate requires dealing with uncertain and ambiguous situations	• Having the responsibility to start something new • Re-organising • Dealing with strategic changes • Responding to rapid changes in business environment	• Launching new product or project • Downsizing • Implementing performance management • Dealing with business crises	• Taking risks • Making decisions • Dealing with ambiguity • Analytical change • Management skills • Strategic analysis
Increased responsibility • Creates high levels of visibility yet has potential to generate exposure and pressure at a high level	• Opportunity to make key decisions that can lead to success or failure	• Managing across geographical locations • Acting-up • Managing assignments with tight deadlines	• Impression management • Influencing upwards • Learning management skills • Building self-awareness and confidence
Managing across boundaries • Dealing with important groups outside the organisation	• Requires the need to work laterally, cross-functionally and the ability to influence others without any coercive powers	• Presenting ideas to senior management • Managing external customer relations • Running a high-profile organisation event	• Exposure to other cultures and points of view • Influencing laterally • Developing referent management skills
Dealing with diversity • Working across cultures and dealing with different races and genders	• Managers are required to deal with the challenges of globalisation and be capable of dealing with employees and customers across the globe	• International assignments • Dealing with international customers • Handling different types of employees	• Learning self-efficacy skills to deal with culture shock • Language skills • Cultural analysis • Building awareness

Factors that Facilitate and Inhibit the Use of Job Assignments for Leadership Development

Woodall and Winstanley (2003) suggested that managers can learn from experience but can sometimes be prevented from doing so. Organisation defensive routines may encourage single-loop learning, which means that if the manager makes a mistake he/she will look for solutions based on restricted options. McCall *et al.* (1998:185) suggested that learning from success can lead to the complacent assumption 'that the same behaviour will result in the same outcomes in all circumstances, and encourages over-confidence in individual ability'. This concept can lead to a 'one-size-fits-all' approach to solving problems and many highly capable managers can be predisposed to using the same approach precisely because it was successful in the past. Properly structured and guided job-based development can provide opportunities to help managers become more effective in current and future roles.

Facilitators of Job Assignments

Organisations can facilitate effective learning from job assignments by ensuring that managers are provided with the necessary support and that there is an appropriate organisation culture and climate that champions the job as a learning and development opportunity. Appropriate human resource strategies need to be deployed to facilitate this development process. The nature of the manager's job needs to be examined in order to build in developmental opportunities and to ensure that the manager is given the necessary time to learn in the job. The willingness of the manager to take responsibility for learning in the job can greatly enhance their skills and capabilities. The individual manager needs to develop awareness of the potential of the job for learning and use appropriate learning strategies to develop in the job.

Table 9.2 summarises various contextual characteristics that will facilitate the effective use of learning strategies.

Table 9.2: Factors that Facilitate the Use of Job Assignments for Leadership Development

The Organisation	• An organisation culture that promotes values of change, creativity, innovation and risk-taking. • A structure that facilitates empowerment of managers. • A developmental climate that values learning and development related to individual and organisational goals. • A sufficient allocation of learning resources, including time. • Strong social support from peers, direct reports and managers. • Synergistic human resource management strategies aligned with development.
The Manager's Job	• The extent to which the job has target- and goal-setting features. • The complexity of the work performed. • The manager's tenure in the role. • The balance of routine and non-routine aspects of the job.
The Individual	• The manager's confidence, self-efficacy and motivation to learn. • The manager's skill to identify and capitalise on learning opportunities. • The manager's self-efficacy and skills to use different learning strategies. • The age and experience of the manager. • The change orientation of the manager and his/her capacity for self-evaluation and reflection.

Van Velsor and Guthrie (1998) placed strong emphasis on preparing the manager to maximise learning from job assignments. Specifically, they offered the following guidelines:

- Assist managers to gain an insight into the learning process and understand the ideal conditions conducive to enhancing their learning.
- Develop an awareness of other strategies that can assist learning, e.g. coaching, use of a reflective journal or use of action learning approaches.
- Develop strong levels of self-esteem and self-efficacy in the manager's ability to learn by using a feedback-intensive programme.
- Analyse and evaluate organisational development systems and decide whether or not they offer the appropriate development opportunities.
- Encourage regular and informal feedback from peers and superiors.
- Create a learning environment which tolerates mistakes and uses them as learning opportunities.

Inhibitors to the Use of Job Assignments

Woodall and Winstanley (2003) highlighted a number of factors that are particularly salient in preventing managers capitalising on the learning potential of job assignments. These are:

- Lack of integration of job-based development initiatives into formal organisational development policies.
- Lack of knowledge, on the part of the manager, that they are engaging in job-based development activity.
- Inadequate practical support from a senior manager who may or may not be aware of the development opportunities provided by the job. Managers may not have been made aware of the potential of the job for development.
- The existence of a formal learning culture, which can lead to a lack of awareness of the potential of job-based opportunities.

Other barriers include the following:

- The climate of the organisation may not be conducive to the recognition of development opportunities.
- There may be too strong a focus on getting the job done. There are fewer opportunities for learning in these circumstances, especially if the culture of the organisation does not recognise or value development.
- The mindset of managers may be anti-development with the focus on getting as much work done as possible.
- Managers might lack the awareness and skills to engage in developmental activities, be set in their ways or lack the initiative to experiment and try new behaviours or ways of doing things.
- Managers may have limited education and self-confidence and have negative experiences of development which cause them to reject opportunities for development.

Table 9.3 suggests how some of the factors highlighted can be minimised or managed to facilitate management and leadership development.

Table 9.3: Factors that Impede Learning from Job Assignments

Impeding Factor	Example	Consequence	Positive Response
Inappropriate and undesirable knowledge and behaviour	Negative, inflexible leadership style exhibited by the individual's manager	Modelling inappropriate leadership style and behaviour	Provide relevant coaching support from expert others to capitalise on learning opportunities
Lack of appropriate or authentic leadership-development opportunity in the assignment	Young managers required experience in strategic awareness yet had limited opportunity to do so	Development limited by lack of appropriate opportunities	Give manager access to strategic project working groups and relevant strategic analysis workshops
Lack of expertise within the organisation to design developmental assignments	No relevant expert to guide specific initiatives relevant to manager	Can lead to frustration and result in making the wrong decisions	Introduce relevant experts from outside the organisation
Increasing complexity of work makes tasks difficult to understand	Difficulties of accessing a rich and deep understanding of the task because the manager cannot access the required knowledge	Leads to arrested development and frustration on the part of the manager	Ensure that manager gains access to knowledge by using innovative interventions, e.g. learning, coaching, mentoring

Ohlott (2004) recommended the need to create an insight into and awareness of the learning opportunities in job assignments and she suggested that this can be achieved through initiating discussions about the potential of developmental job assignments with significant individuals in the organisation tasked with a responsibility/interest in the development of managers. These individuals might be mentors, coaches, relevant bosses or even the manager's peers and employees. She also advocated the use of the job challenge profile (JCP), a robust and useful tool with a key focus on assessing the developmental potential of jobs (McCauley, Ohlott and Ruderman 1999). The JCP questionnaire increases understanding of how the job can contribute to an individual's development.

Job assignments can be used to address development issues in personal development plans. Too often managers are inclined to offer prescriptive training courses to address development issues because they lack the knowledge and skill to design and implement relevant job assignments for their employees. Managers can develop effective skills from job assignments, often through implicit learning processes. Job assignments can also be used to address succession planning issues. There is a requirement in this context to seek out suitable, high-profile job assignments in order to stretch high-calibre employees and expose them to challenges across the organisation. Lombardo and Eichinger (1989) suggested that if managers rely on the application of old skills to tackle new situations, developmental assignments may not result in learning. They recommend, therefore, that if managers are to learn skills and behaviours of significant long-term value they should be required to abandon their usual way of approaching situations. This process, which they describe as transitioning, may include the manager having to do something they may never have done before, such as handling a crisis or dealing with conflict. However, we recommend that in order to maximise learning from assignments the manager must be properly prepared. The manager must also be supported during this process, to help them overcome problems and to ensure that they remain motivated throughout the experience. It is also important to track the effectiveness of job assignments and to ensure that their value is monitored and evaluated over an extended period of time.

Lombardo and Eichinger advocate the following strategies to help managers unpack the learning from job assignments:

- Provide support through cognitive scaffolding by offering feedback and advice to the manager.
- Suggest the need for the manager to keep a learning diary, which gives them an opportunity to record and reflect on their learning.
- Assist the manager to build a learning network to find out how other managers have coped with difficult challenges and to learn from this.
- Advocate the use of effective role models to use for observation purposes and to learn best practice from these opportunities.

Lombardo and Eichinger suggest that the following factors can create blocks to learning from job assignments:

- A tendency to be focused on results, which limits the ability to develop leadership skills.
- Over-reliance on bosses and senior management for advice and the inability to respond to feedback in a positive manner.
- An inclination to use behaviours that were successful in the past and an unwillingness to try out new behaviour.
- A lack of self-awareness and a limited ability to understand one's strengths and development opportunities; limited insight into one's blind spots and one's impact on others.
- A lack of emotional maturity, a tendency to react negatively under pressure and a propensity to blame others for one's failure.
- Excessive focus on the manager's own progression and a failure to develop his/her own employees.

They recommend the following strategies to overcome barriers to learning. The manager needs to:

- Develop leadership skills yet simultaneously focus on the achievement of results.
- Be willing to tolerate ambiguity, to think outside the box and remain open to new and innovative solutions to problems.
- Be capable of breaking with past habits and constantly challenge him/herself to move outside his/her comfort zone.
- Actively solicit feedback and be willing to act on constructive feedback.
- Be focused on developing strong levels of self-awareness and understand how he/she impacts on others.
- Become effective under pressure and remain calm and balanced in difficult situations.
- Understand the need to develop his/her own employees in order to succeed in the job.
- Be willing to learn from failure and mistakes and avoid creating the same problems in the future.

Ohlott (2004) highlights the need to assess the development track records of women and minority managers to ensure that they benefit from a wide variety of career challenges. Research has uncovered a dearth of development opportunities for these managers, which has resulted in limited career opportunities. Woodall and Winstanley (1998) suggested that, at an organisational level, it is important to communicate the importance of job assignments as a leadership development strategy. The value of job assignments needs to be championed by managers. It is important to implement robust leadership development practices so that leaders understand what is involved and what behaviours are expected of whom. The leadership development specialist should clarify the rules of the key individuals who are driving the process, and make sure that they understand what is involved. They must possess the skills to implement job assignment strategies, to take responsibility for the learning process and to be proactive about development.

EXHIBIT 9.2

Job Assignments as a Development Strategy

Guile and Griffiths (2001) propose a typology of perspectives of work experience which explains the role of experience in learning and development for managers.

- The Traditional Model: This form of experience focuses on both adaptation and assimilation. Managers engaged in work are viewed as 'containers' into which various forms of social interaction can be 'poured'. Job assignments in this context can be viewed as a way of developing the novice manager.
- The Experiential Model: This model places emphasis on the manager's interpersonal and social development. It applies Kolb's ideas concerning how managers learn through work experience. This perspective allows the job assignment to take more explicit account of the actual trajectory of the manager's development.
- The Generic Model: This approach requires managers to formulate their own personal action plans. It advocates that managers can reflect critically on their work experience. Managers need to be immersed in ideas as well as the world of experience. Managers use a process of mediation to connect context-specific learning with previously learned ideas and concepts.
- The Work Process Model: The primary role of work experience is to enable managers to adjust themselves more effectively to the changing context of work. This occurs because managers have opportunities to participate in different communities of practice. The development of a manager is influenced by tasks and activities and the context in which the manager is required to operate. Context is also impacted by the manager's development. Managers need to learn about the context in which they are working. They avail of development and learning opportunities by adjusting, amending and varying their performance as required. Work experience is not sufficient in itself to promote the development of work process knowledge.
- A Connective Model: This model is premised on the idea of a reflective theory of learning. Manager learning must take greater account of the influences of context and the organisation of work. It argues for the situated nature of learning. Managers are tasked with conceptualising their experience in different ways. Managers are expected to achieve an understanding of the workplace as an interpersonal activity system and a diverse range of communities of practice. Job assignments, therefore, have value in developing personal, social and behavioural skills that support manager learning.

The Spectrum of Job Assignments

We now focus on five different types of job assignment that may be used to develop managers and leaders: special assignments, projects and hardship experiences, job rotation, shadowing and acting-up. Special assignments cover a cluster of different activities including promotion, working with different people who characteristically resist change initiatives, working with challenging people, both inside and outside the organisation, working on special high-risk projects that involve high-level visibility and potential negative exposure. Job rotation involves moving managers laterally to different roles and tasks, in order to enhance their knowledge and skills. Shadowing allows a manager to observe the performance of new tasks in sometimes unfamiliar settings. Secondment refers to the loan of a manager to another part of the organisation or outside the organisation. Acting-up refers to a situation where a manager assumes responsibility for a more senior position on a temporary basis. Table 9.4 summarises the advantages and disadvantages of these different job assignments. We discuss them more fully in the sections that follow.

Table 9.4: The Advantages and Disadvantages of Alternative Job Assignments

Description	Advantages	Responsibilities
Job Assignments, Special Projects and Hardships Starting a business unit Turning around an underperforming unit Stretch assignments to challenge the manager	Enables the manager to: • Make decisions • Have greater responsibility • Learn new skills • Tolerate ambiguity • Deal with difficult people and situations • Cope with exhausting workload • Assist in decisions relating to succession planning	• The manager requires support as senior management need to give these projects their imprimatur to ensure that they will receive support from relevant others • The manager needs to have the necessary maturity to cope with increased responsibilities • The manager needs to have the requisite interpersonal skills to deal with difficulties • The organisation has a responsibility to ensure that work– life balance is achieved • The organisation needs to ensure that projects are not regarded as dumping work and that tasks are delegated appropriately
Job Rotation/Planned Experiences Moving managers into different roles and tasks to increase knowledge and skill base and provide wider exposure to the organisation	• Flexible approach used to develop graduates and trainees • Opens up the manager's appreciation of what the organisation does • Creates exposure to novel developmental opportunities • Can open up development opportunities for plateaued managers	• Needs proper planning to move the relevant learning • Can result in the manager getting disillusioned if they are not properly rotated • Need to ensure that the manager is assigned relevant roles • Need to ensure that managers do not perceive themselves to be dumped upon

Description	Advantages	Responsibilities
Shadowing Observing new tasks and skills to be carried out in a new and unfamiliar job role 'Sitting by Nellie'	• Gives an in-depth insight into the role and responsibilities of the subject	• Set up the shadowing arrangement by agreeing it with both parties
Secondments Manager is taken out of normal work unit and relocated into a different working environment; or placement in different organisation or in a different part of the organisation	• Acquire knowledge and skills that will be useful to parent organisation • Provide service to the community and thus increase perception of the parent company in the community	• Careful management of exit from project • Expectations of both parties need to be clear • Re-entry of secondees needs to be carefully managed • Requires careful support structures

Acting-Up
• Assume responsibility of a more senior position on a temporary basis
	• Gives the organisation flexibility and allows them to cope with recruitment issues presented by the following challenges:
	  – illness
	  – maternity leave
	  – delayed replacement of departing employees
	• Gives the organisation an opportunity to see how the manager can cope with increased responsibility and if they have the skills to be promoted
	• Gives the manager an opportunity to learn new skills and behaviours and to see if they are suitable for promotion
		• Requires effective delegation to ensure that employee is not dumped on
		• Need to manage the return to previous role efficiently
		• Need to manage the relinquishing of power efficiently

Special Projects, Assignments and Hardship Experiences

Particular types of job assignment foster the development of leadership capabilities more than others. Special projects and assignments are considered to be particularly beneficial in offering development opportunities to managers.

In order to be effective, special projects should provide novelty and be significantly different from the work that the manager is used to. Special projects need to have the capacity to develop a manager's self-awareness and perception yet must also give a manager responsibility for specific aspects of major business projects which involve taking action and, most important, gaining recognition and getting feedback. This will also involve some element of self-reflection. Special projects need to be designed to give a manager the ability to stand alone, make decisions and shoulder responsibility. They should involve: learning new skills; learning to act where there is a high risk of failure; learning to work with difficult people under trying circumstances; and/or learning to cope with an exhausting work load.

McCauley (2002) suggested that special projects need to incorporate elements such as setting direction, creating alignment, adapting to new challenges and sustaining commitment over the duration of the assignment or project. They are based on the assumption that developing the capabilities needed to be a leader requires doing the work of leadership. Special projects provide a rich environment for the development of particular aspects of leadership competency, including: making decisions and initiating actions; observing the consequences of these actions; forming insights and generalisations based on these observations; and testing out these new ideas through taking more refined actions.

Hardship represents a particular type of job assignment. Mumford and Gold (2004) suggested that managers face problems of equivocality in terms of managing employees. It is not often possible to take a structured approach to these issues because this will ultimately result in mistakes. However, they argued that learning from mistakes can be highly beneficial for a manager's development, especially when the tools of reflection and learning are applied and a manager is given the opportunity to examine what has been learned. The organisation needs to embrace the mistake as a learning opportunity and eliminate the tendency to blame. This involves changing the development culture and harnessing the skills of reflection to learn from mistakes rather than dismissing them and moving on.

The organisation, the individual and the line manager have a responsibility to reframe their perception of mistakes and look at ways of learning from them. Table 9.5 examines what each stakeholder can do to learn from mistakes.

Table 9.5: Developing the Manager through Hardships: Some Examples

What the individual can do	What the organisation can do	What the line manager can do
• Recognise limits and blind spots • Accept that they will make mistakes and accept assignments that will challenge and test them • Accept responsibility for mistakes • Push themselves outside their zones of comfort • Develop humility • Find a constructive leadership lesson in leadership • Use self-reflection • Avoid feeling victimised • Adopt a positive approach and rename the mistake or hardship as a learning experience	• Design and facilitate a 'mistake management system' and ensure people don't get punished for mistakes • Define how to handle mistakes when they occur • View risk-taking as innovative • Incorporate recognition for taking on different assignments into performance management system • Assist senior managers to see the value of giving managers challenging assignments where mistakes can be made and learned from • Link hardship experiments to formal assessment processes such as 360 degree or coaching • HR can act as a coach to help the manager cope and reflect	• Reframe concept of hardship from failure to learning opportunity • Avoid allocating punishment for perceived failures • Help employee learn lesson from the hardship • Give appropriate developmental feedback • Make the cause and effect of the mistake clear to the manager

When a manager makes a mistake it should be viewed as a learning opportunity and the focus should be on turning mistakes into vehicles that increase learning and ultimately lead to improvements in performance. This can, in some way, increase self-confidence and self-esteem, develop emotional maturity levels and self-efficacy and lead to a manager taking more risks and becoming more open to change. Managers can use these incidents as learning tools and case studies in their own development interactions with employees. If a manager can admit to making a mistake and can describe the learning consequences to direct reports, this can serve as a learning relationship building exercise. Hardships give a manager an opportunity to evaluate and take stock and reflect on key strengths and weaknesses. They create the need to turn inwards to generate self-reflection, to dig deeper and develop strategies to overcome fear and defeat.

Table 9.6: Examples of Hardships in a Leadership Development Context

Description	Possible Consequences	Appropriate Strategies
Career setbacks or failure to get promotion	• Lack in confidence • Derailment • Attrition	• Support of relevant coaches and mentors • Appropriate and timely feedback to understand the factors impeding progress
Personal trauma such as bereavement, divorce and personal difficulties	• Loss of control • Depression • Loss of self-efficacy • Withdrawal • Attrition	• Skills to cope with emotional difficulties • Counselling • Support from the organisation by giving the individual time to recover • Reduction of pressure and stress in the job on a temporary basis
Dealing with difficult and challenging bosses, peers and employees	• Lack of confidence • Lack of self-efficacy • Withdrawal tendencies	• Develop assertion skills • Flexible conflict management skill • Techniques for managing upwards • Influencing skills
Downsizing in the organisation	• Insecurity • Lack of trust • Suspicion	• Acquire skills to cope with change • Assertiveness skills
Business mistakes and failures	• Blacklisted in the organisation • Loss of faith by organisation in the individual's potential • Serious financial losses • The individual will leave or be fired	• The organisation must assist the manager to take responsibility for the mistake and take ownership • The organisation needs to have risk management strategies to cope with change • The organisation needs to see the potential of failure as a learning opportunity

Job Rotation and Planned Sequences of Experiences

Campion, Cheraskin and Stevens (1994) defined job rotation as a lateral transfer of managers between jobs in an organisation. Job rotation is concerned with moving managers in a planned fashion between jobs over a prescribed period of time in order to broaden knowledge and skill base and provide greater exposure to the organisation. Bennett (2003) suggested two forms of job rotation: the within-function rotation and the cross-functional rotation.

Within-function involves giving the manager exposure to jobs with similar responsibilities within the same operational area. Cross-functional rotation involves moving the manager to different jobs in different parts of the organisation. This approach, also termed the 'helicopter effect' or 'Cook's tour', focuses on giving managers an overall view of what is happening in the organisation to enhance their knowledge and understanding of it. Job rotation can be used as part of a career progression and succession planning approach to give graduates exposure to the organisation. Job rotation can be used as a job development opportunity and can provide the organisation valuable insights concerning a manager's or graduate's capabilities, facilitating job placement.

There are three theories of job rotation (Eriksson and Ortega 2006):

Manager learning theory argues that managers who rotate will accumulate more human capital than other managers, because they are exposed to a wider range of job experiences. Exposure to inter-functional job rotations is valuable in preparing managers for senior positions. At senior levels such rotations enable managers to get a wider understanding of the business at more junior management levels. Intra-functional job rotation is valuable because it makes better use of manager resources.

Employer learning theory argues that organisations learn more about their managers if they have the opportunity to observe how they perform in different roles. This theory argues that organisations gain important information about the manager's abilities and performance. Ortega (2001) highlighted that this information is very valuable for promotion decisions; however, he found that the relative benefits of job rotation are better when the firm knows less about the manager's abilities.

Manager motivation theory argues that managers are motivated by job rotation. They would otherwise grow bored with continuously doing the same tasks. This theory, however, given the variety of tasks that managers perform, may have less application to a manager population.

A job rotation programme typically runs for a year or more and can vary in size and perspective. Job rotation has the potential to create diversity and channel new experiences into a manager's development, avoiding the boredom factor associated with spending too long in the same role. A manager's performance can decrease when the job is mastered and he/she needs stimulation in the form of more interesting job challenges.

Bennett (2003) highlighted the benefits of cross-functional job rotation when it is expanded and offered to managers at all levels in the organisation, not just to graduates and high flyers. These advantages include the following:

- It can result in a strong increase in the knowledge and skills of new managers by contributing to their accelerated development.
- It can increase the potential of high flyers by giving them exposure to valuable knowledge, skills and expertise throughout the organisation.
- It can contribute to an increase in the effectiveness of organisation-wide communication.
- It can enhance cross-functional team development by improving working relationships between teams across the organisation.
- It can enhance the effectiveness of internal customer relationships.
- It can lead to an increase in motivation and a reduction of inertia by exposing employees to new work challenges and skill-development opportunities.
- It can contribute to enhanced levels of individual and collective learning and expertise throughout the organisation and contribute to tacit knowledge retention.

Job rotation does present challenges to organisations because it involves in-depth planning, support and considerable resources in order to be implemented effectively. These challenges include the following:

- The organisation needs to put in place appropriate structures and processes to support job rotation and to ensure that managers are aware of the scope and application of the process. Bennett (2003) argued that the goals of job rotation should be clear and aligned with the organisation's business needs at corporate level, and the benefits of job rotation need to be clear and explicit to all. Armstrong (2006) also advocated that a properly skilled manager should be assigned to the job rotation assignment to ensure that the learning manager is exposed to relevant experience and learning opportunities, and that the learning is reflected on and evaluated before the manager moves on to the next role.
- Managers may resent job rotation as intrusive and time wasting and might not be willing to co-operate with a scheme; they therefore need to be bought-in to the benefits of a job rotation scheme.
- The perception might exist that only managers with high potential will be selected for job rotation and this can contribute to a lack of support by managers for planned job rotation. It is vital, therefore, to give all managers the opportunity to apply for job rotation in a transparent fashion and to use appropriate selection criteria to determine the suitability of the manager.

Job rotation is underused in organisations. Job rotation offers the manager the opportunity to experience the business and become a business partner. Campion, Cheraskin and Stevens (1994) suggested that job rotations can enhance a manager's credibility. Organisations should manage job rotation as a component of their career development systems.

Developing Leaders through Acting-Up

Acting-up can be used by organisations as a strategy to determine whether managers have the capability to be promoted and to work effectively in more senior positions. It gives organisations scope to fill a post quickly if a previous manager goes on maternity leave, is fired, is ill or is offered a new job. However, throwing managers in at the deep end can have disastrous consequences if not managed properly. Acting-up involves taking over a more senior role, which entails developing higher-level skills. Acting-up provides opportunities to cope with challenges and develop higher levels of autonomy and responsibility. Some managers thrive in the acting-up role, but others fail and find it very difficult to cope with the new level of responsibility. What can organisations do to assist managers cope effectively when offered the opportunity to act-up?

Axon (2003) suggested that organisations should consider the following issues if they use acting-up as a development strategy.

- The manager should be made aware of how long he/she will be expected to work in the role and given the opportunity to negotiate a set date when he/she will either return to the previous role or when the current working arrangements will be reviewed
- The manager should be given some time to reflect on how the new role will affect work–life balance and to discuss the implications of this with his/her partner.
- Managers in acting-up roles need to be given the appropriate developmental support by being allocated an appropriate coach or mentor. If they have not managed people before, they should have access to a relevant people management skills programme to gain an insight into how to handle difficult people and situations. A manager's development plan should be reviewed and changed accordingly. Managers should be given advice on how to manage themselves and cope with the stress of an increased workload. Managers need

to have an insight into their strengths and weaknesses in relation to the role and be given an opportunity to learn the skills required to address these weaknesses.

- Managers should also be given the opportunity to liaise with the previous incumbent of the job to discuss the challenges of the role in detail and clarify expectations of the role. This might not always be possible as the previous incumbent might not be available, but it is important to allow the manager to interact with an appropriate manager capable of filling them in on the expectations of the role. Managers should be allowed access to other senior manages as a way of stretching their developmental networks and gaining insights into how to carry out their new role.
- The manager should also be made aware of the impact of this change in role on relationships with colleagues. Managers need to understand that once the acting-up assignment is completed, they might have to go back to their old jobs again and need to maintain relationships accordingly. Managers might be exposed to resentment from some colleagues who might feel they were 'passed over' for this opportunity and this could present challenges in terms of managing future relationships.

Axon (2003) argued that the best approach to acting-up is for a manager to 'own the role'; to take the role seriously and be perceived as being comfortable in the role by management and colleagues at all levels in the organisation. This approach can be used as a strategy to gain respect from others and to show that the manager is capable of fulfilling the role. The acting-up experience has value in increasing a manager's social capital by ensuring access to managers at a higher level in the organisation. It has potential to increase a manager's strategic awareness by giving access to information about activities at a higher organisational level. A manager should be allowed to work with his/her new team and be given time to establish the parameters of the job and the task. The acting-up manager should be briefed on the capabilities of the team and understand their specific competencies and challenges, and should be given the time to bond with the new team and find out who they can delegate to and who they need to monitor.

Organisations need to work on managing the transition back to the previous role when the acting-up project is over. A manager needs to be supported and briefed on how to cope with their changing circumstances. A manager might not feel challenged by the old job and needs to be given the chance to look at new opportunities and review new development needs. The acting-up manager will have to manage relationships with their old team to ensure that they can assume an effective working relationship again.

Acting-up or deputising is an important decision for a manager to make. It is not one that should be made lightly. A number of issues need to be considered.

Table 9.7 Acting-Up: Guidelines for Managers who are Considering Acting-Up Roles

Initial Questions	The following questions need to be asked to clarify the scope of the acting-up role: • How long is the arrangement likely to last? • What is the review date? • What will be expected of the manager in this acting role? • What backfill arrangements will be put in place for the current post? • Will the manager be expected to combine both roles? • What manager reporting arrangements will be in place? • How will the manager's training and development needs be addressed?

Initial Development for the Role	• Formal development opportunities may not be considered at the initial stages because they do not become clear until the manager is in the acting-up role. The acting-up manager should, however, bring up issues concerning training and development expectations for the role. • The acting-up manager should make it very clear if they have concerns about their ability to perform the role. It is also important for the manager to emphasise that he/she is not the 'finished article'.
Negotiation of Relationships	• The acting-up manager needs to consider relationships with colleagues. It is particularly important to negotiate these relationships if the acting-up role requires the manager to have line authority for former peers. The manager will most likely have to revert to being their peer colleague and will need to maintain or re-establish former professional relationships.
Workload and Delegation	• The acting-up role will likely require a significantly increased workload both in range and complexity. This may initially appear daunting; however, the skills of delegation are vitally important. Failure to delegate will probably lead to the manager proving unsuccessful. Where the acting-up manager assumes responsibility for too much, he/she may well become overwhelmed by the workload.
Managing Yourself	• The acting-up manager needs to manage work–life balance issues effectively. This requires him/her to recognise strengths and weaknesses and identify how the characteristics of the new role fit his/her personality and other attributes.
Networking Opportunities	• Acting-up provides significant opportunities for networking. It also requires that the manager think more strategically. These skills can be developed through talking to others in similar roles, who will provide insights into the nature of the job.
After the Acting-Up	• It is important that the manager engages in an evaluation of the acting-up experience. This will include consideration of what went well, what did not go well and what the manager still has to learn. The manager should explore how to take the experience forward either in a new, more senior role, or when he/she returns to the old position. • The manager should have a detailed discussion of development needs and how he/she has changed, and go about identifying further opportunities at the higher level. • The aftermath can be problematic, especially if the manger struggled in the role. The manager should be willing to ask for help and advise the leadership development specialist on how best to prepare managers to act up in the future.

Using Secondments to Develop Managers and Leaders

Mumford and Gold (2004) defined secondments as a strategy that involves taking a manager out of the normal work environment and relocating that person to a different part of the business or to a different organisation. The objective of the secondment is to assist a manager to acquire knowledge and skills that are perceived to be of value to the parent organisation. Secondment is increasingly used as a leadership development strategy. As organisations adopt flatter structures, opportunities for promotion are limited. Secondment offers managers career development opportunities and organisations a chance to enhance their skill base. The CIPD (2004) reported that secondment is one of the top ten most commonly used career management practices. Sixty-seven per cent of companies considered it an effective form of development.

Secondments were associated with downsizing in the 1990s and acquired negative connotations when projects were given to managers without genuine roles in the organisation in order to keep them occupied. However, secondments are now viewed as a viable career development option to assist managers gain in-depth skills and experience in diverse business environments. The secondment has the potential to help a manager gain an insight into how the organisation relates to its external customers.

Secondments can take place within an organisation or externally with another organisation. Secondment within the organisation is a valuable strategy to provide leadership development opportunities. It is also useful for resourcing short-term assignments or projects. A manager potentially gains wider experience and skill without the disruption of relocation, combined with the benefit of continuity of employment. An external secondment involves exposing the manager and the host organisation to different work practices. A key requirement is that the three parties are clear about their responsibilities. Specific questions that need to be answered prior to an external secondment include:

- Is the secondment for a fixed term or for an indefinite period that is subject to notice?
- Although the seconding employer will generally be responsible for basic salary, what are the arrangements for overtime, bonuses, expenses, training, etc.?
- What will happen if long-term absence or persistent short-term absences occur?
- How will supervisory and disciplinary matters be dealt with?
- If the secondment is long-term, how will performance management and development be managed?
- Who will fill the role in the home organisation? How will the secondee maintain contact?

The host organisation should ensure that it does not treat the secondee as an 'employee'.

Table 9.8 Positive and Negative Aspects of Successful Internal and External Secondments

Positive Outcomes	Negative Outcomes
For Secondee	*For Secondee*
• Personal and career development through enhanced managerial professional and technical skills	• Secondee may be treated with suspicion by the host organisation
• Opportunity to achieve clear objectives within a limited time period	• Resistance on the part of the secondee to learning about the culture or developing new skills
• Expanded horizons, which may be of value later in career	• Lack of development opportunities that were promised when secondee joined the organisation
• Increased motivation through wider perspectives and greater understanding of different cultures	• A poorly designed job assignment which does not match the development stage of the manager
• Development of links with other parts of the organisation	
For Host/Seconding Organisation	*For Host/Seconding Organisation*
• Improved communications and networking between host and secondee's organisation	• The perceived loss of an effective manager for a specified period
• Cross-fertilisation of ideas between organisations and sharing of knowledge and expertise	• Potential loss of a manager who may be offered a job in the new organisation
• Insights into the culture and objectives of other organisations	• Resistance of managers in the 'new' organisation to the secondee
• A cost-effective acquisition of special expertise and skills	

A number of important issues need to be addressed if the secondment is to have benefit to the manager as a development opportunity.

Identifying Secondment Opportunities

If secondments are to be successful, they should be based on real opportunities, specifically:

- They should be based on business needs and be part of the organisation's strategic plans.
- They should be regarded as options for developing managerial capabilities which are linked to succession and talent management processes.
- They may emerge through individual development reviews and, if this is the case, the secondment opportunity should be tailored to suit the manager's specific needs.

Preparation for the Secondment

To be successful, secondments require clear objectives and preparation by all of the stakeholders. Specific questions that need to be asked prior to the secondment include:

- Is the secondment for a fixed period or for an undefined period that is subject to notice?
- How will supervisory and reporting issues be addressed?
- If it is long term, how will performance management and development be managed?
- Who will fill in the role in the home organisation? How will the secondee retain contact?
- How will the end of the secondment be managed?

It is important that all stakeholders are clear about their obligations, expectations, accountabilities and performance objectives. It is prudent to set clear learning and performance objectives. The host employer should ensure that the seconded manager is not treated as an 'employee'.

During the Secondment

A number of specific issues are likely to arise during the secondment. These include:

- Monitoring the development requirements and the types of development received.
- Initiating development reviews and providing appropriate managerial support.
- Action planning and regularly evaluating progress.

At the End of the Secondment

It is important that the secondment does not simply come to an end. The host and home organisations should carry out an evaluation of the secondment and, if necessary, complete an exit interview. The manager's reintroduction to the home organisation needs to be carefully managed and any development issues that arise should be addressed.

Mumford and Gold advocate careful management of the secondment. If secondments are to be successful as a leadership development strategy, the following should be considered:

- Secondments have to be based on business need and to be part of the organisation's strategic plans.
- They should be regarded as options for developing future manager capabilities and form part of performance management processes, succession planning and talent development strategies.
- Formal agreements and contracts need to be put in place to facilitate the effective management of the secondment process.

- Organisations need to have a 're-contracting' approach in place when the secondee returns to the old job setting to encourage the manager to utilise his/her new competencies and knowledge and contribute to the effectiveness of the old role.

Job Shadowing and Leadership Development

Shadowing is used to assist managers to gain an in-depth insight into the scope, activities and expectations of a job or role. The focus is on observation and the manager is assigned to a job-holder to help him/her understand the new skills and tasks associated with the job. This is similar to the concept of 'sitting by Nellie': the manager can observe the work of others over days or weeks in order to understand how to perform the role. Young and Khan (2004:20) defined shadowing as a process 'whereby an individual, preferably a non employee who is unfamiliar with the organisation, spends a series of weeks or months observing the daily activities of a manager'. The objective of shadowing is to help this secondee gain an in-depth insight into the work patterns, job description and job role of the manager.

Shadowing can provide managers with an in-depth understanding of the implicit knowledge and skills that are required, beyond formal job descriptions.

Shadowing can provide potential successors with an understanding of all aspects of the job and how to carry it out. There is a need to set up a shadowing arrangement to clarify the objectives of the arrangement and to create a contract outlining the scope and responsibilities. They describe the provisions of the contract as follows:

- A time frame needs to be established for the shadowing process
- A process has to be agreed for asking questions and securing information
- Provisions have to be made for when both parties need a break from the arrangement
- The observer is required to produce a report of what was observed
- The progress of the arrangement needs to be reviewed every two weeks
- A confidentiality agreement needs to be built into the shadowing process.

The observing manager needs to be as unobtrusive as possible and blend into the workplace. It is vital to build trust between the shadow/observer and the subject. Sensitive organisational information is likely to be discussed during the process, so it is vital that the shadow is beyond reproach. The shadow needs to be accepted by other employees and senior management and the reasons for shadowing needed to be communicated clearly to all relevant stakeholders. Young and Khan (2003:23) argued that shadowing 'presents an unparalleled opportunity for organisations to understand their managers, to use and develop their skills to the highest potential and to promote a culture of knowledge sharing and self-awareness in the workplace by providing a grammar of work'.

EXHIBIT 9.3

Perspective from Research: Using Learning Logs to Maximise Learning from Job Assignments

Honey and Mumford (1989) suggested that the best way to learn from experience is to adopt a discipline which requires completion of all four stages of the learning cycle. They recommend keeping a 'learning log' as a means of recording and tracking personal development, which encourages reflection:

The idea is that from writing up what are considered to be significant learning experiences that occur in the form of everyday incidents, the likelihood of actually doing things better in the future will be increased. In this way learning ceases to be a haphazard process, becoming conscious and learner centred.

The format of the learning log should include the following elements:
- An account of what happened, analysing the behaviour of the learner and of any others involved in the situation
- Learning points or conclusions drawn from the experience
- A plan of action for the next time, drawing on the learning from the experience.

This takes in all aspects of the learning cycle. The log should be kept for a specified time period with a specified number of entries about particular events or types of events.

A learning log is thus a means of recording and reflecting on experiential learning, which improves the learning process. It is a flexible method that recognises that learning is a personal, individual process. By planning development activities, it incorporates elements of active self-directed learning and reinforces individual responsibility for development.

Planning for Development

It is only by setting goals and action plans that the learner can become proactive and gain some degree of control over the direction that development takes. It is important, in getting learners to accept 'ownership' of self-development, that individuals should be able to identify relevant opportunities from their own experience. Personal development plans and learning logs can be different for each learner and contingent on each learner's situation, and are therefore seen as relevant and useful. The plan need not be followed slavishly, but used as a guide and modified if necessary. Creating a plan is therefore the first step towards making sure that the development takes place. Creating a plan may be no simple task for many people.

Guidelines

Preparation: Before embarking on your personal development plan, spare some time to assess your present situation, your strengths and weaknesses, and future aspirations. Ask yourself:
- What do I do well in my present job?
- What could I do better?
- Where, and in what roles, do I see my future?
- What new knowledge and/or skills will I need?
- What support might I need from colleagues?
- What constraints or problems do I foresee?
- How could these be minimised?
- What resources are available to me?

The Action Plan: You should now be able to set about creating a personal development plan to address your development goals. Ideally, you should consider:
- The objectives you aim to achieve
- The activities which will allow you to develop the skills identified
- Developing contacts with others who may help (other managers, colleagues, mentors)
- An appreciation of any constraints
- The time by which you will have achieved your objectives.

You should try to carry out and write up one activity per month. You should also review your plan regularly (and discuss and revise it if necessary). In completing the log, the key points to ask yourself are:
- What did I do?
- What did I get from doing it?
- What will I do differently/better as a result?

For each entry the log should:
- Identify the learning/development objectives
- Outline the processes involved
- Analyse the learning and explore any difficulties
- Evaluate how far the objectives were achieved
- Identify areas for future development.

The log should also include an introduction and summary which should include discussion of:
- What you were trying to achieve in your plan at the outset
- How you felt about the elements of the plan
- What aspects of the development activities you most/least enjoyed and why
- What you have learned about your learning style
- What you have learned about your own strengths and weaknesses
- The main areas you need to work on in future.

Making Job Assignments Effective

The most significant challenge for organisations is turning job assignments into learning opportunities. Many managers are able to highlight experiences that are vital for their development, but it is difficult to identify which job experiences have the most to contribute in terms of leadership development.

Ohlott (2004) suggested that the guidelines in Table 9.9 should prove useful in maximising the development potential of job assignments.

Table 9.9: Maximising Leadership Development Through Job Assignments: Key Questions for Organisations

- How many different positions has the manager held prior to his/her assignment to a particular job or role?
- How are the manager's various job assignments progressively sequenced in size and complexity to enable the manager develop significant management and leadership skills?
- What should be the optimum duration of each assignment to ensure significant management and leadership development?
- What criteria should be used to determine who will participate in a job assignment?
- What are the criteria that will be used to assess the effectiveness of a job assignment?
- What particular competencies will the job assignment help the manager to develop?
- How frequently should the manager be assigned?
- How ready and willing is the manager to participate in the job assignment?
- How adaptable is the manager? Will the manager adjust quickly to the new environment?
- Will the job assignment have developmental potential or is it simply being used to get work done?
- Will the job assignment give the manager an insight into potential weaknesses and will it provide an opportunity to develop these weaknesses?
- Will the job assignment provide access to people who can develop the manager's long-term career?
- Will the job assignment be suitable to the manager's personal / family situation?
- Will the job assignment provide opportunities for self-reflection and personal learning?
- Will the job assignment provide the manager with an insight into his or her potential for leadership?

White (1992) recommended that the following strategies can be used to locate job assignments:

- Human resources can conduct surveys of previous job-holders and employees to establish key job challenges

- Interview senior management to determine their view of the most appropriate developmental job assignments
- Customise relevant assignments that are most appropriate for the job
- Analyse collective experiences of job assignments in the organisation and make this available to all managers
- Examine possible developmental experiences that can be incorporated into existing jobs.

Table 9.10 Using Job Assignments to Develop Managers

Type of Job Assignment	Skills Developed	Success Outcome
Small Projects and Start-Ups *Example*: Being tasked with setting up a subsidiary of the company including a start-to-finish mandate with full responsibility for the implementation process	• The ability to persuade and negotiate • The ability to work under pressure • Dealing with diverse groups of people	• Plateaued project engineers reported more recognition, more challenge and more job involvement than non-plateaued colleagues (Hall 1996)
Building and Developing the Team *Example*: Tackling a financial turnaround issue and reducing the reporting time from seven days to three days	• Gaining an understanding of team roles, team dynamics and team facilitation • Dealing with conflict and pressure • Talking a leadership role	• Creating an effective team process where all team members contribute to the best of their ability
Cross-Functional Strategic Assignments *Example*: Setting up a continuous improvement process for the organisation without knowledge, experience or expertise in the area	• Capacity to influence upwards • Willingness to work outside area of expertise and cope with issues such as lack of credibility • Résumé investigation • Building networks • Coping with ambiguity	• Managers move from operating at an operational leval and adopt a strategic perspective. They have enhanced strategic agility
Becoming a Coach/Mentor *Example*: Being asked to coach or mentor an employee without having the relevant skills	• Development of self-awareness and the ability to engage in reflection • Insight into learning styles and strategies • Development of interpersonal skills, active listening and engaging questioning	• Managers are often specialists and they find it difficult to teach others. This assignment helps them to relate to others and build developmental relationships
Off-the-Job Activities *Example*: Acting as chairperson for the local community crèche or playschool; becoming involved in the Chamber of Commerce	• Developing humility and ability to cope with individuals outside the manager's business environment • Learning the patience to influence in a volunteer setting • Learning to learn from others	• The manager has to cope with diverse situations and people and lead without coercive behaviour and be capable of dealing with conflict

Type of Job Assignment	Skills Developed	Success Outcome
Leading a Team of Experts	• Seeking mentoring to help in the management of knowledge experts • Observing the individual and assessing their strengths and development needs • Ability to size people up	• The manager has a better understanding of people differences and the types of strategy that are effective in managing people

Conclusion

Organisations have neglected the rich development opportunities that can be gained by using job assignments in a developmental way. In order to facilitate a climate of learning through job assignments, organisations must become mistake-tolerant and regard mistakes as development opportunities. It is not appropriate to drop managers in at the deep end on difficult assignments in the hope that they can swim. Managers need support to help them learn from the job assignment. Careful analysis must be made of the individual characteristics of managers and their suitability to benefit from particular job assignments. When managers utilise the development opportunities available through the use of job assignments, it can significantly enhance their credibility and capability. Capable managers are developed through diverse and challenging experiences.

A development culture becomes particularly relevant in the context of job assignments. This means that there must be support for managers who are prepared to develop new ways of dealing with problems, and who do not see themselves as entirely bound by existing policy. Finally, such support also needs to be reinforced through rewards and recognition.

Summary of Key Points

- Structured job assignments represent an effective way of developing management and leadership capabilities.
- New situations with unfamiliar responsibilities enable a manager to learn because they take a manager out of his or her comfort zone, they disrupt routine, demand new behaviours and skills and may lead to surprises which have learning implications.
- Special tasks and assignments enable managers to develop specific leadership competencies such as managing change, managing across boundaries and networking.
- High-level and high-latitude responsibilities, where managers take responsibility for specific business activities, profit and loss responsibility and acting-up, enable the manager to stretch capability. High-level assignments expose the manager to complexity, the opportunity to use discretion and to experience risk-taking.
- Job assignments need to be used with developmental intentions; otherwise they are viewed merely as a way of getting additional performance out of managers.
- Job assignments require an effective matching of the individual manager with the assignment. It is important to assess the particular characteristics of the manager and provide the appropriate supports.

■ Discussion Questions

1. Suggest reasons for and against the use of job assignments to develop managers and leaders.

2. Why is learning from hardships considered an appropriate leadership development strategy?

3. How are special projects and job rotation programmes useful for the development of leadership capabilities?

4. Suggest how you could use learning logs to aid learning from job assignments.

5. What factors will facilitate and inhibit the development potential of job assignments?

■ Application and Experiential Questions

1. If you were to design the perfect leadership development job experience or assignment, how would you do so and what would it include? How would you know it was effective?

2. Using yourself or a specific instance of leadership, discuss how particular characteristics of the individual may impact on the effectiveness of job assignments.

3. Having read the material in this chapter, design a development assignment. Share your ideas with someone in class. Your partner should critique your assignment plan using the framework identified in Table 9.9.

Chapter Ten

Using Formal Developmental Relationships to Develop Managers and Leaders

Learning Objectives

After reading this chapter you will be able to:

- Define and explain the nature of formal developmental relationships and their value in the development of managers and leaders.
- Distinguish the various forms of formal developmental relationships that are possible in organisations.
- Explain and evaluate the characteristics of formal mentoring as a developmental relationship and distinguish between hierarchical and peer-mentoring relationships.
- Devise an action plan to implement formal mentoring in organisations.
- Identify and evaluate the main ethical issues associated with formal mentoring.
- Describe the characteristics of coaching and explain the various applications of coaching in a leadership development context.
- Describe the nature and value of sponsorship as a developmental relationship.
- Explain the issues that need to be considered when implementing developmental relationships strategy in organisations.

OPENING CASE SCENARIO

Establishing a Formal Mentoring Programme at Bausch and Lomb Ireland

Bausch and Lomb is an eye health company dedicated to perfecting vision and enhancing life. It is a company with over 150 years of innovation and it focuses on innovation in new materials, new technologies, and in helping people to 'see better'. Its culture is driven by seven core values: a strong focus on the external environment; open and candid dialogue; the achievement of more with less; restless discontent; a laser-like focus on what is important; a disciplined, evidence-based approach to decision-making; and personal accountability in the context of the team. Bausch and Lomb Ireland was established in 1982. It employs more than eight hundred people. Like its parent company, Bausch and Lomb Ireland places a strong emphasis on management and leadership development. The organisation encourages managers to identify their training and development needs. There is an emphasis on specific competency development as well as a focus on increasing the mobility of managers within the organisation. The company has pursued a partnership approach in working with the unions on training and development issues and it has worked on the accreditation of prior learning in conjunction with the Waterford Institute of Technology. The organisation has a strong learning and development culture.

In January 2006, the organisation decided to pilot a formal mentoring programme within the engineering community. The purpose of the programme was to provide engineers with the possibility of developing and broadening their skill base in order to become more flexible and innovative in dealing with the many challenges experienced in the workplace. The mentoring programme consisted of four key elements: identifiying participants; setting development goals; administering and managing the programme; and programme review and evaluation. The organisation formulated a mentoring policy. This policy placed emphasis on structured mentoring, maximising development and ownership for development.

The mentoring programme guide was prepared, which identified and explained the guiding principles of the programme, the key roles, guidelines for mentors and mentees, key considerations in mentoring and the evaluation process. A steering committee was established, which comprised senior engineering managers, a representative from learning and development, and a mentoring programme manager. This committee was given the task of driving the implementation of the mentoring programme. The committee also defined the objectives of the programme and determined its duration (one year). The objectives of the programme emphasised the facilitation and acceleration of the engineering team, the alignment of engineer development with the development of the organisation and business objectives, the establishment of effective relationships to facilitate the construction of helpful feedback and the promotion of discussion outside hierarchical peer relationships.

The committee had a major role to play in the selection of mentors and mentees. It identified mentors who possessed interpersonal skills, experience and a track record that suggested they would perform effectively as mentors. Mentees were identified based on an analysis of their development needs and on who would benefit from a mentoring relationship. The committee discussed a number of ways in which the matching process could be undertaken. The decision was made to use a combination of self-selection and personality profiling to ensure an effective mentor–mentee fit. Participation in the programme was voluntary for both mentees and mentors. A mentee's manager was not selected as a mentor for the programme. The mentoring was viewed as developmental rather than remedial in nature. The mentoring programme manager met formally with each participant to review the mentoring guidelines, give a briefing on the policy and set out and explain key expectations. Concerns and questions were addressed at this meeting and the organisation sought and secured the commitment from selected mentors and mentees to participate in the process. Regular scheduled meetings were held throughout the pilot to monitor progress and provide support. These meetings were documented and the minutes circulated. Follow-up actions were highlighted and specified time frames were put in place to address them.

In order to maximise the effectiveness of the pilot programme, the organisation designed a formal mentoring training programme, which was undertaken by an external provider. Two separate training sessions were delivered (one for mentors and one for mentees) during March 2006. The formal training sessions were highly interactive. Both mentors and mentees completed a mentoring contract that set out responsibilities and expectations within the programme. This formal training was followed by separate, structured one-to-one coaching sessions with mentors, which were designed to address skill gaps and to explore the use of appropriate mentoring techniques and interventions, and when they would be appropriate.

Separate one-to-one feedback sessions were set up for mentees who had completed a personality profile following the training. The pairing process was formalised. The mentoring manager was the primary driver of this process. Mentees were asked to nominate in order of priority at least three mentors with whom they would like to work. This allowed some flexibility in the pairing process. The pairing process was difficult and challenging. Mentors were generally assigned one mentee, but, in some cases, the mentor had responsibility for two mentees. The steering committee reviewed the pairing process. Each mentor and mentee was then informed. Mentees set up an initial meeting with their mentor to discuss how the mentoring relationship should proceed and to focus on establishing specific development objectives and clarifying expectations. The development objectives were also included in the mentor's and mentee's individual development plans. The meeting between mentor and mentee was highly structured and the published mentoring guidelines clearly set out the process to be followed.

Mentees were encouraged to take on primary ownership and management of the process. This meant that they were expected to set up regular meetings with their mentors. Mentors and mentees met on average once every two weeks. Each meeting lasted approximately one to two hours. Once a number of meetings had been held, mentees completed a programme goals and objectives form which described details of their development goals and the development strategies they would use to achieve them. The contents of the programme goals and objectives form was discussed with the mentoring programme manager. This worked on a continuous basis with both mentors and mentees to ensure that the mentoring process was on track and to focus mentees on their development goals. The mentoring manager needed to work closely with both mentors and mentees in order to build and sustain effective mentoring relationships. The manager played a key role in ensuring that problems that were encountered were dealt with quickly. Where a mentoring relationship was clearly not working out, the programme manager would secure another mentor. A key principle of this programme was a 'no fault divorce'.

The programme was reviewed on an ongoing basis. While the steering committee stayed in place over the duration of the pilot, it needed to meet less frequently. The mentoring manager's role was, however, continuous and sustained. The manager also gave inputs on how to solicit and provide feedback, and conducted reviews of the relationships. Each mentor and mentee provided feedback to the rest of the group included in the pilot. These review meetings enabled key learnings to be shared. Feedback was regularly given via the steering committee to the wider engineering community and to the plant leadership team. The mentee also provided feedback to his/her superior. Mentors did not provide feedback or discuss mentee/mentor relationships with their mentee's supervisor unless this was agreed with the mentee beforehand. Mentors found the process challenging and mentees benefited from the range of developmental goals which they had set and from the informal and formal networking dimensions of the programme.

QUESTIONS

Q.1   Critically evaluate the way in which Bausch and Lomb approached the development and implementation of a formal mentoring scheme.

Q.2   Suggest reasons why formal mentoring programmes such as those introduced in Bausch and Lomb might not succeed.

Relationships play a major role in the development of leadership capabilities in organisations. Recent thinking suggests that it is more effective to identify a network of developmental relationships than to rely on the mentor or coach. Supervisors, peers and professional colleagues, both inside and outside the organisation, all have a major role to play in the development of leadership capabilities. We focus in this chapter on formal developmental relationships: relationships created by the organisation to enhance the development of leaders. These relationships are intentional and targeted at managers who have leadership development needs. Formalised relationships ensure that there is more uniform development of leaders.

A manager's development is particularly influenced by the personality, interpersonal skills and learning orientation of their manager. Therefore, the existence of a competent, capable and supportive developmental relationship with their manager is pivotal in terms of the manager's success in their role. It is not always possible to have this kind of relationship with an individual's immediate manager, and the organisation therefore needs to acquire a more in-depth understanding of how other types of developmental relationships can contribute to the success of the manager. It is important to examine other types of developmental relationships that may be used to ensure effective leadership development. We will focus in this chapter on describing the characteristics of four types of developmental relationship: mentoring, formal coaching, sponsoring and peer mentoring. We consider the factors that organisations should discuss and make decisions on when creating developmental relationships in organisations.

The Nature and Scope of Developmental Relationships

The concept of a 'developmental relationship' is a relatively new one in the literature. Higgins and Kram (2001) defined it as a relationship where an individual takes an active interest and action to advance the career of a manager by providing developmental assistance. D'Abate, Eddy and Tannenbaum (2003) used the term 'developmental interaction', which they suggested occurs between two or more people with the goal of personal and professional development. A developmental interaction is a more informal relationship. We use the term 'developmental relationship' to mean a formal relationship created by the organisation. McCauley *et al.* (2006) suggested that formal developmental relationships may be one-off or long-term. They include elements of assessment feedback and the interpretation of feedback from others. They offer alternative perspectives and, in some cases, elements of coaching and counselling. Managers should develop multiple relationships, taking on roles that may include those of a formal mentor, a coach and a peer-mentoring support.

Rock and Garavan (2006) suggest that formal developmental relationships have five important characteristics:

Relationship Type: Molloy (2005) suggests that relationships with developers can be instrumental or expressive or some combination thereof. Instrumental relationships serve the primary purpose of advancing individual career and professional interests (e.g. sponsorship, protection, visibility and access to extended powerful networks). Expressive relationships serve psychological support functions such as encouragement in trying times, a safe outlet for discussion of career troubles, advice about coping with the unique stresses of the job and considerations about work–life balance. Instrumental support functions often occur through direct developer intervention or influence. They may also occur in tandem with psychological support from a single source such as a senior manager. However, the mentor may provide direct intervention or exert network influence. In this case, instrumental outcomes arise indirectly through the developer, offering knowledge and expertise toward a manager's learning about how to navigate organisational structures and exert network influence for themselves. The developmental relationship is proactively focused on instrumental career outcomes. The developer offers visibility and potential access to powerful networks. If this can be achieved successfully, it is likely to increase the manager's self-efficacy and circumvent some of the overdependence or 'side-kick effect' identified by Higgins and Nohria (1999). It may also eliminate the possible negative consequences of role conflict with the manager's direct reporting manager(s).

Developmental relationship types that are proactive in network effect would tend to be instrumental and vice versa. This is because interactions are geared toward enhanced organisational effectiveness or career advancement. For managers in contemporary organisations, networking skills and social-capital accumulation are inextricably linked instrumental outcomes.

Network Effect: Network effect in the context of developmental relationships can be either proactive or passive. The extent of the network effect influences a manager's ability to develop social capital in general and may serve to help extend a manager's developmental network. The developmental relationship can have a direct effect on the manager's ability to increase visibility and establish network contacts. Conversely, this effect could be absent where there is no perceived functional role or focus in the relationship on facilitating networking with others.

A developer with substantial organisational and political knowledge can focus on helping a manager create and capitalise on networking opportunities, leading to career enhancement and increased social capital. However, the developer remains removed from the actual enactment of the learned behaviours, knowledge, skills or attitudes.

A developer can directly influence a developing manager's exposure to key decision-makers. The developer sponsors the learning by acting on the manager's behalf, creates the opportunities and ushers the nascent manager into new and challenging roles and responsibilities.

A developmental relationship with a passive network effect does not focus on sponsorship or learning skills designed to navigate organisational structures or politics successfully. However, developmental relationships that have a proactive network effect will be more instrumental in nature, whereas relationships with a passive network character will tend to be more expressive in nature.

Object of Learning: The object of learning in a developmental relationship can be either task-focused or self-focused (learner-focused). Managers need to develop competencies in the management of both self and career. They need to continually develop task-based competency to improve performance and adaptability and need to acquire greater self-awareness such as changing attitudes and developing and enhancing identity. Therefore, the focal outcomes of a developmental relationship may be either task-focused (having goals to be met and learning how to achieve these goals) or self-focused (learning about how one fits into the bigger picture, becoming aware of available options, and developing intrapersonal competencies).

Time Span of Outcomes: Hall (1996) defined short-term learning as improved skill-based performance on the job (task) and learning about one's personal attitudes concerning current work experiences (self). Long-term learning focuses on acquiring 'metaskills' (i.e. learning how to learn over time and taking a longer-term perspective). In terms of self, this requires learning about one's identity and the construction of views of reality. In terms of task, the long-term view is about improving skills that can develop into and even influence the future by increasing adaptability to changes over time (Hall 1996:11).

Developer Style: This may be either directive or reflective. Directive interactions are likely to focus on immediate matters and be short-term in nature, whereas reflective styles may be appropriate to more complex issues that have a longer-term impact. Directive styles emphasise telling, guidance, and a requirement for action. Reflective styles emphasise self-ownership, exploration, self-management by the learner, and a focus on personal issues. This suggests that the outcomes of the developmental relationship may have a longer-term effect. The developer style can be both reflective and task-focused. For instance, a developer may help a manager to take a helicopter view of the organisation and provide relevant examples from past experiences about how organisations and their actors operate. Then the developer can encourage the manager to apply this knowledge and insight. On the other hand, a developer style can be reflective and self-focused. For instance, the developer can offer some wisdom about past experience relevant to a manager's current situation. This will help the manager gain greater personal clarity about options and decisions that are likely to lead to developing and extending identity.

Categorising Formal Developmental Relationships

Figure 10.1 presents an example of a typology of developmental relationships. We suggest four categories:

- *Organisational Navigator or Mentor*: This type of developmental relationship will be reflective rather than directive in style. The developer provides the manager with assistance that is based on expert knowledge and past experience of what the organisation is about. The developer focuses on helping the manager make sense of what is occurring rather than directing him/her to take specific courses of action. The developmental relationship is characterised as instrumental because it focuses on the extrinsic. The task for the manager is to develop an understanding of how to achieve personal goals through interaction with others. The relationship is proactive in terms of network effect because the role of the developer is to develop in the learner the networking skills necessary to navigate the organisation's structure and political system successfully. The object of learning is task-based. However, the skills developed have a value in the longer term. The developer seeks to facilitate the manager in interpreting and making sense of feedback. This dimension closely aligns with McCauley and Douglas's (1998) 'feedback interpreter'. It also incorporates their 'role model' dimensions to the extent that the developer strives to encourage the manager to move into unfamiliar territory and model skills and behaviours that have worked for the developer. It also includes a support dimension in that the developer is in a strong position to empathise with the manager because he/she is likely to have struggled with similar challenges. The developer is living proof that such skills can be mastered. The primary focus is on learning about organisational structures and politics, and understanding 'what makes people tick'.
- *Sponsor of Development*: This role is most likely to be performed within a traditional boss–subordinate relationship where there is the greatest opportunity to take direct intervention to manage development, performance and overall effectiveness. The developer style is most likely to be directive and it will focus on interpersonal skills, task performance and style issues. The learning objectives are likely to be set by the developer, but it is possible that they may be agreed collaboratively. However, it is likely that once they are agreed, the learner may have difficulty in renegotiating them simply because of the more directive style of interaction adopted by the developer. It is likely that instrumental outcomes will be emphasised, with little room for expressive aspects of the relationship. The relationship will be proactive in network effect and directly intervene to ensure network access and visibility. This may occur in a number of ways, including participation on committees, challenging and stretching assignments, and representation of the department or section in which the leader works at senior levels in the organisation.

Figure 10.1: Developmental Relationship Typology

		Long-Term	Time Span of Outcomes	Short-Term	

(Left margin, top to bottom: Proactive — Tasks; Network Effect — Object of Learning; Passive — Self. Right margin, top to bottom: Instrumental; Relationship Type; Expressive.)

Organisational Navigator or Mentor
Characteristics of the Relationship:
- Developer is perceived as a master in 'how to play the game'
- Developer plays a key role in the process of organisational sense-making
- Developer has the potential to offer another perspective on reality (s/he provides illumination of structure, informal processes and political behaviour
- Developer performs the role of champion and cheerleader
- Most likely to occur in an informal coaching or mentoring context

Characteristics of the Learner:
- Learner has strong self-determination and self-efficacy
- Learner places a lot of value on networking and interpersonal competence
- Learner views developer as a role model for behaviour
- May be ambitious, but also somewhat 'green' and values expert advice

Developmental Benefits:
- Helps the learner read and interpret behaviours and avoid political faux pas
- Helps the learner learn how to learn and develop organisational savvy
- Develops competencies in navigating obstacles and avoiding pitfalls
- Long-term value/task-based/improving adaptability and self-management

Sponsor of Development
Characteristics of the Relationship:
- Most likely to be a boss/senior figure in organisation – likely to be formal
- Developer possesses the capacity to change the rules of the game
- Likely to intervene directly , create opportunities and enhance visibility
- Good opportunity to review leaner performance and give daily feedback
- Reinforces learner actions and provides directive advice

Characteristics of the Learner:
- Willing to assume the challenges provided by the sponsor
- Comfortable with the directive advice and the day-to-day feedback
- Views the developer as a broker who creates opportunities
- Learner is at an early stage of development (nascent or low to mid mgmt)

Developmental Benefits:
- Developer holds a mirror up but also gives directive advice about actions
- Learner is coached on the appropriate interpersonal skills to deal with people in the job and to be an effective networker
- Learner has obstacles removed, facilitating exposure to high organisation levels
- Short-term value/task-based/improving performance

Grandparent or Coach
Characteristics of the Relationship:
- Developer performs a multiplicity of sub-roles including counsellor, listener, storyteller, 'sounding board', empathiser and 'dialogue partner'
- Developer has a breadth and depth of experience to draw from and impart
- Open and personal discussion and reflection about life and career, but the developer remains passive about guidance and direction setting
- Developer is highly skilled in articulating the relevance of the past experience
- Less concerned about networks and more concerned about the individual

Characteristics of the Learner:
- Learner is open to new perspectives, possesses reflective skills and has strong feedback orientation
- Learner views the developer as 'sage'
- Learner has well-established self-concept and development maturity
- Learner is prepared to make changes based on feedback

Developmental Benefits:
- Learner has access to sound advice but action is optional
- It encourages the learner to think, justify, and decide for him/herself
- Provides the learner with personal clarity about options and choices
- Examples provided of what has worked well or not or well in the past
- Enables forging ahead with confidence and informal reassurance
- Long-term value/self-based/developing and extending identity

Friend or Peer
Characteristics of the Relationship:
- Peer to peer or friend to friend – likely to be informal and unstructured
- May be an opportunity to 'vent' anxieties or negative experiences
- Developer offers encouragement and may prod the learner to set and address challenges
- Advice is based on the sharing of reciprocal personal experiences
- The developer is a model or benchmark point of comparison

Characteristics of the Learner:
- Learner is at a similar or slightly less advanced stage of development
- Learner values the friend or peer as a confidant
- Learner values the openness and honesty of the relationship
- Learner has strong trust in the developer

Developmental benefits:
- There is ample opportunity for mutual support behaviours; the developer may benefit significantly from the relationship as well
- Each party may challenge the other to identify opportunities and seize them
- There is likely to be significant confidence-building and reassurance
- Encourages both the developer and learner to be effective self-monitors
- Short-term value/self-based/changing attitudes

		Reflective	Developer Style	Directive	

The developer will provide a significant amount of sponsorship and may emphasise supportive functions where the developer considers that it is important to enhance self-efficacy and where it is not counterproductive to the self-sufficiency of the learner. The object of learning will most likely be task activities that are short-term in nature. It may include some elements of self, such as establishing and enhancing self-identity and identifying and discussing blind spots. The manager will be continuously visible to the developer, with the result that there is ample opportunity for assessment and feedback. The developer is likely to be sufficiently senior so that it is possible to broker cross-functional and cross-organisational assignments. The developer will have ample opportunity to provide support and affirm what the manager has done. The developer will also have the opportunity to provide both intrinsic and extrinsic rewards to the manager. It is likely, for example, that the developer will be in a position to make decisions concerning promotion, transfers and special assignments, either within the department or interdepartmentally.

- *Grandparent or Coach*: The developer as grandparent provides the manager with sufficient space to articulate his or her ideas about work and career. The role of the developer is to help clarify and enhance decision-making by offering wisdom and advice, and communicating stories about highly relevant past achievements and experiences. This relationship has a more expressive quality in that it is largely about the manager seeking personal clarity and gaining a valuable alternative source of advice. This helps the quality of decision-making. The network effect can be characterised as passive in that the developer's primary focus is on the manager and his or her options rather than on establishing contacts and developing networks. The learning focus or object of learning will emphasise self rather than task. The relationship will contribute to the development of self-identity, which has longer-term value to the manager. The developer will adopt a reflective style of intervention and he or she will act as a 'sounding board' or 'dialogue partner'. The developer will nudge the manager to reconsider preconceived strategies and will help fine-tune them before implementation. The developer provides a broad and deep base of experience that enables the learner to be more confident concerning actions that can be taken. It is likely that the developer will adopt many of the skills of non-directive counselling because he or she helps the learner to explore feelings, personal concerns, expectations, career objectives and life plans. This counselling dimension will be of value in helping to develop the manager's self-efficacy, self-identity and increased self-determination or self-regulation. The developer, as counsellor, empathises with the learner and encourages action. The learner takes the lead in this relationship and has complete ownership of work and career decisions. The developer stands back, observes, and analyses the bigger picture while providing sufficient inputs to enable the manager to be self-regulated.

- *Friend or Peer*: The fourth developmental relationship focuses on the friend or peer. The friend or peer identifies with the manager and the relationship may come from some unusual or chance encounter. The developer style is likely to have a directive character because the focus will be on advice-giving about what a manager should do to enhance self and career. The relationship will be based on strong mutual trust, with the developer having a significant amount of experience to offer the manager, who will likely seek this directive advice. However, the relationship will be more expressive than instrumental because the primary focus is on manager behaviours and action. The parties discuss situational dilemmas and explore options and goals. The learner will derive significant intrinsic value from the exchange in and of itself. Therefore, it will not be viewed purely as a means to an end.

The network effect is likely to be more passive than proactive. The developer may refer the manager to other contacts or encourage the him/her to seek out others. However, this networking is likely to be infrequent and play a minor role in the overall relationship. The primary focus will always be on the manager rather than on the development of a wider network. The object of learning focuses on self rather than on task. The developer will act as a 'comparison point' because he/she will be at a similar or slightly more advanced stage of development and may be working towards similar developmental goals. The developer may reciprocally discuss these goals with the manager. The friend may also monitor the manager's progress towards agreed goals and, if necessary, push him/her with both encouragement and challenges. The friend will provide valuable support because of his or her capacity to empathise with the manager, provide examples of obstacles that can be overcome and bolster his/her confidence. We will explore the issues associated with some of these relationships in more detail in the remainder of this chapter.

Formal Mentoring and Leadership Development

Formal mentoring corresponds to our organisational navigator in the typology presented in Figure 10.1. There is a lot of confusion concerning what constitutes formal mentoring. Table 10.1 suggests a number of definitions of mentoring as a process.

Table 10.1: Definitions of Formal Mentoring

Summary of Definitions of Mentoring	Author
'Off-line help by one person to another in making significant transitions in knowledge, work or thinking.'	Clutterbuck and Megginson (1999)
'Mentoring involves primarily listening with empathy, sharing experience (usually mutually), professional friendship, developing insight through reflection, being a sounding board, encouraging.'	Clutterbuck (2001)
'Mentoring is a partnership between two people built on trust . . . addressing issues and blockages identified by the mentee, the mentor offers advice, guidance and counselling and support in the form of pragmatic and objective assistance.'	Clutterbuck (2001)
'A career development life preserver pivotal in assisting individuals weather organisational volatility and steering through an increasingly complex and global environment.'	Bierema and Hill (2005)
'A protected relationship in which experimentation, exchange and learning can occur and skill, knowledge and insight can be developed'	Mumford (1993)
'Mentoring falls into the broader category of developmental relationships that range from one-time career sponsorship (i.e. recommending an individual for a developmental task or promotion) to full-blown mentoring that involves a committed, long-term, mutually beneficial relationship.'	Bierema and Hill (2005)
'The mentoring relationship is confidential . . . For this reason the mentors are rarely in a line relationship.'	Clutterbuck (2001)
'Mentoring is recognised as a key developmental resource for individuals in organisations.'	Noe, Greenberger and Wang (2002)
'Mentors can help individuals reach significant decisions about complex issues . . . Mentors are not there to solve problems, but rather to illuminate the issues and to help find a way through them.'	Clutterbuck (2001)

Summary of Definitions of Mentoring	Author
'The most intense and powerful one-to-one developmental relationship, entailing the most influence, identification and emotional involvement.'	Wanberg, Welsh and Hezlett (2003)
'Mentoring is a positive development activity . . . mentoring has proved to be very effective in transferring tacit knowledge within an organisation, highlighting how effective people think, take decisions and approach complex issues.'	Clutterbuck (2001)
'The developmental assistance provided by a more senior individual within the protégé's organisation.'	Higgins and Kram (2001)
'Mentoring helps mentees and mentors progress their personal and professional growth.'	Clutterbuck (2001)
'A set of role activities, including coaching, support, and sponsorship that upper-level mangers provide to protégés.'	Turban and Dougherty (1994)
'A relationship in which an individual takes a personal interest in another's career and guides or sponsors that person.'	Campion and Goldfinch (1983)
'In order to assist individuals in their development and advancement, some organisations have established formal mentoring programme where protégés and mentors are linked in some way. This may be accomplished by assigning mentors or by just providing formal opportunities aimed at developing the relationship.'	Ragins, Cotton and Miller (2000)

Bard and Moore (2000:356) described mentoring as a means of achieving personal growth and development by using a mentor as a long-term guide, counsellor and friend. Mentoring is regarded as a confidential one-to-one relationship in which a manager uses a more experienced, usually more senior, person as a sounding board and for guidance. Mentoring is a protected, non-judgemental relationship which facilitates a wide range of learning, experimentation and development. The perception of mentoring as being the prerogative of the more senior and experienced employee with the less experienced employee is no longer relevant. Age is no longer viewed as being a defining prerequisite for a successful mentoring relationship. Younger people can also be mentors because they can possess specific expertise and experience in certain areas.

Differences do exist between formal and informal mentoring. Informal mentoring has been described by Noe (1988a, 1988b) as relationships where the mentor and protégé, of their own accord, agree that the protégé will trust the mentor to counsel or teach him/her (Friday, Friday and Green 2004). This relationship can be either intra-organisational (the same organisation) or inter-organisational (different organisations). Informal mentoring evolves from shared interests or mutual admiration which can contribute to the creation of deeper and more personal relationships (Chao and Walz 1992) and can move outside the traditional confines of the workplace. Informal mentoring is seen to be the prerogative of the 'lucky few' (Forret 1996:6) and can also be described as classical mentoring or mainstream mentoring (Kram 1983). Informal mentoring is a longer-term, broader relationship which encompasses career and psychosocial functions and can last up to ten years or more (Rees and McBain 2004).

Formal mentoring was introduced in the 1980s in an effort by organisations to replicate and capitalise on the obvious benefits of informal mentoring (Bahniuk and Kolger Hill 1998). Formal mentoring has been described as secondary mentoring. It can last up to two years and focuses on short-term, less inclusive career functions. The following differences between formal and informal mentoring have been identified in the literature.

> **Formal Mentoring**
> - Organisationally assigned relationship between protégé and mentor
> - Focuses on organisational learning needs and priorities
> - Sometimes described as secondary mentoring
> - Usually short- to medium-term
>
> **Informal Mentoring**
> - Voluntary nature of the evolution of the relationship
> - Protégé perceives informal mentors as more beneficial than formal mentors
> - Informal mentoring provides career support and guidance
> - Described in the literature as classical mentoring
> - Focuses on career and psychological issues

Kram (1983) suggested that mentoring tends to perform two distinct functions: career and psychosocial. Career functions focus on career enhancement and on ensuring that protégés get exposure at senior levels and undertake high-level stretch projects to gain kudos and recognition in the organisation. Psychosocial functions are concerned with enhancing interpersonal skills and work skills and provide mentees with opportunities for self-reflection, dialogue and role modelling. Mentoring has functions in areas such as knowledge sharing, performance enhancement, career development, counselling support, coaching and taking the role of a critical friend. Day (2000) suggested that mentoring relationships are heavily skewed towards support, with less focus on ensuring challenge and very little on assessment. Mentoring is typically considered by organisations as a component of leadership development in context, but the gaps in our knowledge concerning its effectiveness for senior managers are surprising.

E-Mentoring or Virtual Mentoring

Mentoring, as we have asserted, has evolved from the traditional face-to-face concept to incorporate other types of mentoring such as peer mentoring, mentoring circles, professional groups and networking (Bierema and Merriam 2002). However, e-mentoring has emerged as a strong supporter of e-learning and has numerous advantages.

E-mentoring has been defined by Bierema and Merriam (2002:214) as 'a computer mediated, mutually beneficial relationship between a mentor and protégé that provides learning, advising, encouraging, prioritising, and modelling, that is often boundaryless, egalitarian and quantatively different than traditional face-to-face mentoring'. Boyle *et al.* (2001:107) have defined e-mentoring as 'the merger of mentoring with electronic communication that links mentors with protégés independent of geography or scheduling constraints'.

E- or virtual mentoring is useful when face-to-face mentoring is not possible. It has the advantage of being asynchronous, it does not require proximity of premises and can be carried out at any time and in any place (Kirk and Olinger 2003). It can be less costly, flexible, provides opportunities for deliberate reflection and creates a written record of the mentoring process which in turn can enhance writing skills. However, careful training must be carried out to ensure that the managers involved know how to use the technology and have access to the relevant online mentoring tools. The fact that there is a written record of the interaction highlights issues of privacy. Table 10.2 outlines the benefits and challenges of virtual mentoring.

Table 10.2: Benefits and Challenges in Virtual Mentoring

Benefits	Challenges
• Anytime/anyplace mentoring • Continued professional development enabling peak performance • Enables skill development (writing, teamwork, communication) • Enables cross-cultural connections • Continuous learning for all managers • Facilitates the development of manager learning communities	• Technology (cost, access) • Online communication skills • Privacy of the relationship • Training in the use of virtual mentoring • Matching the mentor and the protégé • Sustaining the relationship over time

Source: Bierema and Hill (2005)

Advantages and Disadvantages of Formal Mentoring Relationships for Leadership Development

Formal mentoring has numerous advantages from the perspective of the mentee. Ragins and Cotton (1998) found that individuals who participate in mentoring relationships can benefit from career success and higher compensation levels than individuals who have not benefited from mentoring. However, there are also advantages for the mentor and the organisation. The advantages to the mentor can be encapsulated in the Buddhist belief 'what goes around comes around'. The mentor can experience a sense of personal satisfaction from helping others to contribute to the success of the organisation by contributing to a stronger talent pool (Kram and Isabella 1985; Noe 2006). The typical advantages claimed for formal mentoring include the following: a contribution to succession management and improved manager retention; a chance to offer recognition and status to the mentor; the chance to communicate that the mentor and the mentee are valued by the organisation; and the creation of insight into the organisation's culture for the mentee.

Formal mentoring does have its disadvantages. It is important that the personalities of the mentor and the protégé are compatible. Assigned mentoring relationships may not be as beneficial as naturally occurring informal relationships. There may be a lack of genuine commitment on the part of both the mentor and the mentee, because both parties feel that the relationship is contrived or that they were coerced in some way to participate in the mentoring relationship. There may also be confusion concerning what the mentor role involves. Some mentoring relationships have the potential to be completely ineffective, or even damaging. The mentor may be highly egotistical and use the relationship for control and power purposes. It is possible that the mentor could impede the development of the mentee by ceasing to end the relationship at the appropriate time. It is possible that a strong personal bond can develop between the mentor and the protégé which is dysfunctional in terms of development. The protégé may be developed in an inappropriate manner and mentoring may be regarded as a substitute for the absence of other developmental processes. Mentors can be quite controlling and may not empower the protégé to the right level. They may have developed a dependency on the relationship and be reluctant to disengage from the relationship at the appropriate time, thus creating a co-dependency. The mentoring relationship should not be regarded as a long-term contract and a time will occur when the mentee will have received everything from the relationship and will need to move on. A mentee can become over-reliant on and overshadowed by their mentor and become subject to the 'side-kick effect'. Research highlights the downsides of mentoring relationships that are concerned with creating conditions of dysfunctionality in the relationship (Eby, Butts and Lockwood 2003).

At an organisational level, there may be insufficient corporate resources and support for formal mentoring. Formal mentoring can be a significant drain on development resources and organisations frequently have concerns that it is difficult to assess the quality of developmental relationships and their return to the organisation in terms of enhanced leadership effectiveness.

Table 10.3 provides a summary of both advantages and disadvantages of formal mentoring relationships.

Table 10.3: The Advantages and Disadvantages of Formal Mentoring for the Mentee, Mentor and Organisation

Advantages for the Mentee	Advantages for the Mentor	Advantages for the Organisation
• Increased confidence • Knowledge of what is happening in the organisation • Increased exposure and understanding of power structures • Access to a sounding board • Role model • Opportunity for self-reflection • Increased career mobility and advancement • Personal fulfilment	• Increase in their own learning (Allen and Johnston 1997) • Getting information from protégés (Mullen and Noe 1999) • Gain insight into their own development needs • Insight into how others perceive them at work • Opportunity to develop their management style (Hale 2000) • Assistance on projects	• Developing human resources, improved motivation, job performance, retention, succession planning • Managing organisational culture and contributions and fostering change • Improving organisational communication • Relatively cost-effective strategy
Disadvantages for the Mentee	**Disadvantages for the Mentor**	**Disadvantages for the Organisation**
• Poor match with mentor who lacks the skills and empathy to develop the relationship • Might have high expectations of the relationship which cannot be fulfilled • Can develop a dependence on the mentor • Issues in relation to role conflict can arise between boss and mentor	• May lack the self-awareness, insight and skills to be an effective mentor • May have limited time available to develop the relationship • Might feel organisational pressure to take on role and is not committed to it • Might not understand the mutual benefits of the mentoring role	• No structures and supports in place to ensure the success of the process • Lack of resources to monitor and implement the programme • Lack of knowledge and expertise in terms of developing mentor and protégé relationship • Can create a climate of favouritism

Implementing Formal Mentoring Processes in Organisations

It is important to understand the dynamics of the formal mentoring relationship in order to maximise the impact of formal mentoring processes. Mentees should be actively encouraged to shape their relationships with mentors and not to act as passive recipients. The mentoring relationship will work most effectively where the relationship is allowed to evolve naturally and where rapport – and possibly chemistry and even mutuality – exists in the relationship. Enscher *et al.* (2001) highlighted the need for mentor–protégée reciprocity and that mentors can also learn from their roles. It is important to state clearly at the outset the expectations of the mentoring relationship and to ensure that both mentor and protégé understand their respective responsibilities. The frequency and duration of the interactions need to be outlined clearly. Clutterbuck (2001) suggested that the most successful mentoring relationships are those where the mentees select their own mentor.

Indeed, the formal mentoring relationship can be understood as an arranged marriage where both individuals might not be personally compatible and might even dislike one another. The mentor needs to be aware of the interpersonal skills required to be successful in the relationship. Egan (2005) offered the following guidelines to assist organisations create successful formal mentoring relationships:

- The interpersonal process of mentoring needs to be explored in order to improve mentoring relationships and interpersonal connections need to be made to increase rapport and commitment levels.
- The mentor requires strong interpersonal skills and in-depth self-awareness in order to understand the impression they make on others. They need to understand the learning process and their own approach to learning and how this will impact on the mentoring relationship. They need a strong understanding of their own personality and personality types in general and require the necessary skills to analyse others and be capable of 'thinking like a shrink'.
- The mentor requires strong emotional maturity and must be prepared to facilitate the learning of the protégé rather than leading it. They require authority and the ability to give constructive feedback that is both motivational and developmental.
- There is a requirement to examine the factors that lead to the initiation and maintenance of mentoring relationships and it is possible that organisations might use this research in order to foster an appropriate approach to creating effective developmental relationships.
- The backgrounds and interests of the mentor and protégé have to be matched to ensure commonality of interest and experience.
- The developmental needs of the protégé need to be matched with the expertise of the mentor.
- Learning-goal orientation is a critical factor in creating successful mentoring dyads and individuals with a high-level learning-goal orientation are more likely to be motivated to learn and thrive on challenge than those who have a low learning-goal orientation. If the mentor and the protégé share similarities in their capacity for learning-goal orientation, they are more likely to work well together.

Organisations need to create the right conditions to implement an effective formal mentoring process by getting senior management support to champion mentoring. In other words, they need to engage in the process themselves and create a top-down approach to integrating the concept within their own teams that will cascade through the organisation. The organisation should implement a corporate mentoring strategy and put in place relevant training and development policies and interventions to facilitate mentoring. Managers need to be aware of the benefits of mentoring and not perceive it as another time-waster employed by leadership development specialists to justify their existence. Pegg (2005) suggested a mentoring charter as a useful tool for defining and explaining the role of the mentor by making a business case for mentoring and selling its advantages. Once the benefits of mentoring have been highlighted by the organisation, it is possible to develop a mentoring faculty.

Scaffolding

The mentor or coach is in a position to provide cognitive scaffolding in order to assist the manager become self-aware and develop self-efficacy. 'Scaffolding' is a term used to describe devices or strategies to support learners (Rosenshine and Meister 1992). This process of scaffolding has the advantage of helping the manager to achieve work goals by offering support, feedback and advice. The challenge for the developer is knowing when to take away the scaffold: excessive support can prevent the manager from developing because they become dependent on their mentor or coach. It is recommended that the scaffold is faded or gradually withdrawn until it is no longer needed (van Merriënboer, Kirschner and Kester 2003). The scaffold has the potential to be destructive if not properly managed in that it can create a co-dependency relationship that can hinder progress for the long-term career development of the manager.

Formal mentoring programmes frequently fail because the organisation omits to take into account problems in the rapport between the mentor and the protégé. The mentor may feel that this relationship is being forced on him/her and that he/she does not have the time or interest in the development of the protégé. There may be a complete mismatch between the learning styles and personalities of the mentor and protégé and this will result in the relationship being destroyed even before it starts. The mentor may also lack the interpersonal skills to work effectively with the protégé and needs to be prepared to engage in self-analysis to ensure that conditions of compatibility are created (Friday, Friday and Green 2004). It is strongly advised that in-depth analysis be conducted on the mentor's personality and skills to ensure that he/she is prepared for the mentoring relationship.

Pegg (2005) advocated the need to ensure that protégés choose their own mentor, drive the process and possess the skills to get the best out of the process. Therefore, the protégé will need to develop these skills as part of a relevant training workshop. He also emphasised that it is acceptable for the protégé or mentor to end the relationship at any stage. The core issue is to ensure conditions where the protégé drives the process by setting up the initial meeting and ensuring that both individuals create rapport. Following on from this, it is necessary to make a contract outlining: the goals of the mentoring relationship; the issues and challenges that the protégé needs to explore; clear expectations of the limitations of the relationship; and the structure and frequency of the meetings. The effectiveness of the formal mentoring relationship is dependent on the skills of the mentor and they require support from the organisation in terms of relevant training and feedback on their approach. Rees and McBain (2004) outlined the importance of setting up a mentoring contract and offered the following guidelines:

- Ensure that there is clarification on learning goals and outcomes.
- Decide on the ground rules and the boundaries of the relationship.
- Draw up a schedule of meetings and agree on availability.
- Agree on a process to discuss any difficult issues that arise.
- Agree on the criteria for success and the time frame and closure of the relationship.
- Ensure that there are appropriate checkpoints and implement a systematic evaluation process.

Awareness of Ethical Issues in Formal Mentoring Relationships

Formal mentoring can lead to ethical issues. These have been described by McDonald and Hite (2005) as cultural replication, which involves inculcating the organisation's values, brainwashing and generating unquestioning acceptance. Ethical issues include the exploitation of those who have access to mentoring, and gender and race issues concerning who can avail of mentoring relationships in organisations. Hezlett and Gibson (2005) suggest that the following gender and race issues may arise. Are women (or minorities) less likely than men (or Caucasians) to have a mentor? Do women (or minorities) receive the same kind of mentoring support as others? Do women (or minorities) gain the same favourable outcome from mentoring as men (or Caucasians)?

The misuse of power represents another critical ethical issue. Mentors with long experience may cause imbalance in the relationship, which can result in dysfunctional behaviours such as dependency, exploitation, jealousy and violation of confidences. If this situation arises, it can lead to major problems for the credibility of formal mentoring in organisations.

Table 10.4: Ethical Issues in Formal Mentoring Relationships and Responses of Leadership Development Specialists

Ethical Concerns	Potential Consequences	Role of Leadership Development Specialist
Cultural replication: perpetuates existing power structures	• Lack of independent cultures within the organisation • May reinforce the 'old boy' network	*Organisational Analysis:* • Assess organisation's culture to ensure goals/purposes of formal mentoring programmes are ethical, in line with good organisational practices and beneficial to both parties *Recruitment / Selection:*
Access: limited mentoring opportunities for some individuals	• Denial of an important development activity for under-represented groups • Lack of this activity may lead to fewer opportunities for advancement, salary increases, and so on • Limited success of diversity goals in organisations	• Use a selection process that ensures mentors/protégés have the skills and desire to enter into this relationship • Assist in the matching/pairing process; use selection processes that result in equitable access to mentors • Advocate for alternative forms of mentoring that will provide more opportunities for protégés to be mentored (e.g. peer, team, networks) *Training:*
Power: the inherent imbalance of power found in this type of dyadic relationship	• May result in dysfunctional behaviours such as over-dependency, exploitation, sabotage, jealousy, violation of confidences and harassment • Will ultimately result in lower relationship satisfaction	• Discuss dysfunctional mentoring behaviours in training and provide assistance in ways that detect when a relationship is becoming dysfunctional *Follow-up/Evaluations:* • Follow up with mentors and protégés through periodic meetings, interviews, and/or surveys to determine satisfaction and address issues that may arise; provide ongoing coaching support and training as needed

Formal Coaching and Leadership Development

Formal coaching programmes are frequently used by organisations to develop managers. They represent another type of developmental relationship, which has a number of salient features:

*   There is a one-to-one relationship between the manager and the coach which lasts from six months to more than a year.
*   The process usually begins with the manager completing a battery of personality and self-awareness inventories, as well as interviews by the coach and other individuals in the manager's world of work.
*   The manager and the coach seek to gain a clear picture of developmental needs and how the different components of the process will evolve.
*   The coach and the manager agree to meet regularly to review the results of the feedback and to work on building skills and practising particular behaviours.
*   The immediate boss may perform the role of a coach. This relationship can have different degrees of formality.

Coaching is typically used to improve a manager's performance and to enhance career or work through organisational issues, such as culture change. Table 10.5 presents a summary of coaching definitions found in the literature.

Table 10.5: Definitions of Coaching Found in the Literature

Summary of Definitions of Coaching	Author
'A process that enables learning and development to occur and thus performance to improve. To be successful, a coach requires a knowledge and understanding of process as well as the variety of styles, skills and techniques that are appropriate to the context in which the coaching takes place.'	Parsloe (1999)
'Executive coaching is defined as a helping relationship formed between a client who has managerial authority and responsibility in an organization and a consultant who uses a wide variety of behavioral techniques and methods to assist the client achieve a mutually identified set of goals to improve his or her professional performance and personal satisfaction and consequently to improve the effectiveness of the client's organization within a formally defined coaching agreement.'	Kilburg (2000)
Coaching is concerned with 'developing a person's skills and knowledge so that their job performance improves, hopefully leading to the achievement of organisational objectives. It targets high performance and improvement at work, although it may also have an impact on an individual's private life. It usually lasts for a short period and focuses on specific skills and goals.'	CIPD (2004)
'Coaching is the art of facilitating the performance, learning and development of another.'	Downey (1999)
'A process in which a manager, through direct discussion and guided activity, helps a colleague to solve a problem, or to do a task better than would otherwise have been the case.'	Megginson and Boydell (1979)
'Effective coaching in the workplace delivers achievement, fulfilment and joy from which both the individual and the organisation benefit.'	Downey (2003)
'Someone from outside an organisation uses psychological skills to help a person develop into a more effective leader. These skills are applied to specific present-moment work problems in a way that enables this person to incorporate them into his or her permanent management or leadership repertoire!'	Peltier (2001)
'Coaching is both an assistance and a collaborative construction offered to a person (or a team) through a time-limited intervention or, more often, as support spread over a period of time. This assistance and co-construction is in keeping with a professional situation, and/or managed and/or organisational situation.'	Lenhardt (2004)

Interest in coaching in organisations is attributed to the enormous change taking place in business and the need to develop new skills and competencies quickly and efficiently to cope with relentless change. Kets De Vries (2005:62) argued that, because of the pace of change, 'coaching and commitment cultures have replaced the command, control and compartmentalisation orientations of the past.' Gabriel (1996) suggested that downsizing, delayering and flatter organisational structures have created the need for coaches in organisations. The traditional hierarchical support structures no longer exist for managers and this creates a loneliness which prompts the need to look elsewhere for sounding boards to cope with work pressure and stress and to explore career-planning options. Coaching has been described as a modern success-driven approach to leadership with a focus on helping the individual to improve performance. Goldsmith, Lyons and Freas (2000) suggested that coaching offers an appropriate style of working in the post-management era, which they described as the leadership era, with the capacity to transform managers into leaders. The concept of coaching was originally based in the sports realm and introduced as a legitimate development concept in organisations from the 1970s onwards. Skiffington and Zeus (2003) suggested that research demonstrates significant return on investment for organisations, but they also highlighted that this research is in its infancy and called for methodologically sound studies to evaluate the effectiveness of coaching.

Wright (2005) explored the origins of coaching in psychology, which asserts that the individual has the capacity to change their lives by using appropriate therapy (Rogers 1959,1961), such as cognitive behavioural therapy, to help change self-defeating beliefs. Yet, while coaching and therapy have similar roots, coaching differs from therapy in that coaching 'spends very little time on the past and focuses on developing the person's future. Coaching is wellness versus illness oriented . . .' (Wright 2005:326). Workplace coaching is concerned with improving performance, and coaching focuses on facilitating the learning of the individual. Hall, Otazo and Hollenbeck (1999) argued that, typically, the coach is not the employee's supervisor and does not provide feedback on the organisation's reward system to the employee.

Chan and Latham (2004:261) highlighted the fact that several books with a particular focus on the subject have been written, but limited empirical evidence exists on 'who is most effective as a coach'. They further argued that 'there is, at best, indirect evidence from social psychology based on theories as well as empirical studies, that coaching may change behaviour positively'. Hackman and Wageman (2005) suggest that the most research on coaching exists in the training literature and the main focus is on skill acquisition. Bennett (2003) advocated the need to view coaching as developmental rather than remedial and believed that coaching is based on the principle that the manager is responsible for his/her own learning and that coaching is there to facilitate this learning process. The facilitation process is based on stimulating questioning designed to assist individuals come up with their own solutions to problems in an empowered fashion.

Table 10.6 summarises six particular models of coaching that may have application in a leadership development context.

Table 10.6: Types of Coaching Found in Organisations

Behavioural Coaching		
Objective	**Methods**	**Assumptions**
• To adopt a holistic, multifaceted approach to helping the coachee learn and change and emphasise the necessity of effort, practice and rehearsal to obtain lasting behavioural change	• Uses established laws of learning • Employs a validated stage model of change • Uses a variety of assessment tools	• There is a requirement to use validated behavioural change techniques to influence learning, performance and development

Appreciative Coaching

Objective	Methods	Assumptions
• Coaching focused on affirming existing strengths and competencies and assumes that these executives have achieved considerable success and should focus on enhancing this	• Uses appreciative language • Focuses on self-reflection and self-responsibility	• The solutions sought by the coachee are within themselves • Affirmation and praise can reinforce behavioural change

Reflective Coaching

Objective	Methods	Assumptions
• To help the coachee become aware of how they interpret and make sense of their experiences and to understand their world view	• Understanding the language the coachee uses • The coachee must become self-correcting and self-generating	• The coachee must take action for learning and change to occur

Cognitive Coaching Meta-cognition

Objective	Methods	Assumptions
• To help the coachee develop awareness of their thinking styles, build confidence in these thinking styles and improve conceptual thinking and decision-making	• Uses questions about thinking to develop awareness about the coachees' thinking and guide them through a structured process of decision-making and action	• The coach is prepared to change his/her style to accommodate new approach

Observable Coaching/Live Coaching

Objective	Methods	Assumptions
• To use direct observation or shadowing to get an insight into the coachee	• Collect data and analyse and provide feedback • Develop action plans to enhance personal and professional development and business growth	• Coachees observe their own behaviour to enhance self-awareness • Coaches observe the coachee and give specific feedback

Peer Coaching

Objective	Methods	Assumptions
• To allow coaches to use relationships with their colleagues to gather appropriate developmental feedback • To co-create developmental plans to improve performance	• Collect data from peer colleagues • Build networking relationships with colleagues	• The peer relationships must be strong enough to give the appropriate developmental feedback

Source: Skiffington and Zeus (2003)

Types of Coaching in Leadership Development

The coaching literature highlights a number of different types of coaching that can be used in a leadership development context.

Executive Developmental Coaching: Executive coaching has been defined by Ennis *et al.* (2003:20) as 'an experimental, individualised leadership development process that builds a leader's capability to achieve short-term and long-term organisational goals. It is conducted through one-to-one interactions, driven by data from multiple perspectives, and based on mutual trust and respect. The organisation, the executive and the executive coach work in partnership to achieve maximum learning and impact.' The focus in executive coaching is to develop executives and to assist them to lead and manage effectively. Stern (2004) advised that the executive coach must be considered highly competent and this view was echoed by Cialdini (2001), who believed that the coach must be perceived as having authority, credibility and expertise in order to function effectively in that role and thus bring about behavioural change in the individual being coached. Stern (2004) advocated that the executive coach needs to have essential knowledge and expertise in psychology, business, conflict resolution, team dynamics, career development and organisational behaviour. The executive coach should be more practical than theoretical in his/her interpersonal styles and well matched to the executive being coached. Executive coaching is particularly effective for executive assessment, development and succession planning programmes and is extremely useful in terms of creating high-performance leaders. It can also assist executives to implement performance management efficiently. Executive coaching can also be used to achieve strategic understanding and appreciation, to facilitate executive development, to help conflict resolution and to develop skills on change leadership and change management.

Career Coaching: Career coaching is enjoying unprecedented popularity and has been and is concerned with assisting individuals to make more effective career choices. Bell (1996) viewed career coaches as sounding boards, support systems, chair leaders and teammates. However, Chung and Gfroerer (2003) argued that there is a need to understand the distinction between career coaches and career counsellors and suggested that there should be work on professionalising career coaching.

Remedial Coaching: Remedial coaching, in a management and leadership development context, focuses on helping managers take corrective action to bring performance back on track. It typically explores style issues that are impacting on the performance of the manager or leader. Leadership style issues are important factors in career derailment. In the remedial context, the coach takes on the role of devil's advocate and advisor. The coach will seek to encourage the manager to step back and examine performance and behaviour from the perspective of other organisational members. There may be a need to challenge the assumptions and beliefs of the manager. The key challenges for the coach are to build trust, to handle manager resistance and to get the manager to commit to a performance improvement plan.

Transitional Coaching: Transitional coaching focuses on preparing managers to meet the challenges posed by a new work setting. They may involve on-boarding assignments that are designed to prepare the newly hired manager to cope with a new culture, a new team or division and new performance criteria. The specific roles of the coach in this context are to understand the new organisational setting and culture and to have them communicated to the manager. They also help the manager make sense of the new organisational setting.

Transitional coaching is usually of short duration and the coach needs quickly to understand the differences between the old and new organisational controls. Coaches may also play a role in ensuring that organisational managers support the new leader.

Peer coaching: Peer coaching is recognised as extremely useful where managers need to build up skills rapidly in specific technical or business areas, where there is a need to build cross-functional teams across the organisation and where peers can gain insights and support each other by sharing relevant information.

   Peer coaching is concerned with facilitating managers working with each other to share information, develop skills and support each other by creating a type of performance partnership. McCauley and Douglas (1998) highlighted potential problems including the need for a complementary match between peers, the need for the organisational climate to be conducive to the facilitation of peer communication, and the need for specific time constraints to conduct the coaching.

Team Coaching: Team coaching has been described as an act of leadership. It typically involves the creation of a learning team of four to six people who meet regularly under the guidance of a senior manager (McCauley and Douglas 1998). However, it is far more challenging to coach a team than an individual and it requires higher-order learning facilitation skills. Hackman and Wageman (2005) identified four approaches to team coaching which they describe as follows:

- Eclectic interventions, which are based not on theoretical perspectives but on the practitioner sphere of team facilitation and team dynamics
- Process consultation, where the emphasis is on improving interpersonal communications in order to increase the performance of the team and where the team is responsible for assessing interaction levels and how this impacts on work issues (Schein 1969, 1988)
- Behavioural models, where coaches provide feedback to the team in order to develop more effective team behaviours (Schwarz 1994)
- Developmental coaching, where the coach and team members review the team's purpose, progress and the issues that need to be examined and explored.

Whatever approach is taken to coaching in organisations, it is important to ensure that the coach has the appropriate skills to make the relationship successful. These skills are explored in the next section.

Table 10.7: Advantages and Disadvantages of Different Types of Coaching in a Development Context

Executive Coaching

Objective	Content	Responsibility	Advantages	Disadvantages
Formal in nature. Aimed at up-skilling senior managers by developing a behaviourally specific developmental plan. External to the organisation.	Specific around job responsibilities. Performance-related, involving a formal matching process with goal setting and assessment. Learning is goal setting, feedback and emotional support is 'aiding'.	External to the organisation or from a very senior person from within. On a regular schedule, dyadic in structure.	• Potential to be objective. • Perceived expert in field. • Allows for concentrated effort.	• Private executive coaching may focus on creating a dependency and is constantly raising the bar for the client and pushing for more and thus creating a demand for more support. • Challenging for coach as dealing with top team, i.e. high-achieving confident people.

Peer Coaching

Objective	Content	Responsibility	Advantages	Disadvantages
Learning-related. Object-specific, new perspectives on how other functions operate or to impart new technical knowledge.	Specific. Related to emotional support and 'aiding'. Focuses on expressive dimensions of the relationship	Lateral	• Highlights new perspectives and appreciates how to work and create as new learning. • Participants are on the same level so more open communication around learning needs. • Processes more streamlined and efficiencies evident.	• Organisational climate may not be open enough for communication needed. • Time and motivational difficulties with managers to engage in this.

Career Coaching

Objective	Content	Responsibility	Advantages	Disadvantages
Formal in nature and aimed at assisting the client's personal development in the context of work and career.	Focused on helping the individual make effective career choices.	External to the organisation.	• Highly supportive. • Assists the manager to clarify his/her own expectations.	• Lack of credibility of career coaching as it is not regarded as a legitimate profession. • Very similar to career counselling.

Remedial Coaching

Objective	Content	Responsibility	Advantages	Disadvantages
Job-specific, professional skill/ expertise development	Emphasis on knowledge, skill, attitudes, values and performance.	Line manager responsibility.	• Relationship building increases skill and thus job satisfaction. • Increased visibility thus additional opportunities/ challenging work. • Manager has greater confidence in delegation • Cost-effective means of staff development • Builds self-esteem.	• Resentment by those not participating. • Lack of skills and interest on the part of the coach. • Time issues.

Team Coaching

Objective	Content	Responsibility	Advantages	Disadvantages
To assist teams to learn together and build stronger teams.	Working on job-specific issues and learning through project work.	Senior manager	• Builds strong team ethos. • Increases communication. • Develops strong internal ethos of knowledge sharing. • Builds relationships.	• Needs higher-order team coaching/ facilitation skills • Personality clashes • Some team members may need individual coaching.

Transitional Coaching				
Objective	Content	Responsibility	Advantages	Disadvantages
To assist the manager make a successful transition to a new role.	Working on culture and context issues, the organisation's leadership philosophy and establishing leader credibility in the new organisation.	Internal or external coach	• Enables the new leader adjust elements of style to the new context. • Provides the leader with confidence that he/she can make an impact quickly. • Helps the leader handle sensitive interpersonal situations during the first few months of the new setting.	• Very short time frame to reach coaching goals. • Requires lots of clarity on both organisation settings. • May experience difficulties in getting organisational support for the new manager.

Factors that Impact the Leadership Development Coaching Relationship

Well-designed and well-executed leadership development coaching programmes can lead to significant behavioural change. The effectiveness of a coaching relationship depends on a number of important factors. First of all, the manager being coached must be motivated to change and the coaching relationship must start from the position where the coachee fully understands the benefits of changing behaviours and the consequences that may result if change does not occur. Formal assessments are an important component of the coaching relationship. This provides the coachee with a detailed insight concerning the behaviours that need to be changed, the factors that will drive that change and the ease or difficulty of changing behaviours. The relationship must be built on the understanding that some behaviours cannot be changed, but change is optimised where the coach gets the coachee to practise targeted behaviours. Senior managers should hold coachees accountable for the changes they intend to make. Accountability represents a vital component of an effective coaching relationship and its discussion should not be avoided.

Frisch (2001) examined the issues that impact negatively on the coaching relationship and stressed the need to analyse coaching cases to determine possible debilitating effects. These were described as lack of motivation on the part of the coachee and the avoidance of feedback opportunities on the part of the coach. Frisch grouped these issues into two areas: 1) the organisational context; and 2) the characteristics of the coachee. These issues can seriously compromise the coaching relationship even to the extent that coaching cannot be regarded as a suitable intervention and another approach needs to be considered. The threats to the progress of coaching in the organisational context and the characteristics of the coachee context are summarised in Table 10.8.

Table 10.8: Threats to the Progress of Coaching in the Organisational and Personal Context

The organisational context	Issues that need to be addressed
Equivocal organisational commitment	Is the coaching being used to improve performance or is it being used to establish whether the coachee is suitable for the job? If the coachee feels that their job is under threat, their performance is unlikely to improve.
Sudden changes in the status of the organisation – upheaval	If coachees have fears about their jobs due to conditions of organisational flux, coaching needs to be deferred to a more appropriate time.
Sponsor-coachee relationship	'The sponsor should be an ally for the coachee' • When the boss and coachee are experiencing dissonance due to conflict, lack of respect or avoidance, the coaching relationship will be undermined as a result. • The boss might have limited interpersonal skills and thus be regarded as a poor role model for the coachee. • The coach needs an appropriate coaching sponsor to anchor the learning in the workplace and even use three-way relationship-building meetings to address issues.
Politically charged organisational climate	• Coaching is not successful in highly competitive work environments where revealing developmental issues (weaknesses) can impact negatively on the individual. Cut-throat caustic work environments fuelled by authoritarian leadership styles are not conducive to coaching. Coaching works well in servant–leader organisational cultures.
Coaching as part of a formal programme	• Coaching can be successful if the formal management development programme is considered worthwhile; if it is not, coaching will not be appreciated.
The personal context	**Issues that need to be addressed**
Personal problems	• The coachee might not be able to discuss difficult family issues or personal problems that are impacting on their performance. • Stressful work-related issues can contribute to post-traumatic stress that requires counselling rather than coaching and benefit from the organisation's employee assistance programme instead. • If the coachee is under major work pressure, working long hours and travelling, the coaching intervention might not be used appropriately. The coachee has to be focused and ready to be involved in coaching.
The confidence levels of coachees and their willingness to engage in behavioural change	• The coachee needs to be open to taking the risk of changing their behaviour and might require support from their boss and other professionals as well as the coach. • Lack of confidence, fear and anxiety can undermine an individual's ability to take risks so they must be assured of a safe environment in which a blame culture does not exist. • The self-examination and experimentation required for coaching can be regarded as too challenging for some coachees.
Ability to accept feedback	• Coachees need to understand the benefits of feedback and be capable of coping with the unsettling impact of negative feedback. • Coachees need to tap into their emotional resilience to be able to accept feedback and do something about it.

The personal context *contd.*	Issues that need to be addressed
The coachee needs to develop psychological curiosity and insight	• Coachees need to understand how they impact on others and the effects of this on their work relationships. • They need to be capable of 'thinking like a shrink' and develop insights into how they change their work relationships.
The motivation to change	• The coachee must internalise the feedback to the extent that they want to change and it is in everyone's interest for them to change. The coachee is wholly responsible for changing their behaviour and the coach cannot make this happen. The joke about the psychologist and the light bulb comes to mind: how many psychologists does it take to change a light bulb? One, but the light bulb has to want to change!

Source: Hamlin, Ellinger and Beattie (2008); Grant and Cavanagh (2004)

Core Skills and Behaviours in the Coaching Relationship

Table 10.9: Perspectives on Theory: Models of Managerial Coaching

Model	Description
The GROW Model	The GROW model, developed by Whitmore (1996), starts with his definition of coaching as 'unlocking a person's potential to maximise their performance. It is helping them to learn rather than teaching them.' The purpose is declared as improvement and the process as humanistic or person-centred, so the model fits into the engagement quadrant. Whitmore is seeking to promote coaching using humanistic values. The goals would need to be generated by the client and there would need to be access to emotional material in the coaching process to focus on the humanistic aspects. The GROW model enables the coach to ensure that the client agrees to the organisation goals, to examine the current situation for the client, to discuss possible options and, finally, to establish what action will be taken, when and by whom. Before embarking on the model proper, the coach needs to explore the client's levels of awareness and responsibility. Awareness includes self-awareness. When a client is given a choice, responsibility and improved performance follow. **G** is for goal setting. This will differentiate functionalist activity from evolutionary activity. The client is invited or persuaded to align personal goals with organisational objectives. For executive or life coaching, clients generate their own goals. **R** stands for reality testing. This can be done by Socratic questioning. Open questions are the key to this part of the model, so the coach uses 'What?', 'Why?', 'When?', 'Where?', 'Who?' and, most important, 'How?'. For instance, a report-writing client might be asked 'How will you complete a 5,000-word report in two days?' In order to be able to deploy open questions effectively, the coach will need to have some knowledge about the client's situation and this means listening first, restating in order to check and then being in a position to offer open questions that will test the reality of the given situation. **O** stands for exploring options. This can be done using the key skills for basic coaching: first listen and then restate, question and summarise. For instance, with the report client above, 'You were saying that you have been given too much work. Is that right?' and 'How are you gong to manage the report?' and 'What other options are there?'

Model	Description
The GROW Model *contd.*	**W** stands for verifying the client's will to act This is achieved by restatement and summary. The client may be assenting to an outcome that is outside his or her disposition. The coach should ensure that the summarised outcome is within the client's disposition, and this can be ensured by the coach asking the client to summarise, e.g. 'What have you decided to do, then?' The GROW model is recommended for clients who are willing and co-operative, and is especially suited for functionalist or engagement coaching. The structure ensures that clients are informed about the functionalist purpose of the coaching programme, and there is less potential for disappointment. The GROW process may take six months to achieve or one session, and may be repeated for different projects.

The Flow Model	The Flow Model was developed by Flaherty (1993). He argued that coaching must allow for people to change, to become competent and to become excellent. His five stages are: establish relationship; recognise opening; observe / assess; enrol client and coaching conversations. The first stage, establishing the relationship, is equivalent to a contracting stage, with the emphasis on shared commitment, mutual trust, mutual respect and freedom of expression. If there is no shared commitment, there can be no coaching. If there is an existing relationship, the task at this first stage is to establish how it can be used as the basis of a coaching relationship.
	    The second stage, recognising openings, relates very much to functionalist and engagement coaching, as it is designed to find a time when the client is ready for coaching. The idea of recognising openings is to be ready to take advantage of a moment when the client is experiencing difficulties or having his or her habitual identity questioned and to offer coaching at this stage. The advice for coaches when the client declines coaching is to revert to traditional management techniques of command and control. For evolutionary, executive or life coaches, the relationship supports an egalitarian context where the idea of an 'opening' does not occur.
	    The third stage of observation and assessment also seems to relate very much to functionalist or engagement coaching, and we note again here that the concept of personality inventories and learning styles is inconsistent with coaching, as they present individuals as collections of fixed properties that cannot be changed. However, the interpretation of assessment in this model aims to explore with clients their concerns, their history, their desires and their satisfactions as well as their qualities, skills and commitment to their declared goals.
	    The fourth stage of enrolment is the moment when the client 'buys into' the coaching project, and this again has echoes of functionalist or engagement coaching. The necessity to 'buy in' does not arise in evolutionary coaching, as clients generate their own objectives and the executive or life coaching process addresses them.
	    In the fifth stage, coaching conversations, Flaherty offers us three types of conversation. The first, functionalist, type of conversation is 'clarifying standard for performance', which sets the scene for a dialogue aiming at improvement. The second type of conversation, engagement, takes place over time. Its purpose is to address a client who is, for example, 'not being open to the input of others', which suggests some overcoming of resistance, a characteristic of hidden functionalist objectives to which the client may not have assented. The final type of conversation is 'more profound'; it will bring about 'deeper change' and 'in most business situations there is not very much of an opening' for it.

Model	Description
The SOS Model	The SOS model suggests that coaching should focus on the situation(s), how others feel about the situation(s) and how self(s) can act to progress the issue. **S** stands for the situation in which clients find themselves or the context in which the coaching is taking place, such as clients who seek additional qualification in their work. However, what they have not heard is the client's own 'take' on that situation. **O** stands for others who feature or act in the client's world and these may be colleagues, staff, senior managers, family or friends. The open question, starting with 'Who?', is relevant here and can be followed up by other open questions. For instance, the coach will try to focus on the client's situation as well as the significance of studies in the workplace. **S** stands for self. There is a temptation to identify the failings of clients, highlighting their faults or shortcomings. However, coaches seek to encourage their clients and celebrate their attributes, while seeking to persuade them to adopt the required dispositions. The SOS model is popular with managers because it provides a simple framework, but its effectiveness depends on the skill of the coach.
Rogers Model	Rogers (1986) suggests that coaching is essentially about creating trust, taking stock and choosing options for the future. Rogers suggest six principles that should inform the coaching relationship: 1) the client is resourceful; 2) the coach's role is to spring loose the client's resourcefulness; 3) coaching is holistic and addresses the whole person; 4) the client sets the agenda; 5) the coach and the client are equals; and 6) coaching is about change and action.
Egan's Skilled Helper Model	Egan's (1990) model suggests a linear structure consisting of three stages: 1) the present scenario where the coach helps the client to clarify the existing situation; 2) the preferred scenario, where the coach helps the client to develop goals and objectives based on an understanding of the situation; and 3) action strategies where the coach helps the client to develop strategies for accomplishing goals. In order to identify the present scenario, Egan suggests three strategies: 1) telling the story as the client sees it; 2) recognising unawareness and generally easing the client towards a clearer picture; and 3) a search for what will make a difference. In developing a preferred scenario, the coach can help the client through exploring a range of possibilities, creating viable agendas and making a choice and commitment to a preferred agenda. In developing action strategies and plans, the coach helps the client through brainstorming, repeated questioning, identifying the best strategy and encouraging the client to formulate plans. The model encourages managers to explore their world in detail before moving on to the next stages. It is a very person-centred model which encourages a dialogue and the possibility of change.

The brief solution-focused approach to coaching has its roots in the field of family therapy and counselling. It is founded on the work of De Shazer and Berg in the Brief Therapy Centre, Milwaukee, USA in the 1980s. The original ideas have been applied across many disciplines including coaching, psychology, social work and education. Bill O'Connell, who wrote the book entitled *Solution-Focused Therapy* (2005), is a strong advocate of this approach in counselling and psychotherapy in the UK. The approach focuses on solutions and not problems. It is about getting the client or coachee to identify and take a step in the right direction. In brief, the focus is on solutions (not problems), the future (not the past) and on the competence of the coachee to take immediate action.

The application of the model to a coaching session begins with the coach helping the coachee to be clear and specific about what they want to get from this session. The next step is about building the solution focus through the 'miracle question': 'Something amazing happens in relation to your problem while you are asleep one night; when you wake up in the morning, what will you notice?' The third step is about establishing the coachee's competence to solve similar problems or issues. The fourth step gives the coachee a way of measuring progress on a scale of one to ten. Step five is about helping the coachee to be clear and specific about the next steps that they will need to make to effect change. Finally, the conversation closes with the coach leaving the coachee in charge of the situation.

The coach needs to ensure that the coachee commits to developing the skills required to change by practising and rehearsing these skills. The coach needs to keep the coachee on track to achieve these changes on a permanent basis. Landsberg (1997) describes the elements of an effective coaching relationship as follows:

- Creating a context of trust and understanding. This involves ensuring that the learner can bond with the coach and trust the coach to demonstrate respect and empathy towards him/her. An agreement must also be reached on how the coaching is to be delivered.
- The coach must avoid coming up with solutions and conclusions and work on questioning the learner, thus empowering them to come up with ways to become more effective performers.
- It is also necessary to agree specific goals with the learner in terms of performance improvement and to ensure that these are SMART goals.
- The effective coach must continuously look for ways of giving the learner the opportunity to develop their skills and competence. The coach must seek out relevant skill development opportunities and make the learner conscious of identifying learning opportunities themselves.

In coaching, the importance of regular feedback is vital and involves motivational feedback (catching the learner doing something well) and developmental feedback (giving constructive feedback and being capable of replaying negative actions, highlighting the implications of these and then suggesting a desired outcome which will ultimately lead to improved performance). It is important to ask the individual for their suggestions about how to improve their performance before offering solutions because individuals often have the answers themselves and, when they are given responsibility for coming up with performance improvement strategies themselves, they will be more likely to own this learning, which in turn can lead to lasting improvements. Table 10.10 shows research findings on facilitative coaching behaviours. These studies highlight particular behaviours and skills of effective coaches.

Table 10.10: Perspective on Theory: Understanding Managerial Coaching Behaviours

Ellinger and Bostrom (1999) Managerial Coaching Behaviours in Learning Organisations Study	Beattie (2004) Managerial Learning Facilitative Behaviours Study
Empowering • Question-framing to encourage employees to think through issues: posing outcomes, results-oriented questions or context-specific questions to encourage learners to think through issues themselves • Being a resource – removing obstacles: providing resources, information, materials to learners, and removing roadblocks and obstacles they perceive to be in their way	• Thinking – reflective or prospective thinking, clarification: reflective or prospective thinking through the process of taking time to consider what has happened in the past or what may happen in the future • Informing – sharing knowledge: sharing knowledge through the transmission of information

Empowering *contd.*
- Transferring ownership to employees: not taking over learners' responsibilities and shifting them back to the learners and holding them accountable
- Holding back – not providing the answers: mentally holding back and consciously not providing answers, solutions, or telling learners what to do in certain situations

Facilitating
- Providing feedback to employees: providing observational, reflective and third-party feedback to learners
- Soliciting feedback from employees: seeking feedback from learners about their progress
- Working it out together – talking it through: talking through things together to come up with options, a game plan, or an overall approach
- Creating and promoting a learning environment: organising meetings and activities, using learning plans and creating formal and informal opportunities to help employees grow and develop
- Setting and communicating expectations – fitting into the big picture: setting goals and expectations with learners and communicating their importance to learners
- Stepping into other's roles to shift perspectives: stepping into another person's shoes to experience their perspective
- Broadening employees' perspectives – getting them to see things differently: encouraging learners to think outside the box by helping them to see other perspectives and by providing other perspectives and experiences
- Using analogies, scenarios and examples: role-playing, personalising learning situations with examples, and using analogies and scenarios
- Engaging others to facilitate learning: bringing in others – peers or human resources – to help facilitate learning or sending learners to outside resources

- Empowering – delegation, trust: delegation by giving duties and responsibilities to others, trust and having confidence in someone
- Assessing – feedback and recognition, identifying developmental needs
- Advising – instruction, coaching, guidance, counselling: instruction by directing an individual in a specific task; coaching through discussion and guided activity; guidance by providing advice
- Advising – counselling by helping others take control of their own behaviour and solve problems themselves
- Being professional – role model, standard-setting, planning and preparation: role model by behaving in a manner that people respect and wish to emulate; standard-setting by outlining or encouraging an acceptable level of performance or quality; planning and preparation in terms of organising and structuring learning
- Caring – support, encouragement, approachablility, reassurance, commitment / involvement, empathy: supporting by giving aid or courage; encouraging by inspiring or instilling confidence; demonstrating approachability by being easy to approach; giving reassurance to relieve anxiety; displaying commitment and involvement by giving time (to staff); demonstrating empathy by showing understanding of another's situation
- Developing others – developing developers: developing developers by stimulating the acquisition of skills and knowledge by employees to develop others
- Coaching – challenging: challenging by stimulating people to stretch themselves

The Coaching Assessment Process and Developmental Coaching

A critical component of any coaching engagement involves the assessment of the client's needs. In the developmental coaching context, coaches take on the roles of leadership developers and career planners. Coaches help the client take on more demanding leadership roles. Such a context provides important challenges for the developer to identify the most important leadership skills that are required to succeed in the job. The coach may also be coaching an executive who is making a job transition into a more demanding role. The coach will need to make a judgement concerning whether the difficulties encountered by the executive are related to leadership-style issues or technical skill deficiencies. An assessment interview can provide the coach with the necessary information to make a judgement on each of these issues.

We have emphasised throughout this chapter the need to base developmental interventions on systematic assessment processes. A review of the leader's work history will be useful in helping the coach achieve an understanding of the manager's career path. This review should also be useful in helping achieve an understanding of the factors that have driven the executive's career.

Table 10.11: Conducting an Assessment for Leadership Development Coaching

Interview Component	Developmental Coaching Questions
Gap Assessment	• What leadership challenges are you facing in this new job? • What technical skills are going to be put to the test in this new job? • What aspects of this new job are still a little unknown to you? • What missing pieces still have to be filled in? • What's the single biggest 'jump point' you face? That is, what's going to be the toughest leadership demand or expectation that you're going to have to meet?
History	• Tell me a bit about some of the leadership challenges that you've faced in your previous jobs. • What have you learned from these experiences that you think will translate into your next assignment?
Goals and Priorities	• What goals could we set to help you feel fully prepared for handling your new role? • Among these goals, what is most important? What is most urgent?

Barner (2006) suggests that the coach should adopt particularly professional practices when conducting the assessment, become a reflective practitioner, communicate the approach to the client and be flexible and adaptable. Coaches should reflect on their methods and consider how aligned these methods are in the coaching context. The client and the organisation should understand the purpose of the coaching intervention. It is important to check the mental model of the executive or manager in order to unearth expectations. Coaching methods need to be used in a flexible manner. It is important to match coaching interventions to the clients' needs rather than simply using tried and trusted methods.

Using Internal or External Coaches?

The conventional wisdom in the practitioner literature is that you should use external coaches for senior executive coaching, given the need for confidentiality, the complexity of the coaching task and the need for the coach to have credibility. Frisch (2005) suggested that internal coaches have an important contribution to play in coaching executives. The external coach is usually recommended because of their greater capacity to give valued, honest, accurate feedback about strengths and weaknesses, as well as clear advice about ways to become more effective. External coaches, however, are expensive even when used for a limited time. It is more important to find a coach who is able to establish a good working relationship with the executive while remaining objective and professional than being concerned about whether that coach is internal or external.

Trisch suggests that organisations should consider the merits of an internal coach. He acknowledged that they are more likely to be challenged by confidentiality issues. Where internal coaches are used, it is important to familiarise them with the process, carefully select the coaches and provide ongoing development. Internal coaches need a common philosophy and approach and a mechanism through which they can review their task. The goals of the internal coaching process need to be clearly defined and the organisation should adopt a common set of assessment tools and concepts. Coaches should receive systematic training in their use and application.

Table 10.12: Recommendations to Promote Effective Coaching for Leadership Development

> For coaching to be most effective, top managers and HRD professionals must ensure that:
> - An effective performance management system is operating within the organisation. Among other things, this means that the organisation's recognition and rewards system properly rewards managers and supervisors for effective coaching.
> - All managers and supervisors are properly trained in coaching skills and techniques.
> - A thorough coaching analysis has been done before employee performance issues are discussed with employees.
> - Supervisors prepare in advance for the coaching discussion
> - Supervisors' comments are constructive, helpful and supportive.
> - Supervisors provide specific and behavioural feedback on employee performance.
> - Employees are involved in the coaching discussion.
> - Specific goals are set during the discussion.
> - An action plan is jointly established between the employee and the supervisor.
> - Coaching discussions are followed up to ensure that the employee is following the action plan and to recognise performance improvements when they occur.

Sponsorship as a Form of Leadership Development

Friday, Friday and Green (2004) argued that mentoring and sponsorship tend to be considered as the same concepts, but they believed that there is a need to 'reconceptualize mentoring and sponsorship and to offer them as distinctly different concepts, rather than viewing sponsorships as an inherent sub-function of mentoring'. They argued that clarity is required around these concepts in order to assist managers to make appropriate choices of relevant people who can help them progress in their careers. They highlighted the views of experts that mentors give their protégés both high levels of career support and limited levels of psychosocial support (Higgins and Kram, 2001:269; Chao 1998). Sponsorship is defined by Friday, Friday and Green (2004:631) as 'a developmental relationship in which the sponsor provides instrumental career support by nominating the protégé for promotion and other types of organisational activities that may be supportive of promotion'. Other definitions are presented in Table 10.13.

Table 10.13: Definitions of Sponsorship in a Leadership Development Context

Someone who provides high amounts of career support but low amounts of psychosocial support.	Higgins and Kram (2001)
Those who actively intervene, contriving to get their protégés exposure and visibility through assignments that involve working with other managers and endorsing their protégés for promotions and special projects.	Whitely, Dougherty and Dreher (1991)
A sponsor discovers and fosters individuals for higher placement in other parts of the organisation.	Campion and Goldfinch (1983)
A sponsor functions to generate power in protégés by fighting for and promoting them, by allowing them to bypass the hierarchy and obtain inside information, and by reflected power or power by association.	Campion and Goldfinch (1983)

The literature presents sponsorship as a developmental relationship which focuses on career support and promotion opportunities. Managers should recognise that they need someone to look out for career development opportunities who will work to advance their promotion opportunities in the organisation (Kanter 1977).

Friday, Friday and Green (2004) argued that sponsorship has been subjugated, overshadowed and sidelined by mentoring and can be regarded as a less robust developmental relationship as a result. However, sponsoring is vital in terms of helping a manager move forward in the organisation and it should not be regarded as the poor relation of mentoring because it is a powerful strategy to facilitate career development. Formal mentors typically supply the same psychosocial support as informal mentors, but they do not provide the same amount of career support, which is usually an expected outcome of mentoring. Thus, informal mentors do not supply the appropriate levels of career support. The sponsor's ability to advance the career of the manager is central to establishing a robust distinction between informal and formal mentoring and sponsorship.

Effective sponsors have a number of important characteristics:

- Sponsors facilitate managers by obtaining outside information and helping them bypass the hierarchy
- Sponsors help their managers to fight for their promotions
- The sponsor vouches for, is responsible for or supports a manager or makes a pledge or promise on behalf of another
- Sponsors can assist in helping the manager advance within the organisation.

Peer-Mentoring or Co-Mentoring Processes and Leadership Development

We highlighted peer mentoring in our typology of mentoring earlier in this chapter. This form of developmental relationship is one between two managers that is based on the assumption that the relationship can facilitate learning and growth. It is sometimes called co-mentoring. Peer managers can fulfil a variety of mentoring functions across all stages of life and career and they have the potential to be as good or better than hierarchical mentors.

Rymer (2002) articulated the characteristics of peer or co-mentoring.

- Co-mentors are peers who participate in a multiplicity of beneficial relationships that are based on equality. Co-mentoring represents a collaboration, which serves the needs of both peers. The peers may differ significantly in variables such as age, status, skills and knowledge.
- Co-mentors are typically friends and their relationship focuses on the whole person. They are usually colleague managers who have developed a friendship which has been sustained over a significant period of time. Both peers will share inner thoughts and feelings and the relationship lasts as long as it satisfies both parties. It is premised on a strong emotional connection, mutual knowledge and trust. It will serve both professional and personal needs.
- Co-mentors are focused on the 'others' in the relationship. Peer mentors are fully engaged; they understand each other as people, they demonstrate strong empathy and listening skills, and they share views openly. The aim is not to win arguments but to expand individual perspectives. The exchanges facilitate the development of identity and an understanding of strengths and weaknesses.
- A focus is open dialogue. Co-mentors discuss a multiplicity of things, including careers, professional issues, intellectual questions and personal matters. These conversations are typically open-ended, in-depth and based on a desire to develop new knowledge and, if necessary, change beliefs and values.

- Co-mentorships are multiple relationships. It is unlikely that one relationship could provide all mentoring needs. Managers will typically have several co-mentoring relationships. These may vary in terms of their emotional intensity and will focus on specific interests and professional activities rather than the full spectrum of managerial issues, which may be the case with formal hierarchical mentoring.
- Peer mentoring is focused on development. The manager will typically form a developmental network from which he/she can draw support and counsel. Each co-mentor will likely offer a unique perspective and complement others in the developmental network. The developmental value of this network will depend on its diversity and the range of experiences among the individual co-mentors, as well as cultural and ethical issues.

Peer mentoring has considerable value in a leadership development context. It blends the professional and the personal in a holistic manner. Managers can support each other and deal more confidently with highly complex and ambiguous information. Co-mentors are also a useful resource in handling problems and tasks. Co-mentors represent a valuable form of 'social capital' for the manager. They encourage co-operative interaction, the dissemination of important information and the development of teamwork. McCauley and Douglas (2004) suggested that the key drawback is that the developmental needs of the co-mentors may not complement each other. Some managers may not have the motivation or time to participate in formal peer-mentoring processes. They may not see it as having personal or career benefits.

Creating Developmental Relationships in Organisations

Formal developmental relationships can be designed to achieve important development objectives. They have an important contribution to make to the total leadership development effort. We suggest five key issues that need to be addressed in order to ensure that they are successful:

- *Organisational Support*: Formal developmental relationships should be advocated by senior management and supported by the organisation as a whole. In order for this to happen, the organisation needs clear objectives for leadership development that are linked to strategic goals. Formal developmental relationships must be clearly aligned with other leadership development initiatives and integrated with organisational HR strategies. Senior management should visibly support such initiatives and it is important that the overall development climate is conducive to the behaviours and values associated with formal developmental relationships.
- *Programme Goals and Expectations*: The developmental relationship programme needs to have clearly articulated goals and objectives, which should be agreed in a collaborative fashion, involving the participation of key stakeholders. It is important that goals and objectives are fully understood and that each participant should receive a clear description of their roles, accountabilities and responsibilities.
- *Participant Commitment and Behaviour*: Effective formal developmental relationships require certain commitments and behaviours from both mentors and protégés. Relationships must be based on trust and trust must be earned. Participants must demonstrate openness in sharing thoughts and feelings and asking questions, confronting differences and giving honest feedback. It is also important that there is a commitment to challenge issues and build strong bonds. Participants must be committed to ensuring that conversations and relationships are sustained and that they meet face to face as much as possible. This includes holding meetings at agreed times, exploiting new technology and using the telephone. Participants must be committed to listening empathetically, working collaboratively and managing conflicts that may emerge.

- *Selecting Mentors and Protégés*: Effective matching is a core element of a strong developmental relationship. Managers need to be carefully selected with regard to the leadership development needs identified and the capacity of the relationship to flourish. Organisations may decide to perform the matching through a committee or they may encourage voluntary matching. The criteria used should be published. Typical criteria which organisations use include personality, similarity of interests, accessibility, position in the organisation, strengths of the mentor, functional area, the objectives of the leadership development programme and, a less tangible criterion, the leadership development philosophy of the organisation.
- *Evaluation of the Programme*: The evaluation of formal developmental relationship programmes is complex. It is important to have ongoing monitoring and evaluation in addition to summative evaluation. Leadership development specialists need to consider when the programme should be monitored, the methods that should be used, who to involve in the process and how the programme results and progress are communicated. The overall summative evaluation strategy will depend on the wider learning and development evaluation strategy and the resource considerations that need to be taken into account in order to conduct an effective evaluation.

Conclusion

Formal developmental relationships are increasingly recognised as an effective approach to developing managers and leaders in organisations. They are recognised as cost effective and have application at different levels in the organisation. They have emerged as an important way of complementing other formal development initiatives. Their effectiveness will depend on the match of both mentor and protégé in terms of personality, the amount of interaction, the level of commitment and motivation and the clarity of expectations. Formal developmental relationships can include formal mentoring and coaching, sponsorship and peer mentoring. These need to be selected appropriately to suit the development needs that have been identified.

In order for formal developmental relationships to be successful, they require strong organisational commitment. This typically involves support from the manager's direct boss to ensure that the relevant development opportunities are identified and acted upon. These relationships require a strong development climate and senior managers must be committed to sustaining them.

Summary of Key Points

- Formal developmental relationships represent an important strategy for enhancing management and leadership capabilities in organisations.
- Formal developmental relationships are created by the organisation in order to ensure that they are of benefit to the total manager population.
- Developmental relationships can take the form of formal mentoring, coaching, sponsorship and peer mentoring.
- One-to-one formal mentoring relationships typically involve the assignment of a junior manager to a senior manager outside the direct-reporting relationship.
- Formal coaching is typically used to enable managers enhance their effectiveness and develop capabilities which can be used in the future.
- Sponsorship involves support of the manager in pursuing specific career objectives and identifying career enhancement opportunities.
- Formal peer mentoring involves establishing relationships between manager colleagues at the same level within the organisation.

- Effective formal developmental relationships must have organisational support, clarity of purpose, strong commitment from the key parties, systematic matching and evaluation processes.

■ Discussion Questions

1. What are the main characteristics of formal developmental relationships?

2. Compare and contrast formal mentoring and peer-mentoring relationships.

3. What are the key skills required by a coach to ensure effective leadership development?

4. Describe the conditions necessary to ensure effective formal developmental relationships in organisations.

5. Why might managers be resistant to coaching advice when it involves performance issues?

■ Application and Experiential Questions

1. Based on what you have studied about peer mentoring in this chapter, suggest a list of issues that organisations should consider when designing and implementing a formal peer-mentoring programme.

2. Suggest how you would go about evaluating the effectiveness of a formal developmental relationship. What cost-benefit issues would you consider? At what point would you consider your evaluation and what stakeholders would you include in the evaluation process?

3. Assign groups of students the task of identifying various criteria by which each of the following may be evaluated: coaching, peer mentoring and sponsorship. Each group should try to achieve consensus about the prioritisation of these different criteria. The class as a whole can share their views and identify whether specific criteria apply to the different types of developmental relationships.

Chapter Eleven

Informal and Incidental Management and Leadership Development

Outline

Learning Objectives

After reading this chapter you will be able to:

- Understand, evaluate and explain the role of informal learning processes in the context of management and leadership development.
- List and explain differences between informal and formal management and leadership development processes.
- Understand and evaluate alternative perspectives on informal management and leadership development.
- Identify and explain the importance of organisational and individual factors in facilitating informal management and leadership development.
- Evaluate a number of informal management and leadership development processes.
- Facilitate effective informal management and leadership development processes.

OPENING CASE SCENARIO

Dick Spring: A Case of Informal Learning

Dick Spring is currently a businessman; however, he has had a long and distinguished career as a politician. Dick was born in 1950 in Tralee, County Kerry. His formal education started at the Cistercian College, Roscrea, followed by Trinity College, Dublin, where he studied Law, and King's Inn, Dublin, where he qualified as a barrister. He entered politics in 1979, when he successfully contested the local elections in Tralee and was first elected to Dáil Éireann in 1981, when he secured a seat in Kerry North, previously held by his father, Dan Spring. His rise through the political ranks was swift. He was appointed a junior minister on his first day as a deputy. In 1982 he was elected leader of the Labour Party. Following the November 1982 general election, Labour formed a coalition government with Fine Gael. He was appointed Tánaiste and Minister for the Environment. He played a major role in the negotiations leading up to the Anglo-Irish Agreement in 1986. In 1987 he showed great political courage by withdrawing from the government because of a difference over budget issues. This led to a general election in which he narrowly escaped losing his seat when he was elected by just four votes. Spring was instrumental in having Mary Robinson selected as Labour's candidate in the 1990 presidential election. Robinson was elected, further demonstrating Spring's foresight and willingness to take risks in the interests of change. His most significant political success was in the 1992 general election, when the Labour Party increased its representation from fifteen to thirty-three seats. This has commonly been referred to as the 'Spring Tide'. He led his party into a coalition with Fianna Fáil, he became Tánaiste for the second time and was appointed Minister for Foreign Affairs. He resigned from the government in 1994 following a disagreement with the then Taoiseach, Albert Reynolds, and the Labour Party joined in coalition with Fine Gael and the Democratic Left. He was again appointed Tánaiste and Minister for Foreign

Affairs. After the 1997 general election, Labour returned to opposition. In that year Spring resigned as leader of the Labour Party after having served for fifteen years, one of the longest-serving party leaders in Ireland. Following the loss of his seat as a TD in 2002, he joined the world of business with Fexco.

Dick Spring considered third-level education extremely important and was encouraged to attend university by his mother who was passionate about education and regretted that she had not had the opportunity to go to university herself. She also regarded education as something he could fall back on if his potential political career was not suitable or successful. However, Dick believes that there is little substitute for the University of Life. There is no manual that can teach you how to lead a party or cope with the tumultuous vagaries of political life. It is not possible to develop a formal learning and development plan to help politicians become effective leaders. These skills are developed in the course of one's work. Learning occurs through active participation in everyday political interaction. Leadership in politics and leadership in business are similar in that the leader needs to demonstrate discipline and be capable of initiating and sustaining teamwork through coaching. The leader must be capable of building trust by going that extra mile and respecting others. Networking is an extremely important skill that Spring developed throughout his political life. He believes that it is important to respect all the people one meets as there are extremely small circles in the business world. Political life creates a wide range of contacts and Irish culture promotes an ethic of mutual assistance. Being courteous to people is of great benefit in terms of building coalitions and creating loyalty. A leader needs to work hard, but avoid becoming enslaved to work, and to understand that one gets out what one puts in. One must ensure that one works hard at the right thing. It is important to be capable of seeing the bigger picture and learn to delegate accordingly. Business has taught Spring to set targets and milestones and ensure that he is self-regulating in ensuring that his business goals are being achieved. Politicians are measured every four years, yet business leaders are measured every quarter. Spring's family influenced his learning in that his mother taught him the value of formal education and the need for tenacity, and his father's ethic of hard work and his popularity and respect among his peers demonstrated the need to relate well to others. This capacity to relate well to people at all levels served him well throughout his career.

The role model that has been of most value in Dick Spring's career to date is Nelson Mandela, whom he has met on a number of occasions. Mandela, he feels, is an extraordinary person, charismatic and inspirational, a person who connects and blends with people and allows others to get inside him. The main lesson Spring learned from Mandela is the necessity to forgive in order to move on. Mandela went through a great deal of hardship and came out the other side and his example is a beacon to all who need to develop and move on. Dick Spring was a relative latecomer to the business world and understands that he is challenged with constantly having to learn. In order to learn you always have to be prepared to ask questions and keep an open mind. Fexco has a culture that is conducive to peer-learning. People are willing to act as sounding boards and thresh out ideas. They are willing to share ideas in an open fashion, which assists in terms of understanding projects fully. The business contacts made throughout Dick Spring's political life have been very useful in his current career. He has cultivated informal mentoring relationships with leading-edge business people who generously share their business acumen and time and willingly contribute to his development. He, in turn, has no problem acting as a mentor and coach to younger people who require his assistance and in-depth knowledge of political life. He believes that learning is about sharing knowledge in an unselfish manner and he is prepared to seek knowledge by using his interpersonal skills to build alliances and create business relationships based on mutual respect.

Dick Spring believes that it is possible to learn from every experience: general elections provide amazing learning opportunities because no two are alike. Equally, chasing contracts in the business world can be exhilarating in that tremendous satisfaction can accrue in closing the deal. However, it is important to be capable of evaluating the learning that develops as a result of gaining the contract and capturing it before it evaporates in the warm glow of success. It is important to create a win-win environment to ensure that the client is fully engaged in the process. He believes that it is also possible to learn from setbacks rather than dismissing them as failures and banishing them to the recesses of the subconscious. The first difficult lesson he learned was at university when he thought that one could become captain of the Trinity rugby club without canvassing – in keeping with the gentlemanly code in the institution. He did not canvas and found himself relegated to the sidelines. He learned from his mistake and became captain in 1973–4. Losing his seat in the general election was a devastating blow initially, but he discovered that the 'Lord works in mysterious ways' and, as the door closed on conventional political life, a new and exciting business opportunity opened up for him. The 'school of hard knocks' can be the most effective way to learn, provided you develop the ability to avoid crying over spilt milk and learn from it. Spring's political career yielded numerous opportunities to learn from setbacks and he cites the example of flying back from Washington after some powerful and positive peace negotiations, and putting plans in place to get George Mitchell involved, when an IRA bomb went off in Canary Wharf and all the careful plans and negotiations collapsed like a house of cards. He had no option but to pick himself up, dust himself off and keep at it. This capacity to be tenacious can be innate, yet he feels that it can also be enhanced and developed through sport. If a team are playing a brilliant match yet are beaten in the last minutes, the players need to cope and move on; they need to be able to take setbacks, learn from them, recover quickly and regain their self-confidence to be able to go out the next day and win. Spring has developed a formula for evaluating important decisions: he looks at the positives and negatives of the scenario, which gives him the ability to look around the corner. He has also learned to avoid answering annoying letters straight away. He takes time to reflect and regroup and has learned that perspectives change. He has also learned that when you are tired, it is important to walk away from your desk and chill out because when you are tired, you are no good to anyone. One of the ways he unwinds is by building stone walls. Some days they come together synergistically and other days they disintegrate. It's amazing how it is all about learning, and he believes very strongly that you can learn something new every day.

QUESTIONS

Q.1   What lessons are to be learned from the case scenario about the value of informal and experiential learning?

Q.2   Based on this scenario, how important are role models to managers as far as their development is concerned?

The majority of management and leadership development activities provided in organisations are formal and draw upon rational forms of knowing. Learning is viewed in an instrumental way; it is considered intentional and it is aimed at enhancing managerial effectiveness. This approach is confirmed by the provision of formal, tangible management and leadership development interventions. It is assumed that these interventions will produce changes in managers and ensure increased organisational effectiveness. However, formal management and leadership development processes can be removed from the realities of the workplace; they frequently suffer from learning transfer problems and can be perceived as lacking relevance to the needs of managers. Raelin (1998) suggested that it is important to challenge how we think about management and leadership development. If learning emerges from active participation in everyday work, then it is appropriate to interpret the workplace as an arena of management and leadership development. Informal and incidental development processes are possibly the most important processes in the context of developing managers and leaders. A large proportion of what managers and leaders learn, both inside and outside the organisation, comes in the shape of informal learning processes. Organisations are more frequently seeking to create and sustain a learning culture and climate that facilitates informal development.

The contingent nature of managerial work suggests that management and leadership development should be grounded in the work that managers perform. Knowledge and skills may quickly become out of date. Managers constantly experience mental challenges in their work and home lives. They require complex or integrated knowledge in the workplace. This knowledge and skill is best developed through solving everyday problems in the workplace.

We explore various dimensions of informal management and leadership development in this chapter. The dynamics of informal management and leadership development are complex. They include how work is defined, manager learning styles and preferences, how managers use their time, key issues of learning culture and climate, and the developmental potential of managerial jobs. We evaluate the use and effectiveness of a number of informal development processes, such as reflection, conventions, learning from mistakes, and informal coaching and mentoring.

Characteristics of Informal and Incidental Management and Leadership Development

We have already made a distinction between formal and informal development processes. Informal development processes are viewed as tacit learning processes. They are also perceived as relevant to the manager's needs and involve knowledge and skills that are immediately applicable. They reinforce the acquisition of knowledge more effectively than formal development by providing opportunities for application and experimentation. Informal development is especially relevant to leadership development because it emerges from specific manager needs. Formal development tends to be specific and structured, goal-directed and contrived. For managers, it can, depending on how it is presented, be perceived as irrelevant. Informal development, in the management and leadership development context, is initiated, determined and directed by managers themselves. As a result, it is active, relevant and contextualised.

However, informal development is considered to be not one type of learning, but a category consisting of informal, incidental and implicit learning processes. Marsick and Watkins (1990) provided the following distinctions:

- *Informal Development*: This development is unplanned, ad hoc, with no specified outcomes. It is predominantly experiential and non-institutional. It occurs in a self-directed way and may be derived from networking, trial and error and informal coaching and mentoring processes.

- *Incidental Development*: This consists of development which is unintentional, a by-product of another activity. It represents a sub-category of informal development. Incidental development has a tacit, taken-for-granted character. It is implicit in the manager's assumptions, actions and beliefs and attributions. It also includes internalised meanings about the actions of others.
- *Implicit Development*: This consists of the acquisition of knowledge that occurs 'independent of conscious attempts to learn'. Eraut (2004) suggested that it is development without awareness or explicit knowledge and that the knowledge or skill was acquired. Some commentators, such as Sadler Smith (2000), suggested that implicit development is broadly equivalent to incidental learning, but definitions of incidental learning do emphasise internal awareness.

These three variants of informal development speak of development which occurs outside of the classroom. The two latter categories are interesting in that they envisage that learning is not planned or intentional, whereas informal learning can be both planned and intentional. The insistence, however, on the use of the word 'planned' is considered controversial because it describes the intention to learn rather than the content of the learning.

The concept of control is important to the broad category of informal development. First, managers cannot be forced to learn and they will have choices concerning the nature of work, its organisation, what they should learn and how they can learn. Hales (1993) suggested that managers have scope to exercise four types of control: 1) ante-control, operating before a developmental activity takes place and emphasising the conditions and inputs required for learning; 2) concurrent control, operating during the learning event and focusing on the processes of learning; 3) ex-post control, operating after the event and emphasising the outputs of learning; and 4) meta-control, which they define as operating above the event and focusing on managers' core learning values.

Table 11.1 provides a selection of definitions of informal development and learning.

Table 11.1: Definitions of Informal Learning

Definition	Author
Predominantly experimental and non-institutional.	Conlon (2004)
An integration of work with daily routines, triggered by an internal or external jolt, not highly conscious, it is often haphazard and influenced by chance, inductively occurs through action and reflection and is linked to the learning of others.	Marsick and Volpe (1999)
Interpret the workplace as a suitable locus of learning. If knowledge is viewed as arising as much from active participation in the very apparatus of our everyday life and work, then we have to expand our notions of learning before the classroom.	Raelin (1998)
Learning for which the process is neither determined nor specific and which may take place inside or outside of the classroom.	Livingstone (2001)
'Part of the job' or a mechanism for 'doing the job properly' and is thus rendered invisible as learning.	Boud and Middleton (2003)
Learning resulting from natural opportunities for learning that occur in everyday life when a person controls his or her own learning.	Cseh, Watkins and Marsick (1999)
Recognises the social significance of learning from other people, but implies greater scope for individual agency than socialisation.	Eraut (1994) Knowles *et al.* (1998)

Definition	Author
Shaped by employee emotions, which may react differently to individual circumstances. Emotions are integral to learning as the whole person is involved in the learning process.	Knowles, Holton and Swanson (1998)
Facilitated by helping establish or allowing supportive mentoring relationships to flourish, encouraging communities of practice to dialogue informally on work-related issues or concerns, providing skill development in process and facilitation to support reflective practice and developing a shared set of values which reinforces the organisation's commitment to learning.	Laiken (2003)
Informal (training) forces newcomers to learn on the job.	Cable and Parsons (2001)
Often reactive and directed at short-term, immediate problems rather than development of people.	Hill and Steward (2000)
A value-laden, contextual social process that serves an employer and may oppress workers and employee unions in the name of building cognitive workplace skills.	Rainbird (1988)
Horizontal or everyday (learning).	Bernstein (2000)
Learning through everyday embodied practices, horizontal knowledge, non-educational settings.	Malcolm, Hodkinson and Colley (2003)
Informal learning is [often described as] open-ended, with few time restrictions, no specified curriculum, no predetermined learning objectives, no external certification.	Malcolm, Hodkinson and Colley (2003)

Definitions highlight the importance of experience in informal development. This experience is context-driven. It is learning that is real, direct and occurs naturally as part of day-to-day work. However, if we focus on incidental and implicit variants, it is usually unconscious and not easily observable. Marsick and Watkins (1990) suggested that some types of managerial task are less dependent context, but the majority of managerial and leadership activity is interpersonal and social in nature. Mumford and Gold (2004) suggested that the apparent naturalness of informal development can lead to some impatience on the part of leadership development specialists who seek more discipline and structure. While context is important in creating learning opportunities, managers need first of all to be able to recognise them and, second, to be sufficiently motivated to learn. It is also likely that learning may be inhibited by aspects of the context, such as a culture, which do not allow mistakes.

Understanding Informal Management and Leadership Development Processes in Organisations

We highlight five general perspectives on informal management learning and development: however, they are not mutually exclusive. They focus on action, cognition, reflection, experience and learning space. These perspectives provide a complex context or set of frameworks with which to analyse informal development in organisations.

Action-Focused Informal Management and Leadership Development

Action approaches emphasise the behavioural changes that occur when managers engage in problem-solving. They place a strong focus on managers achieving goal-directed outcomes. This perspective considers informal development to be linear and quantifiable. The emphasis is placed on enabling managers to develop their capacity to identify and prevent errors and to achieve goals successfully. A number of different approaches can be found within the action perspective. These include: Argyris and Schon's single- and double-loop learning; Revan's (1983) action learning approach; Marsick and Watkins' (1997) incidental learning, and Mezirow's (2000) transformational learning theory.

The action perspective was initially put forward by Argyris and Schon (1978). They distinguished between single- and double-loop learning. Single-loop learning occurs when managers seek to correct the mismatches between actions and intended outcomes. Action science theory rests on the idea that managers are guided by tacit assumptions, values and beliefs. Intentions guide actions, but there is often a gap between the espoused intension and what managers actually do. Actions produce outcomes and where there is a significant mismatch, managers may notice this error and seek to learn new ways of correcting errors and achieve intentions. The theory suggests that managers modify their tactics to ensure a better match in the future.

Double-loop learning involves changes in organisational values and assumptions. We highlight some of the fundamental characterics of double-loop learning in Table 11.2. Nielsen (1996) further expanded on Argyris and Schon's action science framework by introducing the concept of triple-loop learning. This concept suggests that managers not only change instrumental actions and drive change in values and assumptions, they also address errors embedded in the organisation that currently shape and constrain individual values and assumptions. Single-loop learning or incremental solutions are relatively easy to achieve and tend to be short term. Double-loop learning is more difficult to achieve because managers have deep-rooted psychological tendencies and strategies designed to avoid threat and embarrassment. Argyris (1996) suggested that certain social virtues exist in organisations which foster positive thinking and respect for others.

Table 11.2: Characteristics of and Barriers to Double-Loop Learning

Characteristics
- Double-loop learning involves radical challenges to managers' value systems or frames of reference.
- A free flow of valid information is a necessary condition for double-loop learning.
- A pre-existing positive emotional context and positive relationships between managers are important to the effective achievement of double-loop learning.
- Barriers to double-loop learning arise as a result of social and psychological factors in individuals.
- Double-loop learning requires a level of tolerance for loss of control, uncertainty and ambiguity.
- Single-loop learning enables managers to build up positive outcomes on which they can base double-loop learning.

Barriers
Emotional
- Double-loop learning can trigger strong negative emotions in managers, such as anger, embarrassment and feelings of being threatened.
- Managers may perceive that double-loop learning represents a profound threat to their psychological and social well-being.
- Managers may engage in defensive reasoning and defensive action behaviours such as protecting, moving against opposition or moving away from a situation.

Political
- The defence mechanisms of various individuals and the organisation may block the flow of information.
- Political processes and the desire to hold on to power may influence the desire to share information. Managers may also modify information to suit their purposes.
- Double-loop learning may undermine the political power balance of the organisational. Coalitions may emerge that are designed to resist double-loop learning.

Mezirow (1981, 1985, 2002) proposed transformational learning theory, which argues that learning is based on assumptions which lead to a fundamental preconceptualisation of experience. The three domains of learning are: instrumental, dialogue and self-reflective. Instrumental learning involves task-oriented problem-solving. Dialogue learning refers to the creation of consensual norms. Self-reflective learning focuses on the way in which managers learn to understand themselves. He suggests that managers often set out to solve a task-related, instrumental problem and end up encountering norms and self-perceptions which result in a questioning of perceptions, interpretations and experiences.

Managers go through various stages of the transformative learning process. First, they experience a disorienting dilemma which results in self-examination and feelings of guilt and shame. They engage in critical assessment of presuppositions. This results in the manager recognising his/her discontent. This begins the process of exploring new roles, relationships and actions and the planning of action. Through the process of action, managers acquire knowledge and skills. They experiment and build competence and self-confidence in these new roles and relationships. They then arrive at a point when these new roles and relationships are reintegrated into their acting. This process requires that the manager is able to see the action and its consequences in perspective. The manager must possess the ability to consider alternatives and to analyse underlying assumptions critically.

Marsick and Watkins (1990) suggested a model of informal and incidental learning and argued that managerial work presents a new life experience that offers a challenge and a problem to be solved. The context within which this experience occurs includes personal, social and cultural aspects, and plays a major role in influencing the way in which a manager interprets the situation, the choices and actions taken and the learning that the manager receives from it. The model suggests that learning begins for the manager with some kind of a trigger, which may be either internal or external, and that signals dissatisfaction. Managers use reflection to become more aware of the situation and to learn new ways to understand and address the problem.

The model suggests that managers diagnose or frame a new experience that they encounter. They engage in a number of processes, including assessing, challenging, comparing and sense-making. Managers perform their diagnosis by deconstructing the context and attending to those elements of context that significantly influence their interpretation. This context is typically political, with multiple actors and a range of social and cultural norms. Managers then lead from interpretation of context to choices about alternative actions. These choices are generally informed by past solutions and a search for new ones. Once the action is taken, the manager is then in a position to assess outcomes and determine how effective the action was. Figure 11.1 presents an outline of the model.

Figure 11.1: Informal and Incidental Learning

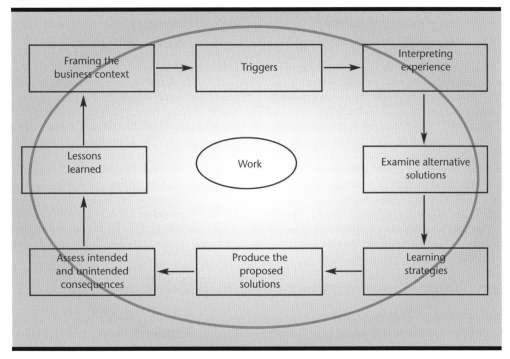

Marsick and Watkins' informal and incidental learning model, as adopted by Cseh. Reprinted with permission from Marsick and Watkins (1990).

Revan's (1978) notion of action learning placed the need for questioning insight before that of instruction. He argued that learning is not solely concerned with the acquisition of programmed knowledge. He proposed that learning is derived from the confrontations of everyday life. He envisaged that managers engage in a reflective process whereby their long-held assumptions are unfrozen, then subjected to scrutiny through action and then temporarily refrozen on a new level. The majority of Revan's ideas have been incorporated into formal action-learning sets in the context of management development, but his ideas are also relevant in explaining action in informal learning processes.

Cognition and Informal Management and Leadership Development

Cognitive approaches to informal development emphasise intra- and inter-personal transformations that occur within and between managers. This perspective focuses on how managers think. Cognitive approaches are particularly concerned with how managers think in a coherent way concerning the work environment and focus on thinking processes such as memory, perception, mental modes, schemas and interpretations. Managers impose meaning on the stimuli that they encounter by attaching these stimuli to their own beliefs, biases and assumptions. This suggests that managers with different sets of assumptions or interpretative schemas will come to different understandings, given identical objective stimuli to interpret.

There is also an interest in how practising managers allocate attention. The attention span of managers tends to be very short and broken by interruptions from others as well as by the managers themselves. It appears that managers pay attention primarily to orally communicated information that is not directly relevant to any particular decision they are in the process of making. Managers' perceptions of organisational reality tend to be fragmented, varied and subject to multiple interpretations. Isenberg (1986) suggested that intuitive processes underlie the actions of managers. These processes help managers to get ideas about what to do and enable them to perform routine, well-learned behaviours.

Managerial understanding and action are intimately related and managers tend to engage in thinking/acting cycles. Managers may take actions based on an incomplete understanding. However, the action feeds back to complete their understanding. Weick (1983) suggested that the actions that managers perform embody thinking and proposed that these actions can be 1) more thoughtful, 2) provoked by thinking, and 3) intensified by thinking. Schön (1983) suggested that an essential element of skilled professional practice is the manager's ability to reflect on actions while performing them.

There is evidence to indicate that managers' cognition and learning are influenced by national culture, function-specific belief systems, perceptions of issues and career backgrounds. It appears that managers draw on a series of frames of reference to make sense of issues. There is a continual interplay between the individual, the context in which the manager operates, the frames of reference related to these contexts and the political and social dynamics of the work place.

Reflection and Informal Management and Leadership Development

Reflection is a widely discussed concept in the context of how managers develop informally. Reflective approaches focus on how managers engage in self-discovery and questioning and how these processes lead them to develop a comprehensive view of managerial practice. Reflective approaches emphasise that, as part of day-to-day work, managers should think critically about their assumptions and beliefs and be emancipated from perspective-thinking assumptions. Managers should achieve a holistic understanding of the situation which enables a better understanding of complexity of work. Proponents of reflection emphasise its role in surfacing power, status and bureaucratic issues. A number of significant contributions in the area of reflection are those of Dewey (1938), Merizow (1991), Schön (1988) and Reynolds (1999).

Dewey had a particular conception of reflection as a coherent system of thoughts and actions. He considered thinking both conscious and involuntary, and suggested four kinds of thinking process: framing, which is the construction of a tentative hypothesis and solution; anticipatory thinking, which is thinking ahead and constructing a working hypothesis; testing the guiding idea for action, reasoning about the result and using one of the hypotheses; and elaboration, which involves the reconstruction of knowledge. Dewey considered reflective thinking as an active, persistent and detailed consideration of both beliefs and knowledge. It arises out of meeting with perplexity, confusion and doubt.

Dewey's ideas were put forward in the 1930s. The notion of reflection does not emerge again in the management learning literature until the mid 1980s. Kolb (1984) was influential in this respect. He incorporated the term 'reflection' into his notion of individual experiential learning. Boud, Keogh and Walker (1985) proposed a model of reflection called 'returning to experience'. This they define as a process in which the manager stands back from the immediacy of the experience and reviews it with the leisure of not having to act on it in real time. Boud, Keogh and Walker separated out the thinking from the action. Returning to experience enables the manager to detect wrong perceptions, to view experience from other perspectives and to examine the event in a wider context than the pressing context in which it was originally situated. They consider reflection a social process in which managers reflect together as they help to detect working perceptions and create new perspectives on experience.

Boud and Middleton (2003) argued that attending to feelings is an important element of reflection. Attending to feelings has two aspects: utilising positive feelings; and revising obstructive feelings. If the manager has negative feelings, he/she cannot make a detailed examination of the experience. Awareness of positive experiences is important in learning. It provides the learner with the impetus to persist in a very challenging situation. Boud also emphasised the need to integrate. He used the term 'revaluating experience' and stated that it represents the most important dimension in relation to reflection at work.

Schön (1988) explored and expanded on the concept of reflection to emphasise that a flow of consciousness and reflection occurs at the time of action. Schön's theory involves an intimate relationship between knowing and action. He defined reflection in action as on-the-spot as opposed to retrospective reflection on action, and viewed it as a process of surfacing, testing and evaluating and of intuitive understanding. Schön contended that, in the real world, problems do not present themselves to managers as given. Managers must construct the situation and define the problem. When managers set and define a problem, they also organise the solution. They set the boundaries of attention to the problem and impose some coherence on the problem, identifying what is wrong and which direction the situation needs to take.

Malinen (2000) suggested that, in managerial reflection, different kinds of experience get in contact with each other and ultimately change each other. Learning is re-learning and the learning process is essentially a reconstruction of knowledge. She suggested two types of experience that interact in the reflection process. First-order experiences are memory experiences and have four important characteristics: they are past, lived, life experiences; they have a task and implicit character; they are always true and authentic; and they are both incomplete and inadequate. Second-order experiences are immediate, here-and-now experiences. They help to unlock some elements of first-order experiences; they have the potential to generate confusion and negative feelings; and they are related to the totality of first-order experiences.

Reynolds (1998) distinguished between the terms 'reflection' and 'critical reflection'. Critical reflection insists on asking questions of purpose and confronting the taken for granted that influences managers' thoughts and actions. The purpose of critical reflection is to examine social processes that have the status of unnoticed or unquestioned certainty. Reynolds suggested that three principles underpin critical reflection: a commitment to questioning assumptions and the taken for granted; a perspective that is social rather than individual; and paying particular attention to the analysis of power relations. Brookfield (2000) suggested that critical reflection makes the assumption that managers are able to engage in an accurate analysis of the world and, as a result, achieve political clarity and self-awareness. It enables managers to subject assumptions to critical scrutiny and identify those that are valued and those that are not. Reynolds acknowledged that the workplace is not an easy context for critical reflection. He suggested that it may be perceived as ineffective and irrelevant to the bottom line. He also indicated that managers are likely to be afraid to reveal shortcomings and faults.

Raelin (2002) advocated that reflection is concerned with social dialogue; it is collective. The process occurs in conjunction with trusted managers in the midst of managerial practice. This conception of reflection has a number of important features: managers periodically step back to ponder the meaning of something that has recently happened; it seeks to illuminate what the self and others have experienced; it provides a basis for action in the future; and it facilitates an understanding of experience that may have been overlooked in practice. Woerkom (2003) expanded on Raelin's ideas. She identified five characteristics that are of relevance:

- *Learning from Mistakes*: Reflection enables managers to be more conscious of mistakes and problems and to interpret faults as a basis for improvement and learning.

- *Vision Sharing*: Managers express the results of reflection by communicating their vision, asking critical questions and suggesting changes.
- *Sharing Knowledge*: The sharing of knowledge promotes learning. It is important that managers also engage in skill disclosing, where they realise more about themselves.
- *Challenging Group Think*: Reflection leads to assumption breaking and prevents ideas being taken for granted.
- *Asking for Feedback*: Feedback is an essential component of informal learning. Some workplaces do not facilitate feedback.

Vince (2002) extended the concept of reflection. He considered it as an organising process that facilitates the creation and sustaining of opportunities for organisational learning. He considered reflection a collective action and took into account issues beyond managers' personal (interpersonal and organisational) taken-for-granted general assumptions. He identified three important issues that contribute to reflection as an organisational process: it should contribute to a collective questioning of assumptions that underpin organising; it provides a 'container' for management of the assumptions that are inevitably raised; and it contributes towards democracy in the organisation. Vince highlighted the questioning of assumptions. This is an integral part of organising and it facilitates the collective capacity to question assumptions. Power relations must be made visible and reflective practices should be able to provide opportunities for building experience and collectively containing anxiety. Vince rested a lot of his arguments on the viewpoint that the focal point of authority in organisations is the individual manager. He suggested that authority needs to be based on their ability to open up leadership and decision-making to the critique and evaluation of others. The overall focus of reflection is to legitimise learning in a management context as a way of freeing managers from socially embedded assumptions.

Experiential Approaches to Informal Management and Leadership Development

Experiential approaches to informal learning are extremely popular. They focus on how managers acquire and transform new experiences and how these experiences lead to development. Experiential approaches emphasise the need for managers to develop a more holistic view of themselves. They conceive knowledge to be largely personal and individual. They place significant value on the manager as a self-directed individual and basically argue that a better person makes a better manager.

EXHIBIT 11.1

Perspectives on Theory: A Summary of Learning Styles Theory

Conceptualising Learning Styles
Learning styles consist of three interrelated elements:
- Information processing – habitual modes of perceiving, storing and organising information (e.g. pictorially or verbally)
- Instructional preferences – predispositions towards learning in a certain way (e.g. collaboratively or independently) or in a certain setting (e.g. time of day, environment)
- Learning strategies – adaptive responses to learning specific subject matter in a particular context.

'Learning styles' is an umbrella term covering a spectrum of modalities, preferences and strategies. Debate arises concerning the extent to which learning styles are stable or hard-wired into learners' brains. Some theorists believe that learning styles are rooted in fixed genetic traits, while others emphasise the influence of experience and context on how students learn. There is little evidence to support the theory that individuals' learning styles are fixed. There is a problem with the reality of the tools (often questionnaires) used to test learning styles: even if learning styles are stable, many of the tools cannot be relied upon to give consistent results from one test to another. Neither is it clear how fixed the characteristics of an individual's brain are. Even if there is a neurobiological basis to an individual's learning style, it may be that the brain's inherent adaptability will allow that style to change over time.

Learning Modalities: Among those who regard learning styles as fixed traits, one of the most widely known and used concepts is that of learning modalities. A modality is a combination of perception and memory – in other words, how the mind receives and stores information. Learning modality theorists argue that all learners have a preference for one or more of the sensory modalities: visual, auditory and kinaesthetic (some theorists also include a tactile modality). Visual learners learn best from pictures or written text, auditory learners prefer the spoken word, and kinaesthetic learners think in terms of actions and bodily movement. While there has been considerable research to support the existence of these modalities, the implications for teaching and learning are far from clear.

Cognitive Styles: Cognitive styles are similar to modalities inasmuch as they are thought to be physiologically based and therefore relatively stable. There are many competing and overlapping theories. Two of the most widely accepted types of cognitive style are the verbal-imagery dimension and the wholist-analytic dimension. Verbalisers represent information in the form of words; imagers tend to think pictorially. Imagers therefore learn best from graphic representations of information, while verbalisers learn best through text or the spoken word. For the wholist-analytical dimension, it is the organisation of information that is the key consideration. Wholists take a global, top-down view of information; analytics break information down into its component parts. Wholists therefore tend to prefer a breadth-first structure which gives an overall view of a topic, thereafter introducing detail. Analytics prefer a depth-first approach, where each topic is explored fully before moving on to the next.

Learning Style Models

There are numerous models; however, they have considerable validity and reliability problems.

Gregorc – Mind Styles Delineator: Two dimensions: concrete-abstract and sequential-random. Most learners prefer a variety of instructional approaches. Issues with validity and reliability. No empirical evidence that using Gregorc's model brings any learning benefits.

Dunn and Dunn – Leaning Styles Questionnaire / Inventory: Four styles: environmental, sociological, emotional and physical. Aims to help teachers identify individual instructional preferences and adapt pedagogy and the learning environment accordingly. Widely used internationally. Lack of independent research to support this model.

Riding – Cognitive Styles Analysis: Two dimensions: wholist-analytic, verbaliser-imager. Evidence of links between cognitive styles and instructional preferences. Need to take working memory into account as well as cognitive styles. Although the model has potential value, Riding's instrument for measuring cognitive styles is not reliable.

Myers and Brigs – Myers-Briggs Type Indicator (MBTI): Based on Jung's theory of personality – four bipolar scales (perceiving / judging, sensing / intuition, thinking / feeling, extraversion / introversion), producing sixteen personality types. Conceived as a tool to categorise personality, not just approaches to learning. Limited evidence that matching teacher and learner types may increase performance.

Apter – Motivational Style Profile: Based on motivational 'states', not fixed types, in four domains: means-ends, rules, transactions and relationships. Theory of personality, not learning style. Although not widely researched, the theory's emphasis on motivation may have considerable relevance for education.

Jackson – Learning Styles Profiler: Four types: initiator, reasoner, analyser and implementer. Mostly used in business. Emphasises the importance of personal development through building up multiple strengths.

Kolb – Learning Styles Inventory: Four styles: active, reflective, abstract and concrete. Learning styles are not fixed personality traits, but relatively stable patterns of behaviour. Students should gain competence in all four learning styles to become balanced, integrated learners.

Honey and Mumford – Learning Styles Questionnaire: Four types: activists, reflectors, theorists and pragmatists. Learning style is defined as 'a description of the attitudes and behaviour which determine an individual's preferred way of learning'. Most people exhibit more than one learning style.

Herrman – Brain Dominance Instrument: Four types: theorists, organisers, innovators and humanitarians. Most people have two or more strong preferences. Although originally based on brain research, this approach considers that social, culture and experiential factors are more important in determining learning preferences. Learners should develop the flexibility to respond to particular learning situations, regardless of their natural preferences. Well established in business.

Allinson and Hayes – Cognitive Styles Index: One bipolar dimension: intuition-analysis. Relatively high level of validity and reliability. Intended primarily for use in business.

Entwistle – Approaches and Study Skills Inventory for Students (ASSIST): Three approaches: deep, surface and strategic. Deep learning is seen as the most effective and beneficial. Intended to characterise approaches, not individuals. Widely used in UK higher education. Offers recommendations for designing instruction to promote deep learning.

Vermunt – Inventory of Learning Styles: Four approaches: meaning-directed, application-directed, reproduction-directed and undirected. Each learning style affects five dimensions: cognitive processing, learning orientation (motivation), affective processes (feelings about learning), mental model of learning, and regulation of learning. Used mainly in higher education. Combines cognitive and emotional aspects. Emphasis on the teaching–learning environment rather than individual differences.

Sternberg – Thinking Styles: Thirteen thinking styles divided into three functions, four forms, two levels, two scopes and two learnings. Distinguishes between styles and abilities – a style is 'a preferred way of using the abilities one has'. Learners have a profile of styles, not just one single style. Profiles of styles may differ according to gender and culture background. Styles are teachable and should fit the context – a variety of teaching and assessment methods is therefore desirable.

Overall there is limited evidence to support any one theory of learning styles. They are generally viewed as one factor of many that should be considered when understanding how managers react to learning situations. Learning style theory does highlight the need to represent knowledge in multiple formats, but it potentially stereotypes learners.

Source: CIPD (2008)

Kolb (1984) is one of the key proponents of the experiential approach. He suggested that the experiential learning process is built on six important propositions:

- *Learning should be understood as a process*: Managers need to be engaged in a process that enhances learning. This includes both feedback and reflection.
- *Learning is about relearning*: Learning is most effective when it draws on and challenges the manager's beliefs and ideas, so that they can be examined, tested and integrated with new, better-formulated ideas.
- *Learning is about the resolution of conflicts*: Managers learn best when they encounter conflict, differences and disagreements. When managers learn, they must move back and forth between reflection and action, feeling and thinking.
- *Learning is holistic*: Learning involves cognition, feeling, perceiving and behaving. It involves a process of adaptation to the world.
- *Learning is derived from the interaction of the manager and the environment*: Environment or context includes the nature of the work performed, the nature of the organisation's culture and the strategic processes.
- *Learning is a process of creating knowledge*: Experiential approaches are strongly constructivist in approach and argue that social knowledge is created and recreated in the personal knowledge of the manager.

The concept of learning style represents a particular contribution to our understanding of what learning is about. Learning style describes individual differences in learning based on the learner's preference in employing different phases of the learning cycle. Kolb posited that learning is a major determinant of development and that managers shape the course of their personal development. His model suggests two didactically related modes of understanding experience and two didactically related modes of transforming experience. Figure 11.2 presents an explanation of these four modes.

Figure 11.2: Understanding the Key Dimensions of Learning Style

Concrete Experience	
An Accommodating Style • Strong ability to learn from hands-on experience • Enjoys carrying out plans and involvement in new and challenging experiences • May act on gut feelings rather than on logical analysis • Relies heavily on people for information rather than their own technical analysis • Prefers to work with others • Gets assignments done, to test out different approaches to completing a project	**A Divergent Style** • Best at viewing concrete solutions from different points of view • Performs best in situations that call for idea generation • Has broad cultural knowledge and likes to gather information • Has a strong interest in people, strong imagination and is emotional • Likes working in groups. Good at listening and has an open mind • Has a strong preference for personalised feedback
A Converging Style • Strong at finding practical uses for ideas and theories • Has the ability to solve problems and make decisions based on finding solutions to questions or problems • Likes to deal with technical tasks and problems rather than social and interpersonal issues • Likes experimenting with ideas, simulations, assignments and practical applications	**An Assimilating Style** • Strong understanding of a wide range of information and good at putting it into concise, logical form • Less focused on people and more focused on ideas and abstract concepts • Likes to have a logical theory rather than have something of practical value • Likes reading, lectures, exploring models and having to think things through
Abstract Conceptualisation	

(Left axis: Active Experimentation — Right axis: Reflective Observation)

Experiential learning, therefore, involves a creative tension among the four learning modes. Kolb suggests that these modes are responsive to contextual demands and that the learner touches all the bases in a responsive process. Initially immediate or concrete experiences are the basis for observation and reflection. The manager assimilates these reflections and distils them into abstract concepts. This enables the manager to derive new implications for application. These implications can be actively tested and serve as guides in creating new experiences.

Table 11.3 presents a summary of criticisms of experiential learning theory.

Table 11.3: Limitations of Experiential Learning Theory in a Leadership Development Context

- It does not consider sufficiently the role of power relations and issues such as gender, social status and culture.
- It does not emphasise or focus on the here and now of information experience and tends to overemphasise retrospective reflection.
- It does not deal adequately with the unconscious learning processes and manager defence mechanisms that inhibit learning.
- It is largely silent on the issue of tacit learning. This concerns questioning the assumptions of communities of managers.
- It needs to be more cognisant of social learning. (Individual learning is inseparable from the social and historical position of the manager.) It needs to consider issues such as argument and rhetoric.
- The cognitive bias of experiential learning theory is considered a problem. It overemphasises the role of the manager and makes insufficient discussion of context.
- The concept of experiential learning does not account for the process nature of experience.

We should not, however, de-emphasise the contribution of Dewey because he stressed the 'ultimate linkages' between the manager's cognitions and the contexts in which they take place. Dewey emphasised that it is important not to separate events and circumstances from their context. In actual experience, 'there is never any such isolated object or event'. The context of learning is not fixed, well defined or stable. It is shaped by the relationship between the manager, his/her activity and the social world that the manager is part of.

Learning Space and Informal Management and Leadership Development

The concept of learning space has emerged as an important dimension of workplace learning and formal learning processes. Its origins can be traced back to Levins' (1969) notion of life space. He argued that person and environment are interdependent variables. Learning space ideas have been influenced by a number of important theoretical contributions.

Vygotsky (1978) suggested an activity theory of social cognition, which conceives of learning as a transaction between the personal and the social environment. He suggested that learning consists of a subject (the individual learner), the object (the managerial or leadership task) and mediating artefacts which include communication and information technology. He also placed emphasis on cultural artefacts, stressing that individuals cannot be understood in isolation from their context.

Lave and Wenger (1991) focused on the idea of situated learning. They argued that well-bounded 'communities of practice' enable managers to acquire knowledge and skills and to develop their understanding of content through contact with more experienced others. They envisaged a community of practice as a particular type of informal group in which practice is grounded on and manifested in everyday work. According to Wenger (1998) the basis for any community of practice is a joint enterprise, a shared repertoire and mutual engagement. Joint enterprise refers to the common purpose that binds a group and guides its development in a work context. A shared repertoire consists of the community's common way of doing things. It represents accumulated, tacit and explicit knowledge. Mutual engagement refers to the activity of managers to interact. An important feature relates to the degree to which managers mutually engage with each other. This process of mutual engagement enables managers to learn the community's shared repertoire. Learning space in this context refers to constructs of the manager's experience in the social environment. Situated learning theory emphasises that learning space is not confined to the classroom. Beach and Vyas (1998), for example, suggested that managers may engage in different forms of learning within a community of practice. They may learn 'on the fly' through making requests for help; they may learn by collaborating; through meeting and talking to other managers and engaging in both routine and stretching activities alongside a more experienced manager; and they may learn by observation.

Engestrom's (2000) activity theory is also of value as a basis for understanding learning space. He emphasised the relationship between context, mediation and development. He concentrated on analysing how learning occurs in situations that are unbounded and unstable. He suggested that managers are expected to act as 'boundary crossers between activity systems'. Managers must therefore possess the ability to contribute to the development of new practice and new forms of knowledge.

Learning network theory also places an emphasis on learning space. Van der Krogt (1989) and Poell (1999) proposed a framework for organising various manager-learning environments at an organisational and group level. They considered learning to be embedded in the everyday work activities of managers, which could be geared more systematically to learning by self-directed managers. They postulated that self-directed managers are part of an organisational learning context, with its own particular history dynamics. To a considerable degree, this context shapes what and how managers are willing and able to learn. This theory proposes that managers are responsible for their own learning and development. It does, however, recognise that structural and cultural barriers may prevent this happening. The theory helps to explain how context shapes managers' learning arrangements. Learning space is therefore vital to promoting effective learning at work. Table 11.4 provides a summary of ideas that organisations can consider to develop effective learning space for managers.

Table 11.4: Creating Learning Space for Informal Leadership Development – Guidelines for Practice

- Focus on the manager's physical and social environment and the quality of relationships.
- Get managers to own and value their experiences.
- Effective learning requires that managers face and embrace differences. The learning space should encourage the expression of differences. Managers need both challenge and support.
- The learning culture or climate must promote trust and experimentation.
- Encourage conversation. Significant learning can occur through conversations. These conversations enable reflection and meaning-making.
- Managers need to act and reflect appropriately. Action is vital because the inside world of reflection comes into contact with the outside world of experience.
- The organisation needs to promote positive feelings, interest and motivation.

Factors Influencing Informal Management and Leadership Development

Three levels of analysis are relevant in explaining the quality of informal management and leadership development for managers. These are the learning environment within the organisation, the learning potential of managerial work and various individual-level factors, including self-efficacy, motivation to learn, learning style and learning strategies. We have already considered the learning potential of managerial work in Chapter Eight.

The Organisation's Learning Environment

The concept of a learning environment refers to both culture and climate characteristics of the organisation (Table 11.5). The culture of an organisation impacts learning in the workplace and can have a strong effect on manager behaviour. It represents the values, beliefs, norms and patterns of behaviour that are shared by employees and which guide behaviour. It is suggested that managers who understand the organisation's culture are better able to interpret organisational events, know what is expected of them and behave appropriately in novel and unfamiliar situations. The climate within the organisation is also an important factor in the success of informal learning. If the climate is not conducive to learning, it will be difficult to achieve learning. If there is evidence of low trust and fewer opportunities to develop, the quality of informal learning will be significantly lower.

Table 11.5: Factors that Influence Informal Development Processes in Organisations

Factor	Descriptions
Openness	When openness to new ideas exists (e.g. where taking a chance is valued and encouraged), individuals are motivated to engage in continuous learning actions.
Opportunities to Learn	When managers are assigned tasks where they can apply what they have learned and are stretched and challenged, this will enhance continuous learning.
Co-worker Support	Co-worker support for learning has a strong influence on whether employees engage in learning opportunities and subsequently apply learning on the job.
High Performance Expectations	Holding employees accountable for learning sends the message that learning is an essential part of being successful.
Supervisor Support	Supervisor support for learning has a strong influence on whether employees engage in learning opportunities and subsequently apply learning on the job.
Toleration of Mistakes	Although detrimental in the short term, mistakes can be valuable learning experiences. An environment in which mistakes are tolerated will increase the chances that learning will be applied on the job.
Situational Constraints	Lack of tools and supplies, insufficient personnel and unrealistic time pressure are a few examples of situational constraints that can influence whether an individual will engage in continuous learning.
Assigns to Avoid Errors	Assigning individuals to tasks in order to avoid errors will not promote learning. A risk-averse organisation can create fear of failure and inhibit learning, initiative and innovation.
Big Picture Awareness	Individuals who understand what the organisation is trying to accomplish and how their unit and job relates to others can better align personal goals and development with organisational goals.

An organisation's culture can both facilitate and act as a barrier to informal learning. Gieskes, Hyland and Magnusson (2002) found that differences between parties in a project development context restricted learning from each other. Pool (2000) found that a supportive organisational culture facilitates quality as well as quantity of learning. Seng, Zannes and Pace (2002) suggested that the cultivation of a positive climate and culture may represent the most important precondition for effective learning.

Some commentators have identified elements of both climate and culture that facilitate learning. Baars (2003), for example, suggested five dimensions of learning climate that are relevant: organisational purposes versus personal development; technical competence versus problem-solving competences; knowledge transfer versus learning from experience; on-the-job versus off-the-job learning; and organisational responsibility versus shared responsibility.

Van den Berg and Wilderom (2004) suggested particular dimensions of organisational culture that facilitate learning: the level of autonomy; the external orientation of the culture; the human resource orientation of the organisation, the extent of interdepartmental co-ordination; and the improvement orientation of the culture. Honey and Mumford (1996) highlighted the role of managers in creating a supportive learning climate. They identify four key activities, including the demonstration of role-model behaviour, acting as learning champion, facilitating learning opportunities and building learning into day-to-day work processes.

Leslie, Aring and Brand (1997) specifically investigated informal learning. They found that organisational culture has a strong impact on informal learning. They highlighted two dimensions of culture: social norms and values; and organisational practices. Sambrook and Stewart (2000) found that learning culture and senior management support were important. They also found that changes in organisational structure and job design features impeded the informal learning processes. Ashton (2004) and Dennen and Wang (2002) suggested a host of factors that impact on informal learning, including space available for learning, a climate of collaboration and trust, communities of practice, task variation, incentives for knowledge sharing and flexible structures. Ellinger (2005) has conducted the most comprehensive study of factors that facilitate and inhibit informal learning. She identified a host of factors, which are summarised in Table 11.6.

Table 11.6: Positive and Negative Organisational Factors Influencing Informal Development Processes in Organisations

Positive Organisational Factors	Negative Organisational Factors
• Managers and leaders who create informal development opportunities • Managers and leaders who serve as developers • Managers and leaders who visibly support and make space for training • Managers and leaders who encourage risk-taking and instil the importance of sharing knowledge and developing others • Managers and leaders who give positive support to others • Openness and accessibility of managers in the organisation	• Unsupportive and disrespectful leaders and managers who do not value learning • Micro leaders and managers who tell direct reports what to do • Organisational distractions that impede informal development • Being territorial and hedging knowledge because of fear of downsizing • A silo mentality and functional wells • Physical architectural barriers • Lack of time because of job pressures and responsibilities • Too much change and not enough learning from learning

Recommendations for Enhancing the Learning Environment

• Select job assignments that enable managers to pursue their interests and enable them to learn new skills
• Establish work schedules that allow enough free time to experiment with new approaches
• Enable managers to develop self-awareness and find new ways to achieve their full potential
• Use symbols and slogans that espouse values such as flexibility, adaptation, self-development, continuous learning and innovation
• Encourage managers to take risks in the selection of job tasks

The Influence of Individual Differences

Psychological dispositions, motivations and learning preferences are important in determining how managers learn and develop. Specific individual differences relevant in the management and leadership context include cognitive ability, learning style, learning motivation and cognitive style. Previous learning experiences and already developed expectations are important in explaining future learning potential. We describe in Exhibit 11.2 a summary of six perspectives on how managers learn. We focus in the following pages on specific individual differences.

EXHIBIT 11.2

Six Perspectives on How Managers Learn

Behaviourism and Leadership Development
There is a strong behaviourist basis to many leadership and management development activities. A behaviourist approach argues that learning depends on certain environmental stimuli to provoke particular types of behavioural change. Management and leadership development programmes frequently specify competencies required for the managerial or leadership role and provide or create conditions in which the learning of these competencies can be encouraged. Lots of management processes, such as management objectives, the setting of behavioural objectives and competency-based training, operate on the premise that behaviour can change if a successful link can be established between the required action and recognition of the stimulus by the manager.

Behaviourist theory has two key implications for the design of leadership and management development programmes.
- *Repetition*: Behaviourism believes that practice makes both perfect and permanent. If you wish to develop a particular management and leadership skill, it is important to practise it frequently. Repetition also helps to memorise key points of knowledge.
- *Objectives*: Setting behavioural objectives is central to the behaviourist approach. The formulation of precise objectives may prove challenging in the leadership and management development situation.

Behaviourist approaches to leadership and management development are considered inflexible and do not match the changing business environment. Behaviourist theories tend to discount the relevance of thoughts, feelings and motives in the learning process.

Cognitive Perspectives on Learning and Leadership Development
Cognitive approaches are primarily interested in internal mental processes. This type of perspective or approach is premised on the human mind's ability to produce knowledge and insight. Particular preoccupations of cognitive theories include perception, insight, memory, imagination, meaning and the importance of language in the manager's thinking processes. They assume that the manager is an active agent who interprets information and gives meaning to events based on prior knowledge, experience and expectations.

Because cognitive approaches place a strong emphasis on information processing and the development stage of the learner, the key learning design challenge is to learn operationally through instructional techniques that match the needs of the learner. Meaningful learning for a manager depends on the concepts or frames that are present in the learner's cognitive structure. Effective learning and development will occur when the learning design takes into account the manager's past history, present needs and learning styles. Cognitive approaches argue for the individualisation of the learning process to match the needs of the total person.

Cognitive approaches offer a number of key principles which should be considered when designing management and leadership learning programmes.

- *Prior Knowledge*: New knowledge of leadership and management must be linked to the manager's prior knowledge and experience.
- *Relationships*: Cognitive approaches operate on the principle that the whole is greater than the sum of the parts. Managers need to see how various concepts and ideas link together. An important element of leadership development, from a cognitive perspective, concerns the development of insight. This occurs when a manager suddenly sees a link between concepts and achieves a deeper understanding of an issue.
- *Organisation*: Cognitive approaches place a strong emphasis on how the material to be learned is organised. Organised materials are easier to learn and remember.
- *Feedback*: Well-timed feedback is a key component of a cognitive approach. Knowledge of progress is an important motivator and an important mechanism to reinforce learning.
- *Individual Differences*: Management and leadership development interventions must take into account the learning style of the manager. Differences in learning style can influence the outcomes of learning.
- *Task Perception*: Learners use different perceptual processes to understand aspects of the environment. Effective programme design should engage as many of the senses as possible.

Humanist Approaches to Leadership Development

Humanist approaches give consideration to both affective and cognitive needs of the manager. They characterise the learning process in terms of discovery, value, acquisition and a hunger for knowledge. A major concern of the humanist approach is the motivational state of the manager. It considers self-actualisation to be the goal of learning. The manager has primary responsibility for learning; however, this approach assumes that the context provides the freedom to learn. Knowles' (1973) conception of andragogy is premised on humanist principles. It places the manager at the centre of the learning process and assumes that learning is driven by internal motives. The primary concern is to address the individual learning needs of the manager. 'Real-life' experiences become the key platform for learning.

Humanist approaches favour collaborative learning approaches. The manager has a key role to play in identifying learning needs, deciding on learning objectives and selecting learning strategies. Humanist approaches favour management and leadership development methods that focus on action, learning, project work, questioning, guided reflection and self-assessment. They assume that managers learn more effectively if they feel secure, respected, esteemed and empowered.

Social Learning Approaches and Leadership Development

Social learning theories place a strong emphasis on interaction with others and observation in a social context. Self-efficacy emerges as a key concept in social learning. Self-efficacy plays an important role in actualising learning processes and in determining motivation to learn. It is assumed that the needs of the learner, the learner's self-efficacy and the social context will vary over time and space. Learning for the manager is, therefore, situational and is derived from his/her interactions.

Social learning theory also incorporates the concept of self-regulation. This suggests that managers can regulate their own behaviour by visualising the consequences of it. It suggests that management and leadership development initiatives should be built around relationships between people. Dialogue is an important aspect of collaborative learning. An important design challenge for management and leadership development is to help managers become more socially effective. Learning is considered an active process; therefore, developmental activities need to incorporate learning from experience and problem-solving. Social learning theory advocates the use of role modelling, mentoring, coaching development relationships, experimentation and personal development interventions that are directed at enhancing the manager's self-efficacy.

Constructivist Approaches to Leadership Development

Constructivist theory suggests that managers construct their own knowledge from their experience, mental models and beliefs. It suggests that meaningful learning is premised on active engagement in planning, problem-solving, communicating and creating. Learning entails the manager making sense of his/her environment and personal history. Berger and Lickman (1966) suggested that constructivist approaches have four important characteristics: a belief in the social construction of reality; the need to be reflective; a socio-cultural focus on the study of learning; and an emphasis on the significance of symbols. Critical reflection represents an important and valuable contribution of constructivist theory. Mezirow (1991) advocated premise reflection. This requires the manager to question the basic assumptions that govern judgements and to consider alternative solutions. This deep reflection has the capacity to lead to changes in meaning structures. Constructivist approaches assume that knowledge is relative rather than absolute. Knowledge must be presented in a meaningful context if effective learning is to take place. The role of the management-development specialist is to act as a learning facilitator. The facilitation role requires that the manager is engaged with the learning process and that the manager seeks out a discourse knowledge.

Constructivist theory underpins experimentation learning, self-directed learning and discovery learning. The manager's life experience is an important learning resource and practical activities, combined with group discussion, form the core of development interventions.

Sense-Making and Leadership Development

Sense-making has emerged as a contemporary perspective in understanding manager learning. Sense-making refers to 'meaning-making' or 'feeling-making'. It incorporates both cognitive and emotional aspects of learning. Meaning-making occurs as a result of the interaction of three components: cues or information from the manager's environment that trigger or signify that meaning is required; a framework or knowledge structure that incorporates elements such as values and roles; and a relationship or what is called a script that links the information to the script. The interaction and awareness of these three elements results in meaning. Sense-making is considered a valuable contribution to learning because it provides an explanation of the connection between cognition and actions. It suggests that this connection is subjective and consists of multiple socially constructive realities and the embeddedness of this process in a context which may be cultural, social or power-based. Weick (1995) suggested that sense-making has seven key principles which distinguish it from other perspectives:

- *Grounded in Identity Construction*: Meaning is assigned to events due to a combination of the self-identify of the manager and the identity of the organisation.
- *Retrospective*: Meaning is assigned after the manager considers what has been experienced.
- *Enaction of Sensible Environment*: Action is considered a fundamental precondition for sense-making.
- *Social*: Sense-making is collective. It is the experience of collective action that enables the manager to create and test meaning.
- *Ongoing*: Sense-making is a messy process. It is ongoing and difficult to say when it stops or finishes.
- *Focused on and by Extracted Cues*: The types of cue that are extracted by the manager are influenced by the language of the organisation, the environmental context and by language in general.
- *Driven by Plausibility*: There is little concern with accuracy. The primary preoccupations are plausibility, pragmatism, coherence and reasonableness. The manager is essentially dealing with reconstructed perceptions that have been edited in various ways.

Sense-making, as a perspective on learning, has major implications for management and leadership development. A key implication concerns 'learning to learn'. This process entails managers engaging in self-reflection and reflective judgement. It requires that the manager examines his/her learning style, assumptions about knowledge and current behaviours. This self-reflection enables the manager to engage in reflective judgement. Sense-making perspectives suggest that it may be useful to develop learning situations where managers flounder. These types of learning situation will enable the manager to confront confusion and deal with contradictions. The approach suggests that management and leadership development must provide managers with the right experiences and conditions, whether in the workplace or the classroom, to enable learning to take place. It essentially requires managers to develop the ability to question and explore their key assumptions.

- **Learning Behaviour:** Learning behaviour is concerned with the way in which a manager approaches the work environment and work experiences. Megginson (1996), for example, found that managers used two kinds of learning behaviour: emergent and planned. Emergent learning is unprecedented learning involving the retrospective exploration of experience. Planned learning, in contrast, is characterised by careful deliberation prior to action. This type of learning is more learning-oriented. Hoeksema, van de Vliert and Williams (1997) suggested an alternative categorisation of learning behaviour: meaning orientation and instruction orientation. Meaning-orientation learning involves retrospective learning. Managers search for the deeper meaning of experiences. The focus is on the learning. Instruction-oriented learning tends to be more instrumental and performance-focused. Managers search for superficial information, guidelines and expectations regarding tasks prior to taking action. Learning behaviour tends to focus on both behavioural and cognitive aspects of learning.

- **Learning-Goal Orientation:** *Learning-goal orientation* is important in explaining what and how managers will learn in a work situation. Vandewalle (2001) suggested that managers may have three types of goal orientation. Some managers have a *performance-goal orientation*; they focus primarily on achieving a successful result and being perceived as successful in the eyes of others. Managers with this type of learning-goal orientation tend to take fewer risks and often forego opportunities to learn new skills. They focus on trying to outperform their colleagues and this is not always conducive to building effective work relationships. Managers may also have an *avoidance-goal orientation*. These managers will focus primarily on finding ways to avoid looking bad to others and are concerned to maintain a particular image rather than focusing on achieving results for the benefit of the organisation. Managers with this goal orientation likewise take fewer risks and they forego opportunities to learn new skills.

  In contrast, some managers have a *learning-goal orientation*. These managers focus primarily on enhancing their competitiveness and are more likely to take in challenging assignments in which they make mistakes while learning new skills. They are more likely to persist when faced with difficult work tasks.

- **Manager Motivation to Learn and Self-Efficacy:** Motivation to learn has been defined as the specific desire of the manager to learn. Colquit, LePine and Noe (2000) demonstrated that this individual difference factor is relevant to a variety of work learning and development outcomes. Noe and Wilk (1993) demonstrated that motivation to learn generally predicts participation in work-learning activities. Motivation is generally perceived as an internal process that regulates learning behaviour. Noe (1986) suggested that motivation to learn comprises three elements: an energiser, which provides the manager with enthusiasm for learning; a director, which guides and directs learning; and a maintainer, which helps the manager to apply the newly acquired knowledge and skills. There is ample evidence that motivation to learn is an important determinant of learning outcomes. Cannon-Bowers *et al.* (1993), for example, found that highly motivated learners are more likely to use their learning on the job.

  Expectancy theory has particular application to informal learning. Expectancy theory argues that for a manager to put effort into learning, there must be a belief that rewards will be derived from the learning. Noe (1988b) applied expectancy theory to learning. He suggested that high effort will lead to more learning, and this learning will lead to better job performance. Better job performance is instrumental in securing desirable career outcomes.

  Noe (2005) suggested that learning is also influenced by a person's self-efficacy. He defines this concept as a manager's judgement about whether he/she can successfully acquire managerial skills. There is evidence to suggest that where a manager has stronger perceived self-efficacy, he/she will set higher goals and be stronger in pursuing these goals. In the context of management and leadership development, it is likely that managers who believe they possess a capacity for learning are likely to give extra effort in pursuit of knowledge and skills. Self-efficacy is therefore related to motivation. Tracey *et al.* (2001) found that self-efficacy is related to strong pre-learning motivation.

- **Learner Attitudes:** Smith and Sadler-Smith (2006) suggest that the attitudes a manager has towards learning represent an important determinant in explaining whether he or she will engage in learning. Clardy (2000) suggested that managers differ in their attitudes to learning. Attitudes to learning are, however, dependent on situational factors rather than being a more or less fixed personality trait. Lim and Chan (2003) suggested that learning attitudes are determined by issues such as self-efficacy, learning-goal orientation and motivation to learn. They also suggested that attitudes to learning are not easy to change.

  Maurer (2002) put forward the notion of development orientation. This suggests that managers who are oriented towards learning tend to have more favourable attitudes to learning. Managers who possess a strong development orientation are likely to view learning opportunities in a positive manner. They are also less likely to experience anxiety and will face difficult work challenges with confidence. Maurer found that high development-orientated managers will show more resilience when faced with difficult work and learning situations. This suggests that feedback may play an important role in enhancing the development orientation of the manager.

- **Cognitive Styles:** Cognitive style has emerged as an important individual difference in explaining learning. The majority of cognitive style categorisations emphasise two cognitive dimensions: the mode of presentation, which may be in the form of words or images; and the mode of organising, which may be in part or in whole. Sadler-Smith and Riding (1999) conducted a number of studies investigating the role of cognitive style in explaining learning and instructional preferences. They found, for example, that individuals who were categorised as holists had a preference for more collaborative and informal learning situations. They are also more likely to be more confident in social situations. They have a stronger capacity to process information simultaneously. There is evidence to indicate that cognitive style is independent of learning style, which is also an important individual characteristic.

- **Learning Preferences and Styles:** Smith and Sadler-Smith (2006) suggest that learning preferences can be distinguished from learning styles. They follow earlier research carried out by Curry (1983), which suggested that learning preferences represent a situation where the manager favours a particular mode of learning over another. Learning style represents the manner in which a manager acquires knowledge, skill and attitudes. Canfield (1980) suggested that learning preferences fit into three categories. The first is conditions of learning, which refers to the manager's preferences in respect of the learning environment. Particular dimensions of the learning environment include the desire to be instructed, individual versus team learning and the level of structure in the learning environment. The second category concerns the manager's preference for working with numeric, qualitative or people-related content. The third category mode focuses on the preferences of the manager for learning through listening, reading, watching or doing.

  Learning style is based on two key dimensions: 1) the manner in which a manager gathers information; and 2) the way in which the manager evaluates and acts on information. The majority of research on learning styles can be attributed to Kolb (1976) and Honey and Mumford (1992). Most American studies have utilised the learning-style inventory developed by Kolb. He suggested that individuals have four basic learning styles: divergent, assimilation, convergent and accommodation.

A manager with a development learning style is strong on concrete experience and reflective observation. This manager works well viewing concrete situations from many different perspectives and in situations that involve idea generation. Managers with a divergent style are interested in people, are emotional and have a strong imagination. They like team learning situations and are very perceptive to personalised feedback.

Managers with an assimilating style tend to be strong on abstract conceptualisation and reflective observation. Managers with this style work well with a wide range of information. They like situations that are concise and logical. They tend to be less interested in people and prefer ideas and abstract concepts. They may be less effective in team learning situations and are cautious because of their desire to think things through.

Managers with a convergent learning style are strong on abstract conceptualisation and active experimentation. Managers who possess this style like the practical, they solve problems by finding solutions to questions and are more concerned with the technical dimensions of a problem. They also have a preference for solo learning.

Managers with an accommodating style tend to focus on concrete experience and active experimentation. They like a hands-on situation and perform very effectively in informal learning situations. Managers who are strong on this style like challenging situations and lots of variety. They tend to act on gut feelings rather than logical analysis. They prefer to work with others and are more likely to set goals.

Hunt (1987) extended this original learning typology. He identified four additional styles: Northerner, Easterner, Southerner and Westerner. The Northerner manager places a lot of emphasis on feelings while balancing acting and reflecting. This manager likes action as well as reflection, but is less effective on conceptualisation. The Easterner manager places strong emphasis on reflection and balances feelings and thinking. This manager likes deep reflection, but also possesses the ability to be conceptual and feeling-oriented. He/she may not be strong on action. The Southerner manager places emphasis on thinking while balancing acting and reflecting and possesses strong conceptual and analytical capabilities but is, however, very weak on feelings. The Westerner manager places emphasis on acting while balancing feelings and thinking. This manager has higher effective action skills and uses intuition, but is less effective on the reflection dimension.

Honey and Mumford (1992) adapted Kolb's four learning styles and named them activist, reflector, theorist and pragmatist. Activist managers learn by doing and are keen to get involved in the action. Reflector managers learn through observation and critical thinking. Theorist managers like concepts and the exploration of relationships. They are not strong on emotional learning situations. Pragmatist managers like to see if and how things can be used in the real world. They work best on practical application.

Cognitive learning strategies generally involve the learner engaging with the material to be learned. They involve rehearsal, organisation and elaboration procedures. Rehearsal is concerned with reflection, where an organisation focuses on the learner creating mental structures. Elaboration involves the manager making connections and looking at implications. Behavioural learning strategies involve the manager engaging in interpersonal help-seeking, finding information in written material and gaining insights from practical application. Self-regulatory strategies involve the manager focusing on the emotional dimensions, which include controlling emotion, staying cool in anxious situations, maintaining motivational control and assessing whether learning goals are achieved.

Smith and Sadler-Smith (2006) suggest that learning strategies are amenable to development. They can be developed through both experience and more structured interventions. The use of learning strategies by managers does not necessarily, however, result in learning, and the application of learning strategies may not be useful for all managers.

It should be highlighted that the notion of learning styles was originally formulated as a dynamic rather than fixed concept. Kolb and Kolb (2005) point out that managers tend to refer to themselves and others as having learning styles which are fixed in nature. The majority of studies have found, however, that no matter what type of problem a manager faces, most use their preferred learning style to approach it. Differences in learning style tend to lead managers to have different decision-making processes (Henderson and Nutt 1980).

Table 11.7: Managers' Personal Learning Strategies

Cognitive Learning Strategies	Reproduction/ Rehearsal	Organisation	Elaboration
• Pintrich and Garcia (1991) • Zimmerman and Martinez-Pons (1990) • Pintrich *et al.* (1993) • Fisher and Ford (1998)	• Intention to reproduce information without reflecting on its meaning • Repetition of information being learned	• Identifying key issues • Creating schemas and grouping information learned • Ferguson-Hessler and de Jong (1990)	• Examining the implications of new material and information in light of existing knowledge
Behavioural Learning Strategies	**Interpersonal Help Seeking/Obtaining Assistance from Others**	**Seeking Help from Written Materials (Zimmerman and Martinex-Ponz (1990))**	**Practical Application**
• Warr, Allan and Birdi (1991) • Karabenick and Knapp (1991)	• Obtaining help from others through coaching, mentoring, networking and team interventions • Practical behaviour • Understanding by seeking help from others rather than receiving information through routine instruction	• Reading relevant information which is applicable to solving problems and developing awareness and self-insight • Manuals, computer e-learning and non-social sources • Non-social analogue of interpersonal help-seeking involving self-generated efforts	• Increasing knowledge by trying things out in practice
Self-Regulation Learning Strategies	**Emotional Control**	**Motivation Control**	**Comprehension Monitoring**
	• Procedures to ward off anxiety by preventing concentration failures caused by the intrusion of anxiety-linked thoughts	• Procedures to maintain motivation and interest despite a limited interest in the task	• Procedures to assess the degree to which learning goals are being achieved and to modify learning behaviour if necessary

- **Managers' Personal Learning Strategies:** The notion that managers utilise different learning strategies has emerged in recent years as another difference beteen individuals. Learning strategies have been variously defined as the practices that individuals use to aid the acquisition of and development of knowledge in any context. Curry (1983), for example, suggested that a learning strategy is a mechanism which enables the learner to cope with a learning environment and makes information meaningful to the individual. Holman, Epitropaki and Fernie (2001) suggested that learning strategies are a relevant concept in understanding manager learning and development. Managers who possess an understanding of learning strategies are more likely to achieve better development in the workplace.

  Research on learning strategies has largely been confined to educational settings. O'Malley and Chamot (1990) focused on language learning. They suggested three separate groups of learning strategy: meta-cognitive strategies, which focus on lower-order skills such as planning, monitoring and evaluating learning; cognitive strategies, which are used to cope with, organise and process information; social/effective strategies, which focus on interaction with others.

  It is important to highlight that learning styles differ from learning strategies in that learning styles are considered to be more generic and consistent ways of processing information and to be less impacted on by context.

  Two studies have focused on the use of learning strategies by managers: Warr and Downing (2000) and Holman, Epitropaki and Fernie (2001) (Table 11.7).

Informal Learning Strategies Used by Managers and Leaders

We focus now on learning strategies that are used by managers in their day-to-day work. The use of the term 'strategies' suggests that they are planned. They are, however, more opportunistic and unstructured.

Learning through Observation of Peers

This is described as a process through which managers internalise professional norms and practices. Cheetham and Chivers (2001) emphasised the role of working alongside more experienced managers. Eraut (2004) and Ohlott (2004) suggested that informal learning from experienced co-managers represents a rich source of learning which is achieved through a form of role modelling. Learning from significant others is perhaps the most important informal learning process for managers. McCauley and Douglas (2004), for example, found that managers valued learning grounded in feedback and relationships with peers. The essence of this learning process concerns observing how others learn. Bandura (1986) suggested four stages of observation: attention, retention, production and motivation. The manager does not learn everything that is seen, but tends to be selective depending on the motivation to learn. The absence or inadequate execution of any of the other elements will lead to ineffective coping. Offerman and Sonnemanns (1998) suggested that managers can learn from their own experience, from imitating successful others and from the experience of others. Boud and Middleton (2003) suggested that participation is a key to informal learning. McCauley and Douglas (2005) suggest that feedback is vital. This may come from one feedback provider who is a source of day-to-day feedback on how a manager is doing and who will likely have the opportunity to observe performance and give in-the-moment feedback. Likewise, managers need a sounding board for their personal strategies and ideas. Managers frequently compare themselves to others in an informal way, consider how they measure up and identify where improvements are needed. Some managers may act as feedback interpreters and help the manager make sense of the feedback received from others. McCauley and Douglas also highlight how learning from significant others may result in the manager moving out of a comfort zone by challenging, thinking and doing things differently. Managers frequently provide support to others and play counselling, cheerleading and championing roles. These are designed to provide emotional support, to encourage and provide affirmation and to empathise in difficult situations.

Learning from Mistakes

Moxley and Pulley (2004) suggested that mistakes are manifest in many work situations. Woerkom (2003) suggested that learning from mistakes involves a process of reflection that leads to 'consequences of undesirable matters'. An experience of incompetence combined with the confidence to take a risk can be the best catalyst for learning. The lessons learned from mistakes are those learned from challenging work activities. Mistakes are not intentional and the lessons they teach are retrospective. They require the manager to take time to reflect on the mistake and gain a perspective on what went wrong. Mistakes have many challenges embedded in them. They may be intensely private, they may involve insecurity and may involve a sense of loss.

Moxley and Pulley (2005) suggest that the sense of loss arising from mistakes can include a loss of credibility, control, self-efficacy or identity. Mistakes can help the manager to be more resilient. Masten (1989) suggested that resilient managers give appropriate purpose or meaning to what has happened; they see things as they are and deal with reality in a constructive way. They have the ability to respond creatively in the moment and they possess a belief that people in their personal and/or professional life will support them through good and bad times.

Learning from mistakes enables the manager to develop his/her own initiative. Senge (1990) suggests that failure represents an 'opportunity for learning'. The manager can learn about inaccurate pictures of current reality, about strategies that did not work as expected and about clarity of issue. Agile managers use mistakes as opportunities to learn the important lessons to grow and change. There is the risk that managers may be hurt by negative experiences even when they learn from mistakes. Self-efficacy appears to be an important antecedent of effective learning from mistakes. A manager is likely to suffer from a learning standpoint where he or she does not possess self-confidence. Learning from mistakes can be significantly enhanced where the cause and effect are clear to the individual involved, the mistake is openly acknowledged and the organisation's position on how mistakes are dealt with is clearly understood. Many organisations suggest that they tolerate mistakes, but this is not always the case.

Learning from Informal Coaches and Mentors

Informal mentoring and coaching are commonplace in organisations, but they are less frequently acknowledged in the management and leadership development literature. Cleveland, Stockdale and Murphy (2000) suggested that a mentor, in the informal sense, is an experienced superior who establishes a relationship with a less experienced manager and assists that manager with his/her personal development. They suggested that the relationship can be initiated either by the protégé manager or by the mentor. Informal mentors typically provide psychological support in the context of development. There is evidence to suggest that mentors provide novice managers with the opportunity to enter into the organisation's informal social network and to establish alliances. Bosses may also play an informal mentoring role in a developmental context, particularly in situations involving career advancement and the opening up of opportunities for special projects or assignments.

Ragins, Cotton and Miller (2000) found that informal mentoring programmes were more effective than formal mentoring processes in facilitating development. Formal mentoring programmes had a difficult time perfecting the strong emotional bonds found in informal mentoring relationships. Most formal mentoring programmes only last for a specified period of time, whereas informal mentoring relationships can last a lifetime. In most cases, mentors seek out protégés, or mentors and protégés seek each other out, to build relationships. Organisations can do a number of things to help improve the likelihood of finding a mentor. The first and most obvious step is for the manager to do his/her job well. Mentors are always looking for talent. They are unlikely to take under their wing someone who appears unmotivated or incompetent. Managers should also seek out opportunities to gain visibility and build social relationships with potential mentors.

Informal coaching can take place anywhere in an organisation and occurs whenever a leader helps another manager to change their behaviour. Petersen and Hicks (1996) suggested that informal coaches follow a five-step process (Table 11.8).

Table 11.8: The Five Steps of Informal Coaching

Forge a Partnership	Coaching only works if there is a trusting relationship between the leader and his or her followers. In this step, leaders also determine what drives their followers and where they want to go with their careers.
Inspire Commitment	In this step, leaders help followers determine which skills or behaviours will have the biggest payoff if developed. Usually this step involves reviewing the results of performance appraisals, 360-degree feedback, values and personality assessment reports, etc.
Grow Skills	Leaders work with followers to build development plans that capitalise on on-the-job experiences and create coaching plans to support their followers' development.
Promote Persistence	Leaders meet periodically with followers in order to provide feedback, help followers keep development on their radar screens, and provide followers with new tasks or projects to develop needed skills.
Shape the Environment	Leaders need periodically to review how they are developing role modelling and what they are doing to foster development in the workplace. Because most people want to be successful, doing this step well will help attract and retain followers to the work group.

Weitzel (2000) suggested that the most effective informal coaches have particular leadership traits and skills. They possess strong listening, relationship-building and assertiveness skills. They use these traits to build trusting relationships with direct reports and they give tough and honest feedback when it is necessary.

Learning through Day-to-Day Experience

We considered formal planned job experiences in Chapter Nine, but here we consider day-to-day experience, which is informal and unplanned. Marsick and Watkins (1990) suggested that three personal characteristics of managers are important in capturing the benefits of day-to-day experiences. These are: proactivity or a readiness to take the initiative in situations; the tendency to reflect; and the capacity to think beyond their normal point of view. Burgoyne (1995) suggested that learning from experience involves 'an active sense-making process which addresses itself to all experience, external events, impinging on the person, sensations of seemingly inner awareness and pre-structured knowledge without the privilege of any of these or any other categories of the learning experience'. Eraut (2004) argued that most learning from experience has implicit elements and that awareness of explicit learning does not mean that implicit learning is not also taking place. Eraut proposed the notion of reactive learning as learning that is intentional, which occurs in the middle of the action with little time to think.

The process of learning through experience tends to overlap with the reflective process. Mumford (1995) suggested that learning from experience is varied and situation-specific because what managers do is substantially different from one situation to another. Mumford (1996) studied 144 managers and found that they use four approaches when learning from experience: intuition, learning from experience but not through a conscious process, in which the manager automatically associates managing with learning; incidental learning, where the manager learns from a bigger event and reviews it afterwards; retrospective learning, which is learning from the experience by looking back after the event, mostly involving reviewing matters of a routine nature and coming to a conclusion about them; and prospective learning by experience, which combines the retrospective elements and planning to learn before the experience takes place.

Informal day-to-day experiences can be valuable if given the necessary attention. Experience is key to the manager's skills. There is a lot of guidance in the literature concerning the processes inherent in learning from experience or experience-based learning.

Experience-based learning is fundamental to the effective development of managers and leaders. Andersen, Boud and Cohen (1995) suggested six defining features of experience-based learning: the involvement of the whole person; the use of relevant prior experiences; continued reflection on prior experiences to achieve a deeper level of understanding; the structure of the experience; the manager's engagement in the experience; and the extent to which the learning outcomes are identified. Boud and Walker (1990) emphasised that effective learning from experience has important constituent elements, including encountering experiential events, reflection during the experience and reflection after the experience.

Experience-based learning is holistic in that it attempts to change the total manager as a person. Experience-based learning has both a structural and a meaning component. Marton and Booth (1997) pointed to the role of the person–world relationship in experience-based learning. They viewed learning as the reconstruction of an already constituted world. Gerber (1997) highlighted important ways in which managers learn through work experience. These include learning in which the manager practises his or her values, learning through problem-solving, learning through planning and learning through being an advocate for colleagues.

In essence, experience-based learning involves risks. We highlighted earlier the specific value of learning from mistakes. Managers who learn from mistakes point out that they had the freedom to take risks. Furthermore, experience-based learning is influenced by the socio-emotional context in which it occurs. It is socially and culturally construed and learners actively construct their own experience.

Learning through Reflection and Conversations with Others

Reflection is an important individual process in informal learning. It is viewed primarily as a key element of problem-solving. Reflection is concerned with questioning assumptions and learning. Cope and Watts (2000) suggested that reflection involves two levels: adjusting rather than learning and assimilation that is transferable from one situation to another. At this level, the manager has a new conception or world view. Wood (1999) suggested that reflection involves taking experience from the outside world, internalising that experience, turning it over, making connections and filtering it through personal biases. This process results in significant learning. Managers experience two kinds of learning: emergent learning, which involves unpremeditated learning and incorporates retrospective exploration of experience; and planned learning, which incorporates careful deliberation prior to action. Learning through reflection provides the potential to combine elements of solo and social learning. Woerkom *et al.* (2002) suggested the concept of double-loop learning, which focuses on the more social aspects of questioning and feedback from others. Wood (1999) suggested that reflection may be conducted solo, with one other person who takes on a 'helper for', or with a small group in which others have experience of the challenges that lead to reflection. Brooks (1989) suggested that the ability to ask critical questions is fundamental to informal, critically reflective learning. He viewed reflection as a mental activity aimed at examining one's own behaviour in a certain situation.

Daudelin (1996) suggested that while the catalyst for reflection is external, the reflection occurs within the mental self. She viewed it as a process of stepping back from the experience to ponder the meaning of the experience to the self. Learning occurs through the creation of meaning from past or current events that focus or guide future behaviour. Reflection, therefore, can be spontaneous and outside a manager's awareness. Spontaneous reflection tends to be stimulated by challenges. Daudelin sees reflection as a four-stage process involving: articulating a problem; analysing that problem formulation; testing a tentative theory; and some form of action. The initial stage consists of a state of doubt or hesitancy. The second stage focuses on the search for possibilities. Stage three seeks to address the problem, and stage four brings closure to the cycle.

Seibert (1999) made an important distinction between coached reflection and reflection in action. Coached reflection is more the concern of Chapter Eight; reflection in action is an unplanned, informal, active and ongoing process. It is conducted by the learner himself or herself and involves a spontaneous mental process intended to make sense of experience. Reflection in action is facilitated where:

- The environment provides freedom and discretion to structure the work as one sees fit.
- There is a flow of information on the results of a manager's actions; information represents the raw material for reflection.
- The manager has an opportunity to encounter skilled and knowledgeable peers and has a caring, interpersonal relationship with at least one person.
- The manager's encounters are with people who are capable of providing new ideas and perspectives.
- The manager experiences significant performance demands due to time constraints, information overload, visibility of the job and importance of the role.
- The manager is provided with the opportunity to be away from work in order to process new information.

Table 11.9 provides a summary of strategies that can be used to create the appropriate conditions for reflection.

Table 11.9: Creating the Conditions for Reflection in Action – Some Strategies for Managers and Leaders

Reflection Condition	Strategies
Autonomy	• Clearly define the scope of the learner's authority in the assignment and define it broadly • Clarify expectations between learning and boss • Genuinely empower the learner
Feedback	• Establish formal and informal mechanisms for obtaining feedback from superiors, peers, customers • Look for feedback in the work itself (financial data, status reports, etc.) • Emphasise the developmental (versus evaluative) nature of feedback
Interacting with Others	
Access to Others	• Connect with customers, functional experts, suppliers, etc. • Pursue breadth in a variety of personal contacts • Make it appropriate to ask naive questions
Connection to Others	• Develop one or two deep relationships at work • Find a superior, peer, mentor or friend who can help support the learner emotionally • Try to build a relationship involving mutual support
Stimulation by Others	• Connect with people who think differently • Embrace diversity in others • Interact with others who will challenge the learner's perspectives and assumptions
Pressure	
Promote Pressure	• Establish stretching deadlines • Immerse the learner in large quantities of new information • Approach decisions decisively
Directive Pressure	• Establish the importance of the assignment to the learner and to the organisation • Publicly announce goals and timetables • Seek opportunities to share the status of the work with people who matter (executives, customers, etc.)

Momentary Solitude	• Use brief moments alone as chances to reflect
	• Reflect while engaged in activities that do not require conscious thought, e.g.
	  – Sitting through unproductive meetings
	  – Eating lunch alone
	  – Travelling

Baker, Jensen and Kolb (2005) suggest that learning conversations can be used by managers to construct new meaning and transform collective experiences in knowledge. They define conversational learning as an 'experimental process of learners constructing meaning from their collective experiences' by using the medium of conversations. Conversations allow this to occur because it is a meaning-making process whereby managers achieve understanding through the interplay of opposites and contradictions.

Conversational learning needs a receptive space or context for it to occur. This could include both temporal and physical space. Conversations can be killed through internal processes where an over-directive monologue crushes other managers. It can also be externally inhibited where a manager demonstrates prejudice or bias and his or her mind is made up. This suggests that managers need to be open to other points of view and reconsider their own point of view. If this does not happen, little conversational learning occurs. The manager must engage and remain open to having prejudices challenged. Van Maanen (1995) argued that it is important for managers to listen and respect rather than control. Managers should not impose a viewpoint just because it serves their purpose. The goal should be learning.

Learning through Common Sense and Intuition

Common sense and intuition are important aspects of informal learning for managers. Forguson (1989), for example, defined common sense as a set of insights that enables a manager to deal with situations that arise during the day. This suggests that managers with common sense have insights into problems, they weigh up different courses of action, form sensible judgements and make responsible decisions. Common sense as a process is not necessarily precise, oriented and scientific. The goal for using common sense is to achieve a practical outcome. Langer (1989) suggested that common sense can be described as acting mindfully. This he defined as the ability to create new categories of knowledge based on the nature of the situation and the content, openness to new information and awareness of more than one perspective. The manager is alert to new ways of doing things, doing things differently and, as a result, develops a better understanding of issues which can then be shared in a peer learning situation.

Managers who use common sense are therefore less likely to panic, are even-handed in judgements of people and their behaviours and they use their intuitive powers frequently and effectively.

Sadler-Smith and Shefy (2004) suggested that managers make significant use of intuition. Isenberg (1984) suggested that intuition enables a manager to sense a problem, achieve an integrated picture, check on rational analyses and bypass relational analysis. Intuition has an important role to play in management and leadership development. It represents an important dimension of learning in the workplace, but the organisational context may be either a facilitator or an inhibitor of intuition. Sadler-Smith and Shefy (2004), for example, suggested that managers may feel under pressure to produce relational analysis to justify decisions. They may not want to admit that decisions they make are based on gut feelings. At the most senior levels, executives may be required to display rationality in order to gain legitimacy for their actions. Sadler-Smith and Shefy define intuition as a form of knowing that manifests itself in a strong awareness of 'thoughts, feelings and bodily sense', which is linked to perception and understanding. This suggests that intuition is a broad concept and includes such ideas as expertise, judgement, implicit learning, feelings and emotions, creative processes and reflection. Executives and managers tend to describe intuition as a feeling that comes from within and the integration of previous experience. Intuition therefore draws on both cognitive and emotional dimensions; knowing and feeling. Intuition as knowing or expertise focuses on organising facts into a meaningful pattern and taking mental shortcuts in order to make a decision. This process works well when the current and previous situation are relatively similar. When this condition does not prevail, it is necessary for the manager to redefine and adjust his/her mental structures in order to account for differences in the situation. Intuition as feeling focuses on the emotional dimension of decision-making. Emotional responses may facilitate the manager in sifting through detail and focusing on the feeling-based signals for or against a particular option. Emotional dimensions may override cognitive dimensions. Intuition has an important role to play in informal learning. It allows the manager to function effectively in a fast-changing environment and can contribute to higher-order learning which can be applied to a wide range of situations.

Learning through Networking

Informal network interaction is an important process through which learning occurs. Informal networks provide important learning resources in addition to benefits such as friendship and social support. They involve discretionary patterns of interaction. The control of the relationship may focus on work or social dimensions or both. Informal networks tend to be much broader than formal networks.

EXHIBIT 11.3

The Value of Networking for Managers and Leaders: A Summary of Research Findings

- Managerial networks can be either instrumental or expressive in nature, or both.
- Instrumental networks focus on the work itself and involve the exchange of information, resources and expertise. They are important in getting challenging and highly visible work assignments. They also focus on development and guidance.
- Expressive networks focus on friendship and social support. They involve high levels of trust and closeness and are less likely bound to formal relationships. They may involve information transfer and decision making.
- Managers need to have an effective network size. The size of the network determines the manager's access to information; however, it may result in redundant information benefits if it is too large.
- A greater number of weak tie relationships (those that have less interaction and affection and a shorter history) provide the manager with a greater amount of diverse information.
- Managers who have a lot of strong ties will benefit less because they possess the same information, and information that is less valuable. Managers with strong ties tend to have a smaller network.
- Managers differ in their ability to benefit from networks. The benefits are dependent on the manager's position in the network.
- Managers need to realise the potential opportunities that networks provide. The motivation of the manager to take advantage of these benefits is important. Managers who have a strong need for cognition are better able to benefit from the benefits of networking.
- Managers with a strong need for cognition are better at seeking out, acquiring and reflecting on information. They have more open minds and they are better at driving out information from the environment.
- Where managers have similar human capital characteristics, they are likely to gain more from networks within the organisation.
- Managers can secure developmental as well as information benefits from both internal and external network ties.

The nature of the network is significant because it has an important role in defining the resource exchanged. Networks have a number of important characteristics which help to explain their value for learning and development. Ibarra (1993) suggested that managers are required to manage tensions between the types of people and relationships that provide access to different kinds of developmental benefits. The characteristics of informal networks that are important for informal learning include the following:

- *Composition of the Network*: The nature and scope of development opportunities depends on the type of people with whom a manager interacts. How organisationally and interpersonally similar are the pairs of individuals? Do the managers share the same world views? Do they have the same interpersonal style? What are the personal attributes of the managers? The more similar the personal attributes, the more networking there will be. How broad is the network? Breadth is an important characteristic because it ensures greater access to information and learning opportunities. Does the network include peers, superiors or superiors' subordinates? This provides more scope for informal learning.
- *Characteristics of the Relationships*: The precise nature of the informal learning is influenced by the strength of relationships, the density of the relationships and the relationships between contacts. The strength of a relationship refers to the amount of time devoted to it and its emotional intensity. Granovetter (1973) suggested that the intimacy of the relationship is important. The multiplicity of the relationship is also very important for learning. This refers to the extent of resources that are exchanged, such as advice, guidance and information. Granovetter made a distinction between weak and strong ties. Strong ties bond similar people, but weak ties are also valuable because they act as a 'bridge' to aspects of the social network that are not connected. It appears that learning will be most valuable in strong-tie relationships. Strong ties provide more assistance in difficult or uncertain situations, but they do require greater effort to develop. An effective learning network will, however, have a balance of strong and weak ties.
- *The Density of the Network*: This is also important for learning. Marsden (1990) suggests that this characteristic refers to the extensiveness of contact among the members of a manager's personal network. The density will be high where there is a great deal of contact between network members. High-density networks provide lots of social support and solidarity, and are conducive to learning.

Learning through External Experiences

Gerber (1998) suggested that learning can also occur outside the workplace. This includes the home, the sporting field and doing the shopping. Mumford (1995) identified domestic life, voluntary work, social committees and reading as sources of learning opportunities available to any senior manager. Schartz and Walker (1998) asked managers which learning experiences mattered most. External experiences were considered most important in the context of career development. These external experiences may also involve encounters with a significant person, committees, sport and ongoing learning through technology. People actively engage in these external situations, thinking consciously about different activities or events and making deliberate decisions during the activity itself. Schartz and Walker (1998) suggested that critical experiences outside the workplace that involve some form of loss often lead to the greatest learning experience or transformation. For learning to occur from personal experiences, managers must be provided with a better understanding of these experiences. However, this may be difficult to achieve in the informal context.

Collective Informal Development Strategies

Raelin (2003) suggested that it is possible to consider informal development as a collective characteristic of organisations. Vince (2000) thought along similar lines. He challenged the extensive focus on individual reflection and suggested that reflection represents a collective capacity to question assumptions. He criticisesd individual reflection because it has the potential to promote detachment from organisational politics and the politics of organisations. He set three conditions for collective reflection: it should contribute to the collective questioning of assumptions; it should make power relations visible; and it should contribute towards struggles for democracy.

Vince suggested four practices to facilitate or organise reflection and connect organising and learning. These are peer consultancy groups, communities of practice, organisational role analysis and group relations conferences. The majority of these operate in an informal way.

Peer consultancy groups are self-managed groups of three managers who share in the analysis and development of real-life work issues. Each member performs a particular role: one member presents an issue, one consults on the issue and the other observes the process of consultation. Such a process is underpinned by friendships, network-building and interpersonal alliance. The participants have the opportunity to question and reflect on the spoken and unspoken dialogue. The observation process enables the participants to gain insights into the processes involved in solving real-life issues. *Organisational role analysis* requires the manager to engage in one-to-one reflection, where he/she makes links between the person, the organisational role and the organisation. It enables the manager to consider the organisational context within which the role is embedded. It focuses the manager's thinking on what is emotional, relational and political about the organisation. *Group relations conferences* are an experiential learning process in which the participants can focus on the complexities of feelings, interactions and power relations that are vital to the process of organising. Managers can begin to reflect on organisational dynamics and how this impacts on their learning. Managers can also focus on how they enact different managerial roles, relational experiences and other psychological processes such as defence and avoidance mechanisms. Participating managers bring to the process an internalised version of the organisation to which they belong. The focus is on both understanding and changing aspects of the organisation.

The fourth practice suggested by Vince is a community of practice. Communities of practice can evolve as managers develop a shared history as well as particular values, beliefs, ways of talking and ways of doing things. They come together through action and learn to construct shared meaning in the midst of confusion and conflict. They begin to rely on one another for mutual assistance. Table 11.10 summarises the concept of a community of practice.

Table 11.10: Characteristics of Communities of Practice

- Communities of practice are informal relationships that emerge as people attempt to solve problems, although they may be influenced by formal roles and relationships.
- Within them, people share tacit knowledge, exchange ideas about work, experiment with new methods and ideas, test and modify theories in use. In so doing, they engage in experiential learning, develop cognitive structures and engage in the formation of culture.
- They represent relationships and activities which embody shared understandings for participants, access to which is related to language and shared meaning.
- They involve complex social processes centred on the construction, maintenance and change of identities.
- They emerge in a historical, political and social context that affects possibilities for learning.
- They give rise to 'situated learning' in that learning and practice occur in a spatial and temporal context.
- Such learning is associated with a person acting in a cultural setting rather than simply through narrowly defined processes of cognitive assimilation.
- Skills learned in communities of practice are socially defined, tacit skills that link formal, technical skills to a particular context.
- Resources for learning are embedded in existing practices, work relations, and other communities of practice.
- By forming and transmitting culture, communities of practice may inhibit change.
- Communities of practice thus embody tensions between forces that encourage learning and those that impede it.

Source: Adapted from Hendry (1996)

Vince (2000) argued that communities of practice contribute to collective learning and promote the experiences of involvement, engagement at the boundaries, and interaction with and presentation of power relationships within the organisation. Communities of practice are necessary for the dissemination of knowledge. Gherardi and Nicolini (2001) suggested that learning and working are closely bound up with each other and therefore communities of practice have the potential to provide an understanding of how managers work and how managerial practice is perpetuated. Communities of practice have a reflective component in that they encourage managers to think and reflect on practice and action, and how that practice develops within the social and power dynamics of the organisation. They provide a valuable organisational context for active reflection. They enable managers to learn about power and about the actions that they should take.

The notion of communities of practice returns learning back to its context. It suggests that informal leadership development is built out of the situation and this is essentially collective.

EXHIBIT 11.4

Perspective on Theory: Researching Managerial Learning in the Workplace – Instruments and Methodological Issues

Instrument	Operational-isation of On-the-Job Learning and Development	Research Goal	Researcher's Role	Instrument Description	Value for Researchers
Critical Reflective Work Behaviour (CRWB) (Woerkom 2003)	CRWB is a set of connected activities, carried out individually or in interaction with others, aimed at optimising individual and collective practices, or critically analysing and trying to change organisational or individual values	To validate the construct of CRWB and examine the relationships specified in the conceptual model (describe and practise)	Informant: constructs conceptual model and collects anonymous information via mail questionnaire	Based on case study, 47 items developed by researcher	Possesses good construct validity and good reliability
Learning Strategies (Holman, Epitropaki and Fernie 2001)	Learning strategies can be defined as the practices that people use to aid the acquisition and development of knowledge in any context	To examine learning strategies in a non-educational organisational setting (explore)	Information: adapts learning strategies that others gathered from literature, and collects data via mail questionnaire	Based on measures developed by Warr and Downing (2000) and in educational setting examined	Very good construct validity and strong reliability

Instrument	Operational-isation of On-the-Job Learning and Development	Research Goal	Researcher's Role	Instrument Description	Value for Researchers
Learning Strategies (Megginson 1996)	Learning strategies are defined as an approach to all experiences, and are not observable or amenable to regulation by others	To measure planned and emergent learning strategies as independent dimensions (explore)	Informant: constructs conceptual model and anonymous mailing	From twenty-five original items, nine were allotted to planned learning and eight to emergent learning. Finally, the best twelve items were kept	Good content validity, but reliability may not be as good
Learning Tactics (Dalton *et al.* 1999)	Learning is approached as a set of behavioural tactics that an individual employs to engage in learning from experience	To measure four kinds of learning tactics in challenging and unfamiliar work assignments in order to increase self-awareness of personal development (action)	Passionate participant: uses inventory as educational tool	Based on conversations with experts, journal entries and literature	Possesses both very good construct validity and strong reliability
Learning at Work Inventory (Hoeksema 1995; Hoeksema, van de Vliert and Williams 1997)	A learning strategy is a combination of related tactics aimed at a change in knowledge and/or behaviour in a specific situation	To examine career success of individual managers as a complex positive or negative function of individual learning strategy and organisational structure (1997)	Informant: constructs hypothetical conceptual model and anonymous mailing	Based on measures by Selmes (1987) of school graduate learning behaviour and tested among 135 students	Questions concerning both the validity and reliability of the inventory
Motivated self-directed learning in schools and companies (Straka 2003)	Learning strategies are part of the behavioural dimensions in a learning event	To test assumption of more dimensionality of self-directed learning based on interest strategies, control and emotion (describe)	Informant: constructs conceptual model and anonymous mailing	Based on a questionnaire originally developed for educational settings by Nenninger (1999) and his research group	Good construct validity, but reliability levels do vary and fall below .70 benchmark

Instrument	Operational-isation of On-the-Job Learning and Development	Research Goal	Researcher's Role	Instrument Description	Value for Researchers
Semi-structured Interviews (Eraut 1998)	Working and learning cannot be separated from each other; a large part of learning is a tacit process, some is explicit. Focused on learning rather than knowledge use	To study what is being learned at work, how it is taking place and what other factors affect the amount and direction of learning in the workplace (describe and explain)	Passionate participants, trying to gather data by interpreting the different voices of the participants, without being distracted by any preconceptions	Relation to theory, pilot test expert or peer review	Questions are well validated, both theoretically and in terms of generalisability
Semi-structured interviews about self-directed learning projects (SDLP) (Clardy 2000)	SDLP operationalised based on Tough (1971), a self-initiated or directed set of activities with the primary purpose of learning about job, vocational or occupational subjects	To explore types and occurrence of SDLP (describe)	Passionate participant in naturalistic research. Inductive, articulate, emergent categories through iterative process of constant comparison. Conceptual categories are grounded in a multi-voice reconstruction	Relation to theory by Tough (1971). Interview was pilot tested and revised. After each interview the researcher would evaluate the interview and make appropriate adjustments for future interviews	Possesses less effective generalisability. Interviewer training is crucial to ensure its effectiveness
Semi-structured interviews combined with observations (Collin 2002)	Learning is understood as a ubiquitous, ongoing activity, though often unrecognised as such (Lave 1991). It is informal, experiential, context-bound participation	To explore conceptions of learning in a work context from a process-oriented perspective (describe)	Reflexivist who continuously elucidates the means by which her own and respondents' values and suppositions guide the framing of theory and fact	According to phenomenolog-ical principles, too many questions or details were not formulated in advance. The point is to establish the phenomenon as experienced and to explore the different aspects of the experience jointly as fully as possible	Question marks concerning the theoretical validity and generalisability of the questions

Instrument	Operational-isation of On-the-Job Learning and Development	Research Goal	Researcher's Role	Instrument Description	Value for Researchers
Critical incident interviews (Billet 2000)	Learning is engagement in everyday activities in the workplace that provide ongoing access to goal-directed activities and support, which are instrumental in assisting individuals constructing or learning new work-related knowledge as well as the strengthening of that learning	To determine whether guided workplace learning can assist the development of skills and knowledge required for workplace performance and understand how that learning can be maximised (explain)	Activist who conducted trials to guide learning strategies and reflects on their effectiveness through interviews with participants	The interview approach focused on three kinds of actual workplace incidents, namely 'high moments', problem situations' and 'low moments'. The approach was modelled on an earlier investigation, which used similar procedures to elicit data grounded in actual workplace problem-solving incidents. Relation to theory, expert or peer review	Possesses very good descriptive and interpretative validity
Stimulated recall interview (Poskiparta, Liimatainen and Kettunen 1999)	Self-reflection in improving communication skills in the areas of listening, interviewing methods, motivation, giving advice and feedback. Self-reflection is seen as a way of learning by doing in normal working processes and consists of seven levels of which four are seen as conscious levels and three as critical conscious levels of reflectivity	To describe nurses' opinions of their communication skills in health counselling situations and analyse the levels of reflectivity in their evaluations according to Mezirow (1981) (describe)	Passionate participant. Besides classification in levels of reflection, the author refers to how the nurses benefit from this method of data-gathering	Stimulated recall interviews based on videotaped counselling and appended written evaluations	Difficult to establish generalisability. Videoing disturbs the intervention

Instrument	Operational-isation of On-the-Job Learning and Development	Research Goal	Researcher's Role	Instrument Description	Value for Researchers
In-depth Interviews (Fenwick 2004)	Learning in general is practice-based and participative. Innovative learning is an interplay of local choice-making and design within social relations constituted by material interests, cultural histories and conflicting discourses	To understand how portfolio workers learn for innovative work and in innovative work (describe)	Reflectivist who continuously elucidates the means by which her own and respondents' values and suppositions guide the framing of theory and reality	Three main topics of the interviews were: work histories; strategies and challenges; and skills and knowledge required. These were fully explored based on narratives of critical incidents and periods of lived experiences	Difficult to comment on the generalisability of the method. May not fully reveal the extent of learning
Informal Learning Project (ILP) Interview (Gear, McIntosh and Squires 1994)	Informal learning is learning that professional people may undertake, in and through their normal work and practice, initially or spontaneously. The method section shows focus on deliberate learning. ILP means spending at least one working day developing some aspect of professional knowledge, skills and competence to the point where some of it could be passed on to a colleague	To explore the pattern of learning in an ILP, the nature of the process and influences (describe and explain)	Informant: the researchers gather information about informal learning	Semi-structured interviews that ensured that all topics were covered in most cases, to minimise interviewer differences, and to provide enough freedom to pursue themes and topics that arose during the interview, in a relatively flexible manner	This interview protocol possesses very good generalisability and good interpretative validity

Instrument	Operational-isation of On-the-Job Learning and Development	Research Goal	Researcher's Role	Instrument Description	Value for Researchers
Narrative (life and work-history interviews) (Valkevaar 2002)	Development of professional expertise is viewed as experienced performance and developed as an interactive constructive process based on the interpretation of experience and narratives in a variety of everyday situations at work as well as in other fields of life	To explore the construction of professional expertise through interpretations of experience in the practice of HRD professionals (describe)	Passionate participant. Regards the interviews as beneficial to the interviewees; they offer space and time for reflection	Narrative (life and work history) interviews to supplement an earlier held survey about the HRD professionals' experience and conceptions in order to examine the quality and development of their expertise in HRD work	Untested in terms of generalisability

Creating Conditions Conducive to Facilitating Informal Management and Leadership Development

We now consider the practices that organisations can introduce to promote informal learning. We suggest a number of guidelines that focus on the individual, the team, the organisation and the strategic environment in which the organisation operates. While various aspects of management policy and practice can enhance the likelihood of informal learning, ultimately it is the individual manager who is key to ensuring that it happens.

The Role of the Individual Manager's Job: It is clear that managers need time to think. Strategies that may help to provide thinking time include time-management strategies and flexible work schedules. Freedom from distractions and time to think need to be combined with the availability of relevant information. Organisations need to consider strategies that incentivise knowledge development. Because learning requires a focus on the work and freedom from distractions (as well as allowing the manager to distribute and relocate effort, depending on changing requirements and emerging opportunities), managerial jobs should be defined in terms of broad activities rather than in terms of administrative requirements. Organisations should allow discretion in structuring work activities. Managers should be allowed substantial discretion in how they allocate time to core tasks. Human resource practices that promote discretion, including flexible work schedules and self-defined work plans, are likely to contribute to informal learning.

Goals and Rewards: Goals and objectives should be defined in broad terms, focusing on learning as well as productivity, and be framed in such a way as to allow managers to pursue a number of different opportunities. Goals should be used as an informative, directional mechanism rather than solely for evaluation purposes. Learning in work is often ambiguous and ambiguity is an important condition for double-loop learning. Organisations should therefore tailor performance objectives to learning and the objectives should recognise that autonomy contributes to learning and that the unique work done by different managers presents different issues. Objectives should be defined collaboratively. The manager should have a significant input into the identification of key objectives. If objectives are linked to the unique work that the manager performs, then evaluating a progress should be made with reference to those objectives. Informal learning calls for both intrinsic and extrinsic motivation, operating in a synergistic way. Rewards of an intrinsic manner should include greater autonomy, rich feedback and additional development opportunities. Extrinsic rewards should focus on advancement.

Content of Informal Development: The careful selection of talented managers is important because informal learning opportunities are likely to be richer amongst a group of talented managers. It is important to highlight that the quality of learning will be higher when managers are allocated tasks consistent with their interests and work systems. It is also possible that competition amongst groups of managers may also enhance learning. Work content is particularly important in shaping informal learning. Job characteristics such as autonomy, skill variety, task feedback and identity and task significance enhance learning in work. Perception of contextual factors may play as important a role as their objective presence. In order to enhance informal learning, it is important for organisations to define work content collaboratively. Managers should be skilled in both identifying and changing context and managing group dynamics.

Learning Culture and Climate: The climate and culture prevailing in the organisation does have a marked influence on informal learning. The culture should, where possible, emphasise risk-taking, challenge, change, competitiveness and the intrinsic enjoyment of work. Organisations can influence their own climate and culture by initiatives designed to audit the culture, encourage collaboration and devise recognition programmes that emphasise collaboration and learning. It is also important to recognise that human resource policies that emphasise training, external education and professional development will also influence informal learning. Policies that promote high-performance work, such as collaborative goal-setting, teamwork, autonomy and ongoing learning, are also effective in contributing to informal learning. At a strategic level, it is important to assess the implications of strategic changes for informal learning. Table 11.11 highlights key human resource policies that facilitate informal learning.

Table 11.11: The Role of Human Resource Policies in Facilitating Informal Management and Leadership Development – Management Guidelines

The Individual	The Group
• Select for breadth and depth of expertise and skill in working with expertise • Provide incentives for ongoing knowledge development • Define job expectations in terms of broad core duties • Allow discretion in structuring work activities • Periodically review work progress	• Select leaders based on management skills as well as expertise • Provide multiple career tracks for advancement • Orient work group planning around learning issues • Allow individuals to develop and maintain a mix of activities and projects • Provide training in the nature and management of learning • Provide team-training focus on collaboration and learning • Ensure awards and recognition are consistent with climate and collaboration requirements

The Organisation	The Environment
• Help prepare staff to support development and implementation • Implement policies that emphasise professional growth and development • Promote high-performance workplace policies • Conduct audits of the learning climate	• Assess the implications of strategic changes for expertise requirements • Monitor workforce capabilities and expertise

Conclusion

Informal management and leadership development takes place in organisations, regardless of whether it is understood or not. There is a strong case to be made for its place in management and leadership development. It is considered the most effective means by which to acquire skills and competencies. Estimates suggest that over ninety per cent of management learning in the workplace occurs through informal learning processes. The distinction between formal and informal development is contested. Each learning situation includes characteristics of both formality and informality, with the balance between them shifting continuously.

Organisations should capture and leverage informal learning and development processes and cultivate the learning abilities of managers. This may require that organisations consider using formal learning processes in a manner that prompts growth in informal learning capacity. Specific spheres focused on fostering an environment conducive to informal learning include the development of a positive learning culture, improving networking and the exchange of information, and encouraging learning in team situations. Ultimately, the effectiveness of informal learning is bound up with the personal characteristics of the manager. These characteristics include motivation and self-confidence to learn, learning styles and preferences and learning goal orientation.

Informal management and leadership development is multidimensional and multifaceted and occurs in different environments. The extent to which informal development is effective, in a management and leadership development context, depends on the broader organisational, social, cultural and political context within which it is located, as well as the learning practices utilised. Its particular feature of interest is the degree of control that the manager has in relation to the development process. Managers have choices over how they learn and in demonstrating motivation in challenging learning situations.

Summary of Key Points

- Informal development takes place randomly. It is unstructured and control is with the manager. It is learning that results from natural opportunity.
- The informal development process is characterised by below-the-surface beliefs, values and assumptions that guide and influence managerial action. Informal development is influenced by how managers frame a situation as a problem. This problem is framed within the boundaries of the manager's context.
- Informal learning includes processes of both action and reflection that have both intended and unintended consequences.
- Informal learning is enhanced by a positive learning culture and climate. Jobs that possess developmental potential and a host of individual managerial characteristics, including motivation to learn, self-efficacy and learning-goal orientation, all enhance informal learning.
- Organisations need to stress positive contextual aspects to help improve informal management and leadership development.

- Managers utilise different informal development processes, including experience-based learning, common sense and intuition, reflection in action, peer learning and learning from external experiences.

■ Discussion Questions

1. Contrast informal and formal learning. How useful is such a distinction?

2. The concept of control is a fundamental component of informal learning. Explain how the concept of control is understood.

3. Distinguish the action and cognition perspectives of informal learning.

4. What actions can an organisation take to encourage reflection in action in the workplace?

5. Distinguish learning goal orientation, learning preferences and learning style. What relevance do they have to informal management and leadership development?

■ Application and Experiential Questions

1. Consider your organisation or select one that you are familiar with and answer the following questions:
   - What is the relative importance of informal development? Explain your answer.
   - How do managers view informal development processes?
   - What contribution does informal development make to leadership development efforts?

2. What actions could you take in your organisation to encourage informal coaching and mentoring? What measures, if any, would you apply to assess the effectiveness of informal mentoring and coaching processes? Justify your answer.

3. In groups of three or four, develop a set of guidelines in respect of the application of informal development in organisations. Prepare guidelines that address both organisational and individual issues. How would you ensure that informal development and formal development can augment each other and integrate synergistically? You have twenty minutes to prepare your presentation to the class.

PART FOUR

Self-Development and Self-Managed Learning

OPENING CASE SCENARIO

Focusing on Individual Development at Ernst and Young Ireland

Ernst and Young is a global leader in professional services and its mission is to ensure that the public has trust in professional service firms and in the quality of financial reporting. Ernst and Young Ireland is one of the leading firms of auditors, tax and business advisers. It employs over fifty partners and approximately 850 staff in Dublin, Cork, Waterford, Limerick and Galway. It has as its clients some of Ireland's largest companies from all sectors of the economy. Globally it has over 100,000 employees in over 140 countries. It has a strong commitment to bold leadership, integrity, quality and value and the development of the potential of its human resources. It provides its managers with a strong programme of professional and management development and ensures that its professionals can plan a successful career with the organisation.

Each year Ernst and Young hires graduates from Irish universities who enter into a contract in conjunction with the Institute of Chartered Accountants. Graduates typically have a contract of between three and three and a half years and are placed in the organisation's audit and tax services divisions. Graduates come to the organisation seeking both a professional training and with the understanding that they will have a robust career and development opportunities. In 2005 Ernst and Young Ireland identified a need to support graduate trainees in identifying their career opportunities with the firm before they came out of contract. This need was prompted by an Ernst and Young Global People Survey conducted in 2005 which highlighted that graduates did not have access to appropriate career guidance and had relatively few meaningful career opportunities available when they completed their contract. Ernst and Young responded to this survey by implementing three specific initiatives to support career planning. These were career planning guides, career planning briefings to support these guides and structured career planning workshops lasting one and a half days. The organisation devised career planning guides for all its service lines such as tax, audit and risk advisory. Briefings on the guides were rolled out across the organisation in late 2005 and 2006. The career planning workshop was mandatory for all graduates coming out of contract. These various career initiatives were designed to: ensure that Ernst and Young retained the right people for the right reason; ensure that graduates had an opportunity to take time out and think about what they want from their careers; and provide graduates with an opportunity to identify their career goals and examine their personal responsibility in managing their careers. These initiatives provided an increased focus in the organisation on longer-term career development and gave partners a greater understanding of graduates' aspirations. Graduates were also provided with a positive experience of the organisation even if they decided to leave.

This career initiative had a number of features which made it unique. The organisation assigned a dedicated career sponsor to each graduate. Each graduate met with a partner on a one-to-one basis for thirty minutes during the career planning workshops to discuss their career. It utilised external facilitators. The facilitator used movies to illustrate points on people's life journeys, challenging situations, facing a crossroads and meeting difficult situations. The workshops utilised a range of exercises focused on building the reputation of the brand of the graduate, the articulation of the graduate's values and how the graduate is perceived by others. During the workshop, a partner talked through his or her life journey and was questioned by an actor for the group. The workshops also focused on self-awareness and taking ownership of career decisions while de-emphasising technical and business issues. Each graduate was required to commit to an action in front of other participants before they completed the workshop.

Prior to the formal workshop, graduates attended a pre-workshop briefing session which was co-facilitated by a representative from training and development and a partner from the graduate's line of business. Sponsors from the business line were identified to support each graduate. Sponsors were typically drawn from senior management or higher and were organisational members with whom the participant would have had little contact. This enabled the partner, as sponsor, to be objective, act as a sounding board and communicate their experience and advice. Graduates met with the sponsor prior to attending the workshop. This meeting provided the impetus to help graduates start focusing on their career aspirations. Each graduate completed a profile outlining their area of interest, which was submitted before the graduate attended the workshop. This profile provided graduates with a foundation to start the career planning process and to provide the organisation with an insight concerning graduates' career expectations. The workshops had distinct objectives including the identification of career paths, a review of the graduate's career to date, the identification of career options, strengths and development needs, the identification of supports available to graduates and the use of career planning tools. Once graduates completed the workshop, they met with their sponsor again to discuss any agreed actions. Actions were discussed during this meeting and the owner of the action was also identified.

These career interventions continually emphasised that it was important for graduates to take time to think about their careers and to plan properly. Graduates needed to understand that their development journey had already started and was not an isolated or one-off event. They needed to take control of their careers. The focus of the programme was on the individual rather than the organisation. Ernst and Young used external facilitators who specialised in career journeys and the programme was about helping graduates make the optimum career choices. The intervention contributed to a number of important individual outcomes. Graduates have moved into different service lines and have been assigned to specific project work if they expressed an interest in doing so. The programme facilitated peer networking and graduates put themselves forward for travel opportunities. Partners achieved a greater understanding of graduates' career aspirations and the challenges they are likely to face. The programme improved morale and had a ripple effect on newer graduates who heard about the programme from peers. Ernst and Young is committed to enhancing the programme. They included alumni-contacts to talk to graduates about their experiences and redesigned the workshop content to match the stage of the graduate's career. The organisation will also incorporate career planning initiatives into the early stages when graduates join the organisation and continue these through their careers with Ernst and Young.

QUESTIONS

Q.1 To what extent does the intervention deigned by Ernst and Young address the development needs of graduates?

Q.2 What are the potential barriers to self-development in organisations?

The post-modern manager can no longer rely solely on the organisation to identify and provide opportunities for development. Managers must be capable of identifying and diagnosing their skills gaps, seeking out proactive development strategies to address these needs and accessing environment rich in learning opportunities. Caproni (2005) argues that the first stage in this learning process is the ability of the manager to be self-aware, coupled with being capable of acquiring self-understanding. These are pivotal in terms of assisting the post-modern manager to survive and adapt in organisations. Managers are expected to accept, take ownership of and engage with development and, most important, to accept that they have learning gaps that need to be addressed in order to achieve their potential.

Fox (1997) suggested that self-development emerged in the 1970s as a way of assisting the individual to augment their natural learning, yet he concurred with the views of Handy *et al.* (1998) that self-development 'was used as a convenient rhetoric for the low spending on education and training by corporations and government in the UK'. Self-development was regarded as a response to management training where providers decided what managers should learn. It was considered a process in which learners took the primary responsibility for choosing what, when and how to learn. Some organisations see self-development as a cost-effective method of developing employees, and others see it as an appropriate organisational response to changing work circumstances.

This chapter examines self-development and self-managed learning. We discuss the nature of development, self-awareness and self-managed learning. We consider the organisational conditions that facilitate and inhibit self-managed learning and describe the role of learning contracts in helping managers to plan self-managed learning processes.

Why the Focus on the Self and Self-Management?

The notion of the self and the need to satisfy individual manager needs has become a major area of academic investigation, as well as a challenge for organisations. Traditional leadership development processes focused primarily on organisational needs. Managers are increasingly advised to manage both their development and their careers. This individualisation of both development and career advocates that managers build appropriate leadership competencies, increase their career portability, and develop and take responsibility for career decisions. This focus on the individual may be in conflict with organisational efforts to build a leadership talent pool, but it is a reality that organisations face. Sturges (2004) suggested that a consequence of this dualism, the main focus of development, may be on what she termed 'near' leadership skills. These are empowering and team-building skills. The emergence of greater diversity has prompted organisations to customise development and career strategies to reflect individual manager priorities. We will focus here on particular processes that have brought a focus on individual development to the fore, such as employability, career self-management and internal career self-management behaviours consisting of networking and development activities. Career self-management challenges managers to be more innovative concerning their development. Miles and Snow (1986) suggested that managers need to develop referral, partnering and relationship management skills. Referral skills focus on the ability to diagnose situations and act as a broker. Partnering skills focus on developing networks and long-term relationships. Relationship management skills focus on the ability to prioritise the needs of both internal and external customers. Inkson and Arthur (2001) focused on the development of career capital. They suggested that it consists of a cluster of competencies: knowing how, knowing why and knowing whom. 'Knowing how' competencies focus on job-related knowledge and include both tacit and explicit knowledge, soft as well as technical skills. 'Knowing why' competencies focus on values, meanings and interests that shape the manager's development, and on self-confidence, motivation and self-assurance. 'Knowing whom' competencies focus on the accumulation of social capital. These competency sets potentially benefit both the individual manager and the organisation.

Individualisation of development and career poses significant challenges for management and leadership development in organisations. It suggests that organisations should give more prominence to self-managed learning and to adopting a set of development processes that can cope with diversity. It is unlikely that organisations can completely abdicate their responsibility for developing managers. At a minimum, they need to put in place the conditions that enable managers to take individual development initiatives.

The Emergence of Employability

The concept of employability has emerged in the management and leadership development literature as a factor driving development initiatives in organisations. It is often considered an elusive term, but the CBI (1999) defined it as the possession by managers of qualities and competencies required to meet the changing demands of employers and customers. This definition envisages that a focus on employability should lead to the manager realising his or her potential. Managerial competencies and skills are a central component of employability. McQuaid and Lindsay (2005) suggest two forms of employability that have relevance to managers:

- *Initiative Employability*: This variant of employability envisages that managers and organisations will accept that successful career management requires the development of leadership competencies that are transferable. It also includes the flexibility to move between roles. Managers have a responsibility to develop skills and networks, and this in turn strengthens their position in the wider labour market.

- *Interactive Employability*: This perspective argues that while managers have a responsibility for development, the employability of a manager is relative to the employability of others. This suggests that managers must be ahead of the game.

Hillage and Pollard (1998) suggest that a manager's employability depends on complex interactions between four key components:

- *Employability Assets*: including baseline assets, such as basic skills and essential personal attributes (for example, reliability and honesty); intermediate assets, such as job-specific, generic and 'key' skills (e.g. communication and problem-solving); and high-level assets, such as those skills that contribute to organisational performance (e.g. teamwork and commercial awareness).
- *Presentation*: defined as the ability to secure an appointment to an appropriate position through the demonstration of employability assets (e.g. through the competent completion of a curriculum vitae or application form, or participation in an interview).
- *Deployment*: refers to a range of abilities including career management skills (e.g. awareness of one's own abilities and limitations, awareness of opportunities in the labour market, and decision-making and transactional skills) and job-search skills.
- *Context Factors or the Interaction of Personal Circumstances and the Labour Market*: the manager's ability to realise that his/her assets and skills will, to some extent, depend upon external socio-economic factors, personal circumstances and the relationship between the two. External conditions, such as local labour market demand and employer attitudes, will impact upon the availability of suitable opportunities, while personal circumstances will affect the ability of managers to seek and benefit from opportunities.

Moss Kanter (1997) was one of the first academics to focus on the relevance of employability for managers. She argued that it was necessary to offer managers a chance to grow in skills and accomplishments so that their value to the current and future employer is enhanced. Managers need to possess: a belief in self rather than in the power of position alone; the ability to collaborate and become connected to new teams in various ways; a strong commitment to the excitement of achievement; and a willingness to keep learning. Martin, Pate and Beaumont (2001) argued that not all organisations have embraced the employability perspective. Directors who reported that employability was an influence on their leadership development initiatives said it was delivered in company-specific areas and did not provide the skills that managers perceive to be relevant to their future career. Organisational practice did not match the rhetoric.

The Emergence of Career Self-Management

Hall (976) identified the individual rather than the organisation as the driver of the career. He proposed the notion of a protean career and highlighted seven important prescriptions for leadership development in organisations: development is managed by the manager, not the organisation; a career is a lifelong series of experiences; development is continuous, self-directed, relational and found in work challenges; development is not about formal development and upward mobility; managers must shift their mindset to one that moves from know how to learn how, from work-self to whole-self, and from an organisational career to one which is self-managed. The role of the organisation is to provide challenging assignments, information on development resources and developmental relationships.

Sturges (2004) suggested the notion of individual career orientation. She argued that these career orientations influence both leader roles and leadership development and suggested four types of individuals in terms of career orientation (see Figure 12.1).

Figure 12.1: Individual Career Orientations of Managers

The Climber	The Expert
• This manager describes career success very much in terms of objective criteria, e.g. hierarchical position. • They aspire to move up the hierarchy and see it as essential for their well-being. • They are very goal-oriented and they set stretching goals and targets. • They have strong competitive instincts. • They adopt more formal leadership roles and value distant leadership.	• They view career success in terms of the competence they achieve and recognition for what they do. • They value positive feedback and being acknowledged for good work. • The context of the job is as important as the hierarchical position and they are not as preoccupied with advancement. • They are very suited to empowering leadership roles and like to lead by example.
The Influencer	**The Self-Realiser**
• Career success is defined as doing things at work which are positive for the organisation. • They value autonomy in what they do, but younger managers may wish to progress up the hierarchy. • Influencers like to network and they gain influence beyond their hierarchical position. • They are well suited to senior leadership roles because of the potential power and influence involved.	• Career success is defined in an informal way. They define it in personal terms. • They are not interested in hierarchical position and like being good at their job. • They value challenging work and they like developing other managers. • They will only accept leadership positions that facilitate a good work–life balance.

Source: Sturges (2004)

The contemporary career literature suggests that both managers and organisations have responsibility for career management. Noe (1996), however, argued that the onus for managing the career has most definitely shifted to the individual. This has resulted in the emergence of career self-management. Kossek *et al.* (1998) suggested that an essential component of this practice involves information gathering and career planning.

EXHIBIT 12.1

Focus on Theory: Understanding the Authentic Leader

The concept of the authentic leader has gained prominence in the recent literature on leadership development. Contributions by George *et al.* (2007) and Avolio and Gardner (2005) have highlighted the importance of this concept to our understanding of leadership. The concept of authentic leadership itself is not yet clearly defined. The notion of authenticity has its roots in Greek philosophy. However, regarding its role in explaining leaderships, Erickson (1995), for example, argued that central to the notion of the authentic leader is the idea that the leader should not engage in any explicit consideration of 'others'. A focus on authenticity requires that the leader pays attention to the self. The self is viewed as operating as a social force in its own right and this self is actively involved in the social construction of reality. The self is shaped by and shapes social exchanges with others. Authentic leaders are described as those who are deeply aware of how they think and behave and are perceived by others as being self-aware. Authentic leaders are said to possess a number of important characteristics, which are enumerated by Avolio and Gardner as follows:

- **Positive Psychological Capital:** Authentic leaders possess a number of positive psychological capabilities such as self-confidence, optimism, hope and resilience. Where the leader operates in a positive organisational context, these capabilities enable the leader to heighten his/her self-awareness and engage in appropriate self-regulating behaviours. These positive psychological characteristics are open to development and change and play an important role in developing a leader's potential.
- **Positive Morale Perspective:** Authentic leadership has a strong morale component. Authentic leaders possess courage and moral capacity and are willing to address ethical issues and ensure the implementation of moral principles. Authentic leaders take actions that are driven by moral principles.
- **Leader Self-Awareness:** The authentic leader possesses heightened levels of self-awareness. Self-awareness is manifest in an increased understanding of one's existence. It is an emerging process in which the leader continually comes to understand his/her unique talents, strengths, values and beliefs and sense of purpose. It also requires the leader to have a clear understanding of his/her knowledge, experience and capabilities.
- **Leader Self-Regulation:** Leaders who are self-regulated possess the capacity to exert self-control by setting internal standards, identifying discrepancies between standards and actual outcomes and identifying actions that can reconcile or reduce these discrepancies. Authentic leaders are effective at aligning their values with their intentions and actions.
- **Leadership Processes/Behaviours:** Authentic leaders lead by example. This is achieved through self-confidence, optimism, resilience, transparent decision-making and consistency between words and deeds. Authentic leaders focus on developing peers by both modelling and supporting self-determination. They also achieve development of follow-through emotional contagion and positive social exchanges. Leaders who possess positive emotions will impact on follow-through social contagion and foster the emotional development of followers. Social exchange helps to ensure that followers will show high levels of trust in the leader and engage in behaviour that is consistent with the values of the leader.
- **Follower Self-Awareness/Regulation:** Authentic leadership helps followers to heighten their self-awareness. In particular, this involves followers developing greater clarity about their values, personal identities and emotions. Followers come to know themselves and self-regulate their behaviour.
- **Follower Development:** Authentic leadership theory argues that both leaders and followers are developed over time and the relationship between them becomes more authentic. Followers internalise the values and beliefs espoused by the leader. This impacts the follower's sense of self. Followers come to know who they are and they become more transparent with the leader. Leaders benefit from this transparency.
- **Organisational Context:** Authentic leadership occurs in a dynamic and emerging context. Particular features of context that are important include open access to information resources, support, equal opportunity to learn, opportunities for empowerment and teamwork. Leaders have a major responsibility to ensure an inclusive and open organisational climate in which followers can continually learn and grow.
- **Sustained Performance Beyond Expectations:** Sustained performance involves persistent high performance and growth over the longer term. This must be achieved by working within ethical values. Performance includes financial, human, social and psychological measures.

George *et al.* suggest that no one can be authentic simply by imitating someone else. They argue that for the leader to develop his or her authentic leadership requires a commitment to the development of self. They suggest seven guidelines that are required to develop authentic leadership:

1. An understanding of the leader's life story, which provides the context for the leader's experiences. Through this life story, the leader can find the inspiration to make an impact on the world. *Question: Which people and experiences in your early life had the greatest impact on you?*

2. Authentic leaders must focus on knowing their authentic self. This requires the leader to be honest and have the courage to open up and examine their experiences. This enables the leader to become more humane and be more willing to be vulnerable. *Question: What tools do you use to become self-aware?*

3. The values that form the basis of authentic leadership derive from the leader's beliefs and convictions. However, the leader will only achieve a full understanding of these values when they are tested under pressure. Where the leader has a solid base of values, it is then possible to develop principles that will be used in leading. *Question: What are your most deeply held values?*

4. Authentic leaders should balance intrinsic and extrinsic motivations. Authentic leaders need to sustain high levels of motivation and keep their lives in balance. Many leaders focus on the extrinsic, but the authentic leader focuses on the inner meaning of what they do. These intrinsic motivations are related to the leader's life story. Examples include personal growth and helping other people. *Question: What motivates you intrinsically and extrinsically?*

5. Authentic leaders focus on developing their support team. They are conscious that a strong team is necessary to enable the leader stay on course. Teams play an important role in supporting the leader, in helping them in difficult times and in helping the leader celebrate success. Teams are important in that they provide the authentic leader with a sense of perspective and may call for corrections when needed. *Question: What kind of support team do you have?*

6. Authentic leaders stay grounded. The authentic leader seeks to bring together key elements of work, family, community and friends, so that the leader is the same in each environment. The authentic leader is steady and confident and shows the same person all the time. They continue to stay grounded. *Question: Is your life integrated?*

7. Authentic leaders focus on empowering people to lead. They recognise that leadership is not about their own success or getting loyal followers. It is about having empowered leaders at all levels in the organisation. *Question: What does being authentic mean to your life?*

Sources: George *et. al.* (2007); Avolio and Gardner (2005)

The Characteristics of Self-Managed Individuals

The concept of self-regulation is important in the context of self-managed learning and development. Self-regulation involves several processes. Higher-order self-regulation involves the strength to overcome natural tendencies and to focus on the longer term. De Waele, Morval and Sheitoyan (1993) suggested that leaders who are effective at self-regulation know their limitations, take care of themselves and recognise how changes around them impact on their lives. Self-managed individuals have four important values: 1) they have confidence and faith in life; 2) they have confidence in their own ability and that of others; 3) they are open-minded and curious; and 4) they have a sense of autonomy and a desire to express their individuality. They are also better at managing themselves and others and are sensitive to their own internal conflicts. De Waele, Morval and Sheitoyan (1993) suggested that leaders who lack good self-management and self-regulation do not believe that their learning process depends on their own participation. Table 12.1 outlines the characteristics of managers with strong self-management attitudes and behaviours.

Table 12.1: Self-Management Attitudes and Behaviours

People who are self-managers . . .
- Take care of themselves physically
- Know where and when to set limits to guard their own well-being
- Are aware of how changes in their lives have an effect on their development
- Are interested in conscious self-development; set development goals and plans, participate in development activities
- Believe that their own learning process depends on their own doing; take control of their learning
- Develop a realistic attitude in coping with life events, especially sudden, possibly stressful changes
- Know when to say no – for instance, refuse to accept an assignment they feel would be beyond their capabilities; make sure they are prepared for the level of responsibility they take on
- Know that there are things in their environment that cannot be changed easily or at all – for instance, others' attitudes
- Accept prior experiences, even if they are painful
- Prepare for the future through professional training or by learning new skills
- Balance the energy they expend on different aspects of life (body, emotion, money, love, work)
- Are able to actively cope with disappointments, deceptions, burnout and depression
- Are aware that at times their failure to self-manage may affect others negatively (e.g. mismanaging money may have repercussions for others)
- In working with others, particularly direct reports, they are simultaneously directive and supportive, rather than corrective or punitive
- Encourage others, particularly direct reports, to manage themselves rather than encourage submissiveness
- Do not wait for the organisation to provide opportunities for self-development, but take charge of their own self-development
- In interaction with others, especially supervisors, are responsive to the group and to authority while also expressing their autonomy
- Set their own standards for success and failure, with knowledge, but not blind acceptance, of others' expectations and standards
- Stay away from ideologies that do not support development of the process

Source: Based on De Waele *et al.* (1993)

Defining Development, Self-Development and Self-Managed Learning

The concepts of development, self-development and self-managed learning are used in different ways in the literature. There is a lack of agreement as to what each term means, and therefore the three terms have multiple meanings. We explore some of these meanings in the following sections.

Alternative Conceptions of Development

Development is perceived as a complex concept. Cunningham (2002), for example, equated development with learning that is not individualistic because 'it occurs within the context of the individual's social and work practice'. He argued that the organisation cannot force its managers to learn and develop and, in fact, managers will make the decision about how and what they learn. He takes issues with the assertion of Van de Sluis and Hoeksema (2001:1) that 'the central challenge of leadership development is to control and measure the learning process of managers'. Managers are adults and intrinsically need to drive their own learning. Knowles (1990) supported the view that it is not possible to control the learning process of adults. Lee (1997) likewise challenged the view that organisations can control what their managers learn. She proposed four notions of development, and warned against the facile labelling of development. These four ideas are:

Development as Maturation: Maturation has been defined as a process of development which is 'stage like, largely predetermined, in a historically rooted way. It presents development as a process of maturation similar to child development or the lifespan development of individuals.' (p.200).

Development as a Shaping Process: Shaping as a development process addresses limitations or gaps in development. Shaping seeks to overcome skills deficiencies by advocating tools or blueprints such as relevant courses to address these weaknesses. The original state of being is regarded as ineffective and the developed state is deemed to be effective.

Development as Voyage: Development is viewed as an exploratory process where the individual is actively engaged in a development process in which they become something different and new without using a clear path or guide.

Development as Emergent: This view is considered emergent in the sense that 'the individual is contextualised within a web of influences and development occurs through mutual negotiations of the boundaries of these influences'.

These categorisations are elaborated on in Table 12.2, below.

Lee (1997:206) suggested that maturation and shaping are goal-driven and bounded approaches to development which support the concept of the predictability of existence. The role of developers here is as experts who can help mould managers and organisations to achieve predetermined objectives. This bounded approach serves to reinforce the status quo. Conversely, voyage and emergent development are considered less bounded and unpredictable approaches with limited emphasis on expertise and 'developers are more like self-deprecating facilitators and co-workers'. This less bounded approach 'supports anarchy and deviance, and questions the existence of organisations and our appreciation of these'. Managers are more likely to view development as a voyage process, whereas senior management consider development as a shaping process. Expert developers are likely to consider development as maturation or shaping. Facilitative developers will view development as voyage or emergent. Despite these different views on development, the general message is that the individual and the organisation need to develop to maintain a competitive edge.

Lee argued that each of these notions of development highlights ethical issues for individuals and organisations. She suggested the following:

- The use and abuse of the power of the expert linked to the maturation and shaping processes of development.
- The manipulative role of development as social engineering associated with shaping and emergent interpretations of development.
- The invisibility of agency in the emergent and voyage interpretation of development, where developers act as co-creators or facilitative supporters of development are, in fact, the opposite to the experts in the maturation and shaping approaches. The success of this approach is dependent on the developers becoming invisible or taking a back seat so that the 'recipients perceive themselves to be the agents of their own development' (Lee 1997: 209). In this situation, the recipients might not grasp the role of the developer in their development and, as a result, will fail to appreciate this role and may not be willing to pay for it. Lee asserts that if developers become too invisible in this role and stick to their principles, they might become unemployable.
- The subversive role of development as destiny where the maturation and voyage interpretations of development have, as their central tenet, the appreciation of development as a journey toward destiny or towards fulfilling unique potential (Lee 1997:210). Lee asked the question, 'By encouraging individuals to work toward their

development potential, are the developers not just creating dissatisfaction, lack of commitment and alienation on the part of the individual?'

Lee (1997) acknowledged that it is not easy to avoid the multiplicity of interpretations of development. She tended to favour the emergent approach, but acknowledged that it is not ethically pure. Developers, therefore, need to be aware of their own motivations and values concerning development and consider whether it is a process that is beneficial to both individuals and organisations.

Table 12.2: Different Conceptions of Development and the Role of Developers

Development as Maturation 'Cycles'	Development as Shaping 'Brainwashing'	Development as a Voyage	Development as Emergent
• Development and management follow inevitable cycles • Predictable reactions to the environment • System seen as a coherent unitary force with clearly defined boundaries • Groups can be labelled and go through inevitable stages of development • Organisations develop along routes that are well understood through expert analysis	• Development and management is a complex phenomenon • Development has end points defined by someone or something external to the process of development • The corporate hierarchy determines the developmental force • Individuals are malleable and can be moulded into the wider system • Empowerment confined as a tool to enhance performance – yet not to question senior management or act as agent provocateur	• Development is a voyage into oneself • No end points to development • Lifelong journey upon unchartered internal routes • Individuals construct their own frames of reference in which they make sense of the world • Active process in which individuals are continually reanalysing their roles • Development is for the individual and occurs through the reflective activities of the individual	• Individual's frames of reference are fluid interpretations and emerge through implicit and explicit negotiation with others • Development is messy, confusing, complex and emergent • Development cannot be driven by any single sub-section • Individuals dynamically alter their actions with respect to the ongoing and anticipated actions of their partners (Fogel 1993:34)
Role of Developers in Maturation	**Role of Developers in Shaping**	**Role of Developers in Voyage**	**Role of Developers in Emergence**
• Understand the parameters of the inevitable development and facilitate this • Act as relatively uninvolved experts who can intervene and help facilitate development • Seen as 'expert' consultants • Can reassure that all will be well	• Developers are the process experts • Help to identify and enhance future and apply tools to ensure future is achieved for all • Help to devise blueprint to achieve end criteria	• Help others to help themselves • Attempt to help individuals to understand their frames of reference • Use expert skills to help individuals recognise self-imposed boundaries and widen their horizons • Do not use the power of expertise	• Act as consultants to widen the group's frames of reference • Catalyse development by confronting the group's version of reality • Act as facilitative interpreters • Do not hold unique or special status • Have no vested interest in political machinations

What is Self-Development?

Having considered the concept of development, we now examine the concept of self-development and how it impacts the learning of a manager. Self-development is an even more elusive concept than development. Cunningham (2004) suggested that self-development is a process which has eight key characteristics:

- *Individual Acceptance of the Need for Change*: Self-development focuses on the manager's self-consciousness. It requires an awareness of the context in which the manager finds himself or herself. This awareness extends to the manager's physical, psychological and spiritual self. Acceptance of the need for change is a necessary component of self-development, because it is not possible to impose it on the individual.
- *Knowledge of Self is Essential for Development*: Self-awareness represents a core component of self-development. This involves knowledge about self, the manager's role and the environment within which this role takes place. We discuss self-awareness in more detail later in this chapter.
- *Managers must take Ownership of their Development*: Managers are expected to take responsibility for their development. This suggests manager interdependence with the organisation. Such a perspective reinforces feelings of self-worth and interdependence. Cunningham, however, acknowledged that employers cannot delegate responsibility entirely to the manager. The employer must accept that each manager is distinctive.
- *Accept that Failure is a Part of Self-Development*: The manager must internalise and accept the reasons why development must occur. The process of self-development opens the possibility that the manager may fail or may be viewed as incompetent. This indicates that the environment needs to be supportive to enable the manager to deal with possible failure.
- *Self-Development Emphasises a Positive Self-Image Combined with a Respect for Human Dignity on the Part of the Organisation*: Self-development will most likely involve mindset or attitude changes for the manager. It will probably include a need to be flexible, to tolerate the unknown, to show a willingness to take risks and to engage in learning that may not have predetermined outcomes.
- *Self-Development Equates with Power for the Manager*: Cunningham envisages that self-development can lead to a redistribution of power in the organisation. This highlights the need for the manager to be willing to take on a new responsibility and to use it in a developmental way.
- *Self-Development is Goal-Focused*: Self-development processes require an articulation of goals. There must also be an acknowledgement that these goals reaffirm the manager's perception of their worth to the organisation.
- *Self-Development requires Resilience and Tenacity*: The manager requires the tenacity to take up new challenges and the resilience to understand that development is an ongoing life-long process of learning and development.

Self-development therefore focuses on the process of developing the self. It requires, as a first step, the recognition that an individual needs to develop. It requires an understanding of personal beliefs and assumptions, an understanding that differences matter and a willingness to be uncomfortable. Self-development places strong emphasis on the values and attitudes of the manager concerning his/her development.

What is Self-Managed Learning?

Many interpretations of development and self-development exist. Likewise, organisations use a multiplicity of approaches to achieve development objectives. The experts have hailed self-managed learning as a flexible and ground-breaking approach to helping managers to up-skill and address learning gaps as they occur in the context of their work practices. The failure of traditional learning has led to the development of self-managed learning (Confessone and Kops 1998; Cunningham 2002). Gilligan (1994) credited Cunningham as the creator of the concept of self-managed learning because he perceived the need to develop 'a holistic learner-centred approach to development and learning'.

Self-managed learning (SML) and self-directed learning are considered to be the same concept (Guglielmino and Guglielmino 2001). They involve a situation where individual learners initiate and promote their own learning. Since these concepts are synonymous they will be treated as such throughout this chapter. There are numerous definitions of self-managed learning found in the literature. Gerber *et al.* (1995) argued that some 'associate self-directed learning with tightly circumscribed activities like programmed learning. Others view SML as much more open-ended, emphasising autonomous or independent learning on virtually any topic by almost any means.' However, experts concur that the variations in interpretation are dependent on the context that theorists and practitioners apply. Straka (2000) argued that there is no common definition of self-directed learning. Carre (1994) discovered twenty terms for self-directed learning and Hiemstra (1996) found over two hundred.

Table 12.3 provides a selection of definitions found in the literature.

Table 12.3: Definitions of Self-Managed Learning

Definition	Author
Self-managed learning includes the learner initiating the learning, making the decisions about what training and development experiences will occur and how the learner selects and carries out their own learning goals, objectives, methods and means by which goals were met.	Chien (2004)
Self-managed learning is one of the most common ways in which adults pursue learning in their lifespan.	Candy (1991)
Self-directed learning, often called self-managed learning, is a process in which the learner is responsible for identifying what is to be learned, when it is to be learned and how it is to be learned. The learner is also responsible for evaluating not only whether the learning occurs but if it is relevant to the learning objective.	Guglielmino and Guglielmino (2001)
Self-managed learning is a process in which 'individuals take the initiative' with or without the help of others in diagnosing their learning needs, formulating learning goals, identifying human and material resources for learning, choosing and implementing appropriate learning strategies and evaluating learning outcomes.	Knowles (1975:18)
Two-shell model of motivated self-managed learning: self-directed learning is a process in which a person approaches a learning subject with an interest as regards the content as well as the proceedings, applies strategies of resource management, of sequencing and of acquisition, controls their application cognitively, meta-cognitively and motivationally as well as evaluating by diagnosing and attributing the achieved learning result.	Straka (2000)
Brookfield outlines two types of self-managed learning: 1. Various techniques such as goal setting, identifying resources, implementing strategies and evaluating progress.	Brookfield (1986:47)

Definition	Author
2. Self-direction can refer to interpsychic changes in which learners come to regard knowledge as relative and contextual, to view the value frameworks and moral codes informing their behaviours as cultural constructs and to use this altered perspective to contemplate ways in which they can transform their personal and social worlds.	Brookfield (1986:50–59)
The self-managed learner pursues 'an understanding and awareness of a range of alternative possibilities' for learning and living where 'critical reflection on the contingent aspects of reality, the exploration of alternative perspectives and meaning systems and the alteration of personal and social circumstances are present'.	Gerber *et al.* (1995)
Self-managed learning occurs when a learner takes responsibility for what is learned and how. Self-directed learning can include the learner recognising the range of available potential sources of learning in the workplace, for example that a colleague has the knowledge or skill required, seeking them out and learning from them.	Smith and Sadler-Smith (2006:89)

Guglielmino and Guglielmino (2001) highlighted four characteristics of self-managed learning:

- *Learning is Self-Managed, not Other Managed*: Each manager is expected to both take responsibility for learning and share relevant learning with other managers. This requires that the role of the leadership development specialist is to act as a resource provider or facilitator of learning rather than taking on the role of an information-giver.
- *Learning is Individualised rather than Predetermined*: Each manager has the opportunity to customise learning to priority needs. The manager may continue this learning through some form of learning contract.
- *Learning is Independent or Interdependent rather than Dependent*: Self-directed or self-managed learning emphasises individual or small group learning. Self-directed learners may seek out other learners with similar needs and use them as opportunities for collaboration and support. This may also facilitate the sharing of experiences, knowledge and resources and the distribution of the learning tasks.
- *Just-in-Time Learning*: Self-managed learning envisages a just-in-time approach where the manager seeks out learning that will assist in solving immediate problems.

A central issue running through these characteristics is recognition by the manager of responsibility to address learning gaps. Robotham (1995:7) argued that 'as organisations operate in increasingly unstable environments that require greater levels of flexibility and adaptability from their employees, then self-direction would appear to be an increasingly desirable attribute'. He described self-managed learning as the 'ability of an individual to select actively from a personal style or skills portfolio' and states that a self-managed learner should be capable not only of deciding the resources and skills required to achieve his/her learning objectives, but also 'how to acquire these specific resources and skills'. It is clear that the individual is responsible for initiating and implementing their self-managed learning, but traditional leadership development practices have disempowered the learner and created conditions of 'learned helplessness' (p. 4), where the manager can become dependent on the trainer to initiate learning activities.

Dealtry (2004:101) suggested that learners are automatically exposed to an environment rich in learning opportunities and that the managerial learner 'in particular has to be increasingly aware and more discriminating in how they spend time and learning energy if they are to arrive where they want to be and at the same time satisfy these process events'.

The effective manager requires a specific learning capability to develop business and management acumen on a continual basis. Some managers innately have this characteristic but other managers need to acquire it. Learning to learn is described as a type of self-direction in learning. Dealtry used Knowles's (1990) theory which describes managers moving from dependency and passivity in their learning approach and evolving into mature, dynamic self-directed learners. This theory concurs with Robotham's (1995) assertion that self-direction in learning evolves from dependency to independence (Figure 12.2).

Dealtry (2004:104) advocated the need for the manager to become an accomplished self-managed learner by achieving 'competency and personal mastery over their personal and situational learning dynamics'. Smith (2002) identified 'the significant commercial value of encouraging managers to become effective self-managed learners in that they can develop and pursue their learning goals and outcomes that contribute to competitiveness without the need for all learning to occur only when there is direct training by an instructor'.

Figure 12.2: Moving from Dependency to Self-Managed

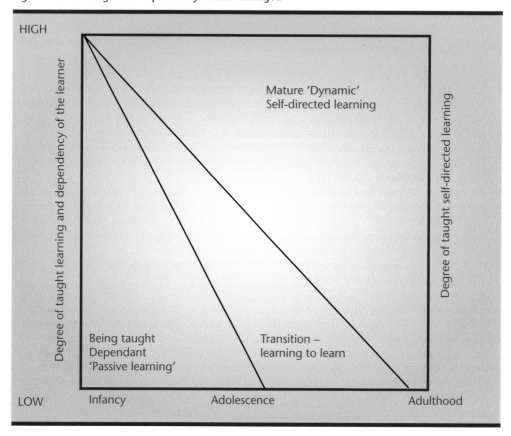

Source: Knowles (1990)

Clardy (2000) suggested that it is best to conceptualise self-directed learning as consisting of three different types. Induced self-directed learning involves a situation where a change occurs in the work environment propels the manager to acquire new skills or knowledge in order to cope with this change. Voluntary self-directed learning describes a situation where the manager is motivated to learn even though it is not required by the organisation.

Synergistic self-directed learning describes a situation where change induces new learning, yet the manager is also highly motivated to learn.

Cunningham (2002) concluded that much confusion exists in terms of what self-managed learning is and is not. Self-managed learning, at a strategic level, requires the learner to have 'thought through their learning goals and then looked at ways of how to meet them'. He believes that 'learners are assisted to develop a coherent strategy for their learning within which various tactics may be appropriate'. He asserted that self-managed learning differs from open learning, distance learning and e-learning in that the learner has an imposed content by using these mediums. The central tenet of self-managed learning is that the learner is responsible for their learning and they can choose the learning methods to achieve their learning objectives. The optimal level of self-directed learning is where the learner controls the learning objectives and means of learning to achieve these objectives. This is critical to distinguish SDL (self-directed learning) as a learning concept from other forms of learning. This provides a basis for Straka's Two-Shell Model of Motivated Self-Directed Learning (1999). It assumes that in SDL the learner takes control of the choice of learning strategy and the evaluation of the process. The learner must accomplish three different levels of control to self-direct their learning, according to Straka (1999, 2000). The first level is 'cognitive' control, e.g. being able to concentrate for the purpose of learning; the second, 'meta-cognitive' control, e.g. being able to monitor, reflect on and regulate the learning; and last, motivational, e.g. what does the learner expect when they achieve their learning goals, and is that of value? This control enables self-direction only when accompanied by motivation on the part of the learner (i.e. interest). Furthermore, this process is conditioned by both internal and environmental conditions, which we consider later in this chapter.

EXHIBIT 12.2

What do Positive Organisation Studies tell us about Leadership Development and Self-Development?

Positive organisation studies (POS) draw on a number of fields such as psychology, organisational behaviour and sociology, and point to the generative dynamics of organisations that facilitate human strength, healing, resilience and development. Where organisations achieve an understanding of the conditions that enable people to excel, this unlocks human potential, reveals possibilities and enables positive organisational functioning. POS has major implications for how we view the process of leadership and the way organisations develop leaders. Spreitzer highlights a number of principles derived from POS.

- It is important to leverage strengths rather than continually focus on performance gaps. Individuals and organisations should focus on identifying what leaders do best and then find how best to organise work and life around these strengths. Where individuals and organisations leverage strengths, they will perform tasks well, they will learn new things and interact with others to create a positive environment.
- Leaders need challenges to get out of their comfort zones. Leaders need positive jolts to enable them to learn. POS defines jolts as triggers that stimulate growth. They primarily consist of personal experiences that cause the leader to pause and reflect about the meaning and implication of a particular action. They jar because they are outside the leader's typical range of experience. Positive jolts are beneficial for leadership development because they give rise to positive emotions which open leaders up to learning and broadening their perspectives.
- The leveraging of strengths does not, however, mean that weaknesses are ignored. Leaders must learn how to manage their weaknesses. This may mean, in some cases, finding someone else to perform tasks that the leader does poorly. A focus on strengths does not mean that the leader

becomes over-confident. Leaders who become over-confident are less likely to learn and they focus on validating their abilities instead of carrying out their tasks effectively. The leader who focuses on strengths will also remain in learning mode and will strive to develop relationships with others who have complementary strengths.

- Traditional leadership development emphasises the need for the organisation to drive the development process. A POS encourages leaders to co-create support through the building of a durable resource base. Leaders are usually more aware of the contexts that are important in developing their potential. Leaders should therefore focus on developing a supportive context which encourages employees at all levels to develop the resources necessary to thrive in the organisation. Employees can draw from four durable resources: shared knowledge, positive meaning, positive emotions and positive connections. The challenge for the leader is to stimulate and nurture these resources. Leaders also have a major role in regulating these resources. If they are excessively high, they may be detrimental to growth and learning.

- POS emphasise the importance of the leader undertaking an assessment called the Reflected Best Self (RBS). This exercise is designed to enhance the leader's self-knowledge, which facilitates the development of increased authenticity. It is premised on the notion that all leaders have blind spots which make it difficult for them to see the full spectrum of strengths and contributions. The RBS assessment asks leaders to obtain short descriptions of who they are and what they do when they are at their best. It focuses on getting views from a diverse array of significant people. When the leader collects these scores or descriptions, he/she is then able to compose a portrait of his/her best self. The RBS assessment is designed to evoke positive emotions. Positive emotions enable the leader to broaden his/her thought-action repertoires and build enhanced capacities to act. An RBS assessment also helps the leader to develop positive relationships with those who provided feedback. It can lead to the development of relational resources that can be drawn on in times of difficulty. RBS assessments also help to produce a heightened sense of agency and efficacy to help the leader move forward, grow, learn and embrace challenges.

Quinn, Dutton and Spreitzer suggested that RBS can be used to achieve four important objectives in the context of leadership development: 1) to generate awareness of how others see the leader when the leader is at his/her best; 2) to enhance the leader's understanding of the kinds of work situations that bring out the best in him/her; 3) to create personal and career development plans and actions based upon the portrait generated from the reflected best self feedback; and 4) to provide the leader with a tool to get back on track when times are difficult.

There are four key steps involved in composing an RBS portrait.

Step 1 – Identify Respondents: A leader should identify ten to twenty people whom he/she knows well. These may be colleagues, friends, family, customers or any individuals who have extended contact with the leader. It is important that these respondents will give an honest opinion. It is also important to have diversity of opinion. RBS requires that the leader achieves a minimum of ten completed responses.

Step 2 – Compose a Feedback Request Form: The leader should compose a feedback request form which asks each respondent to provide three stories of when the leader was at his/her best.

Step 3 – Analyse Feedback: The leader should read all the feedback and take notes on the key insights. It is important to look for commonalities across the responses. The leader should create themes and link those themes to several examples.

Step 4 – Compose the Reflected Best Self-Portrait: The leader then creates a portrait of his/her best self that captures the wisdom of the data.

This process should help the leader to grow. It focuses the leader's attention on what is important and reinforces learning in leadership development. POS advocates that a positive approach to leadership development increases the probability of sustained development and decreases the chances of leader derailment.

Sources: Spreitzer (2006); Quinn, Dutton and Spreitzer (2004); Roberts *et. al.* (2005)

The Role of Self-Awareness in Self-Development and Self-Managed Learning

Effective managers work hard to increase self-knowledge and insight. Caproni (2005:32) argues that the self-aware manager possesses a 'combination of self-confidence, humility and adaptability that enables them to appreciate the views and styles of others and thrive in the ambiguous, imperfect and often stressful world of management'. A lack of self-insight can lead to the 'empty suit phenomenon' where managers operate in a superficial continuum and exhibit 'much style and dress-for-success dash; little substance, skill or managerial accomplishment'. The concept of the empty suit is similar to Kaplan's (1986) description of the expansive manager. The expansive manager, while successful at a superficial level and committed to the success of the organisation, does not consider self-awareness as important for success. They feel an overarching and debilitating need to control and drive for success at the expense of their health and wellbeing and relationships with others. The success generated from this approach is not pervasive and lasting and the need for control is manifested in a propensity to micromanage with a limited capacity to delegate, thus rendering the management style ineffective. The negative effects of this expansive style are detrimental to the relationship between the manager and the employee and contribute to generating a sense of collaborative disempowerment.

The Nature of Self-Awareness

Self-awareness is a difficult concept to explain and define (Table 12.4). It involves self-knowledge, but self-knowledge can act as both a facilitator and inhibitor of development. Self-knowledge serves to provide a basis from which to develop. Although self-knowledge contributes to better managerial and leadership roles, it may lead to stagnation because of the fear of knowing more.

Whetten and Cameron (2005) suggest that managers have a sensitive line, a point where the manager encounters pressure to alter behaviour, or where the manager becomes defensive or protective when he/she encounters information about self that is inconsistent with his/her current self-concept. When individuals are threatened, they become more rigid. Harris (1981) suggested that the way to get over this rigidity is through self-disclosure. A lack of self-disclosure inhibits self-awareness and impacts on managerial skill development, as well as on self-development. Harris recommended that the process of becoming self-aware can be managed. The manager can exercise some control over the type of information he/she receives and can get help from others in the pursuit of self-understanding. The feedback and support from others enables the manager to become self-aware without crossing the sensitivity line.

Table 12.4: Dimensions of Self-Identity Relevant to Management and Leadership Development

Social Identity
This refers to the extent to which a manager identifies himself/herself as a member of a specific social group and the groups that constitute this social identity.

Organisational Identity
This refers to the extent to which a manager identifies with his/her employing organisation.

> **Work, Career Identity and Values**
> This focuses on how a manager perceives his/her skill set, competencies, values and beliefs that are brought to the workplace. Values focus on the things that are important to the manager.
>
> **Personal Identity**
> This refers to the dimensions that a manager uses to perceive himself or herself. Specific aspects include self-confidence or self-efficacy to achieve a particular managerial task and self-esteem, which is a general evaluation of how a manager feels about himself/herself.
>
> **Personal Identity Clarity**
> This refers to how certain the manager is about his/her core values, needs and interests. This identity will probably change over the manager's lifetime.
>
> **Accuracy of Self-Perception**
> This refers to the fit between a manager's self-perception and the perceptions held by others.
>
> **Identity Learning Ability**
> This refers to the skills of a manager in gathering and utilising new information about the self. It includes feedback seeking and learning ability or the capacity to make changes based on the feedback.

Key areas of self-awareness are highlighted as important for managers. Whetten and Cameron (2005) suggested that managers must be aware of their personal values. These are defined as core to explaining the behaviour of the manager. Managers must understand their orientation towards change, which determines how the manager copes with change. Finally, it is important that the manager understands how he/she interacts with other people. Interpersonal orientation helps explain how assertive the manager is, how open he/she is to new ideas and the level of empathy he/she demonstrates in interpersonal situations. These areas are considered core features of self-awareness.

Barriers to Self-Awareness

Caproni (2005) argues that pressure at work limits self-awareness because there is literally no time to stop and think and evaluate. However, there are advantages to creating time for this in terms of acquiring insightful learning in order to address issues. Managers prevent themselves becoming self-aware because they fear that they might lose the winning formula that has contributed to their career success to date. Managers are promoted on the basis of their previous achievements and behaviours. Therefore, they feel that inner-directed change might interfere with their effectiveness. It is often assumed that self-insight is a mystical phenomenon and can be acquired by a process of osmosis from the workplace or can be assumed by acquiring the status of manager, very like King Arthur bestowing instant wisdom on his knights with the sword of Excalibur.

Stressful working conditions catapult managers back into habitual ways of thinking and acting that might not necessarily alleviate the situation. In fact, stress can destroy managerial effectiveness in that the manager might develop some degree of self-awareness and might recognise the need to change, yet when confronted with difficult situations, he/she reverts to type despite a certain degree of self-awareness. This is viewed as the rubber-band effect, in that behaviour that is recognised as ineffective can be inadvertently reverted to in times of pressure.

Daudelin (1996) argued that making the time for self-reflection and self-analysis is the key to self-awareness, but accepted that managers are under constant pressure at work and do not have time for self-reflection. Managers have a natural propensity to dislike self-reflection because it is time-consuming and somewhat invasive and challenging and they can regard it as a threat to self-concept and self-esteem. Mintzberg (2004) argued that this is a result of a manager's propensity to be action-orientated and task- and results- driven and these factors, combined with a fast-paced business environment, contribute to creating barriers to managerial self-reflection.

Strategies to Enhance Managerial Self-Awareness

Managerial self-awareness can be enhanced in a number of ways. Caproni (2005) suggests the following strategies (Table 12.5).

Table 12.5: Strategies to Develop Managerial Self-Awareness

- Celebrate major achievements in the organisation.
- Use developmental relationships, such as mentoring, to help managers become more self-aware.
- Create sources of support to enable managers to feel psychologically secure and nudge the manager along in his or her development.
- Use self-assessment tools to enable the manager to gain insights concerning career values, work orientations, learning styles and leadership practices.
- Use multi-source feedback to provide both performance and development feedback.
- Encourage managers to use reflection techniques such as learning logs after action reviews to enable them build on past experience and recognise future challenges.
- Provide managers with novel and interesting experiences. These enable the manager to engage in self-exploration and learn more about the self.
- Encourage managers to use self-help books.
- Provide personal development workshops where managers can develop an insight into why they act the way they do.

The achievement of self-knowledge is clearly not easy. Managers need to understand the complexities involved. Caproni argues that managerial self-concept is influenced by interactions with others, the signals we receive from others, and how we interpret them. She suggests that managers must see themselves as:

- Bricoleurs (those managers who tend to try one thing, step back, reconsider and try another), who are able to combine taken-for-granted resources in novel ways to address novel situations.
- Managers of meaning, who can unite diverse employees towards common goals by helping employees make sense of the organisation and their roles in it.
- Multiple selves who are comfortable with a multi-faceted, sometimes conflicting self-concept rather than a stable, unified self-concept.

Self-awareness helps the manager become more effective and forces them to adapt their behaviours in order to increase their effectiveness. It enables the manager to identify skills gaps and development needs and encourages them to find development activities to address those gaps.

EXHIBIT 12.3

The Inner Game of Leadership Development: Focusing on the Development of Intrapersonal Skills

The majority of leadership development activities focus on technical and leadership skills but few focus on understanding the underlying drivers of leadership behaviour. Kaizer and Kaplan argue that it is important for leadership development activities to focus on intrapersonal skills, to examine the basic beliefs and assumptions of the leader and the strategies the leader uses to regulate impulses and emotional needs. They suggest an intrapersonal approach to leadership performance problems which is premised on the view that there is a dynamic integration between responding to a particular challenge and the internal state of the self. Leaders may overdo or underdo certain behaviours. The challenge for leadership development is to help the leader to achieve balance between the vices of deficiency and excess.

Kaiser and Kaplan focus on the notion of sensitivities. These are defined as a leader's 'hot buttons' or 'issues'. They consist of emotionally charged beliefs and expectations that help to protect the leader from repeating a painful situation. These sensitivities act as an alarm system and warn the leader when danger is in sight. Sensitivities operate below the threshold of awareness in the non-verbal experiential information-processing system. When a leader carries around a sensitivity, its roots are to be found in a painful experience in the leader's past. The sensitivity is automatically activated by characteristics of the situation. When the sensitivity is triggered, an alarm is sounded and perceptions become exaggerated because self-protection is the key issue. Sensitivities therefore lead to distortions in leadership behaviour. Sensitivities are not visible to the naked eye, because leaders are very effective at masking them.

Leaders are likely to have a number of sensitivities which lead to the 'overdo' or 'underdo' behaviour:
- **Sensitivities to Intellectual Inadequacies:** Leaders may have concerns about their intelligence. This may be a feeling of inferiority resulting from, for example, not having a degree. Leaders may worry about being 'found out'. Feelings of intellectual inadequacy may result in leaders avoiding activities that are associated with intelligence. They may be slower to engage in activities designed to acquire technical knowledge. Leaders may make too many efforts to prove their intelligence. They may dominate conversations and work extra hard to compensate.
- **Sensitivity to Being Weak:** Leaders are typically perceived to be strong, dominant individuals. Some leaders, however, feel a desire to compensate for feelings of inferiority and they are anxious to prove their strength. They may do too much or too little. When they do too much, they talk, they want always to be right and always win and they come across as arrogant. They may do too little by not delegating or empowering, by not seeking advice and not listening and by not praising or giving encouragement. They have trouble stepping back and letting others learn.
- **Sensitivity to Disapproval or Rejection:** Leaders generally have a strong desire to be liked and often find it difficult to give negative feedback and hold people accountable. They may be slow to remove a manager who is not performing effectively and may fail to make difficult decisions. They are less likely to take a stand and are likely to avoid conflict. Leaders may do too much by sugar-coating tough messages and overreacting to constructive criticism. They may be perceived as 'too nice'.
- **Sensitivity to Depending on Others:** Leaders may find it difficult to trust others because they have been let down in the past in a significant way. They experience difficulties in building a team, they don't delegate or seek help, and they are reluctant to collaborate with peers. Alternatively, leaders may micromanage and try to do it all. They become parochial and focus on their own unit at the expense of the organisation.
- **Sensitivity to Authority:** Some leaders find it difficult to engage in dialogue with authority figures. They are frequently too quick to defer rather than engage in debate. Alternatively, they may engage in attack rather than offer another perspective.

Kaiser and Kaplan acknowledge that it is possible to use leadership development interventions to help a leader whose performance is hampered by a sensitivity. They suggest a number of steps that can be taken.

- **Assessment:** They advise that it is important to start off with a detailed assessment of the individual's leadership in the context of his/her life history. This assessment enables the development of the leader's strengths and limitations. The role of the developer is to bring the leader through the dynamics of how sensitivities play out. This process of reflection can enable the leader to come to terms with private fears and to engage with unrealistic assumptions and expectations that are part of these emotions.
- **Managing Expectations:** It is important for the developer to calibrate expectations. The process of outgrowing a sensitivity is a long-term one and demands a significant shift in the mentality of the leader. It takes a sustained effort on the part of the leader to change behaviours. The leader may also experience a relapse and take some time to achieve lasting change.
- **Deciding on the Development Strategy:** Kaiser and Kaplan suggest two parallel approaches to outgrowing a sensitivity: minimise the disruptive effects of the sensitivity; and/or outgrow the sensitivity. The developmental challenge for the first track focuses on managing symptoms to minimise the disruptive impact of a sensitivity. This requires that the leader must first of all become aware of the sensitivity. The leader must acknowledge that the sensitivity exists. This is likely to be challenging because the leader will likely have many rationalisations and defences to ensure that the sensitivity is protected. The leader must then learn how to recognise the signals. Once these signals have been recognised, the leader can then learn how to 'catch themselves' before a fight or flight response kicks in. The leader will then focus on developing skills to calm the mind and body or learn how to redirect the tension. Leaders then move on to developing techniques to manage their energy. They may also enlist help to keep themselves in bounds. This may include the help of a mentor or advisor.

The second track – outgrowing the sensitivity – involves personal growth in the long term. It involves a process of transformational learning that involves changing the leader's mental model. To start this process of mental transformation, the leader must first of all recognise basic beliefs and tacit assumptions concerning the nature of the self, other people and the world. The leader begins to learn when he/she recognises that tacit beliefs are assumptions rather than self-evident truths. The leader learns to distinguish between facts and assumptions. The leader then begins to grow more comfortable with being in situations that he/she found threatening. The leader begins to free himself/herself from inhibitions. This process will occur in small steps and over time the leader will participate in more risky activities that enable fears to be dealt with. To maximise the learning, it is important that the leader takes time out to reflect. This may be done by keeping a diary or journal. This process of reflection enables the leader to see their values in a new light. The leader will also benefit from social support to help bring about the personal transformation. This may be a coaching or mentoring relationship or support from peers. It is also possible to create a learning community in which leaders can work jointly on their development.

Sources: Kaplan (2002); Kaiser and Kaplan (2006)

Facilitating Self-Managed Learning in Organisations

Proponents of self-managed learning view it as an effective form of learning because it allows managers to be in control of learning strategies and to customise their learning to meet personal needs. One might conclude that a self-directed approach is the only way forward. It is important, however, to understand that the advantages are contextualised and that they may not always apply.

Advantages of Self-Managed Learning

Table 12.6 provides a summary of the advantages of self-directed learning and their implications for both managers and organisations. We comment in more detail on some of these advantages.

Table 12.6: Advantages of Self-Directed Learning and its Impact on Organisation and Individual

Advantages	Effect on Organisation	Effect on Individual
Enables employees to resolve dilemmas independently	Improved problem-solving	Improved morale
Greater learner involvement in the learning process	Improved performance	Increased confidence
Increased willingness and motivation to learn	Better staff morale	Increased motivation
Learners enabled to pursue activities that correspond to their learning needs	Increased learning readiness Improved cost-benefit of training expenditure	Increased relevance of the learning content for the learner
Learning from the individual's own work experiences	Increased employee effectiveness in their jobs	Contentment in his/her job
Learning to learn according to the individual's learning style	Training resources used effectively	Increased motivation to learn
Learners learn to help themselves and each other with practical and timely materials	Reduces training costs substantially Improves communication Long-term payback of learning	Enthusiasm Deeper understanding of subject area Fulfils socialisation needs
Time flexibility	Increased flexibility, unlike conventional 'timetabled' training	Learners can plan learning according to their available time – more convenient
Learning is tailored to job needs	Improved productivity	Enthusiasm for learning
Learner reviews own progress	Leaner can change direction of learning as the organisation changes	Encourages self-analysis and continuous development

Cost-effectiveness and flexibility: Managers benefit from increased flexibility in that they can plan learning to tie in with their time schedules and are not burdened with having to attend a traditional timetabled learning process. The cost-effectiveness of self-managed learning is well documented and self-managed learning can distribute the cost of development evenly amongst all employees (Guglielmino and Murdick 1997). Self-managed learning is an attractive option for organisations as it is cost-effective: the traditional learning model is extremely costly to maintain in terms of competitiveness. It offers efficiency and effectiveness by being relevant, flexible and immediate. It can provide highly focused and timely learning, creating huge cost savings by reducing the cost of learning (Guglielmino and Guglielmino 2001).

The use of e-learning can also contribute to the cost-effectiveness of the self-managed learning process. Cunningham (2002), however, argued against using pure e-learning for self-managed learning purposes and highlights Frankola's (2001) assertion that pure e-learning is not always successful and is associated with high drop-out rates and complaints about the boredom factor; and it is easier to assimilate printed material. Cunningham suggested that e-learning can be solipsistic and individualistic in context and can ignore the social nature of learning.

Greater confidence in problem-solving skills: Self-managed learning can give managers the appropriate strategies to solve problems independently. This leads to improved morale and empowerment in solving problems. Guglielmino and Roberts (1992) observed that, as managers become more self-confident, their ability in independent problem-solving increases.

Broader remit of learning opportunities: Self-directed learning has the capacity to equip managers with a broader remit of learning opportunities outside traditional learning methods as there are many transfer issues associated with classroom-bound learning and development activities. Robotham (1995) suggested that traditional, didactic learning is dependent on memory, and in rapidly changing work environments it is not always easy to remember and apply appropriate theoretical solutions to dynamic workplace problems. The involvement of managers in their learning increases the chances of them becoming more motivated and committed to the learning.

Increases learning relevance and motivation: Learners have the freedom to get involved with learning activities that are directly related to their needs. This ensures that there is a greater relevance of learning content for the learner and that they can learn to assist their own and others' learning with practical, relevant and timely development solutions. This serves to increase the manager's readiness to learn. The manager has the capacity to learn from their own work experience and therefore learning is tailored to their specific job needs. This has the advantage of contributing to managers' effectiveness in their jobs and has the added value of ensuring that learning is not divorced from the workplace and is seen as integral to the job. Learning in this context will improve productivity and increase enthusiasm for learning and contribute to a greater understanding of the workplace and the numerous opportunities presented here for development.

Increased self-awareness and self-mastery: The manager develops the skills to become self-aware, engage in self-analysis and be responsible for continuous development. Therefore, managers need to seek out appropriate development opportunities and decide on the relevance of these to their jobs. They must also be capable of evaluating these opportunities in terms of their potential for learning before and after the event. The manager can use self-managed learning to engage with others and seek balanced and structured feedback on their interaction and performance.

Knowledge sharing: Knowledge sharing is an important advantage of SDL because managers decide for themselves where to find the required knowledge. This has positive implications for financial resources in the organisation. Sharing knowledge allows managers to develop a stronger understanding of the issues being learned and fulfils socialisation needs – an important aspect of motivation to work. This is learning from other people's experiences, but in SDL the learner also draws on their own previous learning experiences, whether these are formal or informal on-the-job experiences. This promotes organisational efficiency because the manager recognises what works and what does not and finds ways of doing the job in a more effective way. This is obviously a benefit for the organisation, but it may also be an advantage for the manager.

Disadvantages of Self-Managed Learning

Self-directed learning does have limitations. Organisations may experience difficulties monitoring, analysing and regulating self-managed learning. They frequently do not fully understand what self-managed learning actually means as a concept. Table 12.7 summarises the disadvantages of self-directed learning and their impact on managers and organisations.

Table 12.7: Disadvantages of Self-Directed Learning and its Impact on Organisation and Individual

Disadvantages	Effect on Organisation	Effect on Manager
Looseness and width of the concept	Difficult to find a 'happy medium' in terms of self-direction and support Difficult to monitor	Causes confusion and perhaps complacency
Requires individual to set learning goals	Not working towards correct target	Not gaining new skills or knowledge
Requires individual to identify learning needs	Inefficient use of training resources	Not fulfilling potential to learn
Fear of taking responsibility for learning	Low morale	Reduced self-esteem
Lack of learner willingness	Unmotivated workforce	Lack of personal development
Lack of facilitation for SDL	Hinders flexibility of workforce	Prevents individual learning according to their learning style
Time flexibility	Learners not investing time and effort needed	Not reaping learning and self-development benefits of SDL
SDL unsuitable in certain situations	Traditional training methods required	Reduced ability of individual to manage learning style and adapt it as required

Difficulty in clarifying the concept: The concept and process of SDL can take a variety of forms. This looseness can make it difficult for the organisation to monitor, regulate and decipher exactly what and how much support to provide to the learner. Confusion about its conceptual basis can lead to difficulties in managing SDL processes in organisations. Organisations may not possess the clarity to implement structures to support SDL.

The absence of a facilitator: The role of the facilitator is one that is often forgotten and this can result in unsuccessful learning interventions. Facilitation must be in place, especially at the early stages, to encourage a manager to diagnose his or her learning style correctly and to decide on appropriate learning objectives. Left solely to the individual learner, learning needs may be incorrectly identified. Consequently, the manager does not learn what is necessary and the organisation wastes resources carrying out the learning programme. If the established objectives are not adequately linked to organisational objectives, or if they are over- or underestimated, the manager is less likely to gain new knowledge or work towards appropriate goals.

Individual manager shortcomings: The individual manager can, in some cases, present problems for the successful implementation of SDL, because of an unwillingness to learn or to take on new responsibility. Time flexibility can be a disadvantage because for certain individuals the learning is never actually completed. Organisational learning is not activated through incomplete learning programmes and the learner misses out on the opportunity for self-development. The potential self-managed learner must have the ability to self-diagnose development needs, develop goals to meet these needs and evaluate learning appropriately. These skills are complex and, if potential development needs are incorrectly diagnosed and implemented, this can impact negatively on the type of learning undertaken. Robotham (1995:4) cautioned that inappropriate learning goals may fail to act as a motivator. The learner may also lack the skills required to set up learning infrastructures, particularly in an organisation not culturally disposed towards self-development. The learner may have developed negative attitudes to learning and may exhibit a reluctance to take responsibility for learning. Organisations need to be aware of the disempowering factors that impede an individual achieving self-managed learning.

Table 12.8: Factors that Facilitate the Success of Self-Directed Learning: Organisational and Individual Perspectives

The Organisation	The Individual
• A supportive organisation culture that embraces the concept of a learning culture • Creating relevant support structures to facilitate self-directed learning • Creating relevant workplace learning opportunities to enhance learning transfer • Ensuring the availability of knowledge and experienced facilitators to assist in the self-directed learning process • Enabling the self-directed learner to transfer learning to the workplace to increase motivation • Encourage knowledge sharing by creating a supportive, nurturing environment that promotes learning networks • Developing an equitable, challenging learning environment that does not intimidate • Reward issues; the organisation rewards self-directed learning initiatives and integrates rewards into the performance management system	• An individual who understands the concept of self-directed learning and is skilled in self-directed learning behaviours • An individual who demonstrates high levels of self-efficacy and belief in oneself as a learner • An individual who is self-aware, self-reflective, self-analytical and has the ability to recognise and accept learning gaps • An individual who demonstrates a positive attitude to learning • An individual who is self-motivated and self-disciplined • The individual needs to be capable of moving from traditional approaches to learning and be able to overcome any fears associated with change • The individual needs to be capable of managing their time and ensuring that the organisation gives them the time to learn

Conditions Conducive to Self-Directed Learning

A multiplicity of factors help to explain the success or otherwise of self-directed learning for managers. Table 12.9 summarises these organisational and individual factors.

Table 12.9 Supporting Self-Directed Learning in Organisations: Key Research Findings

- Self-directed learning is an approach to management and leadership development in which the learner takes responsibility for the learning process and content. It allows managers to determine their learning requirements and goals, select resources to achieve the goals, decide upon and employ their preferred learning strategies, and assess the outcomes of the leadership process.
- Research suggests that managers can be allowed to have control over nine learning variables in a management and leadership development context:
  - Identifying leadership development needs
  - Selecting topics and goals for learning
  - Identifying expected learning outcomes
  - Determining what evaluation methods will identify the success or otherwise of the learning
  - Selecting the learning experiences
  - Choosing the learning methods
  - Structuring the learning environment
  - Setting the pace of the learning process
  - Selecting methods to document the learning.
- Self-directed learning may result in greater levels of satisfaction with the development process; however, its effectiveness depends on the maturity level of the manager and the manager's comfort with a self-directed approach.
- Self-directed learning does require that the leadership development specialist is prepared to relinquish control. The specialist needs to be clear about the expectations of each party and to understand the key deliverables.
- A key issue explaining the success of a self-directed approach concerns the variety of learning materials that are available to managers. A range of learning approaches such as chat rooms, 'ask the expert' sessions, and joint problem-solving groups should be available to managers.
- Managers who have particular human capital characteristics are more likely to be more effective self-directed learners:
  - The nature of the manager's job responsibilities are related to self-directed learning readiness.
  - Years of work experience will influence the self-directed learning of managers in a positive way, making them more confident.
  - Self-directedness will be influenced by the manager's participation in educational activities in the past.
  - Managers who are positive about their past career tend to think about their career as something they are able to influence and manage themselves. Managers with a positive past career are more willing to self-direct their learning.
- Personality characteristics are likely to be influential in predicting self-directedness in learning and development. Managers with a proactive personality are more likely to be self-directed. A proactive personality involves a manager actively shaping the situations in which they find themselves.
- Managers with strong career ambition and who pursue knowledge focused on personal skill development are likely to be self-directed. Mobility aspiration is a strong predictor of self-directed learning. Managers who pursue vertical mobility are more likely to self-direct their learning.
- Three organisational characteristics are important in explaining a manager's self-directed learning:
  - A positive learning environment will support the position that every manager in an organisation is in continuous learning mode, searching, trying, sharing ideas and learning from others.
  - The organisation's leadership development policies will also be important. Do policies involve situations where the manager is presented with learning opportunities? Do they set a climate that is favourable to the emergence of self-directed learning practices?
  - The organisation's participation policy is also important. High participation levels and decentralised management stimulate better organisational support for self-directedness in learning processes.
- Self-directed learning behaviours can be facilitated in traditional leadership development programmes through the developer or leadership development specialist adopting a facilitating approach to teaching.

- Instead of asking questions that have a preconceived correct answer, they may probe, while suspending some of their presuppositions about the answer, so as to concentrate their full attention on the student's reasoning.
- Instead of first jumping in to provide their expertise to solve an individual or team problem, they may let managers offer their solutions to each other and acknowledge that their ideas can be mutually enriching.
- Instead of masking their lack of knowledge with an obfuscated answer, they may acknowledge their ignorance, often along with a view on how all might approach the problem at hand.
- Instead of allowing participants to downplay their experience as compared to their own wealth of academic study, they may reinforce the value of their practice knowledge while looking for ways to make it more accessible to participants.
- Instead of over-preparing their lecture presentations to demonstrate their clarity of thought, they may concentrate on how to introduce new material using multiple methods and entry points to appeal to managers' diversity of learning styles.
- Instead of requiring managers to write concept-based reports from their experiences in the field, they may encourage them to journal on these experiences using their own style and idiom but prompted by questions that might include deeper reflections.
- Instead of encouraging managers to offer opinions to one another, they may invite them to ask good genuine questions to bring out the collective knowledge of everyone.
- Instead of seeking consensus on a controversial topic, they may express tolerance for a resolution of indeterminacy in order to promote ongoing reflection on the topic.

An appropriate organisation context: Cunningham (2004) suggested that self-managed learning processes need to mirror organisational development and the demands of work. Furthermore, the organisation's commitment to SDL must be at a philosophical level rather than simply as a programme. There is a need to resolve the conflict between the manager's concern about development and advancement and the organisation's focus on achieving its objective and this requires a negotiated compromise.

Conducive social and cultural norms: Self-directed learning requires value changes within the organisation. It involves an acceptance of diversity. Guglielmino and Guglielmino (2001) argued that an organisation culture that supports learning is vital for the effective implementation of self-directed learning. Self-directed learners need to be exposed to a learning environment that facilitates the transfer of knowledge and allows learners to engage in knowledge sharing and accessing knowledge within and outside the organisation. There also needs to be a safe environment where self-directed learners can discuss their learning problems and needs. Fisher (2002) suggested that the organisation needs to create an environment of openness and trust that is conducive to the development of learning networks which allow the individual the flexibility to develop, evaluate and measure their learning. Creating support structures is particularly important in that the individual needs to avoid the barriers that would naturally impede their learning. The organisation needs to recognise the wealth of learning opportunities provided by the workplace and equip employees with the skills to recognise and harness these opportunities. This gives the learner the satisfaction of successfully transferring the learning to the workplace, which in turn increases motivation.

Rewards: In order to encourage managers to engage in self-directed learning activities, the organisation needs to reward individuals for being involved in the process. Guglielmino and Guglielmino (2001) suggested that the rewards need to be clearly communicated to the learner and be implemented by the organisation. Thompson *et al.* (2001) cautioned that it is important to ensure that rewards are appropriate for the learner to sustain and maintain motivation. These rewards can be many and various, but there must be a relevant motivator for the self-directed learner. Rewards for self-directed learning can include:

- Career advancement related to the learning and skills developed through self-directed learning.
- Status: the manager can be perceived as the subject-matter expert with all the referent power associated with this.
- Financial reward: the organisation can ensure that managers who engage in self-directed learning are suitably rewarded by giving them extra payments in their salaries. This will reinforce the benefits of engaging in self-directed learning to the managers and their colleagues who, in turn, will be more motivated to engage in self-directed learning.

A changed role for leadership development: Self-directed learning requires a different type of role performance from the leadership development specialist. This role involves facilitation. The characteristics of an effective facilitator include a deep knowledge of facilitated learning, skill in motivating and assisting the manager to achieve learning goals without disempowering his/her learning, skill in moving in and out of the learning process as the situation and the manager require, assistance in breaking down learning barriers, developing managers' learn-to-learn skills and empowering managers to evaluate their learning. Smith and Sadler-Smith (2006) suggest the following as possible strategies that can be implemented by the leadership development specialist (Table 12.10).

Table 12.10: Strategies to Facilitate Self-Directed Learning in Organisations

Assistance to managers
- Grounding new learning goals in a context of experience, existing knowledge, and an appreciation of the place of learning in 'becoming' skilled and knowledgeable
- Understand their learning within the broader context of the workplace
- Developing and negotiating learning goals
- Developing and negotiating a learning plan and learning contract, starting with limited contracts prior to developing towards more comprehensive contracts
- Identifying authentic tasks and learning resources through which the learning contract is to be pursued
- Identifying and accessing other experts who can provide demonstration, discussion and guided practice
- Developing a structured approach to completing the learning contract negotiated between the learner and trainer
- Developing monitoring of learning as it proceeds, and the self-evaluation of learning outcomes
- Providing regular discussion with managers on their learning contract
- Recognising and reviewing achievements as learning proceeds, and assistance to modify learning contracts on the basis of that feedback
- Encouraging cognitive and meta-cognitive skills such as anticipation and question-asking, strategy planning and analysis, wider use of learning resources, monitoring of learning processes, and articulation of knowledge
- Providing opportunity within the production schedule for withdrawal to make use of learning resources.

Source: Smith and Sadler-Smith (2006:161)

The characteristics of the manager: The characteristics of the manager are particularly important in explaining whether self-managed learning will be effective. The manager needs to be open to learning opportunities. He/she needs to possess a positive self-concept of learning. The manager must love learning, take responsibility for learning and demonstrate initiative and independence.

Sadler-Smith (2006) argues that older, mature learners are more likely than younger managers to engage with self-directed, self-managed learning. However, given the significant changes that are now a feature of organisations, younger managers are expected to be more motivated to learn.

Robotham (1995) suggested that managers need to be encouraged to develop insights into motivation towards self-direction in learning and to develop self-awareness in how to achieve self-direction in learning. Managers should also gain an understanding of the key processes used by self-directed learners to achieve learning objectives and understand how the social and physical environment impacts and affects learning.

Cunningham (2002) described a strategic approach that self-managed learners can use to initiate self-managed learning.

- *Problems*: Identifying a suitable learning problem to stimulate the learning process, e.g. using the outputs of a 360-degree feedback exercise to address team affiliation problems.
- *Persons*: Using their own personal skills reservoirs and those of other people to learn, e.g. using team dynamics, coaches, communities of practice and their bosses.
- *Patterns*: Identifying inappropriate habits that may be inhibiting their effectiveness as managers and addressing these appropriately, e.g. time management or negative leadership styles.
- *Plans*: Certain issues like globalisation or rapid changes in technology might drive the need for further learning, e.g. new IT.
- *Processes*: The organisation facilitates change by using specific processes of working and coping with change. An individual will have to adapt to these processes and learn how to cope, e.g. learn how to become more flexible and adaptable.

Cunningham (2002) advocated the need to move from 'this "P" word (problems, persons, patterns, plans and processes) to the "S" word, which is characterised by applying solutions to these learning problems by identifying appropriate subjects (academic) and learn skills/systems and specialists to address the "P" issues'. He highlighted the need to move to the 'S' word to become a more effective manager and leader. The most effective managers and leaders must understand how to learn and develop in an organisational context using all the learning tools available to help at the time.

It is possible to determine the manager's ability to self-direct and to quantify this ability using the self-directed learning readiness scale (SDLRS). Designed by Guglielmino and Guglielmino (1992), this instrument measures the manager's willingness and ability to engage in self-directed learning. Research using the scale demonstrated that that the manager's willingness towards self-directed learning positively correlated with job performance. Guglielmino and Guglielmino (2001) found that managers with high SDLRS scores prefer to establish their own learning needs and implement their own learning strategies. Despite having a natural tendency towards empowerment in their learning approach, they are also capable of engaging in structured learning environments. Chien (2004) demonstrated that managers with lower than average SDLRS scores favour more structured traditional learning environments. However, if managers feel that in order to succeed they need to engage in self-directed learning, their readiness for self-directed learning also increases.

The Learning Contract as a Vehicle for Self-Managed Learning

A learning contract is a useful method of helping organisations to support the self-development of their managers. The learning contract is similar to a personal development plan, setting out aims and objectives for learning, outlining which activities will be undertaken and what resources are needed.

A learning contract is a very useful tool to assist in the implementation of self-directed learning. It is a written agreement between a manager, an employee and a facilitator of learning. It is a means of helping learners structure learning projects systematically in order to involve them actively in their own learning. Learning contracts comprise four key interrelated components: objectives, learning plans, implementation and evaluation. Garavan and Sweeney (1994) argued that the advantage of the learning contract is that it keeps the learner focused on the achievement of their learning goals; it empowers them to be responsible for their learning and ensures the application of this learning back in the workplace. The characteristics of effective learning contracts are outlined in Table 12.11.

Table 12.11: Characteristics of Learning Contracts

- Learners will learn more effectively because learning-centred involvement will make them more likely to be committed and motivated to learn.
- Learners are provided with the opportunity to work towards satisfying their own development needs within the organisational context.
- The learner-centred approach of the learning contract implies a willingness on behalf of the employee to take responsibility for his/her own learning and its application to the workplace.
- In order to create a climate where the employee takes on those responsibilities, it is necessary for the trainer to modify his/her role from instructor to teacher to facilitator and become a resource to both the employee and his/her manager.
- Managing the learning climate to facilitate a learning-centred approach involves removing or neutralising the internal (personal) and external (work environment) barriers to learning.
- Learning contracts are comprised of sequential steps that inherently involve a review by the employee of the process as well as the content of the learning. Gold (1990) found this to have significant benefits – not only did it review past activities but also 'it plays a potent part in the build-up of understanding that allows a person qualitatively to enhance the planning of future actions'.
- Learning contracts are based on real organisational problems in a specific workplace context.
- Through the application of learning, employees can see positive results from their efforts. This sense of achievement tends to be a further motivator for learning and improvement.
- Qualitative as well as quantitative objectives can be successfully catered for in a learning contract.

Source: Garavan and Sweeney (1994:19)

A negotiated learning contract can be used by the learner as a development instrument, and the potential benefits for both the manager and the organisation are significant. Nevertheless, if the process is ineffectively managed, the effect of the learning contract may produce a barren and unrewarding learning experience. These potential advantages and disadvantages are illustrated in Table 12.12.

Table 12.12: Advantages and Disadvantages of Learning Contracts

Advantages	Disadvantages
• Support individualised learning and flexible learning • Enhance self-reflection, learning to learn and self-management • Provide learners with clear goals and pathways for achieving these, based on their own learning needs • Make explicit what the learner plans to learn • Promote communication between the learner and the facilitator • Increase learner dedication to learning • Can measure qualitative and quantitative goals • Evaluation of the learner's attainment of learning goals is continuous, thus ensuring correct objectives are met	• Can be inflexible and not take into account changes in learner's needs and goals • Learner may not be learning what is needed to fulfil organisational goals • No guarantees of satisfactory learning outcomes • Deviation can be viewed as not fulfilling goals, even when organisational changes demand it • May result in negative relationship if no agreement is established • May result in the isolation of the learner • Possible ineffective time management for daily tasks by the learner • The importance of goals will depend on the pressure of key stakeholders and not necessarily the individual learner • Time-consuming process

Conclusion

Self-directed learning ideas have emerged to assist organisations keep abreast of rapid change and to ensure that managers enhance their employability. In order to survive and thrive, managers need to develop their capacity for self-awareness by taking time for self-reflection, developing their emotional intelligence and seeking insights and feedback from significant others on their skills, attitudes and behaviours in the workplace. This form of awareness can assist managers to take personal responsibility for their own development and become less reliant on the organisation.

There are a number of interpretations of the concept of development, and organisations take specific approaches depending on their learning orientation. Self-managed learning presents high levels of intellectual and psychological challenge despite the difficulties associated with achieving self-managed learning in organisations.

Self-managed learning involves the manager initiating the learning, making the decisions regarding both the type of learning activity that will take place and how it will take place. Self-managed learning refers not only to the manager having the capability to choose the method of achieving the goal, but also to the manager selecting the goal itself, and the measure for showing attainment. Thus, self-directed learning is very 'tight' on the learning process, on learning how to learn and solving problems, but it is very 'loose' on learning content, on the specific information that is required and how to solve particular problems.

Self-directed or self-managed learning has significant implications for the organisation's leadership and development activities. SDL is not sufficient alone; it is important that organisations recognise this and use SDL in conjunction with other learning strategies. While the responsibility for SDL lies, for the most part, with the manager, failure can occur if not adequately facilitated by the organisation. Thus, the leadership development specialist needs to provide a facilitator throughout the process. The specialist should also ensure that the skills learned are transferable to the manager's working environment. The focal manager must be ready and motivated to learn, as they are the key person in self-directed learning and will take personal responsibility for their own learning.

Summary of Key Points

- Self-development and self-managed learning processes have emerged in response to increased organisational complexity and a desire on the part of managers to manage their own careers and employability.
- The concept of development is understood in a number of different ways. How development is used and discovered depends on the manager's values and attitudes and the organisation's philosophy and approach to development.
- Self-development and self-managed learning are a response to more traditional leadership development approaches which created a dependency relationship between the developer and the manager.
- For the individual manager, self-directed learning emphasises the need to be motivated and ready to learn, to have the self-confidence to learn and to possess the skills to learn effectively. Most important of all, it requires strong self-awareness.
- Learning contracts are a valuable tool to encourage managers to plan and manage their learning. They provide a mechanism to individualise and customise learning and to increase the motivation of the manager to achieve learning goals.

■ Discussion Questions

1. Critically evaluate the various notions of development described in this chapter and outline their implications for self-managed learning.

2. What can an organisation do to encourage self-managed learning processes?

3. Why is self-awareness a fundamental component of self-development processes?

4. What implications does career self-management have for leadership development processes in organisations?

5. How can a learning contract be used to assist in self-managed learning?

■ Application and Experiential Questions

1. Based on what you have learned in this chapter, select two aspects of self-awareness and write a plan concerning how you can think and behave differently.

2. Draft a learning contract. Involve your manager in the discussion and identify your responsibilities and accountabilities under the contract.

3. In groups of three or four, draft a proposal for presentation to the senior management team which sets out a case to include self-managed learning as part of its leadership development strategy. Explain how you will implement this approach in the organisation. You have twenty minutes to complete the task. You will then role play your presentation to the class, who will act as the senior management team.

Chapter Thirteen

Career Management and Development

Outline

Learning Objectives

After reading this chapter you will be able to:

- Explain concepts such as career planning and career management.
- Describe contemporary perspectives on careers, including boundaryless and protean careers.
- Explain what is involved in career management and describe various models of career management.
- Describe career management practices that can be implemented in the organisation.
- Describe and evaluate issues that affect the career development of women and plateaued managers, and career development issues in flat organisations.
- Outline and explain the issues to be considered when designing career development processes in organisation.

OPENING CASE SCENARIO

Mapping Protean Careers: Bono and Mary Robinson

Paul Hewson, otherwise known as Bono, was born in May 1960 in Dublin. He was originally nicknamed 'Bono Vox' by a schoolfriend. He is also known by a number of other alter egos, including the Sonic Leprechaun, the Mother Teresa of Abandoned Songs, the Fly and Mirrorball Man. His father Bobby described Bono as 'a bloody exasperating child' and he soon acquired a reputation as a somewhat absent-minded and argumentative teenager. He was given the nickname 'The Antichrist' by friends and family. He was also considered to be curious and starry-eyed, and he had a tendency to view the world through rose-tinted glasses, while at the same time questioning everything. A significant development in the early life of Bono was the loss of his mother when he was fifteen years old. This significant life event was responsible for Bono's restless and inquisitive nature. At about this time Bono was also drawn to music. His early influences included bands such as Patti Smith, Thin Lizzy, Television and the Ramones. At school he experimented with a variety of artistic mediums and he proved himself to be a strong networker. He was a good painter. While at school he had many girlfriends who admired his romantic nature. He participated in the school theatre group in which he performed as a singer. In 1976 Bono answered an advert he found on a bulletin board in Mount Temple Comprehensive School, which instructed interested performers to come to the house of Larry Mullen Junior. This was the start of the band that became U2, which is now one of the world's most successful and famous rock groups. Bono was initially accepted as part of the group because of his songwriting ability and theatrical persona. Vocally he was not considered a very effective singer and he was not able to play a guitar. However, over the years his voice has evolved and has shown considerable versatility. This is nowhere more evident than when you listen to a succession of albums such as *Boy*, *War*, *The Unforgettable Fire*, *The Joshua Tree*, *Rattle and Hum* and the band's most recent album, *Vertigo*. U2 have gone through many musical changes, but the band has managed to keep its music connected. Bono's music career has been as a socially conscious songwriter. He has used his lyrics to inspire the crowds and he is particularly effective in his live performances. Fans of U2 agree that their live recordings exhibit a particular uniqueness. They demonstrate the ultimate in creative freedom. Bono possesses a tremendous ability to connect with an audience during a concert. The often-cited example of this ability is during the Live Aid concert in 1985 when, during a performance, he leapt off the stage over a security barricade and pulled a woman up from the crowd to dance with her.

To date Bono and U2 have had an exceptionally successful artistic career. They have won more Grammy Awards (nineteen) than any other group in the world and they are the holders of three Best Album awards. Bono is highly respected both within and outside the music industry. Beyond U2, Bono has branched out and pursued other projects and causes. He has emerged as a major social activist and champion of the poor. He has used his many connections, including actors, musicians and politicians, to pursue his many causes. One of his special projects is the campaign to end Third World debt. Bono has a broad network of powerful friends and includes among his numerous acquaintances former US president Bill Clinton, Bill Gates, Sean Penn, Sir Bob Geldof, Mohammad Ali and Jack Nicholson, to name but a few. He is considered to be a genuine and generous person and has exceptional social and interpersonal competence. In 2005 Bono was named by *Time* Magazine as one of the most influential people in the world. He has used his profile and popularity to pursue his vision and champion causes which are not always popular with politicians.

Mary Robinson is an Irish leader who has shown vision and courage throughout her still thriving career. Mary Robinson was born in May 1944 in Ballina, County Mayo. She became a barrister and was appointed Reid Professor of Criminal Law in Trinity College at the age of twenty-five. In 1988, with her husband Nicholas, she founded the Irish Centre for European Law. She was a member of Seanad Éireann from 1969 to 1989 and served on many parliamentary committees. On 3 December 1990 Mary Robinson was inaugurated as the seventh president of Ireland. She significantly changed the focus and nature of the office, bringing a strong sense of justice and compassion to her role as president and placing a strong emphasis on cultural plurality and the recognition of diversity. She has campaigned throughout her career on a wide range of issues including civil rights, the rights of women, homosexuality, law reform, the rights of Travellers, and, in Northern Ireland, the rights of Unionists to be considered in the Anglo-Irish agreement. Throughout her tenure as president she acted as a peacemaker and presented an image of Ireland that was dynamic, imaginative and charitable.

Following an extremely successful tenure as president of Ireland, Mary Robinson served as United Nations Commissioner for Human Rights. She became the first commissioner to visit Tibet despite objections from China. She also travelled to other countries including Cambodia, China, Rwanda and South Africa. Her task during her five years as High Commissioner was to integrate human rights activities into all United Nations activities. She has frequently articulated that her own approach to human rights is based on an 'inner sense of justice'. She championed a multiplicity of causes during this period, including issues concerning development, the rights of indigenous people, gender issues, the rights and empowerment of people with disabilities and the accountability of organisations in furthering human rights. She is considered to have been extremely successful and on many occasions she upset governments that did not have a good understanding of human rights issues. She demonstrated an excellent understanding of diplomacy and her credibility in civil rights issues gave her a strong background to succeed. She was never silenced and she sought nothing less than the enforcement of international human rights laws.

In 2004, Mary Robinson established the Ethical Globalisation Initiative which carries on the human rights advocacy she performed as High Commissioner. She is working to ensure that corporations adhere to the human rights standards that all human beings require to live with dignity. She is also concerned to bring a human rights agenda to the issues of trade, migration and Aids. She is concerned that 'economic and social rights have to go hand in hand with political rights'.

Mary Robinson has received many prizes and honorary doctorates during her career. Among the prizes she has been awarded are the Global Leadership Award of the United Nations Association of New York, the Fulbright Prize for International Understanding, the Erasmus Prize, the Indira Gandhi Peace Prize and the Sydney Peace Prize. She holds doctorates from Cambridge, Harvard, Yale and Columbia, amongst others. She is currently Chair of the Council of Women Leaders and Professors of Practice in International Affairs at Columbia University. She has shown a consistent focus on what is practical, as well as a clear vision, persistence and a strong intellectual credibility. She has, like many great leaders, shown courage, tolerance and an energy to pursue issues which in some cases are unpopular with both governments and corporations.

QUESTIONS

Q.1   What are the similarities between the careers of Mary Robinson and Bono?

Q.2   What particular career metaphors are most useful to describe the careers of Bono and Mary Robinson?

Career management and development are key issues for organisations, especially where managers and leaders are concerned. Like management and leadership development, career management and development focus on the future. A recurring theme throughout this book has been the speed of change in organisations recently and the resulting need for continuous learning at all levels within them. This has had an impact on career systems designed and implemented by human resource professionals, in partnership with line management, with the overall goal of achieving business success. Organisations are beginning to realise that their greatest asset is their people. Academics and practitioners are therefore consumed with 'The War for Talent'. In other words, how do organisations attract, retain and motivate key managers on an ongoing basis?

In this type of environment, career development is a key success factor for the individual and the organisation. As stated by King (2004:10), 'The crucial point to make is that, at a time when many employers are facing recruitment difficulties, developing resources from within is critical for future growth and sustained competitive advantage.' As practitioners in the field will know, it is not always easy to achieve the right balance between individual and organisational goals, and this presents a key challenge in career development within the organisation. The 1980s and 1990s were characterised by organisational downsizing and delayering and these changes, among other factors, have challenged the traditional hierarchical career model. Therefore, organisations and individuals have had to redefine the meaning of the word career and, in particular, the idea of a career for life. Today, career development can mean lateral and downward moves, as well as moving upwards.

These changes have raised a number of important questions for the career development of managers and leaders. Is career development the responsibility of the individual or the organisation? What impact have these changes had on the old psychological contract? Who are the key players in making career management work? These are some of the dilemmas raised in this chapter. Managers have the primary responsibility for developing their careers. Equally, the organisation has a role to play in enabling managers to take ownership of their careers. The balance between meeting individual and organisational needs for career management is at the heart of the issues that we discuss in this chapter.

The Changing Context of Career Management and Development

We discussed in Chapter Two a number of contextual issues that can influence career management and the development of leaders. We summarise here some of the specific issues that impact on the careers of managers. The new employment relationship is characterised by a shift in emphasis away from the notion of entitlement to that of a two-way deal. Traditionally, career development was viewed as primarily an organisational responsibility. The aim was to ensure that managerial ranks were filled with individuals who fitted the organisation's culture and were sufficiently competent. Promotion was primarily from within and career development practices focused on creating a strong internal labour market to meet the future requirements of the organisation. This situation has given way to an organisational context of unpredictability and change, one which Hall (1996) has described as 'permanent white water'.

Cooper (2005) highlighted a number of changes that have significantly impacted on career development processes in organisations. These include, but are not confined to, the following:

*   Increasing workload for individuals, both in terms of hours worked per week and the intensity of effort required during each working hour.
*   Oganisational changes, particularly the elimination of layers of management (delayering) and reductions in the number of people employed (downsizing).
*   Increased global competition, which means that organisations in Western countries need to control costs and also make maximum use of employees' skills and ideas.
*   More team-based work, where individuals with different types of expertise are brought together for a limited period to work on a specific project with clear goals.
*   More short-term contracts, where the length of a manager's employment is specified at the outset. Renewal of the contract when it has expired is the exception, not the norm.
*   More self-employment and employment in small organisations. Nearly half of the people in work in the United Kingdom and Ireland are either self-employed or work in organisations with fewer than twenty employees.
*   Working at or from home. Advances in communications technology and cost-cutting by employers mean that more managers either work from home or are permanently based there.

These changes have resulted in managers thinking differently about their careers and pose more challenges to organisations in terms of managing careers. Some of the more frequently highlighted challenges include:

- A greater need for managers to look ahead and ensure that they update their skills and knowledge in order to remain employable. Development, therefore, is lifelong, not confined to childhood and early adulthood.
- Organisations, too, need to look ahead in order to develop the skills and knowledge required for future survival.
- Less frequent promotions within organisations and (because of delayering) bigger increases in status and responsibility when promotions do happen.
- Less time (and often energy) is left over for a manager to consider his or her future.
- A greater need for managers to make an effort to build up and maintain their networks of contacts.
- A greater need for older managers, as well as younger ones, to initiate and cope with change.
- A greater need for skills of entrepreneurship, self-management and small business management.
- A greater need for managers to be able to handle uncertainty.
- A greater need for managers to be flexible in terms of the work they are prepared to do and the people with whom they are able to work constructively.

There is widespread agreement, in the academic and practitioner literature, that managers need to more fully understand the nature of their employer's business; they must assume responsibility for skill development; and they must consistently demonstrate value to the organisation. Employers are expected to provide development opportunities, to involve managers in decisions concerning careers and to focus on the measurement of performance.

Table 13.1 summarises some of the changes in the nature of career management in organisations.

Table 13.1: The Old Versus the New Career Paradigm in Organisations

New Career Paradigm	Old Career Paradigm
Discrete exchange means:	The mutual loyalty contract means:
• Explicit exchange of specified rewards in return for task performance	• Implicit trading of employee compliance in return for job security
• Basing job rewards on the current market value of the work being performed	• Allowing job rewards to be routinely defined into the future
• Engaging in disclosure and renegotiation on both sides as the employment relationship unfolds	• Leaving the mutual loyalty assumptions as a political barrier to renegotiation
• Exercising flexibility as each party's interests and market circumstances change	• Assuming employment and career opportunities are standardised and prescribed by the firm
Occupational excellence means:	The one-employer focus means:
• Performance of current job in return for developing new occupational expertise	• Relying on the firm to specify jobs and their associated occupational skill base
• Employees identifying with and focusing on what is happening in their adopted occupation	• Employees identifying with and focusing on what is happening in their particular firm
• Emphasising occupational skill development over the local demands of any particular firm	• Forging technical or functional development in favour of firm-specific learning
• Getting training in anticipation of future job opportunities; having training lead to jobs	• Doing the job first to be entitled to new training; making training follow jobs

New Career Paradigm	Old Career Paradigm
Organisational empowerment means: • Strategic positioning is dispersed to separate business units • Everyone is responsible for adding value and improving competitiveness • Business units are free to cultivate their own markets • New enterprise, spin-offs, and alliance building are broadly encouraged	The top-down firm means: • Strategic direction is subordinated to 'corporate headquarters' • Competitiveness and added value are the responsibility of corporate experts • Business unit marketing depends on the corporate agenda • Independent enterprise is discouraged and likely to be viewed as disloyalty
Project allegiance means: • Shared employer and employee commitment to the overarching goal of the project • A successful outcome of the project is more important than holding the project team together • Financial and reputational rewards stem directly from project outcomes • Upon project completion, organisations and reporting arrangements are broken up	Corporate allegiance means: • Project goals are subordinated to corporate policy and organisational constraints • Being loyal to the work group can be more important than the project itself • Financial and reputational rewards stem from being a 'good soldier' regardless of results • Social responsibility within corporate boundaries are actively encouraged

Source: Nelson and Campbell (1997)

Defining Career Development Concepts

Three particular concepts need to be defined in the context of this chapter: career; career development planning and multiple perspectives of a career. Career terms have been subjected to multiple interpretations in the literature. They are also discoursed by managers and leadership development specialists in different ways.

What is a Career?

This is a difficult question to answer. There are many definitions of career in the current literature. These definitions tend to reflect an individual and/or organisational perspective. Woodall and Winstanley (1998:40) suggested that 'much career theory has centered around the individually focused subjective career, whereas most organizational career development activity has centered around career management. This is ironical, as current developments within organisations are challenging conventional assumptions about career management and impelling organizations to devote more attention to individual career planning'. Table 13.2 summarises a number of contemporary definitions.

Table 13.2: Contemporary Definitions of a Career

Definition	Author
The Meaning of Career • Career implies a route to be followed which has direction and purpose. • There is movement over time which has order, logic and meaning between successive points. • In organisations, employers and employees can plan the logical progression through work-related events and experiences. • Over the course of one's life, a career can pass through a number of stages.	Adamson, Doherty and Viney (1998)

Definition	Author
A career refers to the individual sequence of attitudes and behaviour associated with work-related experiences and activities over the span of the person's life. • Career is a process. • Career success or failure is not based on promotion or advancement.	Noe (2005:352)
Career can be defined as the sequence of jobs that a person has during his or her working life. • Career encompasses a wide range of occupational experiences. • Careers don't necessarily involve promotion or progression. • Careers frequently cross occupational and organisational boundaries.	King (2004:6)
Career development is the process used to create opportunities for employees' professional interests and capabilities and to help meet current and future business needs.	Joy-Matthews, Megginson and Surtees (2004:148)
The core concept (career) suggests the experience of continuity and coherence while the individual moves through time and social space . . . However, 'career' refers not only to the observable movement through and experiences in organisations and the social structure generally. That is their objective career, while the personal interpretation they make of those experiences, the private meaning and significance it has for them, is their subjective career.	Beardwell, Holden and Claydon (2004:290)
A career is 'a process of development by (an) employee along a path of experience and roles in one or more organisations'.	Baruch (2004:3)
Career denotes a subjective construction that imposes personal meaning on past memories, present experiences and future aspirations, by weaving them into a life theme that patterns the individual's work life. • Careers do not unfold. • They are constructed as individuals make choices that express their self-concepts and substantiate their goals in the social reality of work roles.	Savickas (2005:43)
Career is the pattern of work-related experiences that span the course of a person's life.	Greenhaus, Callanan and Godshalk (2000)

- Conceptualisations of what constitutes a career have broadened significantly. It traditionally involved a sequence of related jobs, but can now include a significant number of unrelated jobs.
- Career can be viewed as a property of an occupation. This occurs when it is used to describe a manager's tenure in the organisation or the specific occupation in which the manager works, e.g. sales or human resources.
- There is a mutual dependency between the individual and the organisation in terms of enabling a career.
- Career consists of a process or sequence of phases as well as objective and subjective elements.
- Career has traditionally been associated with advancement, but more recent definitions recognise the multiplicity of work-related paths that managers engage in.

The working definition of a career for the remainder of this chapter will be Baruch's (2004) definition, to the effect that a career is '. . . a process of development by [an] employee along a path of experience and roles in one or more organisations'. This definition encompasses all of the key features discussed above.

What is Career Development?

Greenhaus, Callanan and Godshalk (2000) defined the overall process of career development as 'an ongoing process by which individuals progress through a series of stages, each of which is characterised by a relatively unique set of issues, tasks, themes and roles'. They suggest that career development consists of two distinct activities: career planning; and career management.

- *Career Planning*: This is defined as a process consisting of four elements. It is planned and deliberate, it focuses on enhancing the self-awareness of managers, it focuses on career-related goals and it specifies career development experiences designed to enhance career attainment. Greenhaus, Callanan and Godshalk (2000) viewed career planning as an activity performed by individual managers. The role of the organisation is to provide support and assistance.
- *Career Management*: This is defined as an organisational process focused on integrating individual career plans with the organisation's career systems. It may include elements of succession and talent management and is likely to focus on preparing leaders for future positions in the organisation.

Hall (1986) suggested that career management can be viewed along a career development spectrum. He suggested that career management activities vary according to: 1) the amount of influence which the individual manager has on the process; 2) the amount of information which the organisation provides to the individual; 3) the amount of influence that the organisation has on the manager's career; and 4) the amount of information provided by the manager to the organisation (Figure 13.1). We will use the integrated term 'career development' throughout this chapter.

Figure 13.1: The Spectrum of Career Development Activities in Organisations

Employee-Centred: Career Planning			Mutual Focus: Manager-Employee Planning			Organisation-Centred: Career Management
Self-directed workbooks and tape cassettes	Company-run career-planning workshops	Corporate seminars on organisational career	Manager-employee career discussions (includes separate training for managers)	Developmental assessment centres (with feedback)	Corporate talent inventories	Corporate succession planning

Source: Hall (1986)

What Constitutes a Career?

A multiplicity of perspectives exist on what constitutes a career. Although they do not represent theories, they contribute to the debate concerning what the modern career is about. We briefly consider a number of these perspectives here.

Career as Lifestyle: Schein (1996) acknowledged that the 'lifestyle' career anchor had changed the most. There is an increasing interest in the relationship between work and non-work activities. Fletcher and Bailyn (1996) highlighted that the traditional tendency was to keep work and family separate. Eaton and Bailyn (2000) proposed the notion of a career as 'life path'. This suggests that an individual's life choices are increasingly complicated by the career and life choices of his or her partner, and by other domestic and home responsibilities. Career should be viewed as fluid, complicated by a series of choices, concerning not only the individual but also the wider family. This plays out in the employment contract with more mutual and consensual understandings of flexibility.

Baruch offers another dimension of the career as lifestyle perspective. Table 13.3 captures this shift.

Table 13.3: Measures of Career Success

Traditional Concepts	The 'New Careerist'	Contemporary – Individual	Contemporary – Organisation
Formal education	Getting ahead	Self-development competencies	Empowerment
Lifelong employment, job security	Getting secure	Employability	Investment in people
Up the ladder	Getting high	Lateral transitions: spiral movement	New or no career paths
	Getting free	Self-management: entrepreneurial	Flexibility
	Getting balanced	Quality of life; work-family balance	Alternative working arrangements and work–family policies
		New psychological contracts	
		Search for spiritual meaning based on individual consciousness	True, open partnership

Source: Baruch (2004:77)

The younger participants in the workforce (Generation X and those who have followed) are less interested in a job for life and more interested in exploration and doing different kinds of work that will contribute to their self-development. Organisations and leaders must recognise that younger managers will not have the same career motivators as the baby-boomers and traditionalists (Noe 2005:354). It can be quite challenging for managers in their mid-40s upwards to understand why some of their team members (Gen Xers) expect meaningful work, organisational commitment to their development and alternative working arrangements. Managers require a satisfactory balance between work and the rest of their lives. Senior managers need to consider this factor in enabling employees to plan and manage their careers, for optimal individual and team performance.

Career as Employability: We discussed employability in the context of individual and self-managed learning in Chapter Twelve. Kanter (1989) described employability as the 'new security'; if an organisation has invested in managers' employability, they should be employable elsewhere if their job comes to an end. This idea of 'employability' has given rise to a marked emphasis on creating learning cultures in organisations. It also means that managers need to become more proactive and take more responsibility for their careers. An employability perspective is widely discussed in the literature. Some commentators suggest that it offers a relatively simple, optimistic and generic solution to the problem of managing careers. It is also considered to resonate with the rhetoric of learning, but there are questions concerning how it can be applied in practice.

Career as Market Power: Cappelli (1999) highlighted the increased importance of labour markets in shaping careers. Processes such as outsourcing, benchmarking and decentralised responsibility for performance have resulted in employment competition. Furthermore, organisational restructuring has led to more flexibility and permeable organisational boundaries, which have disrupted career prospects and created permanent insecurity. Hendry (1996) argued that the career has been exposed to the logic and the rhetoric of the labour market.

Career as a New Deal: The psychological contract is a content-based idea. There has been a major shift in terms of the psychological contract between employers and employees, as we mentioned in the section on career as employability. The psychological contract is 'the unspoken promise' of what the employer gives and what the employees give in return. It has also been defined by Guest and Conway (2002) as '. . . the perceptions of the two parties, employee and employer, of what their mutual obligations are towards each other'. These obligations will often be informal, imprecise and not present in the small print of the formal, legal employment contract. It is clear that a balanced psychological contract is essential for a continuous, harmonious relationship between an employee and employer.

Traditionally, as part of the psychological contract, employers gave job security, advancement according to tenure, and a 'career for life' if the employee performed. Employees gave the organisation loyalty, commitment and good job performance in return. This traditional deal was based on reciprocity, and a high degree of trust existed between both parties. In this long-term arrangement, the career development of managers was the organisation's responsibility. A major theme in the current literature is how organisational restructuring has undermined employees' trust in their organisation and what actions can be taken to build new bases for employee commitment to the organisation. Baruch (2004) articulated the components of the new or transformed career deal (Table 13.4). A new deal perspective highlights that psychological contracts differ between individuals. It is a two-way exchange rather than a unilateral one and various norms and values will influence the honouring of the deal.

Herriot and Pemberton (1997) suggested that the contractual process consists of informing, negotiating, monitoring and reciprocating. This model is iterative and requires each party to be aware of what it wants and what it is willing to offer. The issue of power is, however, relevant to the dealing process. The dealing process allows individuals to achieve agency and autonomy in their relationships with the organisation. In our experience, it is too simplistic to suggest that today's organisations fit one profile or the other (traditional or transformed deal). Many organisations will have a combination of permanent and flexible workers, with different legal and psychological contracts. This presents challenges in all aspects of people management, including learning and development, human resource planning, leadership development, reward and performance management and career management. In fact, the challenge for the leader is to manage multiple psychological contracts with their corresponding expectations and motivations.

Table 13.4: The Traditional Versus the Transformed Career Deal

Aspect	Traditional Deal	Transformed Deal
Environmental characteristic	Stability	Dynamism
Career choice made	Once, at early age in career	Serially, at different age stages
Main career responsibility lies within	Organisation	Individual
Career horizon (workplace)	Single organisation	Several organisations
Career horizon (time)	Long	Short
Employer expects/employee gives	Loyalty and commitment	Long-time working hours
Employer gives/employee expects	Job security	Investment in employability
Progress criteria	Advancement according to tenure	Advancement according to results and knowledge
Success means	Winning the tournament, i.e. progress on the hierarchy ladder	Inner feeling of achievement
Training	Formal programmes, generalist	On-the-job, company specific, sometimes ad hoc

Source: Baruch (2004:13)

Career as Instrumental and Calculative: Scase and Goffee (1990) argued that managers' jobs, careers and employment prospects are increasingly characterised by greater uncertainty. This has had important implications for the attitudes, commitment and personal lifestyles of managers. Managers have become more cynical; they are shrewder in their attitudes toward their employer and they increasingly calculate the emotional and psychological costs of career success.

These various perspectives highlight the multiplicity of views that exist on the modern career. While each perspective has a unique emphasis, it is possible to derive from them a number of significant implications for managerial careers and career development.

- The individual is now responsible for his/her career, with some organisational support for career management.
- The individual and the organisation must invest in employability (continuous learning and development of competency portfolio).
- Advancement is not guaranteed, so employees need to consider broader forms of development (including lateral and downward moves, job expansion and challenging job assignments).
- Career success is measured by the individual in subjective terms. Therefore, a 'one-size-fits-all' approach to career management within an organisation is not optimal.

Perspective on Theory: Understanding Career Theories

General Career Theories

Social Cognitive Career Theory (SCCT)	Social cognitive career theory focuses on a) personal and physical attributes; b) external environmental factors; and c) overt behaviour. The interactions between these elements are said to be major considerations regarding individual development. SCCT, contextualised within career development (CD) identifies three determinants of CD: self-efficacy, outcome expectations and personal goals. Self-efficacy is viewed as beliefs regarding a specific domain of performance and is developed through learning experiences such as a) personal performance accomplishments; b) vicarious learning; c) social persuasion; and d) physiological states and actions. Outcome expectations are regarded as personal beliefs about anticipated results or the significance of related results. Individuals may be more or less motivated by intrinsic or extrinsic rewards associated with career-related actions. Finally, personal goals are viewed as frameworks for the initiation and maintenance of self-directed behaviour.
Cognitive Information Processing Theory	Focuses on how individuals use information to make CD-related decisions. Cognitive ability is identified as a major element influencing the degree to which individuals take control over their careers and CD. This theory makes ten assumptions: a) CD-related choices are problem-solving activities; b) career choice is a result of affective and cognitive processes; c) individuals approaching CD problems rely on knowledge and cognitive abilities; d) CD-related problem-solving requires high memory load; e) motivation is important to CD-related success; f) CD involves ongoing growth and evolution of cognitive frameworks; g) CD and career identity are dependent on self-knowledge; h) career maturity depends on individual abilities to solve career problems; i) career counselling and/or CD has reached its highest point when information processing skills are facilitated; and j) the ultimate goal of CD-related interventions is to enhance individual abilities associated with problem-solving and decision-making. These assumptions emphasise cognitive ability and frame CD as a learning event that can be catalysed by a CD professional.
Constructivist Career Theory	Constructivist career theory assumes that: a) people create their identities and environments through individual interpretations that inform their decisions and actions – may or may not be useful or beneficial; b) people are meaning-makers and do so in ways that are self-organising – individual life stories and/or constructs are under constant revision; c) multiple meanings and multiple realities are the foundation of the human condition; d) individual fulfilment is the product of individual critical reflection and connection between thoughts, assumptions and actions; and e) regardless of their similarities or differences, individuals are likely to have different perspectives on events. Career practitioners working from this theory often approach their work from a holistic or career life-planning perspective.

General Career Theories *contd.*

Career Decision-Making Theories	Career decision-making theories are based on the notion that individuals are able to make choices from a variety of career options. Career decision events often include: a) problem definition; b) generation of scenarios or alternatives; c) information gathering; d) information processing; e) making plans; f) goal clarification; and g) taking action. Career decision-making theory may emphasise critical life points when actions are taken that have significant influence on career development. Related actions include job and/or career choices, participation in formal education and efforts to enhance work abilities and skills. According to career decision-making theory, our choices are influenced by our awareness of available options and our abilities to evaluate what is presented. In addition, environmental decision-making theories try to account for the complexities in the naturalistic job environment.
Personality-Oriented Theories	Personality-oriented theories assume that managers select their jobs because they see potential for the satisfaction of their needs. Worker needs are seen to connect largely to personality dimensions. Personality-oriented theories additionally hypothesise that job-related experience influences the personalities of employees; so that, for example, information technology employees develop similar personality characteristics – there may also be a chance that the employees had prior similarities.
Self-Concept Theories	Self-concept theories assume that: a) individuals refine self-concepts as they grow older, but self-concepts are influenced by ageing and evolve along with individual perceptions of reality; b) individuals make decisions by comparing their images of the world of work with their self-image; c) the quality of career decisions for individuals depend on the congruence between self-concept and the career roles that are focused on.
Socioeconomic Perspectives	Socioeconomics is the study of the economic and social impact products or services, market interventions, or other related actions have on individuals, organisations and the overall economy. These effects are often measured in numerical terms: overall economic growth, unemployment and job creation, life expectancy or education. These factors may influence consumption patterns, wealth distribution, the manner in which people choose to spend their time and resources and their general quality of life. Socioeconomic theory in the context of CD relates to how individual values and identities associated with social and economic conditions, family background, and other factors outside individuals' control, influence their CD and career-related decisions.
Social Network Theory	Social network theory assumes that individual behaviour in social institutions, such as families or organisations, is affected by the structure of interpersonal relationships. A network is a set of interrelationships that may consist of connections or links between groups or social units. Repeated interaction defines and maintains the links over time. In the case of careers, networks may support or hinder the access to career-related opportunities, career-related information, or even training that may enhance individual careers. When two individuals interact, regarding for instance the information exchanged, it is viewed as a by-product of their relational networks that may consist of family members, friends, co-workers or neighbours. The type and frequency of exchanges between individuals and their relational networks are said to influence possibilities for information gathering and exchange.

General Career Theories *contd.*

Social Systems Theory	Social systems theory assumes that individual control over the impact of events and societal circumstances is limited. In addition, it is held that transactions between social systems and individuals contribute considerably to career development. The primary undertaking confronting individuals is the development of knowledge and skills to cope effectively with the environment. The ambitions or aspirations of individuals may also influence CD and career choice in the context of the social system. Social systems are perpetuated occupational levels and result in the generation of occupational subcultures.
Trait-Factor Theories	Trait-factor theories are the oldest CD-related theories. They assume a match can be made between an individual and the world of work based on the characteristics of the person and the identified needs of the job or career context. A match between job and individual characteristics is believed to resolve the CD needs for any individual. Parsons suggested that career and vocational choices depended on: a) accurate self-knowledge; b) specific understanding of job-related requirements; and c) a capacity to connect self-knowledge with job requirements. Career and vocational testing emerged from the trait-factor approach. Trait-factor theory has been integrated into many other CD approaches. Assumptions associated with trait-factor theory include: a) that job traits and individual attributes can be matched; and b) that job success and satisfaction result, to a great degree, from alignment between individual characteristics and career roles and tasks. These concepts continue to influence present-day CD.

Specific Career Development Theories

Brown's Values-Based Theory	The underlying assumption of Brown's approach to CD is that individual values orientations are a core factor in career decision-making. In fact, values are emphasised as a dominant feature in human development and are viewed as providing direction and guidance towards individual action and reflection on the actions of others. Values are generated through experience and inherited characteristics. Environmental factors are given greater weight in terms of values development. Individuals are bombarded with values-laden messages from early childhood onrward, and values-focused messages begin early in life and lead to individual cognitive, affective and behavioural patterns. These patterns assist in the prioritisation of values toward decision-making in the natural environment. Six propositions were used to support this model: a) individuals focus on and prioritise only a small number of values; b) those values that are of the highest priority to an individual influence CD-related choices; c) values are defined and applied based on learned experience in the environment; d) holistic fulfilment is based on life roles that satisfy all of an individual's core values; e) the salience of a particular role is associated with the level at which essential values are enacted in that role; and f) life role and CD success depend on many facets including affective, cognitive and physical capacities.

Specific Career Development Theories *contd.*

Ginzberg's Developmental Theory	Ginzberg revealed three distinct phases that occur during occupational choice: a) fantasy; b) tentative; and c) realistic. This development process was said to occur between the ages of eleven and seventeen years, or even into early adulthood. During the fantasy period, play was said to become work oriented, generating specific kinds of activities in which various types of occupational roles were played, ultimately leading to specific individual assumptions or preferences about the world of work. The tentative phase had four specific stages: a) the interest stage, when individuals make more specific decisions regarding preferences; b) the capacity stage, whereby individuals make connections between perceived abilities and vocational aspirations; c) the value stage, in which clearer perceptions of occupational style emerge, and the transition stage leading to a vocational choice and alignment regarding the requirements for such a choice. In addition, d) the realistic stage is also characterised by three sub stages: exploration, crystallisation and specification. Exploration involves educational or training preparation for work. During this stage the career focus narrows in scope. Commitment to a particular field and career is solidified during crystallisation. Finally, specification involves the selection of a particular job or defined professional training opportunity.
Holland's Career Theory	Holland's theory stressed the importance of accurate self-knowledge combined with specific career information necessary for career identification and planning. The foundation of this career theory and framework proposed that workplace performance is best considered along with the environment associated with a particular job or career. Holland also developed a set of assumptions associated with the manner in which job choice, job satisfaction, and job and career success occur in context with an extensive set of job and work environments. Holland also assumed that people select careers based on their personalities and that there is a connection between the environment selected and the personality of the individual. He then identified personality type and work environment combinations as realistic, investigative, artistic, social, enterprising and conventional. Holland suggested that satisfaction would be closely linked to the association between the work environment and the individual personality.
Kram's Career Development Function	Kram identified CD to be an essential element for protégés and found that a commonly shared interest between mentor and protégé was the advancement of the protégé's career. In fact, available research has supported that career mentoring is associated with increased pay and promotion. The five essential activities that assist in the promotion of protégé career development include: a) challenging work assignments; b) coaching; c) exposure and visibility; d) protection; and e) sponsorship. By providing or arranging for protégé involvement in challenging work assignments, protégés are supported in the development of critical learning experiences. Coaching is often a central part of the mentoring role. Through the offering of feedback, direction and advice, mentors support protégé development of subject matter, practice, and political abilities necessary for organisational success.

Krumboltz's Social Learning Theory of Career Choice	Krumboltz formulated a career decision-making theory based on social learning, responses to environmental conditions, genetics and learning experiences. Krumboltz suggested that people make career choices based on what they have learned and what particular behaviours are modelled, rewarded and reinforced. Career-related development thus occurs because of learning and the imitation of others. From this perspective, individuals choose careers as an outcome of internalised learning; therefore, individual career choice is the result of innumerable learning experiences enacted through interactions with available persons, organisations and experiences. Key learning experiences direct individuals towards the formation of beliefs about the nature of careers and their prospective life roles based on generalised self-observations. Life experiences and learning that results, especially from observation and interaction with significant role models (e.g. parents, teachers and heroes), are believed to be persuasive in the development, differentiation and execution of career choices. Positive modelling, reward and reinforcement will likely lead to the development of appropriate career-planning skills and career behaviour.
Roe's Needs Theory Approach	Roe emphasised the importance of early experiences, particularly in family life, that influence the definition of and satisfaction with selected careers. Roe explored the relationship between parental decision-making and choices that led to the later adult lifestyles chosen by their children. Roe connected the need structures for individuals to early childhood experiences involving need-related fulfilment and limitations. Occupations were divided into two major areas: person- and non-person-oriented, and identified as rooted in family-related experiences. Roe later modified her theory to include environmental and genetic factors that may also influence CD and career choice.
Schein's Career Anchors	Schein expanded the notion of career to incorporate individual identity or self-concept, including: a) self-perceived talents and abilities; b) basic values; and c) the evolved sense of motives and needs as they pertain to the career. Career anchors evolve only through work-related and life experiences, and the eight main career anchors are: a) technical and/or functional competence; b) general management competence; c) autonomy and/or independence; d) security and/or stability; e) entrepreneurial creativity; f) service and/or dedication to a cause; g) pure challenge; and h) lifestyle.
Super's Life-Span Theory	According to Super, patterns associated with CDE are by-products of socioeconomic factors, mental and physical abilities, personal characteristics and the opportunities to which persons are exposed. His notion of career maturity involves success in tasks associated with age and stage development across the life span. Self-concept is foundational to this model: 'Vocational self-concept develops through physical and mental growth, observations of work, identification with working adults, general environment, and general experiences.' Super named six key elements of vocational maturity: a) awareness of the need to plan ahead; b) decision-making skills; c) knowledge and use of information resources; d) general career information; e) general world of work information; and f) detailed information about occupations of preference.

Tiedman's Decision-Making Model	Tiedman's framing of CD was truly holistic with the emphasis on total cognitive development and related decision-making. Tiedman viewed CD as emergent from general cognitive development in which individuals are constantly evolving in terms of career-related awareness toward action at the appropriate age or time. Tiedman focused on CD in the context of ego and identity development, whereby individuals engage in a self-evaluative process involving differentiation and integration. From this perspective, the CD process is complex and highly individualised. Tiedman focused on evolving self-awareness as key to the career decision-making process. Emphasis is given to influencing change and growth through adjustment to the existing social, interpersonal and career context at hand.

Models of Career and Career Development

Models of career and career development can be divided into those that are individually focused and those that are organisationally focused. Individually focused models include: Super's (1957, 1996) Stages Theory; Schein's (1990) Career Anchor Theory; Greenhaus, Callanan and Godshalk's (2000) Five-Stage Model of Careers; Hall and Moss's (1998) Protean Career; Arthur's (1994) Boundaryless Career Model; and Driver's (1994) Multiple Career Concept Model. Organisationally focused models include Sonnenfeld, Peiperl and Kotter's (1988) Typology of Career Systems, Brousseau *et al.*'s (1996) Pluralist Career Theory, Nicholson's (1996) Systems View of Career Management and Cianni and Wnuck's (1997) Team-Based Career-Development Model. Exhibit 13.3 (page 524) highlights many other metaphors that are valuable in analysing careers in organisations.

Individual-Focused Career Development Theories

Individual-focused models present explanations of how managers experience their career and they contain prescriptions concerning how they can manage their career more effectively. They represent the more traditional theories and have proved useful in explaining the decisions that managers have to make in managing their careers.

Super's Development Theory of Careers: It is widely accepted that a career is a developmental process that spans several stages during the course of an individual's life. Super's developmental theory (1957) has had a major influence on our thinking about careers. His theory shows how individuals implement their inner being and self-concept in one or more career (or vocational) choices during their lives. One of the key ideas in this model, according to Mumford and Gold (2004:202) was that '. . . career maturity was achieved by matching tasks with stages of development over a life-span. Career satisfaction could be obtained if, at the appropriate stage of development, people could choose a work role that allows them to develop their self-concept' (Table 13.5).

Table 13.5: Super's Developmental Theory of Careers: Key Concepts and Propositions

The concept of a one-time vocational choice is no longer relevant as the world has changed. Super's concept of career development was that of progression throughout the entire lifespan. In his original research in the 1960s (Super, Savickas and Super 1996), Super defined five specific life stages related to career development as follows:

Stages
- **Growth**: Under 14. Focus on physical growth, formation of the self-concept and early exploration of interests and abilities.
- **Exploration**: 14–25. Learning about many different areas of work and their requirements. Making a commitment to a specific area of work, getting training for it, and beginning to engage in it.
- **Establishment**: 26-45. Getting firmly settled into an occupational field; making contributions to that field of work and being very productive, perhaps being promoted to higher levels of responsibility.
- **Maintenance**: 46-65. Maintaining the current position in work; updating skills as needed to stay competitive with younger people; planning towards retirement at the end of this period.
- **Disengagement**: 65-?. Slowing down and making a gradual separation from paid employment; engaging in a different lifestyle that includes more leisure, family, and community activities.

These five stages of career development are accompanied, and driven, in Super's theory, by five developmental tasks. These are tasks related to learning and planning that are necessary in order to move through these stages well and at the correct time. These tasks are:

- **Crystallisation:** The process of considering a variety of career options, discarding some, and ultimately limiting the list to a few that most appropriately use one's interests and abilities. The process also involves a clear formation of a vocational identity, or vocational self-concept. In Super's view, this developmental task should optimally occur between the ages of fourteen and eighteen. This task includes understanding the factors that need to be considered when making a vocational choice (interests, abilities, values, self-concept), understanding the factors in the environment that may affect personal goals (the economy, the labour market, hiring practices, etc.), knowing how to set goals and progress toward them, and learning in detail about the occupations under consideration.
- **Specification:** The process of committing to one career over others that have been under consideration. Knowing and engaging in the training needed, feeling confident in the choice, and moving forward with commitment. In Super's view, this developmental task would optimally occur between the ages of eighteen and twenty-one.
- **Implementation:** The process of getting the training for a selected occupation and of getting one's first job in it. This should ideally occur between the ages of twenty-one and twenty-four.
- **Stabilisation:** The process of settling into a field of work, experiencing the benefits of having made a good choice, and making contributions to the field and to the employer (twenty-five to thirty-five).
- **Consolidation:** The process of further commitment to the chosen career or field of work with the seniority and productivity that come with experience. This task continues until retirement from paid employment.

Vocational Maturity
A further concept in Super's theory is that of vocational maturity, which he researched for at least twenty years. In Super's view, vocational maturity can be described simply as accomplishing the above five tasks (and their multiple sub-tasks) 'on schedule', that is, during the age range in which one would optimally do so. According to Super's theory, if an individual does not accomplish these tasks in sequence at the time proposed, he or she may be vocationally immature, that is, not possessing the necessary skills to make informed and satisfying career choices.

Throughout all of these tasks, the individual's self-concept is a central and all-important factor. A second important factor is the ongoing process of the **compromise** between what an individual may **desire** or be able to do and the **opportunities available** to that person due to external forces outside his or her control.

The context in which career choices are made has changed tremendously since Super's first statement of his theory in the 1950s and 1960s. He acknowledged this fact in his later works. Due to the changes, both in the views of people and the views of organisations/corporations, the 'lifetime career' described by Super is much less a reality now than it was in the 1950s and 60s. Thus, Super acknowledged in his later writings that it may be typical for people to go through the life stages (mini-cycles) of growth, exploration and early establishment, and after a short time go back to exploration and make a different career choice, perhaps never reaching the stage of maintenance in a given occupation. He also acknowledged that people may approach these tasks and stages at different ages as a larger percentage of women enter the workforce, larger percentages of people retrain or increase their formal education in the adult years, and corporations continue to 'downsize' or 'right size'.

Baruch (2004) emphasised the ongoing relevance of Super's theory and outlined the fourteen major propositions of the theory as summarised by Super, Savickas and Super (1996).

Table 13.6: Super's Propositions on Careers and Career Development

- People differ in abilities, personalities, needs, values, interests, traits and their self-concepts.
- People are qualified, by virtue of these characteristics, for a number of occupations.
- Each occupation requires a characteristic pattern of personal abilities, traits, etc., with a certain degree of tolerance to allow a variety of occupations for each individual and a variety of individuals for each occupation.
- Vocational preferences and competencies and life and work situations change with time and experience, but the self-concept is relatively stable since it derives from social learning.
- The change processes come in the time frame of the stages described above. Mini-cycles will occur when a career is established.
- The career pattern is determined by paternal socio-economic background, mental ability, education, skills, personality, career maturity and opportunities.
- Success in coping with organisational and environmental demands depends on career maturity.
- Career development is about the development and implementation of an occupational self-concept.
- Development can be guided by external facilitation.
- Career development is about the development and implementation of an occupational self-concept.
- The process of synthesis or compromise between the individual and social factors is one of role-playing and learning.
- Work and life satisfaction depends on finding adequate outlets for one's own qualities.
- Work satisfaction is proportional to ability for the implementation of the self-concept.
- Work and occupation provide a focus for personality organisation for most people. Social traditions, opportunities and individual differences determine performance in the role taken by individuals in all their life spaces.

Source: Baruch (2004:50-51)

Schein's Career Anchors: Schein (1990) developed the idea of people having different career anchors. He defined these as relatively stable orientations to one's organisation and one's career (Exhibit 13.2). Schein distinguished between an internal and an external career. An internal career focuses on how a manager's work life develops over time and how it is perceived by the manager. An external career refers to the actual steps that are required by a particular occupation or an organisation for progress through that organisation. Organisations frequently use career paths which define the discrete steps for a manager to take. Schein's model proposed a set of stages for the external career. The key features of this model are growth, fantasy and exploration. These stages prepare the individual for: entry into a tentatively chosen occupational investment in education and training; entry into the world of work; basic training and socialisation; the development of a meaningful self-image;

becoming a member of an occupation and/or organisation; securing tenure and permanent membership; the experience of a mid-career crisis and reassessment; the maintenance of momentum (and regaining it if it is lost or levels off); disengagement and retirement. Schein does not specify precise durations. He argues that they depend on the individual. The stages can be repeated if the manager changes his or her career. Schein's ideas are widely used to analyse career development and to provide advice to managers. Arthur, Inkson and Pringle (1999), however, suggested that the performance implied in the notion of career anchors may be misplaced. They found that careers lacked the objective rationality that was implied by Schein's anchors, or else they revolved around managers' desire for personal fulfilment or maximisation of their earning or education. This depended on their ambition at a particular point in time.

EXHIBIT 13.2

Schein's Career Anchors

- *Technical/Functional Competencies*: Career choice is based on the technical or functional content of work, and so self-image relates to competence and skill in this area. Task accomplishment and getting the job done are highly valued. Such people avoid general management roles, seeing them as a 'jungle' or 'political arena'. They thus do not want to be promoted out of their area, require challenging work content, want pay commensurate with their experience and expertise rather than their output, prefer a separate professional career stream and value the recognition of professional peers and opportunities for continued professional development.

- *General Managerial Competence*: Career choice is based on the key values and motives of organisational advancement, leadership, contributions to organisational success and high income. Thus, managers view specialisation as a trap. However, to achieve success their values and motivation need to be matched by skills and abilities in three key areas: analytical competence; interpersonal and inter-group competence; and emotional competence. They cannot function without some degree of each of these. Thus, they are attracted to work that gives them organisational status, pay that reflects this and rewards their success, and recognition through frequent promotion to positions of higher responsibility with accompanying financial reward.

- *Autonomy/Independence*: Career choice is determined by the need to avoid the restrictive, irrational and intrusive nature of organisational life. Such people would prefer to stay in their current job if it permits autonomy, rather than move to a better job that involves giving this up. Very often this need stems from high levels of education or professionalism or childhood socialisation. Such people want work with clear goals, but cannot stand close supervision. This often means that they are employed on fixed-term contracts. They avoid 'golden handcuffs' and prefer flexible benefits, seek promotion only on the understanding that it leads to greater autonomy rather than greater responsibility, and respond more to public acknowledgement of their excellence than to change in title, promotion or financial rewards.

- *Security/Stability*: Career choice is guided and constrained by such concerns, so these people often seek jobs in organisations that provide tenure and good human resource practices in exchange for which they are willing to be told what to do. While often giving an impression of a lack of ambition, they can be highly talented people, but ones who prefer jobs that require steady, predictable performance. Thus, job enrichment and challenge are less important to them than good pay and working conditions. They prefer a seniority-based promotion system and want recognition of their loyalty and steady performance.

- *Entrepreneurial Creativity*: Career choice is determined by the need to create new organisations, products or services that can be identified closely with the entrepreneur's own efforts. Typically, this need is developed early in life, and their high motivation is likely to be due to their family socialisation. They differ from those who are 'autonomy' anchored in their drive to prove that they can create businesses, which often means sacrificing both autonomy and stability. They continually seek new challenges, and may lose interest in old ones. Individual ownership is much more important than levels or types of benefits. Power and freedom, public recognition and visibility are major drivers.

- *Sense of Service/Dedication to a Cause*: Career choice is determined by central values that they want to have embodied in their work rather than the area of competence involved. Values such as working with people, serving humanity or environmental protection can be powerful anchors. Thus, there is a need for work that permits them to influence their employing organisation; they want fair pay, but money is not of central importance. They want promotion based on their contribution and recognition and support from both peers and superiors.
- *Challenge*: Some people anchor their careers in the perception that they can conquer anything or anybody. They define their careers as daily combat or a competition where winning is all. Thus, the challenge overshadows concern with the area of work, the pay system, promotion and recognition. A career for such a person has meaning only if competitive skill can be exercised.
- *Lifestyle*: Here the motivation is towards a meaningful career on the condition that it is integrated with a total lifestyle in which there is integration with the needs of the individual, their family, leisure interest, etc. Requirements include flexibility or working hours, employer location and job mobility.

The Protean Career: Hall and Mirvis (1996) advanced the idea of the protean career concept. The idea was first suggested by Hall (1976) as follows: 'The protean career is a process which the person, not the organisation, is managing. It consists of a person's entire experience in education, training, work in several organizations, changes in occupational field, etc. The protean person's own personal career choices and search for self-fulfilment are the unifying or integrative elements in his or her life.'

It is important to point out that the protean concept describes a particular individual orientation to one's career. One can envisage a continuum to describe a range of career orientations, with the traditional organisation orientation at one end and the protean view at the other. Some managers are still very much motivated by having a long career in a particular organisation and are concerned with maximising their chances for achieving promotions, higher pay and greater power within the context. The problem is that this option may or may not be available to the individual, depending on the organisation and the external environment. Managers with a more protean orientation are less concerned with these extrinsic rewards and are more motivated by autonomy, personal values and psychological success (Figure 13.2).

The protean view of careers opens up new ways of thinking about work over time. It encompasses careers marked by peaks and valleys, early or late blooming, movement from one line of work and non-work roles, paid and unpaid work, overlap, and it shapes a person's identity and sense of self. It engenders new ways of thinking about the relationship between the employer and the employee, where the latter takes a more proactive role, taking charge of their own work career rather than depending on the corporation's definition of career development.

The protean view embraces the idea of lifelong learning and personal development as central to effective career development. A career can be conceived as a succession of mini stages of exploration – trial, mastery and exit – as managers move in and out of the various areas. The protean view does not emphasise a manager's chronological age but instead considers the career age important. The career age is the number of years a manager has spent in a particular cycle. The model indicates that career management must be proactive. It is sometimes suggested that while the protean career is liberating, it also has a dark side. The manager may experience fear and uncertainty and find it difficult to cope with the major changes involved.

Figure 13.2: Elements of the Protean Career Concept

1. The career is managed primarily by the person, not the organisation.
2. The career is a lifelong series of experiences, skills, learning, transitions, and identity changes (career age counts, not chronological age).
3. Development is considered to be continuous, self-directed, relational and found in work challenges.
4. Development is not necessarily confined to formal training, retraining or upward mobility.
5. The ingredients for success focus on employability rather than job security, learning how to learn rather than knowledge and know-how, and a focus on the whole self'.
6. The organisation seeks to provide challenging assignments, developmental relationships, information and other development resources.
7. The goal of the protean career is psychological success.

Source: Hall and Moss (1988)

The Boundaryless Career: The concept of the boundaryless career was initially proposed by Arthur (1994). It has proved to be very popular with theorists and practitioners in the field of career development and human resource management. Pringle and Mallon (2003:839) suggested that 'it is, it seems, an idea whose time has come'. The boundaryless career has offered theorists a way to make sense of the apparent chaos in career and career opportunities in destabilised organisations.

In recognition of the changing nature of careers, Arthur has referred to the boundaryless career as the concept of the age. Careers are boundaryless in the sense that, either by choice or necessity, people move across boundaries between organisations, departments, hierarchical levels, functions and sets of skills. Movement across these boundaries is made easier by the fact that they are tending to dissolve anyway. Such movement is necessary for individuals to maintain their employability and for organisations to maintain their effectiveness. Careers are also becoming more like a sequence of short-term episodes rather than a long-drawn-out systematic accumulation of experience.

Sullivan and Arthur (2006) suggested that the boundaryless career should not be considered an 'either/or' proposition. They suggest that it is necessary to consider both physical and psychological mobility dimensions of the boundaryless career. Physical mobility refers to transitions across boundaries, whereas psychological mobility refers to the perception or capacity to make successful transactions. The boundaryless career can be understood in terms of verifying levels of physical and psychological mobility. They identify four possible combinations:

- *Careers characterised by both low physical and low psychological mobility*. These managers may have highly specialised knowledge and low transferability. The job has unique challenges and offers considerable job security.
- *Careers characterised by high physical but low psychological mobility*. Managers may change jobs within the same area, but be less confident about working in another area.
- *Careers with low physical mobility but high psychological mobility*. These managers have high expectations of employability but they do not change employers. They have major opportunities for personal growth outside the workplace and can innovate and change their work practices.
- *Careers with high physical and psychological mobility*. These managers change jobs often and they also change their expectations. The manager may value reflection, and better work–life balance.

Ashkenas *et al.* (1995) wrote about the blurring of boundaries within organisations, noting the following dimensions in particular.

- *Vertical*: Rigid hierarchical structures are in decline.
- *Horizontal*: Different departments and units within organisations are being merged, e.g. HR and marketing, and fluidity exists in terms of organisational restructuring.
- *External*: The distinction between the organisation and the external environment has diminished, e.g. external consultants are viewed as organisational partners; employees may be seconded to key customers.
- *Geographic*: Many organisations do not operate from one specific location today, e.g. many workers may work remotely from the organisation.

One consequence of blurred boundaries is that, for managers, it is more difficult to maintain clear boundaries between work and non-work. In this sense, career management has become a lot more challenging for individuals, their managers and organisations. Thus, the boundaryless career refers to the objective move that a person makes as he or she moves across organisational boundaries, e.g. functions within an organisation, entry and exit from an organisation, movement across industries and sectors. This new career type contributes to a more open and fluid job market. The boundaryless career concept is used interchangeably with the idea of the 'intelligent career' (Baruch 2004).

Briscoe and Hall (2006) highlight the confusion that often exists between the boundaryless and the protean career. The boundaryless career focuses on identifying the strengths and weaknesses of different career orientations, whereas the protean career emphasises a self-directed approach to the career and a career driven by the individual's values. They suggest an interesting typology which combines boundaryless and protean career concepts. They identify eight possible combinations. Table 13.7 provides a summary of these careers and the development challenges that they pose.

Table 13.7: Combining Boundaryless and Protean Careers: A Suggested Typology

Career Type	Characteristics	Development Issues
Trapped/Lost	• This manager is lost in the sense that he/she has no emphasis on inner values or on boundaryless perspectives. • He/she is not in control and, as a result, reacts to issues. • Career success depends on lack of circumstances rather than planning and control.	• Basic career exploration identifying values and enhancing self-efficacy. • Focus on unfreezing the manager and motivating him/her to consider new possibilities. • Make this manager accountable for his/her behaviour and reinforce autonomy. • This manager may avoid experiences and interventions designed to help them.
Fortressed	• This manager has considerable clarity of personal issues. • The manager possesses inflexibility concerning their ability to direct career and change behaviours. • He/she likes stability and predictability in work and career. • Many find it difficult to get different work if organisational circumstances change.	• The career development task is to encourage the manager to become aware of other opportunities. • Focus on reflection in order to assess the current career situation. • Development activities should challenge the manager on their current values.

Career Type	Characteristics	Development Issues
Wanderer	• This manager is willing to link up with whatever opportunities arise. • Does not view geography or organisation to act as barriers. • Does not possess strong values on career and career management.	• Development challenge is to learn how to articulate career values and not be expectant. • This manager is often slow to seek career development. • Scope to help managers in this category to develop clearer career priorities.
Idealist	• This manager is very values driven and can think of new career horizons, but is less effective on self-management. • He/she is less likely to be flexible; places strong emphasis on a career with strong value fit.	• Development challenge is to get this manager outside his/her comfort zone. • Focus on getting the manager to be better at self-managing career. • May use experiences outside the organisation to encourage the manager to be more mobile.
Organisation Man/Woman	• This manager has a strong ability to manage his/her career successfully. • Manager is willing to cross boundaries in a psychological but not a physical sense. • Not interested in physical mobility if he/she can avoid it. • This manager may not realise potential as he/she does not have fully realised values.	• Key development challenge is to get the manager out of comfort zone. • Give manager exposure to new perspectives and challenge values. • Offer support and a buffer of reassurance so that manager will take chances. • Encourage the manager to reflect on issues in order to identify key lessons learned.
Solid Citizen	• This manager is self-directed and values-driven. • Manager has no problem with psychological boundary but is not physically boundaryless. • Will do well in a variety of roles but needs the context to be clearly defined. • Likes autonomy and has a desire to learn.	• Key development challenge is to find interesting learning opportunities. • Manager needs to remain adaptive and to demonstrate continued performance. • Need job matches that are in line with strong values.
Hired Gun/Hired Hand	• This manager is willing to work across physical and psychological boundaries. • He/she is not values-driven and does not have a clear sense of priorities. • Is mobile and adaptive and will respond to external challenges.	• Development challenge is to focus on values and to become a self-leader. • Less likely to be a leader who will drive change, due to lack of well-articulated values.
Protean Career Architect	• This manager actively directs his/her career and is driven by strong personal values. • Demonstrates strong respect for other cultures and focuses on development.	• Major challenge is to identify the best area to realise potential. • Key development challenge is to manage the manager earlier in a constructive way.

Five-Stage Model of Careers: Greenhaus, Callanan and Godshalk (2000) proposed a five-stage model of careers. This model emphasises the notion of an orderly series of career stages linked to age ranges, and places the career in the context of a manager's life. These ideas represent a throwback to the bureaucratic career.

Greenhaus, Callanan and Godshalk suggest that the first career stage can be labelled occupational choice and preparation for work. The main tasks for the individual focus are developing an occupational self-image, assessing alternative occupations, developing initial occupational choices and pursuing the necessary education. These typically occur up to the age of eighteen. The second stage, organisational entry, focuses on the individual's initial job offer, and the selection of an appropriate job based on accurate information. Stage three focuses on the early career. The key priorities are establishment and achievement. The key tasks are learning the job, learning organisational rules and norms, filling into the chosen occupation and organisation, developing competence and pursuing career goals. Stage four focuses on the mid-career which typically occurs between the ages of forty and fifty-five. The main tasks involve reappraising early career and early adulthood, recertifying or modifying career goals, making choices for the next phase of the career, and maintaining the desire to remain productive at work. The late career stage focuses on the maintenance of self-esteem, remaining productive at work and preparation for retirement.

Driver (1994) suggested that it may be more appropriate to consider different career patterns. This model suggests that there are four different patterns, or career concepts, of career experience. These concepts differ in the direction and frequency of movement. The manager will have a different set of motives depending on the concept implemented.

- *Linear:* This career is characterised by consistent and steady movement up the organisational hierarchy, the job holder taking on positions of greater responsibility and authority. The individual is primarily motivated by a need for power and achievement. The linear career is often considered to represent the traditional or typical view of a career.
- *Expert:* This career is characterised by a devotion to a particular occupation. The manager will focus on building knowledge and skill within a speciality. There may be little upward movement. The manager will be strongly motivated by both competence and stability.
- *Spiral:* This career consists of a lifelong progression of periodic moves across related occupations, disciplines or specialities. The manager will spend a sufficient amount of time in the area to achieve a sufficient level of competence before moving on. There is a strong emphasis on creativity and personal growth.
- *Transitory:* This includes a progression of moves across different or unrelated jobs or fields. It is a non-traditional career. The reasons for the moves include variety and independence.

Brousseau *et al.* (1996) argued that these four concepts can be combined to form a wide variety of hybrid concepts. While the traditional model of career has favoured managers with a linear or expert career concept, the shift in thinking about work and work–life balance issues places increased emphasis on managers with transitory or spiral concepts. They argued that organisations and managers need to think differently about career development and that a more pluralistic and flexible approach to managing and developing careers is required.

Organisation-Focused Career Development Theories

Organisation-focused theories are premised on the idea that an organisation's structure and needs should guide its career management systems. Organisation-focused theories have become popular in recent years, and include pluralistic and team-based career development models.

Typology of Career Systems: Sonnenfeld, Peiperl and Kotter (1988) conducted very interesting research in the area of relating career systems and succession planning strategies to different strategic corporate contexts. They found that the most effective career systems in organisations were those that were clearly matched to the organisation's overall strategies. It was shown that a) the competitiveness of the product markets, and b) the openness of the organisation to employment at all levels had implications for career management. Using these two dimensions, Sonnenfeld, Peiperl and Kotter identified four career system types: Fortress; Baseball Team; Club; Academy (Figure 13.3).

The academy has an internal supply flow and an individually based assignment flow. Firms that employ this strategy devote effort to early-career hiring and long-term career development within the company. Career development activities would include: extensive job-specific training; talent management; and elaborate career paths for successful candidates. Examples of this approach are found in large blue chip organisations such as Hewlett Packard and General Motors.

Figure 13.3: A Typology of Career Systems: Linking Career Systems to Competitive Strategy

	FORTRESS	BASEBALL TEAM
External (Supply Flow)	• Human resource orientation: retrenchment • Strategic model: reactor • Typical competitive strategy: cost, e.g. retails, textiles	• Human resource orientation: recruitment • Strategic model: prospector • Typical competitive strategy: focus (based on human skills), e.g. software, houses, advertising, law firms
	CLUB	**ACADEMY**
Internal	• Human resource orientation: retention • Strategic model: defender • Typical competitive strategy: focus (non-competitive), e.g. utilities, government agencies, banks	• Human resource orientation: development • Strategic model: analyser • Typical competitive strategy: differentiation, e.g. pharmaceuticals, car production

The baseball team-type organisation is characterised by external supply flow and individual assignments. The human resource orientation is recruitment, and individuals will be hired in at all levels. The emphasis is on an individual's credentials and expertise. Career development will tend to be on-the-job training with little emphasis on succession planning. This type of organisation will offer highly motivated individuals an opportunity to be a star performer and to be highly rewarded. Typical examples include software houses and advertising firms. Club-type organisations (e.g. utilities and banks) focus strongly on internal supply and on commitment, job security and hierarchy. An early career, general career development, slow progression and reliability are emphasised. The fortress-style organisation encompasses external supply flow and group contribution. This is the type of organisation that is under siege because of market conditions or a specific business crisis. The goal for everyone is survival, and individual commitment is very low. Career development is about trying to retain core talent and knowledge within the company. Typical examples are airlines and retailers.

This model is useful in that it links career development with organisational strategy. However, not all organisations will fit neatly into one category or the other. Woodall and Winstanley (1998) commented that, with the variety that now exists in terms of employment contracts (even within the one organisation), more sophisticated models relating career systems to corporate strategy will be required for the future.

A Pluralist Approach to Careers: Brousseau *et al.* (199:52) introduced the idea of a pluralist career concept against the backdrop of what they describe as 'career pandemonium'. They acknowledge the current 'destabilisation of relationships between people and organisations' and recommend a pluralist approach that takes account of varied amounts of organisational structure with varied career opportunities. Their view (p. 56) is that 'a pluralist framework specifies that there are markedly different approaches to career management and development in organisations'. An organisation's career culture is defined by the organisation's structure, what forms of performance it values and the rewards it offers managers. Its career culture should support its strategic direction. They suggest that an organisation involved in diversification should adopt a spiral career concept culture (Table 13.8).

Table 13.8: Four Career Concepts and Related Organisational Career Cultures

Key Features and Motives				
	Linear	Expert	Spiral	Lateral
Direction of movement	Upward	Little movement	Lateral	Lateral
Duration of stay in one field	Variable	Life	7-10 years	3-5 years
Key motives	Power Achievement	Expertise Security	Personal growth Creativity	Variety Independence

Organisational Career Cultures				
	Linear	Expert	Spiral	Lateral
Structure	Tall pyramid Narrow span of control	Flat Strong functional departments	Matrix Self-directed, interdisciplinary teams	Loose, amorphous structure Temporary teams
Valued performance	Leadership Efficiency Logistics management	Quality Reliability Stability Technical competence	Creativity Teamwork People development	Speed Adaptability Innovation
Rewards	Promotions Management perquisites Executive bonuses	Fringe benefits Recognition rewards Continuing technical training	Lateral assignments Cross training Creative latitude	Immediate cash bonuses Independence and autonomy Special temporary assignments Job rotation

Brousseau *et al.* argued that organisations need to combine varied and different amounts of organisational structure with different career opportunities. They should retain sufficient structure to maintain core leadership competencies, while adopting more flexible arrangements to cope with external change and flux. So, can an organisation manage to sustain two or more career cultures simultaneously? Our experience is that organisations do this, but it may not be planned or systematic. For example, linear and expert career concepts can be managed together very comfortably. Individuals who want to be experts or specialists will not necessarily want to manage teams. Therefore, individuals with general manager aspirations can move up the ladder acquiring more and more people responsibility. Designing and managing pluralist career cultures in a single organisation is challenging but essential if organisations are to attract and retain key performers at all organisational levels.

Operationally, Brousseau *et al.* suggest that organisations should offer three types of career management: counselling, individual career development contracts, and a cafeteria approach that incorporates a variety of career track options, training, development and performance management. A pluralist career model challenges organisations to have an ongoing process of assessing the gaps between the organisations' strategy and managers' career concepts and motives. It should identify the optimal organisational structure and identify and implement strategically aligned career management processes.

A Systems View of Career Management: Nicholson (1996) proposed a career development system that consists of three key elements: people, job market, and management and information systems. The people system involves various activities involved in selecting, developing, motivating and retaining management talent. The job market system includes the structure of development opportunities within the organisation. The management and information system facilitates the exchange of ideas, information and people. The task of career management is to ensure that these three systems are interlinked. This can be achieved by ensuring that career information is accessible and useful and providing development opportunities which are flexible to the needs of individuals. Nicholson suggested that a well-integrated system will ensure that there is better-quality leadership, teamwork, flexibility and capacity to deal with change.

Team-Based Career Development: Cianni and Wnuck (1997) proposed a team-based model of career development. Increasingly, organisations are becoming more team-oriented. Cianni and Wnuck suggest that in these organisations, career development responsibility can be shared between the individual, team and organisation. They identify six characteristics of team-based career development:

- Team members act as role models.
- Teams reward behaviours that enhance team performance and growth. They also encourage personal growth and development.
- The team determines development opportunities for both the team and for individuals.
- The team moves collectively to higher organisational levels.
- Individuals move laterally within the team.
- The organisation evaluates the team and the team evaluates the individual.

The model suggests different development activities depending on the team's stage of development. Stage one development activities are designed to integrate the individuals into the team. They may include team-building, personal style assessment and project management training. Stage two interventions focus on further development of the team, including task rotation, coaching and team problem-solving. Stage three development activities focus on making the team independent and accountable for its performance. These include leadership rotation and leadership potential assessment.

EXHIBIT 13.3

Perspective on Theory: Using Metaphors to Understand Careers

Metaphor	Explanation
Careers as Inheritance	• Individuals have a unique starting point in their careers. • This starting point can be understood and taken account of but may be difficult to change. • Individuals are born with some career inheritances, such as gender, genetic make-up, whereas others result from family and school influences, including values, motivation and beliefs. • An individual's inheritance will predict aspects of career.
Careers as Cycles	• The cycle metaphor emphasises that individuals cannot expect themselves or their context to stay constant. • Life consists of natural patterns which will override predetermined plans. • A career is only one aspect of an individual's life. • In some cases career cycle theories suggest that it is possible to connect particular stages of career to particular age categories.
Careers as Action	• The action metaphor emphasises that individuals are capable of exercising a degree of agency over careers. • Individuals have the capacity to express themselves, to make career decisions and to take proactive steps to manage career. • If individuals are empowered to take responsibility for their own careers and are provided with the information and skills to do so, then they can act in their own careers.
Careers as Fit	• This metaphor highlights the importance of finding a strong fit between the person and the career. • Person–career fit is a necessary precondition for a successful and happy career. • Fit can be enhanced through a process of gathering knowledge about self and the world of work. • Where individuals have a detailed knowledge of each, they will strive to achieve greater fit.
Careers as Journeys	• This metaphor highlights that careers are whole-of-life experiences. • Careers take individuals on unexpected journeys and the destination may not always be clear. • Careers can take a multiplicity of routes to reach a particular destination. • Careers therefore have movement. This may be a path, a ladder, a fast track or a plateau.
Careers as Roles	• Careers involve a multiplicity of stakeholders who will have different views concerning how individuals should conduct their careers. • Careers involve negotiation with others in a work and in a non-work context. • Individuals are required to play multiple roles, which may not be compatible with each other.

Metaphor	Explanation
Careers as Relationships	• Careers are conducted in a social context. They have meaning and effects in relation to other people and institutions. • Careers are largely an expression of the social networks to which people belong. • Connections can be developed purposefully and in a calculated way in order to enhance one's career. • Career networking is a continuous process and networks are reciprocal in nature.
Careers as Resources	• Careers are economic. They have a resource base and a potential to develop other resources. • Careers serve as inputs to organisations. The question arises concerning who owns these resources and how best they can be developed and for what purpose. • Organisation and individual goals may not always be congruent and they are unlikely to be over-identified. • A resource metaphor raises challenging questions concerning who has ownership of a career.
Careers as Stories	• This metaphor highlights that careers are subjective phenomena. • Careers help individuals to understand and express their identities. • Careers allow individuals to find meaning in their work. • Career stories can be used to facilitate the process of career development.

Contemporary Issues in Career Development

Organisations frequently have to address specific career development issues. Those particularly highlighted include career development, issues for women, career plateauing and derailment, and career development that does not involve advancement.

Women's Career Development Issues

It is widely acknowledged that women's careers do not unfold in the same way as traditional 'male' hierarchical career models. The new views of career paths that have emerged, such as downward, lateral, spiral and transitory, are more representative of the typical career paths of women in the workplace. Having said this, it must be noted that women have made progress in hierarchical career terms in the last two decades. Davidson and Burke (2004) showed that there are now more women in executive positions, more female CEOs and more women on corporate boards worldwide. However, this increase in presence at more senior levels within organisations has been shown to be modest. This raises a number of questions in terms of women's careers. For example, do women have different career expectations than men? Do women have different success criteria in terms of their careers? Are women being blocked from getting to the top? Is the proverbial 'glass ceiling' (an invisible but impassable barrier that limits the career development of women) still in existence? O'Neil and Bilimoria (2005) delineate women's careers as unfolding in three distinct phases (Table 13.9):

Table 13.9: Phases in Women's Careers

Career Phase 1: Idealistic Achievement
- Early career (ages 24–35)
- Career choices based on desire for career satisfaction, achievement and success (inner satisfaction)
- Proactive career management
- Unlimited possibilities to 'do and have it all'

Career Phase 2: Pragmatic Endurance
- Mid-career (ages 36-45)
- Pragmatic about careers; doing what it takes to get the job done
- Managing multiple priorities – personally and professionally
- May be questioning centrality of careers in their lives
- Can be dissatisfied and disenfranchised with their workplaces
- Searching for more overall meaning in their lives

Career Phase 3: Reinvent Contribution
- Advanced career (ages 46-60)
- Focused on contributing to their organisations, their families and their communities
- Likely to have a stable, planned career path
- Success is about recognition, respect and living integrated lives
- Seeking for work that makes a meaningful contribution

Source: Adapted from O'Neil and Bilimoria (2005)

This research suggests that if organisations want to retain talented women in the workplace, they need to be flexible, particularly in the mid-career phase when women are balancing multiple work and non-work demands. A linear career model will not fit the needs of the majority of women in the organisation. For example, in the early career phase, women need challenging assignments which will stretch and develop their capabilities. In the second career phase for women, their managers 'must recognize that the careers of these women are embedded in their larger life contexts and work with each individual to identify the necessary resources that will allow them to do their best work' (O'Neil and Bilimoria 2005:185). Finally, organisations have a lot to gain from women at the advanced career stage and this must be recognised and rewarded. These women make excellent coaches and mentors to younger people within the organisation and to younger women in particular.

Ruderman *et al.* (2002) studied how the roles that women play in their personal lives impact on their effectiveness as managers. They identified six aspects of personal lives which enhance professional lives.

- Psychological benefits from overcoming obstacles and taking risks. Success in personal areas enhances self-esteem, self-confidence and courage.
- Opportunity to enrich interpersonal skills. Dealing with children helps them to motivate, respect and develop others' skills. These skills are highly transferable to the workplace.
- Emotional support and advice. Friends and family can act as an effective sounding board and a source of motivation.
- Multi-tasking. Women frequently have to multi-task in the home and are particularly effective in prioritising and planning.
- Leadership opportunities. The family setting provides lots of opportunities for leadership, as does the wider community.
- The personal interests of women provide skills and valuable perspectives for understanding relationships at work.

Madsen (2008) suggested that effective career development for women requires organisations to expand their definitions of effective leadership. Eagly and Carli (2003) identified four considerations for organisations. First, organisations must realise that women themselves have changed and that they have different career aspirations. Second, leadership roles have changed. Third, organisational practices have changed and, finally, culture has changed. These suggest a greater commitment to involvement of women in senior leadership roles.

EXHIBIT 13.4

Kaleidoscope Careers: An Alternative Explanation for Women's Careers

Mainiero and Sullivan (2005) suggest a Kaleidoscope Career Model, which advocates that women's careers need to be perceived as relational. Their career decisions are made as part of a large and intricate web of 'interconnected issues, people and aspects' that come together in a balanced way. Women, according to the model, shift the pattern of their careers by rotating different aspects of their lives and arranging their roles and relationships in new ways. Actions taken by women in their careers have profound and long-lasting effects on others. Women take actions in respect of career having regard to the impact of such actions on others, rather than considering those actions in isolation.

The model highlights three key issues that are relevant to women's careers: authenticity, balance and challenge. Authenticity focuses on the extent to which the woman can be herself and be authentic. Balance focuses on the extent to which a woman can balance the different parts of her life if she makes a particular career decision. Challenge focuses on the extent to which a woman will be sufficiently challenged if she takes a particular career option.

In the early career, women tend to be concerned with goal achievement and challenge. Issues of balance and authenticity are important but they tend to recede into the background while the woman pursues her career. This pattern changes in mid-career. At this stage women are expected to have to cope with issues of balance and family/relational demands. Balance therefore moves to the forefront. Women may wish to experience challenge and authenticity, but these issues are secondary because compromises have to be made in the interest of balance. In the later career stage, women tend to be free of balance issues, so authenticity emerges again as a primary concern. They may also wish to pursue challenge and balance, but authenticity is the primary issue.

This career pattern provides significant career management challenges for organisations. There is ample evidence that women are opting out and organisations are losing a vital human resource. They have, in many cases, experienced a talent drain of women. This has, in some cases, promoted organisations to consider a range of policies and initiatives that fall within the general category of work–life balance issues.

Mainiero and Sullivan suggest specific initiatives that organisations can take in order to accommodate the kaleidoscope model of careers:

- *Flexible Work Schedules*: This could involve the redesign of work so that it is more flexible, and utilising technology so that it is possible for managers to work remotely from their offices 24/7. Organisations may reinforce these behaviours by rewarding and promoting managers who are perceived as role models for others.
- *Challenging Linear Career Paths*: Organisations that accept kaleidoscope career models will implement alternative career paths and provide opportunities for women to 'opt back in'. Organisations need to consider on-ramps as well as off-ramps so that women in particular are able to take career interruptions and return at a later stage. Women who return should, where possible, be rewarded with advancement opportunities.

- *Accountability for Advancement of Women in Organisations*: Organisations should make managers accountable for both retaining and advancing the careers of women. This could involve providing career succession plans that enable women to take career interruptions. Organisations should continuously monitor the number of men and women in the talent 'pipeline'. Some organisations have implemented early field experiences for women who have yet to take a career interruption.
- *Be Innovative in the Use of Reward Systems*: Organisations are encouraged to design reward systems that recognise performance and outcomes rather than face time. They should also take proactive steps to eliminate gender inequalities in training, promotion and financial reward systems. Organisations may also consider the use of multi-source feedback systems that include feedback from family and friends.
- *Focus on Changing the Organisation Culture*: Organisations should strive to create an organisational culture that encourages and promotes the use of family-friendly programmes. The concept of family needs to be redefined to focus on women in care-giving roles. Organisations may also encourage and implement initiatives such as corporate sabbaticals, tuition reimbursement programmes and special programmes for children.

Source: Mainiero and Sullivan (2005)

Career Plateau and Career Derailment Issues

A career plateau as defined by Applebaum and Santiago (1997:13) is a stage when 'after a period of consistent career progression within an organization or several organizations, the individual's role takes on a sameness'. They referred to the measurement norm of five or six years in the same job, noting that this can vary according to the individual and the organisational culture. They drew a distinction between organisational plateaux and personal plateaux. Individuals who are organisationally plateaued may have the ability to perform a job at a higher level, but the openings may not be currently available. This can lead to quite a lot of frustration on the part of the individual who believes that he/she is ready for the next move and it requires skilful management by the leader. Individuals who are categorised as personally plateaued are viewed as not desiring a higher-level job. This individual may have the necessary ability but does not want the responsibility.

A career plateau can be viewed as positive or negative, depending on the individual's outlook. Some commentators would argue that the learning process requires plateaus. Following a period of rapid career enhancement, an individual can benefit from an opportunity to assimilate new knowledge and skills. Others view career plateaux as negative and proffer strategies to avoid getting your career 'in a rut'. From an organisational point of view, individuals need to be encouraged to think of careers in the broadest sense, i.e. multidirectional. Once an employee is learning and developing, he/she should not feel that his/her career has plateaued. Leaders need to demonstrate this learning ethos if it is to permeate the organisation and avoid the potential negative effects of career plateaus; frustration, dissatisfaction and poor performance.

Moving on to career derailment, research indicates that somewhere between thirty and fifty per cent of managers and executives fail (Charan and Colvin 1999; Curphy and Hogan 2004). McCall and Lombardo (1983:23) originally defined derailment as follows: 'A derailed executive is a person who has been very successful in his or her managerial career, but who failed to live up to his or her full potential, as the organisation saw it.' The consequences for this person could be demotion, retirement or a long-term career plateau, depending on the company's HR policy. The outcome of career derailment is the non-voluntary end of career progression within that company. Managers and executives derail for similar reasons across industries and organisations. McCall (1998:36) outlined the dynamics of derailment as follows:

- *Strengths become Weaknesses*: Strengths that enable a manager to succeed in one situation can become liabilities in another, e.g. a team player might be perceived as lacking independent judgement.
- *Blind Spots Matter*: Weaknesses that were not deemed central in the past are now critical. A common blind spot found in McCall's research was insensitivity.
- *Success Leads to Arrogance*: Success goes to a manager's head and he/she begins to think that he/she is infallible and does not need others.
- *Bad Luck*: Derailment can result from a run-in with fate, in combination with one of the other dynamics.

Yukl (2002) suggested that a number of factors explain whether a manager advances or derails. These include:

- *Emotional Stability*: Managers need to be able to handle pressure.
- *Defensiveness*: Successful managers learn from mistakes and move on, i.e. successful managers have the ability to learn and adapt to change.
- *Integrity*: Managers who derail are too ambitious about career advancement at the expense of others.
- *Interpersonal Skills*: Managers who derail are weak at interpersonal skills, especially in terms of team leadership.
- *Technical and Cognitive Skills*: Managers who derail can be technically brilliant at the expense of seeing the bigger picture.

Table 13.10 summarises some of the research on leadership derailment. This table highlights a number of key trends:

- *Inability to Build Relationships*: Derailed managers tend to be very insensitive to the needs of their followers and peers. They are often over-competitive, demanding and domineering. They are also likely to be extremely arrogant and to believe that no one in their organisation is as good as they are. They do whatever is necessary to get the job done, and this often involves stepping on a few toes while doing so.
- *Failure to Meet Business Objectives*: Derailed managers are less successful in handling business issues and fail to meet business goals. Derailed managers tend to engage in finger-pointing and blame others for problems.
- *Inability to Lead and Build a Team*: Derailed managers have a tendency to hire people who are too much like themselves. They frequently want to stay in the limelight and hire team members less capable than they are. They often micromanage their staff even when they are not expert in the tasks involved.
- *Inability to Adapt*: Derailed managers find difficulty in adjusting to new cultures, structures and processes. They persist in acting the same way, even when it is no longer effective. They have a tendency to impose solutions and find it difficult to accept new or innovative ideas.

Table 13.10: Career Derailment in Organisations: Individual and Organisational Factors and Possible Management Interventions

Factor	Managerial Intervention
Individual:	
• Narrow and short-sighted emphasis on immediate results and/or technical expertise	• Design a performance goal system which rewards a broad range of behaviours and outcomes
• A lack of intrinsic motivation due to low task identity, low task variety and low growth need	• Redesign the manager's job to ensure that it contains motivational elements
• Assumption that managers are smarter than everyone else – arrogance which prevents learning	• Provide feedback and enhance the self-awareness of the manager
• Poor listening skills and empathy with peers	• Provide development to the manager to enhance his/her interpersonal skills
• A lack of self-control; self-centredness; poor emotional maturity and resilience	• Intervention to enhance the emotional intelligence of the manager
• Too much focus on personal achievement at the expense of collaboration and teamwork	• Provide the manager with projects and tasks where he/she has to work as part of a team
• Too much of a results focus and, as a result, losing sight of the big picture	• Individual coaching or mentoring intervention
• Placing too much emphasis on perfection with the result that deadlines are missed	• Coaching or mentoring intervention
• Stress and burnout due to role conflict and poor interpersonal relationships in the job	• Better work–life balance; development of interpersonal skills; provide incentives to leave the organisation
Organisational:	
• Slow organisational growth due to poor strategy and management practices	• Consider reduction in the number of managers; encourage sabbaticals
• Organisation assumes that the cream will rise to the top and as a result it does not invest in development	• Design a systematic development process for high potentials which includes stretch job assignments
• Lack of a framework within which to manage the manager's career and poorly selected development assignments	• Devise an appropriate career framework with planned job and developmental moves
• Assuming that an effective manager will work in any position that he/she is promoted to	• Support managers who are floundering in new positions; provide supports and safety nets
• Managers get promoted too quickly without sufficient opportunity to learn from experience	• Give managers time to learn from experience; allow managers to fail; ensure coaching and feedback
• The culture of the organisation does not allow managers to learn from their failures	• Support managers to conduct analysis of why they failed

The following are questions that managers should ask to determine whether they are at risk of career derailment.

1. *Disagreements with Higher Management:* Obviously this is a no-no, even if the manager's point of view is correct. Those who would rather be right than be promoted almost always get their wish.
2. *Problems with Team-Building:* Managers need to be good at spotting talent. Building diversity, developing talent and helping people work together effectively are also core capabilities that a manager cannot do without for very long.
3. *Problems Developing Working Relationships:* If people do not want to be around a manager, that manager's career is in trouble. Bullying, isolation and being out of the loop in various ways all torpedo corporate careers.
4. *Lack of Follow-Through*: When managers consistently forget to follow up on promises and do not attend to important details, people notice and question the wisdom of handing managers anything else to forget.
5. *Problems Moving from a Technical to a Strategic Level:* This is where engineers and other highly technical people can stumble and find themselves unable to go beyond what they know in order to formulate more complex strategies. If managers are on their way up the ladder from a highly technical role to a more managerial one, it is important to ask for feedback on skills that need to be developed.
6. *Assuming that Something Other than Your Own Hard Work and Strategising Will Take You Where You Want to Go*: Being overly dependent on a powerful boss or some other advocate, or even on natural talent, sometimes causes high-potential managers to get a little lazy. Exhibit 13.5 highlights some surreptitious career strategies that are used by managers.

EXHIBIT 13.5

Perspective on Theory: Utilising Surreptitious Career Success Strategies

Obligation Creation and Exploitation	• This strategy involves purposefully forming, maintaining and taking advantage of perceived independencies. • Obligations can be created to advance, promote or defend individuals to secure positions of authority or influence. • Obligations may be created through acquiring and supplying something desired, which may include friendliness. • Obligations may also be created through the gradual supply of small 'gifts'.
Personal Status Enhancement	• This strategy involves actions intentionally designed to improve the perceived standing or position of an individual relative to a competitor. • Efforts may be made by individuals to increase their personal standing by damaging the reputation of others. • Individuals may establish supportive peer relationships or a coalition strategy of improved influence. • Personal status enhancement may be pursued through emotional or sexual association.

Information Acquisition and Control	• This strategy involves the collection of pertinent and advantageous information and its control to the perceived benefit of the individual. • Information may be gathered through subterfuge or surreptitiously from subordinates. • It may also involve the calculated control of obtained data and its release to the benefit of the individual.
Similarity Exploitation	• This involves deliberately taking advantage of similarities with others for the purpose of career enhancement. • Demographic similarity may be used to influence a senior organisational member of similar demographic background. • Similarity may also involve situations where there are shared contacts or associations. • Similarity may involve the sharing of past educational experiences and the use of the old school-tie network. • People may also use intra-firm family contacts to their career advantage. This may constitute a form of nepotism.
Proactive Vertical Alignment	• This involves the deliberate search, identification, pursuit and development of close personal relationships with an individual in a position of authority or influence. • It may involve a form of proactive mentor acquisition or it may involve the acquisition of informal mentors or unofficial mentors. • It may also involve attempts to circumvent an immediate supervisor who is perceived as impeding an individual's career.

Source: Harris and Ogbonna (2006)

Career Motivation and Career Development Without Advancement

One of the most significant challenges for organisations is the development of career motivation. London (1985) suggested that career motivation impacts on how managers choose their careers, how they view their careers, how hard they work on them and how long they stay in them. Noe (2005:349) defines career motivation as 'employees' energy to invest in their careers, their awareness of the direction they want their careers to take, and their ability to maintain energy and direction despite the barriers they may encounter'. London and Mone (1987) pointed out that career motivation consists of career salience, career insight and career identity. Table 13.11 provides a summary of each concept and strategies that can be used to enhance them.

Table 13.11: Facets of Career Motivation and Strategies to Enhance Them

Definitions of the Three Facets of Career Motivation

- **Career Resilience:** The extent to which people resist career barriers or disruptions affecting their work. This consists of self-confidence, need for achievement, the willingness to take risks, and the ability to act independently and co-operatively as appropriate.
- **Career Insight:** The extent to which people are realistic about themselves and their careers and how these perceptions are related to career goals. This includes developing goals and gaining knowledge of the self and the environment.
- **Career Identity:** The extent to which people define themselves by their work. This includes involvement in job, organisation and profession and the direction of career goals (e.g. towards advancement in the organisation).

Strategies to Increase Career Motivation

- **To support career resilience**
  - Build employees' self-confidence through feedback and positive reinforcement
  - Generate opportunities for achievement
  - Create an environment conducive to risk-taking by rewarding innovation and reducing fear of failure
  - Show interpersonal concern and encourage group cohesiveness and collaborative working relationships
- **To enhance career insight**
  - Encourage employees to set their own goals
  - Supply employees with information relevant to attaining their career goals
  - Provide regular performance feedback
- **To build career identity**
  - Encourage work involvement through job challenge and professional growth
  - Provide career development opportunities, such as leadership positions and advancement potential
  - Reward solid performance through professional recognition and/or financial bonus

Source: London (1991)

The modern organisation is increasingly faced with a situation in which there are fewer opportunities for vertical career progression. Organisations, it is suggested, need to focus on an enriched career development strategy. This strategy involves certification, retraining programmes, job transfers and rotation, and development activities that focus on enhancing managers' sense of self-esteem and self-determination in guiding their own careers. We discussed a number of these strategies in detail in Chapters Nine and Eleven.

Designing Effective Career Development Processes

We focus in this last section on the issues that organisations need to consider when designing effective career development systems for managers. These include the manager's key role in career development, the selection of career development practices, individual counselling on career issues and the elements of effective career management.

Roles in Career Management

The manager as developer has a primary responsibility for his/her own career. Hall (1996) emphasised that career management is a lifelong process and argued that managers must become more adaptable. Jones and DeFillippi (1996) identified six competencies that are required by managers to successfully operate the boundaryless career and be effective in networked organisations. These are:

- *Knowing What*: Understanding the industry's key threats and opportunities.
- *Knowing Why*: Understanding the meaning, motives and interests in pursuing a career.
- *Knowing Where*: Understanding the locations and boundaries for entering, developing and advancing within an organisation's career system.
- *Knowing Whom*: Establishing relationships, based on personal attraction and potential to develop social capital, that will gain access to opportunities and resources.
- *Knowing When*: Understanding the timing and choice of development activities to use during one's career.
- *Knowing How*: Understanding and acquiring the skills and competencies required for effective performance in the managerial role.

Our experience in working with individual managers in organisations would suggest that, in order to be successful, managers must develop the skills of managing their own careers, as well as working in a supportive environment. It also follows that the manager must be committed to ongoing learning and career development, as a principle, in order to facilitate effective learning and development for his/her team members. Therefore, the manager needs to role model proactive career management for his/her own sake and overall to enhance organisational success. A very useful model in this regard was presented by Ball (1997). He proposed a model of career self-management competencies which can be adopted by the individual and the organisation as a step towards partnership in career management.

Table 13.12: Ball's Four Overlapping Career Competencies

Competencies	Behaviours
Optimising Career Prospects	• Take a goal-oriented approach to career planning • Gather intelligence across the organisation • Make use of formal or informal mentors • Project a positive self-image • Work alongside colleagues who are seen as high performers • Envision future opportunities, create and make own chances
Career Planning – Playing to Your Strengths	• Take advantage of learning opportunities within work roles • Review – personal review and self-appraisal • Explore – researching options for change or progression • Plan – establishing goals and decisions, based on first two steps • Act – taking actions and reviewing outcomes

Engaging in Personal Development	• Individual employees need to take advantage of whatever development opportunities exist by:
	  – Having sufficient self-awareness to review and identify their development needs
	  – Being an effective learner, with a positive attitude towards the learning process
	  – Finding others to support them in the learning process

Balancing Work and Non-Work	• The required balance is based on individual needs and life stages • 'Lifestyle' is an important career anchor for some individuals

Source: Adapted from Ball (1997:76-79)

What constitutes career success for managers has changed. Career success will be defined differently by individual managers. Therefore, it is important for individual leaders to know what success means for them so that they can strive to achieve it on their terms.

Career success for the individual and the organisation depends on being able to have open, honest dialogue. This accountability must rest with line managers, and line managers therefore need structured career management support from the organisation. Career management, like other HR practices, is a lot more challenging in today's business environment. However, it is an area that must be addressed in a proactive way so that the company's vital assets (people) are aligned with the overall strategic goals.

The Manager as Developer: The manager has a key role to play in the career management of other managers. The manager can provide accurate information about career paths and opportunities within the organisation. The manager supports individual managers' career plans and serves as a source of feedback to managers throughout career progress. Leibowiktz and Schlossberg (1981) suggested four roles that managers need to perform to fulfil their responsibilities as career developers. These roles involve being a coach, an appraiser, an adviser and a referral agent. Coaching focuses on defining managers' career concerns; appraising focuses on clarifying career goals and giving feedback; advising focuses on identifying and evaluating career options; and a referral agent focuses on action planning and linking with key organisational resources and career supports.

The Leadership Development Specialist: The role of the leadership development specialist is to ensure that career development activities help both the organisation and the manager to achieve their goals. Hall (1993) suggested that leadership development specialists must focus on enabling managers become 'masters of their own careers'. This involves paying attention to the following issues:

- Start with the recognition that the manager has ownership of his or her career.
- Provide information support to enable the manager to take career development initiatives.
- Develop expertise on career information and assessment processes.
- Promote career support services and form a career contract with managers.
- Encourage job experience that relates to organisational goals.
- Promote career development through relationships at work.
- Provide support when the manager experiences career roadblocks.
- Promote mobility and the idea that learning is lifelong.
- Develop a mindset of using existing resources for career development.

Enhancing Career Management Processes in Organisations

King (2004) suggested that career management focuses on the design and implementation of organisational processes which enable the careers of individuals to be planned and managed in a way that optimises both the needs of the organisation and the preferences and capabilities of individuals. It is possible to achieve effective career management with appropriate planning in an organisational context. Career development, in contrast, is more challenging to achieve because it is longer-term in nature. For example, it may not be possible for an individual to achieve their long-term career ambitions in their current organisation. It is also very difficult for organisations to plan for competencies that will be required five to ten years hence. Most organisations tend to focus on career management and career management systems matched to current priorities, if they invest in this area at all. It is possible for individuals and organisations to have very productive and honest dialogue in this realm. Long-term career development (next ten years) tends to stay with the individual in terms of ownership and responsibility.

King (2004) suggested that effective career management needs to pay attention to four key issues:

- *Consistency*: Ensure that consistent messages relating to career management are delivered by HR professionals and line managers.
- *Proactivity*: Maintain current capabilities of the organisation whilst building flexibility and agility for the future.
- *Collaboration*: A partnership approach is required between employer and employees.
- *Dynamism*: Flexibility is required from employer and employee as so much can change for both parties over time.

Hirsch and Jackson (1996) suggested that career development can be managed in a number of ways, even within the one organisation (Figure 13.4).

Figure 13.4: The Career Development Continuum in Organisations

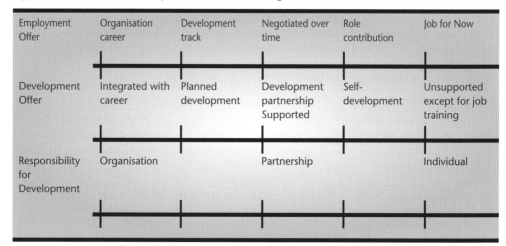

This career development continuum is also interesting from the point of view that full-scale career development, where the organisation is responsible for development, is more the exception than the rule today. This equates to career development where the manager's future goals and life goals are considered by the organisation. The middle of the continuum highlights a career management scenario where current priorities are taken into account on both sides. While a partnership approach to career management is recommended, it is widely acknowledged that this is not easily achieved. This is evident from the way that much of the literature addresses career management and development from the perspective of the individual or the organisation.

Gutteridge, Leibowitz and Shore (1993) argued that organisations should adopt a systems approach when designing a career management system. This involves making clear links between career management and business strategy and aligning the manager and organisational needs. Organisations should endeavour to design systems that link with other leadership development and human resource systems, creating a corporate-wide infrastructure. It is also important to ensure line manager participation; hold them accountable and provide them with skills to fulfil their responsibilities. Finally, it is important to have continuous evaluation and improvement of the system. Table 13.13 summarises some of the approaches to organisational career management and the roles of the various stakeholders.

Table 13.13: Organisational Approach to Career Management and Roles of Key Stakeholders

Role/Activity	Employee	Manager	HR Manager	Organisation
Career Planning and Support	• Self-assessment • Self-development action plan (including career development objectives) • Ask for independent counselling and support	• Support objective-setting process • Provide input to assessment process • Assist employees in setting realistic objectives • Provide access to career counselling or other external resources if required • Request information from other company resources	• Share specialist knowledge on career planning and development • Provide workshop where individual can identify strengths and weaknesses vis-à-vis critical competencies • Provide specialised services, e.g. assessment, counselling	• Decide on approach to career management • Develop system to support career management • Set up career resource centres
Learning and Development (Formal and Informal	• Develop new skills • Maximise all learning opportunities • Actively network • Take personal charge	• Encourage two-way feedback • Provide coaching on the job • Encourage continuous learning	• Provide developmental workshops on topics such as learning styles and accelerated learning • Encourage a culture of continuous learning within the organisation, e.g. 'it's ok to make mistakes'	• Develop culture that supports career management (as part of a learning organisation) • Encourage honest communication • Train managers in coaching skills • Support the set-up of mentoring relationships
Job Performance/ Developmental Assignments	• Create visibility through good performance and relationships • Seek challenging job assignments • Self-market	• Conduct formal appraisal • Encourage employee to take on tough assignments with SMART objectives • Challenge employees	• Support the implementation of the performance management process • Support individuals considering developmental assignments	• Set up effective performance management processes • Market jobs to staff • Set up systems to support secondment, international assignments and career breaks

Role/Activity	Employee	Manager	HR Manager	Organisation
Initiatives aimed at Specific Populations	• Take the opportunity (if offered) • Discuss career progression with line managers	• Support specific initiatives involving specific employees	• Support specific schemes, e.g. succession planning, graduate development centres	• Decide on organisational strategy re same, e.g. succession planning

Career Management Practices in Organisations

Organisations have a wide variety of career management practices to choose from. These tend to fall into the categories of self-assessment tools, individual career counselling, career information and job matching, organisationally focused assessment processes and development programmes. We will focus here on the first four. Development strategies were dealt with in more detail in Chapters Eight to Eleven.

Self-Assessment Tools: These tools focus on providing the manager with a systematic means of identifying capabilities and career preferences. Self-assessment can be undertaken by the individual manager, but it is important that the correct interpretations are made. Smith (1988) suggested that effective self-assessments should set the stage for reflection and help the manager explore values, interests, competencies, resources and goals. Some organisations provide career assessment workshops which enable managers discuss personal information on strengths, weaknesses, goals and values. Workshops are also valuable for reality testing of insights and expectations. Greenhaus and Callanan (1994) highlighted that it is also important to evaluate the environment in order to contextualise career goals.

Individual Counselling: Career-focused counselling involves one-to-one discussions between the manager and a specialist career counsellor. These may be informal or formal and may involve a series of interactions. Managers may also play the career counsellor role, but they must be trained to perform this role and the wider career development process must be clarified. The leadership development specialist may be the most appropriate individual to conduct this counselling. Managers are often reluctant to discuss their career plans with their current bosses or to take advice from a non-professional.

Career Information and Job Matching: Accurate information is an essential element of effective career management. Organisations achieve this task in a number of ways. Job posting involves making open positions known to managers before they are advertised to outsiders. Organisations may also develop specific career paths, which delineate what typically happens in an organisation. Some organisations use dual career paths in which they identify both management and non-management tracks. Skills inventories and competency frameworks are also useful for job matching. These consist of databases that contain information about manager skills, career preferences and education. This information enables organisations to identify capabilities within the leadership population.

Organisation Assessment Processes: Organisations frequently use career assessment centres for particular groups of managers. These assessment processes enable the organisation to secure rich data on managers and to enable the development of plans to address competency issues. We focused on a number of assessment processes in Chapter Seven.

Conclusion

Career management and development are important components of an organisation's leadership development process. Organisations can assist managers by providing information on opportunities in addition to assistance and support. The process of career management and development must accommodate both individual and organisational perspectives. Effective alignment of career goals and expectations is the key aim. Organisations can use a wide spectrum of models and approaches to facilitate the effective management of the careers of managers. Individual managers, managers as developers and the leadership development specialist have key roles to play in career management and development.

Organisations can use a wide variety of career development activities. These include self-assessment processes, career counselling, organisational career assessment centres, job postings and career pathing. These activities provide both managers and organisations with rich information on skills, competencies, requirements, values and career aspirations. They enable the development of realistic career plans and investment in appropriate development strategies.

Organisations can adopt a systems perspective when designing their career management systems. This involves aligning the career management system with strategic goals, establishing needs analysis, and aligning career development with leadership development and human resource strategies. Special considerations apply to the development of female managers, career derailed managers and career development in flat organisations. These require special processes and systems.

Summary of Key Points

- A career is essentially an evolving process, involving objective and subjective elements. There is a mutual dependency between the individual and the organisation in defining and enabling career success.
- Career success is determined by an individual in terms of his/her beliefs and self-concepts. These concepts and beliefs have changed for many managers. Careers for life have been replaced with variable work contracts, lifelong learning and work–life balance.
- Career development is about the development and implementation of an occupational self-concept.
- Career movement can be lateral and downward as well as upward. Organisational strategies for career management need to be aligned with other HR practices within the organisation.
- Line managers should be committed and engaged in proactive career management.

■ Discussion Questions

1. Outline the advantages of defining the term 'career' broadly. How does this differ from a more traditional notion of career?

2. Contrast individual- and organisational-level models of career development. How do they complement each other?

3. How do the ideas of a protean career contribute to our understanding of career development? How do they fit in with your views on career development?

4. Career plateaux and manager derailment are complex and demand special management by organisations. Explain this statement.

5. What special challenges do female leaders provide organisations in the area of career development?

■ Application and Experiential Questions

1. As a manager, describe how you feel about the prospect of becoming a career adviser for other managers. What would your concerns be and what would you like to see an organisation do to ensure that the career counselling experience is a positive one for all concerned?

2. Each student should write a short memorandum in which they answer the following questions: What do I want to be? Where am I now? How am I going to get there?

3. In two groups of three or four students, prepare a case for the following motion: 'The flattening of many organisation structures is forcing many managers to change their perceptions of what career advancement and development is all about.' You will have twenty minutes to prepare your case. Each team will present their case for and against the motion to the class.

Chapter Fourteen

Developing Management Teams, Top Teams and Senior Executives

OPENING CASE SCENARIO

Developing the Top Team Through Executive Education: Avocent Partnering with the Kemmy Business School

The Kemmy Business School, University of Limerick is a leading business school in Ireland and internationally. One of its key strategic objectives is to work with industry in a learning partnership approach in order to develop corporate learning solutions. Successful learning partnerships are based on a clear commitment to co-ownership of the programme, co-involvement of stakeholders and co-investment in programme design, planning, delivery and follow-up. The Kemmy Business School has worked in partnership with the ESB, the Garda Síochaná, FÁS, Abbott Laboratories and, more recently, with Avocent Corporation.

Avocent is a technology company that designs, manufactures and sells console switching systems, digital connectivity solutions, serial connectivity devices, extension and remote access products and display products for the computer industry. The company provides plug-and-play switching systems for a broad range of network administration, management and storage problems faced by corporate customers, data centres and server farms. Its analogue, digital and serial switching systems and extension and remote access products help network administrators manage multiple servers from a single local or remote console consisting of a keyboard, video monitor and mouse. The company also offers visual display products for high-information-content digital display solutions, such as Smartglas technology, which permits the consolidation of information from multiple sources to be displayed on single or multiple flat-panel displays, forming a tilted display solution.

Avocent also offers embedded virtual presence infrastructure, which helps reduce operational costs by offering pre-integrated health monitoring, power control, and virtual media and console access that integrates with Avocent appliances and consoles. Avocent was established in 2000 through the merger of Apex and Cyber Computer Products. In 2001, Avocent acquired Equinox Systems, which was followed by the 2002 acquisition of 2C Computing, and it acquired Soronti in 2003. Soronti was a developer of virtual-presence PC devices for server management and in November 2003 had seven patents pending covering its technology. During January 2004, the acquisition of Crystal Link Technologies was announced. In April 2004, Avocent announced the acquisition of OCA Technologies, a privately held company. Another development in 2004 was the acquisition of Sonic Mobility, a software provider for Palm PCs, Blackberry and Pocket PC platforms. Avocent announced the acquisition of Cyclades Corporate for around $90 million.

Strategically, Avocent operates in a strong dynamic external environment, which includes political, technological, regulatory and competitor forces. Politically, there is an increased globalisation of information technology, and, with the availability of infrastructure and the emergence of strong educated workforces in India and China, there are more companies and users of IT and an increased need for remote connectivity and management tools. Globalisation has led to an increase in the interdependency of business, resulting in greater security and storage requirements. Another key environmental factor influencing the organisation includes open source and standardisation. Open source has accelerated the commoditisation of technologies. Customers are demanding products that can work in a heterogeneous environment. ACIS technology is enabling organisations to have more embedded capabilities and there is a growing trend towards virtualisation, blade servers, multi-core processors, IT management as a service and the alignment of IT to business objectives. On the regulation front, there are significant shifts, such as Sarbanes-Oxley (Sox), which have resulted in stricter regulations and are creating pressure on the operational costs of IT organisations. Avocent has a number of key competitors, including Microsoft, EMC, server vendors such as HP, IBB and Dell, infrastructure vendors such as APC and CISCO and a number of smaller competitors. These competitive dynamics are driving prices down and moving into markets that are targeted by Avocent.

Avocent realised that it needed to start planning how best to respond to these real market, environmental, technological and competitive issues, and to focus on strategies to promote the changes needed to adapt to new technologies and market conditions.

Avocent approached the Kemmy Business School to design a strategic-level intervention for the top team, which would address a number of objectives, including: developing a collective understanding among its senior executives concerning the current business context; analysing the complexity and uncertainty of the external business environment; challenging senior executives to explore current and future strategic stances; and agreeing on a change agenda. Other objectives of the intervention included developing a framework to evaluate the success of the corporate strategy and enhance the teamworking capabilities of the top team.

The partnership began with a discussion about how the Kemmy Business School could help Avocent. This process of discovery involved the KBS learning about the needs of Avocent through undertaking analysis with key stakeholders, working closely with key corporate sponsors and getting in contact with participants in the programme. The next step involved a discussion of the design specifications, which was undertaken consultatively. This involved briefing key faculty members who were likely to be involved in the programme, and clear articulation and agreement on the objectives. Partnership at the pedagogic level was intense and thorough and involved a number of important decisions, including: What type of model or concept should inform the programme? What should be the main components of the learning design? Should the school in- or out-source key faculty? The design process took over three months to complete. The final design agreed was premised on the expectation that the top team of Avocent had a comprehensive understanding of the current context of the organisation and well-formed views concerning how the organisation should develop strategically. The programme was based on an experiential model of learning. This required that executives actively participate in organisation-specific workshops, which required full engagement, discussion of real organisational issues, the management of difference and consensus on how best to proceed. The programme also included formal inputs from experts on specific aspects of the economic, competitive and regulatory environments, designed to provide the top team with multiple perspectives and options and create understanding on contemporary debates and strategic issues. These formal inputs were distributed at key points over the three-day workshop. The workshop utilised the business score-card framework to structure discussions during the workshop activities and ensure that the strategic options generated addressed multiple perspectives, including financial, customer, internal processes and growth.

The partnership theme was also evident during the delivery and review stages. The KBS worked with the human resource department to identify the venue and agree on the various logistics for the programme. The delivery stage involved intensive interaction between Avocent and KBS and required agreement on all the details. The programme was summatively evaluated using a structured questionnaire. Four months after the programme, representatives from both Avocent and KBS had intensive debriefings to identify the key learnings from the partnership and identify how best to work together in the future.

The partnership was based on trust and openness. The design process worked because both partners demonstrated flexibility regarding the achievement of their objectives. It also had strong top management commitment within both Avocent and the KBS and there was a strong chemistry between the key people involved. The KBS sought to develop strong customer focus through learning about the partner organisation, clarifying expectations, understanding needs and dedicating time and effort to a joint design process. It also sought to take into account the point of view of the key stakeholders. The KBS has learned that partnership is possible only if there is a clear management process for co-ordinating and integrating contributions. Partnership is the only effective way to develop integrated, blended and aligned approaches to corporate learning. Full commitment to the partnership is also necessary. However, partnership approaches are demanding. They require significantly more design time than off-the-shelf solutions and they require a continuous development mentality on the part of the business school.

QUESTIONS

Q.1 How can executive education contribute to the development of senior teams and executives?

Q.2 What issues could potentially undermine a partnership approach for top management development?

Teams represent an essential feature of organisations. The proliferation of teams in organisations today has resulted in organisations seeking quick and effective ways of developing them. Effective teamwork does not come about automatically. It is a complex process that is influenced by the organisation's culture, the characteristics of team networks and the nature of the tasks they perform. Team performance requires team members to think, do and feel as a team. When this happens, it is possible to achieve synergies and high levels of team effectiveness.

There is limited agreement on how best to develop teams. Traditional leadership development strategies focused on individual development, which was conducted off-site. Development interventions that enhance team effectiveness increasingly need to be contextualised and to focus on developing both individual and team skills. The development of top teams presents a number of unique challenges. They frequently resist development interventions or claim that they have little time for them. Senior executives also have unique and specialised development needs that require customised responses from the leadership development specialist.

This chapter focuses on the issues that organisations need to consider when developing teams, top teams and senior executives. We examine both the challenges to teamwork and the types of interventions that are appropriate. We identify and discuss strategies and approaches that organisations can use to develop senior or top executives.

Why a Focus on Developing Teams and Senior Executives?

A large number of organisations utilise teams, but teams should not be formed just for the sake of having them. In order to be successful, teams need to have a specific purpose and be formed to accomplish a goal that needs the attention of a large number of people in the organisation. Schwarz (2001) suggested that organisations should consider forming teams in three different situations:

- Where there is a specific goal or set of goals that require a multifaceted group of people who have complementary competencies.
- Where there is a specific project that can best be solved by forming cross-functional and multidepartmental teams that have the potential to offer different perspectives on the project.
- Where there are broad-based strategic perspectives that require teams to implement them successfully in organisations.

Team-based approaches are potentially very effective ways of achieving organisational goals, but the variables which determine team effectiveness are many and complex. Tannenbaum, Beard and Salas (1992) suggested that team effectiveness must be understood as consisting of inputs, processes and outputs (Figure 14.1). They specified four types of input variables that are both related to each other and also influence team processes. Effective team processes are related to performance outcomes, which in turn are recycled as input feedback to the team. This framework points out that training and development interventions may moderate the relationship between inputs, processes and performance outcomes. The model also highlights that various organisational and situational characteristics influence team effectiveness at each of the key stages.

Figure 14.1: Understanding the Dynamics of Team Effectiveness

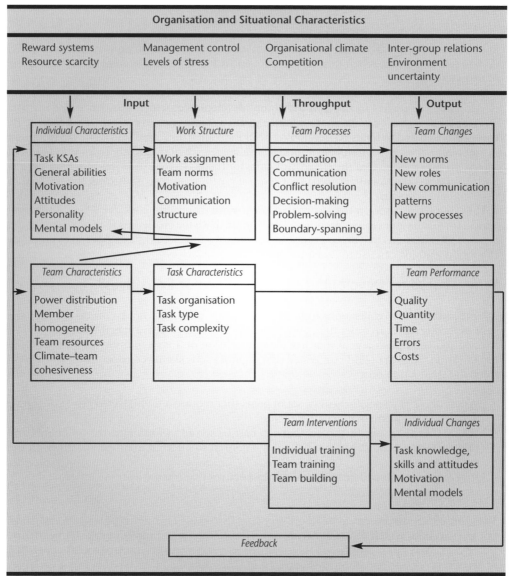

Werner and Lester (2001) identified five variables which they believe explain team effectiveness. These are team structure, team spirit, social support, workload sharing and communications within the team. They emphasise that team development interventions may help team members to understand team goals, define team roles and facilitate the emergence of effective team norms. Development may also be of assistance to individual team members. It may help members achieve confidence in their activities and motivate them to invest energy on behalf of the team.

Team building is a process designed to improve the team's problem-solving abilities and effectiveness. Teams can suffer from dysfunctional issues when they experience problems that members cannot resolve or when they lack the ability to adapt to external changes.

Dysfunctional teams result in a poor team relationship, heightened conflict, lower performance and difficulties in retaining team members.

There is considerable agreement about what constitutes an effective team. Salas, Burke and Stagl (2004) suggested that teams are complex entities that possess a number of characteristics:

- They consist of two or more individuals who interact socially.
- They share a common goal to which all team members are committed.
- Team members have meaningful task interdependencies.
- They are hierarchically structured and will usually have some form of leadership.
- They possess the capacity to adapt and, in some cases, they may have a limited lifespan.
- The expertise and roles of the team are distributed.
- Teams are embedded in an organisational and environmental context.
- Teams have boundaries which are flexible and operate at multiple levels.
- Teams are fluid and dynamic and they possess the potential to evolve.

Teams are premised on members being motivated to pursue goals on behalf of the team. This collective motivation is determined by the cohesion of the team and from the trust that is engendered by team members. The detailed characteristics of what makes teams are beyond the scope of this book, but Table 14.1 summarises some of the more important features.

Table 14.1: Characteristics of Effective Teams: Core Themes in the Literature

Trust
- Team members are more likely to contribute to the team goals when they trust one another.
- Team members must trust the competence and integrity of team members.
- Team members must believe that the human resources and other materials will be available to accomplish the team's goals.
- Team members must be able to rely on consistent and reliable sources of information, both internal and external to the team.
- Trust is derived essentially from the belief that team members will behave in a particular way.

Cohesiveness
- Team members care about the success of other group members because individual goal attainment is linked to the team achieving its collective goals.
- Team cohesiveness enables the team to deal effectively with setbacks and adversity.
- Cohesiveness enables the team to think more smartly about handling setbacks and persisting with the team.

Collective Efficacy
- Collective efficacy reflects the confidence of team members that they can achieve their collective goals.
- Members who have confidence in the overall capability of the team will be more motivated to work on behalf of the team.
- Teams with strong collective efficacy will work on more difficult goals and demonstrate stronger commitment to these goals.

Shared Mental Models
- Mental models focus on mechanisms through which people are able to generate descriptions of the purpose of the team.
- Mental models enable team members to organise information about the team and the environment within which it operates.
- Well-developed mental models enable the team to anticipate the reactions of individual team members better and to predict team performance.
- Shared mental models are essential to create high performance in teams.

Katzenbach and Smith (1993) defined 'a real team' as 'a small number of people with complementary skills who are committed to a common purpose, performance goals and an approach for which they hold themselves mutually accountable'. Sheard and Kakabadse (2004) reviewed the similarities inherent in fifty-two authors' definitions of a team. They identified seven common characteristics described as: common purpose, interdependence, clarity of roles and contribution, satisfaction from mutual working, mutual and individual accountability, realisation of synergies, and empowerment

Mottram (2002) argued that definitions that differentiate groups from teams focus on a number of concepts: reliance on collaboration to achieve both individual and team goals; a focus on individuals working together to achieve more than they could alone; acceptance of common goals; a belief among team members that they are actually a team; a team actually meeting and working together as a team; a strong focus on performance goals; and mutual accountability.

This emphasis on the fusion of attitudes, thoughts and behaviour to achieve a common aim is the direct consequence of creating an alternative to the traditional twentieth-century view of business as an individually orientated entity in which only the cream of managerial ability can rise to the top. A team philosophy contradicts a traditional individualistic view and creates conditions where the rising tide of team ethos can lift all boats. The focus of teams is to mesh together the collective skills, experiences and views of several people so that problems can be solved collaboratively and learning can accrue in the process. Kakabadse, Bank and Vinnicombe (2004:75) suggested that an effective, functioning team is synergistic when it works to create an output that is greater than the sum of its parts.

Teams should not be viewed as a panacea for all problems in organisations. Teamworking is perceived as an effective strategy for harnessing knowledge and skill and as a means of increasing productivity and increasing motivation levels. It is also recognised that today's employees are better educated, more assertive and require more involvement in work organisation. Flood, MacCurtain and West (2001) argued that we are living in a knowledge-based information age, which requires that organisations implement strategies to harness the 'knowledge, skills, experience, attitudes and networks of all their employees in order to assimilate and create the new knowledge required to fuel innovation and new product development'. However, the experts caution against the universal application of teamwork strategies to address all issues in organisations, and research suggests that teamworking is ideally suited to situations that require complex analysis. Procter (2004) asserted that the modern vision of teams requires that a team should be empowered to accomplish tasks and that managers should act as coaches and facilitators to help achieve this. Teamworking can be used to create employee involvement and thus improve performance by increasing benefits to the bottom line.

Types of Teams and their Development Implications

Organisations increasingly use different types of teams to achieve their objectives. Six types of teams are highlighted: problem-solving teams, functional operating teams, cross-functional teams, self-managed teams, virtual teams and top executive teams. We focus on the first five here. We will discuss the characteristics of executive teams later in this chapter.

Problem-Solving Teams

Problem-solving teams tend to be temporary in nature. They are typically composed of five to twelve employees from the same department, who meet every week to discuss quality and efficiency issues. Members share ideas and offer suggestions on how work methods and processes can be improved. These teams may be of a relatively short duration. They require team-building interventions to enable them to function effectively. It is likely that the objectives will be understood and accepted by all members. The team development needs will focus on the development of problem-solving skills, conflict management and prioritising. This development intervention will need to happen in a relatively short period of time.

Another variation of the problem-solving group is what Kakabadse, Bank and Vinnicombe (2004) described as 'hot groups'. These are 'highly charged groups who come together to achieve a dedicated task'. They are typically highly focused, creative, intense, and use laughter and debate to tackle very difficult tasks. These groups can be very useful when the organisation needs to come up with original and creative outputs and are often used in the media to generate new ideas in film and television. The Apple Macintosh computer is reputed to have been created and designed using just such an approach.

Self-Managed Teams

In self-managed work teams, the responsibility and authority of the team is vested in all team members. They are usually responsible for supplying a product or service. Yukl (2002) suggested that self-managed teams usually have members from similar functional backgrounds. Team members rotate tasks and there is collective responsibility.

Self-managed teams require shared leadership. Members will typically need to discuss priority matters and make a team decision. The development challenge is to give team members the confidence to take on the shared leadership role. There may be one team leader who will co-ordinate the implementation of team decisions. This type of team will require coaching and encouragement to get started. The process of team development may last for a considerable period of time. The team facilitator, where there is one, will help ensure that team members gradually assume more responsibility for coaching new members and improving work relationships within the team.

Cross-Functional Teams

Cross-functional teams are increasingly often formed to enhance co-ordination among specialised sub-units. Ford and Randolph (1992) suggested that cross-functional teams should include representatives from different areas of the organisation, in addition to external members. Cross-functional teams have a strong project focus and the membership will be relatively stable over the life of the project. Development of cross-functional teams presents particular challenges to organisations. Team members may have a primary loyalty to their functional units and may be more concerned with protecting their functional turf. Development initiatives will focus on developing the commitment of members to other duties and on handling conflicting loyalties. The team leader will require considerable interpersonal skills.

Mumford *et al.* (2000) found that leadership issues in cross-functional teams are challenging. Challenges include:

- *Technical Expertise*: The team leader needs to possess sufficient expertise on technical matters in order to have credibility with team members from diverse functional backgrounds.
- *Cognitive Skills*: The leader must possess the competencies to solve complex problems that require creativity and systems thinking, and the skills to integrate different functional specialisms that are relevant to the success of the project.
- *Interpersonal Skills*: Cross-functional teams place a premium on interpersonal skills. These include the ability to communicate the team vision, influencing skills, team cohesiveness and conflict-handling skills.
- *Project Management Skills*: The leader must be skilled in planning and organising project activities and handling various functional and technical aspects of the project.
- *Political Skills*: Cross-functional skills are political. They demand skills in building coalitions, securing resources, networking with other functions and dealing with the demands of top management.

Functional Teams

These teams are usually composed of individuals who have specialised skills but are still part of the same function. They usually exist for a considerable period of time and membership will be relatively stable. The leader is usually appointed and will have considerable decision-making authority. The leadership development challenge in functional teams focuses on the individual leader. The effectiveness of the team leader will depend on many of the issues that we discussed in Chapter Three.

EXHIBIT 14.1

Perspectives on Theory: Research Findings on the Dynamics of Teamwork in Organisations

Proposition	Explanation
Demanding performance levels create a team	The desire to achieve high performance is considerably more important to team success than team-building initiatives. Teams often form around challenges without any help from management. Potential teams without significant challenges usually fail to become teams.

Proposition	Explanation
The application of team basics is often overlooked in developing teams	This includes issues such as the size, purpose and goals of the team, and the skills and accountability of team members. Careful attention to these issues creates the conditions conducive to effective teamwork. Deficiencies in the basics will derail a team.
Team performance opportunities exist in all parts of the organisation	The concept of teamwork applies to different groups and levels in an organisation. Each faces different challenges, but they share many features in common.
Teams at the top of the organisations are the most difficult and complex	Top teams have many long-term challenges, e.g. heavy demands on executive time and individualism, which conspire against their effective functioning. Executives are often expected to act in a way that conflicts with effective team performance.
Many organisations intrinsically prefer individual over group accountability	A significant proportion of an organisation's processes, reward systems, job descriptions, career paths and performance management systems focus on the individual. Teams are sometimes perceived as a 'nice to have' category. The shift from individual to team accountability is sometimes difficult to achieve.
Organisations with strong performance standards spawn more real teams than organisations that promote teams	Teams do not become teams simply because we call them teams. Sustainable teams form best when the organisation implements clear performance standards.
High-performance teams are extremely rare	This occurs because the amount of personal commitment required of the members of high-performance teams differentiates them from ordinary team members. High commitment such as this is not easy to achieve; however, it can be exploited where it exists.
Hierarchy and teams go together almost as effectively as teams and performance	The evidence suggests that teams integrate and enhance formal structures and processes. Hierarchical structures are not threatened by teams but they integrate across structural boundaries. Teams are therefore not a replacement for hierarchy.
Teams integrate opportunities for performance and learning	Teams possess the potential to balance short-term performance with longer-term institution learning. Learning that occurs in teams has the capacity to endure.
Teams represent the primary unit of performance for increasing numbers of organisations	Organisations are increasingly challenged by issues such as customer focus, technology change, competitive threats and environmental constraints, which demand a speed and quality of response that is beyond the reach of individual performance. Teams have the capacity to meet these demands

Virtual Teams

Virtual teams are difficult to define. Bell and Kozlowski (2002) defined a virtual team as consisting of multiple actions which are separated by boundaries of time and/or distance and which leverage technology to conduct discrete interpersonal, social and economic exchanges of value to produce an outcome. Salas *et al.* (1992) pointed out that virtual teams share many characteristics with traditional teams, such as communication, and specific roles and structures, but the notion of disposition is fundamental. Mittleman and Briggs (1999) suggested five types of team interaction disposition:

- *Same Time, Same Place*: This represents the traditional team format and corresponds to face-to-face interaction. Some virtual teams make less use of technology and instead use face-to-face interaction.
- *Same Time, Different Place*: In this scenario, teams interact at the same temporal place but are located elsewhere geographically. They use teleconferencing and videoconferencing to communicate.
- *Different Time, Same Place*: Team members are likely to be in a similar location geographically, but at different time intervals. Team members work different shifts and may travel frequently. They use email to facilitate interaction.
- *Different Time, Different Place*: Team members are geographically and temporally dispersed. Team interactions are achieved through technology.
- *Any Time, Any Place*: This scenario describes a situation where team members are continuously on the move and interact entirely through communication technology.

Virtual team members have a common purpose, goal and approach to working together that holds them mutually accountable for their performance. Virtual teams were described by Lipnack and Stamps (2000) as groups of people working in an interdependent way with a shared purpose across space, time and organisational boundaries, using technology to communicate and collaborate. The members rarely meet face to face and can be from different cultures. They are highly skilled people with strong technical expertise rather than softer skills. Table 14.2 summarises definitions of virtual teams found in the literature.

Table 14.2: Definitions of Virtual Teams

Definition	Author
A virtual team is a self-managed knowledge work team, with distributed expertise that forms and disbands to address specific organisational goals.	Kristof *et al.* (1995:230)
A virtual team, like every team, is a group of people who interact through interdependent tasks guided by a common purpose. Unlike conventional teams, a virtual team works across space, time and organisational boundaries with links strengthened by webs of communication technologies.	Lipnack and Stamps (1997:6–7)
A global virtual team is an example of a new organisational form, where a temporary team is assembled on an as-needed basis for the duration of a task, and staffed by members from the far corners of the world.	Jarvenpaa and Ives (1994); Lipnack and Stamps (1997); Miles and Snow (1986)

Definition	Author
In such a team, members 1) physically remain on different continents and in different countries, 2) interact primarily through the use of computer-mediated communication technologies (electronic mail, videoconferencing, etc.), and 3) rarely or never see each other in person.	Knoll and Jarvenpaa (1995); O'Hara-Devereaux and Johansen (1994); Jarvenpaa, Knoll and Leidner (1998:30)
Teams identified as virtual teams usually fall under a more expansive definition of a project or task-focused team that can include inter-organisational members and physical dispersion that is bridged primarily by new communication technologies such as the Internet, faxes, videoconferencing and groupware, which allow for real-time meetings from almost any location	Oakley (1998:4)
Virtual teams are groups of geographically and/or organisationally dispersed co-workers that are assembled using a combination of telecommunications and information technologies to accomplish an organisational task. Virtual teams rarely, if ever, meet in a face-to-face setting. They may be set up as temporary structures, existing only to accomplish a specific task, or may be more permanent structures, used to address ongoing issues such as strategic planning. Further, membership is often fluid, evolving according to changing task requirements.	Townsend, DeMarie and Hendrickson (1998:18)
Virtual teams, composed of geographically dispersed members who communicate and carry out their activities using technologies such as email and videoconferencing, depend upon effective collaborations for their success.	Cohen and Mankin (1999:105)
A virtual team is an evolutionary form of a network organisation (Miles and Snow 1986) enabled by advances in information and communications technology.	Davidow and Malone (1992); Jarvenpaa and Ives (1994)
The concept of virtual implies permeable interfaces and boundaries; project teams that rapidly form, reorganise, and dissolve when the needs of the dynamic marketplace change; and individuals with differing competencies who are located across time and cultures.	Mowshowitz (1997); Kristof et al. (1995); Jarvenpaa and Leidner (1997:791)

While virtual teams offer numerous advantages to organisations, they need to be managed effectively to produce results and require different management approaches from those used by the regular team. Blackburn, Furst and Rosen (2003) suggested that teams need to be co-located or have opportunities for face-to-face contact. Yet, despite lacking the advantage of co-location, researchers advocate that virtual teams are more effective and have higher-level results than individuals (Duarte and Snyder 2001; Cohen and Gibson 2003). If managers understand the complexities inherent in the development of virtual teams and have the relevant strategies to address these issues, they are likely to manage virtual teams to best effect. Blackburn, Furst and Rosen (2003) argued that senior management needs to assess the best opportunities to deploy virtual teams, to pay careful attention to the requirements essential for team success and to establish an organisational climate that supports the performance of virtual teams. The benefits and risks of virtual teams to management practice are outlined in Table 14.3 as follows:

Table 14.3: The Benefits and Risks of Virtual Teams

	Benefits for the organisation	Associated risks	Suggestions
Goal	• Set challenging and innovative goals • Leverage assets from across the business • Develop flexibility and agility across the business	• Difficulties in executing multiple, divergent business goals across cultures and time zones at the same time • Choosing wrong people, strategy or technology • Heavy political, competitive and time pressure	• Focus on strategic clarity • Develop and evaluate alternative solutions • Support the creation of a virtual team culture in the organisation
Communication	• Reduced communication effort through dispersed teams • Improved speed and flexibility of communication	• Unclear loyalties, division of role or tasks within the team • Higher degree of unco-ordinated effort. Remote locations may not have technology infrastructure to support virtual teams	• Team-based planning together with management • Communication audit, team-based decisions on best communication strategies and technologies available
Change	• Quickly react to market and customer requirements • Quickly shift to new technologies	• Speed of work may overwhelm the entire organisation • Wrong solution or technology could be chosen	• Place greater importance on linking results to strategy • Develop and evaluate alternative solutions
Structure	• Organisational structure to support flexibility and responsibility at all levels • Quicker release of resources • Formal authority is replaced with interpersonal, technical and entrepreneurial competencies	• Overburdening virtual team members with organisational structures • Conflict with management over role and priorities for virtual team members • Changing power structure will meet with resistance from some line managers	• Agree boundaries and roles of virtual team members • Choose team members based on reputation and personality in addition to technical skills • Stakeholder management

Source: Rees and McBain (2004)

Virtual teams present some unique leadership and leadership development challenges. There is the major task of securing the commitment of diverse team members. This development challenge is even more complex when members represent different organisations and are located in different time zones and cultures. Virtual teams frequently encounter significant co-ordination problems when the environment is dynamic and when the task is complex. Zaccaro, Ardison and Orvis (2004) suggested that leaders in virtual teams must engage in more boundary spanning. The need to communicate increases dramatically, as do other interpersonal tasks.

Leaders will require skills in sense-making processes, communicating through electronic means and handling conflict issues. Sullivan (1999) highlighted that development interventions for virtual teams must focus on the essential characteristics of virtual teams. They should reflect the complexity which the leader faces and move away from traditional team-training models. Development initiatives should also focus on developing the following competencies:

- Foster awareness of similarities and differences. Development of the virtual team should focus on establishing clear team boundaries, while at the same time giving team members an understanding of relevant cultural differences.
- It is important to have face-to-face meetings at the beginning and at junctures when interdependent working is required. These opportunities should be seen as development opportunities and the leader should use them to develop mutual understanding and more effective team relationships.
- The leadership of a virtual team will require strong people skills in areas such as self-management, interpersonal awareness and communication skills. It is important, however, that this skill development is supported by a collaborative, trusting and people-oriented culture.

Table 14.4 summarises a number of guidelines for leading virtual teams.

Table 14.4: Summary of Prescriptions for Leading Virtual Teams

- Focus on the development of quick trust in virtual teams, especially when team membership and the team's existence is temporary.
- Maximise technology enablement to foster greater interactions among geographically and temporally dispersed teams.
- Routinise the use of email, computer bulletin boards, chat rooms and video and audio conferencing to monitor and record group action and progress.
- Structure and facilitate social, enthusiastic, supportive initial interactions among team members.
- Provide clear role distinctions and role expectations among team members.
- Provide a clear mission and purpose for group action.
- Provide prompt and substantive verification of electronic communications and feedback on team actions.
- Maintain a highly active and proactive action orientation in the team and through team communications.
- Facilitate intensive and supportive interactions, face to face if possible, to address trust violations and repair broken trust.
- Maintain frequent task-oriented communications, especially in physically distant teams.
- Convey enthusiastic messages encouraging collective effort.
- Keep an archive of team interactions and history to minimise disruption of team cohesion by member turnover.
- Emphasise a collective identity instead of an individualised identity among team members, especially in physically distant or culturally heterogeneous teams.
- Develop electronic communication norms that emphasise mutual goals and minimise affective conflict.
- Act as an information hub for the team, encouraging the exchange of information and the identification of distributed expertise among team members.
- Encourage communication that confirms information receipt as well as provides information about local, contextual constraints on team members.
- Act as gatekeepers for all team members and prevent misinterpretations of silence and member non-responsiveness.
- Monitor and encourage full and complete information exchanges, and minimise biased discussions.
- Facilitate continued searches for solution alternatives.
- Prevent premature consensus on solution alternatives.
- Make frequent requests of team members to report on solution implementation.

Effective Team-Building Processes

The development of teams and the use of team-building interventions must not be viewed in isolation. Team development must be considered in context. We will examine this context and then focus our discussion on a number of team-building strategies that have a developmental focus. Table 14.5 suggests a number of issues that contribute to the process of building effective teams.

Table 14.5: Perspective on Theory: Research Findings on the Process of Building Effective Teams in Organisations

Finding	Explanation
Ensure effective interdependencies	Teams are not teams unless there is interdependency within the team. The team must work to meet a shared objective. The organisation of work within the team can create co-dependencies.
Interdependence needs to be reinforced with appropriate goals and feedback processes	Clear goals and effective feedback helps to reinforce interdependencies. Goals direct the team in resource allocation and feedback processes direct teamwork efforts and ensure effective accountabilities. Feedback that is aligned with goals and performance is most effective.
Clearly define the team boundary	Boundaries are essential to effective team functioning. Boundaries provide focus and definition for the team. Leaders have a major role in creating boundaries by, for example, establishing norms, clear lines of communication and team meeting processes.
Clearly define decision-making scope	An effective team understands its authority limits. This requires a careful balancing of empowerment with accountability. The extent of authority depends on the expertise of the team, its purpose and the length of time it is in operation. Team leaders will be challenged to relinquish some level of control in order to allow the team to grow.
Team stability enhances effectiveness	Effective teams have a sense of stability. Team members have long tenure and the teams are more cohesive as a result. Teams with stability are better placed to develop shared cognitive, affective and behavioural resources. They achieve better performance. These shared processes enable teams to deal with both complexity and turbulence in a more effective way.
Articulate a compelling vision for the team	A compelling vision defines direction and motivates members to meet the team goals. To be effective, a vision must be challenging and clear. It must have the capability to guide the actions of team members. Team leaders have the primary role in articulating the vision and making it meaningful to team members.
Challenge the status quo	Effective teams have a consistent capacity to change and work towards the impossible. Team direction and challenge serves to move the team in a new way and to give it the confidence to achieve something special.
Engage team members	Effective teamwork requires engagement. Engagement ensures continued application and commitment by team members. Engaged team members are more likely to apply their expertise and competencies in pursuit of team goals. Engagement engenders extra discretionary performance by team members. It enables team members to address obstacles and helps the team to set higher-level goals.
Promote team self-management	Effective teams usually have a significant component of self-management. This includes discretion concerning the way work is done and a sense of task ownership. Skill variety and task identity are essential components of team self-management. Autonomy may also be created by allowing teams to manage team processes.

Finding	Explanation
Balance the team composition to the needs of the task	Team composition is considered essential. This indicates the size of the team. The optimum number of team members is between four and seven. Other elements of effective teamwork include the mix of knowledge and skill and the style of the leader. The personalities and role types of team members are also important in explaining team performance.
Capitalise on development opportunities	Effective teams capitalise on development opportunities. These may include team briefings, team coaching and the development of collectively shared mental models. Utilise novel tasks to enable the team to experience stretch and work outside its comfort zone.
Initiate team post-action reviews	Post-action reviews represent an important learning opportunity. They enable the team to assess performance and enable team members to share their observations on a team's performance, processes and outcomes. It is a time set aside for significant learning because it is an opportunity to test team members' competence and understanding of issues. It enables the team to generate explanations for its performance. Post-action reviews contribute to the development of strategic knowledge and shared mental models that enable the setting of future performance goals.

Creating a Team Culture and Achieving Effective Team Composition

Harris and Beyerlein (2004) suggested that transforming a traditional organisation into a team-based one is a costly and difficult undertaking. An organisation can, however, develop strategies to support team development and functioning, and help teams thrive and flourish by shifting from being individually orientated to being team-orientated. They suggest the following guidelines for creating team-based organisations:

- Teams must have clarity of purpose and appropriate measures of performance must be used, which must be aligned with the organisation's goals.
- Teams should have the support of top management and top management needs to work as a team in certain appropriate circumstances to be effective role models. Senior leaders must espouse a team-based philosophy and a team ethos should pervade every level of the organisation.
- It is important to identify collective work and individual work and recognise that some tasks are not appropriate for a team.
- A wide variety of team approaches, such as work teams, management teams, task teams or project teams, should be employed.
- A strong effort is required to build on organisation-wide, tacit understanding of the concept of teams. Managers from the top down need to understand how teams operate and develop the skills and attitudes to work in a team situation.
- A concerted effort should be made to improve the approach to teams and adapt this regularly to the changing needs of the organisation.

Senior managers also need to understand how to structure teams to ensure that they are effective. Sheard and Kakabadse (2004) derived a number of general principles that organisations should follow when creating and structuring teams:

- Teams of four to six are most effective.
- Complex tasks are suitable projects for teams to perform.
- Teams should be capable of coming up with a number of relevant solutions.
- Team tasks should be confined to two man years of effort.
- Team members can fear loss of identity, which can prevent them getting involved in teams, and this issue needs to be addressed positively.

- Team members need to feel a sense of affiliation towards the team.
- Organisations should be aware of the impact of change on group membership and the potential it has of initiating an 'annihilation anxiety' which can contribute to active and passive resistance to change.
- Cross-functional teams are a useful way to encourage trans-organisational communication and learning and can contribute to leadership development.
- Develop an understanding of team functions, team roles, and team dynamics.
- Use 'goal-based' planning to contribute to the organisation's problem-solving.
- Teams can contribute to creativity and innovation within the organisation.
- Senior management need to champion the team concept.
- Senior management must be failure-tolerant in order to encourage teams to take risks and thus foster creativity.

Table 14.6 summarises the main findings and principles of effective teamwork.

Table 14.6: Findings on Developing Teams: Principles to Bear in Mind

Findings
- Teamwork and task work are different components of team performance.
- Teamwork is affected by a number of external and internal factors.
- Effective teamwork requires that team members amass competencies for their specific team task before they receive team training.
- There are a number of teamwork skills that are non-exclusive (generic).
- Effective teams exhibit a strong feeling of 'teamness'.
- Teams that are motivated and think about their efficacy will stretch themselves to attain what individuals would not contemplate as possible.
- Effective teams optimise resources.
- Teams develop and transform over time.
- Mature teams are composed of members who can foresee one another's needs.
- Mature teams depend less on overt communication to perform effectively.
- Because all teams are not equal, contextual factors, as well as the task that is facing the team, must be considered when deciding the importance of the various competencies needed within a particular team.
- Teams change over time.

Principles
- Teamwork is influenced by multiple environmental, situational and input factors.
- Teamwork is characterised by a set of flexible and adaptive behaviours, cognitions and attitudes.
- Teamwork requires that members monitor each other's behaviours and action and feel free to provide and accept feedback based on monitoring behaviour.
- Teamwork is characterised by members being willing and able to back up fellow members during operations.
- Teamwork involves clear and concise communication.
- Teamwork requires co-ordination of collective and interdependent action.
- Teamwork requires leadership skills that enable the direction, planning and co-ordination of activities.
- Teamwork involves effective communication among members, which often involves closed-loop communication.
- Teamwork implies the willingness, preparedness and proactivity to back up fellow members during operations.
- Teamwork involves group members collectively viewing themselves as a group whose success depends on their interaction.
- Teamwork means fostering within-team interdependence.
- Teamwork is characterised by a flexible repertoire of behavioural skills as a function of circumstances.
- Teamwork requires team members' expectations and behaviours to be driven by shared and accurate knowledge structures.
- Teamwork requires team members to actively manage conflict in order to create and maintain interpersonal and intra-team relationships.

Team Competencies

Effective teams require particular competencies to be effective. The challenge in managing teams is to understand when and where these team competencies are required. Team members must be capable of harnessing them proactively to achieve team goals. Team building is based on the premise that individuals need to be developed in order to work effectively in teams. The consensus of available evidence is that development interventions can significantly enhance the effectiveness of teams. Salas *et al.* (1999) have investigated four key competencies that are necessary for effective teams.

- *Goal Setting*: This competency focuses on setting objectives and developing individual and team goals, and includes skills in action planning to achieve the goals that have been set.
- *Interpersonal Skills*: This competency focuses on developing skills in sharing ideas, mutual supportiveness and communication. It also involves the development of trust in each team member and confidence in the team as a whole.
- *Problem-Solving*: This competency focuses on developing skills in team problem-solving skills. It involves elements of solution evaluation, as well as the implementation and evaluation of solutions.
- *Role Understanding*: This competency focuses on understanding each team member's prospective role within the team.

Mills and Tyson (2001) produced perhaps the most comprehensive classification of team competencies. This is an empirically derived typology. They identify three sets of competencies:

- *Enabling or Task Competencies*: These focus on skill issues such as communication, integrating, adapting, situation sensing, evolving expertise and creating.
- *Resource or Knowledge Competencies*: These focus on skills such as knowing, contextualising and team wisdom.
- *Fusing or Team Climate Competencies*: These focus on skills and values such as openness, bonding, affiliation, emotional maturity, consulting, inspiring and believing.

Table 14.7: The 16 Team Competencies

Enabling or Task Competencies	
Communicating	How well does the team facilitate effective communication? This includes effective use of formal communication channels, how well team members access and share information, and how effectively information is absorbed by the team.
Integrating	This competency is dependent upon those process elements that enable the team to become integrated to an appropriate level to ensure effective task actions. It includes effective task planning, working to team members' strengths and successfully co-ordinating actions.
Adapting	How competent is the team at enabling flexibility in the face of changing task demands? This includes such aspects as role substitution, finding effective solutions to problems and being able to make radical changes to plans if new situations demand it.

Situational Sensing	How well does the team manage the collective ability to understand the task environment and monitor changes? This competency includes the abilities to see the broad picture, monitor the team's performance and develop a shared understanding of important issues
Evolving Expertise	This competency describes the team's ability to achieve and exhibit domain expertise within the team. How well do team members share expertise, and how effective is the team at ensuring development?
Creating	This competency describes the way the team facilitates creativity. This includes how well the team generates and develops new ideas, how much team members are encouraged to work together to solve problems and how willing the team is to implement new ideas and new ways of working.

Resource or Knowledge Competencies

Knowing	This is a resource competency that encompasses the shared understanding of the knowledge required by the team to achieve a successful task outcome.
Contextualising	How well does the team achieve a collective understanding of environmental and organisational factors that constrain team processes? How well are organisational goals understood? Is there a shared understanding of the structure of the organisation? Does the team access resources from outside itself if required?
Team Wisdom	This describes the level of collective knowledge pertaining to aspects of the team itself and includes knowledge of the strengths and weaknesses of team members, knowing what knowledge team colleagues have and sharing an understanding of the team's structure.

Fusing or Team Climate Competencies

Emotional Maturation	This competency requires processes that enable emotional understanding to develop between members of the team. Such empathy is represented by sensitivity to team members' feelings, ability to share emotional concerns and a willingness to challenge inappropriate behaviour.
Bonding	How well does the team manage to achieve social interaction between team members? This is assisted by such things as a shared sense of humour, feeling a sense of fun from team interaction and having some social contact outside the work environment.
Openness	This competency enables the creation of an environment within the team where members are free to express themselves in a valued way. This requires honesty between team members, assured confidentiality and a willingness to admit personal shortcomings within the team.
Affiliating	The outcome of this competency is a high-level cohesion. Team members express a sense of belonging to, and ownership of, the team. Aspects of this include loyalty to the team, a feeling of being involved with the team's activity and respecting members' contributions.

Committing	How does the team achieve a collective commitment to the task? Important aspects are likely to include how effectively team members feel rewarded for their efforts, how much responsibility the team takes for achieving task outcomes and ensuring equal efforts from all team members.
Inspiring	How does the team achieve a sense of 'wanting to perform' to bring about team success? This is likely to be aided by ensuring interest is taken in the task, ensuring the team feels appreciated for its contribution and generating a sense of fulfilment on task completion.
Believing	This competency describes those factors that facilitate a sense of team efficacy within the team. This is a type of team belief and team confidence, and includes is celebration of success, taking trouble to maintain morale and dealing with criticism in a positive manner.

Source: Mills and Tyson (2001)

Marks, Mathieu and Zaccaro (2001) suggested another conception of team processes and competencies. This emphasises that particular competencies are required at different stages of development, which are displayed in two recursive phases of action and transition. During the team action phase, team members engage in goal-directed behaviour, whereas in the transition phase, the concern is with planning. Interpersonal processes are important at both phases (Table 14.8).

Torrington, Hall and Taylor (2005) highlighted that teams have three areas of development needs:

- *Team Leader and Manager Training*: When team leaders take on a new role they are expected to acquire skills in delegation and time management, as well as the ability to harness the skills of the team.
- *Team Member Training*: This involves all team members, including the leader. It is most likely to focus on the development of general skills such as problem-solving, communication and task management.
- *Team Development*: This development focuses neither on creating a vision nor on the team, but on a future role, developing a team mental model and agreeing on ways of working as a team.

Table 14.8: Team Skill Competencies at Different Phases of Activity

Process Skills	Definition
Transition Processes	
Mission analysis formulation and planning	Interpretation and evaluation of the team's mission, including identification of its main tasks as well as the operative environmental conditions and team resources available for mission execution
Goal specification	Identification and prioritisation of goals and sub-goals for mission accomplishment
Strategy formulation	Development of alternative courses of action for mission accomplishment

Process Skills	Definition
Action Processes	
Monitoring progress towards goals	Tracking task and progress toward mission accomplishment, interpreting system information in terms of what needs to be accomplished for goal attainment, and transmitting progress to team members
Systems monitoring	Tracking team resources and environmental conditions as they relate to mission accomplishment, which involves a) internal systems monitoring (tracking team resources such as personnel and equipment), and b) environmental monitoring (tracking the environmental conditions relevant to the team)
Team monitoring and back-up behaviour	Assisting team members to perform their tasks. Assisting may occur by a) providing a teammate with verbal feedback or coaching, b) helping a teammate behaviourally in carrying out actions, or c) assuming and completing a task for a teammate
Co-ordination	Orchestrating the sequence and timing of interdependent actions
Interpersonal Processes	
Conflict management	Pre-emptive conflict management involves establishing conditions to prevent, control or guide team conflict before it occurs; reactive conflict management involves working through task and interpersonal disagreements among team members.
Motivation and confidence building	Generating and preserving a sense of collective confidence, motivation and task-based cohesion with regard to mission accomplishment.
Affect management	Regulating member emotions during mission accomplishment, including (but not limited to) social cohesion, frustration and excitement.

Source: Marks, Mathieu and Zaccaro (2001)

Team-Building and Learning Strategies

We will focus here on a number of strategies that developers can use to build teams and facilitate team learning. The most commonly highlighted strategies are: after-activity reviews; dialogue sessions; alignment sessions; process consultation; brainstorming and fishbowl techniques; scenario-based development; meta-cognition training, team-building workshops and outward bound workshops; and development of the team leader.

After-Activity Reviews: This idea originated in the USA. It involves a systematic analysis of an important completed task to identify the reasons for success or failure. It involves collective analysis of processes and outcomes achieved and it seeks to identify what can be improved in the future. It involves the team working through a number of steps:

- Team members review their initial plans and objectives for the activity and the procedures used to carry out the activity.
- The team consider any problems or obstacles that they encountered in conducting the activity. They focus on key decisions and outcomes.
- The team then plan how to use what has been learned to improve performance in the future.

The review can be conducted by the team leader or the team may use an outside facilitator. The role of the team leader or facilitator is to guide the team and keep it focused on objectively analysing what happened and on the key learning for future performance. Tannenbaum, Smith-Jentsch and Behson (1998) suggested a number of guidelines that should be followed to ensure that it is an effective team-learning process. It is important at the beginning of the review that each member conducts a self-critique that acknowledges shortcomings. The facilitator should encourage feedback from others to ensure that the self-critique is accepted, and it is also important to ask members to identify effective and ineffective aspects of team performance. It is important that the discussion focuses on behaviours rather than individual team members. The facilitator or team leader may also provide their assessment of team performance. It is important to solicit as many suggestions for improvement as possible and the facilitator should volunteer some if they are not already generated. An outside facilitator is sometimes useful, especially where there is a need to discuss leadership processes. The facilitator may also provide personal one-to-one feedback to the leader.

Dialogue Sessions: McLean (2006) suggests that a dialogue session is an appropriate team development intervention. It is defined as a structured conversation focused on exploring topics around which there is conflict. The aim is to achieve a better collective understanding of the issues. Cannon-Bowers, Salas and Converse (1993) highlighted that team problem-solving is particularly difficult when team members have conflicting assumptions about the nature and causes of the problem. Dialogue sessions enable teams to examine those assumptions and reach some kind of consensus. McLean (2006) provides a very useful set of dialogue session guidelines, which are summarised in Table 14.9.

Dialogue sessions require careful facilitation. The facilitator has to balance advocacy with inquiry. Inquiry focuses on discussing assumptions, articulating implicit assumptions and exploring alternative ways of looking at the issue. The facilitator will encourage members to view each other as colleagues and to ask questions in order to understand, rather than ignore or attack. The facilitator will enable the team to summarise points of agreement and disagreement and encourage them to explore a basis for consensus.

Table 14.9: Guidelines for Conducting Dialogue Sessions

- Identify and clarify the issue that should be the focus of the dialogue.
- Emphasise that all team members are equal and that outside authority should be discounted.
- Reinforce the importance of confidentiality and anonymity. The team should decide whether the dialogue remains within the team or whether it can be shared.
- Each team member should be given space to contribute and articulate their basic assumptions on the issue which is the subject of the dialogue session.
- Individual team members should note their reactions to other members' perspectives.
- Team members should use 'I' statements to express their reaction to what they have heard.
- The facilitator needs to ensure that team members listen to each other. They should not interrupt, argue or persuade.
- The goal of the session is to achieve shared understanding of the issue, not to develop a solution.

Alignment Sessions: Mitchell (1986) suggested that the purpose of an alignment session is to increase mutual understanding among team members. Prior to the session, each team member is given an open-ended questionnaire that focuses on values, concerns and personal objectives. Team members are asked to prepare responses that will help other team members understand and appreciate them. During the session, each team member spends some time describing and explaining their answers. Alignment sessions can facilitate improved relationships within the team.

Process Consultation: Process consultation is also used to improve team effectiveness. It involves a facilitator serving as a mirror to team members, so that they can interact and perform more effectively. McLean (2000) suggested that the facilitator will probably have to re-emphasise the agreed-on ground rules and remind the team of their mutual responsibilities to ensure that they are enforced. The facilitator will observe team activities and processes and conduct a feedback session on those observations at the end of the meeting. McLean (2006) recommends the use of a sociogram to provide specific feedback on how the team communication processes are operating. The key emphasis is on ensuring that team processes are understood and deficiencies are identified.

Brainstorming and Fishbowl Techniques: Brainstorming represents an important strategy for generating ideas within a team. Teams often experience difficulty in generating creative ideas and can be unable to solve complex problems. Brainstorming works on the principle that it is the amount of ideas that counts. All team members are expected to participate in generating ideas. The idea generation process must be spontaneous; off-the-wall ideas are welcomed and the facilitator should encourage team members to build on each other's ideas. Discussion or critique is not allowed until the well of ideas has run dry. The facilitator will record all ideas on a flipchart. McLean suggests that it may be necessary for the facilitator to suggest a few ideas to get things started.

The fishbowl technique is frequently used with large teams. It involves a subset of a team sitting in a circle with the rest of the team sitting around the subset. The outer circle provides the inner circle with feedback on interactions during the activity and discusses the role that each person played.

Scenario-Based Development and Meta-Cognition Training: Scenario-based development enables team members with an integrated series of trigger events to provide team members with multiple opportunities to both practise and receive actionable development feedback. During the development process, team members are exposed to a micro world that mimics the features of the actual team environment. This simulation focuses on encouraging team risk-taking and experimentation. Jacobs and Jaques (1987) reported that these simulations enable team members to develop more accurate cognitive or mental maps of the issues that impact on the performance of the team.

Meta-cognition refers to a thinking skill that focuses on 'thinking about thinking'. Paris and Paris (2001) suggested that there are two dimensions of thinking: a) knowledge about one's own thinking; and b) one's ability to use this awareness to regulate one's own cognitive processes. It is like mission control and has an important role to play in teams. Meta-cognition training can target the development of meta-cognitive skills. This development should enhance the team's ability to solve complex problems. Team members' meta-cognitive skills will regulate how the team performs.

Team-Development Workshops: Hughes, Ginnett and Curphy (2006) suggest that team-development workshops must meet three general requirements to be successful. The first element involves raising awareness. Second, they need some diagnostic, instrument-based feedback in order to provide an understanding of where the team is currently located. Third, each intervention should involve practice. This can be achieved through the use of experiential exercises. These exercises should be as real as possible and the role of the team facilitator is to link the team dynamics back to the real world.

Outward Bound Workshops: Outward-bound workshops involve the use of a set of structured activities in an outdoor environment. The purpose is to focus on the whole team. Badger, Sadler-Smith and Michie (1997) suggested that team tasks can be designed to reflect organisational structures and processes. They afford a safe environment in which the team can experiment and take risks that may not be acceptable in the work environment. Harrison (2000) suggested that outward bound workshops can be used to develop newly formed teams. They can also be used to enable an existing team to spend time away from the workplace in a challenging environment. They also offer effective strategies for developing the skills of the team leader. We highlighted a number of dimensions of outward bound development in Chapter Eight.

Developing the Team Leader: Dyer (1995) suggested a top-down approach to the development of team leaders. He views the leader as the prime driver of team development, and considers leader development to involve three key stages:

- *Leader as Educator*: This involves the leader focusing on developing the team's understanding of what constitutes an effective team and the various roles within the team.
- *Leader as Coach*: This involves the leader intervening at appropriate points to highlight team processes and dynamics.
- *Leader as Facilitator*: This involves the leader achieving an understanding of when not to intervene and encouraging collaborative decision-making.

EXHIBIT 14.2

Focus on Research: Managing Complex Team Interventions

Robert Barner contends that the two main reasons why team events go wrong for organisation development (OD) practitioners are (a) the facilitator is working from a team model that does not fit with the reality of today's team environment; and/or (b) the facilitator is using an approach that is not sophisticated enough for complex team performance issues. Challenging the outdated views of what constitutes a team, there are seven factors that distinguish team myths from current team realities.

A prevailing team myth is the idea of the 'intact team'. The reality is that a team intervention today may or may not involve an intact team, i.e. a team comprised of full-time members. Teams can often be comprised of part-time members who are grouped together to achieve a particular task or project. This type of team can be challenging to facilitate because of its temporary nature and competing priorities. Team-building, therefore, needs to be brief, task-focused and to address issues of team members' accountability and responsibility.

Another old team myth is the idea of the unitary team, operating within a clear reporting structure. Most teams today work in a matrix environment with overlapping reporting structures. This represents an additional challenge for team facilitation and leadership in terms of goal alignment and reporting relationships.

The idea of teams being manager-led is also changing. Increasingly, teams are self-directed or manager-coached. This is challenging for both the team leader and the team members, who are expected to contribute at a higher level. Facilitators must encourage shared ownership of work and role clarity.

Other myths that are being challenged are as follows: that teams are egalitarian; that teams are integrated; and that teams are culturally homogeneous. As teams become more complex entities, facilitators therefore need to take account of subtle power relationships, multi-location teams, different cultural expectations and the wider organisational environment. It follows that as teams become more complex in their make-up and how they operate, OD specialists or team facilitators must up their game. As in the wider training and development arena, *one size no longer fits all teams*.

There is a critical distinction between team development programmes and team interventions, both of which involve the use of an OD practitioner. Team development programmes use a training approach to team building that depends on team exercises and simulations to help team members perform more effectively as a group. These activities work best with new teams that are establishing ground rules or old teams that have acquired a new leader. In contrast, team interventions use a problem-solving approach to team-building that enables intact teams to identify and overcome obstacles and challenges to high-performance teamwork. Team interventions resolve current problems as well as setting out processes for future resolution of issues. This type of intervention requires a higher level of skill from the facilitator than implementing team development programmes.

A combination of the seven factors noted can produce very challenging team situations for the facilitator to explore and resolve. Complex scenarios tend to contain some combination of the following elements:
- Team performance issues that are linked into wider organisational issues
- They require use of multiple team interventions at multiple organisational levels
- The team members have very different weltanschauungs regarding the goals of team-building and their respective roles in the process.

When any of these elements are present, it is imperative that the facilitator takes a helicopter view and reframes the team building as an organisational assessment and intervention. There are six guidelines suggested by Barner to assist in the process:
- Check your assumptions
- Step outside the circle
- Map the organisation
- Determine your path of entry into the intervention
- Use triangulation to explore alternative perspectives
- Understand the context for change.

It is increasingly likely that OD practitioners will be called in to facilitate complex team interventions. For this reason, it is critical that old team models are challenged and that a team development activity is not used by the facilitator where more complex team interventions are required.

Source: Barner (2006)

QUESTIONS

Q.1 How would you begin to devise a team intervention for a complex senior team in your organisation?

Q.2 Of the seven myths outlined, which three have the greatest implications for your practice?

Development Issues for Global Management Teams

Global management teams are an increasingly common feature in multinational organisations. These teams are described as a collection of managers from several countries who must collaborate in order to achieve their goals. Gross, Turner and Cederholm (1987) suggested that international or global management teams must develop a number of skills:

- The communication of the corporate culture and its acceptance by team members
- The development of a global perspective among team members
- Skills to co-ordinate and integrate the global enterprise
- Skills and attitudes to be responsive to local market conditions.

Increasingly, global management teams are virtual. This poses a number of additional development challenges. These include the skills to use technology, to co-ordinate information exchange and communication in order to facilitate knowledge sharing, and to capitalise on twenty-four-hour productivity.

Deresky (2006) suggests that teams comprising managers from different geographical locations are challenged with a number of key problems:

- How to deal with conflicting goals of achieving efficiency, being responsive to local conditions and facilitating organisational learning;
- How to address conflicts that arise because of cultural differences, different local norms and varied time zones.

Joshi, Labianca and Caligiuri (2002) studied global teams of human resource specialists. They found that these teams did facilitate greater competitiveness and greater opportunity for cross-cultural understanding and exposure to a multiplicity of viewpoints. The disadvantages were, however, very significant. They included language, communication and management style differences, more complex decision-making, fewer promotional opportunities for managers, significant personality conflicts and a serious increase in complexity in the workplace.

Global management teams are not always successful. Govindarajan and Gupta (2001) found that a significant number of these teams did not live up to expectations. Five significant factors undermined their effectiveness: 1) difficulties in developing trust among members; 2) problems in overcoming communication barriers; 3) difficulties in aligning the goals of individual managers within the team; 4) lack of clarity about goals; and 5) skill deficiencies that undermined the effectiveness of the team. They made a number of interesting recommendations, many of which have a developmental focus. These included: the rotation and diffusion of team leadership; the building of social networks among managers from different teams; the implementation of development interventions focused on cultivating trust; the scheduling of face-to-face meetings; the rotation of meeting locations in order to connect managers with all team members; and hiring a facilitator to implement team-building initiatives. Table 14.10 provides a list of questions which organisations should ask in order to establish whether or not a development intervention is appropriate.

Table 14.10: How Effectively are Your International Management Teams Performing?

- Do team members have a common purpose? Are all team members committed to it?
- Has the team developed a shared mental model? Does it have a common language?
- Does the team have common processes and procedures for holding meetings?
- Does the team possess the capacity to learn from its mistakes, build on success and conduct after-action reviews?
- Is the team explicit in terms of discussing cultural differences? Is there an openness regarding the cultural origins of team members?
- Do team members demonstrate sensitivity towards other members from different cultural backgrounds?
- What are the levels of trust within the team? How is trust tested and reinforced? Is it possible to voice frustrations?

Salas *et al.* (2004) made a major contribution to understanding the challenges for leaders in global multicultural teams. They put forward eight key propositions:

- *Proposition 1*: The leader must act as a boundary spanner and information gatherer. This requires that the leader understands how his/her cultural frame will affect information gathering and attention giving.
- *Proposition 2*: Leaders will have cultural biases in their own cultural framework. Such biases will impact on the meaning they assign to cues in an external environment.

- *Proposition 3*: Within multicultural teams that are global in nature, the non-verbal aspect may be absent, but it is important for the leader to understand the hidden aspects of culture.
- *Proposition 4*: Shared mental models are difficult to achieve and promote in global multicultural teams. However, it is important to develop such shared mental models because they provide the basis for the assignment of meaning.
- *Proposition 5*: Leaders of global multicultural teams must articulate a direction for the team that aligns with team members' cultural expectations. Cultures differ in the degree to which they tolerate ambiguity and risk. This indicates that goals may need to be set differently.
- *Proposition 6*: Feedback processes must be aligned with team members' cultural lenses. Ting-Toomey (1988) suggested that team members from high-context cultures find it difficult to separate the person from the feedback, whereas those from low-context cultures find it an easier task.
- *Proposition 7*: Team leaders should encourage and facilitate team self-correction behaviours. This proposition focuses on the processes through which team members provide developmental feedback to each other. Managers from more collectivist cultures are more comfortable with team evaluations.
- *Proposition 8*: Multicultural teams may require more interaction by the team leader to achieve team coherence.

Development Issues for Top Teams

The perception exists that senior executives, and particularly the top team, do not require development because of their impressive set of skills, competence and capabilities. Leadership development specialists have a natural inclination to steer clear of suggesting that the senior team requires development because of the obvious political ramifications of such actions. However, as senior executives move higher up in the organisation, they receive less and less developmental feedback as their direct reports are also inclined to edit their feedback (Edelstein and Armstrong, 1993). Jackson, Farndale and Kakabadse (2003) quoted a senior HR employee who believed that highly effective senior executives have achieved their status because of their 'world-class strengths'. Because of these great strengths, however, they may also have extreme levels of weaknesses. Jackson, Farndale and Kakabadse suggested that these managers have succeeded because of their self-sufficiency in relation to their own development, but they may lack clarity about what is expected from them. In today's rapidly changing world, the top team need to be skilled in strategic analysis and capable of assessing the effects of global competition and the evolving corporate needs arising from these competitive threats. They need to have highly evolved interpersonal skills and flexible approaches to managing and leading people. These sophisticated competencies need the application of appropriate development strategies. It is vital, therefore, to assist senior executives to understand what they need to develop and encourage them to take ownership of the process.

A number of barriers exist which make top leadership development difficult:

- *Individualistic Culture of the Top Team*: Top-level executives typically reach the most senior levels because of traits such as decisiveness and independence. Organisational reward structures do not emphasise collaboration and development. Vicere, Taylor and Freeman (1994) found that personal development and organisational learning are not valued by top teams and that executives and senior managers who have earned their positions through getting results and being personally accountable are slow to display any chink in their armour by indicating that a development need exists. Cleveland, Stockdale and Murphy

(2000) suggested that top team members are promoted on individual capability. They are expected to be individually accountable and they are therefore less open to development. Armstrong and Edelstein (1993) found that top team members rarely receive feedback and, as a result, frequently have less self-awareness, which therefore limits their openness to development activities.

- *Ineffective Top Teams*: Dainty and Kakabadse (1992) suggested that top teams can differ in their overall effectiveness. Brittle teams do not have the ability to focus on the vital issues facing the business. They are, however, mature in their interactions and place a high value on expertise, independence, low disclosure and interpersonal values. They are less effective in discipline and integration. Blocked teams, on the other hand, possess the capacity to address business issues, yet their members have difficulty integrating with each other. This team is greatly in need of feedback to address interpersonal issues. The blind team is misguided in its approach to addressing business issues. The blind team may have difficulty in identifying the needs for development and it must be opened up to the need to change. The blended team has the capacity to balance business issues and achieve strong relationships within the team. This team is open to advice and development interventions. It possesses the capacity to develop greater insight into how to improve its performance. Its key challenge is the integration of new team members. Development interventions can enhance the overall competitiveness of the team.
- *The Perceived Applicability of Development*: Four particular perceptions exist concerning the applicability of leadership development to top teams. Executives frequently view development as a strategy to overcome personal weaknesses and believe that it has very little to contribute to the team. Second, leadership development can make some contribution to 'learning at the top', but this is essentially unnatural for top teams. Third, leadership development initiatives do not address core development needs. Executives frequently perceive that leadership development has only one solution to offer, i.e. formal development. Finally, top teams frequently articulate the view that development makes no difference to the effectiveness of the top team. These are difficult issues for the leadership development specialist to cope with.

The Changing Skills and Competencies Required of Top Teams and Senior Executives

Jackson, Farndale and Kakabadse (2003) suggested that top teams require the ability to think of work creatively, 'out of the box', which calls for high levels of cognitive skills. Top team development needs to be perceived as a tool for competitive advantage rather than a means of career development or succession planning and organisational success depends on the top team possessing an appropriate balance of skills, competencies and capabilities. Jackson, Farndale and Kakabadse put forward a strong case for making a direct link between the development of the top team and business strategy where it can be implemented within a strategic framework instead of being divorced and isolated. The competencies of top teams and senior executives need to focus on strategy, value creation, interpersonal skills and leadership capabilities.

Coulson-Thomas (1992) and Kakabadse and Kakabadse (2001) highlighted that top teams and executives need to have the capacity for flexibility and innovation; they must be quality conscious, customer-oriented and constantly improving performance. Strategic awareness, planning and decision-making capabilities are frequently highlighted, as is the capacity to form an all-encompassing vision of the organisation.

Table 14.11: The Evolution of Top Team and Executive Development

The Past	The Present	The Future

• Provenance early 1900s
• University degrees, MBAs
• Company universities, e.g. Motorola University
• Partnerships with universities
• Problems associated with this approach are:
  – Transfer of knowledge back to workforce
  – Difficulty of measuring return on investment
  – Resistance to new ideas from colleagues
  – Lack of conviction in relation to the benefits of formal development
  – Some organisations prefer to use experience on the job to develop executives through job rotation and job assignments
	• Executive development seen as more relevant in response to extreme changes in business environment
	• Present content focused on global issues:
	  – culture
	  – employment conditions
	  – foreign opportunities
	  – globalisation and education
	  – leadership
	  – communication
	  – customer relations
	  – change
	  – winning business strategies
		• Emphasis on creating a culture of constant learning
		• Organisations are requiring leading-edge development strategies
		• Desire exists for customised programmes despite expense
		• Combining development with other organisations in consortia arrangements
		• Using technology and e-learning
		• Use executive education to transform corporate cultures
		• Seen as a requirement rather than nice to do

Source: Adapted from Jackson, Farndale and Kakabadse (2003)

The identification of the skills which should be developed in the top team is complex. A well-developed executive team is required to navigate the complexities evident in business environments today. Yukl (2002) argues that the CEO can no longer possess the broad range of expertise required to function effectively and requires the support of a strong team to help the organisation cope with change. He advocates the need for the top team to possess 'diversity of backgrounds and perspectives to improve the quality of strategic decisions made by a team facing a turbulent, uncertain environment' (Yukl 2005:381). Jackson, Farndale and Kakabadse (2003) highlighted that a major challenge is understanding how the context within and surrounding the organisation determines the shape and nature of executive development for executives and organisations alike. They acknowledge that the breadth of knowledge required by executives is vast and that current approaches to executive development are not sufficiently sensitive in focusing on the array of skills that are essential to effective performance of the executive role.

Katzenbach (1997) argued that it can be extremely challenging to force a group of top-level executives to perform as a team. Team researchers believe that some tasks are not suitable for teams. Therefore, an effective CEO needs to be able to recognise team and non-team opportunities (Katzenbach 1997) and adopt appropriate strategies to address them. Katzenbach described trying to create top teams as an 'unnatural act'. He urged the need to value both team and non-team behaviours and suggested the need to integrate the two to achieve optimum performance. He highlighted particular challenges:

• It is difficult to define a meaningful purpose for the top team because they have to cope with abstract and broad-ranging goals.
• It is difficult to apply tangible performance goals and results-orientated senior executives are not motivated by this ambiguity.

- It is important to have the right mixture of skills, yet selection for the top team is often based on formal positioning rather than on relevant skills.
- Senior teams face major challenges in relation to allocating time for the activities of a real team.
- Senior executives have reached the top by relying on individual accountability for performance, and moving to a position of team accountability can be very challenging. Issues of loss of identity, affiliation and even annihilation anxiety can contribute to even more resistance.
- Power issues can contribute to a lack of comfort in relation to collaboration 'in amorphous groups with overlapping accountabilities'.
- It is much easier to control the activities of a group than a team and an effective leader can usually control and execute the task efficiently in group situations. Real teams need time to shape the task and team process and cognisance must be taken of team dynamics and team facilitation. Senior teams lack the patience and the skills to operate within the structure of a real team and can find the process time-consuming and wasteful.
- Teams are useful, but not in all leadership situations, and should only be utilised where there is a requirement for collective action or work products.

Identifying Competency and Skill Requirements of Senior Executives

Leadership development specialists encounter difficulties when identifying the competency development needs of executives and top teams. Korac, Kakabadse and Kouzmin (2001) highlighted that what constitutes the board or the top team varies considerably from one organisation to another. Furthermore, the tasks of the chairperson, CEO, non-executive and executive directors will also vary. Dulewicz, Macmillan and Herbert (1995) suggested that it is the chairperson who sets the corporate agenda and takes responsibility for developing strategic plans, maintaining a dialogue with the CEO, and implementing operational and financial plans. The CEO is usually the ultimate point of accountability. The CEO can, therefore, easily lose the confidence of the board. Non-executive directors are not involved in the day-to-day activities of the business. They attend board meetings and focus on issues such as corporate governance. Executive directors report to the CEO and usually have responsibility for a part of the business. They are held accountable for their own area of operation. They usually shape strategic priorities, establish corporate policy and focus on the development of management talent within the organisation.

The Institute of Directors UK (1995) found that boards need twelve broad areas of knowledge and six broad areas of competency. The knowledge areas focus on 1) matters related to the board itself, such as roles, relationships, corporate governance and the development of directors; 2) matters related to the external environment, such as strategic issues, political, economic, social and legal influences and key environmental trends; and 3) technical issues such as corporate finance and new business developments. The key competencies include strategic perception, analytical understanding, communication, board management communications and achieving results.

Table 14.12 provides a summary of the issues organisations should consider when designing executive development.

Table 14.12: Getting Started on Executive Development: Key Issues for Organisations

Formulating an Executive Development Strategy
- It is important to have a coherent strategy rather than a set of activities and programmes.
- The strategy must be linked with the competencies that executives require to achieve business goals.

Top-Management Support for Executive Development
- Senior executive involvement in the executive development process is vital to its success.
- Senior executives should be involved in evaluating potential executives, in meeting them and in evaluating their experience-based learning.

Define the Desired Future Executive
- The distinct qualities of the future executive need to be clearly defined.
- The future executive should be strong on capability building and collaborating, demonstrate understanding of the organisation and be comfortable with technology.

Systematic Analysis of Gaps
- The organisation needs to consider key gaps in both quality and quantity of future executives.
- Organisations should profile the key executive trends in the organisation and document key skills necessary for effective performance.

Align Executive Development with Culture
- Executive development activities should align with the corporate culture.
- Development strategies should be culturally acceptable and reflect the core beliefs, values and rituals of the organisation.

Customise Executive Development
- Effective executive development requires a horizontally integrated blend of developmental experience.
- The organisation should avoid sheep-dip approaches which do not address the unique needs of individual executives.

Development Strategies for Top Teams and Executives

Organisations have a number of options available to develop executives and top teams. We focus on three possible interventions here. The first two, executive coaching and executive education programmes, focus on the individual executive, whereas the third, action learning, focuses on the executive team as well as the individual executive.

Executive Coaching

Executive coaching is defined as an individualised leadership development process that focuses on developing an executive's capabilities to achieve both short- and long-term goals. It is typically conducted as a one-to-one interaction and may use the outputs of multisource feedback processes as its foundations.

Executive coaching may be performed by many individuals, including the executive's boss, a leadership development specialist, an executive peer and an external coach. The coach will usually facilitate the executive to learn relevant skills such as handling specific strategic challenges, coping with organisational change, dealing with a difficult board and coping with cross-cultural issues.

Formal executive coaching usually operates in the following manner. The organisation appoints a panel of executive coaches. A professional executive coach will formally contact the executive and agree on a collaborative partnership with him/her. This contract will incorporate agreed ground rules, the expected business results and the executive's learning objectives. What will actually happen in the coaching relationship will be driven by the objectives that are articulated, the preferences of the executive and the organisational context. It is, however, possible to envisage more informal executive coaching which is incorporated into day-to-day interactions between executives.

An effective executive coach will require some specific knowledge and expertise. Stern (2004) suggested that the following are essential requirements:

1. Essential knowledge and expertise in psychology, including adult learning, individual assessment, change management, leadership, interpersonal and group dynamics, motivation and individual differences.
2. Essential knowledge and expertise in business, including strategic and tactical planning, knowledge, organisational communications, business ethics, knowledge of the history of the business.
3. Coaching knowledge and skill, including conflict mediation, video feedback, career development, work–life balance and stress management.

Stern (1998) suggested that most executives are comfortable with more practical, concrete and experientially oriented coaches. The coach needs to care about the organisation as much as the executive and to possess the capacity to move from the big picture issues to those that are more micro. Ennis *et al.* (2003) found that a good executive coach will have a systems perspective and a results orientation. He/she will understand the business, emphasise collaborative partnership, focus on building the competence of both the executive and the organisation, use common sense and good professional ethics.

When selecting an executive coach, organisations need to have a strong understanding of the characteristics of the executive and the specific development challenges. Table 14.13 provides a summary of the more general issues that organisations should consider when selecting an executive coach.

Table 14.13: Issues to Consider when Selecting an Executive Coach

- Does the executive coach possess the required knowledge and skills?
- Does the executive coach have specialist knowledge and experience which is applicable to the specific coaching situation?
- Is the executive coach familiar with the industry, its business function and other factors that are relevant to the executive to be coached?
- Does the executive coach demonstrate good professional coaching principles?
- Will the chemistry between the executive and the coach be effective?
- How will the executive respond to the coach's approach, style and personality?
- Has the coach continually developed his/her knowledge and skills?
- Will the contractual arrangements for the coaching fit with the limits and preferences of the executive?

Cognitive-Behavioural, Psychodynamic and Action Approaches to Executive Coaching

Three particular approaches to executive coaching are cognitive-behavioural, psychodynamic and action-based. Cognitive-behavioural approaches tend to focus on specific issues and delve more deeply into solving them. Ducharme (2004) suggested that a cognitive behavioural approach is useful when the goals of the executive coaching assignment focus on the following issues:

- The provision of honest feedback to the executive
- Exploration of different ways to handle stress
- The development of skills for developing others

- The refinement of specific skills
- The need to ensure sustained change in the behaviours of the executive
- A focus on results and the elimination of ineffective behaviours.

Cognitive-behavioural approaches have proved useful in helping executives manage stress and develop specific skills such as dealing with change. Cognitive-behavioural coaching can provide the executive with three particular areas of skill development: coping skills, problem-solving skills and cognitive restructuring. Coping skills interventions tend to focus on problems that are external to the executive and are, to a degree, beyond the executive's control. Problem-solving skills provide the executive with skills to be able to identify day-to-day executive situations, generate and decide among different courses of action and then implement those actions. Cognitive restructuring involves changing the negative thought patterns of executives. When executives have maladaptive schemas, they develop problems in coping with their lives. This form of coaching is likely to take a considerable period of time to achieve results.

Table 14.14: Situations in which Psychodynamic Issues and Interventions are Relevant Considerations for Executives

Situations in which a client:
- Continues to misbehave or underperform, despite the consciously stated intention and desire to improve and do well;
- Suffers from powerful disorganising and disruptive emotional experiences and reactions for which there are no obvious explanations;
- Faces repeated situations and problems in families, groups and organisations that are incomprehensible and destructive and for which there are no obvious answers or previous intervention efforts have failed;
- Seeks to understand his or her history, goals, motives, and behaviours with a greater degree of psychological sophistication.

or when:
- Things are not happening in the executive's organisation that should be happening;
- Conflict – overt or covert, conscious or unconscious – is possible, impending, detected or explicit;
- Major life course changes are possible, impending or explicit, in the executive, the executive's group, or the executive's family;
- Transitions in human relationships in the organisation or the family are possible, impending, detected or explicit;
- Normal or abnormal crises, regressions or failures in the group, organisation, or market are possible, impending, detected or explicit;
- Knowledge, ability or skills may be insufficient to master a challenge or solve a problem;
- An executive's spouse, key family member, close friend or significant other is in trouble or experiencing problems;
- Performance problems or an inability to do a job are impeding an executive's career;
- Relationship disturbances are imperilling an executive's career or ability to do a job, or are affecting a group or organisation's functional capabilities;
- A trauma or catastrophe strikes an individual executive, the executive's group or the executive's organisation;
- A coach detects significant emotional, cognitive or behavioural responses in him or herself to a client or a client's situation.

Psychodynamic approaches to coaching emphasise the development of self-awareness, the management and containment of emotions, the demonstration of resilience and flexibility, and creating the development of psychological skills and interpersonal relationships.

Psychodynamic coaching helps the executive improve awareness of a wide range of issues that contribute to both personal and professional effectiveness. Kilburg (2004) provides a useful summary of the situations in which it is appropriate to use a psychodynamic approach. He recommends a psychodynamic approach when there is individual behaviour which is dysfunctional and therefore not achieving or not contributing to leadership effectiveness. A psychodynamic approach does demand that the coach is skilled and confident to take the executive through the session. Killburg (2004) recommends that the following stages are followed:

- Coach and client should possess substantial knowledge, skill and ability about: a) the work of leaders; b) the process of changing human behaviour; c) individual, family, group and organisational dynamics; and d) the current challenges in their lives.
- The coach should possess a solid set of concepts that guide his or her work with executive clients.
- Client and coach should generate a diverse and extensive base of information and experience related to both current and past relevant situations.
- Coach and/or client should become aware that there may be a thought, feeling, defence, conflict, compromise formation, or past or present relationship that is having an adverse impact on performance but may have limited information about how it is working in the client's mind.
- Coach should construct tentative hypotheses based on the data collected, the analysis undertaken of the data, and the explicit or implicit underlying models, theories and concepts he or she uses in this work.
- Coach should request permission to use intervention and invite the client to a mutual exploration of aspects of the data that have accumulated.
- Coach should deliver the interpretation in a non-stringent and tender fashion and invite the client's response and participation in making it relevant, meaningful and helpful.
- Client should respond immediately or through time, concisely and unconsciously, verbally and non-verbally, providing data to validate or invalidate the content, structure and timing of the interpretation.
- Client and coach should mutually explore, collaboratively reformulate, and modify the interpretation to make it more meaningful and useful in the client's life.
- Coach and client should reflect individually and collaboratively on the interpretation and its effectiveness in helping the client in his or her work and use the information to further refine and define the coaching work they are doing together or, if necessary, the coaching agreement.

A psychodynamic approach should be used with caution. It is not appropriate where the executive is not interested in the information and where there is insufficient data to confirm observations. The executive coach must be skilled in handling the key stages. If the executive is defensive or if there are conflicts of interest between the self-development of the executive and the needs of the organisation, it is unwise to pursue this approach. It should be used only if there is scope to improve the situation and enable the executive to be more emotionally aware.

Action-focused creative coaching focuses on conditions, means, action results and consequences. Cocivera and Cronshaw (2004) suggested that the conditions focus on the constraints inherent in a situation over which the executive has no immediate or direct control and which need to be considered when giving advice to the executive or when exploring options. The coaching intervention must also explore the enablers within reach and control of the executive so that they can be used to achieve an effective outcome. Action refers to goal-directed behaviour that the executive implements. The result focuses on what the executive has achieved. In a typical practice context, this will involve the following stages:

- *Defining the Job Context*: This involves defining the job context and setting the foundation for the coaching session. This will require the executive coach to work with both the executive client and the organisation to understand the executive's development needs. The definition of the context enables both parties to develop a set of criteria and to formulate an appropriate development plan.
- *Assessing the Individual and Building a Developmental Picture*: This involves the integration of the coach's insights and the results of multi-source data to formulate a statement of the executive's strengths and weaknesses. During this assessment, the executive and the coach can analyse the means to identify what resources are within the control of the executive and what can be developed or strengthened.
- *Providing Feedback and Development Planning:* After the executive has had time to consider the feedback, it is then appropriate for the executive coach to work with the executive to identify the key development issues, the most appropriate development objectives and then to formulate a development plan that identifies appropriate actions and development strategies that will enable the executive to realise the development goals. These actions and results are used, if necessary, to update and adjust the development plan.

EXHIBIT 14.3

Perspective on Theory: Evidence-Based Approach to Developing Executives

Evidence-based management focuses on managerial decisions and organisational practices that are informed by the best available scientific evidence. Evidence-based management education focuses on developing in managers the skills to use evidence and to enhance their expertise throughout their careers. Rousseau and McCarthy highlight six key principles of an evidence-based approach.

- *Principle 1 – Focus on Principles Where the Science is Clear:* The key challenge is to educate managers and executives on principles that are well supported by the research. Managers need to develop the know-what and the know-how. The know-what focuses on the principles, whereas the know-how focuses on the application of those principles. Teaching managers these two dimensions involves the presentation of the principles followed by exercises designed to put them into action. It also involves exploring conditions that would promote or inhibit the application of those principles.
- *Principle 2 – Develop Decision Awareness in Professional Practice:* Managers and executives need to develop an awareness of when they are making a decision. The task of executive education is to enhance the critical thinking capabilities of managers and leaders to reflect on how they would conduct themselves in the work role. The key recognition issue is to understand that any decision is an opportunity to apply evidence. This can be facilitated in the classroom, where managers are encouraged to share their insights with each other. The task of executive education is to ensure that managers consider how they can apply their newly acquired knowledge. This facilitates the transfer process.
- *Principle 3 – Diagnose Underlying Factors Related to Decisions:* Evidence-based executive development focuses on diagnosis. Diagnosis focuses on understanding that a decision has to be made. The challenge for the educator or developer is to ensure that managers ask the appropriate questions. The challenge for executive development is to enhance managers' and leaders' diagnostic skills through such activities as practice reflection and rehearsal. This can be achieved through the use of cases which provide managers with critically important questions, and asking them to collect and apply the evidence.

- *Principle 4 – Contextualise Knowledge Related to Evidence Use:* Managers need to become skilled at adapting their knowledge to settings and their circumstances. Evidence which is not contextualised is of little value. Principles are essentially context-free, therefore managers must question 'can it work?' 'will it work?' and 'is it worth taking action based on the evidence?' Managers in the work situation develop over time the tacit knowledge to ask these questions. In the classroom the challenge for the educator is to devise teaching strategies that facilitate repeated practice opportunities. Practice enables managers to acquire tacit knowledge and it facilitates the development of special competencies that are required to make the decision. Development activities that emphasise practice reflection and feedback are most likely to provide managers with the skills to contextualise the evidence.
- *Principle 5 – Develop Evidence-Based Decision Supports:* Decision supports play a major role in ensuring that managers can identify critical factors, diagnose the most appropriate solution and follow effective procedures. Educators are therefore challenged to provide managers with examples of how decision supports can be developed. This will enable the manager to transfer evidence-based practices into day-to-day decision-making. Decision supports may be unique to the particular context but can include checklists, frameworks and routines.
- *Principle 6 – Prepare to Assess the New Evidence:* Managers are expected continually to update their knowledge by accessing new practice-related evidence at various stages of their careers. Managers are frequently challenged with how best to access evidence. Participation in executive development initiatives on a regular basis is one way to keep up to date.

Source: Rousseau and McCarthy (2007)

Executive Education Programmes

Executive education programmes are major business opportunities for universities and training institutes. Internationally recognised providers of executive education include INSTEAD in France, Management Centre Europe in Belgium and the Centre for Creative Leadership in the USA. Executive MBAs have become extremely popular. These programmes condense or accelerate coursework with course attendance, typically at weekends. Courses typically last two years. Executives tend to be older, and may come from a variety of organisations.

Proponents of executive MBA programmes argue that they provide executives with an opportunity to interact with executives from other organisations, they provide a forum for the discussion of new ideas and there is prestige in having an affiliation with a respected university. Universities typically sell these programmes with the promise that executives will have access to top-quality academics. Most organisations use executive MBAs as one component of their executive development activities and usually combine them with other internal offerings.

Critics of executive MBAs suggest that they do not offer any additional value over other course-based developmental interventions. They are accused of focusing too much on analytical capabilities and neglecting softer skills. Baruch and Peiperl (2000) suggested that they frequently do not give enough focus to teamwork, customer/client relationships, interpersonal skills, listening and entrepreneurial imagination.

Executive MBAs are also frequently criticised because of their generic nature and lack of relevance to the specifics of the executive's organisation. They are a very expensive development option and they require a strong work and time commitment from the individual executive. Executive MBAs are also criticised on the basis that they are merely a watered-down version of a full-time MBA programme and that they frequently offer poor quality of instruction and set low admission standards. The primary goal is sometimes perceived as generating income for the business school rather than providing top-quality executive education. There is relatively limited research to indicate that the executive MBA is an effective development strategy for organisations to invest in. Andrews (1966) and Hollenbeck (1991) did, however, report that executives are generally satisfied with the executive MBA experience, claiming that the programme provided a more strategic and global outlook on the business and broadened their thinking through exposure to new ideas and people. They also reported increased self-confidence in the executive role. It is, however, prudent for organisations who are considering investing in executive MBAs to examine carefully whether they are suitable for the development needs of the executive and whether the executive is prepared to give the commitment necessary to realise the benefits of the programme. Exhibit 14.3 highlighted the characteristics of an evidence-based approach to executive education.

Action Learning for Top Teams

We discussed the key principles of action learning in Chapter Seven. Therefore, we will focus here on its potential value to top-team development. Raelin (2006) suggests that action leaning can benefit the individual executive as well as the executive team. At the individual level, action learning can help the executive to understand that a viewpoint is just a viewpoint. It encourages the executive to be reflective. Bell (1998) found that the reflective executive is open to experience and learning, is less self-absorbed, engages in deep listening, displays tolerance of contrary views and sets realistic expectations. Action learning can increase an executive's capacity to collaborate. This arises because the executive is stimulated by the experience of peer challenge and support, by feeling empowered and by the opportunity to work on personal goals which are outside the executive's comfort zone.

At the level of the executive team, action learning sessions can lead to executives challenging their own values, views and behaviours, and becoming critical about their own and others' actions. They may lead executive teams to focus more on challenging and experimenting with new approaches. Raelin (2006) highlights the important role of the facilitator in this context. He suggests that the facilitator:

* Needs to observe the team during learning team meetings
* Provides feedback to both individual executives and the team as a whole on its interpersonal process
* Seeks to ensure that the team maintains ownership of their own agenda
* Focuses on increasing the executive's capacity for reflection.

Raelin envisages that both individuals' leadership capabilities and the leadership capability of the team can be significantly enhanced through a well-designed and implemented action learning process.

Conclusion

The development of teams, top teams and executives is complex and challenging for leadership development specialists. A key challenge focuses on diagnosing whether the issue is an individual or a team development issue. Executive team development presents an additional challenge. Frequently, many executive issues do not require teamwork at all and the 'team at the top' rarely functions as a collective. The executive team is, however, the only team that can change the organisational agenda. Therefore, it is important to make an impact in terms of strategic development at this level. The top team itself has major scope to facilitate team building at lower levels in the organisation.

Executive and top team development interventions have to cope with a complex context and an understanding that the competencies required by executives are both vast and complex. Many executive development initiatives focus on key knowledge components, but fail to address issues of self-awareness for both individual executives and the larger executive team. The leadership development specialist must be able to speak the language of the boardroom in order to make the case for top team and executive development.

Summary of Key Points

- Team development processes focus on enhancing aspects of team functioning, including their meta-cognition, team relationships and effectiveness.
- Executive and top team development is a key strategy for enhancing the performance and effectiveness of the executive, the executive team and the organisation.
- Executives and top teams demand a multiplicity of capabilities and competencies, simply because their tasks are both complex and potentially conflicting.
- Top teams require an effective balance of competencies in order to be successful.
- Top team and executive level development interventions include executive coaching, executive education programmes and action learning programmes.
- Leadership development specialists frequently encounter difficulties in making the case for executive and top team development.
- Many executive development interventions focus too much on education and not enough on development and self-awareness processes.

■ Discussion Questions

1. What are the key challenges that leadership development specialists face when developing top teams in organisations?

2. What are the leadership development issues in cross-functional and virtual teams? Under what conditions are self-managed teams most likely to flourish?

3. Evaluate the effectiveness of three strategies that can be used to facilitate team building.

4. What development strategies are appropriate to develop executives?

5. Critically evaluate the contribution of executive coaching and executive education programmes to manager performance.

■ Application and Experiential Questions

1. Select one cluster of team competencies presented in Table 14.7. Suggest different methods that you could use to develop each competency in the cluster. Which ones do you consider cannot be developed? Justify your answer.

2. Based on what you have studied in this chapter about the negative perceptions of executive teams concerning the contribution of development, prepare a proposal setting out how you would sell an executive development programme in a selected organisation.

3. In groups of three or four, prepare a strategy to identify the development needs of senior executives. Suggest and justify the methods you would use and indicate how you would communicate the results to executives and get their buy-in for the developmental interventions you propose.

Chapter Fifteen

Leadership Development for Specific Categories and Contexts

Outline

Learning Objectives

After reading this chapter you will be able to:

- Explain why it is necessary to focus on the leadership development issues of specific groups in organisations and different organisational contexts.
- List and evaluate the key issues that arise for the development of female managers and leaders in organisations.
- Explain the management and leadership development issues that arise for managers of race and managers from different ethnic backgrounds.
- Evaluate the continuous professional development issues that arise for specialist managers and leaders.
- Discuss the unique management and leadership development issues that arise for unemployed and mid-career managers.
- Describe and explain the leadership development issues that arise for fast-track or high-potential graduates.
- Describe and explain the leadership development issues that arise in voluntary organisations, small micro enterprises and for entrepreneurs.

OPENING CASE SCENARIO

Developing Graduates at Kerry Group plc

Kerry Group plc was established in 1972 as Kerry Co-op, with Denis Brosnan, Hugh Friel and Denis Creegan as key strategists. It remained a co-op until 1986, when it acquired the status of a publicly owned company. This was its first major step to becoming a multinational company. Since 1980, Kerry Group plc has become a world leader in food ingredients and flavours and it has also become a leading added-value chilled-food company in Ireland and the UK. Currently, Kerry Group supplies over 10,000 foods, food ingredients and flavoured products to customers in 120 countries. Strategically, Kerry Group places a strong emphasis on developing a team of dedicated, innovative and experienced managers. This focus on top-team strength has enabled Kerry Group to pursue a high-risk acquisition strategy. The Group has excelled in its financial management and has consistently sustained its profitability over a twenty-year period. It is responsive to meeting the needs of its customers and emphasises technological creativity, quality and superior customer service as key components of its strategy and organisational culture.

Kerry Group places a strong emphasis on training and leadership development. It has invested in the development of its employee and management skills and competencies, and has created an organisational culture that is capable of generating competitive advantage in local and international markets. The Group has operated a successful graduate development programme for over twenty years, employing and developing graduates in a range of business disciplines. Because the Group's overall strategy is one of expansion through acquisition, graduates are afforded many personal and professional growth opportunities. It adopts a high-potential graduate development strategy, seeks to hire the best and brightest graduates, and is unique in the industry in that it employs a full-time HR manager for graduates. This manager is charged with the task of ensuring that the organisation has a quality pool of high-potential graduates who will successfully complete a two-year graduate development programme. In order to maximise the development of graduates, Kerry Group established a relationship with the IMI in the mid-1990s and created an IMI/Kerry Group management development programme. This programme arose from the need to facilitate the speedy transition of graduates from the world of academia to the world of business. Graduates are drawn from all the Group's business divisions and from all its geographical locations. The overall aim of the programme is to develop the management and leadership competencies of graduates. Participants are awarded a certificate at the end of the first year and a Kerry/IMI diploma on successful completion of the second year.

The graduate development programme is unique in that Kerry Group acknowledges that it is developing graduates for management positions within the organisation as well as making them more marketable outside the Group. This represents a considerable risk. The programme focuses on developing graduates' specific and generic competencies and is designed to provide graduates with insights and skills to enable them to manage business units. It ensures that they acquire a deep understanding of Kerry Group's businesses and key managerial functions. It also focuses on developing the employability of graduates and enhancing their personal managerial capabilities. The programme takes a holistic approach and seeks to balance business and individual development needs.

The programme consists of four key components: graduate socialisation; a structured development programme; mentoring and coaching processes; and planned work experience. Graduates are exposed to an intensive socialisation process that enables them to 'learn the ropes' of the organisation, to understand their role in the organisation and to learn the culture from senior colleagues. The socialisation process combines the formal and the informal. The formal component involves thirty days of formal training and covers content in areas such as strategy, finance, people management, teamworking, understanding culture and structure, and management processes. Classroom training is blended with a small component of e-learning and distance learning. Graduates value the structured components and perceive that these contribute to their work performance and personal development.

The programme also incorporates mentoring and coaching processes. These activities are undertaken by managers within Kerry Group and by IMI faculty. Graduates are encouraged to take responsibility and ownership for their managerial and personal development. They are expected to have open dialogue concerning their career goals and individual motivations. Graduates value the opportunity to learn from colleagues, being shown how to do things and actually performing key tasks. Planned work experience is central to the development process. It is important because it brings the graduate into contact with senior management and it tests the graduate's skills to the limit. It is also an important test of the graduate's decision-making capability and provides the opportunity to take on new challenges. As part of their work experience, graduates are required to undertake specific development projects. These projects are assessed by the Group's chief executive, who engages with each graduate on the strategic analysis that they have undertaken. The endorsement and commitment of the chief executive illustrates the overall importance of the programme to the organisation.

The programme has been systematically evaluated. Graduates are motivated to participate in the programme because they perceive it as an opportunity to plan their career and enhance their employability and future employment prospects, either within or outside the organisation. Kerry Group invests a considerable amount of money in the programme and seeks to gain the graduates' commitment to the organisation. The dual purposes of the graduate development programme may not always be compatible, in that the organisation acknowledges that notions of commitment and employability may not fit easily together. The programme is, however, firmly established as a key component of Kerry Group's strategy to recruit and develop the best graduates. It is a rolling annual programme and has proved instrumental in fast-tracking young managers to positions of responsibility within the Group. The programme has been continuously fine-tuned to ensure an effective balance of development challenges. Graduates most appreciate the work experience element. They value the opportunity for job relocation and working with a variety of managers. However, the Group is conscious that the fast-track programme may be perceived as elitist, leading to resentment among other managers, who may feel that their own careers are being neglected.

QUESTIONS

Q.1 Evaluate the key design features of the graduate development programme in Kerry Group.

Q.2 What do you see as the main advantages and disadvantages of graduate development programmes?

Organisational leadership development provision is not a one-size-fits-all approach. Various groups exist in organisations that pose specific challenges for management and leadership development. Furthermore, different types of organisation have particular management and leadership development challenges. These include voluntary organisations, small firms and entrepreneurial ventures. These different categories and organisational contexts are increasingly acknowledged in the research as having specific management and leadership development needs, as well as requiring more customised and specialised development strategies. Many of the categories we consider in this chapter are, relatively speaking, under-represented in the business world and are often forgotten in discussions of management and leadership development.

Organisations are increasingly requested to realise the importance of embracing diversity. For example, they need to understand the diverse talent and knowledge that resides in female managers and managers of different race or colour. These groups require leadership development specialists to think beyond traditional management and leadership development approaches. Small firms, entrepreneurial ventures and voluntary organisations have particular contextual characteristics that make management and leadership development difficult to understand. There is often a lack of commitment to leadership development in these organisations.

The development of unemployed and mid-career managers' management and leadership capabilities is also an important issue. Widespread restructuring of organisations has led to leaner and less hierarchical structures, resulting in an increase in the number of unemployed managers. Mid-career managers often have unique leadership development needs, as do fast-track graduates who are increasingly employed by multinational organisations.

We discuss these particular categories and contexts in this chapter. We explain the issues they pose for leadership development and outline the appropriateness of different leadership development interventions. The chapter concludes with a discussion of the issues and themes that are common to the different categories as well as the issues that are unique.

Leadership Development Issues for Female Managers

The development of female leaders poses particular challenges for organisations. Ruderman (2004) suggested that gender inequity is a characteristic of modern organisations. We highlighted in Chapter Three that an increasing number of women have entered the management ranks. They are, however, most likely to be found in the junior and middle categories. Morrison (1992) suggested that the reasons for this include prejudice on the part of men and limited exposure of women to developmental assignments, relationships and experiences to prepare them for senior positions. Male managers feel more comfortable dealing with their own kind. Managers take into account their comfort level with a direct report when making a promotion decision. Women have the unique challenge of integrating career and family needs. Women are still more likely, in dual-career situations, to take on most of the responsibility for home and family. These pressures pose challenges for the ways in which leadership development is organised and delivered. Some organisations have provided specific leadership development programmes for women. We consider the arguments for and against these types of programmes in the next section.

Specific Leadership Development Programmes for Women: Good or Bad?

Organisations frequently provide leadership development programmes specifically for women. Mallon and Cassell (1999) suggested that they are provided to support the advancement of women within the management ranks. Leadership development initiatives may also be driven by a need to increase the diversity of the management team. Lewis and Fagenson (1995) suggested that leadership development programmes can help female managers to develop their leadership skills and facilitate them to overcome barriers to advancement.

There are many arguments concerning the value of women-only leadership development programmes versus mixed-gender leadership development programmes. Women-only leadership development programmes can take many forms, but are generally focused on areas where it is believed to be possible to overcome prejudices present in the organisation. Bhavnani (1997) questioned whether or not these programmes have been effective in increasing the number of women in management positions. Hite and McDonald (1995) suggested that women-only leadership development programmes have created a perception that women do not have certain skills that male managers possess. Therefore, they lead to increased stereotyping and gender bias. There is, however, some support for the view that women do benefit on an individual basis from assertiveness training to adapt and cope with power structures and to fit in with the organisation's culture. Women-only leadership development programmes tend to have a double-edged quality. They have the potential to enhance the skills of female managers, but they can also isolate female managers and further emphasise differences from male colleagues.

Mixed-gender leadership development programmes are designed to address the leadership development needs of both genders. These programmes typically develop leadership and team-building skills, negotiation, problem-solving and change management competencies. For female managers, these programmes provide an opportunity to be treated equally in a leadership development context. The impact of mixed-gender leadership development programmes is unclear, but they appear to have more advantages than disadvantages when compared with women-only programmes.

Specialised mentoring and single-identity group feedback-intensive programmes are highlighted as potentially useful for female managers. Mentor availability is highlighted as a significant issue for female managers. Ragins and Cotton (1992) identified several perceived barriers to women obtaining a male mentor. Specifically, female managers have less informal access to a male mentor, and they are reluctant to develop a mentoring relationship with a male manager because of how the relationship may be perceived. Potential male mentors may also be reluctant to act as a mentor to a female manager. Female managers can benefit more from a male than from a female mentor. Ragins and Cotton (1999) found that they were likely to receive greater financial rewards. It appears that female mentors are likely to provide more psychological support. Ragins and McFarlin (1990) found that mentees in a cross-gender mentoring relationship were less likely to engage in social activities with mentors after work. Overall, the question of whether a female or a male mentor is best for women's development and advancement is still unclear.

Ruderman (2004) suggested that there are advantages and disadvantages associated with women-only feedback-intensive programmes. She specifically emphasised that they can validate the experience of being a minority manager in a majority organisation. It is a safe context in which to share experience and it enables the manager to be with others in a similar situation. On the other hand, it can highlight perceived differences and potentially create negative feelings.

Ohlott and Hughes-James (1997) suggested that organisations and individual managers should ask the following questions when considering whether a women-only or a mixed-group developmental intervention is appropriate:

- Does the manager consider that her gender is having an impact on her career?
- How comfortable will the manager feel in a women-only group or in a mixed group of managers?
- Does the manager value having a connection and bonding with female managers who have similar career issues?
- Has the manager already participated in a traditional leadership intervention?
- How are gender-specific developmental initiatives perceived in the organisation?
- What are the specific skill needs of the female manager?
- What is the environment in which the developed skills will have to be applied?

Table 15.1: The Advantages and Disadvantages of Development Interventions Focused on Women-Only and Mixed-Gender Groups

Advantages	Disadvantages
Women-Only Development Programmes	
<ul><li>Provide women with knowledge and opportunity to develop skills and leadership abilities</li><li>Create a forum for support for learning in a prejudice-free environment and allow discussion on the experiences and problems of women in the workplace</li><li>Women become more self-aware of their strengths and weaknesses. They increase confidence and self-image</li><li>Create networking opportunities with other women</li><li>Encourage women to take responsibility for own career</li><li>Motivate women to meet their full capacity</li></ul>	<ul><li>Women viewed as gaining preferential treatment leading to resentment, further alienation and tension</li><li>Support the idea that women must change to fit in with the traditional idea of management, i.e. encourages women to think male and adopt male stereotypes</li><li>Do not reduce stereotyping and bias and support gender reinforcement rather than gender integration</li><li>Decrease chance of gender integration in management</li><li>Women may continue to be excluded and isolated from management</li><li>Often seen as a forum for complaints and not as a developmental opportunity</li><li>Limited opportunity for networking and skill development due to the gender imbalance</li><li>Take place in an unrealistic environment</li><li>Skills learned may be hard to transfer to the workplace</li></ul>
Mixed-Gender Management-Development Programmes	
<ul><li>Improve women's knowledge, skills, qualifications, leadership and managerial abilities</li><li>Do not isolate women from men or label them as different</li><li>Can reduce biases, stereotyping and prejudices of women and sexism (through discussion on the subject)</li><li>Provide forums for managers to network (especially between genders)</li><li>Encourage the development of relationships and support between the sexes</li><li>Act as incentive for female managers to remain in the organisation</li><li>Provide learning environment that reflects the real work environment</li></ul>	<ul><li>Mixed-gender programmes may not be sufficient to get women access to middle and senior management positions</li><li>There is little focus on specific women's needs and experiences</li><li>Women's contributions may be less recognised and seen of less value</li><li>Women tend to be less vocal in mixed-gender forums</li></ul>

Advantages	Disadvantages
Special Mentoring and Feedback-Intensive Sessions for Female Managers	
• Can help women to progress into management positions and to advance their careers • Improve technical, managerial and leadership skills • Help decrease prejudice against women by giving them the opportunity to progress up through the organisation while also alleviating gender and work-related problems • Give access to power channels and information networks • Can focus on issues that are unique to women	• Mentoring may not provide psychological and career-oriented support • Women face obstacles to gaining a suitable mentor • Organisational culture may not support a mentee relationship • Women may be perceived as receiving more favourable treatment • The mentoring and feedback processes do not take place in the real-world context

Tharenou, Latimer and Conroy (1994) pointed out that more men than women participate in leadership development programmes. Women often have to prove their career intent before they are given access to leadership development. Organisations are frequently less likely to provide women with career development interventions; they are then unaware of their development needs. Hite and McDonald (1995) stressed that women may not always be committed to leadership development. They choose not to participate in leadership development opportunities because of the difficulties of achieving work–life balance. Unfortunately, while women have to accept some of the responsibility, organisations still engage in gender bias when designing and implementing leadership development activities.

Multicultural and Race Issues in Leadership Development

Managers from diverse backgrounds experience barriers to management and leadership development as they progress throughout their careers. Giscombe and Mattis (2002) indicated that these problems are not confined solely to the early career stages. Wentling and Palma-Rivas (1998) found that managers from minority groups who experienced negative attitudes, stereotyping and discomfort from other people in the organisation were less likely to advance. The organisational perception of diverse groups and other cultures will probably inhibit their advancement. Lindsay (1994) found that the development potential of a manager from a minority group in the organisation depended largely on the level of discrimination and oppression that the group suffers in the wider society. Management and leadership development initiatives are unlikely, therefore, to be effective if the culture does not support the application of diversity initiatives. This indicates that issues to do with race and cultural background increasingly impinge on leadership development in organisations. Being of a minority ethnic origin, for instance, can be a salient issue in organisations. Because these leaders have a different skin colour, they are frequently assessed differently according to stereotypical notions rather than their effectiveness as leaders.

Organisations are increasingly recognising that it is important to provide ethnic minority managers with developmental assistance to ensure that they can contribute fully to the organisation. Wentling *et al.* (1998) argued that leadership development can provide managers of ethnic minority origin with the opportunity for advancement and it can also help to maximise their potential. Livers and Caver (2004) suggested that when organisations and managers are challenged to deal effectively with ethnic minority, they must still focus on the need for self-development, education and specific diversity initiatives.

Self-Development: Managers need to develop their own thinking concerning their attitudes to managers of a difference race. This involves achieving an understanding of personal beliefs and assumptions. Three particular attitudes are highlighted as important: managers need to understand that differences really do matter; managers who are in the majority need to understand that differences in the workplace are a good thing; they must be willing to be uncomfortable and they must make every effort to avoid misreading situations.

Education: Livers and Caver (2004) argued that education plays an important role in helping managers come to a better understanding of diversity and issues of race. They suggested that managers should learn about their colleagues' background and should seek feedback on how they interact with managers from a different race. They should also learn more about the expectations they have of them and they should achieve an insight into important stereotypes and what lies behind such stereotypes. Organisations can implement a number of initiatives to ensure that there is a greater understanding of the potential contribution of ethnic minority managers.

Table 15.2: Potential Problems with Diversity Training

When trainers . . .	When the training programme . . .
• Use their own psychological issues (e.g. trust or group affiliation) as templates for training • Have their own political agenda • Do not model the philosophy or skills associated with valuing diversity • Are chosen because they represent or advocate a minority group • Are not competent at facilitation and presenting, may have poor credibility with trainees, or are known to be insensitive • Force people to reveal their feelings about other people • Do not respect individual styles of trainees • Pressure only one group to change • Cover too few issues and do not engage participants individually	• Is not integrated into the organisation's overall approach to diversity • Is too brief, too late, or reactive • Is presented as remedial and trainees as people with problems • Does not distinguish the meanings of valuing diversity, equal opportunities, affirmative action and managing across cultures • Does not make a link between stereotyping behaviour and personal and organisational effectiveness • Is based on a philosophy of political correctness • Is too shallow or too deep • Uses outdated esource materials • Has a curriculum that is not adapted to trainees' needs or not matched with the skills and experience of the trainer • Does not allow discussion of certain issues (e.g. reverse discrimination)

Source: Mobley and Payne (1992)

Experiential Development Activities: These are appropriate to achieve more multicultural understanding. Fish (1999) highlighted that an 'on-the-ground' development is a useful learning technique to gain skills and knowledge of the working environment and to develop successful cultural understanding. Active learning occurs in a multicultural environment whereby managers learn through sharing each other's experiences and this is facilitated through acceptance of the concept of diversity. This enables enhanced learning and problem-solving as well as challenging the mindset and beliefs that hinder the acceptance of knowledge. Korac-Kakabadse and Kouzmin (1999) suggested that this intervention, on its own, may be ineffective without a foundation in formal development initiatives.

Targeted Diversity Initiatives: Targeted diversity initiatives can contribute to creating a culture of trust and tolerance. Diversity initiatives, however, frequently fail. They are often initiated because it is the latest fad or because they are recommended by an outside agency. The initiative needs to be custom-made for the organisation; however, they are often off-the-shelf programmes. Many diversity programmes go only so far as awareness training. Managers are not encouraged to practise what they have learned and effective follow-up is not guaranteed. Organisations frequently do not allocate sufficient resources to the initiative.

An effective diversity initiative for leadership development and the success of minorities and people of minority ethnic origin in management positions needs to focus on the culture of the organisation, its strategies, the nature of leadership and leadership development practices. It is important that cultural issues are addressed. Specifically, the culture must foster a sense of belonging, mutual respect and the toleration of differences. It must promote concern for equality, including equal respect for minority and majority groups. It is important that the organisation links diversity to business strategies. Diversity needs to be promoted at all levels in the organisation and, strategically, there must be consequences if diversity is not encouraged. The diversity initiative must not be viewed as a quick fix. Iverson (2000) suggested that leadership practices should take all employees seriously, recognise the capabilities of all employees, support employees, value diverse work teams and respect the cultural beliefs and needs of employees. Organisations' leadership development practices must encourage the promotion of managers from different cultures, provide opportunities for the development of new skills, implement positive action programmes for the promotion of minorities into management positions and ensure access to top management positions. Efforts by the organisation to develop a diverse climate and create multicultural opportunities will not, by themselves, create an organisation that values diversity. It requires that the organisation's top management recognises the capabilities of all managers and supports both minority and majority manager groups.

Networking and Mentoring: Organisations should provide education on the effectiveness of networks and promote and support the development of individual networks. McCarthy, Hukai and McCarthy (2005) noted that networks provide access to development opportunities, provide support mechanisms and help to change the culture of the organisation. Rudderman *et al.* (2005) suggest that structured dialogue sessions between junior and senior managers from diverse backgrounds encourage relationship-building and learning about diversity issues. Minority managers are also likely to benefit from formal mentoring. Managers overcome problems in areas such as developing career strategies for advancement, and gain an introduction to social networks. Experienced mentors can offer feedback on performance as well as encouraging minority managers to achieve high performance. Ruderman *et al.* (1995) suggested that a mentoring relationship which incorporates the use of multisource processes and coach-facilitated feedback can enable minority managers to understand personal assumptions and behaviours. McCarthy *et al.* (2005) highlighted that minority managers often find it difficult to obtain suitable mentors. A lack of diversity amongst senior management inevitably leads to a lack of mentors for this group. This promotes a vicious circle. The following are a number of guidelines which ensure that diversity initiatives are effective:

- Embed diversity management into corporate strategy for best advantage.
- Locate diversity responsibility in the whole organisation (it should not be a purely human resource issue).
- Give diversity an inclusive definition. What values does the definition highlight? Is this in alignment with corporate strategy?
- Create a high-level, visible 'diversity champion', and an organisation-wide 'diversity council'.
- Appoint a diversity director or manager and form a diversity task force to draw up an action plan.
- Allocate a central budget, at least for preliminary initiatives. But remember that training costs should be the responsibility of the delegates' departments, as managers should be

prepared to invest in this training. (If they pay for it, they may be more likely to make the resulting change happen in their department.)

- Assess the current situation: the climate in the organisation, employee satisfaction surveys, focus groups and interviews. Look at the symbolic as well as the real – remember that perceptions are as important as reality in terms of influencing behaviours.
- Design relevant interventions, such as training, to increase awareness and understanding about diversity. Be creative in designing support such as mentoring, coaching and executive education, as well as flexible ways of working. Monitor take-up and outcomes in different minority groups.
- Develop skills that employees can use to deal with diversity in the workplace as well as with diverse customers. Diversity skills should address internal (employee to employee) and external (employee to customer) relationships.
- Create open channels of communication throughout the organisation using new technology.
- Have a local diversity co-ordinator to maintain contact with the central head of diversity so that there is sustainability.
- Hold managers accountable for diversity performance and build diversity management into the competency and capability framework.
- Monitor the diversity of the employee profile at group and organisational levels.
- Measure costs and effectiveness of each component of diversity initiatives (training, taskforce, mentoring, employee networks, and so on) so that appropriate choices can be made for further action
- Be aware that the impetus is easily lost. There may be a change of champion, a loss of passion, other priorities and mergers, and support for the process may dissipate as a result. Diversity management needs to be sustainable through such changes.

Developing Professional Managers and Continuous Professional Development

Organisations frequently employ professionals and specialists who possess particular technical and theoretical expertise that is important for the organisation to achieve its goals. Professionals are usually given a considerable amount of autonomy and freedom. They are usually able to determine their work methods and will follow particular ethical practices. Professionals are increasingly made responsible for the delivery of services and are expected to manage groups of professionals. This has been referred to as the new managerialism. Cooper, Robinson and Arnold (1996) suggested that professionals are increasingly managed as a business. They are expected to be accountable to the organisation for their performance and to focus on strategy and planning. They are also exposed to customer surveys and other feedback mechanisms. Hinings, Greenwood and Cooper (1999) suggested that they have to work within a framework of professional standards and, at the same time, be accountable to line managers for their performance. The development issues for these groups are no different from those of other managers. What is different, however, is their potential to accept the values and practices that underpin management and leadership development. Professional values, beliefs and standards for performance of professionals (e.g. accountants, auditors and engineers) may conflict with the strong organisational focus of management and leadership development. Professionals may reject practices and ideas which are not in line with their professional values.

Specialist managers frequently have continuous professional development (CPD) needs over and above their general management and leadership development requirements. CPD emphasises the acquisition, improvement and updating of professional knowledge, skills and capabilities. It also focuses on qualities that contribute to individuals' performance as professionals. Managers in specialist areas increasingly recognise that their professional attitudes to and engagement with updating their skills are important to their employability and career success. Pazy (1990) highlighted that professional or specialist managers are not immune to obsolescence, and can be negatively impacted on by organisational and technological change. Rusaw (1995) suggested that the shelf life of technical knowledge has diminished considerably. London (1996) argued that the more professional managers are affected by change in their professional knowledge base, the more they need to participate in continuous learning.

The engagement of managers with CPD is not necessarily a given. Taylor (1996) suggested that if managers perceive a lack of need for CPD, they are unlikely to participate. Ownership of CPD must rest with the manager, otherwise they are unlikely to perceive it as valuable.

Defining CPD and its Perceived Value

There are numerous definitions of CPD (Table 15.3). These definitions emphasise that CPD for managers is continuous and systematic, lifelong and long-term. It focuses on maintaining, improving, updating and broadening professional competence, and facilitates the manager in meeting his/her professional commitments through education and training processes.

Megginson and Whittaker (2003) stated that CPD has advantages for a number of organisational stakeholders. For managers, it provides an opportunity to reappraise personal and career goals. For organisations, it helps ensure that managers keep their knowledge and skills up to date and take responsibility for their development. CPD can be valuable in the context of succession planning and retention of professional or specialist managers. Rothwell and Arnold (2005) found that CPD can enhance the employability and career prospects of managers. In our experience, it contributes to enabling managers to cope with the changing nature of work, it helps improve job performance and it impacts on the motivational state of the manager.

Table 15.3: Definitions of Continuous Professional Development (CPD)

Definition	Source
CPD is a personal commitment to keeping your professional knowledge up to date and improving your capabilities throughout your working life. It's about knowing where you are today, where you want to be in the future and making sure you get there.	CIPD (2002)
Any process or activity that provides added value to the capability of the professional through the increase in knowledge, skills and personal qualities for appropriate execution of professional and technical duties, often termed competence. It is a lifelong tool that benefits professional, customer, employer, professional association and society as a whole and is particularly relevant during periods of rapid technological and occupational change.	Professional Associations Research Network (UK)
The systematic maintenance, improvement and broadening of knowledge and skills and the development of personal qualities necessary for the execution of professional and technical duties throughout the practitioner's working life.	Institution of Engineers of Ireland
The maintenance and enhancement of the knowledge, expertise and competence of professionals throughout their careers according to a plan formulated with regard to the needs of the professional, the employer, the profession and society.	Madden and Mitchell (1993)
Continuing Professional Development (CPD) is a term commonly used to denote the process of the ongoing education and development of health care professionals, from initial qualifying education and for the duration of professional life, in order to maintain competence to practice and increase professional proficiency and expertise.	Alsop (2000)

Organisations are likely to invest in manager CPD because of its role in both sustaining and enhancing technical and service quality and ensuring that the needs of internal customers are met. It also represents an important statement of the organisation's commitment to best practice and to the professional career of the manager. This has the potential to enhance the reputation of the organisation.

Types of CPD Activity

Managers can engage in CPD in both formal and informal ways. Rothwell and Arnold (2005) found, for example, that managers used the job context and role to develop their specialist skills, rather than through more generic professional knowledge interventions. The most popular methods were the reading of books and journals, sharing knowledge with colleagues, reading work-related documents, spontaneous learning through work and personal activities, and reflective discussions with colleagues (Table 15.4).

Table 15.4: Methods Used by Managers for CPD

- Regular reading of journals and books relevant to my profession
- Shared knowledge with colleagues
- Reading work-related documents from my organisation
- Acquiring generic transferable skills and competencies related to my job
- Spontaneous learning arising from work or personal activities
- Practising the rules and procedures of my work organisation
- Learning through informal teamwork in the workplace
- Reflective discussions with colleagues that are informal but still relevant to the profession
- Action learning: learning from development projects
- Acquiring knowledge through browsing websites or 'surfing the net'
- Keeping a portfolio record of CPD activities that the manager has undertaken
- External courses the employer has paid for
- Membership of committees at my place of work, e.g. quality, health and safety
- Employer's internal training courses
- Learning professional knowledge, e.g. professional codes of practice
- Reflective discussions with colleagues as part of a formal development review process
- Learning that is carefully planned in advance
- Technical training
- Other personal activities outside work, e.g. hobbies, scouts/guides, community or religious organisations, voluntary activities
- Undertaking academic study that isn't necessarily related to the manger's job or profession
- Authorship of technical papers (internal or external to the organisation)
- Exchanging emails on professional topics with other professional members
- Keeping reflective diary over an extended period
- Participating in internal secondments or transfers at my place of work
- Working towards a vocational qualification sponsored by my employer
- Working towards a vocational qualification which the manager pays for
- Taking part in an online discussion forum relevant to the manager's profession

Source: Rothwell and Arnold (2005) (in order of priority)

Chivers (2003) highlighted two particular methods that are appropriate in a CPD context: learning logs and team reflection.

Learning Logs: Cheetham and Chivers (2001) suggested that encouraging professionals to articulate their work activities in written form is an effective source of learning. Honey and Mumford (1986) further recommend learning logs as a way of recording and tracking professional development and encouraging reflection. Recording how things were done encourages a conscious process of reflection. Barclay (1996) is a strong advocate of learning logs in a professional development context. She suggested that they focus on all aspects of the learning cycle and they help the manager identify what happened, facilitate the articulation of key learning points and encourage a plan of action for the next time the professional issue arises. She emphasised the need to set goals and action plans because they provide a path for CPD and encourage the manager to take ownership for CPD. Barclay found that human resource managers placed particular value on the use of learning logs. Learning logs enhanced self-awareness and made the manager confront their professional strengths and weaknesses. They also motivated managers to seek new experiences and responsibilities, to communicate more effectively with fellow professionals and to be better at recording their development.

The Role of Team Reflection: Learning logs are an important strategy to encourage managers to engage in reflection. Chivers (2003) emphasised that professional managers tend to reflect in isolation, even though a lot of professional work is carried out in teams. He acknowledged that too much individual reflection can be counterproductive and actually lead to reduced professional competence. Individual reflection may, in some cases, encourage managers to become overly critical, more introverted and to lose their self-confidence. He advocates reflecting jointly with others. Kleinman, Siegal and Eckstein (2002) suggested that team-based reflection has value because professional or specialist managers can offer different insights and stimulate individual manager learning. Managers who participated in team reflection were better at communication, they had more effective listening and persuasion skills, and were more informed about how their actions impacted on others. It may also be possible to facilitate web-based reflection. Brosnan and Burgess (2003) studied web-based reflection that was built around a forum. They found that it facilitated a diverse mix of professionals sharing their experiences. Managers were comfortable reflecting online. The communication process was very open and voices that might not be heard in face-to-face interaction were given an opportunity to be heard via a bulletin board. Table 15.5 summarises some of the practice issues that organisations should consider when implementing CPD for managers.

Table 15.5: Best Practice Guidelines for Implementing CPD in Organisations

- In order for CPD to be effective, it should have an element of individual manager self-directed learning. Organisations should ensure that collaborative processes and a support network are in place.
- Reflection should be encouraged through the use of personal development plans, suitable mentors and team-based activities.
- CPD should identify, incorporate and develop competencies, both generic and specific, for the profession in question, encourage experiential and on-the-job learning activities and provide frequent feedback to professional managers on their CPD.
- Organisations should provide time, financial resources and assistance in the development of professional development plans to facilitate any contribution towards business objectives.
- Where there is a mandatory element of CPD, it should set minimum standards of development, but there should also be equal credit for participation in those CPD activities which enhance those competencies outside the minimum requirement of technical expertise.

Development Issues for Unemployed and Mid-Career Managers

Managers have traditionally believed that, in exchange for hard work, competence and loyalty, lifelong employment would follow. This is no longer the case. Fielden and Davidson (1998) suggested that managerial employment has gradually increased since the 1980s.

Fielden (2001) suggested that structural changes in organisations are the main reasons attributed to increased unemployment among management positions. The experience of male and female managers when unemployed is different. Men have lower levels of self-esteem, hostility, and distress. Stokes and Cochrane (1984) found that female managers experienced significantly higher levels of anxiety when unemployed and had a greater need for social support to reduce this anxiety.

The main purpose of leadership development for an unemployed manager is to make the manager more employable and therefore facilitate re-employment. Leadership development activities can increase a manager's self-esteem and motivation. Miller and Robinson (2004) found that organisations who are making managers redundant may provide leadership development activities to project an image that they are socially responsible.

Mid-career managers experience particular career and development issues. Rosen and Jerdee (1990) argued that this is an important stage in the manager's career because it dictates whether the manager will experience further career growth or experience a career plateau or decline. Mid-career managers have a strong desire for development, but this may also lead to feelings of anxiety and depression.

Applebaum and Finestone (1994) found that mid-career managers who experience a career crisis may feel worthless and frustrated, which in turn can have a negative impact on both performance and motivation. Leadership development initiatives can help the manager to overcome these problems. Mid-career managers also suffer career problems such as skill or managerial obsolescence and can find themselves unable to meet the demands of organisational change. Leadership development interventions can be used in these situations to retrain managers and update their skills and knowledge. Organisations often use leadership development as a retention tool for mid-career managers, who are often more likely to leave the organisation at this stage of their career than at any other stage.

Leadership Development Interventions for Unemployed and Mid-Career Managers

A number of leadership development interventions can be used to help unemployed and mid-career managers:

- *Career Interventions*: These interventions can be used to provide managers with advice and structures within which to plan their careers. Career interventions may provide managers with an opportunity to assess their strengths and weaknesses and achieve greater self-awareness.
- *Job Changes and Job Redesign*: Job changes can be used to develop mid-career managers. These might include special projects and job switching. These development interventions can help the manager to develop new ways of working and new ideas and to gain experience in other parts of the organisation. If a job change is not feasible, an organisation may seek to redesign the manager's job by adding new responsibilities, creating challenging activities and allowing the manager to participate in task forces or project teams. Applebaum and Finestone (1994) suggested that job redesign and changes can help to broaden the manager's career options and prevent skill obsolescence. These experiences can also provide the manager with experiences similar to being promoted.
- *Outplacement Activities*: Leadership development can be used as part of an outplacement process. Leadership development can help the manager find a new job. Miller and Robinson (2004) suggested that organisations can provide CV preparation training, job search training, career assessment and interview skills training as part of its leadership development provision. These activities can help the manager to improve job search skills such as interviewing, negotiating and networking. Saam and Wodtke (1995) suggested that organisations can also include a cognitive-based stress-reduction programme as part

of its leadership development. This provides managers with advice on how to manage stress, anxiety, anger and frustration. It should also help the redundant manager cope with morale problems.

- *Mentoring*: Formal mentoring can assist unemployed and mid-career managers with specific advice and guidance. It has a particularly important role to play in facilitating networking, the provision of psychological support and enhancement of the manager's feelings of self-worth and motivation.

Leadership Development for High-Potential Graduates

Organisations frequently hire 'high-flier', 'fast-track' or high-potential graduates. They are considered a major investment by organisations. They are potentially the managers of the future. Fast-track graduates typically expect fast career progression and major development opportunities. Structured fast-track development programmes are provided by organisations so that graduates quickly realise their potential and achieve career advancement. Well-organised fast-track development programmes can benefit both the graduate and the organisation. They provide the graduate with significant career and work benefits and the organisation with a pool of potential leaders and lots of succession potential. Table 15.6 summarises the typical features of fast-track graduate leadership development programmes.

Table 15.6: Summary of Typical Features of Fast-Track Graduate Leadership Development Programmes

Type of Development Activity					
Dimension or Difference	*Formal Training Courses*	*Work-Based/ Coaching/Job Assignment/ Action-Learning Projects*	*Career Planning Activities*	*Performance Reviews/ Feedback Mechanisms*	*Developmental Support Strategy*
Voluntary to Mandatory	Generally mandatory	Primarily mandatory but some elements of discretion	Can be either voluntary or mandatory	Usually mandatory	Frequently voluntary
Formal to Informal	Highly formalised and structured	Varies in format and structure. Evidence indicates that they may be informal, incremental and highly unstructured	More likely to be formal if driven by organisation; graduate may engage in informal career planning	Highly formalised and structured. Evidence of informal performance evaluation	Varies in formality - tends to be more informal.
Current to Future Orientation	Primarily a current focus and priority	Emphasis on both current and future orientation	A mix of current and the future; stronger emphasis on the future	Focus on both current performance and future performance expectations	May emphasise current as well as future needs

Type of Development Activity					
Dimension or Difference	Formal Training Courses	Work-Based/ Coaching/Job Assignment/ Action-Learning Projects	Career Planning Activities	Performance Reviews/ Feedback Mechanisms	Developmental Support Strategy
Job to Non-Job Focus	Strong focus on job-related competences	Primary focus is on job and generic managerial competencies	May focus on job or the broader career	Primary focus is job with some consideration of development needs for career	May focus on the job or alternatively the person and/or career
Group to Individual Development Activities	Group focus	Individual or group focus depending on the strategy	Primarily an individual focus	Primarily an individual focus	Primarily a focus on the individual
Work to Non-Work Time	Primarily occurs in work time; funded courses may occur in non-work time	Primarily occurs in work time; action learning may occur outside work time	May occur in work or non-work time	Primarily occurs in work time	Generally occurs in work time but could be either

Graduate Competencies

Organisations typically require graduates to demonstrate excellent communication, work effectively with teams, and be quick to take sound decisions, be highly motivated and possess the capacity to motivate others. Organisations' expectations of graduate competencies fall into four categories: knowledge and skills; capacity to learn; flexibility and adaptability; and capacity for change.

- *Knowledge and Skills*: Harvey and Green (1994) suggested that it is difficult to identify the precise nature of the specialist knowledge that employers expect graduates to possess. They tend to rate specialist knowledge low on their list of priorities. Interpersonal skills are considered by employers to be the most important skill requirement. Organisations also place considerably more emphasis on thinking and decision-making skills, as well as communication skills. They do expect that the graduate will have a strong ability to learn. Finally, they also expect graduates to possess the capacity to be good leaders and to possess leadership skills.
- *Ability and Willingness to Learn*: Harvey and Green (1994) found that an ability and willingness to learn is far more important than a stock of knowledge. Dillon (1992) and Johnson, Pere-Verge and Hanage (1993) suggested that organisations hire graduates because of their self-reliance and ability to work productively at an early stage. Smaller organisations typically want graduates to make an immediate contribution to the organisation's success, whereas larger organisations provide graduates the time to learn in order for them to make a more long-term contribution. Organisations are increasingly concerned with their talent strength and therefore expect the graduate to grow and develop quickly.
- *Flexibility and Adaptability*: Organisations expect graduates to be both flexible and adaptable and to exhibit a range of intellectual skills. They expect graduates to have open, enquiring minds and a breadth of view. Darby (1993) argued that organisations expect

graduates to be accepting of change, to recognise and seek out opportunities for change, to possess the confidence to ask questions and the ability to suggest better alternatives. Dillon (1992) found that graduates need to be strong on synthesis, to think laterally and to cope with uncertainty by learning how to deal with problems.

- *Transformative Potential*: Graduates are frequently hired because they bring a fresh and creative mind to the organisation. They can learn quickly, question assumptions and cope with change. Smaller organisations, however, tend to be less clear in what they demand of graduates. They want the graduate to bring an outsider's view. The notion of transformative potential is somewhat elusive; it does not facilitate the specification of exact requirements.

In summary, it is clear that organisations have major expectations of graduates.

Individualised Versus Group-Focused Fast-Track Graduate Development Programmes

Organisations generally provide development programmes that range in focus from the individual to the group. Individualised programmes are based on the assumption that each high-potential graduate has a different set of skill development needs that require a unique set of development experiences (Arnold 1989). Group-focused programmes assume that a group of graduates has a common or core set of development needs that can be met through a group-level intervention. Table 15.7 highlights the advantages and disadvantages of group-focused programmes.

Table 15.7: Group-Focused Graduate Development Programmes: Advantages and Disadvantages

Advantages	Disadvantages
• Consistent quality of delivery throughout the organisation • All graduates get the opportunity to participate in the programme • Group-focused programmes can help build team support as well as establish a sense of competition • They provide an opportunity for the organisation to expose graduates to its culture in a consistent manner • Programmes can be organised by a central leadership development function • Group learning situations enable the graduate to share experiences and build a network of contacts • Group learning may result in cost savings for the organisation	• Potential for cliques forming and preventing the graduate from integrating effectively in the organisation • Other managers may not have the same development opportunities • There may be a loss of flexibility and timing to meet the needs of the individual graduate • Some graduates with higher levels of education may become demotivated because not everyone moves at the same speed • Managers may not take their own development responsibilities to the graduates seriously • Fast-track programmes can engender negativity and jealousy from other managers in the organisation

Group-focused fast-track graduate development programmes vary, but these are examples of objectives they may have:

- To familiarise graduates with the organisation's history, structure, people, policies and procedures.
- To enable graduates to make an early contribution to the organisation.
- To develop the graduate's ability to perform a managerial role.
- To enable both the graduate and the organisation to explore career opportunities and choose appropriate job assignments.

- To provide new graduates with job and project variety and allow them to work on different assignments.
- To enable graduates to build a network of relationships and understand the principles and ethos of teamwork.

Fast-track development programmes are a useful strategy for organisations to adopt if they hire a large number of graduates. They enable the graduate to integrate quickly and contribute to the development of graduate maturity. Organisations can make more considered decisions concerning the appropriate career and work experience path of the graduate. They are not, however, without drawbacks. Organisations frequently encounter difficulties in organising appropriate job assignments for the graduate. Managers may not take their development responsibilities seriously. The programme may not live up to expectations and graduates may leave the organisation feeling disengaged and demotivated.

Graduate Development Strategies, Initial Work Assignments, Career Development, Feedback, Mentoring and Support and Formal Job Placement Strategies

Ghoshal, Moran and Bartlett (1996) argued that because graduates are a scarce resource, organisations utilise accumulation mechanisms, including continuously graduates' enhancing skills, to ensure that graduates are ready for advancement within the organisation. Organisations also use linking mechanism such as development opportunities, the development of formal and informal networks and job assignments in order to ensure change and innovation. Finally, organisations are finding mechanisms to enhance the mutual attraction of both the organisation and the graduate towards each other. These bonding mechanisms include personal development, advanced leadership development, feedback processes and reward strategies.

Development Strategies: There are five alternative approaches that organisations adopt to train and develop graduates.

- *Sink or Swim*: The sink or swim approach involves giving the graduate a degree of responsibility, with nominal support and guidance from superiors. The outcomes of such an approach depend primarily on the skills and abilities of the graduate.
- *The Upending Approach*: The graduate is introduced to organisational realities from the very beginning of work life in an effort to ensure a realisation that working life is the antithesis of academic life and that psychological and practical adjustments must be made to deal with the realities of working life.
- *Training while Working*: A training while working approach is similar to an apprenticeship in that the graduate has a significant degree of responsibility but there is a supervisor or manager available to take full responsibility for job outcomes.
- *Working while Training*: The graduate pursues either full-time or part-time training combined with real-life projects and is evaluated on these projects. Alternatively, the graduate is rotated through departments or different projects while simultaneously pursuing a training and development programme.
- *Full-Time Training*: The graduate is assigned full time to the training department and completes projects for different departments that are of little consequence to the organisation if they are unsuccessfully completed.

Hogan (1994), in a survey of 2,700 graduates, found that, in practice, training and development consisted of several elements. Seventy-six per cent of graduates indicated that their programme consisted of learning through job assignments, seventy-four per cent mentioned experience in different departments, sixty-three per cent of graduates had training in interpersonal skills and fifty-six per cent had exposure to some kind of mentoring system. Only nine per cent of graduates received any foreign language training. Almost all the organisations surveyed reported that the main aim of the graduate training and development programme was to produce future managers. Graduates tended to perceive it in the same way.

Initial Work Assignment Strategies: One specific aspect of managing development concerns the initial job assignment. It is in the area of job duties that the new graduate may experience the greatest discrepancy between expectations and organisational reality. A graduate who is given a challenging first job is more likely to internalise high standards and positive attitudes. This, in turn, encourages the organisation to give the graduate increased opportunities to demonstrate competencies, leading to organisational rewards and reinforcement of high performance.

The work assignment should involve a situation where the graduate is not merely living through a set of experiences, but is also reflecting on and learning from that set of experiences. Table 15.8 presents possible aims of the initial work assignment for graduates.

Table 15.8: Possible Aims of the Fast-Track or High-Potential Graduate Work Assignment

- Enhancing: to enable the graduate deepen understanding of concepts and skills learned in college
- Motivational: to make the training and development programmes more meaningful and significant to the graduate
- Motivational: to facilitate the graduate's personal and social development
- Investigative: to enable the graduate to develop an understanding of the world of work
- Expansive: to broaden the range of jobs that the graduate is prepared to consider in terms of personal career planning
- Sampling: to enable the graduate to test vocational preferences before committing him/herself to a particular job
- Preparatory: to help the graduate acquire skills and knowledge related to a particular occupational area
- Anticipatory: to enable the graduate to experience some of the strains of work so that they will be able to manage the organisational transition more comfortably
- Placing: to enable the graduate to establish a relationship with a particular employer which may lead to an offer of a full-time job on completion of the training programme
- Custodial: to transfer some areas of responsibility to a graduate for a specified period of time

Doherty, Viney and Adamson (1995) found that some organisations move graduates around in the initial stages of their development within the organisation, offering a variety of initial work experience and, in some cases, international experience, although this was the exception rather than the rule. Connor, Strebler and Hirsch (1990) found that the type of initial job experiences varied considerably, depending on the purpose, length and type of graduate training and development programme. These included:

- Positions as junior members of a permanent business or project team in a real job contributing to mainstream activities of the business.
- Short assignments to departments or branches where the graduate spends most of the time observing work or working on projects.
- Job rotation to experience different jobs within a specific function or in a particular location.
- Secondments to special project teams where the graduate can work for a short period as part of a team with more senior staff in a highly stimulating environment.
- Periods spent shadowing managers in specific posts to gain experience of a range of different positions, to learn about the business and be more visible to senior management.

Some graduates have a choice in their first job placement or are able to make a return visit to a particular department of their choice towards the end of the training programme. In other organisations, the graduate is placed in one department for the totality of the programme and he/she has limited choice in the scheduling of initial assignments. Better-performing graduates are more successful in exercising individual choice on initial job assignments.

Job assignments are an extremely valuable aspect of graduate development, but their effectiveness can be undermined through poor planning, moving through a host department and a lack of flexibility concerning the duration of the placement. Graduates express considerable enthusiasm for job-placement strategies which allow lateral career development. Arnold and Mackenzie-Davey (1994) found that graduates reported being under-utilised on their work assignments. Graduates were frequently expected to perform routine tasks. The level of discretion increased with tenure. In terms of work volume, graduates reported that it was moderately high and on very few occasions that they had nothing to do. Long hours are not the norm. Many graduates reported that job assignments brought them into contact with senior management and involved decision-making, but they were unsure about the significance of their work in terms of its impact on other jobs and whether there was a supervisory dimension to the job. The supervisory dimension increased with job tenure.

Career Development Strategies: Career issues are important for the high-potential graduate because career aspirations are high, especially at the outset, and the graduate can take some time to adjust to the reality of organisational life. Poor career management during training and development programmes is often cited as one of the reasons for high graduate turnover. Many career problems arise because the career expectations of the graduate do not match the reality of what they experience. High-potential graduates often have inflated career expectations prior to entry, which sow the seeds of dissatisfaction.

On fast-track programmes, there is a tendency to lay out clearly the types of placement to which the graduates will be assigned. Organisations offering graduates opportunities on fast-track programmes place symbolic messages in their recruitment literature to the effect that the graduate would fill a real position, using the language of 'opportunity', 'added value', 'marketability' and 'employability' as hooks for graduates. They are selling not progression but development as the attraction for graduates. Such changes are directed at a subtle redefinition of the psychological contract on the organisation's part. Career development systems for high-flier programmes are geared towards the graduate assuming responsibility for career and career development. This is achieved by encouraging open dialogue about career development opportunities, aspirations and alternatives.

The main issues for longer-term high-flier programmes relate to the gradual clarification of career expectations in terms of the types of jobs chosen and an idea of when career goals might be met. There is also the issue of how job choices and sequencing of placement on the programme relate to subsequent career options. Arnold and Mackenzie-Davey (1992) found that graduates could not see clear career paths within their employing organisation. They tended to think that the company offered attractive career paths, but found it difficult to identify exactly what they were. There was also confusion as to what factors determined career prospects within the organisation. Graduates in the first year of their programme viewed work performance as most important, followed by being liked by the right people and being in the right place at the right time. Graduates with one or more years of training experience viewed all three factors as equally influential.

Feedback and Performance Management: Many organisations view performance management strategies as a key element of a successful graduate development programme. Arnold and Nicholson (1991) suggested that, at the beginning of their careers, graduates generally seek feedback of all types from many different people. This allows the graduate to develop confidence that the right course of action is being taken and that the potential exists to relate current tasks to the 'bigger plan'. An effective performance management system provides the graduate with the opportunity to monitor work and personal development which, in turn, creates a sense of security that the career path of the graduate is proceeding as planned. Doherty, Viney and Adamson (1995) found that organisations generally viewed a performance management system as integral to the process of graduate development. Some organisations used computer tracking to provide a means of pinpointing where graduates were in the organisation and for monitoring their progress relative to possible alternative positions.

Graham and McKenzie (1995) found that graduates received feedback from many formal and informal sources, including:

- *Training Programme Assessments*: This is perceived by organisations and graduates to be a useful way of informing the graduate how they are perceived and it is generally understood to be a good indicator of how well a graduate has developed particular competencies. Graduates considered this source of feedback useful, although it is somewhat subjective in nature. Managers, on the other hand, perceived it as more significant because it highlighted attributes that needed to be strengthened and provided the line manager with a second opinion. Although not feeding directly into performance management processes, it was perceived as significant in setting the overall tone of the relationship.
- *Project Progress Reviews*: These are primarily used to ensure that a graduate project is on track and that graduates within a project team are managing their component of the project satisfactorily.
- *End-of-Assessment Reports:* These tend to be utilised where the graduate has undertaken a series of jobs in different departments or a number of project-based assignments. Performance is generally assessed at the end of the assignment and future learning needs discussed. Graham and McKenzie (1996) found that this process tends to be very formal and, in some cases, leads to the setting of new salary levels or future work appointments at a particular location.
- *Appraisal Systems*: Graham and McKenzie (1996) and Doherty, Viney and Adamson (1995) found that at the very early stages of graduate training and development programmes, the objective of the appraisal system is generally developmental, designed to encourage the graduate to acquire the knowledge that will enable him/her to improve performance. After the initial period, the appraisal system tends to move towards the appraisal of job performance.

Support Strategies: Organisational support strategies are commonly used on graduate development programmes as a means of giving graduates constructive coaching and facilitating graduates to develop clear career plans and secure a better understanding of strengths and weaknesses. A number of key people are involved in supporting graduates: the manager as coach and counsellor, the mentor, the peer group, the individual graduate and other graduates.

The manager of a new graduate is the person the graduate is assigned to work with for the duration of an assignment, project, placement, job or training programme. In practice, he/she may be a line manager, a project supervisor or a branch manager. The manager has the responsibility to ensure that the graduate understands the particular job, project or assignment, that the graduate fully understands their role as a participant on a graduate training and development programme. The manager, additionally, has a responsibility to ensure that the graduate is developed and plays an effective role within the organisation. The line manager plays a pivotal support role because of the day-to-day influence on the job satisfaction of the graduate. The manager is the first person through whom the graduate will experience work within the organisation. Managers have a role in assessing the performance of the graduate and will probably have to answer the graduate's questions. It is possible to have effective management of new graduates provided that managers are able to develop both skill and confidence. In particular, effective managers can develop graduates to perform effectively and feel good about themselves.

A study by Garavan and Morley (1997) found that effective managers of new graduates have a number of important characteristics:

- The manager accepts ownership for the development of the graduate and provides the necessary development opportunities.
- The manager has the capacity to resolve conflicts between what the manager thinks and what the graduate has been taught. The manager fully understands what has been discussed on training programmes provided by the organisation.
- The manager accepts full responsibility for managing the project or assignment the graduate is undertaking. The research suggests that it is common practice, where the development programme consists of projects and assignments, for a situation to arise where the manager is not responsible for the results of the project. Such a dilution of responsibility can be dangerous because it leaves the graduate confused as to who is accountable.

The coaching relationship is determined by three variables: the nature of the work situation, the characteristics of the graduate and the characteristics of the manager. Effective coaching of graduates depends on three important foundations:

- The skills of the manager as coach to recognise that the graduate has joined the organisation for the purpose of facilitating the organisation to achieve its goals and that the graduate also has goals which he/she wishes to achieve. There is a process of dovetailing involved: understanding the needs and aspirations of the graduate; and relating them to the assignment or project.
- The coaching relationship should be formalised to the extent that, at the end of each coaching session, both graduate and manager are clear about what the results should be.
- An effective coach must demonstrate the ability to listen effectively and receptively. Such a process provides the graduate with confidence and enhances the supervisor–graduate relationship.

Effective graduate coaching leads to increased job satisfaction for the graduate which, in turn, leads to a greater individual and team contribution from the graduate. It can enhance graduate commitment levels to the organisation and enhance the graduate retention process.

Final Placement Strategies: Final job placement, or end-of-training placement, is a fundamental component of a high-potential graduate development programme. Final job placement strategies generally give the graduate an opportunity to continue to learn about the organisation by working in different environments and developing special skills. Such experience provides the graduate with an opportunity to form personal contacts with managers whom they are likely to need in their future career and to be assessed by different managers.

Graduate job experience can play an important role in helping the graduate choose a career direction, and provides experience of a number of different positions. Some of these functions are given greater emphasis in the design of graduate training and development programmes and are more visibly recognised in some organisations than others. Some graduates are often unsure about why particular job placements are chosen although they are, in general, aware of the overall rationale behind the selection of job placements.

A major concern for graduates who participate in a graduate training and development programme is what happens at the end of it. Graduates may view it as the starting point of their career, or it may be their first real job where they lose the label 'graduate trainee'. Doherty, Viney and Adamson (1995) found that graduates are surprised that they have to compete with other employees for vacancies as they arise or that they cannot obtain their preferred position. Significant problems can arise if human resource planning systems are poor or if the number of jobs envisaged at the recruitment stage are no longer available. If a number of graduates come off the development programme at the same time, the placement problem can be accentuated. The essential problem in terms of final job placement appears to be one of balancing the preferences of the graduate with the needs of the organisation.

Leadership Development Issues in Small Enterprises, Entrepreneurial Ventures and Voluntary Organisations

These three types of organisation are challenging contexts for management leadership development activities. The purposes of management and leadership development are the same as for larger organisations: what differs is the context. The context is characterised by a range of organisational and individual factors that inhibit management and leadership development processes.

Voluntary Organisations

Voluntary organisations have a unique context in that their members are, in the main, unpaid and transitory. They face the challenge of relying heavily on a small group of permanent staff in an environment that faces increasing demands for more effective organisational structures and greater accountability to stakeholders. Wilensky and Hansen (2001) pointed out that staff members in voluntary organisations are generally hired for their area of expertise, rather than their management and leadership skills, and are motivated by factors outside the normal working experience, such as challenge, stimulation and meaningful achievement.

Myers and Sacks (2003) suggested that the profile of the voluntary sector has changed. More professionals are drawn to the sector. They found that a significant proportion of executive-level staff in voluntary organisations come from outside the humanitarian sector. This has the potential to bring about a clash of core values and ideology. Voluntary organisations can take a number of different stances on management tools and techniques. These are: the view that management techniques have a place in the private sector; a copycat stance, where they adopt a short-term strategy; a focus on fads and off-the-shelf, blanket solutions; a contextual approach which suggests adapting management techniques to suit the context and the purposes of the organisation; and, finally, an innovative stance involving the development of approaches that are suitable to the organisation.

Some commentators question whether there exists a set of generic management skills that managers of diverse non-profit organisations require to perform their roles effectively. Wilensky and Hansen (2001) suggested that managers in non-profit organisations believe that their authority is derived from the ability to implement change and to motivate people towards achieving organisational assignments, rather than financial control. Drucker (1989) suggested that voluntary organisations require a solid mission supported by managers who are accountable, results-oriented and have an openness to change.

Management and leadership development activities in voluntary organisations can facilitate the organisation to develop staff with management potential and, for those already in a management role, develop their altruistic management skills. Volunteers typically view development opportunities as occasions to take on more challenging assignments and responsibilities. Some voluntary organisations have responded to this challenge by providing specific career ladders within which leadership development plays a key role. Wilensky and Hansen (2001) suggested that executives on the boards of voluntary organisations are increasingly realising the importance of developing management and leadership capability in order to achieve the mission of the organisation.

Small, Micro and Entrepreneurial Ventures

Mumford and Gold (2004) emphasised that most small organisations are managed by one or two key individuals. Many entrepreneurial ventures start out with one key individual having responsibility for managing the organisation. These organisations present a number of important challenges for management and leadership development:

- There is frequently an absence of a wider human resource management strategy and a corresponding lack of formal policy in leadership development.
- Owner-managers may not always be committed to leadership development. Thomson *et al.* (1997) and Garavan, Hogan and Cahir-O'Donnell (2003) found that owner-managers will support leadership development if they perceive it as in line with their interests.
- Small and micro businesses vary considerably, making it difficult to identify generic competencies which owner-managers should acquire. Perren and Grant (2001) reported that SME managers and entrepreneurs highlighted general business competences such as finance, accounting, marketing and people management.
- There is a strong emphasis on informal development in small and micro organisations. Owner-managers will value more formalised development activities provided they are customised. Devins and Gold (2000) found that they valued an external coach who worked on issues such as succession planning, work reorganisation and innovation. It did, however, take a considerable amount of time for the coach to gain the trust of the owner-manager.

Generic management and leadership development interventions for owner-managers, therefore, may not be the most effective strategy. Paton and Brownlie (1991) and Cohen (1998) found that off-the-shelf leadership development programmes are often perceived to be inadequate. They are unable to address the specific skill development needs and long-term strategies of the small enterprise. They also found that they were conducted by developers and trainers who had less effective skills than the managers who were participating. Carrier (1999) found that most of the owner-managers he surveyed valued traditional, lecture-based programmes. They also found large class-based programmes to be ineffective.

Garavan and O'Cinneide (1994a, 1994b) found that many traditional management and leadership development programmes placed too much emphasis on rationality and analytical skill components over the more creative aspects of the entrepreneurial personality. They found that more participative and individualised development strategies, such as workshops and practical case studies, were better suited to their needs.

Tailored management and leadership development programmes that enable owner-managers to maintain successful control over their businesses were more appropriate. O'Dwyer and Ryan (2000) found that strong management skills are critical for owner-managers to successfully expand their business and remain competitive. The lack of management skills and experience is one of the most significant causes of small business failure. The objective of management and leadership development activities initially is to develop the self-confidence and self-efficacy of owner-managers. Garavan and O'Cinneide (1994a, 1994b) found that leadership development could facilitate owner-managers in working beyond boundaries and developing creative problem-solving capabilities.

Leadership development interventions must, initially at least, focus on specific competencies. Paton and Brownlie (1991) found that small firms rarely took action to develop skills of their managers that were not directly applicable to specific intra-firm problems. Management and leadership development programmes were chosen for their practicality, and owner-managers had to be concerned about the payback for the business before deciding to participate.

O'Dwyer and Ryan (2000) suggested that, given the array of experience and skill needs of owner-managers, the most appropriate strategy is to select developers who can act as learning facilitators. This will allow the use of techniques such as role play, structured management exercises, feedback, one-to-one and group discussion. The developer's knowledge and experience of the owner-manager issues will enhance the credibility of leadership development. Carrier (1999) found that coaching was a successful development strategy to meet the needs of entrepreneurs and owner-managers. She suggested that experienced entrepreneurs from the manager's sector could act as a coach. O'Dwyer and Ryan (2000), however, reported that owner-managers did not actively seek out mentors because of their lack of perceived value. They reported concerns about the confidentiality associated with the mentor and that the mentor might impose ideas and management processes that were too sophisticated for the organisation. Garavan and O'Cinneide (1994a, 1994b) suggested that action learning may be an effective development intervention, but not at the initial stage of the development process. In summary, this is a challenging group to develop.

Key Challenges for Management and Leadership Development

It is widely accepted that management and leadership development represents a keystone in the performance of the individual manager and the organisation. Management and leadership development, therefore, has the same purpose, irrespective of the context. Each of the categories and contexts discussed in this chapter present unique challenges for management and leadership development.

Meeting the Needs of the Group and the Context: For managers of small and micro enterprises and entrepreneurs, the specific context of management and leadership development plays an integral part in their decision to value it or not. Management and leadership development frequently lack credibility for owner-managers. They can frequently be influenced by the more traditional approaches and relationally based skills. Voluntary or not-for-profit organisations have different objectives and therefore different leadership development needs. Female managers have particular perspectives and views on what development interventions are appropriate. Minority managers frequently want to participate in leadership development, but find that organisations are not sufficiently flexible in their provision. Graduates value leadership development because it enhances their employability and facilitates quick career progression.

Resources and Commitment: Effective leadership development activities require both resources and commitment. These issues are pertinent to each of the categories discussed in this chapter. In the case of the entrepreneur and small and micro businesses, the development of the owner-manager in reality represents the development of the business itself. Small and micro businesses tend to have limited resources for development and, as a result, they focus on short-term development interventions. Owner-managers are slow to see the value of management and leadership development. In order to justify the investment, owners need to see development activities contributing to the expansion of the business. Voluntary organisations are less likely to view management and leadership development in business terms. They often consider investment in management and leadership development to be a misuse of resources. The boards of voluntary bodies may also be slow to commit resources.

Management and leadership development programmes for women are generally not viewed by organisations as a top priority. Women have only recently begun to enter the top echelons of organisations. Therefore they have not acquired the networks or the top management influence to secure resources for specialist development activities for women. The financing of management and leadership development for managers who are being made redundant is problematic. There is ambiguity concerning who is in the best position to help this group of managers. Is it the managers themselves, or the organisation that contributed to their unemployment, or a state body? Fast-track graduate development programmes require a major investment in resources. They are costly development interventions and are less likely to be an option for many smaller organisations, which lessens the organisation's attractiveness as an employer of graduates.

Common Application of Leadership development Interventions: Leadership development methods can be targeted and customised to the specific development needs of different groups. Mentoring interventions have value for the development of women and minority managers, unemployed and mid-career managers, small business owner-managers and fast-track graduates. Women and minority groups frequently encounter difficulties in gaining access to suitable mentors, and this represents a significant barrier to progression to senior management in organisations. Owner-managers are sometimes sceptical of the value of an external mentor. They frequently perceive that the mentor is too sophisticated and does not understand the needs of the business. Mid-career managers may be slow to avail of mentoring because of their lack of self-confidence. Mentoring is, however, a flexible leadership development intervention which has many applications.

Networking is emphasised as an important leadership development activity which has value for each group and context discussed in this chapter. The key challenge for female managers is that they find themselves excluded from networks. Male managers are more likely to benefit from networking activities. Networking can be used to improve the career development of minority and mid-career managers. Networking can break down barriers and enable managers to share experiences with more experienced managers.

Management and leadership development interventions that are generic in nature are less valued. Generic courses assume that there is a set of needs which can be addressed by a common programme. Generic programmes have little applicability to small and micro businesses. Owner-managers perceive that generic programmes are of little value. Female managers frequently argue that generic programmes do not address their needs. Customised programmes have significantly greater value. These programmes can address the specific needs of the group or context and, if they are designed on the basis of a systematic identification of needs, they are likely to be more effective.

Management and leadership development activities address both individual and organisational needs. Management and leadership development can enhance the motivation, self-confidence and career prospects of many different groups of managers. Unemployed and mid-career managers who avail of management and leadership development report greater confidence, increased motivation and more clarity concerning career issues. Female managers and managers from minority groups also derive personal and career benefits from development activities. Voluntary organisations frequently use management and leadership development to retain high-performing managers and to encourage them to challenge their careers. Managers of small micro organisations and entrepreneurs derive both individual and organisational benefits from development. It enhances owner-managers' self-belief in their abilities and it builds the core competencies of the organisation. Graduates view management and leadership development as a career enabling strategy. It facilitates both high performance and faster career progression.

Overall, management and leadership development contributes to a variety of individual and organisational needs. There are particular issues in relation to some groups of managers. These issues require customised responses from those responsible for leadership development in organisations.

Conclusion

The demographics of the workforce have changed significantly. Organisations now have managers from diverse ethnic backgrounds. Female managers are also more common in organisations. Owner-managers make up a significant proportion of the managerial population, and there is a significant growth in voluntary sector managers. High-potential graduates are increasingly employed by organisations as a pool of potential future managers. Similarly, managers who reach mid-career experience unique development and career challenges. These different groups impact on the application of management and leadership development. Some organisations have begun to embrace diversity and have made changes to their management and leadership development policies to reflect these new challenges.

Leadership development specialists are challenged to provide development solutions which address the unique needs of these groups. They will need to develop their own competencies to understand and work effectively with diverse groups and needs. They need to understand the multiplicity of issues that managers from particular groups face and the perspectives from which they are coming. Leadership development specialists have a major role in educating and influencing top management on the importance of providing resources for management and leadership development initiatives customised to unique needs and situations.

Ultimately, however, there are no differences in terms of the purposes and the processes used in management and leadership development. The challenge for diverse groups is involved in implementing management and leadership interventions and achieving the appropriate level of customisation.

Summary of Key Points

- Management and leadership development interventions have application to different groups and contexts. Their purposes are the same, to enhance individual and organisational effectiveness.
- Context can impose barriers or provide opportunities for the provision of management and leadership development.
- Female managers can utilise development activities to overcome stereotyping and prejudice in organisations.
- There are contrasting views on whether leadership development activities should be gender-specific or mixed-gender in focus.
- Managers from ethnic minorities or managers of colour also face stereotyping and exclusion from management and leadership development activities.
- Organisation-wide diversity initiatives can help to contribute to making an organisation more sensitive to differences.
- Professional and specialist managers have development needs related to their technical areas of expertise. CPD activities are an important component of a specialist manager's development.
- Organisations provide fast-track graduate development programmes to accelerate the development of graduates and develop a pool of talented future leaders.
- Managers in small, micro and voluntary organisations have unique management and leadership development challenges. They perceive management and leadership development in a very short-term business-focused way.

■ Discussion Questions

1. What are the arguments for and against having separate leadership development interventions for women?

2. What role can management and leadership development play to support ethnic minority managers?

3. What role does CPD play in enhancing the competence of specialist or professional managers?

4. Why do owner-managers frequently reject management and leadership development initiatives? What responses can be made in order to make management and leadership development more relevant?

5. Why should organisations implement a fast-track development programme for graduates? Should it design a group-focused or a more individualised approach? Justify your answer.

■ Application and Experiential Questions

1. You have received a request to design a diversity initiative to raise awareness of differences in organisations. How would you start to go about this activity? What issues would you consider? What should you include in the initiative?

2. Your organisation has just hired twelve graduates into a range of functions and disciplines in the organisation. You are the leadership development specialist. You have been tasked with responsibility to design a one-year fast-track development programme. What learning objectives would you consider appropriate? What development strategies would you include in the programme? How would you evaluate its effectiveness?

3. Divide your class into groups of three. Brainstorm the issues that female managers encounter during their careers in organisations. How do these impact on management and leadership development? What actions should be taken so that management and leadership development activities can play a significant role in addressing those issues? Prepare a presentation based on your findings.

Chapter Sixteen

An Organisational Learning Approach to Leadership Development

Outline

Learning Objectives

After reading this chapter you will be able to:

- Understand and explain the value of an organisational learning approach to leadership development in organisations.
- Explain and evaluate the concept of organisational learning and its contribution to the development of leaders.
- Explain the various issues that need to be addressed in order to facilitate organisational learning.
- Explain the characteristics of an expansive development environment and how it can be managed.
- Describe the characteristics of a learning organisation and their implications for leadership development.
- Evaluate how knowledge management concepts influence thinking on leadership development.
- Describe and evaluate different ways in which organisational development interventions can be used for collective leadership development.

OPENING CASE SCENARIO

Managing Strategic Change Through Business Score Card and a Workshop: Processes at Sonopress

The Bertelsmann Media Group was formed in Germany in 1835 and today is the fourth largest media company in the world with annual sales of approximately €18 billion. The company has significant interests in all areas of media – including book, magazine and newspaper publishing, music, television, online, film and radio – with more than 400 individual companies. Bertelsmann currently employs more than 80,000 people in fifty-one countries across six divisions: RTL Group – the leading European broadcasting and production company; Gruner & Jahr – Europe's premier magazine publisher; Sony BMG – the world's third largest music publisher; Random House – the world's largest book publishing company; Arvato – which provides services for 35 million consumers worldwide; and Direct Group – which has 55 million customers and members worldwide.

Sonopress was founded in 1956 as a pressing plant for vinyl records and today replicates various types of digital data carriers, including all CD and DVD formats. Sonopress has worldwide production capabilities of 3.5 million optical discs (CD/DVD) per day and almost fifty years of expertise in media manufacturing, packaging and supply-chain services as a leading provider of content delivery to the market.

The Irish operation was established in 1994 and operates out of facilities in Balbriggan and Swords, County Dublin. Sonopress Ireland currently employs 345 people, serving approximately twenty major blue-chip clients in the IT and games industries with daily local production capacity exceeding 300,000 disks per day.

Sonopress Ireland offers its customers an array of services, from content management and manufacture to print, packaging and assembly, procurement, order management, warehouse fulfilment and distribution. In the on-demand world, digital media must move from content creators to consumers faster than ever before. By implication, the technology and customer requirements are ever-changing; therefore, constant investment is required in a sector where margins are being eroded daily. Despite constant price pressure on both the customer and the material side, together with increased competition from plants in Eastern Europe and Asia, Sonopress Ireland has been successful in meeting its financial objectives year on year.

While the last decade has brought many difficult challenges, Sonopress Ireland has grown in a local Irish market where many of its competitors have not survived; of the five replicators operating in Ireland in 1994 none has survived, and Sonopress believes that the next decade poses challenges beyond what it has previously encountered. Its traditional areas of key focus of complete and on-time delivery (COTD); short lead times; quality, security, and flexibility; and front-end support will no longer be enough to sustain the business.

In recognition of the challenges facing Sonopress internationally, a vision for the organisation was composed, which was aligned with the Bertelsmann vision. It was focused on a five-year period of operation, and encompassed strategies for growing the business organically and by acquisition; developing a presence in new markets; diversifying the manufacturing and service portfolio; growth of non-core activities and establishing best practice within the group and modelling these best practices throughout the group.

The strategy commenced with strategies operating on an international level, and each local operation was tasked with finding their 'best fit' local strategy. In Ireland, Sonopress began that process with a strategic review of their current capability; growth of non-core activity; the establishment of a management development centre focused on key leadership skills; and the development of a balanced score card to ensure all parts of the organisation are moving in unison towards the strategic goals.

Vision 2010, which was set out by Bertelsmann, committed the organisation to becoming a one-billion company by 2010. In order to achieve this vision, the organisation should build on its core strengths of a customer-driven mentality, an international network and human resources who are highly qualified and motivated. As a corporation, Bertelsmann seeks generally to be a value-added business, to have strong growth in global key accounts, strong DVD video growth and an increased presence in Asia. This vision is premised on the view that there would be increased customer needs for integrated solutions. Sonopress Ireland was mandated to take this vision and adopt the goals appropriate to its business strengths and weaknesses. These included the requirement to increase gross margin per employee, to generate significant revenues from value-added services and to achieve growth in key accounts. These goals were: reduction in overheads; productivity growth; purchasing and IT synergies; identification of opportunities; key account management; on-time delivery; and a strong emphasis on training and quality. This vision provided the context and the framework for the year-long workshop process. The process was facilitated by an external consultant and initially involved an assessment of the teamworking effectiveness of the top team. Members completed a team effectiveness profile which assessed the effectiveness of the team using five criteria: mission; planning and goals; group roles; group processes; group relationships and inter-group relationships. This analysis highlighted gaps in functioning. The team, facilitated by the external consultant, produced an action plan which it committed to implementing over the duration of the workshop process and at its weekly work meeting.

The strategic analysis and business score card process took place thereafter. The organisation's readiness for change was indicated by senior management's commitment to Vision 2010. The managing director and the managers of each division provided time, support and commitment. The workshop process involved the organisation engaging in a diagnostic process that examined key strategic goals, strategies and performance measures, as well as the organisation's human reward strategies and organisational culture. The results of the strategic analysis evolved over a series of intensive workshops. Understanding the culture and the extent of teamwork were important characteristics of the analysis process. In 2002, Sonopress had adopted a unique vision and philosophy that outlined the values that should guide individual behaviour. To reinforce these values, a significant investment in management and leadership development was made. The cultural vision and philosophy had a distinctive vocabulary.

During the workshop process, the top team worked through the Kaplan and Norton business score card framework. This started with a discussion of what should be the strategic priorities of the organisation in terms of cost reduction and revenue growth opportunities. This part of the process challenged the team to consider what its real priorities, resources and capabilities were, as well as challenging division managers to consider how they could contribute to each of the goals and to commit to these goals for a specified period of time. The top team was asked to stand in the future and describe the organisation that would be necessary to achieve the goals. This required them to consider organisation resources such as information systems, relationship culture, structure, work design and human resource systems. They had to think about an organisation that could operate with a cost focus but could also exploit growth opportunities.

The strategic workshop process generated considerable energy and enthusiasm. Team members were frequently challenged by the facilitator and by peers. They had to think outside their functional areas. This was an important first step towards the 2010 vision.

QUESTIONS

Q.1 To what extent can a strategic review process contribute to organisational learning?

Q.2 What are the potential barriers to organisational learning highlighted in the case scenario?

Leadership development is often criticised because it separates learning from the job and organisation context. An alternative perspective suggests that the most effective approach is to merge organisation and individual development by ensuring that as much development as possible is in context-driven. The concepts of organisation learning, the learning organisation and organisation development are well established in the literature. They are potentially elusive concepts and, in some ways, they have reinvented themselves under a number of different terms and ideas.

Managers and leaders are increasingly expected to adopt more proactive views of organisations and their positions as managers. They must view organisations as entities in a state of continuous change. Managers and their activities are not fixed or static. Organisations are increasingly highlighted as changing, evolving entities that are 'living'. These complex conditions potentially challenge the way in which organisations view leadership and leadership development. Organisational learning approaches to management and leadership development highlight the importance of the organisation as a living system that reflects a plurality of viewpoints.

In this chapter we focus on a number of organisational-level perspectives on management and leadership development. We explore and explain the concepts of organisational learning, the learning organisation and expansive learning environments. We discuss the concept of knowledge management and explain how it influences thinking on leadership development. The final section of the chapter discusses the application of various concepts from organisation development to leadership development.

Why an Organisational Learning Approach to Leadership Development?

Increasingly, academics and practitioners alike focus on the collective features of the organisation as an important component of the leadership task. O'Connor and Day (2002) suggested that organisational members share particular beliefs concerning what constitutes effective leadership. Where leaders do not act in ways consistent with these beliefs, then leaders will not be effective. O'Connor and Quinn (2004) argued that organisational systems and practices represent sources of leadership. In fact, they explain how leadership is enacted.

Vardimen, Houghton and Jinkenson (2006) propose a contextual model of leadership development in which they argue that effective leadership is derived from an interplay of organisational or environmental characteristics and individual leader characteristics. This interplay determines both the effectiveness and development of the leader. The suggest that focusing on the individual level of analysis provides an incomplete picture. They define an organisational environment that is supportive of leadership as one that consists of a culture that values and actively encourage the process of leadership development. Ruvolo, Peterson and LeBoeuf (2004) suggested that a learning culture is similar to a learning organisation in that it empowers employees, facilitates change, encourages collaboration, creates opportunities for learning and promotes the development of leaders.

Various researchers have emphasised that leadership is increasingly a shared responsibility. It is frequently the task of many rather than the designated work of a few. Raelin (2006) highlights, for example, that collaborative leadership is increasingly valued in organisations. Organisations need to unlock the capacity of all people to contribute. O'Connor and Quinn (2004) suggested that the leadership task is progressively ambiguous, complex and unprogrammed. Leaders, therefore, require access to multiple knowledge bases and practices to create effective alignment and strategic direction. These imperatives increasingly make individualised leadership redundant. They require the enactment of collective leadership but do not, however, eliminate the need for individual leadership.

Ideas such as the learning organisation and organisational learning highlight that effective leadership requires that all individuals are ready to learn at every opportunity. This postulates that effective organisations are able to tap both the commitment and capacity to learn at all levels in the organisation. Senge (1990) suggested that a new range of skills is needed in the 'new work' of leaders, who are required to create and sustain a learning organisation. They fulfil three key roles: designer, leader and steward. He advocated that leaders in learning organisations must be skilled at disseminating knowledge, encouraging staff to share their specialised talents and facilitating knowledge transfer. Argyris and Schon (1996) indicated that learning that results from organisational inquiry must be embedded in the images of organisational members, its artefacts and the organisational environment. It requires a leadership vision and commitment to organisational learning systems.

Another strand of research highlights the importance of developing a learning culture before focusing on developing a learning organisation. A particularly important component of a learning culture concerns trust. Davenport and Prusak (1998) highlighted the importance of developing a common language for building trust and the role of trust in facilitating knowledge transfer. Pillai, Schriesheim and Williams (1999) identified the key role of followers' perceptions of trust and fairness in determining leadership effectiveness. Shared values are also an important factor in creating trust. The level of trust in leadership is therefore very important in determining the effectiveness of organisational learning and the learning organisation. A related idea, suggested by Van der Krogt (1998), is that a key element of a learning culture focuses on care. When care is high, members are freer with information; it generates trust and enables the active exploration of ideas and knowledge.

These various strands in thinking are useful, therefore, in understanding leadership processes in organisations. Some of the ideas that are discussed in the following sections are not always conceptually clear. In Figure 16.1 we highlight a number of important distinctions and their relationship to each other.

Figure 16.1: Understanding Collective Leadership Development Processes in Organisations

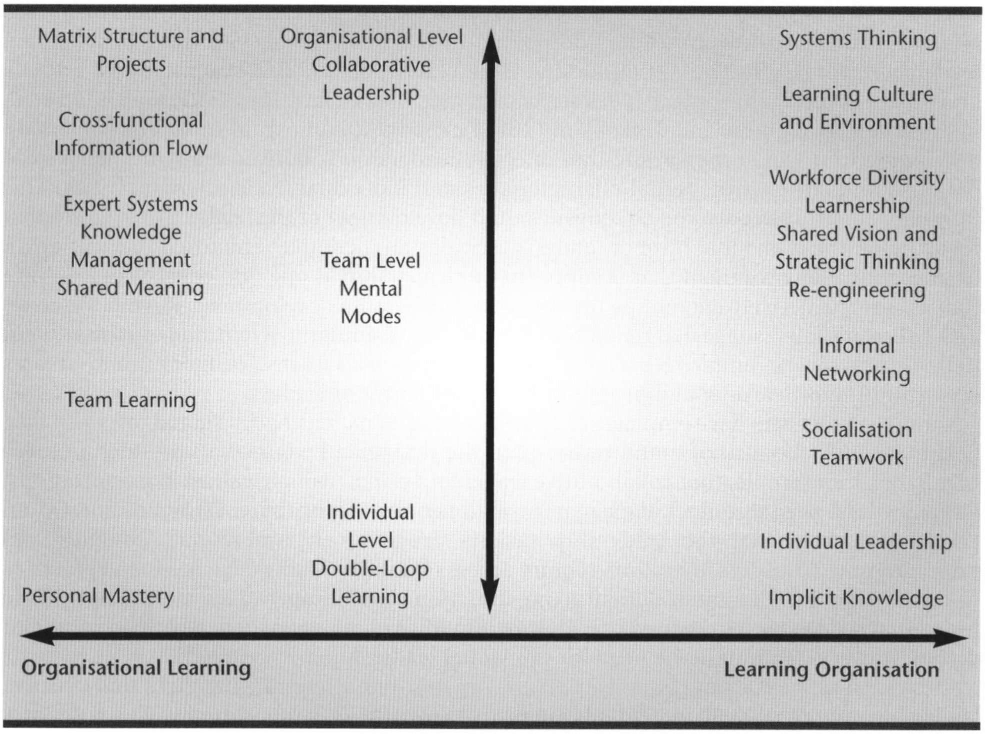

Many of the ideas presented in Figure 16.1 emphasise connectivity and complexity. Connectivity focuses on the means by which members of the organisation work in a collective manner. Strategic planning and visionary processes represent an explicit form of connectivity. Other processes, such as shared meaning and team learning, are more implicit. The concepts mapped out are all potential responses to organisational complexity. Complexity requires organisations to think about novel ways to solve problems and to move away from an emphasis on individual leadership. They emphasise the creation of social capital, interpersonal influence and the need to create shared meaning. These collective activities enable organisations to manage both differentiation and integration and to solve other organisational dilemmas and problems.

What is Organisational Learning?

Organisational learning is a complex topic. There is much debate concerning how it differs from the learning organisation and knowledge management. Organisational learning and the learning organisation are concepts which are frequently used interchangeably. 'Organisational learning' is often used to describe learning activities that occur in organisations, whereas 'the learning organisation' is proposed as a particular type of organisation.

Organisational Learning Versus the Learning Organisation

Yeo (2005) suggested that organisational learning is a process that seeks to answer the question of how learning occurs in organisations. It is a dynamic and organic process. The term 'learning organisation' represents a collective entity that seeks to answer the question: 'What particular characteristics of organisations enable them to learn?' It emphasises the idea that an organisation is an open system. Murray (2002) suggested that the learning organisation focuses on the process of gaining, sharing and using knowledge. It seeks to explain how individuals in organisations transfer knowledge to facilitate the achievement of organisational goals. Individuals experience learning and they are the means through which it is communicated. It is transferred because of the strong social and interactive relationships between people.

Stewart (2001) proposed that organisational learning is a type of collective cognition. He envisaged that individuals are constantly seeking to understand their environment and negotiate each other's learning experience. Learning occurs at multiple levels and is integrated into everything people do. It is a central component of the work that leaders perform and not an 'add-on' or deliberate process. Organisational learning assumes the co-operation of members, both in one-to-one relationships and in team processes. Table 16.1 presents some differences between organisational learning and the learning organisation. It suggests that organisational learning is descriptive, whereas the learning organisation is prescriptive. Organisational learning is concerned with identifying gaps in learning capacity and with structures that generate new information, whereas learning organisations expand their capability to learn and ensure a continuous capacity to transform themselves.

Table 16.1: Main Differences Between Organisational Learning and the Learning Organisation

Organisational Learning	The Learning Organisation
Descriptive	Prescriptive
Asks 'How does an organisation learn?'	Asks 'How should an organisation learn?'
Draws from psychology and OD; management sciences; sociology and organisation theory; strategy; production management; cultural anthropology. Each of these disciplines represents its own ontology and is problematic.	Originates mainly from management science and OD disciplines. First tradition (Senge 1990; Garvin 1993; Nevis, DiBella and Gould 1995) starts from management science perspective and then adds insights from organisational development. Second tradition (Dixon 1994; Hawkins 1994; Nonaka 1994; Torbert 1994; Swieringa and Wierdsma 1994) takes, as a starting point, models of human development and emancipation, and then distinguishes between cyclical and evolutionary models of learning.
Authors focus on conceptualisation and answering questions such as: What does OL mean? How is OL at all feasible? What kinds of OL are desirable, and for whom and with what chance of actual occurrence? Concept is intentionally distant from practice and value-neutral.	Authors focus on continuous improvement, competence acquisition, experimentation, boundary spanning and specific organisational outcomes. They stress the need for visible commitment from managers to learning by incorporating in it and giving it symbolic expression.

Source: Adapted from Argyris and Schon (1996: 181–8), Easterby-Smith (1997:1087–1107), Tsang (1997:74–6).

Organisational learning literature tends to de-emphasise practice and to remain value-neutral. The learning organisation literature stresses the application of its ideas to practice. Table 16.2 reveals that although this distinction does not always hold up in practice, it does capture the notion of levels of learning.

Table 16.2: Key Themes in the Organisational Learning and Learning Organisation Literature

Stages of Learning			
Circular and cyclical approach (Garratt 1987; Swieringa and Wierdsma 1992)	• Level I: Single-loop learning • Activities are at the individual level • Concerned with existing rules and systems • Activities are routine and repetitive	• Level II: Double-loop learning • Activities at the team/group level • Concerned with changing rules and systems • Activities are non-routine and complex	• Level III: Triple-loop learning • Activities are at the company level • Concerned with company's vision, aims, identity and business direction • Activities are complex and deal with external environments

Hierarchy of Learning			
Three-stage conceptual hierarchy (Griffey 1998)	Level I: Pre-personal learning	Level II: Personal wisdom	Level III: Trans-personal enlightenment
Levels of Learning			
Treble-loop learning (Hawkins 1991)	Level I: Efficiency Operations Independent view	Level II: Effectiveness strategy Helicopter view Connected to level I by a business 'brain'	Level III: Evolutionary need Service Satellite view Connected to level II by a business 'soul'
Processes of Learning			
Systemic approach and five disciplines (Senge 1990, 1992)	Level I: Individuals Mental models and personal mastery Change front-line workers, work towards continual improvement, removing impediments and support new practices	Level II: Teams Team learning Improve the way people work, think and interact with a focus on managers	Level III: Organisation Systems thinking and shared vision Institutionalise learning as an inescapable way of life
Levels of Interaction			
Team-building approach (Watkins and Marsick 1993)	Level I: Individuals Promote inquiry Create continuous learning opportunities	Level II: Sub-group/teams Collaborate and share the gains	Level III: Management Empower people Integrate quality and quality of work life Create free space for learning

Understanding Organisational Learning

The concept of organisational learning is a somewhat elusive term. It is defined in a variety of ways in the literature. Heraty (2004) suggested that it has more recently tended to be defined in terms of organisational processes and structures. Learning is embedded in organisational policies, cultures and routines. Organisational learning is influenced by individual learning processes, but it involves, in a collective sense, the capacity of the organisation to use experience to enhance its performance.

Table 16.3: Approaches to the Study of Organisational Learning

Approach	Contributions	Perceived Problems Facing Organisational Learning
Psychology		
• Hierarchy of learning • Cognitive processes of learning • Experiential learning • Learning styles • Difficulties of learning	• The existence of different hierarchical levels of individual learning • The recognition of the importance of context • The assumption that ideas concerning individual learning can be adjusted to relate to organisational learning • The recognition of importance of cognitive maps and frames of thinking • The recognition of the interrelationships between thinking and action	• How to move from learning by individuals to collective learning • How to overcome the defensive reactions of individuals and groups • How to improve poor communication between organisational members
Management Science		
• Information gathering and processing • Systems thinking • Organisational knowledge	• An understanding of the creation and dissemination of information • The development of the concept of organisational knowledge • The promotion of progressive levels of learning • A holistic view of organisational learning	• How to overcome the distorting effect of organisational politics • How to overcome other forms of non-rational behaviour • How to reconcile conflicts between short-term and long-term agendas • How to 'unlearn' previous behaviours
Sociology and Organisation Theory		
• Functional views • Contingency theory • Learning as social construction • Critical views	• Different types of learning according to contingent factors • The exploration of the processes of social construction that underpin organisational learning • The study of politics and conflict as inevitable organisational processes that affect learning • Questioning whose interests are served by organisational learning • A fundamental questioning of the nature of organisational learning	• How to facilitate dissemination of information between hierarchical levels and through political barriers • How to reconstruct knowledge following perceived discontinuities in organisational functioning • Questioning who is to direct organisational learning; whose knowledge is to be privileged; whose interests are served • Questioning whether organisational learning should be a lever to be pulled at the behest of senior executives

Approach	Contributions	Perceived Problems Facing Organisational Learning
Strategy		
• Competitive advantage • Environmental alignment • Population-level learning	• Organisational learning produces competitive advantage • Contribution to the debate concerning whether organisations can adapt to their environments • Further explication of levels of learning, the importance of direct experience and tacit knowledge in organisational learning • Exchange of knowledge and technology transfer between organisations	• How to facilitate higher-level learning in highly complex and ambiguous contexts • Whether organisational learning will have an impact on the environment or whether the environment selects out organisations • How to facilitate technology transfer between organisations • How to facilitate organisational learning when members are tied to strict deadlines • Whether ideas from countries such as Japan can be transferred to different cultures
Production Management		
• Learning curve • Exogenous effects on organisational learning • Technology and working arrangements	• The use of productivity to measure organisational learning • The concept of the learning curve • The debate about exogenous and endogenous factors in organisational learning • The role of organisational design in facilitating organisational learning	• How to compare learning across national boundaries and cultural differences • How to assess organisational learning in the absence of longitudinal studies • How to overcome methodological weaknesses of comparative research
Culture		
• Organisational learning in Japanese firms • Organisational learning as shared meanings • Organisational learning as embedded in a context	• Focus on values and beliefs • Investigation of how culture affects organisational learning • Whether some cultures have an advantage in facilitating organisational learning	• How to transfer tacit knowledge which cannot be articulated • How to change cultures that do not generate organisational learning
Learning Organisation		
• Organisational development • Human development • Action research	• Identification of success factors associated with organisational learning • How to implement organisational learning • Cyclical and evolutionary modes of organisational learning	• Problems of implementation • How to address different levels or types of learning • How to overcome utopian recommendations in the literature

Source: Adapted from Easterby-Smith (1997)

Easterby-Smith (1997) suggested that organisational learning is a multi-perceptual concept (Table 16.3). It derives its justification from psychology, sociology, organisation theory, strategy and organisation culture. Tables 16.3 and 16.4 summarise various views of organisational learning. It can be defined in terms of the acquisition of knowledge, the modification of conceptual maps, the sharing of relevant organisational knowledge, adaptation and change, the construction of meaning, changes in culture and the institutionalisation of learning. There is a strong assumption that organisations can learn collectively, and it is also clear that the learning must involve a fundamental shift in understanding and the emergence of shared meaning.

Table 16.4: Views of Organisational Learning

- Organisational learning as acquiring knowledge that is recognised as potentially useful to the organisation
- Organisational learning as knowledge acquisition, information processing and distribution, information interpretation and organisational memory
- Organisational learning as knowledge acquisition (the development of skills, insights and relationships); knowledge sharing and dissemination; and knowledge utilisation (the integration of learning to make it widely available and generalisable to new situations)
- Organisational learning as the assumption-sharing modification of cognitive maps
- Organisational learning as the development of knowledge about action-outcome relationships, including the effectiveness of past and future actions and the impact of the environment on these relationships
- Organisational learning as the enhanced ability to perform in accordance with a changing environment through the search for strategies to cope with those contingencies, and the development of appropriate implementation systems and structures
- Organisational learning as systems that acquire, communicate and interpret organisationally relevant knowledge of use in decision-making and which transform individual knowledge into an organisational knowledge base
- Organisational learning as a different response to the same stimulus
- Organisational learning as adaptation and change
- Organisational learning as the process of improving actions through better knowledge and understanding
- Organisational learning as a process where known objects and phenomena acquire new meaning
- Organisational learning as acquiring, sustaining and changing the meanings embedded in the organisation's cultural artefacts through collective action
- Organisational learning as the construction of meaning from a wide range of materials, including social and physical circumstances and the histories and social relations of the people concerned
- Organisational learning as the development of organisational efficiency through the creation and organisation of knowledge and routines around and within organisational activities and cultures
- Organisational learning as institutionalised experiences

Sources: Adapted from Shrivastava (1983); Fiol and Lyles (1985); Duncan and Weiss (1979); Brown and Duguid (1991); Huber (1991); Cook and Yanow (1993); Nevis, DiBella and Gould (1995); Nicolini and Meznar (1995); Thatchenkery (1996); Boland and Tenkasi (1996)

Levinson and Asahi (1995) suggested there are four distinct phases of organisational learning. The first phase involves becoming aware of and identifying knowledge. This involves questions concerning how the environment is scanned, how new knowledge is identified, what sources and forms of knowledge are considered legitimate, and the types of filters that are used to screen out potential new knowledge. Phase two involves the transfer and interpretation of new knowledge. Questions for organisations at this phase include identifying ways in which knowledge is transferred across different parts of the organisation, the transfer of tacit knowledge, the interpretation of knowledge, the problem of multiple interpretations, and the processes through which interpretations are deemed legitimate. Phase three involves using knowledge through the adjustment of behaviour. The key challenges for organisations are understanding how knowledge is transformed into action, the capacity of the organisation to absorb new ideas, the initiation of collective action and the strategies that are used to address resistance to change. Phase four involves institutionalising knowledge. The key considerations for organisations involve identifying how knowledge can be institutionalised, how knowledge can be deposited and what the impact of knowledge institutionalisation will be on future learning.

Table 16.5: Types of Organisational Learning

- **Single-Loop Learning:** The correction of error within a given set of governing variables, norms, policies, objectives, etc. Those activities that add to the knowledge base and specific competencies of the organisation.
- **Double-Loop Learning;** The correction of error in ways that change the governing variables themselves. Changes to the knowledge base and competencies.
- **Deutero Learning:** When organisations reflect on previous episodes of learning to discover what facilitated or inhibited it, develop new strategies for learning, and evaluate what these new strategies have produced. A consideration of why and how to change.
- **Lower-Level Learning:** Routine learning that occurs through repetition within a given set of organisational rules and structures to produce behavioural outcomes, including the institutionalisation of formal rules, adjustments in management systems, the development of problem-solving skills.
- **Higher-Level Learning:** Takes place within an ambiguous context and involves changing rules and norms that govern behaviours and activities through the use of heuristics and insights to produce new missions, new agendas, problem-defining skills.
- **Generative Learning:** Addresses the underlying causes of behaviour at a level that enables patterns of behaviour to change through the redesign of underlying systems.
- **Adaptive Learning;** Focuses more on short-term and surface issues, which may lead to some changes in behaviour but not to system change.
- **Reliable Learning:** Produces shared understandings of experiences and shared, public and stable interpretations of those experiences.
- **Valid Learning:** Enables organisations to understand, predict and control their environment.
- **Exploitation:** Refinement and extension of existing competencies, technologies and paradigms producing positive, short-term predictable returns.
- **Exploration:** Experimentation with new alternatives whose returns are uncertain, distant and possibly negative.
- **Analytical Learning:** Methodical learning in an unconstrained environment that takes place mainly at upper echelons through relational analysis of environment and organisation; uncertainty and conflict are relatively low; criteria and standards are clearly defined; relies on and produces largely explicit knowledge.
- **Systematic Learning:** Emergent learning in an unconstrained environment that takes place mainly at upper echelons whereby individuals' creative capabilities allow them to see patterns and opportunities in conditions of high uncertainty where others only see a mumble of elements; criteria and standards are aesthetic and subjective; relies on and produces primarily tacit knowledge; outcomes are likely to be radical.
- **Experimental Learning:** Methodical learning that takes place at middle levels of the organisation where actions are constrained; small experiments circumvent some of the constraints that limit organisation-wide action and help overcome high uncertainty about how best to achieve goals; effects of learning are applied locally.
- **Interactive Learning:** Emergent learning that takes place at middle levels of the organisation where actions are constrained; negotiations between individuals circumvent political constraints on learning and high levels of conflict regarding both goals and the means to achieve them.
- **Structured Learning:** Highly constrained, in terms of both action and thought, methodical learning which is embodied in organisational routines that guide – and circumscribe – learning throughout organisations.
- **Institutional Learning:** Highly constrained, in terms of both action and thought, emergent learning that derives from institutionalised practices and ideologies that affect all organisational members.

Source: Adapted from Shrivastava (1983); Fiol and Lyles (1985); Argyris (1986); Senge (1990); March, Sproull and Tamuz (1991); Dodgson (1993); Miller (1996)

Similarly, Slater and Narver (1995) envisaged that the processes of organisational learning involve a process of knowledge codification. They explain it in terms of the following stages:

- *Acquisition*: Organisations acquire information beyond their formal systems. Such information can be secured through benchmarking, networking, strategic alliances and customer interaction.
- *Encoding and Storage*: Organisations need to encode and store the new knowledge in their collective memory. Processes that organisations use to achieve this include the preparation of mission statements, standard operating procedures and information systems. These represent the more explicit aspects of knowledge. The challenge is to capture organisational learning which is tacit in nature.
- *Sharing*: Sharing is a complex process. Kim (1993), for example, suggested that organisations construct shared mental models which enable them to address issues in a particular way. Ben-Horin Naot, Lipshitz and Popper (2004) suggested that organisations develop mechanisms which enable them to collect, store and share information. This involves an interplay between individual and organisational-level learning. The process of making individual models explicit enables the creation of shared mental models. These allow the organisation to use its memory to achieve organisational goals.
- *Interpretation and Incorporation*: The sharing of learning leads to interpretation and its incorporation into different schemas. Interpretation represents a vital component of organisational learning because without it, learning will remain embedded in the mental models of a small number of organisational members. Organisation-level interpretation allows organisation members to identify tensions and conflicts and to contribute to the development of a shared mental model. This process of interpretation may need to be facilitated in order to produce functional outcomes. It is possible that organisational members may not be able to achieve an interpretation which is acceptable to all. The development of a shared mental model can be helped along by encouraging a climate of openness, by allowing multiple perspectives to be discussed and conflicts to be resolved, and by creating a shared perception of a performance gap.

Facilitating Organisational Learning and Collective Leadership

A multiplicity of factors facilitate or inhibit organisational learning and the emergence of collective leadership. Patterns that facilitate organisational learning include: the hiring of key leaders; development and continuous education; continuous improvement initiatives; environmental scanning; commitment to learning by leaders; decentralised structures and the diffusion of information; strong levels of organisational trust; and the adoption of systems perspectives. Hardy and Dougherty (1997) and Easterby-Smith (1997) stressed that organisations should: possess a high absorptive capacity, an ability to pick up new ideas, a willingness to experiment; implement strategies to facilitate experimentation and benchmarking; and use customer input.

Table 16.6: Perspective on Theory – Leaders and Organisational Learning: A Summary of Propositions

- Leaders play a major role in helping individuals realise what they have learned. They manage meaning and frame experience.
- Leaders facilitate employees in setting the context in which learning can be meaningful.
- Leaders use metaphors to make issues relevant to followers. Metaphors allow learners to frame their learning and align it with organisational goals.
- Leaders have an important role in driving the process of interpretation and enabling a shared understanding to emerge.

- When leaders communicate vision, they embed their vision in a context and therefore make it more attractive to employees.
- Leaders will impact the intuition of employees by creating particular cultures and climates that encourage intuition. Leaders who support the ideas of employees encourage transformative learning.
- Leaders have the potential to provide the shared understanding to enable employees integrate new and existing learning.
- Leaders obtain the necessary resources for learning to occur.
- Leaders provide the guidance that enables employees to cross organisational boundaries and integrate what is learned.
- Leaders help to ensure that learning is institutionalised. They achieve this through a process of teaching.

Sources: Berson *et al.* (2006); Bass and Avolio (1993)

The barriers to organisational learning include constant pressure to meet deadlines, a lack of resources and incentives for learning, top-down leadership processes, conflicting strategic practices, lack of experimentation with multifunctional teams and communication bottlenecks. Nevis, DiBella and Gould (1995) and Beer and Eisenstat (1996) highlighted the existence of defensive routines in organisations. These are manifest in situations where people say they learn but it is not always evident in their behaviour. They are unable to deal with inconsistency and are unwilling to challenge the status quo. Such organisations encounter significant difficulties in dealing with tacit knowledge and possess cultures that do not facilitate risk-taking or the making of mistakes and have cultures which are highly institutionalised.

Argyris (1993) suggested that leaders and managers must free themselves of the conceptual frameworks in which they are imprisoned. They must be helped to differentiate between their espoused theories and their theories in use and confront the differences which arise. Leaders need to change their theories in use rather than defend them. Isaacs (1993) suggested that managers should use dialogue to identify disparities and enhance organisational learning. Dialogue enables managers to reflect on their ways of knowing, the language they use and what constitutes meaning. It helps managers to bring to the surface fundamental assumptions and to open up to alternative perspectives. Through dialogue, managers share tacit understanding and then focus on how their shared meaning needs to be altered. Isaacs envisaged that dialogue could be used to build trust, confront assumptions, find common ground and ultimately lead to a new shared mental model.

O'Connor and Quinn (2004) advocated that collective leadership involves a similar process of dialogue. It requires the emergence of a new shared mental model that recognises the need to shift thinking to a need to build organisational capacity for leadership, rather than focusing on individual leader development. Collective leadership requires that an organisation addresses complex questions concerning how it deals with complexity, how it understands the challenges that it currently faces, how it facilitates or inhibits collective learning and connectivity and how leaders behave. It also involves a detailed consideration of the organisation's overall readiness for change. Table 16.7 sets out the questions that organisations need to answer when considering how to develop their collective capacity for leadership.

Table 16.7: Developing Collective Leadership: Key Questions for Organisations

Complex Challenges
- What are the complex challenges facing your organisation for which there are no ready solutions, tools or responses?
- What leadership orientation characterises the approach your organisation is taking to address these challenges?
  - Is top leadership expected to deal with the challenges?
  - Are members throughout the organisation trying to influence the adoption of certain approaches over others?

- Have cross-functional, cross-level groups come together to try to make sense of the challenges and collectively develop an approach?
- Have there been efforts to assess systemic factors within the organisation that may be shaping the approach to the challenge?
- What is not working in the approach being taken? What are the limitations?
- Are there resources or perspectives not being brought to bear? Why?
- What evidence do you have that the organisation is facing the challenge in ways that will help it to learn and develop? How might it integrate more learning into dealing with the challenges?

Leadership Tasks

- How are setting direction, creating alignment and maintaining commitment accomplished in your organisation?
- Does your organisation exhibit different leadership orientations for accomplishing this work in different contexts or situations (in the context of a new venture, addressing strategic versus operational issues, in time-pressured situations, and so forth)?
- Does this work happen similarly in different parts of the organisation?
- How might your organisation become more versatile in achieving direction, alignment and commitment? What might that look like?

Targets for Development

- What forms of capital (human, social, organisational) do your practices tend to recognise as valuable and target for development? Why?
- Who in your organisation has access to developmental opportunities?
- Who in your organisation is influential in determining which approaches to development will be supported? How are these determinations made?
- To what degree is development embedded in the leadership work?
- How might your organisation develop more versatility in assessing and addressing relevant targets for development?

Outcome Orientation

- Has your organisation articulated outcomes regarding the complex challenges it is currently facing? Are they primarily focused on performance? On learning? On development or change? On a blend of these?
- In what ways are outcome expectations in these situations influencing the approaches your organisation takes to address challenges?
- To what degree are multiple outcomes understood, evaluated and learned from in these situations?
- Do certain contexts or situations pit desired outcomes against each other? For example, are performance outcome expectations in conflict with learning outcome expectations? Why?

Connectivity

- How interconnected are members of the organisation? Groups in the organisation? The organisation and its primary stakeholders?
- How is interconnectedness (or disconnectedness) demonstrated in your organisation? What is happening or not happening when members address leadership tasks?
- Does your organisation demonstrate greater connectivity while addressing some leadership tasks (setting direction, creating alignment or maintaining commitment) than others? Why might this be so?
- Does your organisation experience greater connectivity when involving certain individuals or groups compared to others? Why might this be the case?
- In leadership situations in which a high level of connectivity has been experienced, what were the resulting benefits?
- What kinds of practices and beliefs support connectivity?
- What kinds of practices and beliefs hinder connectivity?

The Learning Organisation

It is clear from our discussions so far that the concept of the learning organisation is an elusive one. Table 16.8 presents a selection of definitions of the learning organisation. They emphasise that the learning organisation is predominantly viewed as an outcome. The outcome particularly valued is enhanced organisational performance. It is clear that the learning organisation concept draws heavily on the organisational learning concept to explain its rationale.

Palmer and Hardy (2000) suggested that organisations that deliberately develop strategies to enhance learning can be called learning organisations. Learning organisations are considered to be skilled at acquiring information, sharing it and using it to achieve their strategic objectives. Garvin (1993) suggested that a learning organisation has the capacity to create, acquire and transfer knowledge. The characteristics of the learning organisation are many and varied. Watkins and Marsick (1993) and Ulrich, Von Glinow and Jick (1993) have highlighted some of the more pertinent characteristics, including: a learning approach to strategy, participative policy making, decentralised decision-making, and the development of leaders who are role models for risk-taking and experimentation.

Table 16.8: Definitions of the Learning Organisation

Themes	Theorists	Definitions
Theory in Action	Argyris (1993)	In a learning organisation, individuals are the key where they are acting in order to learn, or where they are acting not to produce a result. All the knowledge has to be generalised and crafted in ways in which the mind and brain can use it in order to make it actionable.
Renewal	Braham (1996)	Organisational learning is learning about learning. The outcome will be a renewed connection between employees and their work, which will spur the organisation to create a future for itself.
Organisational Change	Denton (1998)	Organisational learning is the ability to adapt and utilise knowledge as a source of competitive knowledge. Learning must result in a change in the organisation's behaviour and action patterns.
Action Learning	Garratt (1995)	A learning organisation is linked to action-learning processes where it releases the energy and learning of the people in the hour-to-hour, day-to-day operational cycles of business.
Technological	Marquardt and Kearsley (1999)	A learning organisation has the powerful capacity to collect, store and transfer knowledge and thereby continuously transform itself for corporate success. It empowers people within and outside the company to learn as they work. A most critical component is the utilisation of technology to optimise both learning and productivity.
Growth and Survival	Pedler, Burgoyne and Boydell (1997)	A learning organisation is like a fountain tree where the image of energy and life is characteristic of growth and survival. Organisational members are constituents of this fountain tree.
Cultural	Schein (1996)	The key to organisational learning is helping executives and engineers (groups representing basic design elements of technology) learn how to learn, how to analyse their own cultures, and how to evolve those cultures around their strengths.

Themes	Theorists	Definitions
Systems	Senge (1990)	Organisational learning involves developing people who learn to see as systems thinkers see, who develop their own personal mastery, and who learn how to surface and restructure mental models collaboratively.
Team-Building	Watkins and Marsick (1993)	A learning organisation is one that learns continuously and transforms itself where the organisational capacity for innovation and growth is constantly enhanced.
Organisational and Management Practices	Liu and Vince (1999)	Learning organisations are those that identify and measure the essential organisational characteristics and management practices that promote organisational learning.

Structural and cultural factors are also highlighted as indicative characteristics of learning organisations. These include a learning culture, a commitment to learning, inter-company learning through networks and alliances, idea sharing across vertical, hierarchical, external, geographic and temporal boundaries, enabling structures to facilitate learning and learning-based information systems. Various human resource and leadership development activities are emphasised, such as flexible rewards, human resource practices that encourage learners to take risks, collaborative and team learning processes, the provision of opportunities to learn from experience, continuous learning opportunities, self-development and the use of learning strategies that facilitate inquiry and dialogue. Poell (1999) used many concepts of organisational learning to describe the learning organisation. He highlighted the notion of a shared vision, empowerment, continuous learning, single- and double-loop learning, knowledge distribution and collective dialogue.

Heraty (2004) highlighted the prescriptive and contradictory nature of the learning organisation literature. She viewed it as a catch-all phrase that has multiple meanings. This idea is also complemented by the view that the learning organisation is a work in progress. Pfeffer and Sutton (2000) shared the view that the concept of the learning organisation represents no more than aspiration and prescriptions. This indicates why it is very popular with leadership development practitioners.

Models of the Learning Organisation

We focus in this section on explaining and evaluating a number of models of the learning organisation that are found in academic and practitioner literatures. These are Senge's (1990) notion of five disciplines; Pedler, Burgoyne and Boydell's (1997) learning company model; Steiner's (1998) learning model; Reynolds and Ablett's (1998) molecular development model; Buckler's (1996) learning process model and Thomas and Allen's (2006) multilevel learning organisational framework. We have selected these models because a number of them have something to say about the role of leadership.

Senge's Five Disciplines: Senge is very popular with practitioners because he devised a set of principles which he believes should be implemented. He suggested that the learning organisation consisted of five disciplines:

- *Personal Mastery:* The capacity of organisational members continually to clarify and implement their personal visions.
- *Mental Models*: The processes whereby individuals open up their internal personal pictures of the world and have them scrutinised by others.
- *Shared Vision*: The development of a shared mental model for the future and strong commitment to it.

- *Team Learning*: The capacity of organisation members to think together and achieve synergies for the benefit of the organisation.
- *Systems Thinking*: This represents the integrating vision and brings the other principles into a coherent whole.

Steiner (1998) suggested that these disciplines prove to be ineffective in reality because of a multiplicity of barriers. These include shared mental models that are not meaningful and the fact that the building of a shared vision is very difficult to achieve. Team learning is often not necessary, and structural deficiencies can prevent organisations thinking in a systems fashion. We will return to Steiner's suggested model later in this section.

Pedler, Burgoyne and Boydell's Learning Company Model: Pedler, Burgoyne and Boydell (1997) proposed a learning company model which is similar in many respects to that suggested by Marquardt and Reynolds (1994). Pedler *et al.* suggested that a learning company possesses five key characteristics. These are:

- *A Focus on the External*: Organisational members have contracts with customers and suppliers. They scan the environment and bring information back into the organisation. Learning through joint ventures and benchmarking is also a possibility.
- *Strategy Processes*: Learning companies adopt a learning approach to strategy. This suggests that strategy is emergent and experiential.
- *Organisational Structures*: Structures are sufficiently flexible to enable change and adaptation.
- *Learning Opportunities*: The learning company fosters a climate of learning. It supports a culture of questioning, feedback and support. It encourages members to engage in self-development activities and promotes the resources necessary to pursue such activities.
- *Information Flow*: Learning companies facilitate information flow, internal exchange, formative accounting and control and ensure recognition of employee flexibility.

Marquardt and Reynolds (1994) had a similar prescription for a global learning organisation. They emphasised characteristics such as appropriate strategies, environmental scanning, strategy and vision, learning and networking, knowledge creation and transfer and a corporate learning culture.

Steiner's Learning Model: Steiner (1998) started from the proposition that Senge's original principles are not easily applied in practice due to the interaction of the internal and external business environments. In particular, she suggested that the individual employee represents a significant barrier to the learning organisation. This occurs because employees do not understand the language of management; they do not possess sufficient competency; they have an inability to think and talk in the same way as managers and leaders; and employees may not wish to be part of the organisation's decision-making processes. Organisation structures are also inhibitors because they emphasise hierarchy, they encourage balkanisation and they emphasise divisions rather than co-operation. Management actions, such as poor information flows, mixed messages and poorly articulated vision, restrict the capacity of the organisation to develop a learning organisation.

Steiner suggested a holistic model of learning where organisations consider the big picture, organisational goals are articulated and managers think differently about their role. She suggested that the new role for the manager in a learning organisation is to be a tutor and a helper. She highlighted the need for an approach to learning which is systemic and which helps to bridge the perceived dysfunction between the five disciplines proposed by Senge.

Buckler's Learning Process Model: Buckler (1996) suggested that reflection is the key driver that facilitates single- and double-loop learning. He proposed a model of the learning organisation which places reflection as the highest level of learning (Figure 16.2). He considers the six components of learning (ignorance, awareness, understanding, commitment, evaluation and reflection) to represent the complete cycle of learning. Organisations that have the capacity to move through these various stages are more likely to be successful. Buckler placed specific emphasis on the role of leadership. Leadership is viewed as a catalyst for the creation of shared vision. Organisational leaders have a key role to play in the communication of shared vision. They formulate strategic direction and they are best placed to have it shared throughout the organisation.

Figure 16.2: Buckler's Learning Model

No.	Stages	Common Responses	Leadership: Develop ownership and remove barriers	Desired Responses
6.	Reflection	None	What have we learned? How have we learned it?	I now have a better understanding
5.	Enactment	I'm not good enough to do this	Enable	I want to know more
4.	Commitment	I don't believe this will work	Allow risk-taking	I want to try this
3.	Understanding	This isn't my job	Develop shared vision: 'whys'	I want to know about this
2.	Awareness	I don't need to change	Develop shared vision: 'whats'	I need to know about this
1.	Ignorance	I don't know and I don't care	Question	I ought to know about this

Reynolds and Ablett's Molecular Development Model: Reynolds and Ablett (1998) integrated many of the ideas proposed by Senge and other writers on the learning organisation. In particular, they focused on five key attributes: team building, business focus, human resource integration, commitment and internal energy. They argued that human resource development, leadership development and organisation development each make an important contribution, but these need to be integrated. The concept of business focus clearly places their model's emphasis on business success. This represents the catalyst for the integration of organisational learning practices.

Thomas and Allen's Multilevel Model of the Learning Organisation: Thomas and Allen (2006) argue that it is necessary to move away from looking at isolated events and focus instead on the system as a whole (Figure 16.3). They identified a number of important attributes of the learning organisation, including mental models, implicit and explicit knowledge and shared vision. Their model incorporates organisational learning ideas and highlights the specific role of leadership. The model proposes that organisations make a generative response which is shaped by emergent strategy.

Figure 16.3: The Learning Organisation Multilayered System of Causal Attributes

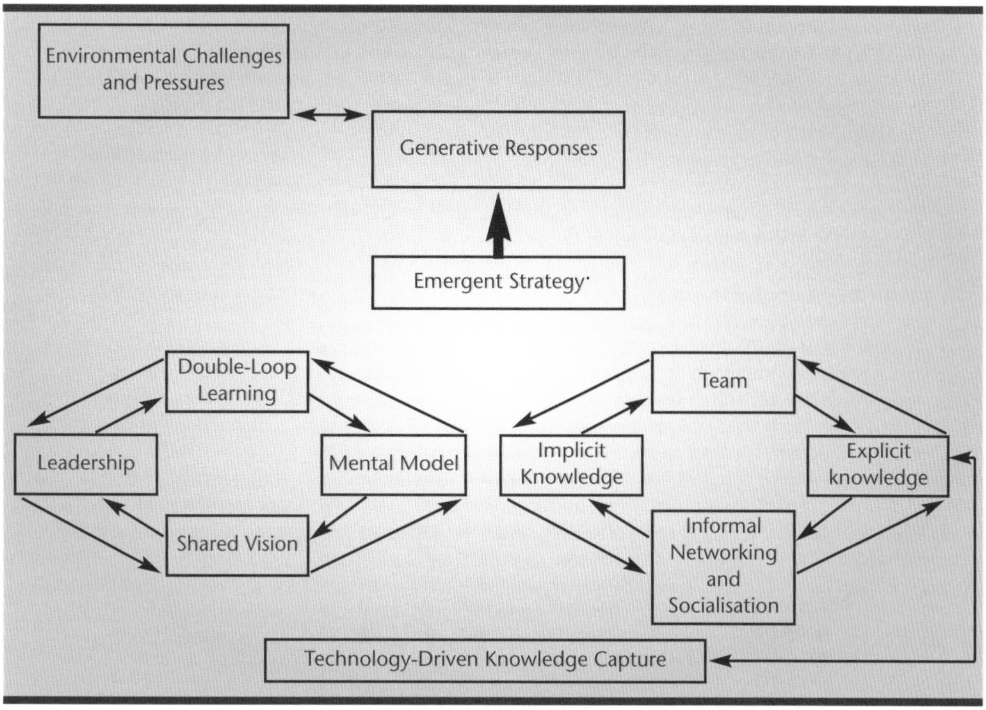

Thomas and Allen stressed, in particular, that there are two loops and that each of the team factors identified are both cause and effect. Nothing is solely influenced in one particular direction. The individual's mental model and implicit knowledge serves as the connection between both loops. These links are reciprocal and reinforcing. Thomas and Allen emphasised that leadership is responsible for creating an environment that nurtures double-loop learning. Leadership leads to shared vision and this positively reinforces the act of leadership. Leadership processes, however, can impact negatively on shared vision. The model indicates that implicit knowledge is likened to both team and informal networking and socialisation. This implicit or tacit knowledge is made explicit through collaborative learning and sharing information.

Table 16.9: Perspective on Practice: Guidelines for Implementing the Concept of a Learning Organisation

- View learning as work and work as learning. Learning appears in many contexts, resulting in many opportunities to learn that might not be recognised in a traditional context. When everyday work situations can be viewed as learning opportunities, the organisation and its employees can increase learning dramatically.
- Informal learning is more likely than formal learning to result in benefits. Because of the large number of potential informal learning opportunities, and because informal learning occurs alongside actual work, it is extremely important that an organisation encourage situations that enhance informal learning, such as informal collaboration.
- Because informal learning often takes place in informal communities, it is important that all employees have access to these communities. For instance, if a female manager is excluded from networks because of her gender, she will not be able to learn from community interaction in the workplace. Consequently, it is necessary to identify any blocks to individual participation in these communities.
- Learning should match practice as much as possible. Because informal learning communities are often

concerned with the sharing and development of tacit knowledge and its real-life application, it is important that any formalised learning follow a similar pattern: the application of theory in everyday, work-based situations.

- Communities of practice should be treated as assets. Because informal learning communities are often based on mutual interest and the desire to improve performance, they are extremely important for the development of innovative ideas and practices that are of direct benefit to the organisation. Encouraging their formation and collaboration should be a priority.
- Because participation in knowledge communities is usually voluntary, it is important to reward members for their involvement above and beyond their regular work remuneration.
- General mechanisms for ideas and innovations developed in communities of practice are to be utilised. If the fruits of informal learning need to be formalised before they can be accepted or used in everyday work situations, it is unlikely that they will be developed, and the community will reduce its organisational input. Consequently, by making it easy for knowledge communities to apply their ideas, managers are harvesting valuable human capital.
- Recognise that the informal learning within knowledge communities does not always look like work (e.g. 'watercooler moments'). Despite the value of ideas and innovations developed in informal gatherings, managers often see these interactions as time away from 'real work'. When managers encourage constructive, informal collaboration, they are enhancing organisational learning by allowing the dissemination and development of tacit knowledge within the firm.
- Recognise that new practices emerging from knowledge communities might, at first, appear to be unrelated or incompatible with current practices. However, given time, these new ideas can dramatically alter the effectiveness of a given system or method. Consequently, it is important that managers allow time for new ideas to show their merit.
- Encourage interaction between separate knowledge communities. Although knowledge communities are informal and flexible, they are often limited to the interests of their members. By encouraging interaction between groups, when ideas that were of little value in isolation are exposed to different ways of thinking, they can grow to become valuable organisational contributions.
- Allow informal learning communities to direct their own learning. If groups of employees are interested in learning new skills, make sure they have the resources to access the information they require, and the time to learn and apply their learning to everyday work.
- Let employees know that their learning efforts are appreciated, and that they are enhancing the organisation through their learning efforts.

Conceptualising Organisational Learning Environments

Various characteristics of organisations will have an indirect and moderating effect on collective leadership development. Various models and concepts have emerged which seek to describe characteristics of the organisation which facilitate learning and development. Four particular notions are of relevance to collective leadership development: expansive and restrictive learning environments; organisational climate for leader development; organisational climate for learning; and organisation-led learning.

Expansive and Restrictive Learning Environments

Fuller and Unwin (2004) developed a model of the learning environment which, although developed in an apprenticeship context, has relevance to collective leadership development. They focused on three particular dimensions of learning in organisations that are important in explaining the effectiveness of development. These are: opportunities for engagement in multiple communities of practice at and beyond the workplace; access to a multidimensional approach to the acquisition of experience through the way in which work is organised; and the opportunity to pursue qualifications and courses related to work (Figure 16.4).

Fuller and Unwin indicated that organisations who are closer to the expansive side of the spectrum are better at integrating the personal and organisational development of employees and managers. Particular characteristics of the expansive learning environment relevant to collective leadership development include: access to learning fostered by cross-organisational experience; organisational recognition of and support for the manager's career; managers as facilitators of individual development; cross-boundary collaboration and teamwork; and a multidimensional view of expertise. The model serves as a valuable diagnostic tool which allows organisations to map where their organisation stands. It suggests issues that need to be addressed in order to effectively promote collective leadership development.

Figure 16.4: Expansive and Restrictive Learning Environments

Expansive	Restrictive
Participation in multiple communities of practice inside and outside the workplace	Restricted participation in multiple communities of practice
Primary community of practice has shared participative memory; cultural inheritance of workforce development	Primary community of practice has little or no participative memory; little or no tradition of apprenticeship
Broad: access to learning fostered by cross-company experiences	Narrow: access to learning restricted in terms of tasks/knowledge/location
Access to range of qualifications including knowledge-based VQ	Little or no access to qualifications
Planned time off the job for knowledge-based courses and for reflection	Virtually all on the job; limited opportunity for reflection
Graduate transition to full, rounded participation	Fast – transition as quick as possible
Vision of workplace learning; profession for career	Vision of workplace learning; static for job
Organisational recognition of and support for career	Lack of organisational recognition of and support for employees as learners
Workforce development is used as a vehicle for aligning the goals of developing the individual and the organisational capability	Workforce developments used to tailor individual capability to organisational need
Workforce development fosters opportunities to extend identity through boundary crossing	Workforce development limits opportunities to extend identity; little organisational boundary crossing experienced
Reification of 'workplace curriculum' highly developed (e.g. through documents, symbols, language tools) and accessible to apprentices	Limited reification of 'workplace curriculum'; patchy access to reificatory aspects of practice
Widely distributed skills	Polarised distribution of skills
Technical skills valued	Technical skills taken for granted
Knowledge and skills of whole workforce developed and valued	Knowledge and skills of key workers/groups developed and valued

Expansive	Restrictive
Teamwork valued	Rigid specialist roles
Cross-boundary communication encouraged	Bounded communication
Managers as facilitators of workforce and individual development	Managers as controllers of workforce and individual development
Chances to learn new skills/jobs	Barriers to learning new skills/jobs
Innovation important	Innovation not important
Multidimensional views of expertise	Unidimensional top-down view of expertise

Organisational Climate for Leadership Development and Learning

Klein and Ziegert (2004) proposed the concept of an organisational climate for leadership. They defined it as leaders' shared summary perceptions concerning the extent to which leader development is expected, supported and rewarded within an organisation. The perceptions that leaders have are derived from a multiplicity of events, including the organisation's development-related events, policies, procedures and statements on development. They are also determined by both the intensity and consistency with which the organisation has communicated to organisational leaders that their development is high on the organisation's priorities.

The more development opportunities that an organisation offers its leaders, the stronger the climate for leader development. Day (2000) suggested that organisations that provide coaching, mentoring and feedback activities will have a positive impact on the perceived climate for leader development. Organisations that visibly reward those managers who develop their leadership skills have a more positive climate for development. Locke and Latham (2002) found that an organisational climate for leader development has an indirect impact on leadership development. It tends to support the availability of novel and creative development experiences. It communicates to leaders that development is rewarded, that they will advance more quickly and it heightens their sensitivity and openness to learning. There can be dysfunctional consequences of the climate for leader development. Leaders may become too focused on developmental goals over their job-based goals. This may lead to competition, with some leaders trying to outshine others in their demonstration of leadership skills.

Organisational climate for learning is a broader concept that equally has relevance to collective leadership activities. It focuses on the general perceptions of employees that learning is supported, expected and valued. Its effect is to motivate employees to broaden their skills, enhance their job performance and contribute to business performance. Garvin (2000) highlighted that learning can be fostered through after-action reviews and action-learning projects. A positive climate for learning facilitates job transfers, communities of practice and cross-boundary learning initiatives. These developmental opportunities provide employees with novel learning opportunities. Table 16.10 provides a list of questions that organisations can ask to determine the openness of their learning climate.

Table 16.10: Assessing an Organisation's Learning Climate: Key Questions for Organisations

- Does the organisation provide feedback to employees on performance?
- How often is feedback provided and is it a typical activity in the organisation?
- Do managers suggest ways in which direct reports can develop?
- Do managers provide opportunities for direct reports to participate in novel developmental activities?
- Do managers encourage employee initiatives and creativity?
- Do managers provide opportunities for participative goal setting and planning?
- How are organisational goals used in a developmental context?
- What are the consequences of a mistake or failure to meet performance goals?
- Is learning confined to formal settings only?
- Do managers inspire direct reports to do their best?
- Does a clear sense of vision and mission exist within the organisation?

Organisation-Led Learning Model

Heraty (2004) suggested an architecture model of organisation-led learning. She identified a number of specific elements that facilitate organisational learning and, by extension, a collective leadership development capability. An organisation-led learning architecture is embedded in a wider managing framework where key roles are specified for leaders, leadership development specialists and organisation members as a whole. The specification of roles is extremely important because it links key actors and helps share the organisation's strategic intent. In the context of leadership development, the specialist with overall responsibility will envision and manage leadership development. Managers will have a key role in enabling collaboration, in facilitating solutions to emerge and in working with the leadership development specialist in creating the learning infrastructure for leadership development.

The organisation-led learning model proposes seven elements of the learning structure. We briefly comment on each and its relevance to an organisation's collective capacity for leadership.

- *Experiential Learning*: Experiential learning is likely to flourish where there is a willingness to share information and share tacit knowledge. It requires that the climate provides both space and time for learning.
- *Teamwork and Facilitating Structures*: The work that leaders perform represents an important opportunity for development. Some organisations contrive teamwork activities in order to enable leaders to utilise their collective skills to solve problems. Notions such as teamwork have extended to virtual and cross-boundary contexts.
- *Learning as an Incentive*: Learning must be perceived as an incentive or opportunity. It should be viewed as an opportunity to enhance the manager's employability and career-advancement opportunities.
- *Learning Alliances and Networks*: Alliances and networks represent an important context for the development of leadership. They extend the opportunities for development outside the organisation. Networking facilitates the sharing of tacit knowledge, problem-solving, the generation of new knowledge and the development of leadership and organisational competencies.
- *Formalised Learning*: These programmes are an important part of the architecture and contribute to organisational as well as individual learning.
- *Certification of Learning*: Certification of learning has become more relevant in the era of employability. Certification can be organisational and individual-based. Organisation-level certification facilitates continuous improvement and opportunities to capture tacit knowledge.

- *Vision Communication*: The final element of the architecture focuses on the articulation of a collective vision and its value in sustaining motivation to learn and develop. Shared vision determines learning values and facilitates the development of a learning climate. Communication processes facilitate the diffusion of development practices, collaboration and the emergence of communities of practice.

Collaborative Leadership Development and Learnership

Two interesting concepts which fit within the general concept of collective leadership are collaborative leadership and learnership. Collaborative leadership is defined by Raelin (2006a) as true participation in leadership and decision-making. Learnership, as proposed by Cooksey (2003), suggests a fusion of leadership and learning, where responsibility for learning and leading is progressively diffused from a few individuals to a critical mass of organisational members.

Raelin (2006a) suggests that collaborative leadership is based on a number of key ideas:

- *The Notion of a Stake in the Process*: When people have a stake in a process they will demonstrate commitment to achieving it.
- *Non-Judgemental Inquiry*: The members of the organisation are expected to engage in a process of non-judgemental inquiry.
- *Critical Scrutiny*: Members must be prepared to submit their ideas to the critical scrutiny of others.
- *Unique Ideas from Mutual Inquiry*: Members need to understand the idea that mutual enquiry may lead to something new.

Raelin (2003; 2006a) suggests four perspectives that collaborative leadership needs to adopt in order to become what he calls 'leaderful' proof.

- *Concurrent Leadership*: This idea suggests that it is possible to have more than one leader operating at the same time. It requires that leaders are willing to share power with others.
- *Collective Leadership*: Leadership derives from a process through which people work together to achieve a common purpose. It is not about influence. Collective leadership accommodates a situation where anyone can arise and meet a team's leadership needs. It suggests that decisions are made by whoever has the relevant responsibility. It is possible for leaders to emerge at any point in the organisation. It is possible to have an initiator, but that initiator can share leadership.
- *Mutual Leadership*: This idea advocates that all members may speak for the organisation. They may have a point of view which can contribute to the good of the organisation. Mutual leadership requires sensitivity to the views and feelings of others and consideration of all perspectives as equally valued. It requires a public dialogue and a realisation that everyone counts.
- *Compassionate Leadership*: Leaders are expected to demonstrate compassion. This is defined as preserving the dignity of others. It suggests a priority concern for diversity. Views of members are valued, regardless of the characteristics of the person who makes them. Raelin argues that leaders are required to adopt the stance of a learner who views organisational change as dependent upon the contribution of others. Compassionate leadership realises that values are an intrinsic component of activity. Democratic participation is the most central value. This requires full participation in organisational decisions.

Raelin (2006a) views collaborative leadership as very much in line with the changing paradigm of organisations, where individualism is less important than teamwork. He highlights the need to think differently about the development of leaders. He rejects the value of formal education and corporate development programmes that emphasise the formal, the explicit and the individual. He suggests that it should be possible for organisational members to co-construct their practice environments and their learning environments. He is a particularly strong advocate of action-learning ideas. Table 16.11 summarises how action-learning ideas may be applied to develop collaborative leadership.

Table 16.11: Using Action-Learning Principles to Develop Collaborative Leadership

Dimension	Action-Learning Application
Concurrent Leadership	• Action learning requires the involvement of facilitators to assist teams in their development. • Facilitators can explore readiness issues such as: How prepared are members to share leadership? Will they rely on one person to assume the leadership role? How will the team resources be maximised? Who will be concerned with fostering collaboration? • Each team member has a responsibility to develop himself/herself with the help of other team members. • Contribution to an understanding of group dynamics, reflective processes and participation in decision-making.
Collective Leadership	• Helps sustain collective leadership through reflective process. • Members can question one another about their professional and personal experiences. • Action helps members come to understand learning as a collective process that extends beyond the individual. • The questioner can learn as much as the speaker. • Learning is structured and it endorses the practice of double-loop learning.
Mutual Leadership	• Action learning models non-judgemental enquiry. Participants are encouraged to express curiosity and to avoid maintaining hidden interests. • Members submit their own ideas for critical scrutiny. • Members are encouraged to adopt the viewpoint that new perspectives or ideas may emerge. • Action learning encourages members to question their world views in pursuit of a much more important common goal. • Action learning facilitates collaborative inquiry. It requires that members engage by challenging the status quo.
Compassionate Leadership	• Action learning emphasises democratic values such as sustainability and humility. • Participants achieve a better understanding of context in which they are embedded. • They are part of a social transformation process.

Cooksey's (2003) idea of leadership was similarly premised on the ideas of complexity, dynamism and uncertainty. He referred to organisational environments as messy and viewed the challenge of the organisation as one of adoption. His solution was the culmination of leadership, defined as the developed capacity to 'know when, where and how to best engage in the collective learning process' to ensure organisational adoption and success. He viewed learnership as a meta-cognitive concept in that members achieve a knowledge about learning combined with the doing of this learning. He had particular prescriptions for our understanding of the role of leaders and their development.

- *Setting the Context for Learning*: Leaders are charged with facilitating a supportive environment for learning. They are expected to empower others, serve as role models and create and share meanings for the business and its members.
- *Dynamic Component of Leadership*: Leadership is a dynamic component of effective organisational learning. Leadership is an energising force underpinning learning. This embeddedness of learning ensures that organisational members develop leadership as a capability.
- *Learners become Leaders*: Learnership suggests that learners evolve to become leaders in their own right. Leadership roles are less vested in a few people and instead become diffused amongst all members of the organisation.

Ultimately, Cooksey (2003) envisaged a situation where the organisation has achieved true self-organising status. The distinction between leaders and learners becomes redundant and double-loop learning becomes possible. The model does, however, pose a number of significant challenges for organisational members. Specifically, they are expected to become boundary spanners and to focus on the larger organisation. They should establish and extend the boundaries for learning at specific points in time and space. They must understand that the learning context is multidimensional and that all organisational members have unique strengths and weaknesses.

EXHIBIT 16.1

Focus on Research: Competent Jerks, Lovable Fools and the Formation of Social Networks

In companies people are brought together for the variety of their skills which are needed to carry out complex activity, and this leads to fragmentation along the lines of specialised knowledge. Organisations are designed to facilitate the interaction between people that is necessary to get their jobs done, but informal relationships play a major role.

When given a choice of people to work with, the selection is based on various factors that come down to two main criteria: competence and likeability. 'Does Joe know what he's doing, and will he be enjoyable to work with?'

Competencies and likeability combine to produce four main archetypes: the competent jerk, who knows a lot but is unpleasant to work with; the lovable fool, who doesn't know much but is a delight to be around; the lovable star, who's both smart and likeable; and the incompetent jerk who's incompetent and unlikeable. These archetypes are caricatures. Organisations usually weed out both the truly incompetent and the socially inept.

Research showed that everybody wanted to work with the lovable star and nobody wanted to work with the incompetent jerk. Things got more complicated when faced with the choice between the lovable fool and the competent jerk. While people initially claimed that competence trumped likeability, the reverse was true in practice, and if somebody is widely disliked people will not want to work with them regardless of competence. In contrast, if someone is liked people will use every bit of competence they have to offer.

Clearly, then, some likeability goes a long way. We may shun the jerk simply to deny him the satisfaction of lording his knowledge over us. Sometimes it can be difficult to get the needed information out of him, and since obtaining knowledge often needs explanation and interaction this is difficult with a jerk. In contrast the lovable fool will be happy to share his (limited) skills and knowledge and help others put them to use.

Studies in psychology have shown that we like people who are similar and familiar to us, who have reciprocal positive feelings towards us and who are attractive in appearance or personality. When we work with these people their similar values, logic and communication styles help things to flow smoothly. On the other hand there are disadvantages to working with these people: it can dampen debate with the limited perspectives on an issue, and the group might be too busy having fun to achieve anything.

To leverage the power of liking there are three main approaches: first, manufacture liking when possible, second, carefully position likeable people to bridge organisational divides, and third, work on the jerks.

To manufacture liking, you can promote familiarity. Research has shown that increased proximity generates the comfort and pleasure of interaction. This can be achieved by mixing up the workspaces, creating water-cooler type areas to foster informal chats, and office get-togethers outside the office can also be helpful. Redefining familiarity by integrating different specialisms in new teams can also prove effective. Bonding can also be fostered on off-site team-building exercises.

To leverage the likeable people, first identify them and their contribution, perhaps with a social network analysis with questions equipped to gather information about the relationships. Then protect them; their skills are sometimes deemed less important than those with technical skills and they are often victims of downsizing to the detriment of the company. Third, position them strategically to link people in different parts of the organisation who might be slow to collaborate or share ideas.

Competent jerks are wasted as much of their expertise remains untapped. To work on them, begin by reassessing their contribution in terms of their individual effort and within the company overall. If their contributions are significant it is worth working on them by rewarding their good behaviour and punishing bad behaviour. Socialise and coach by explaining the effects of the bad behaviour through incentive-based coaching or interpersonal coaching. If these strategies fail, it may be best to reposition them in a role where they work independently.

Obviously the questions of whether a person is liked or disliked does not prove their worth in an organisation, but building an environment in which people like one another can help all employees work more happily and productively and encourage the formation of strong and smoothly functioning social networks.

Source: Casciaro and Lobo (2005)

QUESTIONS

Q.1   What value does networking have in an organisation?

Q.2   Is it possible to develop managers to be better networkers?

Organisations are ultimately expected to work towards dissolving the distinction between leader and follower. These circumstances are likely to prove challenging for the organisation. They challenge much of what we understand by traditional leadership. Table 16.12 provides a set of questions that organisations should consider when analysing readiness for the development and diffusion of learnership.

Table 16.12: Diagnostic Trigger Questions for Detecting Readiness to Pursue the Development and Diffusion of 'Learnership'

Diagnostic Category	Trigger Questions
Systems Thinking	• Are there people in the business who exhibit systems-thinking capabilities and can see the big picture? • Does such systems thinking typically show a balance between inward and outward focus, from both the business and people points of view?
Leadership	• Can people occupying the formal leadership roles be predominantly characterised using such descriptions as facilitating, mentoring, rewarding, and empowering? • Do the people occupying the formal leadership roles tend to work actively to create and spread shared meanings within the business? • Do the people occupying the formal leadership roles tend to connect actively and productively with the other people in the business?
Questioning	• Are organisational members generally willing to ask difficult, potentially upsetting and destabilising questions in order to stimulate problem solving and lateral thinking? • Is critical questioning typically rewarded? • Is there a generally shared awareness of the critical assumptions that underpin the current business activities, coupled with a willingness to question and perhaps discard those assumptions in favour of new ones?
Empowerment	• Is participating at a range of levels actively encouraged and rewarded? • Can the empowerment of most employees be considered genuine and actionable? • Is there a generally shared awareness of what people in the business (including those in formal leadership roles) can and cannot control within the context and environment they inhabit?
Feedback and Evaluation	• Are there systems in place to gather feedback from inside and outside the organisation? • Is the resulting feedback explicitly and periodically audited and reviewed in order to ascertain meanings and implications? • Is the evaluation of feedback and of possible future actions open, critical and contributed to by many in the business rather than a few? • Does learning from feedback, both individually and collectively, tend to be valued and actively pursued?
Communication	• Is the shadow side of communication activities generally well understood, managed and harnessed so that members actively and openly contribute to thinking and action? • Is shared meaning for activities and goals easily established without creating pockets of ignorance and resentment? • Are communication networks predominantly laterally oriented and open in nature rather than being vertically oriented and closed?
Culture	• Is risk-taking and experimentation by individual members and/or groups explicitly encouraged and rewarded? • Is failure typically viewed as an opportunity to learn rather than as an occasion to blame and punish? • Is there a culture of trust between the people in formal leadership roles and the other people in the business as well as amongst the people themselves? • Can people's attitudes within the business generally be characterised by an overt appreciation of diversity and pluralism?

Diagnostic Category	Trigger Questions
Collective Focus	• Does collective effort in the pursuit of goals tend to be actively valued and encouraged? • Is the organisation generally sensitive to when and how teamwork might effectively be harnessed to achieve important goals?
Creativity	• Are time, freedom and resources generally made available to enable employees to engage in creative thinking and activities? • Does lateral thinking tend to be actively encouraged and rewarded?
Growth and Development	• Is individual as well as collective personal growth and development consistently encouraged and resourced? • Are organisational members generally willing to take responsibility for their own learning?

Knowledge Management and Leadership Development

Knowledge management has emerged as a significant offshoot of organisational learning. Knowledge management and organisational learning are used interchangeably to apply to a broad set of activities through which organisations learn and organise knowledge. Table 16.13 suggests a number of conceptual distinctions.

Table 16.13: Distinguishing Organisational Learning from Knowledge Management

Organisational Learning	Knowledge Management
• Emphasises organisational structures and social processes that enable organisations to learn and share knowledge • Draws heavily on the social sciences for conceptual grounding • Tends to emphasise interventions such as structural alignment, employee involvement and teamwork processes • Organisationally, OL activities are associated with human resource management and development functions	• Knowledge management focuses on the tools and techniques that enable organisations to collect, organise and translate information into knowledge • Relies heavily on information and computer sciences • Emphasises electronic forms of knowledge storage and transmission • Organisationally, knowledge management applications are located in information systems functions

Organisational learning and knowledge management are related. Interventions derived from organisational learning address how organisations can promote effective learning and how learning processes can be enhanced. Knowledge management interventions focus on the outcomes of organisational learning processes and on how it is possible to organise strategically important knowledge to achieve organisational goals.

A major outcome of organisational learning processes is to produce organisation knowledge. Knowledge management interventions tend to focus on three key components of the knowledge management process.

• *Knowledge Generation*: Organisations are required to make decisions concerning the types of knowledge that are of strategic value. Organisations then need to devise mechanisms to acquire or create that knowledge. This suggests a range of possibilities, including external consultants and experts, internal acquisitions through communities of practices, informal networks and teamwork activities.

- *Knowledge Organisation*: These activities focus on converting valued knowledge into forms that organisational members can use. They can do this in two ways: codification and personalisation. Hansen, Nohria and Tierney (1999) highlighted that codification requires sophisticated information technology and involves the use of databases. It is appropriate only where the knowledge is explicit and can be easily extracted. Personalisation strategies focus on people who develop knowledge and on how they share it on a one-to-one basis. The emphasis is on tacit knowledge which cannot be shared and codified. Tacit knowledge is accessed through ongoing dialogue, personal conversations and direct contact.
- *Knowledge Distribution*: The task for knowledge management is ultimately to ensure that organisational members have access to knowledge in order to make decisions. Davenport and Prusack (1998) suggested that the task for distribution can be achieved through self-directed distribution, facilitated transfer, knowledge services and networking. Self-directed methods place emphasis on the employees and managers who initiate and control knowledge distribution. Knowledge services and networks require the provision of helpdesks, information systems, special units and roles that scan the flow of information. Some organisations use knowledge networks to facilitate sharing knowledge and learning from one another. Such networks can be electronic or personal.

Knowledge management concepts have major implications for collective learning and development efforts in organisations. Harrison and Kessels (2004) identified four key implications:

- It is essential to ensure that employees possess skills in both learning and knowledge processes. Individual and team competence facilitates knowledge sharing. Employees impact on the knowledge process.
- Learning environments need to develop sensitivity to employee involvement in learning and knowledge development. The organisation needs to be sufficiently confident to allow employees develop knowledge in their own way. It is important that leaders do not impose strategies and processes.
- Leadership development should focus less on uniform instructional content and more on individualised approaches. Learning and development should be within the workplace or communities of practice. Organisations should encourage leadership communities to work together in order to strengthen overall knowledge sharing.
- Organisations should facilitate the development of practical judgement. Practical judgement is vital for learning, knowledge creation and sharing knowledge, and it involves experience, character, alertness and flexibility.

Knowledge management calls into question the value of traditional command and control approaches to leadership development. It requires that leaders as learners are emancipated to participate in self-managed communities of practice.

Eisenhardt and Santo (2002) suggested that managers and leaders should focus on transferring only the most strategically valuable knowledge. They believe that managers need to be made aware of knowledge transfer opportunities. Organisational rules and routines support knowledge integration. Knowledge management reinforces the interrelationships between work and leadership development. Tapcott (1999) suggested that when knowledge is the basis of value creation, it follows that work and development are one and the same. Leonard-Barton (1995) found that in a knowledge management and innovation context, learning and development are woven throughout the organisation. They may take a variety of forms, including complex problem solving or knowledge creation through experimentation. Leaders are expected to be curious information seekers.

EXHIBIT 16.2

Perspective on Theory: A Typology of Organisational Learning

Shipton (2006) suggests that the concept of organisational learning is both complex and confusing. She suggests a typology which focuses on two key dimensions: whether the focus is on individual learning within an organisational context or whether it is focused on organisation-level learning; whether the approach to organisational learning is normative/prescriptive or explanatory and descriptive.

The prescriptive/normative literature takes as a premise the idea that it is possible to detect a positive relationship between organisational learning and performance. Performance is usually defined as profitability, productivity, flexibility and innovation. The prescriptive/normative approach assumes that organisations have lots to gain from implementing learning processes. The explanatory/descriptive approach focuses on understanding how organisational learning happens and identifies the factors that facilitate and inhibit it. The explanatory approach envisages that organisational learning can have negative outcomes.

The individual level of analysis focuses on understanding how individuals and the teams to which they belong enhance learning. The priority is on how individuals transfer their learning into the organisation. The organisational level makes a distinction between those who argue that organisations learn as entities and those who suggest that the individual represents the starting point.

Quadrant	Example Definitions	Example Scholars	Research Objectives	Implications for Leadership Development
1. Individual learning within an organisational context: the prescriptive/normative perspective	• A learning organisation is one which facilitates the learning of all its members and consciously transforms itself and its context (Pedler, Burgoyne and Boydell 1999) • Places where people continually expand their capacity to create the results they truly desire (Senge 1990)	• Argyris and Schon (1978) • Argyris (1990) • Armstrong and Foley (2003) • Garvin (1993) • Pedler *et al.* (1999) • Senge (1990) • Watkins and Marsick (1993)	• To highlight the processes by which individuals implement their learning to promote organisation-level outcomes. • To investigate further in empirical terms whether or not measures designed to promote learning are associated with increased organisational effectiveness and performance	• Develop managers and leaders to implement their learning in the organisation

Quadrant	Example Definitions	Example Scholars	Research Objectives	Implications for Leadership Development
2. Organisation-level focus: the normative perspective	• The principal means of achieving the strategic renewal of an enterprise (Crossan, Lane and White 1999) • In order to measure OL we should operationalise changes in individual learning as well as in organisational elements such as social structure, technology and goals... (Lahteenmaki, Toivonen and Mattila 2001) • Organisational learning involves more than individuals becoming better at their particular jobs (Argote, Beckman and Epple 1990)	• Argote, Beckman and Epple (1990) • Arthur and Aimant-Smith (2001) • Birdi *et al.* (2004) • Bontis *et al.* (2002) • Crossan *et al.* (1999) • Lahteenmaki, Toivonen and Mattila (2001) • Shipton *et al.* (2005)	• To highlight further what desirable outcomes one might expect to find where organisational learning is working well, and develop robust scales to capture these dimensions • To examine further the importance of tacit knowledge and investigate the situations within which tacit knowledge exchange underpins organisational learning effectiveness	• Use leadership development interventions to help leaders learn collectively and acknowledge the importance of tacit development
3. Organisation-level focus: the explanatory perspective	• OL is an adaptive process through which firms respond to environmental changes by readjusting their goals, attention rules and search rules (Cyert and March 1963) • OL is the processing of information that changes the range of the organisation's potential behaviours (Huber 1991)	• Huber (1991) • Levinthal and March (1993) • Levitt and March (1988) • March (1991) • McGrath (2001) • Hedberg (1981) • Nevis, DiBella and Gould (1995) • Shrivastava (1983)	• To highlight what measures are likely to mitigate the dysfunctional aspects of organisational learning (such as strategic myopia or contemporary traps) • To consider under what conditions codification enables rather than inhibits organisational learning effectiveness	• Use leadership development to address competency traps in the organisation and encourage sharing of knowledge

Quadrant	Example Definitions	Example Scholars	Research Objectives	Implications for Leadership Development
4. Individuals learning within an organisational context; the explanatory/des criptive perspective	• All learning takes place inside human heads and an organisation learns in one of two ways: by the learning of its members or by ingesting new members who have knowledge that the organisation didn't previously have (Simon 1991) • Working, learning and innovating are interrelated and compatible (Brown and Duguid 2001)	• Brown and Duguid (1991, 2001) • Huysman (1999, 2000) • Lam (2000) • Scott and Yanow (1993) • Simon (1991) • Sims *et. al.* (1994) • Weick and Roberts (1993)	• To clarify through further empirical study what social environments foster the learning of individuals and the communities to which they belong • To identify the circumstances where it may or may not be appropriate explicitly to articulate tacit knowledge and the mechanisms most likely to facilitate this process	• Use leadership development to create a learning culture in which learners shape learning and utilise tacit learning processes

Source: Shipton (2006)

Organisation Development and Leadership Development

McLean (2006) suggests that organisation development is interdisciplinary and focused on the enhancement of organisational effectiveness. In a leadership development context, it potentially provides a wider range of interventions than the more conventional approaches to leadership development. We suggest that a number of approaches and interventions, within the broad field that is organisational development, can contribute to the development of collective leadership capability in organisations. Particular interventions that are of value include mission, vision and values interventions, strategic planning, large group interventions and re-engineering.

Mission, Vision and Values Interventions

Mission, vision and values interventions can be occasions for significant collective development of leaders. The development of vision statements represents one of the most frequent activities by senior leaders in organisations. A vision generally describes the core values and purposes of the organisation, and generally specifies an envisioned future towards which the organisation is moving. McLean (2006) distinguishes between vision statements and mission statements. Mission statements articulate the purpose of the organisation, whereas vision statements articulate how the organisation will look at a particular point in the future. Values tend to focus on four or five core values that articulate basic principles and beliefs that are 'in use'. They inform organisational members about what is important in the organisation.

The preparation of vision and mission statements requires the active participation of leaders. They play a key role in describing the desired future for the organisation and in generating commitment to the vision. The process of creating the vision and mission statements taps into the creative and intuitive thought processes of leaders, and it requires that special conditions are created in the form of workshops to stimulate their creative thinking. This helps to strengthen and change the mental models of leaders. Collins and Porras (1994) suggested that this demands of leaders the skills to produce descriptions of envisioned futures and to prepare passionate and engaging statements intended to motivate organisational members.

Strategic Planning and Collective Leadership Development

Organisation-development interventions can make a significant contribution to what is called 'traditional strategic planning'. Organisation development emphasises that strategic planning should be a highly participative process involving both senior and middle managers. Worley, Hitchin and Ross (1996) identified three features of an OD approach to strategic planning:

- Strategy and organisational design are considered as an integrated whole.
- Organisational leaders need to focus on ensuring that when strategic plans are created, they are also working on gaining commitment for them, devising implementation plans and ensuring execution.
- Individuals and teams throughout the organisation are a fundamental part of the strategic process.

Cummings and Worley (2001) highlighted four key phases in achieving an integrated strategic planning process:

Conducting a Strategic Analysis: Organisation leaders begin with a strategic analysis, which focuses on readiness to change and the appropriateness of the current strategy and organisation structure. It will also examine whether senior management are ready to engage in the change process. Greiner and Schein (1988) suggested that it is important to address whether the leader of the organisation is committed to change and whether or not the senior team is committed and has the ability to follow the initiative of the leader. Where this commitment is absent, an organisation-development intervention that focuses on team building may prove valuable.

The organisation-development consultant and facilitator will then work with the team in analysing the current strategy and organisational design. Strategic analysis should also involve organisation members in the process, as well as people from outside the organisation. It may include customers and suppliers. The goal is to build commitment for and ownership of the analysis.

McLean (2006) recommends that the consultant can use SWOT (strengths, weaknesses, opportunities, threats), PEST (political, economic, social and technological) and scenario planning. Scenario planning focuses on identifying all possible changes that are likely to take place in the business environment and factoring them into the analysis. The organisation then develops strategic responses for each possible alternative.

Making Strategic Choices: The task for the organisation is to come to an understanding of the strategic orientation, the current environment and the performance of the organisation. The strategic analysis will probably reveal misfits when they become inputs for the workshop process. The consultant will then work with senior management in formulating a vision and identifying strategic objectives and strategies to achieve these objectives. While it is desirable to involve members of the wider organisation in this process, the most significant learning and responsibility rests with the senior team. Senior executives are well placed to evaluate the strategic options from a wider perspective. Lower-level managers are likely to have a narrower focus.

Designing a Strategic Plan: Effective learning and development of collective leadership capability involves the design of a plan to achieve the strategic vision and objectives. The plan will specify the changes to be implemented and will likely address culture, power and learning issues.

Implementation of the Strategic Plan: This component of the process is ongoing and will focus on a multiplicity of issues including team working, organisational and personal learning and structural alignment. Senior managers will become champions of the strategic plan. They will initiate actions, commit resources, set goals and provide feedback for performance. Strategic implementation requires that leaders are accountable for change. They may have to change the plan to ensure that unforeseen events are addressed.

Large Group Interventions and Leadership Development

Organisation development places a strong emphasis on system-wide process interventions. Weisbord (1993) and McLean (2006) suggest that these can be variously called 'large-scale interactive events', 'search conferences', 'open-space meetings' and 'open-systems planning'. This category of intervention focuses on issues that impact on the wider organisation. Specific characteristics of this category of intervention include the following:

- The purpose of these interventions includes solving organisational problems that are operational or strategic.
- They may involve fewer than fifty participants, or as many as two hundred.
- They consist of representatives from all parts of the organisation and consultants frequently want to achieve an optimum mix of organisational members.
- They typically last for two to three days and are relatively unplanned and unstructured. They will, however, have elements of uniformity.
- They may involve a succession of meetings designed to accomplish system-wide change.
- They operate along democratic lines where each participant has an equal chance to contribute.
- They are frequently used to break down organisational silos and focus on the future direction of the organisation.

Cummings and Srivastava (1977) suggested that in order for this type of intervention to be effective, the members of the organisation must have a common view of the organisation's environment. This collective perception must be accurate and realistic and the members must accept that organisations must create their environment as well as adapt to it. Table 16.14 provides guidelines for conducting large group interventions.

Table 16.14: Using Large Group Interventions: Guidelines for Implementation

- The meeting requires a compelling focal point or purpose.
- Senior leaders need to communicate very clearly what the meeting is about. Ambiguity concerning its purpose will undermine the effectiveness of the meeting.
- As many organisation members as possible should be invited to the meeting to ensure that organisation members who have a stake in the issues and who are energised and committed to achieving its purpose are present.
- The tasks to be completed must be within the competence of the group to address.
- Select an appropriate framework within which to conduct the meeting.
- Participants should be able to provide information freely and the role of the facilitator is to ensure that trust is maintained and that task, team and individual needs are met.
- Leaders, as well as the OD consultant, will need to spend time on the implementation phase following the meeting.

Large group processes tend to use two frameworks to achieve their objectives: open-systems methods and open-space methods. Open-systems methods assume that organisations are open systems and that they interact in different ways with the external environment. Open-systems methods begin with a diagnosis of the existing environment and how the organisation relates to it. The open-systems approach then focuses on developing possible future environments and action plans. Open-space methods de-emphasise the need for a formal structure. The meetings 'self-organise' participants around interests and topics associated with the large group meeting.

Table 16.15: OD Consultant Actions for both Open-Systems and Open-Space Approaches

Open-Systems Methods	Open-Space Methods
<ul><li>The meeting identifies and prioritises different parts of the environment.</li><li>Participants then describe each domain or expectations for how the organisation should behave.</li><li>Participants then describe how the organisation currently addresses environmental expectations.</li><li>Participants then focus on the purpose or core mission of the organisation.</li><li>Participants then project the organisation and its environment into the near future and answer the question: what will happen if the organisation continues to operate as it does at present?</li><li>Participants' responses are combined to develop a likely organisation future assuming no change.</li><li>Participants then create alternative, desirable futures. They fantasise about desired futures.</li><li>Participants will then identify specific actions that will move both the environment and the organisation towards the desired future.</li></ul>	<ul><li>Set the conditions for self-organising.</li><li>Decide the themes for the session and the norms that govern it.</li><li>Inform participants that the group norms should observed.</li><li>Develop a road map for the remainder of the meeting.</li><li>Ask participants to describe a topic related to the conference theme that they are interested in discussing.</li><li>The topic is adopted and the person announcing the topic convenes the meeting.</li><li>This process continues until everyone who wants to define a topic does so.</li><li>Participants sign up for as many sessions as they have an interest in.</li><li>During the conference, participants meet as a community to announce new topics and to share observations and learning.</li><li>The role of the meeting convenor is to produce one-page summaries of what happened and the key recommendations.</li></ul>

These large-scale group interventions have the potential to engender enhanced feelings of community, an ability to see the bigger picture, in increased speed of change and enhanced leadership capability.

Re-engineering as Collective Leadership Development

Re-engineering is frequently used by organisations to achieve major improvements in organisational performance. Hammer and Champy (1993) and Champy (1995) suggested that re-engineering is based on a number of principles of change:

- It focuses on transforming how organisations traditionally produce and deliver goods and services. It breaks down specialised work units and focuses on achieving more integrated cross-functional work processes.
- Work processes become faster, more flexible and more responsive to changing competitive conditions and customer demands.
- It addresses fundamental issues concerning the purpose of the organisation and its ways of doing things.
- It questions the assumptions that organisations make concerning how they operate and challenges managers and organisation members to think more radically about their work activities.
- It challenges the vertical orientation of organisations and the tendency to be solid.

Table 16.16 summarises the key characteristics of re-engineered organisations.

Table 16.16: Characteristics of Re-engineered Organisations

- *Work units change from functional departments to process teams*: Following re-engineering, the department organised around cross-functional pre-sale teams aimed at developing and building customer relationships and post-sale teams that maintain them.
- *Jobs change from simple tasks to multidimensional work*: The post-sale team was responsible for a field-support process called licensing and contracting. Under the old structure, this was a sixteen-step effort that involved nine people in different departments and on different floors in principal's home office. Following re-engineering, the process consists of only six steps and involves only three people who are cross-trained to perform various tasks.
- *People's roles change from controlled to empowered*: The re-engineering effort resulted not only in changed jobs and processes, but in increased employee involvement as well. Production teams meet twice daily to discuss problems; hiring decisions are made by a four-person team of employees; major equipment purchases are jointly determined by management and employees; and the manufacturing group plays a big role in deciding whether to bid on new jobs.
- *The focus of performance measures and compensation shifts from activities to results*: Re-engineered organisations routinely collect and report measures of customer satisfaction, operating costs and productivity to team and then tie these measures to pay. In this way, teams and their members are rewarded for working smarter and harder.
- *Organisation structures change from hierarchical to flat*: The favoured structure of the re-engineered organisation is process-based. Rather than having layers of management, the organisation has empowered, cross-functional and well-educated process teams that collect information, make decisions about task execution and monitor their performance.
- *Managers change from supervisors to coaches; executives change from scorekeepers to leaders*: In process-based structures, the role of management and leadership changes drastically. A new set of skills is required, including facilitation, resource acquisition, information sharing, supporting and problem-solving.

Kaplan and Murdock (1991) suggested that re-engineering makes considerable demands of leaders. It begins with a clarification and assessment of the organisation's context. The organisation's strategy and vision will determine the focus of the re-engineering and will highlight the business processes that are imperative for high business performance. Leaders are required to rethink the ways in which work is done. Organisations which initiate re-engineering activities will create cross-functional teams to analyse core business processes, define performance objectives and design new processes. The teams proceed on the basis that all processes must address the needs of customers. They must not be constrained by past practice, make the assumption that work gets done right the first time, focus on both technical and social aspects of processes, and simplify processes by combining or eliminating steps. Re-engineering initiatives can help organisations clarify their function and vision, engender top management involvement and commitment and help in sharing learning, and can contribute to organisational learning as well as leader development.

Conclusion

Organisations increasingly face challenging issues that demand that they think differently about leadership development. Learning is viewed as a contextualised idea which cannot be separated from work. Leadership development takes place in context and therefore collective approaches to leadership development have become more prominent in the academic context, if less so in practice. In this chapter, we discussed and explained various aspects of a collective leadership approach. Collective leadership approaches focus on enhancing organisational learning, enhancing connectivity between organisation members, taking a multidimensional approach to leadership and developing more inclusive leadership approaches.

Concepts such as organisational learning, the learning organisation, knowledge management and collaborative leadership provide significant challenges for leadership processes as well as opportunities to think differently about how to develop leadership capability on an organisation-wide basis.

Organisational learning environments, or learning climates, can facilitate or inhibit collective leadership development. Facilitative or positive learning environments promote teamwork, access to development opportunities, certification of learning, organisational recognition of and support for managerial careers, cross-boundary collaboration and the promotion of risk and experimentation. Positive learning environments facilitate the integration of the individual and organisational development of leaders. Organisational development interventions that focus on organisation-wide initiatives, such as strategic planning, visioning, large group interventions and re-engineering, challenge organisational leaders to integrate leadership development into wider strategic decision-making, and to develop shared mental models and collective leadership capability.

Summary of Key Points

- Leadership has evolved from a focus on the individual to a partner who nurtures the contribution of all organisation members.
- Changing organisational conditions demand that organisations think differently about leadership. Organisations are more diverse and can no longer be managed using bureaucratic approaches.
- Formal leadership development activities that are decentralised and individualised are increasingly of less value. Leaders are required to co-construct their learning environments.
- Organisational learning requires that leaders collectively reflect on experience, that they learn with each other and that they agree on shared mental models.
- Leadership must increasingly be open to a multiplicity of interpretations and world views and all organisational members must have the capacity to lead and learn.
- A collective approach to leadership development requires strong organisational commitment, opportunities for experiential learning, teamwork, the use of learning networks and incentives for learning.

- Organisation-development interventions provide an opportunity to facilitate leadership development in the context of strategic and change initiatives. These include large group interventions, strategic planning, visioning and business process re-engineering.

■ Discussion Questions

1. How do you define 'organisational learning'? What does your definition focus on? Why is organisational learning so challenging to define?

2. Differentiate the 'learning organisation' from knowledge management. Why are they challenging to define and differentiate clearly?

3. How does organisational climate for leadership climate differ from organisational climate for learning? What impact do they potentially have on collective leadership development activities?

4. Explain how action learning can be used to develop collective leadership.

5. What is the relative importance of tacit and explicit knowledge in the context of knowledge management initiatives? What role do leadership processes have for knowledge management?

■ Application and Experiential Questions

1. Draft a set of proposals to take to top management on how to build a learning environment that will be conducive to collective leadership development. Propose specific actions to ensure that managers identify opportunities for collective leadership.

2. Your organisation has decided to launch a knowledge management initiative. As a leadership development specialist, outline the kinds of leadership development policies and practices that you feel are essential to sustain the knowledge management initiative.

3. In teams of three, reflect on your organisation or select one from the business literature. Refer to the various characteristics and definitions of a learning organisation set out in this chapter and consider whether the organisation is a learning organisation. What critical success factors make it a learning organisation? What changes would you make to enhance learning in the organisation?

Chapter Seventeen

Developing Leaders for International and Global Roles

Outline

OPENING CASE SCENARIO

Developing a Global Virtual Learning and Development Team within Hewlett Packard

Hewlett Packard (HP) provides technology solutions to customers, businesses and institutions globally. Its offerings are spread across information technology (IT), infrastructure, personal computing and access devices, consulting services and imaging and printing. HP's products include desktops and workstations, notebooks and tablet personal computers, printing and multifunction and other related devices. HP organises its operations into five key business areas: imaging and printing; personal systems; enterprise storage and services; HP services and HP financial services; software and corporate investment. The imaging segment offers imaging and printing systems for printer and scanning devices. The personal systems segment focuses on commercial personal computers, consumer PCs, workstations, hand-held computing devices, digital entertainment systems and other accessories. The enterprise storage and services segment focuses on both low-end servers and high-end scalable servers. The HP services segment provides a portfolio of seventeen multi-vendor services, including technology services, consulting services and integration and managed services. The financial services segment offers financial services to support HP product and service solutions. The software segment provides management software solutions, and the corporate investments segment includes HP labs and business invention projects.

HP has a strong corporate culture and a core set of business objectives that focus on customer loyalty, profit, market leadership and growth, employee commitment, leadership capability and global citizenship. HP places a strong value on ensuring that employees share in the company's success. Employment opportunities are based on performance. This performance starts with motivated employees. Their loyalty to the company is considered to be paramount. The corporate culture places strong trust in employees and believes that everyone has something to contribute. The culture emphasises diversity, a safe and exciting work environment and placing responsibility for lifelong learning on employees. HP places particular emphasis on the development of leaders at every level in the organisation. Leaders are accountable for the exemplification of core values and the achievement of business results. HP has a unique philosophy on the role of leaders. Leaders are expected to inspire, foster collaboration and turn vision into strategy, to be effective coaches, to demonstrate strong self-awareness, accept feedback, and continually develop. They speak with one voice and they are expected to measure people on the results they achieve against goals.

HP is a global company which places a strong emphasis on managing virtually and developing virtual teams. Virtual teams provide HP with the possibility of leveraging expertise globally, eliminating duplication and overlap, driving standard process and achieving cost savings, drawing higher levels of innovation and leveraging diversity, accelerating the implementation of change and the centralisation of infrastructure to ensure maximum business impact. There is a concerted drive to move to a strategic investment model rather than focus on local affordability.

The P6 supply chain and manufacturing workforce development (WD) team focuses on development issues, programme consulting and performance improvement consulting for 8,000 employees worldwide. The virtual team is led by an Irish manager. It provides over 380 learning solutions and ensures that training and development solutions are leveraged on a global basis. This team was established in 2001. Over a period of five years, it had a very significant impact on workforce development within HP. The organisation moved from having six independent site training organisations to one global workforce development team. Similarly, it moved from having six local learning models, driven by local needs and affordability, to a worldwide training and investment plan, driven by the organisation's business strategy and targeted towards ROI. This resulted in the reduction of the number of learning solutions from over 800 to one single global portfolio, with 350 learning solutions. It also resulted in a single systematic training methodology rather than six different approaches and sets of practice. Prior to the creation of the team, the organisation had multiple vendors with different costs and local-only contracts. Now there is a single global vendor base which allows global leverage and has, in turn, driven down training costs. This has had a major impact on the careers of training and development professionals, who are now part of a global job family which provides greater opportunities for development, career advancement and broadening of job scope. It is also possible to have global calibration of performance, to recognise top talent and reward high performers. The move to becoming a global virtual workforce development team has brought about a significant improvement in business partner satisfaction, a rationalisation of the training investment budget to ensure better spend, a reduction of the headcount from thirty-seven to twenty-two, and sustainment of the number of training days delivered.

Training and development specialists have been challenged by the move to a virtual team, but they have benefited in a number of specific ways. They have gained new skill sets that are not restricted by local use. They have a much broader perspective and knowledge of the business. There is increased communication between specialists and greater sharing of knowledge. It has also provided specialists with greater opportunities to specialise and grow careers in the learning and development profession, and opportunities to lead or participate in global programmes. It has challenged specialists to develop and enhance their teamworking and technology skills. They are required to communicate more frequently and use email effectively. They have to be more flexible in terms of time and approach to assignments and they are expected to leverage their expert knowledge and apply it across boundaries. In some cases, specialists have been challenged to take risks to solve problems and add value to manage ambiguity, while at the same time achieving significant stretch goals.

Cultural awareness and trust have emerged as two important dimensions facilitating the work of the development team. Specialists have had to realise that cultural stereotypes are problematic and should not be relied upon. They have had to talk to people in other locations in order to understand their culture and to show respect for core rules of the national culture. A significant element of learning has involved recognition that when an initiative is not going to plan, it is most likely because the specialist is doing something that is not aligned with the culture. Trust is an important component of an effective work relationship. Specialists have had to become familiar with each other's competence and unique personal attributes. They have had to spend time working on relationships, and have had to take account of difference and understand that it can add value to the business.

The workforce development team within HP has significantly altered the way in which development is undertaken, the resource base required to achieve objectives and the competencies and skills of learning and development professionals. It has increasingly emphasised the role of technology in connecting the team, the importance of cultural learning, and the leadership development capability required of the managers of virtual teams.

QUESTIONS

Q.1 **What do you see as the main challenges in establishing a global virtual learning team?**

Q.2 **What skills are required of management and leadership development specialists who work in a global virtual environment?**

Organisations are increasingly challenged to develop leadership talent for international and global roles. The entire landscape of how international organisations operate has changed and this, in turn, has changed the role of the international manager. The international manager is no longer synonymous with the expatriate manager. This is not to say that the expatriate manager assignment no longer exists. Organisations are increasingly faced with challenges in persuading dual-career couples to relocate and have to consider alternative international manager assignments such as 'commuter assignments' and 'virtual assignments'. Research indicates that the development of leaders for global roles is one of the most significant issues in explaining the effectiveness of the multinational corporation. To remain competitive, companies must continually develop their leaders to be successful in global tasks and activities. Both academics and practitioners are increasingly focused on the challenges that leadership development poses for global organisations. The goal of this chapter is to provide an overview of the issues involved in developing global leaders.

In this chapter, we distinguish between the roles of the expatriate, the international manager and the global manager. There are aspects of these roles that are similar, but the global manager's role is complex; managing across multiple time zones, country infrastructures, and cultural expectations, whilst co-ordinating performance results, business knowledge and technological advances. The global manager requires a very specific set of competencies, including the ability to develop a global mindset. To use a popular phrase, he/she needs to think global and act local. An expatriate manager assignment, in contrast, may represent the first step to a global management career.

We explore the various ways in which organisations can develop a global management cadre. To do this successfully, organisations need to formulate their own international management development strategies based on their unique requirements. This involves deciding on the set of international leadership competencies that drives their recruitment, selection, reward and development processes. We discuss the vital role of training before, during and after international assignments. This chapter concludes with practice recommendations for the effective development of international managers.

The Emergence of the Global Organisation

The term 'global organisation' increased in popularity in the nineties, with CEOs of multinational corporations (MNCs) declaring that their organisations were global. There is much debate concerning what constitutes a global organisation. However, there is general agreement that an organisation moves through distinct stages as it becomes global. The four key phases are illustrated in Table 17.1.

Table 17.1: Globalisation and Human Resource Management Issues

	Phase I Domestic	Phase II International	Phase III Multinational	Phase IV Global
Primary orientation	Product or service	Market	Price	Strategy
Strategy	Domestic	Multidomestic	Multinational	Global
Worldwide strategy	Allow foreign clients to buy product/service	Increase market internationally, transfer technology abroad	Sourced, produced and marketed internationally	Gain global strategic competitive advantage
Staffing expatriates	None (few)	Many	Some	Many
Why sent		To sell, control or transfer technology	Control	Coordination and integration
Who sent		OK performers, salespeople	Very good performers	High-potential managers and top executives
Purpose	Reward	Project 'to get job done'	Project and career development	Essential for executive suite
Career Impact	Negative	Bad for domestic career	Important for global career	Essential for executive suite

	Phase I Domestic	Phase II International	Phase III Multinational	Phase IV Global
Professional re-entry	Somewhat difficult	Extremely difficult	Less difficult	Professionally easy
Training and development	None	Limited	Longer	Continuous throughout career
For whom	No one	Expatriates	Expatriates	Managers
Performance appraisal	Corporate bottom line	Subsidiary bottom line	Corporate bottom line	Strategic positioning
Motivation assumption	Money motivates	Money and adventure	Challenge and opportunity	Challenge, opportunity, advancement
Rewarding	Extra money to compensate for foreign hardship		Less generous, global packages	
Career fast track	Domestic	Domestic	Token international	Global
Executive passport	Home country	Home country	Home country, token foreigners	Multinational
Necessary skills	Technical and managerial	Plus cultural adaptation	Plus recognising cultural differences	Plus cross-cultural interaction, influence and synergy

Source: Adler and Ghadar (1990).

Adler and Ghadar (1990) illustrated how an organisation's strategy towards human resource management, in a global organisation, evolves in line with the product life-cycle. As the organisation moves along the continuum from domestic to global, there is a corresponding increase in the complexity of its human resource management and leadership development systems, structure and strategy.

- *Phase 1 - Domestic*: The primary emphasis of this phase is on the home market. The products and services are unique, competition is minimal and therefore the product pricing is high relative to cost. The worldwide strategy is to allow the product/service to be sold outside the domestic market, without adaptation. HR systems are not demanding in international terms.
- *Phase 2 – International*: Competition increases in relation to the product or service offering and the international markets become more critical for profit generation. The focus changes from domestic product development (R&D) to either exporting or developing assembly and production facilities in global markets. The development of cultural sensitivity is imperative in terms of the organisation being able to implement corporate strategies. However, control and decision-making will tend to stay with the parent company. At this stage of the organisation's development, HR plays a critical role in managing local operations. Home country managers/employees are used to transfer their technology and management systems into other countries. However, the impact on a home country manager's career of taking up a long-term international role can be negative.

- *Phase 3 – Multinational*: The primary strategic orientation for this phase of the organisation's development is price. The product or service offering has reached maturity and competition abounds. Domestic and global operations are integrated into worldwide lines of business, and services and products are largely standardised. At this stage, strong organisational performers are selected for international roles in order to reduce costs and increase profits. The role that these individuals play in the organisation is valued and it is easier for them to repatriate on successful completion of assignment. International experience is recognised in terms of the individual's potential global career. As the organisation's culture is seen as more important than national culture at this stage, selection of international managers tends to be biased towards those who are familiar with the parent culture.
- *Phase 4 – Global*: A key characteristic of this phase is that global organisations operate across national boundaries, simultaneously achieving global integration while retaining local differentiation (Bartlett and Ghoshal 1989). In order to achieve global integration, systems, structure and strategy must be determined by the task. It follows, therefore, that some of the organisation's activities will be organised geographically, some by function and others by product line. Domestic and foreign operations are integrated into worldwide lines of business and products are mass-customised for local markets. According to Adler and Ghadar (1990:240), this requires the organisation to build 'complex networks of joint ventures, wholly owned subsidiaries and organisational and project defined alliances.' This is the type of organisation that requires sophisticated global leaders.

This model is criticised because it emphasises the role of the expatriate manager, and management expertise in general, to the detriment of other employee groupings. Milliman and Von Glinow (1990:28) also criticised its narrow emphasis, as they perceived it, on the product life-cycle of the organisation as the key strategic dimension. They highlighted the importance of defining the nature of international HRM vis-à-vis the inter-relationships between the parent and subsidiary as follows: 'The degree to which the corporate business and human resource strategies affect the SBU's [Strategic Business Unit] strategic choices and practices depends on a number of fundamental characteristics of the MNC, such as its organisational culture, management style, and control systems.'

The global strategy (Phase IV), as already described, can also be referred to as a transnational strategy. Deresky (2006:292) states that the transnational strategy is 'to maximise opportunities for both efficiency and local responsiveness by adopting a transnational structure that uses alliances, networks, and horizontal design formats'. Operating in this type of complex, interdependent global environment can be very challenging for managers/leaders.

Edwards and Rees (2006) propose four forms of strategy and structure relationship in international firms: the multinational form (a decentralised federation); the global form (a centralised hub); the international form (a co-ordinated federation); and the transnational form (an integrated network). Table 17.2 summarises the implications of these forms for human resource management and leadership development.

Table 17.2: International Forms and their HR and Leadership Development Implications

Edwards and Rees (2006)	Multinational Form	Global Form	International Form	Transnational Form
Description	Collection of national companies that manage their local businesses with minimal direction from headquarters.	Creation of 'mini-replicas' of home-country operations. Foreign units are closely modelled on domestic ones. Standardised products are produced in a highly efficient way.	This strategy is based mainly on transferring and adapting the parent company's knowledge or expertise to foreign markets. Less centralised than global firms since local management can vary nature of products/services to the national market.	Manages the simultaneous pressures of: being locally responsive, achieving efficiency through a global scale and sharing innovation and learning across sites. This strategy involves the creation of an integrated network with large flows of people, resources and knowledge across interdependent units.
HR and Leadership Development Implications	• Very little influence on people practices from HQ • Strategic decisions decentralised • Unlikely to be a large number of expatriate managers • Little requirement for knowledge and expertise to be diffused across borders	• Key positions in subsidiaries are filled by parent country nationals (i.e. expatriates). • Distinctive parent company approach to HRM. • Strategic decisions are centralised. • The parent company has a high degree of control over the subsidiaries' operations.	• Strategic decisions are guided by the centre. • Medium operational controls. • Managers at local level are responsible for ensuring that the knowledge transferred from the centre is harnessed and deployed.	• International assignees will not originate from parent company alone, i.e. best person selected for the job. • Best practice is shared and implemented across the globe, regardless of where it originates. • High cadre of managers roaming from site to site, sharing knowledge and expertise.
Classification of mindsets	Polycentric mindset: focus on the host country's values and ways of operating.	Ethnocentric mindset: focus on home country values and ways of operating.	Hybrid of polycentric and ethnocentric	Geocentric mindset: global values and ways of operating.

Source: Edwards and Rees (2006:70–6)

Edwards and Rees's description of the global form as a centralised hub would not mirror the common understanding of or references to the successful global organisation today. The transnational form, as described by Edwards and Rees, is the one that most global organisations aspire to achieve. In this chapter, we use the terms global organisation and transnational organisation interchangeably to mean the following:

> *A global/transnational organisation operates across national boundaries, simultaneously achieving global integration while retaining local differentiation. The organisation is aligned along three broad dimensions: strategy and structure, corporate culture and people. Best practice is shared and implemented across the globe, regardless of where it originates. In this way, the organisation achieves global competitive advantage.*

Suutari (2002) argued that being global is not just about operating around the world. It also involves being able to integrate and act as a co-ordinated network; the organisation must have resources that flow through the business; it must be able to leverage in order to eradicate unnecessary duplication; and it must balance local repressiveness with global repressiveness. It needs to think local and act global. This complex process requires considerable leadership capability. It makes significant demands on global leaders to manage complexity, change and be effective in ambiguous global environments. Bartlett and Ghoshal (2003) indicated that global leaders respond to this complexity by conceiving strategies on a global basis, expanding business into corporate markets and managing and motivating geographically dispersed and diverse teams. These demands pose significant challenges for the development of leadership competencies.

Defining Expatriate, International and Global Managerial Roles

We focus here on distinguishing between the roles of expatriate, international and global managers in an international context. These terms are frequently used interchangeably. Organisations typically create these positions for three key reasons:

- *Position Filling.* The organisation has a managerial need at a particular level and will either identify a suitable candidate locally or transfer in a suitable manager (expatriate).
- *Leadership Development.* Managers can be transferred to another part of the organisation for learning and development purposes as part of an overall career development plan. This offers the manager and the organisation the opportunity to develop international management expertise.
- *Organisation Development.* Managers are transferred so that the company can meet its strategic objectives, i.e. need for control, transfer of skills and knowledge or company values and practices.

The reasons for international assignments will vary, depending on the manager and the organisation. Dowling and Welch (2004) suggested that managers may participate in international assignments for a varying length of time. Assignments may be short-term or extended, usually up to one year, or long-term assignments of one year or more. The longer-term assignments will usually involve a specific managerial role. Dowling and Welch define this as the traditional expatriate assignment. They also identify a number of standard international assignments. These may involve any one of the following types:

- *Commuter Assignments*: Manager commutes from home country on a weekly or bi-weekly basis to their place of work in another country.

- *Rotational Assignments*: Manager commutes from the home country to a place of work in another country for a short, set timeframe followed by a break in the home country (e.g. oil rigs).
- *Contractual Assignments*: Manager with specific skills vital to an international project is assigned to the project for a limited duration, e.g. six to twelve months.
- *Virtual Assignments*: Manager manages from home base and has international responsibilities for a part of the organisation in another country, as opposed to relocating to host location.

The duration and purpose of the assignment will determine the various roles played by the manager.

The Expatriate Manager

The traditional expatriate role tended to serve the organisation's needs in terms of position-filling. Significantly, the expatriate manager is based in the host country for a specified period. Dowling and Welch (2004) suggested that this manager can perform a number of roles. These include the following:

- *Agent of Direct Control*: The primary role for the expatriate manager can be that of ensuring compliance through direct supervision of employees in host country.
- *Agent of Socialisation*: This role is related to the use of the corporate culture as an informal control mechanism. Companies hold an implicit expectation that expatriate managers will facilitate the transfer of parent company values and beliefs.
- *Network Builder*: International assignments are an opportunity for the individual to foster international networks and contacts that can be used for informal control and communication purposes. The duration of the assignment will affect the strength of the network developed.
- *Boundary Spanner*: The expatriate manager can engage in activities that bridge internal and external organisational contexts. Expatriates can collect host country information, act as representatives of their organisations in that country and influence external agents.
- *Language Node*: An expatriate manager who has spent time in a foreign location and has learned some of the host language may be used by his/her colleagues on return to home base as a communicator with others in the corporation.
- *Transfer of Competence of Knowledge*: Dowling and Welch (2004) highlighted that there are obvious elements of competence and knowledge transfer in all the roles they identified for expatriates.

Organisations typically have high expectations that the expatriate manager will deliver. This is usually the first step in the manager's international career. Adler and Bartholemew (1992) highlighted the key differences between the expatriate manager and the international and global/transnational manager (Table 17.3). The key point to make is that the expatriate manager is concerned with a single foreign country and is usually managing the relationship between the home country headquarters and the host country. It is a less complex role than that of the international or global manager. The expatriate manager adjusts to residence in the host country, but only focuses on learning about a single culture. The role of the expatriate manager is to successfully carry out the assignment on behalf of the corporation.

Table 17.3: Comparison between Expatriate, International and Global/Transnational Manager Roles

	Expatriate Manager	International Manager	Global/Transnational Manager
Increasing Levels of Role Complexity ⟶			
Global Perspective	Concerned with a single foreign country and on managing the relationship between home country headquarters and host country. Based in host country for a specified period.	Concerned with an understanding of the international business environment. Responsible for a number of countries; may be based at home country headquarters with requirement for international travel. This person may also be based in a host country.	Concerned with the understanding of the transnational business environment, with a global mindset. This person can be based in any company location and his/her job will involve a lot of travel.
Local Responsiveness	Gains extensive knowledge relating to one cultural environment	Acquires understanding of a few cultures	Acquires understanding of numerous cultures
Synergistic Learning	Learns from and works within one single culture at a time	Learns from and works within a few cultures at a time	Learns from and works within many cultures simultaneously
Adjustment to Culture	Adjusts to residence in host culture	Adjusts to various cultures as required for the role	Adjusts to living across numerous cultures and nations
Cross-Cultural Interaction	Cross-cultural interaction with host-country nationals through skills developed in expatriate training	Use of cross-cultural interaction skills pertinent to international role	Use of cross-cultural interaction skills continually throughout his/her career
Collaboration	Interaction with foreign (host country) personnel within specific hierarchical boundaries	Interaction with foreign colleagues as equals	Interaction with foreign colleagues as equals
Foreign Experience	Role as an expatriate is to carry out the necessary assignment successfully on behalf of his/her company	International role used to develop future global managers as well as fulfilling organisational requirement	Role as a global manager for both career and organisational development

Source: Adapted from Adler and Bartholomew (1992)

The International Manager

We have made the distinction between the international manager and the global manager. The international manager was not originally included in Adler and Bartholomew's model (1992). In our experience, this reflects practice in a number of multinational corporations.

The international manager is concerned with an understanding of the international business environment. He or she is responsible for a number of countries and may either be based at home country headquarters with requirement for international travel, or in a host country. The key difference between the international manager and the global manager is that the latter has developed a global mindset and is operating at a much higher strategic level, i.e. he/she can work effectively across organisational, functional, geographic and cross-cultural boundaries. Global managers value sharing knowledge, information and experience and can balance competing country, business and functional priorities. Pucik (1998:41) suggested that 'the definition of an expatriate/international manager is linked to the location of the assignment, whereas the global manager is defined by his or her frame of mind'.

Pucik (1998) used the terms 'expatriate manager' and 'international manager' interchangeably, but we distinguish between them. Dowling and Welch (2004) defined an expatriate manager as one who is transferred from a home base to some part of the firm's international operations. In contrast, an international manager might not be transferred out of the home base.

Sparrow (1999) offered an interesting typology:

- The home-based manager who has a central focus on different markets and players; a multicultural team that works on a series of international projects;
- Internationally mobile managers who undertake frequent but short visits to numerous overseas locations while remaining loyal to the parent culture;
- Specialist management roles that involve international activity or transfer of knowledge (e.g. sales, training, buying, engineering);
- Expatriates who carry the parent organisational culture, but who undertake lengthy assignments representing the parent in a limited number of host countries;
- Transitional managers who move across borders on behalf of the organisation, but are relatively detached from any organisational headquarters (i.e. global managers).

The role of the international manager is therefore quite varied in terms of location and overall responsibility.

The Global Manager: Myth or Reality?

It is clear that organisations that seek to be successful on a global stage must develop leaders to take on complex global roles.

Deresky (2006) defines global management as a process of delivery strategies, designing systems and working with human resources on a global basis to ensure sustained competitive advantage.

There are many views concerning 'the global manager' and whether or not such a leader exists. Ayman, Kreicker, and Masztal (1994:64) distinguished between an international manager and a global manager as follows:

> *International refers to an exchange across nations, whereas global represents a sense of unity across multiple borders. A global orientation is represented by a more collective awareness and inclusive perspective than is international, but international may be a precursor to global.*

In contrast, Bartlett and Ghoshal (1989) proposed that a universal global manager cannot exist as the nature of global work is so complex. Supporting this view, Dowling and Welch (2004:84–5) referred to 'the myth of the global manager' by challenging four assumptions linked to this view. They argue, first, that there is not necessarily a universal approach to management. Second, it is unlikely that all managers can acquire multicultural adaptability and behaviours. Third, not all international managers share common characteristics; and fourth, there are significant impediments to mobility. We acknowledge these arguments and make the distinction that a global manager is defined by the complexity of his or her position across a number of dimensions, in contrast with a definition of global managers who all behave in the same way and possess similar traits. McCall and Hollenbeck (2002) described a global manager as one whose job is cognitively and emotionally complex; there is no single type of global executive. Deresky (2006:12–13) agrees that the role of the global leader is a multifaceted one.

> *This complex role demands a contingency approach to dynamic environments, each of which has its own unique requirements. Within the larger context of global trends and competition, the rules of the game for the global manager are set by each country: its political and economic agenda, its technological status and level of development, its regulatory environment, its comparative and competitive advantages, and its cultural norms. The astute manager will analyze the new environment, anticipate how it may affect the future of the home company, and then develop appropriate strategies and operating styles.*

Deresky (2006) suggests that the global manager's role is impacted by a multiplicity of factors, including the macro or wider environment, the host country environment and the operating environment. It is therefore appropriate to view the role of the global manager as contingent and open to a variety of influences, over some of which the manager has little control.

It is now clear that the role of the global leader is very complex and, because of this, it is more difficult to stipulate a single overarching model. Global managers have to operate across the dimensions of geographic distance, country infrastructures and various cultural expectations simultaneously. This requires flexibility, adaptability and willingness to learn on an ongoing basis.

Pucik (2003) made the point that many global managers are most likely to have performed an expatriate role at some point in their careers. Many expatriate managers do not, however, make the transition to being a successful global manager.

EXHIBIT 17.1

Perspective on Theory: Understanding the Leader's Role in an International Business Context

The Role Perspective	The role perspective considers the leader's role as the key determinant, and suggests that today's international business climate creates an organisational need for three groups of 'highly specialised yet closely linked' global leaders to manage the 'transnational' organisation. One group includes the business manager, who is needed to further the company's global scale efficiency and competitiveness. This requires the perspective to recognise opportunities and risks across national and functional boundaries. The business manager's primary goal is to capture the full benefit of integrated worldwide operations. This first group has evolved as business has shifted from an international to a global orientation where business activity in multiple countries has to be co-ordinated and controlled, for example by a global supply chain manager.

The Role Perspective	The second is the country manager, who plays a crucial role in meeting local customer needs, satisfying a host government's requirements and defending their company's market position against local and external competition. The country manager's primary responsibility is to be sensitive and responsive to the local market. Historically, the country manager – for example, Intel's country manager for China or Danone's Eastern European regional manager – was the most common cross-border assignment and is the one we know the most about.

The third is the functional manager, whose primary responsibility is to build an organisation that uses learning to create and spread innovations. This requires transferring specialised knowledge while also connecting scarce resources and capabilities across national borders. The emergence of this third group is a reflection of one of the key drivers of globalisation, the complexity of technology with which organisations now grapple – global product management or global technology management are functions representative of this role. |
| The Context-Driven Perspective | The Corporate Leadership Council's (CLC) 'new' global general manager exemplifies the context-driven perspective on cross-cultural leadership, one that emphasises the strength of the contemporary global reality. A 'new' global general manager is one with the skills and abilities needed in the global competitive environment. Specific responsibilities for new general managers include entering new markets, launching operations in new geographies, making acquisitions and alliances, managing joint ventures and stewarding new business initiatives. New general managers are responsible for driving operations along both product and geographical lines within an organisational matrix. These new global leaders' responsibilities can be for all corporate operations within a particular country or for a particular product line within a region that includes several countries. From this perspective, the nature of the job itself determines cross-cultural leadership skills, abilities and competencies that are the building blocks of organisational effectiveness. |
| The Interactive Perspective | The interactive perspective is based on a hierarchical notion of cross-cultural leadership captured in the 'mobility pyramid'. The mobility pyramid is built around the merging of the leader's ability or willingness to relocate and the organisation's need for a leader in the foreign location. Multinationals are encouraged to manage their international human resource requirements, giving consideration to employees' mobility preferences and realities and the company's needs. Five different kinds of mobility-based assignments exist: Glopats, Globals, Regionals, Mobile Local Nationals and Rooted Nationals, each with distinct geographic, cross-cultural and task considerations. *Glopats* are leaders with a world perspective, who can 'fit in' and contribute wherever the organisation operates, and are frequently on the move tackling short- and medium-term assignments. Glopats need the most sophisticated, expert cross-cultural leadership competencies, skills and abilities, which might best be referred to as transcultural. They rarely have the time or the need to master the local culture. The transcultural demands mean that Glopats must learn how to learn culture quickly. *Globals* are leaders who move around the world on medium-term assignments. Globals need advanced cross-cultural leadership proficiency, but enjoy a longer time frame than Glopats to develop proficiency in the specific local culture. *Regionals* accept short-, medium- or long-term assignments within a geographic region and/or at a regional headquarters. Regionals need |

The Interactive Perspective *contd.*	cross-cultural competence and have a long time frame to master regional cultures, one of which is usually the Regional's home culture. If they are not local, they may be mistaken for local because of their depth of localised cross-cultural knowledge and effectiveness. Regionals are capable of assuming the 'cultural mentor' role for Globals and Glopats. *Mobile Local Nationals* are functional experts and regional managers prepared for cross-border task-force membership, short-term projects and training assignments abroad. These include commuter assignments – one of the fastest growing forms of expatriate mobility in Europe. Mobile Local Nationals need both cross-cultural awareness and communication skills and virtual teaming skills, at least at the 'advanced beginner' level. *Rooted Local Nationals* are functional experts and general managers tied to their home base. Rooted Local Nationals need an awareness level of cross-cultural skills that would be characterised as a novice skill level.
The Behavioural Perspective	A behavioural perspective highlights that cultural forces influence many aspects of leadership. The GLOBE study looked at leadership by examining 'prototypical requisites for leadership positions: privileges, power and influence granted to leaders; degree to which leadership roles are filled by ascription or achievement; model leaders' behaviour patterns; preferences for an expectations of leaders; and follower and subordinate reaction to different kinds of leader behaviour.' The research identified ten culture clusters of 'culturally endorsed implicit leadership theory', leadership profiles that help delineate culture-specific boundaries of acceptable, effective leader behaviours and practices. The GLOBE researchers found that the typical American manager communicates using direct and explicit language anchored in facts, figures and rational thinking. Russian and Greek managers communicate using indirect and vague language. Facts and figures are suspect and are not taken seriously when available because they are hard to come by. Additionally, Greek managers believe effective communication is discussion and exploration of issues without any commitment or explicit results. For the Swedish manager, effective communication is in-depth dialogue that focuses on the content of the communication. Managers in the Philippines and Malaysia avoid conflict and communicate in a caring and paternalistic manner with followers. South Korean male managers believe that one-way paternalistic communication that they initiate is appropriate. The expectations of Russian, Greek, Swedish, South Korean, Filipino, or Malaysian followers of effective communications are worlds apart from the typical American communication style. Unless the American leader is sensitive to these realities and adjusts his or her style, miscommunication will be the most likely outcome. There is not one single kind of cross-cultural leader; they vary in the scope of their responsibilities, the content of their work, the complexity of their work, the location of their work, their willingness and ability to travel globally, the expectations of their followers, their emotional maturity, their career stage, and their own developmental needs. Cross-cultural leaders cross cultures and contexts regularly in their work; they must be able to manoeuvre across these multiple boundaries that are fraught with multiple local expectations, and their reflective capacity enhances the ability to do this well.

Key Competencies of International and Global Managers

Caligiuri (2006) suggests that international and global managers have to perform ten key tasks. These tasks have important implications for their personality, knowledge, skills, abilities and competencies (Table 17.4).

There is a strong body of research concerning the competencies that international and global managers should possess. Schneider and Barsoux (2003) suggested that international managers need competencies for managing differences both abroad and at home (Table 17.4).

Table 17.4: Tasks and Competencies of International and Global Managers

Global Leaders do the following:
- work with colleagues from other countries
- Global leaders interact with external clients from other countries
- Global leaders interact with internal clients from other countries
- Global leaders may need to speak in a language other than their mother tongue at work
- Global leaders supervise employees who are of different nationalities
- Global leaders develop a strategic business plan on a worldwide basis for their unit
- Global leaders manage a budget on a worldwide basis for their unit
- Global leaders negotiate in other countries or with people from other countries
- Global leaders manage foreign suppliers or vendors
- Global leaders manage risk on a worldwide basis for their unit

Competencies for Managing Differences Abroad (Expatriates & International Managers)	Additional Competencies for Managing Differences at Home (International Managers)
<ul><li>Interpersonal skills</li><li>Linguistic ability</li><li>Motivation to live abroad</li><li>Tolerance for uncertainty and ambiguity</li><li>Flexibility</li><li>Patience and respect</li><li>Cultural empathy</li><li>Strong sense of self (or ego strength)</li><li>Sense of humour</li></ul>	<ul><li>Understand business interdependencies</li><li>Respond to multiple cultures simultaneously</li><li>Recognise the influence of culture 'at home'</li><li>Be willing to share power</li><li>Demonstrate cognitive complexity</li><li>Adopt a 'cultural-general' approach</li><li>Rapidly learn and unlearn</li></ul>

Sources: Schneider and Barsoux (2003:190–8); Caligiuri (2006)

Schneider and Barsoux (2003) also highlighted linguistic ability as a key success factor. A willingness to communicate in the other's language is more critical than actual competence in the host language. International and global managers must, as an essential requirement, simultaneously develop cultural awareness, empathy with and an ability to cope in multinational cultures. Dalton and Ernst (2004) identified five essential managerial competencies for all managers and four potential capabilities that are uniquely related to global managers. The five essential capabilities are: the ability to manage people; the ability to manage action; the ability to manage information; the ability to cope with pressure – emotional stability; and core business knowledge.

Dalton and Ernst (2004) make a very interesting distinction in relation to this set of capabilities. They report that global leaders need to play the same roles as domestic leaders (such as managing people) but the behaviours may need to be different in different settings. In other words, just because a manager is good at managing people in an Irish context he or she will not necessarily be good at managing people in the USA, unless he or she adjusts behaviours. As Dalton and Ernst stated (2004:367):

This need to do the same things in different ways can be a real source of tension for the practising manager. Managers are often promoted to complex global jobs because they are highly effective at what they do. However, without modifications for globally complex situations, the behaviours that lead to success in a domestic role will lead to failure in a global role.

The four pivotal capabilities identified by the Centre for Creative Leadership for success as a global manager are presented in Table 17.5.

Table 17.5: Pivotal Competencies for Success as a Global Leader

International Business Knowledge	• Know how business is conducted in each country and culture where the leader has responsibilities • Know employing organisation's core business and how to leverage that business across borders
Cultural Adaptability	• Act on knowledge of cultural differences • Use that knowledge to enable effective interaction with people from different cultures • Assume differences until similarity is proven
Perspective-Taking	• Take the perspective of others • See and understand the views of others of how things are and how they should be • Popular idiom: 'Walk a mile in my shoes' • Cultural empathy: knowing, understanding and acting in line with deeply held beliefs and values of cultures other than the leader's own culture
Innovation	• This is the most crucial of the pivotal capabilities • It is about going beyond managing the complexity of a global role to turning that complexity into an advantage, e.g. taking the best of two or more cultures and creating a new policy, procedure, product, service or practice.

Source: Adapted from Dalton and Ernst (2004:367–71)

Caligiuri (2006) provides a detailed conceptualisation of the knowledge, skills and abilities required by global managers as follows:

Knowledge: Caligiuri suggests that global managers need to possess culture-general knowledge, culture-specific knowledge and international business knowledge. Culture-general knowledge focuses on knowledge of the societal level, values and norms on which most cultures differ. Culture-specific knowledge includes an understanding of a given country's specific values, norms, beliefs and behaviours. International business knowledge focuses on topic-specific knowledge necessary to conduct business globally and includes such aspects as labour relations, international finance and law.

Skills and Abilities: Caligiuri suggests that skills are amenable to development but are limited by natural ability and personality. She suggests three core skills: intercultural interaction skills, foreign language skills and cognitive abilities. Intercultural skills focus on foreign negotiation skills and skills in cross-national conflict resolution. Foreign language skills refer to competence in a given language. Cognitive abilities include problem-solving and the ability to perceive and interpret behaviours across different cultural contexts.

Some competencies suggested by the various researchers are easier to develop than others. The extent to which they can be developed depends on the openness of the leader, his or her abilities and the nature and extent of the organisation's leadership development activities.

Issues in Developing a Global Management Cadre

The development of a global management cadre focuses on enhancing the organisational competence of managers to perform international roles and contribute to the strategic success of the corporation. In order to accomplish this task, organisations need to formulate an international leadership development strategy, appropriately select managers for internal assignments, and devise systems to manage expatriate managers.

Formulating an International Management and Leadership Development Strategy

The CIPD (2005) argue that each organisation must develop its own unique approach to developing an international or global management cadre. The approach taken will depend on a number of factors, such as:

- *The Level of Senior Management Involvement* in developing and delivering on the IMD strategy. The more involvement by the CEO and the senior team, the better the talent pool will be.
- *Alignment with Global Strategy* – The business requirements will strongly shape the IMD strategy, whether that is headquarters-oriented or globally-oriented.
- *HR and Line Capabilities* – A strong HR capability is required to lead the design and implementation of leadership competencies, selection procedures and learning interventions and to put developmental relationships in place (coaching and mentoring). Line managers also need strong capabilities in identifying and nurturing talent and to think beyond their own current resourcing requirements.
- *Talent Management* – The IMD strategy needs to be part of a wider talent-management strategy. Organisations need to consider the balance that they will require between home-grown and acquired talent in creating their senior management team.

Other critical success factors for an organisation in defining a global leadership development strategy include:

- Defining a set of international leadership competencies (organisation-specific)
- Using an international competency framework that is integrated into recruitment and selection, reward and development processes across all global business units
- Planning diversity in leadership teams
- Planning development interventions
- Evaluating the IMD strategy and its implementation.

In defining the IMD strategy for an organisation, it is useful for leadership development specialists to be aware of the extent to which such practices should reflect the country of origin, the countries of operation (host countries) or a combination of both. Ferner, Quintanilla and Varul (2001) found that German MNCs adopted 'Anglo-Saxon-style' human-resource practices as opposed to a completely Germanic model. For example, these MNCs engaged in international management development, adopted global performance management systems and used culture as a formal tool. However, some distinctly German HR practices remained, e.g. policies were developed systematically in great detail. Schneider and Barsoux made the point that there needs to be a discussion on how much similarity or variation is necessary when IMD strategies and policies are being developed.

Selection of Managers for International Assignments

This is an obvious point, but it is one worth making: it is vital to select the right managers for international assignments in the first place. Dowling and Welch (2004) suggested that this process is sometimes conducted in an ad hoc manner. Harris and Brewster (1999) called the approach to international selection the 'coffee-machine system'. They suggest that the selection process can begin in an informal way around the coffee machine (or water cooler), which is very worrying considering the frequency of expatriate manager failure.

Dalton and Ernst (2004:372) highlighted personality factors that should be assessed for global leaders, because they have learned that 'certain personality traits are covariant with certain pivotal capabilities'. For example, they found a statistically significant relationship between high emotional stability and high capability in terms of international business knowledge and cultural adaptability. They stressed that the purpose of personality assessment is to flag the potential global leader in terms of which pivotal capabilities (a) he or she needs to work on, or (b) the organisation need to hire into the team. They do not expect a global leader to master all the pivotal capabilities.

Caligiuri (2006) highlighted five personality traits of effective global leaders:

- *Extroversion*: Global leadership tasks have a major social component. Extroverts have a greater natural ease and are more effective at interacting with people from different cultures.
- *Agreeableness*: She argues that leaders who deal with conflict in a collaborative manner, are less competitive and strive for mutual understanding are more effective at cultural adjustment and are likely to be more effective global leaders.
- *Conscientiousness*: Managers who are more conscientious will demonstrate greater effort and task commitment.
- *Emotional Maturity*: Leaders with stronger emotional maturity tend to be more successful in global roles.
- *Openness or Intellect*: The ability of the global leader to assess the social environment quickly is an important attribute of effectiveness. Individuals who are more open are more accepting of diverse cultures.

Deresky (2006) suggests that there are five main factors for success in expatriate assignments: job factors; relational dimensions such as cultural empathy and flexibility; motivational state; family situation; and language skills. She points out that the relative importance of each of these success factors is dependent on the situation. Therefore, when recruiting managers for international assignments, the organisation needs to consider such questions as:

- What are the needs of head office from the international assignee/expatriate?
- What sort of role does the international assignee need to play?
- How long will they be required for this role?
- How mobile are the candidates?

In summary, selection of a manager for a particular international assignment must be based on the particular role definition that is required of the assignee.

The Role of Country Culture in Developing International and Global Managers

Managing country culture is a process that will impact upon every international manager. We have already discussed the competencies of the international manager in terms of being able to manage effectively within and across various cultures. The international and global manager, and potentially his/her family, must also manage the feeling of 'culture shock'. This is a state of disorientation and apprehension about not knowing how to behave in a new culture. The process of adjusting to a foreign culture can progress through four stages, as described by Oberg (1960):

1. *Honeymoon*: Positive attitudes and expectations; excitement and optimism prevail.
2. *Irritation and Hostility*: The crisis stage, when cultural differences result in problems at work, home and in daily living.
3. *Gradual Adjustment*: The culture begins to make sense; patterns of behaviour can be predicted.
4. *Biculturalism*: Person can operate effectively in two cultures.

Figure 17.1: Dealing with Cultural Differences

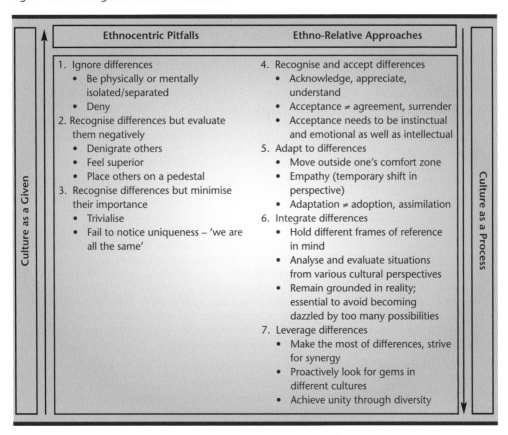

Source: Adapted from Rosinki (2003:30)

The objective of most cross-cultural training programmes for international managers is to get the managers past stage two, so that they will be able to operate effectively in the new environment. Schneider and Barsoux (2003) state that the phrase 'culture shock' is misleading as it tends to suggest a sudden impact, whereas the feeling of real frustration can result from a series of minor incidents. They also make an interesting observation that returning home from abroad can result in a greater culture shock than going away in the first place. We will return to this and how to manage this issue later in the chapter.

The international manager who wants to be successful on the global stage must deal with their own culture shock (if their job is in a new location) and become effective in dealing with cultural differences within their teams. Rosinski (2003) presents an interesting model for the development of intercultural sensitivity, based on the work of Milton Bennett (1993). This is a seven-stage model with the ultimate goal of 'leveraging cultural differences' (Figure 17.1). In some ways, this model mirrors Oberg's staged reactions to culture change. Rosinski's model is useful as a guide for the development of international managers because, to become a truly global leader, it is not enough to recognise, adapt to or integrate differences. A global leader needs to leverage differences and achieve unity through diversity.

EXHIBIT 17.2

Perspective on Practice: Enhancing the Cultural Intelligence of International Managers – Suggested Guidelines

Guideline	Implications of Guideline
Organisations should focus on a broader selection of suitability criteria	A movement away from the tendency to select solely on technical competence and thus incorporate empathy along with other interpersonal skills, which ensures the global or expatriate manager can become more integrated in the host country ethos and impose corporate culture values.
Effective use of CD-ROM programmes for interested future expatriate	These programmes aid individuals in self-learning and self-assessing, but as we see it allow individuals to self-nominate themselves for the expatriate role, which can aid problems of selection and suitability assessment for the human resource department.
The human resource department should understand the knock-on effects and culture shock that can affect the family	This would imply a package based on responding to family concerns, which would more readily meet the needs of the spouse and family and lessen family culture shock as a cause of premature expatriate return.
Language adjustment programme	Facilitation of greater opportunity to localise and gain the relevant benefits of networking and social relationships that can aid the success of the overseas assignment.
Communicate the value of the assignment and lessen the distance between the expatriate and home country	The assignee will feel a sense of value and worth and will be more closely aligned with company goals, alleviating any resentment that may be caused if they thought that the company simply wanted them out of the way. This also communicates top management support.

Guideline	Implications of Guideline
Ease of readjustment for repatriates through incorporating into their position a duty to act as a coach and give seminars on expatriation and overseas adjustment	This would meet the repatriates' need for appreciation of skill, experience and knowledge gained, while simultaneously aiding an enhanced pre-departure training scheme for future expatriates. This can be collectively beneficial for the repatriate and the organisation, as each extends their employment contract, commitment and beneficial service to the other.
Need for greater stress on the methods that enhance cultural intelligence	This implies a greater cultural awareness and interaction ability with host country manager and subordinates, thus aiding social relationships and networking, and the development of expatriate and global managers to work in foreign environments.
Do not get too consumed by the debate that mature managers are more revered than younger managers in many societies	We propose that this issue is specific to a location rather than a general finding and that selection will become more focused on taking younger managers who have few family commitments on board.
More investigation and focus should be given to the scope of broadening one's mental mind-map and thinking about others' outlooks and perspectives	Through further developing methods of mapping, bridging and integrating one can better adjust to the nuances of the host country, which can aid ability to co-operate and collaborate with foreign nationals more effectively.
Programmes should focus on improving the cognitive ability of managers (in terms of thinking about thinking, lateral thinking and thinking outside the box)	This would facilitate development of global managers through adjusting mindsets to more open-mindedness, facilitating a capacity to integrate with various cultures in a timely fashion.
Allowance of expatriates to localise	Expatriates should be given freedom to make their own way at times and to localise. If expatriates are not allowed to localise and are instead given a forum with other expatriates, it can hinder localising and adaptation as it provides a medium for complaint in relation to differences from home.
Ensure appropriate measures are taken for the repatriation process	Failure to properly deal with repatriation issues can result in future reluctance of volunteering expatriates.

Managing Expatriate Managers Effectively

Much of the existing knowledge on international and global management is derived from studies of expatriates, as this was considered the traditional international assignment. There is a vast body of knowledge available on expatriate failure and how organisations can avoid it. Expatriate failures are defined as managers who do not remain abroad for the duration of their assignment. There are some key learnings from this literature and research which can guide the development of international and global managers.

Figure 17.2: The Expatriate Manager Transition Process

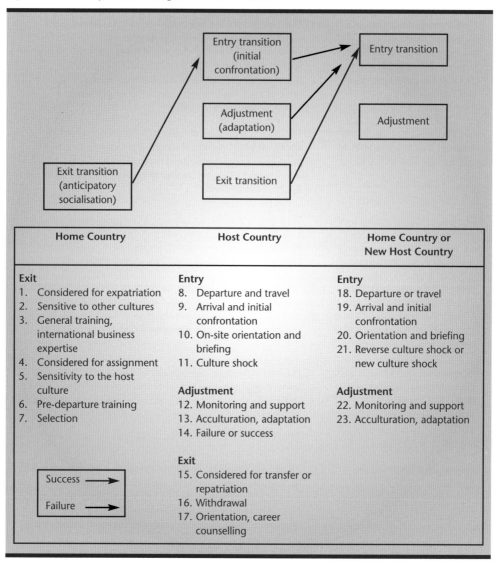

Source: Asheghian and Ebrahimi (1990:470)

Three key phases of transition and adjustment must be managed effectively in order to retain managers with increasing international experience and skills:

- *The exit transition from the home country*: The quality of preparation for exit, including training and development, is a key success factor here.
- *The entry transition to the host country*: The level of monitoring and support received will determine successful acculturation to host country (or early exit).
- *The entry transition back to the home country or to a new host country*: The preparation and support at previous stages will determine the level of reverse culture shock (return shock) and the ease of re-acculturation.

There are significant benefits to both expatriate managers and their organisations of managing this process effectively. Managers who are considering international assignments, particularly in an expatriate role (extended period), need to agree their return strategy with the organisation before they leave.

Brewster and Scullion (1997) highlighted three problems that lead to unsuccessful repatriation:

- *Loss of status*: This may arise because the expatriate returns to a position held prior to the international assignment or takes on a new position that is less prestigious than the assignment position.
- *Loss of autonomy*: International assignments will tend to give an individual a high degree of autonomy, especially if it involves heading up new operations at a distance from the parent company. This autonomy may be withdrawn when the expatriate returns home.
- *Loss of career direction*: The international experience may not be valued in career advancement terms by the parent company. The expatriate may feel frustrated that their new competencies are under-utilised by the company.

Deresky (2006) suggests that the main causes of expatriate manager failure result from: selection criteria being based on headquarters' issues, rather than the needs of the assignment; inadequate preparation, training and orientation prior to assignment; alienation or lack of support from headquarters; inability of the manager to adapt to the local culture and working environment; insufficient compensation and financial support; poor programmes for career support and repatriation; and poor family adaptation.

These difficulties suggest that a planned approach is necessary. Black and Gregersen (1992) found that companies that reported a high degree of job satisfaction and strong performance, and that experienced limited turnover, used the following practices for international assignments:

- They focused on knowledge creation and global leadership development.
- They assigned overseas posts to people whose technical skills were matched or exceeded by their cross-cultural capabilities.
- They ended expatriate assignments with a deliberate repatriation process.

Deresky (2006) suggests that organisations should 'begin with the end in mind'.

EXHIBIT 17.3

Developing Globally Responsible Managers and Leaders

The Globally Responsible Leadership Initiative argues that globally responsible leaders face four key challenges. They are expected to think and act in a global context; they should broaden their corporate purpose to reflect accountability to society across the globe; they must act ethically; and business educators and organisations should transform their education and leadership development activities to give corporate global responsibility to ensure they are at the centre.

Globally responsible leadership is defined as 'the global exercise of ethical values-based leadership in the pursuit of economic and social progress and sustainable development'. Globally responsible leadership is based on the view that the world is highly interconnected and advancement is required on three fronts: economic, societal and environmental. It demands that managers and leaders have the vision and courage to place decision-making and management practices in a global context.

Business ethics and corporate global responsibility need to be at the centre of all business decision-making. This is currently not the case, which is due to a number of barriers. Managers and leaders face increasing time constraints and are in some cases not prepared to take the perceived risks in order to be socially responsible. Managers may fear that corporate responsibility will not be rewarded. It is viewed as a cost rather than as an investment. Guiding principles that represent a starting point for the development of globally responsible leadership include fairness, freedom, honesty, transparency, responsibility and sustainability. These behaviours need to be continually refined and developed.

The Globally Responsible Leadership Initiative recognises that there is a need to broaden the purpose of corporations. It argues that while profitability is a necessary goal, it is not sufficient: there is also a need for accountability to the needs of society. Corporations are value-creation entities in society and they provide employment, growth and healthy work conditions. However, they also contribute to corruption and environmental degradation. Leadership development has a major role to play in nurturing and developing desired leadership behaviours. It can contribute to:

- Transforming the culture of the organisation by changing attitudes and behaviours
- Understanding the purpose of change
- Designing change management processes
- Rewarding globally responsible behaviour
- Developing stakeholder engagement skills such as careful listening and the ability to engage in dialogue
- Tuning into the societal and environmental business context.

Leadership development and business education needs to be transferred. There is a prevailing view that much development and education does not prepare managers and leaders to handle fraud and mismanagement. Business ethics is not considered a core component of development and education. The initiative argues that globally responsible behaviour must be internalised in the conduct and activities of the organisation. Development and education initiatives for managers and leaders need to broaden their agenda to reflect a global business environment.

Six key issues are highlighted as key learning needs for globally responsible leaders:

- Skills in the analysis of political, social, intellectual, technological and environment trends
- Skills in the analysis of ethical codes and understanding of how to successfully implement organisational ethical codes and principles
- The development of key personal skills such as integrity, empathy, compassion, dialogue and self-awareness
- Enhancement of cross-cultural understanding and language skills
- Understanding sustainable business practices
- Understanding social and environmental accounting and reporting.

The Globally Responsible Leadership Initiative acknowledges that it does not have the answers; however, it seeks to create a situation whereby managers and leaders have the courage to question and change how things are done. Globally responsible leadership is viewed as a process which is 'participative, iterative and inclusive, open to all concerned stakeholders'.

Source: European Foundation for Management Development (2005)

Development Interventions for International and Global Managers

Organisations have a number of decisions to make concerning the types of development assignments to use to develop global managers. These include, but are not confined to, the following: How can the development assignment be used as a developmental tool? What other types of international development experiences can be used? What types of training and development interventions are appropriate to prepare managers for international assignments, for when they arrive on the assignment and for effective repatriation? We will explore these issues in the following sections.

Using International Assignments as a Development Tool

Schneider and Barsoux (2003) suggested that an early international assignment can be used to develop potential international managers. Early challenges and varied international experiences can help to develop cultural sensitivity and a flexible mindset.

An international assignment allows a manager the opportunity to learn what he/she does not know, increase his/her self-awareness and interpersonal skills and learn to take the perspectives of others on board. Oddou, Mendenhall and Ritchie (2000:160) explained that international assignments help individuals 'to learn in-depth the international operation, understand the links between domestic and international operations, better manage diversity, and develop other personal and managerial abilities'. They provide an opportunity to share learnings from abroad when the manager returns.

EXHIBIT 17.4

Possible International Development Experiences for Managers

- *Short-Term International Travel*: This gives an individual an appreciation of cultural differences within a business context. An early appreciation of how business works in various countries can be very useful in building up a global mindset.
- *Working as a Member of a Cross-Cultural Team*: This can give an individual a very good insight into the complexities of managing a global workforce. For example, there can be real challenges in arranging teleconferences across time boundaries and competing priorities.
- *Managing a Major Multi-Country Project*: This type of project provides an individual with an opportunity to work across multiple countries, cultures and distances. There is an excellent learning opportunity in terms of managing virtual teams.
- *Assignments with Regional Responsibilities*: Regional assignments tend to be in a functional area such as sales, human resources or finance. They will involve working simultaneously in more than one culture such as the Middle East or Europe or the Americas. This is a great learning channel in terms of managing cultural differences, local laws and regulations and global company objectives.
- *Global Responsibility for a Product*: This is a complex global assignment, requiring all of the global competencies that we mentioned earlier in the chapter. The person who takes on this task needs to have a highly developed global mindset, i.e. can work effectively across organisational, functional and cross-cultural boundaries.

There is no doubt that an early international experience can have a positive impact on the individual's developing global mindset. However, there can be significant costs for organisations in adopting this approach. It needs to be planned and be part of an overall talent-management strategy. Oddou, Mendenhall and Ritchie (2000) suggested that the following are disadvantages:

- Managers frequently reject international assignments for personal reasons (e.g. fear of living overseas; educational needs; special family needs).
- Managers often reject international assignments due to dual-career issues and the perception that this experience is not valued by the organisation.
- In a prosperous economy, managers have many career options. The offer of an international assignment may cause a good manager to leave the company.
- Overseas assignments are now frequently filled by host nationals.

Development assignments should therefore be used with some caution. While returning managers report significant enhancement of skills, organisations often under-utilise their newly developed skills and activities. Organisations should consider other variants of the international assignment as a development experience (Exhibit 17.4).

Development Interventions for Use with International and Global Managers

Caligiuri, Lazarova and Tarique (2005) have categorised development interventions that are appropriate for developing international and global leaders into three types: didactic learning interventions; experiential opportunities; and intensive experiences.

Didactic Learning Opportunities: Didactic learning opportunities include cross-cultural training, diversity training and language training. Culture-specific cross-cultural training can help improve managers to behave in a more culturally appropriate manner and help managers identify suitable ways of performing their tasks with people from a given culture or a given country. General cross-cultural training may help managers to develop methods of coping with uncertainty when working with people from different cultures or in foreign countries, and may help managers form realistic expectations for their cross-national interactions and experiences.

Diversity training can facilitate the leader to cope with the tasks involving intercultural interaction. It is designed to help employees work successfully with a diverse workforce. It can help individuals become more aware of group-based differences and of negative stereotyping and prejudice. Foreign language training complements both cross-cultural training and diversity training in that it provides employees with language skills that are needed to communicate with co-workers and individuals in other countries.

Formal education programmes provide managers with foundational knowledge on cultural dimensions, project management processes and language training. They include self-study courses offered electronically, off-site courses offered by academic institutions, in-house or on-site company seminars offered by subject matter experts and company-sponsored management development programmes.

Experiential Opportunities: These opportunities are effective in developing the skills associated with global leadership tasks. Organisations use experiential opportunities, such as individualised coaching, mentoring and immersion programmes. These programmes are tailored to the individual's strengths and developmental needs for global leadership tasks and frequently provide opportunities for contact with individuals from different countries.

Some organisations offer immersion programmes in foreign cultures to help managers gain increased cultural sensitivity and cultural knowledge. They provide managers with an extensive understanding of the local culture and involve sending them to live in communities in foreign countries where they have to interact extensively with individuals from the local culture. Immersion programmes are also used to improve individuals' foreign language skills. These experiential interventions are effective for improving skills and abilities, but also tend to be cost and time intensive.

Intensive Cultural Experiences: Intensive cultural experiences are experienced by leaders while living and working in another country. They are often called 'rotational programmes', with the stated purpose of global leadership development. It is typical for managers on these programmes to spend between one and two years in a foreign country before moving to the next location. These rotational programmes are offered early in managers' careers in order to provide the manager with the knowledge, skills and abilities necessary to manage and lead successfully anywhere in the world.

Rotational assignees report that they develop an appreciation for new things, become culturally sensitive and learn to respect values and customs different from their own. They frequently report that they have developed valuable skills through their international experience, and that these newly developed skills have greatly enhanced their expertise in both the domestic and the international context.

Training and Development for International Assignments

We must emphasise that training is one fundamental part of an overall HR strategy in managing international managers. In itself, it will not guarantee success for the international assignee. A number of other factors are also at play, such as suitability for role, family factors, openness to new experiences and motivational state. However, effective training and development delivered in a timely manner can help an international assignee to prepare for each of the three stages of the appropriate transition process.

Pre-Departure Training and Development: At the pre-departure stage, the manager has been successfully selected for the new role and this role fits with the individual's and the organisation's objectives. All of the literature in this field refers to the criticality of cross-cultural awareness training and development. Caligiuri *et al.* (2001:358) stated: 'Success on a global assignment is greatly influenced by an expatriate's cross-cultural adjustment to the host country. For example, cross-cultural adjustment is positively related with performance on the assignment and negatively related to the premature termination of the assignment.' Caligiuri *et al.* state that the objectives of cross-cultural training (CCT) are threefold:

1. To help expatriates to determine apt cultural behaviours and appropriate ways of performing job-related tasks in the host country.
2. To help expatriates cope with unanticipated events in the host culture and reduce conflict/ambiguity.
3. To create reasonable expectations for expatriates with regard to living and working in the host country.

In terms of cross-cultural training, it is vital to note that 'one size will not fit all'. Black and Gregersen (1992) advised that the leadership and development specialist should assess the training needs of the expatriate and of his or her family for each global assignment in terms of the culture of the host country, the language of the host country, and the difficulty of the employee's new job.

The difficulty of the new job will be determined by rules and norms for communicating in the host country, expected frequency of the expatriate's communications with the locals, nature of the communication required by the job, and duration of the assignment. Therefore, cross-cultural training will need to be customised for each international assignment, depending on the individual manager and his/her competencies vis-à-vis the specific new role.

Mendenhall, Dunbar and Oddou (1987) developed a very useful model for cross-cultural training that takes a number of factors into account: training methods; levels of training rigour; duration of training relative to degree of interaction; and culture novelty. Obviously, for lengthy assignments (one to three years), it is worth investing in: assessment centres for selection; simulations; field trips; and in-depth language instruction. For short-term international travel (one month or less), survival-level language training and cultural briefings are more than adequate preparation.

There is widespread agreement that cross-cultural training that is customised is more effective than a generic programme (CIPD 2005). The IOMA's report (2005) on preparing expatriate employees for cross-cultural work environments recommended including the following in a training programme: basic facts about the country of assignment; behaviour modification; business etiquette; communication issues; cultural biases; increased awareness; cultural contrasts; and an individually based cultural profile.

Systematic identification of training needs is vital for pre-departure training. In the case of international assignments, the organisation needs to consider the following questions:

- What are the strategic plans for the business?
- How will the organisation manage its talent pool? What is the next role for this person?
- Which competencies are critical for international roles?
- Which specific competencies will this role require?
- What are the language and cross-cultural requirements for this role?
- What assistance will the selected assignee require in terms of new language, cross-cultural adjustment and managerial and technical skills?

Having answered these questions, the organisation can begin to set up an individualised programme. There are numerous options in terms of delivery of pre-departure training. Melkman and Trotman (2005) suggested the following: internal tailor-made course; internal standard course; external course; distance learning; e-learning; coaching/mentoring and self-study.

The approach adopted will need to suit budgets, ease of implementation, culture and trainee profiles. For example, if a manager is going to France for three years, he/she will require extensive language training (unless he/she is already a fluent French speaker). He/she will also require cross-cultural training which may be best delivered on a one to one basis with a native French person. It would not be appropriate to ask this person to attend standard language classes at a language school, which would not be customised to the business environment and the specific business need.

EXHIBIT 17.5

Developing Global Managers: The Challenge of Learning about Cultures

Nordon and Steers (2008) argue that the major challenge facing the global manager is understanding cultural differences. Different cultures represent a difficult challenge because managers tend to have preconceived notions both about the world and about how people should behave. These ideas are influenced by the manager's personal experiences and the culture in which he/she grew up. Managers approach intercultural interactions with a combination of 'perception, beliefs, values, biases and misconceptions' about what is likely to happen. As a result, when they engage with other cultures they often find that particular behaviour patterns result in unanticipated consequences. The traditional approach to global assignments has emphasised three particular development challenges: the development of cultural fluency; learning culture on the fly; and the development of a global mindset.

Cultural Fluency: Managers are generally advised to prepare for the global assignment by mastering the culture and language of the country to which they are assigned. Managers are developed to interact more effectively with people from other cultures and they may also receive training in the local language and be briefed on key features of the local culture. When managers take up global assignments they learn more about the new culture and develop mechanisms to cope with it. This approach to development is considered valuable when the manager is expected to work in a particular country for a significant period of time. It is less effective when the global manager has to do business across countries and cope with multiple cultures.

Developing a Global Mindset: The concept of a global mindset involves managers expanding their knowledge and understanding of multiple cultures. The precise level of knowledge required is difficult to specify; however, it must be adequate to enable the manager to cope with cross-cultural challenges. The content of the global mindset focuses on developing an understanding of personal and business performance issues that is not driven by the assumptions of a single culture or context. Global mindsets focus on cognitive structure, and enable the manager to possess knowledge about many cultures. This type of knowledge enables managers to use multiple cultural frameworks and recognise what is appropriate in a particular situation.

Learning Cultures on the Fly: Nordon and Steers argue that today's complex global environment demands that managers learn about culture on the fly rather than at a distance. They suggest two reasons for the 'learning on the fly' approach: inter-cultural encounters typically happen at short notice and as a result the manager is left with little time to learn about the new culture to which he/she must adapt; and many inter-cultural interactions are virtual rather than face to face. Managers must therefore learn how to learn. They are required to make sense of multiple and varied business environments.

Nordon and Steers make an important distinction between individual and interdependent learning. Individual learning focuses on the experiential learning cycle. Managers will initiate their learning process at different points in the cycle. This process does not, however, account for the essentially social nature of learning and it largely ignores the role of learning from and with others. Learning is essentially interactive and interdependent. Applied to the cultural context, intercultural interaction provides an opportunity for interdependent learning. This learning process consists of four key stages or areas of learning: negotiating identity; negotiating meaning; negotiating new rules; and negotiating new behaviours.

- *Negotiating Identity:* A manager's self-identity focuses on characteristics that are central, enduring and distinctive to that manager. The process of engaging with a new culture may lead to these assumptions, values and beliefs being questioned. Managers may find that their self-worth is challenged. Effective inter-cultural interaction requires that managers preserve their own identity while at the same time respecting and preserving the identity of the manager from the other culture. These processes require that managers develop self-awareness and empathy toward others. Self-awareness focuses on understanding who the manager is, whereas empathy focuses on the ability of the manager to identify and understand the motives and feelings of others. The development challenge is for managers to be open-minded and willing to suspend judgement.
- *Negotiating Meaning:* Meaning in this context refers to the interpretations that managers give to things. Meaning is constructed through interactions and the exchange of information. The negotiation of meaning focuses on uncovering hidden cultural assumptions and achieving an understanding of how culture shapes perceptions, assumptions, evaluations and behaviour. Managers need to engage in inquiring and advocacy in order to negotiate meaning. Inquiry focuses on the exploration and questioning of reasoning by the manager and others; advocacy focuses on expressing

and standing up for what a manager thinks and desires. These processes are, however, challenging because they involve the manager exposing him/herself and having to change his/her perceptions, and because the manager has to listen carefully. Effective negotiation of meaning places emphasis on developing learning skills in both information gathering and information analysis.

- *Negotiating New Rules:* Managers then move on to negotiate new rules that inform and guide future relationships. The development of new rules requires that managers gain learning skills in both the integration and the transformation of information. Integration of information focuses on the manager's ability to assimilate information gathered and develop a coherent theory of action. Information transformation focuses on the creation of a theory of action based on the information the manager possesses.
- *Negotiating New Behaviours:* The final stage involves the negotiation of new behaviours. This involves the development of behavioural flexibility and the ability to engage in different behaviours. Managers need to be attentive to what they and other parties are feeling during the interaction. Managers reach a high level of self-awareness.

Source: Nordon and Steers (2008)

As an organisation becomes more global, there is a greater need to develop specialists within the leadership development function who will be responsible for the development of the international managers. Much of the literature suggests that multinationals do not allow sufficient time or resources for pre-departure training (Dowling and Welch 2004; IOMA 2005).

Post-Arrival Development Programmes: It is critical to continue with development activities after the manager has taken up the international assignment. Cross-cultural training will probably be even more effective after the manager has taken up his/her post. Mendenhall and Stahl (2000) warned about the dangers of 'expatriate myths' which may form when expatriates advise each other. They recommended in-country training that responds to international assignees' specific needs and concerns in a timely manner.

There are a number of options for delivery of post-arrival training and development. One is the traditional training route of gathering all of the expatriates together at regular intervals for a set programme. Mendenhall and Stahl (2000:253) suggested that this provides them with 'more in-depth knowledge of the idiosyncrasies, complexities, and paradoxes of the host culture than was given in their pre-departure training experience'. A limitation of this approach is that everyone receives the same content, whether it is required or not.

Other options for delivery of post-arrival training and development include:

- Action learning: Assignees tackle real organisational problems that they encounter in small groups, aided by an expert learning facilitator.
- One-to-one coaching (line manager and/or external): this involves the international manager being coached on issues/challenges specific to his/her new role by his/her line manager or an external coach.
- Strategic sponsorship from home country: international assignees will perform more effectively when they know that they have not been forgotten in the home country. This vital and formal link with the home country in the form of a strategic sponsor helps the process of settling into the new role.
- Host country mentoring: it is very useful to have an assigned mentor in the host country, particularly in the early stages of the assignment.
- Team development: specific team processes can be facilitated by an external facilitator to allow maximum learning to take place. Maznevski and DiStefano (2000) summarised the critical global team processes as mapping, bridging and integrating.

- International assignee network: this can be a great support mechanism as well as a tool for peer learning. This network can be formal or informal.
- Self-training via software and the Internet: lots of products are available on the market as well as in-company software and intranets.

In our experience, a combination of methods is best for post-departure training. However, we have found that the most critical support for an international assignee is in the form of developmental relationships. Therefore, it is imperative for the organisation to set up a coach, mentor and/or sponsor for the international manager.

Repatriation Training and Development: Repatriation should be planned as part of the manager's overall career development plan. This helps to minimise the effect of reverse culture shock (shock of returning home) and avoids loss of career direction or status. Training and development for repatriation needs to be customised according to the individual's needs and the role to which he/she is returning. If it involves a promotion or moving to a new area within the company, specific knowledge training may be required.

Dowling and Welch (2004) suggested a list of topics that should be covered by a repatriation programme:

- Physical relocation and transition information
- Financial and tax assistance
- Re-entry position and career-path assistance
- Reverse culture shock (including family disorientation)
- School systems and children's education and adaptation
- Workplace changes (e.g. corporate culture and decentralisation)
- Stress management and communication-related training
- Establishing networking opportunities
- Help in forming new social contacts.

A lot of these topics are concerned with enabling the repatriated manager and his family to integrate back into the cultural and social system that they left. This underlines the fact that settling back can be challenging for repatriates and their families. If it is managed well, the company will retain the repatriate as a valued employee who has gained additional knowledge. On the other hand, if it is not carefully managed, there is a strong chance that the repatriate will leave the company or become demotivated. This is very costly for organisations in the long term.

An effective practice used in some companies is to assign the expatriate to a mentor. This is usually a person who is more senior than the expatriate in the sending work unit. The mentor can fulfil a number of functions for the organisation and the expatriate if he/she is properly briefed and/or trained. For example, the mentor can be a dialogue partner, assignment broker and role model, providing challenge and support for the expatriate. Firms in a Price Waterhouse survey (1998) described the duties of mentoring for international assignees as follows:

- Maintaining contact with the expatriate during the assignment
- Ensuring that expatriates are kept up to date with developments in the home country
- Ensuring that expatriates are retained in existing management- development programmes
- Assisting expatriates with the repatriation process, including helping them with a repatriation position.

In other words, the mentor can alleviate the perception (and sometimes reality) of 'out of sight is out of mind'. The mentor ensures that the international assignee is not forgotten when there are restructuring or promotions at base. He/she can also maintain a flow of informal communication so that there are no major surprises on re-entry.

The CIPD report on international management development (2005) highlights the following best practices regarding repatriation: pre-departure career discussions; a named contact person in the home country organisation; a mentor at the host location; re-entry counselling; family repatriation programmes; employee debriefings; and succession planning. Another useful tactic for organisations is to request that the repatriated manager mentors another international assignee. This obviously makes the repatriated manager feel that he/she is a valued resource and part of an important international management cadre. McCauley and Van Velsor (2004) highlighted a number of dimensions of development relationships in the context of the development of global leaders.

Table 17.6: The Contribution of Developmental Relationships to Global Leadership Development

Element	Role	How to Achieve in a Global Context
Assessment	Feedback Provider	• Key role here for international assignee's line manager • Feedback can be structured on an ongoing basis vis-à-vis the competencies assessed for selection for international assignment
	Sounding Board	• Line manager • Peers in host country
	Comparison Point	• Peers in host country • Successful international managers
Assessment *contd*	Feedback Interpreter	• Internal or external coach (assigned to the individual by HR) • Trusted colleague
Challenge	Dialogue Partner	• Internal or external coach • Host country or home country mentor
	Assignment Broker	• Sponsor/mentor in home country (keeping an eye on possible next assignment for individual) • Line manager
	Accountant	• Line manager and/or internal coach support achievement of development goals
	Role Model	• Successful international or global leader within the company (mentor)
Support	Counsellor/Cheerleader	• Internal or external coach helps individual to see what is making the learning difficult and boosts belief that success is possible
	Reinforcer	• Line manager gives formal rewards for progress towards goals
	Companion	• Peers on similar assignments

Source: Adapted from McCauley and Van Velsor (2004)

Key Challenges in Developing a Global Management Cadre

We focus in this final section on the issues that challenge organisations when developing a cadre of global managers. These are family issues, the issues of women in international assignments, managing genXpats and the retention of expatriate managers.

Family Issues and Global Leader Development

A growing trend over the last ten years has been increased reluctance of employees to take on expatriate assignments due to family concerns, which can include spouse's career, children's schooling or ageing parents (Expatica 2004). Interestingly, the GMAC-GRS 2005 survey cites spouse's career as the major factor in assignment refusal by managers. Another interesting trend is that nineteen per cent of employees surveyed in 2005 embarked on international assignments without their spouses or partners, compared to the historical average of fourteen per cent. Notwithstanding this factor, organisations are increasingly offering programmes and services to help ease the transition to a new location. GMAC Global Relocation Services found that forty per cent of companies surveyed offered education and training support for employees' families in 2003, compared to only fifteen per cent offering similar support in 1993 (Expatica 2004).

Even when managers overcome their family concerns and get to their new destination, sixty-seven per cent of survey respondents (GMAC 2005) reported spouse or partner dissatisfaction as the top reason for assignment failure. The worldwide increase in the number of dual-career couples is the driver of this very significant challenge for firms who require overseas assignees. If one partner accepts a traditional expatriate assignment, this has a major impact on their spouse's career (assuming that the spouse travels with their partner). A trailing spouse (as they are called in the literature) may be leaving both career and established social networks behind.

Multinationals seem to have three approaches to the dual-career issue.

- Ignore it: not very effective in the short to medium term.
- Offer alternative assignment arrangements, such as: short-term assignments; commuter assignments or 'commuter marriages'; unaccompanied assignments; business travel instead of expatriation; and virtual assignments.
- Develop family-friendly policies such as: inter-company networking (spouse can get job with another multinational); job-hunting assistance (including help with securing work permits); on-assignment career support (e.g. educational support, career counselling); and other networking opportunities.

Obviously, international organisations cannot afford to ignore the needs of the assignees' spouses. Providing support for spouses is not simply a 'nice-to-do'; it is essential for the retention of key talent within the international organisation.

Women and International Assignments

The GMAC-GRS survey 2005 reports that 'the world's expatriate workforce is becoming increasingly female. Women accounted for 23% of international assignees in 2004, the first time they have accounted for more than 20% of the total expatriate workforce'. This number will continue to increase as international experience becomes an essential criterion for career progression in global firms. According to Deresky (2006), women and minorities represent a large resource for international assignments that is under-utilised by companies. There have been many theories put forward on why that is the case. For example, Fischlmayr (2002) conducted some interesting research into the barriers to females taking international assignments and identified both external and self-established barriers (Table 17.7).

Table 17.7: Barriers to Females Taking International Assignments

External Barriers	Self-Established Barriers
• HR managers reluctant to select female candidates • Culturally tough locations or regions preclude female expatriates • Those selecting expatriates have stereotypes in their minds that influence decisions	• Some women have limited willingness to relocate • The dual-career couple • Women are often a barrier to their own careers by behaving according to gender-based role models

Source: Based on the literature reviewed in Fischlmayr (2002)

Adler (1997) made three specific recommendations for enhancing the role of women in international assignments: avoid assuming that a female executive will fail because of the way she will be received or because of problems experienced by female spouses; avoid assuming that a woman will not want to go overseas; give female managers every chance to succeed by giving them the titles, status, and recognition appropriate to the position, as well as sufficient time to be effective.

Managing GenXpats

A new term abounds in the literature to describe a particular age-group of expatriates: GenXpat. This group is defined as 'a member of Generation X, born between 1964 and 1981, who is also an expatriate or expat; that is one who decides to live and pursue a career abroad'. According to the GMAC-GRS survey (2005), in addition to the increase in female expatriates, the typical expatriate manager is also getting younger. The survey found that fifty-four per cent of expatriates in 2004 were between the ages of twenty and thirty-nine, compared to a historical average age of forty-one since the survey began in 1994. The needs of this generation have created a shift in traditional expatriate policies and procedures.

The case of Lego (the toy manufacturer) in Denmark in an interesting one. Lego started hiring more young designers from overseas for positions at their headquarters. The company needed to design a different policy from the traditional expatriate policy for these young professionals. Their package now includes tax advice for the first two years, language training, cultural awareness training and removal costs, as well as an extra month's salary at the beginning of the assignment so that these young designers can afford to rent an apartment.

In general terms, it seems that GenXpat compensation packages are less lucrative than traditional ones. This may be due to several factors, such as eagerness for international experience, less experience in negotiating and a more self-reliant attitude. This can create a win-win situation for both companies who are trying to keep international assignment costs down and individuals who want to travel. Obviously, for this generation, the training outlined in this chapter is vital. Companies may need to consider switching their investment from lucrative packages into more creative training and support for GenXpats.

Retention of Expatriate Managers

This is probably the single most challenging issue for corporations in developing their global management cadre. According to the GMAC–GRS survey (2005):

> *Retaining expatriate talent remains a considerable challenge for companies and attrition rates were at least double the rate of non-expatriate employees. While respondents reported an attrition rate of 10% among the general employee population, they indicated that 21% of expatriate employees left their companies in the midst of international assignments. Another 23%, meanwhile, left within one year of returning home from one.*

Stroh (1995) found that the best predictors of repatriate turnover were whether or not the company had a career development plan and whether the company was undergoing major change, such as downsizing. Forster (1994) highlighted five predictors for repatriation maladjustment: length of time abroad; unrealistic expectations of job opportunities in the home company; downward job mobility; reduced work status; and negative perceptions of the help and support provided by employers during and after repatriation.

The GMAC–GRS survey highlighted several explanations for the expatriate attrition rate:

- Expatriates are more marketable because of their international experience
- Expatriates find overseas compensation packages more generous than home packages and move from company to company to maintain/enhance their packages and status
- Expatriates anticipate a lack of attractive positions in the home company
- Expatriates feel out of place and dissatisfied both during and after an assignment, causing them to search for new employment.

Conclusion

The development of international and global managers is a significant challenge for international organisations. An international management and leadership development strategy should be part of an overall management and leadership development strategy within an organisation. Leading-edge global organisations have successfully integrated international leadership development with business strategies. They grow their leaders in parallel with the business. The starting point for the development of international leaders is the identification of a core set of leadership competencies with some specific competencies for global leaders. This set of competencies drives the agenda for selection, training and development, and overall remuneration.

The role of the international assignment has changed. The traditional expatriate assignment involved relocating to another country for a period up to three years. International assignments today can involve commuting (country to country on a weekly or bi-weekly basis), short-term assignments (up to six months), cross-region project work or virtual assignments. The emergence of the global manager is a recent phenomenon, leading some researchers to question whether or not such a person can exist. We highlighted key differentiating factors between the three roles of expatriate, international and global manager.

It is important that organisations invest in training and development for assignees and their families before, during and after an international assignment. Development interventions serve many purposes, including preparation for the role, minimising culture shock, increasing the probability of retaining the employee and helping the spouse and family to settle. Organisations that aspire to become global players cannot afford to ignore the development of their international management cadre. They do, however, face challenges. Women and GenXpats will have to be supported and encouraged with flexible HR policies.

Finally, organisations will have to become a lot more cognisant of not losing key managerial talent that has had excellent international experience.

Summary of Key Points

- Global management and leadership development is a vital component of implementing an effective global strategy. It is a major determinant of success or failure in international business.
- It is possible to make distinctions between the expatriate, international and global manager based on the scope and geographical spread of the role.
- Development activities play a major role in enabling the expatriate process to function.
- Expatriate failure can result from poor selection for the assignment, inadequate preparation, alienation from headquarters, poor programmes of development and career support and an inability of the manager or family to adapt.
- Organisations can use a combination of didactic, experiential and intensive development experiences.
- Organisations should have both a leadership development strategy and a plan in place for the development of international managers.
- Global leadership development activities must be integrated with performance management, succession planning and talent management processes.
- Global leadership development should be integrated with global business goals and the organisation's global human resource system.
- Organisations should approach global leadership development in a strategic and comprehensive manner.

■ Discussion Questions

1. Why should organisations invest in the development of international and global managers? What steps can organisations take to maximise the effectiveness of expatriate manager assignments?

2. What can organisations do to facilitate the repatriating of managers? How can they leverage the skills they have gained while on assignment to the benefit of. the organisation?

3. What difficulties do women encounter on international assignments? What steps can organisations take to deal with these difficulties?

4. What are the key characteristics and competencies of effective global managers? Is it possible to develop these competencies?

5. Analyse the advantages and disadvantages of using international assignments as a development tool for leaders.

■ Application and Experiential Questions

1. Interview two managers who have participated in an international assignment. Explore with the managers their experience of the working assignment and the foreign culture. How did their family adjust? How did they find the renting process and what impact has the international assignment had on the career progression of the manager?

2. Research an organisation with business operations in several countries. Find out what kinds of training, development and preparation are provided to expatriates and how the effectiveness of these initiatives are evaluated.

3. In groups of four, choose a country to research and create a cultural profile of that country. What implications do these cultural factors have for the selection and development of an international manager?

Chapter Eighteen

Management and Leadership Development: Country Comparisons and World Views

Outline

Learning Objectives

After reading this chapter you will be able to:

- Describe and evaluate the institutional approach to management and leadership development.
- Understand the role of different institutional processes in explaining management and leadership development practices in organisations.
- Describe the concept of a national management and leadership development system.
- Compare and contrast a number of different national models of management and leadership development.
- Evaluate the extent of convergence and divergence in management and leadership development practices.
- Describe management and leadership development practices in a number of developed countries.
- Define the concept of world view and explain its relevance to understanding management and leadership development practices.
- Evaluate the policy and practice implications of both institutions and world-view perspectives for management and leadership development.

OPENING CASE SCENARIO

Excellence Through People: Implementing a National Standard for Learning and Developing in Ireland

Excellence Through People (ETP) is an Irish human resource development standard designed to recognise and promote effective training and development practices, including leadership development. The standard seeks to link investment in learning and development activities with improved organisational performance. It has the potential to act as a 'significant point of leverage' in enhancing productivity and competitiveness in Irish companies. The standard is specifically focused on ensuring that organisations continually improve their approach to learning and development, that they foster development activities in accordance with business needs, and will ultimately link ETP to other awards, so Irish companies can progress towards other international awards.

The original Excellence Through People standard was implemented in 1995 and it focused on giving recognition to organisations that had achieved excellence in training, development and involvement of human resources. A revised standard was introduced in 2005. The revised standard includes eight core criteria: business planning and quality improvement; effective communication and people involvement; leadership and people management; planning of learning and development; training and lifelong learning; review of learning; recruitment and selection; and employee wellbeing. The revised standard reflects a significant change in emphasis. The original standard focused almost exclusively on training and development and human resource development. The new standard is broader in scope and focuses on wider aspects of human resource management.

The reasons why organisations seek ETP accreditation are many and varied. The standard commits organisations to a culture of continuous improvement through investment in human resources. ETP provides a framework which facilitates the development of a learning culture and nurtures employees. It may also contribute to effective diversity practices in the organisation. The standard requires that organisations create opportunities to ensure that employees fully contribute to the organisation. More fundamentally, ETP requires a direct linkage between business strategies and training plans to ensure that there is a genuine return on investment from HRD. ETP requires continuous investment in employee development, which helps to raise employee human capital levels. This investment in human capital should enable firms to achieve greater performance from their employees. ETP helps to ensure that organisations take a proactive approach to training and development and that learners have access to a diverse range of learning methods.

The process of achieving ETP accreditation is complex and involves considerable focus on and investment in resources. As a starting point, it is vital that the values inherent in the ETP award are fully understood by and have the support of all stakeholders in the organisation. Some organisations create a steering group, representing the interests of employees, and set up focus groups to elicit their views. The organisation will also have to perform an initial review to identify how far it meets the standards and to specify the gaps. Having identified the areas in which it falls short, it will then be able to devise appropriate action plans. Management buy-in and leadership from the top is vital for the accreditation to be achieved. It is likely that organisations who have experience of quality systems will have a strong foundation for the attainment of ETP. Experience suggests that where a strong commitment exists with quality certification experience, the process is easier to manage and implement. The standard seeks the interlinking of business planning, training needs analysis, identification of training needs and staff development plans as vital components of the ETP process.

The effective implementation of a plan to achieve ETP accreditation requires that organisations invest heavily in communication. There is a definite requirement for clear and consistent communication about what is required, when and by whom and, most important of all, clarity regarding who is responsible for what. The organisation will need to allocate sufficient resources to relevant personnel to ensure that they can work to plan. The size of the organisation is likely to present particular challenges. Organisations that are regionalised will probably experience problems in ensuring consistency of standards and processes. The resources required to prepare for ETP assessment will vary depending on the nature and level of adherence to existing quality and other systems that exist within the organisation. It is likely, in larger organisations, that different sections will have varying experience of quality systems and standards. This will require different levels of effort to ensure that the organisation is prepared for ETP assessment.

The results of the external assessment process can highlight areas in which organisations are less successful in meeting aspects of the standard. These might include: the lack of training specifications for training programmes, workshops and courses; the lack of defined and well-specified objectives for training programmes and courses; the lack of comprehensive, signed, training records for all trainees; the lack of follow-up procedures to ensure that the actions resulting from evaluation processes are implemented; the lack of an individual with appropriate qualifications who can co-ordinate the assessment preparation process; and the lack of comprehensive training and development plans. It is also important to give sufficient time to achieve the standard. Experience indicates that it requires at least one full year of systematic and intensive preparation.

For most organisations, the natural home for the project management of ETP is the HR department or, where one exists, a learning and development department. These departments will have the necessary links with other areas of the organisation, and understand the various policies and structures that will support the process. Some organisations allocate the process to an internal change agent. The ultimate aim is to ensure that ETP becomes embedded in the HR process throughout the organisation. The standard should represent a strong strategic fit with the overall business strategy and the organisation's HR strategy. The ETP standard is ultimately concerned with the diffusion of HRD norms and values among organisations. It is a prescriptive standard and adopts a one-size-fits-all approach. It is likely that organisations will adopt the standard because it offers significant technical benefits, but its ultimate value will be determined by the level of take-up by industry and service sectors.

QUESTIONS

Q.1   What reasons would you put forward to explain why organisations should seek ETP accreditation?

Q.2   How might a national standard such as ETP enhance the quality of management and leadership development in organisations?

Management and leadership development is increasingly viewed through both institutional and world-view lenses. An institutional perspective focuses on country context and highlights the extent to which there is divergence or convergence in management and leadership development practices across countries. A world-view lens focuses on a particular philosophical orientation which is related to a religion. This does not, however, eliminate the possibility that the notion of a world view can be independent of religion.

Institutional and world-view lenses facilitate the examination of country differences in management and leadership development and highlight the implicit models of management and leadership development in different world views. Specifically, a country-level approach enables the identification and discussion of the priority given to management and leadership development between firms in different countries. It also highlights the similarities or differences in management and leadership development strategies and the effectiveness of these strategies. A country-level analysis also emphasises the role of national management and leadership development systems. Different world views have within them particular perspectives on learning, leadership and development. The majority of writings on management and leadership development emphasise a traditional Western view of development. However, other world views suggest an alternative viewpoint concerning both the nature of leadership and the leadership development process. In this final chapter, we move beyond the individual and organisational focus of previous chapters to identify the key learning that can be derived from country and world-view levels of analysis.

Institutionalism, Management and Leadership Development

Powell (1991) urged that organisations are deeply embedded in wider institutional environments. Therefore, organisational management and leadership development practices are frequently either direct reflections of, or responses to, the structures, rules and processes built into these institutional environments. Institutional theory suggests that organisational actors do not necessarily make rational decisions and that societal expectations of appropriate organisational action will influence the types of decision that organisations make concerning management and leadership development. Jaffee (2001:231) suggested that organisational policies and practices on management and leadership development potentially become infused with value beyond the technical requirements of the task at hand. Organisations, therefore, plan their management and leadership development activities in response to a combination of factors, but are not always confident of conditions in the labour market and competitive pressures. They also respond to institutional pressures from regulatory agencies, societal expectations and the actions of leading organisations.

Greenwood and Hinings (1996) argued for new institutionalism, which suggests that organisations conform to contextual expectations in order to gain legitimacy and enhance their chances of growth. It further suggests that decision-makers make their organisations increasingly similar as they try to change them. This is described as isomorphism. DiMaggio and Powell (1983) stated that isomorphism is a constraining process that forces one organisation to resemble other organisations that are exposed to the same set of environmental conditions. There are two forms of isomorphism – competitive and institutional. Competitive isomorphism assumes that organisations are rational and strive to achieve 'fit' with the wider environment. Institutional isomorphism highlights three mechanisms that can influence the decisions that organisations make concerning management and leadership development:

- *Coercive Mechanisms*: These stem from political influence and the problem of legitimacy, and may be derived from the role of state agencies that demand that organisations invest in management and leadership development, or where it is a requirement of customers and suppliers. These pressures can be informal or formal.
- *Mimetic Mechanisms*: These stem from the uncertainty of the environment and the tendency to adopt practices that have been successful for other organisations operating in that particular environment.
- *Normative Mechanisms*: These are forces or pressures associated with the need to be professional or to professionalise the organisation. These professional networks may consist of professional training bodies or universities that develop and reproduce organisation norms among professional managers.

Institutional theory is, therefore, useful in explaining the adoption and diffusion of management and leadership development practices by organisations. Adoption concerns the decision to make full use of management and leadership development as the best course of action possible. Diffusion happens when a particular management and leadership development practice is communicated through various channels and becomes accepted practice. Rogers (2003) suggested that technical requirements are likely to be the main reason for diffusion in the early stages, but the desire to achieve legitimacy becomes more important at later stages of diffusion. As a management and leadership development practice spreads, a threshold is reached beyond which its adoption contributes to legitimacy rather than to improving the compliance and performance of managers and the organisation.

Monahan, Meyer and Scott (1994) suggested that management and leadership development represents an important and sensitive barometer of the changing relationships between managers and organisations. They identified three overlapping phases in the evolution of management training. These are the market, technical and citizenship phases. Countries and governments increasingly offer public recognition to organisations for their commitment to training and development. The extent to which management and leadership development practices become institutionalised depends on the length of time the practices have been in existence and their level of acceptance in firms. Scott (2001) suggested the notion of an organisational field which consists of key suppliers, resources and product, consumers, regulatory agencies and other organisations that produce similar services and products. An organisational field takes into account the totality of relevant actors. In the context of management and leadership development, there are a number of relevant actors. These include the state, firms, professional associations, employer bodies and trade unions. Within organisations, relevant actors include boards of directors, senior managers, leadership development practices and managers who participate in management and leadership development. The more diffused the management and leadership development practices become, the more legitimate they become and the more likely it is that other organisations will adopt them. On the other hand, where there is little diffusion of management and leadership development practices, other organisations are less likely to adopt them. Alberga, Tyson and Parsons (1997) found that a critical factor in the adoption of HR practices involves their take-up by organisations. Considerable take-up is required before such practices become legitimate.

Adoption of Management and Leadership Development Practices: Institutional Perspectives

Institutional theory suggests a number of factors that are associated with the adoption of management and leadership development by organisations. Organisational size is important. Larger companies are more likely to adopt management and leadership development practices early. They have greater access to resources, they have greater visibility than small organisations and they are more differentiated. Monahan, Meyer and Scott (1994) found that larger firms were more likely, first, to offer training and, second, to offer a greater variety of development opportunities. Larger firms are also more likely to have a specialist leadership development function. The presence of such a function is associated with the adoption of leadership development practices.

Organisations are also influenced by the linkages they have with the wider environment. Organisations that operate in highly interconnected environments are more likely to be exposed to new practices. When environmental conditions are uncertain, organisations will seek guidance from other reference organisations via social comparison. Mizuchi and Galaskiewicz (1994) suggested that social contagion processes facilitate diffusion. These occur when two firms use one another as a reference point when deciding to adopt a particular practice. Organisations are directly linked through social cohesion and indirectly linked through structural equivalence. Social cohesion focuses on firms or actors coming to a normative understanding of the value of a management and leadership development practice through direct contact between organisations. Structurally equivalent organisations are identically positioned in the social structure and have similar relationships with third parties. These organisations use one another as reference points to determine their relative strengths.

Organisations do, however, respond differently to institutional norms. Scott (1987), for example, suggested that private sector organisations are more influenced by efficiency gains, whereas legitimate reasons are more important in the public sector. Public sector organisations are not necessarily compelled to conform, but do so voluntarily. Private sector organisations are more likely to be responsive to technical arguments, whereas public sector organisations are more responsive to institutional factors. Public sector firms are more likely than private firms to achieve accreditation of their learning.

Institution theory is also useful in explaining why some organisations adopt early and others adopt late. Early adopters actively choose to adopt management and leadership development practices, whereas late adoptors adopt leadership development practices because of a perceived pressure to do so. This is often called a bandwagon effect. Early adoptors are also more likely to customise their leadership development initiatives in order to ensure the maximum technical benefits. They are also more likely to reduce or eliminate the uncertainty that may be associated with the particular practice.

Institutional Theory and Change in Management and Leadership Development Practices

Institutional theory, therefore, suggests that it is reasonable to assume that management and leadership development practices will be similar in different countries. We will establish in later sections whether or not this is the case. However, institutional theory is now also used to explain change in organisational practices. Greenwood and Hinnings (1996) suggested that some organisations may decouple from the institutional context. This, however, depends on three things:

- The kind and degree of commitment to change within the organisation
- The power structures and conditions favouring or opposing organisational change
- The capacity to implement change and manage the transition process from one set of practices to another.

Oliver (1991) suggested that certain accepted practices may become eroded or discredited. This may happen as a result of internal or external pressures. The internal pressures may include the recruitment of new members, a decline in performance, power shifts within the organisation and new organisational goals. These changes may call into question various patterns of management and leadership development activity. External factors include increased competition, changes in the business environment, new government regulations and incentives, changes in professional opinion concerning particular practices and dramatic events or crises. Table 18.1 summarises a number of strategic responses to institutional processes in a management and leadership development context.

Table 18.1: Strategic Responses to Institutional Processes in a Management and Leadership Development Context

Strategy	Tactics	Examples
Acquiesce	Habit	Follow taken-for-granted views on management and leadership development
	Imitate	Copy best practices because they are perceived to work
	Comply	Obey the requirements of key institutions for management and leadership development
	Balance	Balance the expectations of different stakeholders in management and leadership development provision
Compromise	Pacify	Accommodate and placate the requirements of suppliers, customers, etc.

Strategy	Tactics	Examples
Compromise contd.	Bargain	Negotiate with institutional stakeholders such as regulatory bodies
	Conceal	Take steps to disguise the fact that the organisation does not invest in management and leadership development
Avoid	Buffer	Reduce dependency on relationships that demand investment in development
	Escape	Change goals or activities or move into another space or domain in order to avoid management and leadership development
	Dismiss	Ignore the norms and demands of key actors in the organisational field
Defy	Challenge	Contest the requirement for management and leadership development
	Attack	Consult the sources of institutional pressure and diminish their credibility
	Co-op	Get influential constituents to support the organisation's point of view
Change	Influence	Shape the values and priorities of the organisational field
	Control	Set the agenda for a new set of management and leadership development practices

Our discussion of institutional theory as it applies to management and leadership development highlights the potential of both similarities and differences across countries on the basis of differences and similarities in context, including political, historical and economic functions. The institutional perspective suggests that history and processes of institutionalisation are important. Various levels, such as national industry and corporate, interact to produce potential differences and institutionalism brings abut homogeneity, stability and legitimacy, as well as change.

Comparative National Management and Leadership Development Systems

Thomson *et al.* (2001) highlighted that management and leadership development systems are deeply embodied in a multiplicity of contexts including culture, labour markets, educational systems and history. As a result, we have differences in the management and leadership development options of different countries. These differences are likely to explain differences in how organisations in different countries approach management and leadership development practices, even though institutional theory would make arguments in favour of convergence. Firms in different countries are not self-sufficient or independent. They are shaped by institutional arrangements which influence the way management is construed in different countries and how management talent is nurtured and developed. We first consider a generic typology of national management and leadership systems and follow this up with a brief discussion of specific country models.

Models of National Management and Leadership Development

Cho and McLean (2004) suggested a categorisation of national training and development systems consisting of five variants, which have relevance in illuminating management and leadership development practices. They highlighted that it is not possible to identify a 'pure' model. Each country, while having one dominant model, will bring in components from other models and countries.

- *Centralised Models*: Countries that adopt this type of model have a top-down approach to education, training and development. The central government has a key role to play in planning, implementing and evaluating policies and strategies on education and management development. A centralised model discourages firms from taking individual initiatives and few agencies, beyond the government, have any responsibility for setting policy on management and leadership development. Management and leadership development initiatives will have a strong social dimension and emphasise long-term planning. Governments with this type of model play a major role in economic development and the corporate sector is relatively insignificant in shaping economic policy.
- *Transitional Model*: This model best describes countries that are evolving from a centralised model to a more decentralised one. It will typically accommodate the involvement of key stakeholders such as the government, employers' bodies and trade unions in the formulation of policies on education, training and development. Policy formulation and implementation may be distributed amongst a number of agencies and the role of the government will involve coordination and effective use of resources. These tasks will probably be undertaken by a government minister for education and development.
- *Government Initiated Model towards Standardisation*: This model places emphasis on the government's establishment of development initiatives that are based on the needs of the economy and of the views of different stakeholders. A variety of bodies work to satisfy needs. It allows for flexibility of provision and helps to ensure that there is standardisation across the different sectors and actors.
- *Decentralised or Free-Market Model*: This model emphasises that the extent of management and leadership developments are determined by the competitive market. It is a vocational model, in that management and leadership development are regarded as activities that occur at enterprise level. The private sector has a major responsibility for training and development, but it may be supported by the state in a number of indirect ways. Managers are considered responsible for their own learning and development.
- *Small-Nation Models*: Small nations may not have the resources to develop their own management and leadership development infrastructure. Countries that would normally be in competition with one another have to co-operate, pool resources and share best practices. It is a participative model in that key stakeholders get involved in policy making.

National management development systems differ in the degree to which they are regulated, the extent to which there are legally binding regulations, the involvement of the social partners, the responsibilities placed on individuals and firms and the concern of the country for standardisation of development initiatives. Cho and McLean (2004) suggested that there is no 'right' way for a country to approach management and leadership development. They highlighted that national systems must be sufficiently flexible, be able to respond to changes in the wider environment and ensure a good balance between centralised planning and enterprise and individual-level initiatives. It is also important that these systems have a vision for development and tailor their initiatives to take account of particular features of context. Table 18.2 summarises the features of the five national development systems and gives particular examples.

Table 18.2: Characteristics of National Management and Leadership Development Models

Model	Key Driver	Dominant Approach	Particular Features	Examples
Centralised	National government	Top-down, collective approach	• Development has strong moral and social implications • Education and development are important for industrialisation • Government drives economic development	• China • France
Transitional	National government Tripartite	Co-ordinated and inter-ventionist	• Policies on development are derived from a tripartite approach • Government co-ordinates development initiatives at national level	• Germany • Singapore • Ireland
Structured	Government	Consultative and framework-oriented	• Co-ordination of the activities of key stakeholders • Various initiatives to ensure standardised initiatives across sectors • Difficulty is to balance standardisation with sensitivity to context	• UK
Free market	Firms and individuals	Competitive and decentralised	• Firms and individuals are responsible for development • State will support the private sector in indirect ways	• USA • Canada
Small Nation	Governments from several small countries	Co-operative	• Resource limitations require co-operation between countries • Strong involvement of stakeholder	• Caribbean Islands

Examples of National Management and Leadership Development Models

Handy (1987) carried out pioneering analyses of four national management and leadership development models, which he considered were distinct in particular ways. He focused on their historical, cultural and economic characteristics and how these impacted on approaches to management and leadership development. We will briefly consider five systems here (US, German, French, Japanese and UK), in addition to explaining the characteristics of the Irish system.

The US Model: The US model places strong emphasis on individualism and free enterprise, and managers are considered an important social and economic group. Education and development are considered an investment in credentials, employability and self-management. Managers are expected to take proactive steps to plan their own development. A significant number of managers in the USA possess a degree and have invested in continuing their own development.

The MBA is one of the most important contributions that the USA has made to management and leadership development. Although MBAs differ greatly in their content and teaching approach, they are based on the assumption that managers have an understanding of business and general management. They initially emphasised the harder skills but have in recent years shifted towards development of the softer management and leadership skills. A specific MBA has emerged for executives which focuses on strategic and leadership issues. Business schools also provide non-qualification-oriented executive development programmes.

Individual firms invest a considerable amount of resources in management and leadership development. Many of the larger corporations have established corporate universities that run their own MBA and postgraduate programmes; in-house development tends to be organisationally focused and designed to address strategy. They invest considerably in softer skills development. Organisations are, however, increasingly aware that managers place a strong emphasis on mobility within the labour market.

The German Model: The German management development system places a strong emphasis on understanding specialised tasks and on understanding economics. Business education is not equated with management development. Managers from technical and legal backgrounds can also pursue managerial careers. The German system places a strong emphasis on the role of the professional. Education plays a major role in providing future managers with broadly based and vocationally oriented development. Potential managers undertake a long apprenticeship and participate in job rotation programmes. German management education and development is not very global or internationally focused.

Within the firm, the responsibility for development lies with the individual manager and his/her immediate manager. The HR or leadership development function plays an indirect role. There is a strong emphasis on in-house development and organisations are reluctant to send managers on MBA programmes and public programmes. Universities, as a rule, do not offer management and leadership development programmes and there are relatively few private providers. Chambers of commerce, however, have an important role in management development policy. People tend to stay in a particular professional area, which is a product of technik (the creation of useful objects), and there is low mobility of managers due to strong paternalism and regional loyalties.

The French Model: The French model of management and leadership development is both centralised and elitist. This can be traced back to the influence of the *grandes écoles*, which were created to provide administrators and engineers to run the state. The focus, therefore, is on the intellectual, on problem-solving and on the 'hard' skills of management. Engineers dominate the managerial ranks, especially the top management positions, and are prevalent in non-technical sectors such as banking and finance. Thomson *et al*. (2001) suggested that while universities have a key role to play in the education of managers, they are treated with suspicion by employees. Universities have, in recent years, taken steps to develop programmes that are in line with the needs of industry.

Organisations do accept responsibility for management and leadership development. There is a statutory requirement to prepare training and development plans and discuss them with works committees. Leadership development functions do not have significant prestige or influence in French industry. Responsibility for management development generally rests with department managers. The *grandes écoles* produce managers who are often too generalist and intellectual; therefore, organisations have to spend a considerable amount of time on the development of specialist skills. There is some evidence of management mobility and that France is becoming more globalised in its approach to management and leadership development. French managers are increasingly concerned with the development of portable competencies and the development of a global perspective on management.

The Japanese Model: Development and education are highly valued in Japanese society. There is a strong collective focus on management and Japanese managers are required to invest time in their own development. Universities play a major role in the development of managers, but they do not have undergraduate degree programmes. Companies play a major role in the development of managers and they place a strong emphasis on the hiring of high-potential graduates. Development is considered a long-term process and the Japanese labour market places strong emphasis on lifelong employment, strong labour markets and intensive on-the-job development. Managers are expected to demonstrate strong commitment to the organisation and to accept authority. In contrast to the American system, individualism is considerably less valued. Organisations have a requirement that each manager should have a formal mentor.

The Japanese system emphasises a strong link between development and the manager's career. Managers are typically given intensive induction and socialisation, planned job experiences or job rotation and planned job assignments. Japanese organisations utilise a rigid system of decision-making that facilitates learning and development. There is a strong emphasis on monitoring performance, so managers are very conscious of their development needs. Managers generally seek to get a broad base of multifunctional experience early in their careers. They are expected to be generalists rather than specialists. Off-the-job development is used, but it appears to be significantly less valued than on-the-job development.

The UK Model: Lee (2004) suggested that the UK model is diverse and multifaceted, and that it is largely a political and economic process in that the government has concentrated on up-skilling and the promotion of lifelong learning. The majority of national initiatives are directed towards organisations and the development of managers in the workplace. NVQs (national vocational qualifications) are a core feature of the UK system and the implementation of 'Investors in People' has placed management and leadership development formally on the agenda of large organisations.

Thomson *et al.* (2001) highlighted that responsibility for development has shifted from national to enterprise levels at various times, with the result that there is a lack of continuity. The creation of the Council for Excellence in Management and Leadership, formed in 2000, has brought leadership development to the centre of the national agenda. This body has responsibility for the co-ordination of development efforts and the development of a national strategy for management and leadership development. Business schools play a major role in the development of managers and a significant proportion of UK managers possess master's degrees. Professional institutes also have a major role to play in management development. However, these institutes tend to concentrate on functional skills and provide specialist qualifications to managers.

The UK management development system places a strong emphasis on standardisation. Lee (2004) considered this to be risky in the long term, because it may lead to inflexibility. The UK system is frequently criticised when international comparisons are made, but it has placed a strong emphasis on encouraging the individual manager to take responsibility for development.

The Irish Management and Leadership Development System

The Irish management and leadership development system can best be described as transitional. In the last thirty years, government policy has focused on attracting foreign direct investment to Ireland. The development of managers in Ireland has not, however, always been high on the agenda of various governments. The first significant move in increasing its priority came with the publication of the Galvin Report in 1998. This report called for the professionalisation of management. Three of its recommendations were particularly relevant. It acknowledged the urgent need for an increased commitment at national level to management development; it advocated that the providers of business education should offer a broadly common curriculum; and it endorsed the need to develop a code of good practice on management and leadership development. The Galvin Report acknowledged the need for a national mindset change. Heraty and Morley (2003) pointed out that the volume of management development increased significantly during the boom years of Ireland's 'Celtic

Tiger' economy. In 2000, the Open University Business School reported that some aspects of management development had improved significantly. Various government reports have highlighted the need to further strengthen management development efforts. The Enterprise Strategy Group Report (2004) emphasised the need to develop management capability as an essential condition for the success of Ireland's enterprise strategy.

The government, organisations, universities and private providers play a major role in the development of managers. Government initiatives have primarily focused on economic and labour market initiatives, but they have facilitated employers to meet their responsibilities (through the provision of financial subsidies to small and medium-sized enterprises) to meet development needs and skill sets which drive the adoption of best practice in management and leadership development.

A system of national partnerships has operated in Ireland since 1987 that involves government, trade unions, employer organisations and other interest groups. This has resulted in a series of three-year national agreements which, although they have no legal standing, have contributed to the enhancement of lifelong learning and development. Table 18.3 provides an illustration of the varying interests and priorities of different stakeholder groups and the extent to which there is a coherent set of policy objectives.

Table 18.3: The Policy Objectives of Different Stakeholders in the Irish National Management Development Plan

Objective	Stakeholder						
	Government	FÁS	Education Providers	HETAC / FETAC	Employers	Trade Unions	Individual Managers
To overcome labour shortages	Med.	High	High	Low	High	High	Med.
To promote workforce development	Med.	Med.	High	High	High	Med.	Low
To support economic and social development through labour market policy	High	High	High	High	Low	High	Low
To contribute to development of a co-ordinated NHRD strategy	High	High	Low	Med.	Low	Low	Low
To promote access to, and participation in, training programmes	High	High	High	High	Low	High	Low
To deliver optimum return on resources	High	High	High	High	High	High	Low
To improve relationships with all stakeholders	Med.	High	High	High	Med.	Med.	Med.
To foster professionalism, intellectual and social needs of the individual	High	Low	High	High	Low	Low	High
To promote quality assurance and relevance of programmes offered	High	Med.	High	High	Med.	Med.	Low

Source: Adapted from Limerick Institute of Technology (2006); FÁS (2005); FETAC (2005); and IBEC (2004)

The EU has also had a major impact on the development of the Irish management and leadership development system. It expects that member states will treat capital investment and investment in human resources on an equal footing. It emphasises the need for increased collaboration between education and business sectors and it encourages the acquisition of new knowledge.

Heraty (2004), however, contended that the training and development system in Ireland is still lacking a cohesive overarching policy and does things in an unplanned, unco-ordinated and ad hoc manner. It is generally acknowledged that Ireland has yet to develop a framework for management and leadership development systems that facilitates learning opportunities on a lifelong and life-wide basis and that recognises and supports individual and national autonomy and ensures flexibility in the implementation of policy. Table 18.4 summarises key strengths and weaknesses of the Irish management development system.

Table 18.4: Strengths and Weaknesses of the Irish Management Development System

Strengths	Weaknesses
National Qualifications Authority of Ireland (NQAI) established: • Articulation and co-ordination of policies on, for example, quality assurance, transfer and progression and standards of awards based on learning outcomes European Credit Transfer System (ECTS): • Attempt to establish equivalency within a transnational context National Framework for Qualifications (NFQ) launched: • Outcomes-based approach for validation and certification of informal and non-formal learning Provider improvements: • Increase in policies by providers in relation to transfer and/or progression routes within formal learning systems • Recognition of prior learning for entry to programmes and access to awards • Increased linkages between industry and providers of development to ensure relevance of programmes and awards • Increased focus on social aspects of human resource development Legislation: • Teaching Council Act (2001) to promote teaching as a profession • Overall Plan for RD emphasising in-career development opportunities Resources: • Increased investment in learning and development initiatives Tripartite Approach: • Increased opportunities for interaction, dialogue, consultation and involvement enhances the process of policy development and improves decision-making	• Overlap in remit of the awarding councils • Inefficient use of limited resources • No history of ECTS within the system, therefore low levels of understanding and absence of a defined infrastructure • Policies and procedures do not necessarily result in increased participation • Inherent difficulties assessing knowledge acquired outside formal learning systems • Danger that by focusing on the needs of learners, the needs of industry will be overlooked • Multiplicity of providers (for example, FÁS, VECs and IoTs provide an extensive range of ACE) results in duplication of objectives and competition for similar target groups of learners • Lack of parity of esteem regarding traditional classical academic orientation at all levels of education impacts negatively on training and development • Differing qualification systems for providers of education • Financial rather than output control is the norm • Multiplicity of stakeholders slows down decision-making process

Source: Adapted from: Deane and Watters (2004a, 2004b); Fox (2004); Fox and McGinn (2000); Garavan, Costine and Heraty (1997); Gunnigle, Herary and Morley (2000); Heraty, Morley and McCarthy (2000)

Management and Leadership Development Practices in Selected Countries

We will now focus on the types of management and leadership development practices that organisations implement in different countries. Mabey and Ramirez (2004) suggested that in most countries managers are considered the carriers of firm-specific knowledge. They play a major role in capturing the tacit knowledge of the firm and contribute to competitive advantage. We address whether there is convergence or divergence in organisations in a number of European countries concerning the way they develop managers. We give specific attention to Ireland, but also describe organisation-level management and leadership development practices in the UK, France, Germany, Spain, Norway and New Zealand. These countries represent the diversity of national management and leadership development systems that we considered earlier in this chapter.

Management and Leadership Development Practices in Irish Organisations

A number of studies have been published on leadership development in Ireland. These include studies by Garavan, Barnicle and O'Suilleabhain (1999), Heraty and Morley (2003), Open University (2000), O'Connor, Mangan and Cullen (2006) and the CIPD study (2007). These studies highlight a number of consistent themes and trends. We focus here on the following issues: the volume of management and leadership development activity; the drivers of management development; the policy dimensions of management and leadership development; management development practices; and the effectiveness of management and leadership development activity.

Volume of Management and Leadership Development: The amount of money invested in management and leadership development has increased significantly in the last fifteen years. Heraty and Morley (2003) analysed CRANET data and found a steady increase in investment between 1992 and 1999. In the 1999 survey, seventy per cent of managers received between one and five days' management training and development, compared with fifty per cent of managers in 1995 and forty-four per cent in 1992. O'Connor and Mangan (2004) found that junior and middle managers received six days' management training, whereas senior managers received 5.9 days. The CIPD study (Garavan and Carbery 2008) found that the average was 6.2 days for all managers. This data, however, needs to be interpreted with caution. It is likely that some organisations will over-report their investment. Furthermore, there are major differences across company size. O'Connor and Mangan (2004) found that organisations with between 251 and 1,000 employees invested in more management development than is the case for smaller organisations. A report by the Expert Group on Future Skills Needs (2005) found that Irish SMEs do not invest in a significant amount of management and leadership development. The CIPD (2007) study found that organisations with fewer than one hundred employees spent considerably less on formal management and leadership development. Managers in such firms spend approximately three days on formal management training and development.

The form and content of management and leadership development is as important as the number of training days. The majority of studies reveal that Irish organisations tend to rely on formal programmes that focus on personal skills training and management training. There is a strong emphasis on seminars, but significantly less investment in coaching and mentoring programmes, self-awareness activities and personal profiling. Customised management and leadership development activities are more frequently found in large organisations. These programmes represent a more focused and organisation-specific investment in managers and leaders.

The Drivers of Management and Leadership Development: The factors that drive management and leadership development are complex. Heraty and Morley (2003) found that both structural and policy variables may explain management development provision in Irish organisations. The key structural factors that appear to be relevant include size, sector and ownership. These factors, while important, are of themselves insufficient. Policy reasons appear to be more important. These include: a drive for business efficiency; the need to support organisational strategy and culture; demands from managers themselves of the business; the need to achieve training rewards; and the strong buy-in of senior managers. These were coupled with a strong HR strategy. We will now discuss these reasons in a little more detail,

The various studies highlight, however, that management and leadership development in Ireland tends to be on a needs basis and to be reactive in nature. This is particularly the case in SMEs. Larger organisations tend to adopt a more integrated approach in which management and leadership development is considered an integral part of strategy and is linked to the specific context of the roles that managers perform. Table 18.5 summarises the main objectives of leadership development programmes.

Table 18.5: Key Objectives of Irish Organisations' Leadership Development Activities

Objective	% of Organisations
Developing high-potential individuals whom the organisation values	79
Improving the skills of leaders to think in a more strategic and future-focused way	77
Enabling the achievement of the organisation's strategic goals	78
Changing the leadership style across the organisation	62
Improving relationships with external or partner organisations	41
Producing a common standard of behaviour for those in leadership roles	49
Accelerating change within the organisation	49
Changing the prevailing organisational culture	56
Addressing the current underperformance of leaders	41

Organisation strategy is a key influence on management and leadership development. It emerges as a key driver in all the major studies. Typically, organisations achieve a link between management and leadership development and organisation strategy through such processes such as performance reviews, competency frameworks, succession management and multisource feedback. This reflects our discussion in Chapter Eleven concerning the proactive behaviours of managers in managing their careers and employability. This has contributed to an increase in management development activity undertaken. Organisations that have robust HR processes and systems to evaluate the impact of management and leadership development are increasingly likely to invest in management and leadership development. Training awards such as FÁS, Excellence Through People and the National Training Award are highlighted as other factors driving investment in the studies conducted by O'Connor and Mangan (2006) and Garavan and Carbery (2008).

The Policy Dimension of Management and Leadership Development: We emphasise here the existence of written policies, the level at which policies are made and the impact of these policies on management and leadership development activity. The various studies highlight a mixed picture with respect to policy formulation on management and leadership development. Heraty and Morley (2003) focused on the impact of having formal policies on management-development activity. They found that organisations with a written policy undertook significantly more management and leadership development than organisations that did not have one. Second, they found that organisations with an explicit HR strategy also invested more in management and leadership development. They found that the level at which the policy is formulated does not make a difference.

O'Connor and Mangan (2004) investigated the context of management and leadership development policy in addition to its objectives. Policy objectives in Irish organisations typically focus on developing managerial styles, creating an organisational vision and culture, securing competitive advantage for the organisation and facilitating succession planning. Organisations with divisional structures tend to have autonomy at a country or plant level in some aspects of management development. Larger corporations, however, tend to have a more centralised approach, especially in respect of senior management and top team development. Divisions within a large multinational will have autonomy to develop more customised initiatives while, at the same time, adopting some corporate-driven management development initiatives. Policy and practice in the development of middle and more junior managers tends to be more decentralised and business-unit driven. Few Irish organisations have a specific budget for management and leadership development and they find it difficult to separate expenditure on management development from general training and development expenditure.

Management development policy tends to be driven from central HR or a centralised leadership development function. Line functions have an increasing role to play in implementing leadership development policy and individual learners will also have a major input into their own development. Irish organisations experience a number of barriers in implementing management and leadership development policy. These include, in priority order: lack of support and commitment from senior leaders; lack of financial resources; ineffective linkage with business and/or HR strategy; an inappropriate organisation culture and a perception that management and leadership development is not an essential activity.

Management and Leadership Development Practices: Irish organisations utilise a wide range of practices. There is evidence of increased sophistication and customisation of practices. Heraty and Morley (2003) found that the use of methods such as career plans, international experience and succession plans has an impact on the amount of management development undertaken. They found that organisations did not use assessment or development centres and high-flier management-development programmes. The CRANET study also found that the process of vacancy filling leads to an increased violation of management and leadership development processes and performance management systems are likely to lead to more formal management and leadership development activity. Performance appraisal is commonly used in Irish organisations to identify the development needs of managers.

O'Connor and Mangan (2004) found that organisations rely, to a considerable degree, on formal management development practices. Formal development methods typically include short and long programmes, seminars and conferences. Garavan and Carbery (2008) found that there was a disparity between the use of the method and the perceived effectiveness of the method for leadership development purposes. Table 18.6 summarises the key findings of the CIPD (2007) study. Irish organisations use formal programmes extensively, and they are considered to be the most effective. Internal and external coaching is increasingly used and it is perceived to be an effective development method. Multisource feedback, psychological assessment, development centres and formal mentoring programmes are less frequently used by Irish organisations, but they are considered to have greater impact than more formal methods. Executive education programmes receive a mixed rating in terms of their perceived effectiveness. They are, however, increasingly used by organisations. This finding is similar to that made in the equivalent UK survey. Organisations in Ireland tend to favour more traditional leadership development activities. These activities are considered to be moderately effective. Increasingly, multinational organisations are experimenting with more alternative methods or a broader range of approaches. These are rated as more effective.

Table 18.6: Usage and Perceived Effectiveness of Different Leadership Activities

Method	Usage of Method	Perceived Effectiveness of Method
External seminars and conferences	3.25	3.10
In-house leadership development programmes	3.75	1.65
Visiting speakers and experts	2.45	3.75
Internal executive coaching	3.04	3.45
External executive coaching	3.35	3.65
Development centres	2.45	3.35
Formal mentoring schemes	3.15	3.65
Development review as part of appraisal	2.85	2.80
External secondments, exchanges and visits	1.75	2.35
Internal secondments/project assignments	2.95	3.25
Psychological assessment with feedback	2.65	3.45
360-degree feedback programmes	2.84	3.35
Leadership courses at external institutions (e.g. business schools)	2.85	2.90
Courses leading to a management/business qualification (e.g. MBA)	2.95	3.10
Corporate universities	1.25	3.45

The Effectiveness of Management and Leadership Development: The various surveys reveal that there is widespread recognition among larger companies of the importance of leadership development as a contribution to long-term business performance. In the CIPD (2008) study, sixty-one per cent of organisations indicated that they were satisfied with their overall leadership development strategy. A significant proportion of organisations indicated that they were dissatisfied. This suggests that some organisations have a desire to achieve more, to be more innovative and to achieve a better integration of leadership development with business strategy.

The study findings also highlight that the true value of leadership development is less well understood by senior executives. They are also less well informed on development processes. Irish organisations are less effective in distinguishing between short- and long-term development. The thinking of leadership development and HR specialists on leadership development is often not in line with that of senior managers with regard to its overall value and the value placed on particular leadership approaches. Leadership development specialists are concerned that organisations do not take it seriously enough.

Irish organisations and leadership development professionals perceive that management and leadership development activities have a positive impact on both individuals and organisations, but they have difficulty in making the case. A significant proportion of organisations in the CIPD study do not evaluate management and leadership development in terms of return on investment, but almost ninety per cent of respondents indicated that they think well-designed leadership development activities can have a positive impact on the bottom line. The majority of organisations do not perceive generic leadership development programmes to be a waste of money. However, they do believe that organisations focus on management in the short term and that it is not an essential activity in terms of economic orientation.

O'Connor and Mangan (2004) indicated that many organisations experience difficulties in evaluating management and leadership development. A significant barrier is that the outcomes of management and leadership development take time to materialise. Organisations experience difficulties in generating real-time indicators that show the impact of the programme as it unfolds. Irish organisations rely too much on the subjective measures of success. These methods are useful, but they are often insufficient to convince senior management of the value of management and leadership development.

Table 18.7 highlights some of the practice guidelines that emerge from the study of management and leadership development in Ireland.

Table 18.7: Trends in Management and Leadership Development in Ireland: Implications for Practitioners

- Leadership development specialists must challenge simplistic views of leadership development to reflect current context and challenges.
- Organisations should use leadership development approaches that are appropriate for induction needs.
- Organisations should not rely solely on traditional approaches. They should be prepared to be innovative and to experiment.
- It is important to integrate leadership development initiatives with business strategy and take proactive steps to demonstrate how they contribute to business performance.
- Organisations should not, however, get preoccupied with large-scale evaluations. Development specialists should focus on quick wins, place less emphasis on reaction and evaluation and identify specific initiatives to evaluate and demonstrate return on investment.
- Organisational leadership development specialists should focus on impacts and benefits rather than on barriers.
- Organisations should benchmark their leadership development efforts against organisations of a similar size.
- Organisations should evaluate the internal and external factors that are facilitating or inhibiting management and leadership development.
- Organisations should focus on ensuring that they evaluate how those responsible for leadership development are carrying out their roles.
- Leadership development specialists should combine qualitative and quantitative approaches to evaluate management and leadership development activities.

Management and Leadership Development Practices in Countries other than Ireland

We now focus on six countries that demonstrate a variety of management and leadership development practices and from which it is possible to derive insights into organisational practices that are effective and those that are ineffective. Klarsfeld and Mabey (2004) argued that there is little evidence of analysis of management and leadership development through a comparative or cross-cultural lens. Mayrhofer *et al.* (2004) suggested that comparative analysis is difficult because of the multitude of differences in work context.

New Zealand: Ruth (2006) has investigated management and leadership development practices in New Zealand. He points out that the New Zealand government is increasingly concerned that more attention be paid to management and leadership development capability. New Zealand organisations tend to perceive a good manager as an individual who has acquired job experience in the workplace, has internal ability and responsibility, has acquired external management education and has participated in in-house development. Organisations perceive that they have primary responsibility for management and leadership development. Organisations in New Zealand face drivers of and inhibitors to management and leadership development that are similar to those experienced in organisations in Ireland. Ruth found that the most significant drivers were business changes and external changes. HR strategy, goals and practices are also significant drivers. Internal structural changes and individual demand are significant factors driving development in New Zealand organisations. The most significant barriers to management and leadership development include the need to cover for absent managers, a lack of enthusiasm from managers themselves, a lack of support from the board and line managers, and the cost of management development.

In comparison with Ireland, a significant number of New Zealand organisations do not have an explicit policy on management and leadership development. Organisations do, however, have difficulties in communicating management development policy throughout the organisation. Managers do not always accept responsibility for management and leadership development and a significant proportion of organisations do not give high priority to management and leadership development. New Zealand organisations do not evaluate their management and leadership development initiatives. Evaluation is frequently conducted in an ad hoc manner. There is a strong emphasis on the use of subjective, self-report measures. They also use informal processes and rarely conduct cost-benefit analyses.

Overall, management and leadership development in New Zealand is not sufficiently strategic. New Zealand has, like Ireland, a large percentage of small companies who spend significantly less on management development than larger companies. New Zealand organisations have a non-integrated approach to management and leadership development and rely on more traditional development methods. They place little emphasis on systematic evaluation and cost-benefit analysis.

France: Mabey and Ramirez (2004) investigated management and leadership development practices in France. French management and leadership development activities are broad in scope and include issues such as team management, communications and interpersonal skills, management processes and systems and company-specific development. Most management development activities are company-wide, apply to all managers and are delivered by external providers as well as by internal development specialists. There is significantly less emphasis on job-based development, planned job experiences, mentoring and shadowing and more emphasis on informal development processes.

The precise drivers of management and leadership development in France are difficult to determine. The majority of management and leadership development provision tends to be driven by external changes, whereas HR strategy is the least significant factor. A significant proportion of French organisations have a specific training and development budget, due primarily to a legislative requirement, but a significant proportion of organisations do not have a written management-development policy. Organisations in France are less likely to use career-planning processes, fast-track development programmes and individually focused development initiatives. The management development ethos in French organisations tends to be mixed. They are less likely to use competency frameworks and to take responsibility for development. They are also less likely to develop for potential, to focus on long-term development and to retain managers for more than five years.

Organisations in France spend significantly less on management and leadership development than those in other European countries. They do, however, spend more than is the case in Ireland, the UK and Spain. The systematic evaluation of management and leadership development is not a major priority for French organisations. They are less likely to benchmark their management and leadership development efforts and to assess the impact of management development on the organisation. They do not systematically assess whether or not they achieve their management development objectives.

Mabey and Rameriz (2004) suggested that the value systems of top managers have a major impact on management and leadership development activities. They highlighted a strong respect for well-being and openness and an insistence that management development helps the individual. There is, on the negative side, a view of leadership which focuses on charisma and an emphasis on unsystematic and unplanned management and leadership development. Overall, French management and leadership development practices fall behind those of some of their European competitors and they pay significantly less attention to systematic and strategically integrated approaches. This may explain French organisations' lack of competitiveness.

Table 18.8: Patterns of Management and Leadership Development in Europe: A Typology

	In-House/Specific Skills	**External/Generalist Skills**
Short-Term/Lower Career Focus	• Strong focus on internal development activities designed to enhance organisation-specific competencies • Managers do not focus on the development of portable and generic skills • Limited promotion structures and less value placed on external qualifications and MBAs • Development is short term with limited focus on managerial careers • **Examples:** France and Spain	• Strong emphasis placed on broad work experience as a means of developing managers • Strong focus on the use of external development programmes. Some elements of internal development • Significant value placed on professional management qualifications and the MBA • Tendency to view management and leadership development as a short-term activity due to a perceived lack of job security • Managers seek generic skills in order not to get locked into specific skills development • **Examples:** UK, Ireland and New Zealand
Long-Term/High Career Focus	• Strong focus on the long-term development of managers in a specific organisational context • Strong emphasis on company experience and in-house formal programmes • Little or no use of external qualification programmes and MBAs • Strong assumption that managers are interested in long tenure with their organisation • Development takes a considerable amount of time and career progression is slow • **Examples:** Norway and Germany	• Strong emphasis on developing the careers of managers • Dominant view is that development is a long-term activity • Strong value placed on external management qualifications and MBA programmes • Focus on the development of managerial skills that are portable and applicable to different contexts • Development can be achieved using a multiplicity of methods • **Examples:** Denmark

Germany: Management and leadership development practices in German organisations have a distinctive character. They place a strong emphasis on unilateral management and leadership development activities and, as a result, invest considerably in management and leadership development activities. Management and leadership development practices in large German organisations are closely linked with strategy. They view management and leadership development activities as mechanisms to shape the strategies of the organisation. Mabey and Ramirez (2004) found that responsibility for management and leadership development is well positioned in German organisations. It is closely linked with senior management and there is usually a dedicated budget and a key manager driving the process.

Leadership development in German organisations is considered a long-term activity and managers are expected to stay in a particular role for a considerable period of time. However, the effects of globalisation have led to shorter terms and stronger lateral mobility. German organisations tend to promote from within and they expect that managers will stay with the organisation for a considerable period of time. They are also likely to train for potential. A large number of German CEOs hold PhDs and there is an almost total focus on formal development processes. Although they also place emphasis on the development of managers' technical abilities, management is viewed as a relatively inflexible process.

German organisations utilise a variety of management and leadership development practices. They use formal appraisal processes, career planning activities and some aspects of fast-track development. They are, however, less likely to evaluate leadership development activists. Formal mentoring and coaching processes are less common, but they view development as an important component of an effective manager. Compared to other European countries, they place less emphasis on the possession of management qualifications such as the MBA. German organisations consider the general impact of management and leadership development on the organisation and they are likely to benchmark their performance with other companies. These activities are, however, undertaken in a very subjective and impressionistic way. They have not demonstrated a strong capacity to use scientific development approaches.

Overall, management and leadership development activities in German organisations tend to reflect German culture, which emphasises order, structure and high power distance and, as a result, German organisations have not come to appreciate the value of informal development processes. Responsibility for development is a top-down approach, with the developer taking on a major role. It is difficult to say how effective German management development efforts are due to the lack of systematic evaluation.

United Kingdom: Management and leadership development activities in the UK are something of a mixed bag. A significant proportion of organisations consider management and leadership development important and the level of investment in management development has increased since the mid-1980s. Individual managers are increasingly concerned with enhancing their employability and larger organisations are more successful in aligning individual and organisational needs. Mabey and Ramirez (2004) found that UK organisations struggle with balancing the priorities for development with the need to meet day-to-day objectives. Some organisations, therefore, are reluctant to offer qualification-based programmes such as MBAs, because they create expectations that the organisation may have difficulty in meeting. In some cases, these organisations will lose management talent.

There are question marks concerning the strategic nature of management development practices in UK organisations. They are less likely to view human resources as a source of competitive advantage and human resource activities are less likely to be linked to business strategy than in other countries. There is a considerable degree of scepticism concerning the strategic contribution of leadership development activities. Management and leadership specialists frequently do not have a voice at the top table and a relatively small percentage of UK organisations have an explicit policy statement on management and leadership development. A significant proportion of UK organisations (twenty-five per cent) do not have a budget for training and development.

UK organisations use a variety of management and leadership development practices. Performance appraisal is relatively commonplace and development needs are discussed at appraisal time. Career planning is less frequently used, but fast-track development programmes are used in larger organisations. UK organisations have, however, less systematic approaches than those in other countries for selecting managers to participate in management development. UK organisations encourage promotion from within and they expect managers to have long tenure with the organisation. They sometimes train for potential, but they do not necessarily focus on long-term development and may not always take responsibility for development. UK managers receive, on average, nine days' development per year. This is more than France and compares favourably with Germany.

Overall, a view exists in UK organisations that to be effective a manager needs a combination of job experience, innate abilities and personality, as well as in-company training. In-company development is more valued than formal education, but UK managers have continued to invest in qualification-based programmes and, due to demand for employability, MBA programmes remain popular there.

Spain: Management and leadership development in Spain differs from that in other countries in that there is a strong focus on having distinct career paths for managers, and MBAs are considered a popular development strategy for senior managers. Spain, like Ireland, is dominated by SMEs and, as a result, there is a significant lack of uniformity in management and leadership development initiatives. Larger organisations are significantly more likely to develop their managers when compared to smaller organisations (those employing fewer than 200 people).

Spain, like France, places strong emphasis on internal management and leadership development and there is a strong individual demand for management development. In larger organisations, management and leadership development is clearly linked to business strategy and HR plays an important role in business strategy formulation. Unlike the UK and France, Spanish organisations are more likely to view the quality of managers and leaders as a source of competitive advantage. Spanish organisations use an interesting mix of development strategies. Performance appraisal is not popular, but they do have some career planning activities. There is little formal discussion of development needs and the evaluation of management and leadership development is not commonplace. Mabey and Ramirez (2004) found that Spanish organisations scored lowest on organisational responsibility for development and they were less likely to focus on long-term development or to develop for potential. Spanish managers, however, participate in a lot of formal development, but their organisations are less likely to have a formalised or explicit policy on leadership development or to have a budget for training and development. This is an interesting conflict given that, in Spanish organisations, individual demand for leadership development represents a dominant trigger. Managers are motivated to develop their skills and to advance their careers.

Managers have considerable mobility in Spain and, as a result, there is a strong tendency for organisations to adopt more reactive approaches to leadership development and to be less concerned with employability. Management and leadership development activities have a low priority in SMEs. They are reluctant to invest in management development out of fear that managers will leave or be poached by career organisations. Organisations that have a high number of managers with degrees are more likely to invest in development because of the increased demand and the complexity of the work that these managers perform.

Norway: Management and leadership development activities in Norway are explained by both globalisation and professional values. Mabey and Ramirez (2004) pointed out that Norwegian managers have a strong focus on professionalism. They participate in professional networks and attend external seminars. They tend to be more open to new ideas, creativity and experimentation. Like Ireland, the UK and Spain, Norway has a predominance of small organisations (fifty employees or fewer). However, large organisations employ the majority of the workforce. Therefore, management and leadership development is generally confined to larger organisations.

Norway has a strong collaborative culture. It places a strong emphasis on consensus, involvement, participation, flexibility and integration. It focuses on relationships. These cultural values have, however, been influenced by globalisation and the need to adopt more global management techniques. There is a widespread expectation amongst Norwegian managers that they will have opportunities for management and leadership development. Norwegian organisations are likely to view leadership capability as a source of competitive advantage. Organisations are more likely to have a clear business strategy. However, HR is less likely to play an active role in business strategy formulation. This is despite the fact that HR will, in a significant number of organisations, have representation on the board.

Norwegian organisations use regular performance appraisal and there is some formal discussion of development needs. They make significant use of fast-track development programmes and also utilise career planning processes. They are likely to take responsibility for management and leadership development and to use some form of competency framework. There is a strong emphasis on promotion from within, development for potential and a focus on long-term development, but less of an expectation that managers will have long tenure with the organisation. Norwegian organisations are, however, placing more emphasis on developing their internal labour markets. Norwegian organisations compare favourably in terms of the amount of leadership development provided, but place a strong emphasis on external management training and qualification-based programmes provided by business schools.

The majority of management and leadership development provision in Norway focuses on the individual rather than the team or the organisation. There are relatively few attempts to evaluate the impact of investment in management and leadership development on business performance. Mabey and Ramirez (2004) suggested that it is used more as a strategy for stability than for change. It emphasises consistency, stability and commitment rather than focusing on change, new opportunities and diversity. Norwegian managers gain value from the process of development rather than the outcomes.

Denmark: Managers in Denmark have the advantage of a strong institutional system that places emphasis on both general and specific development. Danish organisations place a strong focus on the development of managers and leaders. It is a system which is open to new practices and managers are encouraged to be entrepreneurial. Unlike a number of other countries, in particular Germany, it places a strong emphasis on the informal and experiential development of managers and leaders. Danish organisations have strong and well-articulated development strategies, linked to business strategy, and leadership capability is viewed as a source of competitive advantage. Human resource functions do not, however, play a major role in the strategy formulation process. However, HR has representation on the boards of a significant proportion of Danish organisations.

Management and leadership development activities in Danish organisations are not always put on a sound footing. Mabey and Ramirez (2004, 2005) highlighted that, unlike those in France, Germany and Norway, Danish organisations are less likely to have a budget for training and development and less than one-third of organisations have an explicit management and leadership development policy. However, Danish organisations implement career planning processes and regular performance appraisals, but there is less focus on discussing development needs. They make significantly less use of fast-track development programmes and there are relatively few attempts to evaluate management and leadership development efforts.

The management and leadership development ethos in Danish organisations is moderate. They are likely to promote from within, to expect long managerial tenure and to focus on long-term development. They make less use of competency or skills frameworks, but managers take responsibility for development. Danish organisations place a strong emphasis on informal development, including informal coaching and mentoring, and they provide managers with significant formal opportunities for development. They spend a considerable amount on leadership development and their development efforts are less likely to emphasise hierarchy, formality and status. Larger organisations invest in management and leadership development in order to promote a corporate culture, to enhance corporate image and to raise the level of managerial competence. Danish organisations are willing to sponsor managers who wish to undertake qualification-based management programmes. They are successful in evaluating the contribution of investment in management development to organisational performance.

Table 18.9 summarises the main characteristics of management and leadership development in a number of countries.

Table 18.9: Comparing Management and Leadership Development Practices in Different European Countries

Country	Main Features	Skills Type & Career Paths	Strengths	Obstacles/ Challenges
Denmark	• Multi-method approach, including experiential, vocational and general MD • MD is informal and formal	• Managers develop strong practical skills with a good theoretical grounding • Careers are internally focused, with many opportunities for progression	• Danish MD is flexible and open-minded • Public training and developmental institutions are highly regarded • Takes the best aspects of equal treatment and entrepreneurialism	• Little attempt has been made to formally establish a link between MD and performance
France	• Influential professional educational institutions • Formal internal career structures • Firms legally obliged to spend 2% of annual payroll on training	• Occupational skills originate from *les grandes écoles* • Internal job hierarchies and labour markets • Possibly lose career status when changing jobs	• A *grande école* education is regarded as being of a high standard, as it is closely aligned to and originated from the business world	• *Grande école* is difficult to access due to its high expense • Approach to MD is not strategic, despite 2% training budget requirements

Country	Main Features	Skills Type & Career Paths	Strengths	Obstacles/ Challenges
New Zealand	• Major capability deficiencies among New Zealand managers • Predominant focus on external and internal leadership development programmes • Strong emphasis on generalist skills	• Strong emphasis on promoting from within • Strong focus on developing individual potential • Strong focus on long-term development	• Increased attention by New Zealand government on the development of managers • Evidence that top managers are increasingly committed to developing their managers • HR plays an active role in business strategy	• A high proportion of small firms that do not invest in leadership development • Modest integration of leadership development with business strategies • Very low overall spend on management and leadership development
Germany	• Internal, formalised MD structures • Many CEOs have a PhD- level education	• Vocational education training for managers in technical and scientific skills • Career planning is internal • Low inter-firm employee transfer	• VET has a high status amongst managers • Managers are company loyal	• Rigidity of the German MD structures stifles their effectiveness • Organisations need to make MD more flexible to encourage managers to develop a more diverse skills portfolio
Norway	• Training is both internal and external, formal and informal • Inclusive community spirit and ethos • Performance is not individually rewarded to a great degree	• Skills are derived from both vocational and organisational training • Managers are becoming increasingly mobile between firms • Managers are highly committed to the organisation in the long term	• Managers' high expectations with regard to the amount and quality of MD they will receive are generally well met by the organisation • Managers regard MD as having positive outcomes	• Norwegian MD needs to develop and encourage higher individual risk management and innovation, while preserving the stability and equal opportunities that it already promotes
Spain	• Internal • Takes place in large companies and MNCs • Number of managers in Spain has been limited by the prevalence of SMEs	• Learn skills internally, with good opportunities for internal career path • Foreign assignments are associated with career progression	• MNCs and other large organisations have introduced MD systems	• Numerous difficulties associated with persuading SMEs to implement MD programmes • MD is too reactionary, with a short-term focus

Country	Main Features	Skills Type & Career Paths	Strengths	Obstacles/ Challenges
United Kingdom	• External vocational education and training • Generalist • Poor career structures • TNA through appraisals	• Flexible skills and career • High emphasis on employability rather than firm-level progression	• Amount of MD in the UK has increased extensively over the last twenty years	• MD is not aligned to strategy • MD is too short-term in its orientation • National policy structure is poorly connected
Ireland	• Strong focus on values of education and credentials • Combination of in-house and formal qualifications • Level of investment in MD development	• Increasing emphasis on employability and leadership for competitive advantage • Increased use of competency frameworks and development of career paths • Focus on the soft skills in addition to technical skills of management • Has increased significantly in the last ten years	• Multinational companies have positively impacted on management and leadership development • State provides encouragement for investment in management and leadership development • Excellence Through People standard encourages organisations to enhance their leadership development effort	• Major deficiencies in MD in SMEs • Too much emphasis on traditional management and leadership development methods • Relatively few attempts at systematic evaluation • Lack of strategic integration and strategic positioning of leadership development

Source: Adapted from Mabey and Ramirez (2004) and Ramirez (2004)

EXHIBIT 18.1

Management Development in SMEs in Ireland

- Management and leadership development for SMEs is considered a high priority for the Irish government.
- Problems arise because the design of management development is increasingly supply- rather than demand-led. Demand is often latent and unfocused.
- Owner-managers are the key to management and leadership development in the Irish SME sector. Where they are committed, it is more likely that the organisation will invest in management and leadership development activities.
- Irish SMEs frequently fail to understand the benefits of management and leadership development. They also focus on the short term, have fears that managers will be poached and have insufficient financial resources for leadership development.
- Informal management and leadership development activities have an important role to play. Owner-managers and entrepreneurs have a strong preference for informal development approaches.

- The population of Irish SMEs is not uniform. It varies considerably in size, sector and level of management skill. Smaller SMEs have more senior management skill problems than larger ones. Many SMEs have managers who do not come from professional management backgrounds and many owner-managers have little engagement with or commitment to management and leadership development.
- SMEs should be prepared to finance management and leadership development, but there is a role for state subsidies in encouraging small firms to invest in management and leadership development and where the lack of skills prevents the development of the industry.
- SMEs experience difficulties in gaining information on learning resources for managers, in identifying learning needs and designing appropriate development interventions.
- SME owner-managers do not perceive existing management development initiatives in Ireland to be relevant or to offer value for money. They do not see significant benefits from investment in management development and, as a result, they are not prepared to incur the cost of development.

Source: Expert Group on Future Skills Needs (2005)

Convergence and Divergence in Management and Leadership Development Practices

A major issue concerns whether management and leadership development practices in Europe converge or diverge. It is commonplace to compare Europe and the USA, but Brewster (2004) suggested that the potential differences within Europe are more significant. Mayrhofer *et al.* (2004) pointed to the inevitability of heterogeneity and diversity. This diversity can be attributed to a multitude of factors, such as the size of Europe, the use of different languages and the specific and unique historical, political and economic backgrounds of each country. Proponents of convergence of management and leadership development practices argue that there is a need for organisations worldwide to become more efficient as a response to the intensification of global competition. Boxall and Purcell (2003), for example, posited that the adoption of a standardised best-practice framework for management and leadership development is the only solution if organisations seek to achieve competitive advantage. A convergence thesis argues that, irrespective of national context, firms will move towards adopting common management and leadership development practices that have proved successful for other companies in different countries. Morley (2004) suggested that there are technological, institutional and external market forces driving convergence, not least the influence of the European Union.

Proponents of divergence in management and leadership development practices acknowledge the existence of many common challenges in European business systems, but they contend that the responses of firms in different countries will be influenced by historical, cultural and institutional factors. Brewster *et al.* (2004) suggested that the resultant diverse responses to these factors prevent the efficient operation of a set of universal management and leadership development practices. Ramirez (2004) suggested that institutions often reflect national developments and these tend to be multiple and interlinked with the characteristics of the business environment in that country. However, institutions are forced to make changes in response to these external pressures.

It is acknowledged that the societal systems in which managers live and work will have a significant influence on management and leadership development. Ramirez (2004) suggests that there will be significant diversity in the types of specific skills that organisations want their managers to develop, the way in which managers subsequently use these skills and managers' perceptions of their own development. National culture will also play a major role. Culture is likely to lead to variations across countries and impact on the diffusion of management and leadership development practices. Cultural differences will affect management and leadership development practices. Table 18.10 summarises key areas of convergence and divergence in management and leadership development practices across Europe.

Table 18.10: Convergence and Divergence in Management and Leadership Development Practices in Europe

Factor	Convergence	Divergence
Investment in MD	• Increase in amount of MD activity in all countries	• Amount spent on MD varies greatly and the instruments used to measure this are not consistent across countries • Variation in spending by firms within countries
Trigger for Investment	• Most countries regard changes in the external environment as the primary trigger	• Spain and Romania see individual demand as being the main trigger for MD investment
Constraints on MD	• The biggest limitation of MD across Europe is practical or logistical difficulties	• Spanish organisations found that a low interest in MD, combined with logistics, was the biggest constraint on MD
Methods of MD Development	• Consensus about the top three ways of developing managers: internal skills training, external public courses and mentoring/coaching • Low utilisation and understanding of e-learning across Europe	• Norway, Denmark, UK and Ireland mainly use external development, while Spain, Germany and France prefer internal methods • Denmark and the UK use qualifications-based MD more than other European countries
Strategy	• There is a clear belief that HR management can lead to competitive advantage • Management and leadership development should be linked to business strategy	• France and the UK do not appear to acknowledge a link between HR and business strategies and therefore are not likely to approach MD strategically • Lack of influence of the HR function
Institutions and Government	• Strong influence on educational and political factors in all countries	• Government support of MD in Denmark is high compared to Spain, Germany and Ireland • France is the only European country to have legislation pertaining to training budgets • There is a lack of continuity of institutions and policies within the UK
Evaluation and Performance Link	• All countries surveyed used business measures as a preferred reference point for MD evaluation • There is a general belief across Europe that MD is positively linked to operational performance outcomes • Feedback is the second most popular evaluation method	• There is generally little or no evaluation in France, the UK and Denmark • Countries vary in their preference for formal or informal evaluation • Certain countries, such as Norway and France, believe that MD is linked more with individual than organisational outcomes

Factor	Convergence	Divergence
Career Planning	• Some evidence of an increase in career-planning activities to manage employability	• UK has an unstructured approach to careers, while Danish firms are seen as paternalistic in this respect • Labour mobility is low in countries such as France and Germany, and higher in the UK and Norway
Focus on Development	• Constant tension between an individual and the organisation in the short and long term	• Spain and France are sceptical about long-term management retention and as a result are mainly interested in short-term MD • Spain and France also prefer to use external labour markets; Norway, Denmark and Germany develop internal labour markets; the UK uses a combination of both
What makes an Effective Manager?	• Managers are understood as co-ordinators of resources. They possess a combination of generalist and specialist skills. Managers are encouraged to be risk takers.	• Some countries, such as the UK, consider managers to be 'gifted amateurs'. They learn as they go along.

EXHIBIT 18.2

Perspective on Theory: Discourses on Management and Leadership Development

The literature on management and leadership development is replete with alternative discourses on what management and leadership development is about. Mabey and Finch-Lees (2008) make a distinction between grand discourses and meso-discourses. Grand discourses focus on broader explanations of management and leadership development that are not context-specific, whereas meso-discourses are language and social practices whose meaning is more context-specific, but which provide a potential explanation of management and leadership development.

Grand Discourses

Functionalist Discourse: A functionalist discourse on management and leadership development emphasises the objective. The primary goal of management and leadership development is productivity and efficiency. It is assumed that organisations exist primarily to accomplish strategic goals. These rational goals should prevail over personal preferences. The purposes of management and leadership development are primarily viewed as interventions to address performance gaps and to achieve a strong fit between management and leadership capability and the organisation's strategic goals. The identification of management and leadership development needs can be undertaken in an objective way. The nature and extent of those needs are unlikely to be contested. Organisations should implement actions to evaluate the performance impact of management and leadership development. It is assumed that the outcomes of management and leadership development are mutually beneficial for both employers and managers alike. These outcomes can be measured in an objective fashion.

Constructivist Discourse: A constructivist discourse focuses on understanding the emergent processes associated with management and leadership development and makes a number of important assumptions concerning management and leadership development. Organisations are understood as spaces for individual and team learning, and for mutually beneficial leaning. The nature of learning and development processes are contextual, but there is a drive towards coherence and mutuality. Managerial competence is situational and context-dependent. A manager's development arises from a subjective framing of learning needs and experience of work. Formal management and leadership development initiatives have relatively little to contribute, whereas day-to-day experience, discovery and challenges are of much greater value. Management and leadership development is about shared processes of observation, personal accounts and story-telling. A constructivist discourse does not necessarily assume alignment between strategy and managers' competence. The organisation's culture has a major role to play in explaining the significance of development initiatives. It suggests an approach to development that emphasises the building of management potential and the capability of managers and teams. Management and leadership development contributes to sense-making.

Dialogic Discourse: A dialogic discourse draws attention to multiple voices, politics and the language that surrounds management and leadership development in organisations. Managers should be considered as social constructions rather than having objective certifiable characteristics. How managers think and speak is unique. Their identity is fragmented, multiple, negotiable and continually changing. Development processes must also be considered in this way. Dialogic discourse places particular emphasis on the language used to describe management and leadership development. This is the means by which managers construct reality. The context of management and leadership development is socially constructed and historically situated. Development processes can be used to help form managerial identity. Power and politics lie at the heart of management and leadership development. They are bound up in constructions of knowledge and what constitutes competency.

Critical Discourse: A critical discourse highlights how management and leadership development can provide organisations with a way of maintaining control, order and predictability. Management and leadership development is concerned with knowledge and power, and is tied to the locus of decision-making in the organisation. It challenges functionalist discourse and asks a number of fundamental assumptions: Is management and leadership development beneficial overall, as is generally assumed? What moral and ethical issues are attached to management and leadership development? Whose voices do we not hear in management and leadership development? Critical discourse proposes a set of tools that enable individuals to expose situations where managers and others are suppressed or marginalised as a result of management and leadership development or the lack of it. It questions whose interests are served and which groups might be disadvantaged by management and leadership development practices. Critical discourse encourages reflexivity, in which managers critique their own knowledge. Managers are expected to be critically aware of their values, motivations and assumptions. This also applies to those who organise management and leadership development activities.

Meso-Discourses

Best Practice Management and Leadership Development Practice: Best practice is frequently advocated as a rationale for management and leadership development. Best practice approaches reflect a functionalist discourse and argue that the alignment of management and leadership development with strategic priorities is highly desirable. They promote off-the-shelf solutions; however, there is a major danger that organisations may not appropriately diagnose the situation. Failure to analyse the situational factors that shape management behaviour will result in poor results for particular management and leadership development activities. There is also confusion concerning whether the adoption of best practice management and leadership development practices makes a difference to organisational performance.

Institutional Approaches to Management and Leadership Development: An insititutionalist discourse is valuable in understanding country systoms of management and leadership development. It focuses on formal and informal institutional factors. Formal institutional processes include how firms are constituted and labour markets are structured. Informal processes include custom and practice, social norms, traditions and unwritten rules. This institutional context reflects the relationship between interest groups and facilitates the mediation of conflicts. Institutions concerned with management and leadership development play a major role in ensuring that managers and employees are incentivised to invest in management and leadership development.

Management and Leadership Development Diversity: Management and leadership development activities can be viewed from a diversity perspective. Its starting point is the view that the bulk of the literature on management and leadership development is written in a very abstract way that takes no account of differences in race and gender. Management and leadership development activities are considered to perpetuate traditional paternal structures and power relations. Only recently has the literature focused on minorities and it has for the most part been gender-blind. A diversity approach advocates that management and leadership development should promote organisational inclusion and equality.

Sources: Alvesson and Deetz (2000); Mabey and Finch-Lees (2008); O'Donnell, McGuire and Cross (2006)

A number of particular aspects of convergence and divergence are apparent in management and leadership development practices. We will highlight a number of these areas here.

Triggers for Investment in Management and Leadership Development: One of the most important external triggers for management and leadership development is the state of the external environment. This suggests that organisations across Europe are increasingly using management and leadership development to cope with changes in the environment. Other common triggers include business requirements, HR strategy, increased flexibility and diversity in skills. Individual demands for management and leadership development have emerged as an important trigger across Europe. The emergence of the knowledge worker, changing psychological contracts and requirements for employability and marketability are also important triggers. Internal changes, such as work design innovations, require managers to be flexible and adaptable. Mabey (2004) suggested that management and leadership development may also be linked to the supply of training programmes.

While there is considerable convergence on the triggers or drivers of management and leadership development in Ireland, the UK and Germany, the requirements of an organisation's HR strategy drive demand for management and leadership development. External demands drive provision particularly in France, whereas in Spain individual dimensions are the most significant trigger.

Amount of Management and Leadership Development and its Priority: Comparisons of the amount of management and leadership development interaction by organisations in different countries must be approached cautiously due to differences concerning what constitutes a day's development. There is a gap between high-performing and lower-performing countries within the EU. The evidence suggests an increase in training and development activity in different countries. Spain, Denmark and Germany provide significant levels of development to managers in terms of expenditure. Germany, Denmark and Norway spend the most on management and leadership development. Spain, UK and Ireland fall below the European average. Expenditure on management and leadership development needs to be considered in relation to the costs of development in specific countries. Costs are higher in Germany, Ireland and the UK. In terms of priority, the Mabey and Ramirez studies reveal that Germany places the highest priority on management and leadership development. It is lowest in France and the UK. Ireland is somewhere in the middle, but there is relatively little difference in the overall level of priority.

Usage of Different Management and Leadership Development Methods: There is a strong reliance on internal development programmes in European countries. External qualification programmes are most popular in Ireland, the UK and Denmark. These countries place a strong emphasis on external accreditation and achieving management qualifications. Coaching and mentoring processes are also widely used in European organisations, but there are significant variations in the use of job-based methods and informal development. Denmark places a lot more value and emphasis on informal development. German companies favour highly structured internal programmes, as do larger organisations in Spain. In France, there is a strong emphasis on internal programmes, but significantly less on job rotation, experiential and informal development.

Strategic Integration of Management and Leadership Development: The linkage of management and leadership development to business strategy is increasingly recognised as important. In various European countries, organisations seek to make explicit links. Espedal (2004) suggested that Norwegian organisations perceive that it is a strategic goal to improve the effectiveness of the organisation through leadership development. Hjalager, Larsen and Bojesen (2003) found that Danish organisations focused on linkages between management development and organisation strategy. Seebacker *et al.* (2003) found in German organisations an increased awareness of the need to link management development to corporate strategy, but some organisations view it as a cost rather than a driver of strategic value.

Variations are evident in the strategic contribution of human resources to strategy and the specific contribution of HR to strategy formulation. HR specialists have an impact in Ireland, Denmark and Germany and, to a lesser extent, in the UK. French and British managers are less likely to perceive human resource management practices as a source of competitive advantage. In Ireland, organisations are more positive on the contribution of HR practices. The key message emerging is that HR specialists need to have a more strategic role in order for the link between leadership and HR and business strategy to be more evident.

Perception of Managers' Development: There is a considerable degree of convergence concerning what makes an effective manager. Managers are expected to be decision-makers and to possess a range of task-focused and interpersonal competencies. Managers perform a range of management and leadership functions. Organisations across Europe generally perceive that in-house development and work experience are important components of management and leadership development. Experience tends to be more highly valued in the UK and Ireland. There is a strong focus on the general development of skills in both countries. German and Norwegian organisations place emphasis on more formal experience as a means to develop effective managers. Formal qualifications can act either as a screening mechanism or as a strategy to improve managerial skills. Ireland, Denmark and the UK place emphasis on qualifications, but in the UK this is perhaps more for screening than for the development of skills.

A key dimension of divergence concerns the commitment of the organisation to the manager and whether there is a career structure in the organisation. Irish organisations are increasingly committed to career development. In Spain and France, there is less emphasis on long-term retention, whereas in Denmark, Germany and Norway there is a focus on the longer term. The situation in the UK is that a significant proportion of organisations do not have career structures for managers.

Evaluation of Management and Leadership Development: The overall commitment to the evaluation of management and leadership development is weak across European organisations. Espedal (2004) suggested that Norwegian organisations link management and leadership development with individual performance, but not with organisational performance. There are few attempts to evaluate management and leadership development in German organisations, but they believe that management and leadership development can contribute to organisational performance. Seebacker *et al.* (2003) suggested that German organisations rely on performance appraisal and informal evaluation. Danish organisations seek to evaluate management and leadership development. Hjalager (2003) indicated that Danish organisations use balanced scorecards, multisource feedback and satisfaction surveys. They do not, however, conduct ROI studies. Irish and UK organisations carry out relatively little formal evaluation and few ROI studies. They espouse the belief that management and leadership development contributes to individual and organisational performance. Irish and UK organisations rely on feedback questionnaires, informal feedback and career tracking. Spanish organisations carry out relatively little leadership development evaluation. Le Deist *et al.* (2004) suggested that French organisations have mixed opinions concerning the impact of management and leadership development. Organisations that conduct evaluation typically use performance appraisals, debriefing sessions, development plans and progress reports. They use these methods to claim that management and leadership development positively impacts on business performance. However, French organisations that do not carry out such evaluations make similar claims.

Institutions and Government: Countries differ in terms of the role of institutions and the government on management and leadership development activities in individual firms. The German government, for example, has become increasingly active in the provision of vocational education and training. They have implemented a number of significant structural reforms and government spending has increased by twenty-one per cent over a seven-year period. It launched a major vocational training and education initiative in 2002. Despite these significant initiatives by the government, responsibility for management and leadership development in Germany is left to companies themselves.

The Danish Ministry of Industry and Trade has focused on the need for upgrading skills and competencies. The Danish government has placed a strong emphasis on the enhancement of management skills. In Denmark, there are many publicly provided management-development programmes which are held in high esteem by employers and managers. Mabey and Ramirez (2004) suggested that public development is required in Denmark due to the predominance of small companies who lack the expertise and resources to develop their managers effectively.

In Ireland, the launch of a revised Excellence Through People Standard and the formulation of a National Workplace Strategy have increasingly highlighted the need for increased government initiatives to enhance managerial skills in Irish organisations. Excellence Through People is a national human resource standard designed to enhance the quality of training and development activities, including leadership development activities. The accreditation process distinguishes between standard, global and platinum certification. These various types of certification enable certified organisations to make continuous improvements to their leadership development activities (Jenkinson 2004). The revised standard includes a specific standard on leadership and people management. This standard emphasises the need for organisations to lead and manage their human resources in a competent and effective way. Table 18.11 sets out the different requirements at the three levels of certification. The standard envisages, at the platinum level, that organisations will have an integrated approach to leadership development, including clearly defined competencies, effective succession and career management processes, integration of leadership development with business plans and an approach to leadership which empowers people.

Table 18.11: The Excellence Through People Standard: Requirements for Leadership and People Management

		Leadership and People Management: The organisation leads and manages its people and their performance to predetermined objectives in a competent and effective manner	
STANDARD	3A	Managers can describe how the organisation plans and implements development to enhance their skills in line with the Business Plan and can provide examples of how they have applied the learning acquired	20
	3B	The organisation can show that all people and managers undergo a formal performance review at least once per year and can provide examples of how the review has impacted on their success in their job	10
	3C	Managers and people can provide examples of how they have been developed to participate effectively in a performance review discussion	15
	3D	People have clearly defined job objectives with measurable goals and targets	10
	3E	The organisation can demonstrate to all people that it values them as individuals and their input to business success	10
GOLD	3F	Groups of people have clearly defined team/department objectives with measurable goals and targets	10
	3G	The organisation can show that all managers and people undergo a formal and interim performance review every year	5
	3H	The organisation can show that its management performance review process is effective at measuring the progress of managers carrying out their staff development responsibilities	10
	3I	The organisation effectively communicates its key selection criteria for management positions in order to facilitate internal promotion opportunities	10
	3J	People throughout the organisation can describe how their manager is effective at motivating them	10
PLATINUM	3K	People can describe how they contribute to the performance review process	5
	3L	The organisation can show improvements made to their performance review process as a result of people's feedback	5
	3M	The organisation has clearly defined competencies that underpin manager and people performance	10
	3N	The organisation has a clear vision and values that directly link to the performance indicators at individual, team and organisation level	5
	3O	The organisation can show that it has an effective succession planning and career development plan in place	5
	3P	The organisation can show that changes to its business plan have an effect on manager and people competencies where applicable	5
	3Q	The organisation can show that its approach to leadership and people management is effective at improving performance	5
		Total Points	**150**

The National Workplace Strategy places considerable emphasis on the development of skills, including the development of management skills. This strategy calls for proactive and cohesive management at a policy level and at the level of the enterprise. The strategy emphasises that the education sector has a major role to play in management and leadership development and encourages the accreditation of work-based management and leadership development. It recommends that the National Training Fund should support a wider range of workplace training and development initiatives, focused on enterprise needs and, if possible, leading to an accredited award. The activities of skill sets will focus on the development of managers in SMEs. The strategy advocates a partnership approach at a national level with a commitment to increased investment in in-company development activities.

Thomson *et al.* (2001) suggested that, at national level, there is a lot of uncertainty concerning policy frameworks for organisational learning and development. This has led to considerable confusion, with a lack of certainty concerning how best to facilitate organisations and encourage leadership development. The Spanish institutional context is especially challenging. Spanish legislation effectively discourages companies from allocating financial resources to training plans and other development activities. Many Spanish businesses are family-run and, as a result, managers have only begun to emerge in the last fifty years or so. The Spanish government has been less successful in integrating management development into business activities. The French government and the French employers' association (MEDEF) have sought to raise awareness of the importance and impact of management and leadership development. The French government has adopted a tripartite approach and, in conjunction with trade unions, has sought to change attitudes towards the development of young and other managers.

There are, therefore, many commonalities in organisational approaches to management and leadership development in Europe. There is strong convergence on the use of management and leadership development methods and the overall level of investment in management and leadership development. Each country does, however, have certain unique practices resulting from the influence of national institutions and culture. Brewster, Mayrhofer and Morley (2004) suggested that management and leadership development practices and meanings vary across borders and it is difficult to identify a standard set of best practices for management and leadership development. Klarsfeld and Mabey (2004) argued that the variation in approach to management and leadership development reflects that all practices are influenced by specific national cultures. There is evidence of directional convergence, but not final convergence. Table 18.12 summarises a number of practice issues and guidelines that emerge from the comparative analysis of management and leadership development activities and practices. In terms of approaches, organisations in Europe tend to adopt management and leadership development practices that emphasise the short or long term, have a lower or higher career focus, focus on organisation-specific skills or generic managerial skills, and are carried out exclusively in house and/or external to the organisation, in business schools and training institutions.

Table 18.12: Comparative Management and Leadership Development Practices: Implications for Organisations and Best Practices

- Management and leadership development can make an important contribution to manager self-confidence, individual accountability and empowerment.
- Organisations should communicate realistic expectations concerning management and leadership development. Expectations should be clearly articulated and any potential conflicts addressed openly.
- Management and leadership development is best positioned to deliver in the long term. Organisations need to demonstrate patience before it can contribute to strategic value.
- Leadership development practitioners need to fully understand context and to analyse organisational barriers to learning transfer.

- Human resource and leadership development specialists need to be assertive in articulating their contribution to management and leadership development and in interpreting the implications of business strategies into actionable policies and practices.
- The evaluation of management and leadership development is problematic but should not be ignored. Evaluation strategies should involve key stakeholders and the results should be published.
- Organisations and leadership development specialists must focus on developing a strong ethos for management and leadership development, as well as developing appropriate systems.
- Effective management and leadership development requires a shared agenda, a sense of realism about the contribution of management and leadership development and needs to ensure that the managers understand the strategic intent underpinning management and leadership development.

World Views of Management and Leadership Development

The majority of literature on leadership and leadership development is written from a Western perspective. Leadership development, as practised in organisations, is not associated with any religious tradition. The use of religion in organisations is, however, potentially divisive as it may encourage distrust. It can become divisive because people within the organisation may not share the same religious tradition. We believe, however, that there is value in considering the topics of leadership and leadership development from the perspectives of a number of world views. World views derived from Christian, Hindu, Buddhist, Islamic, Judaic and Confucian thinking have the potential to enrich our understanding of management and leadership development. World views are important because they direct how we think about issues. Ruona and Lynham (2004) suggested that how people think about the world shapes their actions and this, in turn, influences how people see the world. World views are useful devices in which to frame, explore and understand leadership processes and management and leadership development. Kriger and Seng (2005) suggested that world views have the potential to deepen our understanding of the practice of leadership and leadership development in organisations. Leadership and leadership development is often a result of 'subtle invisible feelings, thoughts and intuitions' (Badaracco 2002). Therefore, world views have the potential to highlight a range of beliefs, values and paradigms and to shape thinking, beliefs and behaviours in managers. We will focus in this last section of the book on six world views and highlight their implications for our thinking about leadership and leadership development. These are Christianity, Judaism, Islam, Buddhism, Hinduism and Confucianism. Table 18.13 provides a summary of the implications for leadership and leadership development of each of these world views.

A Christian World View of Leadership Development: Reagan (2000) and Elias and Merriam (2005) argued that Western people tend to trivialise religion, make reference to God as a formality but do not allow religion to enter discussions concerning how organisations function. The Ten Commandments are central to a Christian world view. These commandments do not deal with work or leadership in a direct way. They represent fundamental human values that are worded in a very abstract way. They represent idealised guidelines that are designed to perfect human beings. God is perfect, therefore man can be perfect. This pursuit of the ideal may induce believers to give priority to spiritual duties and neglect other duties.

As principles, the Ten Commandments in Christianity are universal in nature. They place a strong emphasis on avoiding conflict and on full obedience to authority. These commandments have major implications for leadership behaviour in organisations and suggest a model of leadership behaviour. Ali and Gibbs (1998) suggested that the Ten Commandments have a number of implications for leaders (page 727):

Table 18.13: World View Perceptions for Leadership and Leadership Development

World View	Views of Leadership	Views of Leadership Development
Christianity	• The leader is a role model for thinking and behaviour • The thoughts of the leaders focus on love and peace • Moral leadership is based on moral virtues • Leadership wisdom is derived from the Old and New Testaments • The core vision of leadership is love	• Leadership development focuses on developing appropriate role model behaviours • Develop leaders to think of their role as that of servants. Focus on developing the whole person • Leaders need to develop the reliance to transform the organisation, to stay on course and to create good for society • Development is a lifelong process of openness to change, humility, personal reflection and meditation
Judaism	• The leader is a teacher and asker of questions • The leader focuses on meaning-making • Leaders show perseverance • The core vision of the leader is oneness • The basis for moral leadership is the Mishrak or 610 rules of correct behaviour	• Development should encourage the use of discussion questions and a search for meaning • Mentoring relationships should be open, intense, challenging and based on strong emotional bonds • Development should be on a strong work ethic and diligence in the performance of duties • Development should seek to balance the work life and the private life • Leadership development can be achieved through small group activities, communities of practice and collective learning activities
Islam	• The leader is a servant of God and his creators • The thinking of the leader is embodied in the 99 names of God • The core vision of the leader is surrendering to God • The key source of wisdom from leaders is the Qur'an • The basis for moral leadership is the law or Sari'ah	• A strong emphasis on continuous learning and collective learning • Development should emphasise justice and equity in the workplace • Leadership development should focus on teamwork and collaboration • Development can take place through informal interaction and collaborative activity • Development processes should emphasise memorisation and the acquisition of knowledge

World View	Views of Leadership	Views of Leadership Development
Buddhism	• Leader is essentially a teacher and role model • The process of leadership focuses on being an example • The leader engages in meditation and investigation of awareness • The leader demonstrates wisdom and compassion • The basis for moral leadership is the leader's mind fitness • The source of wisdom for leaders is investigation of the inner self	• Leadership development is a process inquiry, but it is not dogma • Leadership development should focus on the message and not the teacher • Learning involves a search for meaning, not rote methods • Meditation is a key component of leadership development. It helps leaders to become aware of their thinking • The leader becomes his or her own teacher, becomes more independent, self-confident and learns from all life experiences • Leaders possess a unique potential to develop • The development of the leader is a joint responsibility of the individual and the organisation
Hinduism	• The leader is a role model of the 'gods' • The leader demonstrates leadership through examples and stories • The leader should demonstrate awareness and perception • The core vision of the leader is liberation and quality • The basis for moral leadership is meditation, worldly success, liberation and rebirth	• Leaders possess a unique potential to develop • The development of the leader is a joint responsibility of the individual and the organisation • Organisations facilitate the realisation of self through the activities that leaders perform • Leadership development is continuous, holistic and occurs in different stages • Leadership development activities should discourage introspection, self-study based on personal experience • Organisations can facilitate introspection through providing a learning environment, providing appropriate learning experiences and developing learn-to-learn skills
Confucian	• Leaders are essentially good and are changeable • Leadership is about multiple realities and interpretation of the world • Leaders strive to achieve learning and group orientation. Harmony is more important than the leader's growth • Leaders engage in action, thinking and being • Moral leadership is demonstrated through sympathy and self-control • Leaders promote stability through following traditional social hierarchy	• Leadership development should emphasise unity between theory and practice • Development should focus on using a strong trainer-centred approach • Learning should focus on reflection, systematic approaches and questioning • Leadership development should emphasise harmony, paternalism, respect and avoidance of conflict or disagreement • Knowledge related to leadership is certain, unambiguous and unchanged • Leadership development can be achieved through collective and group-focused development activities

- The negotiation of settlements to solve business problems is a virtue. Leaders should pursue compromise, listen to and understand the views of others.
- A strong understanding of motives and needs will facilitate better leadership and relationships with others. Sincere relationships are a vital component of leadership.
- Confidence in and trust of others facilitates better leadership.
- Leaders should avoid work conflicts and compromises.
- Leaders should rely on sound judgement and personal sympathy, avoid conflict with others and tolerate their aggressiveness.
- Leaders should pursue fairness and due process. These are essential components of Christian leadership.

Delbecq (1999) suggested that the Christian world view informs leadership in a number of ways: leadership should be viewed as a calling to service rather than a job or a career. All creation is redeemable and good; therefore, the leader participating in co-creation can be viewed as being involved in an act of love. The private and public life of the leader are integrated rather than separate. Leadership is therefore a role worthy of the highest form of servant leadership.

The Christian world view advocates that leaders are expected to have courage, they are required to stay on course, demonstrate dignity when they encounter challenge and continually strive to implement a vision which is bold and courageous. Leaders from this world view are also expected to be flexible, to be open to change and to maintain a detachment from what is comfortable and familiar.

Leadership development, therefore, focuses on the development of role models. Christianity requires that leaders model the way and that they walk the walk. They need to be skilled to create a climate for truth within the organisation. It is not enough to espouse values; they must practise them. Daft and Lengel (1998) suggested that the development of imagination, inspiration and mindfulness are the key challenges for leadership development. These are necessary to enable leaders to feel what others are feeling, to see what is about to be created out of the list of possibilities and to show persistence when things are not going as planned. Organisations should strive to create developmental activities that develop the whole person. Leadership development should not be about exploiting talents and strengths. This suggests that leaders are not owned by the organisation and therefore leaders' continued employability is a key concern for organisations. Development activities should affirm the basic humanity of the leader.

An Islamic World View of Leadership and Leadership Development: An Islamic world view places a strong emphasis on the building of community, a concern for social justice and the equality of voice. Kriger and Seng (2005) argued that the community has a particular significance in Islamic thinking. This sense of community is strengthened by the Five Pillars of Islam. These Five Pillars consist of 1) affirmation of the oneness of God and that Mohammad is God's messenger; 2) the requirement to pray five times daily with a communal, noon prayer on Friday; 3) the conduct of acts of charity and the giving of alms to the poor; 4) fasting during the month of Ramadan; and 5) the performance of a pilgrimage to Mecca. These Pillars emphasise that all people are created equal and that, as leaders, they must strive for balance and harmony.

An Islamic world view also emphasises the transcendent and the immanent (the visible universe). There is a strong belief that each individual is responsible for his or her own actions. The individual must constantly balance the needs of the individual and the needs of the community. Leaders are expected to enhance and further the common good. Economic activity is a means to a spiritual end and prosperity is concerned with living a virtuous life. An Islamic world view has a lot to say about business conduct and day-to-day activities in business. Ali and Gibbs (1998) suggested that Islamic teaching has important implications for leadership behaviours. These include:

- Unity of direction and a respect for competent and accepted authority
- Respect for employees with longevity, respect for human dignity and a concern for justice and equity
- A concern not to ignore agreed-on contracts, and to fulfil promises to others.

Akdere, Russ-Eft and Eft (2006) argue that learning, knowledge and education are central to the Islamic world view. Knowledge provides the basis for truth, ethics and wisdom. Knowledge is achieved through studying the holy texts. The Qur'an is considered pivotal and the hallmark of learning. A strong emphasis is placed on memorising, as well as understanding. Education is concerned with enabling the development of the individual, increasing an understanding of society and its rules, and the transmission of knowledge. An Islamic world view places a strong emphasis on autonomous learning, informal learning and collective learning. Work plays a central role in Islamic teachings. It is viewed as a means of achieving spiritual growth and individuals are expected to be accountable for their work and to maximise their abilities. Discrimination is not permissible. There is a strong emphasis on developing a profession and leaders are expected to engage in an apprenticeship process through which they will eventually become professional leaders.

Leadership development activities should focus on teamwork and collaboration. Leaders are encouraged to interact with each other, to develop and acquire new skills and to be open to continuous learning. Islamic teaching gives strong recognition to informal leadership development. A central concept of Islamic teaching involves a situation where adults sit in learning sets and interact with each other and a teacher. This concept has application to organisations in that learners acquire new skills through interaction and facilitate organisational learning. Ultimately, while the leader is part of a larger community, he is responsible for his or her own learning. Leaders are leaders in their own lives and to those around them.

The Buddhist World View of Leadership and Leadership Development: Central to the teachings of Buddhism is the idea that the personal self is empty of reality. This suggests that the leader within the Buddhist world view 'thinks, feels, serves and observes the changing aspects of the world and the inner contents of the mind, along with feelings and sensations' (Kriger and Seng 2005:783). Therefore, the concept of the ego or self so prominent in Western psychology is considered to be negative and a fundamental cause of unhappiness. Buddhist thinking advocates selflessness or no-self, the idea that there are no distinctions between ourselves and others. The challenge for leaders, according to Buddhist teachings, is to become a balanced and aware individual. Goldstein and Kornfield (1987) highlighted that within Buddhist teaching, leaders can achieve enlightenment through effort and energy, mindfulness, investigation, interest, concentration, tranquillity and equanimity. When these are developed, the leader has the potential to be more energised and empathetic. Leaders are, however, hindered by an aversion to people, an attachment to sense of pleasure, laziness of the body and mind, doubt and restlessness in behaviour and mind. These hindrances can result in negative emotions and decreased leadership effectiveness.

Buddhist teachings emphasise four immeasurable states of mind: love, compassion, joy and equanimity. This suggests that a leader will be effective only if he/she practises and embodies these four positive states of mind. Kriger and Seng (2005) suggests that this highlights a dynamic moment-by-moment view of leadership. It focuses on inner spiritual practice as well as outward behaviour. Buddhists make a commitment to follow rules, or principles, which are vows made to oneself. These precepts advocate that all individuals abstain from killing, stealing, unwholesome sexual contact, incorrect speech and intoxicants.

A Buddhist world view proposes some interesting ideas for the development of leaders. Johansen and Gopalakrishna (2006) suggest that it promotes enquiry and questioning. Leaders are encouraged not to accept leadership ideas as dogma. Ideas should be tested before they are accepted and all ideas need to be verified. Hanh (1998) suggested that leaders should not necessarily focus on the teacher; learning should focus initially on basic concepts and then build up towards more complicated concepts; learning processes should promote deep learning and meaning; and inductive and deductive approaches to learning should be used. Developers have particular responsibilities. Kelly, Sawyer and Yareham (2005) suggested that they must check understanding, demonstrate self-discipline, be well versed in their discipline and demonstrate compassion and understanding for the learner.

Meditation is considered a key component of effective leadership development. Das (1997) suggested that meditation is a way to create mindfulness and to help leaders be aware of what their conscience is telling them. An important outcome of meditation is the development of self-confidence and independence. It enables leaders to be mindful of the key learning from all life experiences. Leadership development activities need to focus on the entire person. Buddhist teaching states that leadership does not exist in isolation. It involves interaction with other things and people. Leadership development practices have implications for the wider organisation, in particular for the well-being of the organisation. Buddhist thinking encourages experiential learning, the active testing of ideas in the workplace and reflection on how those ideas work in practice.

A Judaic World View of Leadership and Leadership Development: Judaism commands that people work six days a week. Because God left his work unfinished, it is up to man to finish that work. According to Judaism, work has duality in life, spirituality and worldly affairs. Work can take various forms, but the desire to achieve and to excel in life is considered a religious duty. Jewish teachings place a strong emphasis on good behaviour, honesty, faithfulness and respect for authority figures. Individuals are expected to show loyalty to authority, to place an emphasis on appearance and the value of good impressions. There is a strong emphasis on literal meaning and on contractual relationships. Leaders are expected to promote honesty as a virtue, to promote conflict resolution in a frank and businesslike way, treat partnerships as necessary for business growth, engage in activities that strengthen relationships within the community, promote respect for seniority in the organisation and promote commitment.

Judaism considers learning to be an end in itself, an essential part of being Jewish. Beck (2006) suggests that Jewish children learn about religious traditions and practices at home and in synagogue. Jews are expected to ask questions and to wonder continually. Jewish teachings emphasise dialogue, questioning, mentoring and workplace learning. Schuster (2003) suggested that Judaic learning focuses on the use of discursive questioning techniques and striving for meaning. Jews have a healthy scepticism and are comfortable with self-managed learning processes. Judaism emphasises the important role of mentoring, the creation of emotional bonds between developee and developer and a process of intense argumentation. The role of the mentor is to be challenged in discussion and to be flexible in dialogue. The mentoring relationship is therefore expected to be intense and open, and to further both individual and corporate needs. Learning and development in Jewish teaching is strongly linked to the workplace. The workplace can take many forms, including the community and wider society. Meir (2005) suggested that individuals should work for a living, but work to live rather than live to work. Leaders are expected to be diligent and to serve both the organisation and, ultimately, God. Interestingly, Judaism recognises that self-interest plays a major role in ensuring moral leadership. Leaders should focus on encouraging long-lasting relationships which are based on honesty.

Judaism has a lot of interesting ideas that inform leadership development. It highlights the value of structured coaching and mentoring relationships, the facilitation of interaction amongst colleagues and the use of small group learning activities. These ideas could also support a community of practice or learning organisation approaches. The emphasis on questioning and the development of shared meaning represent important components of collective approaches to leadership development.

A Hindu World View of Leadership and Leadership Development: A Hindu world view places strong emphasis on a holistic approach to leadership and leadership development. Leadership behaviour is determined by the interaction of individual, organisation, society, the universe and the cosmos. The process of development therefore facilitates the leader to achieve self-realisation and to achieve insights concerning the relationship between the various elements of organisations, society, and the wider world. Hinduism proceeds from the principle that all individuals have unique potential.

Hinduism says that each individual is wrapped up within five sheaths called Koshas. Ashok and Thimmappa (2006) summarise these as relating to body, breath, mind, intellect and bliss. The bodily sheath determines the strength and overall health of the human body. The bodily sheath is the reservoir of vital energy. The mental sheath governs intelligence, whereas the intellectual sheath is the source of ultimate knowledge and self-realisation. The bliss sheath contains the source of divine bliss which is defined as a state of mind leading to ultimate spiritual realisation. These Koshas are hierarchical and a leader may operate from any one of them at a particular time. Leadership development activities, therefore, have a major role to play in enabling the individual leader to understand and unfold each sheath and to achieve personal growth and development.

Hinduism argues that growth and development occurs in stages. Hiriyanna (2002) suggested that each stage is associated with a particular set of goals: childhood/duty, youth/wealth, adult/desire, recluse/liberation and self-realisation. Hinduism advocates that yoga is a way of life rather than a set of exercises. It provides the leader with stability, self-realisation and skilfulness. Yoga focuses on restraints, observances, bodily posture, breathing mechanisms, withdrawal of senses, credibility and global absorption. The ultimate challenge is to ensure that the leader becomes one with the true self. In such a state of mind, the leader and the object of perception achieve a true unity.

Hindu teaching has important implications for the process of leadership development. It suggests the following propositions: 1) leadership development is a joint responsibility between the individual and the organisation; 2) yoga facilitates the leader to understand inner potential and realise oneself and it also enables the leader to achieve realisation of self through work; 3) development is a continuous process; 4) formal development activities enable the leader to acquire knowledge and skills that can be implemented to the benefit of both the individual and the organisation; 5) experiential methods, such as action, reflection, introspection and personal experience, are central to effective leadership development; 6) organisations can facilitate leadership development through the creation of an appropriate learning environment; 7) development activities should focus on reducing the egocentric or self-centred nature of people; and 8) various learning practices, including yoga, help leaders to meet both individual and organisational needs.

The leadership development process is essentially one of self-realisation at the individual level. For organisations, the key challenge is to provide a learning environment which fosters development and, in particular, introspection, self-realisation and discovery, and which achieves cosmic unity.

A Confucian World View of Leadership and Leadership Development: Confucianism represents traditional Chinese culture and stands for a philosophical system which is over two thousand years old. Yang, Zheng and Li (2006) highlight six dimensions of Confucian teaching. These are as follows: 1) harmony is the ultimate goal of society; 2) the individual is less valued than perceived collective interest; 3) a strong priority is given to doing, thinking and being; 4) individuals must demonstrate self-control and sympathy; 5) an emphasis on the past; and 6) a strong emphasis on stability, harmony and tradition. Harmony is considered much more important than the growth of the individual.

Confucianism assumes that people have the capacity to be good and to change. Unlike many other world views, it does not believe in a single superpower, and knowledge is viewed as subjective and having an instrumental function. It is possible to have multiple realities and an interpretative approach to leadership. Change is a cyclical process and concerned with the maintenance of equilibrium. The essence of humankind is in the spirit and, as a result, people should focus on the spiritual rather than the material. It does acknowledge that people can fall prey to the material world, but they need to exercise control.

Confucian teachings have a strong influence on thinking about learning and development. Education is highly valued. It is designed to ensure that potential leaders have intelligence and knowledge, good courage, consistency, benevolence, maturity, talent and faculty. Learning and development processes serve society rather than the individual. Leaders are expected to fulfil social responsibilities. Education should facilitate equilibrium and ensure that there is a balance between people and the environment. Confucian teaching places a strong emphasis on the integration of theory and practice. There is less emphasis placed on problem-solving and critical thinking. Learning occurs in didactic settings with little time for discussion and debate. Tsang, Paterson and Packer (2002) highlighted the strong emphasis on knowledge as a linear process and that learners should be passive, compliant and respect leaders.

There is a strong focus in Confucian teachings on developer-centred approaches. Learning and development can best be achieved through the transmission of knowledge. The developer has to spend time explaining issues and the notion of interactive or learner-centred development is less valued. Learners are not expected to challenge their superiors and the same dynamic occurs in the context of leadership development. Leaders are reluctant to pursue two-way communication and leadership development strategies such as coaching and mentoring are difficult to accommodate within a Confucian perspective.

Conclusion

There is much to be learned from comparative and world view perspectives of management and leadership development. The comparative study of management and leadership development provides useful insights concerning what makes an effective manager, the factors that drive and constrain management and leadership development in different countries, the overall level of investment in management and leadership development, the various types of management and leadership development practices, which practices are favoured, the strength of the ethos for management and leadership development in different countries and the extent of divergence and convergence in both policy and practice.

Institutional theory suggests that, ultimately, organisations within a particular organisational field will converge in terms of their practices due to the impact of isomorphic tendencies. Other institutional approaches argue that social and institutional arrangements within individual countries are critical in shaping the types of management and leadership development practices that are adopted. These factors influence how the processes of management and leadership development are understood and they shape organisations' views on how best to develop leadership talent.

The majority of writings on management and leadership development espouse a Western perspective. However, given the processes of globalisation, it is appropriate to consider how different world views consider management and leadership development processes. These world views suggest a diversity of thinking concerning how best to develop leaders and the role of leaders in both organisations and the wider society. World views challenge leadership development specialists and academics to question the assumptions they make about leaders from different cultural and religious backgrounds. They also highlight the need to accommodate multiple perspectives and to realise that management and leadership development is a complex and diverse process.

Summary of Key Points

- Institutional theory argues that management and leadership development practices will converge and organisations will imitate practices which give them legitimacy in the wider environment.
- The extent to which management and leadership development practices become institutionalised depends on the length of time the practice has been in existence and its level of acceptance by organisations.
- Countries differ in terms of their approaches to management and leadership development. Some countries focus on short-term development, whereas others take a long-term view. Some countries place more value on internal development processes, while others focus on external qualifications. Others emphasise specific rather than generic managerial competencies.
- Managers are considered to be a source of competitive advantage and to be carriers of specific knowledge. However, countries differ in the level of commitment they give to management and leadership development, the amount of money invested and the level of responsibility that organisations take for the development of managers and leaders.
- Investment in management and leadership development in Ireland has grown steadily during the last fifteen years. Multinationals have had a major influence on investment levels and a significant impact on the practices of indigenous organisations. Management and leadership development practices in Irish SMEs are significantly below the standard of larger organisations.
- World views provide an additional lens through which to consider management and leadership development processes. They highlight the diversity and complexity of thinking in the role of leaders and the types of practices and approaches that organisations should adopt to develop managers and leaders.

■ Discussion Questions

1. How do institutional processes explain management and leadership development practices in organisations?

2. To what extent is there convergence in management and leadership development practices across Europe?

3. What are the key strengths and weaknesses of management development systems in Ireland?

4. How strategic is management and leadership development in Europe and what influence does human resource strategy have on management and leadership development practices?

5. Compare and contrast three of the six world views presented in this chapter in terms of their ideas about management and leadership development.

■ Application and Experiential Questions

1. Conduct research on two countries with which you are familiar. Examine the key institutional and labour market factors that potentially influence management and leadership development practices. How do these influence the management and leadership development practices of individual firms?

2. Select a multinational corporation with which you are familiar. Interview the leadership development specialist and/or the human resource manager in a particular operation. Consider the following issues: How does the operation manage the interface with headquarters? What role has management and leadership development played at different stages of the organisation's internationalisation? What factors have constrained the MNC to determine management and leadership development practices across national borders?

3. Divide the class into groups of three or four students. Each group should take one of the world views presented in this chapter and devise a set of management and leadership development policies which would reflect that world view. They should also consider ways in which the leadership development specialist can accommodate world views in their management and leadership development practices.

Bibliography

Adair, J. (2003): *The Inspirational Leader: How to Motivate, Encourage and Achieve Success*. London: Kogan Page.

Adamson, S. J., Doherty, N. and Viney, C. (1998): 'The meanings of career revisited: implications for theory and practice', *British Journal of Management*, 9:4, 251–259.

Adler, N. J. (1997): *International Dimensions of Organizational Behavior*. Cincinnati, OH: South-Western College Publishing.

Adler, N. J. and Bartholomew, S. (1992): 'Managing globally competent people', *Academy of Management Executive*, 6:3, 52–65.

Adler, N. J. and Ghadar, F. (1990): 'Strategic Human Resource Management: A Global Perspective', in Pieper, R. (ed.), *Human Resource Management: An International Comparison*. Berlin: Walter de Gruyter.

Adler, N. J. and Izraeli, D. N. (1988): *Women in Management Worldwide*. Armonk, NY: M.E. Sharpe.

Aitchison, C. (2004): 'Succession planning at the Dixons Group', *Strategic HR Review*, 3:5, 24–27.

Akdere, M., Russ-Eft, D. and Eft, N. (2006): 'The Islamic worldview of adult learning in the workplace', *Advances in Developing Human Resources*, 8:3, 355–363.

Alberga, T., Tyson, S. and Parsons, D. (1997): 'An evaluation of the investors in people standard', *Human Resource Management Journal*, 7:2, 47–60.

Albers, S. A. (2008): 'Leading change', *Leadership Excellence*, 25:10, 5–5.

Alden, J. and Kirkhorn, J. (1996): 'Case Studies', in R. L. Craig (ed.), *The ASTD Training and Development Handbook* (4th edn). New York: McGraw-Hill.

Ali, A. J. and Gibbs, M. (1998): 'Foundation of business ethics in contemporary religious thought: The ten commandment perspective', *International Journal of Social Economics*, 25:10, 1552–64.

Alimo-Metcalfe, B. (1995): 'An investigation of female and male constructs of leadership', *Women in Management Review*, 2:2, 36–44.

Allen, J. and Johnston, K. (1997): 'Mentoring', *Context*, 14:7, 15.

Allred, B., Snow, C. and Miles, R. E. (1996): 'Characteristics of managerial careers in the 21st century', *Academy of Management Executive*, 10:4, 17–27.

Alsop, A. (2000): *Counting Professional Development in Health-Care: A Guide for Therapists*. Oxford, UK: Blackwell Science.

Alvesson, M. and Deetz, S. (2000): *Doing Critical Management Research*. London: Sage.

Andersen, L., Boud, D. and Cohen, R. (1995): 'Experience-Based Learning', in G. Foley (ed.), *Understanding Adult Education and Training*. Sydney: Allen and Unwin.

Andrews, E. S. and Noel, J. L. (1986): 'Adding life to the case study method', *Training and Development Journal*, 40:2, 28–29.

Andrews, K. R. (1966): *The Effectiveness of University Management Development Programs*. Boston, MA: Harvard University.

Antonacopoulou, E. P. (1999): 'Training does not imply learning: the individual's perspective', *International Journal of Training and Development*, 3:1, 14–33.

Antonacopoulou, E. P. and Fitzgerald, L. (1996): 'Reframing competency in management education', *Human Resource Management Journal*, 6:1, 27–48.

Appelgate, L. M. (1995): '*Designing and managing the information age organization*', Harvard Business School, note # 9-196-003, pp. 14–15.

Applebaum, S. H. and Finestone, D. (1994): 'Revisiting career plateauing: same old problems – avant-garde solutions', *Journal of Managerial Psychology*, 9:5, 12–21.

Applebaum, S. H. and Santiago, V. (1997): 'Career development in the plateaued organization', *Career Development International*, 2:1, 11–20.

Ardts, J., Jansen, P. and van der Velde, M. (2001): 'The breaking in of new employees: effectiveness of socialisation tactics and personnel instruments', *Journal of Management Development*, 20:2, 159–167.

Argote, L., Beckman, S. L. and Epple, D. (1990): 'The persistence and transfer of learning in settings', *Management Science*, 36, 140–154.

Argyris, C. (1976): *Increasing Leadership Effectiveness*. New York: Wiley-Interscience.

Argyris, C. (1980): 'Some limitations of the case method: Experiences in a management development program', *Academy of Management Review*, 5:2, 291–298.

Argyris, C. (1986): 'Reinforcing organizational defence routines: An unintended human resources activity', *Human Resource Management*, 25:4, 541–555.

Argyris, C. (1993): *Knowledge for Action: A Guide to Overcoming Barriers to Organizational Change*. San Francisco: Jossey-Bass.

Argyris, C. and Schon, D. A. (1978): *Organizational Learning: A Theory Of Action Perspective*. Reading, MA: Addison-Wesley.

Argyris, C. and Schon, D. A. (1996): *Organizational Learning II: Theory, Method and Practice*. Reading, MA: Addison-Wesley.

Armstrong, A. and Foley, P. (2003): 'Foundations for a learning organization: organization learning mechanisms', *The Learning Organization*, 10:2, 74–82.

Armstrong, D. J. and Edelstein B. C. (1993): 'A model for executive development', *Human Resource Planning*, 16:4, 51–64.

Armstrong, M. (2006): *A Handbook of Human Resource Management Practice* (8th edn). London: Kogan Page.

Arnold, J. (1989): 'Career decidedness and psychological well-being: A two-cohort longitudinal study of undergraduate students and recent graduates', *Journal of Occupational Psychology*, 62, 163–176.

Arnold, J., Cooper, C. L. and Robertson, I. T. (1997): *Work Psychology: Understanding Human Behaviour in the Workplace*. London: Pitman Publishing.

Arnold, J. and Mackenzie-Davey, K. (1992): 'Self-ratings and supervisor ratings of graduate employees' competencies during early career', *Journal of Occupational and Organisational Psychology*, 65:3, 235–250.

Arnold, J. and Mackenzie-Davey, K. (1994): 'Graduate experiences of organisational career management', *International Journal of Career Management*, 6:3, 14–18.

Arnold, J. and Nicholson, N. (1991): 'From expectation to experience: Graduates entering a large corporation', *Journal of Organisational Behaviour*, 12, 413–429.

Arons, R. M. and Ruh, R. (2004): American Hospital Supply Corp: An Historic Incubator of Leadership Talent, Korn Ferry International Monograph.

Arthur, J. and Aimant-Smith, L. (2001): 'Gainsharing and organizational learning: an analysis of employee suggestions over time', *Academy of Management Journal*, 44:4, 737–754.

Arthur, M. B. (1994): 'The boundaryless career: A new perspective for organizational inquiry,' *Journal of Organizational Behaviour*, 15:4, 295–306.

Arthur, M. B., Inkson, K. and Pringle, J. K. (1999): *The New Careers: Individual Action And Economic Change*. Thousand Oaks, CA: Sage.

Asheghian, P. and Ebrahimi, B. (1990): *International Business*. New York: Harper Collins.

Ashkanasy, N. M. and Daus, C. (2002): 'Emotion in the workplace: The new challenge for managers', *Academy of Management Executive*, 16:1, 76–86.

Ashkenas, R., Ulrich, D., Jick, T. and Kerr, S. (1995): *The Boundaryless Organisation*. San Francisco: Jossey-Bass.

Ashok, H. S. and Thimmappa, M. S. (2006): 'A Hindu worldview of adult learning in the workplace', *Advances in Developing Human Resources*, 8:3, 329–336.

Ashton, C. and Morton, L. (2005): 'Managing talent for competitive advantage', *Strategic HR Review*, 4:5, 28–31.

Ashton, D. (2004): 'The impact of organizational structure and practices on learning in the workplace', *International Journal of Training and Development*, 8:1, 43–53.

Ashton, D., Easterby-Smith, M. and Irvine, C. (1975): *Management Development: Theory and Practice*. Bradford: MCB.

Avolio, B. J. (1999): *Full Leadership Development: Building the Vital Forces in Organizations*. Thousand Oaks, CA: Sage.

Avolio, B. J. and Gardner, W. L. (2005): 'Authentic leadership development: Getting to the root of positive forms of leadership', *Leadership Quarterly*, 16(3), 315–388.

Axon, D. (2003): 'Act up, don't crack up: A manager's guide to deputizing', *Nursing Management*, 11:8, 19–21.

Ayman, R., Kreicker, N. A., and Masztal, J. J. (1994): 'Defining global leadership in business environments', *Consulting Psychology Journal*, 46:1, 64–77.

Baars, M. (2003): 'Learning Climate: The Cultural Dimension of Learning in Organisations'. Unpublished Doctoral Dissertation. The Netherlands: Tilburg University.

Badaracco, J. L., Jr (2002): *Learning Quietly: An Unorthodox Guide to Doing the Right Thing*. Boston, MA: Harvard Business School Press.

Badger, B., Sadler-Smith, E. and Michie, E. (1997): 'Outdoor management development: Use and evaluation', *Journal of European Industrial Training*, 21:9, 318–325.

Bahniuk, M. H. and Kolger Hill, S. (1998): 'Promoting career success through mentoring', *Review of Business*, 19:3, 4–7.

Bailey, C. and Austin, M. (2006): '360-degree feedback and developmental outcomes: The role of feedback characteristics, self-efficacy and importance of feedback dimensions to focal managers' current role', *International Journal of Selection and Assessment*, 14:1, 51–66.

Baker, A. C., Jensen, P. J. and Kolb, D. A. (2005): 'Conversation as experiential learning', *Management Learning*, 36:4, 411–27.

Baldwin, T. T. and Padgett, M. Y. (1994): 'Management Development: A Review and Commentary', in C. L. Cooper, I.T. Roberts and Associates (eds), *Key Reviews in Managerial Psychology: Concepts and Research for Practice*. Chichester, UK: Wiley.

Baldwin, T., Wagner, R. and Roland, C. (1991): 'Effectiveness of outdoor challenge on group and individual outcomes'. Unpublished manuscript, University of Wisconsin, Center for Research in Experiential Training, Whitewater, WI.

Balkundi, P. and Kilduff, M. (2005): 'The ties that lead: A social network approach to leadership', *Leadership Quarterly*, 16:6, 941–961.

Ball, B. (1997): 'Career management competencies – The individual perspective', *Career Development International*, 2:2, 74–79.

Bandura, A. (1986): *Social Foundations of Thought and Action*. Englewood Cliffs, NJ: Prentice-Hall.

Bandura, A. (1990): 'Conclusion: Reflection On Nonability Determinants Of Competence', in R. J. Sternberg and J. Jr Kolligian (eds), *Competence Considered*. New Haven, CT: Yale University Press.

Bandura, A. (1995): 'Exercise of Personal and Collective Efficacy in Changing Societies', in A. Bandura, (ed.), *Self-efficacy in Changing Societies*. Cambridge: Cambridge University Press.

Bandura, A. and Locke, E. (2003): 'Negative self-efficacy and goals effects revisited', *Journal of Applied Psychology*, 88:1, 87–99.

Barclay, J. M. (1996): 'Learning from experience with learning logs', *Journal of Management Development*, 15:6, 28–43.

Bard, M. and Moore, E. (2000): 'Mentoring and self-managed learning: Professional development for the market research industry', *International Journal of Market Research*, 42:3, 255–275.

Barid, L. and Meshoulam, I. (1988): 'Managing the fits of strategic human resource management', *Academy of Management Review*, 13:1, 122–123.

Barker, R. (1997): 'How can we train leaders if we do not know what leadership is?', *Human Relations*, 50:4, 343–362.

Barner, R. (2006): 'The targeted assessment coaching interview: Adapting the assessment process to different coaching requirements', *Career Development International*, 11:2, 96–107.

Barnett, R. (1994): *The Limits of Competence*. Buckingham: Open University Press.

Baron, R. A. (1988): 'Negative effects of destructive criticism: Impact on conflict, self-efficacy, and task performance', *Journal of Applied Psychology*, 73:2, 199–207.

Barrett, G. V. and Depinet, R. L. (1991): 'A reconsideration of testing for competence rather than for intelligence', *American Psychologist*, 46, 1012–1024.

Bartlett, C. A., and Ghoshal, S. (1989): *Managing Across Borders: The Transnational Solution* (1st edn). Boston: Harvard Business School Press.

Bartlett, C. A. and Ghoshal, S. (1997): 'The myth of the generic manager: New personal competencies for new management roles', *California Management Review*, 40:1, 92–116.

Bartlett, C. A. and Ghoshal, S. (2001): *Managing Across Borders: The Transnational Solution* (2nd edn). Harvard Business School Press Books.

Bartlett, C. A. and Ghoshal, S. (2003): 'What is a global manager?', *Harvard Business Review*, August 2003.

Baruch, Y. (2004): *Managing Careers: Theory and Practice*. England: Pearson Education Ltd.

Baruch, Y. (2006): 'Career development in organizations and beyond: Balancing traditional and contemporary viewpoints', *Human Resource Management Review*, 16:2, 125–38.

Baruch, Y. and Peiperl, M. A. (2000): 'The impact of an MBA on graduate careers', *Human Resource Management Journal*, 10:2, 69–90.

Bass, B. M. (1990): *Handbook of Leadership: A Survey of Theory and Research*. New York: Free Press.

Bass, B. M. and Avolio, B. J. (1993): 'Transformational Leadership: A Response to Critiques', in M. M. Chemers and R. Ayman (eds), *Leadership Theory and Research*. Orlando, FL: Academic Press.

Bass, B. M. and Avolio, B. J. (eds) (1994): *Improving Organisational Effectiveness through Transformational Leadership*. Thousand Oaks, CA: Sage.

Batt, R. (2000): 'Strategic segmentation in front-line services: Matching customers, employees and human resource systems', *International Journal of Human Resource Management*, 11:3, 540–561.

Batt, R. and Moynihan, L. (2004): 'The viability of alternative call centre production models', *Human Resource Management Journal*, 12:4, 14–34.

Battu, H. and McMaster, R. (2002): 'Tenure and employment contracts: An empirical investigation', *Journal of Economic Studies*, 29:2/3, 131.

Baumgarten, K. (1997): 'The Training and Development of Staff for International Assignments', in A. Harzing and J. Van Ruyssevldt (eds), *International Human Resource Management*. London: Sage.

Beach, K. and Vyas, S. (1998): *Light Pickles and Heavy Mustard: Horizontal Development Among Students Negotiating How to Learn in a Production Activity*, Paper Presented at the Fourth Conference of the International Society for Cultural Research and Activity Theory, University of Aarhus, Denmark.

Beach, R., Muhlemann, A. P., Price, D. H. R., Paterson, A. and Sharp, J. A. (2000): 'Manufacturing operations and strategic flexibility: Survey and cases', *International Journal of Operations and Production Management*, 20:1, 7–30.

Beardwell, I., Holden, L. and Claydon, T. (2004): *Human Resource Management: A Contemporary Approach* (4th edn). Essex: Pearson Education Ltd.

Beattie, R. S. (2004): 'Line Managers, HRD and Ethics', in J. Woodall, M. Lee and J. Stewart (eds), *New Frontiers in Human Resource Development*. London: Routledge.

Beck, J. K. (2006): 'Jewish adult learning and the workplace', *Advances in Developing Human Resources*, 8:3, 364–372.

Becker, B. E. and Huselid, M. A. (1998): 'High performance work systems and firm performance: A synthesis of research and managerial implications', *Research in Personnel and Human Resource Management*, 16, 53–101.

Beer, M. and Eisenstat, R. A. (1996): 'Developing an organization capable of implementing strategy and learning', *Human Relations*, 49:5, 597–619.

Bell, B. S. and Kozlowski, S. W. (2002): 'A typology of virtual teams: Implications and effective leadership', *Group and Organization Management*, 27, 14–49.

Bell, J. (1993): *Doing Your Research Project: A Guide For First-Time Researchers In Education and Social Science* (2nd edn). Buckingham; Philadelphia: Open University Press.

Bell, J. and Dale, M. (1999): *Informal Learning in the Workplace*. DfEE Research Report RR134. Sheffield: DfEE.

Bell, P. (1996): 'Business Coaches: Consultants for the 90s'. *Las Vegas Sun*, 18 March.

Bell, S. (1998): 'Self-reflection and vulnerability in action research: Bringing forth new worlds in our learning', *Systemic Practice and Action Research*, 11:2, 179–191.

Ben-Horin Naot, Y., Lipshitz, R. and Popper, M. (2004): 'Discerning the quality of organizational learning', *Management Learning*, 35:4, 451–472.

Bennett, B. (2003a): 'Developmental coaching: Rejecting the remedial approach', *Development and Learning in Organisations*, 17:4, 16–19.

Bennett, B. (2003b): 'Job rotation: Its role in promoting learning in organizations', *Development and Learning in Organizations*, 17:3, 7–9.

Bennett, M. (1993): 'Towards Ethnorelativism: A Developmental Model of Intercultural Sensitivity,' in R. M. Paige (ed.), *Education for the Intercultural Experience*, Intercultural Press.

Bennis, W. (1997): *Why Leaders Can't Lead: The Unconscious Conspiracy Continues*. Los Angeles, CA: Jossey-Bass.

Bennis, W. G. and Nanus, B. (1985): *Leaders: The Strategies for Taking Charge*. New York: Harper and Row.

Bergenhenegouwen, G. J. (1996): 'Competence development – a challenge for HRM professionals: Core competencies of organizations as guidelines for the development of employees', *Journal of European Industrial Training*, 20:9, 29–35.

Berger, L. A. and Berger, D. R. (eds) (2004): *The Talent Management Handbook: Creating Organizational Excellence by Identifying, Developing and Promoting your Best People*. New York: McGraw-Hill.

Berger, P. L. and Lickman, T. (1966): *The Social Construction of Reality: A Treatise In the Sociology of Knowledge*. Garden City, NY: Doubleday.

Bergeron, C. (2004): 'Build a talent strategy to achieve your desired business results', *Handbook of Business Strategy*, 5:1, 133–9.

Bernstein, B. (2000): *Pedagogy, Symbolic Control and Identity*. Lanham, MD: Rowman Littlefield.

Bernthal, P. and Wellins, R. (2006): 'Trends in leader development and succession', *Human Resource Planning*, 29:2, 31–40.

Bernthal, P. and Wellins, R. S. (2003): *Leadership Forecast: 2003–2004*. Retrieved 25 March 2004, from http://www.ddiworld.com/pdf/CPGN50.pdf

Berry, J. K. (1990): 'Linking management development to business strategies', *Training and Development Journal*, 44:8, 20–22.

Berson, U., Nemarich, L. A., Waldman, D. A., Galvin, B. M. and Keller, R. J. (2006): 'Leadership and organisational learning: A multiple levels perspective', *Leadership Quarterly*, 17, 577–595.

Bhavnani, R. (1997): 'Personal development and women's training: transforming the agenda', *Women in Management Review*, 12:4, 140–149.

Bierema, L. L. and Hill, J. R. (2005): 'Virtual mentoring and HRD', *Advances in Developing Human Resources*, 7:4, 556–568.

Bierema, L. L. and Merriam, S. (2002): 'E-mentoring: Using computer-mediated communication to enhance the mentoring process', *Innovative Higher Education*, 26, 211–227.

Billet, S. (2000): 'Guided learning at work', *Journal of Workplace Learning*, 12:7, 272–285.

Birdi, K., Wood, S., Patterson, M. and Wall, T. (2004): 'Individual, Team and Organizational Learning Practices and Organizational Performance'. Paper presented at the Academy of Management Conference, New Orleans.

Black, J. S. and Gregersen, H. B. (1992): 'The other half of the picture: Antecedents of spouse cross-cultural adjustment', *Journal of International Business Studies*, 22/3, 461–477.

Blackburn, R. and Benson, R. (1993): 'Total quality and human resource management: Lessons learned from Baldrige award-winning companies', *Academy of Management Executive*, 7:3, 49–66.

Blackburn, R., Furst, S. and Rosen, B. (2003): 'Building a Winning Virtual Team. KSA's Selection, Training, Evaluation', in C. B. Gibson and S. G. Cohen (eds), *Virtual Teams that Work. Creating Conditions for Virtual Team Effectiveness*. San Francisco: Jossey-Bass.

Blanchard, P. N. and Thacker, J. W. (2007): *Effective Training: Systems Strategies and Practices* (3rd edn). Upper Saddle River, NJ: Prentice Hall.

Bloch, D. P. (2005): 'Complexity, chaos and non-linear dynamics: A new perspective on career development theory', *The Career Development Quarterly*, 53:1, 194–207.

Block, P. (1993): *Stewardship: Choosing Service Over Self-Interest*. San Francisco: Barrett Koehler Publishers.

Boal, K. B. and Hooijberg, R. (2000): 'Strategic leadership research: Moving on', *Leadership Quarterly*, 11:4, 515–549.

Boam, R. and Sparrow, P. (eds) (1992): *Designing and Achieving Competency*. London: McGraw-Hill.

Boje, D. M. and Dennehey, R. (1999): *Managing in the Post-Modern World*. Dubuque, IA: Kendall-Hunt.

Boland, R. J. and Tenkasi, R. V. (1996): 'Perspective making and perspective taking in communities of knowing', *Organization Science*, 4:6, 350–372.

Bolman, L. and Deal, T. (1997): *Reframing Organizations*. San Francisco: Jossey-Bass.

Bolton, R. and Gold, J. (1994): 'Career management: Matching the needs of individuals with the needs of organisations', *Personnel Review*, 23:1, 6–24.

Boon, J. and Van der Klink, M. (2001): 'Scanning the concept of competencies: How major vagueness can be highly functional', 2nd Conference on HRD Research and Practice across Europe, University of Twente, Enschede, January.

Boris, B. and Jemison (1989): 'Hybrid arrangements as strategic alliances: Theoretical issues in organisational combinations', *Academy of Management Review*, 14:2, 234–249.

Bos, E. S. (1998): *Competentie: Verheldering van een Begrip* [Competence: Clarification of a Concept]. Heerlen: Open University of the Netherlands, Educational Technology Expertise Center.

Bossidy, L. and Charan, R. (2002): *Execution: The Discipline of Getting Things Done*. New York: Crown Business.

Boud, D., Keogh, R. and Walker, D. (1985): 'Promoting Reflection in Learning: A Model', in D. Boud, R. Keogh and D. Walker (eds), *Reflection: Turning Experience into Learning*. London: Kogan Page.

Boud, D. and Middleton, H. (2003): 'Learning from others at work: Communities of practice and informal learning', *Journal of Workplace Learning*, 15:5, 194–202.

Boud, D. and Walker, D. (1990): 'Making the most of experience', *Studies in Continuing Education*, 12:2, 61–80.

Boudreau, J. W. and Ramstad, P. M. (2005): 'Talentship and the new paradigm for human resource management: From professional practices to strategic talent decision science', *Human Resource Planning*, 28:2, 17–26.

Boudreau, J. W. and Ramstad, P. M. (2002): *Strategic I/O Psychology and the Role of Utility Analysis Models*. Ithaca, NY: Cornell University.

Boxall, P. and Purcell, J. (2003): *Strategy and Human Resource Management*. Hampshire: Palgrave MacMillan.

Boyatzis, R. (1982): *The Competent Manager – A Model for Effective Performance*. New York: Wiley.

Boyatzis, R. E., Smith, M. L. and Blaize, N. (2006): 'Developing sustainable leaders through coaching and compassion', *Academy of Management Learning and Education*, 5:1, 8–24.

Boydell, T., Burgoyne, J. and Pedler, M. (2004): 'Suggested development', *People Management*, 10:4, 32–34.

Bracken, D., Timmreck, C. and Church, A. (eds) (2001): *Handbook of Multisource Feedback*. San Francisco: Jossey-Bass.

Bradford, D. L. and Cohen, A. R. (1984): *Managing for Excellence: The Guide to Developing High Performance Organizations*. New York: John Wiley.

Braham, W. G. (1996): *Creating a Learning Organization*. London: Kogan Page.

Breene, T. and Nunes, P. F. (2004): 'Is bigger always better?', *Outlook Journal*, October 2004. http://www.accenture.com.

Brett, J. M. (1984): 'Job Transition and Personal Role Developments', in K. M. Rowland and G. R. Ferris (eds), *Research in Personnel and Human Resources Management*. Greenwich, Conn: JAI Press.

Brew, K. and Garavan, T. N. (1995): 'Eliminating inequality: Women only training, part 2', *Journal of European Industrial Training*, 19:9, 28–32.

Brewster, C. (2004): 'Developing managers in Europe', *Advances in Developing Human Resources*, 6:4, 399–403.

Brewster, C., Mayrhofer, W. and Morley, M. (2004): *Human Resource Management in Europe: Evidence of Convergence?* Oxford: Elsevier Ltd.

Brewster, C. and Scullion, H. (1997): 'A review and an agenda for expatriate HRM', *Human Resource Management Journal*, 7:3, 32–41.

Briscoe, J. P. and Hall D. T. (2006): 'The interplay of boundaryless and protean careers: Combinations and implications', *Journal of Vocational Behavior*, 69, 4–18.

Bromnell, J. (2006): 'Meeting the competency needs of global leaders: A partnership approach', *Human Resource Management*, 45:3, 309–336.

Brookfield, S. (1986): *Understanding and Facilitating Adult Learning*. San Francisco: Jossey-Bass.

Brookfield, S. D. (2000): 'The Concept of Critically Reflective Practice', in Wilson (ed.), *Handbook of Adult and Continuing Education*. San Francisco: Jossey-Bass.

Brooks, A. (1989): '*Critically Reflective Learning within a Corporate Context*', Unpublished doctoral dissertation, New York: Teachers College, Columbia University.

Brosnan, K. and Burgess, R. C. (2003): 'Web based continuing professional development – a learning architecture approach', *Journal of Workplace Learning*, 15:1, 24–33.

Brousseau, K. R., Driver, M. J., Eneroth, K. and Larsson, R. (1996): 'Career pandemonium: Realigning organizations and individuals,' *Academy of Management Executive*, 10:4, 52–66.

Brown, A. D. (1997): 'Narcissism, identity and legitimacy', *Academy of Management Review*, 22:3, 642–643.

Brown, J. S. and Duguid, P. (1991): 'Organizational learning and communities-of-practice: Toward a unified view of working, learning and innovation', *Organization Science*, 2, 40–57.

Brown, P. (2004): 'Seeking success through strategic management development', Northampton Business School, University College Northampton. Unpublished.

Brown, P. and Hesketh, A. (2004): *The Mismanagement of Talent: Employability and Jobs in the Knowledge Economy*. Oxford: Oxford University Press.

Brown, R. B. (1993): 'Meta-competence: A recipe for reframing the competence model', *Personnel Review*, 22:6, 25–36.

Bryman, A. (1992): *Charisma and Leadership in Organizations*. London: Sage.

Buckingham, M. (2006): 'What great managers do', *Harvard Business Review OnPoint*, Winter, 96–105.

Buckingham, V. and Vosburgh, R. (2001): 'The 21st century human resources function: It's the talent, stupid', *Human Resource Planning*, 24:4, 17–23.

Buckler, B. (1996): 'A learning process model to achieve continuous improvement and innovation', *The Learning Organization*, 3:3, 31–39.

Bunker, K. A. and Webb, A. D. (1992): *Learning How to Learn From Experience: Impact of Stress and Coping*. Greensboro, NC: Center for Creative Leadership.

Burack, E., Hochwarter, and Mathys, N. (1997): 'The new management development paradigm', *Human Resource Planning*, 20:1, 14–21.

Burgoyne, J. (1988): 'Management development for the individual and the organisation', *Personnel Management*, June, 40–44.

Burgoyne, J. (1989): 'Creating the managerial portfolio: Building on competency approaches to management development', *Management Education and Development*, 20:1, 56–61.

Burgoyne, J. (1993): 'The competence movement: Issues, stakeholders and prospects, *Personnel Review*, 22:6, 6–13.

Burgoyne, J. (2002): 'Trying To Create Linked Individual And Organisational Learning From The Base Of An In-Company MBA', in J. Nasi (ed.), *Cultivation of the Strategic Mind*, Kelsinki WSOY.

Burgoyne, J., Hirsch, W. and Williams, S. (2003): *The Value of Business and Management Education*, Working Paper. Lancaster: Department of Management Learning, Lancaster University Management School, http://www.lums.co.uk/publications.

Burgoyne, J. and Jackson, B. (1997): 'The Arena Thesis: Management Development as a Pluralistic Meeting Point', in J. Burgoyne and M. Reynolds (eds), *Management Learning: Integrating Perspectives in Theory and Practice*. London: Sage.

Burgoyne, J. and James, K. (2003): *Towards Best or Better Practice in Corporate Leadership Development: Issues in Mode 2 Research*, Working Paper. Lancaster: Department of Management Learning, Lancaster University Management School.

Burgoyne, J. and Mumford, A. (2001): *Learning from the Case Method*. Lancaster: Lancaster University.

Burgoyne, J. and Reynolds, M. (1997a): 'Introduction', in J. Burgoyne and M. Reynolds (eds), *Management Learning*. London: Sage.

Burgoyne, J. and Reynolds, M. (eds) (1997b): *Management Learning: Integrating Perspectives in Theory and Practice*. London: Sage.

Burgoyne, J. G. (1995): 'Learning from experience: From individual discovery to meta-dialogue via the evolution of transitional myths', *Personnel Review*, 24:6, 62–73.

Burgoyne, J. G. and Stewart, R. (1976): 'The nature, use and acquisition of managerial skills and other attributes', *Personnel Review*, 5:4, 19–29.

Burke, M. J. and Day, R. R. (1986): 'A cumulative study of the effectiveness of management training', *Journal of Applied Psychology*, 71, 232–245.

Burke, R. J. and Ng, E. (2006): 'The changing nature of work and organizations: Implications for human resource management', *Human Resource Management Review*, 16:2, 86–94.

Burke, W. W. (1997): 'The new agenda for organization development', *Organizational Dynamics*, 26:1, 1.

Burns, J. M. (1978): *Leadership*. New York: Harper & Row.

Cable, D. and Parsons, C. (2001): 'Socialization tactics and person–organization fit', *Personnel Psychology*, 54:1, 1–23.

Cairns, H. (1997): 'Study of current practice in assessing the impact of management development in international organizations', paper presented to the UNICON Conference, Creating the Future of International Executive Development Together: A Visioning Process, Lausanne, 2–5 April.

Caligiuri, P. (2006): 'Developing global leaders', *Human Resource Management Review*, 16:2, 219–28.

Caligiuri, P., Lazarova, M. and Tarique, I. (2005): 'Training, Learning and Development in Multinational Organizations', in H. Scullion and M. Linehan (eds), *International Human Resource Management: A Critical Text*. Palgrave Macmillan.

Caligiuri, P., Phillips, J., Lazarova, M., Tarique, I. and Burgi, P. (2001): 'The theory of met expectations applied to expatriate adjustment: The role of cross-cultural training', *International Journal of Human Resource Management*, 12:3, 357–372.

Callaghan, G. (1997): 'Here's looking at me kid', *The Australian Magazine*, 25–26 October, 12–17.

Cameron, K. S., Freeman, S. J., and Mishra, A. K. (1991): 'Best practices in white-collar downsizing: Managing contradictions', *Academy of Management Executive*, 5:3, 57–72.

Campion, M., Cheraskin, L. and Stevens, M. (1994): 'Career-related antecedents and the outcomes of job rotation', *Academy of Management Journal*, 37:6, 1518–1542.

Campion, M. A. and Goldfinch, J. R. (1983): 'Mentoring among hospital administrators', *Hospital and Health Services Administration*, 28, 77–93.

Candy, P. (1991): *Self-Direction for Lifelong Learning*. San Francisco: Jossey-Bass.

Canella, A. A., Jr. and Shen, W. (2001): 'So close and yet so far: Promotion versus exit for CEO heirs apparent', *Academy of Management Journal*, 44, 252–270.

Canfield, A. A. (1980): *Learning Styles Inventory Manual*. Ann Arbor, MI: Humanics Media.

Cannon-Bowers, J. A., Salas, E. and Converse, S. A. (1993): 'Shared Mental Models in Expert Team

Decision-Making', in N. J. Castellan, Jr. (ed.), *Current Issues in Individual and Group Decision Making*. Hillsdale, NJ: Lawrence Erlbaum Associates Inc.

Cannon-Bowers, J. A., Salas, E., Tannenbaum, S. I. and Mathieu, J. E. (1993): 'Toward theoretically-based principles of training effectiveness: A model and initial empirical investigation', *Military Psychology*, 7, 141–164.

Capaldo, G., Iandoli, L. and Zollo, G. (2006): 'A situationalist approach to competency management', *Human Resource Management*, 45:3, 429–448.

Cappelli, P. (1999): *The New Deal at Work*. Boston, MA: Harvard Business School Press.

Cappelli, P. (2000): 'A market-driven approach to retaining talent', *Harvard Business Review*, 78:1, 103–111.

Cappelli, P. and Singh, H. (1992): 'Integrating Strategic Human Resources and Strategic Management', in D. Lewin, O. Mitchell and P. Shewer (eds), *Research Frontiers in Industrial Relations and Human Resources*. Madison University of Wisconsin: Industrial Relations Association.

Caproni, P. J. (2005): *Management Skills for Everyday Life. The Practical Coach* (2nd edn). Upper Saddle River, NJ: Pearson Education.

Cardy, R. L. and Miller, J. S. (2005): 'e-HR and Performance Management: A Consideration of Positive Potential and the Dark Side', in H. G. Gueutal and D. L. Stone (eds), *The Brave New World of e-HR: Human Resources Management in the Digital Age*. San Francisco: Jossey-Bass.

Carre, P. (1994): 'Self-Directed Learning in French Professional Education', in *New Ideas About Self-Directed Learning*, pp. 139–148. Oklahoma: Oklahoma University Press.

Carrier, C. (1999): 'The training and development needs of owner-managers of small businesses with export potential', *Journal of Small Business Management*, 37:4, 30–41.

Carroll, S. J. and Gillen, D. J. (1987): 'Are the classical management functions useful in describing managerial work?' *Academy of Management Review*, 12:1, 38–51.

Casciaro, T., and Lobo, M. S. (2005): 'Competent jerks, lovable fools and the formation of social networks', *Harvard Business Review*, 83:6, 92–99.

Casio, W. (1993): 'Downsizing: what do we know? What have we learned?', *Academy of Management Executive*, 7, 95–104.

Cedefop (2001): *Training and Learning for Competence*. Thessaloniki: Cedefop.

Champy, J. (1995): *Reengineering Management: The Mandate for New Leadership*. New York: Harper Collins.

Chan, S. C. and Latham, G. P. (2004): 'The relative effectiveness of external, peer, and self coaches', *Applied Psychology: An International Review*, 53:2, 260–278.

Channer, P. and Hope, T. (2001): *Emotional Impact: Passionate Leaders and Corporate Transformation*. New York: Palgrave.

Chao, G. T. (1997): 'Mentoring phases and outcomes', *Journal of Vocational Behavior*, 51, 15–28.

Chao, G. T. (1998): 'Invited reaction: challenging research in mentoring', *Human Resource Development Quarterly*, 9:4, 333–338.

Chao, G. T. and Walz, P. M. (1992): 'Formal and informal mentorships: A comparison on mentoring functions and contrast with non-mentored counterparts', *Personnel Psychology*, 45, 619–636.

Chappelow, C. T. (1998): '360-Degree Feedback', in C. D. McCauley, R. S. Moxley and E. Van Velsor (eds), *The Centre for Creative Leadership Handbook of Leadership Development* (1st edn). San Francisco: Jossey-Bass.

Charan, R., Drotter, S. and Noel, J. (2001): *The Leadership Pipeline: How to Build the Leader-Powered Company*. New York: Jossey-Bass.

Charin, R. and Colvin, G. (1999): 'Why CEOs Fail', *Fortune*, 139:12, 69–78.

Cheetham, G. and Chivers, G. (1998): 'The reflective (and competent) practitioner: A model of professional competence which seeks to harmonise the reflective practitioner and competence-based approaches', *Journal of European Industrial Training*, 22:7, 267–276.

Cheetham, G. and Chivers, G. (2001): 'How professionals learn in practice: An investigation of informal learning amongst people working in professions', *Journal of European Industrial Training*, 25:5, 248–292.

Chemers, M. M. and Ayman, R. (eds) (1993): *Leadership Theory and Research: Perspectives and Directions*. San Diego, CA: Academic Press.

Cheng, M., Dainty, A. and Moore, D. (2003): 'The differing faces of managerial competency in Britain and America', *Journal of Management Development*, 22:6, 527–537.

Chia, R. (1996): *Organisational Analysis as Deconstructive Practice*. Berlin: de Gruyter.

Chien, M. H. (2004): 'The relationship between self-directed learning readiness and organizational effectiveness', *The Journal of American Academy of Business, Cambridge*, 4:1/2, 285–288.

Child, J. (2005): *Organization: Contemporary Principles and Practice*. Malden, MA: Blackwell Publishing.

Child, J. and McGrath, R. G. (2001): 'Organizations unfettered: Organizational form in an information-intensive economy', *Academy of Management Journal*, 44:6, 1135–1148.

Chivers, G. (2003): 'Utilising reflective practice interviews in professional development', *Journal of European Industrial Training*, 27:1, 5–15.

Chivers, W. and Darling, P. (1999): *360-Degree Feedback and Organisational Culture*. London: Institute of Personnel and Development.

Cho, E. and McLean, G. N. (2004): 'What we discovered about NHRD and what it means for HRD', *Advances in Developing Human Resources*, 6:3, 382–393.

Chung, B.Y. and Gfroerer, C.A.M. (2003): 'Career coaching: Practice, training, professional and ethical issues', *The Career Development Quarterly*, 52:2, 141–152.

Cialdini, R. B. (2001): 'The science of persuasion', *Scientific American*, 284, 76–81.

Ciampa, D. (2005): 'Almost ready: How leaders move up', *Harvard Business Review*, 83:1, 46–53.

Cianni, M. and Wnuck, D. (1997): 'Individual growth and team enhancement: Moving towards a new model of career development', *The Academy of Management Executive*, 11:1, 105–115.

CIPD, Chartered Institute of Personnel and Development (2001): *The Case for Good People Management: A Summary of the Research*. London: CIPD.

CIPD, Chartered Institute of Personnel and Development (2002a): *Developing Managers for Business Performance*. Executive Briefing. London: CIPD.

CIPD, Chartered Institute of Personnel and Development (2002b): *Sustaining Success in Difficult Times: Research Summary*. London: CIPD.

CIPD, Chartered Institute of Personnel and Development (2003): *HR Survey: Where We Are, Where We're Heading*. London: CIPD.

CIPD, Chartered Institute of Personnel and Development (2004): *Career Management*. London: CIPD.

CIPD, Chartered Institute of Personnel and Development (2005a): *International Management Development: A Guide*. London: CIPD.

CIPD, Chartered Institute of Personnel and Development (CIPD) (2005b): *Latest Trends in Learning, Training and Development: Reflections on the 2005 Training and Development Survey*. London: CIPD.

CIPD, Chartered Institute of Personnel and Development (CIPD) (2007): *Management Development in Ireland*. London: CIPD.

CIPD, Chartered Institute of Personnel and Development (2008): *Learning Styles: Factsheet*. London: CIPD.

Ciulla, J.B. (2003): *The Ethics of Leadership*. Belmont, CA: Thomson Wadsworth.

Clardy, A. (2000): 'Learning on their own: Vocationally oriented self-directed learning projects', *Human Resource Development Quarterly*, 11:2, 105–126.

Clark, L. A. and Lyness, K. S. (1991): 'Succession Planning as a Strategic Activity at Citicorp', in L. W. Foster (ed.), *Advances in Applied Business Strategy*. Vol. 2. Greenwich, Conn.: JAI Press.

Clarke, M., Butcher, D. and Bailey, C. (2004): 'Strategically Aligned Leadership Development', in Storey, J. (ed.), *Leadership in Organizations: Current Issues and Key Trends*. London: Routledge.

Clegg, S. R. (1990): *Modern Organization: Organization Studies in the Post-Modern World*. London: Sage.

Clements, C., Wagner, R. J. and Roland, C. C. (1995): 'The ins and outs of experiential learning', *Training and Development*, 49:2, 52–56.

Cleveland, J. N., Stockdale, M. and Murphy, K. R. (2000): *Women and Men in Organizations: Sex and Gender Issues at Work*. London: Lawrence Erlbaum Associates.

Clutterbuck, D. (2001): *Everyone Needs a Mentor*. London: CIPD.

Clutterbuck, D. (2005): 'Succession Planning', *Development and Learning in Organisations*, 19:5, 11–13.

Clutterbuck, D. and Megginson, D. (1999): *Mentoring Executives and Directors*. Oxford: Butterwoth-Heinman.

Cocivera, T. and Cronshaw, S. (2004): 'Action frame theory as a practical framework for the executive coaching process', *Consulting Psychology Journal: Practice and Research*, 56:4, 234–45.

Cockerill, T. (1989): 'The kind of competence for rapid change', *Personnel Management*, September, 52–56.

Cockerill, T. and Hunt, J. (1995): 'Managerial competencies: Fact or fiction?', *Business Strategy Review*, 6:3, 26–34.

Cohen, L. and Manion, L. (1989): *Research Methods in Education* (3rd edn). London: Routledge.

Cohen, S. (1998): 'Big ideas for trainers in small companies', *Training and Development*, 27–30 April.

Cohen, S. G. and Gibson, C. B. (2003): 'In the Beginning: Introduction and Framework', in C. B. Gibson and S. G. Cohen (eds), *Virtual Teams That Work: Creating Conditions for Effective Virtual Teams*. San Francisco: Jossey-Bass.

Cohen, S. G. and Mankin, D. (1999): 'Collaboration in the Virtual Organization', in C. L. Cooper and D. M. Rousseau (eds), *Trends in Organizational Behavior, Vol. 6: The Virtual Organization*. New York: John Wiley.

Cohn, J. M., Khurana, R. and Reeves, L. (2005): 'Growing talent as if your business depended on it', *Harvard Business Review*, 83:10, 62–70.

Cole, G. (2002): *Personnel and Human Resource Management* (5th edn). London: Continuum.

Collin, A. (1989): 'Managers' competence: Rhetoric, reality and research', *Personnel Review*, 28:6, 20–5.

Collin, K. (2002): 'Development engineers' conceptions of learning at work', *Studies in Continuing Education*, 24, 133–152.

Collingwood, H. (2001): 'Personal histories', *Harvard Business Review*, December, 27–38.

Collins, D. B. and Holton, E. F. (2004): 'The effectiveness of managerial leadership development programs: A meta-analysis of studies from 1982–2001', *Human Resource Development Quarterly*, 15:2, 217–48.

Collins, J. and Porras, J. (1994): *Built to Last*. New York: Harper Business.

Collins, J. C. (2001): *Good to Great: Why Some Companies Make the Leap and Others Don't*. New York: Harper Collins.

Colquit, J. A., LePine, J. A. and Noe, R. A. (2000): 'Toward an integrative theory of training motivation: A meta-analytic path analysis of 20 years of research', *Journal of Applied Psychology*, 85, 678–707.

Confederation of British Industry (CBI) (1999): *Making Employability Work: An Agenda for Action*. London: CBI.

Confessone, S. and Kops, W. (1998): 'Self-directed learning and the learning organisation: Examining the connection between the individual and the learning environment', *Human Resource Development Quarterly*, 9:4, 365–375.

Conger, J. (1993): 'The brave new world of leadership training', *Organisational Dynamics*, 21:3, 46–59.

Conger, J. A. (1992): *Learning to Lead*. San Francisco: Jossey-Bass.

Conger, J. A. (1999a): 'Charismatic and transformational leadership in organizations: An insider's perspective on these developing streams of research', *Leadership Quarterly*, 10:2, 145–179.

Conger, J. A. (1999b): 'The new age of persuasion', *Leader to Leader*, Spring, 37–44.

Conger, J. A. (2004): 'Developing leadership capability: What's inside the black box?', *Academy of Management Executive*, 18:3, 136–139.

Conger, J. and Benjamin, B. (1999): *Building Leaders: How Corporations are Developing the Next Generation*. San Francisco: Jossey-Bass.

Conger, J. A. and Kanungo, R. (1987): 'Toward a behavioural theory of charismatic leadership in organizational settings', *Academy of Management Review*, 12, 637–647.

Conger, J. A. and Toegel, G. (2003): 'Action Learning and Multirater Feedback: Pathways to Leadership Development?', in S. E. Murphy and R. E. Riggio (eds), *The Future of Leadership Development*, Mahwah, NJ: Lawrence Erlbaum Associates.

Conlon, T. J. (2003): 'A Review of Literature, Theory and Practice of Informal Learning in Developing Professional Expertise', in P. Kuchinke (ed.), *Proceeding of the Academy of Human Resource Development Conference* (pp. 303–307). Bowling Green, OH: Academy of Human Resource Development.

Conlon, T. J. (2004): 'A review of informal learning literature, theory and implications for practice in developing global professional competence', *Journal of European Industrial Training*, 28:2/3/4, **283–295.**

Connor, A., Strebler, N. and Hirsch, W. (1990): *You and Your Graduate: The First Few Years*. Report No. 1, Institute of Manpower Studies, Brighton.

Contractor, F. J. and Lorange, P. (1988): 'Why Should Firms Cooperate? The Strategy and Economic Basis for Cooperative Ventures', in F. J. Contractor and P. Lorange (eds), *Cooperative Strategies in International Business*. New York: Lexington Books.

Conway, N. and Guest, D. (2002): 'Organizational Change and the Psychological Contract: A Single Organization Case Study', paper presented at British Academy of Management conference, London.

Cook, S. D. and Yanow, D. (1993): 'Culture and organizational learning', *Journal of Management Inquiry*, 2:4, 373–390.

Cooksey, R. W. (2003): 'Learnership in complex organisational textures', *Leadership and Organization Development Journal*, 24:4, 204–14.

Cooper, C. L. (ed.) (2005): *Leadership and Management in the 21st Century: Business Challenges of the Future*. Oxford: Oxford University Press.

Cooper, C. L. and Jackson, S. E. (1997): *Creating Tomorrow's Organizations. A Handbook for Future Research in Organizational Behavior*. West Sussex: Wiley.

Cooper, C. L., Robinson, I. T. and Arnold, J. (1996): *Work Psychology: Understanding Human Behaviour in the Workplace* (2nd edn). London: Pitman Publishing.

Coopey, J. (1995): 'Managerial culture and the stillbirth of organizational commitment', *Human Resource Management Journal*, 5:3, 56–76.

Cope, J. and Watts, G. (2000): 'Learning by doing: An exploration of critical incidents and reflection in entrepreneurial learning', *International Journal of Entrepreneurial Behaviour and Research*, 6:3, 104–124.

Corporate Executive Board (2006): *Leaders who Develop Leaders: Strategies for Effective Leader-Led Development*. London: CEB.

Corporate Leadership Council (2000): *The Next Generation: Accelerating the Development of Rising Leaders*. Washington, DC: Corporate Executive Board.

Corporate Leadership Council (2001): *Voice of the Leader: A Quantitative Analysis of Leadership Bench Strength and Development Strategies*. Washington DC and London, UK.

Coulson-Thomas, C. (1992): 'Developing competent directors and effective boards', *Journal of General Management*, 11:1, 39–49.

Crossan, M. M., Lane, H. W. and White, R. E. (1999): 'An organizational learning framework: From intuition to institution', *Academy of Management Review*, 24:3 (July), 522–537, http://www.jstor.org/stable/259140. Accessed 8 January 2009.

Crotty, P. T. and Soule, A. J. (1997): 'Executive education: Yesterday and today, with a look at tomorrow', *Journal of Management Development*, 16:1, 4–21.

Cseh, M. (2003): 'Facilitating learning in multicultural teams', *Advances in Developing Human Resources*, 5:1, 26–40.

Cseh, M., Watkins, K. E. and Marsick, V. J. (1999): 'Informal and incidental learning in the workplace', in G. A. Straka (ed.), *Conceptions of Self-Directed Learning: Theoretical and Conceptual Considerations*. Munster, Germany: Waxman.

Cummings, T. and Srivastva, S. (1977): *Management of Work: A Socio-Technical Systems Approach*. San Diego: University Associates.

Cummings, T. G. and Worley, C. G. (2001): *Organization Development and Change* (7th edn). Cincinnati, OH: South-Western College Publishing.

Cunningham, I. (1986): 'Self-managed learning', in A. Mumford (eds), *Handbook of Management Development*. Gower: Aldershot.

Cunningham, I. (2002): 'Individual Development and Self-Managed Learning', **in M. Pearn (ed.), *Individual Differences and Development in Organizations*. West Sussex: John Wiley and Sons Ltd.**

Cunningham, P. (2004): 'The transformation of work and self-development', *Problems and Perspectives in Management*, 3, 170–180.

Currie, G. and Darby, R. (1995): 'Competence-based management development: Rhetoric and reality', *Journal of European Industrial Training*, 19:5, 11–26.

Curry, L. (1983): 'An organization of learning style theory and constructs', ERIC Document Retrieval Service, TM 830 554.

Cyert, R. M. and March, J. G. (1963): *A Behavioral Theory of the Firm*. Englewood Cliffs, NJ: Prentice Hall.

D'Abate, C. P., Eddy, E. R. and Tannenbaum, S. L. (2003): 'What's in a name? A literature-based approach to understanding mentoring, coaching and other constructs that describe developmental interactions', *Human Resource Development Review*, 2:4, 360–384.

Daft, R. L. and Lengel, R. H. (1998*): Fusion Leadership: Unlocking the Subtle Forces that Change People and Organizations*. San Francisco: Berrett-Koehler Publishers.

Dainty, P. and Kakabadse, A. P. (1992): 'Brittle, blocked, blended and blind: Top team characteristics that lead to business success or failure', *Journal of Managerial Psychology*, 7:2, 4–17.

Dalton, M., Swigert, S., Van Velsor, E., Bunker, K. and Wachholz, J. (1999): *The Learning Tactics Inventory: Facilitator's Guide*. San Francisco, CA: Jossey-Bass/Pfeiffer.

Dalton, M. A. and Ernst, C. T. (2004): 'Developing Leaders for Global Roles,' in McCauley, C. D. and Van Velsor, E. (eds), *The Centre for Creative Leadership Handbook of Leadership Development* (2nd edn). San Francisco: Jossey-Bass.

Dansereau, F., Yammarino, F. J., Markham, S. E., Alutto, J. A., Newman, J. and Dumas, M. (1998). 'Individualized leadership: A new multiple level approach', in F. Dansereau and F. J. Yammarino (eds), *Leadership: The Multiple Level Approaches: Part A*. Stamford, CT: JAI Press.

Darby, C. (1993): '*Quality Assessment and Employer Satisfaction*', Keynote Presentation at the QHE 24-hour Seminar, Scarman House, University of Warwick, 16–17 December.

Das, S. D. (1997): *Awakening the Buddha Within*. New York: Broadway Books.

Datta, D. K. and Guthrie, J. P. (1994): 'Executive succession: Organizational antecedents of CEO characteristics', *Strategic Management Journal*, 15:7, 569–577.

Daudelin, M. (1996): 'Learning from experience through reflection', *Organizational Dynamics*, 24:3, 36–48.

Davenport, T. H. and Prusack, L. (1998): *Working Knowledge: How Organizations Manage What They Know*. Boston: Harvard Business School.

Davidow, W. H. and Malone, M. S. (1992): *The Virtual Corporation: Structuring and Revitalizing the Corporation for the 21st Century*. New York: Edward Burlingame Books/ Harper Business.

Davidson, M. J. and Burke, R. J. (2004): *Women in Management World-Wide: Facts, Figures and Analysis*. Aldershot: Ashgate Publishing Company.

Davidson, M. J. and Cooper, C. L. (1992): *Shattering the Glass Ceiling: The Woman Manager*. London: Paul Chapman.

Davies, J. and Easterby-Smith, M. (1984): 'Learning and developing from managerial work experiences', *Journal of Management Studies*, 21:2, 169–183.

Day, D. V. (2000): 'Leadership development: A review in context', *Leadership Quarterly*, 11:4, 581–613.

Dealtry, R. (2004): 'Professional practice: The savvy learner', *Journal of Workplace Learning*, 16:1/2, 101–109.

Deane, C. and Watters, E. (2004a): 'Towards 2010 – Common themes and approaches across higher education and vocational education and training in Europe', *Background Research Paper for the Irish Presidency Conference*, 8 March.

Deane, C. and Watters, E. (2004b): 'Towards 2010 – Common themes and approaches across higher education and vocational education and training in Europe', *Conference Report for the Irish Presidency Conference*, 8 March.

Dearden, L., Reed, H. and Van Reenen, J. (2000): *Who gains when workers train? Training and corporate productivity in a panel of British industries*. The Institute for Fiscal Studies, Working Paper 00/04.

Dechant, K. (1990): 'Knowing how to learn: The "neglected" management ability', *Journal of Management Development*. 9:4, 40–49.

Delahaye, B. L. (2000): *Human Resource Development: Principles and Practice*. Milton, Qld: Wiley and Sons.

Delbecq, A. L. (1999): 'Christian spirituality and contemporary business leadership', *Journal of Organizational Change Management*, 12:4, 345–349.

Deloitte & Touche (2000): 'Characteristics of good corporate leadership', *News*, January, www.dtlus.com.

Denmark, F. (1993): 'Women, leadership and empowerment', *Psychology of Women Quarterly*, 17, 343–356.

Dennen, V. P. and Wang, M. (2002): 'The keyboard-based job coach: Informal learning via the Internet', *Advances in Developing Human Resources*, 4:4, 440–450.

Denton, J. (1998): *Organizational Learning and Effectiveness*. London: Routledge.

Deresky, H. (2000): *International Management: Managing Across Borders and Cultures* (3rd edn). Englewood Cliffs, NJ: Prentice-Hall.

Deresky, H. (2006): *International Management: Managing Across Borders and Cultures* (5th edn). New Jersey: Pearson Prentice Hall.

Derous, E. (2000): '*The C story: Clarifying stories… actual approaches and threads in competence literature*', Retrieved from, http://users.skynet.be/vocap/

Descy, P. and Tessaring, M. (2001a): *Training and Learning for Competence*. Thessaloniki: Cedefop.

Descy, P. and Tessaring, M. (2001b): *Training and Learning and Competence. Second Report on Vocational Training Research in Europe: Synthesis Report*. CEDEFOP Project. Luxembourg: CEDEFOP.

Devins, D. and Gold, J. (2000): 'Cracking the tough nuts: Mentoring and coaching the managers of small firms', *Career Development International*, 5:4/5, 250–255.

De Waele, M., Morval, J. and Sheitoyan, R. (1993): *Self-Management in Organizations: The Dynamics of Interaction*. Toronto: Hogrefe and Huber.

Dewey, J. (1938): *Experience and Education*. New York: Collier Books.

Dillon, P. A. (1992): 'What business expects from higher education', *College Board Review*, 164, 22–25.

DiMaggio, P. and Powell, W. (1983): 'The iron cage revisited: Institutional isomorphism and collective rationality in organisational fields', *American Sociological Review*, 48, 147–160.

Dixon, N. M. (1994): *The Organizational Learning Cycle: How can we Learn Collectively?* London: McGraw-Hill.

Dodgson, M, (1993): 'Organizational learning: A review of some literatures', *Organization Studies*, 14:3, 375–394.

Doherty, N., Viney, C. and Adamson, S. (1995): *Managing the Fast Track Graduate: Contemporary Concerns and Developments*. Cranfield: Cranfield University.

Dorfman, P. W. (2003): 'International and Cross-Cultural Leadership Research', in B. J. Punnett and O. Shenkar (eds), *Handbook for International Management Research* (2nd edn). Ann Arbor, MI: University of Michigan.

Dorfman, P. W., Howell, J. P., Hibino, S., Lee, J. K., Tate, U. and Bautista, A. (1997): 'Leadership in Western and Asian countries: Commonalities and differences in effective leadership processes across cultures', *Leadership Quarterly*, 8:3, 233–274.

Dowling, P. J. and Welch, D. E. (2004): *International Human Resource Management: Managing People in a Multinational Context*, (4th edn). London: Thompson Learning.

Downey, M. (1999): *Effective Coaching*. London: Orion Business Books.

Downey, M. (2003): *Effective Coaching*. New York: Texere.

Downs, A. (1997): *Beyond the Looking Glass: Overcoming the Seductive Culture of Corporate Narcissism*. New York: Amacom.

Doyle, M. (1995): 'Organisational transformation and renewal: A case for reframing management development', *Personnel Review*, 24:6, 6–18.

Doyle, M. (1997): 'Management Development', in Beardwell, I. and Holden, L. (eds), *Human Resource Management: A Contemporary Perspective* (2nd edn). London: Pitman.

Doyle, M. (2000): 'Managing development in an era of radical change: Evolving a relational perspective', *Journal of Management Development*, 19:7, 579–601.

Drew, E., Murphy, C. and Humphreys, P. (2003): *Off the Treadmill: Achieving Work/Life Balance*. Dublin: Family-Friendly Framework Committee.

Drew, E. and Murtagh, E. M. (2005): 'Work/life balance: Senior management champions or laggards?', *Women in Management Review, 20*:4, 262–278.

Dreyfus, S. E. and Dreyfus, H. L. (1986): *Mind Over Machine*. Oxford: Basil Blackwell.

Driver, M. (2003): 'United we stand, or else? Exploring organizational attempts to control emotional expression by employees on September 11, 2001', *Journal of Organizational Change Management*, 16:5, 534–546.

Driver, M. J. (1994): 'Workforce Personality and the New Information Age Workplace', in J. A. Auerbach and J. C. Welsh (eds), *Aging and Competition: Rebuilding the US Workforce* (pp.185–204). Washington, DC: National Council on Aging and the NatioPlanning Association.

Drucker, P. (1996): 'Foreword: Not Enough Generals Were Killed', in F. Hesselbein, M. Goldsmith and R. Beckhard (eds), *The Leader of the Future*. San Francisco: Jossey-Bass.

Drucker, P. F. (1989): 'What business can learn from non-profits', *Harvard Business Review*, July–August, 88–93.

DTI White Paper (1995): *Competitiveness: Forging Ahead*, CM2867. London: HMSO.

DTZ Pieda Consulting (1998): *Evaluation of the Business Benefits of Management Development*. Research Report No. 66. DfEE.

Duarte, D. L. and Snyder, N. T. (2001): *Mastering Virtual Teams: Strategies, Tools and Techniques that Succeed* (2nd edn). San Francisco: Jossey-Bass.

Duarte, D. L. and Snyder, N. T. (2006): *Mastering Virtual Teams* (3rd edn). New York: Jossey Bass.

Ducharme, M. J. (2004): 'The cognitive-behavioral approach to executive coaching', *Consulting Psychology Journal: Practice and Research*, 56:4, 214–24.

Dulewicz, V. and Higgs, M. (2002): 'Emotional Intelligence and the Development of Managers and Leaders', in M. Pearn (ed.), *Individual Differences and Development in Organizations*. West Sussex: John Wiley and Sons Ltd.

Dulewicz, V. and Higgs, M. J. (2003): 'Design of a new instrument to assess leadership dimensions and styles'. *Henley Working Paper Series,* HWP 0311. Henley-on-Thames, UK: Henley Management College.

Dulewicz, V., MacMillan, K. and Herbert, P. (1995): 'Appraising and developing the effectiveness of boards and their directors', *Journal of General Management*, 20:3, 5–8.

Duncan, R. and Weiss, A. (1979): 'Organizational Learning: Implications for Organizational Design', in B. Staw (ed.), *Research in Organizational Behaviour*. JAI Press.

Dyer, W. G. (1995): *Team Building: Current Issues and New Alternatives*. Reading, MA: Addison-Wesley.

Eagly, A.H. and Carli, L.L. (2003): 'The female leadership advantage: An evaluation of the evidence', *The Leadership Quarterly*, 14:6, 807–834.

Eagly, A. H., Karau, S. J. and Makhijani, M. G. (1995): 'Gender and the effectiveness of leaders: A meta-analysis', *Psychological Bulletin*, 117, 125–145.

Eagly, A. H. and Wood, W. (1991): 'Explaining sex difference in social behavior: A meta-analytic perspective', *Personality and Social Psychology Bulletin*, 17, 306–315.

Easterby-Smith, M. (1997): 'Disciplines of organizational learning: Contributions and critiques', *Human Relations*, 50:9, 1085–1106.

Eaton, S. C. and Bailyn, L. (2000): 'Careers as Life Paths in Firms of the Future', in Peiperl, M., Arthur, M. B., Rob Goffee, R. and Morris, T. (eds), *Career Frontiers: New Conceptions of Working Lives* (pp. 177–198). Oxford: Oxford University Press.

Eby, L., Butts, M. and Lockwood, A. (2003): 'Predictors of success in the era of the boundaryless career', *Journal of Organisational Behaviour*, 24:6, 689–709.

Edelstein, B. C. and Armstrong, D. J. (1993): 'A model for executive development', *Human Resource Planning*, 16:4, 51–64.

Edwards, T. and Rees, C. (2006): *International Human Resource Management: Globalization, National Systems and Multinational Companies*. England: Pearson Education Ltd.

Effron, M., Greensdale, S. and Salob, M. (2005): 'Growing great leaders: Does it really matter?', *Human Resource Planning*, 28:3, 18–23.

Efimova, L. (2002): 'Mathamagenic: Giving birth to learning', Retrieved from http://blog.mathemagenic. com/stories/2002/08/29/phdideas.html

EFMD, European Foundation for Management Development (2005): *Globally Responsible Leadership: A Call for Engagement*. Brussels: EFMD.

Egan, G. (1990): *The Skilled Helper: A Systematic Approach to Effective Helping* (4th edn). Pacific Grove, CA: Brooks/Cole.

Egan, T. M. (2005): 'Factors influencing individual creativity in the workplace: An examination of quantitative empirical research', *Advances in Developing Human Resources*, 7:2, 160–181.

Eichinger, R. W. and Lombardo, M. (2002): *The Leadership Machine*. Lominger.

Eisenhardt, K. M. and Santos, F. M. (2002): 'Knowledge-based View: A New Theory of Strategy?', in A. Pettigrew, H. Thomas, and R. Whittington (eds), *Handbook of Strategy and Management*. London: Sage.

Elias, J. and Merriam, S. (2005): *Philosophical Foundations of Adult Education*. Malabar, FL: Krieger.

Ellinger, A. D. (2005): 'Contextual factors influencing informal learning in a workplace setting: The case of "reinventing itself company"', *Academy of Human Resource Development*, 16:3, 389–416.

Ellinger, A. D. and Bostrom, R. P. (1999): 'Managerial coaching behaviors in learning organizations', *Journal of Management Development*, 18:9, 752.

Ellström, P. E. (1998): 'The Many Meanings of Occupational Competence and Qualification', in W. J. Nijhof and J. N. Streumer (eds), *Key Qualifications in Work And Education* (pp. 39–50). Dordrecht: Kluwer Academic Publishers.

Engeström, Y. (2000): 'Activity theory as a framework for analyzing and redesigning work', *Ergonomics*, 43:4, 960–974.

Ennis, S., Stern, L. R., Yahanda, N., Vitti, M., Otto, J., Hodgetts, W. (2003): *The Executive Coaching Handbook*. Wellesley, MA: The Executive Caching Forum.

Enos, M., Kehrhahn, M. and Bell, A. (2003): 'Informal learning and the transfer of learning: How managers develop proficiency', *Human Resource Development Quarterly*, 14:4: 369–387.

Enscher, E. A., Thomas, C. and Murphy, S. E. (2001): 'Comparison of traditional, step-ahead and peer mentoring on protégés' support, satisfaction, and perceptions of career success: A social exchange perspective', *Journal of Business and Psychology*, 15:3, 419–38.

Enterprise Strategy Group Report (2004): *Ahead of the Curve: Ireland's Place in the Global Economy*. Dublin: Forfas.

Eraut, M. (1994): *Developing Professional Knowledge and Competence*. London: Falmer Press.

Eraut, M. (2000): 'Non-Formal Learning, Implicit Learning and Tacit Knowledge', in F. Coffield, *The Necessity of Informal Learning*. Bristol: Policy Press.

Eraut, M. (2004): 'Informal learning in the workplace', *Studies in Continuing Education*, 26:2, 247–273.

Eraut, M. F. (1998): *Development of Knowledge and Skills in Employment*. Brighton: University of Sussex Institute of Education.

Eriksson, T. and Ortega, J. (2006): 'The adoption of job rotation: testing the theories', *Industrial and Labor Relations Review*, 59:4, 653–666.

Espedal, B. (2004): 'Management and leadership development in Norway: Discrepancies between talk and action', *Advances in Developing Human Resources*, 6:4, 470–485.

Eurich, N. (1990): *The Learning Industry: Education for Adult Workers*. Princeton, NJ: The Carnegie Foundation for the Advancement of Teaching.

Ewert, A. (1989): *Outdoor Adventure Pursuits: Foundations, Models, and Theories*. Scottsdale, AZ: Publishing Horizons.

Expatica (2004): 'Companies respond to "family concerns" of potential assignees', News article dated 26 October 2004. Retrieved from http://www.expatica.com.

Expert Group on Future Skills Needs (2005): *SME Management Development in Ireland*. Dublin: FÁS, Enterprise Ireland.

Farnham, D. (2005): *Managing in a Strategic Business Context*. London: CIPD.

FÁS, Foras Áiseanna Saothair (2005): *The Irish Labour Market Review 2005: A FÁS Review of Irish Labour Market Trends and Policies*. Dublin: FÁS.

Fayol, H. (1916): *Administration Industrielle et Generale*. Storrs, London: Sir Isaac Pitman and Sons.

Feldman, D. (1996): 'Managing careers in downsized firms', *Human Resource Management*, 35:2, 145–161.

Feldman, D. C. and Lankau, M. J. (2005): 'Executive coaching: A review and agenda for future research', *Journal of Management*, 31:6, 829–848.

Felstead, A., Jewson, N., Phizackleg, A. and Walters (2002): 'Analysing the opportunity to work at home in the context of work–life balance policies and practices', *Human Resource Management Journal*, 12:1, 54–76.

Fenwick, M. (2004): 'On international assignment: Is expatriation the only way to go?', *Asia Pacific Journal of Human Resources*, 42:3, 365–377.

Ferguson-Hessler, M. G. M. and de Jong, T. (1990): 'Studying physics texts: Differences in study processes between good and poor performers', *Cognition and Instruction*, 7, 41–54.

Ferner, A., Quintanilla, J. and Varul, M. Z. (2001): 'Country of origin effects, host-country effects, and the management of HR in multinationals: German companies in Britain and Spain', *Journal of World Business*, 36:2, 107–127.

FETAC, Further Education and Training Awards Council (2005): *First Review of the FETAC Strategic Plan for 2005–2007*. Dublin: FETAC.

Fiedler, F. E. and Garcia, J. E. (2005): 'Leadership in a Non-Linear World', in C. L. Cooper (ed.), *Leadership and Management in the 21st Century: Business Challenges of the Future*. Oxford: Oxford University Press.

Fiegener, M. K., Brown, B. M., Prince, R. A. and File, K. M. (1994): 'A comparison of successor development in family and non-family businesses', *Family Business Review*, 7:4, 313–329.

Fielden, S. L. (2001): 'Stress and gender in unemployed female and male managers', *Applied Psychology: An International Review*, 50:2, 305–335.

Fielden, S. L. and Davidson, M. J. (1998): 'Social support during unemployment: Are women managers getting a fair deal?', *Women in Management Review*, 13:7, 264–273.

Fielden, S. L. and Davidson, M. J. (2000): 'Stress and the Unemployed Woman Manager – A Comparative Approach', in M. Davidson and R. Burke (eds), *Women in Management: Current Research Issues*, Vol. 2. London: Sage Publications.

Fielding, N.G. (1988): 'Competence and culture in the police', *Sociology*, 22, 45–64.

Fineman, S. (ed.) (1993): *Emotion in Organizations*. London: Sage Publication.

Fiol, C. M. and Lyles, M. (1985): 'Organizational learning', *Academy of Management Review*, 10, 803–813.

Fischlmayr, I. C. (2002): 'Female Self-Perception as Barrier to International Careers?', *International Journal of Human Resource Management*, 13:5, 773–783.

Fish, A. (1999): 'Cultural diversity: Challenges facing the management of cross-border business careers', *Career Development International*, 4:4, 196–205.

Fisher, S. L. and Ford, J. K. (1998): 'Differential effects of learner effort and goal orientation on two learning outcomes', *Personnel Psychology*, 51, 397–420.

Fisher, S. R. and White, M. A. (2000): 'Downsizing in a learning organization: Are there hidden costs?', *Academy of Management Review*, 25:1, 244–251.

Fisher, T. D. (2002): 'Self-directedness in adult vocational education students: Its role in learning and implications for instruction', *Journal of Vocational and Technical Education*, 12:1, 1–12.

Flaherty, J. (1993) 'Coaching: Evoking excellence in others'. San Francisco, CA: Unpublished manuscript.

Flanagan, J. C. (1954): 'The critical incident technique', *Psychological Bulletin*, 51, 327–358.

Fletcher, J. K. and Bailyn, L. (1996): 'Challenging the Last Boundary: Reconnecting Work and Family', in M. B. Arthur and D. M. Rousseau (eds), *The Boundaryless Career. A New Employment Principle For A New Organizational Era* (pp. 256–267). Oxford: Oxford University Press.

Fletcher, J. K. and Kaufer, K. (2003): 'Shared Leadership: Paradox and Possibility', in C. L. Pearce and J. A. Conger (eds), *Shared Leadership: Reframing the Hows and Whys of Leadership*. Thousand Oaks, CA: Sage Publications.

Fletcher, S. (1992): *Competence-Based Assessment Techniques*. London: Kogan Page.

Flood, P., MacCurtain, S. and West, M. (2001): *Effective Top Management Teams*. Dublin: Blackhall Publishing.

Flood, P. C., Rammorthy, N., Sardessai, R. and Slattery, T. (2005): 'Determinants of innovative work behaviour: Development and test of an integrated model', *Creativity and Innovation Management*, 14:2, 142–150.

Fogel, A. (1993): *Developing Through Relationships: Origins of Communication, Self and Culture*. Hemel Hempstead: Harvester Wheatsheaf.

Ford, J. K. and Noe, R. A. (1987): 'Self-assessed training needs: The effects of attitudes toward training, managerial level, and function', *Personnel Psychology*, 40, 39–53.

Ford, R. C. and Randolph, W. A. (1992): 'Cross-functional structures: A review and integration of matrix organization and project management', *Journal of Management*, 18, 267–294.

Forguson, L. (1989): *Common Sense*. London: Routledge.

Forlin, J.R. and Dans, C. S. (1997): 'Challenges of leading a diverse workforce', *Academy of Management Executive*, August, 32–44.

Forret, M. L. (1996). 'Issues facing organizations when implementing formal mentoring programmes', *Leadership and Organizational Development Journal*, 17(3), 27–30.

Forster, N. (1994): 'The forgotten employees? The experiences of expatriate staff returning to the UK', *International Journal of Human Resource Management*, 5:2, 405–425.

Foster, R. N. and Kaplan, S. (2001): *Creative Destruction*. New York: Doubleday.

Fournies, F. F. (1978): *Coaching for Improved Work Performance*. Bridgewater, NJ: F Fournies & Associates.

Fowler, J. L. and O'Gorman, J. G. (2005): 'Mentoring functions: A contemporary view of the perceptions of mentees and mentors', *British Journal of Management*, 16:1, 51–57.

Fox, R. (2004): *The Vocational Education and Training System in Ireland: Short Description*, CEDEFOP Panaroma Series, 83. Luxembourg: Office for Official Publications of the European Communities.

Fox, R. and McGinn, K. (2000): *The Financing of Vocational Education and Training in Ireland: Financing Portrait*. Thessaloniki: European Centre for the Development of Vocational Training (CEDEFOP).

Fox, S. (1997): 'From Management, Education and Development to the Study of Management Learning', in J. Burgoyne and M. Reynolds (eds), *Management Learning: Integrating Perspectives in Theory and Practice*. London: Sage Publications.

Frankola, K. (2001): 'Why online learners drop out', *Workforce*, 80:10, 53–58.

Freedman, D. H. (1992): 'Is management still a science?', *Harvard Business Review*, 70:6, 26–38.

Friday, E. and Friday, S. S. (2002): 'Formal mentoring: Is there a strategic fit?', *Management Decision*, 40:2, 152–157.

Friday, E., Friday, S. S. and Green, A. L. (2004): 'A reconceptualization of mentoring and sponsoring', *Management Decision*, 42:5, 628–643.

Frisch, M. H. (2001): 'The emerging role of the internal coach', *Consulting Psychology Journal: Practice and Research*, 53:4, 240–250.

Fry, L. (2005): 'Toward a Theory of Ethical and Spiritual Well-Being, and Corporate Social Responsibility Through Spiritual Leadership', in R. A. Giacalone and C.L. Jurkiewicz (eds), *Positive Psychology in Business Ethics and Corporate Responsibility*. Greenwich: Information Age Publishing.

Fuller, A. and Unwin, L. (2004): 'Expansive Learning Environments: Integrating Organizational and Personal Development', in H. Rainbird, A. Fuller and A. Munro (eds), *Workplace Learning in Context*. London: Routledge.

Fuller, L. and Smith, V. (1996): 'Consumers' Reports: Management by Customers in a Changing Economy', in C. L. Macdonald and C. Sirianni (eds), *Working in the Service Society*. Philadelphia: Temple University Press.

Gabel, S. (2002): 'Leading from the middle', *Leadership and Organizational Development Journal*, 23:7.

Gabriel, T. (1996): 'Personal Trainers to Buff the Boss's People Skills'. *The New York Times*, 28 April, Section 3, p 1.

Gallagher, C. (1996): *Windows in the Glass Ceiling: The Importance of Professional Relationships*, Unpublished Dissertation. Almeda: California School of Professional Psychology.

Gangani, N. T., McLean, G. N. and Braden, R. A. (2004): 'Competency-based human resource development strategy', *Academy of Human Resource Development Annual Conference*, Austin, TX, 4–7 March, Proceedings Vol. 2, 1111–1118.

Garavan, T. N., Barnicle, B. and O'Suilleabhain, F. (1999): 'Management development: Contemporary trends, issues and strategies', *Journal of European Industrial Training*, 23:4/5, 191–201.

Garavan, T. N. and Carbery, R. (2008): *Management Development in Ireland*. Limerick: University of Limerick.

Garavan, T. N., Collins, E. and Brady, S. (2004): *Training and Development in Ireland: A Study of Training and Development Practices*. Dublin: CIPD Ireland.

Garavan, T. N., Costine, P. and Heraty, N. (1997): *Training and Development in Ireland: Context, Policy and Practice*. Dublin: Oak Tree Press.

Garavan, T. N., Hogan, C. and Cahir-O'Donnell, A. (2003): *Making Training and Development Work: A Best Practice Approach*. Cork: Oak Tree Press.

Garavan, T. N. and Morley, M. (1997): 'The socialization of high-potential graduates into the organization: Initial expectations, experiences and outcomes', *Journal of Managerial Psychology*, 12:2, 118–137.

Garavan, T. N., Morley, M., Gunnigle, P., and McGuire, D. (2002): 'Human resource development and workplace learning: Emerging theoretical perspectives and organisational practices', *Journal of European Industrial Training*, 26:2/3/4, 60–71.

Garavan, T. N. and O'Cinneide, B. (1994a): 'Entrepreneurship, education and training programmes: A review and evaluation – part 1', *Journal of European Industrial Training*, 18:8, 3–12.

Garavan, T. N. and O'Cinneide, B. (1994b): 'Entrepreneurship, education and training programmes: A review and evaluation – part 2', *Journal of European Industrial Training*, 18:11, 13–21.

Garavan, T. N., Shanahan, V. and Carbery, R. (2008): *Training and Development in Ireland: Results of the 2007 National Survey of Benchmarks*, Dublin: CIPD Ireland.

Garavan, T. N. and Sweeney, P. (1994): 'Supervisory training and development: The use of learning contracts', *Journal of European International Training*, 18:2, 17–26.

Garonzik, R., Nethersell, G. and Spreier, S. (2006): 'Navigating through the new leadership landscape', *Leader to Leader*, Winter, 26:39, 30–39.

Garratt, B. (1987): *The Learning Organization*. Worcester: Gower.

Garratt, B. (1995): 'Helicopters and rotting fish: Developing strategic thinking and new roles for direction-givers', in B. Garratt (ed.), *Developing Strategic Thought: Reconsidering the Art of Direction-giving*. London: McGraw-Hill.

Garvey, B. and Williamson, B. (2002): *Beyond Knowledge Management*. Harlow: Pearson Education.

Garvin, D. A. (1993): 'Building a learning organisation', *Harvard Business Review*, July–August, 78–97.

Garvin, D. A. (2000): *Learning in Action: A Guide to Putting the Learning Organization to Work*. Boston: Harvard Business School.

Gear, J., McIntosh, A. and Squires, G. (1994): *Informal Learning in the Professions*. Hull: School of Education, University of Hull.

Gedro, J. A., Cervero, R. M., Johnson-Bailey, J. (2004): 'How lesbians learn to negotiate the heterosexism of corporate America', *Human Resource Development International*, 7:2, 181–195.

Gendron, G. (1995): 'The real female advantage', *Inc.*, 17:5, 16.

George, G., Sims, P., McLean, A. N. and Mayer, D. (2007): 'Discovering your authentic leadership', *Harvard Business Review*, 85:2, 129–138.

Gerber, R. (1997): 'Understanding how Geographical Educators Learn in their Work: An Important Basis for their Professional Development'. Paper presented to *Geographical Association Conference*, April, London.

Gerber, R. (1998): 'How do workers learn in their work?', *The Learning Organization*, 5:4, 168–175.

Gerber, R., Lankshear, C., Larsson, S. and Svensson, L. (1995): 'Self-directed learning in a work context', *Education and Training*, 37:8, 26–32.

Gherardi, S. and Nicolini, D. (2001): 'The Sociological Foundations of Organizational Learning', in M. Dierkes *et al.* (eds), *The Handbook of Organizational Learning and Knowledge*. London: Sage.

Ghorpade, J. (2000): 'Managing five paradoxes of 360-degree feedback', *Academy of Management Executive*, 14:1, 140–150.

Ghoshal, S., Moran, P. and Bartlett, C. A. (1996): *Employment Security, Employability and Sustainable Competitive Advantage*. London: London Business School.

Gibb, S. (2003): 'Line manager involvement in learning and development: Small beer or big deal?', *Employee Relations*, 25:3, 281–93.

Gibbons, A. (1993): 'Motivation is the key to professional development', *Personnel Management Plus*, August 1993.

Gibbs, G., Habeshaw, S. and Habeshaw, T. (1992): *53 Interesting Things to do in your Lectures* (4th edn). London: Technical and Education Services Limited.

Gibson, S. K. (2004): 'Organizational Politics and Culture: An Essential Attribute of the Mentoring Experience for Women Faculty', in T. Egan (ed.), *Proceedings of the Academy of Human Resource Development Research Conference* (pp. 218–225). Bowling Green, OH: Academy of Human Resource Development.

Giddens, A. (1984): *The Constitution of Society. Outline of the Theory of Structuration*. Cambridge: Polity Press.

Gieskes, J. F. B., Hyland, P. W. and Magnusson, M. G. (2002): 'Organizational learning barriers in distributed product development: Observations from a multinational corporation', *Journal of Workplace Learning*, 14, 310–319.

Gill, R. (2006): *Theory and Practice of Leadership*. London: Sage.

Gilligan, J. H. (1994): 'Evaluating self-managed learning, part 1: Philosophy, design and current practice', *Health Manpower Management*, 20:5, 4–9.

Gilmore, T. (1988): *Making a Leadership Change: How Organizations and Leaders Can Handle Leadership Transitions Successfully*. San Francisco, CA: Jossey-Bass.

Giscombe, K. and Mattis, M. (2002): 'Leveling the playing field for women of color in corporate management: Is the business case enough?' *Journal of Business Ethics*, 37, 103–119.

Gist, M. E. and McDonald-Mann, D. (2000): 'Advances in Leadership Training and Development', in C. L. Cooper and E. A. Locke (eds), *Industrial and Organizational Psychology: Linking Theory With Practice*. Oxford: Blackwell.

GMAC, Global Relocation Services (2005): Annual Global Relocation Trends Survey. Retrieved from http://www.gmacglobalrelocation.com/survey.html.

Godshalk, V. M. and Sosik, J. J. (2003): 'Aiming for career success: the role of learning goal orientation in mentoring relationships', *Journal of Vocational Behavior*, 63:3, 417–437.

Goel, M. L. (1988): *Political Science Research: A Methods Handbook*. Ames: Iowa State University Press.

Goffee, R. and Scase, R. (1992): 'Organizational change and the corporate career. The restructuring of managers' aspirations', *Human Relations*, 45, 363–385.

Gold, J. (1990): 'Learning to learn through learning contracts', *Training and Management Development Methods*, 4:4.

Goldman, D. (1995): *Emotional Intelligence: Why it Can Matter More Than IQ*. New York: Bantam Books.

Goldsmith, M., Lyons, L. and Freas, A. (2000): *Coaching for Leadership: How the World's Greatest Coaches Help Leaders Learn*. San Francisco: Jossey-Bass/ Pfeiffer.

Goldstein, J. and Kornfield, J. (1987): *Seeking the Heart of Wisdom: The Path of Insight Meditation*. Boston, MA: Shambhala Publications Inc.

Goleman, D. (2000): 'Leadership that gets results', *Harvard Business Review*, 78:2, 78–90.

Gonzi, A., Hager, P. and Athanasou, J. (1993): *The Development of Competency-Based Assessment Strategies for the Professions: National Office of Overseas Skills Recognition, Research Article No. 8*. Canberra: Australian Government Publishing Service.

Govindarajan, V. and Gupta, A. K. (2001): 'Building an effective global business team', *MIT Sloan Management Review*, 42:4, 63.

Graham, C. and McKenzie (1995): 'Delivering the promise: Developing new graduates', *Education and Training*, 37:2, 16–29.

Granovetter, M. (1973): 'The strength of weak ties', *American Journal of Sociology*, 6, 1360–1380.

Grant, A., and Cavanagh, M. J. (2004): 'Toward a profession of coaching: Sixty-five years of progress and challenges for the future', *International Journal of Evidence-based Coaching and Mentoring*, 2:1, 1–16.

Gratton, L., Hailey, V. H., Stiles, P. and Truss, C. (1999a): 'Linking individual performance to business strategy: A people process model', *Human Resource Management*, 38:1, 17–31.

Gratton, L., Hailey, V. H., Stiles, P. and Truss, C. (1999b): *Strategic Human Resource Management*. Oxford: Oxford University Press.

Greenhaus, I. H. (1987): *Career Management*. New York: CBS College Publishing.

Greenhaus, J. H. and Callanan, G. A. (1994): *Career Management*. London: Dryden Press.

Greenhaus, J. H., Callanan, G. A. and Godshalk V. M. (2000): *Career Management* (3rd edn). Fort Worth: Dryden Press.

Greenleaf, R. K. (1977): *Servant Leadership: A Journey Into the Nature of Legitimate Power and Greatness*. Nahwah, NJ: Paulist Press.

Greenwood, R. and Hinings, C. R. (1996): 'Understanding radical organizational change: Bringing together the old and the new institutionalism', *Academy of Management Review*, 21, 1022–1055.

Greer, C., Youngblood, S. and Gray, D. (1999): 'Human resource management outsourcing: The make or buy decision', *The Academy of Management Executive*, 13:3, 85–96.

Greiner, L. and Schein, V. (1988): *Power and Organizational Development: Mobilizing Power to Implement Change*. Reading, MA: Addison-Wesley.

Griffey, S. (1998): 'Conceptual frameworks beyond the learning organization', *The Learning Organization*, 5:2, 68–73.

Grint, K. (2005a): 'Twenty-First Century Leadership – The God of Small Things; or Putting the "Ship" back into "Leadership"', in C. L. Cooper (ed.), *Leadership and Management in the 21st Century: Business Challenges of the Future*. Oxford: Oxford University Press.

Grint, K. (2005b): *Leadership: Limits and Possibilities*. Hampshire, Palgrave MacMillan.

Gross, T., Turner, E. and Cederholm, L. (1987): 'Building teams for global operations', *Management Review*, June, 32–36.

Groysberg, B., McLean, A. and Nohria, N. (2006): 'Are leaders portable?', *Harvard Business Review*, May.

Groysberg, B., Nanda, A. and Nohria, N. (2004): 'The risky business of hiring stars', *Harvard Business Review*, May, 92–100.

Guest, D. E. and Conway, N. (2002): *Pressure at Work and the Psychological Contract*. London: CIPD.

Guest, D., Michie, J., Sheehan, M., Conway, N. and Metochi, M. (2000): *Effective People Management, Initial Findings of the Future of Work Study*. London: Institute of Personnel and Development.

Guglielmino, P. and Murdick, R. (1997): 'Self-directed learning: The quiet revolution in corporate training and development', *SAM Advanced Management Journal*, 62:3, 10–18.

Guglielmino, P. J. and Guglielmino, L. M. (2001): 'Moving toward a distributed learning model based on self-managed learning', *SAM Advanced Management Journal*, 66:3, 36–43.

Guglielmino, P. J. and Roberts, D. G. (1992): 'A comparison of self-directed learning readiness in US and Hong Kong samples and the implications for job performance', *Human Resource Development Quarterly*, 3:3, 261–271.

Guile, D. and Griffiths, T. (2001): 'Learning through work experience', *Journal of Education and Work*, 14:1, 113–31.

Gunnigle, P., Heraty, N. and Morley, M. J. (2002): *Human Resource Management in Ireland* (2nd edn). Dublin: Gill and Macmillan.

Guthrie, V. A. and Kelly-Radford, L. (1998): 'Feedback-Intensive Programs', in C. D. McCauley, R. S. Moxley and E. Van Velsor (eds), *The Center for Creative Leadership Handbook of Leadership Development* (pp. 66–105). San Francisco: Jossey-Bass.

Gutteridge, T. G., Leibowitz, Z. B. and Shore, J. E. (1993): *Organizational Career Development: Benchmarks for Building a World-Class Workforce*. San Francisco: Jossey Bass.

Guzzo, R. A. and Noonan, K. A. (1994): 'Human resource practices as communications and the psychological contract', *Human Resource Management*, 33, 447–462.

Hackman, J. R. and Wageman, R. (2005): 'A theory of team coaching', *Academy of Management Review*, 30:2, 269–287.

Hailey, V. H., Farndale, E. and Truss, C. (2005): 'The HR department's role in organisational performance', *Human Resource Management Journal*, 15:3, 49–66.

Hakim, C. (1996): *Key Issues in Women's Work: Female Heterogeneity and the Polarisation of Women's Employment*. London: Athlone Press.

Hale, R. (2000): 'To match or mis-match? The dynamics of mentoring as a route to personal and organisational learning', *Career Development International*, 4:4/5, 223–234.

Hales, C. (1993): *Managing Through Organisation*. London: Routledge.

Hales, C. (1999): 'Why do managers do what they do? Reconciling evidence and theory in accounts of managerial work.' *British Journal of Management*, 10:4, 335–350.

Hall, D. T. (1976): *Careers in Organizations*. Glenview, IL: Scott, Foresman.

Hall, D.T. (1986): 'An Overview of Current Career Development Theory, Research and Practice', in D.T. Hall and Associates (eds), *Career Development in Organisations* (4). San Francisco: Jossey-Bass.

Hall, D. T. (1996): *The Career is Dead – Long Live the Career*. San Francisco: Jossey-Bass.

Hall, D. T. and Mirvis, P. H. (1996): 'The New Protean Career: Psychological success and the Path with a Heart', in D. T. Hall and Associates, *The Career is Dead – Long Live the Career: A Relational Approach to Careers* (pp. 15–45). San Francisco: Jossey Bass.

Hall, D. T. and Moss, J. E. (1998): 'The new protean career contract: Helping organizations and employees adapt', *Organizational Dynamics*, 26:3, 22–37.

Hall, D. T., Otazo, K. L. and Hollenbeck, G. P. (1999): 'Behind closed doors: What really happens in executive coaching', *Organisational Dynamics*, 27:3, 39–52.

Hamlin, R. G., Ellinger, A. D. and Beattie, R. S. (2008): 'The emergent "coaching industry": A wake-up call for HRD professionals', *Human Resource Development International*, 11:3, 287–305.

Hammer, M. and Champy, J. (1993): *Reengineering the Corporation: A Manifesto for Business Revolution*. New York: Harper Business.

Hammond, R. (1989): *Verbal presentation to IPM Bedford branch*, November.

Hammonds, K. H. (2005): 'Why we hate HR', *Fast Company*, 97: August, 40–46.

Handfield-Jones, H., Michaels, E. and Axelrod, B. (2001): 'Talent management: A critical part of every leader's job', *Ivey Business Journal*, 66:2, 53–58.

Handy, C. (1987): *The Making of Managers*. London: NEDC, MSC and the BIM.

Handy, C. (1992): 'The Language of Leadership', in M. Syrett and C. Hogg (eds), *Frontiers of Leadership*. Blackwell.

Handy, C. (1995a): *Beyond Certainty: The Changing Worlds of Organization*. Hutchinson.

Handy, C. (1995b): *The Gods of Management*. Arrow.

Handy, C., Gordon, C., Gow, I. and Randlesome, C. (1998): *Making Managers*. London: Pitman.

Handy, C., Gow, I., Gordon, C., Randlesome, C. and Moloney, M. (1987): *The Making of Managers*. London: National Economic Development Office.

Hanh, T. N. (1998): *The Heart of the Buddha's Teaching*. New York: Broadway Books.

Hansen, M., Nohria, N. and Tierney, T. (1999): 'What's your strategy for managing knowledge?', *Harvard Business Review*, March–April 1999, 106–116.

Hardy, C. and Dougherty, D. (1997): 'Powering product innovation', *European Management Journal*, 15:1, 16–27.

Harris, C. L. and Beyerlein, M. M. (2004): 'Team-Based Organization: Creating an Environment for Team Success', in M. A. West, D. Tjosvold and K. G. Smith (eds), *The Essential of Teamworking: International Perspectives*. West Sussex: Wiley.

Harris, H. and Brewster, C. (1999): 'The coffee-machine system: How international selection really works', *The International Journal of Human Resource Management*, 10:3, 488–500.

Harris, L. C. and Ogbonna, E. (2006): 'Approaches to career success: An exploration of surreptitious career-success strategies', *Human Resource Management*, 45:1, 43–65.

Harris, S. (1981): *Know yourself? It's a paradox*, 6 October, Associated Press.

Harrison, R. (2000): 'Learning, knowledge productivity and strategic process', *International Journal of Training and Development*, 4:4, 244–258.

Harrison, R. (2005): *Learning and Development* (4th edn). London: CIPD.

Harrison, R. and Kessels, J. (2004): *Human Resource Development in a Knowledge Economy: An Organisational View*. London: Palgrave Macmillan.

Hart, S. L. (1992): 'An integrative framework for strategy-making processes', *Academy of Management Review*, 17:2, 327–351.

Harvey, L. and Green, D. (1994): *Quality in Higher Education Project: Employer Satisfaction*. Birmingham: The University of Central England.

Harvey, M. (1997): 'Dual career expatriates: Expectations, adjustment and satisfaction with international relocation', *Journal of International Business Studies*, 28:3, 627–658.

Harvey, R. (1991): 'Job Analysis', in M. Dunnette and L. Hough (eds), *Handbook of Industrial and Organizational Psychology* (Vol. 2). Consulting Psychology Press: Palo Alto.

Hassard, J. (1993): 'Postmodernism and Organisational Analysis: An Overview', in F. Hassard, and M. Parker (eds), *Postmodernism and Organisations*. London: Sage.

Hawkins, P. (1991): 'The spiritual dimension of the learning organization', *Management Education and Development*, 22:3, 172–187.

Hawkins, P. (1994): 'Organizational learning: Taking stock and facing the challenge', *Management Learning*, 25:1, 71–82.

Hay Group, Towers Perrin, Hewitt Associates LLC, M. William Mercer Inc. and American Compensation Association (1996): *Raising the Bar: Using Competencies to Enhance Employee Performance*. Scottsdale, AZ: American Compensation Association.

Heifetz, R. (1994): *Leadership Without Easy Answers*. Cambridge, MA: Belnap Press of Harvard University Press.

Heifetz, R. A. and Laurie, D. L. (1997): 'The work of leadership', *Harvard Business Review*, January–February, 124–134.

Held, D., Goldblatt, D. and Parraton, J. (1997): *Global Transformations*. Cambridge: Polity Press.

Henderson, I. (1993): 'Action learning: A missing link in management development', *Personnel Review*, 22:6, 14–24.

Henderson, J. C. and Nutt, P. C. (1980): 'The influence of decision style on decision-making behavior', *Management Science*, 26:4, 371–386.

Hendry, C. (1995): *Human Resource Management, A Strategic Approach to Employment*. Oxford: Butterworth-Heinemann.

Hendry, C. (1996): 'Understanding and creating whole organisational change through learning theory', *Human Relations*, 49:5, 621–641.

Heppner, P. P., and Peterson, C. H. (1982): 'The development and implications of a personal problem-solving inventory', *Journal of Counseling Psychology*, 29, 66–75.

Heraty, N. (2004): 'Towards an architecture of organization-led learning', *Human Resource Management Review*, 14:4, 449–72.

Heraty, N. and Morley, M. J. (2003): 'Management development in Ireland: The new organizational wealth', *Journal of Management Development*, 22:1, 60–82.

Heraty, N., Morley, M. J. and McCarthy A. (2000): 'Vocational education and training in the Republic of Ireland: Institutional reform and policy developments since the 1960s', *Journal of Vocational Education and Training*, 52:2, 177–198.

Herling, R. W. (2000): 'Operational definitions of expertise and competence', *Advances in Developing*

Human Resources, 5, 8–21.

Herriot, P. and Pemberton, C. (1997): 'Facilitating new deals', *Human Resource Management Journal*, 7:1, 45–56.

Herzenberg, S. A., Alic, J. A. and Wial, H. (1998): *New Rules for a New Economy: Employment and Opportunity in Postindustrial America*. New York: Cornell University Press.

Hezlett, S. and Gibson, S. (2005): 'Mentoring and human resource development: Where we are and where we need to go', *Advances in Developing Human Resources*, 7:4, 446–469.

Hiemstra, R. (1996): 'What's in a word? Changes in self-directed learning language over a decade', paper presented at the 10th International Self-Directed Learning Symposium, West Palm, Florida.

Higgins, M. and Nohria, N. (1999): 'The sidekick effect: Mentoring relationships and the development of social capital', in R. Leenders and S. Gabbay (eds), *Corporate social capital and liability* (pp. 161–179). Boston: Kluwer.

Higgins, M. C. and Kram, K. E. (2001): 'Reconceptualizing mentoring at work: A developmental network perspective', *Academy of Management Review*, 26:2, 268–288.

Higgs, M. and Dulewicz, V. (1999): *Making Sense of Emotional Intelligence*. Windsor: NFER-Nelson.

Higgs, M. J. and Rowland, D. (2001): 'Developing change leadership capability: The impact of a development intervention', *Henley Working Paper Series*, HWP 2001/004.

Hilgert, A. D. (1995): 'Developmental outcomes of an executive MBA programme', *Journal of Management Development*, 14:10, 64–76.

Hill, R. and Stewart, J. (2000): 'Human resource development in small organizations', *Journal of European Industrial Training*, 24: 2/3/4, 105.

Hillage, J. and Pollard, E. (1998): *Employability: Developing a Framework for Policy Analysis*. London: Dfee.

Hinings, C. R., Greenwood, R. and Cooper, D. (1999): 'The Dynamics of Change in Large Accounting Firms', in D. M. Brock, M. J. Powell and C. R. Hinings (eds), *Restructuring the Professional Organization*. London: Routledge.

Hiriyanna, M. (2002): *Essentials of Indian Philosophy*. Varanasi, India: Banarasidas.

Hirsch, W. (2000): *Succession Planning Demystified*. Brighton: Institute for Employment Studies.

Hirsch, W. and Jackson, C. (1996): *Strategies for Career Development: Promise, Practice and Pretence*. Brighton: Institute of Employment Studies.

Hirsch, W. and Jackson, C. (1997): *Strategies for Career Development: Promise, Practice and Pretence*. Report 305. Brighton: Institute of Manpower Studies.

Hirsch, W. and Reilly, P. (1999): *Planning for Skills*. Strategic Planning Society Seminar. London, 18 March.

Hislop, D. (2004): *Knowledge Management: A Critical Introduction*. Oxford: Oxford University Press.

Hite, L. M. and McDonald, K. S. (1995): 'Gender issues in management development: Implications and research agenda', *Journal of Management Development*, 14:4, 5–15.

Hjalager, A., Larsen, H. and Bojesen, J. (2003): *Management Training and Development in Denmark: A Case of Serious Playfulness*. Leonardo Project, London: Chartered Management Institute.

Hochschild, A. (1990): 'Ideology and Emotion Management: A Perspective and Path for Future Research', in T. Kemper (eds), *Research Agendas in the Sociology of Emotions*. New York: SUNY Press.

Hochschild, A. (1997): *The Time Bind: When Work Becomes Home and Home Becomes Work*. New York: Metropolitan Books.

Hoeksema, L. H. (1995): *Learning Strategy as a Guide to Career Success in Organizations*. Leiden: DSWO Press, Leiden University.

Hoeksema, L. H., van de Vliert, E. and Williams, A. R. T. (1997): 'The interplay between learning strategy and organisational structure in predicting career success', *International Journal of Human Resource Management*, 8:3, 307–327.

Hofstede, G. (1992): 'Motivation, Leadership, and Organization: Do American Theories Apply Abroad?', in H. W. Lane and J. J. DiStefano (eds), *International Management Behaviour* (2nd edn). Boston: PWS-Kent Publishing Co.

Hogan, C. (1994): *A Study of Graduate Training Programmes*. Limerick: University of Limerick.

Hogan, R. (2000): *Hogan Leadership Forecast. Leadership Advisor Report*. Tulsa, OK: Hogan Assignment Systems.

Hogan, R., Curphy, G. J. and Hogan, J. (1994): 'What we know about leadership: Effectiveness and personality', *American Psychologist*, 49:6, 493–504.

Hogan, R. and Warrenfeltz, R. (2003): 'Educating the modern manager', *Academy of Management Learning and Education*, 2:1, 74–84.

Holbeche, L. (1999): *Aligning Human Resources and Business Strategy*. Oxford: Butterworth-Heineman.

Holbeche, L. (2004): *Politics for the Greater Good*. Roffey Park Institute.

Holbeche, L. (2008): 'Great performance occurs when people know what is expected and why that matters', *People Management*, 14:22, 24–27.

Holland, R. (1980): 'Learner characteristics and learner performance: Implications for instructional placement decisions', *Journal of Special Education*, 16, 7–20.

Hollenbeck, G. P. (1991): 'What did you learn in school? Studies of a university executive program', *Human Resource Planning*, 14:4, 247–260.

Hollenbeck, G. P. (1994): *CEO Selection: A Street-Smart Review*, Greensboro, NC: Center for Creative Leadership.

Hollenbeck, G. P., McCall, M. W. and Silzer, R. F. (2006): 'Leadership competency models', *Leadership Quarterly*, 17:4, 398–413.

Holman, D., Epitropaki, O. and Fernie, S. (2001): 'Understanding learning strategies in the workplace: A factor analytic investigation', *Journal of Occupational and Organizational Psychology*, 74, 675–681.

Holmes, L. and Joyce, P. (1993): 'Rescuing the useful concept of managerial competence: From outcomes back to process', *Personnel Review*, 22:6. 37–52.

Holton, E. F. and Lynham, S. A. (2000): 'Performance-driven leadership development', *Advances in Developing Human Resources*, 6, 1–17.

Honey, P. and Mumford, A. (1986): *Using Your Learning Styles*. Maidenhead: Peter Honey.

Honey, P. and Mumford, A. (1989): *The Manual for Learning Opportunities*. Maidenhead: Peter Honey.

Honey, P. and Mumford, A. (1992): *Manual of Learning Styles* (3rd edn). Maidenhead: Peter Honey Publications.

Honey, P. and Mumford, A. (1996): *How to Manage Your Learning Environment*. Maidenhead: Peter Honey.

Horowitz, F. M., Heng, C. T. and Quazi, H. A. (2003): 'Finders, keepers? Attracting, motivating and retaining knowledge workers', *Human Resource Management Journal*, 13:4, 23–44.

Horwitz, M. (1996): 'Executive development: Facing the new realities', *Journal of European Industrial Training*, 20:4, 11–16.

House, R. J., Hanges, P. J., Javidan, M., Dorfman, P. W., Gupta, V. and Associates (2004): *Leadership, Culture, and Organizations: The GLOBE Study of 62 Societies*. Thousand Oaks, CA: Sage.

House, R. J. and Shamir, B. (1993): 'Toward an integration of transformational, charismatic, and visionary theories', in M. Chemers and R. Ayman (eds), *Leadership Theory and Research Perspective and Directions*. Orlando, FL: Academic Press, 1993, 577–594.

House, R. S. (1996): 'Classroom Instruction', in R. L. Craig (ed.), *The ASTD Training and Development Handbook* (4th edn). New York: McGraw-Hill.

Howell, J. P., Bowen, D. E., Dorfman, P. W., Kerr, S. and Podsakoff, P. M. (1990): 'Substitutes for leadership: Effective alternatives to ineffective leadership', *Organizational Dynamics*, 19, 21–38.

Hube, K. (1996): 'A coach may be the guardian angel you need to rev up your career', *Money*, 25, 43–46.

Huber, G. P. (1991): 'Organizational learning: The contribution processes and the literatures', *Organizational Science*, 2, 88–115.

Hughes, R. L., Ginnett, R. C. and Curphy, G. J. (2006): *Leadership: Enhancing the Lessons of Experience* (5th edn). New York: McGraw-Hill.

Hunt, D. E. (1987): *Beginning with Ourselves in Practice, Theory and Human Affairs*. Cambridge, MA: Brookline Books.

Hunter, L., Beaumont, P. and Lee, M. (2002): 'Knowledge management practice in Scottish law firms', *Human Resource Management Journal*, 12:2, 4–21.

Hurley, A. E., Fagenson-Eland, E. A. and Sonnenfeld, J. A. (1997): 'An investigation of career attainment determinants'. *Field Report*, Autumn.

Huselid, M. A. (1995): 'The impact of human resource management practices on turnover, productivity, and corporate financial performance', *Academy of Management Journal*, 38:3, 635–672.

Hussey, D. (1988): *Management Training and Corporate Strategy – How to Improve Competitive Performance*. London: Pergamon.

Hutchison, S., Kinney, N. and Purcell, J. (2002): '*Bringing policies to life: Discretionary behaviour and the impact on business performance*'. Paper presented at the Bath Conference, University of Bath School of Management, 10–11 April.

Ibarra, H. (1993): 'Personal networks of women and minorities in management: A conceptual framework', *Academy of Management Review*, 18:1, 56–87.

IBEC, Irish Business and Employers' Confederation (2004): *Education Policy Document, July 2004: Education for Life – the challenge of the Third Millennium*. Dublin: IBEC.

IDS, Incomes Data Services (2003): *Leadership development*. IDS Study 753. London: IDS.

Illinitch, A. Y., D'Aveni, R. A. and Lewin, A. Y. (1996): 'New organizational forms and strategies for managing in hypercompetitive environments', *Organization Science*, 7, 211–230.

Industrial Society (1999): *Liberating Leadership*. London: The Industrial Society.

Inkson, K. and Arthur, M. (2001): 'How to be a successful career capitalist', *Organizational Dynamics*, 30:1, 48–58.

Institute of Directors (1995): *Standards of Good Practice for UK Board of Directors*. London: IoD

Institute of Management and Administration (IOMA) Report (2005): *'How to Prepare Your Expatriate Employees for Cross-Cultural Work Environments'*, IOMA's Report on Managing Training and Development, February 2005, New York.

International Labour Organisation (ILO) (1998): 'Women in management: It's still lonely at the top', *World of Work Magazine*, No.23.

Ireland, R. D. and Hill, M. A. (2005): 'Achieving and maintaining strategic competitiveness in the 21st century: The role of strategic leadership', *Academy of Management Executive*, 19:4, 63–77.

Isaacs, W. (1993): 'Dialogue, collective thinking and organizational learning', *Organizational Dynamics*, Fall, 24–39.

Isenberg, D. J. (1984): 'How senior managers think', *Harvard Business Review*, November/December: 81–90.

Isenberg, D. J. (1986): 'Thinking and managing: A verbal protocol analysis of managerial problem-solving', *Academy of Management Journal*, 29:4, 775–88.

Iverson, K. (2000): 'Managing for effective workforce diversity: Identifying issues that are of concern to employees', *Cornell Hotel and Restaurant Administration Quarterly*, 41:2, 31–37.

Jackson, C. and Yeates, J. (1993): *Development Centres: Assessing or Developing People?* Sussex: Institute of Manpower Studies.

Jackson, S., Farndale, E. and Kakabadse, A. (2003): 'Executive development: Meeting the needs of top team and boards', *Journal of Management Development*, 22:3, 185–265.

Jackson, S. E. and Schuler, R. S. (1990): 'Human resource planning: Challenges for industrial/ organizational psychologists', *American Psychologist*, 45:2, 223–239.

Jacobs, R. (1989): 'Getting the measure of management competence', *Personnel Management*, June, 32–37.

Jacobs, T. O. and Jaques, E. (1987): 'Leadership in Complex Systems', in J. Zeidner (ed.), *Human Productivity Enhancement: Organizations, Personnel and Decision Making*. New York: Praeger.

Jaffee, D. (2001): *Organization Theory: Tension and Change*. New York: McGraw-Hill.

Jarvenpaa, S. and Ives, B. (1994): 'The global network organization of the future: Information management opportunities and challenges', *Journal of Management Information Systems*, 10:4 25–57.

Jarvenpaa, S. L., Knoll, K., and Leidner, D. E. (1998): 'Is anyone out there? Antecedents of trust in global virtual teams', *Journal of Management Information Systems*, 14, 29–64.

Jarvenpaa, S. L. and Leidner, D. E. (1999): 'Communication and trust in global virtual teams', *Organization Science*, 10, 791–815.

Jenkinson Consulting (2004): *Excellence Through People Standard Review*. Dublin: FÁS.

Jeris, L. and Johnson, K. (2004): 'Speaking of competence: Toward a cross-translation for human resource development and continuing professional education', Academy of Human Resource Development Annual Conference, Austin, TX, 4–7 March, Proceedings Vol.2, 1103–1110.

Johansen, B. P. and Gopalakrishna, D. (2006): 'A Buddhist view of adult learning in the workplace', *Advances in Developing Human Resources*, 8:3, 337–345.

Johnson, D., Pere-Verge, L. and Hanage, R. (1993): 'Graduate retention and the regional economy', *Entrepreneurship and Regional Development*, 5, 85–97.

Johnson, S. (2001): *Emergence*. London: Penguin.

Jones, C. and DeFillippi, R. J. (1996): 'Back to the future in film: Combining industry and self-knowledge to meet career challenges in the 21st century', *The Academy of Management Executive*, 10:4, 89–103.

Joshi, A., Labianca, G. and Caligiuri, P. M. (2002): 'Getting along long distance: Understanding conflict in a multinational team through network analysis', *Journal of World Business*, 125, 1–8.

Joy-Matthews, J., Megginson, D. and Surtees, M. (2004): *Human Resource Development: MBA Masterclass*. London: Kogan Page.

Jubb, R. and Robotham, D. (1997): 'Competencies in management development: Challenging the myths', *Journal of European Industrial Training*, 21: 4/5, 171–177.

Judge, T. A. and Bono, J. E. (2000): 'Five-factor model of personality and transformational leadership', *Journal of Applied Psychology*, 85, 751–765.

Judge, T. A., Locke, E. A. and Durham, C. C. (1997): 'The dispositional causes of job satisfaction: A core evaluation approach', *Research in Organizational Behaviour*, 19, 151–88.

Kabst, R. and Strohmeier, S. (2006): 'Virtualization: Boundaryless Organizations and Electronic Human Resource Management', in H. Holt Larsen and W. Mayrhofer (eds), *Managing Human Resources in Europe*. London: Routledge.

Kaiser, R. B. and Kaplan, R. E. (2006): 'The deeper work of executive development: Outgrowing sensitivites', *Academu of Management Learning and Education*, 5 (4), 463–483.

Kakabadse, A. and Anderson, S. (1993): 'Top teams and strategic change', *Management Development Review*, 11:2, 10–22.

Kakabadse, A., Bank, J. and Vinnicombe, S. (2004): *Working in Organisations: The Essential Guide for Managers in Today's Workplace* (1st edn). Aldershot: Gower.

Kakabadse, A. and Kakabadse, N. (2001): *The Geopolitics of Governance: The Impact of Contrasting Philosophies*. Basingstoke: Palgrave.

Kakabadse, N. and Kakabadse, A. (2005): 'Discretionary Leadership: From Control/ Co-ordination to Value Co-Creation', in C. L. Cooper (ed.), *Leadership and Management in the 21st Century: Business Challenges of the Future*. Oxford: Oxford University Press.

Kamoche, K. (1996): 'Strategic human resource management within a resource capability view of the firm', *Journal of Management Studies*, 33:2, 213–34.

Kanfer, R. (1996): 'Self-Regulatory and Other Non-Ability Determinants of Skill Acquisition', in J. A. Bargh and P. M. Gollwitzer (eds), *The Psychology of Action: Linking Cognition and Motivation to Behavior* (pp. 403–423). New York: Guilford.

Kanter, R. M. (1977): *Men and Women of the Corporation*. New York: Basic Books.

Kanter, R. M. (1989): *When Giants Learn to Dance*. New York: Simon & Schuster.

Kanungo, R. and Misra, S. (1992): 'Managerial resourcefulness: A reconceptualization of management skills', *Human Relations*, 1311–1331.

Kanungo, R. N. and Mendonca, M. (1996): *Ethical Dimensions of Leadership*. Thousand Oaks, CA: Sage.

Kaplan, R., Drath, W. and Kofondimos, J. (1985): *High Hurdles: The Challenge of Executive Self-Development* (Technical Report No. 25). Greensboro, N.C.: Center for Creative Leadership.

Kaplan, R., Drath, W. H. and Kofodimos, J. R. (1991): *Beyond Ambition: How Driven Managers Can Lead Better And Live Better*. San Francisco, CA: Jossey-Bass.

Kaplan, R. and Murdock, L. (1991): 'Core process redesign', *McKinsey Quarterly*, 2, 27–43.

Kaplan, R. E. (2002): 'Know your strengths', *Harvard Business Review*, 80, 20–21.

Karabenick, S. A. and Knapp, J. R. (1991): 'Relationship of academic help seeking to the use of learning strategies and other instrumental achievement behaviors in college students', *Journal of Educational Psychology*, 83, 221–230.

Kates, A. (2006): 'Re-designing the HR organization', *Human Resource Planning*, 29:2, 22–30.

Katz, R. L. (1955): 'Skills of an effective administrator', *Harvard Business Review*, 33:1, 33–42.

Katzenbach, J. R (1997): 'The myth of the top management team', *Harvard Business Review*, 75:6, 83–91.

Katzenbach, J. R. (2000): *Peak Performance: Aligning the Hearts and Minds of Your Employees*. Boston: Harvard Business School Press.

Katzenbach, J. R. and Smith, D. K. (1993): *The Wisdom of Teams*. Boston: Harvard Business School Press.

Keen, K. (1992): 'Competence: What is it and How can it be Developed?', in J. Lowyck, P. De Potter and J. Elen (eds), *Instructional Design: Implementation Issues* (pp. 111–122). Brussels: IBM International Education Center.

Kelleher, D., Finestone, P. and Lowy, A. (1986): 'A managerial learning: First notes from an unstudied frontier', *Group and Organization Studies*, 11:3, 169–202.

Kellerman, B. (2006): 'When should a leader apologise and when not?', *Harvard Business Review*, 84:4, 72–81.

Kelly, J., Sawyer, S. and Yareham, V. (2005): *Sigalovada's Sermon*. Retrieved 9 December from http://www.accesstoinsight.org/canon/sutta/digha/dn-31-ksy0.html.

Kent, T. W., Crotts, J. C. and Aziz, A. (2001): 'Four factors of transformational leadership behaviour', *Leadership and Organization Development Journal*, 22:5/6, 221–229.

Kenton, B. and Yarnall, J. (2005): *HR – The Business Partner*. Oxford: Butterworth-Heinemann.

Kerr, S. and Jermier, J. M. (1978): 'Substitutes for leadership: Their meaning and measurement', *Organizational Behavior and Human Performance*, 22, 375–403.

Kesler, G. and Kirincic P. (2005): 'Roadmaps for developing general managers: The experience of a healthcare giant', Human Resource Planning, 28:3, 24–37.

Kester C. C. (2004): 'Why the leadership bench never gets deeper: Ten insights about executive talent development', *Human Resource Planning*, 27, 32–44.

Kets De Vries, M. F. R. (2005): 'Leadership group coaching in action: The zen of creating high performance teams', *Academy of Management Executive*, 19:1, 61–76.

Keys, B. and Wolfe, J. (1988): 'Management education and development: Current issues and emerging trends', *Journal of Management*, 14:2, 205–229.

Kilburg, R. R. (2000): *Executive Coaching: Developing Managerial Wisdom in a World of Chaos*. Washington, DC: American Psychological Association.

Kilburg, R. R. (2004): 'When shadows fall: Using psychodynamic approaches in executive coaching', *Consulting Psychology Journal: Practice and Research*, 56:4, 246–268.

Kim, D. (1993): 'The link between individual and organizational learning', *Sloan Management Review*, 35:1, 37–50.

King, Z. (2004): *Career Management: A Guide*. London: CIPD.

Kirk, J. J. and Olinger, J. (2003): *From Traditional to Virtual Mentoring*. Washington, DC: Eric.

Kirkbride, P. S. (2003): 'Management development: In search of a new role', *Journal of Management Development*, 22:2, 171–80.

Kirkpatrick, S. A. and Locke, E. A. (1991): 'Leadership: Do traits matter?', *Academy of Management Executive*, 5, 48–60.

Klarsfeld, A. and Mabey, C. (2004): *Management Development in Ireland: Do National Models Exist?* Retrieved from http://www.emj.eu.com/currentissue.html.

Klein, K. J. and Ziegert, J. C. (2004): 'Leader Development and Change Over Time: A Conceptual Integration and Exploration of Research Challenges', in D. V. Day, S. J. Zaccaro and S. M. Halpin (eds), *Leader Development for Transforming Organisations*. Mahwah, NJ: Lawrence Erlbaum Associates.

Kleinman, G., Siegal, P. and Eckstein, C. (2002): 'Teams as a learning forum for accounting professionals', *Journal of Management Development*, 21:6, 427–460.

Klink, M. R., Van Der Boon, J. and Bos, E. (2000): 'The investigation of distinctive competencies within professional domains', *Proceedings of the First Conference of HRD Research and Practice across Europe* (pp.105–114), Kingston-upon-Thames: Kingston University.

Knoll, K. and Jarvenpaa, S. (1995): '*Learning to Work in Distributed Global Teams*', Proceedings of the 28th Hawaii International Conference on System Sciences, p.92, 4–7 January 1995.

Knowles, M. S. (1973): *The Adult Learner: A Neglected Species*. Houston, Texas: Gulf Publishing Company.

Knowles, M. S. (1975): *Self-Directed Learning: A Guide for Learners and Teachers*. Chicago Association Press: Follett Publishing Company.

Knowles, M. S., Holton, E. F. and Swanson, R. A. (1998): *The Adult Learner: The Definitive Classic in Adult Education and Human Resource Development*. Woburn, MA: Butterworth-Heinemann.

Kolb, A. Y. and Kolb, D. A. (2005): 'Learning styles and learning spaces: Enhancing experiential learning in higher education', *Academy of Management Learning and Education*, 4:2, 193–212.

Kolb, D. (1984): *Experiential Learning*. Englewood Cliffs: Prentice Hall.

Kolb, D. A. (1976): *Learning Styles Inventory: Technical Manual*. Boston, MA: McBer and Company.

Konrad, A. M., Kashlak, R., Yoshioka, I., Waryszak, R. and Toren, N. (2000): 'What do managers like to do? A five-country study', *Group & Organization Management*, 26:4, 401–432.

Korac-Kakabadse, N., Kakabadse, A. K. and Kouzmin, A. (2001): 'Board governance and company performance: Any correlations?', *Corporate Governance*, 1:1, 24–30.

Korac-Kakabadse, N. and Kouzmin, A. (1999): 'Designing for cultural diversity in an IT and globalising milieu: Some real leadership dilemmas for the new millenium', *Journal of Management Development*, 18:3, 291–319.

Kossek, E., Roberts, K., Fisher, S. and Demarr, B. (1998): 'Career self-management: A quasi-experimental assessment of the effect of a training intervention', *Personnel Psychology*, 51, 935–962.

Kotter, J. P. (1988): *The Leadership Factor*. New York: Free Press.

Kotter, J. P. (1990): *A Force for Change*. New York: Free Press.

Kotter, J. P. (1996): *Leading Change*. Boston, MA: Harvard Business School Press.

Kotter, J. P. and Heskett, J. L. (1992): *Corporate Culture and Performance*. Free Press.

Kram, K. E. (1983): 'Phases of the mentor relationship', *Academy of Management Journal*, 26, 608–625.

Kram, K. E. and Isabella, L. A. (1985): 'Mentoring alternatives: The role of peer relationships in career development', *Academy of Management Journal*, 28, 110–32.

Kretovics, M. (1999): 'Assessing the MBA: What do our students learn?', *Journal of Management Development*, 18:2, 125–136.

Kriger, M. and Seng, Y. (2005): 'Leadership with inner meaning: A contingency theory of leadership based on the worldviews of five religions', *Leadership Quarterly*, 16:5, 771–806.

Kristof, A. L., Brown, K. G., Sims, H. P., Jr. and Smith K. A. (1995): 'The Virtual Team: A Case Study and Inductive Model', in M. M. Beyerlein, D. A. Johnson and S. T. Beyerlein (eds), *Advances in Interdisciplinary Studies of Work Teams: Vol. 2. Knowledge Work in Teams*. Greenwich, CT: JAI.

Kudish, J. D. and Ladd, R. T. (1997): *Factors related to participants' acceptance of developmental assessment centre feedback*. April 1997. Paper presented at the Annual Conference of the Society for Industrial and Organizational Psychology, St Louis, MO.

Kudish, J. D., Ladd, R. T. and Dobbins G. H. (1997): 'New evidence on the construct validity of diagnostic assessment centres: The findings may not be so troubling after all', *Journal of Social Behavior and Personality*, 12, 129–144.

Kuhl, J. (1984): 'Volitional Aspects of Achievement Motivation and Learned Helplessness: Toward a Comprehensive Theory of Action Control', in B. A. Maher (ed.), *Progress In Experimental Personality Research* (Vol. 13, pp. 99–171). New York: Academic Press.

Lahteenmaki, S., Toivonen, J. and Mattila, M. (2001): 'Critical aspects of organizational learning and proposals for its measurement', *British Journal of Management*, 12, 113–129.

Laiken, M. (2003): 'Models of organizational learning: Paradoxes and best practices in the post-industrial workplace', *Organization Development Journal*, 21:1, 8.

Landsberg, M. (1997): *The Tao of Coaching*. London: HarperCollins Business.

Langer, E. (1989): *Mindfulness*. Reading, MA: Addison-Wesley.

Lauterbach, B., Vu, J. and Weisberg, J. (1999): 'Internal versus external successions and their effect on firm performance', *Human Relations*, 52:12, 1485–1504.

Lave, J. (1991): 'Situated Learning in Communities of Practice', in J. B. Resnick, J. M. Levine and S. D. Teasley (eds), *Perspectives on Socially Shared Cognition*. Washington, DC: American Psychological Association.

Lave, J. and Wenger, E. (1991): *Situated Learning: Legitimate Peripheral Participation*. Cambridge: Cambridge University Press.

Lawler III, E. E., Boudreau, J. W., Mohrman, S. A. and Associates (2006): *Achieving Strategic Excellence: An Assessment of Human Resource Organizations*. Stanford, CA: Stanford University Press.

Lawler, E., Mohrman, S. A. and Ledford, G. E. (1995): *Creating High Performance Organizations*. San Francisco: Jossey-Bass.

LeDeist, F., Dutech, A., Klarsfeld, A., Lafoucriere and Winterton, J. (2004): *Management Training and Development in France*. London: Chartered Management Institute.

Lee, M. (2004): 'National human resource development in the United Kingdom', *Advances in Developing Human Resources*, 6:3, 382–393.

Lee, M. M. (1997): 'The Developmental Approach: A Critical Reconsideration', in J. Burgoyne and M. Reynolds (eds), *Management Learning: Integrating Perspectives in Theory and Practice*. London: Sage.

Leedner, R. (1996): 'Rethinking Questions of Control: Lessons from McDonalds', in C. L. McDonald and C. Sirianm (eds), *Working in the Service Society*. Philadelphia: Temple University Press.

Lees, S. (1992): 'Ten faces of management development', *Journal of Management Development*, 23:2, 89–105.

Lefkowitz, J. (2006): 'The constancy of ethics amidst the changing world of work', *Human Resource Management Review*, 16:2, 245–268.

Legge, K. (2005): *Human Resource Management: Rhetorics and Realities*. London: Palgrave MacMillan.

Leibman, M. (1996): 'Succession management: The next generation of succession planning', *Human Resource Paintings*, 19:3, 16–29.

Leibowitz, Z. and Schlossberg, N. (1981): 'Training managers for their role in a career development system', *Training and Development Journal*, 35:7, 72–79.

Lenhardt, V. (2004): *Coaching for Meaning: The Culture and Practice of Coaching and Team Building*. Basingstoke, UK: Palgrave MacMillan.

Leonard-Barton, D. (1995): *Wellsprings of Knowledge: Building and Sustaining the Sources of Innovation*. Boston: Harvard Business School Press.

Leonhardt, D. (2000): 'A matter of degree? Not for consultants'. *New York Times*, 1 October.

Lepak, D. P. and Snell, S. A. (1999): 'The human resource architecture: Toward a theory of human capital allocation and development', *Academy of Management Review*, 24, 31–48.

Leslie, B., Aring, M. K. and Brand, B. (1997): 'Informal learning: The new frontier of employee and organizational development', *Economic Development Review*, 15:4, 12–18.

Levins, R., (1969): Some demographic and genetic consequences of environmental heterogeneity for biological control', *Bulletin of Ecological Society of America*, 15, 237–240.

Levinson, N. and Asahi, M. (1995): 'Cross-national alliances and inter-organizational learning', *Organizational Dynamics*, 24:2, 50–63.

Levinthal, D. A. and March, J. G. (1993): 'The myopia of learning', *Strategic Management Journal*, 14, 95–112.

Levitt, B. and March, J. G. (1988): 'Organizational learning', *Annual Review of Sociology*, 14, 319–340.

Lewis, A. E. and Fagenson, E. A. (1995): 'Strategies for developing women managers: How well do they fulfil their objectives?', *Journal of Management Development*, 14:2, 39–53.

Lewis, L. H. and Williams, C. J. (1994): 'Experiential Learning: Past and Present', in L. Jackson and R. S. Caffarella (eds), *Experiential Learning: A New Approach*. San Francisco: Jossey-Bass.

Lewis, R. E. and Heckman, R. J. (2006): 'Talent management: A critical review', *Human Resource Management Review*, 16:2, 139–54.

Lim, G. S. and Chan, A. (2003): 'Individual and situational correlates of motivation for skills upgrading: An empirical study', *Human Resource Development International*, 6:2, 219–242.

Limerick Institute of Technology (2006): *Strategic Plan 2006–2010*. Limerick: LIT.

Lindsay, C. (1994): 'Things that go wrong in diversity training', *Journal of Organizational Change Management*, 7:6, 18–33.

Lipnack, J. and Stamps, J. (1997): *Virtual Teams: Reaching Across Space, Time, and Organizations with Technology*. New York: John Wiley & Sons.

Lipnack, M. and Stamps, J. (2000): *Virtual Teams: People Working Across Boundaries with Technology*, (2nd edn). New York: Wiley.

Littler, C. R. (2000): 'Comparing the Downsizing Experiences of Three Countries: A Restructuring Cycle?', in R. J. Burke and C. L. Cooper (eds), *The Organization in Crisis*. Oxford: Blackwell.

Liu, S. and Vince, R. (1999): 'The cultural context of learning in international joint ventures', *Journal of Management Development*, 18:8, 666–675.

Livers, A. B. and Caver, K. A. (2004): 'Leader Development Across Race', in C. D. McCauley and E. Van Velsor (eds), *The Centre for Creative Leadership: Handbook of Leadership Development* (2nd edn). San Francisco: Jossey-Bass.

Livingston, J. S. (1971): 'The myth of the well-educated manager', *Harvard Business Review*, 49, 79–89.

Livingstone, D. W. (2001): 'Adults' informal learning: definitions, findings, gaps and future research'. Retrieved from http://www.oise.utoronto.ca/depts/sese /csew/nall/res/21adultsifnormallearning.htm.

Locke, E. A. and Latham, G. P. (2002): 'Building a practically useful theory of goal setting and task motivation: A 35-year odyssey', *American Psychologist*, 57, 705–717.

Loden, M. (1996): *Implementing Diversity*. Chicago, IL: Irwin Professional Publishing.

Lombardo, M. M. and Eichinger, R. W. (1989): *Eighty-Eight Assignments for Development in Place*. Greensboro, North Carolina: Centre for Creative Leadership.

London, M. (1985): *Developing Managers*. San Francisco: Jossey-Bass.

London, M. (1991): 'Career Development', in K. N. Wexley and J. Hinrichs (eds), *Developing Human Resources* (pp. 5–159). Washington, DC: BNA Books.

London, M. (1996): 'Redeployment and continuous learning in the 21st century: Hard lessons and positive examples from the downsizing era', *Academy of Management Executive*, 10:4, 67–79.

London, M. (2002): *Leadership Development*. Mahwah, NJ: Lawrence Erlbaum Associates.

London, M. and Mone, E. N. (1987): *Career Management and Survival in the Workplace*. San Francisco: Jossey-Bass.

Longenecker, C. O. and Fink, L. S. (2000): 'Improving managerial performance in rapidly changing organizations', *Journal of Management Development*, 20:1, 9–18.

Luoma, M. (2005): 'Managers' perceptions of the strategic role of management development', *Journal of Management Development*, 24:7, 645–55.

Luthans, F., Hodgetts, R. M. and Rosencrantz, A. A. (1988): *Real Managers*. Cambridge, MA: Ballinger.

Lynton, R. and Pareek, U. (2000): *Training for Organisational Transformation: Part 1 for Policy Makers and Change Managers*. London: Sage.

Mabey, C. (2002): 'Mapping management development practice', *Journal of Management Studies*, 39:8, 1139–1160.

Mabey, C. (2003): 'Reframing human resource development', *Human Resource Development Review*, 2:4, 430–452.

Mabey, C. (2004): 'Developing managers in Europe: Policies, practices and impact', *Advances in Developing Human Resources*, 6:4.

Mabey, C. and Finch-Lees, T. (2008): *Management and Leadership Development*. London: Sage.

Mabey, C. and Ramirez, M. (2004): *Developing Managers: A European Perspective*. London: Chartered Management Institute.

Mabey, C. and Ramirez, M. (2005): 'Does management development improve organizational productivity? A six-country analysis of European firms', *International Journal of Human Resource Management*, 16:7, 1067–82.

Mabey, C. and Salaman, G. (1995): *Strategic Human Resource Management*. Oxford: Blackwell.

Mabey, C. and Thomson, A. (2000): 'The determinants of management development', *British Journal of Management*, 11(Special Issue), 3–16.

Madden, C. A. and Mitchell, V. A. (1993): *Professions, Standards and Competence: A Survey of Continuing Education for the Professions*. University of Bristol.

Madsen, S. R. (2008): *On Becoming a Woman Leader: Learning from the Experiences of University Presidents*. San Francisco, CA: Jossey-Bass.

Mainiero, L. A. and Sullivan, S.E. (2005) 'Kaleidosope careers: An alternative explanation for the "opt-out" revolution', *Academy of Management Executive*, 19 (1) 106–123.

Malcolm, J., Hodkinson, P. and Colley, H. (2003): 'The interrelationships between informal and formal learning', *Journal of Workplace Learning*, 15:7/8, 33–42.

Malinen, A. (2000): *Towards the Essence of Adult Experiential Learning: A Reading of the Theories of Knowles, Kolb, Mezirow, Revans and Schon*. Finland: SoPhi, University of Jyvaskyla.

Mallon, M. and Cassell, C. (1999): 'What do women want? The perceived development needs of women managers', *The Journal of Management Development*, 18:1, 137–152.

Malone, T. (2004): *The Future of Work: How the New Order of Business Will Shape Your Organization, Your Management Style, and Your Life*. Boston: Harvard Business School Press.

Management Charter Initiative (1990): *Management Competencies: The Standards Project*. London: MCI.

Mangham, I. L. (1990): 'Managing as a performing art', *British Journal of Management*, 1:2, 105–115.

Manz, C. C. and Sims, H. P., Jr. (1989): *Superleadership: Leading Others to Lead Themselves*. Englewood Cliffs, NJ: Prentice Hall.

Manz, C. C. and Sims H. P. (1992): 'Becoming a Super Leader', in R. Glaser (ed.), *Classic Readings in Self-Managing Teamwork*. King of Prussia, PA: Organization Design and Development Inc.

March, J. (1991): 'Exploration and exploitation in organizational learning', *Organization Science*, 2:1.

March, J. G., Sproull, L. S. and Tamuz, M. (1991): 'Learning from samples of one or fewer', *Organization Science*, 2:1, 1–13.

Marchington, M., Grimshaw, D., Rubery, J. and Willmott, H. (2004): *Fragmenting Work Blurring Organizational Boundaries and Disordering Hierarchies*. UK: Oxford University Press.

Margerison, C. J. and Kakabadse, A. (1984): *The American chief executive's management development survey*. New York: American Management Association.

Markham, S. E. and Markham, I. S. (1998): 'Self-Management and Self-Leadership Re-Examined: A Levels of Analysis Perspective', in F. Dansereau and F. J. Yammarino (eds), *Leadership: The Multiple-level Approaches, Classical and New Wave*. Stanford, CT: JAI Press.

Marks, M. A., Mathieu, J. E. and Zaccaro, S. J. (2001): 'A Temporally Based Framework and Taxonomy of Team Process', *Academy of Management Review*, 26, 356–376.

Marquardt, M. and Reynolds, A. (1994): *The Global Learning Organization: Gaining Competitive Advantage through Continuous Learning*. Burr Ridge, IL: Irwin.

Marquardt, M. J. and Kearsley, G. (1999): *Technology-Based Learning: Maximising Human Performance and Corporate Success*. Boston, MA: St Lucie Press.

Marsden, P. V. (1990): 'Network Data and Measurement', in W. R. Scott (ed.), *Annual Review of Sociology*, 16, 435–463. Palo Alto CA: Annual Reviews.

Marsh, H. W., Richards, G. E. and Barnes, J. (1986): 'Multidimensional self-concepts: The effect of participation in an Outward Bound program', *Journal of Personality and Social Psychology, 50*, 195–204.

Marsh, H. W., Richards, G. E. and Barnes, J. (1987): 'Multidimensional self-concepts: A long-term effect of participation in an Outward Bound program', *Personality and Social Psychology Bulletin*, 12, 475–492.

Marsick, V. J. (1990): 'Experience-based learning: Executive learning outside the classroom', *Journal of Management Development*, 9:4, 50–60.

Marsick, V. J. and O'Neil, J. (1999): 'The many faces of action learning', *Management Learning*, 30:2, 159–176.

Marsick, V. J. and Volpe, M. (1999): 'The nature and need for informal learning', *Advances in Developing Human Resources*, 3, 1–9.

Marsick, V. J. and Watkins, K. (1990): *Informal and Incidental Learning in the Workplace*. London: Routledge.

Marsick, V. J. and Watkins, K. E. (1997): 'Lessons from Informal and Incidental Learning', in J. Burgoyne and M. Reynolds (eds), *Management Learning: Integrating Perspectives in Theory and Practice*. London: Sage.

Marsick, V. J. and Watkins, K. E. (2001): 'Informal and incidental learning', in S. Merriam (ed.), *The New Update on Adult Learning Theory*. San Francisco: Jossey-Bass.

Marsick, V. J., Watkins, K. E. and Wilson, J. A. (2002): 'Informal and Incidental Learning in the New Millenium: The Challenge of Being Rapid and/or Being Accurate', in M. Pearn (ed.), *Individual Differences and Development in Organizations*. West Sussex: John Wiley and Sons Ltd.

Martin, A. (2007): *The Changing Nature of Leadership*, Greensboro, NC: Center for Creative Leadership.

Martin, G. (2006): *Managing People and Organizations in Changing Contexts*. Oxford: Butterworth-Heinemann.

Martin, G., Pate, J. and Beaumont, P. (2001): 'Company-based education programmes: What's the pay-off for employers?', *Human Resource Management Journal*, 11:4, 55–73.

Marton, F. and Booth, S (1997): *Learning and Awareness*. Mahwah, NJ: Lawrence Erebaum.

Masten, A. S. (1989): 'Resilience in Development: The Roots of Resilience as a Focus of Research', in D. Cicchetti (ed.), *Rochester Symposium on Development Psychopathology: The Emergence of a Discipline*, Vol. 1. Mahwah, NJ: Erlbaum.

Maurer, T. J. (2002): 'Employee learning and development orientation: Toward an integrative model of involvement in continuous learning', *Human Resource Development Review*, 1:1, 9–44.

Mayer, J. D. and Salovey, P. (1995): 'Emotional intelligence and the construction and regulation of feelings', *Applied and Preventive Psychology*, 4, 197–208.

Mayrhofer, M., Mayer, M., Iellatchitch, A. and Schiffinger, M. (2004): 'Careers and human resource management: A European perspective', *Human Resource Management Review*, 14:4, 473–498.

Maznevski, M. L. and Chudoba, K. M. (2000): 'Bridging space over time: Global team dynamics and effectiveness', *Organization Science*, 11:5, 473–492.

Maznevski, M. L. and DiStefano, J. J. (2000): 'Global leaders are team players: Developing global leaders through membership on global teams', *Human Resource Management*, 39:2/3, 195–208.

McCall, M. and Lombardo, M. (1983): *Off the Track: Why and How Successful Executives Get Derailed*, Technical Report No. 21. Greensboro, NC: Center for Creative Leadership.

McCall, M. W. (1998): *High Flyers: Developing the Next Generation of Leaders*. Boston: Harvard Business School Press.

McCall, M. W. (2004): 'Leadership development through experience', *Academy of Management Executive*, 18:3, 127–130.

McCall, M. W. and Hollenbeck, G. P. (2002): *Developing Global Executives: The Lessons of International Experience*. Boston: Harvard Business School Press.

McCall, M. W., Lombardo, M. M. and Morrison, A.M. (1988): *The Lessons of Experience: How Successful Executives Develop on the Job*. Lexington, MA: Lexington Books.

McCall, M. W., Jr., Morrison, A. M. and Hannan, R. L. (1978): *Studies of Managerial Work: Results and Methods,* Technical Report No. 14. Greensboro, NC: Center for Creative Leadership.

McCarthy, A. M. and Garavan, T. N. (2001): '360-degree feedback processes: Performance improvement and employee career development', *Journal of European Industrial Training*, 25:1, 5–32.

McCarthy, A. M. and Garavan, T. N. (2006): 'Postfeedback development perceptions: Applying the theory of planned behaviour', *Human Resource Development Quarterly*, 17:3, 245–267.

McCarthy, K. C., Hukai, D. and McCarthy, C. E. (2005): 'Building diversity in the pipeline to corporate leadership', *Journal of Management Development*, 24:2, 155–168.

McCauley, C., Ohlott, P. and Ruderman, M. (1999): *Job Challenge Profile: Facilitator's Guide*. San Francisco: Jossey-Bass.

McCauley, C., Ruderman, M., Ohlott, P. and Murrow, J. (1994): 'Assessing the developmental components of managerial jobs', *Journal of Applied Psychology*, 79:4, 544–560.

McCauley, C. D. (2002): 'Developing Individuals for Leadership Roles', in M. Pearn (ed.), *Individual Differences and Development in Organizations*. West Sussex: John Wiley and Sons ltd.

McCauley, C. D. and Douglas C. A. (2004): 'Developmental Relationships', in C. D. McCauley and E. Van Velsor (eds), *The Centre for Creative Leadership: Handbook of Leadership Development* (2nd edn). San Francisco: Jossey-Bass.

McCauley, C. D., Drath, W. H., Palus, C. J., O'Connor, P. M. G., Baker, B. A. (2006): 'The use of constructive-developmental theory to advance the understanding of leadership', *Leadership Quarterly*, 17:6, 634–653.

McCauley C. D. and Van Velsor, E. (eds) (2004): *The Centre for Creative Leadership: Handbook of Leadership Development* (2nd edn). San Francisco: Jossey-Bass.

McClelland, D. (1973): 'Testing for competence rather than for "intelligence"', *American Psychologist*, 28:1, 1–14.

McClelland, R. (2002): *'Web-based delivery of degree modules using blackboard: A university strategy'*, Liverpool Business School, Liverpool John Moores University. Conference on New Patterns of Learning in H.E.

McClelland, S. (1994): 'Gaining competitive advantage through strategic management development', *Journal of Management Development*, 13:5, 4–13.

McCrimmon, M. (2005): 'Thought leadership: A radical departure from traditional positional leadership', *Management Decision*, 43:7/8, 1064–70.

McDonald, K. S. and Hite, L. M. (2005): 'Ethical issues in mentoring: The role of HRD', *Advances in Developing Human Resources*, 7:4, 569–582.

McDougall, M., Solomon, S. (1993): *'Continuous Professional Development: A Survey of IPM Members' Attitudes and Practices'*, Unpublished report. Glasgow Caledonian University.

McEvoy, G., Cragun, J. and Appleby, M. (1997): 'Using outdoor training to develop and accomplish organizational vision', Human Resource Planning, 20:3, 20–28.

McGivney, V. (1999): *Informal Learning in the Community: A Trigger for Change and Development*. Leicester: NIACE.

McGrath, R. G. (2001): 'Exploratory learning, innovative capacity and managerial oversight', *Academy of Management Journal*, 44:1, 118–131.

McLagan, P. (1997): 'Competencies: The next generation', *Training and Development*, 51:5, 40–47.

McLean, G. N. (2006): *Organization Development: Principles, Processes, Performance*. San Francisco: Berrett-Koehler.

McQuaid, R.W. and Lindsay, C. (2005): 'The concept of employability: Transcending the orthodoxies of supply and demand', *Urban Studies*, 42:2, 197–219.

Megginson, D. (1996): 'Planned and emergent learning', *Management Learning*, 27:4, 411–428.

Megginson, D. and Boydell, T. (1979): *A Manager's Guide to Coaching*. London: British Association for Commercial and Industrial Education.

Megginson, D. and Whittaker, V. (2003): *Continuous Professional Development*. London: CIPD.

Meir, A. (2005): The Jewish ethicist: Ethical work. *JCT Center for Business Ethics*. Retrieved 5 December 2005 from http://www.aish.com/societyWork/work /The_Jewish-Ethicist.

Meir, A. (29 April 2005): No work/family firewall in Israel. *Jerusalem Post*. Retrieved 5 December 2005 from http://www.besr.org/ethicist/jpost/4.22.2005.html

Meldrum, M. and Atkinson, S. (1998): 'Is management development fulfilling its organisational role?', *Management Decision*, 36:8, 528–532.

Melkman, A. and Trotman, J. (2005): *Training International Managers: Designing, Deploying and Delivering Effective Training for Multi-Cultural Groups*. Aldershot: Gower.

Mellahi, K. and Wood, G. (2003): *The Ethical Business: Challenges and Controversies*. Basingstoke: Palgrave.

Mendenhall, M., Dunbar, E. and Oddou, G (1987): 'Expatriate selection, training and career-pathing: A review and critique,' *Human Resource Management*, 26:3, 331–345.

Mendenhall, M. E. and Stahl, G. K. (2000): 'Expatriate training and development: Where do we go from here?', *Human Resource Management*, 39:2/3, 251–265.

Merton, R. K., Fiske, M. and Kendall, P. L. (1990): *The Focused Interview: A Manual of Problems and Procedures* (2nd edn). London: Collier MacMillan.

Mezirow, J. (1981): 'A critical theory of adult learning and education', *Adult Education*, 32:1, 3–24.

Mezirow, J. (1985): 'A Critical Theory of Self-Directed Learning', in S. Brookfield (ed.), *Self-Directed Learning: From Theory to Practice. New Directions for Continuing Education* (No. 25). San Francisco: Jossey-Bass.

Mezirow, J. (1991): *Transformative Dimensions of Adult Learning*. San Francisco: Jossey-Bass.

Mezirow, J. (2000): *Learning as Transformation: Critical Perspectives on a Theory in Progress*. San Francisco: Jossey Bass.

Mezirow, J. & Associates (2000): *Learning as Transformation*. San Francisco: Jossey-Bass.

Micco, L. (1996): *Women outmuscle men in management tasks, study finds*. HR News Online. Retrieved 30 September 1996 from http://www.shrm.org/hrnews/

Michaels, E., Handfield-Jones, H. and Axelrod, B. (2001): *The War for Talent*. Boston: Harvard University Press.

Miles, R. E. and Snow, C. C. (1986): 'Organizations: New concepts for new forms', *California Management Review*, 18:3, 62–73.

Miller, D. (1996): 'A preliminary typology of organizational learning: Synthesizing the literature', *Journal of Management*, 22:3, 485–505.

Miller, P. (1991): 'A strategic look at management development', *Personnel Management*, August, 45–47.

Miller, V. M. and Robinson, C. (2004): 'Managing the disappointment of job termination – outplacement as a cooling-out devise', *The Journal of Applied Behavioural Science*, 40:1, 49–65.

Milliman, J. F. and Von Glinow, M. A. (1990): 'A life-cycle approach to strategic international human resource management in MNCs,' *Research in Personnel and Human Resources Management*, Supplement 2, 21–35.

Mills, T. and Tyson, S. (2001): *Organisational Renewal: Challenging Human Resource Management*, presented on 15 November 2001 at the HRM Network Conference, Nijmegen School of Management, the Netherlands.

Mintzberg, H. (1973): *The Nature of Managerial Work*. New York: Harper and Row.

Mintzberg, H. (1975): 'The manager's job: Folklore and fact', *Harvard Business Review*, July/ August.

Mintzberg, H. (1994a): *The Rise and Fall of Strategic Planning*. London: Prentice Hall.

Mintzberg, H. (1994b): 'Rounding out the manager's job', *Sloan Management Review*, 37:1, 23.

Mintzberg, H. (2004): *Managers not MBAs: A Hard Look at the Soft Practice of Managing and Management Development*. San Francisco: Brett-Koehler.

Mirabile, R. (1997): 'Everything you wanted to know about competency modeling', *Training and Development*, 51:8, 73–77.

Mitchell, R. (1986): 'Team building by disclosure of internal frames of reference', *Journal of Applied Behavioural Science*, 22:1, 15–28.

Mittleman, D. and Briggs, R. O. (1999): 'Communication Technology for Traditional and Virtual Teams', in E. Sundstrom (ed.), *Supporting Work Team Effectiveness*. San Francisco: Jossey-Bass.

Mizuchi, M. S. and Galaskiewicz, J. (1994): 'Networks of Interorganizational Relations', in S. Wasserman and J. Galaskiewicz (eds), *Advances in Social Network Analysis: Research in the Social and Behavioral Sciences*. Thousand Oaks: Sage.

Mobley, M. and Payne, T. (1992): 'Backlash', *Training and Development Journal*, 46:12, 45–52.

Molander, C. (1986): *Management Development*. Bromley: Chartwell-Bratt.

Molander, C. and Winterton, J. (1994): *Managing Human Resources*. London: Routledge.

Mole, G. (2000): *Managing Management Development*. Buckingham: Open University Press.

Mole, G. W. (1996): 'The management training industry in the UK: An HRD director's critique', *Human Resource Management Journal*, 6:1, 19–26.

Molloy, J. C. (2005): 'Development network: Literature review and future research', *Career Development International*, 10:6/7, 536–547.

Monahan, S. C., Meyer, J. W. and Scott, W. R. (1994): 'Employee Training: The Expansion of Organizational Citizenship', in W. R. Scott and J. W. Meyer (eds), *Institutional Environments and Organizations: Structural Complexity and Individualism*. Thousand Oaks: Sage.

Montoya-Weiss, M. M., Massey, A. and Song, M. (2002): 'Getting it together: Temporal coordination and conflict management in global virtual teams', *Academy of Management Journal*, 44:6, 1251–1262.

Morgan D. L. (1997): *Focus Groups as Qualitative Research* (2nd edn). London: Sage Publications.

Morley, M. J. (2004): 'Contemporary debates in human resource management: Context and content', *Human Resource Management Review*, 14, 353–364.

Morris, J. (1971): 'Management development and development management', *Personnel Review*, 1:1, 30–43.

Morris, J. A. and Feldman, D. C. (1997): 'Managing emotions in the workplace', *Journal of Managerial Issues*, 9:3, 257–275.

Morrison, A. M. (1992): *The New Leaders: Guidelines on Leadership Diversity in America*. San Francisco: Jossey-Bass.

Moser, C.A. and Kalton, G. (1971): *Survey Methods in Social Investigation*. London: Heinemann Educational Books.

Moss Kanter, R. (1997): *The Frontiers of Management*. Boston: Harvard Business School Press.

Mottram, R. (2002): 'Teamworking and the Implications for Individual Development', in M. Pearn (ed.), *Individual Differences and Development in Organisations*. West Sussex: Wiley & Sons Ltd.

Mowshowitz, A. (1997): 'Virtual organization', *Communications of the ACM*, 40:9, 30–37.

Moxley, R. S. and Pulley, M. (2004): 'Hardships', in C. D. McCauley, and E. Van Velsor (eds), *The Centre for Creative Leadership Handbook for Leadership Development* (2nd edn). San Francisco: Jossey-Bass.

Mulder, M. (1998): 'Het begrip competenties: enkele achtergronden en invullingen' [The concept of competence: Some backgrounds and interpretations]. *Opleiding en Ontwikkeling, 10*, 5–9.

Mullen, E. J. and Noe, R. A. (1999): 'The mentoring information exchange: when do mentors seek information from their protégés?', *Journal of Organizational Behaviour*, 25:4, 233–242.

Mumford, A. (1989): *Management Development Strategies for Action*. London: Institute of Personnel Management.

Mumford, A. (1993): *How Managers Can Develop Managers*. Aldershot: Gower.

Mumford, A. (1995): *Learning at the Top*. Maidenhead: McGraw-Hill.

Mumford, A. (1996): 'Effective learners in action learning sets', *Journal of Workplace Learning*, 8:6, 3–10.

Mumford, A. (1997a): *How to Choose the Right Development Method*. Maidenhead: Honey Publications.

Mumford, A. (1997b): *Management Development: Strategies for Action*. London: CIPD.

Mumford, A. (2002): 'Choosing a Development Method', in M. Pearn (ed.), *Individual Differences and Development in Organizations*. West Sussex: John Wiley and Sons Ltd.

Mumford, A. and Gold, J. (2004): *Management Development Strategies for Action* (4th edn). London: CIPD.

Mumford, M. D., Marks, M. A., Connelly, M. S., Zaccaro, S. J. and Reiter-Palmon, R. (2000): 'Development of leadership skills: Experience and timing', *Leadership Quarterly*, 11:1, 87–114.

Mumford, M. D., Scott, G. M., Baddis, B. and Strange, J. M. (2002): 'Leading creating people: Orchestrating expertise and relationships', *Leadership Quarterly*, 13, 705–750.

Mumford, M. D., Zaccaro, S. J., Harding, F. D., Jacobs, T. O. and Fleishman, E. A. (2000): 'Leadership skills for a changing world: Solving complex social problems', *Leadership Quarterly*, 11:1, 11–35.

Mumford, T. V., Campion, M. A. and Morgison, F. (2007): 'The leadership skills strataplex: Leadership skills requirements across organisational levels', *The Leadership Quarterly*, 18, 154–166.

Murray, P. (2002): 'Cycles of organizational learning: A conceptual approach', *Management Decision*, 40:3, 239–247.

Myers, J. and Sacks, R. (2003): 'Tools, techniques and tightropes: The art of walking and talking private sector management in non-profit organisations, Is it just a question of balance?', *Financial Accountability and Management*, 19:3, 287–305.

NCVQ, National Council for Vocational Qualifications (1997): *Criteria for National Qualifications*. London: Qualifications and Curriculum Authority.

Nelson, D. L. and Campbell, J. (1997): *Organisational Behavior* (2nd edn). Thomson/South-Western.

Nenninger, P. (1999): 'On the role of motivation in self-directed learning: The "Two–shells-model of motivated self-directed learning" as a structural explanatory concept', *European Journal of Psychology of Education*, 14, 71–86.

Nevis, E., DiBella, A. and Gould, J. (1995): 'Understanding organisations as learning systems', *Sloan Management Review*, 36:2, 73–85.

New, G. E. (1996): 'Reflections: A three-tier model of organisational competencies', *Journal of Managerial Psychology*, 11:8, 44–52.

Nicholson, N. (1996): 'Career systems in crisis: Change and opportunity in the information age', *The Academy of Management Executive*, 10, 40–51.

Nicholson, N. and West, M. A. (1998): *Managerial Job Change: Men and Women in Transition*. Cambridge: Cambridge University Press.

Nicolini, D. and Meznar, M. B. (1995): 'The social construction of organizational learning: Conceptual and practical issues in the field', *Human Relations*, 48:7, 727–746.

Nicoll, D. (1986): 'Leadership and Followership', in J. D. Adams (ed.), *Transforming Leadership*. Alexandria, VA: Miles River Press.

Nielsen, R. P. (1989): 'Changing unethical organizational behavior', *Academy of Management Executive*, 3:2, 123–130.

Nielsen, R. P. (1996): *The Politics of Ethics: Methods for Acting, Learning and Sometimes Fighting with Others in Addressing Problems of Organizational Life*. New York: Oxford University Press.

Niven, D. (1993): 'When times get tough, what happens to TQM?', *Harvard Business Review*, 71:3, 20–34.

Noe, R. (1986): 'Trainees, attributes and attitudes: Neglected influences on training effectiveness', *Academy of Management Review*, 11:4, 251–261.

Noe, R. (1996): 'Is career management related to employee development and performance?', *Journal of Organizational Behaviour*, 17, 119–133.

Noe, R. A. (1988a): 'Women in mentoring: A review and research agenda', *Academy of Management Review*, 13:1, 65–78.

Noe, R. A. (1988b): 'An investigation of the determinates of successfully assigned mentoring relationship', *Personal Psychology*, 41, 457–479.

Noe, R. A. (2006): *Employee Training and Development*. New York: McGraw-Hill Irwin.

Noe, R. A., Greenberger, D. B. and Wang, S. (2002): 'Mentoring: What We Know and Where We Might Go', in G. R. Ferris (ed.), *Research in Personnel and Human Resource Management* (Vol. 21, pp. 129–174). Oxford, UK: Elsevier Science.

Noe, R. A. and Wilk, S. A. (1993): 'Investigation of the factors that influence employees' participation in development activities', *Journal of Applied Psychology*, 78, 291–302.

Nonaka, I. (1994): 'A dynamic theory of organizational knowledge creation', *Organizational Science*, 5:1, 14–37.

Nordhaug, O. (1998): 'Competencies specificities in organisations', *International Studies of Management and Organisation*, 28:1, 8–29.

Nordhaug, O. and Grunhaug, K. (1994): 'Competencies as Resources in Firms', *International Journal of Human Resource Management*, 5:1, 89–106.

Nordon, L. and Steers, R. M. (2008): 'The new global manager: Learning cultures on the fly', *Organisational Dynamics*, 37 (1) 47–59.

Northouse, P.G. (2004): *Leadership: Theory and Practice* (3rd edn). London: Sage Publications Ltd.

O'Brien, M. (1994): 'The managed heart revisited: Health and social control', *Sociological Review*, Vol. 43 No.2, 393–413.

O'Connell, B. (2005): *Solution-Focused Therapy* (2nd edn). Sage Publications.

O'Connor, M. and Mangan, J. (2004): *Management Development in Ireland*. Dublin: Irish Management Institute.

O'Connor, M., Mangan, J. and Cullen, J. (2006): 'Management development in Ireland: Justifying the investment', *Journal of Management Development*, 25:4, 325–49.

O'Connor, P. M. G. and Day, D. V. (2002): 'Tapping your organization's leadership reserve', *Leadership in Action*, 22:1, 3–7.

O'Connor, P. M. G. and Quinn, L. (2004): 'Organizational Capacity for Leadership', in C. D. McCauley and E. Van Velsor (eds), *The Centre for Creative Leadership: Handbook of Leadership Development* (2nd edn). San Francisco: Jossey-Bass.

O'Donnell, D., McGuire, D. and Cross, C. (2006): 'Critically challenging some assumptions in HRD', *International Journal of Training and Development*, 10 (1) 4–16.

O'Dwyer, M. and Ryan, E. (2000): 'Management development issues for owners/managers of micro-enterprises', *Journal of European Industrial Training*, 24:6, 345–353.

O'Hara-Devereaux, M. and Johansen, R. (1994): *Globalwork: Bridging Distance, Culture and Time*. San Francisco: Jossey Bass.

O'Malley, J. M. and Chamot, A. U. (1990): *Learning Strategies in Second Language Acquisition*. Cambridge: Cambridge University Press.

O'Neil, D. A. and Bilimoria, D. (2005): 'Women's career development phases: Idealism, endurance and reinvention', *Career Development International*, 10:3, 168–189.

Oakley, J. G. (1998): 'Leadership processes in virtual teams and organizations', *Journal of Leadership Studies*, 5:3, 3–17.

Oberg, K. (1960): 'Culture shock: adjustments to new cultural environments', *Practical Anthropology*, 4, 177–182.

Oddou, G., Mendenhall, M. E. and Ritchie, J. B. (2000): 'Leveraging travel as a tool for global leadership development', *Human Resource Management*, 39:2/3, 159–172.

Offerman, T. and Sonnemans, J. (1998): 'Learning by experience and learning by imitating successful others', *Journal of Economic Behavior and Organization*, 34, 559–575.

Ohlott, P. J. (2004): 'Job Assignments', in C. D. McCauley and E. Van Velsor (eds), *The Centre for Creative Leadership Handbook for Leadership Development* (2nd edn). San Francisco: Jossey-Bass.

Ohlott, P. J. and Hughes-James M. W. (1997): 'Single-gender and single-race leadership development programmes: Concerns and benefits', *Leadership in Action*, 17:4, 8–12.

Ohlott, P. J., Ruderman, M. N. and McCauley, C. D. (1994): 'Gender differences in managers' developmental job experiences', *Academy of Management Journal*, 37:1, 46–67.

Oliver, C. (1991): 'Strategic responses to institutional processes', *Academy of Management Review*, 16:1, 145–179.

Olsen, R. (2000): 'Harnessing the internet with human capital management', *Workspan*, 43:11, 24–27.

Open University Business School, PriceWaterhouseCoopers and Forfás (2000): *Management Development in the Republic of Ireland: Pattern and Trends*.

Ortega, J. (2001): 'Job rotation as a learning mechanism', *Management Science*, 47:10, 1361–1370.

Overmeer, W. (1997): 'Business integration in a learning organisation: The role of management development', *Journal of Management Development*, 16:4, 245–261.

Paauwe, J. and Williams, R. (2001): 'Seven key issues for management development', *Journal of Management Development*, 20:2, 90–105.

Palmer, I. and Hardy, C. (2000): *Thinking About Management*. London: Sage Publications.

Paris, S. G. and Paris, A. H. (2001): 'Classroom applications of research on self-regulated learning', *Educational Psychologist*, 36, 89–101.

Parker, S. K., Wall, T. D., Jackson, P. R. (1997): 'That's not my job: Developing flexible employee work', *Academy of Management Journal*, 40:4, 899–929.

Parry, K. W. (1998): 'Grounded theory and social process: A new direction for leadership research', *Leadership Quarterly*, 9:1, 85–105.

Parry, S. B. (1996): 'The quest for competencies', *Training*, 33:7, 48–54.

Parsloe, E. (1999): *The Manager as Coach and Mentor*. London: CIPD.

Pascal, C. (2004): 'Foreword', in A. Schweyer (ed.), *Talent Management Systems: Best Practices in Technology Solutions for Recruitment, Retention and Workforce Planning*. Canada: Wiley.

Passfield, R. (2002): 'Creating innovation and synergy through a parallel action learning structure', *The Learning Organization*, 9:4, 150–158.

Patching, K. (1998): *Management and Organisation Development*. London: MacMillan.

Paton, R. and Brownlie, D. (1991): 'Strategy formulation in small enterprises: A developmental approach', *Journal of European Industrial Training*, 15:4, 3–8.

Paton, R., Taylor, S. and Storey, J. (2004): 'Corporate Universities and Leadership Development', in J. Storey (ed.), *Leadership in Organizations: Current Issues and Key Trends* (pp.103–124). London: Routledge.

Patterson, M. G., West, M. A., Lawthom, R. and Nickell, S. (1997): *Impact of People Management Practices on Performance*. London: Institute of Personnel and Development.

Pazy, A. (1990): 'The threat of professional obsolescence: How do professionals at different career stages experience it and cope with it?', *Human Resource Management*, 29:3, 251–269.

Pearce, C. L. and Conger, J. A. (2003): 'All Those Years Ago: The Historical Underpinnings of Shared Leadership', in C. L. Pearce and J. A. Conger (eds), *Shared Leadership: Reframing the Hows and Whys of Leadership*. Thousand Oaks, CA: Sage Publications.

Pedler, M. (ed.) (1997a): *Action Learning in Practice* (3rd edn). Aldershot, England: Gower.

Pedler, M. (1997b): 'Interpreting Action Learning', in J. Burgoyne and M. Reynolds (eds), *Management Learning: Integrating Perspectives in Theory and Practice*. London: Sage Publications.

Pedler, M., Burgoyne, J. and Boydell, T. (1978): *A Manager's Guide to Self-Development*. Maidenhead: McGraw-Hill.

Pedler, M., Burgoyne, J. and Boydell, T. (1997): *The Learning Company: A Strategy for Sustainable Development* (2nd edn). London: McGraw-Hill.

Pegg, M. (2005): 'Sowing the seeds of success', *Strategic HR Review*, 4:2.

Peltier, B. (2001): *Psychology of Executive Coaching: Theory and Applications*. New York: Brunner-Routledge.

Perren, L. and Grant, P. (2001): *Management and Leadership in UK SMEs*. London: CEML.

Peters, L. H., Hartke, D. D. and Pohlmann, J. T. (1985): 'Fiedler's contingency theory of leadership: An application of the meta-analysis procedures of Schmidt and Hunter', *Psychological Bulletin*, 97, 274–285.

Peters, R. S., Smith, D. B., Martorana, P. and Owens, P. D. (2003): 'The impact of chief executive officer personality on top management team dynamics: One mechanism by which leadership affects organisational performance', *Journal of Applied Psychology*, 85:5, 795–808.

Petersen, D. and Hicks, M. D. (1996): *Leader as Coach*. Minneapolis, MI: Personnel Decisions.

Pfeffer, J. (1994): *Competitive Advantage Through People*. Boston: Harvard University School Press.

Pfeffer, J. (2001): *Fighting the War for Talent is Hazardous to Your Organization's Health*, Research Paper Series (No. 1687), Stanford: Graduate School of Business, Stanford University.

Pfeffer, J. and Fong, C. (2002): 'The end of business schools? Less success than meets the eye', *Academy of Management Learning and Education Journal*, September.

Pfeffer, J. and Sutton, R. I. (2000): *The Knowing-Doing Gap: How Smart Companies Turn Knowledge into Action*. Boston: Harvard Business School Press.

Phillips, J. J. (1997): 'Measuring ROI: Progress, Trends and Strategies', in J. J. Phillips (eds), *In Action: Measuring Return on Investment* (Vol. 1). Alexandria, VA: American Society for Training & Development.

Pickard, J. (1998): *Externally Yours. People Management*, 23 July.

Pillai, R., Schriesheim, C. and Williams, E. (1999): 'Fairness perceptions and trust as mediators for transformational and transactional leadership: A two-way study', *Journal of Management*, 25, 897–933.

Pintrich, P. R. and Garcia, T. (1991): 'Student Goal Orientation and Self-Regulation in the College Classroom', in M. Maehr and P. R. Pintrich (eds), *Advances In Motivation And Achievement* (Vol. 7, pp. 371–402). Greenwich, CT: JAI Press.

Pintrich, P. R., Smith, D. A. F., Garcia, T. and McKeachie, W. J. (1993): 'Reliability and predictive validity of the Motivated Strategies for Learning Questionnaire (MSLQ)', *Educational and Psychological Measurement*, 53, 801–813.

Podsakoff, P. M., Dorfman, P. W., Howell, J. P. and Todor, W. D. (1986): 'Leader Reward and Punishment Behaviors: A Preliminary Test of a Culture-Free Style of Leadership Effectiveness', in R. N. Farmer (ed.), *Advances in International Comparative Management*, Vol. 2. Greenwich, CT: JAI Press, 95–138.

Poell, R. (1999): 'The Learning Organization: A Critical Evaluation', in J. P. Wilson (ed.), *Human Resource Development: Learning and Training for Individuals and Organisations*. London: Kogan Page.

Poell, R. F., Van Dam, K. and Van Den Berg, P. T. (2004): 'Organising learning in work contexts', *Applied Psychology: An International Review*, 53:4, 529–540.

Pofeldt, E. (2002): *Jumping off the corporate ladder*. Retrieved 8 December 2002 from http://www.fortune.com

Pool, S. W. (2000): 'The learning organization: Motivating employees by integrating TQM philosophy in a supportive organizational culture', *Leadership and Organization Development Journal*, 21, 373–378.

Popper, M. and Mayseless, O. (2003): 'Back to basics: Applying a parenting perspective to transformational leadership', *The Leadership Quarterly*, 14:1, 41–66.

Porter, M. E., Schwab, K. and Lopez-Claros, A. (2005): *The Global Competitiveness Report 2005–2006: Policies Underpinning Rising Prosperity*. London: Palgrave MacMillan.

Poskiparta, M., Liitmatainen, L. and Kettunen, T. (1999): 'Nurses' self-reflection via videotaping to improve communication skills in health counselling', *Patient Education and Counselling*, 36, 3–11.

Powell, W. W. (1991): 'Expanding the Scope of Institutional Analysis', in P. J. DiMaggio and W. W. Powell (eds), *The New Institutionalism in Organizational Analysis*. Chicago: University of Chicago Press.

Powers, E. (1987): 'Enhancing managerial competence: The American Management Association competency programme', *Journal of Management Development*, 6:4, 7–18.

Prager, H. (1999): 'Cooking up effective team building', *Training and Development*, 53:12, 14–20.

Prahalad, C. K. and Hamel, G. (1990): 'The core competences of the corporation', *Harvard Business Review*, 68:3, 79–91.

Price Waterhouse Europe (1998): *International Assignments: European Policy and Practice*. Europe: Price Waterhouse International Assignment Services.

Pringle, J. (1994): 'Feminism and Management: Critique and Contribution', in A. Kouzmin, V. Still and P. Clarke (eds), *New Directions in Management*. Sydney: McGraw-Hill.

Pringle, J. K. and Mallon, M. (2003): 'Challenges for the Boundaryless Career Odyssey', *International Journal of Human Resource Management*, 14:5, 839–853.

Procter, S., Fulop, L., Linstead, S., Mueller, F. and Swell, G. (2004): 'Managing Teams', in S. Linstead, L. Fulop and S. Lilley (eds), *Management and Organisation: A Critical Text*. Palgrave: Macmillian.

Pucik, V. (2003): 'Developing Global Leaders', in S. Chowdhury (ed.), *Organization 21C*. Englewood Cliffs, NJ: Prentice-Hall.

Pucik, V. and Saba T. (1998): 'Selecting and developing the global versus the expatriate manager: A review of the state-of-the-art', *Human Resource Planning*, 21:4, 40–54.

Purcell, K. and Pitcher, J. (1996): *Great Expectations: The New Diversity of Graduate Skills and Aspirations*. IER for AGCAS and CSU, Manchester, GSU.

Quader, M. S. and Quader, M. R. (2008): 'A critical analysis of high performing teams: A case study based on the British Telecommunication (BT) PLC.' Journal of Services Research, 8:2, 175–216.

Quinn, R. E., Dutton, J. E and Spreitzer, G. M. (2004): 'Reflected best self exercise'. Michigan: Centre for Positive Organisational Scholarship, Ross School of Business.

Quinn, R. E., Hildebrandt, H. W., Rogers, P. S. and Thompson, M. P. (1991): 'A competing values framework for analyzing presentational communication in management contexts', *Journal of Business Communication*, 28:3, 213–232.

Raelin, J. (2006a): 'Does action learning promote collaborative leadership?', *Academy of Management Learning and Education*, 5:2, 152–68.

Raelin, J. (2006b): 'The role of facilitation in praxis', *Organizational Dynamics*, 35:1, 83–95.

Raelin, J. A. (1998): 'Work-based learning in practice', *Journal of Workplace Learning*, 10:6/7, 280–283.

Raelin, J. A. (2002): '"Don't have time to think" versus the art of reflective practice', *Reflections*, 4:1, 66–79.

Raelin, J. A. (2003): *Creating Leaderful Organizations: How to Bring Out Leadership in Everyone*. San Francisco: Berrett-Koehler.

Raelin, J. A. and Cooledge, A. S. (1995): 'From generic to organic competencies', *Human Resource Planning*, 18:3, 24–33.

Ragins, B. R. (1997): 'Diversified mentoring relationships in organisations: a power perspective', *Academy of Management Review*, 22, 482–521.

Ragins, B. R. (1999): 'Gender and Mentoring Relationships: A Review and Research Agenda for the Next Decade', in G. N. Powell (ed.), *Handbook of Gender and Work*. Thousand Oaks, CA: Sage.

Ragins, B. R. and Cotton, J. (1991): 'Easier said than done: Gender differences in perceived barriers to gaining a mentor', *Academy of Management Journal*, 34:4, 939–951.

Ragins, B. R. and Cotton, J. (1999): 'Mentor functions and outcomes: A comparison of men and women in formal and informal mentoring relationships', *Journal of Applied Psychology*, 84, 529–549.

Ragins, B. R., Cotton, J. L. and Miller, J. S. (2000): 'Marginal mentoring: The effects of type of mentor, quality of relationship, and program design of work and career attitudes', *Academy of Management Journal*, 43:6, 1177–1201.

Ragins, B. R. and McFarlin, D. B. (1990): 'Perception of mentoring roles in cross-gender mentoring relationships', *Journal of Vocational Behaviour*, 37, 321–339.

Ragins, B. R., Townsend, B., and Mattis, M. (1998): 'Gender gap in the executive suite: CEOs and female executives report on breaking the glass ceiling', *Academy of Management Executive*,12, 28–42.

Rainbird, H. (1988): 'New Technology, Training and Union Strategies', in R. Hyman and W. Streek (eds), *New Technology and Industrial Relations* (pp.174–185), Oxford: Blackwell Publishing.

Ramirez, M. (2004): 'Comparing European approaches to management education, training and development', *Advances in Developing Human Resources*, 6:4, 428–450.

Reagan, T. (2000): *Non-Western Educational Traditions: Alternative Approaches to Educational Thought and Practice*. Mahwah, NJ: Lawrence Erlbaum.

Reber, A. S. (1993): *Implicit Learning and Tacit Knowledge: An Essay on the Cognitive Unconscious*. New York: Oxford University Press.

Redford, K. (2005): 'Shedding light on talent tactics', *Personnel Today*, September, 20–22.

Rees, D. and McBain, R. (2004): *People Management: Challenges and Opportunities*. Palgrave: MacMillan.

Revans, R. W. (1978; reprinted 1995): *The A. B. C. of Action Learning: A Review of 25 Years of Experience*. Salford: University of Salford.

Revans, R. W. (1980): *Action Learning: New Techniques for Management*. London: Blond and Briggs.

Revans, R. W. (1982): *The Origins and Growth of Action Learning*. Bromley: Chartwell-Bratt.

Revans, R. W. (1983): *The ABC of Action Learning*. Bromley, Kent: Chartwell Bratt.

Reynolds, M. (1998): 'Reflection and critical reflection in management learning', *Management Learning*, 29:2, 183–200.

Reynolds, M. (1999): 'Critical reflection and management education: Rehabilitating less hierarchical approaches', *Journal of Management Education*, 23:5, 537–553.

Reynolds, R. and Ablett, A. (1998): 'Transforming the rhetoric of organizational learning to the reality of the learning organization', *The Learning Organization*, 5:1, 24–35.

Richard, O. (2000): 'Racial diversity, business strategy, and firm performance: A resource-based view', *Academy of Management Journal*, 43, 164–177.

Richardson, R. and Thompson, M. (1999): *The Impact of People Management Practices on Performance: A Literature Review*. London: Institute of Personnel and Development.

Roberts, L. M., Dutton, J. E., Spreitzer, G. M., Heaphy, E. D. and Quinn, R. E. (2005): 'Composing the reflected best self portrait: building pathways for becoming extraordinary in work organisations', *Academy of Management Review*, 30(4), 712–736.

Robinson, S. L. and Rousseau, D. (1994): 'Violating the psychological contract: Not the expectation but the norm', *Journal of Organisational Behaviour*, 15, 245–259.

Robotham, D. (1995): 'Self-directed learning: the ultimate learning style?', *Journal of European Industrial Training*, 19:7, 3–7.

Rock, A. D. and Garavan, T. N. (2006): 'Reconceptualizing developmental relationships', *Human Resource Development Review*, 5:3, 1–25.

Roehling, M. V., Cavanaugh, M. A., Moynihan, L. M. and Boswell, W. R. (2000): 'The nature of the new employment relationship: A content analysis of the practitioner and academic literatures', *Human Resource Management*, 39:4, 305–320.

Rogers, A. (1986): *Teaching Adults*. Maidenhead, UK: Open University Press.

Rogers, C. R. (1959): 'A theory of therapy, personality and interpersonal relationships, as developed in the client-centred framework', in S. Koch (ed.), *Psychology: A Study of a Science*, Vol. 3: *Formulations of the Person and the Social Context*. New York: McGraw Hill.

Rogers, C. R. (1961): *On Becoming a Person*. Boston, MA: Houghton Mifflin.

Rogers, E. M. (2003): *Diffusion of Innovations* (5th edn). New York: Free Press.

Rosen, B. and Jerdee, T. H. (1990): 'Middle and late career problems: Causes, consequences and research needs', *Human Resource Planning*, 13:1, 59–70.

Rosener, J. (1990): 'Ways women lead', *Harvard Business Review*, 68:6, 119–125.

Rosenshine, B. V. and Meister, C. (1992): 'The use of scaffolds for teaching less-structured cognitive tasks', *Educational Leadership*, 49(7): 26–33.

Rosinski, P. (2003): *Coaching Across Cultures: New Tools for Leveraging National, Corporate and Professional Differences*. London: Nicholas Brealey Publishing.

Rossett, A. (1987): *Training Needs Assessment*. Englewood Cliffs, NJ: Educational Technology Publications.

Rothwell, A. and Arnold, J. (2005): 'How HR professionals rate continuing professional development', *Human Resource Management Journal*, 15:3, 18–32.

Rothwell, W. J. (1994): *Effective Succession Planning: Ensuring Leadership Continuity and Building Talent from Within*. New York: Amacom.

Rothwell, W. J. (2005): *Effective Succession Planning* (3rd edn). Broadway, NY: Amacom Books.

Rothwell, W. J. and Kazanas, H. C. (2003): *The Strategic Development Of Talent* (2nd edn). Amherst, MA: HRD Press.

Rousseau, D. M., Ho, V. T. and Greenberg, J. (2006): 'I-deals: Idiosyncratic terms in employment relationships', *Academy of Management Review*, 31:4, 977–994.

Rousseau, D. M. and McCarthy, S. (2007): 'Educating managers from an evidence-based perspective', *Academy of Management Learning and Education*, 6 (1), 84–101.

Ruderman, M. N. (2004): 'Leader Development Across Gender', in C. D. McCauley and E. Van Velsor (eds), *The Centre for Creative Leadership: Handbook of Leadership Development* (2nd edn). San Francisco: Jossey-Bass.

Ruderman, M. N., McCauley, C. D. and Ohlott P. J. (1999): *Job Challenge Profile*. San Francisco: Jossey-Bass.

Ruderman, M. N., Ohlott, P. J. and Kram, K. E. (1995): 'Promotion decisions as a diversity practice', *Journal of Management Development*, 14:2, 6–23.

Ruderman, M. N., Ohlott, P. J., Panzer, K. and King, S. N. (2002): 'Benefits of multiple roles for managerial women', *Academy of Management Journal*, 45:2, 369–386.

Ruona, W. E. A. and Lynham, S. (2004): 'A philosophical framework for thought and practice in human resource development', *Human Resource Development International*, 7:2, 151–164.

Rusaw, C. A. (1995): 'Learning by association: Professional associations as learning agents', *Human Resource Development Quarterly*, 6:2, 215–226.

Ruth, D. (2006): 'Frameworks of managerial competence: Limits, problems and suggestions', *Journal of European Industrial Training*, 30:3, 206–26.

Ruvolo, C. M., Peterson, S. A. and LeBoeuf, J. N. G. (2004): 'Leaders are made, not born: The critical role of a developmental framework to facilitate an organizational culture of development', *Consulting Psychology Journal: Practice and Research*, 56:1, 10–9.

Rymer, J. (2002): 'Only connect: Transforming ourselves and our discipline through co-mentoring', *The Journal of Business Communication*, 39:3, 342–363.

Saam, R. H. and Wodtke, K. H. (1995): 'A cognitive stress-reduction program for recently unemployed managers', *Career Development Quarterly*, 44:1, 43–52.

Sadler, P. (2003): *Leadership* (2nd edn). London: Kogan Page.

Sadler-Smith, E. (2006): *Learning and Development for Managers*. Oxford: Blackwell Publishing.

Sadler-Smith, E. and Riding, R. (1999): 'Cognitive style and instructional preferences', *Instructional Science*, 27, 355–371.

Sadler-Smith, E. and Shefy, E. (2004): 'The intuitive executive: Understanding and applying gut feel in decision-making', *Academy of Management Executive*, 18:4, 76–91.

Sagie, A. and Magnezy, R. (1997): 'Assessor type, number of distinguishable dimension categories and assessment centre construct validity', *Journal of Occupational and Organizational Psychology*, 70, 103–108.

Salas, E., Burke, C. S. and Stagl, K. C. (2004): 'Developing Teams and Team Leaders: Strategies and Principles', in D. V. Day, S. J. Zaccaro and S. M. Halpin (eds), *Leader Development for Transforming Organisations*. Mahwah, NJ: Lawrence Erlbaum Associates Inc.

Salas, E., Burke, C. S., Wilson-Donnelly, K. A. and Fowlkes, J. E. (2004): 'Promoting Effective Leadership Within Multicultural Teams: An Event-Based Approach', in D. V. Day, S. J. Zaccaro and S. M. Halpin (eds), *Leader Development for Transforming Organisations*. Mahwah, NJ: Lawrence Erlbaum Associates Inc.

Salas, E. and Cannon-Bowers, J. A. (1997): 'A Framework for Developing Team Performance Measures in Training', in M. T. Brannick, E. Salas and C. Prince (eds), *Team Performance Assessment and*

Measurement: Theory, Methods, and Applications (pp.45–62). Mahwah, NJ: Lawrence Erlbaum Associates Inc.

Salas, E., Dickinson, T. L., Converse, S. A. and Tannenbaum, S. L. (1992): 'Toward an Understanding of Team Performance and Training', in R. J. Swezey and E. Salas (eds), *Teams: Their Training and Performance*. Norwood, NJ: Ablex.

Salas, E., Rozell, D., Mullen, B., and Driskell, J. E. (1999): 'The effect of team building on performance', *Small Group Research*, 30, 309–329.

Sambrook, S. (2004): 'A critical time for HRD?', *Journal of European Industrial Training*, 28:8/9, 611–624.

Sambrook, S. and Stewart, J. (2000): 'Factors influencing learning in European learning-oriented organizations: Issues for management', *Journal of European Industrial Training*, 24:2, 209–221.

Sandberg, J. (1994): *Human Competence at Work: An Interpretative Approach*. Goteborg: Bas.

Sandberg, J. (2000): 'Understanding human competence at work: An interpretative approach', *Academy of Management Journal*, 43:1, 9–25.

Sandowsky, D. (1995): 'The charismatic leader as a narcissist: Understanding the abuse of power', *Organizational Dynamics*, 24:4, 57–71.

Savickas, M. L. (2005): 'The Theory and Practice of Career Construction', in S. Brown and R. Lent (eds), *Career Development and Counselling: Putting Theory and Research to Work*. New Jersey: Wiley.

Savickas, M. L. and Lent, R. W. (1994): *Convergence in Career Development Theories: Implications for Science and Practice*. Palo Alto, CA: Consulting Psychologists Press.

Scandura, T. A., Von Glinow, M. A. and Lowe, K. B. (1999): 'When East Meets West: Leadership "Best Practices" in the United States and Middle East', in W. H. Mobley, M. J. Gessner and V. Arnold (eds), *Advances in Global Leadership*. Stamford, CT: JAI Press, pp.235–248.

Scase, R. and Goffee, R. (1990): 'Women in management: Towards a research agenda', *International Journal of Human Resource Management*, 1:1, 107–125.

Schartz, M. and Walker, R. (1998): 'Towards an ethnography of learning: Reflection on action as an experience of experience', *Studies in Cults, Organisations and Society*, 4, 197–209.

Schein, E. (1990): *Career Anchors: Discovering Your Real Values*. San Francisco, CA: Pfeiffer & Co.

Schein, E. H. (1969): *Process Consultation: Its Role in Organization Development*. Reading, MA: Addison-Wesley.

Schein, E. H. (1978): *Career Dynamics Matching Individual and Organizational Needs*. Reading, Massachusetts: Addison Wesley.

Schein, E. H. (1988): *Process Consultation, Vol. 1*. Reading, MA: Addison-Wesley.

Schein, E. H. (1996a): 'Three cultures of management: The key to organizational learning', *Sloan Management Review*, 38:1, 9–20.

Schein, E. H. (1996b): *Career Anchors Revisited: Implications for Career Development in the 21st Century*, MIT Sloan School of Management, February 1996. Retrieved from http://www.solonline.org/repository/download/10009.html?item_id=507557

Schmeck, R. R. (1983): 'Learning Styles of College Students', in R. F. Dillon and R. R. Schmeck (eds), *Individual Differences In Cognition* (Vol. 1, pp. 233–279). New York: Academic Press.

Schneider, S. C. and Barsoux, J. (2003): *Managing Across Cultures*. England: Pearson Education Ltd.

Schoenfeldt, L. F. and Steger, J. A. (1990): 'Identification and Development of Management Talent', in G. R. Ferris and K. M. Rowland (eds), *Organizational Entry* (pp 191–251). Greenwich, CT: JAI Press.

Scholte, J. A. (2000): *Globalization: A Critical Introduction*. London: MacMillan.

Schön, D. A. (1983): *The Reflective Practitioner*. New York: Basic Books.

Schön, D. A. (1988). 'Coaching Reflective Teaching', in P. P. Grimmett and G. F. Erickson (eds), *Reflection in Teacher Education*. New York: Teachers College Press.

Schuster, D. T. (2003): *Jewish Lives, Jewish Learning: Adult Jewish Learning in Theory and Practice*. New York: UAHC Press.

Schwarz, D. (2001): 'Making art of work', *Journal for Quality and Participation*, 24:1, 54.

Schwarz, R. (1994): *Team Facilitation*. Englewood Cliffs, NJ: Prentice-Hall.

Scott, W. R. (1987): 'The adolescence of institutional theory', *Administrative Science Quarterly*, 32:4, 493–511.

Scott, W. R. (2001): *Institutions and Organizations*. Thousand Oaks: Sage.

Scribner, S. and Cole, M. (1973): 'Cognitive Consequences of Formal and Informal Education', *Science*, 182, 553–59.

Seebacker, U., Kwiecinski, B., Matthews, R., Meng, C. and Pabst, V. (2003): *Management Development in Germany*, USP Consulting GmbH, Leonardo Program Final Report, June 2003, London: Chartered Management Institute.

Seibert, K. W. (1999): 'Reflection in action: Tools for cultivating on-the-job learning conditions', *Organizational Dynamics*, Winter, 54–65.

Seibert, K., Hall, D. and Kram, K. (1995): 'Strengthening the weak link in strategic executive development', *Human Resource Management*, 34:1, 549–567.

Sellers, P. (2002): 'True grit', *Fortune*, October 14, 101–112.

Selmes, I. (1987): *Improving Study Skills*. London: Hodder and Stoughton.

Selznick, P. (1957): *Leadership and Administration*. New York: Harper & Row.

Seng, C. V., Zannes, E. and Pace, R. W. (2002): 'The contribution of knowledge management to workplace learning', *Journal of Workplace Learning*, 14, 138–147.

Senge, P. M. (1990): *The Fifth Discipline: The Art and Practice of the Learning Organisation*. London: Doubleday.

Senge, P. M. (1992): 'Building learning organizations: The real message of the quality movement', *Journal of Quality and Participation*, 15, 30–36.

Shamir, B., House, R. J. and Arthur, M. B. (1993): 'The motivational effects of charismatic leadership: A self-concept based theory', *Organization Science*, 4, 1–17.

Sheard, A. G. and Kakabadse, A. P. (2004): 'A process perspective on leadership and team development', *The Journal of Management Development*, 23:1, 7–106.

Shefy, E. and Sadler-Smith, E. (2006): 'Applying holistic principles in management development', *Journal of Management Development*, 25:4, 368–85.

Shipton, H. (2006): 'Cohesion or confusion? Towards a typology for organisational learning research', *International Journal of Management Review*, 8 (9), 233–252.

Shipton, H., Fay, D., West, M., Patterson, M. and Birdi, K. (2005): 'Managing people to promote innovation', *Creativity and Innovation Management*, 14:2, 118–128.

Shrivastava, P. (1983): 'A typology of organizational learning systems', *Journal of Management Studies*, 20:1, 7–28.

Shroder, H. M. (1989): *Managerial Competence: The Key to Excellence*. Iowa: Kendall-Hunt.

Siebert, K. and Hall, D. (1995): 'Staffing policy as a strategic response: A typology of career systems', *Academy of Management Review*, 13:4, 568–600.

Silzer, R. (2002a): 'Selecting Leaders at the Top: Exploring the Complexity of Executive Fit', in R. Silzer (ed.), *The 21st Century Executive: Innovative Practices for Building Leadership at the Top*. San Francisco: Jossey-Bass.

Silzer, R. (2002b): *The 21st Century Executive: Innovative Practices for Building Leadership at the Top*. San Francisco: Jossey-Bass.

Simmons, R. (2005): 'Designing high performance jobs', *Harvard Business Review*, July–August.

Skiffington, S. and Zeus, P. (2003): *Behavioural Coaching: How to Build Sustainable Personal and Organizational Strength*. McGraw-Hill.

Slater, S. F. and Narver, J. C. (1995): 'Market orientation and the learning organization', *Journal of Marketing*, 59, 63–74.

Sloan, E. (2001): *The Contribution of University-Based Executive Education to Corporate Talent Management Results*. Minnesota: Personnel Decisions International Corporation.

Smith, A., Whittaker, J., Loan Clark, J. and Boocock, G. (1999): 'Competence-based management development provision to SMEs and the providers' perspective', *Journal of Management Development*, 18:6, 557–572.

Smith, C. B. (1988): 'Designing and Facilitating a Self-Assessment Experience', in M. London and E. M. Mone (eds), *Career Growth and Human Resource Strategies: The Role of the Human Resource Professional in Employee Development* (pp. 157–172). New York: Quorum Books.

Smith, K. G., Smith, K. A., Sims, H. P., Jr, O'Bannon, D. P., Scully, J. A. and Olian, J. D. (1994): 'Top management team demography and process: the role of social integration and communication', *Administrative Science Quarterly*, 39 (3), 412-438.

Smith, P. and Sadler-Smith, E. (2006): *Learning in Organizations: Complexities and Diversities*. London and New York: Routledge.

Smith, P. B., Misumi, J., Tayeb, M., Peterson, M. and Bond, M. (1989): 'On the generality of leadership styles across cultures', *Journal of Occupational Psychology*, 62, 97–107.

Smith, P. J. (2002): 'Modern learning methods: Rhetoric and reality – further to Sadler-Smith *et al.*', *Personnel Review*, 31:1/2, 103–113.

Snell, R. S. (2000): 'Studying moral ethos using an adapted kohlbergian model', *Organization Studies*, 21:1, 267–295.

Snell, S. A. and Dean, J. W., Jr. (1992): 'Integrated manufacturing and human resource management: A human capital perspective', *Academy of Management Journal*, 35, 467–504.

Snow, C. C., Miles, R. E. and Coleman, H. J., Jr. (1992): 'Managing 21st Century Network Organizations', *Organizational Dynamics*, 20:3, 5–20.

Sonnenfeld, J. A. and Peiperl, M. A. (1988): 'Staffing policy as a strategic response: A typology of career systems', *Academy of Management Review*, 13:4, 568–600.

Sonnenfeld, J. A., Peiperl, M. A. and Kotter, J. P. (1988): 'Strategic determinants of managerial labour markets: A career systems view', *Human Resource Management*, 27:4, 369–388.

Sparrow, P. (1999): 'International Recruitment, Selection, and Assessment', in P. Joynt and R. Marlin (eds), *The Global HR Manager: Creating the Seamless Organisation*. London: CIPD.

Sparrow, P. (2002): 'To Use Competencies or Not to Use Competencies? That Is the Question', in M. Pearn (ed.) *Individual Differences and Development in Organizations* (pp. 107–129). Chichester: Wiley.

Sparrow, P. R. (1996): 'Careers and the psychological contract: Understanding the European context', *The European Journal of Work and Organizational Psychology*, 5:4, 479–500.

Sparrow, P. R. (1998): 'New Organizational Forms, Processes, Jobs and Psychological Contract: Resolving the HRM issues', in P. R. Sparrow and M. Marchington (eds), *Human Resource Management: The New Agenda*. London: Financial Times/ Pitman Publishing.

Sparrow, P. R. (2002): 'Globalization as an Uncoupling Force: Internationalization of the HR Process?', in P. Gunnigle (ed.), *The John Lovett Lectures: A Decade of Development of Human Resource Management in Ireland*. Dublin: Liffey Press.

Sparrow, P. R. and Cooper, C. L. (2004): *The Employment Relationship: Key Challenges for HR*. Oxford: Butterworth-Heinemann.

Sparrow, P. R. and Marchington, M. (eds) (1998): *Human Resource Management: The New Agenda*. London: Financial Times/ Pitman Publishing.

Speaker, A. W. (2000): 'A strategic typology of human resource activities', Alpharetta GA: Synhrgy HR Technologies. Unpublished.

Spencer, L. and Spencer, S. (1993): *Competence at Work: A Model for Superior Performance*. New York: Wiley.

Spencer, L. M. (1983): *Soft Skills Competencies*. Edinburgh: Scottish Council for Research in Education.

Spreitzer, G. M. (2006): 'Leading to grow and growing to lead: Leadership development lessons from positive operational studies', *Organisational Dynamics*, 35 (4), 305–315.

Starkey, K. and Tempest, S. (2005): 'Late Twentieth-Century Management, the Business School, and Social Capital', in C. L. Cooper (ed.), *Leadership and Management in the 21st Century: Business Challenges of the Future*. Oxford: Oxford University Press.

Staufenbiel, T. and Kleinmann, M. (1999, May): *Does P-O fit influence the judgments in assessment centers?* Paper presented at the Annual Conference of the Society for Industrial and Organizational Psychology, Espoo-Helsinki, Finland.

Staunton, M. and Giles, K. (2001): 'Age of enlightenment', *People Management*, 7:15, 30–33.

Steiner, D. D. (1997): 'Attributions in leader-member exchanges: Implications for practice', *European Journal of Work and Organizational Psychology*, 6, 59–71.

Steiner, L. (1998): 'Organizational dilemmas as barriers to learning', *The Learning Organization*, 5:4, 193–201.

Stern, L. R. (1998): 'Five types of executives in search of coaching', *The Manchester Review*, 3:2, 13–19.

Stern, L. R. (2004): 'Executive coaching: A working definition', *Consulting Psychology Journal: Practice and Research*, 56:3, 154–162.

Stewart, D. (2001): 'Reinterpreting the learning organization', *The Learning Organization*, 8:4, 141–152.

Stewart, R. (1975): *Contrasts in Management*. Maidenhead: McGraw-Hill.

Stewart, R. (1991): *Managing Today and Tomorrow*. London: Macmillan.

Stewart, T. A. (1997): *Intellectual Capital: The New Wealth of Organisations*. New York: Double Day/ Currency.

Stiles, P. (1999): 'Transformation at the Leading Edge', in L. Grattan, V. Hope Hailey, P. Stiles and C. Truss (eds), *Strategic Human Resource Management*. Oxford: Oxford University Press.

Stogdill, R. M. (1974): *Handbook of Leadership*. New York: Free Press.

Stokes, G. and Cochrane, R. (1984), 'A study of the psychological effects of redundancy and unemployment', *Journal of Occupational Psychology*, Vol. 57, 309–322.

Stone, D. L. and Stone, E. F. (1985): 'The effects of feedback consistency and feedback favorability on self-perceived task competence and perceived feedback accuracy', *Organizational Behavior and Human Decision Processes*, 36:2, 167–85.

Stone, D. L., Stone-Romero, E. F. and Lukaszewski, K. (2003): 'The Functional and Dysfunctional Consequences of Human Resource Information Technology for Organizations and their Employees', in D. Stone (ed.), *Advances in Human Performance and Cognitive Engineering Research*. Greenwich, CT: JAI Press.

Stone, D. L., Stone-Romero, E. F. and Lukaszewski, K. (2006): 'Factors affecting the acceptance and effectiveness of electronic human resource systems', *Human Resource Management Review*, 16:2, 229–44.

Stoof, A., Martens, R. L., Van Merrienboer, J. and Bastiaens, T. (2002): 'The boundary approach of competence: A constructivist aid for understanding and using the concept of competence', *Human Resource Development Review*, 1:3, 345–365.

Storey, J. (1989a): 'Management development: a literature review and implications for future research Part 1: Conceptualisations and practices', *Personnel Review*, 18:6, 2–15.

Storey, J. (1989b): 'Management development: a literature review and implications for future research Part 2: Profiles and contexts', *Personnel Review*, 19:1.

Storey, J. (1995): *Human Resource Management: A Critical Text*. London: Routledge.

Storey, J., Edwards, P. and Sisson, K. (1997): *Managers in the Making: Careers, Development and Control in Corporate Britain and Japan*. London: Sage Publications.

Storey, J., Mabey, C. and Thomson, A. (1997): 'What a difference a decade makes', *People Management*, 3:12, 28–30.

Straka, G. A. (1999): 'Perceived work conditions and self-directed learning in the process of work', *International Journal of Training and Development*, 3:4, 240–249.

Straka, G. A. (2000): 'Conditions promoting self-directed learning at the workplace', *Human Resource Development International*, 3:2, 241–51.

Straka, G. A. (2003): 'Modelling a More-dimensional Theory of Self-Directed Learning', in G. A. Straka (ed.), *Conceptions of Self-Directed Learning*. Munster: Waxmann.

Stringer, R. A. (2002): *Leadership and Organisational Climate*. Englewood Cliffs: Prentice Hall.

Stringer, R. A. and Cheloha, R. S. (2003): 'The power of a development plan', *Human Resource Planning*, 26:4, 10–17.

Stroh, L. K. (1995): 'Predicting turnover among expatriates: Can organizations affect retention rates?', *International Journal of Human Resource Management*, 6:2, 443–456.

Sturges, J. (2004): 'The Individualization of the Career and its Implications for Leadership and Management Development', in J. Storey (ed.), *Leadership in Organizations: Current Issues and Key Trends*. London: Routledge.

Sullivan, G. (1999): 'Foreword: From Theory to Practice', in J. G. Hunt, G. G. Dodge and L. Wong (eds), *Out of the Box Leadership: Transforming the Twenty-First Century Army and Other Top-Performing Organizations*. Stamford, CT: Jal.

Sullivan, S. E. and Arthur M. B. (2006): 'The evolution of the boundaryless career concept: Examining physical and psychological mobility', *Journal of Vocational Behavior*, 69, 19–29.

Sundstrome, E., De Meuse, K. P. and Futrell, D. (1990): 'Work teams: Applications and effectiveness', *American Psychologist*, 45:2, 120–133.

Super, D. E. (1953): 'A theory of vocational development', *American Psychologist*, 8, 185–190.

Super, D. E. (1957): *The Psychology of Careers*. New York: Harper and Row.

Super, D. E., Savickas, M. L. and Super, C. M. (1996): 'The Life-Span, Life Space Approach to Careers', in D. Brown and L. Brooks (eds), *Career Choice and Development* (3rd edn). San Francisco: Jossey-Bass.

Suutari, V. (2002): 'Global leader development: An emerging research agenda', *Career Development International*, 7:4, 218–233.

Swieringa, J. and Wierdsma, A. (1992): *Becoming a Learning Organization*. Wokingham: Addison-Wesley.

Talbot, C. (1997): 'Paradoxes of management development – trends and tensions', *Career Development International*, 2:3, 119–46.

Tannenbaum, S. I., Beard, R.L. and Salas, E. (1992): 'Team Building and its influence on Team Effectiveness: An Examination of Conceptual and Empirical Developments', in K. Kelley (ed.), *Issues, Theory, and Research in Industrial/Organizational Psychology* (Vol. 82). Amsterdam: Elsevier Science Publishing Company.

Tannenbaum, S. I., Smith-Jentsch, K. K. and Behson, S. J. (1998): 'Training Team Leaders to Facilitate Team Learning and Performance', in J. A. Cannon-Bowers and E. Salas (eds), *Making Decisions Under Stress: Implications for Individual and Team Training*. Washington, DC: American.

Tapscott, D. (1999): 'Introduction', in D. Tapscott (ed.), *Creating Value in the Network Economy*. Boston: Harvard Business School Publishing.

Tavuchis, N. (1991): *Mea Culpa: A Sociology of Apology and Reconciliation*. Stanford: Stanford University Press.

Taylor, E. W. (1911): *The Principles of Scientific Management*. New York: Harper and Row.

Taylor, N. (1996): 'Professionalism and monitoring CPD: Kafka revisited', *Planning Practice and Research*, 11:4, 379–389.

Teece, D. J. (1990): 'Firm capabilities, resources and the concept of strategy: Four paradigms of strategic management', *CCC Working Paper*, 90–98.

Tharenou, P., Latimer, S. and Conroy, D. (1994): 'How do you make it to the top? An examination of influences on women's and men's managerial advancement', *Academy of Management Journal*, 37, 899–931.

Thatchenkery, T. (1996): *Post-modern Management and Organization Theory*. Thousand Oaks, CA: Sage.

Thesing, G. (1998): 'The missing sex: Women in corporate Ireland', *Business and Finance*, April 23–29.

Thomas, A. S. and Ramaswamy, K. (1996): 'Matching managers to strategy: Further tests of the miles and snow typology', *British Journal of Management*, 7:3, 247–261.

Thomas, K. and Allen, S. (2006): 'The learning organisation: A meta-analysis of themes in literature', *The Learning Organization*, 13:2, 123–39.

Thompsom, M. (2000): *The competitiveness challenge, Final report, The bottom line benefits of strategic human resource management*. UK Aerospace People Management Audit.

Thomson, A., Mabey, C., Storey, J., Gray, C. and Iles, P. (2001): *Changing Patterns of Management Development*. Oxford: Blackwell Business.

Thomson, A., Storey, J., Mabey, C., Gray, C., Farmer, E., and Thomson, R. (1997*): A Portrait of Management Development*. London: IM.

Thomson, R. and Mabey, C. (1994): *Developing Human Resources*. Oxford: Butterworth-Heinemann.

Thornton, G. C. and Byham, W. C. (1982): *Assessment Centres and Managerial Performance*. New York: Academic Press.

Thornton, G. C. and Cleveland, J. N. (1990): 'Developing managerial talent through simulation', *American. Psychologist*, 45, 190–199.

Thornton III, G. C., Larsh, S., Layer, S. and Kaman, V. (1999): *Reactions to attribute-based feedback and exercise-based feedback in developmental assessment centres*. Paper presented at the Annual Conference of the Society for Industrial and Organizational Psychology, May, Atlanta, GA.

Ting-Toomey, S. (1988): 'Intercultural Conflict Styles: A Face Negotiation Theory', in Y. Y. Kim and W. B. Gudykunst (eds), *Theories in Intercultural Communication*. Newbury Park, CA: Sage.

Toegel, G. and Conger, J. (2003): '360-degree assessment: Time for reinvention', *Academy of Management Learning and Education*, 2:3: 297–311.

Tolley, G. (1987): 'Competency achievement and qualifications', *Industrial and Commercial Training*, September/October, 6–8.

Tonge, A., Greer, L. and Lawton, A. (2003): 'The Enron story: you can fool some of the people some of the time', *Business Ethics: A European Review*, 12:1, 4–22.

Torbert, W. R. (1994): 'Managerial learning, organizational learning: A potentially powerful redundancy', *Journal of Management Learning*, 1, 57–70.

Torrington, D., Hall, L. and Taylor, S. (2005): *Human Resource Management* (6th edn). London: Prentice Hall.

Tough, A. M. (1971): *The Adult's Learning Projects*. Toronto: Ontario Institute for Studies in Education.

Townsend, A., DeMarie, S. and Hendrickson, A. (1998): 'Virtual teams: Technology and the workplace of the future', *Academy of Management Executive*, 12, 17–29.

Tracey, J. B., Hinkin, T. R., Tannenbaum, S. and Mathieu, J. E. (2001): 'The influence of individual characteristics and the work environment on varying levels of training outcomes', *Human Resource Development Quarterly*, 12, 5–23.

Training Standards Agency (2000): Definition as in Horton, S., 'Introduction – the competency movement: Its origins and impact on the public sector', *International Journal of Public Sector Management*, 13:4, 7–14.

Tsang, E. W. K. (1997): 'Organizational learning and the learning organization: A dichotomy between descriptive and prescriptive research', *Human Relations*, 50:1, 73–89.

Tsang, H. W. H., Paterson, M. and Packer, T. (2002): 'Self-directed learning in fieldwork education with learning contracts', *British Journal of Therapy and Rehabilitation*, 9:5, 184–189.

Tsoukas, H. (1994): 'What is management? An outline of a metatheory.' *British Journal of Management*, 5:4, 289.

Turban, D. and Dougherty, T. (1994): 'Role of protégé personality in receipt of mentoring and career success', *Academy of Management Journal*, 37:3, 688–702.

Turnbull, S. (2002): 'Bricolage as an alternative approach to HRD theory building', *Human Resource Development Review*, 1:1.

Turner, D. and Crawford, M. (1994): 'Managing Current and Future Competitive Performance: The Role of Competence', in G. Hamel and A. Heene (eds), *Competence-Based Competition* (pp.241–263). Chichester: John Wiley & Sons.

Tyre, M. J. and Von Heppel, E. (1997): 'The situated nature of adaptive learning in organisations', *Organisational Science*, 1, 71–83.

Tyson, S. (1995): *Human Resource Strategy*. Pitman.

Tyson, S. and Ward, P. (2004): 'The use of 360-degree feedback technique in the evaluation of management development', *Management Learning*, 35:2, 205–223.

Ulrich, D. (1995): 'Shared services: From vogue to value', *Human Resource Planning*, 18:3, 12–23.

Ulrich, D. and Beatty, D. (2001): 'From partners to players: Extending the HR playing field', *Human Resource Management*, 40:4, 293–307.

Ulrich, D., Von Glinow, M. A. and Jick, T. (1993): 'High-impact learning: Building and diffusing learning capability', *Organizational Dynamics*, 22:2, 52–66.

Ulrich, D., Younger, J. and Brockbank, W. (2008): 'The twenty-first-century HR organisation', *Human Resource Management*, 47:4, 829–850.

Useem, M. (1998): *The Leadership Moment*. New York: Times Business Books.

Vaill, P. B. (1989): *Managing as a Performing Art: New Ideas for a World of Chaotic Change*. San Francisco, CA: Jossey-Bass.

Vaill, P. B. (1996): *Learning as a Way of Being*. San Francisco: Jossey-Bass.

Valerio, A. M. (1990): 'A Study of the Developmental Experiences of Managers', in K. E. Clark and M. B. Clark (eds), *Measures of Leadership*. West Orange, NJ: Leadership Library of America.

Valkevaara, T. (2002): 'Exploring the construction of professional expertise in HRD: Analysis of four HR developers' work histories and career stories', *Journal of European Industrial Training*, 26, 183–195.

Van de Sluis, E. C. and Hoeksema, L. H. (2001): 'The palette of management development', *Journal of Management Development*, 20:2, 1–8.

Van den Berg, P. T. and Wilderom, C. (2004): 'Defining, measuring and comparing organisational cultures', *Applied Psychology: An International Review*, 53, 570–582.

Van der Krogt, F. J. (1998): 'Learning network theory: The tension between learning systems and work systems in organizations', *Human Resource Development Quarterly*, 9, 157–178.

Van der Wagen, L. (1994): *Building Quality Service with Competency-Based Human Resource Management*. Oxford: Butterworth Heinemann.

Van Maanen, J. (1995): 'Style as theory', *Organization Science*, 6:1, 133–143.

Van Ments, M. (1999): *The Effective Use of Role Play* (2nd edn). London: Kogan Page.

Van Merriënboer, J. J. G., Kirschner, P. A. and Kester, L. (2003): 'Taking the load off a learner's mind: Instructional design for complex learning', *Educational Psychologist*, 38(1): 5–13.

Van Velsor, E. and Guthrie, V. A. (1998): 'Enhancing the Ability to Learn From Experience', in C. D. McCauley, R. S. Moxley and E. Van Velsor (eds), *The Centre for Creative Leadership Handbook of Leadership Development* (1st edn). San Francisco: Jossey-Bass.

Van Woerkom, M., Nijhof, W. J. and Nieuwenhuis, L. F. M. (2002): 'Critical reflective working behaviour: A survey research', *Journal of European Industrial Training*, 26:8, 375–383.

Vandewalle, D. (2001): 'Goal orientation: Why wanting to look successful doesn't always lead to success', *Organizational Dynamics*, 30, 162–171.

Vardiman, P. D., Houghton, J. D. and Jinkerson, D. L. (2006): 'Environmental leadership development: Toward a contextual model of leader selection and effectiveness', *Leadership and Organization Development Journal*, 27:2, 93–105.

Veres, J. G., Locklear, T. S. and Sims, R. R. (1990): 'Job Analysis in Practice: A Brief Review of the Role of Job Analysis in Human Resource Management', in G. R. Ferris, K.M. Rowland and R. M. Buckley (eds), *Human Resource Management: Perspectives and Issues*. Boston, MA: Allyn & Bacon.

Vernon, P., Philips, J., Brewster, C. and Ommeren, J. (2000): *European Trends in HR Outsourcing*. Report for William M. Mercer and the Cranfield School of Management.

Vicere, A. A., Taylor, M. W. and Freeman, V. T. (1994): 'Executive development in major corporations: A ten-year study', *Journal of Management Development*, 13:1, 4–22.

Vickers, M. H. (2000): 'Australian police management education and research: A comment from outside the cave', *Policing: An International Journal of Police Strategies and Management*, 23:4, 506–525.

Vince, R. (2000): 'Learning in public organisations in 2010', *Public Money and Management*, 20:1, 39–44.

Vince, R. (2002): 'Organizing reflection', *Management Learning*, 33:1, 63–78.

Viney, C., Adamson, S. and Doherty, N. (1997): 'Paradoxes of fast-track career management', *Personnel Review*, 26:3, 174–186.

Vinnecombe, S. and Colwill, N. L. (1995): *The Essence of Women in Management*. London: Prentice-Hall.

Von Krogh, G. (1998): 'Care in knowledge creation', *California Management Review*, 40:3, 133–153.

Vygotsky, L. S. (1978): 'Mind in Society: The Development of Higher Psychological Processes', in M. Cole, V. John-Steiner, S. Scribner and E. Souberman (eds), Cambridge, MA: Harvard University Press.

Wade, M. (2006): 'Developing Leaders for Sustainable Business', in T. Maak and N. M. Pless (eds), *Responsible Leadership*. New York: Routledge.

Wagner, R. J., Baldwin, T. T. and Roland, C. (1991): 'Outdoor training: Revolution or fad?', *Training and Development Journal*, 45:3, 50–57.

Wajcman, J. (1999): *Women and Men in Corporate Management*. Cambridge: Allen & Unwin.

Walker, A. G. and Smither, J. W. (1999): 'A five-year study of upward feedback: What managers do with their results matters', *Personnel Psychology*, 52:2, 393–423.

Walton, J. (1999): *Strategic Human Resource Development*. London: Prentice Hall.

Wanberg, C., Welsh, E. and Hezlett, S. (2003): *Mentoring Research: A Review and Dynamic Process Model*, Vol. 22, Oxford: Elsevier.

Ward, P. (1997): *360-Degree Feedback*. London: Institute of Personnel and Development.

Ware, J. (2005): 'The changing nature of work: Technology'. The future of work blog [online]. Retrieved 15 September 2005 from http://www.thefutureofwork.net/blog /archives/000317.html.

Warr, P. and Allan, C. (1998): 'Learning Strategies and Occupational Training', in C. L. Cooper and I. T. Robertson (eds), *International Review of Industrial and Organizational Psychology* (Vol. 13, 83–121). Chichester, UK: John Wiley and Sons.

Warr, P. and Downing, J. (2000): 'Learning strategies, learning anxiety and knowledge acquisition', *British Journal of Psychology*, 91, 311–333.

Warr, P. B., Allan, C. and Birdi, K. (1999): 'Predicting three levels of training outcome', *Journal of Occupational and Organizational Psychology*, 72, 351–375.

Watkins, K. and Marsick, V. (1993): *Sculpting the Learning Organisation*. San Francisco: Jossey-Bass.

Watkins, K. E. and Marsick, V. J. (2003): 'Demonstrating the value of an organization's learning culture: The dimensions of the learning organization questionnaire', *Advances in Developing Human Resources*, 5:2, 132–151.

Watson, T. J. (1994): 'Management "flavours of the month": their role in managers' lives', *International Journal of Human Resource Management*, 5:4, 893–909.

Weick, K. (1983): 'Managerial Thought in the Context of Action', in S. Srivastava (ed.), *The Executive Mind* (221–242). San Francisco: Jossey-Bass.

Weick, K. E. (1995): *Sensemaking in Organizations*. Thousand Oaks, California: Sage Publications.

Weisbord, M. (1993): *Discovering Common Ground*. San-Francisco: Berrett-Koehler.

Weitzel, S. (2000): *Feedback that Works*. Greensboro, NC: Center for Creative Leadership.

Wenger, E. (1998): *Communities of Practice: Learning, Meaning, and Identity*. New York: Cambridge University Press.

Wentling, R. M. and Palma-Rivas, N. (1998): 'Current status and future trends of diversity initiatives in the workplace: Diversity expert's perspective', *Human Resource Development Quarterly*, 19:3, 236–251.

Werner, J. M. and Lester, S. W. (2001): 'Applying a team effectiveness framework to the performance of student case teams', *Human Resource Development Quarterly*, 12, 385–402.

West, M. and Patterson, M. (1997): *The Impact of People Management Practices on Business Performance*, IPD Research Paper No. 22. London: IPD.

Westwood, R. (1992): *Organizational Behaviour: South East Asian Perspectives*. Hong Kong: Longman.

Wharton, A., (1996), 'Service With a Smile: Understanding the Consequences of Emotional Labor', in C. L. Macdonald and C. Sirianni (eds), *Working in the Service Society*. Philadelphia: Temple University Press.

Whetten, D. A. and Cameron, K. S. (2005): *Developing Management Skills* (6th edn). Upper Saddle River, NJ: Pearson Education.

Whetten, D.A. and Cameron, K.S. (1995): *Developing Management Skills* (3rd edn). New York: Harper-Collins.

White, R. P. (1992): 'Job As Classroom: Using Assignments to Leverage Development', in D. H. Montross and C. J. Shinkman (eds), *Career Development: Theory and Practice*. Springfield, IL: Thomas.

White, R. P., Hodgson, P. and Crainer, S. (1996): *The Future of Leadership*. Lanham, MD: Pitman.

Whitely, W., Dougherty, T. W. and Dreher, G. F. (1991): 'Relationships of career mentoring and socioeconomic origin to managers' and professionals' early career progress', *Academy of Management Journal*, 34:2, 331–351.

Whitmore, J. (1996): *Coaching for Performance* (2nd edn). Nicholas Brealey.

Wilensky, A. and Hansen, C. (2001): 'Understanding the work beliefs of non-profit executives through organizational stories', *Human Resource Development Quarterly*, 12:3, 223–238.

Wilkinson, A. and Wilmot, H. (eds) (1995): *Making Quality Critical: New Perspectives on Organizational Change*. London: Routledge.

Wilson, D. (1996): 'The future for development centres', *Career Development International*, 1:6: 4–11.

Wilson, F. (1995): *Organisational Behaviour and Gender*. London: McGraw-Hill.

Wimer, S. (2002): 'The dark side of 360-degree feedback: The popular HR intervention has an ugly side' – Human Resources. Retrieved from www.findarticles.com.

Winne, P. H. (1995): 'Inherent details in self-regulated learning', *Educational Psychologist*, 30, 173–187.

Winstanley, D., Woodhall, J. and Heery, E. (1996): 'Business ethics and human resource management', *Personnel Review*, 25:6.

Winterton, J. and Delamare-Le Deist, F. (2004): *Extended Outline of the Study on Developing Typologies for Knowledge, Skills and Competencies*, CEDEFOP Project, Thessaloniki: CEDEFOP (21 June).

Winterton, J. and Jackson, C. (1999): *Riding the Wave*. Career Innovation Research Group.

Winterton, J. and Winterton, R. (1996): *The Business Benefits of Competence-Based Management Development*. Dfee Research Studies, R516, London: HMSO.

Winterton, J. and Wintertorn, R. (1997): 'Does management development add value?', *British Journal of Management*, 8, 65–76.

Winterton, J. and Winterton, R. (1999): *Developing Managerial Competence*. London: Routledge.

Woerkom, M. (2003): 'Critical Reflection at Work: Bridging Individual and Organisational Learning'. PhD Thesis, Twente University, Enschede: Print Partners, Ipskamp.

Wong, C-S. and Law, K. S. (2002): 'The effects of leader and follower emotional intelligence on performance and attitude: An exploratory study', *Leadership Quarterly*, 13, 243–274.

Wood, M. (2005): 'The fallacy of misplaced leadership', *Journal of Management Studies*, 42:6, 1101–1021.

Wood, S. (1999): 'Family-friendly management: Testing the various perspectives', *National Institute for Economic Research*, 168, April 2/99, 99–116.

Woodall, J. (2000): 'Corporate support for work-based management development', *Human Resource Management Journal*, 10:1, 18–32.

Woodall, J., Edwards, C. and Welchman, R. (1997): 'Organisational restructuring: A challenge or a threat to equal opportunities?', *Gender, Work and Organisation*, 4:1, 2–12.

Woodall, J. and Winstanley, D. (1998): *Management Development: Strategy and Practice*. Oxford: Blackwell Business.

Woodall, J. and Winstanley, D. (2003): *Work-Based Management Development Methods: Informal and Incidental Learning*.

Woodruffe, C. (1993): *Assessment Centres: Identifying and Developing Competence* (2nd edn). London: IPM.

Woodruffe, C. (2000): *Development and Assessment Centres* (3rd edn). London: Chartered Institute of Personnel and Development.

Woodruffe, C. (2001): 'Promotional intelligence', *People Management*, 7:1, 26–29.

Worley, C., Hitchin, D. and Ross, W. (1996): *Integrated Strategic Change: How OD Builds Competitive Advantage*. Reading Mass: Addison-Wesley.

Wright, J. (2005): 'Workplace coaching: What's it all about?' *Work*, 24:3, 325–328.

Wynne, B. and Stringer, D. (1997): *A Competency-Based Approach to Training and Development*. Boston, MA: Pitman Publishing.

Yang, B., Zheng, W. and Li, M. (2006): 'Confucian view of learning and implications for developing human resources', *Advances in Developing Human Resources*, 8:3, 346–354.

Yeo, R. K. (2005): 'Revisiting the roots of learning organization: A synthesis of the learning organization literature', *The Learning Organization*, 12:4, 368–82.

Young, G. and Khan, A. (2004): 'Using shadowing to build creativity and continuity: Gaining insight into key roles in San Francisco city government', *KM Review*, 7:3, 20–23.

Yukl, G. (2002): *Leadership in Organizations* (5th edn). Upper Saddle River, NJ: Prentice-Hall.

Yukl, G., Wall, S. and Lepsinger, R. (1990): 'Preliminary Report on Validation of the Managerial Practices Survey', in K. E. Clark and M. B. Clark (eds), *Measures of Leadership*. West Orange NJ: Leadership Library of America.

Zaal, J. N. (2002): 'Development Centres: A Neglected Perspective', in M. Pearn (ed.), *Individual Differences and Development in Organizations*. West Sussex: John Wiley and Sons Ltd.

Zaccaro, S. J., Ardison, S. D. and Orvis, K. L. (2004): 'Leadership in Virtual Teams', in D. V. Day, S. J. Zaccaro and S. M. Halpin (eds), *Leader Development for Transforming Organisations*. Mahwah, NJ: Lawrence Erlbaum Associates Inc.

Zajac, E.J. and Westphal, J.D. (1996): 'Who shall succeed? How CEO/board preferences and power affect the choice of new CEOs', *Academy of Management Journal*, 39:1, 64–90.

Zaleznik, A. (1992): 'Managers and leaders: Are they different?', *Harvard Business Review*, 70:2, 126–136.

Zand, D. E. (1997): *The Leadership Triad: Knowledge, Trust and Power*. New York: Oxford University.

Zhao, J., Rust, K. G. and McKinley, W. (1997): *A socio-cognitive interpretation of organizational downsizing: Toward a paradigm shift*. Paper presented at the 23rd European International Business Academy Conference on Global Business in the Information Age, Stuttgart, 14–16 December.

Zimmerman, B. J. and Martinez-Pons, M. (1990): 'Student differences in self-regulated learning: Relating grade, sex and giftedness to self-efficacy and strategy use', *Journal of Educational Psychology*, 82, 51–59.

Zuber-Skerritt, O. (1995): 'Developing a learning organization through management education by action learning', *The Learning Organization*, 2:2, 36–46.

Index

ability, distinct from
   competency, 235
abstract conceptualisation, 23–
   4, 25
   learning and, 427, 437
accommodating style of
   learning, 427, 437
accountability for leadership
   development, 174, 278
accountability, social, 67–8
accountability, span of, 82
accumulation mechanisms, 598
achievement and
   overachievement, 278–9
acquiescence, 694
acquisitions and mergers, 84
acting mindfully, 445
acting up, 359, 360, 364–6
action-focused creative
   coaching, 575–6
action learning model, 24, 336–
   8, 421
   collaborative leadership, 635
   fast-track graduate
      development, 595–6
   learning organisation, 625
   programmes, 336–8
   top teams, 578
action science framework, 418–
   21
activist managers, 437
activity theory of social
   cognition, 428, 429
adaptive learning, 621
administrative expertise style,
   22–3
adoption, 692, 693–4
adventure learning
   programmes, 326–8
advisory board, 171
advisory roles of managers,
   237–40
Aer Lingus, 96–7
affiliative leaders, 120, 279
ageing workforce, 70, 73
agency theory, 42–3
agenda-driven model, 103

agent for change role, 23
AIB (Allied Irish Banks), 263
   development centres, 317–19
   multisource feedback, 314–16
alignment sessions in teams,
   563
allegiance, project/corporate,
   501
alliances, 72, 84–6
   case study, 52–4
ambiguity, and learning, 455
AMIS, 37
AMT (advanced manufacturing
   technology), 79
analytical learning, 621
andragogy, 433
anticipatory thinking, 422
anxiety, 123
apologies from leaders, 135–6
Apple Macintosh, 549
appreciative coaching, 394
arena thesis, 30–2
Argyris and Schon's action
   science framework, 419
arrogance, 529, 530
assessment, 14
   of coaching, 404–5
   of competencies, 246–50
   of development potential, 47–8
   of graduates, 601
   of needs, 211–15
   of talent, 272, 276, 283–7
   of teams, 562–4
   strategic analysis, 644–5
assessment/development centres,
   214–15, 229, 328–31
   career development, 538
   case studies, 186, 317–19
   in Ireland, 705
   needs identification, 214–15
assignments see job
   assignments
assimilating style of learning,
   427, 437
ASSIST (Approaches and Study
   Skills Inventory for
   Students), 426

assumptions, ix–x, 152–4, 174
   competencies, 174, 246
   talent and succession
      management, 269, 271
attention span of managers,
   421–2
attitudes and competency, 234
attitudes to learning, 436
attitudinal structuring, 20
audit, training and
   development, 317
authentic leaders, 467–9
authoritarian leaders, 120, 124
autonomy, 64, 431, 455
   career choice, 515
Avocent, 542–4
avoidance-goal orientation, 435

BA (British Airways), 96, 97
bandwagon effect, 694
barriers to SMLD, 172–4
BARS (behaviourally anchored
   rating scales), 251–2
Bausch and Lomb, 376–8
Beardwell and Holden Model,
   22–3
Bear Stearns, 308
behavioural coaching, 393,
   399
behavioural competencies, 231,
   232
   AIB case study, 315
behaviourist theory, 432, 438
   cross-cultural leadership, 664
beliefs see values and beliefs
benchmarking, 148
bench strength, 290
Bennett, Stephen, 37
Bertelsmann Media Group,
   610–12
best practice, 170–1, 718
   talent management, 277–8,
      300, 302
Board of Directors, viii, 32
   CEO succession, 301–2
   competency and skill
      requirements, 571

cognitive information
processing theory, 507
cognitive skills, 17, 18, 110,
116, 119, 241
collaborative leadership, 613,
634–9
action-learning principles,
635
competencies and roles, 237–
40
defined, 634
in Norway, 711
collective leadership, 622–4,
634–6, 643–8
expansive/restrictive learning
environments, 630–2
large-group interventions,
645–6
re-engineering, 647–8
strategic planning, 644–5
collective reflection, 447–9
co-mentoring, 382, 383–4, 408–
9
command mode, 159
common sense, and learning,
445–6
communication, 288, 690
cultural differences, 664
communities of practice, 428,
448–9, 630
commuter assignments, 653,
658–9, 664
compassionate leadership, 634,
635
compensation purpose, 16
competency, 24, 225–59
advantages/disadvantages of
competency approach,
244–6
assessing and measuring,
246–53
assumptions, 174, 246
competency clusters (case
study), 3
conflicts with other
strategies, 254
core competencies, 231
defining, 230–44
domains, 241
individual/distributed, 232
inside-out/outside-in
approach, 231–5
integrated competency
model, 101
job assignments and, 353
leadership and management
compared, 7–8
levels of, 233

likeability and, 636–7
model selection, 253–5
performance and, 229–30,
234, 244, 246–7, 255
person/task-orientated, 232
rationalist/constructivist
approaches, 235–44
social/personal
competencies, 118, 241
specific/general, 232–3
task and skill taxonomies,
212
work/worker-oriented, 235–
41, 246, 247, 251
competing values framework,
104, 105
competitive strategy, 155–6
compromise, 694–5
conceptual-based programmes,
323–6
conceptual model, 177
concrete experience, 24, 25
learning style, 427, 437
concurrent leadership, 634, 635
conferences, search
conferences, 645–6
Confucianism, 726, 730–1
connectivity, 615, 624
constrainers, 119
constructivist theories, 433–4,
718
career theory, 507
competency and, 242–4
consultancy, internal, 189
contingency theory, 111–13, 131
continuous professional
development, 590–3
contract, psychological, 41, 83–
4, 505
contracting out, 196 see also
outsourcing
control, concept of, 417
control, span of, 82
convergence, international,
715–24
convergent style of learning,
427, 437
conversational learning, 444–5
corporate allegiance, 501
corporate citizenship, 157
corporate memory, 60
corporate social responsibility,
67–8, 116–17
global, 673–4
corporate universities, 342–4
Ireland, 705
cost reduction strategies, 155,
156, 158

counselling, 383, 538
courseware, 219, 220–1
CPD (continuous professional
development), 590–3
CRANET study, 702, 704
creative thinking, 16, 47
and learnership, 639
critical incident technique,
248–9, 452
critical reflection, 423
critical reflective work
behaviour (CRWB), 449
critical theory perspective, 37–
9, 718
cross-functional teams, 550,
558, 648
culmination of leadership, 635
culture and diversity, 77, 587–
90, 715–16
communication, 664
cross-cultural leadership,
136–9, 660, 662–4, 666,
670–1
cultural adaptability, 666
culture shock, 668–70, 672,
681
global organisations and, 78,
566–8, 660, 662–4, 666,
668–72
training, 675–82
international practices, 77,
715–16, 719
job assignments, dealing with
diversity, 353, 669
leveraging, 669, 670
mentoring, 390–1, 589–90,
606
networking, 589–90
organisational learning, 619
religion, 724–31
culture of organisation, 63, 112,
643–4
assessing climate for
leadership development,
154, 632–3
career development, 520–3,
530
case studies, 2, 262, 348,
651–3, 582
double-loop learning, 419–20
learnership, 638
learning environment and,
63, 64, 196, 429–31, 447–
9, 455, 489, 613, 614
mission statements, 643–4
multicultural issues, 589–90
questioning assumptions,
419, 421, 424

DATE DUE 5/'09

REFERENCE ONLY
NOT FOR ISSUE

Demco, Inc. 38-293